Medical Pharmacology

7th Edition

Review
of
Medical
Pharmacology

FREDERICK H. MEYERS, MD

Professor of Pharmacology
School of Medicine
University of California, San Francisco

ERNEST JAWETZ, MD, PhD

Professor of Microbiology and Medicine
School of Medicine
University of California, San Francisco

ALAN GOLDFIEN, MD

Professor of Medicine
Departments of Medicine and
Obstetrics & Gynecology
and Cardiovascular Research Institute
School of Medicine
University of California, San Francisco

Illustrated by LAUREL V. SCHAUBERT

Los Altos, California 94022   **LANGE Medical Publications**

A Concise Medical Library for Practitioner and Student

Current Medical Diagnosis & Treatment 1980 (annual revision). Edited by M.A. Krupp — 1980
and M.J. Chatton. 1116 pp.

Current Pediatric Diagnosis & Treatment, 6th ed. Edited by C.H. Kempe, H.K. Silver, — 1980
and D. O'Brien. 1122 pp, *illus.*

Current Surgical Diagnosis & Treatment, 4th ed. Edited by J.E. Dunphy and L.W. Way. — 1979
1162 pp, *illus.*

Current Obstetric & Gynecologic Diagnosis & Treatment, 3rd ed. Edited by R.C. Benson. — 1980
1001 pp, *illus.*

Review of Physiological Chemistry, 17th ed. H.A. Harper, V.W. Rodwell, and — 1979
P.A. Mayes. 702 pp, *illus.*

Review of Medical Physiology, 9th ed. W.F. Ganong. 618 pp, *illus.* — 1979

Review of Medical Microbiology, 14th ed. E. Jawetz, J.L. Melnick, and E.A. Adelberg. — 1980
593 pp, *illus.*

Basic & Clinical Immunology, 3rd ed. Edited by H.H. Fudenberg, D.P. Stites, — 1980
J.L. Caldwell, and J.V. Wells. 782 pp, *illus.*

Basic Histology, 3rd ed. L.C. Junqueira and J. Carneiro. 504 pp, *illus.* — 1980

Clinical Cardiology, 2nd ed. M. Sokolow and M.B. McIlroy. 718 pp, *illus.* — 1979

General Urology, 9th ed. D.R. Smith. 541 pp, *illus.* — 1978

General Ophthalmology, 9th ed. D. Vaughan and T. Asbury. 410 pp, *illus.* — 1980

Correlative Neuroanatomy & Functional Neurology, 17th ed. J.G. Chusid. 464 pp, *illus.* — 1979

Principles of Clinical Electrocardiography, 10th ed. M.J. Goldman. 415 pp, *illus.* — 1979

Handbook of Obstetrics & Gynecology, 7th ed. R.C. Benson. 808 pp, *illus.* — 1980

Physician's Handbook, 19th ed. M.A. Krupp, N.J. Sweet, E. Jawetz, E.G. Biglieri, — 1979
R.L. Roe, and C.A. Camargo. 758 pp, *illus.*

Handbook of Pediatrics, 13th ed. H.K. Silver, C.H. Kempe, and H.B. Bruyn. 735 pp, *illus.* — 1980

Handbook of Poisoning: Prevention, Diagnosis, & Treatment, 10th ed. R.H. Dreisbach. — 1980
578 pp.

Table of Contents

PART IV. SYSTEMIC DRUGS

PART V. ENDOCRINE DRUGS

PART VI. AGENTS USED IN THE TREATMENT OF NUTRITIONAL & METABOLIC DERANGEMENTS

PART VII. CHEMOTHERAPEUTIC AGENTS

Preface

In preparing the seventh edition of this book, the authors have again attempted to emphasize those aspects of pharmacology that serve the clinical needs of the student and practitioner in medicine, dentistry, nursing, and pharmacy. As in previous editions, the discussion of certain theoretical and research aspects of pharmacology has been drastically limited in order to keep the size and cost of the book within reasonable limits.

Because learning how to think clearly about drugs is one of the student's most obvious and most difficult duties, one of the chief aims of this book is to foster a skeptical attitude toward all new drug claims. We hope the clinician will maintain a close working familiarity with the general and specialty sources of current information on new drugs listed on pp 3 and 30 of this text as well as the promotional literature supplied by the manufacturer. The physician should check with the pharmacist when necessary to determine what dosage forms and sizes are available locally.

We wish to express our thanks to all who have helped with the preparation and upkeep of this *Review* and particularly Drs. Mervin J. Goldman, Paul F. White, and Richard D. Mamelok. We appreciate hearing from our readers, and we welcome suggestions from students and others who may have ideas for making the book more accurate and useful. We are pleased to be able to say that this book has achieved a substantial readership out of the country in both the English language editions and in German, Italian, Japanese, Portuguese, and Spanish translations, with French and Chinese translations also in preparation.

The Authors

San Francisco
September, 1980

Part I. General Information

Introduction | 1

Pharmacology, for the purpose of this book, is considered to be the body of information that underlies the effective and safe use of drugs in the diagnosis, prevention, or treatment of disease. However, pharmacology includes many controversial areas, and opinion begins to diverge with the very definition of the field. From the point of view of the practicing physician and medical student rather than the research specialist, pharmacology is a derived or applied science. Understanding how drugs are used and progress in drug therapy require the application and development of special information from many areas, especially organic and analytical chemistry, biochemistry, physiology, and the various clinical specialties.

Many research- and laboratory-oriented pharmacologists prefer to regard pharmacology also as a basic science and view it as a valid field of investigation independent of its immediate applications. Their approach would emphasize some of the headings in the outline below and minimize others. The emphasis of this book reflects the teaching responsibility of pharmacologists toward students in the professions rather than the needs of research pharmacologists. It deliberately blurs any distinction between pharmacology and therapeutics.

The discussion of most of the groups of drugs in the following chapters of this book is organized according to the outline that begins below. However, several chapters on general pharmacologic or therapeutic subjects precede the chapters in which the drug groups are discussed. Whether these general discussions should be read before or after a store of specific pharmacologic information is acquired depends upon the individual student. The following brief review of the conventionalized outline of what a practitioner should consider before using a particular drug should allow study of the general chapters to be deferred if desired.

History

Information about the history of the development or introduction of a drug group to therapy is not essential to its proper use. The history, however, is usually interesting and often important in the formation of attitudes toward current problems. The brief history of pharmacology at the end of this chapter divides the subject somewhat arbitrarily into periods. The histori-

cal sketches that appear in some chapters are usually selected to illustrate one of the generalizations presented in the outline of the history.

Chemistry

Data on the structure and chemical properties of compounds used as drugs have different relevance to different workers and may be of greater or lesser interest to different workers. One interested in the synthesis of new drugs requires information of a different kind from what is needed by a person whose ultimate interest is biologic and practical.

A. Chemical and Pharmacologic Classification: A key problem or concept that will be repeatedly emphasized is that the many hundreds of available drugs can be classified into a reasonable number of drug groups and subgroups rather than as so many individual agents. The most important function of the information on chemical structure given in the tables or figures is to demonstrate the similarity of related drugs within a group and to suggest a basis for establishing subgroups when important differences are present. In a few cases, minor changes in chemical structure may lead to major changes in the nature or specificity of biologic effect. However, the proliferation of drugs within most groups is not necessarily due to the synthesis of significantly different compounds but is related to the marketing of compounds that are merely imitative of the prototype in the group or subgroup.

B. Structure-Action Relationships: A few drugs have been "designed" in the sense that chemical theory predicted a desired biologic effect. For example, most of the antimetabolites introduced since the sulfonamides are compounds whose pharmacologic effect and usefulness were predicted. However, the great majority of drugs now in use derive from prototypes that were natural products and from later synthetic counterparts whose chemistry was patterned after the natural product. Drugs whose discovery was purely accidental or stemmed from the empirical preparation and screening of a large number of compounds without a justifiable theoretic basis also contribute to currently used drugs. Much structure-action speculation is retrospective and is of limited practical importance. The application of structure-action theory to the problems of the mechanisms of drug action, on the other hand, represents one of the ultimate goals of pharmacologic thought. The tentative data available are discussed along with the relevant drugs.

Absorption, Distribution, Metabolism, & Excretion

These properties—(1) absorption from the gastrointestinal tract or injection site, (2) distribution of the drug intra- or extracellularly throughout the body, (3) metabolism or biotransformation of the drug, and (4) its excretion—are discussed together because there are several unifying chemical concepts. The lipid barrier model suggests that the barrier to distribution provided by cells or the cell wall will allow the transfer of lipid-soluble, nonpolar molecules preferentially to water-soluble substances. A more lipid-soluble substance would enter parenchymal cells, but its excretion would be slowed because it would also be well reabsorbed at the renal tubules. The metabolism or biotransformation of drugs by conjugation or chemical alteration converts them to more polar, more water-soluble metabolites that can be more rapidly excreted. The metabolites are usually inactive—ie, drug action is terminated by metabolism—in which case the details of the transformation are of limited practical importance except in following the rate of excretion. However, some metabolites are active or toxic. Some of the possible metabolic pathways are discussed in Chapter 2.

Pharmacologic Actions

A. Mechanisms of Action: Discussions of the mechanisms of action of a drug usually involve separate discussions at the physiologic and biochemical levels. For most drugs, it will be possible to make some statement about the mechanism of action at the level of the organ or functional system or tissue. The site of action, for example, may be localized to an organ such as the spinal cord or even to a functional system such as internuncial or polysynaptic pathways. In a number of cases, drug action can be explained by an action on chemical mediators liberated by the cell.

Below the organ or tissue level, at the biochemical or subcellular site of drug action, information is available in only a few cases. Some drugs are known to be inhibitors of specific enzymes; a few are metabolic antagonists; and several other biochemical mechanisms have been defined. For most drugs, however, the ultimate mechanism of action is unknown.

It is frequently said that an understanding of mechanism of action is a prerequisite to the rational use of drugs. Such understanding is certainly the goal. However, drugs used in the absence of such information will continue to act after the mechanism of action has been defined exactly as they have during the period of their empirical use.

B. Effects: The observed effects on as many organ systems and tissues as are influenced—ie, the descriptive pharmacology—is the crucial part of the discussion of each drug group, since it underlies and explains most of the therapeutic and toxic actions of the drug.

Clinical Uses

The possible therapeutic applications of a drug group cannot simply be listed. Not all of the suggested or even commonly accepted indications for the use of a drug are supported by convincing clinical studies. One cannot even assume that all of the marketed drugs are active. The problems of the clinical evaluation of drugs are discussed in a general way in Chapter 3. For the individual drug groups, the indications are listed, and some discussion of the methods of establishing usefulness and therapeutic effectiveness is given.

Adverse Reactions

The use of drugs is not without many dangers and discomforts. Before any drug or combination of drugs is used, the possible toxic effects must be considered, so that the physician can be prepared to treat toxic reactions and so that some judgment can be made about the possible benefits as compared with the possible toxic effects. A general discussion of the toxicity of therapeutic agents is presented in Chapter 6. In the discussion of each drug, adverse reactions are listed under one or more of the following categories:

A. Side-Effects: Under this category are discussed effects that are often unavoidable if adequate doses of the drug are given.

B. Overdosage Toxicity: Toxic effects of this type are dose-related—ie, their incidence increases as the dose level is increased.

C. Allergic Reactions: These reactions are not dose-related but depend upon the altered reactivity or hypersensitivity of the patient, usually induced by prior contact with the drug that has acted as an antigen.

D. Drug Abuse: A special form of toxicity is the use for nontherapeutic purposes of drugs that act on the central nervous system. The misuse of the individual drug is discussed in the relevant chapters (eg, alcohol; see Chapter 24), but the general problem of drug abuse and habituation is discussed in Chapter 7.

Contraindications & Cautions

For each drug, there are situations in which its use invites disaster. Most of the contraindications to the use of a drug are predictable from its effects and are easily remembered. Some are unexpected or easily overlooked. For each drug, therefore, a list of contraindications and cautions is presented. This checklist in a text or in the physician's mind should be reviewed before a drug is ordered for any patient.

Most contraindications are disease entities or altered physiologic states—eg, morphine is contraindicated in head injury. In other situations, the possible interaction of a drug with one previously administered dictates caution. Drug interactions are discussed at this point in each chapter, and a general discussion of the topic is presented in Chapter 6.

Preparations, Choice of Drug, & Dosage

In many chapters, all of the drugs in a group will be discussed as if there were no differences between them or as if the newer compounds did not differ from the prototype. In many cases, it does not matter which of a large number of similar compounds is selected for use. In most drug groups, however, there will be compounds or subgroups of compounds that are more efficacious for a particular purpose than others, and these will be discussed when such difference does exist. The importance of the general principles of the technic of drug administration discussed in Chapter 4 will be apparent to the practitioner. These principles should be reviewed by the student when the selection and ordering of drugs for patients becomes one of his or her responsibilities.

An especially confusing factor is the multiplicity of names involved. Each drug has a generic or public name—eg, penicillin G—but in addition may be given a protected or trademark name by one or by many different manufacturers or distributors.

The dosages included in this text are in most instances those that are generally accepted or those suggested by the manufacturer. In some cases, a more conservative position on dosage has been adopted. When drugs are known to cause frequent or dangerous toxic reactions; when establishment of a maintenance dose is difficult, when parenteral administration requires special precautions, or when the drug is unfamiliar to the prescriber, the manufacturer's package insert or other current FDA-monitored sources of information should be consulted before the drug is administered.

References

A. Chapter References: The references at the end of each chapter are chosen to guide the student to further reading in areas that are judged to be rapidly changing, controversial, or unfamiliar. The emphasis is on the clinical aspects of the drug group, and most of the references are chosen from a few of the most readily available journals. The best source of additional reading or references depends on the library facilities available and on whether the seeker's interest is primarily in the clinical or laboratory aspects of the subject.

B. General References: The following texts contain comprehensive discussions of specific drug groups and of the general problems of pharmacology:

Goldstein A, Aronow L, Kalman SM: *Principles of Drug Action,* 2nd ed. Wiley, 1974. [Highly recommended when rigorous theoretical approach is needed.]

Goodman LS, Gilman A (editors): *The Pharmacological Basis of Therapeutics,* 5th ed. Macmillan, 1975. [Comprehensive text.]

Sollman T: *A Manual of Pharmacology,* 8th ed. Saunders, 1957. [Useful for data on old and obscure drugs.]

Access to the current research aspects of pharmacology is often provided by one of the following annual or serial publications:

The *Annual Review of Pharmacology* catalogs the literature by subject area. Comprehensive, research-centered reviews may be located by searching

the indices of the following publications or their equivalents in specialized areas: *Pharmacological Reviews, Advances in Pharmacology and Chemotherapy, Progress in Drug Research,* and *Progress in Medicinal Chemistry.*

C. Clinical Evaluation: The clinical application and evaluation of drugs require the use of a literature distinct from the above. The journals of the several specialties and the better general medical journals are most useful, and the general problem is discussed in Chapter 3.

HISTORY OF PHARMACOLOGY

The discussion of some of the specific drug groups in the following chapters will begin with the history of their use or discovery. A survey of the history of drug therapy at this point serves as a way of outlining or organizing the entire subject. The data presented in subsequent chapters will illustrate the ideas outlined in this section.

Prescientific Period

The prototypes of many modern drug classes derive from natural products that have a long history of folk use. Scholars enjoy searching the records of the oldest cultures for references that can be interpreted as establishing the first use of a drug still used today. It is often assumed that our present more or less rational use of drugs and their natural progenitors in therapy grew out of the primitive experience. Actually, however, only a few folk remedies or contributions of the medicine of earlier cultures have been taken over directly. Most of the active natural products were used originally not as medicines but as magic tools, as arrow poisons in hunting or combat, as cosmetics, or even as a means of committing murder. The properties of opium have certainly been exploited for 3 millenniums, but the specific use of most natural products is based on the intervention of a relatively recent worker. In many cases, modern use could occur only when a sufficient nosologic basis had been developed—eg, only after fevers and dropsy were classified could cinchona bark and digitalis be used properly. Most of the drugs used in therapy prior to the modern period were abandoned along with bleeding and purging.

Therapy to 1800

The development of medicine and biology lagged far behind that of the other sciences. For medieval authoritarian systems, the physical sciences substituted observation, quantitative analysis, and the experimental method. Medicine actually regressed from Hippocratic empiricism and even late in the 18th century was scholastic and dependent on pure logic rather than observation. Many systems of medicine were developed, usually with a single pathologic process to explain all disease. These attempts to reach a system of Newtonian unity and comprehensiveness actually inhibited observation and therefore progress.

There are more than a few exceptions to the above generalization, and medicine did have its great individuals. Vesalius, Paré, and Paracelsus were physicians of the Renaissance who trusted their own observations and experience.

More important to the history of therapy are the 17th century Englishmen—eg, Harvey and especially Sydenham—whose empiricism presaged the British clinical school.

First Applications of Experimental Method

At the time of the French Revolution, then, medicine was barely into its descriptive period, only anatomy having reached any maturity. Even general biology was still structural and taxonomic. François Magendie (1783–1855), an instructor of anatomy in Paris, then introduced the experimental method to medicine and biology. He studied the absorption of strychnine in order to challenge some of the vitalistic teaching of the period. A Javanese arrow poison (nux vomica) was administered by various routes and the resulting convulsions and asphyxia described. After studying the action in animals with the cord sectioned or destroyed, Magendie and his collaborating medical student accurately concluded that the spinal cord was the site of action of the active component, which was subsequently isolated and named strychnine. They presented their work in 1809 to the Paris Academy.

Magendie studied many other drugs and physiologic problems. His students isolated a number of alkaloids, and he published a formulary based on only pure, single compounds. His demonstration of the value of the experimental approach was influential.

Not the least of Magendie's contributions was to hire and encourage Claude Bernard (1813–1878). Unlike Magendie, who resisted all generalizations and compared his function as data collector to that of a junkman, Bernard not only contributed to every area of physiology but reflected on the methods of "experimental medicine," as the undifferentiated field of physiology-pharmacology-biochemistry was then called.

Clinical Research

For the development of modern medicine, a revolution in clinical medicine to restore the primacy of observation was as necessary as the application of the experimental method, and it too took place in France. After the Revolution, when all sciences broke with tradition and a new intellectual life was encouraged, the medical schools of the old regime (together with all universities) were simply abolished and new schools established within a few large hospitals. Clinical observations, especially those arising from the new technics of physical diagnosis, were correlated with autopsy data. Progress in the study and classification of disease entities was extremely great during the period 1825–1850. Cabanis, Pinel, and Bichat were the

philosophic progenitors of the medical revolution, and Broussais should perhaps be called the founder of the Paris clinical school.

Progress in therapy was not equally rapid. Ineffective remedies had first to be eliminated. The resulting nihilistic attitude toward drugs and the emphasis on diagnosis have persisted. P.Ch.A. Louis (1787–1872), a successor to Broussais and Laennec, introduced his "numerical," or statistical, method of describing the natural history of disease and of evaluating therapy. His recognition of observer bias and other still current problems was especially influential in the USA through Oliver Wendell Holmes and others.

Germany & the Rise of the University

Not only were the French ideas immediately very influential in neighboring Germany, but, in response to the imperialism of Napoleon, the unification of Germany began during the period just described. Soon thereafter, the influence of the German university appeared, and by 1850 the Germans led the world in research. The German universities were provincial rather than national, and governmental support was increased because of interprovincial competitiveness. Students and faculty moved freely between schools, and the faculties were large enough so that time for research as well as teaching was available.

Experimental medicine differentiated into the separate basic sciences. In 1846, Rudolph Buchheim established the first laboratory for experimental pharmacology in Dorpat (Tartu), Estonia. His student, Oswald Schmiedeberg (1838–1921), together with the great physiologist Ludwig, became preeminent and trained many of the pioneers of modern pharmacology—whether German, American, British, or other.

American Pharmacology

It has not been many years since it was almost true that syphilis and general anesthesia were the only contributions of the New World to medicine. American medical education initially followed the British provincial pattern, which meant that most practitioners were trained by apprenticeship. However, as British medical training improved during the 19th century with the dominance of hospital schools, American training deteriorated as proprietary and sectarian (eg, homeopathic, chiropractic) undergraduate schools proliferated. Each state controlled licensing of its practitioners, and degrees of doubtful validity were accepted as licenses. A few superior or privileged men were trained at Edinburgh, Paris, and, later, in Germany, but little investigational medicine existed.

In the years just prior to 1890, the State Boards of Medicine began to move against the worst incompetents in medicine, and a few isolated universities began to respond to the social need. The first American pharmacologist, J.J. Abel, returned from his training in Germany to an appointment at the University of Michigan.

An important stimulus to scientific medicine in

the USA was provided by Johns Hopkins University. A graduate school more or less patterned after the German university was opened in 1876, and soon thereafter the hospital (1889) and a medical school (1893) were established. J.J. Abel moved from Michigan to Hopkins and trained most of the academic leaders in pharmacology for the next generation.

The reorganization of the American Medical Association in 1901 and the dramatization of the situation by the Flexner Report (1910) led to the disappearance of the proprietary schools and the emergence of the university-associated medical school. Clinical and laboratory research finally appeared in respectable amounts in the USA.

American pharmacology continued to lag in its development until after World War II, when unprecedented amounts of money were made available for research, first by voluntary agencies and then by the National Institutes of Health. Graduate programs made it possible for a student to enter pharmacology with a research degree rather than an MD, resulting in an increase in the numbers of pharmacologists but also in an alienation from medicine. Finally, the American drug industry expanded to match in size if not in originality its European counterpart.

•   •   •

References

Ackerknecht EH: *Medicine at the Paris Hospital, 1794–1848*. Johns Hopkins Univ Press, 1967.

Ackerknecht EH: Medical education in 19th century France. J Med Educ 32:148, 1957.

Flexner S, Flexner JT: *William Henry Welch and the Heroic Age of American Medicine*. Viking, 1941.

Leake CD: *An Historical Account of Pharmacology to the 20th Century*. Thomas, 1974.

Olmsted JMD: *François Magendie*. Schuman, 1944.

Olmsted JMD, Olmsted EH: *Claude Bernard and the Experimental Method in Medicine*. Collier Books, 1961.

Shryock RH: European backgrounds of American medical education. JAMA 194:709, 1965.

Shryock RH: *Medicine in America: Historical Essays*. Johns Hopkins Univ Press, 1966.

Silverman M: *Magic in a Bottle*. Macmillan, 1941.

2 | Drug Biodisposition & Interactions

The metabolism of each drug or drug group must be studied separately. However, the discussion of this aspect of drug information in subsequent chapters can be greatly shortened by a preliminary general consideration here, since the several processes that occur between the time of administration of the drug and the termination of its activity are closely related. The absorption, the distribution within the body, and the excretion of a drug are related processes, since they all depend upon the passage of the drug across a series of cellular membranes of similar properties. These plasma membranes or ''lipid barriers'' are more permeable to uncharged, lipid-soluble drugs than to ionized, water-soluble molecules. The biotransformation or metabolism of drugs is generally a process by which drugs are rendered more water-soluble, less subject to renal tubular reabsorption, and, therefore, more readily excreted.

In the qualitative, descriptive account presented here, it may seem that absorption, distribution, metabolism, and excretion are sequential processes. This is true only in retrospect after the drug has been excreted and its effect finally dissipated. At any given moment, a drug and a variety of metabolic products may be distributed in many compartments—eg, the drug in the lumen of the intestine, the drug and perhaps a conjugate within the cells of the intestinal mucosa, drug and metabolites in the plasma, etc—until excretion occurs in bladder urine, expired air, or feces. Each transfer or metabolic change occurs at its own rate and has its own equilibrium constant. As drugs are ordinarily given—ie, with the exception of a continuous intravenous infusion—a steady state is not achieved. The multiple and complex processes acting simultaneously and interdependently can be assessed by (1) quantitative determination of factors such as changes in plasma concentration with time and (2) kinetics of volume distribution, functional half-life clearance, metabolic alterations, etc of the drug.

DISTRIBUTION OF DRUGS WITHIN THE BODY

Unit Membrane or Plasma Membrane
The distribution of drugs within the body is hin-

dered by a series of membranes. Some of these membranes, like the skin or a mucosal surface, may be many cells thick; but the barrier to distribution resides in the cell membrane, and some generalities about transport across this membrane apply to many sites.

A. The Lipid-Sieve Model: The unit or plasma membrane surrounds or forms the boundary of all cells and surrounds the nucleus and organelles. Fig 2–1 presents a model of the lipoprotein membrane based on chemical analysis and electronmicroscopic and x-ray diffraction technics. Studies of the permeability of this membrane lead to the conclusion that it is a fluid mosaic with at least 3 functional components. The major component, for drugs if not for most physiologically important substances, is the lipid membrane that is permeable to lipid-soluble molecules and impermeable to polar, water-soluble substances. The membrane must in addition contain pores that permit the passage of small water-soluble molecules such as urea, alcohol, electrolytes, and water itself. Finally, the membrane contains channels through which substances can move after they have combined with a specific carrier.

B. Mechanisms of Transfer Across Membrane:

1. Passive transfer–Transfer or transport is said to be passive when the membrane need not generate energy to carry out the process.

a. Filtration, as across the capillary wall, is not

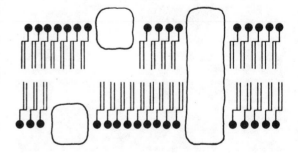

Figure 2–1. Hypothetical model of plasma membrane. The matrix of the membrane is a double layer of phospholipid molecules oriented with the polar heads in contact with intra- and extracellular water. Globular protein masses are embedded in the phospholipid bilayer with charged ionic residues projecting from the surface into water.

an important factor in limiting drug distribution.

b. Simple diffusion–If the rate of transfer across a membrane is proportionate to the concentration gradient, one infers that the process is one of simple diffusion. A water-soluble drug of low molecular weight such as alcohol may diffuse through the aqueous pores of the membrane. Water-soluble drugs of greater molecular weight either do not cross the membrane or are transported by an active process. Transfer by simple diffusion is then an important process for the distribution of lipid-soluble drugs. Many drugs—eg, ether or digitoxin—have a lipid solubility or oil-water partition coefficient that favors their transfer regardless of the pH of the medium. However, many drugs are either weak acids or weak bases, and the fraction of molecules present as the lipid-soluble un-ionized form to which the cell is preferentially permeable varies depending on the drug's pKa and the pH of the system. The pH within cells or of extracellular fluid cannot, of course, vary greatly. In order for a substance that is not actively transported to act intracellularly, it must either be lipid-soluble at all pHs or, if it is an amine or weak base, it must be largely in the un-ionized form at the pH of the body. It is possible, however, to alter the absorption or excretion of drugs by varying the pH of the gastric contents or the renal tubular urine.

c. Carrier-facilitated diffusion–In this process, the substance to be transported combines with a carrier molecule at one membrane surface and dissociates from it at the other surface. The carrier, a protein, is specific for the transported ion or larger water-soluble molecule that would not otherwise traverse the membrane. The process is still one of diffusion, and a substance cannot be moved against a concentration gradient. Exchange diffusion is a common variation of carrier-facilitated diffusion in which the carrier combines with one substance at the outer surface to transport it inward and, having dissociated from the first substance, picks up a generally similar molecule at the inner surface and carries it to the outside.

2. Active transport–Active transport is carrier-facilitated but is able to move the substance against a chemical or electrical gradient. Performance of such work or active transport requires energy which is known, in the common examples, to be generated by the action of membrane ATPase. There are a variety of channels or pumps of this type. Each transports a specific chemical type—eg, sodium, organic acids—and related compounds compete for the capacity of the mechanism. Interference with the supply of energy inhibits the system noncompetitively.

Absorption

A. From the Gastrointestinal Tract: This discussion applies to the absorption of drugs after oral administration.

Small, neutral water-soluble molecules—eg, alcohol and water itself—are absorbed from the stomach, although the amount absorbed is limited by its rapid emptying time. The absorption of other drugs will vary depending on the pH, which is a function of the secretory state of the stomach. Aspirin, the most commonly used drug, is a weak acid that exists almost entirely in the non-ionized lipid-soluble form at the pH of the secreting stomach and is well absorbed from the stomach (Fig 2–2). Giving aspirin with a base or with food in order to reduce gastric irritation would increase the fraction present as the salt or water-soluble form

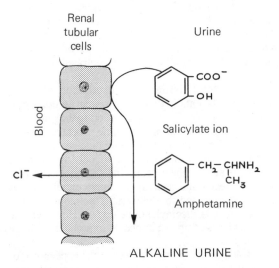

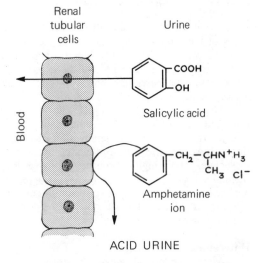

Figure 2–2. The influence of the pH of the medium on the diffusion of aspirin (acetylsalicylate) and amphetamine across a cellular barrier illustrated with a diagram of the renal tubule. The excretion of salicylic acid, a metabolite of aspirin, is increased if the renal tubular fluid is alkaline because it then exists as the ionized, less lipid-soluble salt form. The excretion of amphetamine, a weak base, is increased in an acid urine because it then is present as the salt rather than the lipid-soluble free base.

and slow its absorption to the rate normally observed in the small intestine.

The intracellular and luminal pH influences movement in both directions. Thus, weak bases given by parenteral injection can appear in the gastric contents via a reverse ion-trapping mechanism.

In the alkaline medium of the small intestine, those drugs that are weak bases exist as the free base and are well absorbed.

B. From the Urinary Tract: The pH of the urine is determined by the acid-base status of the patient, and alterations affect the ionization of drugs in a manner analogous to what takes place in the stomach. Examples of a weak acid (salicylic acid) and a weak base (amphetamine) are shown in Fig 2–2.

C. From Injection Sites: The rate of absorption from a subcutaneous or intramuscular injection site is related to the water solubility of the injected substance as well as the local blood flow. The rate of absorption can be slowed and the duration of action of a water-soluble drug prolonged by injecting it as an insoluble complex—eg, procaine penicillin or protamine zinc insulin.

D. From the Skin: The keratinized layer of the skin is a much less permeable barrier than the ordinary cell membrane, and the skin conforms to the lipid barrier model only if the keratinized layer is removed. Absorption of drugs after application to the skin or even penetration for a local effect is difficult to achieve and is discussed separately in Chapter 5. On the other hand, many drugs are well absorbed from the non-keratinized epithelium of the mucous membranes of the mouth or pharynx.

Transport Within the Vascular Compartment

Drugs readily leave the vascular compartment to enter the interstitial fluid. Lipid-soluble drugs pass across the entire membranous surface, but even large, water-soluble molecules are filtered through the large pores of the capillary membrane with the aid of hydrostatic pressure. Thus, distribution of a drug to a particular region of the body will be determined by blood flow to that part rather than by the rate of transfer across the capillary membrane.

Many drugs combine loosely with plasma albumin, and such protein binding reduces the amount of freely diffusible drug and thereby slows its distribution. However, the drug-protein complex rapidly dissociates, and a high concentration of free drugs is maintained. A few clinically important applications are known—eg, the ability of sulfonamides to displace bilirubin from the binding sites on plasma protein and intensify jaundice in the newborn.

Differential Distribution

A. To the Central Nervous System: The factors that determine whether or not a drug can reach and act on an intracellular site are similar throughout the body. The central nervous system is unusual in that drugs can reach extracellular sites only after passing through glial cells.

Capillaries in the central nervous system ("within the blood-brain barrier") cannot filter plasma into the interstitial space, because interstitial space is very limited in extent and the supporting glial cells are closely opposed to the capillary wall. Drugs that act on peripheral nerve tissue, presumably at an extracellular site, may not reach parenchymal central nervous system cells if the drugs are in a charged, lipid-insoluble form because of the so-called blood-brain barrier. Quaternary ammonium derivatives such as curare or acetylcholine, for example, exist entirely in the salt form at body pH and, after intravenous injection, do not act on the central nervous system however great their effect on peripheral nerve. They act on brain and spinal cord only if applied directly.

B. To Other Special Sites:

1. To lipid depots and other storage sites— Drugs with high intrinsic lipid solubility and low water solubility may accumulate in high concentration in the adipose tissues of the body—eg, thiopental or the chlorinated hydrocarbon type of insecticide. (The accumulation of thiopental in fat is discussed again below as an example of redistribution as a mechanism of terminating drug action.)

Some other examples of selective accumulation depend upon factors other than blood: tissue compartment coefficients. Colloidal and particulate drugs are taken up by the cells of the reticuloendothelial system; heavy metals concentrate in bone. Physiologically important substances may also accumulate by mechanisms unrelated to solubility—eg, cobalamin (vitamin B_{12}) in the liver or norepinephrine in the specific granules of adrenergic nerve. The concentration of the antimalarial drug quinacrine in parenchymal tissues is several thousand times that in plasma.

2. To sites of metabolism or excretion—The drug and its more water-soluble metabolites will accumulate at the sites of metabolism and excretion: in the liver if that is the site of biotransformation; in the intestinal contents if secretion is into the bile; or in the kidney if the metabolites are concentrated in tubular urine.

3. To fetal tissues—The distribution of drugs across the placenta is dependent primarily upon passive diffusion. The fetal tissues covering the villi are in contact with maternal blood. Some substances move back and forth across this membrane as if it were conforming to the lipid barrier model. The general anesthetic agents, the narcotic analgesics, and the barbiturates reach and depress the fetal central nervous system as expected, but quaternary ammonium compounds such as succinylcholine do not. However, the fetal barrier is at times permeable to particles as large as red cells.

4. To milk—In animal studies, the appearance of drugs in milk appears to be predictable by reference to the lipid barrier model. Since milk is slightly more acidic than plasma, basic compounds may be concentrated in milk. Small neutral molecules (alcohol) appear in milk in the same concentration as in plasma. Acidic drugs such as penicillin appear in milk (pH 6.6) in concentrations less than in plasma, and bases (erythromycin) are more concentrated in milk.

Verified reports of toxic reactions in nursing infants due to drugs ingested by the mother are few. Drugs that have bad demonstrable effects include the nicotine in cigarettes, bromides, cascara and purified anthraquinones, antithyroid drugs, and phenindione (but not the other anticoagulants). Heroin—but not morphine or codeine—is said to act on the infant. Many drugs—eg, radioactive agents and antimetabolites—are almost certainly dangerous.

TERMINATION
OF DRUG ACTION

The processes that terminate drug action determine the duration of effect of a drug. If they are altered by disease or concurrent administration of other drugs, the intensity and duration of drug effect may be altered.

ELIMINATION OF UNCHANGED DRUG
OR METABOLITE

Elimination by the Lungs

The gases and volatile liquids used as general anesthetics are absorbed and excreted across the pulmonary alveolar membrane. Many other volatile drugs—eg, alcohol or paraldehyde—appear in the expired air but have other more important routes of excretion or metabolism. However, the content of alcohol and certain industrial solvents in alveolar air reflects plasma levels in a consistent way and can be used to quantify the degree of intoxication.

Elimination by the Kidneys

Drugs and their metabolites or conjugates appear in the urine as a result of 2 processes: (1) They appear in the glomerular filtrate, and (2) an additional fraction is then secreted or reabsorbed through the renal tubular cell. The reabsorptive process is also an example of passive diffusion. The more lipid-soluble the material, the greater the degree of reabsorption. The more water-soluble the material, the greater the fraction that remains in the urine. The excretion of the unmetabolized, lipid-soluble drug can be altered by acidification or alkalinization of the urine. (Fig 2–2.) For example, intoxication with salicylates or barbiturates (both weak acids) is treated by maintaining a high volume of alkaline urine. The weak acids then exist largely in the salt form or the ionized, water-soluble form, and reabsorption is greatly decreased.

The renal tubule is also able to actively transport or secrete organic anions and cations through separate channels.

Other Routes of Elimination

Drug and drug conjugate may appear in the feces subsequent to excretion in the bile or secretion by the colon. Specific drugs may also appear in saliva or sweat in significant amounts.

TERMINATION OF DRUG ACTION BY
PROCESSES NOT INVOLVING
ELIMINATION OF DRUG

The action of a drug may terminate even though a major portion of the drug is still present in the body. Conversely, if the change caused by the drug requires a long period for compensation, the effect may persist long after the drug has been eliminated from the body.

Redistribution

The differential distribution of a drug (see above) may be a mechanism for terminating its activity. For example, when the anesthetic thiopental is injected intravenously, a high plasma level is immediately achieved. The subsequent distribution of thiopental depends upon its high lipid solubility and the blood flow to the various tissues. An effective amount of thiopental is immediately carried to the central nervous system and other vessel-rich tissues. However, over the subsequent 10–120 minutes, the less well perfused tissues, eg, muscle and adipose tissue, take up enough thiopental to bring about its withdrawal from the central nervous system and the termination of its anesthetic action. In somewhat the same manner, the action of injected epinephrine or norepinephrine is terminated mostly because the amine enters sympathetic nerve and can no longer act on smooth muscle.

Repair of Drug-Induced Changes

Some drugs that disappear from the body after a few hours cause changes that may take many days for correction. For example, after prothrombin synthesis is inhibited by a coumarin anticoagulant, the effect persists until new protein is synthesized.

Antagonism

The effect of a drug may be terminated by giving its competitive or physiologic antagonist—eg, the sedative and analgesic effects of morphine can be antagonized by nalorphine, while the physiologic effect of histamine can be partially antagonized by epinephrine.

Physiologic Compensations

Some adaptations or compensations by the organism may decrease or completely abolish the effects of a drug. Other compensations may modify only certain prominent responses such as pulse rate or blood pressure but give the impression of a decreased overall response to the drug.

The familiar compensatory reflexes originating from a change in pressure within the carotid baroreceptor areas are activated whenever a pressor or depressor drug is given. These reflexes may not modify a drug-induced rise in pressure but can cause a reflex bradycardia that obscures the drug's primary effect. Vasoconstrictor drugs (norepinephrine, ephedrine, angiotensin) can reduce cardiac output by increasing the amount of work needed to move the same volume of blood. A long-acting vasoconstrictor such as ephedrine may limit cardiac output enough to limit the rise in blood pressure that it causes. Such a state of reduced response of the blood pressure when the vasoconstricting and other actions are maximal is called tachyphylaxis.

Limited tolerance to the effects of other drugs arises from other compensatory mechanisms. Administration of the potent antihypertensive agents—eg, guanethidine, hydralazine, or methyldopa—results in an expanded plasma volume, and the dose of the drug may have to be increased to maintain the effect unless other supplemental drugs are used.

Tolerance of a qualitatively different kind follows the administration of organic nitrates or the narcotic analgesics. In this case, larger and larger doses must be given to maintain the effect, and tolerance can be made absolute—ie, many previously lethal doses can be given without danger or even much effect.

BIOTRANSFORMATION; ENZYMATIC ALTERATION

Many pharmacologists feel that it is impossible to overemphasize the importance of drug metabolism; others feel that this has already been achieved. In a few cases—eg, the study of cholinesterase or of monoamine metabolism—important information about the mechanism of drug actions and drug interactions has developed. Usually, however, the action of enzymes on drugs, unlike the study of the action of drugs on enzymes, does not often provide information about the mechanism of action of drugs. The process of biotransformation usually reduces or destroys the activity of the drug and hastens its excretion (reduces renal tubular reabsorption) by converting it to a more water-soluble form. More often than not, the process will consist of conjugation or of hydroxylation followed by conjugation. The process of biotransformation of drugs is often called detoxification.

Biotransformation can modify the effects of the drug administered in several ways:

(1) By forming an inactive metabolite from an active drug: This is the most common mechanism of drug inactivation. The metabolite may itself be further transformed and a mixture of metabolites and conjugates excreted, or the fragments may be lost in the metabolic pool.

(2) By forming an active metabolite from an initially inactive drug: For example, the cholinesterase inhibitor parathion must have a sulfur atom replaced by an oxygen atom before it is active; and the antimalarial chlorguanide and the alpha-adrenergic blocking agent phenoxybenzamine must cyclize before they can become active. (See Fig 11–1 for the reaction that converts phenoxybenzamine to a cyclic compound.)

(3) By forming an active metabolite from an initially active drug: Enzymatic transformation of a drug does not always terminate its action—eg, heroin is converted to morphine, and phenacetin is metabolized to an equally potent analgesic, acetaminophen (Fig 27–2).

(4) By forming a toxic metabolite from an initially less toxic drug: An example is isoniazid, which is acetylated to produce an intermediate compound that is the likely cause of hepatic necrosis, particularly in those in whom acetylation is rapid. The metabolism of phenacetin yields small quantities of ethoxyaniline, which is capable of converting hemoglobin to methemoglobin and occasionally produces methemoglobinemia of clinical importance.

CLASSES & EXAMPLES OF METABOLIC REACTIONS

The metabolism of specific drugs will be discussed in subsequent chapters. In the following paragraphs, the general classes of metabolic reactions will be described briefly and some of the many specific reactions will be cited as examples. Because the conjugation reactions apply to so many drug groups and because the oxidative enzymes of liver microsomes are important in drug interactions, they should be especially noted.

Conjugation Reactions

The conjugation reactions (also often called syntheses or transfer reactions) will be discussed first to emphasize their dual function. They can modify not only the original drug but also common metabolites formed by the reactions listed below. In the latter case, the polarization or increase in water solubility begun by one reaction is intensified by conjugation.

A. Glucuronide Formation: Each of the conjugation or synthetic reactions can be represented by the following reaction:

$$Ab + CD \xrightarrow{\text{Transferase}} AC + bD$$

where Ab is a drug or drug metabolite with functional group b, and C is the donor molecule activated by combination with D (UDP in the case of glucuronic acid). For example,

Salicylic acid + Uridine diphospho-glucuronic acid	UDP – Glucuronyl transferase →	Glucuronic acid conjugate of salicylic acid + UDP

If the activated glucuronic acid (UDPGA) reacts with a phenolic or alcoholic hydroxyl group, the resulting conjugate is an ether glucuronide; carboxylic acids react to form ester glucuronides.

Ether glucuronide
of salicylic acid

Ester glucuronide
of salicylic acid

B. Sulfate Formation: Phenols, alcohols, and aromatic amines can be converted to sulfates or sulfanilic acid derivatives. Active sulfate is provided by adenosine-3-phosphate-5-phosphosulfate (PAPS).

Sulfate of phenol

C. O-Methylation: A methyl group from S-adenosylmethionine converts a phenolic or alcoholic hydroxyl group to a methoxy group. This reaction is shown in Fig 10–5, since O-methylation is the most important enzymatic step in the biotransformation of epinephrine and norepinephrine, the chemical mediators released by the sympatho-adrenal system. The reaction is also important in relation to the pharmacologic actions of corticosteroids.

D. N-Methylation: A methyl group from activated methionine (S-adenosylmethionine) replaces a hydrogen on an amine function or is added to the nitrogen to convert the parent drug to a quaternary amine. The N-methylation of histamine is shown in Fig 19–1.

E. N-Acetylation: The acetyl moiety from acetylcoenzyme A replaces a hydrogen on an amine or amide group under the influence of various acetyl or acyl transferases. Histamine (Fig 19–1) and the sulfonamides are important examples of drugs that may be acetylated.

F. Other Conjugation Reactions: Glycine and glutamine (and, rarely, serine and lysine) may conjugate with acids. A few toxins may form mercapturic acid derivatives.

Oxidation by Liver Microsomal System

The enzymes in the liver microsomes govern a large number of reactions important in drug metabolism. Furthermore, the activity of the drug-inactivating enzymes is increased during the administration of many long-acting, lipid-soluble drugs. Administration of a drug may therefore increase its own rate of metabolism or decrease the effect of another concurrently administered drug by hastening its oxidation.

The enzymes are contained in the smooth endoplasmic reticulum of liver cells. Rough endoplasmic reticulum—ie, that with ribosomes on its surface—is not involved. Smooth endoplasmic reticulum increases in amount as enzyme activity is induced.

Microsomal enzymes convert lipid-soluble substances to more easily excreted and less active water-soluble metabolites. The first step in the process, prior to conjugation, is usually hydroxylation. Hydroxylation or oxidation of aromatic rings or alkyl side chains occurs at a cytochrome (designated P450 on the basis of its absorption characteristics) where atmospheric oxygen is activated by NADPH and the drug is oxidized by active oxygen. In other words, these enzymes—unlike the dehydrogenases of intermediary metabolism—require NADPH and oxygen. There is little substrate specificity beyond the requirement that the foreign substance be lipid-soluble.

Enzyme induction—or the increase in activity following chronic administration of, for example, phenobarbital or phenytoin, or exposure to DDT—depends upon the synthesis of new enzyme.

A variety of reactions are governed by hepatic enzymes, but all can be considered as hydroxylation of the substrate or the direct incorporation of oxygen into the substrate molecule. The reactions in this group include the following:

(1) Hydroxylation of aromatic rings.

(2) Oxidation (hydroxylation) of alkyl side chains.

(3) N- and O-dealkylation.

(4) Oxidative deamination: The microsomal enzyme should not be confused with mitochondrial MAO (monoamine oxidase), which is the important enzyme in the transformation of the physiologically important amines—eg, epinephrine, norepinephrine, tyramine, serotonin, and histamine. Microsomal MAO acts on amphetamine, ephedrine, and other phenylisopropylamines only if their excretion is slowed.

(5) Sulfoxidation: Oxygen may be added to sulfur in a ring structure such as that in chlorpromazine.

In addition to the oxidative reactions, liver microsomes catalyze other reactions—eg, hydrolysis of esters and amides, glucuronide conjugation, and reduction of nitro groups. The activity of these microsomal enzymes can also be modified by the prior or simultaneous administration of other drugs.

Other Oxidations

Other oxidative enzymes are important in the metabolism of relatively few and specific pharmacologic compounds. Detailed reactions are shown in the relevant chapters. These reactions include the following:

(1) Alcohol dehydrogenase of mammalian liver converts ethanol and other simple alcohols to the corresponding aldehydes (see Chapter 24).

(2) Aldehyde dehydrogenase converts simple aldehydes, eg, acetaldehyde derived from the oxidation of ethanol, to the corresponding acids. Disulfiram (Antabuse) inhibits this enzyme, and acetaldehyde toxicity results when alcohol is ingested by patients receiving disulfiram.

(3) Xanthine oxidase governs the final steps in the synthesis of uric acid. Inhibitors of xanthine oxidase (eg, allopurinol) are discussed in Chapter 40.

(4) Monoamine oxidase of mitochondria converts simple monoamines to their corresponding aldehydes, which are then further oxidized to acid or reduced to alcohol (Fig 10–6).

(5) Diamine oxidase is also a mitochondrial flavoprotein but will oxidatively deaminate only compounds with 2 amine functions relatively close together, eg, histamine. (Fig 19–1).

Hydrolysis

Many physiologically important enzymes are hydrolytic—eg, proteases, peptidases, or phosphatases. Acetylcholinesterases that inactivate an important neurohumor—acetylcholine—have also been well studied (see Chapter 8). There are, in addition, microsomal esterases and others that have been less well characterized. Esters such as procaine and meperidine are examples of drugs whose activity is terminated by hydrolysis to an alcohol and acid. Amides—eg, procainamide and lidocaine—are hydrolyzed at a much lower rate. The inactivation of penicillin G depends upon the hydrolytic opening of the lactam ring.

Hydrogenation (Reduction)

This mechanism is not commonly encountered in studies of drug metabolism. Nitrobenzene derivatives—eg, chloramphenicol—may in part be reduced to the amine.

DRUG INTERACTIONS

Drugs administered simultaneously or sequentially may simply act independently of each other or may interact to augment or diminish the expected response or to cause unanticipated toxicity. Adverse reactions are directly proportionate to the number of drugs given and the duration of administration. Epidemiologic studies have demonstrated that the rate of adverse drug reactions increases from 4% when fewer than 5 drugs are administered to over 45% when 20 or more are prescribed. (The average in-patient receives 6 drugs daily.) Obviously, the possibility of drug interactions should be considered before the drugs are ordered rather than after therapeutic failure has occurred or dangerous toxic effects have been precipitated.

The stereotyped outline followed in discussing each drug group in the following chapters contains a section on "Contraindications and Cautions." This outline (see Chapter 1) represents a kind of checklist that the prescriber should review before ordering a drug. The best way of anticipating drug reactions is to consciously review all of the drugs being administered before adding another. It probably follows that drug interactions are best discussed and learned as each drug group is studied.

However, it has recently become advisable in the opinion of many to discuss drug interactions as a general problem separate from the properties of the individual drugs. This attitude has probably developed because 2 factors have led to an increase in the number and severity of drug reactions: (1) more different and more potent drugs are in use each year, and (2) physician attitudes are such that drug use is not carefully monitored. The current enthusiasm has perhaps overemphasized a few reactions of more theoretical than real importance. Nevertheless, the problem is real, and the following cautions will help prevent dangerous interactions:

(1) Be aware of the general reactions outlined below in this chapter, and either know or review the cautions that apply to each drug or drug group before prescribing it.

(2) Make certain that the history elicits a record of all drugs being taken, including those from other doctors, nonprescription drugs, and medications for chronic disease taken so regularly that the patient finds them unnecessary to mention. Office patients may receive prescriptions from more than one physician and have them filled at several pharmacies.

(3) Keep careful records and tabulate drugs in use separately from the running record. In hospital patients especially, the number of drugs ordered may build up surprisingly.

(4) The response to the initiation of drug treatment or a change in treatment should be followed with at least as much interest as the steps in the diagnostic process. Physicians rarely administer the drugs, and days or weeks may elapse before a response is

evaluated. Especially in the case of those drugs whose dosage must be carefully titrated to individual need, a change in patient status, including the addition of a new drug to the regimen, may require a rapid change in medication to avoid problems.

A few categories of drug interactions (with examples) are presented in the following paragraphs. An interaction may be the result of (1) direct physical or chemical interactions; (2) altered absorption from the gastrointestinal tract; (3) competition for protein-binding sites or receptors; (4) alterations in drug metabolism via induction, activation, or inhibition of drug-metabolizing enzymes; (5) alterations in acid-base equilibrium; and (6) hemodynamic changes that influence drug distribution and excretion.

Additive or Antagonistic Pharmacologic Effects

By far the most common type of drug interaction in which the magnitude of the change reaches clinically significant levels is that due to simple addition or antagonism of pharmacologic effects. The unwitting administration of 2 sedatives—eg, alcohol and a barbiturate—or any combination of central nervous system depressants can produce depression of an unexpected and dangerous degree. An example of specific antagonism would include the interaction between naloxone and various narcotic analgesics.

Interference With Absorption

If certain drugs are given orally without an adequate interval between their administration, they may react chemically or physically to decrease the absorption and, therefore, the bioavailability of one or both drugs. The combination of 2 drugs present in the same segment of the gastrointestinal tract at one time is the equivalent of incompatibilities that occur in the prescription bottle or infusion flask.

Representative examples (all of which are discussed again in the appropriate chapters) include the following: Cholestyramine (Cuemid, Questran) is an exchange resin that combines with bile salts in the intestinal lumen and prevents their reabsorption. Many drugs taken within 1 or 2 hours of cholestyramine are also rendered less soluble and less absorbable. The tetracyclines will chelate divalent cations (magnesium, calcium) present in antacids or milk and be less well absorbed themselves. Conversely, the chelating properties of the tetracyclines may interfere with the therapeutic effect of orally administered iron or calcium.

Drugs may react in the intestine with ingested foodstuffs. An example is the inhibition of folate deconjugase by phenytoin, primidone, methobarbital, and the oral contraceptives. Thus, the absorbable folic acid monoglutamate is not released from polyglutamates, and folate deficiency results.

Displacement From Binding Sites

Many drugs are reversibly bound to plasma protein during transport, and chemically related drugs may compete for the same binding sites on albumin. Many acids (eg, phenylbutazone, indomethacin, and sulfonamides) are capable of displacing the anticoagulant warfarin from its binding sites and increasing plasma levels and, subsequently, its anticoagulant effect. The total amount of anticoagulant delivered to the site of action in the liver, however, is not increased over a longer period.

Chemical Combination

In a few cases, 2 agents may combine in plasma or extracellular fluid, but this reaction has provided more antidotes than examples of interaction between therapeutic agents—eg, heparin neutralized by protamine, lead or calcium by edetate, copper or lead by penicillamine.

Augmentation of Drug Metabolism

Hepatic microsomal oxidases (see above) govern the hydroxylation reactions that are commonly the initial steps in the metabolism of drugs. A wide variety of lipid-soluble drugs and toxins can increase the enzymic activity following chronic exposure. Such enzyme induction is accompanied by an increase in the amount of smooth endoplasmic reticulum in the hepatocyte, representing the synthesis of new enzyme protein.

Administration of many drugs metabolized at the liver microsomes can therefore accelerate their own metabolism and the metabolism of other drugs similarly metabolized. Thus, the same dosage of a coumarin anticoagulant or of phenobarbital will give lower plasma levels and a lesser biologic effect if it is given to a subject after pretreatment with enzyme inducers, eg, phenobarbital, glutethimide (Doriden), meprobamate, phenytoin, phenylbutazone, griseofulvin, or 3,4-benzypyrene.

The clinical applications of enzyme induction are fewer than predicted by laboratory studies. The effect is dose-related, and a high concentration must be maintained in the liver for a certain time. The reaction in humans is variable and not often clinically significant. The drugs listed above—especially phenobarbital and phenytoin—can alter the rate of metabolism of each other and of the coumarin anticoagulants. These anticoagulants may be used for extended periods, and their dosages must be carefully adjusted to prevent hemorrhage. Addition or deletion of one of the above drugs may alter the dose of coumarin anticoagulant required.

Inhibition of Drug Metabolism

Some drugs—eg, cholinesterase inhibitors, MAO inhibitors, and xanthine oxidase inhibitors (allopurinol)—act by inhibiting the enzyme responsible for the metabolism of some endogenous substance. When a drug or toxin related to the substance is administered, the exogenous compound may not be destroyed and may cause an intense reaction. For example, after MAO (monoamine oxidase) inhibitors are given, the effects of a great variety of drugs are intensified. Tyramine, a constituent of certain fermented cheeses and wine, is ordinarily oxidatively deaminated with great rapidity; however, in the presence of an MAO inhibitor, it becomes a long-acting pressor drug.

A more common example is the toxicity following alcohol ingestion in patients taking disulfiram (Antabuse) and other drugs that inhibit alcohol dehydrogenase (eg, metronidazole, nitrofurans).

Interaction at Receptors

To summarize drug interactions of this type would require repetition of much of the material from each subsequent chapter. Most often the relation is between pairs of agonists and antagonists. Sometimes, however, it is less easily anticipated. For example, the effect of guanethidine is antagonized by other compounds that block norepinephrine reuptake, including the antipsychotics and antidepressants, certain antihistamines (eg, phenylpropanolamine in over-the-counter cold remedies), and even cocaine.

Inhibition or Facilitation of Excretion

One drug may alter the excretion of another. A number of acidic drugs or metabolites share the same mechanisms of secretion and reabsorption in the renal tubule. Thus, probenecid may prolong the action of penicillin by blocking its excretion or decrease the level of uric acid by blocking its reabsorption.

• • •

References

Adverse interaction of drugs. Med Lett Drugs Ther 19:5, 1977.

Bennett WM: Principles of drug therapy in patients with renal disease. West J Med 123:372, 1975.

Blaschke TF: Protein binding and kinetics of drugs in liver diseases. Clin Pharmakokinet 2:32, 1977.

Gelehrter TD: Enzyme induction. (3 parts.) N Engl J Med 294:522, 589, 646, 1976.

Greenblatt DJ, Koch-Weser J: Clinical pharmacokinetics. (2 parts.) N Engl J Med 293:702, 964, 1975.

Hansten PD: *Drug Interactions,* 2nd ed. Lea & Febiger, 1973.

Hug CC Jr: Pharmacokinetics of drugs administered intravenously. Anesth Analg (Cleve) 57:704, 1978.

Koch-Weser J: Bioavailability of drugs. (2 parts.) N Engl J Med 291; 233, 503, 1974.

Koch-Weser J, Sellers EM: Drug interactions with coumarin anticoagulants. (2 parts.) N Engl J Med 285:487, 547, 1971.

LaDu BN, Mandel HG, Way EL: *Fundamentals of Drug Metabolism and Disposition.* Williams & Wilkins, 1971.

Piafsky KM & others: Theophylline disposition in patients with hepatic cirrhosis. N Engl J Med 296:1495, 1977.

Rubin AL, Stenzel KH, Reidenberg MM (editors): Symposium on drug action and metabolism in renal failure. Am J Med 62:459, 1977.

Schanker LS: Passage of drugs across body membranes. Pharmacol Rev 14:501, 1962.

Shand DG: Drug disposition in liver disease. N Engl J Med 296:1527, 1977.

Singer SJ, Nicolson GL: The fluid mosaic model of the structure of cell membranes. Science 175:720, 1972.

Smith JW & others: Studies on the epidemiology of adverse drug reactions. Ann Intern Med 65:629, 1966.

Stowe CM: Extrarenal excretion of drugs and chemicals. Annu Rev Pharmacol 8:337, 1968.

Wilkinson GR, Schenker S: The effect of liver disease on drug disposition in man. Biochem Pharmacol 25:2675, 1976.

Williams RT: Detoxication mechanisms in man. Clin Pharmacol Ther 4:234, 1963.

Over the centuries, many ineffective treatments have been confidently prescribed, with results that were satisfactory as judged by patient responses. Bleeding and purging were abandoned in spite of predictions of disaster by many physicians, just as present-day efforts to remove ineffective drugs from the market are protested by physicians convinced of the usefulness of even demonstrably inactive substances. The clear lesson is that symptomatic improvement or even cure of disease following the administration of a drug is not evidence that the drug played any role in the clinical result. The evaluation of any therapeutic experience must take into account the variable course of the disease, patient responsiveness even to inactive medication, and possible inadequacies (including bias) of the observer. The principles of clinical drug evaluation apply not only to all areas of medical treatment but to nondrug therapy as well.

The practitioner, responsible for patient care rather than therapeutic research, is rarely able to make adequate measurements and comparisons of drug effects but must depend to a large extent upon the research of other physicians. However, the clinical evaluation of drugs is one activity in medicine that has been dealt with in less than an optimal manner, a fact recognized by recent legislation as well as by current thinking within medicine. In this chapter, the origin of the problems surrounding the evaluation of therapy will be examined; some practical steps in the preliminary evaluation of the large number of available drugs and preparations will be suggested; and, most importantly, the characteristics of an acceptable clinical evaluation of drug efficacy will be outlined.

Origin of the Problems Related to Drug Evaluation

A. Great Progress in Drug Therapy: The remarkable progress in drug therapy during the past 30–40 years has posed a real problem in the evaluation of drugs for both the practitioner and the student. The revolutionary changes in medical practice that have occurred since World War II are largely the result of a revolution in drug therapy. A great many potent and effective therapeutic agents have become available to modern practitioners during their years of practice — ie, subsequent to their formal medical training. The current leaders in medical practice and medical education have observed since medical school the development of most of the new antibacterial and antileukemic agents, antihypertensive drugs, antihistamines, oral antidiabetic agents, the anti-inflammatory steroids, the phenothiazine tranquilizers, and other important groups of drugs.

B. Influence of the Diagnostic Orientation of Medicine: The failure to collect and present all of the data needed to evaluate old and new agents is in part due to the traditional diagnostic orientation of medicine carried over from the period of therapeutic nihilism. The elaborate and sophisticated scientific approaches that are applied to diagnostic and physiologic problems in medicine have not been employed in the evaluation of treatment methods. This is a problem not only with drug therapy but with other types of therapy as well. For example, after many years of experience, we are still unable to compare the effectiveness of the several possible treatments for carcinoma of the breast, and the direct relationship between the amount of surgical care provided and the amount available also suggests that some other practices need validation.

C. Economic Factors: The unavoidable problem created by progress in drug therapy is intensified by unnecessary problems that derive from economic factors associated with the use of drugs. Sales of the American "ethical" (prescription) drug industry are estimated at $17 billion per year at manufacturers' prices. As a result, there has been a great proliferation of drugs and dosage forms as manufacturers compete for a share of the market. There has also been competition between professional sources of drug information and information provided by pharmaceutical industry sources.

D. Governmental Pressure: During the past several years, many episodes of drug toxicity have attracted public attention; the public has concluded that drug costs are in general unreasonably high; and there have been violations of ethics in the course of the clinical evaluation of drugs. For these reasons, the conclusion has been reached both inside and outside the medical profession that the clinical evaluation of drugs poses a special problem. This has resulted in legislative pressure on the pharmaceutical industry, on the profession, and on the government regulatory agencies to provide additional protection against toxic or ineffective drugs and to encourage price competition.

Recognition of the problem and the availability of special funds have led to the emergence of clinical pharmacology as a specialized area of medical research intended to increase the number of acceptable clinical evaluations. Clinical pharmacology so defined will cease to have a function when workers in each clinical specialty undertake the responsibility to carry out acceptable studies on the drugs used by its practitioners. It now appears that clinical pharmacology will come to mean human pharmacology—in contrast to the molecular pharmacology that is developing in the traditional departments.

Evaluation of Drugs by Physicians: Preliminary Steps

A. Maintain a Skeptical Attitude: Physicians vary in their attitudes toward new drugs. A cautious attitude would seem to be justified on a statistical rather than emotional basis by the fact that 100–400 new preparations—new single drugs or new mixtures and dose forms—are introduced each year, whereas only a few are genuinely new or useful. The genuinely new advances quickly find wide recognition within the profession. No one will miss a useful new drug by maintaining a reasonably skeptical attitude, and time will be saved for the study of real problems in drug usage rather than of the unnecessary problem posed by the proliferation of "new" preparations.

B. Acknowledge and Assess the Economic Factors Involved: The drug industry has an essential function to perform and has made outstanding contributions to the health of the world population. However, it is an industry, and one must expect commercial rather than professional attitudes in some representations from its members. The conservative point of view is to regard any commercial source of information as biased whether it is in printed form or presented verbally by pharmaceutical manufacturers' representatives.

Subtle as well as obvious forms of advertising should be recognized and in part discounted. These include unsolicited journals and other literature, the distribution of samples that persuade the physician and patient to use trademarked preparations, and use of the lay press to introduce or publicize a drug.

The volume and easy availability of such information can easily distract the physician from the professionally oriented sources of information listed in the following chapter.

Some apparently technical matters—eg, the use of proprietary mixtures, prescribing by trade name, and the use of special dosage forms—may actually be competitive devices.

These matters of drug economics are further discussed in the section on prescription writing.

C. Drugs Can Be Put in Groups: If each new drug or preparation presented under an attractive but meaningless name were to be regarded as a new problem in evaluation, the burden of drug evaluation would become overwhelming even for the person with a special interest in drugs. Usually, the new agent can be related to a familiar drug, and much information and experience already at hand become relevant. For example, many of the drugs said to have new effects and to represent an advance in psychopharmacology are actually closely related to familiar sedative-hypnotics. Even in the genuinely new drug groups— eg, the antipsychotics or the thiazide diuretics—the many compounds available differ only slightly one from another.

D. Laboratory Versus Clinical Results: There is no question that most current progress in medicine originates in laboratory research. However, laboratory data are directly transferable to the clinic only to the extent that the basic work is complete and accurate and to the extent that the laboratory models imitate the condition of the diseased human. The applicability of a new product of research cannot be assumed but must be determined by a test in the clinical situation. For example, studies of the effect of vasodilator drugs on animals (or even normal human volunteers) are not directly applicable to patients with hypertension or coronary artery disease. This final caution, that the problems of drug evaluation cannot be solely approached in the laboratory, emphasizes our dependence on a well-executed clinical trial.

THE CLINICAL TRIAL

The fact that a patient improves after a drug is given does not necessarily mean that the drug was responsible for the change. Before a conclusion about therapeutic usefulness can be reached, the investigator must take into account, measure, or allow for 3 factors other than a pharmacologic effect that can explain an apparent response to medication.

(1) The variable course of the disease process: Colds resolve, ulcers heal and recur, and other diseases run their variable courses whether drugs are used or not. Before an effect can be related to any treatment, a control group must be available and be studied in conjunction with the group receiving the drug. This control group should have received a placebo or a standard drug.

Data for the control group should be collected at the same time as that for the treated group. Control groups selected from the published experience of others ("literature controls") or from earlier experience by the same investigator or at the same hospital are rarely satisfactory. They may be used when a control group is not necessary or justifiable—eg, in the case of a rapidly and uniformly fatal disease.

(2) Patient suggestibility or bias: The reaction of patients or subjects to administered medication does not result entirely from the pharmacologic effect of the active drug contained in the particular dose. The expectation of the patient—generated by the status or the words of the physician; the magic of drugs, especially new drugs in a research setting; and other factors inherent in the personality of the individual—may lead to improvement or deterioration of a symptom or clinical state or to the appearance of side-effects. The nonspecific effects of drugs may be very great on pain, sleep, mood, autonomic functions such as blood pressure, and many other subjective and objective effects.

A physician treating a patient may wish to exploit nonspecific drug effects, but the clinical investigator must measure and evaluate them. A group given no medication will react differently than a group given some medication that might be active or inactive.

The control group in an acceptable clinical trial is, therefore, given a placebo (Latin *placebo* "I shall please"), or dummy medication indistinguishable in every way from the active medication. The patient, of course, is not told whether the preparation is active or inactive but simply that it is investigative and a placebo may be used.

For many symptoms and signs, including most subjective responses, a favorable placebo reaction to single doses is seen in about 40% of a group. With continued administration of a placebo for a chronic complaint, the percentage of placebo responses decreases rapidly and progressively.

When a symptom or disease state has been well studied and a standard treatment measured and evaluated against a placebo, such standard drug should be used instead of a placebo in further testing of related drugs.

The concept of placebo reactions—and all of the concepts discussed in this section—apply to nondrug therapy as well.

(3) Physician or observer bias: An investigator need not be dishonest to be influenced by preconceptions and unconscious bias. In a proper study, which patient is in the control group and which in the treated group is unknown; therefore, all patients are viewed similarly. When neither the patient nor the observer knows the distribution of subjects into control or treated groups, the study is said to be "double-blind, placebo-controlled."

Well-controlled clinical evaluations reflecting the above ideas are not the invariable rule in practice today. Indeed, some resistance to the very concept often arises. The traditional authoritative attitudes held by most physicians make it difficult for them to believe that they cannot put complete trust in their individual judgments but must defer to the conclusions of some investigator unknown to them. However, the individual physician combining the responsibilities of evaluation with those of patient care is easily misled by "mere experience." An acceptable evaluation can be done only by executing a carefully prepared experimental design.

The concept of rigidly controlled experimental drug evaluation studies is an important part of current medical philosophy that is now embodied in federal legislation governing the introduction of new drugs.

Characteristics of an Acceptable Clinical Trial

The goal of the double-blind clinical trial is to assay the effectiveness of a drug or other form of treatment against a specific disease or symptom. The trial is carried out after adequate animal toxicity testing has been done and after preliminary experience in humans has established the dosage and provided other pharmacologic data.

Following the usual sequence and ignoring some of the permissible variations, the characteristics of a good clinical trial would include the following:

A. Careful Planning: The clinical trial must be carefully planned not only to increase the possibility of forming a useful conclusion but also to protect the subject. More than one investigator is usually involved, and the contributions of a clinician, an investigator with a special interest in the clinical pharmacology of the drug involved, and even a statistician are needed. This kind of experiment cannot be modified while the data are being gathered but must be carried out as initially planned in order for the results to be valid.

The planning should be reviewed by a disinterested group whose primary interest is the protection of the subject—an institutional review board or human subjects protection committee. They would consider the possible dangers to the subject, the relationship between possible dangers and possible benefits, and the adequacy of the consent form. Review by such a committee is now required by most institutions, granting agencies, and supervisory bodies.

B. Control Groups: A control group of untreated subjects matched to the group receiving therapy is necessary in order to avoid attributing to the treatment effects that are due to variations in the natural course of the disease or symptom. However, the control group is not adequate unless the subjects receive either an inactive or a standard reference medication indistinguishable in its appearance, texture, taste, etc, from the active drug. Administration of such a dummy medication or placebo provides control over the nonspecific effects of therapy. The more subjective the response, the more important is the effect of patient expectation and responsiveness.

C. Double-Blind Procedure: The placebo control loses its usefulness unless patients are unaware of whether they are in the control group (the placebo group) or the treatment group. (However, they must by law be told that they are involved in an experimental study in which an active drug and placebos are included.) In addition, physicians or technicians evaluating the results of treatment must also be unaware of which group the subjects are in. Any conscious or unconscious bias on the part of observers is thus controlled.

When the response is completely objective—eg, blood levels of uric acid, creatinine, or similar measurement—control groups would still be necessary but placebo administration would not be required.

D. Random Assignment of Patients to Groups: The control and treated groups must be exactly equivalent. If one group differs from the other in age, severity of disease, willingness to cooperate, or other variables, the effects of treatment will be influenced accordingly. Assignment of patients to groups is best done from a table of random numbers rather than by any device subject to manipulation. If large enough numbers of subjects are used, the groups will be equivalent. In any case, a measure of comparability of the groups is necessary. This is presented by tabulations of age, number of patients with a given symptom in each group, etc.

When a homogeneous group cannot be selected—ie, when the subjects vary widely in some characteristic that will alter their response to the drug being tested—individuals or groups may be paired or matched before the experiment. They are then randomly given the active drug and the placebo or standard. For example, subjects may be matched by placing in subgroups selected for sex, age, or severity of disease.

The technic is varied when it is possible or desirable to test 2 or more medications on the same subject. When this kind of paired comparison is done, the patient becomes his or her own control. The order of drug administration must then be randomized so that some patients receive the control medication first and others receive it after the "crossover." The drug or placebo is then randomly assigned to subjects within each subgroup.

E. Statistical Analysis of Data: To establish that a difference between groups is not merely due to variability in response, some statistical measure of variability and significance must be presented. The nature of the analysis is dependent on the design of the experiment and should be established before the drug testing is done. The assistance of a qualified statistician will be necessary for most investigators.

Limitations of the Placebo-Controlled Double-Blind Assay

There are data that the type of evaluation described above cannot provide. These limitations must be discussed explicitly, since they often are used not as a critique of the double-blind method but as an excuse for not doing a proper trial.

The function of the double-blind study is to establish therapeutic effectiveness and compare the effectiveness of different drugs or other forms of treatment. Such experiments in drug evaluation will not provide information about the general pharmacology of the drug or information about the disease entity being treated. In fact, adequate prior information on dosage and other pharmacologic factors is necessary before a clinical evaluation can be carried out. It is also certainly true that a quantitatively minor drug effect may be missed using the methods just discussed. However, most criticisms of the double-blind studies are actually rationalizations of an unwillingness to perform one of these stereotyped studies. For example, the conventionalized method of evaluation may seem invalid on its face if it cannot be used to establish a drug effect the

investigator *knows* to exist but which cannot be affirmed by other investigators. Another frequent comment is that a double-blind study cannot be carried out because patient and staff will identify the active compound from the effects on the patient. An example of how such an objection was circumvented is provided by the study discussed in Chapter 25 on the effectiveness of phenothiazine tranquilizers on an institutionalized population in which an "active placebo" was used—ie, the control group received atropine and phenobarbital, a combination that had no therapeutic effect but mimicked the side-effects of the antipsychotic tranquilizer being tested. And, of course, in most studies comparison with a standard drug rather than with an inert placebo is done.

A final objection that must be seriously considered is that it is not proper to deprive a patient of optimal treatment for research purposes. There are very few situations in which the new drug is so dramatically superior to the accepted treatment with which it is being compared that this objection causes real ethical concern. Drug evaluation can be carried out parallel to patient care but must be planned separate from it. One must believe that a definitive evaluation is so valuable that the inconvenience (but never harm) to the patient is justified.

Ethical & Legal Restraints on Human Trials

Important ethical questions arise whenever an investigator uses a human subject. The situation that we are first concerned with relates to the investigational use of chemical substances that are not yet approved for sale as drugs. Because the public health and safety are so clearly involved and because both physicians and manufacturers were sometimes involved in questionable practices, the Federal Food, Drug, & Cosmetic Act was amended in 1962 to establish additional controls. Under the regulations of the Food & Drug Administration (FDA), a new chemical substance may be investigated as a potential drug in the following steps.

A. Preclinical Study: The regulations governing preclinical testing of new drugs are designed to provide as much protection against toxic reactions in humans as possible. (See Chapter 6, Toxicity of Therapeutic Agents.)

B. Clinical Testing of New Drugs: The initial clinical testing of drugs is governed by FDA regulations as well as by the established procedures of clinical pharmacology. Considerable variations are tolerated, but the following stages are defined:

1. Phase I–Following adequate animal studies, the first trials in humans may be undertaken. This stage is not designed to establish or compare usefulness but to establish dosage, duration of action, and other preliminary factors. These tests may in most cases be carried out on normal volunteers, and the investigator may demonstrate confidence in the preliminary studies and satisfy what some believe to be an ethical obligation by being one of the first subjects. There are perhaps situations where this is not necessary, eg, use

Declaration of Helsinki* (Recommendations Guiding Doctors in Clinical Research)

Introduction. It is the mission of the doctor to safeguard the health of the people. The doctor's knowledge and conscience are dedicated to the fulfillment of this mission.

The Declaration of Geneva of the World Medical Association binds the doctor with the words "The health of my patient will be my first consideration" and the International Code of Medical Ethics, which declares that "Any act or advice which could weaken physical or mental resistance of a human being may be used only in his or her interest."

Because it is essential that the results of laboratory experiments be applied to human beings to further scientific knowledge and to help suffering humanity, the World Medical Association has prepared the following recommendations as a guide to each doctor in clinical research. It must be stressed that the standards as drafted are only a guide to physicians all over the world. Doctors are not relieved from criminal, civil, and ethical responsibilities under the laws of their own countries.

In the field of clinical research a fundamental distinction must be recognized between clinical research in which the aim is essentially therapeutic for a patient, and the clinical research the essential object of which is purely scientific and without therapeutic value to the person subjected to the research.

I. Basic Principles

1. Clinical research must conform to the moral and scientific principles that justify medical research and should be based on laboratory and animal experiments or other scientifically established facts.

2. Clinical research should be conducted only by scientifically qualified persons and under the supervision of a qualified medical professional.

3. Clinical research cannot legitimately be carried out unless the importance of the objective is in proportion to the inherent risk to the subject.

4. Every clinical research project should be preceded by careful assessment of inherent risks in comparison to foreseeable benefits to the subject or to others.

5. Special caution should be exercised by the doctor in performing clinical research in which the personality of the subject is liable to be altered by drugs or experimental procedure.

II. Clinical Research Combined With Professional Care

1. In the treatment of the sick person, the doctor must be free to use a new therapeutic measure, if in his or her judgment it offers hope of saving life, reestablishing health, or alleviating suffering.

If at all possible, consistent with patient psychology, the doctor should obtain the patient's freely given consent after the patient has been given a full explanation. In case of legal incapacity, consent should also be procured from the legal guardian; in case of physical incapacity the permission of the legal guardian replaces that of the patient.

2. The doctor can combine clinical research with professional care, the objective being the acquisition of new medical knowledge, only to the extent that clinical research is justified by its therapeutic value for the patient.

III. Nontherapeutic Clinical Research

1. In the purely scientific application of clinical research carried out on a human being, it is the duty of the doctor to remain the protector of the life and health of that person on whom clinical research is being carried out.

2. The nature, the purpose, and the risk of clinical research must be explained to the subject by the doctor.

3a. Clinical research on a human being cannot be undertaken without free consent after he or she has been informed; if the subject is legally incompetent, the consent of the legal guardian should be procured.

3b. The subject of clinical research should be in such a mental, physical, and legal state as to be able to exercise fully his or her power of choice.

3c. Consent should, as a rule, be obtained in writing. However, the responsibility for clinical research always remains with the research worker; it never falls on the subject even after consent is obtained.

4a. The investigator must respect the right of each individual to safeguard his or her personal integrity, especially if the subject is in a dependent relationship to the investigator.

4b. At any time during the course of clinical research the subject or the subject's guardian should be free to withdraw permission for research to be continued.

The investigator or the investigating team should discontinue the research if in their judgment it may, if continued, be harmful to the individual.

*Resolution [34] adopted at the 18th World Medical Assembly, June, 1964, by the World Medical Association, of which the American Medical Association is a member. Modified slightly.

of a potential antineoplastic agent may be justified only by the presence of a life-threatening disease.

2. Phase II—When phase I has eliminated the probability of a dangerous or disastrous experience, and when adequate data on dosage are available, the drug is tested for therapeutic effect during a phase of controlled evaluation trials. The law requires demonstration of efficacy as well as an evaluation of toxicity, and the FDA requires double-blind, placebo-controlled studies. In actual practice, comparison with standard agents already available is almost always more useful than comparison with a placebo.

3. Phase III—Phase II studies establish the efficacy of the drug in specific therapeutic situations and identify such adverse reactions as appear in the comparatively small number of patients used. Phase III studies are then carried out to provide data from wide use in larger numbers of patients under conditions simulating the actual conditions of use after marketing.

4. Phase IV—At this point, upon application from the manufacturer, the FDA approves the New Drug Application (NDA), and the drug may be marketed and advertised for use in the specific indications for which efficacy has been established. At the same time, post-marketing surveillance is supposed to be carried out to identify toxic reactions which occur with a very low incidence, those which resemble naturally occurring disease, or those which for other reasons can be correlated with administration of the drug only after wide use or special epidemiologic study.

C. Who Can Carry Out New Drug Investigations: Before a new chemical compound can be tested in humans, it must be exempted from the laws forbidding its use as a drug. A sponsor—almost always the company that hopes to market the compound—submits to the FDA a Notice of Claimed Investigational Exemption for a New Drug (IND) summarizing what is known of the compound from prior animal and clinical studies. The sponsor may then proceed with the clinical trials necessary to collect the information required before permission to sell the drug is granted. An individual investigator who wishes to use in research a drug not yet marketed in the USA or to use a marketed drug in a new therapeutic application may act as sponsor by preparing a brief letter.

The sponsor then supplies the drug to physicians for clinical pharmacology investigation (phases I and II) or clinical trial (phase III). The sponsor must collect information from the investigators establishing their competence and must also secure the researcher's agreement to obtain consent from the subjects receiving the drug.

Principle of Informed Consent

When a patient voluntarily visits a physician, implied consent is given to the performance of usual and expected procedures. Administration of drugs accepted for use does not require special permission from the patient unless the drug is unusually hazardous, in which case the patient or a representative of the patient should participate in making the decision to use the drug.

When a new drug is used or when a familiar drug is used as part of an investigation, the patient must give an informed, voluntary consent. Informed consent means that the patient is given all of the information necessary to form a responsible opinion. The information must be provided in understandable (nontechnical) language, and an opportunity for questions and discussion must be offered. Possible adverse effects as well as the possible benefits to others must be described; it must be made clear that the experiment is separate from ordinary treatment.

A consent is voluntary when there is no duress that makes it difficult or impossible for the subject to refuse to participate. The inducement should not be too strong—eg, the fee should be nominal, and the participation of a prisoner (a doubtful practice) should not be made a condition for parole. Both the law (in the case of new drugs) and the consensus of ethical attitudes in the profession make the exceptions necessary for special situations.

"THE DRUG LAG"

In the USA, increased governmental regulatory control of the development, production, marketing, and dispensing of drugs has led to some inevitable controversies involving the FDA, the pharmaceutical industry, the medical profession, and the general public. These disagreements seem at times to be philosophically and practically insuperable. Public demand for new and effective drugs is not always easy to reconcile with the necessity for reasonable product safety and low cost. Impatience engendered by knowledge of "spectacular new drugs" available elsewhere in the world but not in the USA is only partially tempered by unfavorable reports such as adverse drug reactions, improper human experimentation, malpractice actions, and the like.

The so-called "drug lag" in the USA—compared to other industrialized countries—has been the subject of considerable recent controversy. Lengthy delay in approval of the beta-blocker propranolol, for example, has been cited as an instance of unwarranted FDA conservatism and failure to respond to needs. Some useful drugs are withdrawn from the market because drug firms find them to be unprofitable—either because of inability or unwillingness to meet FDA regulations or because of fear of product liability. On the other hand, public pressure to produce drugs considered to be useless or unsafe by the scientific community (eg, Laetrile) has resulted in patchwork permissive special legislation in some states of the USA.

•   •   •

References*

Barron BA, Bukantz SC: The evaluation of new drugs: Current Food and Drug Administration regulations and statistical aspects of clinical trials. Arch Intern Med 119:547, 1967.

Beecher HK: *Measurement of Subjective Responses: Quantitative Effects of Drugs*. Oxford Univ Press, 1959.

Beecher HK: *Research and the Individual: Human Studies*. Little, Brown, 1970.

Byar DP & others: Randomized clinical trials: Perspectives on some recent ideas. N Engl J Med 295:74, 1976.

Gray BH: *Human Subjects in Medical Experimentation: A Sociological Study of the Conduct and Regulation of Clinical Research*. Wiley, 1975.

Hill AB: *Principles of Medical Statistics*, 10th ed. Oxford Univ Press, 1977.

Ingelfinger FJ: Ethics of human experimentation defined by a national commission. N Engl J Med 296:44, 1977.

Isselbacher KJ, Cole P: Saccharin—the bitter sweet. N Engl J Med 296:1348, 1977.

Jick H: The discovery of drug-induced illness. N Engl J Med 296:481, 1977.

Kennedy D: A calm look at the "drug lag." JAMA 239:423, 1978.

Kennedy D: Creative tension: FDA and medicine. N Engl J Med 298:846, 1978.

Kennedy D: Ten medical myths about FDA. West J Med 127:529, 1977.

Ladimer I, Newman RW: *Clinical Investigation in Medicine: Legal, Ethical and Moral Aspects. An Anthology and Bibliography*. Boston University Law-Medicine Research Institute, 1963.

Lasagna L: The controlled clinical trial: Theory and practice. J Chronic Dis 1:353, 1955.

Lasagna L, Meier P: Experimental design and statistical problems. Chapter 4, pp 37–60, in: *Clinical Evaluation of New Drugs*. Waife SO, Shapiro AP. Harper, 1959.

Lewis CE: Variations in the incidence of surgery. N Engl J Med 281:880, 1969.

Relman A: Laetrilomania—again. N Engl J Med 298:215, 1978.

Ryan KJ: The FDA and the practice of medicine. N Engl J Med 297:1287, 1977.

Tukey JW: Some thoughts on clinical trials, especially problems of multiplicity. Science 198:679, 1977.

Van Woert MH: Profitable and non-profitable drugs. N Engl J Med 298:903, 1978.

Wolf S: The pharmacology of placebos. Pharmacol Rev 11:689, 1959.

*See also references for Chapters 4 and 6.

4 | Technics of Drug Administration

The subject matter covered in this chapter is often called "prescription writing," but much more is involved than the mere form of the order to the pharmacist. Whether the drug is ordered by prescription or by entry in a hospital chart or dispensed directly by the physician, prescribing drugs requires much more than simply a knowledge of drug action. The patient whose doctor is skilled in the practical applications of pharmacy and pharmacology will receive the benefits of drug treatment with greater convenience and effectiveness and at less expense and discomfort.

Prescription writing as such has become less complicated as progress in drug therapy has provided more and more specific remedies. The complex and ineffective mixtures of many crude drugs that were the mainstay of the 19th century pharmacy have been largely replaced by pure agents ordered in a simple prescription written in English.

To the patient, the act of prescribing is of great psychologic import, and nothing should be done to minimize the impact of what is felt to be the climactic part of an office visit.

This chapter deals with the administration and prescribing of drugs used for their systemic effects. The topical application of drugs is discussed in Chapter 5.

REVIEW OF FACTORS MODIFYING DRUG ACTION

Most of the factors modifying drug action are discussed in other chapters. They are summarized here because of their importance at the time a specific drug is selected and its dose and method of administration prescribed.

Patient Cooperation or Compliance

Partial or complete failure to take a prescribed drug is perhaps not properly called a factor modifying drug action. It does, however, cause more frequent and quantitatively more important deviations from expected responses and expected blood levels than the other factors outlined in this chapter and for that reason deserves to be emphasized.

The physician who prescribes a drug cannot as-sume that the drug will be taken as directed, that the prescription will even be filled or refilled, that the patient will persist in its chronic use if that is what is wanted, or that the patient, even if warned not to do so, will not take other medication that might alter the action of the prescribed drug.

Even generally cooperative patients may be drug defaulters because of poverty, unconcern, forgetfulness, lack of confidence in the medication, fear of its toxicity, or a subjectively unpleasant reaction to taking it. Failures of cooperation are usually not reported because of embarrassment, indifference, or courtesy to the physician.

Patients who are old, hostile, or schizophrenic are usually unable or unwilling to cooperate with the physician in the drug treatment program. The tendency to noncompliance is especially great during the treatment of chronic problems such as tuberculosis, congestive heart failure, and schizophrenia, when relapse occurs only after a delay and when the initial treatment leaves the patient "feeling fine."

Responsibility for failure of compliance does not lie with the patient alone. The doctor can help solve the problem of noncompliance by involving a member of the family or some other responsible attendant in administering the drug or supervising its daily ingestion; by arranging the simplest possible treatment regimen; and, most importantly, by spending more time carefully and repeatedly explaining the treatment plan to the patient and asking about responses to drugs.

Individual Variation

As is true of all biologic responses, the response of any given patient to a drug will be subject to individual variation—ie, the therapeutic dose will be different for different individuals, and toxic effects will also appear at different dosage levels in different patients. With some drugs—eg, penicillin or aspirin—the margin between the therapeutic and the toxic dose is so wide that it is always possible to give a dose greater than necessary to achieve a response in the most insensitive patient. With most drugs, however, this is not possible, and each drug administration becomes an exercise in bioassay to establish the dose that will have a therapeutic effect without intolerable or dangerous toxic effects. The average dose is thus a statistical abstraction from which the individual dose varies in a manner described by a normal curve of distribution.

In contrast to this individual variation are unexpected drug responses that depend not upon the dosage of the drug but upon the altered reactivity or allergic sensitization of the patient. (See Chapter 6.)

Absorption

The intensity and duration of the response to a single dose of a drug of a certain size will vary depending upon the rapidity with which blood or tissue levels are achieved. Factors modifying absorption include the following:

A. Solubility: One property of drugs that can be modified to provide a longer duration of effect is their solubility when given by subcutaneous or intramuscular injection. For example, unmodified water-soluble penicillin must be injected as often as 6 times a day to maintain constant therapeutic levels. If the penicillin is combined with procaine and thus rendered less soluble, its absorption from the injection site will continue for more than 12 hours. The solubility of insulin is altered in a similar fashion to increase the duration of effect and, therefore, the convenience to the patient. Drugs administered orally may, however, be well absorbed even though they are insoluble in water.

B. Chemical Properties: A drug may be dispensed in different chemical forms suitable for different routes of administration—eg, for topical use, local anesthetics or antihistamines may be dispensed as the lipid-soluble free base rather than the water-soluble salt.

Route of Administration

A. Oral: Oral administration is painless, convenient, and economical, and ''per os'' is therefore the most frequently used route. The onset of action after oral administration is delayed in comparison with the effect after parenteral administration. The major limitations of the oral route are that the drug may not be well absorbed from the gastrointestinal tract; the irritating drugs may cause many local side-effects; the flavor may be unpleasant; and some drugs, such as proteins digested in the stomach or corticosteroids inactivated by the liver, do not reach the general circulation after oral administration. In an emergency situation, when rapid onset of action is important, or if the patient is unable to swallow, another route must be chosen.

B. Rectal: Certain drugs can be given by suppository or, less commonly, by enema. Drugs that may be irritative when given orally are better tolerated when given by this route, and nausea does not prevent giving the drug.

Those routes of administration listed from this point on are **parenteral,** by which is meant any route of administration that does not require absorption across an enteric membrane into the portal circulation and immediate transport to drug metabolizing sites in the liver.

C. Subcutaneous: Solutions or suspensions of drugs can be injected into the subcutaneous areolar

tissue. When small volumes are injected, the skin overlying the deltoid or triceps muscle is lifted, and the needle enters the tent thus formed. When larger volumes are given, the inner surface of the thighs or the back over the thoracic spine (in infants) is preferable. Large volumes of isotonic fluid are absorbed from these sites, and such an injection is often referred to as a hypodermoclysis or clysis. Irritating solutions are more painful if given by this route than if given intramuscularly or intravenously.

D. Intramuscular: Muscle is more vascular and less sensitive than subcutaneous tissue, and irritant solutions or suspensions are better tolerated when given intramuscularly. Absorption from the intramuscular site is somewhat more rapid than from subcutaneous injection sites. Small volumes (2 mL or less) are given into the deltoid. Small or large volumes (up to 10 mL) are given into the gluteal mass underlying the upper outer quadrant of one buttock or the other. The vastus muscle underlying the lateral surface of the thigh is an alternative area.

E. Intravenous: The intravenous route makes possible accurate control of dosage, rapid dilution of caustic material, and an onset of action that is even more rapid than after intramuscular or subcutaneous administration. The volume of fluid that can be injected intravenously is also greater than is possible by other parenteral routes. Even if the volume and rate of injection are carefully controlled, the intravenous route is far more hazardous than other routes of administration because of the high local concentration of drugs that can result.

F. Intra-arterial: Drugs may be injected into the artery perfusing a specific area of the body in order to achieve a high local concentration in the area before dilution by the entire plasma volume occurs. The injection of x-ray contrast media in arteriography is the most common example of the use of this route. Vasodilators may be given intra-arterially during the vasospastic state following an acute arterial occlusion.

G. Intradermal: A small amount (less than 0.5 mL) of an isotonic material can be injected into the skin. If the injection is properly superficial—ie, into the epidermis only a few cell layers deep—a wheal is formed. Antigens for skin tests are injected in this way. Local anesthetics injected in this manner provide an insensitive area through which a larger needle can be passed without pain for the deeper injection of a local anesthetic.

H. Oral Mucous Membrane: Tablets containing drugs may be placed under the tongue (sublingual) or between the gingival and buccal mucosa. The barrier of the mucous membrane is present, but absorption is much more rapid than after the drug is swallowed. In addition, drugs absorbed from this site enter the systemic rather than the portal circulation. Nitroglycerin, ergot, methyltestosterone, and isoproterenol are examples of drugs conveniently administered in this way.

I. Inhalation: In addition to the volatile anesthetics, microcrystals or aerosols may be rapidly absorbed after inhalation. The effect may be most intense upon the tissues of the lung, but the effect is systemic—ie, absorption is rapid.

J. Intrathecal: X-ray contrast media and spinal anesthetics are frequently given intrathecally. In rare circumstances, a chemotherapeutic agent may be administered in this way.

K. Topical: Drugs may be applied topically, ie, upon the surface of the body. This route is discussed separately in Chapter 5. The important distinction here is between application to the skin and application to a mucosal surface. Drugs are well absorbed across the mucosal surface and a therapeutic effect is easily obtained. The intact skin, in contrast, is a barrier to the absorption of most drugs, including many of those suggested for use in this way. Some drugs (eg, the corticosteroids) and some toxins are absorbed after topical application. Important systemic drugs with frequent or dangerous allergic reactions—eg, penicillin—should not be used topically, since sensitization frequently occurs.

Interaction With Other Drugs

Two drugs administered simultaneously or sequentially may simply act independently of each other, or they may interact to augment or diminish the expected responses. Obviously, these possible drug interactions should be considered before the drugs are ordered rather than after toxicity or therapeutic failure has occurred.

Examples and details of such drug interactions are discussed in Chapter 2.

Presence of a Disease State

Patients may be unusually sensitive or unusually resistant to a specific drug in the presence of a particular pathologic state. Hypothyroidism, head injury, potassium depletion, respiratory insufficiency, and other states often mentioned as contraindications to drug use alter the sensitivity of the patient.

Drugs that are detoxified by the liver (eg, barbiturates)—or, more importantly, drugs that are excreted by the kidneys—have an extended duration of action or more intense effect if these organs are diseased.

Tolerance

Drug tolerance necessitating an increasing dosage to maintain the initial effect is of several types and is discussed with the individual drugs: narcotic analgesics, sedative-hypnotics, nitrates, the postural hypotensive drugs, and others.

Age & Weight; Pediatric Dosage

When drugs are given to adults, the weight of the subject is only rarely considered in determining the initial dose to be given. Whenever the relative toxicity of the drug permits, a dosage is chosen that is greater than the minimal effective dose for all patients. The dosage of many drugs is that which produces the optimal therapeutic effect or that beyond which intolerable side-effects or toxicity appears. Factors other than body weight are more important sources of variability of response.

In children, however, dosage must be adjusted to body size. The optimal dosage is most dependably determined from the experience of prior investigators or prescribers of the drug. Several general rules are available for calculating pediatric dosage. These are based on age, weight, or body surface area.

A. Age: Young's rule is the most satisfactory of the guides to dosage that are based on age:

$$\frac{\text{Age}}{\text{Age} + 12} = \text{Fraction of adult dose to be used}$$

Thus, a 12-year-old child would receive half of the adult dose:

$$\frac{12}{12 + 12} = 1/2$$

This child might, however, weigh more or less than the average 12-year-old.

B. Weight: Clark's rule approximates the pediatric dosage as 1/150 of the adult dose per pound body weight or 1/70 of the adult dosage per kilogram.

C. Surface Area: Since both of the above rules underestimate the dosage for infants and young children, and since Young's rule also underestimates the dosage for older children, total body surface area provides a better index of the need for drugs and nutrients. Table 4–1 shows the surface area at several ages and the ratio of surface area at these ages to adult surface area—ie, the fraction of the adult dose to be used.

Nomograms from which surface area can be determined are shown facing the inside back cover. A rough rule for children is

$$(0.7 \times \text{weight in lb}) + 10 = \% \text{ of adult dose}$$
$$\text{or}$$
$$(1.5 \times \text{weight in kg}) + 10 = \% \text{ of adult dose}$$

Table 4–1. Determination of drug dosage from surface area.*

Weight		Approximate Age	Surface Area (m^2)	Percentage of Adult Dose
kg	lb			
3	6.6	Newborn	0.2	12
6	13.2	3 months	0.3	18
10	22	1 year	0.45	28
20	44	5.5 years	0.8	48
30	66	9 years	1.0	60
40	88	12 years	1.3	78
50	110	14 years	1.5	90
65	143	Adult	1.7	102
70	154	Adult	1.76	103

*Reproduced, with permission, from Silver HK, Kempe CH, Bruyn HB: *Handbook of Pediatrics,* 13th ed. Lange, 1980.

Doses based on experience are much better than those calculated from any of the above rules. The sensitivity or resistance of children to drugs varies with factors other than age or size. In the sections on narcotic analgesics, atropine, amphetamine, and a few other drugs, pediatric dosage will be discussed further.

PREPARATIONS & DOSAGE FORMS

Most drugs are synthetic in origin. A few are minerals or are extracted from the organs or body fluids of animals, but many are still derived from plants. A **crude drug** is simply that part of the plant containing the drug, untreated except for drying or powdering. Belladonna is an example of a crude drug still in wide use. If an effort is made to partially purify the drug by extraction of the active fraction with water or alcohol, the various extracts and tinctures are known as galenicals—after Galen, who was an influential herbalist in addition to his other accomplishments. The active compound may be purified from the crude drug and used as a **purified preparation**—eg, atropine or digitoxin from belladonna root or digitalis leaf.

Regardless of the source of the drug, it may be available in a variety of forms and containers.

A **tablet** (the most common preparation for oral use) is made by compressing the drug and an inert binder such as starch or lactose into a hard mass that disintegrates in water. A tablet containing a minimum amount of soluble binder suitable for making a solution for injection is called a tablet triturate or "hypo tablet." These tablets are rarely used today for their original purpose but may be used for sublingual administration. Drugs that are gastric irritants may be "enteric-coated" with a substance that will not dissolve until the tablet has entered the intestine. The dependability of these tablets is variable. (Sustained-release tablets, designed to release their contents over an extended period, are discussed below.)

A **pill** is an obsolete dosage form made by rolling the drug and a binder into a sphere.

Troches and **lozenges** are flavored tablets intended to dissolve slowly when held in the mouth. The released drug acts in the mouth or throat.

Capsules are drug containers made of gelatin that will disintegrate in water.

An **ampule** is a glass container in which solutions of drugs (or dry powder or crystals) can be sterilized and protected until administration. It usually contains a single dose.

Multiple-dose vials are rubber stoppered containers from which several doses can be withdrawn, using aseptic technic, without contaminating the solution.

A **solution** is an aqueous preparation of a drug.

An **elixir** is a sweet, aromatic, dilute alcoholic solution of a drug.

A **syrup** contains the drug in a concentrated sugar solution.

A **tincture** is an alcoholic extract of a drug.

Suppositories contain the drug in a waxy or fatty medium that liquefies and liberates the drug after insertion into the rectum or vagina.

A **gel** may be a colloidal suspension of a drug—eg, aluminum hydroxide—or a solution or suspension of a drug in a thickened vehicle. In the latter case, the intent may be to keep the drug in contact with the oral or pharyngeal mucosa or to achieve a demulcent effect. In the past, gums were used and the preparation was called a mucilage.

Insoluble drugs may be suspended in water for oral administration—eg, milk of magnesia. The thick suspension or the finely divided, amorphous (rather than crystalline) solid may be called a **magma** or mass.

Suspensions of insoluble drugs may also be injected intramuscularly or subcutaneously—eg, procaine penicillin. **Emulsions** are ordinarily only used topically or orally, but one emulsion (vitamin K) is given intravenously.

THE FORM OF A PRESCRIPTION

The form of the practitioner's order to the pharmacist is dictated by tradition, by usage that varies with the locale, and by legal requirements that vary depending upon the drug and the locale.

A prescription may, must, or should include some of the following parts (Fig 4-1):

(1) The date the prescription is written should always be included.

(2) Name of patient.

(3) The patient's address is required only on prescriptions for narcotic and "controlled" drugs (see below).

(4) The age of a young patient may be included to allow the pharmacist to recheck the correctness of the dose.

(5) Superscription: The R (Latin *recipe* "take thou of") was modified to ℞ by adding a symbol invoking the aid of Jove.

(6) Inscription: The name of the drug, dose form, and amount per dose. Until recently, the inscription sometimes included multiple ingredients and, theoretically, was adjusted to the individual patient. The pharmacist was then required to "compound" the prescription—ie, to mix the ingredients and manufacture the dose form. The compounding function has been taken over almost completely by the drug manufacturer.

(7) Subscription: The directions to the pharmacist are now limited to the number of doses to be dispensed.

(8) Signature: This is the instruction to the patient that the pharmacist will transcribe or translate onto the label of the prescription container. This is an important part of the prescription and should be carefully written. To simply state "as directed" is to court misunderstanding or toxicity. Many physicians instruct the

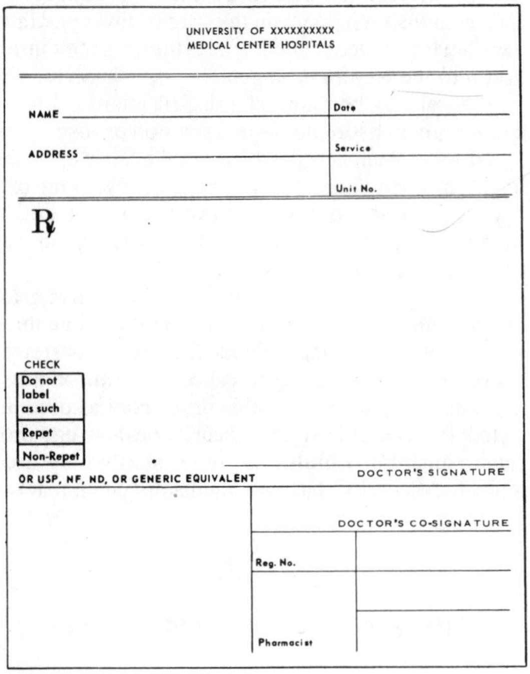

UNIVERSITY OF XXXXXXXXXX
MEDICAL CENTER HOSPITALS

NAME ______ Date ______

ADDRESS ______ Service ______

Unit No. ______

℞

CHECK
Do not label as such
Repet
Non-Repet

OR USP, NF, ND, OR GENERIC EQUIVALENT — DOCTOR'S SIGNATURE

DOCTOR'S CO-SIGNATURE

Reg. No.

Pharmacist

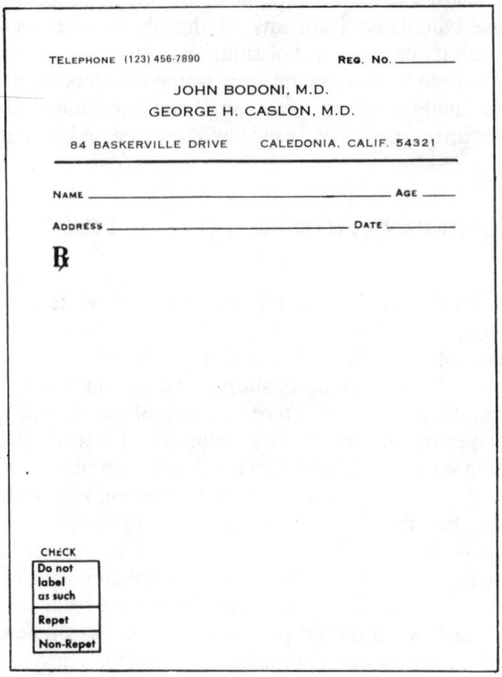

TELEPHONE (123) 456-7890 REG. NO. ______

JOHN BODONI, M.D.
GEORGE H. CASLON, M.D.

84 BASKERVILLE DRIVE CALEDONIA, CALIF. 54321

NAME ______ AGE ______

ADDRESS ______ DATE ______

℞

CHECK
Do not label as such
Repet
Non-Repet

Figure 4–1. Examples of 2 prescription forms in use today. Note that the institutional form specifically authorizes generic name dispensing; that each form reminds the physician to record instructions about refills; and that the name of the drug and dosage will appear on the label unless the physician objects.

pharmacist to "label as such" so that the drug can be identified in case of toxicity or change of doctors, and this practice is generally commended.

(9) Instructions regarding refilling of the prescription: Some indication of the physician's desires about refills should be routinely included in the prescription. These instructions not only are a convenience and courtesy to the patient and pharmacist but also give the physician control over the continued use of a drug. The prescription blank usually offers the prescriber some convenient way of permitting or proscribing refills. Refills may be approved for a certain number of times or through a given date.

Prescriptions for controlled drugs of schedule II (narcotics, amphetamine, and short-acting barbiturates listed in the table on the Inside Front Cover) cannot be refilled. Refills of prescriptions for certain other dangerous drugs may be refilled 5 times in the 6 months after the prescription is written if the physician so indicates on the original prescription or later gives permission on the telephone to the pharmacist.

(10) Signature of the licensed practitioner: The prescription must be signed with the doctor's name and degree. The body of the prescription need not be in the physician's handwriting, but routine prescriptions that are typed, printed, or stamped may be interpreted as "impersonal" by the patient. The address and phone number of the prescriber will almost always be printed on the prescription blank but is required only as noted below. The physician's federal registration number should not be printed on the blank and should be added only on prescriptions for controlled drugs.

WEIGHTS & MEASURES

There are 2 systems of measurement with which the physician must be familiar. The apothecary system is an older one based on arbitrary and unrelated units—eg, grains, ounces. The metric, or decimal, system is based on related and rationally derived units—eg, centimeters, milliliters or cubic centimeters, grams. Because of the use of the metric system by other sciences, the easier calculations it involves, and its greater accuracy and flexibility, the metric system has been adopted by all official agencies and most teaching hospitals in the USA, the British Commonwealth, and many other areas.

The transition from the apothecary to the metric system in medicine is not yet complete, and it is still necessary to be familiar with both systems. This duplication is necessary principally because physicians trained to use the apothecary system will assume or expect a familiarity with the obsolescent scale, and some hospitals still retain it as the local standard. In addition, the dosage forms of some older drugs are understood by reference to the older system. Atropine, for example, is available in tablets containing odd doses in milligrams (0.3, 0.4, 0.6 mg rather than 0.5 and 1 mg) because they derive from fractional grain doses (1/200, 1/150, 1/100 gr).

Prescriptions for liquids should be written to fit the containers available, and waste is avoided if it is remembered that bottles are still manufactured to contain ounce measurements rather than milliliters (5, 30, 60, 120, 240, and 480 mL are standard bottle sizes).

Newer drugs are dispensed in conformity with the metric system, so that practitioners who try to hold to the apothecary system will find themselves ordering morphine, gr 1/8, but meperidine, 100 mg (Table 4–2).

For practical purposes, conversion can be accomplished by remembering that—

1 grain (gr) = 0.065 gram (g) (or 60 mg for
                the usual approximations)
1 gram (g)   = 15 gr
1 ounce (oz) = 30 mL

An ordinary teaspoon will deliver 5 mL, and liquid preparations often contain one dose in 5 mL. In the past, the teaspoon contained 4 mL (1 dram). A tablespoon holds 15 mL (½ oz). A calibrated medicine glass available in many households measures 1 oz (30 mL).

Table 4–2.

Conversion factors.

1 mg	=	1/60 or 1/65 gr
1 g	=	15 or 15.5 gr
1 kg	=	2.2 lb
1 L	=	1.06 quarts
1 gr	=	60 or 65 mg
1 fluid ounce	=	30 or 29.57 mL
1 quart	=	1000 or 946.3 mL

Apothecary system (volume).

1 minim	=	1 drop
60 minims	=	1 fluid dram
8 fluid drams	=	1 fluid ounce
16 fluid ounces	=	1 pint
32 fluid ounces	=	1 quart

Metric system prefixes.

mega (M)	10^6
kilo (k)	10^3
deci (d)	10^{-1}
centi (c)	10^{-2}
milli (m)	10^{-3}
micro (μ)	10^{-6}
millimicro, nano (mμ)	10^{-9}
micromicro, pico ($\mu\mu$)	10^{-12}

When the strength of a solution is expressed in percentage, the meaning is that the solution contains so many parts of solute by weight per 100 parts of solution (W/V). A 5% solution contains 5 g of solute, with solvent added to make 100 mL.

ABBREVIATIONS

Prescriptions today are no longer written in Latin, but the classical influence persists in a number of abbreviations. The use of these abbreviations is not obligatory or even recommended, but they are wisely used in the signature of the prescription and in orders on hospital charts and are certainly preferable to individual or local coinage.

A few common abbreviations:

$\overline{aa}$, of each (ana)
ac, before meals (ante cibum)
ad lib, freely (ad libitum)
bid, twice a day (bis in die)
$\overline{c}$, with (cum)
gt (plural, gtt), drop(s) (gutta)
g or **gm**, gram
gr, grain
h, hour(s)
hs, at bedtime (hora somni, "hour of sleep")
mcg, μ**g**, microgram, 1/1000 mg
mg, milligram, 1/1000 g
non repet, not to be repeated (refilled) (non repetatur)
pc, after meals (post cibum)
prn, as the need arises (pro re nata)
q, every (quaque); eg, q 4 h, "every 4 hours"
qid, 4 times a day (quater in die)
qs ad, a quantity sufficient to make (quantum sufficiat ad)
repet, to be repeated (repetatur)
$\overline{s}$, without (sine)
sig, write on label (signa).
ss, one-half (semis)
stat, immediately (statim)
tid, 3 times a day (ter in die)

SPECIAL REGULATIONS APPLIED TO THE PRESCRIPTION OF CONTROLLED DRUGS IN THE USA

Drugs with a significant potential for abuse are subject to special regulation not only of their prescription but also of their possession and use in hospital, office, emergency, and research situations. The federal laws codified in the Controlled Substances Act of 1970 cover narcotics, cocaine, amphetamines, hallucinogens, marihuana, and the barbiturates and other sedatives.

Responsibility for control and enforcement is assigned to the Drug Enforcement Administration (DEA) of the Department of Justice, and many of the rules outlined below can be changed by administrative order.

Annual Registration

A practitioner (physician, dentist, veterinarian, or other) may apply for federal permission to dispense and prescribe controlled drugs after receiving a state license to prescribe and administer drugs. A registration number that must appear on each prescription for a controlled drug is then assigned. The registration must be renewed each year.

Schedules of Controlled Drugs

Controlled drugs are placed in different schedules to which different regulations apply. The original listings were established by legislation but are changed by administrative action of the Attorney General as new drugs or new problems appear.

Schedule I consists of drugs whose use is forbidden under all but research conditions—ie, heroin, the hallucinogens, and marihuana. These are substances considered to have a high potential for abuse and no currently accepted use in treatment; their safety has not been established even when they are used under medical supervision.

The usual annual registration and number applies only to drugs in schedules II–V. A separate registration for research with schedule I substances must be completed before the drugs can be obtained. Since these drugs are investigational, clearance from the Food & Drug Administration must also be provided. Hallucinogens are legally available only from the National Institute of Mental Health.

Schedule II includes substances with high potential for abuse but with currently accepted use in treatment whose use may lead to severe psychologic or physical dependence—ie, the potent analgesics (formerly called class A narcotics), cocaine, the more widely used amphetamines, and some short-acting sedatives.

The physician cannot authorize refill of a prescription for any of these drugs; a new prescription must be written each time.

In a further effort to prevent misuse, the Department of Justice is authorized to fix the total amounts of these drugs that may be legally manufactured.

Telephoned prescriptions for schedule II drugs cannot be honored by the pharmacist since a prescription must be on file to account for the drugs dispensed. The order may be phoned to the pharmacist and the prescription delivered to the pharmacy or left at the home of the patient, to be given to the pharmacist when the narcotic is delivered.

In the case of a bona fide emergency when no other treatment is possible, the pharmacist may (under federal law) allow the physician 72 hours to deliver the written prescription.

Schedule III is defined as a category for drugs with a potential for abuse less than that for substances in schedules I and II. The narcotics included are paregoric and the former "class B narcotics"—

notably, mixtures of codeine and aspirin, which are widely used mostly because prescribing them is more convenient.

The physician may give prescriptions for drugs in schedules III and IV to the pharmacist by telephone. A new prescription must be provided after 5 refills (if refills are authorized by the physician) or after 6 months.

Schedule IV does not differ from schedule III insofar as prescribing practices are concerned but does differ in other matters, eg, penalties for illegal possession.

Schedule V includes drugs formerly called exempt narcotics. Federal law permits the sale of these mixtures without a prescription, but state laws are more restrictive in some cases. A doctor dispensing any of these preparations must keep a record for 2 years.

Office Supplies

A practitioner is authorized to keep a supply of controlled drugs on hand to use in emergencies and to dispense to patients.

The drugs listed in schedule II (potent narcotics and amphetamines) cannot be ordered from a pharmacist on a regular prescription or from a wholesaler on an ordinary order form. A special federal form in triplicate must be used.

A record must be kept of all controlled drugs received and an inventory made every 2 years. A record must be kept documenting the dispensing of schedule II and III **narcotics**. Entries on the patient's record are adequate documentation of the use of other controlled drugs.

Office and emergency supplies of these drugs must be stored in a locked cabinet.

Form of the Prescription

The information required on prescriptions for narcotics or dangerous drugs differs in different states and for different classes of drugs. The prescription should include the date, the address and full name of the patient, and the signature, address, and registry number of the practitioner. It should be written in ink or typewritten. Some states require that if the prescription is written, it must be entirely in the doctor's handwriting. The signature of the prescription should indicate the use intended—eg, "q 4 hours prn cough" or "prn pain, no oftener than q 4 hours"— and not merely, "q 4 hours" or "as instructed." The doctor must keep a record of each prescription for 2 years. This record is most easily maintained by making a carbon copy of each narcotics prescription. Some states require special prescription blanks that facilitate auditing and prevent forgeries.

State Regulations

Some states have added regulations more restrictive than the federal law. Several states require that narcotics prescriptions be written on special triplicate forms.

LEGAL & ECONOMIC FACTORS IN PRESCRIBING (USA)

Medicine and related professions are subject to licensing and other regulations out of concern for the public health. Similarly, most societies conclude that drugs are different from other commodities and impose special regulations on their manufacturer and distribution. Most of these regulations are designed to protect the safety of the patient.

Statutory Regulation of Prescriptions

There are certain common sense obligations associated with prescribing. Regardless of the nature of the drug prescribed, the physician should keep a record of the prescription. This may be in the form of a duplicate of the prescription, but more commonly the prescription is copied into the patient's record. This is essential for the evaluation of therapy and also protects the physician against legal action in the event of misunderstanding or error in use of the medication.

The federal regulations on prescribing are contained largely in the Durham-Humphrey Amendment to the Food, Drug, & Cosmetic Act (1952) and the Controlled Substances Act discussed above.

The first statute defined "legend drugs," ie, drugs that must bear the label, "Caution: Federal law prohibits dispensing without prescription." The FDA defines permissible over-the-counter (OTC) drugs, but drugs may be made legend drugs if the manufacturer does not wish the OTC classification.

In the USA, drugs classified as "legend drugs" cannot be refilled unless the refill is authorized by the prescriber. For this reason, it is convenient to include on the prescription a statement of the prescriber's desire concerning refills. Lacking this, the pharmacist must obtain permission from the physician for a refill. Such permission is usually obtained by phone.

Telephoned prescriptions are authorized if they are immediately reduced to writing by the pharmacist.

Additional administrative regulations influencing prescribing are issued by the US Food & Drug Administration as the need arises. Drugs may be withdrawn from the market when unexpected toxicity occurs, or special restrictions may be placed on special drugs. For example, the antineoplastic agents methotrexate and triethylenemelamine may be dispensed by the pharmacist only to a physician, not to a patient.

Drug Prices

The total sales of the US drug industry in 1980 were in excess of $31 billion at manufacturers' selling prices. Prescription drugs for humans exceeded $17 billion at manufacturers' prices.

In meeting the need for prescription drugs, the drug industry performs several essential functions. It is, however, an industry rather than a profession, and its competitive efforts have led to several controversial practices. The interaction between the physician and the drug industry becomes most apparent when the physician chooses a specific preparation and gives the patient no alternative but to buy and pay for that specific product. The following would be regarded by many as an outline of sound practice in selecting and ordering a drug, but attitudes vary widely.

A. Prescribe by Generic Rather Than Brand Names: An individual (or company) developing a new drug in the USA can secure a patent on the new substance or on the process for producing it. The patent holder is then entitled to exclusive control of the patented substance or process for 17 years. During this period of freedom from competition, developmental costs can be recovered. In anticipation of expiration of the patent or when the product is not genuinely new, the distributor may attempt to improve its competitive position by advertising a trade name that remains its exclusive property almost indefinitely. The expense of establishing such a protected or registered name invariably increases the cost of the drug. Once the protected name is successfully established, prices can be increased. The wholesale price of an unprotected drug available as a "generic preparation" is usually low, but when the drug is sold under its trade name, the cost will be high—sometimes exorbitantly so. At present, for example, reserpine, 0.25 mg tablets, is offered as a generic preparation at $2.05 per 1000 tablets, but the most familiar brand name preparation costs $39.50 per 1000. Prescribing by generic rather than brand names can therefore result in savings on drug costs if the drug is no longer patented, ie, if price competition is possible.

The argument against generic name prescribing is that only by stipulating the manufacturer can the physician be sure that patients will receive a preparation of the best quality. However, drugs are different from most other commodities in that legal standards of potency, purity, etc are established and only limited variations are permitted. The quality of marketed drugs is monitored by the FDA with expanded facilities; by competing companies; and, during this period of controversy, by individual investigators. All of these efforts now employ blood level studies as well as tablet analysis to establish therapeutic as well as chemical equivalence. Antibiotics are assayed before marketing, and each batch is individually certified by the FDA. With rare exceptions, there have been no important variations among the products of different suppliers. Generic and brand name drugs may actually come from the same manufacturer.

The physician who prescribes only the products of the largest manufacturers (ie, those that spend most on advertising) will not protect patients from the rare variations in quality but will greatly increase the cost of medication not only immediately but in the long run by allowing the drug industry to be dominated by a few large companies.

In private practice, the community pharmacist enters the distributive chain, and in some communities pharmacists may be reluctant to pass on to patients the savings made possible by generic name prescribing. However, as medical care becomes more centralized and institutions and government agencies contribute more to the cost of medical care, the 5% of the medical care dollar being spent on drugs is subject to more and more control. Many institutions reserve the right to substitute generic for protected names unless the physician offers prior objection. (See the specimen prescription, Fig 4–1.) Generic name prescribing is thus an accomplished fact in a large area of medical practice.

Generic name prescribing can be a burden, since the names are chosen to be as difficult as the registered names are euphonious eg, chlordiazepoxide or Librium, prochlorperazine or Compazine. Generic names are proposed by the manufacturer and approved by the United States Adopted Names (USAN) Council, a committee of the American Medical Association, the American Pharmaceutical Association, and the *United States Pharmacopeial Convention.*

Drug Combinations: A patient may often require more than one drug, but only in rare instances should they be given as mixtures of fixed composition; their varied dosages and durations of action usually require that they be given separately. A few common mixtures are official and used for good medical reasons—eg, trisulfapyrimidines USP, oral contraceptives, dermatologic medications—but more are trademarked. Many such combinations have their origin in economic rather than scientific considerations, since they provide a way of developing a proprietary interest in a combination of drugs that would be priced competitively if marketed individually. Atropine and phenobarbital, for example, offer no way for a distributor to establish a brand name individually, but as combinations they can be marketed with the advantage (higher prices) inherent in a trademarked or otherwise protected commodity.

In some cases, use of the combination can be rejected on the grounds that the mixture is therapeutically irrational—ie, that the 2 drugs are not commonly indicated as part of the same treatment regimen (eg, anti-inflammatory steroid plus a sedative)—or that the combination adds a risk without adding a benefit (eg, some antibiotic combinations and antibiotic plus anti-inflammatory steroid ophthalmic topical agents).

However, even when one concedes that each drug in a combination is indicated, it does not follow that they are best given as a combination. The optimal dose of phenobarbital for most patients may vary between 8 and 30 mg/dose. The dosage of anticholinergics must be so individualized that at least a few physicians still prefer to adjust it dropwise, using tincture of belladonna. A combination product with a fixed proportion of phenobarbital and atropine cannot be given with the same precise therapeutic benefit.

Other preparations irrationally combine drugs with slow onset of action and long duration of action (eg, amphetamine) with drugs whose effects are comparatively brief (eg, aspirin, amobarbital).

In most cases, the combinations are more expensive than their separate constituents, a consideration of importance both to the patient and to the agency subsidizing the medical care.

The Food & Drug Administration, acting upon the advice of a NAS–NRC review board, has removed a number of fixed combinations from the market (see Appendix). They propose to require substantial evidence that in fixed combinations of drugs each component contributes to the effect claimed and that the dosage (amount and interval of administration) of each component be appropriate. The evaluation will be gradually extended to include over-the-counter remedies.

C. Prolonged-Action Drugs for Oral Administration: Many drugs are available in dosage forms designed to provide sustained action or repeated release of the drug. The idea of reducing the number of doses that have to be taken per day is attractive, and there is no reason why such preparations should not eventually be developed. However, until the technology is improved, these dosage forms must be regarded as nothing more than competitive devices. Most types, notably the coated bead or Spansule type, release the entire dose at almost the same rate as the ordinary tablet. Others allow some of the drug to traverse the gastrointestinal tract unabsorbed and thus reduce the amount of each dose actually available. Specific data on the behavior of some of these preparations are presented in the discussions of the individual drugs, eg, aspirin, iron, antipsychotic tranquilizers.

REFERENCE SOURCES IN PHARMACOLOGY: ABBREVIATIONS

AMA-DE	*American Medical Association–Drug Evaluations*
BP	*British Pharmacopoeia*
FDA	Food and Drug Administration (Dept of HHS)–Serial drug bulletin
HHS	Department of Health & Human Services (formerly Health, Education & Welfare [HEW])
NF	*National Formulary*
OTC	Over-the-counter (drugs)
PDR	*Physicians' Desk Reference*
USAN	*United States Adopted Names*
USD	*United States Dispensatory*
USP	*United States Pharmacopeia*

SOURCES OF CURRENT INFORMATION ON NEW DRUGS

Chapter 1 lists the most authoritative sources of general pharmacologic information. In the area of prescribing practices, many physicians feel they should have special help in evaluation from the medical literature because of the many new drugs and preparations that continuously appear on the market. Having been told they should reject industrial sources of information, they look for an authoritative source that will enable them to recognize important new drugs and reject the others. As in other areas of medicine, summary authoritative pronouncements should be less influential than a study of the underlying data and experience.

The general and specialty journals publish good drug studies. Several special aids are available for the physician or pharmacist. *Medical Letter* publishes evaluations of current therapy every 2 weeks. Brief discussions represent the consensus of several physicians who have experience with the drug or drug group evaluated.

AMA Drug Evaluations, 4th ed (1980), is the latest in a series of volumes prepared by the AMA headquarters staff. Most of the space is devoted to discussions of individual agents, including the dosage and available preparations. However, the drugs are grouped according to use, some general discussion is provided, and adverse as well as favorable judgments are expressed. For these reasons, *AMA Drug Evaluations* appears preferable to PDR.

Physicians' Desk Reference (PDR) is an annual publication in which manufacturers may buy space to present prescribing information about their products. The material included is similar to the package insert accompanying the product. Toxic reactions and precautions are presented in sufficient detail to shift more responsibility onto the physician than is the case with the usual advertisement. PDR is a convenient source of information about dosage forms.

The *United States Pharmacopeia* (USP) and the *National Formulary* (NF) establish standards of purity, tablet disintegration times, and other criteria of acceptability for a product, and these standards are binding upon the courts. The physician will rarely have occasion to consult these official compendia for prescribing information, but they have some indirect importance to physicians. Now that the FDA is empowered to require testing of efficacy and is involved in the widespread testing of drugs for biologic availability as well as mere tablet content, the importance of the traditional pharmacopeia is waning. Plans to consolidate USP and NF are now going forward.

For additional current information on new drugs, see references below.

DRUG INCOMPATIBILITIES

The term "incompatibility" is carried over from the period when individually compounded mixtures could contain ingredients that were chemically, pharmaceutically, or therapeutically incompatible. Therapeutic incompatibilities are now discussed as drug interactions, but an occasional problem of chemical incompatibility arises when drugs for parenteral injection are mixed either in the syringe or in a larger volume of parenteral fluid to be given by continuous intravenous drip.

When acidic and basic solutions of drugs are mixed in the same syringe, one component may be precipitated. For example, the barbiturates are acids and are prepared for injection as very basic sodium salts—ie, as the salt of a weak acid and strong base. The narcotic analgesics and the atropine alkaloids are bases dispensed as acidic solutions of the hydrochloride or sulfate. If these are mixed in a small volume for intramuscular administration, some of the barbiturate is precipitated. It is true that many injections of such cloudy solutions have been given. In this case, since the ultimate solubility is determined by the pH at the injection site, the effects of the components of the mixture are not altered. However, a variable amount of the drug may adhere to the syringe.

When drugs are added to the contents of the infusion bottle for administration over a period of hours, problems of stability as well as solubility may arise. It is actually difficult to conceive of situations in which more than one drug must be added to an infusion fluid. When a continuous intravenous infusion is being given, drugs can usually be injected slowly into the tubing or side arm of the infusion set with few concerns about chemical incompatibility. Examples of a few drugs that do pose problems are as follows:

(1) Tetracycline: Solutions of tetracycline for parenteral use contain large amounts of ascorbic acid. The acid solution hastens the hydrolysis of penicillin and precipitates a number of antibiotics and other drugs. Further examples involving antibiotics are shown in Table 48–3.

(2) Phenytoin for injection is solubilized with sodium hydroxide.

(3) Heparin is a large, acidic molecule and complexes with many other drugs.

(4) Proteins: Whole blood, protein hydrolysates, and biologicals should not have drugs added because of the theoretical possibility of inactivation by binding.

• • •

References

General

Hoover J (editor): *Remington's Pharmaceutical Sciences,* 14th ed. Mack Printing Co, 1970.

Jerome JB, Sagan P: The USAN nomenclature system. JAMA 232:294, 1975.

Patient Compliance

Blackwell B: Patient compliance. N Engl J Med 289:249, 1973. [See also editorial, p 267, in same issue.]

Gillum RF, Barsky AJ: Diagnosis and management of patient noncompliance. JAMA 228:1563, 1974.

Roth HP, Caron HS: Accuracy of doctor's estimates and patient's statements on adherence to a drug regimen. Clin Pharmacol Ther 23:361, 1978.

Drug Economics

Feldman EG: Brand versus generic drugs. J Am Pharm Assoc 9:8, 1969.

Harris R: *The Real Voice.* Macmillan, 1964. [Summary of Kefauver hearings.]

Hastings GE, Kunnes R: Predicting prescription prices. N Engl J Med 277:625, 1967.

Leprowski WC: Medicinal chemicals: Economic and social forces bring changes. Chem Eng New, pp 100–104, Sept 1, 1969.

May CD: Selling drugs by "educating" physicians. J Med Educ 36:1, 1961.

Silverman M, Lee PR: *Pills, Profits and Politics.* Univ of California Press, 1974.

Steele H: Monopoly and competition in the ethical drugs market. J Law Econ 5:131, 1962.

Sources of Current Drug Information

Facts and Comparisons. Kastrup EK (editor). Facts and Comparisons, Inc. [Loose-leaf compilation of dosage forms with monthly supplements.]

FDA Drug Bulletin. Department of Health & Human Resources. [Appears 4–5 times per year.]

Handbook of Non-Prescription Drugs, 5th ed. American Pharmaceutical Association, 1977.

New Names. [A list of non-proprietary names adopted by the United States Adopted Names (USAN) Council; appears regularly in JAMA.]

Pelissier NA, Burgee SL Jr: Guide to incompatibilities. Hosp Pharm 3:15, 1968. [Also package insert for each drug.]

Shirkey HC (editor): *Pediatric Therapy,* 3rd ed. Mosby, 1968.

Wilson CO, Jones TE: *American Drug Index.* Lippincott. [Annual. A listing of virtually all drugs and preparations.]

Dermatologic Application | 5

The discussion of the technics of medication in Chapter 4 emphasizes factors important in ordering drugs used for their general systemic effect. The application of drugs to the skin involves the concepts already mentioned as well as additional matters of technic. For example, the application of drugs to the skin requires consideration not only of the pharmacologic effect of the active agent but also the physical form of the preparation, which may itself have a therapeutic or adjuvant effect. The present chapter, therefore, defines some pharmaceutical preparations used for topical application and lists some of the possible drug actions. The detailed discussion of some topically active drugs and the discussion of drugs used systemically for the treatment of dermatologic manifestations of disease—eg, corticosteroids, antibiotics, antihistamines—will be found in later chapters.

At one time the ability of the physician to order and of the pharmacist to compound individualized prescriptions was very important. With the availability of specific and potent drugs such as the topical and systemic steroids, antibiotics, parasiticides, and fungicides, dermatologic therapy is both simpler and more effective than in the past. As is true also of other areas of medicine, the pharmaceutical industry now prepares most of the standard preparations.

ABSORPTION OF DRUGS THROUGH THE SKIN

A few substances—eg, the cholinesterase inhibitors used as nerve gases and insecticides—are rapidly absorbed after application to the skin. However, such examples are few in number, and it is the impermeability of the skin, which is physiologically essential, that is most impressive in drug studies.

The rate-limiting barrier to percutaneous absorption is the stratum corneum of the epidermis. This dense layer of dead, flattened cells filled with the fibrous protein keratin resists the diffusion of both water-soluble and lipid-soluble substances. In its absence, as when the skin is denuded by some disease process or even after stripping off part of the epithelium by repeated applications of cellophane tape, the deeper layers of living cells of the epidermis function as a lipid barrier similar to other membranes.

Absorption of drugs across the skin is increased if the drug has low solubility in the vehicle and high solubility in lipids. Hydration of the cornified layer of the epidermis also increases penetration of some drugs, especially the anti-inflammatory steroids. Such a change in the epidermis is accomplished by covering the part with an occlusive dressing such as a polyethylene film. The use of ointments also macerates the underlying skin and is an older technic for improving the absorption of drugs into the skin.

If drugs are dissolved in solvents that are miscible with both water and lipids, their absorption may be enhanced. The investigative drug DMSO (see p 38) provides the only significant application of this idea.

FORMS OF TOPICAL APPLICATION

Topical medication can be applied to the skin dissolved or suspended in a variety of media ranging from simple solutions to greasy ointments. The medium or pharmaceutical form of application has by itself an effect on the skin lesion, and selection of the form in which a topical medication is applied is determined as much by the acuteness or chronicity of the dermatosis as by its specific cause. Acute (recent) lesions are red, burning, blistered, swollen, and weeping. A subacute stage is represented by the subsidence of the above acute changes. In chronic (long-standing) lesions, the skin is thickened by the underlying process or by scratching and is crusted or scaly. A greasy ointment that prevents drainage and drying is unsuitable for application to an acute, weeping lesion; and a powder placed on the surface of a grossly thickened or crusted skin will have little effect. The relation of the preparation selected to the acuteness of the dermatosis is shown in Table 5–1.

Wet Preparations
Baths, soaks, and wet dressings are therapeutically equivalent, the variation selected depending upon the area and extent of involvement. Wet preparations may be used for their inherent cleansing or

Table 5—1. Types of topical formulations used in acute, subacute, and chronic skin lesions.

	Acute Lesions (weeping, hot, edematous, crusting, recent)	Subacute Lesions (edematous, hot, chapped)	Chronic Lesions (scaling, lichenified, crusting)
Wet preparations (baths, soaks, wet dressings)	X		
Powders, shake lotions	X	X	
Emulsions	X	X	X
Creams	X	X	X
Pastes		X	X
Ointments			X

antipruritic action or may be medicated to achieve additional antipruritic, astringent, or other effects. In either case, continued contact with water is cleansing, maintains drainage from the affected areas, and is a convenient way of heating the skin and causing vasodilatation. Water is keratolytic, leading initially to softening and maceration, but water is ultimately drying in its effect on the skin. Medicated baths are suitable for application in the most acute lesions.

Some examples of wet preparations are shown in Table 5–2.

Powders

Powders such as zinc oxide, talc (magnesium silicate), and titanium dioxide reduce friction and absorb moisture. In practice, powders are most often applied to the body in the form of shake lotions (see below). Powders as such are used in intertriginous areas (between the toes, in the groin, beneath the breasts) or as inert carriers of antiparasitic (DDT) or fungistatic agents.

Shake Lotions (Table 5–3.)

Strictly defined, a lotion is a solution or suspension of a medication. It is better to use the term "solution" for the first case and avoid confusion with cosmetic and other uses of the term.

Shake lotions, so called because it is essential to shake well before using, are suspensions of fine powders. They provide a convenient way of applying a powder with good contact and adherence to the surface. The benefit of the application is due to the mechanical properties of the powder and to the effect of added agents—eg, 1% phenol for an antipruritic action. The disadvantages of shake lotions are that they may be excessively drying when applied to acute lesions and that they do not penetrate thickened chronic lesions as well as creams or ointments.

Calamine lotion is a familiar example of a shake lotion. Calamine lotion and calamine lotion with phenol are both official (USP) preparations and are available without a prescription. Calamine was originally a zinc carbonate ore colored pink by iron salts

Table 5—2. Wet preparations: for baths, soaks, and wet dressings.*

Indications: For acute, red, swollen, itching, infected, weeping, or vesicular lesions.
Technic: (1) Baths: Lukewarm or cool baths for 30 minutes 2—3 times daily as needed. Dry by blotting, not rubbing. The usual home tub contains 20 gal (75 L) when half-filled. (2) Basin soaks (2—5 quarts of solution) for hands and feet: Soak for 15 minutes twice daily. Solutions must be applied cool (hot for infections). (3) Wet dressings (for localized lesions): Use a Turkish towel; keep saturated with solution. Frequent applications are necessary (eg, 30 minutes 2—4 times a day). Covered dressings should not be used.

Agent	Action†	Range of Concentrations Used	Most Common Strength Used	Preparation of Solution of Most Commonly Employed Strength
Plain tap water		...	...	...
Starch bath	Antipruritic	...	...	2 cups starch or Linit to tub
Proprietary bath oils (Alpha-Keri, Nivea, Lubath, Demol, etc)	Antipruritic	...	...	5—25 mL to tub
Sodium chloride		0.6—1.5%	0.9%	2 tsp/quart water
Sodium bicarbonate	Antipruritic	2—5%	3%	8 tsp/quart water
Magnesium sulfate (Epsom salts)	Antipruritic	2—4%	3%	8 tsp/quart water
Aluminum subacetate solution	Astringent	0.5—10%	5%	Domeboro powder, 2 tsp/quart, or Burow's solution, 50 mL/quart water
Potassium permanganate	Antipruritic, oxidizing, antiseptic, astringent	0.01—0.25%	0.01%	One 0.3-g tablet to 3 quarts water or one 0.1-g tablet to 1 quart water

*Modified, with permission, from Krupp MA, Chatton MJ (editors): *Current Medical Diagnosis & Treatment 1980.* Lange, 1980.
†All of the solutions listed have a drying, soothing, and cleansing action also.

Table 5—3. Lotions and emulsions.*

Liquid mixtures containing medicaments in solution or suspension are useful in a wide variety of localized and generalized skin lesions because they are easy to apply and remove. They often have a marked drying effect and must not be used if this effect is undesirable. The following are some useful well-known lotions. The composition is given for information only; the preparation would not be compounded upon prescription but would be dispensed as a proprietary preparation.

Lotion and Action	Composition		Instructions and Remarks
Calamine lotion (soothing, drying)	Prepared calamine	8	Apply locally 3—4 times daily or as needed. Use for acute dermatitis. Avoid excessive drying due to prolonged use of this lotion (as with other nonoily lotions). Add 1% phenol for antipruritic effect.
	Zinc oxide	8	
	Glycerin	2	
	Magma of bentonite	25	
	Lime water, qs ad	100	
Starch lotion (anti-pruritic, soothing, drying)	Corn starch	24	Apply locally twice daily or as needed for acute dermatitis. This is a useful basic lotion to which other agents may be added.
	Zinc oxide	24	
	Glycerin	12	
	Lime water, qs ad	120	
Coal tar lotion (soothing, drying, keratoplastic)	Coal tar solution	12	Apply locally at night; scrub in morning. Use for subacute dermatitis. A useful mild stimulating lotion. Do not use on hairy or infected areas.
	Zinc oxide	24	
	Starch	24	
	Glycerin	36	
	Water, qs ad	120	
Oily lotion (soothing, drying, lubricating)	Zinc oxide	10	Apply locally 3—4 times daily or as needed for acute dermatitis. Less drying than calamine and starch lotions.
	Olive oil		
	Lime water $\overline{aa}$, qs ad	120	

*Modified, with permission, from Krupp MA, Chatton MJ (editors): *Current Medical Diagnosis & Treatment 1980.* Lange, 1980.

present as impurities. Calamine lotion is now prepared from zinc oxide and "prepared calamine," which is actually zinc oxide to which a small amount of ferric oxide has been added for color.

Emulsions

Oil in water emulsions are less drying than lotions, and an oily calamine shake lotion (calamine liniment) may be substituted for calamine lotion.

Creams or Hydrophilic Ointments

Creams should be considered in contrast with the heavier greasy ointments (described below). Their properties are intermediate between the properties of drying preparations (wet dressings, lotions) and ointments.

Creams contain a high percentage of water but are semisolid in consistency. Hydrophilic ointments are petrolatum in water emulsions stabilized with a detergent such as sodium lauryl sulfate. Polyethylene glycols are more commonly used today than the older hydrophilic ointments. These polymers have the consistency of an oil, cream, or wax, depending upon their molecular weight, but are water-soluble and dissolve most water-soluble drugs.

Creams are water-washable and do not leave the greasy residue that is present after use of an ointment. They are able to absorb fluids from the skin and bring any dissolved medication into good contact with the skin.

Pastes

A paste, in the present context, is a suspension of a powder such as zinc oxide in a greasy ointment base.

Pastes are thicker and drier than ointments. They do not penetrate as well as ointments but are less occlusive.

Ointments

Ointments are preparations in which a drug is suspended or dissolved in a grease or oil. Petrolatum, liquid petrolatum (mineral oil), olive oil, lanolin, or other animal fats may be used.

Ointments provide mechanical protection to the underlying skin and penetrate thickened lesions well with their contained medication. They are emollient—ie, they lubricate and soften the surface of the skin and overlying crusts or scales. They do not permit drainage or evaporation from the skin, and continued application (by trapping moisture) causes maceration. They should not be used in hairy areas, where their penetration to the base of the follicle may lead to folliculitis.

Direct Application of Drugs

In some situations the most efficacious means of applying a drug may be as a simple solution, tincture, paint, suspension, or as crystals.

PHARMACOLOGIC ACTIONS OF DRUGS APPLIED TO THE SKIN

The form of the topical medication may itself have important pharmacologic effects—eg, the drying or emollient action of the aqueous or greasy preparations, or the antipruritic effect of baths or soaks. In addition, drugs may be incorporated into the vehicle to exert a variety of local actions.

Antipruritic Actions

The mechanical properties of many of the above vehicles may relieve itching by protecting the skin from the stimulation of scratching, friction, or changes in temperature or by moistening or drying the skin as necessary. In addition, several phenols that may be added to lotions reduce itching by an action on sensory reception. Whether the action is local anesthesia or the substitution of one sensation for another (counterirritation) is not clear.

Lotions, creams, and ointments containing local anesthetics and antihistamines are available, but, unless the skin is badly denuded of epithelium, they are poorly absorbed and have little effect other than that inherent in their mechanical properties. Antihistamines given for their systemic effect are highly useful in treating urticarial lesions, but they have no effect on itching due to other causes. The anti-inflammatory steroids (see below) relieve itching by suppressing the underlying process.

Astringent Actions

Astringents are mild protein precipitants that form a thick coagulum on the surface of an area of acute damage (eg, the alcohol in after-shave lotion) or coagulate and remove overlying debris (eg, the zinc chloride in a mouth wash).

Aluminum subacetate, aluminum acetate (Burow's solution), and potassium permanganate are astringents used in the concentrations shown in Table 5–2.

Keratoplastic Actions

Many chemicals cause an apparent destructive (keratolytic) or stimulant (keratoplastic) action on the epidermis depending upon the concentration used. The process is comparable to the more familiar results of constant rubbing or other trauma to an area of the skin. The trauma may denude an area or, if it is continued for a longer time, may result in stimulation of the basal layers and produce a much thickened cornified layer, which is apparent as a callus. Keratolytic drugs, therefore, are those that remove the cornified layer by chemical damage. A keratoplastic effect is seen when the drug does not produce rapid destruction and desquamation but a slower or milder process that increases basal layer activity and a thickened cornified layer.

Keratoplastic drugs include the following: (1) salicylic acid, 1–2%; (2) coal tar and other tars; and (3) those substances grouped together as reducing agents—eg, sulfur, chrysarobin, and pyrogallic acid in low concentrations.

Keratolytic Actions

Keratolytic drugs act to damage the cornified layer of the skin, which is then sloughed off to whatever depth the agent has acted. The very strong agents such as the caustics used on warts or calluses act by dehydrating the horny tissue. Ointments act by hydrating (macerating) the cornified layer, which then separates and is thrown off.

Those drugs listed above as keratoplastic are keratolytic when used in greater concentrations. These and other keratoplastics are salicylic acid, 5–20%; resorcin (resorcinol), 2–30%; chrysarobin, 0.1–10%; and anthralin, 0.1–5%.

Topical agents used in the treatment of **eczema, psoriasis,** and **seborrheic dermatitis** are often discussed as separate groups. The management of these difficult problems has been somewhat simplified by some recently introduced drugs, but definitions of a few old irritants and antiseptics are introduced here.

A. Tar: Crude coal tars are prepared by the destructive distillation of coal, gas, shale, or wood. Their composition is variable.

Tars are keratoplastic and keratolytic. Their effect is intensified by ultraviolet light, which itself alters the epidermis.

Tars have been displaced to a large extent by the corticosteroids but are still used against persistent psoriatic lesions.

Crude coal tar is used in 5–10% concentrations in antiseborrheic shampoos and applied in a thin layer directly to psoriatic lesions. Liquor carbonis detergens is a solution of coal tar with detergent. Ichthammol is tar prepared from fossil fish remains in shale. It is a mild, water-soluble tar. Unless one has a special interest in and experience with these drugs, proprietary preparations of tar should be used.

B. Chrysarobin and Anthralin: These very irritant substances are mentioned for identification and because they suggest the nature of the active component in tar. Chrysarobin is a mixture of hydroxylated polycyclic substances—eg, emodin—from a South American tree. It irritates normal skin, must not be used near the eyes, and stains clothing, hair, and skin.

Anthralin is a pure substance, a trihydroxy anthracene, comparable to chrysarobin but more potent and without its staining properties.

C. Sulfur: Sulfur in fine enough particles (microcrystalline or precipitated and colloidal) is an anti-infective agent and also reduces the activity of the sebaceous glands and dries the skin. Its principal remaining use is in the treatment of acne. Many proprietary acne creams, cakes, and lotions contain 4–8% sulfur together with the keratolytic resorcin.

D. Ammoniated Mercury: This is aminomercuric chloride ($HgNH_2Cl$). It was once used as a 5% ointment as a topical antiseptic and is still occasionally used in psoriasis.

E. Vitamin A Acid: Tretinoin (retinoic acid, vitamin A acid, Aberel) is a more irritating keratolytic.

Antibacterial Actions

Antibiotics should be used topically only for the most superficial infections—eg, impetigo or superficial folliculitis or pyoderma. The antibiotic used should have a low sensitizing potential and should preferably not be one of those commonly used systemically.

Systemic antibiotics can profoundly alter dermatologic diseases, including some that are not primarily infectious in origin. In acne, for example, tetracycline, 250 mg 1–2 times daily, will not only reduce pustule formation but also reduce duct obstruction by altering the bacterial flora and reducing the formation of free fatty acids from the triglycerides present in the sebum. A topical tetracycline was recently approved by the FDA for the treatment of acne.

Anti-inflammatory Corticosteroids

The availability of corticosteroids for systemic and topical application has made the treatment of many dermatologic problems much simpler and much more effective. This important drug group is discussed in detail in Chapter 35, where the corticosteroids most commonly used by topical application are listed.

Antifungal Actions

The deep mycoses require treatment with systemically acting drugs such as the antibiotics discussed in Chapter 55. The superficial mycotic infections may also be treated with an orally administered antibiotic, griseofulvin, but the most common fungal infections of the skin are treated with topical agents. The topical antifungal agents may act on the infecting organism to inhibit its growth or may alter the condition of the cornified layer of the epithelium in which the fungus grows.

A. Dermatophytosis (Athlete's Foot): The prevention and treatment of mild cases of athlete's foot depend upon careful drying of the feet after bathing and the use of dusting powders. Very acute lesions with fissuring and pain may require astringent soaks (see aluminum subacetate in Table 5–2) until the acute process subsides. Thereafter, zincundecate ointment, half-strength Whitfield's ointment, or tolnaftate solution may be used until careful personal hygiene and powders are again adequate.

B. Tinea Capitis (Ringworm of Scalp): Griseofulvin (Grisactin, Grifulvin) is an antibiotic that is deposited in keratinous structures and apparently acts

Table 5–4. Some representative dermatologic preparations not detailed in text. For topical antibiotics and corticosteroids, see Index.

Common Name	Prescriptions		Instructions and Remarks
Sulfur-salicylic acid ointment	Sulfur	1–3	Apply locally as needed. A potent fungicide. *Note:* Not for acute or subacute lesions.
	Salicylic acid	1–3	
	Petrolatum, qs ad	100	
Ointment of benzoic and salicylic acid (Whitfield's)	Benzoic acid	6	Apply locally at bedtime. Fungicide. Often prescribed in ½–¼ strength. Not for acute or subacute lesions.
	Salicylic acid	3	
	Polyethylene glycol ointment, qs ad	100	
Alcoholic Whitfield's solution	Salicylic acid	2	Apply locally. Effective fungicidal combination. May substitute bay rum for alcohol.
	Benzoic acid	4	
	Alcohol, 40%, qs ad	120	
Antiseborrheic shampoo	Selsun, Fostex, Sebulex, Capsebon, Alvinine, Sebical		Contain detergents, salicylic acid, sulfur compounds, tar and allantoin, or quinolone. Some may cause excess oiliness.
Ammoniated mercury ointment	Ammoniated mercury	4	Apply locally as required for seborrheic dermatitis and psoriasis.
	Liquid petrolatum	3	
	Petrolatum, qs ad	100	
Acne lotion	Sulfur, ppt		Apply locally at night for acne.
	Zinc sulfate a̅a̅	3.6	
	Sodium borate		
	Zinc oxide a̅a̅	6	
	Acetone	30	
	Camphor water		
	Rose water, a̅a̅, qs ad	120	
Fungicidal			
Tolnaftate solution	Tinactin solution, 10 mL		Apply twice daily for dermatophyte (tinea) fungal infections.
Miconazole (MicaTin)	2% cream		Ineffective for onychomycosis.
Haloprogin (Halotex)	Solution and cream, 1%		
Amphotericin B (Fungizone)	Fungizone lotion, 30 mL		Apply twice daily and as needed for mucocutaneous candidiasis.
Nystatin (Mycostatin)	Nystatin, 100,000 units/g dusting powder, 15 g		Dusting powder twice daily for candidiasis.
Gentian violet	1% aqueous solution		Antiseptic (gram-positive organisms) and fungicide (candidiasis).
Acrisorcin cream	Akrinol cream, 50 mL		Apply twice daily for tinea versicolor. Avoid eyes and genitalia.
Sodium thiosulfate	10% aqueous solution		Fungicide (especially for tinea versicolor).
Parasiticidal			
Gamma benzene hexachloride (1%) (lindane)	Kwell cream, 60 mL		Apply each night for 3 nights. Useful scabicide and pediculicide.
Chlorophenothane (DDT)	10% in talc (also 2% emulsion)		Not available in USA.

by interfering with reproduction of the fungal elements.

Griseofulvin is employed orally against dermatophyte or "ringworm" fungal infections. It is most effective for ringworm infections of the scalp and quite effective for involvement of the face, neck, and trunk; reasonably effective against ringworm of the groin; and much less effective for involvement of the hands and feet. Nail infections respond only very slowly to griseofulvin therapy, but local treatment is ineffective.

For ringworm of the scalp, microcrystalline griseofulvin (Grisactin, Grifulvin, and generic) should be given for at least 2 weeks in doses of 0.125 or 0.25 g 2 times daily. With extensive involvement, the initial daily dose may be 1 g. The dosage for children is safely predicted on the basis of weight—ie, approximately 10 mg/kg/d.

C. Tinea Corporis (Body Ringworm):
1. Griseofulvin as for tinea capitis.
2. Tolnaftate (Tinactin), haloprogin (Halotex), miconazole (Monistat, MicaTin), and clotrimazole (Lotrimin, Canesten) are topical agents that can be used in place of griseofulvin unless the infection involves the nails.
3. Sulfur–salicylic acid ointment. (See Table 5–4.)

Parasiticidal Actions

A. Scabies: Infestation with this mite is easily treated with gamma benzene hexachloride (lindane, Kwell cream). Benzyl benzoate and crotamiton are also effective.

B. Pediculosis: Benzene hexachloride, available as a shampoo as well as cream and lotion (Kwell), is also useful against body, head, or pubic lice. When, as in body lice infestations, it is necessary to treat bedding or clothing, a powder (lindane) from the garden supply store can be used.

Pigmenting Action

The response of the skin to ultraviolet light, especially long wave (320–400 nm) ultraviolet light, can be increased by the use of psoralen compounds. The topical or systemic use of methoxsalen (Oxsoralen) or trioxsalen (Trisoralen) prior to exposure to ultraviolet radiation augments the deposition of melanin in the skin and also increases the inflammatory response.

The psoralens have been used to increase tolerance to sunlight and to facilitate repigmentation of areas of vitiligo. For the latter purpose, the psoralens must be topically applied in the office, with a timed subsequent exposure to a proper ultraviolet lamp.

The current increased interest in the psoralens stems from their use investigatively in the treatment of psoriasis. The patient is given oral methoxsalen and exposed to calibrated, graded doses of long-wave ultraviolet radiation from a bank of lamps. The results of repeated treatments given at 48-hour intervals have thus far been impressive.

• • •

DIMETHYL SULFOXIDE (DMSO)

DMSO, $(H_3C)_2=S=O$, is a colorless liquid used as a solvent in the paint and other industries. It is highly polar and dissolves a great variety of both water-soluble and lipid-soluble substances. It has had investigational use as a vehicle for drugs and by virtue of its own properties.

DMSO applied topically in concentrations of 70% or greater has an anti-inflammatory action that has been used experimentally for the relief of symptoms associated with arthritis, bursitis, and scleroderma.

Drugs dissolved in DMSO penetrate the keratinized layer of the skin far more rapidly than when they are dissolved in other vehicles. The increased rate of absorption has been shown by measuring both systemic and local effects and is observed with drugs that are water- or lipid-soluble, charged or neutral.

DMSO has a very low acute systemic toxicity and does not alter the toxicity of drugs injected in DMSO rather than in aqueous solutions. Applied topically, especially in greater concentrations (90%), it is a histamine liberator and may cause redness or whealing.

In 3 of the animal species so far studied (dogs, rabbits, and pigs), the chronic administration of large doses of DMSO alters the optical properties of the central area of the lens. The refractive power of the lens becomes more like that of the aqueous than that of the cortical area of the lens, creating the effect of a lens within the lens. Because of this toxic effect (and perhaps also because the clinical investigation of DMSO had become undisciplined in many cases), the drug was briefly deprived of even its investigational status. It is now again available for investigational studies in humans, and a 50% solution (Rimso-50) is marketed for bladder installations for treatment of interstitial cystitis.

Dimethylacetamide and dimethylformamide are solvents with properties similar to DMSO.

• • •

References

Arndt KA: *Manual of Dermatologic Therapeutics.* Little, Brown, 1978.

Cunliffe WJ & others: Tetracycline and acne vulgaris: A clinical and laboratory investigation. Br Med J 4:332, 1973.

Desoximetasone (Topicort) and other topical corticosteroids. Med Lett Drugs Ther 19:85, 1977.

Domonkos AN: *Andrew's Diseases of the Skin,* 6th ed. Saunders, 1971.

Hunter JAA: Structure and function of skin in relation to therapy. Br Med J 4:340, 1973.

Kligman AM: Topical pharmacology and toxicology of dimethyl sulfoxide. (2 parts.) JAMA 193:796, 923, 1965.

Lerner MR, Lerner AB: *Dermatologic Medications,* 2nd ed. Year Book, 1960.

Rubin LF, Mattis PA: Dimethyl sulfoxide: Lens changes in dogs during oral administration. Science 153:83, 1966.

Smith JG Jr, Wehr RF, Chalker DK: Corticosteroid-induced cutaneous atrophy and telangiectasia. Arch Dermatol 112:1115, 1976.

Stern RS & others: Risk of cutaneous carcinoma in patients treated with oral methoxsalen photochemotherapy for psoriasis. N Engl J Med 300:809, 1979.

Stoughton RB, Fritsch W: Influence of dimethyl sulfoxide (DMSO) on human percutaneous absorption. Arch Dermatol 90:512, 1964.

Watson W, Farber EM: Controlling psoriasis. Postgrad Med 61:103, June 1977.

6 | Toxicity of Therapeutic Agents

The toxic effects of specific drug groups and individual drugs vary widely, as would be predicted from their diverse pharmacologic effects. The adverse reactions that may occur are discussed for individual drugs in the subsequent chapters. There are, however, some aspects of toxicity relevant to all drugs, and these will be discussed here. The toxicity of common environmental—ie, nontherapeutic—agents is discussed separately (see Chapters 64–66).

The topics to be discussed in this chapter are: (1) the general evaluation of drug toxicity (especially of new drugs) and the problem of identifying and measuring risk; and (2) allergic reactions to drugs.

SIGNIFICANCE OF ANIMAL TOXICITY STUDIES

There are many reasons why toxicity data from experiments on normal animals cannot be directly extended to diseased human beings. Nevertheless, these data do have considerable predictive value, and it is essential that they be collected before a new drug is tried in humans. Dose-related toxicity can usually be predicted in this way, and the potency of a new drug can be compared with that of older drugs to the extent that the toxic effect is an extension of the desired pharmacologic action.

In most countries, the animal toxicity studies that must precede trials of new drugs in humans are to some extent determined by law or the administrative orders of a regulatory agency. The details mentioned below reflect one suggested set of requirements for preclinical testing.

Acute Toxicity

Acute toxicity is measured by the median lethal dose, or LD_{50}. This is the dose that will kill 50% of a group of animals under stated conditions—ie, it is a statistical expression of the dose that will kill an animal of average sensitivity to the drug. The LD_{50} is an assay, not a measurement. It is not an absolute value but will vary from laboratory to laboratory and even when the assay is repeated in the same laboratory. The experimental conditions of the assay must be stan-

dardized. Both the species and the strain of the animals should be recorded, as well as the route of administration, the vehicle in which the drug is dissolved or suspended, and the concentration and volume of the solution injected. Diet, ambient temperature, season, and other variables are not easily controlled; for this reason, a standard related drug should be studied for comparison. In the USA, 4 species must be used, including one nonrodent form. The routes of administration must be those that are to be used in humans.

Subacute & Chronic Toxicity

Preliminary to an extended chronic toxicity test, a subacute toxicity experiment is usually the second step in preclinical toxicity testing. It extends for 14–21 days and establishes the minimal toxic and maximal tolerated dose as well as a possible role of cumulation and tolerance. It is essential to the design of an extended toxicity test.

The chronic toxicity experiment is the third step. The drug is given to animals of 2 species for 90 days in at least 3 dosage levels, one of which is the predicted therapeutic level and one the level at which at least minimal toxicity occurs. Growing animals are used for this test, and weight gain during the experiment is compared with that of a control group. Gross and histopathologic examinations are done at the conclusion of the experiment. The chronic toxicity test in dogs must (in the USA) continue for 1 year, but early clinical trials may be initiated after 3 months of testing.

Other Toxicity Tests

Depending upon the anticipated use of the drug, special toxicity tests may be required. If the drug is to be recommended for use in women of childbearing age, possible teratogenicity must be studied. For this purpose the drug is given to both male and female rats prior to the first mating and extending through the production of 2 litters. The results of these animal studies are of questionable validity with respect to the possible effects of the same drug on the human fetus, and for this reason most recently introduced drugs are still considered to be of unestablished safety for use early in pregnancy.

Other drugs may need to be studied in newborn animals or, if they are to be used topically, must be studied for possible irritant effects on the skin. Prospective anesthetic agents are administered for 3 hours a day for at least 5 consecutive days in lieu of the above chronic toxicity tests.

Prediction of Toxicity by Pharmacologic Grouping

While the toxicologic data are being collected, general pharmacologic observations are being made. These usually allow a new drug to be placed in a general chemical or therapeutic drug class and thus frequently permit the prediction of adverse effects by analogy with familiar drugs.

Therapeutic Index

Absolute toxicity is less important than the ratio between the toxic and the therapeutic dose. Reference is often made to a median effective dose (ED_{50})—ie, the dose that is therapeutically effective in 50% of a population similar to that on which the median lethal dose (LD_{50}) was determined. The ratio LD_{50}/ED_{50} is then calculated as a "therapeutic index." However, in very few drug groups is a therapeutic effect measured in animals that is comparable to the desired effect in human beings. Furthermore, because the physician hopes to avoid even an isolated fatility due to direct drug toxicity, the dosage that produces the dose-limiting side-effect or first dangerous toxic sign is of greater importance than the therapeutic index. The concept of a therapeutic index thus has value mainly as an abstraction emphasizing that toxicity is relative rather than absolute.

EVALUATION OF TOXICITY IN THE HUMAN

Investigative Drugs

The first trials on human beings of a potentially useful pharmacologic agent may begin while the chronic animal toxicity tests are still in progress. These earliest human studies are done as part of the phase I testing of a new drug as defined in Chapter 3 and are usually performed on healthy volunteers. This experience serves to uncover any marked toxic effects of the drug that were not apparent during administration to animals and to establish dose, duration of action, and other factors necessary to design further clinical investigations. Further studies on larger groups of patients with the disease or symptom against which the drug is to be used then serve to prove or disprove the usefulness of the preparation. At the same time, they begin to uncover adverse reactions that occur with a low incidence. The number and severity of allergic reactions especially—which cannot be predicted on the basis of animal studies—can be accurately evaluated only after hundreds or thousands of subjects have received the drug.

After this stage in the evaluation of a new drug, a judgment is made by the Food and Drug Administra-

tion about whether the possible usefulness of the drug outweighs its possible dangers, and permission to market the drug is given or denied.

Quantitation of Risk of Agents in General Use

When a new drug is released for general use, information about its toxicity may be incomplete. The total number of cases in which the drug has been used, and the number of cases seen by any one investigator, may have been too small to identify dangerous adverse reactions that occur in only one out of hundreds or thousands of patients. A drug remains under "post-marketing surveillance" for an indefinite period and may be withdrawn from the market if unexpected untoward reactions are encountered. However, there are 2 questions about many drugs that remain unanswered even after years of widespread use: (1) the absolute incidence of adverse reactions, and (2) whether all reactions are recognized or only those that cause obscure rather than familiar signs of disease.

A. Incidence of Reactions: To make an accurate statement about the frequency with which a particular reaction occurs, it is necessary to know the size and characteristics of the population at risk and the number of reactions. A closed group—eg, those patients on a particular service in one hospital—may be studied, but this group is not necessarily representative of all patients in and out of the hospital who are receiving the drug. Furthermore, the reporting of drug reactions is grossly inadequate. Reactions are often not recognized as drug-induced, or they may not be reported because of the feeling that a professional error is involved or because of the fear of legal action. Monitoring of hospital populations has shown that adverse reactions occur many times oftener than are recognized and recorded.

What is needed is a report of all untoward effects of a drug given to a representative sample of patients of diverse types. Such a system is not now available or in prospect in spite of the efforts of the FDA to establish one.

Case reports and registries of drug reactions—eg, the now abandoned registry of adverse reactions of the AMA—are not adequate for quantifying the risk with any degree of accuracy. Such registries depend upon volunteered information, and there is no way of knowing what fraction of the total experience is represented. Certainly it is a very small fraction. Adequate epidemiologic studies are available in only a few situations. The example presented in Fig 6–1 has unavoidable limitations but suggests a relation between the amount of a drug used and the incidence of a particular toxic reaction.

In this book, therefore, the attempt to quantitate the frequency of drug reactions will necessarily be expressed in somewhat vague terms—eg, rare, infrequent, common—simply because more precise wording—eg, 9 cases of agranulocytosis per 100,000 administrations—is not forthcoming from the facts at hand.

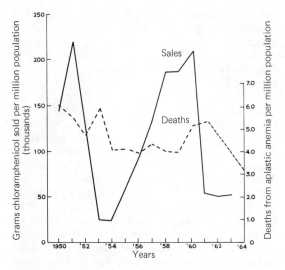

Figure 6–1. The data on the annual sales of chloramphenicol in California illustrate the transient decrease in the prescribing of a drug following public alarm about its toxicity. The increase in the number of cases of aplastic anemia following each sales peak suggests the conclusion (established by more definitive studies) that the use of chloramphenicol is associated with an incidence of aplastic anemia 13 times greater than that seen in the total population. (Redrawn, with additional figures, from California State Department of Health, Report to State Senate: *Chloromycetin—A Study of Antibiotic Drugs.* 1963.)

B. Identification of Reactions: The foregoing suggests that, even in those cases where a causal relation is established between the administration of a drug and the appearance of a toxic effect, information about the absolute incidence of the reaction is often lacking. Another concern is that the causal relation may not be recognized if the reaction occurs infrequently, especially if the toxic reaction resembles a common complaint.

Association of a rare toxic effect of a drug with that drug cannot be accomplished by the study of single cases but only by refined epidemiologic technics. (Consider the similarity with the problem of establishing a causal relationship between cigarette smoking and cancer of the lung.) If the epidemiologic method consists merely of the accumulation of isolated case reports, uncommon toxic effects resembling a common disease would not be recognized and reported as drug-related. If a previously rare disease suddenly occurs more frequently and occurs in clusters in populations or areas of high drug use, the connection is more easily made—eg, phocomelia and thalidomide, renal papillary necrosis and phenacetin, or retroperitoneal fibrosis and methysergide. If thalidomide had merely added to the total of common congenital defects, recognition of its toxicity would have been delayed or its toxicity might not have been recognized at all. The problem of assigning responsibility for a toxic effect is made more difficult by the fact that individuals, whether patients or merely members of

the total population, rarely have contact with a single drug. A degree of conservatism in adopting new chemical types of drugs is therefore justified.

Not all therapeutic misadventures are due to factors inherent in the drug itself. Prescribing and nursing errors, usually but not invariably minor, occur in a surprisingly high percentage of administrations.

ALLERGIC REACTIONS TO DRUGS

The occurrence of most adverse reactions to drugs is related to the amount taken or administered, and the exact nature of the toxic effect is determined by the properties of the drug molecule. A given patient may be unusually sensitive or resistant to a particular drug effect, but all patients will respond if the dose is great enough, and the variation in sensitivity or reactivity is normally distributed—ie, if patient response is plotted against the logarithm of the dose, the response values will be symmetrically distributed about the mean.

In contrast, allergic or hypersensitivity reactions depend on reactivity of the patient altered by prior contact with a drug that functions as an allergen or antigen. Signs and symptoms of the allergic reaction are unrelated to the pharmacologic effect of the drug but resemble instead those of other allergic reactions.

Drug molecules (except for those few that are proteins) cannot function as complete antigens but only as haptens—ie, they must react chemically with some homologous protein after administration or contact. The altered body protein is antigenic and the haptenic drug confers specificity. Fortunately, most drugs do not react as readily with protein as the simple molecules used by immunochemists in their experiments. Penicillin is a well studied example of a drug with a reactive metabolite (penicilloic acid) that is responsible for its antigenicity.

Not all allergic reactions to drugs have been categorized immunochemically. Indeed, there are a few that have not been clearly characterized as either dose-related or allergic. Depending upon the amount of study that a particular reaction has attracted, one or more of the following criteria may be used to establish the allergic nature of an adverse reaction: (1) Circulating or cellular antibodies to the suspect drug can be demonstrated. (2) The process conforms to a known allergic pattern—eg, hives, skin rash, anaphylaxis. (3) After recovery, the process can be precipitated again in its same form by a single test dose. (4) The reaction occurs most frequently after a sensitizing period of administration. (5) The reaction is not related to dosage level (per day) or total amount administered. (The amount of antigen is important in causing sensitization, but thereafter small doses may induce the reaction.) (6) The reaction is relieved by sympathomimetics, antihistamines, or anti-inflammatory steroids.

Some examples of allergic reactions to drugs are discussed in the following section.

Immediate Allergic Reactions

Immediate allergic reactions to drugs depend upon the formation of immunoglobulins of the IgE class. The IgE (reaginic, or tissue-fixed) antibody specific for the drug hapten is bound to the surface of tissue mast cells or blood basophils. When the drug is subsequently reintroduced, the sensitized cells are degranulated by the reaction of antigen and antibody on their surface, releasing histamine and other substances and causing an anaphylactic or urticarial reaction.

At the same time, antibodies of the IgG and IgM (circulating) classes are also formed. These may combine with antigen administered later to keep antigen from reaching tissue-fixed (IgE) antibody and thus block anaphylaxis, or the antigen-antibody complex may be deposited in blood vessels to cause serum sickness or vasculitis. The reaction may appear soon after absorption of the drug or may be delayed for several weeks; the name "immediate" is applied because the reaction to a skin test appears within minutes in those situations in which it is positive.

A. Anaphylaxis: Anaphylaxis is a rare but potentially lethal drug reaction. Anaphylaxis is inherently very dangerous, and delay in recognition, hesitancy in treatment, or lack of preparation for treatment greatly increases the possibility of death.

Anaphylaxis, unlike most other allergic reactions, can be easily studied in animals, and its characteristics are similar in the laboratory and in clinical situations. A sensitizing dose or doses must be given. After a certain minimal period without additional antigen being given, a small challenge dose of antigen causes a reaction due almost entirely to mast cell degranulation. Mast cells of different species contain varying proportions of histamine or serotonin, and the anaphylactic state will vary depending upon which amine is present and upon the reaction of different target organs in different species. Mast cells also contain heparin, kinins, and SRS (slow-reacting substance), which may also contribute to the anaphylactic reaction.

In humans, histamine release leads to bronchiolar constriction; localized edema, often in the laryngeal and glottal region; and vasodilatation with consequent hypotension and shock. Respiratory obstruction due to one or both of the first 2 effects is the cause of death in human anaphylaxis. Urticaria usually appears along with the more dangerous signs.

The treatment of anaphylaxis is outlined in Chapter 19, where the pharmacology of histamine and antihistamines is discussed. In summary, the immediate treatment consists of the injection of epinephrine, 0.5 mL of 1:1000 solution or 0.5 mg intravenously or intramuscularly. This sympathomimetic amine acts as a physiologic antagonist of histamine—ie, it has effects opposite to those of histamine and leads to vasoconstriction, bronchiolar dilatation, and resorption of edema. The antihistamines block further action of histamine but do not reverse changes that have already occurred. The anti-inflammatory steroids inhibit the allergic reaction and suppress allergic in-

flammation just as they suppress other types of inflammation. Their action is too slow for this situation, however.

Oxygen is of little value, since the airway is obstructed. Tracheostomy is often mentioned as advisable, especially when intubation fails. In at least some cases, however, bronchiolar constriction prevents effective respiration even after tracheostomy.

The threat posed by an anaphylactic reaction depends upon the speed with which the reaction occurs after administration of the antigen. Treatment—ie, epinephrine—must be immediately available. If the reaction is delayed as much as 30 minutes after an injection, the situation is less threatening and an antihistamine can be used instead of epinephrine.

Almost all drugs that are injected intravenously and many that are given intramuscularly or subcutaneously have caused anaphylactic reactions. Biologicals containing horse serum and other protein drugs (chymotrypsin, penicillinase, etc) are, of course, most dangerous. Because of its wide use and pronounced allergenicity, intramuscularly administered penicillin was the most common cause of anaphylactic incidents until the adoption of oral penicillin. Anaphylaxis has been reported after oral penicillin and other orally administered drugs, but far less frequently and usually with a slow appearance and progression of signs, permitting effective treatment.

Anaphylaxis is in part mimicked by another process that occurs after rapid intravenous injection and is described as speed shock or nitritoid crisis. Almost any drug, but notably x-ray contrast media today and arsenicals in the past, can, when injected rapidly, alter the blood somehow—presumably by acting on the plasma proteins or other colloids—and cause profound vasodilatation.

B. Other Immediate Reactions: Other immediate allergic reactions are uncommon but not so rare as anaphylaxis. They neither present the same dangers nor require the same instant treatment.

1. Urticaria and angioneurotic edema–Hives and localized edema are caused more often by food allergens than by drugs. Some drugs such as morphine, codeine, and their relatives are able to liberate histamine by a direct action on mast cells. The urticaria thus produced is not allergic in origin.

2. Asthma and rhinitis–These rare reactions to drugs usually occur in patients with other allergies. Some of the gums—eg, acacia and tragacanth—were frequently involved in this reaction in the past. Aspirin, quinine, sulfonamides, penicillin, and other drugs have also caused isolated cases.

3. Serum sickness–Serum sickness involves IgG as well as IgE and is conventionally designated as a type III, or complex-mediated, reaction. It appears in response to an antigen with a plasma half-life so long that antigen is still circulating when antibody titers rise. The antibodies build up during an incubation period of 5–14 days. There is then a sudden decrease in the amount of circulating antigen as soluble antigen-antibody complex is formed. The complex initiates serum sickness by activating mediators of clotting and inflammation. Whether or not the drug is still being administered, there will be the sudden appearance of fever, skin rash, adenopathy, and arthralgia. The state may persist for several days to several weeks and require corticosteroids for its relief.

Biologicals containing horse serum—eg, antivenoms—most regularly produce serum sickness, but penicillin, sulfonamides, phenytoin, streptomycin, and others have also been causal agents.

It appears that the same process can lead to a vasculitis distinguishable from periarteritis by its involvement of smaller vessels and a reversible course.

4. Drug fever–A variant of serum sickness is the sudden appearance of fever to 104 F or higher 7–21 days after the use of a drug. Drug fever has become less common as antibiotics have replaced the sulfonamides. It is most puzzling when it occurs following treatment of an infection, and a distinction must be made between a possible drug reaction and an apparent relapse. The fever usually lasts 2–3 days after the drug has been discontinued.

C. Autoimmune Reactions:

1. Thrombocytopenic purpura–The mechanism of this reaction has been established for quinidine. It is not actually autoimmune in that neither platelets nor other homologous proteins function as the antigen. The antigen-antibody complex formed subsequent to the administration of quinidine to a sensitive patient is adsorbed onto the platelets, and they are suddenly agglutinated. Bleeding into the skin may occur, but recovery is rapid, since the problem is one of peripheral destruction rather than depression of production.

2. Disseminated lupus erythematosus–The long-continued administration of a number of drugs—especially hydralazine and procainamide but also phenytoin, trimethadione, isoniazid, and others—may be followed by the appearance of a state indistinguishable clinically and in the laboratory from spontaneously occurring lupus. It is usually mild and usually regresses when the drug is discontinued. A few cases have resulted in permanent damage.

3. Hemolytic anemia–Drugs may cause hemolytic anemias by several mechanisms. They may act directly to cause hemolysis—eg, phenylhydrazine. In patients with an inherited deficiency of glucose-6-phosphate dehydrogenase in the erythrocytes, administration of many drugs—eg, primaquine, nitrofurantoin—will cause an oxidative hemolysis. Finally, at least one drug, methyldopa, can cause hemolytic anemia. In many patients, the interaction of methyldopa and some ordinary red cell antigen is apparent as a positive Coombs test—ie, the presence of antibody globulin on the surface of the erythrocyte is established. In a smaller number of patients, actual hemolysis and anemia occur. The process is reversed upon discontinuance of the drug and, if necessary, treatment with corticosteroids.

4. Agranulocytosis–Some cases of agranulocytosis are associated with an aplastic bone marrow, are not associated with demonstrable antileukocyte antibodies, and are not controlled by corticosteroid administration. Agranulocytosis presumed to be an allergic reaction to the administration of a drug is due to the abrupt peripheral destruction of granulocytes, is associated with a cellular marrow, and usually responds promptly to treatment with corticosteroids and discontinuance of the drug responsible.

The onset of the process is abrupt and immediately severe—ie, it is not a continuation of any dose-related leukopenia and cannot be anticipated even by weekly blood counts.

Treatment other than steroids consists of antibiotics to treat the infections that develop in the absence of granulocytes. The mortality rate is still estimated to be 20% or higher.

Delayed Allergic Reactions

In the development of delayed hypersensitivity reactions, the drug-protein combination is identified by small lymphocytes (antigen recognition [AR] cells) as foreign. Immune cells differentiate from these AR cells and return to the skin or other antigen-containing tissue to initiate an inflammatory reaction. The inflammatory process precipitated by a delayed reaction reaches a peak only after 24–48 hours.

A. Cutaneous Reactions: Drugs acting as antigens after systemic administration can cause a great variety of skin reactions. Most are delayed and may be in the form of a minor morbilliform rash or resemble atopic or eczematous dermatitis or progress to an exfoliative dermatitis.

Applied to the skin, drugs may act as primary or direct chemical irritants. However, many drugs function as antigen when applied topically. The occurrence of sensitization depends upon the patient, the drug, and the duration of exposure. For some drugs—eg, penicillin and sulfonamides—the incidence of sensitization is so high that topical use has had to be abandoned.

B. Aplastic Anemia: No mechanism for this process has been established. Whether it is allergic or not, an association with the use of certain drugs is quite clear. Of 700 cases of aplastic anemia reported to the AMA Registry in one 7-year period, 45% of the patients had received chloramphenicol and 20% had received no other drug. Phenylbutazone, mephenytoin, gold salts, and chlorinated hydrocarbon insecticides were also implicated.

The condition is one of bone marrow depression, and leukopenia and thrombocytopenia accompany the anemia. Recovery is very slow, and mortality is variously estimated at 50–80%. The reaction may be more easily reversible if detected early. Treatment includes transfusions, antibiotics, and androgens or other anabolic steroids.

Radiation and antimetabolites cause aplastic anemia by a more direct kind of depression. In a fraction (perhaps one-third) of the cases of aplastic anemia, no association with drugs or environmental toxins can be suggested.

• • •

References

General

Jick H: The discovery of drug-induced illness. N Engl J Med 296:481, 1977.

Jick H & others: Comprehensive drug surveillance. JAMA 213:1455, 1970.

Karch FE, Lasagna L: Adverse drug reactions. JAMA 234:1236, 1975.

Meyler L: *Side Effects of Drugs.* Vol 7. Excerpta Medica Foundation, 1972.

Mintz M: *The Therapeutic Nightmare.* Houghton-Mifflin, 1965.

Moser RH: *Diseases of Medical Progress,* 2nd ed. Thomas, 1964.

Shapiro S & others: Fatal drug reactions among medical inpatients. JAMA 216:467, 1971.

Smith JW, Seidl LG, Cluff LE: Studies on the epidemiology of adverse drug reactions. 5. Clinical factors influencing susceptibility. Ann Intern Med 65:629, 1966.

Whipple HE (editor): Evaluation and mechanisms of drug toxicity. Ann NY Acad Sci 123:1, 1965.

Drug Allergy

Corbascio AN: Countermeasures for anaphylactic reactions. Drug Ther 6:101, July 1976.

Drug-induced anaphylaxis: A cooperative study. JAMA 224:613, 1973.

Garratty G, Petz LD: Drug-induced immune hemolytic anemia. Am J Med 58:398, 1975.

Huguley CM Jr: Hematological reactions. JAMA 196:408, 1966.

James LP Jr, Austen KF: Fatal systemic anaphylaxis in man. N Engl J Med 270:597, 1964.

Lichtenstein LM, Norman PS: Human allergic reactions. Am J Med 46:163, 1969.

Parker CW: Drug allergy. (3 parts.) N Engl J Med 292:511, 732, 957, 1975.

Tan EM: Drug-induced autoimmune disease. Fed Proc 33:1894, 1974.

Wallerstein RO & others: Statewide study of chloramphenicol therapy and fatal aplastic anemia. JAMA 208:2045, 1969.

7 | Drug Abuse

Because the drugs subject to misuse present a variety of hazards, there is no single "drug problem" but a variety of problems. However, a few concepts are applicable to the misuse of drugs of all classes. By reviewing them at this point, overemphasis on drug factors can be avoided and individual and social factors stressed. The pharmacology of marihuana and the hallucinogens is discussed in this chapter also.

It is difficult to rationalize the use of any drug for nontherapeutic purposes. Even drugs that are generally pleasurable and safe and whose use is not only socially approved but in some groups almost mandatory—eg, alcohol—become destructive when used by many individuals. Thus, insofar as personal use of drugs is concerned, the physician should both practice and advise the greatest caution in even experimenting with drug use. However, drug use promises to remain widespread in spite of contrary advice. In fact, the amount of experimentation with drugs—especially among the young—and the variety of agents involved have recently increased greatly, creating both social and pharmacologic problems. The health professional, invested with a presumption of technical expertise and a degree of automatic leadership, must influence the development of attitudes toward users of both old and new drugs so that the damage from both drug effects and the societal reaction can be minimized.

Patterns of Drug Abuse

Drugs are used in different patterns, which may vary in their effect on the individual from benign to totally destructive. The terms "addiction" (physical and psychologic dependence) and "habituation" (psychologic dependence) were used in the past to describe some patterns of use, but these inadequate terms have been abandoned even by the expert committees that defined them. The current more or less official terminology (ie, "dependence of the ———type") is even less satisfactory because it obscures the fact that a given drug may be used in a variety of patterns.

In describing and evaluating the hazards of drug use, the following terms allow for the variety of patterns seen, imply a process of progression, and relate drug use to other social and psychologic processes.

A. Experimental Use: Drug use or abuse must begin with experimental or exploratory use, after which the individual may reject the use of the drug or progress to one of the patterns of use described below. This concept is obvious but important. If our goal is abatement rather than treatment of drug problems, our efforts should be aimed at discouraging experimentation with drugs.

B. Social Use: Social drugs are used in groups, and the common examples—alcohol (see Chapter 24) and marihuana—are sedatives that relieve anxiety and facilitate group interaction. When cigarettes, coffee, or soft drinks are used as social drugs, the separation of drug and social factors becomes more complex.

The danger of the social use of drugs, like the danger of experimentation with drugs, is that it exposes those individuals who are vulnerable to a more destructive pattern of use.

C. Episodic Abuse: Excessive amounts of a drug may be used periodically. If the drug is alcohol or another sedative, users may in disinhibited states damage themselves and others. The abuse is, however, still elective rather than compulsive.

D. Compulsive Abuse: In a number of individuals who have experimented with one drug or another, its use becomes a compulsion—ie, an act based on emotion rather than volition, recognizably irrational even to the user but senselessly repeated to avoid the anxiety that appears without the compulsive act.

The hazard of developing such a compulsive pattern of use depends in part upon the personality of the individual. However, considering the fraction of the population that at some time adopts a compulsion—eg, cigarette smoking, coffee drinking, nail-picking, or adolescent masturbation—the vulnerability must be so widely distributed that it escapes being called abnormal.

The probability of a given act becoming a compulsion also depends upon the sensory or pharmacologic reward that reinforces the behavior. Thus, injected opiates and injected amphetamine carry a great hazard because of the rush, or feeling of orgasm, that occurs at the time of injection. The mild central nervous system stimulating properties of nicotine make cigarettes a common vehicle of compulsion; statistically, 85% of adolescents who smoke more than one cigarette become regular smokers and cannot substitute nicotine-free cigarettes. Relief of anxiety by sedatives must also be an important reward or reinforcing factor. The percentage of alcohol drinkers who become compulsive alcoholics is less than the percentage of heroin users or cigarette smokers who become that dependent, but the wide use of alcohol ensures a huge number of chronic alcoholics.

The compulsive drug user (''addict'') has difficulty giving up the habit even when given maximal assistance.

E. Ritual Abuse: Drugs may be used with a philosophic basis or preconception—eg, LSD may be used with the expectation of achieving a religious or psychotherapeutic experience. The ritual pattern of use is not a part of the above sequence—ie, it does not develop from social use or progress to compulsive abuse. Ritual drugs are not selected to provide some hedonistic reward, and if the user is protected by other group members during the drug effect, the dangers are minimal. One is not committed by such a judgment to agreement with the philosophic basis for the use of the drug or to sympathy with any associated life style.

Factors in the Development of Drug Abuse

Drugs are generally misused because they alter mood or behavior, and an understanding of their properties is important to an understanding of their abuse. However, if drug abuse depended entirely on the properties of the drugs, everyone would be using the same drug to the same extent. To understand the geographic, cultural, and temporal variations in the epidemiology of drug use, factors other than the unchanging pharmacologic effects of the drugs must be considered.

A. Individual (Psychologic) Factors in Drug Abuse: Alcohol, the most commonly misused drug, is freely available to all members of our culture, but our patterns of alcohol use vary widely. Some individuals never drink; some drink temperately and intermittently to relieve anxiety or to facilitate participation in social situations; some drink episodically to excess; and a tragically large number develop a compulsive pattern of alcohol misuse that destroys their own and other lives. The same variability occurs in response to contact with other drugs when the personality of the individual is the only variable in the situation. Yet it has not been possible to define a ''user personality.'' Even compulsive users of ''hard'' drugs do not differ greatly from the nonusing members of the groups from which they come until they have lived in the drug world for many years. In the case of some drugs, notably alcohol and cigarettes, the dominant culture encourages experimentation to such an extent that we can guarantee that the vulnerable individuals will be located and damaged. Since individual vulnerability cannot be predicted, the most appropriate attitude toward drug use is that experimentation with all drugs must be avoided.

B. Group (Sociologic) Factors: Individuals form attitudes and react as members of groups. The attitudes and problems of their group will condition their use of drugs and their reaction toward people who choose to use drugs.

The social factors that interact with the properties of drugs and the individual personality can be simplified into 2 categories: (1) the attitudes of the dominant group in the culture, and (2) the often conflicting attitudes of members of the several subgroups in our society.

The attitudes of the dominant group are reflected in the laws. In western society, the laws are generally permissive of alcohol and tobacco, which are actually quite harmful, but often impose severe penalties for the mere possession of other drugs.

There are, of course, subgroups of our pluralistic society who feel that the prohibitions against their social drugs are arbitrary and unjustified by the actions of the drug. Conflict between these groups and the dominant group is inevitable.

The youthful subculture, for example, has been adopting marihuana as a social drug comparable to alcohol. The essential similarity of these 2 drugs is discussed below, yet the use of one is treated by the older generation as a serious crime and the use of the other is more than tolerated.

Other groups, at first mature intellectuals but later middle-class young whites, experimented with LSD and other ''psychedelics'' and formed the ''hippie'' group, many of whom then became nominally ''criminal'' in their possession and use of illegal drugs but had wide influence on music, art, dress, and the attitudes of the young toward the dominant culture.

In societies such as those in the USA, most of the ''drug problem'' is actually a conflict between the mores of the dominant culture and the 2 subcultures that have recently gained identity: the blacks and the emerging generation.

Finally, general economic and social factors can act through the individual. Minority groups and the economically distressed contribute disproportionately to the problem of heroin use in the USA, and one opinion holds that they are vulnerable because of their poverty and repression. There have been few paths out of the ghetto, and heroin provides transient escape along with relief of aggressive feelings. The peace in Harlem had been maintained, according to James Baldwin, by Jesus and junk. An alternative opinion holds that the availability of heroin in the central city explains its wider use there; that blacks and other ethnic groups living in large cities at the time of the first epidemic of heroin use (1949–1951) were not more vulnerable, merely more exposed. The recent epidemic (1968–1972), with its involvement of more diverse groups, supports the concept. In either case, the groups involved were exposed to the societal reaction mentioned below.

C. Drug Factors: For each drug class and individual drug, the possible patterns of misuse, the effect of abuse on the individual, and the effect on society must be considered. Each of the drug classes used as therapeutic agents is discussed in other chapters. Fuller discussions will be provided here about marihuana and the hallucinogens, since these agents have no therapeutic usefulness and are not considered elsewhere.

1. Narcotics or opiates–Heroin, morphine, other alkaloids of opium, and various synthetics are quite dangerous for the individual because of their potential for compulsive misuse. Nevertheless, with society having now expressed its willingness to provide heroin users with huge daily doses of another narcotic, it can no longer be argued that the opiates are inherently and inevitably destructive. The heroin user is either depressed by the drug or shows no effect if "maintaining" on a habit of unvarying size. The addict is driven to antisocial acts not by the drug effect but by a compulsive need to guarantee the availability of the next fix. The dangers and the objections of society must be based on the associated criminal activity resulting from the illegality and expense of heroin—ie, the societal reaction rather than the drug effects.

Tolerance to and physical dependence on the opiates are less important than might be predicted because heroin (owing to its expense) is supplied in diluted form.

Fear of withdrawal is a factor in maintaining the habit and is the first barrier to treatment. However, withdrawal is repeatedly imposed on the average user, by either detention or therapy, but is not curative. Heroin users, like alcoholics, often revert to their compulsion after prolonged periods of abstinence (as during incarceration) when physical withdrawal sickness cannot be present.

2. Major sympathomimetic stimulants–Cocaine and the "diet pills" (discussed in detail in Chapter 28) cause a pleasurable stimulation or euphoria that leads to their frequent misuse.

Cocaine is generally inhaled or sniffed and rapidly absorbed across the pharyngeal mucosa. It is currently used as a party or "spree" drug, but its expense limits its use.

Amphetamine, methamphetamine, and other diet pills (Table 28–2) are prescribed in huge amounts as anorectic agents. They soon lose their effectiveness for this purpose, but patients and others are persistent in their efforts to maintain a continuing supply of the medication. They are obviously being used as euphoriants rather than anorectics. Amphetamine abuse after oral administration is not usually a difficult therapeutic problem, but an occasional case of compulsive oral misuse has followed therapeutic administration. The cause of greatest concern, however, is that when injected intravenously, methamphetamine ("speed," "crystal") causes an immediate pleasurable experience that imposes a hazard of compulsive abuse comparable to that of heroin.

An epidemic of intravenous methamphetamine abuse occurred in the young people's ghettos (eg, the Haight-Ashbury neighborhood of San Francisco) during 1967–1969. Not only was the effectiveness of the drug-dominated individual destroyed, but much violent behavior was generated by the drug effect and by the new, poorly disciplined, illegal marketplace. The user found heroin an effective drug to terminate the speed "run," and through this experience progressed to heroin use, probably initiating the present epidemic. Abuse of intravenous amphetamines continues, but comparatively few people are now involved.

3. Minor stimulants–Central nervous system stimulants, such as the nicotine in cigarettes and the caffeine in coffee, are listed here for 2 purposes: first, to point out that there are drugs that have been accepted as social or recreational agents; and second, to suggest that an understanding of the problem and the treatment of compulsive drug misuse is perhaps best developed by studying similar compulsive acts in those who do not regard themselves as "drug users." The compulsive use of cigarettes, for example, is, like heroin use, an act senselessly repeated despite the certainty of damage to health. Use continues not so much out of a desire to smoke as because the confirmed smoker cannot face the resulting intense, if transient, anxiety.

4. Sedative-hypnotic drugs–The dangers of misuse—ie, the effect of use on the individual and, through the individual's altered behavior, on society—are greatest for alcohol or other sedatives. Not only may the altered psychomotor capability and impaired judgment result in irresponsible and criminal acts if the drug acts long enough, but the hazard of developing a compulsive pattern of use is also present. It must be emphasized again that misuse of alcohol is by far the greatest problem in drug abuse.

Sedative-hypnotics that are misused include the following: (1) Alcohol. (2) Barbiturates, meprobamate, glutethimide, diazepam, and other sedatives ordinarily given by prescription. (3) General anesthetics such as ether, nitrous oxide, and phencyclidine (PCP) or the closely related ketamine. Ketamine is used as a general anesthetic and is discussed in Chapter 20; the chemical structure of PCP is also shown there. PCP, whether smoked or taken by mouth, is long-acting. (4) Many hydrocarbons other than the familiar general anesthetics. Gasoline and solvents in model airplane glue are the older examples. More recently, the propellants in aerosol spray cans have been used. The fluorinated hydrocarbons, or Freons, are comparable to halothane or chloroform. (Freon 11 is trichloromonofluoromethane.) The propellants are inhaled from a plastic bag filled from the spray can, and a high initial concentration is inhaled, sometimes causing the cardiac arrest predicted by experience with other halogenated hydrocarbons. Well over 100 fatalities have been documented as a result of this practice. (5) Marihuana (see below).

CANNABIS
(Marihuana, Hashish)

Marihuana is discussed separately from the other sedative-hypnotics because it is not a therapeutic agent and because of the controversy surrounding it. Part of the controversy is generated by the biases of those occupying 2 poles of thought: the dominant feeling that marihuana is a frighteningly dangerous drug in no way comparable to any accepted social drug, and the often equally emotional claim by groups of increasing size that it is a purely beneficent drug in no way comparable to any acceptable social drug.

Additional reluctance to summarize the pharmacology of marihuana stems from the assumption that research on its pharmacology is scant, dated, and of poor quality. Certainly, huge amounts of research remain to be done. However, the clamor for more research is in part a device to defer the changes in the laws that will inevitably come as the emerging generation becomes the majority. Furthermore, the present inability to present a consistent formulation of the pharmacology of marihuana may not be due so much to lack of data as to failure to apply some unifying concept to the fragmentary information available.

The specific data presented below suggest that marihuana is a sedative-hypnotic comparable in its effect to alcohol but without alcohol's organic toxicity.

Source & Chemistry

The various products that are smoked or ingested

derive from one species of easily cultivated hemp, *Cannabis sativa*. The active principle occurs in all leaves but is especially concentrated in the flowering tops of the female plant, where a resin many times as potent as the leaves is exuded. The resin, which may be collected in concentrated form, is known as hashish in the Middle East or charas in India. The term marihuana is used in the western hemisphere to mean the mixed leaves and flowering tops of *Cannabis*. In the USA, the term marihuana (by legal definition) embraces all parts and preparations of *Cannabis,* including the pure resin.

The active constituent of *Cannabis* is probably one of several isomeric tetrahydrocannabinols (THC). Delta^9-THC (Fig 7–1) reproduces the effects of the natural product.

THC is synthesized with difficulty and is not available as an illegal or street drug. The material currently being sold as THC is another sedative, phencyclidine.

Pharmacologic Actions

A. Mechanisms of Action: The effects described

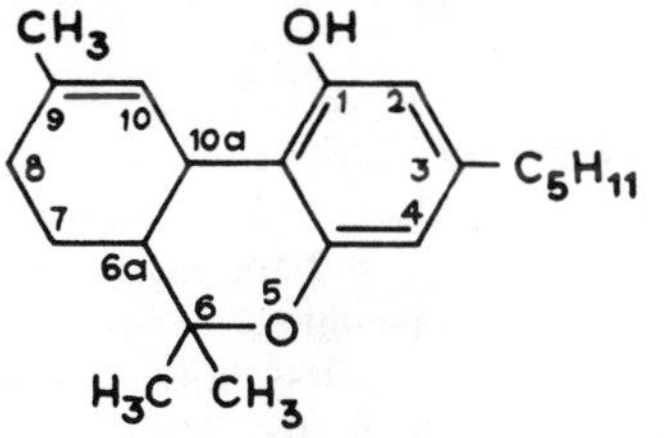

Δ^9-Trans-tetrahydrocannabinol
(Δ^9-THC)

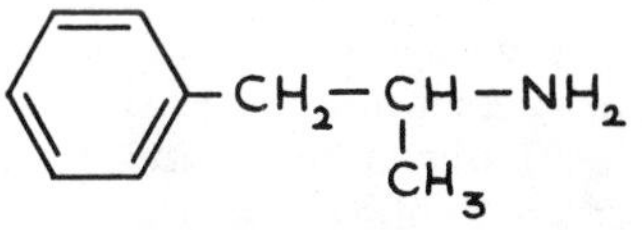

Amphetamine

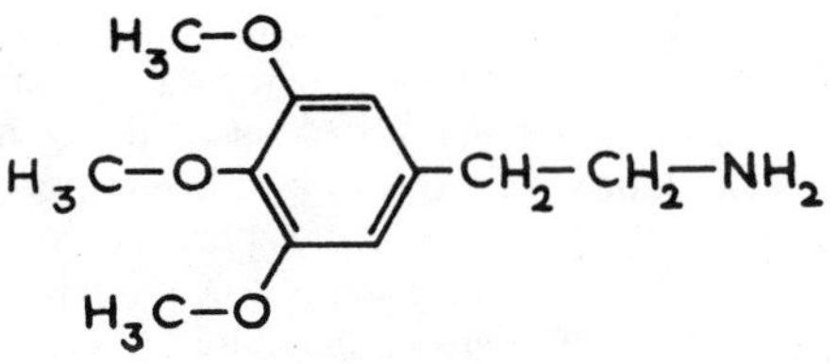

Mescaline

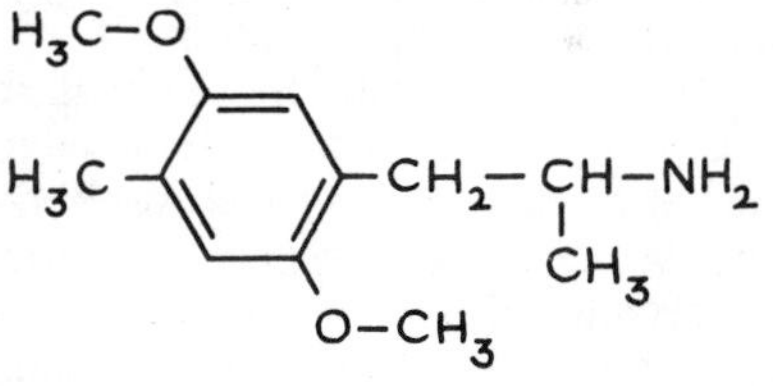

2,5-Dimethoxy-4-methylamphetamine
(STP)

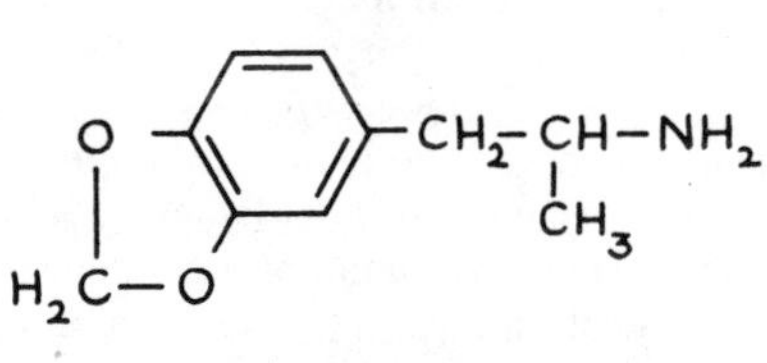

Methylenedioxyamphetamine
(MDA)

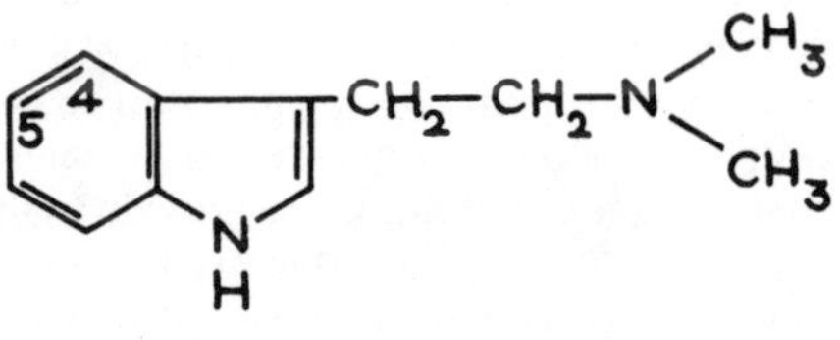

Dimethyltryptamine
(DMT)

Figure 7 –1. Chemical structures of certain drugs subject to misuse. THC is an active constituent of marihuana. Amphetamine is shown for comparison with 3 ring-substituted sympathomimetic amines used as hallucinogens. DMT is a representative tryptamine derivative (see also Fig 19–3). The structure of LSD is shown in Table 14–1.

below establish that marihuana exerts the same diffuse depression of the central nervous system as the barbiturates. The ascending reticular activating system is especially sensitive to the action of marihuana; in studies on cats with electrodes implanted in the midbrain reticular formation and some of its rostral connections, the actions of an analog of THC and thiopental cannot be distinguished.

B. Effects: The effects common to all sedative-hypnotics that provide a basis for classifying a drug as a sedative are discussed in Chapter 23 and summarized in Table 23–2. Marihuana has been shown to exert all of these effects. The actions cannot all be demonstrated after smoking the comparatively weak preparation of the leaves but are demonstrable in experiments using pure THC or synthetic analogs. They are also described in cultures where the more potent hashish is available.

1. Effect of graded doses–Marihuana or other preparations of hemp may cause sedation and can also cause a disinhibited, excited state comparable to intoxication with alcohol or barbiturates or to stage II of anesthesia. The "high" is accompanied by ataxia and impaired performance on tests of psychomotor skills. As with alcohol, one must distinguish between manifest changes in behavior (excitement) and the pharmacologic effect (depression of the central nervous system). Large enough doses cause a loss of consciousness (general anesthesia), and animals given lethal doses die of respiratory depression.

2. Physical dependence and withdrawal–Clinical observations of hashish smokers suggest that withdrawal symptoms are unusual or mild. Experimentally—ie, for purposes of classification—withdrawal can be shown. After 26–31 days on large doses of a synthetic analog of THC (synhexyl), abrupt discontinuance of the drug was followed on the third day by a hyperexcitable state relieved by the drug. In another experimental situation, great numbers of marihuana cigarettes were smoked for 39 days, but withdrawal symptoms were not observed after smoking was discontinued.

3. Dreamy state–An additional area of confusion or controversy is introduced when marihuana is characterized as a "mild hallucinogen." The effect referred to is better described as a dreamy state with an increased tendency to fantasize and to accept suggestion. Such a dreamy, hypnagogic state can be induced with alcohol or almost any one of the sedatives or anesthetics under appropriate conditions. The state is most easily produced with nitrous oxide and was a problem during the use of this gas to provide analgesia for dental procedures. Additional examples are the thiopental interview, the street use of phencyclidine, and the transient "hallucinatory" state described during the therapeutic use of chlordiazepoxide (Librium).

If marihuana is classified as a "mild hallucinogen," it will be invested with the mystic values of LSD and rational discussion of its use will become even more difficult.

4. Other effects–Various preparations of *Cannabis* have been shown in animals and humans to be anticonvulsants and to depress polysynaptic spinal cord reflexes—effects that are not important in its use but emphasize the similarity to other sedatives. The drug increases the appetite and has a minor vasodilating effect often apparent as injection of the conjunctiva. Strong preparations may cause vomiting after inhalation. Cross-tolerance with alcohol has been demonstrated in animals.

Absorption, Metabolism, & Excretion

When any *Cannabis* preparation is smoked, the effect quickly reaches a maximum but persists for only a short time—ie, even though the drug remains in the body for a longer period, the effect quickly passes from excitement to a lesser sedative effect. Redistribution of the lipid-soluble THC occurs rapidly, as with thiopental. When larger amounts are ingested by mouth, absorption is slower, the duration of action is longer—the half-life of THC is 12–24 hours—and the similarity to alcohol becomes more apparent.

Uses

Cannabis has no therapeutic applications, and the problem of its use as a social drug would not be altered if it did.

Adverse Reactions

A. Disinhibited Behavior: The brief duration of the high achieved by smoking marihuana minimizes the problem of drug-induced criminal activity, but social missteps do occur. Psychomotor performance is impaired if large enough doses are taken. As after the use of alcohol, the manifest behavioral change in any one individual—eg, sedation or excitement—will depend upon the individual and the setting. The Assassins, a radical Islamic sect, used hashish and carried out political assassinations, but the assassinations were elaborately planned, not carried out in a drunken state.

B. Potential for Abuse: Marihuana as currently available in the USA ("grass") appears to have a low potential for the development of a compulsive pattern of use. If one looks outside our culture to the Moslem world, it appears that a compulsive pattern of use of hashish, with results comparable to those of chronic alcoholism, is indeed possible. Alcohol is forbidden in the Moslem world, but hashish is available.

C. Anxiety Reactions: Practically all of the complaints brought to the physician by marihuana smokers are manifestations of anxiety. Experienced users are unconcerned and confident of their ability to minimize overt changes in their behavior. Other individuals may fear the loss of inhibition or may feel guilt. The tendency of the youthful subculture to regard marihuana as "psychedelic" increases anxiety by suggesting toxic effects similar to those popularly ascribed to LSD.

D. Legal: A nonpunitive, understanding attitude will often be interpreted as permissive. Any discussion of marihuana must in fairness, therefore, include a warning about the extreme penalties imposed in most areas for the mere possession of even small amounts of the drug.

E. Progression to Use of Other Drugs: The punitive attitudes toward marihuana users are maintained in part by the excuse that, even if marihuana is not inherently extremely dangerous, its use leads to abuse of heroin and other hard drugs. Virtually all heroin users have had experience with marihuana prior to their use of heroin. They have also had prior contact with alcohol and many other factors for which no causal relationship is suggested. Considering that marihuana use involves millions and is increasing and that heroin abuse involves far fewer people and has not increased correspondingly, no correlation or progression can be claimed.

Marihuana use can lead to experimentation with other drugs to the extent that criminalization of marihuana use encourages association with neighborhoods, individuals, and subcultures that favor experimentation.

THE HALLUCINOGENS

Drugs from several pharmacologic classes are able to disorganize neural function and produce a toxic psychosis or acute brain syndrome. The toxic state is characterized by alterations in perception that culminate in hallucinations. These agents have been called hallucinogenic, psychotomimetic, or psychedelic drugs. Except for some uncommon ritualistic uses, these drugs were primarily of toxicologic interest until recently, when 2 factors led to an increase in interest concerning them.

The first factor was the assumption that the drug-induced hallucinatory state provided a model of schizophrenia. It was reasoned that if these chemical agents can cause an altered state that accurately mimics the spontaneously occurring psychosis, they might be useful in the investigation of a postulated biochemical basis for schizophrenia or that descriptions of the experience after experimental induction in volunteers might contribute to our understanding of psychotic behavior. The second reason for renewed interest is that some individuals have attributed great personal value to the "consciousness-expanding" effect of the hallucinogens.

1. LSD
("Acid")

Lysergic acid diethylamide is a chemically modified ergot alkaloid (Table 14–1). Pharmacologically, LSD is unusual in its potency—100 μg causes observable changes in behavior—and in its ability to cause the desired changes in perception with a minimum of

sympathomimetic effects. The total duration of its effect is approximately 8 hours. Tolerance develops after a single dose, and the effects cannot be duplicated within 2–3 days.

Pharmacologic Effects

A. Altered Perception: The intensity of behavioral changes depends upon the dose and time since ingestion. Initial effects or the effects of small doses may be limited to variable degrees of euphoria or anxiety and feelings of depersonalization. Subsequently, there is progressive alteration of perception of tactile, visual, and auditory stimuli. Colors and sounds develop unexpected qualities, or objects change appearance. Delusions occur—ie, objects or sounds actually present are falsely perceived. Finally, in a rare person after a large dose, hallucinations may occur—ie, voices or objects are perceived in the absence of any stimuli. At this time, paranoid ideation and panic are common.

When acid or other hallucinogens are knowingly ingested, the subject recognizes that the symptoms are drug-induced—ie, the ability to test reality is retained to a greater or lesser degree, and the drugs do not mimic a true schizophrenic experience.

B. Meaning to the Individual: In the absence of preconditioning or philosophic preparation, the LSD experience is anxiety laden and only an occasional person will use the drug repeatedly for amusement or for the minor euphoria induced. If an individual accepts instruction from an enthusiast or proselytizer, the experience may develop one of 2 meanings, a mystical one or a psychotherapeutic one. Both groups believe that the altered perception extends to abstract ideas as well as to stimuli from physical sources.

Some individuals use LSD to achieve mystical understanding. The nature of this psychedelic or "consciousness-expanding" effect of LSD is no more susceptible to description than other mystical or religious experiences. Indeed, the analogy to religious conversion first suggested for other drugs by William James is impressive: The requirements are an individual with a need to change; an experience that serves to mark the change; and, afterward, the continued support of a like-minded group.

Another group uses LSD as a substitute or accelerating technic in a process visualized as being close to psychotherapy or psychoanalysis.

Proselytizing for the use of acid has become less effective, and the use of LSD has declined since its peak in 1967.

C. Sympathomimetic Effects: LSD causes a minor elevation in blood pressure, tachycardia, pupillary dilatation, hyperglycemia, tremulousness, awakening, and euphoria.

Clinical Uses

Suggestions that LSD can facilitate psychotherapy or be useful in the treatment of chronic alcoholism are not supported by any controlled studies.

Adverse Reactions

The reaction of an individual to LSD will be strongly conditioned by the predrug personality, expectations of the drug, companions, and the setting. The common adverse reactions (''bad trips'') are manifestations of anxiety.

A. Anxiety Reactions During the Drug Effect: Somatic feelings of depersonalization, distorted perception, and the content of delusional material may be very alarming and lead to anxiety that may be minor in degree or may lead to panic and uncontrolled excitement at the peak of the drug effect. These reactions are most likely to occur in inexperienced users, in disturbing or threatening environments, or in subjects who have ambivalent attitudes toward the drug experience. Most bad trips are handled within the group of users rather than by a physician.

Treatment usually requires only reassurance that the subject will return to normal when the drug effect dissipates and explanation that the symptoms are drug-related. LSD induces a suggestible or hypnagogic state that makes it easy to inadvertently suggest a bad reaction but also makes it easy to establish the relationship between the drug and the symptom. If the patient cannot be ''talked down,'' drugs may be used. A sedative (anti-anxiety) agent usually is preferable. In a few subjects, the panic may be so intense that it is necessary to terminate the reaction with chlorpromazine (50 mg orally or intramuscularly) or similar major antipsychotic tranquilizer.

B. Flashbacks: Flashing (the sudden recurrence of perceptual distortions experienced during a drug experience) is a common occurrence. Flashing is commonly precipitated by the use of other drugs or by some stimulus that reminds the person of the previous experience, but the flashback may be spontaneous. Experienced users recognize them as learned behavior and do not present them as complaints. Patients who are anxious about their drug use, fearing lasting brain damage or other consequences promised by the literature of drug education, may bring the complaint to the physician.

These states do not arise from any pharmacologic effect of LSD but from anxiety and misinterpretation or exaggeration of ordinary perceptions. They can almost always be treated by reassurance and explanation. If drug treatment is necessary, a sedative such as phenobarbital rather than an antipsychotic tranquilizer should be used.

C. Prolonged Psychotic Episodes: There are many reports of prolonged psychotic episodes after LSD use. However, all drug-using communities attract many disturbed people, and it is difficult to separate direct drug effects from episodes precipitated or preordained in the already ill. Acid cannot be exculpated, but it is a mistake to focus on the drug if such interest obscures the underlying problem.

It is similarly difficult to apportion responsibility for suicide among users of ''psychedelics.'' Only a few of the suicide attempts take place while the drug is acting, and the coexistence in the same personality of the tendency toward suicide, drug use, and religious conversion was described long before LSD was used.

D. Chromosomal Damage: LSD has been shown to increase the number of chromosomal breaks in cultured white cells and in cells from skin biopsies. Mutagenic chemicals known to be carcinogenic or teratogenic have the same effect. So, however, do a number of common drugs used without special concern—eg, alcohol, caffeine, menadione, and ergonovine. There are no epidemiologic data that associate LSD with an increased incidence of congenital defects.

The early laboratory studies were probably overinterpreted, but there is no reason to except LSD from the rule that only essential drugs be used during the first trimester of pregnancy. LSD is an ergot derivative capable of contracting the pregnant uterus. Anecdotal evidence suggests that this effect has caused fetal death, so that the caution should actually extend throughout pregnancy.

2. OTHER AGENTS

All of the drugs listed below cause a similar toxic psychosis. The several drugs may also have distinctive side-effects—eg, LSD and the sympathomimetics cause anxiety, pupillary dilatation, and similar sympathomimetic effects; and the parasympatholytic agents add amnesia for the experience. Most of these drugs are discussed in other chapters (see Index).

Sympathomimetic Stimulants

All of these drugs cause side-effects such as anxiety, tremulousness, elevated blood pressure, and pupillary dilatation to a greater extent than does LSD.

A. Methamphetamine, Amphetamine, Cocaine, and Others: Drugs related to amphetamine are misused for their euphoriant effect but not for their hallucinogenic effects. Most individuals who use huge amounts of amphetamine by mouth (up to 2 g/d) or who use methamphetamine intravenously have experienced the hallucinatory state. Except during a most severe paranoid reaction, they recognize the drug origin of their hallucinatory or euphoric state and avoid hospitalization.

B. Hallucinogenic Amphetamine Congeners: Amphetamine congeners with a lipophilic substituent on the ring may act more rapidly and more intensely on the central nervous system. Several of these have been used as substitutes for LSD—eg, STP and MDA (Fig 7-1). STP and MDA have properties similar to those of LSD.

C. Peyote and Mescaline: Buttons from a small cactus that grows in the Sonoran Desert have long been chewed to derive the effect of the active principle, mescaline. Use of peyote has been incorporated into the religious rituals of some American Indians. Mescaline (chemically related to epinephrine) was popularized as a hallucinogenic agent in the cities in the early 1950s, and its use paved the way for LSD. Recently, the drug sold as mescaline has been STP.

D. Tryptamine Derivatives: Serotonin or 5-hydroxytryptamine (see Chapter 19) occurs in several areas of the brain. Exogenous serotonin does not reach the cells of the central nervous system, but a number of other tryptamine derivatives are active as stimulants and hallucinogens and have been used ritually in the past and are now used as LSD equivalents. Psilocybin is the phosphate ester of psilocin (4-hydroxydimethyltryptamine) isolated from a Mexican mushroom and active after oral administration. DMT (dimethyltryptamine) and DET (diethyltryptamine) must be smoked rather than ingested and have a brief duration of action. They were used earlier in the form of ground seeds or cohoba snuff.

Parasympatholytics

Large doses of atropine, scopolamine, and related therapeutic agents cause a toxic psychosis characterized by an unusual degree of excitement, intensely uncomfortable side-effects, and amnesia for the experience. Occasionally, someone intrigued by the publicity given the psychedelic experience but lacking access to the usual drugs will use belladonna or an over-the-counter asthma remedy containing stramonium leaves to achieve an unsatisfactory, uncomfortable effect. Antihistamines and scopolamine (as in nonprescription sleeping tablets) occasionally cause the same excited hallucinatory state.

Sedative-Hypnotics & General Anesthetics

Toxic psychoses resulting from repeated administration of bromides are still seen. However, withdrawal rather than continued administration of hypnotics is the more common cause of delirium. Alcohol is, of course, the most commonly involved drug.

If a protracted stage like that of stage II of anesthesia (disinhibition or excitement) can be induced with one of these drugs—eg, nitrous oxide or phencyclidine—a dreamlike state suggestive to some subjects of the hallucinatory experience may occur. Volatile anesthetics have been used in the past to reach such a state, and marihuana is sometimes called a "mild hallucinogen" on the same basis.

Other Drugs & Causes of Hallucinatory States

Drugs such as narcotic antagonists (nalorphine, etc), anti-inflammatory corticosteroids, disulfiram, amantadine, and methysergide, and many disease states such as infections, dehydration, sodium depletion, and any cause of hypoxia may cause a toxic psychosis, with characteristics similar to those deliberately induced. The delusions that appear during a toxic psychosis caused by disease or by a therapeutically administered drug are more varied, are not so easily related to the precipitating cause by the patient, and are typically worse at night or in a strange place such as a hospital.

TREATMENT & ABATEMENT OF DRUG ABUSE

The treatment and control of drug abuse is a problem that involves public policy and concerns the entire community rather than just the patient and physician or other therapist. Emotional involvement with this subject is intense, and rational discussion is correspondingly difficult. Present public policy in the USA appears inconsistent to many in that it is unduly permissive toward the use of some drugs and unduly punitive in relation to other socially unapproved drugs.

The Punitive Attitude & Its Influence

This attitude accepts the judgment of the dominant culture about which drugs are acceptable and legislates vigorously against all others. Acts that do no harm to persons or property are defined as criminal, and these "crimes without victims" are punished severely—eg, it is a serious crime to merely possess certain drugs, to possess the equipment to use drugs, or to simply be in a place where drugs are kept or to be with people who possess drugs. There now seems to be a growing public and professional awareness of some of the limitations of this approach.

(1) Most important, the punitive attitude has had limited effectiveness. Prior to the enactment of the Harrison Narcotic Act in 1914, narcotics were easily available even without prescription and were misused by large numbers of people. Opiate use decreased sharply thereafter, and no one advocates a return to the unregulated availability of narcotics. However, the old pattern of oral use of narcotics was comparatively benign when compared with the subsequent patterns of intravenous use in a criminalized scene, and the punitive approach has obviously not prevented the increased use of marihuana, LSD, and other drugs.

(2) The laws are inconsistent. The public has been taught to regard narcotic addiction as a terrible crime. Other drugs, some more dangerous and some less so, are uncritically lumped together as narcotics in the law, and penalties inconsistent with the properties of the drug or the possible social consequences of their use are imposed.

(3) No distinction is made between criminal activity inherent in drug misuse—which, except for alcohol, is quantitatively negligible—and associated criminal activity. By associated criminal activity is meant the provision of illegal drugs and the criminal activity into which the user, to maintain the habit, is forced by restrictive laws.

(4) Enforcement of the drug laws is possible only by the use of informers, entrapment, and search and seizure procedures that are of doubtful constitutional validity and are offensive to some citizens. The laws are not uniformly applied, and the heavy penalties prescribed, together with other defects in the system of criminal justice, make the drug laws vehicles for harassment and repression of certain ethnic groups, neighborhoods, or life-styles.

(5) Labeling almost the entire emerging generation as deviant because it is experimenting with grass and acid has intensified the alienation of that group.

Treatment Problems & Technics of Management

A. Individuals Who Acknowledge No Illness: During the foreseeable future, there will continue to be a large number of drug users who regard themselves as neither criminal nor ill. Social drinkers see no reason for telling their physicians or other advisors about their occasional use of alcohol, and the young users of marihuana view themselves in the same way.

B. Problems Unrelated to Drug Abuse: To the extent that drug use is symptomatic of individual and social ills, expansion of general treatment facilities and social and economic change will have an impact on drug use.

C. Acute Drug Reactions: Acute intoxication with stimulants or depressants, adverse reactions to LSD or other hallucinogens, or withdrawal should be treated as medical problems rather than as police problems. Not only is such care safer and more effective, but, more important, more patients could then be induced to accept aftercare from a medical facility.

D. Compulsive Drug Use: The special treatment procedures applicable to the compulsive use of alcohol and narcotics are discussed in the relevant chapters. The general types of treatment can be summarized as follows:

1. Psychotherapy–Conventional psychotherapy is not impressive in this context. Once the compulsive user acknowledges a need to change and solicits treatment, a number of different medical or self-help facilities have significant success. The patient learns, usually slowly, to give up the compulsion and is helped by the supervision of peers and by removal from a threatening environment. The size of the problem is such that community-based facilities rather than the usual medical institutions must be used.

2. Pharmacologic blockade–The use of alcohol becomes intolerably sickening after the administration of disulfiram (Antabuse). Neither the immediate nor the delayed effects of injected heroin appear if a patient is maintained on continuous doses of methadone or a narcotic antagonist.

3. Regulated access–Since neither the purely punitive nor the purely medical approach offers a high rate of success in the case of narcotic use, a third alternative embodying the concept of regulated access to the drug is used in some countries. Such a program continues to impose jail sentences for criminal activity but not for mere use or possession. Addicts must identify themselves and accept treatment and supervision. However, in cases of treatment failure, it offers an alternative to jail by providing maintenance doses of drugs if that is the only way users can remain within the community. This form of treatment removes users from those associations that initiated or perpetuated their addiction. Such a program is repugnant to many citizens because it tolerates the "stabilized addict."

British law permits dispensing narcotics even for intravenous use to an addict, and the British experience is usually mentioned in this context. The British population has characteristics different from that of the USA, but the fact remains that in 1970, with a population of 50 million, there were only 1430 known heroin addicts in England (compared with a conservative estimate of 200,000 in the USA). The associated criminal activity in England is negligible when compared to that in the USA.

In the USA, the nearest equivalent is the provision of a daily oral dose of methadone, a narcotic discussed in a later chapter.

Education & Counseling

If the goal of society's effort in this area is control and prevention rather than retribution, only education and counseling offer any real hope. Dissemination of authoritative information would probably reduce experimentation with drugs, but the following cautions must be observed:

(1) The effectiveness of such efforts will be limited by the extent to which drug use is symptomatic of underlying social and individual problems, including frustration due to apparently unalterable economic conditions, ineffective families, and lack of personal goals or resources.

(2) The information presented must be scrupulously accurate and scientifically derived even if it is in conflict with the preconceptions of the teacher. The "students" will have had personal experience with drugs or will be in contact with others who have. If information from a professional source about one drug is known by the experimenters to be inaccurate, they will subsequently reject more accurate data about another drug. Again, marihuana is the drug of central importance because, if our professional proclamations about it to our young people are judged to be palpably inaccurate, our warnings about methamphetamine or heroin will also be rejected. Personal experimentation with drugs is thus encouraged, since it is judged to be the individual's only dependable source of drug information. The consequences, already apparent, have been the epidemic of methamphetamine abuse followed now by the occurrence of compulsive heroin use among white, middle-class youth. It is the professional drug expert's obvious duty to maintain credibility among those groups who are most apt to need advice. This must be done even at the risk of disapproval from others in the community who might hope that their proscriptions against all drugs will be uncritically heeded. Unfortunately, the young people who must be dealt with in this context are already partially alienated from the establishment we represent, and they have reserved to themselves the decision about what to believe.

(3) Drugs accepted by the older dominant culture must be examined as objectively as the new drugs. Alcohol and cigarettes must be acknowledged as major problems and condemned as freely as marihuana.

• • •

References

General

Brecher EM: *Licit and Illicit Drugs*. Consumers Union, 1972.

Chappel JN: Attitudinal barriers to physician involvement with drug abusers. JAMA 224:1011, 1973.

Davis F: Heads and freaks: Patterns and meanings of drug use among hippies. J Health Soc Behav 9:156, 1968.

Diagnosis and management of reactions to drug abuse. Med Lett Drugs Ther 19:13, 1977.

Eastman JW, Cohen SN: Hypertensive crisis and death associated with phencyclidine poisoning. JAMA 231:1270, 1975.

Flowers NC, Horan LG: Nonanoxic aerosol arrhythmias. JAMA 219:33, 1972.

Goldstein A: Heroin addiction and the role of methadone in its treatment. Arch Gen Psychiatry 26:291, 1972.

Greenblatt DJ, Shader RI: Drug abuse and the emergency room physician. Am J Psychiatry 131:559, 1974.

Greene MH & others: Evolving patterns of drug abuse. Ann Intern Med 83:402, 1975.

Kramer J, Manoguerra A, Schnoll SH: Drug abuse: Treating the overdose victim. Patient Care 11:76, Jan 15, 1977.

Peterson RC, Stillman RC (editors): *Cocaine: 1977*. US Department of Health, Education, & Welfare, 1977.

Russell MAH: Cigarette dependence. (2 parts.) Br Med J 2:330, 393, 1971.

Shick JFE, Smith DE, Meyers FH: Patterns of drug use in the Haight-Ashbury neighborhood. Clin Toxicol 2:1, 1970.

Smith DE, Wesson DR: Diagnosis and treatment of adverse reactions to sedative-hypnotics. National Institute on Drug Abuse, US Department of Health, Education, & Welfare, 1974.

Wikler A: Dynamics of drug dependence. Arch Gen Psychiatry 28:611, 1973.

Marihuana

Boyd ES, Meritt DA: Effects of barbiturates and a tetrahydrocannabinol derivative on recovery cycles of medial lemniscus, thalamus and reticular formation in the cat. J Pharmacol Exp Ther 151:376, 1966.

Cohen S, Stillman RC (editors): *The Therapeutic Potential of Marihuana*. Plenum Press, 1977.

Hollister LE, Richards RK, Gillespie HK: Comparison of tetrahydrocannabinol and synhexyl in man. Clin Pharmacol Ther 9:783, 1968.

Kaplan J: *Marijuana: The New Prohibition*. World, 1970.

Kreuz DS, Axelrod J: Delta-9-tetrahydrocannabinol: Temporal correlation of the psychologic effects and blood levels after various routes of administration. N Engl J Med 286:685, 1972.

Louria DB: The marihuana debate: Doubts about legalization. Page 753 in: *Controversy in Internal Medicine II*. Ingelfinger FJ & others. Saunders, 1974.

Newman LM & others: Δ^9-Tetrahydrocannabinol and ethyl alcohol: Evidence for cross-tolerance in the rat. Science 175:1022, 1972.

Way EL, Isbell H (editors): Symposium: Marihuana and its surrogates. Pharmacol Rev 23:263, 1971.

Williams EG & others: Studies on marijuana and pyrahexyl compounds. Public Health Rep 61:1059, 1946.

Part II. Autonomic & Cardiovascular Drugs

8 | The Autonomic Nervous System & Cholinergic (Parasympathomimetic) Agents

This and the following 3 chapters deal with drugs that either mimic, intensify, or block the effects of the sympathetic and parasympathetic divisions of the autonomic nervous system.

The 4 most general types of drug actions are
(1) Parasympathomimetic (cholinergic), acting like mediators of parasympathetic nerve activity, eg, methacholine.
(2) Parasympatholytic (anticholinergic), blocking the effects of parasympathetic nerve activity, eg, atropine.
(3) Sympathomimetic (adrenergic), acting like sympathetic nerve or adrenal medullary activity, eg, epinephrine.
(4) Sympathoplegic (adrenergic blocking), acting by a variety of mechanisms to decrease sympathetic activity, eg, propranolol.

These drug groups appear first in this survey of classes of drugs because alterations of autonomic nervous system function are also produced by most of the drugs discussed in subsequent chapters even if the drugs do not act primarily on the autonomic nervous system.

FUNCTIONAL ORGANIZATION OF THE AUTONOMIC (PERIPHERAL) NERVOUS SYSTEM

The term autonomic nervous system is convenient but inaccurate, since it is the peripheral organ rather than the nervous system that is autonomic. The "autonomic nervous system" consists of the nervous and humoral mechanisms that modulate and integrate the functions of the autonomous, automatic, or vegetative organs. These organs or functions include heart rate and force of contraction; the caliber of blood vessels; the contraction or relaxation of the smooth muscle of the gut, bladder, and bronchioles; visual accommodation and pupillary size; secretion from exocrine glands, and others.

The widespread interest in drugs modifying these functions is understandable. A significant fraction of all disease entities or altered physiologic states involve the autonomous end organs. Even in those instances

where the etiology of the disease is not yet clarified, as in hypertension, the effective treatment may be with drugs acting on the autonomic nervous system. The large group of symptoms or disease entities that may be behavioral or psychologic in origin (migraine, asthma, peptic ulcer, neurotic conversion symptoms) must be mediated by the autonomic nervous system and are usually more amenable to drug therapy than to psychotherapy.

The classification and mechanism of action of drugs that act on autonomic tissues is in large part understandable from the correlation of the anatomy of the autonomic nervous system with the data on chemical transmission of nerve impulses.

Chemical Transmission

Transmission along a nerve fiber is by the spread, or propagation, of the wave of depolarization. There is an ultramicroscopic discontinuity, or cleft, between the terminations of one nerve and the cell body or processes of the next, or between the nerve and the muscle or glandular cells innervated. Transmission across this discontinuity (neuroeffector junction) is not electrical but chemical. A chemical mediator or neurohumor is liberated by the proximal nerve and acts postsynaptically to depolarize the next cell in the series to excite it to conduct, contract, or secrete. Or, if it is an inhibitory agent, it may hyperpolarize the next cell and delay depolarization.

Mediators are stored within the axon close to the site of release into the synaptic cleft. Norepinephrine is stored within adrenergic granules with a central core that appears dark on electron microscopy; acetylcholine is stored in agranular vesicles. In addition, there are presumed purinergic nerves that contain large, opaque granules and may release adenosine triphosphate (ATP). Other mediators—eg, dopamine, as discussed in Chapter 30—are not concentrated into specific granules.

If the autonomic nervous system is divested of the anatomic complexity that it actually possesses, it can be represented as in Fig 8–1. Such a simplification allows correlation of chemical transmission and anatomic site. In summary, it will be seen that (1) norepinephrine is the mediator liberated by sympathetic nerve endings and by a few chromaffin cells; (2) epinephrine and a small fraction of norepinephrine are

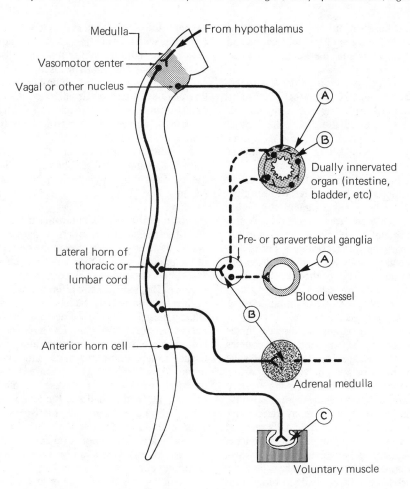

Figure 8–1. Functional organization and chemical transmission in autonomic and somatic efferent nerves. Fibers of cholinergic neurons are shown by solid lines. Fibers of adrenergic neurons are shown by dashed lines. The anatomic basis for the diagram is discussed in the text. The diagram should also be used to visualize the sites of action of the drugs discussed in this and the next 4 chapters. For example, cholinergic drugs act at the following sites: *A:* On muscarinic receptors on the effector tissue to contract nonvascular smooth muscle and stimulate exocrine glands but to relax vascular smooth muscle. *B:* On nicotinic receptors at ganglionic synapses where acetylcholine is also the mediator. Postganglionic sympathetic activity is increased, which constricts blood vessels and stimulates the heart. The adrenal medulla is also activated by agents that mimic the effect of preganglionic activity, and epinephrine is released into the circulation. *C:* On receptors on the motor end-plate of voluntary muscle to initiate contraction of single units. Cholinesterase inhibitors act at *A,* *B,* and *C* by allowing the accumulation of acetylcholine, but not at *A* in blood vessels, since no acetylcholine is liberated that can be protected from hydrolysis.

liberated by the adrenal medulla; and (3) acetylcholine is the mediator at all (both sympathetic and parasympathetic) ganglionic synapses of the autonomic nervous system, at parasympathetic nerve endings, and at the voluntary nerve-muscle junction.

Sympathetic or Thoracolumbar Division of Autonomic Nervous System

A. Sympathetic Nerves: The cell bodies of the preganglionic fibers, comparable to the anterior horn cells of the somatic nervous system, lie in the lateral horn of the spinal cord from T1 through L2 (hence the older designation, thoracolumbar). The myelinated (white) fibers leave the cord over the motor root but run

only a short course before synapsing with the post-ganglionic fiber.

The collection of terminations of the first neuron in the series and the processes and cell bodies of the second neuron is called a sympathetic ganglion. These ganglion cells lie in the ganglia of the paravertebral chain or in the unpaired prevertebral ganglia.

Mediation of the impulse from pre- to post-ganglionic cell is by the liberation of acetylcholine. The preganglionic fiber is cholinergic, a term applied to nerve fibers that work by liberating acetylcholine.

The properties of the postganglionic fibers explain the diffuse effect of sympathetic nerve activity. There are many more postganglionic than preganglionic fibers, and the distribution of both types of fibers is not segmental, allowing for amplification and a diffuse rather than segmental distribution of postganglionic fibers.

Furthermore, the postganglionic fiber is adrenergic, ie, it exerts its influence on the effector tissue by liberating norepinephrine. This amine, like the epinephrine that enters the circulation from the adrenal medulla, is destroyed comparatively slowly (in minutes) and can exert effects distant from its site of liberation.

A further anatomic fact explains the greater effect of chemical sympathetic block compared with surgical sympathectomy. Not all sympathetic ganglion cells are located in the pre- and paravertebral ganglia. A significant number of ganglion cells lie along an embryologic migratory path between cord and periphery. These intermediate ganglia are accessible to drugs but are not removed by the usual sympathectomy, which is based partly on excision of grossly visible ganglia.

The termination of the postganglionic sympathetic fibers involves at least 2 patterns.

Some smooth muscle organs are directly innervated. The sympathetic postganglionic fiber courses parallel to the smooth muscle cells, and at intervals the nerve fiber swells to form a slight varicosity where adrenergic granules are concentrated. As the wave of depolarization passes down the fiber, there is a diffuse release of norepinephrine from the many varicosities along the nerve. Single smooth muscle cells respond by depolarization or hyperpolarization, the effect spreading through junctions between cells to activate a bundle of cells. Some smooth muscle tubes—eg, the vas deferens—are densely innervated. In blood vessels, sympathetic fibers appear only in the adventitia, which suggests that the contractile elements of the media are more likely to be acted upon by circulatory amines.

The smooth muscle of some organs may not have direct sympathetic innervation. At least in the case of the intestine and bladder, the postganglionic adrenergic neuron, identified by its content of fluorescent granules of mediator, terminates in close relation to the cholinergic synapses of the parasympathetic division—ie, the effect of norepinephrine on these tissues is probably due not to an action on smooth muscle but to an inhibitory effect on the intrinsic nerves of the organ.

B. The Adrenal Medulla as a Sympathetic Ganglion: The cells of the adrenal medulla have the same embryologic origin, similar staining reactions, and the same innervation by cholinergic sympathetic preganglionic neurons as the sympathetic ganglia. The adrenal medulla can thus be thought of as a sympathetic ganglion made up of cell bodies without axons or postganglionic fibers. As expected, therefore, the secretion of the adrenal medulla (epinephrine) is similar to that of the sympathetic nerves (norepinephrine). It will also be necessary to speak of sympathoadrenal discharge, since preganglionic discharge will activate both the sympathetic nerves and the adrenal medulla.

Epinephrine, since it enters the bloodstream and exerts a diffuse, widespread effect, is called a hormone rather than a neurohumor—an unimportant distinction.

C. Other Chromaffin Tissue: Other chromaffin cells containing stores of norepinephrine that can be liberated by drugs occur in functionally significant numbers in blood vessels and in the atria. The term "intrinsic amine" is sometimes applied to these stores.

Additional data on sympathetic neurons and neuromediators are given in Chapter 10. The suprasegmental control of sympathetic neurons is discussed in Chapter 11.

Parasympathetic or Craniosacral Division

The preganglionic fibers of the parasympathetic nerves arise from cell bodies in the motor nuclei either of the brain stem or of the sacral segments of the cord. They run to or almost to the organ innervated without synapse. Parasympathetic efferent fibers make up part of the oculomotor (III), facial (VII), glossopharyngeal (IX), vagus (X), and pelvic nerves. The first 3 cranial nerves listed (III, VII, and IX) have ganglia close to but outside of the eye. However, all of the autonomic tissues except the uterus have ganglion cells within them. These may be well organized, as in the submucosal and myenteric plexuses of the intestine; or diffuse, as in the bladder, blood vessels, etc. The preganglionic parasympathetic fibers terminate in close relation to the ganglion cells. These ganglionic synapses are acted upon by ganglion stimulant and depressant drugs in the same manner as are the sympathetic ganglia.

It is an oversimplification to say that acetylcholine is the mediator at the parasympathetic postganglionic endings, since there may be multiple synapses within the plexus between the preganglionic fiber and the neuroeffector junction.

Concept of Sympathetic-Parasympathetic Antagonism

The development of the concept of chemical mediation and the study of drugs related to the mediators have led to the assumption that drug effects necessarily define the physiologic mechanism. Pharmacologic data have been influential in strengthening the hypothesis that the activity of autonomous organs is controlled by the balance between sympathetic and parasympathetic influences. Sympathomimetic and parasympathomimetic drugs do have generally opposite actions, but the following cautions should be observed in translating that pharmacologic fact into physiologic theory.

Drugs that mimic the effects of mediators act independently of innervation. Acetylcholine acts on tissues that have no parasympathetic innervation. Each of the mediators acts more intensely on denervated effector tissue and will act on noninnervated smooth muscle such as that in umbilical vessels.

Many tissues are not dually innervated. The ciliary body has only parasympathetic innervation.

The nictitating membrane, most blood vessels, and uterine muscle have only sympathetic innervation. The salivary glands, which grossly are innervated by both sympathetic and parasympathetic nerves, are made up of 2 cell types, and individual cells are singly innervated.

The response to drugs said to block one or the other division of the autonomic nervous system is not necessarily the same as the response to extrinsic nerve section. Cutting the parasympathetic "motor" nerves does lead to cardiac acceleration and decreased motility of the fundus of the stomach, but many organs, notably the bladder and pylorus, respond by disastrously heightened activity, and some, such as the small intestine, are not affected at all. Atropine or other drugs that diminish the intensity of all of these functions uniformly must therefore be acting on an intrinsic mechanism distal to the surgically accessible nerves.

The autonomic nervous system is by definition an efferent system, but the autonomous organs have a rich sensory innervation and many "autonomic" nerves such as the vagus and pelvic nerves are predominantly sensory. Consideration of the reflex regulation of smooth muscle organs is necessary to understand the difference between the effect of blocking drugs and nerve section—eg, bladder contractions are inhibited by atropine but greatly increased by cutting the pelvic nerves, which nerves include sensory fibers from the bladder that are essential to maintain normal, reflexly generated, sympathetic inhibiting tone.

CHOLINERGIC (PARASYMPATHOMIMETIC) DRUGS

Drugs that act like acetylcholine would be expected to stimulate or mimic the effects of stimulating the vagus or other parasympathetic nerve. The therapeutic usefulness of drugs of this group does indeed depend upon their **parasympathomimetic** actions. The term "parasympathomimetic" is, therefore, satisfactory at the practical level. However, acetylcholine is the mediator at sites other than parasympathetic neuroeffector junctions, and cholinergic drugs have effects other than parasympathomimetic. These additional effects are either sympathomimetic or involve voluntary muscle. Drugs that act like acetylcholine (cholinergics) differ in the proportion of parasympathomimetic effects and sympathomimetic and voluntary muscle effects that they exert.

The following 4 groups of cholinergic drugs discussed in this chapter differ largely in this manner, although one—the cholinesterase inhibitors—has a different mechanism of action: (1) choline esters, (2) cholinesterase inhibitors, (3) old alkaloids that act like acetylcholine, and (4) nicotine and other facilitants of ganglionic transmission.

CHOLINE ESTERS

These drugs, exemplified by methacholine (Mecholyl) and bethanechol (Urecholine), are comparable to the physiologic mediator acetylcholine but are longer acting.

Chemistry: Structure & Resistance to Hydrolysis

However important acetylcholine may be physiologically, its action is too brief for it to be a useful drug. When released from nerve endings, it is hydrolyzed within milliseconds to acetate and virtually inactive choline. If this were not so, it could not mediate the rapidly repetitive movement of a voluntary muscle or even the alteration between accommodation for near and distant vision.

Compounds resistant to hydrolysis by cholinesterase have therefore been prepared. These synthetic drugs have the advantage over some of the older long-acting cholinergic alkaloids of being relatively more active as parasympathomimetics and having relatively fewer sympathomimetic actions.

The chemical structure of some of the choline esters in use is shown in Fig 8–2. Addition of a beta-methyl group to acetylcholine slows the rate of destruction. The resulting drug, methacholine (Mecholyl), acts several times as long as acetylcholine but is not long-acting enough to be active when given by mouth. It is occasionally administered by injection.

Esterification of choline with carbamic acid rather than acetic acid yields a compound, carbachol, that is no longer hydrolyzed by true cholinesterase and whose longer life in the body permits its oral administration. Addition of the beta-methyl substituent in such a carbamate results in bethanechol (Urecholine), the most widely used member of this group.

Pharmacologic Actions

A. Mechanisms of Action: The choline esters act directly on postganglionic neurons and on effector tissues. The effectors that will be sensitive or responsive to acetylcholine can be predicted in part from knowledge of the sites at which acetylcholine is the chemical mediator. Acetylcholine is released at parasympathetic (postganglionic) neuroeffector junctions, at ganglionic synapses, and at the voluntary nerve-muscle junction. Corresponding to these 3 sites are 3 general effects:

1. Parasympathomimetic (muscarinic)—The choline esters act on the gut, bladder, and other nonvascular smooth muscle and on exocrine glands to increase activity much as would parasympathetic nerve stimulation. Long before the concept of chemical mediation was developed, the effects referred to here as parasympathomimetic were observed to occur after the administration of muscarine, an alkaloid from a mushroom (Fig 8–6); hence the term **muscarinic,** which still persists.

To exert their parasympathomimetic or muscarin-

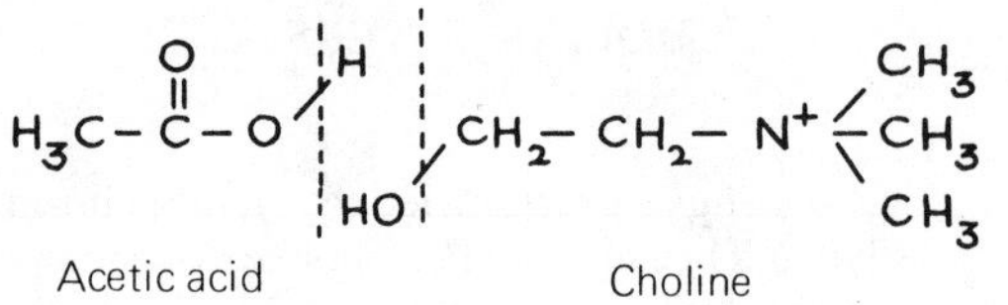

Acetic acid   Choline

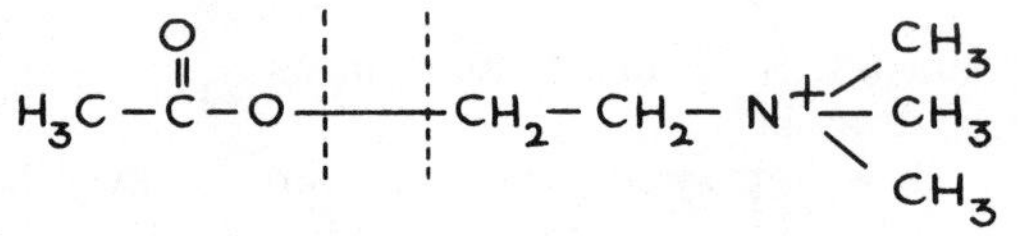

Acetylcholine

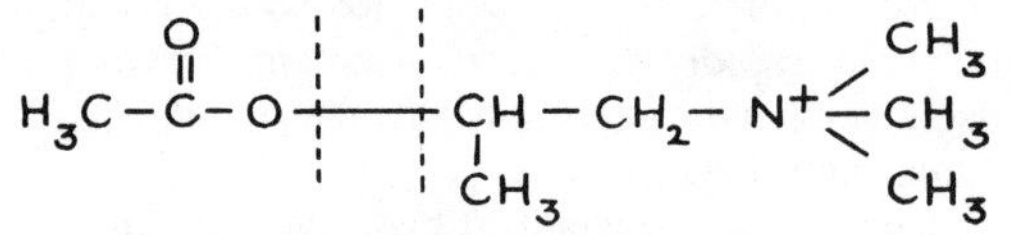

Methacholine
(acetyl-β-methylcholine)
(Mecholyl)

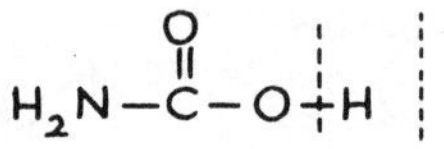

Carbamic acid

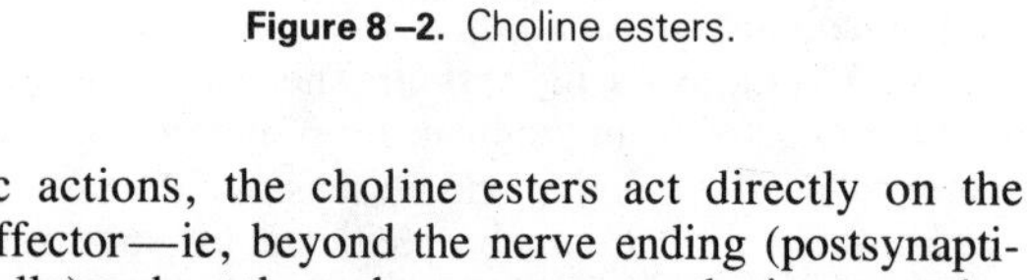

Bethanechol
(carbaminoyl-β-methylcholine)
(Urecholine)

Figure 8–2. Choline esters.

ic actions, the choline esters act directly on the effector—ie, beyond the nerve ending (postsynaptically) and not through any parasympathetic nerves that may be present. Chronic denervation of parasympathetically innervated organs does not decrease the response to choline esters. On the contrary, sensitivity is increased following degeneration of the extrinsic nerves. (At this point, our interest is in the mechanism of action of acetylcholine. Note, however, that denervation supersensitivity is a more general phenomenon. Whenever a damaged nerve degenerates, the next nerve or tissue [effector] in the chain of cells becomes unusually sensitive to the mediator.)

Tissues lacking parasympathetic innervation may respond to choline esters. For example, blood vessels are dilated by choline esters, and the action is quantitatively far greater than can be explained by the cholinergic dilator mechanism demonstrated for some vascular beds.

2. Sympathomimetic (nicotinic)–Simultaneously with their parasympathomimetic action, all of the cholinergic drugs will exert some sympathomimetic effects—eg, vasoconstriction and cardiac stimulation—that are the opposite of the parasympathomimetic action. The sympathomimetic effects were first described for the tobacco alkaloid nicotine. The term **nicotinic** is usually used to encompass also effects on voluntary muscle and the central nervous system. Since there is some confusion and ambiguity in the use of the term, it is probably better to stipulate whether sympathomimetic, voluntary muscle, or central nervous system actions are meant. However, the term nicotinic is in use and should be recognized.

The origins of the sympathomimetic effects of the choline esters are as follows:

a. Facilitation of transmission across sympathetic ganglia–Parasympathetic postganglionic fibers are also stimulated, but such action merely reinforces the parasympathomimetic effect.

b. Liberation of adrenal medullary amines–The adrenal medulla is innervated by cholinergic, preganglionic sympathetic neurons, and cholinergic drugs cause the liberation of epinephrine and smaller amounts of norepinephrine.

c. Liberation of norepinephrine from chromaffin tissue in the atria and blood vessels.

d. Reflex sympathoadrenal discharge stimulated by the fall in blood pressure caused by vasodilatation or decreased force of cardiac contraction.

3. Voluntary nerve-muscle junction (nicotinic)–As ordinarily used, the choline esters have negligible effects on voluntary muscle. Their ability to act like acetylcholine at the voluntary nerve-muscle junction can be demonstrated by special technics such as injection into an artery close to the muscle perfused.

The effects of acetylcholine on voluntary muscle are more important in understanding cholinergics other than the choline esters. The cholinesterase inhibitors allow the accumulation of high concentrations of acetylcholine, and nicotine acts like a persistent cholinergic.

Cholinergic drugs act to cause striated muscle contraction in lower concentrations and to cause muscle paralysis when present in greater amounts. Small amounts act to depolarize the motor end-plate—a specialized membrane at the site where nerve endings approach the muscle. Depolarization of the motor end-plate spreads to the membranes of the muscle cell, and contraction follows. If the acetylcholine effect is intense, depolarization persists; and if repolarization of the motor end-plate does not occur, a flaccid paralysis results.

B. Effects: The parasympathomimetic (muscarinic) actions of these drugs are predominantly on nonvascular smooth muscle, exocrine glands, and the eye; effects on the cardiovascular system are the resultant of the parasympathomimetic and sympathomimetic (nicotinic) actions. The consequences of these diametrically opposed effects cannot always be predicted even if specific drugs and dosages are stipulated.

1. Nonvascular smooth muscle is stimulated to contract. Propulsive gastrointestinal activity is increased; the bladder is contracted; the bronchioles are constricted; the pupils are decreased in size by contraction of the sphincter of the pupil; and the ciliary muscle is contracted to accommodate the eye for near vision (Fig 9–1).

2. Exocrine glands–An increase in salivation and perspiration and in the secretions of the mucosa of the respiratory tract occurs. The secretion of pepsin and mucus is increased, but gastric acid secretion is not augmented. Cholinergic agents do, however, sensitize parietal cells to the effect of gastrin and perhaps other humoral stimuli.

3. Cardiovascular–The direct effect of choline esters on blood vessels is to dilate them. At the same time, the sympathomimetic mechanisms described above cause vasoconstriction. The net effect is unpredictable; however, even when a net increase in total peripheral resistance occurs, the superficial vessels of the skin usually dilate and a flush and a feeling of warmth is noted. Cardiac rate may also change in either direction. The profound slowing or cardiac arrest so easily demonstrated in animals by the rapid intravenous injection of a choline ester is rare in humans. It has, however, occurred during the treatment of atrial tachycardia with methacholine. The force of cardiac contraction is reduced demonstrably in the laboratory, but clinically the effect is more apt to be the opposite, because of sympathoadrenal discharge, or to be negligible. The slowing of the rate of atrioventricular conduction—ie, prolongation of atrioventricular conduction time—is also not prominent under the usual conditions of clinical use.

The mixed vasomotor and cardiac effects lead to a variable blood pressure response until the dose is increased, when a fall in blood pressure regularly appears. Of the choline esters in common use, methacholine gives the mixed effect, and bethanechol, in the usual oral doses, has minor cardiovascular effects.

Clinical Uses, Preparations, & Dosages

These are discussed below in the section on cholinesterase inhibitors.

Adverse Reactions

Allergic reactions have not been reported.

A. Side-Effects: Side-effects are cramps (abdominal or epigastric, resembling hunger contractions), urinary urgency, a feeling of warmth, nausea, faintness, sweating, or excess salivation.

B. Overdosage Toxicity: Toxicity due to excess doses of choline esters is uncommon, and most cases have followed the injection of methacholine. Syncope (especially with the patient in the upright position), asthma, dyspnea, and atrioventricular block have been reported. These drugs are not innocuous, and in one incident 15 deaths occurred as a result of the mistaken injection of an ophthalmic preparation of confusingly labeled carbachol before the labeling was changed.

Treatment of overdosage consists of the prompt injection of atropine, the specific antagonist.

CHOLINESTERASE INHIBITORS

The choline esters just discussed and the alkaloids with an equivalent effect act directly on nerve and effector tissues. The cholinesterase inhibitors act indirectly by inhibiting the enzyme that hydrolyzes acetylcholine, allowing its accumulation at those sites where it is normally liberated.

Source, Chemistry, & Classification

The cholinesterase inhibitors are divided into 3 general groups based upon the reversibility of their combination or chemical reaction with cholinesterase and consequent duration of action.

A. Reversible Inhibitors: These compounds are

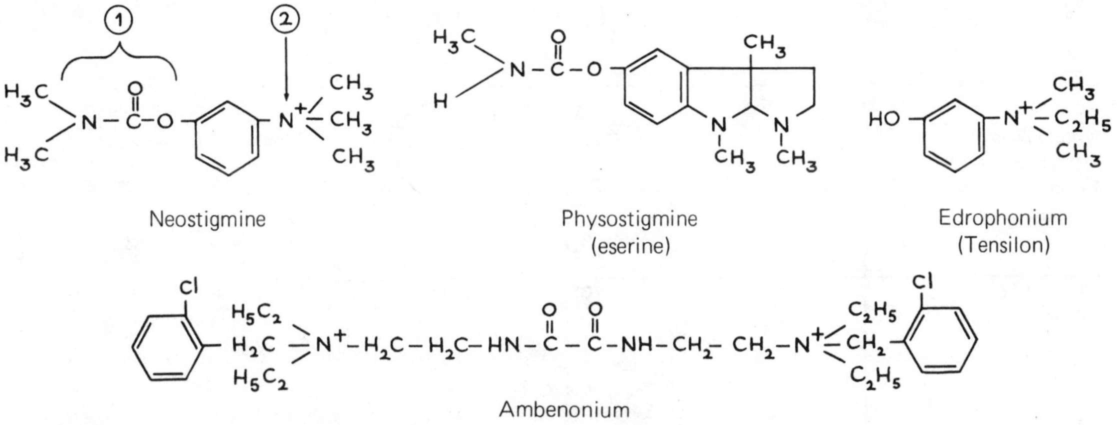

Neostigmine   Physostigmine   Edrophonium
                     (eserine)   (Tensilon)

Ambenonium

Figure 8–3. Reversible cholinesterase inhibitors. Neostigmine exemplifies the typical compound that is an ester of a substituted carbamic acid [①] and a phenol bearing a quaternary ammonium group [②]. Physostigmine, the naturally occurring prototype, is a tertiary amine. The remaining 2 compounds are not esters and, for reasons given in the text, have distinctively shorter and longer durations of action.

Table 8–1. Summary and comparison of effects of choline esters (and old alkaloids) and of cholinesterase inhibitors.

	Choline Esters	Cholinesterase Inhibitors
Nonvascular smooth muscle	Contracted	Contracted
Exocrine glands	Stimulated	Stimulated
Vascular smooth muscle	U*	Contracted
Blood pressure		
Systolic	U*	Elevated
Pulse pressure	U*	Widened
Heart rate	U*	Slowed

*Unpredictable in therapeutic dosages depending upon preponderance of parasympathomimetic or sympathomimetic effects.

esters of carbamic acid that react with the enzyme surface to form a carbamylated enzyme that is regenerated by hydrolysis at a slow rate compared to recovery of the enzyme that has reacted with acetylcholine. The duration of their effect (about 4 hours) is brief only by comparison with the second group, the organophosphates.

1. Physostigmine (eserine)–The prototype of this drug group was introduced into medicine, as is true for many drug classes, following the study of a natural product used in folk practice. Physostigmine was isolated from a Calabar (Nigeria) ordeal bean. (As a test of guilt, a suspect was made to swallow the beans. If death ensued, the suspect was guilty. Perhaps if the beans were eaten rapidly, because the suspect was confident of being innocent, vomiting would occur promptly. The test has never been validated.) Physostigmine is a tertiary amine and crosses cellular barriers better than the quaternary analogs named below. It is, therefore, still applied as drops for a local effect on the eye and is the cholinesterase inhibitor used when

central nervous system effects are desired—eg, for antagonism of the central nervous system effects of atropine and related drugs.

2. Neostigmine and analogs–Neostigmine (Prostigmin), pyridostigmine (Mestinon), benzpyrinium (Stigmonene), and demecarium (Humorsol) are synthetic quaternary analogs of physostigmine.

B. Irreversible Inhibitors; Organophosphates: A large number of widely used insecticides; potential war gases; and one therapeutic agent, isoflurophate, are included in this category. The P–X bond shown in the type structure in Table 8–2 is opened following combination with cholinesterase. The moiety represented by X—eg, fluoride or paranitrophenoxy—is excreted, but the remainder of the molecule reacts with and irreversibly inactivates cholinesterase.

C. Truly Reversible (Short-acting) Inhibitors: Edrophonium (Tensilon) consists, in effect, of only the base contained in neostigmine or other substrate for cholinesterase. It combines with cholinesterase only briefly and does not react with it chemically.

Ambenonium (Mytelase) is a biquaternary compound—ie, it is not an ester and is not split by cholinesterase. It attaches persistently to cholinesterase.

Pharmacologic Actions
A. Mechanisms of Action:
1. Cholinesterases–The cholinesterase most importantly related to the chemical mediation of nerve activity is called acetylcholinesterase, or true cholinesterase. It occurs in neurons known to be cholinergic—ie, it is concentrated in nerve terminals and also in the postsynaptic site if it is part of a cholinergic neuron. The neuromuscular junction is also rich in cholinesterase postsynaptically. It is distributed through the central nervous system in a pattern presumed to iden-

Table 8–2. Representative organophosphorus cholinesterase inhibitors.

$$R_2 - \overset{\overset{\displaystyle R_1}{|}}{\underset{\underset{\displaystyle O}{\|}}{P}} - X$$

	X	R_1	R_2	Related Compounds
Isoflurophate (Floropryl, DFP)	—F	$-O-C_3H_7$	$-O-C_3H_7$	Mipafox, sarin, soman
Tabun	—CN	$-N=(CH_3)_2$	$-O-C_2H_5$	
Paraoxon	$-O-\langle\rangle-NO_2$	$-O-C_2H_5$	$-O-C_2H_5$	Parathion,* ethyl p-nitrophenyl benzenethionophosphonate (EPN)*
Malathion*†	$-S-R_3$	$-O-CH_3$	$-O-CH_3$	Echothiophate (Phospholine)‡
Tetraethylpyrophosphate (TEPP)	R_1 $-O-P-R_2$ $\parallel$ O	$-O-C_2H_5$	$-O-C_2H_5$	Octamethyl pyrophosphoramide (OMPA)

*Sulfur analogs.

†$R_3 = -\underset{\underset{\displaystyle CH_2-COO-C_2H_5}{|}}{CH}-COO-C_2H_5$

‡$R_3 = -CH_2-CH_2-N^+\equiv(CH_3)_3$

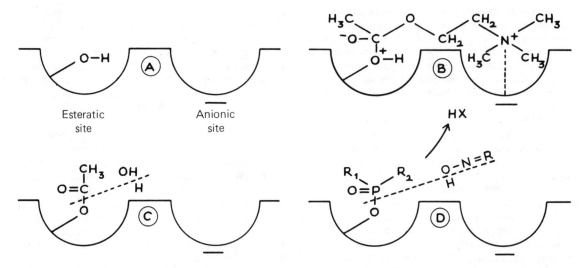

Figure 8–4. Combination of substrate or inhibitor with acetylcholinesterase enzyme. *A:* Representation of the 2 active sites on enzyme. *B:* Acetylcholine is adsorbed to active sites. *C:* Choline is released by hydrolysis and acetylated enzyme formed. Active enzyme is regenerated by hydrolysis of its acetamido derivative. Neostigmine or other reversible inhibitor combines similarly but is more slowly hydrolyzed. *D:* Irreversible inhibitor reacts to form phosphorylated enzyme. Hydrolysis and regeneration of enzyme do not occur in presence of water, but enzyme may be regenerated by reaction with hydroxylamine derivatives.

tify cholinergic neurons and is present in red blood cells. The red cell content of cholinesterase can be measured and provides a clinically useful test for intoxication with cholinesterase inhibitors.

True cholinesterase is distinguished from pseudocholinesterase, or butyrylcholinesterase, which is found in plasma and in glial rather than neuronal cells of the central nervous system. True cholinesterase hydrolyzes acetylcholine more rapidly, whereas pseudocholinesterase hydrolyzes butyryl-choline more rapidly. True cholinesterase, furthermore, hydrolyzes methacholine but not benzoylcholine; the reverse is true for the pseudo enzyme. The function of pseudocholinesterase is unknown. Both forms are inhibited by the drugs being discussed.

2. Reversible or irreversible inhibition–The action of cholinesterase in hydrolyzing acetylcholine is one of transesterification. The properties of the enzyme surface are conventionally represented as shown in Fig 8–4A, which assumes that the reactive group at the esteratic site is the hydroxyl group of serine.

In the process, the ester (Ach) is first physically attached to the enzyme (E), as diagrammed in Fig 8–4B.

$$E + Ach \rightarrow EAch$$

The substrate is hydrolyzed, and the base is released from its attachment to the enzyme surface. The acetyl group, however, reacts at the esteratic site to form an acetamido derivative of the enzyme:

$$EAch \rightarrow EA + ch$$

The acetylated enzyme is rapidly (1 ms) hydrolyzed to regenerate the enzyme:

$$EA \rightarrow E + A$$

The comparatively short-acting, reversible inhibitors such as neostigmine are esters that participate in the transesterification sequence, but a carbamylated rather than an acetylated enzyme is formed that is only slowly hydrolyzed to regenerate the enzyme.

The irreversible inhibitors (organic phosphates) react to form a stable, phosphorylated enzyme. There is almost no regeneration of the enzyme by hydrolysis, and the pharmacologic effect persists until new enzyme is synthesized.

The compounds (edrophonium, ambenonium) characterized above as truly reversible inhibitors are not substrates for the enzyme and act by occluding the site of hydrolysis.

3. Role of acetylcholine–The cholinesterase inhibitors, then, act indirectly through acetylcholine liberated in the organism. In therapeutic or mildly toxic doses, their effects will appear only at sites where acetylcholine is being liberated. Only with the most severe intoxications will acetylcholine be blood-borne and exert a diffuse effect. Thus, blood pressure will be well maintained after cholinesterase inhibition because only a few vessels have cholinergic innervation and most will, therefore, be constricted because of the sympathomimetic effects.

B. Effects: Inhibition of cholinesterase activity will allow the accumulation of acetylcholine at all of the sites where it is liberated. The cholinesterase inhibitors will, therefore, show a mixture of parasympathomimetic (muscarinic) and sympathomimetic and voluntary muscle (nicotinic) effects, as was described above for choline esters. The few differences between the effects of choline esters and cholinesterase inhibitors depend upon the fact that the latter act only where acetylcholine is being liberated. (See Table 8–1.)

1. Nonvascular smooth muscle–All nonvascular smooth muscle (of gut, bladder, bronchioles, constrictor of pupil, ciliary muscle) is contracted. The resulting effects are as described above for the choline esters.

2. Exocrine glands–Salivation and sweating are most sensitive to the stimulant effect of cholinomimetic agents. Increased secretions along the respiratory tract (manifest earliest as rhinorrhea) and lacrimation are also seen. Gastric acid secretion is not increased, but mucus and pepsin secretion is.

3. Cardiovascular–Blood pressure is elevated. A bradycardia is produced at the same time and causes a widened pulse pressure. Thus, systolic pressure rises more than diastolic.

The rise in blood pressure is maintained even in severe intoxications almost until the subject is terminal and acetylcholine actually enters the blood. Facilitation of ganglionic transmission and adrenal medullary stimulation play a part in causing the elevation of blood pressure, but in experimental animals central nervous system stimulation, by increasing sympathetic outflow, is more important.

Cardiac rate is regularly slowed. The slowing is more regularly seen after administration of cholinesterase inhibitors than after the administration of choline esters because there is no fall in blood pressure to evoke compensatory reflexes.

4. Voluntary muscle–Cholinesterase inhibitors will act on striated muscle as described above for the choline esters, and a few drugs of the neostigmine type will in addition act directly on muscle to increase the force of contraction.

a. Initial stimulation–The common effect of the accumulation of acetylcholine is to mimic or intensify the effects of motor nerve stimulation. Therapeutically, this action is apparent as an amelioration of the weakness or fatigability of voluntary muscle in patients with myasthenia gravis (see below). In toxic doses, the depolarization of the motor end-plate by acetylcholine leads to involuntary, incoordinate contraction of small muscle units. These fasciculations are apparent as retraction or undulation of the overlying skin. Only rarely will they be gross enough to briefly lift a limb or turn the head. They are finer and more discrete than preconvulsive jerks but easily apparent compared to fibrillation, the contraction of denervated single fibers, which usually requires electromyography for its demonstration.

b. Depolarization block–The accumulation of very large amounts of acetylcholine prevents repolarization of the motor end-plate. In the case of organophosphate intoxication, paralysis occurs very late and central respiratory and other muscle paralysis is usually also present. During the therapeutic use of neostigmine and related compounds in the treatment of myasthenia gravis, it is possible to cause depolarization block (cholinergic crisis) by an overdose. Since atropine may already have been given to reduce the muscarinic actions of the drug, the differentiation of cholinergic crisis from inadequately treated disease is difficult.

c. Direct effect–Neostigmine and comparable cholinesterase inhibitors—ie, the reversible inhibitors, excluding physostigmine—act to increase the force of voluntary muscle contraction by a mechanism independent of cholinesterase inhibition. This direct, or acetylcholinelike, effect of neostigmine is shown by its action on denervated muscle and after complete inhibition of cholinesterase by an organophosphate. The quantitative clinical importance of this effect has not been established.

5. Central nervous system–The central nervous system effects are demonstrable after administration of reversible inhibitors but are most important in toxic reactions to the organophosphorus type of insecticide. Here again, the actions consist of an initial stimulation followed by depression.

The medullary stimulant effects are manifest as increased respiratory volume and elevated blood pressure. The electroencephalogram shows a desynchronized or awakening pattern, presumably due to facilitation in the reticular activating system (RAS), which is activated by both cholinergic and sympathomimetic drugs. The behavioral correlates of the initial stimulation are anxiety, restlessness, dreaming and nightmares, and insomnia. In animals, sleeping time after a barbiturate is shortened.

With larger doses—ie, with virtually complete inhibition of cholinesterase—the effects include depression, drowsiness, confusion, slurred speech, ataxia, coma, and convulsions. Medullary depression leads to vasodilatation and lowered blood pressure and respiratory paralysis.

Some of the early central nervous system effects of cholinesterase inhibition are antagonized to some extent by atropine.

Clinical Uses

This section and the subsequent discussions of adverse reactions, contraindications, and preparations and dosages apply to choline esters as well as cholinesterase inhibitors.

A. Postoperative Ileus and Urinary Retention: Following surgical procedures done under general or spinal anesthesia, and especially if intra-abdominal manipulation is necessary, patients may have difficulty in urinating and in restoring gastrointestinal activity. These postoperative changes are due to smooth muscle atony, not to obstruction, and the present discussion does not apply if mechanical obstruction of the gastrointestinal or urinary tract is present.

The decrease in propulsive activity is due to drugs such as morphine and atropine used preoperatively and to an increase in inhibitory sympathetic tone generated by peritoneal irritation and distention by swallowed air. Treatment does not necessarily involve drugs, but measures such as gastric suction designed to reduce distention may be supplemented by cholinergic drugs. If parenteral administration is necessary, neostigmine (0.25–0.5 mg subcutaneously) is usually used. If oral medication is possible, as in the case of urinary retention without ileus, bethanechol (Urecholine), 20 mg 3–4 times daily, is used.

B. Glaucoma: Parasympathomimetic drugs constrict the pupil by stimulating the smooth muscle arranged concentrically around the pupil. The miosis so induced pulls the iris away from the anterior chamber angle, facilitates drainage of aqueous humor, and is, therefore, useful in the treatment of glaucoma. At the same time, the ciliary muscle is also contracted and the eye accommodated for near vision. The effect of autonomic drugs on the eye and the treatment of glaucoma are discussed in more detail in association with Fig 9–1.

C. Termination of Curare Action: The use of drugs that weaken or paralyze voluntary muscle as adjuncts to general anesthesia is discussed in Chapter 21. These curariform drugs are of 2 general types. One type acts like a large dose of acetylcholine to cause a depolarization block. The second type, exemplified by the curare alkaloids, acts as a competitive antagonist to acetylcholine at the voluntary nerve-muscle junction. It is often desirable to terminate the action of curare at the conclusion of a surgical procedure and restore the patient's ability to breathe unassisted. For this purpose and in the case of the curare type of blocker, a neostigmine type of cholinesterase inhibitor is used. The mechanisms are to allow the accumulation of acetylcholine and to act directly on muscle as acetylcholine would. Edrophonium (Tensilon) has a brief duration of action and is supposed to have more of the direct action on muscle. It is the most widely used drug in this application.

D. Myasthenia Gravis: Myasthenia gravis is an autoimmune neuromuscular disorder that, like curare poisoning, is characterized by profound weakness and fatigability of voluntary muscles. Normally, at the voluntary nerve-muscle junction, acetylcholine is released in quanta that reflect the amount held in each presynaptic vesicle: about 10,000 molecules. One or 2 of these vesicles fuse with the cell membrane and release their contained acetylcholine into the synaptic cleft each second. Micro end-plate potentials result, but the muscle does not contract. (See Fig 21–2.) When a wave of depolarization arrives, the nerve may liberate a much greater amount of acetylcholine (several hundred quanta) and depolarize the postsynaptic membrane of the motor end-plate. The amplitude of depolarization—and therefore the effectiveness of the neuromuscular transmission—depends on the number of acetylcholine molecules that interact with receptor molecules. Current data suggest that, in myasthenia gravis, acetylcholine is liberated in normal amounts but that fewer acetylcholine receptors are present in the motor end-plate. The changes in muscular function in myasthenia gravis are similar to those described for curare: The strength of a repetitive or sustained muscle contraction cannot be maintained. The muscles are affected in the same order as during the development of a curare effect—ie, muscles innervated by cranial nerves (external ocular, facial, palatal, pharyngeal, laryngeal, neck) and small muscles earliest and only later the limbs, intercostals, and diaphragm.

The mechanism of production of myasthenia gravis is related to the concept of acetylcholine receptor as an antigenic postsynaptic substance with which acetylcholine combines to exert its effect. The receptor can be experimentally marked and partially purified because it combines specifically with isotopically labeled alpha-bungarotoxin, a snake venom. Myasthenic muscles show a significant reduction in number of available acetylcholine receptors per neuromuscular junction by this technic. Animals injected with acetylcholine receptor from the electric organ of the eel develop antibodies to the receptor and signs resembling human myasthenia gravis. Plasma and the thymus gland of patients with myasthenia contain immunoglobulins that react with the receptor. The current formulation holds that myasthenia is a cell-mediated autoimmune disease. The immune complex (IgG and C3) does not block access to acetylcholine but speeds the degradation of receptor substance and reduces the amount present.

1. Effect of cholinesterase inhibitors–From the above, it would seem that the mere accumulation of acetylcholine subsequent to cholinesterase inhibition and the direct action of the reversible inhibitors would be of limited value. Nonetheless, muscle strength is increased by use of these agents in most myasthenic patients. Some patients (and other patients at some time in the course of their disease) have an acetylcholine-insensitive type of block that does not respond to cholinesterase inhibitors.

The several drugs now in use are listed in Table 8–3. The irreversible, organophosphorus type of inhibitors—eg, DFP—have been less satisfactory than the reversible inhibitors listed. The irreversible

Table 8–3. Cholinesterase inhibitors used in treatment of myasthenia gravis.

	Single Adult Dose	Approximate Duration of Action*
Neostigmine bromide (Prostigmin)†	15 mg orally	3 h
Neostigmine methylsulfate (Prostigmin)†	1 mg IM or subcut	2 h
Pyridostigmine (Mestinon)	60 mg orally	4 h
Ambenonium (Mytelase)	10 mg orally	8 h
Edrophonium (Tensilon)	10 mg IV	‡

*Treatment begins with 4 doses each day and is adjusted individually thereafter.
†Generic preparation available.
‡Used as diagnostic test only.

inhibitors did have the advantage of persisting in their effect overnight and leaving the patient with greater strength in the morning. Should DFP or a similar compound be used, it must not be given when neostigmine is acting, since the enzyme will be occupied and the organophosphate metabolized before it can act on the enzyme.

Because atropine does not antagonize the voluntary muscle effects of acetylcholine, parasympathomimetic side-effects (eg, nausea and vomiting, abdominal cramps) can frequently be ameliorated with atropine. Surprisingly, less than half of the patients treated will require atropine.

2. Other drugs–It would be predicted that the anti-inflammatory steroids would be useful if myasthenia is an autoimmune state. Corticosteroids and corticotropin have proved to be clinically useful in the treatment of myasthenia gravis. Alternate-day prednisone therapy in combination with anticholinesterase drugs can be very effective, particularly in older male patients. Other immunosuppressive drugs (eg, azathioprine) have had limited use in those patients who have failed to respond to the above measures.

Ephedrine, 25 mg 2–3 times daily, may enhance the effectiveness of anticholinesterase drugs.

Some drugs can induce myasthenia in patients with no preexisting muscular disorder (See Table 8–4). These drugs may unmask or intensify the symptoms of myasthenia gravis. Narcotic analgesics and sedatives should be used in smaller doses than usual, especially if the patient is having difficulty in swallowing or breathing.

E. Other Uses: The organophosphorus cholinesterase inhibitors are widely used as insecticides and are potential chemical warfare agents.

Supraventricular tachycardias may be converted to a normal sinus rhythm by drugs and maneuvers that augment vagal influences on the atria. Edrophonium, because of its prompt, brief action, is sometimes used intravenously for this purpose.

Contraindications & Cautions

Parasympathomimetics should not be used in the presence of obstructive rather than paralytic or hypotonic ileus or urinary retention. Other situations requiring caution are (1) asthma, because of the risk of added bronchiolar constriction; (2) hyperthyroidism, because paroxysmal atrial fibrillation may be precipitated; and (3) peptic ulcer, because the increased motility may cause increased pain.

Adverse Reactions

A. Side-Effects: When cholinesterase inhibitors are used for their parasympathomimetic action, they may cause gastrointestinal cramps or diarrhea, nausea, sweating, or excess salivation. These side-effects cannot always be blocked by atropine without at the same time blocking the therapeutic effect, and their uncommon occurrence must often be controlled by changing the dosage or using a different preparation.

During the treatment of myasthenia gravis, excessive dosage may cause depolarization block and increased muscle weakness or paralysis. Several methods are available to differentiate "cholinergic crisis" from an exacerbation of the disease. The toxic state may be treated in a number of ways. The dosage of cholinesterase inhibitor can be reduced (with mechanical support for respiration), observing for either improvement or deterioration. An injection of a short-acting inhibitor—eg, edrophonium, 1 mg intravenously—will result in short-lived intensification of weakness due to overdosage or improvement of weakness due to myasthenia gravis. In theory, pralidoxime, a cholinesterase reactivator described below, could be used to antagonize an excess of neostigmine or other carbamate, but it is not indicated for this purpose.

Table 8–4. Clinical syndromes of drug-induced neuromuscular blockade and the drugs implicated.

Clinical Presentation	Antibiotics	Cardiovascular Drugs	Antirheumatic Drugs	Psychotropic Drugs	Anticonvulsants	Hormonal Agents	Other Drugs
Postoperative respiratory depression	Clindamycin Colistin Kanamycin Lincomycin Neomycin Streptomycin Tobramycin	Lidocaine Quinidine Trimethaphan	Chloroquine	Lithium Phenelzine Promazine			Aprotinin Cholinesterase inhibitors Oxytocin
Aggravation or unmasking of myasthenia gravis	Colistin Kanamycin Streptomycin Tetracyclines	Procainamide Propranolol Quinidine	Chloroquine (?)	Chlorpromazine Lithium	Phenytoin	ACTH Corticosteroids Thyroid hormones	Acetylcholinesterase inhibitors Methoxyflurane
Drug-induced myasthenic syndrome	Colistin Gentamicin Kanamycin Neomycin Polymyxin B Streptomycin	Oxprenolol Practolol Trimethaphan	D-Penicillamine		Phenytoin Trimethadione	Oral contraceptives (?)	Tetanus antitoxin

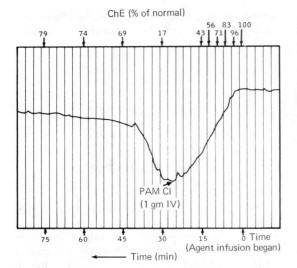

ChE (% of normal)

Figure 8–5. A continuous record of the circulating cholinesterase of a volunteer subject. At zero time, 4 μg/kg of sarin was given intravenously. At 27 minutes, blood cholinesterase had fallen to 17% of normal. Pralidoxime given at this time (very soon after administration of the inhibitor) restored the cholinesterase level to 80% of control in 50 minutes. (Reproduced, with permission, from Sim: Diagnosis and therapy for anticholinesterase poisoning. JAMA 192:404, 1965.)

B. Acute Accidental Toxicity: The problem of acute toxicity exists almost entirely because of the use of organophosphate and carbamate inhibitors as insecticides in the agricultural industry. The most widely used insecticides are of 2 general types. The chlorinated hydrocarbons—DDT, chlordane, lindane, aldrin, dieldrin, toxaphene, etc—are chemically stable, water-insoluble but fat-soluble dusts that are persistent contaminants. Their acute toxicity (central nervous system stimulation) to humans is usually low, but some unresolved concern exists about their chronic toxicity, since residues on food are concentrated in body fat.

The second class of insecticides, the cholinesterase inhibitors, are volatile and chemically labile in the presence of moisture, but, under proper weather conditions, the residue on sprayed vegetation may be dangerous for 1–2 weeks. Parathion is water-insoluble and persists for as long as 3 weeks under usual conditions. They are more likely to present immediate treatment problems to the physician than are the chlorinated hydrocarbons.

Examples of the organophosphates involved would include parathion, TEPP, Phosdrin, Thimet, and Systox. Malathion deserves special mention. It is metabolized rapidly by the mammalian and avian body to an inactive derivative, but in insects is converted to the oxy analog, which is an active metabolite. It is the least toxic of this group and is permitted even in household insecticides. A few insecticides—eg, carbaryl (Sevin) and Prophan—are carbamates comparable to

neostigmine in that the carbamylated enzyme is rapidly regenerated. The toxic effects persist for only about 2 hours. The effect of the organophosphates lasts so long that widely spaced exposures have a cumulative effect.

Exposure may be from inhalation, skin contamination, or ingestion. Handlers—eg, aircraft operators, mixers, sprayers—are most likely to be exposed, but drift from an air spray, contamination from work clothes, or unusual and unpredictable circumstances may lead to toxicity in persons not occupationally exposed.

The toxic effects can be anticipated from the parasympathomimetic, sympathomimetic, voluntary muscle, and central nervous system effects discussed above. The order and occurrence of a given symptom will depend upon the dosage and rate of administration of the toxin. The possible findings may be summarized as follows:

1. Autonomic effects–Nausea, cramps, diarrhea, tenesmus; miosis, ciliary spasm (blurred or painful vision); sweating, salivation, rhinorrhea, lacrimation; bronchial constriction and hypersecretion, with wheezing and dyspnea; urinary frequency and urgency; elevated blood pressure until terminal; and slowed pulse.

2. Voluntary muscle effects–Fasciculations in eyelids, tongue, face, neck, extraocular muscles; generalized fasciculations; and weakness.

3. Central nervous system effects–Dreams and nightmares, giddiness, restlessness, anxiety, tremulousness, fatigability, ataxia, tremors, confusion, paresthesias, convulsions, coma, and central respiratory failure.

The diagnosis can be verified in the clinical laboratory by demonstrating depression of red blood cell cholinesterase. Treatment of an acute intoxication should not await this information, but in chronic, less intense exposures with minimal symptoms it may be useful. Many workers show laboratory evidence of exposure to cholinesterase inhibitors. In the case of parathion, exposure can be quantitatively evaluated by measuring urinary paranitrophenol.

C. Treatment of Acute Toxicity: (See also Chapter 64.) As soon as an airway is assured and respiration assisted and maintained if necessary, remove the patient's clothing and decontaminate the skin as necessary by thorough washing with soap and water.

1. Atropine–The most important part of treatment is atropine, which antagonizes the parasympathomimetic effects, but huge doses may be needed. One effective routine is to give 2–4 mg intravenously every 5–10 minutes until some sign of atropine effect (eg, pupillary dilatation, tachycardia) appears.

2. Pralidoxime (a reactivator of cholinesterase)–Inhibition of cholinesterase by phosphorylation is theoretically reversible by hydrolysis. The phosphorylated cholinesterase is actually regenerated by hydrolysis but at a rate so slow as to be unimportant. Wilson noted that the rate of regeneration was more rapid when the reaction was with hydroxylamine rather than water. He then developed quaternary ammonium compounds that fitted the anionic site on the enzyme and also contained nucleophilic groups that reacted with the phosphorus and broke the enzyme-phosphorus bond (Fig 8–4D). Pralidoxime (2-PAM; pyridyl-2-aldoxime; Protopam) is the available activator of cholinesterase.

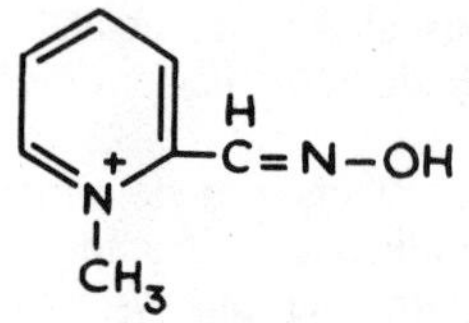

Pralidoxime

The activity of pralidoxime depends on the nature of the inhibitor—eg, it is quite active after parathion, inactive after octamethyl pyrophosphoramide (OMPA)—and on the time elapsed since exposure. As the phosphorylated enzyme "ages," presumably by loss of an alkyl group, it is less readily regenerated. It is most active when used within 24 hours after exposure and is not ordinarily of any value after 36–48 hours. Because of the variables that alter the response, a trial of therapy is advisable in patients with moderate or severe intoxication.

Pralidoxime is most active against the effects of cholinesterase inhibition on voluntary muscle. It is far less effective than atropine against autonomic effects. It is, therefore, a useful supplement to atropine and artificial respiration and often causes dramatic further improvement.

The dosage of pralidoxine is 1 g intravenously, well diluted and given over at least 5 minutes; this amount may be repeated in 30 minutes. In children, the dose is 25–50 mg/kg.

Dosages

Some dosages are listed under Clinical Uses

(above) or, in the case of pralidoxime (Protopam), under the treatment of adverse reactions to cholinesterase inhibitors.

OLD ALKALOIDS

MUSCARINE

Muscarine occurs in a mushroom, *Amanita muscaria,* and thus has toxicologic significance on rare occasions. Its primary significance is historical. It has the parasympathomimetic properties of acetylcholine but lacks the sympathomimetic and voluntary muscle effects. It was isolated and studied by Schmiedeberg, one of the founders of experimental pharmacology, in 1869. Not until 1914 did the studies of Dale on acetylcholine begin to suggest the importance of that ester. As a consequence, even today the parasympathomimetic effects of acetylcholine are described as "muscarinic."

It should be briefly emphasized that *Amanita muscaria* contains an atropinelike toxin as often as it contains the cholinomimetic muscarine. The effects of the very dangerous *Amanita phalloides* are due to a hepatotoxin with a delayed onset of action rather than to any autonomic changes.

PILOCARPINE

Pilocarpine, isolated from a South American shrub, is a tertiary amine with cholinergic properties. It has the parasympathomimetic effects described above

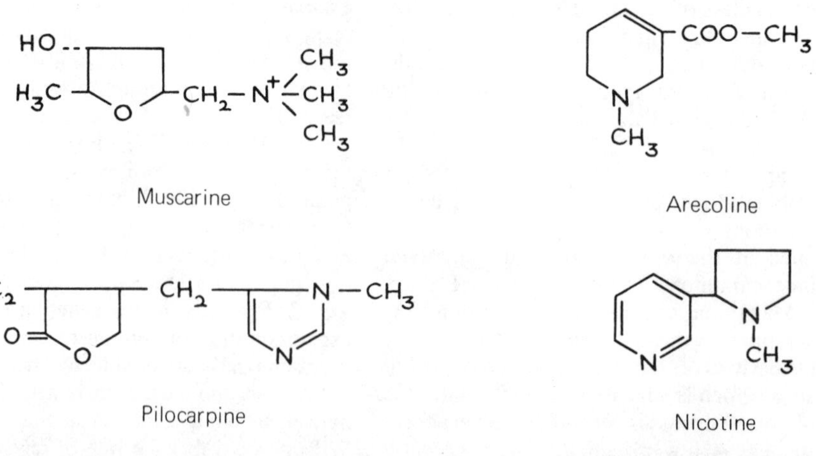

Muscarine

Arecoline

Pilocarpine

Nicotine

Figure 8–6. Chemical formulas of some additional cholinergic compounds.

for acetylcholine but is orally active and especially potent in producing salivation and sweating. Blood pressure and pulse rate changes often show the sympathomimetic or nicotinic effect of pilocarpine. The ganglionic facilitant action is easily blocked by atropine and is therefore often described as nonnicotinic—ie, acting on receptors other than those for acetylcholine.

Pilocarpine has now been almost entirely superseded for systemic use by the drugs mentioned above. It is still the drug most commonly applied topically to the eye in the treatment of glaucoma. In those rare situations in which salivary stimulation is desired, it is also the preferred drug.

ARECOLINE

Arecoline is an alkaloid with predominantly parasympathomimetic effects. It must have some nicotinelike central nervous system stimulant action, however, to explain its habitual use in a manner comparable to tobacco. For this purpose, a slice of the nut of a particular palm, *Areca catechu,* is mixed with lime from burned shell and the leaf of a pepper, *Piper betel.* The lime hastens absorption by keeping arecoline in the form of the free base. The pepper contributes the name, betel nut, to the quid.

NICOTINE & OTHER GANGLION STIMULANTS

Nicotine and a few other comparatively unimportant drugs are often discussed as a separate class of drugs, ganglion stimulants. However, their properties are exactly the same as the nicotinic or sympathomimetic properties of cholinergic drugs.

NICOTINE

Summary of Pharmacology
Nicotine is an alkaloid isolated from tobacco. The free base is a clear liquid that becomes brown upon exposure to air. It is well absorbed from all body surfaces.

Nicotine exerts a sympathomimetic effect by the same mechanisms as acetylcholine—ie, facilitation of transmission across sympathetic ganglia, adrenal medullary stimulation, and release of norepinephrine from chromaffin tissue in the cardiac atria and arterioles. Muscarinic or parasympathomimetic effects due

to stimulation of parasympathetic ganglia occur, especially on the gastrointestinal tract and eye. Acute central nervous system effects are as described above for cholinesterase inhibitors—ie, mild central stimulation followed by depression and culminating in convulsions. As would be expected from its similarity to acetylcholine, nicotine in larger doses causes paralysis of ganglionic transmission and of voluntary muscle. Nicotine is able to stimulate the release of antidiuretic hormone from the pituitary, an action that can influence urine volume in a hydrated subject. It is also very active in stimulating chemoreceptors of the carotid sinus; thus, initial effects on blood pressure and respiration are due to this action.

Laboratory Uses
Nicotine applied locally blocks ganglionic transmission, and the early mapping of the autonomic nervous system utilized nicotine. In addition, the systemic action of smaller doses on ganglia is used to test for the occurrence of ganglionic blockade.

Toxicology
Nicotine was at one time widely used as an insecticide. As long as it was used as an insecticide, it was stored about the house and garden as a 40% solution and was responsible for serious accidental intoxications. Newer insecticides have now replaced it.

Tobacco as a Drug
Tobacco, like the many drugs discussed in Chapter 7, is subject to various degrees of use or misuse. It may be used casually or with the same compulsiveness as the socially unacceptable drugs.

One must assume that the mild central stimulant (euphoriant, awakening) properties of nicotine are important in perpetuating its usage, since nicotine-free cigarettes cannot be substituted and since providing cigarettes with a high nicotine content has been shown to reduce the total number of cigarettes smoked by a given individual. The nicotine dependence hypothesis of the tobacco smoking habit, however, has been challenged in the light of recent experimental studies. Tolerance (except to the nauseant effect) is of a minor degree, and a withdrawal state widely claimed by tobacco smokers is not clearly established and is mostly the anxiety of individuals deprived of their compulsive act.

The clearly established carcinogenic effect of cigarette smoking is unrelated to nicotine, resulting instead from contact with the products of slow combustion (eg, tars). Unburned tobacco—eg, snuff—is also mildly carcinogenic.

OTHER GANGLION STIMULANTS

The following compounds are listed for identification rather than because of any therapeutic importance. Lobeline, an alkaloid from Indian tobacco, resembles nicotine but is even more active in stimulating chemoreceptors. It was used in the past to measure arm-to-carotid artery circulation time. Coniine (propyl piperidine) is the toxic component of hemlock and has more central nervous system depressant properties than nicotine. DMPP (dimethylphenylpiperazinium) and TMA (trimethylammonium) are laboratory drugs used as ganglion stimulants alternatively to electrical stimulation or to nicotine.

•   •   •

References

General

Argov Z, Mastaglia FL: Disorders of neuromuscular transmission caused by drugs. N Engl J Med 301:409, 1979.

Barchas JD & others: Behavioral neurochemistry: Neuroregulation and behavioral states. Science 200:964, 1978.

Burnstock G, Bell C: Peripheral autonomic transmission. In: *The Peripheral Nervous System.* Hubbard JI (editor). Plenum Press, 1974.

Cooper JR, Bloom FE, Roth RH: *The Biochemical Basis of Neuropharmacology,* 3rd ed. Oxford Univ Press, 1978.

Gabella G: *Structure of the Autonomic Nervous System.* Wiley, 1976.

Ganong WF: Neural centers regulating visceral function. Chapter 14 in: *Review of Medical Physiology,* 9th ed. Lange, 1979.

Hillarp N: Peripheral autonomic mechanisms. Vol 2, Chap 38, pages 979–1006, in: *Handbook of Physiology.* Section 1. Field J, Magoun HW, Hall VE (editors). American Physiological Society, 1960.

Hoffman BB, Lefkowitz RJ: Alpha-adrenergic receptor subtypes. N Engl J Med 302:1390, 1980.

Ingram WR: Central autonomic mechanisms. Vol 2, Chap 38, pages 951–978, in: *Handbook of Physiology.* Section 1. Field J, Magoun HW, Hall VE (editors). American Physiological Society, 1960.

Kunos G: Adrenoceptors. Ann Rev Pharmacol Toxicol 18:291, 1978.

Kutt H: *Clinical Neuropharmacology.* Vol 4 in: *Monographs in Clinical Pharmacology.* Livingstone, 1979.

Lefkowitz RJ: β-adrenergic receptors: Recognition and regulation. N Engl J Med 295:323, 1976.

Meyers FH: A critique of the concept of sympathetic-parasympathetic antagonism. J Am Geriatr Soc 7:120, 1959.

Molinoff PB, Axelrod J: Biochemistry of catecholamines. Annu Rev Biochem 40:465, 1971.

Osdin E, Kopin IJ (editors): *Catecholamines: Basic and Clinical Frontiers.* Pergamon, 1979.

Otsuka M, Takahashi T: Putative peptide neurotransmitters. Annu Rev Pharmacol Toxicol 17:425, 1977.

Rang HP: Acetylcholine receptors. Q Rev Biophys 7:283, 1975.

Cholinergic Agents

Drachman DB (Chairman): Immunopathology of receptors. Fed Proc 38:2606, 1979.

Drachman DB: Myasthenia gravis. (2 parts.) N Engl J Med 298:156, 186, 1978.

Dreisbach RH: Cholinesterase inhibitor insecticides. Chapter 7 in: *Handbook of Poisoning,* 10th ed. Lange, 1980.

Euler US von (editor): *Symposium on Tobacco Alkaloids and Related Compounds.* Pergamon Press, 1964.

Gadoth N, Fisher A: Late onset of neuromuscular block in organophosphorus poisoning. Ann Intern Med 88:654, 1978.

Koelle GB (editor): Cholinesterases and anticholinesterase agents. *Handbuch der experimentellen Pharmakologie.* Vol 15. Springer, 1963.

Kumar R & others: Is nicotine important in tobacco smoking? Clin Pharmacol Ther 21:520, 1977.

Milby TH: Prevention and management of organophosphate poisoning. JAMA 216:2131, 1971.

Peoples SA, Maddy KT: Organophosphorus pesticide poisoning. West J Med 129:273, 1978.

Root WS, Hofmann FG (editors): *Physiological Pharmacology.* Vol 3. Academic Press, 1967. [See also general references, p 3 of this book.]

Smoking and Health: Report of the Advisory Committee to the Surgeon General of the Public Health Service. US Department of Health, Education, & Welfare, 1964.

Wynder EC, Hoffman D: Tobacco and health: A social challenge. N Engl J Med 300:894, 1979.

Anticholinergic (Parasympatholytic) Drugs | 9

Atropine and many related drugs have the ability to block the parasympathomimetic (muscarinic) effects of acetylcholine. They act distal to the parasympathetic nerve ending to prevent the action of acetylcholine on smooth muscle, glands, and heart. Their ability to decrease the activity of smooth muscle and exocrine glands, along with incidental central nervous system effects, accounts for the wide and varied medical uses of this group of drugs. There are other drugs that act through anticholinergic mechanisms but are not as specifically parasympatholytic as atropine and its congeners. The curare alkaloids, discussed later, block acetylcholine liberated at the voluntary nerve-muscle junction, and the ganglion blocking agents are antagonists to the acetylcholine acting as a mediator of ganglionic transmission. Botulinus toxin blocks the liberation of acetylcholine at all sites, and the signs of botulism thus combine the effects of curariform and parasympatholytic drugs.

Source, Chemistry, & Classification

The wide use of the parasympatholytics and the ease with which the chemist can synthesize analogs of the naturally occurring molecule have led to the marketing of a great number of compounds. Furthermore, other drug classes also have atropinelike actions. The need to consider each one of the many drugs individually can be largely avoided by grouping the many available preparations into 4 principal classes:

A. Natural Alkaloids: Atropine (DL-hyoscyamine) is extracted from a nightshade shrub, *Atropa belladonna*. The specific name, belladonna, is important to remember because tincture and extract of belladonna are still widely used. Scopolamine (L-hyoscine) occurs in the henbane, *Hyoscyamus niger*. Jimson (Jamestown) weed *(Datura stramonium)* must also be mentioned as a source of L-hyoscyamine because it is a rare cause of intoxication and because stramonium powder is still used.

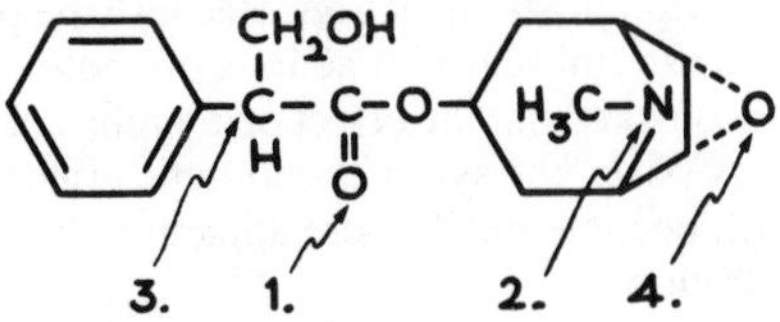

In the structure of atropine shown below, note that it is an ester (1) and a tertiary amine (2) and that there is an asymmetric carbon at (3). Scopolamine contains the epoxy structure at (4).

The L-isomers are more potent in their effects on both the peripheral and central nervous systems.

B. Synthetic Esters With Tertiary Amine Function in the Alcohol: A great number of synthetic esters closely related to atropine were marketed in the past. With a few exceptions (listed in Table 9–1), they have been replaced as systemic parasympatholytics by members of the next class (C). However, parasympatholytics used topically in the eye as pupillary dilators or cycloplegics are tertiary amines because they penetrate the corneal epithelium and endothelium better than the quaternary amines. Drugs used in the treatment of parkinsonism—benztropine (Cogentin) is an ether of this class—exert their therapeutic effect on the central nervous system. To reach the central nervous system, they too must be tertiary amines.

C. Quaternary Analogs of A and B: The number of parasympatholytic compounds has been further increased by the conversion of esters of tertiary amino alcohols of the types described in paragraphs A and B above to their quaternary analogs. Thus, atropine may be converted to the methylnitrate or scopolamine to the methylbromide, and many other esters of amino alcohols may be quaternized. Examples include homatropine methylbromide and propantheline (Pro-Banthine). Others are listed in Table 9–1.

In contrast to the tertiary amines just discussed, these quaternary amines are strong bases. The ionization of a weak base such as atropine is diagrammed in Fig 2–2. Quaternary amines remain in the salt or ionized form at any pH existing in the organism. Only in strongly alkaline solutions is the free base formed:

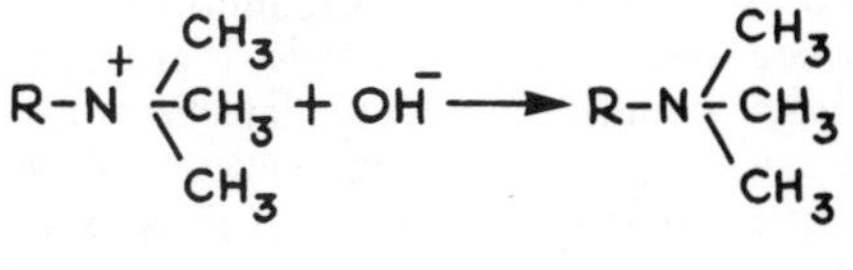

Atropine. Scopolamine contains the oxygen shown at (4).

At the pH of the body, these compounds are always in the ionic form and have low lipid solubility. In this form they cannot cross the blood-brain barrier—the barrier of glial cells interposed between the vascular compartment and the neurons of the central nervous system. Since they cannot reach or enter neurons of the central nervous system, the parasympatholytics that are quaternary amines do not have any central nervous system effects. In contrast, atropine or another parasympatholytic that is a tertiary amine is a weak base that can exist in the body in part as the lipid-soluble, free base. As such, it can reach neurons of the central nervous system and cause behavioral changes.

These amines are active after oral administration. They are also slightly more active as ganglion blocking agents than is atropine itself. These drugs cannot be substituted for atropine in any situation where the central effects are important, but they are potent parasympatholytics.

A representative compound of this class is propantheline (Pro-Banthine):

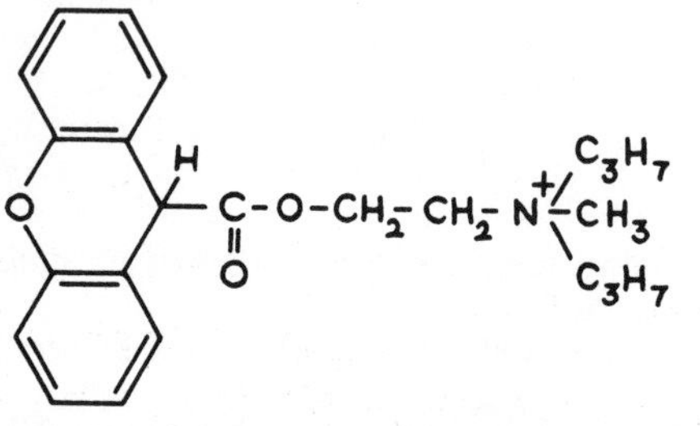

D. Antihistamines, Antipsychotics, Antidepressants, and Antiparkinsonism Drugs: The ester structure emphasized above is not essential for atropinelike activity. The large blocking group may be connected to the amine function by a variety of connecting groups isosteric with the ester grouping, and some of the atropine substitutes listed in Table 9–1 are not esters. Chemically similar structures may be antihistamines, antipsychotics, or antiparkinsonism drugs but retain atropinelike side-effects. Similarly, the central effects of atropine may be expected to be similar to those of the antipsychotics or antihistamines.

Pharmacologic Actions

A. Mechanism of Action: Peripherally, atropine and all of the related parasympatholytic drugs act as competitive antagonists to choline esters and the parasympathomimetic alkaloids discussed above at sites where acetylcholine exerts a parasympathomimetic or muscarinic effect. Thus, following the administration of atropine, acetylcholine—whether injected or neurally liberated—still exerts its sympathomimetic or nicotinic effects and still acts at voluntary muscle. However, the effect of the acetylcholine that acts beyond parasympathetic postganglionic endings is blocked. Heart rate, for example, is ordinarily slowed by vagal stimulation or by the injection of methacholine or a similar parasympathomimetic. When atropine is acting, the bradycrotic effect is blocked and

tachycardia reflects the now unopposed sympathomimetic action.

Acetylcholine release is not altered. Atropine acts beyond the nerve ending on the acetylcholine receptors of the effector organ. Nerve function, including liberation of the mediator, is not altered, but because the receptor is now occupied by atropine, acetylcholine can no longer act to depolarize the cell and initiate contraction or secretion. Atropine then has a greater affinity for the receptor site than does acetylcholine but much less efficacy in initiating activity.

The atropine-acetylcholine relation is competitive—ie, when acetylcholine and atropine are present, the resultant effect depends upon the ratio between the concentrations of the agonist and antagonist. Atropine block can be overcome by increasing the concentration of acetylcholine, eg, by administering a cholinesterase inhibitor. That fraction of atropine attached to the effector cell is in equilibrium with the atropine in the extracellular fluid. As atropine is excreted, the unaltered receptor again responds to the relatively larger concentration of acetylcholine present. Equilibrium block of this type contrasts with the situation in which the antagonist reacts to irreversibly alter the receptor or enzyme.

Atropine acts only where acetylcholine is being liberated or when a parasympathomimetic has been injected. The effect of atropine on some tissues can be demonstrated only by the altered response to a challenge of injected acetylcholine, since no cholinergic influence is present physiologically. Most blood vessels, for example, are not under a tonic cholinergic influence and do not dilate following atropine administration. Yet they are dilated by injected acetylcholine, and such dilatation is blocked by prior administration of atropine. This example also demonstrates that muscarinic receptors are distributed independently of parasympathetic innervation.

Atropine has specificity of action in the usual doses. The response of smooth muscle to acetylcholine can be blocked with amounts of atropine that do not block the response to histamine or other stimulant. This specificity of action has led to the concept of specific and separate receptors for different agonists and their antagonists.

The action of atropine is also specific in the sense that it has no blocking action at voluntary nerve-muscle junctions except in special experimental situations. It has a transient and quantitatively minor action in blocking acetylcholine at ganglionic synapses. In therapeutic dosage, the quaternized analogs do have some ganglion blocking action. Because the parasympathomimetic (muscarinic) actions of cholinomimetic drugs are blocked but the effect on ganglia and adrenal medulla persists, the sympathomimetic effects of such drugs will become much more apparent after atropine administration.

The mechanisms underlying the effects of atropine on the central nervous system are not established. Acetylcholine is certainly one central transmitter, and some of the central effects of atropine are reversed by physostigmine, a cholinesterase inhibitor; but the temptation to relate the central effects of atropine, the tranquilizers, and the antiparkinsonism drugs to a central cholinolytic effect cannot yet be justified by any direct evidence.

B. Effects:

1. Cardiovascular–

a. Heart rate is determined by the balance between vagal slowing and sympathetic accelerator influences acting on the intrinsic rate and is one of the very few examples where the concept of control of function by the balance between sympathetic and parasympathetic influences holds. Vagal blockade with atropine would be expected to cause tachycardia. Tachycardia does appear when the dose is large enough. However, in smaller doses, atropine causes bradycardia before cardioacceleration, or bradycardia may be the sole reaction. The effect of atropine on the unanesthetized human is unpredictable unless dosage and route of administration are stipulated. Bradycardia has been shown by vagal nerve and brain stem section experiments to be due to the stimulation of medullary vagal centers.

The tachycardia that atropine induces in dogs is greater than that which follows vagal section and can only be abolished by sympathectomy, adrenal medullectomy, and vagal section. This indirect sympathomimetic effect of atropine has not been demonstrated in humans, but the extremely rapid rates seen after toxic doses of atropine suggest that it does occur.

b. Blood pressure in the recumbent patient may be slightly elevated after the injection of atropine because of a minor increase in cardiac output accompanying the tachycardia. Postural hypotension may occur with the patient in the erect position. These changes may occur after injection of atropine but are negligible in the patient receiving chronic oral medication.

2. Smooth muscle–All nonvascular smooth muscle is relaxed, ie, its motility is decreased, by atropine or other parasympatholytics. It is an oversimplification to relate this effect to blockade of the influence of extrinsic parasympathetic nerves, since section of these nerves does not have the same effect of smooth muscle relaxation and since atropine demonstrates a similar action on the spontaneous activity of isolated smooth muscle tissues and of noninnervated tissue. The acetylcholine that is antagonized must be that responsible for the intrinsic motility of the involved organ—perhaps that related to the intrinsic ganglia contained in every automatic tissue.

Large doses of atropine depress the response of smooth muscle not only to acetylcholine but to all stimuli.

The claim is still made that some of the atropine substitutes, even in small doses, depress activity of the intestinal or urinary tract by a "musculotropic" effect, ie, an effect on smooth muscle independent of acetylcholine antagonism. Experimentally, this conclusion was based on the ability of the drug to reduce the contractions of isolated muscle caused by barium ion as well as those caused by acetylcholine. However,

barium acts in isolated preparations by stimulating ganglionic transmission, and its effect is equivalent to the addition of acetylcholine. Because of the frequency of smooth muscle dysfunction, the parasympatholytics are still often referred to as "spasmolytics."

3. Secretions–The secretory activity of the exocrine glands is decreased. The effect is marked on the glands of the respiratory tract, the gastric and salivary glands, and sweat glands (except those of the apocrine type). Experimentally, the effect on pancreatic secretion, control of which is largely humoral, is minimal.

4. Central nervous system–The quaternary amine type of compounds described as class C above and listed in Table 9–1 does not act on the central nervous system. If the quaternaries are excluded, the behavioral and neurophysiologic effects of atropine, scopolamine, and all of their synthetic congeners can be discussed together.

Drugs of this class are depressants insofar as manifest behavioral change is concerned, ie, they cause a particular kind of sedation or slowing. However, the depression is accompanied by signs that the underlying neurophysiologic mechanism is stimulation. The same statement will have to be repeated in the discussions of the antihistamines and the antipsychotic tranquilizers. The parasympatholytics cause excitement and hallucinations more commonly, but the behavioral effects of the 3 drug groups are otherwise very similar.

If a series of increasing doses of a parasympatholytic drug are given to a human subject, the following successive changes occur: (1) Sedation—not of the pleasant alcohol or barbiturate type, but rather a slowing apt to be described as unpleasant and accompanied by dizziness and fatigue. (2) Excitement or delirium—ie, hyperreactivity or misinterpretation of stimuli. Hallucinations occur with large doses. (3) Profound depression or coma. (4) Amnesia for the period of intoxication. (5) Convulsions. (6) Respiratory depression only with very large doses.

Scopolamine and atropine are often said to have different behavioral effects, but the manifestations of the action of these drugs on the central nervous system vary greatly with the dose. The conclusion that atropine is a "stimulant" (causes excitement) but scopolamine a sedative was originally suggested because these drugs were not compared over a wide range of doses but only at randomly selected—ie, clinically used—dosages. Scopolamine (L-hyoscine) is 3–10 times more potent than atropine in its central nervous system effects. At the usual nontoxic doses, scopolamine is more apt to cause sedation. If the drugs are compared over a range of doses, the above changes occur with atropine, scopolamine, and the related synthetic drugs.

The parasympatholytics cause electroencephalographic changes (ie, bursts of high-voltage, slower frequency activity) similar to those seen during normal or drug-induced sleep. These changes persist even when behavioral excitement occurs.

5. Respiration–The parasympatholytic drugs

are bronchiolar dilators even in normal, ie, nonasthmatic, subjects. In addition, atropine and scopolamine have in the past had central respiratory stimulating properties ascribed to them. Atropine was formerly used in the treatment of depression induced by morphine, and scopolamine was favored in preanesthetic medication because it was thought to partially antagonize the respiratory depression caused by morphine. Scopolamine, like the phenothiazine antipsychotics, can cause additional sedation without causing additional respiratory depression when combined with morphine, but neither atropine nor scopolamine is a respiratory stimulant in clinically applied doses. The control of respiration does involve cholinergic paths; thus, the respiratory arrest caused by toxic doses of cholinesterase inhibitors can be delayed by atropine.

Pharmacokinetics

The natural alkaloids are completely absorbed across all mucosal surfaces. Absorption across the cornea is limited, but any fraction of a dose instilled into the eye that traverses the nasolacrimal duct into the pharynx will be completely absorbed. The quaternary analogs are less completely (about 25%) and less regularly absorbed.

In the human, hydrolysis of these esters is an unimportant factor in the termination of their activity. Most of the natural alkaloid appears in the urine unchanged. Their maximal effect is reached about 1 hour after oral administration and is dissipated in 3–4 hours after single doses. With large or repeated doses, the effect is prolonged. Pupillary changes are the last to diminish and may outlast the other effects of atropine and related drugs by hours or, after large doses, days.

Clinical Uses

The clinical uses of atropine and its relatives are based upon their effects either on smooth muscle and secretions or the central nervous system. The parasympatholytic effects described above can all be demonstrated in humans if large doses are used. However, in evaluating the uses listed below and in comparing the many compounds available, it must be borne in mind that these drugs must often be used for extended periods. Therefore, the results observed following a single large dose are not necessarily of value in determining the usefulness of much smaller doses that can be given 3–4 times daily without producing disturbing or disabling side-effects.

A. Peptic Ulcer: The belladonna alkaloids have been widely used for many years as part of the treatment of peptic ulcer. There is a theoretic basis for this practice, but no benefit from treatment with chronically tolerated doses has ever been satisfactorily demonstrated. Gastric, duodenal, or marginal ulcer does not occur in the absence of free acid in the gastric secretion, and a part of the pain is related to smooth muscle contractions. All of the parasympatholytic drugs that we have listed can suppress basal (fasting) secretion and even the secretion stimulated by the presence of food in the stomach. Thus, there is a clear rationale for the use of parasympatholytic drugs in the treatment of peptic ulcer. However, the question whether atropine has a favorable effect on the rates of healing or recurrence of peptic ulcer can be answered only by observing the results of a controlled clinical trial. The process has a variable course and responds to other drugs and to nonspecific treatment; therefore, the clinical trial must include control groups. If reports of uncontrolled experiments are eliminated, the clinical trials published to date do not validate the use of parasympatholytics in the ulcer regimen. Some physicians feel that an anticholinergic at bedtime to suppress basal nocturnal acid secretion is an important part of the treatment program. If gastric retention is present, the possibility of pyloric obstruction outweighs any possible benefits.

The histamine H_2-receptor antagonist cimetidine has assumed an important place in the treatment of peptic ulcer and can be given in combination with an anticholinergic drug.

B. Functional Gastrointestinal Disturbances: A wide variety of symptoms of disturbed motor function of the gastrointestinal and biliary tract are treated with the parasympatholytic drugs and usually with sedatives and explanation as well. Cramping pain, pylorospasm, epigastric discomfort, and diarrhea are examples of such complaints that are not associated with any underlying organic disease. The parasympatholytics do appear to be effective in the short-term relief of these symptoms. The treatment of diarrhea associated with irritative lesions is discussed in Chapter 26.

C. Relaxation of Other Smooth Muscle: Parasympatholytics decrease the strength of contraction of the bladder wall and relieve the pain and tenesmus that accompany cystitis. Contraction of the ureter and of the bile ducts can be inhibited in the investigative situation. Clinically, however, ureteral and biliary colic usually require narcotic analgesics for their relief.

D. Acute Pancreatitis: There are several reasons why atropine might be useful in treating acute pancreatitis. A reduction of gastric acid secretion with consequent reduction of acid stimulation of the duodenum should prevent the release of secretin and stimulation of pancreatic secretion. Nasogastric suction can also prevent the entry of acid gastric contents into the duodenum and is evidently much more useful. Blockade of the vagal stimulus to pancreatic secretion and relaxation of the sphincter of Oddi are other theoretic reasons for the use of atropine, but its use in acute pancreatitis must be regarded as unestablished or controversial.

E. Ophthalmologic Uses of Autonomic Drugs: The parasympatholytic drugs have important uses deriving from their effects on pupillary diameter, on accommodation, and on intraocular pressure. The effects of other autonomic agents on these functions will also be introduced at this time.

1. Pupillary size—The iris contains circularly arranged, parasympathetically innervated smooth muscle that responds to cholinomimetic and cholinolytic drugs. Contraction of this sphincter muscle by parasympathomimetic drugs causes pupillary constriction, whereas relaxation by parasympatholytic drugs causes dilatation.

Some investigators describe a pupillary dilator muscle, a minute amount of radially arranged muscle on the posterior surface of the iris, that dilates the pupil by contracting when stimulated by sympathomimetics. The radially coursing blood vessels of the iris also influence pupillary size by their constriction or by internal pressure changes. Whether the effect of the dilator muscle or the blood vessels is predominant has no practical significance, since both act to dilate the pupil in response to sympathetic influences.

Mydriasis (pupillary dilatation) occurs following systemic or topical application of atropine and other parasympatholytic drugs that relax the sphincter muscle. The effect is useful in facilitating ophthalmoscopic examination and when prolonged dilatation of the pupil is desired—eg, in iritis, to prevent adhesions of the iris to the lens (synechias). When only a brief

effect is needed, sympathomimetics may be used to achieve dilatation, as for ophthalmoscopy, without interfering with accommodation.

Miosis (pupillary constriction) is utilized in the treatment of glaucoma (see below) to facilitate the outflow of aqueous from the anterior chamber.

2. Accommodation—The ciliary muscle has only parasympathetic innervation and responds solely to parasympathomimetic and parasympatholytic drugs. When relaxed or when paralyzed by parasympatholytics (cycloplegics), the ciliary body is distended by the turgidity resulting from its vascularity and by its natural elasticity. The relaxed ciliary body moves away from the visual axis of the eye, exerting tension on the suspensory ligament of the lens, and thus flattens the lens to accommodate for distant vision. To emphasize—in the relaxed state of the ciliary muscle, the eye is accommodated for distant vision.

When the ciliary muscle contracts, the radial fibers shorten toward the attachment at the scleral spur and the circumferential fibers also move the ciliary body toward the lens (Fig 9–1). The reduced tension

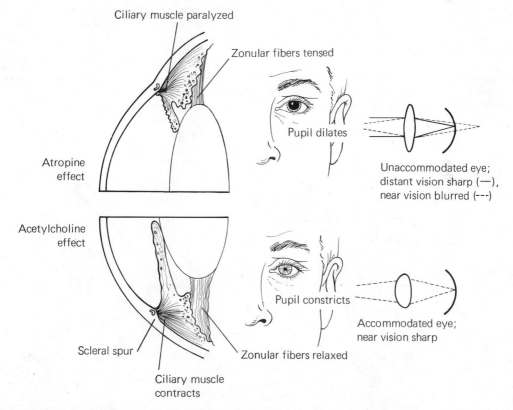

Figure 9–1. Accommodation and pupillary size. In the upper half of the figure, the eye is shown with the ciliary muscle and the sphincter muscle of the pupil relaxed by atropine. Below, these muscles are contracted by a cholinergic drug or by parasympathetic nerve activity. Contraction of both the circular and radial fibers of the ciliary muscle moves the ciliary body toward the optical axis, loosening the fibers of the suspensory ligament and allowing the lens to become more convex. The radial fibers are fixed to the scleral spur, and shortening (contraction) has the same effect as contraction of the circular fibers. Under parasympathetic influence, the eye is thus accommodated for near vision. The pupil is constricted by the contraction of the sphincter muscle of the pupil. Constriction of the pupil—ie, movement of the iris toward the optical axis—pulls the structures away from the angle and facilitates drainage of aqueous.

on the suspensory ligament allows the lens to become rounded by its own elasticity and thus accommodate for near vision.

Cycloplegic drugs (atropine and its relatives) permit the measurement of refractive error without interference by the accommodative ability of the eye. With age, the lens loses much of its elasticity and cycloplegic drugs are not necessary for an accurate refraction.

Ciliary spasm is produced by the parasympathomimetic drugs as a toxic effect or as a consequence of the use of miotics. The effect is blurring of distant vision.

3. Intraocular pressure–Glaucoma or increased intraocular pressure is not only treated with drugs, but its presence also provides a contraindication to the use of parasympatholytic drugs.

Aqueous humor is formed by filtration and by active secretion at the ciliary processes (shown at 1 in Fig 9–2). Fluid passes through the pupil into the anterior chamber and is reabsorbed through the trabecular meshwork, a specialized area of the cornea at the angle.

Primary glaucoma, ie, glaucoma that is not secondary to other ocular disease, is most commonly of the chronic simple, or open-angle, type. Degenerative changes occur in the reabsorbing area, and, with continued production of aqueous, a destructive increase in pressure develops. Miotics—eg, pilocarpine or physostigmine—increase the outflow of aqueous. The effect is probably due to the ciliary muscle pulling on the scleral spur and opening outflow paths in the meshwork. Sympathomimetics or beta-adrenergic blocking drugs may also be used, and the formation of aqueous may be reduced by the use of acetazolamide.

In acute, or angle-closure, glaucoma, the anterior chamber is shallow and the trabecular area at the angle appears to be occluded by the sharply angulated iris. However, the factor that makes the treatment situation so urgent is that some initial pressure change bulges the iris in such a way that the passage of aqueous through the pupil is blocked. The process may be precipitated by locally applied parasympatholytics. Immediate treatment utilizes pilocarpine or other miotic and an osmotic diuretic such as glycerol. If a response is not apparent within a few hours, the pupillary block must be surgically corrected (shown at 4 in Fig 9–2).

The following are the drugs referred to above that lower intraocular pressure:

a. Miotics–Pilocarpine, 2%, is still the most widely used topical miotic. The therapeutic effect on pressure lasts for about 4 hours, although pupillary constriction may persist for 24 hours after a single application. Physostigmine (0.1–1%) is a tertiary amine that is well absorbed and longer acting. Like the other less popular cholinesterase inhibitors (DFP, echothiophate, demecarium), it causes more ciliary spasm, with discomfort and blurred vision, and also blepharospasm because of the effect on striated muscle.

b. Carbonic anhydrase inhibitors—eg, acetazolamide (Diamox) and others—are usually classed as diuretics and are discussed in Chapter 17. They greatly suppress the formation of aqueous.

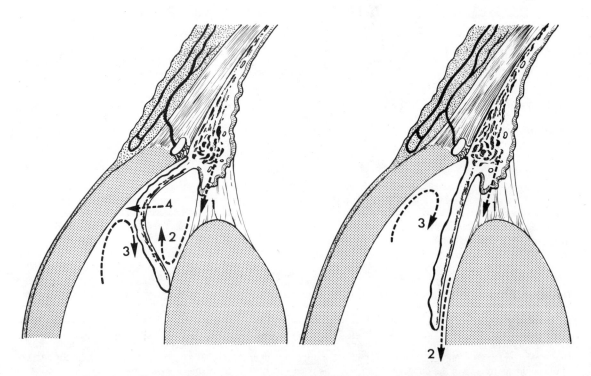

Figure 9–2. Circulation of aqueous in acute (closed-angle) and chronic (open-angle) glaucoma.

c. Sympathomimetics (epinephrine) act both by increasing aqueous outflow and by inhibiting the formation of aqueous.

d. Beta-adrenergic blocking drugs, after systemic or topical administration, lower intraocular pressure in open-angle glaucoma by a mechanism as yet unclarified. Timolol (Timoptic) is available as ophthalmic drops (see Chapter 11). Like other drugs applied to the conjunctival surface, it is absorbed and may cause systemic effects.

e. Hypertonic solutions of osmotic diuretics given intravenously will withdraw fluid from the eye as from other tissues. Glycerol, mannitol, or urea may be used in acute glaucoma. (See Chapter 17.)

F. Treatment of Parasympathomimetic Toxicity: The use of atropine as a partial antagonist to the effects of the organic phosphates and other parasympathomimetics has already been discussed. A variation of this use is in the management of the side-effects associated with the administration of cholinesterase inhibitors given for their effect on voluntary muscle—eg, during the treatment of myasthenia gravis or when a cholinesterase inhibitor is used to abolish residual curarization postoperatively. The undesired parasympathomimetic effects may be eliminated with atropine without blocking the desired effect on voluntary muscle, emphasizing that atropine antagonizes acetylcholine at smooth muscle and glands but not at skeletal muscle.

G. The Common Cold: The traditional cold powders and some modern over-the-counter cold remedies contain belladonna alkaloids. The drying effect does provide some symptomatic relief, and this is probably the explanation of any minor effectiveness that over-the-counter remedies containing antihistamines may have in the treatment of colds. The sympathomimetics are much more effective nasal decongestants.

H. Asthma: Atropine is usually said to be contraindicated in the treatment of asthma because the drying of secretions may add an obstructive element to the bronchiolar constriction. However, proprietary asthma remedies—especially those based on the inhalation of fumes from burning stramonium powder—are claimed by many patients to be effective.

I. Preanesthetic Medication: Preanesthetic medication with atropine or scopolamine is used prior to all but a few general anesthetics to reduce secretions and block vagally mediated bradycardia, which may occur during induction. The reduction in secretions prevents obstruction by the secretions in the airway and also, by preventing droplets of secretion from stimulating the larynx, helps to prevent laryngeal spasm. Other aspects of preanesthetic medication are discussed in Chapter 20.

J. Obstetric Analgesia and Amnesia: Scopolamine in combination with morphine or other narcotic analgesics was at one time widely used to provide analgesia during labor. Many patients became excited rather than sedated by the medication, but the scopolamine did produce amnesia for the experience.

K. Parkinsonism and Other Pathologic Extrapyramidal States: See Chapter 30.

L. Motion Sickness and Nausea and Vomiting: Scopolamine is the prototype of drugs active in preventing motion sickness and, with lesser effectiveness, it is used to reduce nausea and vomiting due to other causes. Drugs more closely related to the antihistamines have largely replaced the parasympatholytics in this use. This indication is therefore discussed with the antihistamines. (See Chapter 19.)

Adverse Reactions

A. Side-Effects: Dry mouth (with thirst or difficulty in swallowing), blurred vision, urinary retention in older men, dizziness or light-headedness, and fatigue are common side-effects that limit the amount of parasympatholytics tolerated during chronic use.

B. Toxicity: A patient is easily made uncomfortable with these alkaloids, but it is very difficult to cause truly dangerous toxicity except in children. Eye drops that traverse the nasolacrimal duct and are absorbed from the nasopharyngeal mucosa are an occasional cause of the signs of acute toxicity described below. Jimson weed, proprietary sleeping medications, and the use of belladonna as a hallucinogen are rare causes of poisoning.

Intoxication results in the expected parasympatholytic signs: pupillary dilatation, dry mouth, tachycardia, urinary retention, constipation, and blurred vision. The sequence of behavioral changes described above is seen: sedation, delirium, hallucinations, coma, and, with huge doses, convulsions or respiratory depression. An effect of toxic doses not predicted by the pharmacologic effects outlined above is a dry flushed skin, especially in the blush area. A great rise in body temperature may occur because of the inhibition of sweating, especially in children. Such hyperpyrexia can be controlled by maintaining a low environmental temperature and by the application of cold baths and sponges.

The manifestations of acute toxicity may persist for a few hours or several days. Treatment includes control of environmental temperature, catheterization if necessary, protection of exposed mucosal surfaces, support of respiration when indicated, and avoidance of overtreatment of the convulsions. Experience with the treatment of organic phosphate intoxication and with a now obsolete form of therapy for psychotic patients has established that the lethal dose in adults is more than 0.5 g of atropine and more than 0.2–0.3 g of scopolamine.

Cholinesterase inhibitors—eg, neostigmine—and other parasympathomimetic drugs are not often used in the treatment of poisoning with atropinelike drugs. A miotic—eg, physostigmine or pilocarpine—may be used if photophobia from pupillary dilatation is a prominent complaint. However, the actions on the central nervous system rather than the peripheral effects are the dangerous actions in poisoning in adults.

A cholinesterase inhibitor that is able to enter the

central nervous system will antagonize the central nervous system effects of atropine. Physostigmine (eserine) is a tertiary amine and is active; quaternary amines such as neostigmine are not. The effectiveness of physostigmine was established because of interest in a potent, synthetic atropine analog as a potential chemical warfare agent ("BZ"). Such agents cause delirium and hallucinations and are potential incapacitating agents.

Contraindications & Cautions

Parasympatholytic drugs should not be used in the presence of glaucoma except for single, small doses such as are used in preanesthetic medication. In addition, cycloplegics instilled into the eye can precipitate glaucoma. They should not be used in patients over age 35 years unless the existence of a shallow anterior chamber is excluded. Pupillary dilatation for routine ophthalmoscopic examination can be accomplished with sympathomimetics.

Gastric retention and urinary retention secondary to prostate hypertrophy are more commonly encountered contraindications to the use of these drugs.

Selection of Drug

When parasympatholytics are used for clearly established indications and when a potent effect is necessary, atropine or scopolamine will usually be used rather than one of the synthetic substitutes. After rejecting claims based upon uncontrolled experiments and assays that are not necessarily applicable to the clinical situation, it would seem that many of the synthetic modifications are potent drugs but that none have any demonstrated superiority over atropine or scopolamine. There is no basis for any claim that one of the parasympatholytics acts selectively on a specific smooth muscle organ such as the bladder.

The matter of drug selection should be simplified by avoiding the many mixtures of atropine substitutes with phenobarbital or other sedatives. Both parasympatholytic and sedative drugs require dosage adjustment on an individual basis, and a mixture with a fixed proportion of ingredients makes this impossible.

Some of the preparations available are listed in Table 9-1.

The maximum tolerated dose must be determined for each patient during chronic administration of a parasympatholytic drug. This is more easily accomplished with the natural products because of the

Table 9–1. Parasympatholytic drugs.

Natural alkaloids
  Atropine (DL-hyoscyamine)*
  Belladonna extract (mostly L-hyoscyamine)
  L-Hyoscyamine
  Scopolamine (L-hyoscine)*
  Tincture of belladonna
Synthetic esters analogous to natural alkaloids (tertiary amines)
  Cyclopentolate (Cyclogyl)†
  Dicylomine (Bentyl)‡
  Eucatropine†
  Flavoxate (Urispas)
  Homatropine hydrobromide†
  Methixene (Trest)§
  Oxyphencyclimine (Daricon)
  Piperidolate (Dactil)
  Thiphenamil (Trocinate)
  Tropicamide (Mydriacyl)†
Synthetic esters that are quaternary amines
  Anisotropine (Valpin)
  Clidinium (Quarzan)
  Diphemanil (Prantal)§
  Glycopyrrolate (Robinul)
  Hexocyclium (Tral)§
  Homatropine methylbromide
  Isopropamide (Darbid)§
  Mepenzolate (Cantil)
  Methscopolamine (Pamine)‡
  Oxyphenonium (Antrenyl)
  Pipenzolate (Piptal)
  Propantheline (Pro-Banthine)‡
  Tridihexethyl (Pathilon)§

*For ophthalmic and systemic use.
†For ophthalmic use only.
‡Generic preparations available.
§Not an ester. See paragraph D under Source, Chemistry, & Classification.

more flexible and varied dosage forms available. In fact, one of the oldest preparations, tincture of belladonna, permits the most accurate titration of dose. The liquid preparation is, however, inconvenient for many patients. Atropine itself or extract of belladonna may also be used.

One of the quaternary derivatives should be used if central nervous system effects—eg, dizziness or tiredness—rather than a peripheral effect limits the tolerated dosage.

The dosage for children more than 1 month of age may be calculated on the basis of weight.

•   •   •

References

Bachrach WH: Anticholinergic drugs: Survey of the literature and some experimental observations. Am J Dig Dis (New Series)3:743, 1958.

Bowers J, Forbes J, Freston J: Effect of nighttime anisatropine methylbromide (AMB) on duodenal ulcer healing: A controlled trial. Gastroenterology 72:1032, 1977.

Crowell EB, Ketchum JS: The treatment of scopolamine-induced delirium with physostigmine. Clin Pharmacol Ther 8:409, 1967.

Eger EI: Atropine, scopolamine, and related compounds. Anesthesiology 23:365, 1962.

Ellis PP, Smith DL: *Handbook of Ocular Therapeutics and Pharmacology,* 4th ed. Mosby, 1973.

Epstein SE, Redwood DR, Smith ER: Atropine and acute myocardial infarction. Circulation 45:1273, 1972.

Feldman M & others: Effect of low-dose propantheline on food-stimulated gastric acid secretion: Comparison with an "optimal effective dose" and interaction with cimetidine. N Engl J Med 297:1427, 1977.

Fordtran JS: Placebos, antacids and cimetidine for duodenal ulcer. N Engl J Med 298:1081, 1978.

Galin MA, Zweifach MD: Glaucoma. (2 parts.) N Engl J Med 267:237, 291, 1962.

Gowdy JM: Stramonium intoxication: Review of symptomatology in 212 cases. JAMA 221:585, 1972.

Johnston D, Goligher JC, Duthie HL: Medical vagotomy: An assessment. Br Med J 2:1481, 1966.

Langer E: Chemical and biological warfare (II): The weapons and the policies. Science 155:299, 1967.

Leopold IH (editor): *Ocular Therapy.* Mosby, 1968.

Longo VG: Behavioral and electroencephalographic effects of atropine and related compounds. Pharmacol Rev 18:965, 1966.

Miller RD & others: Measurement of atropine-induced vascular pooling. Circulation 10:423, 1954.

Richman S: Adverse effect of atropine during myocardial infarction. JAMA 228:1414, 1974.

Zimmerman TJ & others: Timolol plus maximum-tolerated glaucoma therapy. Arch Ophthalmol 97:278, 1979.

10 | Adrenergic (Sympathomimetic) Drugs

Drugs that partially or completely mimic the effects of sympathetic nerve stimulation or adrenal medullary discharge make up a group that is very complex. This complexity is due to the great amount of investigative effort that these drugs have received and to the great number of compounds included in the group. The intense research activity in this area is a reflection of the interest in the naturally occurring neurotransmitters that are the prototypes of the drugs. Epinephrine and norepinephrine (arterenol, levarterenol) would be of great interest even if they had no therapeutic usefulness because of their physiologic importance and their relationship to the action of other drug types. The interest in and the proliferation of available compounds is increased by the fact that the sympathomimetics are therapeutically useful in a variety of common chronic clinical disorders, notably asthma.

The introduction of ephedrine from Chinese folk medicine in 1924 provided an orally active agent and suggested the synthesis of compounds in which various effects could be selectively increased or decreased. In contrast with some drug groups, these differences in effect are real and clinically significant, permitting individual sympathomimetic drugs to be selected for particular clinical purposes.

The classification used in this discussion (summarized in Table 10–1) hardly seems a simplification, but it does organize the many drugs available into a manageable few pharmacologic categories. Each of the classes of sympathomimetics is discussed separately below.

THE CATECHOLAMINES: EPINEPHRINE, NOREPINEPHRINE,* & ISOPROTERENOL

Three catecholamines—dopamine, epinephrine, and norepinephrine—occur in the body as part of the synthetic pathway shown in Fig 10–4. Isoproterenol is a synthetic catecholamine.

In order to simplify this presentation, consideration of the cardiovascular effects of dopamine is given in the discussion of shock (see p 87). The importance

*The official name has been changed. Formerly levarterenol.

Table 10–1. Summary classification of the sympathomimetics.

1. **Catecholamines:** Phenylethylamines that act directly on the effector cells. Norepinephrine is a pure vasoconstrictor. Isoproterenol is a pure vasodilator. Epinephrine causes mixed dilatation and constriction. All are similar in cardiac stimulant and smooth muscle relaxant effects. Dopamine causes additional splanchnic vasodilatation by a separate mechanism of action.

2. **Ephedrine and other phenylisopropylamines:** Orally active, long-acting compounds that act indirectly through catecholamines of the body.

3. **Amphetamine and related central nervous stimulants:** Variants of ephedrine which are selectively more potent as CNS stimulants and comparatively less active on cardiovascular function. (See Chapter 28.)

4. **Indirect-acting vasodilator amines:** Phenylisopropylamines with indirect action. Effects are similar to those of isoproterenol but of longer duration, eg, nylidrin or isoxsuprine.

5. **Incomplete sympathomimetics:** Varied chemical types used as vasoconstrictors on nasal mucosa but otherwise lacking many properties of the true sympathomimetics listed above.

6. **Tyramine:** Acts entirely by liberating norepinephrine from labile pool in nerve and chromaffin tissue.

of dopamine and its precursor dopa in the central nervous system is discussed in Chapters 25 and 30.

The remaining 3 amines differ qualitatively from each other only in that individual drugs may cause pure vasoconstriction (norepinephrine), pure vasodilatation (isoproterenol), or a mixture of vasodilatation and vasoconstriction (epinephrine).

Chemistry (Table 10–3.)

These drugs are phenylethylamines that act directly on the effectors. The phenylisopropylamines

Table 10–2. Some drugs that affect sympathetic activity.* Only the principal actions of the drugs are listed. Note that guanethidine is believed to have 2 principal actions.

Site of Action	Drugs That Augment Sympathetic Activity	Drugs That Depress Sympathetic Activity
Sympathetic ganglia	**Stimulate postganglionic neurons** Acetylcholine Nicotine Dimethphenylpiperazinium **Inhibit acetylcholinesterase** DFP (diisopropyl fluorophosphate) Physostigmine (eserine) Neostigmine (Prostigmin) Parathion	**Block conduction** Chlorisondamine (Ecolid) Hexamethonium (Bistrium, C-6) Mecamylamine (Inversine) Pentolinium (Ansolysen) Tetraethylammonium (Etamon, TEA) Trimethaphan (Arfonad) High concentrations of acetyl-choline, anticholinesterase drugs
Endings of postganglionic neurons	**Release norepinephrine** Tyramine Ephedrine Amphetamine	**Block norepinephrine synthesis** a-Methyl-*p*-tyrosine **Interfere with norepinephrine storage** Reserpine Guanethidine (Ismelin) **Prevent norepinephrine release** Bretylium tosylate (Darenthin) Guanethidine (Ismelin) **Form false transmitters** a-Methyldopa (Aldomet)
a Receptors	**Stimulate a receptors** Norepinephrine (levarterenol; Levophed) Epinephrine Metaraminol (Aramine) Methoxamine (Vasoxyl) Phenylephrine (Neo-Synephrine)	**Block a receptors** Phenoxybenzamine (Dibenzyline) Phentolamine (Regitine) Ergot alkaloids
β Receptors	**Stimulate β receptors** Isoproterenol (Isuprel) Epinephrine Norepinephrine	**Block β receptors** Propranolol (Inderol) Practolol (blocks β_1) Butoxamine (blocks β_2)

*Reproduced, with permission, from Ganong WF: *Review of Medical Physiology,* 9th ed. Lange, 1979.

introduced below exert their effect indirectly through epinephrine and norepinephrine present in the organism. The 3 common amines have 2 phenolic hydroxyl substituents and are grouped together as catecholamines.

Epinephrine (adrenaline is a generic name in most

Table 10–3. Formulas of the catecholamines and congeners.

	R_1	R_2	R_3
L-Epinephrine (Adrenalin)*	HO–	HO–	–CH_3
L-Norepinephrine (Levophed)	HO–	HO–	–H
Phenylephrine (Neo-Synephrine)*	H–	HO–	–CH_3
Isoproterenol (Isuprel)*	HO–	HO–	–C_3H_7
Salbutamol	HO–	HO–H_2C–	–C_4H_9

*Trade names of these old drugs are provided for identification only. They are available from many suppliers under their generic names.

countries, but Adrenalin is a protected name in the USA) was originally an extract of adrenal medulla consisting of approximately 80% epinephrine and 20% norepinephrine. It is now prepared from pure synthetic L-epinephrine. The other 2 are also synthetic. The L-isomer is the active form in each case.

Phenylephrine is not a catechol but is a direct-acting amine comparable to norepinephrine.

Pharmacologic Actions

A. Mechanisms of Action: The catecholamines act directly on receptors on the effector tissues (smooth muscle, gland, or heart). Sympathetic innervation is not necessary for their action; on the contrary, denervation increases the sensitivity of effectors to these direct-acting amines.

The various effects of the sympathomimetics can be placed into 2 categories and described as being due to an action of the drug on alpha and beta receptors in the effector tissue, alpha receptors mediating vasoconstriction and beta receptors initiating vasodilatation, cardiac stimulation, and relaxation of the nonvascular smooth muscle of gut, bronchioles, etc.

The concept of receptors is suggested by the fact that a given tissue may respond to closely related sympathomimetic amines by either relaxation or contraction, and each of these opposing effects can be selectively eliminated by appropriate blocking agents. Thus, the blood vessels within voluntary muscle respond to norepinephrine by contraction, and the vasoconstriction is blocked by alpha-adrenergic blocking agents such as phenoxybenzamine. Epinephrine or isoproterenol causes vasodilatation in the same vascular bed, and the response is prevented by propranolol or other beta blocking agents but is not altered by phenoxybenzamine.

The ability of the same cell to respond oppositely to closely related molecules suggests that some process or structure intervenes between the drug and the contractile mechanism. The concept of receptors is strongly supported by the availability of compounds that selectively block one agonist and leave the effector tissue able to respond to the related agonist and to other unrelated drugs. For example, propranolol will block the dilatation caused by epinephrine but leaves unaltered not only the vasoconstrictor response to norepinephrine but also the dilating effects of histamine or acetylcholine (which can, however, be blocked by other specific agents). Recently, a membrane glycoprotein that has all the characteristics of a beta receptor has been isolated and purified.

The important and possibly the only effect of alpha receptor activation is vasoconstriction. There are 3 other excitatory effects, of which pupillary dilatation is the one seen clinically. In addition, in the laboratory situation, alpha agonists cause retraction of the nictitating membrane and contraction of smooth muscle organs such as the uterus and genitourinary tract. The contraction in intact animals is brief and precedes inhibition. In isolated tissues, the stimulation may be persistent under conditions that increase vascularity or increase the effect of vascular contraction in proportion to the effect of relaxation of nonvascular smooth muscle—ie, alpha agonistic effects may all be due to vasoconstriction.

All of the other sympathomimetic actions are due to activation of the beta receptor and are blocked by propranolol or other beta-adrenergic blocking drugs. These "inhibitory" actions include vasodilatation, stimulation of cardiac rate and force of contraction, and relaxation of nonvascular smooth muscle. The alpha and beta receptor concept cannot be applied to the metabolic and central nervous system effects of the sympathomimetic amines.

Some amines, notably isoproterenol, are pure beta agonists. Phenylephrine and methoxamine (Vasoxyl) are almost pure alpha agonists. Most sympathomimetic drugs—eg, epinephrine, norepinephrine, ephedrine, and amphetamine— have mixed effects.

B. Effects: (Table 10–4.)

1. On blood vessels–The basic difference between the catecholamines (from which the other differences in cardiovascular effects derive) is that nor-

Table 10–4. Summary of effects of sympathomimetic prototypes.

+ = Function increased or stimulated, eg, vasoconstriction
− = Decreased or relaxed
0 = No change
? = Unpredictable

	Norepi-nephrine	Isopro-terenol	Epi-nephrine
Blood vessels			
Of skin and splanchnic area	+	−	+
Of muscle	+	−	−
Net (TPR)*	+	−	−
Cardiac muscle			
Force of contraction	+	+	+
Minute volume (CO)*			
Direct	+	+	+
Indirect	−	+	+
Net	0 or −	+	+
Blood pressure			
Diastolic	+	−	?
Systolic	+	?	+
Cardiac rate (NSR)*			
Direct	+	+	+
Reflex	−	+	−
Net	?	+	?
Other (nonvascular) smooth muscle	−	−	−

*TPR = total peripheral resistance; CO = cardiac output; NSR = normal sinus rhythm.

epinephrine constricts all blood vessels; isoproterenol causes no vasoconstriction but is a pure vasodilator; and epinephrine constricts blood vessels in the skin and splanchnic area but dilates arterioles in voluntary muscle. Because the vascular effect of epinephrine that is most easily observable is blanching of the skin, this drug is often thought of as a vasoconstrictor. Actually, however, epinephrine exerts both constrictor and dilator effects, and in its net effect the dilatation is greater. The teleologic concept of Cannon that sympatho-adrenal discharge prepares for "fight or flight" is a useful device for remembering that epinephrine constricts the blood vessels of the skin and splanchnic area but dilates those of muscle (thus shunting blood from the noncritical to the active organs).

The vasoconstrictor action of epinephrine on the superficial vessels is easily apparent from the skin blanching that follows its administration and is verified by the fall in skin temperature. Direct quantitation of constriction or dilatation in other vascular beds is more difficult and is usually inferred from the resistance to flow, ie, R = P/F (resistance equals pressure divided by flow), a relation that is valid only over a narrow range of change, since the relation of flow to pressure is not linear over a wide range of pressures and flows. "Total peripheral resistance" (TPR), obtained by dividing mean arterial blood pressure by cardiac minute volume, is an index, however approximate, of the sum of vasomotor changes in all beds in either direction. TPR falls when epinephrine is infused—ie, it is a net

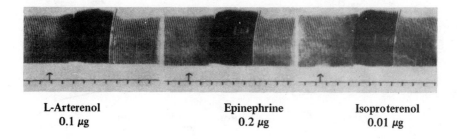

L-Arterenol	Epinephrine	Isoproterenol
0.1 µg	0.2 µg	0.01 µg

Figure 10–1. The effect of epinephrine, L-arterenol, and isoproterenol on the ventricular kymogram of the isolated perfused rabbit heart. Time in 10-second intervals. The drug was injected at arrow (↑). (Reproduced, with permission, from Lands & Howard: A comparative study of the effects of L-arterenol, epinephrine, and isopropylarterenol on the heart. J Pharmacol Exp Ther 106:71, 1952.)

vasodilator, and pressure falls even though cardiac output is increased. Norepinephrine increases TPR, ie, an increase in pressure occurs even though minute volume does not change significantly.

2. On the heart as a pump–Each of the catecholamines increases the force of ventricular contraction. The effect is demonstrable in isolated hearts that are independent of other hydrodynamic influences (Fig 10–1). It is demonstrable in the intact subject with a strain gauge attached to the ventricle and by other technics. The increased force of contraction following the administration of epinephrine or isoproterenol results in a great increase in minute volume. However, although the force of contraction is increased by norepinephrine, the cardiac output (minute volume) is unaltered or even slightly decreased.

The different effects of the amines on cardiac output are explained by their different vasomotor effects. Because norepinephrine is a potent vasoconstrictor, it increases resistance to ejection, ie, increases the amount of work required to elevate intraventricular pressure to the level of aortic diastolic pressure and the work necessary to accelerate and move a given volume of blood against the higher pressure. Norepinephrine is thus stimulating the heart to more forceful contraction and the heart is performing more work, but this action is not manifested as increased cardiac output because the increase is in "pressure work" rather than "volume work."

3. On blood pressure–Blood pressure is a derived function that depends upon peripheral resistance, cardiac output, and cardiac rate. In general, the pulse pressure (the difference between systolic and diastolic pressures) reflects stroke volume, and diastolic pressure is altered by vasoconstriction and vasodilatation.

Norepinephrine, therefore, does not alter pulse pressure greatly because it does not significantly affect stroke volume. (Stroke volume will be increased and pulse pressure widened if reflex slowing of the heart rate occurs, which is usually the case.) Diastolic and systolic pressures will rise proportionately.

Epinephrine acts to widen the pulse pressure and to elevate systolic pressure by increasing stroke volume. The vasodilatation that it also causes may actu-

ally lower diastolic pressure or, if it rises, the elevation will be less than the rise of systolic pressure.

(The differences described above are demonstrable only if the drugs are infused or otherwise slowly administered. Following an instantaneous intravenous injection, as in some laboratory exercises, the distinctions between epinephrine and norepinephrine will not be apparent.)

Beginning with the fact that isoproterenol is a pure vasodilator, its other cardiovascular effects may be accurately predicted. The heart is greatly stimulated, and a resultant increase in cardiac output is possible because total peripheral resistance has been decreased. Pulse pressure is increased. Diastolic pressure is decreased because more run-off of blood from arteries to tissues can take place through the dilated arterioles. Systolic pressure is maintained to some degree by the increased stroke volume, rising slightly or falling less than does the diastolic.

In discussing epinephrine and norepinephrine, the term vasomotor was used without careful definition. Arteriolar constriction was the predominant factor, but venous constriction, by increasing return to the heart, would also elevate blood pressure by increasing cardiac output. In the case of isoproterenol, venous dilatation can lead to peripheral pooling with a consequent decrease in venous return, leading to a decrease in cardiac output that in turn leads to a decrease in blood pressure. This is the sequence of events in some asthmatics taking isoproterenol sublingually while reclining in bed who become dizzy or faint when they arise suddenly because of venous pooling and postural hypotension.

The differential effect on blood pressure of the 3 amines, again assuming a constant heart rate, can be diagrammed (Fig 10–2).

4. On heart rate–The effect of epinephrine and norepinephrine on the heart rate is the resultant of their direct action (increasing the rate) and of reflex slowing due to the rise in blood pressure. This direct action can be demonstrated in isolated hearts (Fig 10–1) or in intact animals or humans following abolition of the efferent arm of the bradycrotic reflex by vagal section or by atropine.

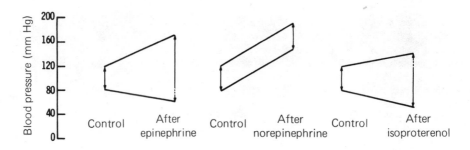

Figure 10–2. Effect of epinephrine, norepinephrine, and isoproterenol on blood pressure.

The net effect depends upon the dosage and other circumstances. We have all been alarmed by slow, very forceful beats attending fright or anger only to note a furiously rapid rate a moment later. After injection of levarterenol, reflex bradycardia almost invariably predominates. (A consistent explanation for the reflex slowing due to catecholamines depends upon demonstrating the effect of the amines on the walls of the pressure-sensitive areas.)

Isoproterenol can only lead to tachycardia, since the direct and reflex influences act in the same direction.

Tachycardia will narrow the pulse pressure and bradycardia will widen it and disturb the idealized blood pressure responses described above.

5. On smooth muscle–In general, nonvascular smooth muscle is relaxed by the sympathomimetic drugs. The effect is generalized—eg, the force of contraction of the bladder may be reduced after systemic doses of long-acting sympathomimetics such as ephedrine—but the effect most used in therapy is bronchiolar dilatation.

Norepinephrine is relatively less potent than epinephrine in its effect on smooth muscle. Isoproterenol causes more prominent effects on smooth muscle not because of greater absolute potency but because of its slightly longer duration of action.

Bronchiolar dilatation is a beta-agonist action, but it is possible to synthesize isoproterenol analogs that retain the ability to relax vascular and bronchiolar smooth muscle but have relatively less effect on the heart. Such compounds have recently been called beta$_2$-agonists on the assumption that different receptors (beta$_1$ and beta$_2$) are present in smooth muscle and in the heart. When used as bronchodilators with minimal (but not absent) cardiac effects, they are similar to isoproterenol. Metaproterenol, for example, is an isomer of isoproterenol with both hydroxyl groups in the meta position, and terbutaline is the tertiary butyl analog of metaproterenol. The relationship of isoproterenol to salbutamol (albuterol, Ventolin), a drug still investigational in the USA, is shown in Table 10–3.

There are many situations in which smooth muscle organs react like vascular smooth muscle—ie, they contract in response to sympathomimetic drugs and the contraction is blocked by alpha-adrenergic blocking agents. The pupillary dilator muscle of the eye (if it exists distinct from blood vessels of the iris) is contracted, causing wider dilatation of the pupil than that achieved by relaxation of the circular muscle of the iris by atropine. The nictitating membrane in animals is also contracted and retracted to the inner canthus by sympathetic or sympathomimetic activity. The closely related smooth muscle that inserts into the lids is also contracted. This change explains the widened palpebral fissure or lid slit, or the staring eyes, of the sympathetically stimulated subject. These changes are often interpreted as establishing the presence of alpha receptors in nonvascular smooth muscle. However, in each of these tissues the blood vessels are so arranged that contraction can cause the observed change—ie, the apparent stimulation may be due to vasoconstriction.

6. On exocrine glands–These effects are discussed to add physiologic rather than therapeutic information.

a. Salivation–The salivary glands contain 2 cell types and functionally respond as 2 separate organs. One type, comprising the parotid gland and the serous cells of the submaxillary gland, receives only parasympathetic innervation. The mucus-secreting cell type of the submaxillary and sublingual glands receives only sympathetic innervation. Epinephrine and the longer-acting amines such as ephedrine would not be expected to alter the secretion of serous saliva but to increase the amount of viscid saliva secreted. Such an effect can be demonstrated in humans. However, the vasoconstriction and reduction in blood flow caused by the sympathomimetics usually decreases secretion, and dry mouth is a common side-effect. Atropine decreases the volume of secretion from both types of glands by acting on the intrinsic mechanism of the glands.

b. Sweating–Sweating also involves 2 types of glands. Apocrine sweat glands open onto hairs in the axillas and genitocrural region. The humoral mechanism controlling these glands has not been clarified. Although they are not stimulated by sympathetic nerve stimulation or by sympathomimetic amines, sympathomimetic influences may give the impression of transient stimulation by emptying the glands. This emptying is brought about by contraction of myoepithelial cells and is equivalent to pilo-erection.

Eccrine sweat glands produce a watery rather than

a cellular sweat and are stimulated in the human by sympathetic postganglionic fibers that are, however, cholinergic. Thus, any stimulus leading to sympathetic nervous system activation—eg, hypotension or anxiety—will cause sweating but sympathomimetic amines will not, although they may also empty the eccrine glands as described above for apocrine glands. The situation may be quite different in other species.

7. Metabolic effects–The catecholamines (norepinephrine is less potent than epinephrine and isoproterenol) increase liver glycogenolysis and thereby elevate blood glucose levels. Increased muscle glycogenolysis, which generates glucose-6-phosphate but not glucose, elevates blood lactic acid. Plasma potassium also rises. Triglycerides are hydrolyzed with a resulting increase in plasma free fatty acids.

The receptor concept is applicable only with difficulty. Blockade of hepatic glycogenolysis requires administration of both alpha and beta receptor blocking agents. Skeletal muscle glycogenolysis and, less dependably, the lipolytic effect require a beta blocker.

The mechanism by which epinephrine elevates blood glucose is important because it may also explain the action of epinephrine at other sites of action. Epinephrine stimulates or activates adenylate cyclase, thus accelerating the formation from ATP of cAMP, an activator of phosphorylase (Fig 10–3).

Cyclic AMP is probably involved in the action of many other drugs and hormones and is further discussed in Chapter 33. The xanthines discussed in Chapter 13, for example, inhibit phosphodiesterase, the enzyme that removes cAMP. Accumulation of AMP results.

FFA (unesterified or free fatty acids) are released

Adenine   Ribose   Cyclic phosphate

Cyclic adenosine-3′,5′-monophosphate
(cAMP)

from adipose tissue by sympathomimetic drugs, causing the level of FFA in the blood to be elevated.

The number of eosinophils in peripheral blood decreases after catecholamine administration. In humans at least, the eosinopenia provides no reliable information about pituitary or adrenal function.

The catecholamines also have a "calorigenic" effect, ie, oxygen consumption is increased. This action is the sum of many of the above effects and not due to a general increase in the metabolic rate of all cells.

8. Central nervous system stimulation–Endogenous epinephrine or exogenous epinephrine or isoproterenol in sufficient amounts can lead to alerting, tremulousness, and respiratory stimulation. (Rapid epinephrine injections in the laboratory may inhibit respiration by acutely elevating blood pressure.) Manifest anxiety and tremulousness appear as side-effects during the use of epinephrine and isoproterenol. Norepinephrine is so much less active in this respect that blood pressure may be greatly elevated by

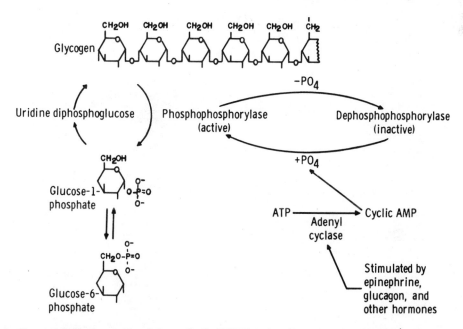

Figure 10 –3. Glycogen formation and breakdown. Cyclic AMP phosphorylates phosphorylase, and a number of hormones increase the formation of cAMP by increasing the activity of adenylate cyclase, the enzyme complex catalyzing cyclic AMP formation from ATP. (Reproduced, with permission, from Ganong WF: *Review of Medical Physiology,* 9th ed. Lange, 1979.)

infusion of the drug without subjective complaints of anxiety.

The apparent central nervous system stimulation is, however, largely if not entirely due to a peripheral action of epinephrine. The amount of afferent activity reaching the reticular activating system (RAS) is augmented by the changes in blood pressure, and the alerting effect of epinephrine is reduced by denervating pressure-sensitive areas.

Central stimulant effects are more clearly seen when the longer-acting compounds such as ephedrine are used. Their effect is clearly central in origin.

Absorption, Metabolism, & Excretion

A. Synthesis and Storage: The synthesis and storage of the catecholamines not only have important implications for their own pharmacologic activity; they are also important to an understanding of the mechanism of action of some sympathomimetic drugs that are not catecholamines and the mechanism of action of the drugs that decrease sympathetic activity.

The synthetic pathway is summarized in Fig 10–4. Most synthesis takes place at the storage sites; however, sympathetic nerves and chromaffin cells can take up preformed norepinephrine, an important process in terminating the action of norepinephrine. Preformed norepinephrine cannot reach the intracellular storage sites in the brain; synthesis must occur from precursors that can enter the parenchymal cells of the central nervous system.

Epinephrine and norepinephrine are stored within the granular vesicles and the cytoplasm of post-ganglionic sympathetic neurons; chromaffin cells of the adrenal medulla, heart, and arterioles; and specific areas of the central nervous system. In sympathetic nerve, norepinephrine is held in 2 functional pools: a labile pool from which it is liberated by nerve stimulation, and a storage pool in equilibrium with the labile fraction. Stored norepinephrine is held within the specific granules protected from enzymatic degradation by the limiting membrane of the vesicle and by combination with other substances. The norepinephrine of these storage granules is in equilibrium with that in similarly appearing granules that are part of the labile pool equilibrating with cytoplasmic norepinephrine. Tyramine acts to deplete only the labile pool, but reserpine acts on both pools.

B. Termination of Catecholamine Action: The process most important in terminating the action of catecholamines liberated from nerve or chromaffin tissue or injected is reentry or uptake by the sympathetic nerve, a process elucidated by following the disposition of tritium-labeled amine. At the same time, the metahydroxyl group may be methylated through

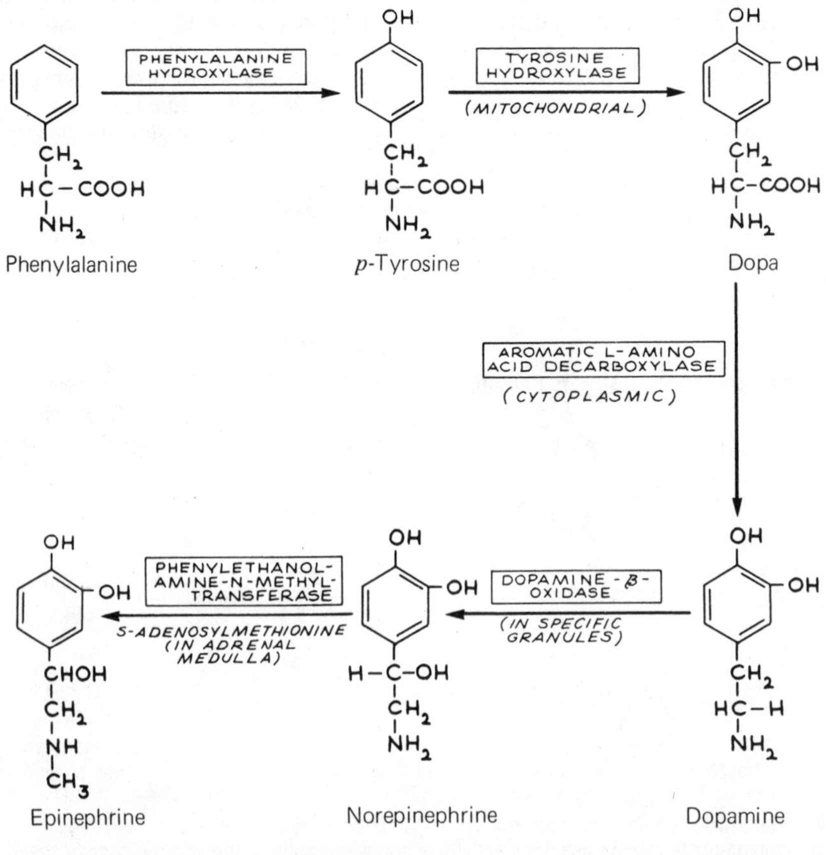

Figure 10–4. Biosynthesis of catecholamines. Dopa, dihydroxyphenylalanine; dopamine, dihydroxyphenylethylamine.

the action of catechol-O-methyltransferase (COMT) and both reentry and activity terminated (Fig 10–5). A significant amount of norepinephrine enters the bloodstream unchanged and, together with adrenal medullary epinephrine, causes the diffuse effects of sympatho-adrenal discharge. As a later process, occurring at a distance from the site of action (principally in the liver), either the unaltered catecholamines or the methylated metabolites may be oxidatively deaminated by monoamine oxidase (MAO), a mitochondrial enzyme. Only the small fraction of circulating or urinary catecholamines that escapes unaltered by either COMT or MAO is an index of sympathetic nerve activity. The other metabolites may be derived from the storage pool as well as from neuronal activity. If both MAO and COMT act on epinephrine or norepinephrine, the substance formed is 3-methoxy-4-hydroxymandelic acid or vanillolformic acid. The clinical laboratory analysis most commonly available for assay of catecholamine liberation determines the amount of this substance in urine. It is conventionally if confusingly referred to as vanillylmandelic acid or VMA.

Reuptake of norepinephrine is an active process inhibited by cocaine, phenoxybenzamine, and all of the antipsychotic tranquilizers and antidepressants.

C. Metabolism of Storage Catecholamines: The pool of catecholamines resistant to liberation is slowly metabolized and replaced. Intracellular MAO acts prior to any other process. The aldehyde formed as the first product of oxidative deamination may subsequently be reduced or oxidized to an alcohol or acid, and these products may or may not be methylated by COMT before excretion (Fig 10–6). Catecholamines in the central nervous system are metabolized in the same way.

Clinical Uses

A. Allergic Reactions: Immediate allergic reaction is due to the liberation of histamine from stores within the body. The antihistamine drugs act as competitive antagonists to histamine much as atropine acts as a competitive antagonist to acetylcholine. They can therefore prevent the further effects of histamine in some situations but cannot reverse histamine effects already established. The sympathomimetics are not "antihistamines" in the same sense but are physiologic antagonists to histamine, ie, the effects of the sympathomimetics are opposite in direction to those of histamine. For this reason, they can actively reverse the bronchiolar constriction, vasodilatation, and edema that accompany an immediate allergic reaction.

The primary treatment of an anaphylactic reaction (see Chapter 6) is the injection of epinephrine (0.3–0.5 mg [0.3–0.5 mL of 1:1000] intramuscularly or intravenously). Other immediate allergic reactions such as urticaria, angioneurotic edema, or serum sickness may be more effectively treated by the administration of ephedrine and the antihistamines (see Chapter 19). The delayed type of allergic reaction cannot usually be treated with the sympathomimetics or antihistamines, but the anti-inflammatory steroids suppress such allergic inflammations.

B. Chronic Obstructive Pulmonary Disease: Bronchodilators are useful in treating conditions characterized by increased expiratory resistance, whether this be due to the acute, easily reversible changes of asthma or the chronic changes of emphysema or chronic bronchitis.

Acute asthmatic attacks—those requiring emergency medical care—will usually occur in patients who have already used maximal dosages of the sympathomimetic asthma medication that they keep on hand and will resist the action of epinephrine. The treatment that is usually effective is the slow intravenous injection of aminophylline.

The treatment of chronic asthmatic wheezing involves choosing among many drugs, and their relative popularity is based as much on patient acceptance as the preference of the physician. Epinephrine or isoproterenol may be used by inhalation of an aerosolized solution or of microcrystals. Isoproterenol is also available for sublingual administration, but side-effects such as anxiety and palpitation are usually more prominent. Ephedrine may be given chronically by mouth, usually combined with a small dose of phenobarbital to counteract the central stimulant effects of chronic administration.

Bronchial asthma (in contrast to cardiac asthma) is due initially to bronchiolar constriction, but inflammatory edema and inspissated secretions may intensify the obstruction as the process continues. Treatment involves more than one drug group, but the sympathomimetics are probably the most important. Aminophylline, a xanthine type of smooth muscle relaxant, may be useful as an alternative to the sympathomimetics. Expectorants such as potassium iodide or water are also often used. The anti-inflammatory steroids may be used in persistent and difficult cases.

C. Hypotension: By reducing the intensity of sympathetic outflow, spinal anesthesia and many drugs may cause a hypotension that is predominantly postural. Since vascular smooth muscle is still responsive to the mediators in this situation, any sympathomimetic can be used to restore blood pressure. It should be emphasized that hypotension is not necessarily the same as shock. If cardiac output and tissue perfusion are well maintained, hypotension does not require vigorous treatment. Preventing the pooling of blood (by keeping the patient recumbent), which is responsible for hypotension, is a more rational and satisfactory way of combating hypotension than adding another drug.

D. Shock: Shock is a complex acute cardiovascular syndrome that results in a critical reduction of perfusion of vital tissues and a wide range of systemic effects. Signs and symptoms of shock usually include arterial hypotension, tachycardia, altered sensorium, pallor, thirst, and oliguria. If untreated, shock usually progresses steadily toward a refractory state and, finally, death.

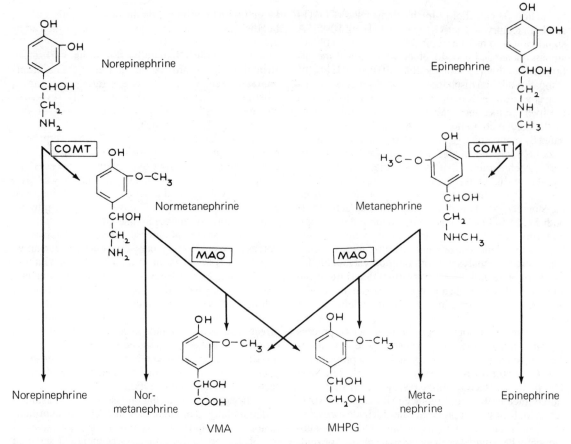

Figure 10–5. Metabolism of free catecholamines. Urinary excretion products appear on the lowest line. Excretion products may be conjugated with glucuronide or sulfate. COMT, catechol-O-methyltransferase; VMA, 3-methoxy-4-hydroxymandelic acid; MHPG, methoxyhydroxyphenylglycol; MAO, monoamine oxidase.

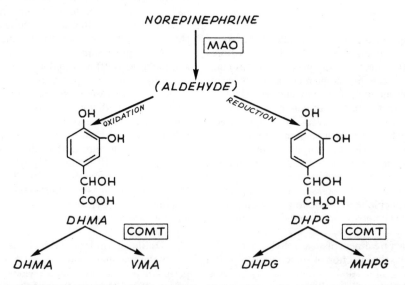

Figure 10–6. Metabolism of norepinephrine of storage pool and central nervous system. Urinary excretion products are shown in lowest line. Excretion products may be conjugated with glucuronide or sulfate. MAO, monoamine oxidase; DHMA, dihydroxymandelic acid; DHPG, dihydroxyphenylglycol; COMT, catechol-O-methyltransferase; VMA, 3-methoxy-4-hydroxymandelic acid; MHPG, methoxyhydroxyphenylglycol.

Table 10–5. Adrenergic stimulating drugs used in hypotensive states.*
(Effects graded on a scale of 0–5.)

Drug	Vasomotor Effect		Cardiac Stimulant (Inotropic Effect)	Cardiac Output	Renal and Splanchnic Blood Flow
	Vasoconstriction	Vasodilatation			
Mixed alpha- and beta-adrenergic					
Metaraminol (Aramine)	3	2	1	Reduced	Reduced
Epinephrine (Adrenalin)	4	3	4	Increased	Reduced
Dopamine (Intropin)†	2	2	2	Usually increased	Increased
Beta-adrenergic					
Isoproterenol (many trade names)	0	5	4	Increased	Usually reduced

*Reproduced, with permission, from *Current Medical Diagnosis & Treatment 1980.* Krupp MA, Chatton MC (editors). Lange, 1980.
†Claimed to have a special (dopaminergic) receptor.

The 3 major pathophysiologic mechanisms in the production of shock are hypovolemia (low blood volume), cardiac insufficiency (pump failure), and altered vascular resistance (vasoconstriction or vasodilatation). Several hemodynamic mechanisms may be at work simultaneously in any given type of shock. The hypotension of shock due to any cause greatly augments sympathetic activity. If continued for long periods, this results in reduced tissue perfusion and loss of intravascular plasma volume. Hypovolemia, therefore, is encountered not only in the shock that one might expect from blood loss; it also occurs in cardiogenic, vascular, and allergic shock.

Early volume replacement is the mainstay in the therapy of many types of shock. Volume replacement is usually accomplished by intravenous administration of crystalloid solutions (eg, physiologic saline) or of colloidal solutions (blood and its derivatives and substitutes).

Vasopressor drugs are not considered to be a primary form of therapy in shock, although they were formerly (and, in retrospect, unwisely) used for this purpose. Vasoactive agents are usually reserved for patients in whom plasma expansion is not achieved after adequate volumes of fluid have been given. Specific pharmacologic effects of certain currently available agents, however, can be utilized to advantage in both primary and adjunctive therapy of shock (see Table 10–5). Epinephrine, for example, is the most important agent in the initial or emergency treatment of allergic shock. Metaraminol is of value in treatment of neurogenic shock.

Vasoconstrictors appear illogical, since infusions of norepinephrine and other pressor amines further reduce plasma volume and since animals can be driven into lethal shock by infusing an adequate dose. Thus, shock and norepinephrine toxicity are simply different points of entry on the same cyclic process (at right).

Experimental and clinical data have suggested that vasodilators are useful in the treatment of shock. On the assumption that blockade of the sympathetic system was necessary, a mixture of chlorpromazine and promethazine, which have beta agonist effects, has been used. Phenoxybenzamine (Dibenzyline), by blocking the vasoconstrictor effects of endogenous epinephrine and norepinephrine, also acts as a vasodilator and has been used as an investigative drug.

Dopamine, which is an adrenergic drug with both vasopressor and vasodilator effects, is currently widely used for the treatment of shock. To explain its vasodilating effects, a distinctive dopaminergic action must be considered, in addition to the alpha- and beta-adrenergic actions that this catecholamine also exhibits.

Infused in small amounts (1–2 μg/kg/min), dopamine dilates renal and splanchnic vessels through an action that is not influenced by beta blockers. With these small doses, there is only a minimal increase in heart rate and less dilatation of vessels in skeletal muscle than occurs with isoproterenol.

With larger doses of dopamine, alpha and beta sympathomimetic effects appear. Cardiac output and heart rate are elevated, and, above a certain dosage, the vasoconstrictor and hypertensive effects of dopamine are indistinguishable from those of norepinephrine.

Dopamine is used in the treatment of shock, including cardiogenic shock, sometimes in combination with isoproterenol. It may also be used in low doses in refractory congestive heart failure to achieve an increase in cardiac output and sodium excretion beyond what is possible with the usual treatment.

More recently, it has been reported that a new catecholamine, dobutamine, is superior to dopamine for treatment of low output heart failure and shock, but experience with the drug has been limited.

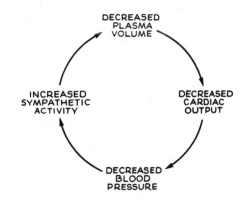

E. Complete Atrioventricular Block: The slow idioventricular rate that accompanies the usual atherosclerotic heart block is not necessarily symptomatic, but it, or a shift in cardiac rhythm, may cause syncope. The implantation of a pacemaker is usually the optimal treatment. However, ephedrine or isoproterenol may be used in the interim or even as definitive treatment.

F. Nasal Congestion: Vasodilatation and edema of the nasal mucosa (''nasal congestion'') is an inflammatory reaction that is commonly infectious in origin although it may be due to allergy or may be of unknown etiology (eg, when it accompanies chronic sinusitis). Regardless of the cause, the vasoconstrictor action of the sympathomimetics provides transient relief. If the complaint is due to an immediate allergic reaction (hay fever), the antihistamines will also be effective.

The sympathomimetics can be applied topically in the form of nose drops or spray or by the inhalation of a volatile salt of an amine. The addition of corticosteroids or antibiotics to the spray does not add to its effectiveness. The antihistamines are better given systemically.

Effective systemic use of vasoconstrictors as nasal decongestants is more difficult. The dosage of phenylephrine (Neo-Synephrine, etc) usually given for this purpose is certainly far below the amounts needed. Other sympathomimetics, if given in adequate doses, cause frequent side-effects but are effective. Ephedrine, pseudoephedrine, and other drugs shown in Table 10–6 cause, in addition, a pleasurable subjective response because of their euphoriant effect.

G. Other Uses: The following applications of the sympathomimetics either are infrequent or are discussed more fully in other parts of this book.

1. With local anesthetics–(See Chapter 22.) The superficial vasoconstriction caused by the addition of epinephrine to solutions of injected local anesthetics delays absorption and thereby decreases toxicity and prolongs the action of the local anesthetic.

2. Topical hemostatic–Epinephrine may be applied locally to a traumatized surface to reduce bleeding from small vessels. It is occasionally still so used in dental practice and in professional sports.

Adverse Reactions

A. Side-Effects: Epinephrine and isoproterenol induce feelings of anxiety, tremulousness, and a frightening awareness of a forceful or rapid heart beat. Following epinephrine administration, patients will appear pallid and sweaty; in contrast, after receiving isoproterenol they may be flushed. L-Norepinephrine causes less anxiety, and, as it is ordinarily used, side-effects are not common. The adrenergic drugs, especially isoproterenol, can cause serious ventricular arrhythmias. Rare cases of peripheral gangrene have been reported with dopamine.

B. Overdosage Toxicity: The most common reported cause of epinephrine toxicity is the accidental injection of a dose 10 times larger than that ordered. Such a dose given subcutaneously usually causes the side-effects listed above in an intense form plus headache and substernal pain. Fatal cases have usually shown acute pulmonary edema due to the extremely high arterial and left atrial pressures. Isolated cases of intracranial bleeding have also been reported. When no cause of death is apparent, it is presumed to be due to ventricular fibrillation. Serious arrhythmias are a more common problem if the epinephrine is injected (or liberated during excitement or asphyxia) in a patient sensitized by prior administration of a halogenated hydrocarbon type of anesthetic.

Table 10–6. Formulas of ephedrine, amphetamine, and related drugs.*

	R₁	R₂	R₃	R₄	R₅	R₆
Ephedrine, pseudoephedrine				HO—		—CH₃
Amphetamine						
Methamphetamine						—CH₃
Mephentermine (Wyamine)					—CH₃	—CH₃
Phenylpropanolamine† (Propadrine, norephedrine)				HO—		
Hydroxyamphetamine† (Paredrine)	HO—					
Metaraminol (Aramine)		HO—		HO—		
Methoxamine (Vasoxyl)		H₃C—O—‡	H₃C—O—‡	HO—		

*When no group is indicated as substituted for R, it is assumed that it is an H atom.

†Generic preparations available. Trade names included for identification only.

‡Methoxy substituents are in 2, 5 positions.

Isoproterenol does not cause the same extreme hypertension, and its acute toxicity in animals is less than that of epinephrine. Nevertheless, the number of sudden, unexpected deaths among young asthmatics has increased as isoproterenol aerosols have come into wide use. The increase in mortality rates was most striking in Great Britain, where preparations stronger than those permitted in the USA and Canada were used. The epidemic was terminated in England and Wales by reducing the concentration of isoproterenol and making the asthma medications subject to prescribing rules. Isoproterenol given by inhalation exerts an effect for at least 1 hour. The patient should be cautioned against repeating inhalation too often, especially from pressurized aerosols.

The serious toxicity of prolonged infusion of norepinephrine was mentioned under the treatment of shock. In addition, the intense vasoconstricting effect of norepinephrine can cause local necrosis when a continuous infusion does not enter a rapidly flowing venous channel. If extravasation occurs or ischemic changes are apparent, an alpha-adrenergic blocking agent such as phentolamine should be infiltrated into the area (see Chapter 11).

Contraindications & Cautions

The catecholamines should be used with great care in patients with angina, hypertension, and hyperthyroidism.

EPHEDRINE & OTHER PHENYLISOPROPYLAMINES

The clinically important properties of ephedrine and the many related phenylisopropylamines are their longer duration of action and the fact that they can be given orally. The effects of ephedrine resemble those of epinephrine and norepinephrine, but central nervous system stimulant properties are more prominent. Some phenylisopropylamines—eg, amphetamines—are used for their central nervous system stimulant effects. The central nervous system stimulant drugs are discussed in Chapter 28, but the present section describes their cardiovascular pharmacology.

Chemistry

The mechanisms described above for terminating the action of the catecholamines are not available for this group. The phenylisopropylamines are poor substrates for monoamine oxidase—in fact, they are inhibitors of that enzyme. Ring substituents may be introduced to increase the reactivity and thus reduce the duration of action, but in the absence of ring substituents the duration of action is prolonged. Ephedrine and many of its analogs are stable enough to be active after oral administration for a period of many hours.

In all drugs of this group the alpha carbon is asymmetric. If, in addition, the beta carbon bears a hydroxyl group, it also is asymmetric and 2 pairs of isomers are possible. Thus, a D- and an L-ephedrine and a D- and an L-pseudoephedrine exist, as shown below:

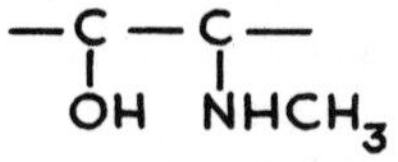

(−) Ephedrine 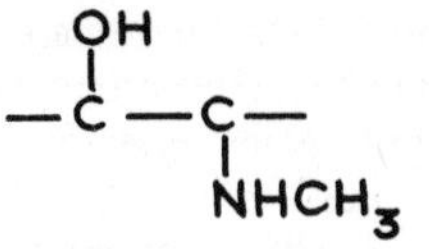   (+) Pseudoephedrine

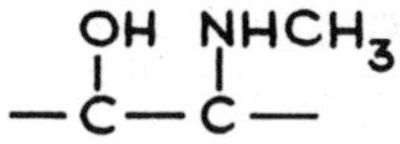

(+) Ephedrine 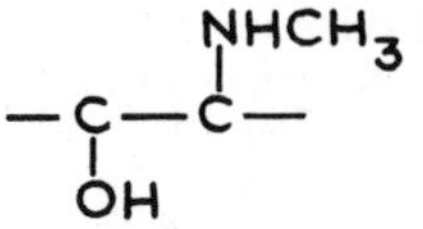   (−) Pseudoephedrine

Ephedrine as used clinically is now a synthetic form of the naturally occurring L-ephedrine. These bases are dispensed as the water-soluble salts of some simple acid, ie, as the hydrochloride or sulfate.

Pharmacologic Actions

A. Mechanisms of Action: The ephedrine molecule does not itself act upon smooth muscle or other effector. Its effect is indirect through the action of endogenous epinephrine and norepinephrine present in the organism. Two separate mechanisms are present.

The first mechanism is the liberation of norepinephrine from storage sites in nerve and chromaffin tissue. However, if the source of these intrinsic amines is eliminated by prior treatment with reserpine, the effects of ephedrine persist and may, as in the case of the blood pressure response, be augmented. Elimination of the ephedrine effect requires not only pretreatment with reserpine but denervation of the organ or tissue being studied.

The second (and quantitatively more important) mechanism, therefore, depends upon sympathetic nerve activity but cannot be more clearly defined than by saying that it depends upon an intensification and prolongation of the effect of amines that are already acting. Both in the laboratory and in the clinic, the intensity and duration of response to injected or liberated epinephrine or norepinephrine are increased by prior treatment with ephedrine.

This discussion of mechanism of action applies to the peripheral effects of ephedrine but not necessarily to its central nervous system stimulating actions. Central effects are not eliminated by reserpine pretreatment sufficient to deplete the brain of catecholamines and serotonin.

B. Effects:

1. Cardiovascular–The cardiovascular effects of ephedrine cannot be equated with those of either epinephrine or norepinephrine. The response is variable, and a degree of controversy therefore exists. If ephedrine acts through epinephrine or norepinephrine already acting in the organism, the variability becomes understandable. In the laboratory, using animal preparations with high epinephrine levels due to barbiturate anesthesia, asphyxia, or shock, the similarity between the effects of ephedrine and those of epinephrine is demonstrable. In unanesthetized, calm humans, the response is closer to that of norepinephrine, ie, cardiac output increases very slightly and vasodilatation is minimal.

2. Other effects–The other effects of ephedrine are qualitatively similar to those described for the catecholamines (above) but are of longer duration. Smooth muscle is relaxed and the pupils dilated. The manifestations of central nervous system stimulation may be marked.

Absorption, Metabolism, & Excretion

Ephedrine and related phenylisopropylamines are not substrates for COMT. Only a small amount is oxidatively deaminated in the human. A large fraction of a dose of ephedrine, amphetamine, etc, is excreted unchanged or with minor chemical change. Since they are slowly metabolized and well absorbed, they are active after oral administration.

Clinical Uses

Ephedrine is substituted for epinephrine in those situations where its longer duration of action or activity after oral administration are advantageous—eg, the nonemergency treatment of allergic reactions, asthma, hypotension during spinal anesthesia, AV block, and as a nasal vasoconstrictor or decongestant. Ephedrine may also be added to the treatment regimen of a patient with myasthenia gravis to improve voluntary muscle function.

Adverse Reactions

A. Side-Effects: The side-effects of ephedrine are similar to those of epinephrine but longer acting. Anxiety, tremulousness, palpitation, and insomnia are common when ephedrine is given 3 or 4 times each day as in the treatment of asthma. Difficulty in initiating urination may be experienced by an older man due to relaxation of the bladder musculature.

B. Overdosage Toxicity: Ephedrine is capable of causing the behavioral changes described after large doses of amphetamine. However, the feelings of anxiety and awareness of heart action are so much more intense after ephedrine that it is not misused. Acute toxicity is seldom encountered, because single large doses do not maintain the blood pressure at greatly elevated levels for the entire period of drug action. Vasoconstriction persists, but cardiac output is lowered and plasma volume is decreased as during norepinephrine infusions. The acute tolerance that develops to the pressor effects of ephedrine is called tachyphylaxis.

Side-effects and overdosage effects of ephedrine are treated by sedation with barbiturates.

Preparations & Dosages

A. Oral: When a continued effect is necessary,

ephedrine sulfate (or, uncommonly, the hydrochloride) is given 3 or 4 times daily. The usual initial dose is 25 mg. Side-effects are common, but ephedrine may be administered in combination with phenobarbital to minimize central nervous system stimulation. Local application of other sympathomimetics, as by nose drops or inhalation of an aerosol, is substituted for oral ephedrine whenever possible.

B. Injection: 25–50 mg of ephedrine may be injected intramuscularly or subcutaneously. Ampules containing 25 or 50 mg of ephedrine sulfate in 1 mL are available.

Congeners of Ephedrine

Many compounds chemically related to ephedrine have been synthesized and studied. It is possible to exaggerate or diminish some of the pharmacologic properties of ephedrine in these new molecules and to alter the duration of action. In amphetamine and related drugs, the central nervous system stimulant properties are more prominent and the cardiovascular actions slightly less. In others, the potency as vasoconstrictors is increased, and the resulting pressor agents are suggested as substitutes for norepinephrine in the treatment of shock. Methoxamine (Vasoxyl) is practically a pure alpha agonist, but the usefulness of such drugs in shock and hypotension is now questioned. It has also been possible to synthesize indirect-acting amines that lack vasoconstrictor effects—ie, act only on beta receptors. These are listed separately, below.

The theoretic optimum for a patient with asthma—a bronchodilator drug devoid of central nervous system stimulant and cardiovascular effects—is not available.

A. Hydroxyamphetamine (Paredrine): This compound is prepared synthetically for use as a drug but is also a (para-hydroxylated) metabolite of amphetamine. It is almost lacking in central nervous system stimulating effects and, in general, is a poor vasoconstrictor although it acts on the heart as ephedrine does. It has been suggested for systemic use in complete heart block, but its common use is as a nasal decongestant and mydriatic. For these last purposes hydroxyamphetamine (Paredrine) is supplied as a 1% nasal solution and 1% ophthalmic solution.

B. Phenylpropanolamine (Propadrine): Similar to ephedrine but possibly with less central nervous system stimulant effects at the usual dosages, this drug is available without prescription, usually in combination with an antihistamine, in many cold remedies.

C. Mephentermine (Wyamine): This compound has a long duration of action and is predominantly a beta agonist. Inhalers containing the free base and 0.5% nasal solution are available for use as nasal decongestant, showing that it is not devoid of vasoconstricting ability. Even though mephentermine is said to be a weak central nervous system stimulant, the contents of the inhaler are sometimes used in lieu of amphetamine.

D. Metaraminol (Aramine, Pressonex): This drug must be separated from other phenylisopropylamines because of the important information on its mechanism of action. Studies with isotopically labeled metariminol show that it is taken up by granules in sympathetic nerve endings, replacing norepinephrine. Subsequent sympathetic nerve activity does not liberate norepinephrine but metaraminol or an active metabolite, the false mediator. The concept of a false mediator has important application to other drugs and is further discussed in Chapter 12 in relation to methyldopa.

The effects of metaraminol are similar to those of norepinephrine, and its use is as a pressor agent. It may be given intramuscularly in doses of 5 or 10 mg, or diluted and given as an intravenous infusion at a rate sufficient to attain the desired blood pressure. Since its duration of action (1 hour) is much longer than that of norepinephrine, intravenous infusion must be started slowly.

INDIRECT–ACTING INHIBITORY AMINES

Nylidrin, isoxsuprine, and ritodrine (Premar) are similar to ephedrine in that they are phenylisopropylamines, but the nitrogen bears a substituent that is bulkier than the usual methyl group.

Qualitatively, the effects of these compounds are similar to those of isoproterenol. They are potent stimulators of cardiac rate and force of contraction and are pure vasodilators. They are effective in relaxing smooth muscle and as central stimulants. Their net effect, therefore, is as described for isoproterenol.

However, these drugs have a much longer duration of action than isoproterenol and may be given orally. In addition, their mechanism of action is indirect, ie, they act to increase the cardiac stimulant and vasodilating properties of ephedrine already acting in the organism.

Nylidrin and isoxsuprine are vasodilators, but they are not useful in chronic arterial insufficiency (see Chapter 13). All have been used as investigational drugs to suppress uterine contractions and defer labor.

INCOMPLETE SYMPATHOMIMETICS

The amines listed below are used only as topical vasoconstrictors of the nasal mucosa or conjunctiva. For these reasons they are usually discussed with the sympathomimetic drugs, but they have few other properties in common with this group. The imidazole derivatives, for example, are vasoconstrictors but have no effect on the myocardium, and, although they relax the intestine, they do not act on the smooth muscle of the bronchioles.

These drugs are familiar in the form of nose drops, inhalers, or in plastic spray bottles. When the latter form is used in children who are reclining rather than upright, a stream rather than a spray may be ejected. In such cases a toxic reaction can occur with hypotension and central depression rather than the expected epinephrinelike effects.

TYRAMINE

Tyramine originates physiologically from the decarboxylation of tyrosine. It has no therapeutic applications, but its mechanism of action is important in understanding certain other drugs and drug interactions.

Tyramine acts as a sympathomimetic by displacing norepinephrine from the labile pool in sympathetic nerve and other chromaffin cells without blocking uptake or synthesis. Its effects are therefore exactly like

p-Tyrosine   Tyramine

Nylidrin (Arlidin)
(Isoxsuprine [Vasodilan] has an oxygen in
place of the CH$_2$ group shown by the arrow.)

those of norepinephrine, but may be more persistent if the amount of tyramine is large or continuously present. The action of tyramine is completely prevented by pretreatment with agents, such as reserpine, known to deplete the organism of norepinephrine.

Tyramine is inactivated entirely by MAO. If this enzyme is inhibited by a MAO inhibitor type of central stimulant, the tyramine response is prolonged and intensified. Tyramine ingested in cheese or other fermented foods by patients receiving a MAO inhibitor has caused serious hypertensive episodes leading in a few cases to cerebral hemorrhage.

• • •

References

Asthma deaths: A question answered. Br Med J 4:443, 1972.

Axelrod J: Noradrenaline: Fate and control of its biosynthesis. Science 173:598, 1971.

Catecholamines. Br Med Bull 29:91, 1973.

Cohn JN: Comparative cardiovascular effects of tyramine, ephedrine, and norepinephrine in man. Circ Res 16:174, 1965.

Gilbert RP, Hohf R: Hemodynamic basis of norepinephrine shock. Proc Soc Exp Biol Med 116:43, 1964.

Goldberg LI: Dopamine: Clinical uses of an endogenous catecholamine. N Engl J Med 291:707, 1974.

Goldberg LI, Hsieh Y-Y, Resnekov L: Newer catecholamines for treatment of heart failure and shock: An update on dopamine and a first look at dobutamine. Prog Cardiovasc Dis 19:327, 1977.

Greiss FC Jr, Crandell DL: Therapy for hypotension induced by spinal anesthesia during pregnancy. JAMA 191:793, 1965.

Himms-Hagen J: Sympathetic regulation of metabolism. Pharmacol Rev 19:367, 1967.

Hoffman BB, Lefkowitz RJ: Alpha-adrenergic receptor subtypes. N Engl J Med 302:1390, 1980.

Kardos GG: Isoproterenol in the treatment of shock due to bacteremia with gram-negative pathogens. N Engl J Med 274:868, 1966.

Karliner JS: The use of dopamine in patients with cardiogenic shock. Med Digest 21:13, Nov 1975.

Loeb HS, Bredakis J, Gunnar RM: Superiority of dobutamine over dopamine for augmentation of cardiac output in patients with chronic low output failure. Circulation 55:375, 1977.

Moore JI, Moran NC: Cardiac contractile force responses to ephedrine and other sympathomimetic amines in dogs after pretreatment with reserpine. J Pharmacol Exp Ther 136:89, 1962.

Schmutzer KJ, Rasschke E, Maloney JV: Intravenous L-norepinephrine as a cause of reduced plasma volume. Surgery 50:452, 1961.

Smith HJ & others: Hemodynamic studies in cardiogenic shock: Treatment with isoproterenol and metaraminol. Circulation 35:1084, 1967.

Tarazi RC: Sympathomimetic agents in the treatment of shock. Ann Intern Med 81:364, 1974.

Webb-Johnson DC, Andrews JL Jr: Bronchodilator therapy. (2 parts.) N Engl J Med 297:476, 758, 1977.

Weil MH, Shubin H, Carlson R: Treatment of circulatory shock: Use of sympathomimetic and related vasoactive agents. JAMA 231:1280, 1975.

Wurtman RJ: Catecholamines. (3 parts.) N Engl J Med 273:637, 693, 746, 1965.

Zaimis E: Vasopressor drugs and catecholamines. Anesthesiology 29:732, 1968.

Adrenergic Blocking (Sympathoplegic) Drugs | 11

The sympathoplegic drugs are those that block the action of sympathomimetic amines or limit sympathetic outflow. There are now many groups of drugs that decrease sympathetic activity and that have many applications in the treatment of hypertension, coronary artery disease, cardiac dysrhythmias, and other important diseases. Their effects will be referred to as sympathoplegic, since the alternative term sympatholytic was used for many years to refer to just one of the drug classes that is now called, with more precision, the alpha-adrenergic blocking agents.

Summary & Classification

Below are listed all of the drug types that can reduce sympathetic influences on blood vessels and other effectors. This general classification is based on site and mechanism of pharmacologic action. The first 3 classes are discussed in this chapter. The postural hypotensive agents and the central sympathoplegics are presented in Chapter 12 in the discussion of the treatment of hypertension.

A. Alpha-Adrenergic Blocking Agents: Drugs that act on the effector organ, beyond the nerve ending (postsynaptically), to block the vasoconstricting action of epinephrine or norepinephrine. Exemplified by phentolamine (Regitine) or phenoxybenzamine (Dibenzyline).

B. Beta-Adrenergic Blocking Agents: Drugs that act on the effector organs, postsynaptically, to block the cardiac and vasodilating actions of epinephrine and the cardiac effects of norepinephrine. Propranolol (Inderal) is an example.

C. Ganglion Blocking Agents: Drugs that block transmission across both the sympathetic and parasympathetic ganglia, eg, hexamethonium or mecamylamine (Inversine). They were useful postural hypotensive drugs but have been replaced by the postganglionic blocking drugs. They are still useful in the animal laboratory to provide chemical denervation of autonomic tissues.

D. Adrenergic Neuron or Postganglionic Blocking Agents: Guanethidine (Ismelin) and other drugs that prevent the liberation of norepinephrine from sympathetic nerve endings. They act proximal to the effector but distal to the ganglion. Guanethidine is a widely used, potent hypotensive agent.

E. Central Sympathoplegics: Reserpine, methyldopa, clonidine, and probably propranolol— drugs important in the treatment of hypertension— reduce the sympathetic outflow by differing actions on suprasegmental centers, presumably hypothalamic.

F. MAO Inhibitors: Some members of this class have more potent hypotensive effects and less potent central nervous system stimulant and sympathomimetic effects than others. Pargyline (Eutonyl) is the only one used as a sympathoplegic or hypotensive drug.

G. Veratrum Alkaloids: These drugs increase afferent activity reaching the brain stem from thoracic and other chemo- and pressoreceptors. They inhibit sympathetic outflow and augment vagal influences. They are now rarely used as hypotensive agents.

H. Others: Phenothiazine type antipsychotics cause postural hypotension that is often attributed to alpha-adrenergic blockade. The vasodilatation is more probably due to an intensification of the beta agonist effects of epinephrine. The antipsychotic tranquilizers also reduce sympathetic outflow by a central effect.

Similarly, hydralazine (Apresoline) is not a sympathoplegic drug; its mechanism of action is to increase the vasodilating and cardiac-stimulating effects of epinephrine.

ALPHA–ADRENERGIC BLOCKING AGENTS

Drugs of this class act on vascular smooth muscle to block the vasoconstricting effects of epinephrine and norepinephrine. Vasodilatation and other actions of the sympathetic mediators persist after alpha-adrenergic blocking agents are given. Following the administration of an adrenergic blocking agent, the hypertensive effect of epinephrine is reversed, ie, pressure falls rather than rises. Since norepinephrine lacks the vasodilating action, its effect is blocked but not reversed. The only functions other than vasoconstriction that are blocked are pupillary dilatation, lid retraction, and, in the animal laboratory, nictitating membrane contraction.

Chemistry, Classification, & Mechanism of Action (Fig 11–1)

A. Competitive, Short-Acting Antagonists: The combination of phentolamine (Regitine) with the

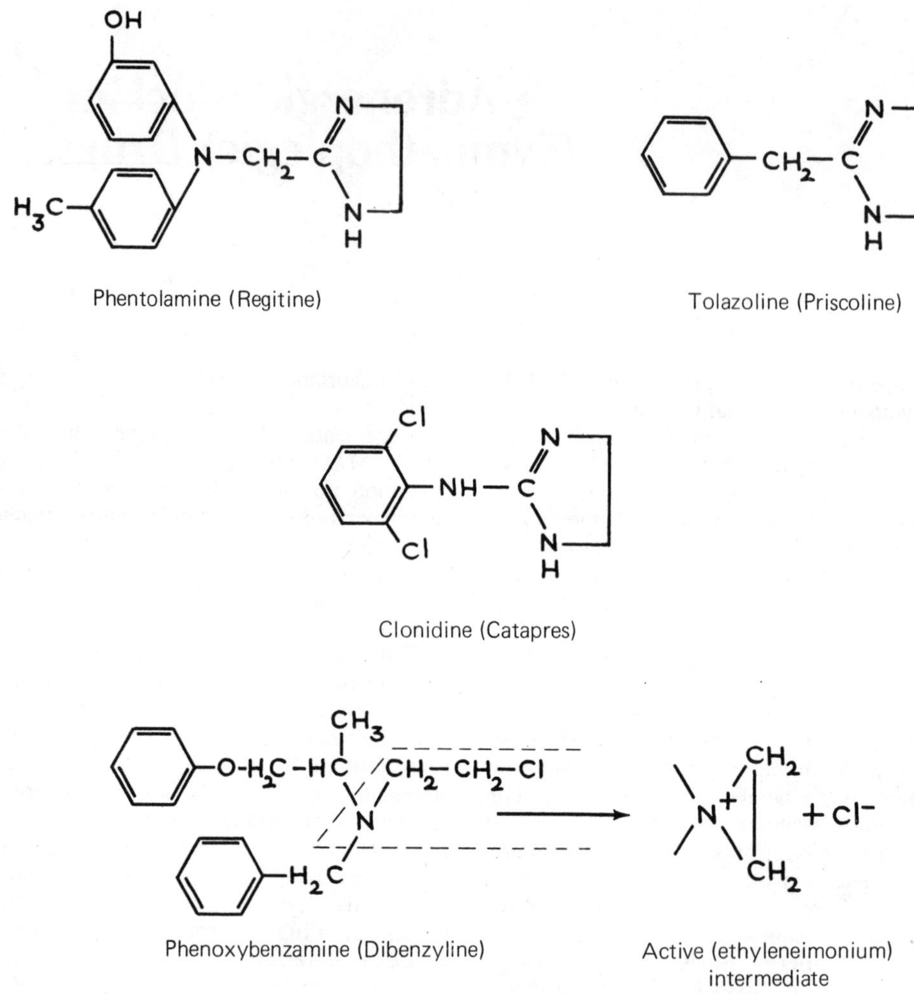

Phentolamine (Regitine)

Tolazoline (Priscoline)

Clonidine (Catapres)

Phenoxybenzamine (Dibenzyline)

Active (ethyleneimonium)
intermediate

Figure 11–1. Structure of alpha-adrenergic blocking agents and of clonidine, a central sympathoplegic.

receptor that mediates vasoconstriction is reversible. This drug is therefore said to produce equilibrium blockade, ie, the free drug and drug-receptor combination are in equilibrium and the blockade disappears as the free drug is destroyed. The blockade is competitive in that it can be overcome by a large amount of epinephrine or norepinephrine.

B. Noncompetitive, Long-Acting Antagonists: Phenoxybenzamine (Dibenzyline) and Dibenamine, an earlier drug now encountered only in the experimental literature, are beta-haloalkylamines related to the other nitrogen mustards discussed later as alkylating agents in cancer chemotherapy. Their onset of action is gradual over a period of several hours, during which time the cyclization reaction shown in Fig 11–1 occurs. The receptor responsible for vasoconstriction is altered chemically. The blockade is not of the equilibrium type; it outlasts the presence of phenoxybenzamine, is noncompetitive, and persists for several days.

C. Ergot Alkaloids: Reversal of the effect of epinephrine on blood pressure was first noted after

administration of ergot. Henry Dale (1906) had first rejected one lot of epinephrine as inactive on the basis of a bioassay and subsequently approved the same lot when it was resubmitted. The apparent inactivity of the first lot was due to his having used an animal that had been given ergot. For many years thereafter, the nonhydrogenated ergot alkaloids were the only alpha-adrenergic blocking agents available. The effect can be demonstrated only in anesthetized animals, however, and should no longer be regarded as an important pharmacologic action of these drugs. The ergot alkaloids are discussed as vasoconstrictors in Chapter 14.

D. Other Drugs With Incidental Alpha-Adrenergic Blocking Action: Tolazoline (Priscoline) and azapetine (Ilidar) are alpha-adrenergic blocking agents in the animal laboratory. They also have actions similar to those of histamine, acetylcholine, and epinephrine. Their action as vasodilators is based on their direct effect on vascular smooth muscle and is discussed in Chapter 13.

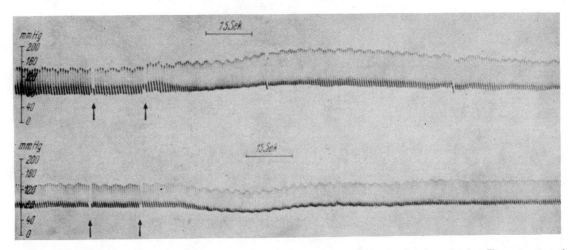

Figure 11–2. Reversal of epinephrine effect on femoral arterial pressure in the human by phentolamine. The upper record shows the control response to epinephrine, 0.2 μg/kg, injected intravenously during the interval marked by the arrows. The lower record shows the response to the same dose of epinephrine after phentolamine, 0.35 mg/kg, was injected intravenously. (Reproduced, with permission, from Bernsmeier & others: Hemmung und Umkehr der Adrenalin-Blutdrucksteigerung am Menschen. Z Ges Exp Med 121:435, 1953.)

Pharmacologic Actions

A. Mechanisms of Action: See above.

B. Effects: The effects of alpha-adrenergic blocking agents depend not only upon the dosage and the amount of sympatho-adrenal activity present but also on the fact that circulating amines from the adrenal are more easily blocked than neurally liberated norepinephrine. The long-acting compounds can block both circulating and neurogenic amines and cause postural hypotension in both normal and in hypertensive subjects in those few cases where an effective dose is tolerated.

Small doses of the short-acting blocking agents have little effect on the blood pressure of normal subjects or patients with essential hypertension, but they lower the blood pressure when it is maintained by circulating amines liberated from a pheochromocytoma. In the presence of shock, if volume replacement is inadequate, phenoxybenzamine will further lower blood pressure.

Other effects of the sympathomimetic amines, notably tachycardia and cardiac stimulation, are usually said to be unaltered by these drugs. Actually, cardioacceleration is in part antagonized by alpha-adrenergic blocking agents, an action minimized in the pharmacologic literature but important in the management of patients with pheochromocytomas.

Clinical Uses

A. Diagnosis and Treatment of Pheochromocytoma: Tumors that arise in chromaffin tissue may release epinephrine and norepinephrine into the general circulation and cause paroxysmal or even sustained hypertension. Such tumors are rare, but essential hypertension is very common, and tests to exclude the existence of pheochromocytoma must be frequently performed to establish an etiologic diagnosis

of hypertension. Any patient with a history of paroxysmal episodes of hypertension or signs of episodic or continuous catecholamine effect (anxiety, sweating, heat intolerance, hypermetabolism, etc) should be tested for this form of surgically curable hypertension. Measurements of urinary or plasma catecholamines reflect the amounts liberated. The principal urinary metabolite of epinephrine and norepinephrine, VMA (see Chapter 10), is more simply determined. It may be necessary to precipitate an increase in the amount of catecholamines liberated from the tumor as described below and to measure the change over a short period rather than determine the content in a 24-hour collection.

Pharmacologic tests for the diagnosis of pheochromocytoma are used infrequently today. The tests are mentioned principally because of their pharmacologic interest.

1. Provocative test with histamine–*Extremely hazardous and very rarely necessary!* (For use during the normotensive phase.) Liberation of catecholamines can be provoked in a patient in the interval between paroxysms by several drugs, but the histamine test is the best standardized. Histamine in a dose of 0.025–0.05 mg of the base is given intravenously. Ordinarily, this amount of histamine—a vasodilator—will cause a fall or slight rise in the blood pressure. An increase of 60/30 mm Hg is interpreted as a positive test if that rise exceeds that caused by the cold pressor test.

2. Phentolamine test–(For use during the hypertensive phase.) In patients with sustained hypertension, the ability of the alpha-adrenergic blocking agents to block circulating catecholamines in smaller doses than are required to block neurally liberated norepinephrine can be utilized. Phentolamine (Regitine), 5 mg intravenously, usually causes only a

Table 11–1. A summary of the effects of administration of adrenergic receptor agonists and antagonists.

Receptor	Tissue or Function	Effect of Receptor Stimulation	Effect of Receptor Blockade
Alpha	Vascular smooth muscle	Vasoconstriction	Vasodilatation
Beta₁	Heart*		
	SA node	Heart rate increased	Pulse rate decreased
	AV node	Conduction more rapid	P–R prolongation to complete AV block
		P–R shortened	
	Force of contraction	Increased; cardiac output increased	Cardiac output reduced
	Metabolic	Lipolysis	. . .
Beta₂	Vascular smooth muscle	Vasodilatation	Transient constriction†
	Other smooth muscle	Relaxed, eg, bronchiolar dilatation	Bronchiolar constriction
Beta (uncharacterized)	Metabolic	Increased insulin release	Slight potentiation of insulin hypoglycemia
		Increased renin release	Renin levels decreased

*Exclusive of quinidinelike effects present in available beta-adrenergic blocking agents.
†Exclusive of vasodilatation and slight fall in blood pressure due probably to central nervous system effect.

minor fall in blood pressure in essential hypertension. A fall of 35/25 mm Hg within 2 minutes is presumptive evidence of pheochromocytoma.

3. Preoperative management–Administration of an alpha-adrenergic blocking agent will prevent the precipitation of acute hypertensive episodes during studies undertaken to localize the tumor and will reverse the changes caused by the chronic release of the catecholamines. As is the case with patients given norepinephrine infusions, these patients have a reduced plasma volume and may become seriously hypotensive when the tumor is removed. Preoperative adrenergic blockade allows restoration of blood volume. Phenoxybenzamine is effective and conveniently administered only once a day. Oral doses of 10–20 mg/d may be increased at intervals of 3 or 4 days to allow for evaluation of the cumulative effect of the long-acting drug on blood pressure. Patients with pheochromocytoma may be treated for weeks to permit election of the proper time for surgery. An alternative drug is phentolamine, which must be administered by mouth every 4 hours. Initial doses of 12.5 mg are given, increasing to 50–100 mg every 4 hours as blood pressure measurements justify.

Beta-adrenergic blocking agents may be used when tachycardia is a persistent problem. Alpha blockers usually ameliorate cardiac effects, however.

An alternative treatment of pheochromocytoma utilizes alpha-methyltyrosine (metyrosine, Demser), an inhibitor of tyrosine hydroxylase. The conversion of tyrosine to dopa (see Fig 10–4) is the rate-limiting step in the synthesis of catecholamines, and the amount of amine in the tumor is reduced by this drug, which can be used in the preoperative management of a patient or substituted for surgery if necessary. Side-effects include sedation and extrapyramidal signs.

B. Other Uses: Phentolamine (Regitine) is used to prevent the local necrosis that may follow the accidental paravenous injection of norepinephrine (Levophed) during the treatment of shock. In the latter instance, the drug is infiltrated locally.

Phenoxybenzamine (Dibenzyline) is a postural hypotensive agent; however, its use is limited by the

occurrence of emesis and by its probable carcinogenicity, and hypertension is treated with other agents. Prazosin (Minipress) is an alpha-blocker recently introduced for the treatment of hypertension.

In those patients in shock who remain hypotensive following more than adequate volume replacement, phenoxybenzamine is one of the vasodilators now being used to mobilize sequestered fluid and restore blood pressure. (See Chapter 10.)

BETA–ADRENERGIC BLOCKING AGENTS

The beta-adrenergic blocking agents (beta-blockers, beta-adrenoreceptor blocking agents) are among the newest of drug groups but have a surprisingly wide spectrum of usefulness.

The beta receptor, defined in detail in Chapter 10, mediates all of the sympathomimetic effects except vasoconstriction.

Chemistry

The available beta-blockers all resemble isoproterenol (the type compound of the beta-agonists) in that they are N-isopropyl amines. The other end of the molecule is bulkier than the phenyl ring of isoproterenol. The antagonists resemble the agonist enough to occupy the receptor but lack efficacy—ie, cannot activate the next reaction in the series.

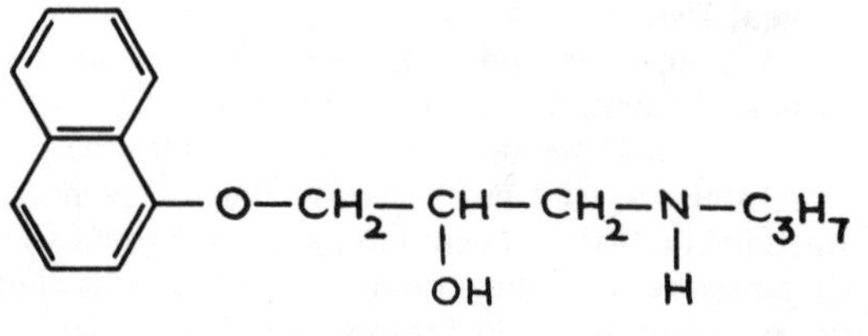

Propranolol (Inderal)

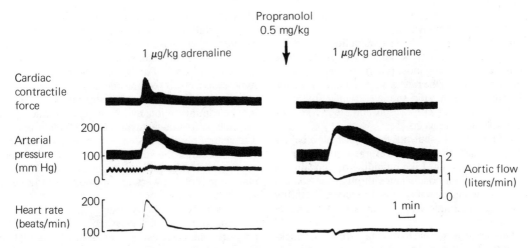

Figure 11 –3. The effect in an anesthetized dog of the injection of epinephrine before and after propranolol. In the presence of a beta-receptor blocking agent, epinephrine no longer augments the force of contraction (measured by a strain gauge attached to the ventricular wall) nor increases cardiac rate. Blood pressure is still elevated by epinephrine because vasoconstriction is not blocked. (Reproduced, with permission, from Shanks: The pharmacology of beta sympathetic blockade. Am J Cardiol 18:312, 1966.)

The several beta-blockers differ in properties, but the classification of the different types must be based on pharmacologic effects rather than chemical structure.

Pharmacokinetics

All of the available beta-blockers are active after oral administration. Propranolol has an unusually high "first pass" clearance by the liver (50%), and its effects are intensified by liver or kidney insufficiency. Its nominal half-life is only 2–3 hours, but that figure increases with chronic administration. With the usual high dosages, administration 2 times a day is sufficient.

Pharmacologic Effects

A. Classification: The beta-adrenergic receptor is not homogeneous but can be separated into beta$_1$ receptors that predominate in the heart and beta$_2$ receptors that mediate relaxation (dilatation) of vascular and other smooth muscle. Among the sympathomimetic drugs, isoproterenol acted unselectively on heart and smooth muscle, whereas the beta$_2$ agonists (eg, metaproterenol) act—in low dosages, at least—predominantly on the extracardiac sites. Similarly, there are **nonselective** beta-blockers (propranolol, nadolol) that affect cardiac, vascular, and bronchiolar function, and **cardioselective** blockers that, until larger doses are given, act only on the beta$_1$ receptors of the heart.

In addition, most of the beta-blockers have a membrane-stabilizing effect that endows them with properties similar to those of quinidine, lidocaine, or other local anesthetics—a property unrelated to their beta blocking action. Finally, all available beta-blockers have central nervous system effects similar to those of reserpine or the antipsychotics.

Beta-blockers are generally nonselective and quinidinelike and have central nervous system effects. One nominal cardioselective agent lacking quinidinelike effects (metoprolol) is marketed, and other combinations exist among the many investigative drugs.

B. Mechanisms of Action: Propranolol blocks almost all of the effects of injected catecholamines except vasoconstriction: Those effects described above as due to activation of beta-receptors—cardiac acceleration, increased force of contraction, vasodilatation, and smooth muscle relaxation—are blocked (Fig 11–3). The action of the blocking agent is postsynaptic, ie, on the effector tissue, and neural function is not altered. The antagonism between propranolol and the catecholamines is competitive.

The effect of administering a drug such as propranolol will depend upon the amount of constant sympathetic tone maintained on the organ or tissue observed. Thus, since the regulation of cardiac function depends upon variations in sympathetic tone, propranolol will cause marked changes in cardiac function.

C. Effects:

1. Cardiac–Blockade of the constant, excitatory sympathetic influences on the heart leads to changes in cardiac function even during the basal state. Moreover, the response of the heart to exercise or other stress is markedly decreased and the expected increase in rate and output does not occur. The effects of propranolol on the heart include the following:

a. A decrease in the rate of normal sinus pacemaker and of other atrial foci present during arrhythmia. The rate of depolarization during diastole is slowed, and a longer interval occurs before the threshold for propagated depolarization is reached. This action slows the rate of a rapid supraventricular focus, but conversion of atrial flutter or fibrillation is not ordinarily accomplished.

b. Atrioventricular (AV) conduction is slowed because the vagal action on the atrioventricular node predominates. Like digitalis, propranolol can produce a graded decrease in the rate of ventricular contraction in the presence of a rapid supraventricular rhythm.

c. The force of contraction and, therefore, the minute volume is reduced.

d. Propranolol—but not the other beta-blockers marketed—has the action referred to above as membrane-stabilizing. Like quinidine or lidocaine, it can reduce sodium conductance through the sodium channel of the cell membrane and reduce excitability and slow conduction, giving it an antiarrhythmic effect and usefulness.

This action is not due to its beta-adrenergic blocking ability. The isomer of propranolol most active in correcting ventricular arrhythmias is a less active beta-blocker. The rate of intraventricular conduction is also slowed, and this action also reflects a coincidental quinidinelike effect rather than a result of sympathetic blockade.

2. Nonvascular smooth muscle–Of the smooth muscle structures other than the blood vessels, only the bronchioles are of significance in relation to the beta-blockers. Even in normal subjects, the administration of propranolol causes bronchiolar constriction. Patients with asthma or other obstructive respiratory disease are especially susceptible and may respond to even the cardioselective beta-blockers with a dangerous degree of bronchiolar constriction.

Clinical Uses

The uses of the beta-blockers are listed below. However, in subsequent chapters—eg, those on the treatment of hypertension, angina, or cardiac dysrhythmias—the beta-blockers are discussed in a larger context.

A. Prevention of Anginal Pain: In controlled studies, the beta-blockers reduce the number of anginal attacks and increase exercise tolerance in treadmill tests. The beneficial effect is due to a reduction in the increment of cardiac work that accompanies exercise or other causes of sympatho-adrenal discharge.

The dosage of whichever drug is used is often large and variable and must be determined for each patient. Side-effects are frequent and sometimes serious, and a fraction—perhaps one-tenth—of patients have reduced exercise tolerance after treatment. Propranolol is nevertheless useful in many (70%) patients who have frequent anginal attacks. Nitroglycerin need not be discontinued.

B. Treatment of Hypertension: Propranolol or another beta-blocker is widely used in the treatment of essential hypertension as a second drug after a thiazide diuretic, very much as reserpine or methyldopa is used. It is not used in the treatment of hypertensive emergencies. The hypotension achieved is not postural, is small in degree, and appears after chronic administration of large doses. At least 2 possible

mechanisms are being considered.

The fall in blood pressure achieved by the use of propranolol alone is usually slight, not postural, and its effect must be supplemented by a thiazide diuretic and often a third drug. Large doses are required, ie, the hypotensive effect requires more drug than the cardiac effect; the hypotensive effect appears only after prolonged administration; and the hypotensive action outlasts the peripheral sympathoplegic effect of the drug. The central nervous system side-effects are similar to those seen after the administration of reserpine or an antipsychotic tranquilizer, suggesting the likelihood that propranolol lowers blood pressure by a central sympathoplegic action.

A second possibility is suggested by the observations that propranolol is most active in lowering blood pressure when pretreatment renin levels are high and that the hypotensive effect is correlated with the ability of the drug to inhibit renin release.

The beta-blocker would act by interrupting the following sequence: Renin from the kidney releases angiotensin from plasma. Angiotensin is a vasoconstrictor, but, probably more important, it acts on the adrenal cortex to increase aldosterone elaboration, which leads to sodium retention and an increase in plasma volume that can cause hypertension. The process is seen as resulting in hypertension when the feedback mechanism that usually limits renin release is defective, as occurs, perhaps, in malignant and renovascular hypertension. Among the several objections to this theory is the observation that nadolol (Corgard) is effective in lowering blood pressure even though its ability to block renin is apparently limited.

C. Cardiac Arrhythmias: In the presence of a cardiac arrhythmia, propranolol may act either because it is a beta-adrenergic blocking agent or because of a coincidental quinidinelike action in suppressing ectopic pacemaking areas.

When given to patients with atrial fibrillation or flutter, propranolol decreases ventricular rate—especially the elevation that follows exercise. The atrial rate remains rapid, and the beneficial action on ventricular rate is the result of prolongation of the refractory period of the atrioventricular node due to blockade of catecholamine effect.

The quinidinelike effect is more often apparent with ventricular than with atrial arrhythmias, although the rate of the ectopic focus responsible for an atrial tachycardia is slowed by propranolol.

1. Digitalis-induced arrhythmias–Arrhythmias due to digitalis toxicity appear to be better controlled by propranolol than by supplementary potassium, although any possible potassium deficit should be repaired. Propranolol may be used against digitalis-precipitated atrial tachycardia, ventricular tachycardia, or ventricular ectopic beats judged to be premonitory of a tachycardia.

2. Ventricular tachycardia–Ventricular tachycardia that is not a consequence of the use of digitalis is now most commonly treated by DC countershock (cardioversion). As an alternative treatment—eg, when equipment is not available—propranolol is as effective as quinidine.

3. Atrial flutter or fibrillation—Propranolol rarely converts these arrhythmias and offers no advantage over digitalis in slowing the ventricular rate. It will not, of course, correct any associated congestive failure. A beta-blocking agent may be used when digitalis is discontinued in anticipation of conversion by countershock.

D. After Myocardial Infarction: Animal experiments suggested the possibility that the size of the eventual infarct could be reduced by early treatment with a drug that would reduce cardiac work and that the beta-blockers might also be useful in reducing the number of serious ventricular arrhythmias. Trials to date have shown no value in the period immediately following an infarct except for one trial using intravenous administration. There are, however, at least 2 acceptable collaborative studies in which the beta-blocker (practolol or alprenolol) was given for 2 years after the acute phase with a significant reduction in overall mortality rate and in the number of sudden deaths. In the larger trial, benefit was limited to patients with anterior infarcts.

E. Control of Thyrotoxicosis: The peripheral effects of thyrotoxicosis—eg, tachycardia, elevated systolic blood pressure and widened pulse pressure, increased cardiac output, tremulousness, elevated body temperature, and the resulting increase in oxygen consumption—are strikingly similar to the effects of epinephrine and have been treated experimentally with several sympathoplegic drugs. Propranolol is the most effective of these agents for this purpose. The beta-blockers can be used alone or with propylthiouracil—as treatment or as preoperative preparation. They are the treatment of choice in the rare patient with thyroid storm.

F. Glaucoma: The agents used in the treatment of glaucoma are discussed in Chapter 9, where the use of pilocarpine and epinephrine drops as treatment for chronic open-angle glaucoma was mentioned. The beta-blockers are evidently as effective as pilocarpine in this form of glaucoma. They cause fewer side-effects than epinephrine causes but more than does pilocarpine.

Timolol (Timoptic) is a nonselective blocker marketed as ophthalmic drops for this purpose. It has minimal local anesthetic properties; it need be given no oftener than twice a day; and, like epinephrine, it appears to decrease production of aqueous humor. Oral propranolol is also useful and may be used when hypertension or angina is also present—not an unheard of circumstance in this group of patients.

G. Prevention of Migraine Attacks: Of the several central sympathoplegics that have been used to prevent episodes of migraine, propranolol is best established at this time and pending further experience with clonidine. One generalization promises a 50% reduction in the number of attacks in 50% of patients (see also Chapter 14).

H. Other Uses: Symptoms precipitated by exercise in the rare patient with hypertrophic subaortic stenosis are reduced.

Essential, familial, or senile action tremors are relieved.

The importance of the use of alpha-adrenergic blocking agents in patients with a catecholamine-producing tumor before and during surgery has been discussed in the preceding section. A beta-blocker may be used in the management of the patient if persistent tachycardia requires its use. An alpha-blocking agent must always be used first, lest an epinephrine-producing tumor cause even greater hypertension following blockade of the vasodilating effects.

Of interest in categorizing the central nervous system effects of propranolol is its antipsychotic effect. It is not useful in the treatment of anxiety, although it may modify some of the somatic signs of anxiety.

Adverse Reactions

A. Side-Effects: Side-effects are common early in treatment but, with continued administration, disappear or are greatly reduced. They may include dizziness, tiredness and depression, increased dreaming, gastrointestinal disturbances (nausea, diarrhea), paresthesias, muscle aching, and asthmatic wheezing. Transient falsely high responses to tests of liver (SGOT) and kidney (blood urea nitrogen) function occur.

B. Overdosage Toxicity: The toxic effects of propranolol are due to an extension of the effects of beta-adrenergic blockade on the heart, on bronchioles, and on glycogenolysis. They are (1) congestive failure in a patient with limited cardiac reserve, (2) hypotension, (3) atrioventricular block, (4) a dangerous degree of bronchiolar constriction, and (5) an intensified hypoglycemic response in diabetic patients receiving insulin or oral hypoglycemic agents.

In the absence of severe ventricular damage or of the contraindications mentioned below, the beta-blockers are comparatively safe. Schizophrenic patients without cardiac disease have tolerated 3000 mg/d.

Intravenous administration is, however, hazardous. The drug must be given in small increments over a long period to avoid bradycardia, hypotension, and atrioventricular block with a very slow idioventricular rate.

Since the agonist-antagonist relation is competitive, hypotension can be treated with isoproterenol infusions. The bradycardia is in part relieved by atropine. Bronchospasm responds to isoproterenol or aminophylline.

C. Allergic Reactions: Skin rashes and thrombocytopenic purpura have been reported following propranolol administration.

D. Withdrawal: Abrupt discontinuance of propranolol in some patients with angina has led to increased angina, arrhythmias, and myocardial infarction. In other patients, a precipitous hypertension has appeared. In patients with angina and in probably all older patients, the drug should be reduced over a 2-week period. Abrupt withdrawal of propranolol from patients with known or unsuspected hyperthyroidism can cause an exacerbation of thyrotoxicosis.

Contraindications & Cautions

The reasons for the following contraindications to propranolol follow from the discussion of adverse effects: (1) Manifest or impending congestive heart failure. (2) Hypotension unless associated with an arrhythmia requiring treatment. Because of the suggestion that beta-blockers be used in the period immediately following a myocardial infarction, cardiogenic shock should be mentioned as a specific contraindication. (3) Complete heart block. (4) Asthma or other obstructive pulmonary diseases.

Propranolol should be used with special care in patients receiving any of the following: (1) insulin or oral hypoglycemic drugs, since the hypoglycemia may in theory be intensified; in practice the changes have been minor; (2) other sympathoplegic drugs—eg, reserpine, guanethidine, or methyldopa—because the effects are additive; and (3) various pressor drugs—sympathomimetic amines, ergot, MAO inhibitors—because, as in the treatment of pheochromocytomas, the augmented alpha-agonist effect may lead to hypertension.

Preparations

Propranolol (Inderal) is the nonselective beta-blocker with a wealth of recorded experience behind it. Nadolol (Corgard) is a propranolol congener with a longer duration of action.

Metaprolol (Lopressor) is cardioselective but only relatively so—ie, with larger doses, beta$_2$ blockade appears.

Among the beta-blockers that are marketed outside the US and will appear in reports of studies from those countries are acebutolol (Sectral), alprenolol, atenolol, oxyprenolol (Trasicor), pindolol (Visken), and sotalol.

Practolol, prominent in the early literature, has been abandoned because of its prohibitive noncardiac toxicity.

GANGLION BLOCKING AGENTS

The ganglion blocking agents are included in the group of sympathoplegic drugs even though they block transmission across both sympathetic and parasympathetic ganglia. Since they do achieve a chemical denervation of autonomic organs, the ganglion blockers are still useful laboratory tools. Until recently they were the most widely used and the most potent of the hypotensive drugs, and they must be mentioned to explain their prominent place in all but the most recent literature on the treatment of severe hypertension.

Chemistry, Classification, & Metabolism

The duration of action and usefulness following oral administration of the ganglion blocking agents are correlated with their chemical structure and provide a basis for classification.

A. Monoquaternary Ammonium and Sulfonium Compounds: Tetraethylammonium (TEA) and trimethaphan (Arfonad) are both filtered and actively secreted by the kidneys, and their duration of action is brief. When trimethaphan is used to produce a controlled postural hypotension, it is, therefore, given by continuous infusion. TEA is no longer used.

B. Bisquaternary Compounds: Many of these drugs were introduced for the treatment of hypertension and were of great value until replaced by newer agents—first by mecamylamine and then by guanethidine. Hexamethonium (C6) was the prototype drug, and pentolinium (Ansolysen) was probably the most widely used. As can be predicted by the fact that these quaternary amines are permanent cations—ie, always in ionized form at body pH—their absorption is incomplete and variable. The variability is increased by their action in decreasing intestinal motility.

C. Secondary Amine: Mecamylamine (Inversine) replaced the bisquaternaries and was widely and effectively used until the postganglionic blocking drugs appeared. Absorption is regular and complete.

D. Sparteine: Sparteine (Spartocin, Tocosamine) is an alkaloid isolated from broom top *(Cytisus scoparius)* (Fig 11–4).

Pharmacologic Actions

A. Mechanisms of Action: In the presence of a ganglion blocking drug, acetylcholine is still released by the preganglionic fiber. However, the postsynaptic membrane of the postganglionic fiber is not depolarized. This mechanism contrasts with the failure of repolarization caused by cholinomimetic drugs such as nicotine that can also block transmission at the ganglia (see Chapter 8).

B. Effects: The hypotension caused by the ganglion blocking agents is similar to that described in detail for the postganglionic blocking agents. In the normal human or experimental animal, arteriolar dilatation and venous dilatation both occur as a result of decreasing sympathetic control. In the hypertensive human, venous dilatation with peripheral pooling and a failure of venous return account for the decrease in cardiac output and consequent fall in blood pressure.

In humans and in unanesthetized animals, the pulse rate increases because the high vagal tone maintaining a slow rate is removed by parasympathetic ganglion blockade. In anesthetized animals with high initial pulse rates, the rate falls after administration of a ganglion blocking agent.

A decrease in gastrointestinal motility (sometimes to the point of ileus), urinary retention, dry mouth, loss of power of accommodation, pupillary dilatation, and impotence are side-effects due to parasympathetic blockade.

The effector tissues are still able to respond to

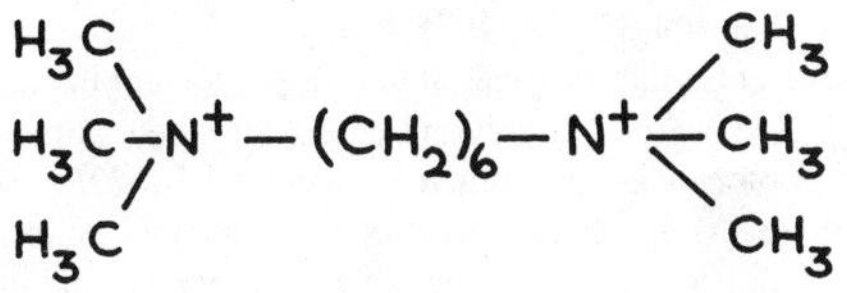

Hexamethonium (C6)

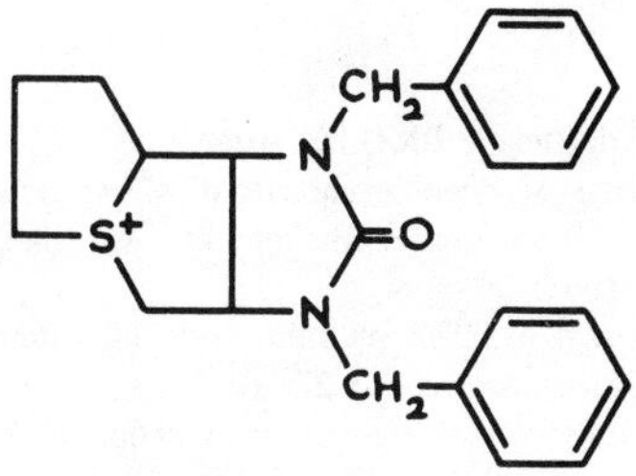

Trimethaphan (Arfonad)

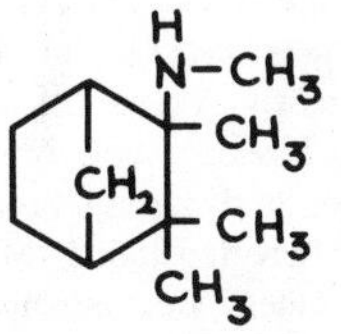

Mecamylamine (Inversine)

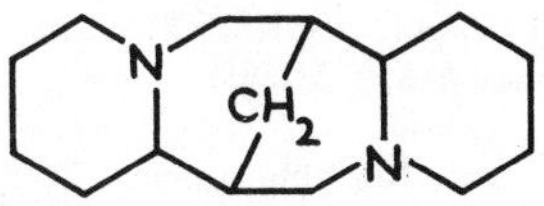

Sparteine
(Spartocin, Tocosamine)

Figure 11–4. Structures of some ganglion blocking agents.

mediators, and the decrease in gastrointestinal motility, for example, may be treated with neostigmine or bethanechol.

Sparteine blocks ganglionic transmission but also has curariform effects and acts directly on the heart to slow the rate. It is used to stimulate uterine activity at term—an action that also occurs, though possibly less intensely, with the other ganglion blocking agents and with other procedures—eg, spinal anesthesia—that reduce sympathetic influences on the uterus.

Clinical Uses

A. Hypotension During Anesthesia: Trimethaphan is sometimes used by continuous intravenous infusion to induce a controlled postural hypotension and so reduce bleeding during surgical procedures on the head and neck.

B. Induction or Augmentation of Uterine Contractions: Sparteine is used as an oxytocic agent, but preferable alternative drugs—ie, oxytocin and ergonovine—are available.

C. Hypertensive Emergencies: In cases of malignant (accelerated) hypertension, when immediate treatment is judged necessary, the ganglion blocking agents are still sometimes used by injection.

D. Investigative Uses: These agents are used investigatively to reduce or abolish all nervous influences on an autonomic tissue. Interpretation of such experiments should recognize that ganglionic synapses, intrinsic as well as extrinsic to the tissue, are blocked. In addition to blocking ganglionic transmis-

sion, TEA and, to a lesser degree, trimethaphan in large or repeated doses show effects due to the release of catecholamines from the adrenal medulla and from adrenergic nerves.

Contraindications & Cautions

The ganglion blocking agents should not be used when a precipitous fall in blood pressure would be dangerous—eg, in the presence of vascular disease.

Dosages

Trimethaphan is the principal drug of this group. Occasions for the use of other ganglion blocking agents are unusual.

Trimethaphan camphorsulfonate (Arfonad): Dilute in 500 mL of saline solution and adjust the rate of infusion to achieve the desired fall in blood pressure.

Mecamylamine hydrochloride (Inversine): When mecamylamine is used in the treatment of hypertension, a diuretic and reserpine should also be used (as when guanethidine is used). The initial dose of 2.5 mg twice daily orally is increased by increments of 2.5 mg of the daily dose every 2–3 days until the desired response is achieved. Control of the dosage must allow for the postural nature of the hypotension and the development of a limited degree of tolerance. All of the suggestions and cautions discussed for the use of guanethidine (Ismelin) or other potent hypotensive drugs (see Chapter 12) apply to mecamylamine also.

•   •   •

References

Alpha-Adrenergic Blocking Agents

Goldfien A: Pheochromocytoma: Diagnosis and anesthetic and surgical management. Anesthesiology 24:462, 1963.

Nickerson M: The pharmacology of adrenergic blockage. Pharmacol Rev 1:27, 1949.

Ross EJ & others: Preoperative and operative management of patients with phaeochromocytoma. Br Med J 1:191, 1967.

Scott HW Jr & others: Pheochromocytoma: Present diagnosis and management. Ann Surg 183:587, 1976.

Sokolow M, McIlroy MB: Systemic hypertension. Chap 9 in: *Clinical Cardiology,* 2nd ed. Lange, 1979.

Sullivan JA, Solomon HS: The diagnosis of pheochromocytoma. JAMA 231:618, 1975.

Beta-Adrenergic Blocking Agents

Bühler FR & others: Propranolol inhibition of renin secretion. N Engl J Med 287:1209, 1972.

Connolly ME, Kersting F, Dollery CT: The clinical pharmacology of beta-adrenoceptor-blocking drugs. Prog Cardiovasc Dis 19:203, 1976.

Feek CM & others: Combination of potassium iodide and propranolol in preparation of patients with Graves' disease for thyroid surgery. N Engl J Med 302:883, 1980.

Kosman ME: Timolol in the treatment of open-angle glaucoma. JAMA 241:2238, 1979.

Miller RR & others: Efficacy of beta adrenergic blockade in coronary heart disease: Propranolol in angina pectoris. Clin Pharmacol Ther 18:598, 1975.

Miller RR & others: Propranolol-withdrawal rebound phenomenon. N Engl J Med 293:416, 1975. [Also Am J Cardiol 35:162, 1975.]

Multicentre International Study: Improvement in prognosis of myocardial infarction by long-term beta-adrenoreceptor blockade using practolol. Br Med J 3:735, 1975.

Roland JM & others: Effect of beta-blockers on arrhythmias during six weeks after suspected myocardial infarction. Br Med J 2:518, 1979.

Scriabine A: Beta-chemoreceptor blocking drugs in hypertension. Ann Rev Pharmacol 19:269, 1979.

Toft AD & others: Propranolol in the surgical treatment of thyrotoxicosis: A report of 100 cases treated with propranolol before operation. N Engl J Med 298:643, 1978.

VA Cooperative Study Group: Propranolol in the treatment of essential hypertension. JAMA 237:2303, 1977.

Wright AD & others: Beta-adrenoceptor-blocking drugs and blood sugar control in diabetes mellitus. Br Med J 1:159, 1979.

Wright P: Untoward effects associated with practolol administration: Oculomucocutaneous syndrome. Br Med J 1:595, 1975.

Yorkston NJ: Propranolol in the control of schizophrenic symptoms. Br Med J 4:633, 1974.

Zonszein J & others: Propranolol therapy in thyrotoxicosis: A review of 84 patients undergoing surgery. Am J Med 66:411, 1979.

Ganglion Blocking Agents

Paton WDM, Zaimis EJ: The methonium compounds. (3 parts.) Pharmacol Rev 2:60, 1950; 4:219, 1952; 6:59, 1954.

Drug Treatment of Essential Hypertension | 12

In Chapter 11, drugs that limit sympathetic influence on blood vessels and other tissues were classified according to their pharmacologic mechanism of action. In this chapter, several of the sympathoplegic drugs are discussed in greater detail, but the classification and emphasis are in terms of their therapeutic use. This apparent inconsistency conforms to common usage and emphasizes the great importance of hypertension as a problem in therapeutics.

Essential hypertension (ie, hypertension of unknown cause) is by far the most common form of elevated blood pressure. Hypertension may also be due to renal or endocrine causes for which specific surgical or medical treatment is available. The drugs available will lower elevated blood pressure regardless of the cause, but they obviously should not be used as a substitute for specific treatment of a correctable underlying disorder.

The elevated blood pressure of essential hypertension is due to arteriolar constriction and related to volume overload and elevated plasma renin levels. The mortality and morbidity rates are not directly related to the arteriolar disorder, however, but to the effect of the sustained high blood pressure. A sustained elevation of blood pressure accelerates the rate of progression of the atherosclerotic process in larger arteries; causes additional arteriolar damage; and greatly increases the work of the heart. Consequently, essential hypertension is damaging because of the development of cardiac hypertrophy and of coronary artery, cerebrovascular, retinal, and renal arteriolar disease with subsequent congestive heart failure, myocardial infarction, strokes, renal failure, and uremia. It is important to point out that lowering blood pressure with drugs will slow the progression of all of the above processes. Some—eg, congestive failure—will regress with treatment of hypertension.

It does not follow that the lowering of blood pressure with drugs is necessarily accomplished by reversing the disease process that caused the elevation. However, if blood pressure is lowered by any mechanism, great benefits result. After the individual drugs have been discussed, the problems of clinical evaluation of the drugs used in the treatment of hypertension will be outlined and the benefits that have resulted from treatment will again be mentioned.

Essential hypertension is a process of variable course and severity. The intensity of the treatment required will be correspondingly variable. However, the variation in intensity is not achieved, as in most situations, by increasing the dose of one drug but by adding stepwise or "layering" additional drugs as required to return blood pressure to normal. Depending upon the needs of the specific patient, one or more of the following drug classes will be used: (1) Thiazide or similar diuretic: Treatment is invariably initiated with a diuretic of the thiazide or other type. Except in the mildest cases, a drug from the following class must be added to the regimen. (2) Central sympathoplegics: These include drugs such as reserpine, methyldopa, propranolol, or clonidine that act on the central nervous system to reduce sympathetic outflow. If the blood pressure has still not been restored to a normal level, a drug from either of the next 2 classes must be added. (3) Potent or postural hypotensive drugs such as guanethidine, an adrenergic neuron blocker. (4) Drugs such as hydralazine that are vasodilators due to a peripheral effect rather than a sympathoplegic action. (5) Angiotensin blocking drugs such as captopril.

THIAZIDES & OTHER DIURETICS

The general pharmacology of the diuretics is discussed in Chapter 17, where emphasis is placed on the ability of the thiazides and other sodium diuretics to decrease the renal tubular reabsorption of sodium. The resultant ability of the thiazides to prevent the sodium retention caused by all of the hypotensive drugs discussed below is one reason for their invariable use in the treatment of hypertension. However, they also have a weak arteriolar dilating effect that is not directly linked to their ability to increase sodium excretion.

The above 2 ideas will be expanded here, but Chapter 17 should be reviewed for additional information.

A. Hypotensive Effect of Thiazides: Thiazides do not lower blood pressure in normotensive humans. In patients with essential hypertension, blood pressure may be decreased 10% or more. For a brief period after diuretic therapy is instituted, plasma volume is decreased, and the fall in blood pressure during this

Table 12–1. Reserpine and related drugs: Chemical structures and preparations available.

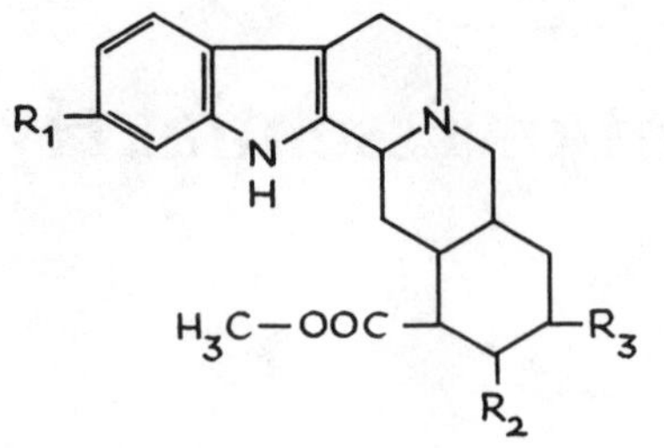

	R$_1$	R$_2$	R$_3$	Usual Daily Adult Dose
Reserpine	–O–CH$_3$	–O–CH$_3$	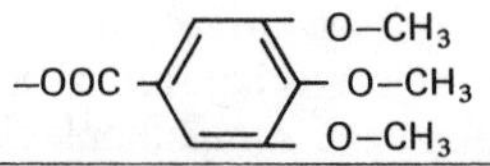 –OOC (trimethoxybenzoyl: O–CH$_3$, O–CH$_3$, O–CH$_3$)	0.25 mg
Deserpidine (Harmonyl)	–H	–O–CH$_3$	(Same as reserpine)	0.25 mg
Rescinnamine (Moderil)	–O–CH$_3$	–O–CH$_3$	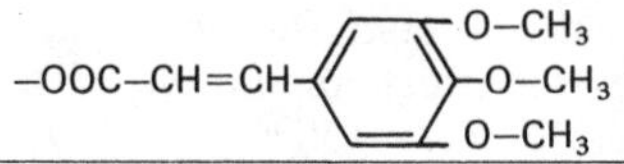 –OOC–CH=CH– (trimethoxycinnamoyl: O–CH$_3$, O–CH$_3$, O–CH$_3$)	0.5 mg
Yohimbine	–H	–OH	–H	*
Crude root (Raudixin, etc)				100 mg

*No therapeutic applications.

period is explained by a decrease in cardiac output rather than by any decrease in total peripheral resistance. After 1–4 weeks, plasma volume and cardiac output return almost to control values and the fall in blood pressure is then due primarily to arteriolar dilatation. At this time, plasma reexpansion by transfusion does not abolish the hypotensive effect.

The mechanism by which these drugs cause arteriolar dilatation is not simply a loss of either sodium or potassium but may be some undefined ion shift at the smooth muscle of blood vessels. Supplementary potassium does not reverse the hypotensive action, and some of the diuretics listed in Chapter 17 are hypotensive but do not increase potassium loss. Sodium loss may not be essential, since a chemically related compound, diazoxide, is an even better hypotensive agent than the thiazides even though it is not a sodium diuretic.

B. Thiazide Diuretics in Combination With Other Drugs: The thiazide diuretics by themselves lower blood pressure slightly and prevent the progression of essential hypertension in many or most cases. When they are given concomitantly with one of the hypotensive drugs discussed below, the effect becomes quite significant. In cases requiring the use of additional hypotensive agents, the thiazides act to reduce the amount of the second drug necessary (and, therefore, its side-effects). They act both through their inherent hypotensive action and through their ability to prevent the expansion of plasma volume.

Chronic administration of the thiazides is well tolerated in this situation; their toxic effects are discussed in Chapter 17. If the response to the usual doses of a thiazide—eg, hydrochlorothiazide, 50–100 mg daily—is not adequate, nothing is gained by increasing the dosage and a second drug must be added to the treatment regimen.

CENTRAL SYMPATHOPLEGICS

1. RESERPINE

One of the drugs that is often added to a thiazide is reserpine. By itself, reserpine is only a weak hypotensive drug, but it is extremely useful in combination with a diuretic or postural hypotensive agent.

Source & Chemistry

Reserpine is the purified alkaloid of *Rauwolfia*, or snakeroot. It occurs in many plants of the genus *Rauwolfia* (Apocynaceae, or dogbane family), but *Rauwolfia serpentina,* the Indian snakeroot, is the usual source. A number of natural and semisynthetic alkaloids other than reserpine are available, but reserpine is the one in widest use. The chemical structures are shown in Table 12–1.

Pharmacologic Actions

A. Mechanisms of Action: Reserpine is an antipsychotic and reduces sympathetic tone. Studies stimulated by the finding that reserpine depletes the organism of norepinephrine, dopamine, and serotonin

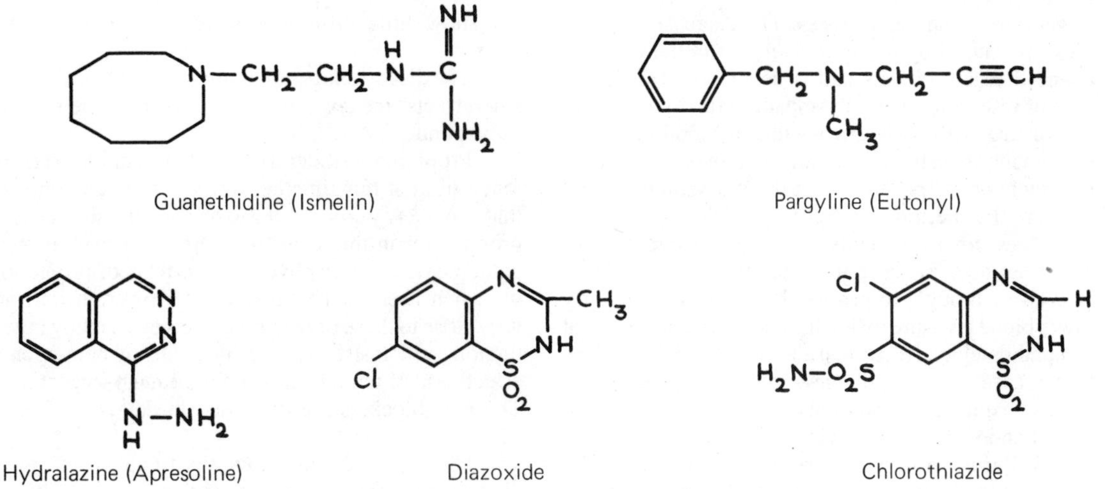

Figure 12-1. Chemical structures of certain hypotensive drugs discussed in this chapter.

have contributed information about the mechanism of action of many drugs.

1. Amine depletion–Norepinephrine is stored in granules within sympathetic nerves, in chromaffin cells in the atria and blood vessels, and in some areas of the central nervous system, notably the hypothalamus. Serotonin (5-hydroxytryptamine, discussed further in Chapter 19) is stored in granules in mast cells, in platelets, in argentaffin cells distributed along the gastrointestinal tract, and in the central nervous system in association with norepinephrine. Dopamine occurs in association with norepinephrine and also without accompanying norepinephrine in the substantia nigra and basal ganglia. Reserpine administration is followed at first by evidence of liberation and elevated circulating levels of these 3 amines or their metabolites; subsequently, the amounts of the amines found in brain, sympathetic nerves, and other sites of storage are reduced. Reserpine exerts a persistent effect in preventing the reaccumulation of amines in storage granules. It is tempting to conclude at once that the sympathoplegic effect of reserpine is due to depletion of norepinephrine from sympathetic nerves and that its tranquilizing effect is due to decreased levels of norepinephrine or serotonin in the hypothalamus. However, the phenothiazine tranquilizers exert behavioral effects almost identical with those of reserpine but have no effect on amine storage or metabolism. The sympathoplegic effect of reserpine, at least in therapeutic dosages, may be central rather than peripheral in origin.

2. Central or peripheral sympathoplegic action–Early experimental work ascribed the sympathoplegic effect of reserpine to a central nervous system (probably hypothalamic) site of action. Current pharmacologic opinion, however, considers that the peripheral effect on sympathetic nerve may also be important.

There are practical reasons for regarding this question as unsettled. Most importantly, although reserpine does reduce sympathetic influences on blood vessels, it does not cause postural hypotension in usual oral doses. All other drugs that effectively block sympathetic activity peripherally do cause postural hypotension. After reserpine administration, some of the reflexes responsible for maintaining blood pressure in the face of a change to the erect position remain intact, which suggests that cord or medullary centers are still able to exert an effect through sympathetic nerves.

In experimental animals, sympathetic nerve retains some functional ability after all but the very largest doses of reserpine. Perhaps the site of the sympathoplegic action of reserpine can be agreed upon only if the dosage is stipulated. In any case, in the dosages used clinically, most sympathetically mediated reflexes are retained, even when unequivocal evidence of decreased sympathetic effects on organs is also present.

3. Sympathoplegic or parasympathomimetic action–The therapeutically useful sympathoplegic effects of reserpine are accompanied by side-effects that can be interpreted as due to a loss of sympathetic inhibitory tone. Augmented parasympathetic activity has been proposed as an alternative explanation, and reciprocal action on the "ergotropic" and "trophotropic" areas of the hypothalamus has also been suggested. The experiments underlying this interpretation are all based on the idea that a side-effect blocked by atropine or by a ganglion blocking agent must originate from the action of extrinsic parasympathetic nerves. As has been discussed in earlier chapters, both atropine and the ganglion blocking agents act on intrinsic automaticity and have actions distinct from those of parasympathetic nerve action.

B. Effects:

1. Sympathetic inhibition–The sympatholytic action of reserpine results in a limited amount of vasodilatation that may be apparent as a flush, a feeling of warmth, or nasal stuffiness. The decrease in blood pressure caused by reserpine is minor in humans and unanesthetized animals and is never postural. In the case of reserpine, then, a sympatholytic effect cannot be equated with a significant fall in blood pressure, presumably because the central site of action allows the retention of postural reflexes maintaining blood pressure. Furthermore, increasing the dosage of reserpine does not appreciably increase the hypotensive effect but does increase the side-effects.

Even though reserpine does not significantly lower blood pressure by itself, it does have a persistent sympathoplegic effect. Its usefulness lies in its ability to increase the effectiveness of other hypotensive agents, reducing the amounts of the other agents required and so reducing their side-effects.

2. Parasympathetic predominance–The side-effects of reserpine can be ascribed to loss of sympathetic inhibitory influences and consequent predominance of intrinsic or parasympathetic activity. These include increased gastrointestinal motility, manifested as cramps or diarrhea; increased gastric acid secretion; bradycardia; and pupillary constriction.

3. Antipsychotic type of behavioral depression–Reserpine can be used to control psychotic behavior but was very early replaced by the phenothiazine tranquilizers in the institutional practice of psychiatry. Reserpine does, however, cause a type of sedation or depression characteristic of the antipsychotic or major tranquilizers (see Chapter 25).

4. Central nervous system stimulation–As is true also of the drugs used primarily for their antipsychotic effect, the tranquilizing action of reserpine in high doses is accompanied by signs of central nervous system stimulation. Extrapyramidal signs and convulsions do not occur with the small doses of reserpine used today, but were demonstrated in the past. Even when given in the doses used in the treatment of hypertension, reserpine may cause nightmares or a change in sleep pattern.

Absorption, Metabolism, & Excretion

Reserpine itself—but not necessarily all of its analogs—is well absorbed after oral administration.

Following discontinuance of reserpine medication, the tranquilizer effects persist for about 2 days and the autonomic actions for about 7–10 days. It may be a month before serotonin blood levels return to normal.

Clinical Uses

When the response to a thiazide alone is not adequate, one of the central sympathoplegics is sometimes added to the regimen. Which of the 4 available agents is chosen first is a matter of individual judgment, preference, and familiarity.

Clinical comparisons of reserpine, propranolol, methyldopa, and clonidine would ideally compare equivalent doses or a range of doses of the central sympathoplegic drugs used in combination with a constant dose of thiazide. Such studies are few in number

but show little difference in efficacy among the 4 drugs.

The disadvantages of methyldopa are the frequent side-effects, the cost, and the failure of some patients to respond.

Propranolol (Inderal) and other beta-blockers are much used at this time because of theoretic concerns that, for a few years, tended to obscure the similarity of propranolol in this context to the other central sympathoplegics. Descriptively, the effects of propranolol, when used in the treatment of hypertension, are very close to those of reserpine. However, many investigators still insist that the blockade of beta-agonist effects and of renin release are of primary importance. The beta-blockers are discussed in detail in Chapter 11.

Clonidine (Catapres) causes frequent and more diverse side-effects than do the other 3 classes. Its use is more difficult for the patient and the physician, and it should probably be tried only if the other 3 are not tolerated.

A given patient may tolerate one drug better than another, but in general the patient who finds the depression unpleasant will be intolerant of all drugs of this class.

Reserpine is used in small doses, eg, 0.1–0.25 mg orally per day. Another hypotensive agent may be given concurrently.

Adverse Reactions

Since allergic reactions to reserpine have not been reported and since the acute toxicity is extremely low, all adverse effects can be considered side-effects. There is no advantage to increasing the dose above 0.25 mg/d, and at these dosage levels side-effects are infrequent.

Of the side-effects related to autonomic function, bradycardia and miosis are persistent. Feelings of warmth, salivation, stomach cramps or diarrhea, and nasal congestion are usually transient complaints. Reserpine augments gastric acid secretion and can activate or initiate peptic ulcer. Even this action is minimal at daily doses of 0.25 mg or less.

Behavioral side-effects are seen even with small doses. The "tranquilizing" effect is not pleasant—as is the sedation following the use of alcohol or other sedatives, which is pleasant or euphoriant—and many patients complain of a lethargic feeling when taking reserpine. A rare patient will experience a depression in mood sufficiently severe to represent a suicidal risk, and this risk is greatly increased with larger doses. Increased appetite and dreaming are common; nightmares are infrequent complaints. Excitement, extrapyramidal motor disorders, and convulsions occurred following the administration of the huge doses required in psychiatric practice in the past.

Sodium retention with edema occurs occasionally, and nonpuerperal lactation rarely.

Contraindications & Cautions

Reserpine is contraindicated in the presence of

depression in the behavioral or psychiatric sense; when, as in ulcerative colitis, increased gastrointestinal motility would be harmful; and in any patient with a history of peptic ulcer. The latter is not an absolute contraindication if the recommended small doses (0.25 mg/d or less) are used and an ulcer regimen is provided.

Administration of an anesthetic to a patient receiving reserpine may lead to hypotension. This can be avoided by discontinuing reserpine for 2 weeks before elective surgery. However, the hypotension can be reversed by sympathomimetics of both the direct-acting—eg, norepinephrine—and indirect-acting—eg, ephedrine—types. The response to a given dose of sympathomimetics may be greater than expected.

Preparations Available (Table 12–1)
Reserpine, known also by many trade names, is the standard drug of this group. It is inexpensive unless ordered by certain brand names. Combinations of reserpine and a thiazide diuretic in fixed proportions are available and may provide an example of justifiable use of such combinations provided that inexpensive generic preparations are ordered.

No advantage has been established clinically for the alternative preparations listed in Table 12–1.

2. METHYLDOPA
(Aldomet)

The place of methyldopa in the treatment of hypertension has been confused by the undue influence of shifting theories concerning its mechanism of action. Heralded at first as an agent as potent as guanethidine but causing little or no postural hypotension, its similarity to reserpine in effects, potency, and side-effects is now recognized.

Chemistry
Fig 10–4 shows the relation of methyldopa (alpha-methyldopa) to the precursors of norepinephrine.

Pharmacologic Actions
A. Mechanisms of Action: Norepinephrine is synthesized through the reaction steps tyrosine → dopa → dopamine → norepinephrine. Methyldopa differs from dopa in that, like ephedrine or amphetamine, it bears an added methyl group on the carbon that adjoins the amine group.

Methyldopa—like dopa, which is discussed in Chapter 30 as a precursor of dopamine, used in the treatment of parkinsonism—enters the central nervous system and exerts sympathoplegic and behavioral depressant effects similar to those of reserpine. Sympathetic nerve reactivity is retained—ie, as described for reserpine (above), the site of action is high enough in the central nervous system that reflex sympathetic ac-

tivity is retained and postural hypotension is not severe when it occurs.

The mechanism of the central nervous system effect is not known, but 2 theories are still discussed. The drug was originally synthesized as one of a series of decarboxylase inhibitors, ie, agents such as those discussed in Chapter 30, that would prevent the decarboxylation of dopa to dopamine. However, the limited effectiveness of methyldopa in this regard has no relation to its hypotensive action.

Another hypothesis suggests, with some experimental basis, that methyldopa must be metabolized in the central nervous system to alpha-methylnorepinephrine. The metabolite then interacts somehow with norepinephrine, possibly by acting as a "false transmitter"—eg, a substance replacing norepinephrine in the central nervous system and liberated in place of it but lacking its mediating property.

Alpha-methylnorepinephrine is a potent vasoconstrictor, so that the concept of the false neurotransmitter cannot be applied to peripheral sympathetic nerve.

B. Effects: In the usual dosage, methyldopa is as effective as reserpine. The fall in blood pressure is probably explained by a decrease in cardiac output and a fall in systemic vascular resistance. In addition, methyldopa has sedating effects.

Absorption, Metabolism, & Excretion
Methyldopa is well absorbed after oral administration, but the onset of its action is delayed for 4–6 hours after oral administration and for 1–2 hours even after intravenous administration. The effect of a single dose may last for 24 hours, and it takes 2–3 days to determine the effect of a particular dosage regimen. Methyldopa is excreted in the urine largely unchanged, and its use can interfere with tests for urinary catecholamines.

Clinical Uses
Methyldopa is one of 4 central sympathoplegic, hypotensive agents added as a second step in treatment when the effect of a thiazide is not adequate. The difficulty in choosing among the 4 is discussed above under clinical uses of reserpine.

Adverse Reactions
A. Side-Effects: Methyldopa sometimes causes the expected bradycardia, diarrhea, dry mouth, and failure of ejaculation. It also causes many of the central nervous system effects seen with reserpine or other antipsychotics: unpleasant sedation, depressed mood, nightmares, and even, in a few instances, lactation and extrapyramidal effects. Tiredness and fatigability may be extreme enough to force discontinuance of the drug in 10–20% of patients.

B. Allergic Reactions: Drug fever is a rare result of treatment with methyldopa. A mild, reversible elevation of hepatic enzymes in serum with biopsy evidence of cellular damage can also occur, often in association with drug fever, myocarditis, or other evidence of an allergic reaction. In addition, methyldopa can lead to a positive direct Coombs test and, rarely, to hemolytic anemia.

Contraindications & Cautions

Because of the effects on liver function mentioned above, methyldopa should not be used in the presence of hepatitis of any kind. Its depressant effects intensify the action of sedatives and are additive to the action of other antipsychotics, including the other 3 hypotensives of the class.

Dosages

The usual initial dose of methyldopa (Aldomet) is 250 mg twice daily. When methyldopa is given in combination with a diuretic, little is gained by increasing the dose above 500–750 mg/d. Dosages as high as 2 g/d may be used, but with great increase in the number and intensity of side-effects. Methyldopate hydrochloride (Aldomet ester hydrochloride), is available in ampules for intravenous administration.

3. BETA–ADRENERGIC BLOCKING AGENTS

Propranolol (Inderal) is frequently used in the treatment of hypertension, always in combination with a thiazide and often with a third drug added to the regimen. The possible mechanisms of its hypotensive effect are discussed in Chapter 11, where it is emphasized that propranolol has actions similar to those described for reserpine or methyldopa.

4. CLONIDINE (Catapres)

Chemistry

The structure of clonidine is shown in Fig 11–1 to emphasize its relationship to tolazoline (Priscoline), another imidazoline with multiple and complex pharmacologic effects.

Pharmacologic Actions

A. Mechanism of Action: Clonidine, like reserpine and methyldopa, acts on an undefined site in the central nervous system to reduce outflow along the sympathetic nerves. It is one central sympatholytic for which a demonstration of its suprasegmental site of action in humans is available in that the hypotensive effect is not seen in individuals with spinal cord transections above the origin of the sympathetic outflow. It is an alpha-adrenergic agonist and causes a brief initial rise in blood pressure if given intravenously.

B. Effects: By itself and given chronically, clonidine may produce little hypotensive effect. Since single doses do lower blood pressure, the limited effect of chronic administration probably reflects the expansion of plasma volume caused by any hypotensive drug except the diuretics. Combined with a diuretic, it is as efficacious as methyldopa, ie, blood pressure is lowered when the patient is supine, and hypotension is only slightly augmented in the erect position. Other effects are listed under adverse reactions, below.

Clinical Uses

Clonidine is used as an alternative to reserpine, propranolol, or methyldopa when those drugs are not tolerated. See further discussion under clinical uses of reserpine, p 108.

It has demonstrated effectiveness in reducing the number of attacks of migraine. The dosage used (0.025 mg twice daily) is smaller than the amounts used in hypertension.

Another careful trial establishes that small doses are also useful in reducing the vascular instability (and flushing) associated with the menopause. Reserpine and propranolol have also been suggested for these investigative uses.

Adverse Reactions

A. Side-Effects: Reported side-effects include the bradycardia, dry mouth, and failure of ejaculation predicted by the sympathoplegic action, and constipation and headache.

Sedation (drowsiness, depression) is frequent and, because the unpleasant feeling may be quite intense shortly after ingestion of a dose, is more troublesome than with the other central sympathoplegics.

B. Withdrawal State: The administration of clonidine must be maintained on a rigid schedule. If chronic medication is abruptly discontinued—ie, if a single dose is missed—the patient may experience a state of hyperexcitability with restlessness, insomnia, headache, tremulousness, ventricular ectopic activity, and a rapid rise of blood pressure to or above pretreatment levels. Deaths have been reported. Readministration of clonidine may not terminate the episode, and an alpha-blocking agent (phentolamine) may be required. A similar but very mild withdrawal state is seen after abrupt cessation of treatment with guanethidine but not with any other hypotensive agent.

Contraindications & Cautions

The physician must be willing to monitor the effect of individual doses of clonidine until a stable response is established. The patient must understand and agree to comply with the need for uninterrupted dosage. Withdrawal—ie, to change medication or in anticipation of surgery—must be anticipated and carried out over about 1 week.

Additive effects with other depressants are as described for reserpine and methyldopa.

Dosages

The initial dose of clonidine (Catapres) is 0.1 mg/d given at bedtime. Dosage is gradually increased to the usual level of 0.2–0.8 mg/d given in 2 doses.

Clonidine has a duration of action that is brief in comparison with the other central sympathoplegics. The effect is most evenly maintained by giving the drug 3–4 times each day. Under such a regimen, side-effects may be maintained as constantly as the desired effect, and most patients prefer to decrease their discomfort during the day by taking a full dose of clonidine at bedtime and a half dose in the morning.

POSTURAL HYPOTENSIVE DRUGS

The thiazide diuretics alone may suffice for the treatment of the mildest hypertensive patients. Reserpine combined with a thiazide will meet the needs of another large group. For the more severe treatment problems, however, additional drugs must be employed.

1. ADRENERGIC NEURON BLOCKING AGENTS

Drugs of this class are also known as postganglionic blocking agents. As these designations suggest, these drugs act to prevent the release of norepinephrine from the sympathetic nerve endings.

Chemistry

Guanethidine (Ismelin) is currently the important member of this class (Fig 12–1). Several similar drugs are available elsewhere but not marketed in the USA. They are bethanidine (Esbatal) and debrisoquin (Declinax). Bretylium, the first drug of this class, is now available for treatment of ventricular arrhythmias.

Pharmacologic Actions

A. Mechanism of Action: Guanethedine prevents the liberation of mediator by postganglionic sympathetic neurons. Sympathetic or adrenergic influences on blood vessels are reduced, and venous dilatation results.

During the guanethidine action, the effector tissue is still responsive to injected mediator, but electrical stimulation of the postganglionic fibers is without effect. Transmission across the ganglionic synapse is unimpaired. Because of the order in which the drugs were introduced, it was convenient to distinguish these postganglionic blocking agents from the ganglion blocking agents, used earlier, but the phrase "adrenergic neuron blocking agents" more clearly describes the activity that is limited to the sympathetic division of the autonomic nervous system.

Guanethidine is taken up by sympathetic nerve through the same pathway utilized for the reentry of norepinephrine. It replaces some norepinephrine in granules, and perhaps it becomes a false transmitter, ie, is liberated in place of norepinephrine. Whatever the mechanism, the interference with norepinephrine release develops very rapidly.

After chronic administration of guanethidine, sympathetic nerve is depleted of norepinephrine. However, the process is too slow to explain the action of guanethidine, especially since the equivalent drugs bethanidine and debrisoquin do not deplete the adrenergic neuron of its mediator but do prevent its release.

The fact that norepinephrine reentry and guanethidine uptake utilize a common pathway has 2 consequences: First, the same agents that block norepinephrine reentry—sympathomimetics of the ephedrine type, phenoxybenzamine, cocaine, tricyclic antidepressants, and antipsychotics—can prevent or reverse the action of guanethidine. In addition, blockade of norepinephrine re-uptake by guanethidine causes a transient initial sympathomimetic effect that is apparent in humans only after intravenous administration.

Central nervous system amines are not altered, since the polar guanethidine does not reach parenchymal central nervous system cells.

B. Effects:

1. Hypotension–The fall in blood pressure caused by guanethidine can be made as intense as desired with the patient in the upright position. When the patient is recumbent, the decrease in blood pressure is much less marked.

2. Mechanism of postural hypotension–In the hypertensive human, the decrease in blood pressure induced by guanethidine is not due to arteriolar dilatation but to dilatation of veins with peripheral pooling, a decreased venous return, and consequent decrease in cardiac output.

Mean arterial blood pressure (MAP) depends upon stroke volume (V_{St}) and upon total peripheral resistance (TPR), ie, the resistance to flow provided by the arterioles as blood flows from the elastic arteries into the tissues. Stroke volume depends upon force of contraction and also upon venous return, which can vary inversely with the size of the capacitance vessels and with the plasma volume available to fill them:

$$MAP \propto V_{St} \cdot TPR$$

Following administration of guanethidine (and other postural hypotensive agents) to hypertensive humans, cardiac output (CO) falls to a degree sufficient to explain the fall in blood pressure. The ratio of MAP/CO—ie, TPR—is not significantly altered. Only in normal humans or experimental animals whose arterioles have not been damaged by hypertension does a decrease in TPR as well as a decrease in CO occur, establishing the occurrence of arteriolar dilatation.

That venous pooling is an important factor in the

action of guanethidine was predicted by clinical observations on the effect of posture and the ability of bandages on the lower extremities or immersion of the patient to abolish the hypotension. Bandages and immersion would be expected to collapse veins but not to alter the caliber of the arterioles with their higher internal pressures.

3. Tolerance–A limited degree of tolerance develops early during treatment with guanethidine. To continue to achieve the same hypotensive effect, it may be necessary to slowly increase the dose as much as 10-fold. In about 2 weeks, however, a dosage plateau is reached and no additional increase is necessary. It was observed that sensitivity to guanethidine could be restored by bleeding or by the simultaneous administration of a sodium diuretic, and that sensitivity could be decreased—ie, tolerance induced—by infusion of plasma or other fluid. Direct measurements then established that the patient's plasma volume increases concurrently with the development of guanethidine tolerance. Whatever the mechanism by which dilatation of the capacitance vessels leads to an increase in plasma volume, the increase does not continue beyond 10–12%, and the degree to which tolerance develops is correspondingly limited. Concomitant administration of a diuretic also limits tolerance.

4. Other effects–Pulse rate is slowed, and an increase in gastrointestinal motility is seen. The hypersecretion of gastric acid that occurs with reserpine does not occur with guanethidine, but diarrhea is common. The excessive motility appears most commonly after eating, and the postprandial diarrhea may be explosive and embarrassing. It can usually be controlled with atropine. With large doses, ejaculation may be delayed or prevented, but—in contrast with the action of the ganglion blocking drugs—erection is not impaired. Muscle weakness or tremor of unknown origin also appears, more commonly with the now rarely used bretylium than after the usual doses of guanethidine. Guanethidine causes a marked decrease in intraocular pressure in glaucomatous eyes.

Absorption, Metabolism, & Excretion

Guanethidine is variably absorbed after oral administration, but the pharmacologic effect develops slowly. On a given daily dose, a stable, maximum effect is reached in 2–3 weeks, and an interval of at least that length should be allowed between changes in dosage schedule.

Guanethidine is excreted by the kidneys, mostly without chemical change.

Clinical Uses

Guanethidine is used in the treatment of severe hypertension. Combinations of diuretics, vasodilators such as hydralazine, and beta-adrenergic blockers have superseded the use of guanethidine in almost all cases.

Adverse Reactions

The side-effects of guanethidine are listed above.

Postural hypotension is not a side-effect but is the primary action of the potent hypotensive drugs. Faintness and fainting are undesirable effects that can be minimized by reducing the amount of guanethidine required by concomitant treatment with reserpine and a thiazide. Any vasodilating influence will intensify the postural hypotension and increase the likelihood of fainting. For example, prolonged standing, alcohol, or heat may cause fainting (especially after exercise).

Contraindications & Cautions

The patient should be instructed about factors that intensify postural hypotension and warned against getting up suddenly from a lying position.

Guanethidine and all of the drugs that decrease sympathetic outflow—ie, all those discussed in this chapter except the diuretics and hydralazine—can decrease cardiac output and cause sodium retention and edema in a patient already verging on congestive heart failure. Concurrent administration of a diuretic will prevent this effect. Edema appears early in the treatment of hypertension before the benefits of lowering blood pressure act on the heart.

Treatment with all of the hypotensive drugs should be initiated very cautiously in the presence of even early renal failure, since an abruptly lowered perfusion pressure could temporarily further reduce renal function.

Guanethidine and other agents that have an initial sympathomimetic effect should not be used if pheochromocytoma is possibly present.

Guanethidine effects are reversed by antidepressants, tranquilizers of the phenothiazine type, amphetamine, and cocaine.

Dosages

In general, guanethidine should replace rather than be added to reserpine or methyldopa when these drugs are ineffective. The initial dose of 10 mg orally is gradually increased at weekly intervals, allowing for the development of tolerance, until the desired response is maintained. The dose should be adjusted on the basis of blood pressure readings taken after the patient has been in the erect position for about 10 minutes. Dosage adjustments are usually in 10- or 12.5-mg increments to a total of 25–50 mg/d. The dose is reduced if severe diarrhea occurs even if an optimal lowering of blood pressure has not been obtained.

2. MAO INHIBITORS

The monoamine oxidase (MAO) inhibitors are central nervous system stimulants discussed in Chapter 28. The postural hypotension described in that context as an adverse reaction is selectively increased in pargyline (Eutonyl), which is utilized infrequently in the treatment of hypertension.

The site and mechanism of the hypotension are not established, but it is not clearly related to MAO inhibition. The hypotension is postural.

All of the data presented in Chapter 28 on the other effects of MAO inhibition are relevant to pargyline. It is a central nervous system stimulant, may in certain circumstances elevate blood pressure, and may interact with many other drugs and some foods.

Pargyline is an effective postural hypotensive agent, but alternative agents are more potent and not so unpredictable in their toxic effects.

The manufacturer's labeling imposes many restrictions and obligations on the physician, and it should be reviewed for dosage and other information if the use of this drug is contemplated.

The dosage of pargyline varies from 25 to 100 mg daily given as a single dose.

Because of the wide availability of other effective drugs, and because of the many interactions of MAO inhibitors with natural products and with other pharmacologic agents, MAO inhibitors should almost never be used.

VASODILATORS

1. HYDRALAZINE
(Apresoline)

Hydralazine (Apresoline) is a hydrazine derivative (Fig 12–1) and, like many other substituted hydrazines, is a MAO inhibitor, although this activity has no clinical importance.

Pharmacologic Actions

A. Mechanism of Action: Hydralazine intensifies the vasodilating action of epinephrine and isoproterenol, and in the laboratory this effect is blocked by the prior administration of propranolol. The mechanism of its hypotensive action thus appears to be similar to that of chlorpromazine (see Chapter 25) and is better described as intensification of beta-sympathomimetic effects rather than sympathoplegic.

B. Effects: Hydralazine causes vasodilatation but also a reflex-induced tachycardia.

Renal blood flow, which is generally unchanged by the hypotensive drugs already discussed, is increased by hydralazine unless pressure is greatly lowered. Plasma volume expansion occurs unless a thiazide is used concurrently.

Clinical Uses

The early experience with hydralazine utilized large doses, and frequent and serious toxic effects resulted. When hydralazine is used in combination with other drugs, hydralazine can be given in smaller dosage with less toxicity. Many clinicians add hydralazine to the regimen when the response to treatment with a thiazide plus sympathoplegic is not sufficient.

It may also be given parenterally in the treatment of a hypertensive emergency, although other agents such as nitroprusside and diazoxide are more commonly used.

Adverse Reactions

A. Side-Effects: Headache (common and often persistent), nausea, weakness, palpitations (rapid, forceful beat), anorexia, sweating, and flushing are frequent side-effects of the usual doses. The tachycardia and cardiac stimulation may precipitate anginal pain, although such effect is rare with small doses and when hydralazine is used in combination with any of the sympathoplegics.

B. Allergic: Hydralazine, given in dosage above a certain threshold, may cause a state indistinguishable from spontaneously occurring systemic lupus erythematosus except that the drug-induced lupoid state is reversible upon discontinuation of the drug or even upon a reduction in dose. Irreversible damage may occur during the active process. Skin rashes and drug fever are also reported. In dosages of 400 mg/d or more, it causes this reaction in 10% of patients. The reaction is rare if dosage is 200 mg/d or less.

In one group of patients with the "hydralazine syndrome," the incidence of malignancy was disturbingly high.

Hydralazine also causes a neuropathy that may be reversed by pyridoxine. The neuropathy probably results because the hydrazine reacts with pyridoxal, as is discussed in the section on isoniazid (see Chapter 52).

Dosages

The oral dosage of hydralazine is 12.5–50 mg 4 times daily. The parenteral dosage of 10–40 mg is used in hypertensive emergencies and can be repeated every 4–6 hours until oral medication becomes effective.

2. PRAZOSIN
(Minipress)

Prazosin is an alpha-adrenergic receptor blocking agent comparable to phentolamine or similar drugs discussed in Chapter 11. The hypotension it causes has a postural component, and the compensatory changes (tachycardia, increased cardiac output) that accompany the fall in blood pressure are minimal.

Side-effects may include a precipitous fall in blood pressure, sometimes with tachycardia and loss of consciousness, following the first dose.

Prazosin (Minipress) is given in combination with a thiazide diuretic and central sympathoplegic. The initial dose of 1 mg 3 times daily is slowly increased to 10 mg twice daily.

Table 12—2. Oral treatment of hypertension (adult dosages).*

	Initial and Incremental Dose (mg)	Doses Per Day	Usual Oral Daily Dose (mg)	Interval Between Increment of Doses
Commonly used mild diuretics				
Hydrochlorothiazide (Hydrodiuril, Esidrix, Oretic)	25, 50	1—2	25—100	2 weeks
Chlorothiazide (Diuril)	250, 500	1—2	250—1000	2 weeks
Bendroflumethiazide (Naturetin, Benuron)	2.5	1—2	2.5—10	2 weeks
Chlorthalidone (Hygroton)	50	1	50—100	2 weeks
Metolazone (Zaroxolyn)	2.5	1	2.5—10	2 weeks
Potassium-sparing diuretics				
Triamterene (Dyrenium)	50	1—2	50—200	2 weeks
Spironolactone (Aldactone)	25	1—3	25—150	2 weeks
Potent diuretics				
Furosemide (Lasix)	20—80	1—3	20—300	1 week
Ethacrynic acid (Edecrin)	25, 50	1—3	25—200	1 week
Adrenergic inhibitors				
Reserpine (Serpasil)	0.1	1	0.1—0.25	4 weeks
Methyldopa (Aldomet)	250	2—4	500—2000	1 week
Guanethidine (Ismelin)	10	1	10—200	1 week
Mecamylamine (Inversine)	2.5	1—4	10—100	1 week
Pentolinium (Ansolysen)	20	1—4	80—200	1 week
Propranolol (Inderal)	10	2—4	20—320	1 week
Clonidine (Catapres)	0.1	1—2	0.1—0.6	1 week
Vasodilators				
Prazosin (Minipress)	0.5—1.0	2—4	10—15	1 week
Hydralazine (Apresoline)	10	2—4	100—200	1 week
Minoxidil	2.5	2—4	5—20	1 week

*Reproduced, with permission, from Sokolow M, McIlroy MB: *Clinical Cardiology*, 2nd ed. Lange, 1979.

Table 12—3. Parenteral treatment of hypertension (adult dosages)*†

	Initial Dose and Route	Onset of Action	Duration of Action (Before Repeat Dose)
Adrenergic inhibitors			
Methyldopa (Aldomet)	250—500 mg IV	2—4 hours	4—12 hours
Trimethaphan camsylate‡ (Arfonad)	1—4 mg/min IV infusion	Seconds to minutes	As long as infused
Reserpine (Serpasil)	0.5—1 mg IM or IV bolus, slowly	2—6 hours	6—12 hours
Propranolol (Inderal)	1 mg bolus, slowly	Minutes	4—6 hours
Pentolinium (Ansolysen)	1—2.5 mg bolus, slowly	10—30 minutes	2—6 hours
Vasodilators			
Diazoxide‡ (Hyperstat)	75—300 mg rapidly IV	1—5 minutes	5—12 hours
Hydralazine (Apresoline)	10—20 mg bolus slowly, IV or IM	15—30 minutes	1—4 hours
Sodium nitroprusside§ (Nipride)	0.5—8 µg/kg/min IV by infusion of 5% dextrose and water, not by direct injection	Immediate; can increase infusion rate every 5—10 minutes as needed	As long as infused
Diuretics			
Furosemide (Lasix)	40—80 mg IV bolus	15—30 minutes	8—12 hours
Ethacrynate sodium (Edecrin)	50 mg IV bolus	15—30 minutes	8—12 hours

*Reproduced, with permission, from Sokolow M, McIlroy MB: *Clinical Cardiology,* 2nd ed. Lange, 1979.
†Information regarding products, precautions, and methods of administration of all agents being given parenterally should be reviewed in the *Physician's Desk Reference* prior to use in patients if the physician is not using the drugs frequently.
‡Requires closely monitored supervision and titration for proper dose.
§Photosensitive—should be protected from light.

3. OTHER VASODILATORS: THE TREATMENT OF HYPERTENSIVE CRISES

It is rarely necessary to rapidly lower the blood pressure of a hypertensive patient. The above agents, given by mouth and acting within 1–2 days, are ordinarily adequate treatment. However, there are a few urgent situations, eg, hypertensive encephalopathy, aortic dissection, and malignant (accelerated) hypertension, that require injection of rapidly acting drugs until the oral agents become effective or oral administration becomes possible.

Diazoxide

Diazoxide (Hyperstat) is a thiazide (Fig 12–1) that is also discussed in Chapter 37 as an investigational hyperglycemic agent. It is probably the preferred agent for the treatment of those hypertensive crises that are so severe that an immediate effect is essential. Given intravenously, diazoxide has a direct effect on smooth muscle and causes arteriolar dilatation and an immediate fall in blood pressure. The effect lasts for about 12 hours.

Diazoxide is not a diuretic; in fact, it causes sodium retention and is used in combination with a thiazide that is a diuretic.

Diazoxide is available in ampules, and the oral dosage form is used in hypoglycemic states (Chapter 37).

When diazoxide was first used, it was recommended that a bolus of 300 mg be given rapidly. However, it is now known that smaller doses can be given in a cumulative fashion. Efficacy is not sacrificed, and there may be less chance of a precipitous fall in blood pressure. The hypotensive effect persists for 4–12 hours, at which time the dose may be repeated.

Minoxidil (Loniten)

Minoxidil is generally comparable to diazoxide but can be given by mouth. Like diazoxide, it dilates arterioles independently of innervation and lowers total peripheral resistance. Since it has no sympathoplegic action, it can cause reflex tachycardia, increased cardiac output, and renin release with prominent sodium and water retention. It should be used with a thiazide diuretic or furosemide and a beta-blocker such as propranolol. It also causes an excessive growth of body hair in perhaps 80% of patients, but not as an endocrine effect. Marketing was delayed for years because of hemorrhagic lesions in the atria of dogs, but these have not appeared in humans.

Minoxidil has been evaluated in small numbers of patients, usually with end-stage renal disease unresponsive to previous drug therapy. It is marketed only for use in that situation: severe hypertension with target organ damage and not otherwise manageable.

Nitroprusside

Nitroprusside is another mainstay of treatment of hypertensive emergencies. The dose usually is 0.5–1.5 μg/kg/min, although higher doses may occasionally be needed. The onset and cessation of action are very fast, which allows for rapid titration of dose to the response. The use of this drug requires constant monitoring of blood pressure.

Other Vasodilators

The ganglionic blocking agent trimethaphan (see Chapter 11) and sodium nitroprusside, a vasodilator similar to nitroglycerin (see Chapter 13), are used by constant intravenous infusion. The central sympatholytics are available in injectable form, but no advantage over oral administration is apparent. Hydralazine is also sometimes given by injection, but side-effects are frequent.

• • •

CLINICAL EVALUATION OF HYPOTENSIVE DRUG THERAPY

Two separate problems must be considered in evaluating hypotensive therapy in arterial hypertension. One is the relatively simple matter of comparing the ability of various drugs and drug combinations to lower blood pressure. The other is to determine whether effective hypotensive therapy significantly decreases mortality and morbidity in hypertensive patients.

Effect of Drugs on Blood Pressure

Blood pressure is not a fixed and invariable measurement. In addition to the usual double-blind technics, 2 special cautions must usually be observed in evaluating drugs proposed for use against hypertension: (1) A control period is necessary before medication is started. The measured blood pressure will often fall as the patient becomes accustomed to the procedure of measuring blood pressure and benefits from reassurance. A drug administered during this period will be falsely credited with effectiveness that is actually due to nonspecific factors. (2) Blood pressure must be measured regularly, not casually, and the physician is probably not the best person to take the blood pressure. Nurses, family members, or the patients themselves not only record lower and less variable pressures but can take pressures at times best suited to assist in adjusting the dose of drug.

The results of studies carried out after adequate planning can be briefly summarized: Reserpine by itself lowers blood pressure more than does a placebo but no more than other mild agents such as phenobarbital. The thiazides do lower blood pressure, and the combination of a thiazide and reserpine is very useful. When a potent (postural) agent is used, blood pressure in the erect position can be lowered to any desired

Table 12—4. Adverse effects of antihypertensive agents.*

Diuretics	Nausea, muscle cramps, hypovolemia, hypokalemia, hyponatremia, hyper-uricemia, hyperglycemia, rash
Potassium-sparing diuretics	Hyperkalemia, gynecomastia
Adrenergic inhibitors	
Methyldopa	Drowsiness, dry mouth, impotence, hepatitis, postural hypotension, hemolytic anemia, fever
Reserpine	Somnolence, nasal congestion, nightmares, mental depression
Guanethidine	Postural hypotension, diarrhea, retrograde ejaculation, weakness on exertion
Propranolol	Bradycardia, left ventricular failure, asthma, Raynaud's syndrome, central nervous system symptoms, sodium retention
Mecamylamine and trimethaphan	Postural hypotension, parasympathetic blockade with constipation and paralytic ileus, loss of visual accommodation
Clonidine	Dry mouth, drowsiness, rebound hypertension if drug stopped abruptly
Vasodilator agents	
Prazosin	Tachycardia, headache, postural weakness and hypotension
Hydralazine	Lupuslike syndrome, headache, tachycardia, angina
Minoxidil	Tachycardia, hirsutism, headache, sodium retention
Diazoxide	Hyperglycemia, tachycardia, angina, sodium retention
Sodium nitroprusside	Excess hypotension, acute tubular necrosis, thiocyanate toxicity

*Reproduced, with permission, from Sokolow M, McIlroy MB: *Clinical Cardiology,* 2nd ed. Lange, 1979.

level. The dosage required is reduced by simultaneous use of reserpine and a diuretic.

Effect of Hypotensive Therapy on the Course of Hypertension

The quickest method of demonstrating the effect on survival and morbidity of radically lowering blood pressure is to treat patients with the most severe (Keith-Wagener IV) hypertension. This is one situation where withholding treatment from a control group cannot be justified, and the results in treated groups must be compared with mortality rates predicted from "literature controls." If patients with severe renal damage are not included, the predicted 5% survival after 4 years will be increased to more than 70%. Cardiomegaly, congestive failure, and retinopathy can regress.

A number of studies on patients with less severe hypertension have now given clear evidence of the benefits of treatment in deferring disabling complications and death. The following data from Veterans Administration cooperative studies are consistent with the results from at least 4 other countries using other drug regimens.

A group of 380 mildly hypertensive men (diastolic pressure 90–114 mm Hg) were divided into a placebo control group and a group treated with hydrochlorothiazide, reserpine, and hydralazine and followed for an average period of 3.3 years. The results were as follows:

	Controls	Treated
Deaths	56	22
Cardiovascular complications	19	8

Complications included, for example, strokes, congestive heart failure, renal insufficiency, and accelerated hypertension.

Groups of more severely hypertensive men (diastolic pressure 115–129 mm Hg) were followed for 16 months (70 controls) and 21 months (73 treated):

	Controls	Treated
Deaths	4	0
Cardiovascular complications	24	2

A more recent NIH study added information from a group with lower initial diastolic pressure. From 159,000 people age 30–69 years, several groups were isolated, including 7800 persons with diastolic pressure of 90–104 mm Hg. These subjects were randomly assigned either to optimal "stepped care" in their community or simply returned to their usual source of medical care for routine treatment. Other data from the study suggest that routine care neglects treatment of hypertension in this group. After a 5-year follow-up, there was a 20% reduction in the total number of deaths in the stepped care group (231 deaths versus 291 deaths in the routine care group). All males and black women benefited—ie, only in white women was there no difference between groups.

Clearly, there is now an obligation to identify those hypertensive individuals in whom treatment is justified. One generalization would suggest treatment for all men and all women below age 40 whose diastolic pressure is above 90 mm Hg. For women beyond that age, a diastolic pressure of 100 mm Hg would be tolerated. A smaller group of physicians treat lesser and unsustained elevations, arguing that arresting progression is a valid goal.

•   •   •

References

General

Bulpitt CJ, Dollery CT: Side effects of hypotensive agents evaluated by a self-administered questionnaire. Br Med J 3:485, 1973.

Goldberg AD, Raftery EB, Wilkinson P: Blood pressure and heart rate and withdrawal of antihypertensive drugs. Br Med J 1:1243, 1977.

Hodge JV, McQueen EG, Smirk FH: Results of hypotensive therapy in arterial hypertension based on experience with 497 patients treated and 156 controls, observed for periods of one to eight years. Br Med J 1:1, 1961.

Hypertension Detection and Follow-up Program Cooperative Group: Five-year findings of the Hypertension Detection and Follow-up Program. 1. Reduction in mortality of persons with high blood pressure, including mild hypertension. JAMA 242:2562, 1979.

Hypertension Detection and Follow-up Program Cooperative Group: Five-year findings of the Hypertension Detection and Follow-up Program. 2. Mortality by race-sex and age. JAMA 242:2572, 1979.

Onesti G: Renal pharmacodynamics of antihypertensive drugs: Clinical applications. Am J Cardiol 17:668, 1966.

Report of the Joint National Committee on Detection, Evaluation, and Treatment of High Blood Pressure. JAMA 237:255, 1977.

Sokolow M, McIlroy MD: *Clinical Cardiology*, 2nd ed. Lange, 1979.

Veterans Administration Cooperative Study Group on Antihypertensive Agents: Effects of treatment on morbidity in hypertension: Results in patients with diastolic blood pressures averaging 115 through 129 mm Hg. JAMA 202:1028, 1967.

Veterans Administration Cooperative Study Group on Antihypertensive Agents: Effects of treatment on morbidity in hypertension: Results in patients with diastolic blood pressures averaging 90 through 114 mm Hg. JAMA 213:1143, 1970.

Diuretics (See also Chapter 17.)

Green MA & others: Mechanisms by which chlorothiazide potentiates the vasodepressor effect of a ganglion blocking agent. Am J Med 36:87, 1964.

Leth A: Changes in plasma and extracellular fluid volumes in patients with essential hypertension during long-term treatment with hydrochlorothiazide. Circulation 42:479, 1970.

Villareal H & others: Effects of chlorothiazide on systemic hemodynamics in essential hypertension. Circulation 26:405, 1962.

Wilson WR, Okun R: Acute hemodynamic effects of diazoxide in man. Circulation 28:89, 1963.

Winer BM, Lubbe WF, Colton T: Antihypertensive actions of diuretics: Comparative study of an aldosterone antagonist and a thiazide, alone and together. JAMA 204:775, 1968.

Reserpine

Coffman JD: Persistence of reflex sympathetic nervous system activity in man on guanethidine or reserpine. Circulation 35:339, 1967.

Schlittler E, Plummer AJ: Tranquilizing drugs from rauwolfia. In: *Psychopharmacological Agents*. Vol 1. Gordon M (editor). Academic Press, 1964.

Shapiro AP, Teng HC: Technic of controlled drug assay illustrated by a comparative study of *Rauwolfia serpentina*, phenobarbital and placebo in the hypertensive patient. N Engl J Med 256:970, 1957.

Sheldon MB, Kotte JH: Effect of *Rauwolfia serpentina* and reserpine on the blood pressure in essential hypertension: A long-term double-blind study. Circulation 16:200, 1957.

Guanethidine

Mitchell JR, Arias L, Oates JA: Antagonism of the antihypertensive action of guanethidine sulfate by desipramine hydrochloride. JAMA 202:973, 1967.

Prichard BNC & others: Bethanidine, guanethidine, and methyldopa in treatment of hypertension: A within-patient comparison. Br Med J 1:135, 1968.

Ronnov-Jessen V: Blood volume during treatment of hypertension with guanethidine. Acta Med Scand 174:307, 1963. [Or see Lancet 2:669, 1960.]

Well JV, Chidsey CA: Plasma volume expansion resulting from interference with adrenergic function in normal man. Circulation 37:54, 1968.

Methyldopa

LoBuglio AF, Jandl JH: The nature of the alpha-methyldopa red-cell antibody. N Engl J Med 276:658, 1967.

Mullick FG, McAllister HA: Myocarditis associated with methyldopa therapy. JAMA 237:1699, 1977.

Onesti G & others: Pharmacodynamic effects of alpha-methyl dopa in hypertensive subjects. Am Heart J 67:32, 1964.

Weil MH, Barbour BH, Chesne RB: Alpha-methyl dopa for the treatment of hypertension: Clinical and pharmacodynamic studies. Circulation 28:165, 1963.

Clonidine

Jain AK & others: Efficacy and acceptability of different dosage schedules of clonidine. Clin Pharmacol Ther 21:382, 1977.

Reid JL & others: The central hypotensive effect of clonidine: Studies in tetraplegic subjects. Clin Pharmacol Ther 21:375, 1977.

Reid JL & others: Clonidine withdrawal in hypertension. Lancet 1:1171, 1977.

Others

Clayden JR, Bell JW, Pollard P: Menopausal flushing: Double-blind trial of a non-hormonal medication. Br Med J 1:409, 1974.

Devine BL, Fife R, Trust PM: Minoxidil for severe hypertension after failure of other hypotensive drugs. Br Med J 2:667, 1977.

Kosman ME: Evaluation of a new antihypertensive agent (Minoxidil). JAMA 244:73, 1980.

Moser M & others: Pargyline treatment of hypertension: Experience with a nonhydrazine amine oxidase inhibitor. JAMA 187:192, 1964.

Pennisi AJ & others: Minoxidil therapy in children with severe hypertension. J Pediatr 90:813, 1977.

Schirger A, Sheps SG: Prazosin—new antihypertensive agent. JAMA 237:989, 1977.

Schirger A, Spittell JA: Pharmacology and clinical use of hydralazine in the treatment of diastolic hypertension. Am J Cardiol 9:854, 1962.

13 | Vasodilator Drugs: Drug Effects on Regional Blood Flow

Many of the drugs discussed in Chapter 12 as useful in the treatment of hypertension have a diffuse dilating effect on all blood vessels. The additional vasodilators introduced in this chapter are sometimes alleged to have a selective vasodilator action on the coronary, cerebral, and peripheral vascular beds. They are also general vasodilators but, unlike the drugs used in the treatment of hypertension, they do not block the outflow of the sympathetic nervous system as part of their effect.

From our discussion of the treatment of hypertension, 2 concepts must be carried over to clarify the discussion of this group of drugs: (1) Drugs may relieve the manifestations of a disease by acting through a mechanism different from that which caused the disease; and (2) drug action in a normal subject may be different from that in a diseased subject. In addition, whereas hypertension is a disease of arterioles, the states to be discussed here involve larger vessels—the arteries.

This chapter covers the following subjects: (1) Nitroglycerin and other drugs used in the treatment of the pain of coronary insufficiency. (2) Drugs suggested for use in peripheral vascular insufficiency in the limbs. (3) Cerebral blood flow. (4) The xanthines, a group of agents with many effects other than peripheral vasodilation (arbitrarily included in this chapter).

NITROGLYCERIN & OTHER "CORONARY VASODILATORS"

When atherosclerosis or other occlusive disease of the coronary arteries progresses far enough or when spasm of the coronary arteries occurs, a disproportion develops between the myocardial need for oxygen as required by cardiac work and the amount of oxygen available from coronary blood flow. Myocardial ischemia is manifested by pain of characteristic nature (pressing), intensity (severe), location (usually substernal), and radiation (usually to left shoulder and upper arm). The resulting sensation of a life-threatening, throttling pain in the chest led to the name **angina pectoris.** The unpredictability and variability

of the occurrence makes the evaluation of drug treatment difficult.

Since the drugs discussed in this section have limited utility, it is important to treat causal and precipitating factors—eg, atherosclerosis, hypertension, obesity, anemia, and emotional factors. However, treatment is often by means of drugs.

Chemistry & Definitions

Drugs used for the relief of angina are usually either nitrates or nitrites—ie, salts or mixed esters of either nitric or nitrous acid. They include the following:

(1) Organic nitrates: Nitroglycerin.
(2) Inorganic nitrites: Sodium nitrite.
(3) Organic nitrites: Amyl nitrite.

Nitroglycerin (glyceryl trinitrate) is by far the most important drug to be discussed. Table 13–1 lists a number of other nitrated polyhydric alcohols that are often called "long-acting nitrates."

Actually, the most important difference among all of these vasodilators is in their rate of absorption. Amyl nitrite is rapidly absorbed after inhalation, and the effect of the small amounts used is quickly dissipated. Small amounts of nitroglycerin can be used sublingually. The "long-acting" nitrates such as those

Table 13–1. Dosages of nitrates other than nitroglycerin.

	Oral Dose* (Every 6 Hours)	Sublingual Dose
Erythrityl tetranitrate† (Cardilate)	15–60 mg	5 mg
Pentaerythritol tetranitrate† (Peritrate, PETN)	40–80 mg	...
Isosorbide dinitrate† (Isordil, Sorbitrate)	10–60 mg	2–5 mg
Mannitol hexanitrate	30–60 mg	...
Trolnitrate (triethanolamine trinitrate, Metamine)	20 mg‡	...

*Dose given every 6 hours before meals and at bedtime. The initial dose should be smaller. As tolerance develops (ie, as headache disappears), increase at intervals up to the dosage listed above. Sustained-release preparations are available.

†Generic preparation available. Trade name given for identification only.

‡Sustained-release.

listed in Table 13–1 appear to be so only because they are slowly absorbed after oral administration. When they are given sublingually, as is possible for all but pentaerythritol tetranitrate, they appear to be similar to nitroglycerin similarly administered. Nitroglycerin given orally in large amounts is slowly absorbed and so becomes long-acting.

(4) Sodium nitroprusside is not used for the relief of angina but has actions very similar to those of nitroglycerin. Unlike nitroglycerin, it is easily available in injectable (intravenous) form.

(5) Calcium antagonists: A variety of drugs that inhibit transmembranous currents mediated by fluxes of Ca^{2+} are becoming useful for the treatment of spasm of the coronary arteries.

Pharmacologic Actions

A. Smooth Muscle Relaxation: Nitroglycerin relaxes all smooth muscle regardless of its location or innervation.

1. Cardiovascular effects–Generalized vasodilatation occurs, but "postarteriolar" or venous dilatation is a prominent and important factor in the blood pressure response to nitroglycerin. Plethysmographic studies established this fact before the postural hypotensive agents became available and before venous dilatation was recognized as an important factor in explaining the therapeutic effect of nitroglycerin.

The vasodilator effect of nitroglycerin is more readily apparent on specific vascular beds. The blush area—the skin from the clavicles up—is particularly sensitive, and an objective flush and a subjective feeling of warmth in the area are present unless the fall of blood pressure is great enough to cause reflex release of vasoconstrictive catecholamines. Vascular smooth muscle relaxation causes the meningeal or intracranial vessels to lose their ability to resist distention, so that with each pulse they become distended and pull on receptors in the meninges. This is sensed as a throbbing headache synchronous with the pulse, a common side-effect of the vasodilator drugs. The coronary vessels certainly are dilated in animals and in normal humans, but whether this occurs in patients with coronary insufficiency is a question discussed in detail below.

Secondary to the generalized vasodilatation, blood pressure is decreased. The effect is similar to that of the gravity-assisted or postural hypotensive agents discussed in Chapter 12 with the important difference that, since the sympathetic nervous system is not blocked, tachycardia and other evidences of sympatho-adrenal discharge may appear. The extent of the hypotensive effect thus depends not only on the dose used but also on the position of the patient. If the patient is upright and immobile, the effect will be intensified. This explains the syncope that may be induced by vasodilators. Furthermore, since the perfusion pressure to the coronary arteries may be reduced, nitroglycerin can (rarely) increase the electrocardiographic signs of myocardial ischemia. If the effect is intense enough, the patient may faint or feel dizzy, but at this point the reflex activation of the sympathetic nervous system will lead to tachycardia and the patient will appear pale, tremulous, and anxious. Nitroglycerin has no direct effect on heart rate or contractility.

2. Other smooth muscle is transiently relaxed, but this effect has limited therapeutic usefulness.

3. Mechanism of pain relief–The prototype of this drug group, amyl nitrite, was introduced (1867) by Lauder Brunton on the premise that a decrease in blood pressure would reduce cardiac work and therefore would relieve anginal pain. However, since it is easy to demonstrate dilatation of the coronary bed in animals, Brunton's theory (but not the use of the drug) was generally rejected for many years. A few investigators found good reason to reject the concept of coronary dilatation. First of all, angina is usually a disease of the larger coronary arteries, and at least one of the major branches is nearly always occluded. It seemed unlikely to these early critics of the coronary vasodilatation theory that drugs could act upon these structurally abnormal arteries, and it was reasoned that ischemia severe enough to cause pain should be a maximal stimulus to dilatation of arterioles, as it probably is to the development of collateral channels. The importance of the venous dilatation in the relief of pain had been demonstrated earlier in studies of the hypotensive effect of nitroglycerin and the relief of responses to standing immobile in the erect position.

Other treatments for angina, such as lowering of associated hypertension or weight reduction, are effective because they reduce the work of the heart. Cardiac catheterization technics made it possible for Gorlin and co-workers to test the hypothesis that nitroglycerin does not act in diseased humans as a coronary dilator but acts to reduce cardiac work. These workers detemined cardiac output and blood pressure by the usual methods. A catheter placed in the coronary sinus allowed them to sample mixed venous blood from the myocardium. (The coronary sinus is assumed to return a constant fraction of the coronary flow.) They also measured myocardial oxygen consumption. From cardiac output and arterial pressure, cardiac work was calculated. From coronary blood flow and central arterial pressure—ie, perfusion pressure—coronary vascular resistance was calculated. From coronary blood flow and central arterial pressure—ie, perfusion pressure—coronary vascular resistance was calculated. In the 10 normal patients studied, nitroglycerin was shown to double the coronary blood flow and to decrease the calculated (pressure/flow) coronary vascular resistance. In patients with angina, however, the values for total coronary flow and coronary vascular resistance remained fixed. However, effects on distribution of blood to the coronary microcirculation could not be detected. By using technics that can detect such changes in regional flow, investigators have provided evidence that nitroglycerin can normalize abnormal flow to ischemic regions. A consistent effect of nitroglycerin in the patient with a history of angina was to decrease cardiac output, blood pressure, and ventricular end-diastolic volume, thereby decreasing cardiac work. The decreased cardiac output responsible for part of the fall in blood pressure presumably is due to venous dilatation and pooling since the subjects showed a fall in systemic and pulmonary venous pressures. Thus, although the relief of angina that follows treatment with nitroglycerin is probably due primarily to decreased cardiac work, the effect of the drug to alter the intracardiac flow of blood cannot be entirely discounted as having therapeutic benefit.

From the concept that nitroglycerin does not act selectively on the coronary bed, it follows that many generalized vasodilators would be useful in relieving angina. Those drugs classified as useful in the treatment of hypertension, for example, should also relieve angina in the normotensive patient. They have been used primarily in hypertensive patients, and relief of angina does occur under these circumstances. It has also been reported that these drugs relieve angina in the normotensive patient with coronary disease, as would also be predicted.

Other vasodilators such as alcohol, MAO inhibitors, and quinidine have been used, but they have no present clinical usefulness in the treatment of angina.

The beta-adrenergic blocking agents defined in Chapter 11 clearly act to prevent anginal attacks by reducing cardiac work. Their effectiveness has probably been important in furthering the reclassification of nitroglycerin as a general rather than a coronary vasodilator.

B. Tolerance: Tolerance to nitroglycerin has been of concern to clinicians for a long time. However, although tolerance probably does develop in some patients so that the clinician should be alert to its development, it does not seem to be a common clinical problem. Also, the abrupt discontinuation of nitroglycerin should be avoided in order to diminish the potential for withdrawal syndrome characterized by increased attacks of angina.

Uses & Clinical Evaluation

A. Suggested Uses of Vasodilators: The following therapeutic objectives must be separately evaluated in patients with angina: (1) Relief of an attack of angina when it occurs. (2) Prevention of an attack of angina by administering the drug before exercise or other stimulus known to induce pain. (3) Decrease in the number of anginal attacks by chronic administration of the drug. (4) Afterload reduction in cardiac failure. (5) Reduction of cardiac load in treatment of cardiac failure (to be discussed below).

B. Problems and Methods of Clinical Evaluation: The evaluation of agents designed to relieve angina is difficult for several reasons. First of all, laboratory assessment in animals or even evaluation in volunteer normal human subjects is impossible; only humans with the spontaneously occurring disease are suitable subjects for drug evaluation.

The symptom is not often regular and predictable in its occurrence. The exercise tolerance of a given

patient is not fixed but varies from day to day and at different times during the same day, and angina can be precipitated or influenced by environmental factors other than activity.

A third problem in the evaluation of anti-angina drugs is the fact that the placebo response is great in this disease. This is true not only with drug treatment but with other types of treatment also. For example, to evaluate a surgical procedure (internal mammary artery ligation) alleged to be effective in relieving angina, it was necessary to compare its effects with those of a sham operation. Both procedures gave measurable but transient good results.

Any assay of an anti-anginal effect must, therefore, be conducted with placebo controls and double-blind observation. The specific technics available are the following:

1. Patient reports–A drug alleged to have prophylactic value in decreasing the number of attacks during chronic medication can be evaluated by having trained patients record and report the number of attacks experienced. An alternative is to record the amount of nitroglycerin used to relieve pain as an indication of the number of attacks experienced—ie, a prophylactic drug should reduce the need for nitroglycerin. This is the test most immediately and confidently applicable to the actual conditions of general use.

2. Electrocardiographic response to exercise–The ability of vasodilators to prevent angina or the electrocardiographic signs of ischemia during exercise can be used to test the efficacy of nitrates. Under carefully standardized conditions, the patient is exercised until pain appears or until signs of ischemia appear on the ECG. The patient is subsequently exercised after receiving a placebo or the drug, and any differences in exercise tolerance are noted. There are several problems in extrapolating results from such a study to the treatment of angina in the general population. It is difficult to equate a minor increase in exercise tolerance with a clinical response to spontaneously occurring pain. Also, there may be no fixed relationship between the occurrence of pain and the electrocardiographic changes. Finally, only a small percentage of patients with angina are suitable for this type of testing.

C. Conclusions: The ability of nitroglycerin to relieve an attack of angina after the pain has begun and to prevent exercise-induced pain has not been demonstrated in controlled experiments on a group of randomly selected patients. The patient experiencing angina is forced to immobility, and the pain is likely to terminate even without the drug. A definitive trial would therefore compare the duration of an attack after nitroglycerin and after a placebo. However, a long clinical experience with this drug has established it as the cornerstone of anti-angina therapy.

Adverse Reactions

A. Adverse Reactions During Therapeutic Use: The occurrence of headache and hypotension with dizziness or fainting is unusual. The hypotensive effect has in a few cases led to permanent cerebral damage. The headache is usually transient and requires no treatment, although an occasional individual may require aspirin or other mild analgesics. The hypotension should be immediately treated by placing the patient in a supine position.

B. Methemoglobinemia: The nitrites—only amyl nitrite and sodium nitrite of the agents mentioned thus far—are able to convert hemoglobin into methemoglobin. The hemoglobin with the iron in the ferric (oxidized)—rather than the ferrous—form loses its oxygen-carrying capacity; if the process is intense enough, hypoxic anemia can result. Methemoglobinemia does not occur during the therapeutic use of any of the vasodilators thus far discussed. It may rarely occur in newborn infants following the ingestion of nitrates in water used for preparation of formulas. The nitrates are reduced to nitrites in the intestine.

Amyl nitrite or even sodium nitrite may be used to deliberately induce methemoglobinemia in the treatment of cyanide intoxication. Cyanide is toxic because it inactivates cytochrome oxidase. Methemoglobin removes cyanide from solution by combining with it to form cyanmethemoglobin. Since the amount of methemoglobin is large in comparison with the amount of cytochrome oxidase, the enzyme is protected. The cyanide slowly liberated from cyanmethemoglobin is converted to thiocyanate (SCN^-) if thiosulfate has been provided by injection.

If it is necessary to treat methemoglobinemia, methylene blue, 1–2 mg/kg intravenously over a period of 5 minutes, is effective.

Preparations & Dosages

A. Nitroglycerin: Nitroglycerin is the drug to which other drugs must be compared.

Nitroglycerin is available as tablets containing 0.15, 0.3, 0.4, 0.5, or 0.6 mg. The intermediate doses are most commonly used. The position of the patient is as important as dose in controlling the intensity of the effect. When administered sublingually, the drug is absorbed very rapidly, and the drug effect appears in about 30 seconds. The patient is told to place one tablet under the tongue upon the appearance of pain. After the precipitating factors have been discussed in detail, the patient may also be taught to use nitroglycerin in anticipation of angina.

Nitroglycerin tablets dispensed in glass or polyethylene containers with an airtight lid retain their potency for years unless stored at elevated temperatures. Supplies that are carried by the patient in such a way as to be kept near body temperature might possibly lose potency sooner.

Nitroglycerin may be applied topically as a 2% ointment in a lanolin base (Nitrol ointment). The ointment is spread onto a premeasured (0.5 cm) strip of paper and secured to the skin with an adhesive. The usual dosage is 1.5–3 cm every 4 hours. Nitroglycerin applied topically is about as effective as when given sublingually, and the prolonged action makes it useful

Nitroglycerin
(glyceryl trinitrate)

Isosorbide
dinitrate

Pentaerythritol tetranitrate
(Peritrate, etc.)

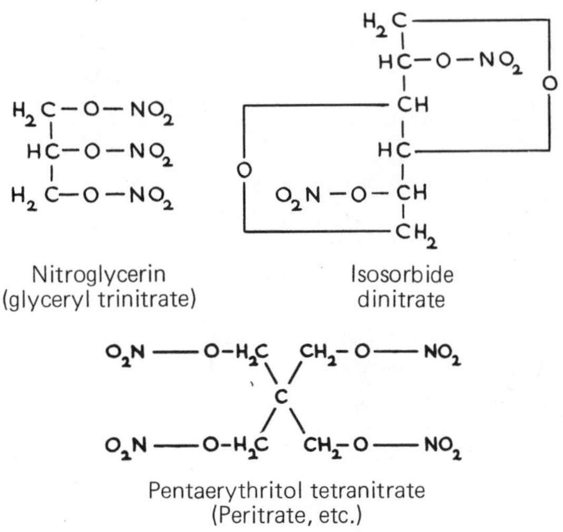

Figure 13–1. Examples of a nitrite and nitrates.

for the prevention of angina pectoris.

B. Amyl Nitrite: Amyl nitrite is equivalent or superior to nitroglycerin in effectiveness and even more rapid in onset of action. It is a liquid dispensed in easily crushed ampules provided with a woven cover. The ampule is broken and 2–3 inhalations of the vapor are used. The use of amyl nitrite is conspicuous and the odor objectionable, and it is, therefore, virtually never used.

C. Other Nitrates: Until recently, nitroglycerin, with its brief duration of action, was the only significantly effective drug treatment for angina. Many efforts were made to develop a long-acting ''coronary vasodilator'' that could be used to prevent attacks of angina. Most of these efforts centered on the organic nitrates.

The ''long-acting nitrates'' are listed in Table 13–1. Whether 3 or 6 alcohol groups are esterified is less important than the route of administration and whether a continuous, prolonged effect is attempted. When these drugs are swallowed, they become long-acting because they are slowly absorbed. The so-called long-acting nitrates have a large first pass effect; ie, a large percentage of an oral dose is metabolized in the liver and never reaches the systemic circulation. When the efficacy of these drugs was first investigated, relatively low doses were used. It has become apparent that if larger doses are used, enough drug is available to result in a therapeutic effect.

Initial doses may indeed cause generalized vasodilatation. With repeated dosage, however, tolerance may develop (see discussion above). There is a difference in the duration of action of the various nitrates:

Sublingual nitroglycerin	20–30 minutes
Sublingual isosorbide	Up to 90 minutes
Oral isosorbide	Up to 3 hours
Nitropaste	Up to 3–4 hours

Table 13—2. Drugs suggested as peripheral vasodilating agents.

	Recommended Doses
Generalized, direct smooth muscle relaxing effect:	
Papaverine	30—60 mg IV every 3—4 hours
Cyclandelate (Cyclospasmol)	100—300 mg orally 4 times daily
Cutaneous vasodilators, primarily in blush area:	
Nicotinic acid (niacin)	50—150 mg orally 3 times daily
Beta-pyridyl carbinol (nico-tinyl alcohol, Roniacol)	50—150 mg orally 3 times daily after meals
Alpha-adrenergic blocking agents: (See Chapter 11.)	
Phenoxybenzamine (Dibenzyline)	
Tolazoline (Priscoline)	
Azapetine (Ilidar)	
Sympathomimetics comparable to isoproterenol:	
(See Chapter 10.)	
Nylidrin (Arlidin)	
Isoxsuprine (Vasodilan)	

D. Other Vasodilators: (See Table 13–2.) A number of nonnitrate generalized vasodilators have given some evidence of usefulness in the treatment of angina even in normotensive patients. None are suggested for use at this time.

E. Beta-Adrenergic Blocking Agents: These drugs—eg, propranolol (Inderal) and the cardio-specific beta-blockers that are still investigational—have been discussed in Chapter 11. The beta-blocking drugs reduce the effects of endogenous epinephrine and norepinephrine on cardiac rate and force of contraction. The increment in cardiac work that precipitates pain after exercise or other stimulus is therefore correspondingly increased.

The material in Chapter 11 will not be duplicated here, but the brevity of the discussion in this chapter should not lead the reader to underestimate the usefulness or possible dangers of the beta-blockers.

CALCIUM ANTAGONISTS & SPASM OF THE CORONARY ARTERIES

In recent years it has become well accepted that spasm of coronary arteries can lead to reversible decreases in myocardial perfusion. Spasm has been shown to cause variant (Prinzmetal) angina, and, on occasion, spasm may lead to frank myocardial infarction. Many patients with this syndrome can be treated satisfactorily with nitrates. Beta$_2$-adrenergic blockers may be detrimental, since such blockade eliminates opposition to the vasoconstrictor effects of stimulated alpha receptors. In addition to nitrates, a new class of drugs known as "calcium antagonists" is being used for treatment of spasm. The name "calcium an-

tagonist" refers to the ability of these drugs to inhibit a Ca^{2+}-mediated current that depolarizes the atrioventricular node. However, the mechanism by which these drugs relieve spasm of the coronary arteries is not well described.

Both verapamil and nifedipine are being tested in the USA and are being used in Europe. The oral dose of verapamil for relief of spasm is 160–360 mg/d in 4–6 divided doses. The oral dose of nifedipine ranges from 40 to 80 mg every 6 hours.

USE OF VASODILATOR DRUGS IN TREATMENT OF CARDIAC FAILURE

Cardiac failure results in abnormally low perfusion of organs and tissues. As a diseased heart fails, various physiologic responses occur that tend to maintain cardiac output and systemic blood pressure at an adequate level. In the absence of therapy, cardiac output is maintained by an increased end-diastolic volume of the ventricle (preload) and an increased heart rate. As these mechanisms become inadequate and cardiac output continues to fall, peripheral vascular resistance increases, so that the perfusion pressure of vital organs is maintained. The increased end-diastolic pressure results in pulmonary and systemic congestion and edema. The increased peripheral vascular resistance decreases left ventricular forward stroke volume. All of these adaptations occur at the price of an increased work load of the heart. As the heart becomes progressively less able to do work, the physiologic responses progressively require more work. Ironically, the adaptive responses ultimately become overtly maladaptive. Thus, the objectives of treatment of heart failure are: (1) to improve cardiac performance (contractility), (2) to decrease ventricular end-diastolic pressure (preload), and (3) to decrease systemic vascular resistance (afterload). The decreased systemic vascular resistance facilitates ejection of blood from the left ventricle, which, in turn, increases stroke volume and reduces ventricular diastolic volume and filling pressure; in this way, pressure in the systemic and pulmonary venous beds is reduced.

Numerous studies have been done that attest to the ability of vasodilating drugs to improve severe heart failure by decreasing peripheral vascular resistance and by increasing venous capacitance. During acute therapy with parenterally administered medicines, therapy is guided according to the responses of cardiac output, blood pressure, and systemic and pulmonary venous pressures, all of which must be closely monitored.

Sodium Nitroprusside

Nitroprusside is a very effective vasodilator that relaxes both venous and arterial smooth muscle. Nitroprusside is the vasodilator of choice in the acute treatment of severe heart failure. The dose is titrated to the hemodynamic response and may range from 15 to 400 μg/min.

Nitroprusside is metabolized to cyanide, which is further metabolized to thiocyanate. Although the toxicity of both of these metabolites has been of great concern, the incidence of actual toxicity is not known. Although recommendations regarding maximal doses of nitroprusside have been made, there are few clinical data to support their widespread use. Cyanide toxicity is associated with metabolic acidosis and an increasing mixed venous P_{O_2} concentration. However, both of these signs are difficult to assess, since severe congestive heart failure can cause metabolic acidosis, and improved cardiac output, resulting from therapy, would tend to increase the mixed venous P_{O_2}. Thiocyanate can cause miosis, toxic psychosis, hyperreflexia, and convulsions. The half-life of thiocyanate is about 1 week in patients with normal renal function and is increased in patients with renal failure. Because of the long half-life of thiocyanate, accumulation of thiocyanate will occur for at least 28 days if a constant dose of nitroprusside is maintained. Although plasma levels could be checked in patients receiving prolonged therapy and in those with renal failure, the ability to predict toxicity based on these levels has not been firmly established.

Phentolamine

This is an alpha-adrenergic blocking drug that affects arterioles. There is relatively little effect on the venous system. The dose is 0.2–2.0 mg/min. Reflex tachycardia may occur more often than with nitroprusside, which limits the appeal of phentolamine.

Trimethaphan

Trimethaphan is a ganglionic blocker that relaxes venous and arterial smooth muscle. However, because of tachyphylaxis and undesired effects of ganglionic blockade, such as ileus and retention of urine, nitroprusside is much preferred.

Nitroglycerin

This drug has been used when increased venous capacitance and decreased venous pressures are the main therapeutic goals, since the drug's effect on systemic vascular resistance is minimal. Topically applied, nitroglycerin (see above) may prove useful for chronic management of congestive heart failure. Oral isosorbide dinitrate may also be useful.

Hydralazine

Hydralazine is a vasodilator that affects the arterial system almost exclusively. Although tachycardia is a common side-effect when hydralazine is used as an antihypertensive, this effect is not prominent in congestive heart failure when an increased cardiac output ensues from therapy. Hydralazine in combination with furosemide or nitroglycerin has been effective in the long-term treatment of severe congestive heart failure.

VASODILATORS IN PERIPHERAL VASCULAR DISEASE

Generalized vasodilation can lower blood pressure, with great benefit to the hypertensive patient, and can reduce the work of the heart and thus relieve anginal pain. However, generalized vasodilatation is not helpful and may actually be harmful in the treatment of chronic arterial insufficiency of the extremities.

Vasodilators in Chronic Atherosclerosis Obliterans

The most common type of occlusive vascular disease results from an atherosclerotic process in the large arteries. As in the case of coronary artery disease, one can anticipate certain reasons why drug therapy might be ineffective. The vessels might be structurally unresponsive, and the ischemia manifested by claudication should have already been accompanied by maximal dilatation. Most importantly, any generalized vasodilator effect that lowers systemic blood pressure (which supplies the perfusion pressure to a limb) could easily cause a reduction in regional blood flow.

However, such a priori reasoning is always inconclusive in pharmacology, and the only way of establishing or disproving the therapeutic usefulness of vasodilators in peripheral vascular disease is the clinical trial. On this basis, it must be emphasized that properly conducted trials designed to discount results that may be referable to spontaneous variations in the occurrence of claudication have not established any usefulness for vasodilators in peripheral vascular disease. Indeed, in measurements of blood flow in humans with atherosclerotic disease of the limbs, vasodilators of several types have been shown to actually reduce flow through the affected region. The use of drugs to predict the usefulness of sympathectomy in producing localized vasodilatation has also not been successful.

Peripheral Vasospastic Disorders

Acrocyanosis and livedo reticularis are ordinarily benign processes but in some cases may be treated with one of the drugs listed in Table 13–2. Here the vasodilators are used with the more plausible goal of increasing blood flow through the skin rather than through muscle, as in the presence of claudication.

CEREBRAL BLOOD FLOW

The intracranial blood vessels do not respond to the same neural and humoral influences that control other vascular beds. Vascular tone is regulated by the intrinsic contractility of the vessels modified by the pressure perfusing them and by changes in CO_2 tension. They do not respond to drugs that mimic or block autonomic nervous system effects. Total cerebral blood flow thus remains constant throughout most disturbances in the circulatory system with the notable exception of reduced perfusion pressure, which results in fainting or more serious changes from hypoxia.

Because cerebrovascular disease is such an important problem, the effect of drugs on *regional* intracranial blood flow is of investigative—if not yet practical—interest. There is no reason to expect that the chronic effects of occlusions can be modified here any more than in the coronary or limb beds. If any element of vasospasm were present, it could perhaps be modified by drugs. Generalized vasodilators could have a deleterious effect because of the postural hypotension induced.

Hydergine is a mixture of 3 dihydroergot alkaloids persistently advertised for use in cerebrovascular insufficiency. No acceptable trials show an effect on cerebral circulation, but some trials do appear to show an effect on behavior. As is pointed out in Chapter 14, the dihydroergots are best classified as congeners of reserpine. The effects on behavior—and the side-effects of nasal stuffiness and diarrhea—are similar to those of an antipsychotic tranquilizer such as reserpine.

Vasoconstrictors such as ergotamine that act on meningeal vessels rather than vessels to the parenchyma are discussed in relation to migraine in Chapter 14.

Carbon Dioxide

Carbon dioxide is a cerebral vascular dilator, and a 5% or even 10% mixture in oxygen can increase cerebral blood flow as much as 75%. (Hyperventilation has the opposite effect; when it occurs in an anxious patient, it can increase the possibility of fainting when vasodilators are used.) Other blood vessels are also dilated, so that total peripheral resistance falls even though CO_2 inhalation causes a generalized sympathoadrenal discharge. Cardiac output and pulse rate increase. Respiration is increased in rate and depth. At CO_2 concentrations of 2%, the effect is measurable; at 5%, the patient is aware of the effect but not uncomfortable; at 10%, a maximum increase occurs and the patient is hyperpneic. Carbon dioxide is a general depressant at lower concentrations and a general anesthetic at great (50%) concentrations. With intermediate levels, convulsions may occur.

The uses of CO_2 are few. It has been used postoperatively to stimulate breathing and prevent atelectasis, and in the treatment of carbon monoxide poisoning and to interrupt persistent hiccup. Better alternative methods are available in each case. Continuous petit mal episodes sometimes respond favorably to CO_2 inhalations. Carbon dioxide in high concentration is used as a general anesthetic for animals by meat packers.

THE XANTHINES

Each of the 3 common xanthines has some pharmacologic importance. Caffeine and theobromine are ingredients of many popular beverages. Theophylline in combination with ethylenediamine (aminophylline) is a commonly used drug.

The xanthines have multiple effects and will be referred to in several other chapters, but the outline of their pharmacology will arbitrarily be placed here.

Chemistry

The xanthines are purine bases. The chemical structure and the close relation of the 3 xanthines of importance are shown below. Caffeine is present in significant amounts in tea and coffee; theobromine is a component of cocoa. Aminophylline, the most commonly used drug form of the xanthines, is theophylline solubilized by the addition of ethylenediamine. These compounds occur naturally, but their source as drugs is synthetic. Unlike other exogenous purines, the xanthines are not metabolized to uric acid but to incompletely demethylated metabolites.

Pharmacologic Actions

The effects of each of the 3 compounds are qualitatively the same, but each affects the central nervous system or the cardiovascular system to a different degree. For example, the administration or ingestion of caffeine leads first to cerebrocortical stimulation, the cardiovascular and diuretic actions appearing as "side-effects." Theophylline is a less potent central stimulant than caffeine, and in therapeutic doses the cardiovascular smooth muscle and diuretic effects are exerted without significant central stimulation. The differences among the 3 xanthines are further described in the discussion of therapeutic use (below).

A. Central Nervous System Stimulation:

1. Cortical–The xanthines can produce wakefulness (or, in a fatigued patient, arousal) and improved psychomotor performance but not necessarily improved mentation. These effects are much more difficult to demonstrate than those of amphetamine. Whether the effect is actually due to direct cortical stimulation or to indirect cortical stimulation via the reticular activating system is not known.

2. Medullary–Large doses can lead to stimulation of respiration. However, the specific effect of abolishing the Cheyne-Stokes pattern of respiration is due not to the xanthine used but to the ethylenediamine used to solubilize theophylline.

Stimulation of the vasomotor center in the medulla, causing peripheral vasoconstriction, would lead to an elevation of blood pressure were this action not usually antagonized by the direct peripheral effects described below.

Stimulation of the medullary vagal (cardioinhibitory) center leads to a decrease in pulse rate, but this is often overridden by increased cardiac automaticity, ie, sinus tachycardia and ectopic rhythms.

Purine

Xanthine
(2,6-dioxopurine)

Ethylenediamine

(Caffeine is 1,3,7-trimethylxanthine; theobromine, 3,7-dimethylxanthine;
and theophylline, 1,3-dimethylxanthine)

In laboratory animals, the xanthines are also stimulants or facilitants of spinal cord transmission and can lead to convulsions of the spinal type.

B. Cardiovascular Effects:

1. On the myocardium–The normal sinus rate, ectopic impulse formation, and force of cardiac contraction are all increased. As a result, the vagal slowing described above will be in part masked; extrasystoles or major ventricular arrhythmias may be produced; and cardiac output will be regularly increased. These are all direct effects on the myocardium independent of innervation.

2. Peripheral dilatation–Since the xanthines are direct smooth muscle relaxants, blood vessels will be dilated. This effect would tend to decrease blood pressure, but it is minimized by the pressor effects of medullary and cardiac stimulation.

3. Coronary circulation–The xanthines dilate coronary vessels in animals. The effect is probably due to a direct action on the smooth muscle of the arteries. However, coronary vasodilatation would also result from increased cardiac work occasioned by the direct myocardial stimulation. The xanthines were used years ago in the treatment of angina without their usefulness being clearly established. On the basis of recent studies on the mechanism of pain relief in patients with angina, the peripheral vasodilatation caused

by the xanthines might be expected to act by reducing cardiac work, but the increased cardiac rate and force of contraction would act in an unfavorable direction.

C. Smooth Muscle Relaxation: The xanthines are direct smooth muscle relaxants which, as mentioned above, lead to vascular dilatation. Other smooth muscle is also relaxed, but only the effect on bronchiolar smooth muscle is of therapeutic importance. The bronchodilator effect is extremely important, and therefore aminophylline is often effective in the treatment of bronchial asthma and chronic obstructive lung disease.

D. Diuresis: The xanthines block renal tubular reabsorption of sodium and were once used as diuretics in the treatment of congestive heart failure. However, they have been replaced by other diuretics.

E. Gastric Secretion: The xanthines stimulate gastric acid secretion and enzyme production. However, both regular and decaffeinated coffee stimulate acid secretion more than caffeine alone, which suggests that the important constituent in coffee is something other than caffeine.

Clinical Uses

The usefulness of the xanthines is limited by 2 factors: Their potency is limited when compared with recently developed agents, and chronic oral adminis-

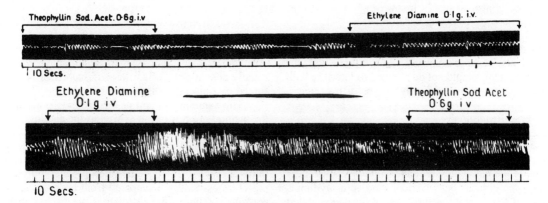

Figure 13 –2. The effect of aminophylline on Cheyne-Stokes respiration in patients with left ventricular failure. Theophylline solubilized with sodium acetate is without effect. Ethylenediamine regularized respiration *(above)* and stimulated it *(below).* (Reproduced, with permission, from Marais & McMichael: Theophylline-ethylene-diamine in Cheyne-Stokes respiration. Lancet 2:437, 1937.)

tration of adequate doses is unsatisfactory in most patients because of the occurrence of nausea and vomiting.

A. Asthma: In the discussion of the uses of sympathomimetic agents in Chapter 10, the treatment of asthma was arbitrarily divided into 2 problems: (1) the control of chronic recurrent wheezing in nonemergency situations, and (2) the treatment of the acute asthmatic attack the patient is unable to control with drugs carried for that purpose. Daily control of chronic asthma is usually most easily achieved with the sympathomimetic drugs. When aminophylline is tolerated by the patient, it is often effective. Theophylline has been solubilized with many agents other than ethylenediamine, and several such preparations are on the market.

Aminophylline finds its most common use in the treatment of the acute asthmatic attack and for chronic use in any patient with bronchospasm. Many patients will be promptly relieved by intravenously administered aminophylline.

B. Acute Pulmonary Edema: In congestive heart failure, pulmonary edema results when intravenous pressure overcomes opposing forces of oncotic pressure of plasma and the permeability of the capillary wall. The sudden transudation of fluid into the alveoli occurs in association with other pathologic states as well. Morphine and furosemide are the principal pharmacologic agents used to treat pulmonary edema. Small intravenous doses (see below) of aminophylline are used occasionally in this setting, but other inotropic agents are usually preferred. Oxygen should be given also.

C. Other Uses: Several other uses of the xanthines are discussed in other sections of this book. Their use in angina pectoris has virtually disappeared. Aminophylline is still rarely used as a supplement to diuretics. Because of the ability of caffeine to constrict cerebral vessels, it is combined with ergotamine in some mixtures suggested for use in the treatment of migraine. Caffeine is added to mild analgesic mixtures but without acceptable clinical evidence of usefulness. Caffeine is also available in over-the-counter proprietaries used to maintain wakefulness.

Except as contained in beverages, the xanthines should not be considered important or useful central stimulants. In the treatment of drug intoxication, for example, they should not be allowed to interfere with more specific or more effective forms of treatment.

Adverse Reactions

In adults, oral aminophylline in chronic effective doses often causes nausea and vomiting. It should be given slowly when used intravenously to avoid headache, fall in blood pressure, and subjective awareness of a forceful heart beat. Serious cardiac arrhythmias have followed the intravenous use of the concentrated solution intended for intramuscular administration.

More serious and even fatal reactions have occurred in children, often when the dose was determined by simply using an available preparation rather than by calculation on the basis of weight. Central nervous system effects cause agitation, convulsions, coma, and respiratory and vasomotor collapse. Regardless of the route of administration, vomiting can occur and may signify toxic levels.

Dosage

Theophylline has an oral bioavailability of 80–90%. Aminophylline is 85% theophylline by weight. The apparent volume of distribution of theophylline is 0.46 L/kg. When theophylline is given intravenously, the loading dose should be administered over 30 minutes. The clearance of theophylline is 50 mL/kg/h, and there is a large variability between patients. The half-life is about 6 hours. Severe pulmonary insufficiency, congestive heart failure, and hepatic dysfunction are associated with lower than average clearances, and the maintenance dose must be reduced in these settings. Cigarette smokers have greater than average clearances. Less than 10% of theophylline is eliminated unchanged by the kidneys.

Beverages Containing Xanthines

A variety of xanthine-containing beverages are used habitually in different cultures. Drug factors in this habituation are present in that the drink contains amounts of xanthine adequate to cause mild central nervous system stimulation.

Compared with amphetamine, caffeine effects are mild and transient. Wide variations in individual sensitivity to alteration in the sleep pattern are established by objective studies as well as by subjective reports. Caffeine can in some subjects delay and lighten sleep.

Physical dependence and withdrawal have been demonstrated in controlled experimental situations. The habitual coffee drinker may experience mild headaches about 18 hours after being deprived of caffeine. The occurrence of such headaches has been verified in controlled experimental situations. The user (5 cups or more daily) responds to morning caffeine—but not to a placebo—with positive subjective feelings, whereas the abstainer becomes dysphoric.

A single cup of coffee can elevate pulse rate and systolic blood pressure slightly (5–10 mm Hg). Larger amounts may cause ventricular ectopic beats. Other arrhythmias—eg, paroxysmal atrial tachycardia—usually appear only when the caffeine effect is reinforced by tobacco, fatigue, or alcohol.

The xanthine content of the drink depends upon the method of preparation as well as the alkaloid content of the crude product. Coffee ordinarily contains about 100 mg of caffeine per cup, although higher values are found. Instant coffee contains only two-thirds as much, and "caffeine-free" products only 3–6 mg. Tea, especially if prepared from tea bags, rarely contains 100 mg caffeine per cup. Cola drinks contain 50 mg caffeine per 12-oz can. Cocoa drinks contain theobromine, which is virtually devoid of central nervous system stimulating effects, in 200- to 300-mg amounts.

•   •   •

References

Angina Pectoris, Heart Failure,
& Vasodilators

Abrams J: Nitroglycerine and long acting nitrates. N Engl J Med 302:1234, 1980.

Aronov WS: Drug therapy: Management of stable angina. N Engl J Med 289:516, 1973.

Chatterjee K & others: Oral hydralazine in chronic heart failure: Sustained beneficial hemodynamic effects. Ann Intern Med 92:600, 1980.

Cohn JN, Franciosa JA: Vasodilator therapy of cardiac failure. (2 parts.) N Engl J Med 297:27, 254, 1977. [See also editorial on p 331.]

Hillis LD, Braunwald E: Coronary artery spasm. N Engl J Med 299:695, 1978.

Mason DT, Braunwald E: Effects of nitroglycerin and amyl nitrite on arteriolar and venous tone in the human forearm. Circulation 32:755, 1965.

Mellen HS, Goldberg HS, Friedman HF: Therapeutic effects of pentaerythritol tetranitrate in the immediate postmyocardial-infarction period. N Engl J Med 276:319, 1967.

Opie LH: Calcium antagonists. Lancet 1:808, 1980.

Robinson BF: Mode of action of nitroglycerin in angina pectoris: Correlation between hemodynamic effects during exercise and prevention of pain. Br Heart J 30:295, 1968.

Schelling JL, Lasagna L: A study of cross-tolerance to circulatory effects of organic nitrates. Clin Pharmacol Ther 8:256, 1967.

Tinker JH, Michenfelder JD: Sodium nitroprusside: Pharmacology, toxicology, and therapeutics. Anesthesiology 45:340, 1976.

Cerebral Blood Flow

Eckenhoff JE (editor): Symposium on carbon dioxide. Anesthesiology 21:585, 1960.

McHenry LC Jr: Cerebral blood flow studies in cerebrovascular disease. Arch Intern Med 117:546, 1966.

Sokoloff L: The action of drugs on the cerebral circulation. Pharmacol Rev 11:1, 1959.

Peripheral Vascular Flow

Abramson DI: Drugs used in peripheral vascular diseases. Am J Cardiol 12:203, 1963.

Barcroft H (editor): Peripheral circulation in man. Br Med Bull 19:97, 1963.

Gillespie JA: The case against vasodilator drugs in occlusive vascular disease of the legs. Lancet 2:995, 1959.

Xanthines

Cohen S, Booth GH Jr: Gastric acid secretion and lower-esophageal-sphincter pressure in response to coffee and caffeine. N Engl J Med 293:897, 1975.

Colton T, Gosselin RE, Smith RP: The tolerance of coffee drinkers to caffeine. Clin Pharmacol Ther 9:31, 1968.

Goldstein A, Kaizer S, Whitby O: Psychotropic effects of caffeine in man. 4. Quantitative and qualitative differences associated with habituation to coffee. Clin Pharmacol Ther 10:489, 1969.

Mitenko PA, Ogilvie RI: Rational intravenous doses of theophylline. N Engl J Med 289:600, 1973.

14 | Vasoconstrictors & Oxytocics

The vasoconstrictors already discussed —ie, the sympathomimetic amines and the facilitators of ganglionic transmission such as nicotine—have many other actions, including some degree of vasodilatation, relaxation of nonvascular smooth muscle, and cardiac stimulation. Their effects are explicable by reference to the physiology of the autonomic nervous system.

The present chapter discusses agents that stimulate the contraction of vascular or uterine smooth muscle through mechanisms unrelated to the innervation of the smooth muscle. The ergot alkaloids, the hormones of the posterior pituitary gland, the polypeptide angiotensin, and the prostaglandins are in this category.

ERGOT ALKALOIDS

History

The history of ergot over many centuries is the history of the epidemics (see Adverse Reactions, below) due to the ingestion of flour from smutted rye. The abortifacient action of toxic amounts of ergot suggested its use to hasten labor. European midwives of the 18th century adopted it and, in a crude way, standardized its dosage. An American physician, John Stearns (1770–1848), apparently learned of the use of ergot from German immigrants to New York State, and his reports (1808) led to its use by regular medical as well as folk practitioners. Used to hasten labor, it often caused excessive uterine contraction and caused ischemia damaging to the child; its present use (to prevent postpartum bleeding only) evolved slowly. The work of the British obstetrician Chassar Moir from 1932 to 1944 led to the isolation and established the use of **ergonovine.** He had noted that crude ergot had effects that were more favorable than those of pure ergotamine, which had been assumed by most workers to be the single active principle.

Source, Chemistry, & Classification

The ergot alkaloids still ultimately originate in the fungus or smut *Claviceps purpurea,* grown on kernels of rye. The growth is today carried out in fermentation vats in factories rather than in the field. Minor chemical modifications of the basic structure are possible, and the following classification separates the native (naturally occurring) alkaloids from 2 chemical modifications.

A. Native Alkaloids: The important naturally occurring alkaloids are ergotamine and ergonovine. Methylergonovine and methysergide are semisynthetic derivatives (see Table 14–1 for structure). Ergotoxine is a mixture of ergocristine, ergocryptine, and ergocornine, but these natural alkaloids are not therapeutically important.

Table 14–1 shows the structure common to all ergots. All compounds of interest are amides of lysergic acid (see Table 14–1). Ergotamine is referred to as an amino acid alkaloid because the amide nitrogen bears the condensation product of 3 amino acids. Ergonovine and the other alkaloids have simpler substituents. The amino acid alkaloids are poorly absorbed in comparison with ergonovine. However, the differences between the 2 are quantitative, and all of the natural alkaloids, the potent smooth muscle activators, retain the double bond shown at 2, ie, they are not hydrogenated.

B. Hydrogenated Alkaloids: Saturation of the double bond at C9-10 (shown at 2 in Table 14–1) reduces the smooth muscle constricting activity of the alkaloids but intensifies their vasodilating action. Dihydroergotamine and a hydrogenated mixture of the natural alkaloids (Hydergine or Deapril) are examples.

C. LSD: Lysergic acid *(Saure)* diethylamide (LSD) is also derived from ergot. The smooth muscle contracting effect of the other ergots is still present in LSD but is not always seen, since very small doses produce the feelings of depersonalization or the hallucinatory state sought by users. LSD is further discussed in Chapter 7 as one of several drugs producing a toxic psychosis. In Table 14–1, the indole moiety formed by rings A and B is shown at 3. Such a structure suggested to a few investigators a relationship between serotonin and LSD effects, but this relationship has never been established.

D. Bromocriptine (Parlodel): Bromocriptine is a semisynthetic derivative of ergocryptine with a bromine added at 4 as shown in Table 14–1. It acts like dopamine on the pituitary and on nigrostriatal systems and can be used to suppress lactation and to treat parkinsonism. It is discussed in Chapter 30 with other drugs that act on dopamine receptors and in Chapter 38.

Table 14—1. Chemical formulas of the ergot alkaloids.

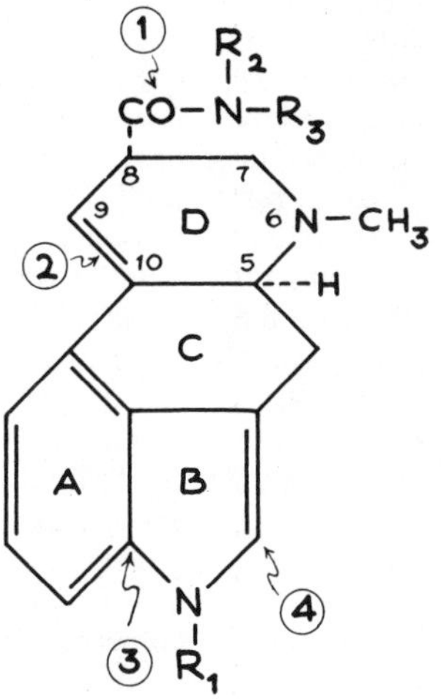

	R_1	R_2	R_3
Lysergic acid diethylamide (LSD)	—H	—C_2H_5	—C_2H_5
Ergonovine (ergometrine)	—H	—H	—C_3H_6OH (Propanol)
Methylergonovine	—H	—H	—C_4H_8OH (Butanol)
Methysergide (Sansert)	—CH_3	—H	Butanol
Ergotamine	—H	—H	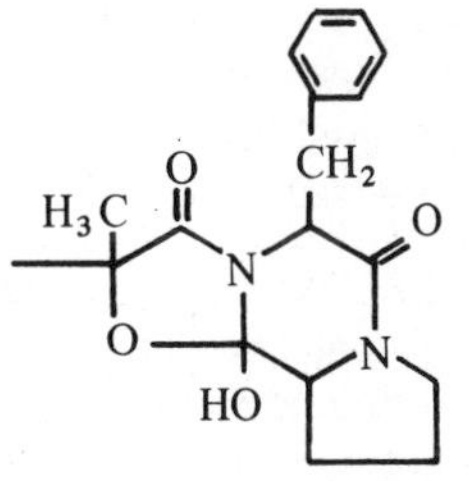 (Hydroxyalanine, phenylalanine, proline)
Lysergic acid	—H	R_2—N—R_3 replaced by —OH	

Absorption, Metabolism, & Excretion

Absorption of ergotamine, the amino acid alkaloid, after oral administration is incomplete and irregular. The oral dose is approximately 10 times the parenteral dose. Onset of action is delayed for 20 minutes or longer even after intramuscular or subcutaneous injection. Intravenous or sublingual administration gives a more rapid effect. Ergonovine acts rapidly and more predictably than ergotamine.

The smooth muscle stimulating actions of ergot persist for several hours. Because toxic effects occur more frequently in patients with liver disease, metabolism is presumed to take place in the liver.

Pharmacologic Actions

A. Mechanisms of Action: These alkaloids have diverse and in part contradictory effects. What little is known about their mechanism of action is mentioned in the discussion of their effects.

B. Effects:

1. Smooth muscle stimulation–All smooth muscle, vascular or nonvascular, is contracted. The action is a direct one on smooth muscle—ie, there is no relation to innervation or to any of the chemical mediators. The actual mechanism is not known.

The smooth muscle excitant action is pronounced in the natural alkaloids but greatly reduced in the hydrogenated derivatives.

a. Oxytocic effect–Only at term is uterine muscle more sensitive to ergot than is other smooth muscle. In the absence of pregnancy or early in pregnancy, dangerous amounts of ergot are required to demonstrate the uterine stimulating effect, and even then the cervix is more affected. Ergot cannot therefore be used in any context as an abortifacient. During the third trimester, the sensitivity of the uterus gradually increases, and ergonovine can be used to induce labor and contract the uterus postpartum. For the induction and stimulation of labor, it is much easier to adjust the dosage of oxytocin than that of an ergot alkaloid. For the prevention of postpartum bleeding, however, ergonovine or methylergonovine is most commonly used. The hemostasis is due to contraction of the uterine wall around the bleeding vessels of the placental site.

b. Vasoconstriction–The blood vessels in all vascular beds are constricted. Arteriolar constriction elevates systolic and diastolic blood pressures, but the effect is not great. Larger arteries are more sensitive. The dilatation of an artery by each pressure pulse is decreased while ergot is acting, and localized narrowings or even occlusion may be shown with arteriograms. The constriction of intracranial arteries is useful in the treatment of migraine, but the decreased flow through peripheral, mesenteric, or coronary arteries may cause ischemia of the tissues perfused by the artery.

2. Adrenergic blockade–Alpha-adrenergic blockade, the ability of a drug to block the vasoconstricting actions of the catecholamines, is discussed in Chapter 11. Adrenergic blockade was first produced by ergotamine and ergotoxine, and for many years these ergot alkaloids were the only such agents available for laboratory use. The blockade appears only after hypertensive doses in anesthetized animals and is unrelated to the therapeutic actions of ergot.

3. Central nervous system actions–

a. Vasodilatation due to central sympathoplegic action–Only the dihydrogenated alkaloids produce a reduction of sympathetic outflow and a reduction of sympathetic influences on blood vessels. A minor fall in blood pressure (not postural or gravity assisted) and bradycardia are produced. This action has not proved useful in the treatment of hypertension. Dihydroergotamine does retain some smooth muscle stimulating properties and is still used occasionally in the treatment of migraine. The other hydrogenated ergots are virtually obsolete.

The sympathoplegic and tranquilizer actions of the dihydroergots closely resemble those of reserpine. Their usefulness in treating hypertension and their mechanisms of action have not been restudied since the information generated by the study of reserpine has been available.

b. Behavioral–The dihydroergots have behavioral effects comparable to those of antipsychotic tranquilizers and in the past were used successfully in the treatment of agitated psychotics before the concept of tranquilizer drugs was recognized.

Clinical Uses

A. Ergotamine in Treatment of Migraine: The clinical picture of migraine is often not classic, but a typical sequence is as follows: A patient with particular genetic and personality traits develops a headache— often in response to a perceived environmental stimulus. The first phase of this recurrent problem is due to intracranial vasoconstriction and is manifest as a prodrome of visual signs and malaise. If not aborted by drug therapy, the period of vasoconstriction is succeeded by a phase of vasodilatation—the intracranial vessels become dilated and flaccid, and the resulting traction on meningeal receptors with each pressure pulse is felt as a unilateral, throbbing headache accompanied by nausea and vomiting and even prostration.

Ergot alkaloids are effective in treatment to the extent that they are vasoconstrictors and prevent the rhythmic distention of arteries (Fig 14–1). If they are given during the prodrome, the attack may be completely aborted.

Ergotamine tartrate (one of several trade names is Gynergen) is the most effective ergot alkaloid. Dihydroergotamine, a dihydroergot that retains some vasoconstrictor action, has also been suggested; however, it offers no advantage if equipotent doses are compared with ergotamine, and it can only be given by injection.

The results of ergotamine treatment may be spectacularly good, or the patient may use the amount of drug allowed per day or week without relief. In the latter case this is often because the drug is used too late in the attack, but it may be because of reliance upon oral ergotamine, which is not dependably absorbed. Oral administration may be tried, but if relief is not obtained, other routes of administration must be used before concluding that ergotamine is ineffective. Rectal suppositories are widely used, but sublingual administration or inhalation is effective and convenient. Subcutaneous injection is the most dependable route of administration of ergotamine and should be used when the drug is given as a therapeutic test.

Whatever the method of administration, a limit must be placed on the amount of drug used—eg, 1–2 mg orally may be repeated up to a total of 6 mg in 1 day and 12 mg in 1 week.

A number of proprietary mixtures are available on prescription, but their advantages over ergotamine alone given by the same route have not been demon-

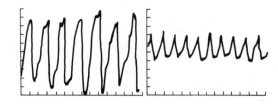

Figure 14 –1. Left temporal artery pulse volume tracing during left hemicrania *(left)* and after parenteral administration of 0.5 mg ergotamine tartrate *(right)*. Subjective response in 8½ minutes; objective response in 10 minutes. (Reproduced, with permission, from Friedman: Studies in the pharmacology of headache. Neurology 13:27, 1963.)

strated. Caffeine is added to one popular mixture (Cafergot) because it is a vasoconstrictor of intracranial vessels.

Ergotamine is not always required for the treatment of migraine. Sedatives such as phenobarbital and nonnarcotic analgesics or even codeine may be useful and preferable.

B. Prevention of Migrainous Attacks:

1. Methysergide (Sansert)–Methysergide (N-methylergonovine), a less potent form of ergonovine, is completely unsatisfactory for the treatment of acute attacks of migraine, but when administered continuously it is useful in preventing headaches. This prophylactic use has been reserved for patients with "cluster headaches" or for occasions that regularly precipitate migraine in a particular patient—eg, menstrual periods or weekends.

Methysergide has measurable value in selected patients. However, its toxicity must be considered in judging its usefulness. The adverse reactions discussed below have occurred frequently after the use of methysergide, and the drug appears to be not qualitatively different from ergotamine but merely a less potent vasoconstrictor.

2. Propranolol (Inderal)–(See Chapter 11.) Propranolol is effective in a large proportion (50–80% of cases in reducing the number of migrainous attacks. It is not useful for cluster headaches.

That the effect is due to a central nervous system effect of propranolol rather than its beta blocking action is suggested by the effectiveness of other behavioral depressants such as the antipsychotics, the antidepressants, cyproheptadine (a sedative antihistamine), and the belladonna alkaloids. Clonidine (Catapres) actually appears more promising at this time.

C. Ergonovine as an Oxytocic: For the induction of labor, oxytocin (Pitocin) is the preferred drug. For the prevention of postpartum bleeding, either ergonovine or methylergonovine is routinely used. Ergonovine may be given prophylactically even before the delivery of the placenta, in which case one parenteral dose is given followed by repeated oral doses; or the drug may be withheld until the first sign of bleeding is seen. After complete or incomplete abortion, ergonovine becomes less effective and slightly larger doses must be used.

Hypertension is the important side-effect of ergonovine. It is especially likely to occur after vasoconstrictors have been used in conjunction with regional anesthesia or in an eclamptic patient. Oxytocin does not have this effect.

Methylergonovine (Methergine) is widely used because it is supposed to cause less elevation of blood pressure. This is probably true, although equally potent oxytocic doses have not always been compared.

Adverse Reactions

This discussion of toxicity does not apply to ergonovine, which causes a moderate elevation of blood pressure but no serious toxic reactions in the usual

doses. If it were used chronically, as its methyl derivative (methysergide) is, it probably would cause more undesirable effects.

A. Side-Effects: The action of ergotamine on gastrointestinal smooth muscle may cause nausea and vomiting, abdominal cramps or epigastric discomfort, and diarrhea. Paresthesias, cold extremities, and claudication are early arteriospastic effects.

Methysergide causes the above side-effects, and its chronic administration may also cause weight gain, edema, loss of hair, and behavioral changes. Behavioral changes are similar to those associated with reserpine and include drowsiness or insomnia, restlessness, and feelings of depersonalization.

These side-effects may be severe enough to force discontinuance of the drug, a decision that is as often made by the patient as by the physician. As many as 20% of patients cannot tolerate methysergide; the rejection rate for ergotamine is probably much lower.

B. Overdosage Toxicity: Arteriospastic disease, the dangerous toxic effect of ergot derivatives, occurs in 2 forms.

1. Acute arterial occlusion–Many patients note transient coldness of the extremities after using ergotamine. In rare cases, the arteriospasm is general (rather than segmental) and persistent. Blood flow through the artery ceases completely. Blood flow may be resumed with no permanent damage, or tissue may become gangrenous before the process reverses itself. The reaction usually involves the legs and is often bilateral but not symmetric; the extent of damage may vary from loss of a toe to loss of an entire leg. During the reaction, blood pressure is elevated and there are electrocardiographic changes consistent with those of myocardial ischemia.

Of the many drugs and maneuvers tried, only nitroprusside infusions have shown any promise in altering the duration of the vasospastic state. In experimental situations, sympathectomy actually intensifies the gangrene.

The occurrence of gangrene is usually due to excessive dosages, but gangrene has occurred following therapeutic doses and even after doses that had previously been tolerated by the patient. The reaction is very rare, but the exact incidence is impossible to express. Most cases are not reported in the medical literature but do become known as the subject of litigation.

2. Retroperitoneal fibrosis–Both methysergide and ergotamine may cause acute arterial insufficiency. In addition, the chronic use of methysergide has been associated with retroperitoneal fibrosis, a previously extremely rare syndrome. In reported cases, the fibrosis has developed after use of the drug for 6 months to 4 years. Retroperitoneal fibrosis leads to ureteral obstruction with hydronephrosis and eventually loss of renal function. It is accompanied in some cases by pleural and pulmonary fibrosis and by changes in the cardiac valve rings, resulting in cardiac murmurs and disturbed dynamics of blood flow, with cardiac enlargement. If the drug is discontinued in time, the process is usually reversible. Surgical intervention and retrograde urologic studies which may precipitate complete obstruction, should therefore be delayed.

This reaction is assumed to be due to the chronic arterial constrictive action of methysergide. Reversible mesenteric artery occlusion after giving methysergide has been demonstrated by arteriography.

Patients receiving methysergide should be told to report promptly dysuria or back or pleural pain and should be seen at least 3–4 times a year for questioning and examination. In addition, a drug-free interval should be provided periodically. The manufacturer recommends 1 month without treatment after 6 months of drug administration; some physicians experienced with the drug recommend interruption of treatment every 2 months.

C. Epidemic Ergotism: Ergot poisoning from contaminated flour is not a current problem in drug toxicity but occurred during the Middle Ages. Rye was the bread grain of the poor in continental Europe, and rye is especially susceptible to attack by *Claviceps purpurea,* the fungus that produces ergot alkaloids. Among the ripe grains of rye, sclerotia—hard, spur-shaped masses of mycelium—are formed. These may be milled with the grain or fall to the ground to germinate and produce spores that perpetuate the infestation. Ingestion of smutted grain caused 2 types of ergotism.

1. Gangrenous ergotism–This form of ergotism occurred largely in France from the 9th to 14th centuries, and is comparable to the acute arteriospastic reaction described above. A foot or leg—less commonly, an arm—became inflamed, and the victim experienced feelings of cold alternating with severe burning pains (St. Anthony's fire). Numbness and dry gangrene followed, with painless loss of tissue varying in extent from nails to whole limbs. Rapidly fatal visceral gangrene also occurred.

The epidemics decreased in seriousness as wheat replaced rye and as agricultural technics such as drainage and deeper plowing developed. Rye can be cleaned of ergot, and legal standards now exist; but in the past the choice was often between eating contaminated grain or starvation. A comparatively minor outbreak was reported in France as recently as 1953.

2. Convulsive (spasmodic) ergotism–In northern Europe and Russia, another form of epidemic ergotism has occurred since the late 16th century. The most prominent sign was a painful spasmodic or spastic contraction of voluntary muscles accompanied in severe cases by convulsions. About 10–20% of those affected died, and many of those who survived suffered residual mental dullness or dementia. Primitive epidermiologic studies suggest that the occurrence of this type of ergotism was determined by a lack of dairy and meat products in the diet, and there is experimental evidence suggesting a relation to vitamin A deficiency. The last epidemic of significant extent occurred in Russia in 1926.

Contraindications & Cautions

The ergot alkaloids should not be used during pregnancy or in the presence of vascular disease (peripheral or coronary). Impaired liver function must now be considered a contraindication to the use of ergot even though ergotamine was once used to relieve the itching associated with jaundice. In view of the experience with methysergide, pulmonary and valvular disease should probably also be considered contraindications.

The drugs should be administered with careful limitation of the total dose, and intervals free of drug treatment should be provided.

Ergot alkaloids are dispensed as salts of organic acids. Both the chemical and trade names are listed to avoid the confusion arising from the trade names.

Dosages

A. Ergotamine Tartrate (Gynergen; many other trade names): Available routes of administration and one example of dose limitation in each case are as follows:

1. Subcutaneous or intravenous–0.25 mg; may repeat one time.

2. Rectal–One 2-mg suppository; may repeat same dose twice at hourly intervals.

3. Buccal or sublingual–1- or 2-mg tablet; may repeat to a total of 6 mg in 1 day and 12 mg in 1 week.

4. Inhalation (Medihaler)–A promising technic for rapid absorption that has been incompletely evaluated for safety.

5. Oral–1–2 mg; may repeat to 6 mg in 1 day and 12 mg in 1 week.

B. Methysergide (Sansert): The dosage of methysergide is 2 mg 3 (or at the most 4) times a day. Treatment should begin with a lower dose.

C. Ergonovine Maleate (Ergotrate) and Methylergonovine (Methergine): The dosage of one or the other of these drugs is usually standardized on a given obstetric service. An example is 0.2 mg intramuscularly or intravenously at the end of the second stage of labor; may repeat once; then 0.2–0.4 mg 2–4 times daily for 2–3 days.

ANGIOTENSIN

The physiologic role of angiotensin may be of great importance. It does not, however, have any established therapeutic usefulness even though a synthetic angiotensin is marketed as a pressor agent.

Source & Chemistry

Angiotensin amide (Hypertensin) is a synthetic octapeptide corresponding to the amide of bovine angiotensin II—ie, 1-L-asparagine-5-L-valyl angiotensin octapeptide. Angiotensin II is formed in the organism by the splitting of 2 amino acids from the decapeptide, angiotensin I. Inactive angiotensin I, in turn, is a fragment split off from angiotensinogen, an alpha$_2$ globulin, by renin elaborated by the juxtaglomerular cells of the kidney.

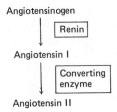

Pharmacologic Effects

Angiotensin amide, after intravenous injection, acts as a very potent but briefly acting vasoconstrictor. Peripheral resistance is greatly elevated, but the heart is not stimulated. Consequently, a larger amount of cardiac work is expended as "pressure work" and a smaller fraction is available to pump a volume of blood—ie, cardiac output falls. Thus, even though both diastolic and systolic pressures rise, tissue perfusion of all extracranial areas is impaired rather than augmented.

Adverse reactions—other than the probability that prolonged infusion is harmful in patients with shock—are secondary to an excessive elevation of blood pressure.

Angiotensin Antagonists

To the extent that angiotensin and renin are important in maintaining vasoconstriction, antagonism of the angiotensin effect by drugs could be useful in the treatment of hypertension or other vasospastic states. Two classes of antagonists are available as investigational drugs, but neither can be said to offer great promise at this time.

Saralasin (sarcosine-1, alanine-8 AII) differs from angiotensin II (AII) in its terminal amino acid and competes with angiotensin II at receptor sites. Blood pressure lowering is inconsistent in hypertensive patients, and the pressure is elevated in normal individuals by a residual agonist effect.

A second class of antagonists acts by inhibiting peptide hydrolase, or converting enzyme. Teprotide and captopril are examples. The latter compound is active after oral administration and has been used in congestive heart failure in the same way as the vasodilators mentioned in Chapter 13. It appears at this time to have prohibitive toxicity.

PROSTAGLANDINS

The prostaglandins are local hormones that function importantly in the platelet phase of clotting and in augmenting the effects of mediators of inflammation. They are therefore important in relation to antithrombotic and anti-inflammatory drugs and are further discussed in Chapters 18 and 27. They are promising abortifacients, but their other uses are still investigational.

Source & Chemistry

The prostaglandins are a family of naturally occurring, lipid-soluble acids and many synthetic congeners. Their structure and nomenclature are presented in Fig 14–2. They derive their name from the high concentrations found in seminal fluid, but they are found in virtually all tissues. Those used as drugs are prepared synthetically.

The differing effects of the various prostaglandins are sometimes even opposite in direction. Specificity of effect is achieved in part by the synthesis of different prostaglandins in different tissues. Several of the common pathways are shown in Fig 18–5.

Pharmacokinetics

The prostaglandins are not stored in the tissues in anticipation of need but are synthesized within seconds in response to various perturbations. Synthesis occurs rapidly as the precursor, usually arachidonic acid, is liberated from combination with other lipids. The synthesis, which is governed by a microsomal enzyme, prostaglandin synthetase, stops within a few seconds after the stimulus ends. Prostaglandin synthetase is inhibited by aspirin and many related drugs.

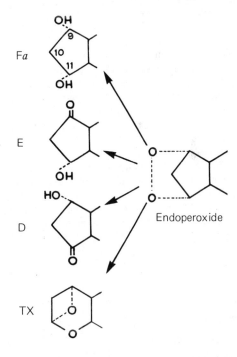

Figure 14 –2. Prostaglandins (PGs) are synthesized in the organism from arachidonic or closely related fatty acids. The prostaglandins are named as derivatives of a hypothetical compound, prostanoic acid. The 5-membered ring is variously modified to give the lettered type prostaglandin (PGA through PGI). A thromboxane (TX) has a 6-membered ring. A subscript indicates the number of unsaturated bonds in the side chains. PGE_2 is shown. In a first step in the biosynthesis of PGs, a PG endoperoxide (PGG or PGH) is generated. See also Fig 18–5.)

The prostaglandins act in very low concentrations but are destroyed quickly—in one circulation time if they enter the blood and reach the lung or kidney. They act for a few minutes when elaborated physiologically. To achieve a therapeutic effect, large amounts (milligrams) must be applied locally.

Effects

The prostaglandins are usually liberated coincidentally with other mediators or local hormones and, as a tentative generalization, may be thought of as inhibiting or, in a few situations, augmenting the effects of other mediators. Like many other mediators, they stimulate adenylate cyclase activity and increase tissue levels of cAMP.

At this time, prostaglandins of the E and F series appear most likely to be applied therapeutically, and their effects are emphasized below.

A. On Vascular Smooth Muscle: Prostaglandins of the E and A series are vasodilators and may lower blood pressure as well as produce a flare if they are injected intradermally. Prostaglandin F (PGF) constricts arterioles and veins, but blood pressure is not usually changed in humans.

B. On Other Smooth Muscle: Prostaglandin E (PGE) and PGF will initiate or augment uterine contractions throughout pregnancy, not only at term, as is the case with oxytocin or the ergot alkaloids. Intestinal motility is increased. PGE dilates bronchioles, whereas PGF precipitates asthma.

C. Other Effects: PGE inhibits gastric secretion stimulated by histamine or food. The prostaglandins block the lipolytic effect of the catecholamines, decrease adrenergic neuron activity, and cause a minor increase in the force of cardiac contraction.

Pathophysiologic Significance

The number of functions of prostaglandins in the organism suggested at the moment is implausibly large. Two well-established functions are referred to at this point (and discussed in more detail in Chapters 18 and 27) because they contribute to an understanding of 2 effects of aspirin and other compounds.

Inflammation is in part mediated by PGE_2, which is released during inflammation after histamine and bradykinin. It contributes to pain and vasodilatation. Aspirin relieves pain by inhibiting the synthesis of PGE.

Similarly, aspirin reduces platelet adhesiveness and agglutination at the onset of thrombus formation, in part by preventing the release of the prostaglandin that accelerates platelet clumping.

Clinical Uses

A. Second Trimester Abortion: As abortifacients during the first trimester, the prostaglandins are less satisfactory than suction curettement simply because of the total time (10–24 hours) required. After 15–16 weeks, the use of PGF_2 or PGE_2 may prove preferable to intra-amniotic injection of hypertonic saline. The prostaglandin is more rapid in effect and causes fewer major complications. There are still questions about the relative incidence with the 2 technics of retained placenta and subsequent curettement.

B. Investigational: The prostaglandins, mostly as PGF_2 and PGE_2, are being evaluated in the treatment of peptic ulcer, asthma, hypertension, and hypercalcemia, among others. They have been less satisfactory than available methods in the induction of labor and as a "morning-after" contraceptive.

Side-Effects

Signs of stimulation of smooth muscle of the gastrointestinal tract—nausea and vomiting, cramps, and diarrhea—are common. In addition, hypotension with fainting, hypertension, headache, asthma, and electroencephalographic abnormalities with convulsions may occur in susceptible individuals.

Preparations

Dinoprost or $PGF_{2\alpha}$ (Prostin F2 Alpha) is available for intra-amniotic injection to terminate pregnancy in the second trimester. Prostaglandin E2 (Prostin E2) is available as vaginal suppositories for the same purpose.

●   ●   ●

References

Ergot

Andersen PK: Sodium nitroprusside and epidural blockade in the treatment of ergotism. N Engl J Med 296:1271, 1977.

Barger G: *Ergot and Ergotism.* Gurney & Jackson (Edinburgh), 1931.

Saper JR: Migraine. II. Treatment. JAMA 239:2480, 1978.

Angiotensin

Davis R & others: Treatment of chronic congestive heart failure with captopril, an oral inhibitor of angiotensin-converting enzyme. N Engl J Med 301:117, 1979.

Hollenberg NK: Pharmacologic interruption of the renin-angiotensin system. Annu Rev Pharmacol 19:559, 1979.

Peart WS: Renin-angiotensin system. N Engl J Med 292:302, 1975.

Vasoactive peptides. (Symposium.) Fed Proc 27:49, 1968.

Prostaglandins

Clayman CB: The prostaglandins. JAMA 233:904, 1975.

Cuthbert MF (editor): *The Prostaglandins: Pharmacological and Therapeutic Advances.* Lippincott, 1973.

Flower RJ: Drugs which inhibit prostaglandin biosynthesis. Pharmacol Rev 26:33, 1974.

Mathé AA & others: Aspects of prostaglandin function in the lung. (2 parts.) N Engl J Med 296:850, 910, 1977.

Wilson DE (editor): Symposium on prostaglandins. Arch Intern Med 133:29, 1974.

Congestive heart failure is frequently reversible even when the underlying cardiovascular disease that causes it may not be treatable; a properly managed patient may have decades of active and comfortable life after the first appearance of symptoms. Digitalis therapy is an important part of the therapeutic regimen in association with indicated restrictions of sodium intake and physical activity and the use of diuretics. The proper use of digitalis is thus a common and important demand on the physician.

Digitalis administration requires close attention. The margin between therapeutic and toxic doses is small, and in most patients there is no reliable index of optimal dosage. Toxicity is therefore frequently encountered, and many details of digitalis action thus become very important.

History

The use of squill (a sea plant now known to contain digitalislike glycosides) was advocated by the ancient Egyptians and described in the Eber's papyruses as a form of therapy for dropsy. William Withering in 1785 published his treatise, ''An Account of the Foxglove and Some of Its Medical Uses.'' Early in his practice in Shropshire, Withering was asked to evaluate a folk remedy containing 20 or more herbs that had been effective in relieving the edema of a prominent personage after the regular practitioners had failed. Withering (1741–1799), who became a preeminent British botanist as well as a master physician, recognized that all of the ingredients except foxglove (digitalis) were medically useless, and that, if the remedy were active in the treatment of dropsy (edema), digitalis must be the active ingredient. At this time he recognized the diuretic effect of digitalis and also appreciated that it could slow the pulse and produce undesirable effects such as nausea, vomiting, and diarrhea. This led to his recommendation that the medication be given in sufficient dosage until it produced an effect on the kidney, the pulse, the stomach, or the bowel.

During his lifetime, Withering saw digitalis come into wide use. Soon thereafter, however, the indications for the use of the drug became confused and the slowing effect on heart rate began to be emphasized, leading to such characterizations as ''cardiac depressant'' and ''opium of the heart.''

The undue emphasis on the slowing of cardiac rate caused by digitalis was intensified by the work of another great physician, James Mackenzie (1853–1925). Mackenzie was a general practitioner who began to sort out for us the common cardiac arrhythmias. His practice included much obstetrics, and many of these patients had rheumatic heart disease with atrial arrhythmias, especially the lasting arrhythmia that he called ''auricular paralysis'' (fibrillation). In such cases digitalis is especially effective, and its action is accompanied by a graded slowing of ventricular rate. The emphasis upon slowing of the rate rather than correction of failure independent of an effect on rate thus became more firmly established.

Parenthetically, after 25 years of general practice, Mackenzie became a London cardiologist and, to his disappointment, became better known for the invention of a polygraph for the simultaneous recording of the venous and arterial pulse waves than for his careful studies of the natural history of the arrhythmias.

One person appreciative of Mackenzie's work was Arthur Cushny (1866–1926). Like Withering and Mackenzie, Cushny trained at Edinburgh, but he did not continue his research in the clinical tradition of the United Kingdom. He was more influenced by his experience in the laboratories of German universities. Cushny deserves credit for the development of the descriptive pharmacology of digitalis and for providing leadership in the development of modern pharmacology at Ann Arbor, London, and Edinburgh.

Early in this century, progress was made in the isolation and characterization of many cardiotonic glycosides from digitalis, and this progress in the chemical area was accompanied by progress in clinical cardiology such that by the mid 1920s another indication for the use of digitalis—congestive heart failure—was clear to the leaders in the profession. Additional clinical progress is mentioned later, but it will become apparent that, except for a clearer understanding of the indications for the use of digitalis and its glycosides, limited progress has occurred since the time of Withering.

Source & Chemistry

The term ''digitalis'' is used for convenience to include a large number of naturally occurring steroid glycosides and derived products, all of which have the same beneficial and toxic effects on the heart.

The most common source of these drugs (which cannot be synthesized) is the crimson or royal purple foxglove or the white foxglove *(Digitalis purpurea or Digitalis lanata)*. *Strophanthus gratus* and *S kombé* (African plants) and squill *(Urginea maritima or indica)* must also be mentioned as sources of glycosides. The remaining botanical sources are many, and there is even one animal source, the secretion of the glands in the skin of toads.

Each of the cardioactive principles contains the familiar steroid nucleus (Figs 15–1 and 15–2). At C17 is a lactone ring that is essential for cardioactivity. To the C3 hydroxyl is added, through a series of glycosidic links, a sequence of sugars that influence the physical properties of the compound. The steroid-lactone system freed of the sugars by hydrolysis—ie, with a free hydroxyl at C3—is called an **aglycone** or **genin.**

A. Common Glycosides: By following the stepwise hydrolysis diagrammed in Fig 15–1, the commonly used glycosides can be identified.

The leaves of *D lanata* contain a mixture of 3 glycosides. The sequence of sugars and acetyl groups is also diagrammed in Fig 15–1. One of the native glycosides, lanatoside C (Cedilanid), is available for oral use, but rarely used because of unreliable absorption. If the acetyl group is removed, the resulting deslanoside (Cedilanid-D) is obtained. If the glucose is then hydrolyzed off, a "purified glycoside," digoxin, results. The properties of these 3 are quite similar. If the sequence of hydrolysis is altered and only the glucose removed, acetyldigitoxin, an uncommonly employed glycoside, is prepared. From the other lanatosides, digitoxin and gitoxin are prepared.

Digoxin is 12-hydroxydigitoxin and gitoxin is 16-hydroxydigitoxin. These minor changes increase water solubility and decrease duration of action.

Digitalis folia (the whole leaf preparation), digitoxin, gitoxin, and gitalin are derived from *D pur-*

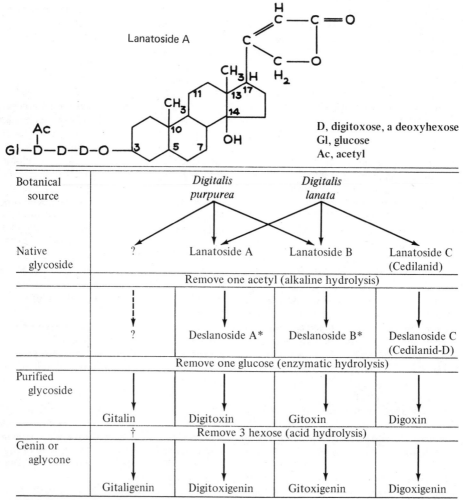

Lanatoside A

D, digitoxose, a deoxyhexose
Gl, glucose
Ac, acetyl

Botanical source	*Digitalis purpurea*	*Digitalis lanata*		
Native glycoside	?	Lanatoside A	Lanatoside B	Lanatoside C (Cedilanid)
	Remove one acetyl (alkaline hydrolysis)			
	?	Deslanoside A*	Deslanoside B*	Deslanoside C (Cedilanid-D)
	Remove one glucose (enzymatic hydrolysis)			
Purified glycoside	Gitalin	Digitoxin	Gitoxin	Digoxin
	† Remove 3 hexose (acid hydrolysis)			
Genin or aglycone	Gitaligenin	Digitoxigenin	Gitoxigenin	Digoxigenin

*Clinically unimportant.
†Preparation of gitaligenin involves removal of 2 hexoses (digitoxose) by acid hydrolysis from gitalin.

Figure 15 –1. Derivation of the common cardiac glycosides by progressive hydrolysis of the glycosides present in the leaf.

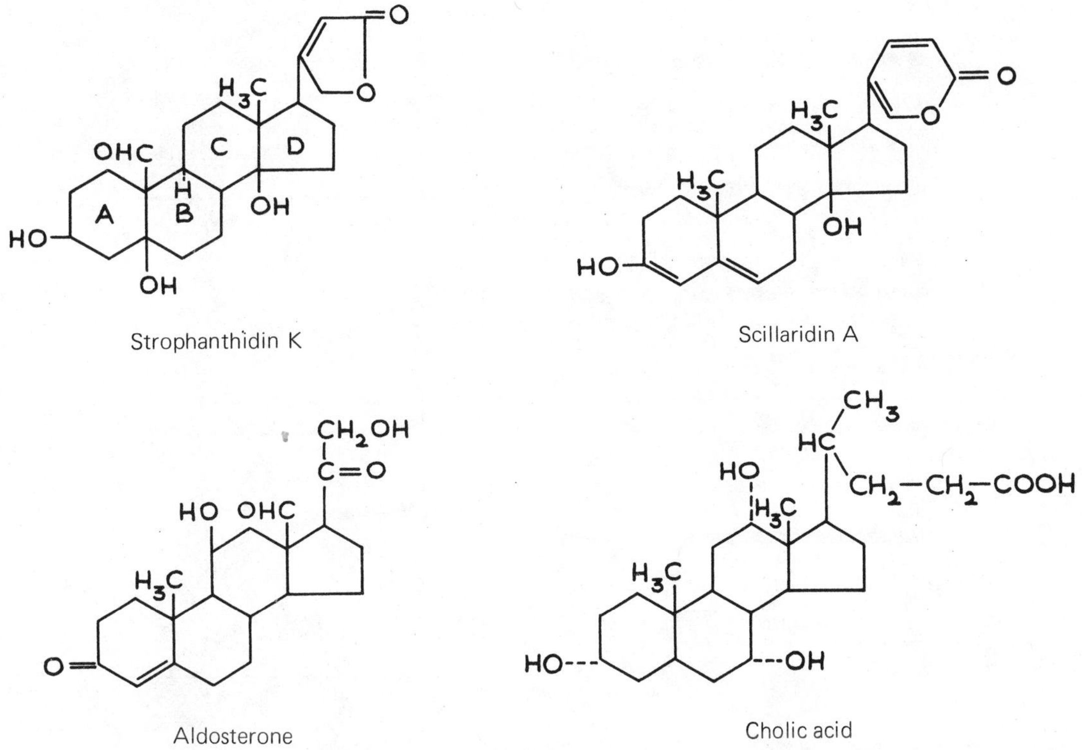

Strophanthidin K

Scillaridin A

CH₂OH

Aldosterone

Cholic acid

Figure 15 –2. Structures of 2 additional aglycones of cardiac glycosides and 2 possibly related steroids for comparison. Strophanthidin is the genin derived from a strophanthin—eg, ouabain or strophanthin G. Scillaridin A from squill contains a 6-membered lactone ring.

purea. The sequence of hydrolysis is similar, but the purpurea glycosides do not bear the acetyl group. Ouabain, or strophanthidin G, is the purified glycoside from *S gratus* and must be distinguished from strophanthidin K (from *S kombé*). The aglycone of a strophanthin is called a strophanthidin.

B. Structure-Action Relationships: The lactone ring is essential for cardiotonic activity. Digitalis contains steroid glycosides—ie, steroid plus sugars but without the lactone ring—that are not cardiotonic. The lactone ring always has an α,β unsaturation but may be 5 or 6 membered (Fig 15–2). The β-hydroxyl at C14 is distinctive and probably essential. The stereochemistry (at C8, 9, 10, 13, and 17) is like the sterols or bile acids rather than the endocrine steroids. Unlike the sterols, however, in digitalis the orientation of the C/D rings is cis.

The several glycosides, genins, and semisynthetic modifications vary in their absolute potency and in rapidity of action. No qualitatively different variant has been identified, ie, it has not been possible to selectively increase therapeutic effect without increasing the toxic effect. It may be that this important goal is unattainable, but it is equally likely that, since the common bioassay methods measure a toxic response, any selectively less toxic compound would be discarded as inactive.

C. Bioassay: The crystalline glycosides, being pure substances, are assayed chemically, prescribed by weight, and have a constant potency. The digitalis leaf preparations, rarely used currently, vary in the amounts of glycosides present. Each batch of the leaf must, therefore, be calibrated against an international standard of the leaf, so that a tablet of given weight will contain the same activity from batch to batch and from manufacturer to manufacturer.

The various methods that have been used all depend on the fact that a continuous infusion of a dilute tincture of digitalis will lead to cardiac arrest in systole or in ventricular fibrillation, depending upon the species. Frogs and cats were formerly used in the official assay, but the current USP recognizes the difficulty of securing enough cats and substitutes the pigeon for the assay.

A human assay method compares the T wave flattening produced by an unknown dose with the graded lowering produced by a series of standard doses of digitalis. The correlation of this assay (which uses nontoxic doses in humans) with animal assays is poor. However, the chemically determined digitoxin content of the leaf correlates well with the activity determined by bioassay in humans. For these reasons, animal assays using toxic (lethal) doses are skeptically regarded in physiologic work, although they do suffice to provide leaf preparations of constant potency. The therapeutic application of digitalis is a difficult exer-

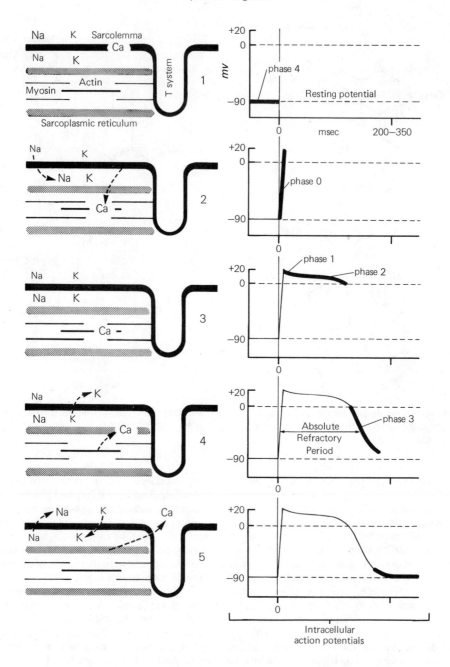

Figure 15 –3. Summary of aspects of myocardial physiology on which glycosides may act. *(1)* Resting state. Na⁺ is in higher
concentration extracellularly, K⁺ is concentrated within the cell, and Ca²⁺ is concentrated in the region of the sarcolemma
and its invagination, the transverse tubule. Membrane resting potential (phase 4) is maintained by relative impermeability of
cell membrane to Na⁺ and permeability to K⁺. *(2)* When a wave of depolarization reaches the unit or when the resting
potential rises to a threshold value in pacemaker tissue, sodium rapidly enters the cell, neutralizing the resting potential.
Calcium moves from storage sites, and its concentration with the cell rises. Troponin is attached to actin and inhibits
actin-myosin interaction—ie, contraction. Calcium binds to troponin and removes the inhibition of bridge formation between
actin and myosin. Digitalis is assumed to increase intracellular Ca²⁺ secondary to a change in step 5 below, and increased
binding of troponin leads to a greater rate of tension development. *(3)* Plateau of action potential. Na⁺ entry slows and K⁺
efflux is delayed, leading to a long refractory period in comparison with nerve or skeletal muscle. *(4)* K⁺ efflux occurs and
restoration of intracellular negativity begins. Calcium is actively transported into sarcoplasmic reticulum, allowing relaxation
to occur. *(5)* The sodium-potassium pump returns Na⁺ to the outside and K⁺ to the inside of the cell. Calcium diffuses from
sarcoplasmic reticulum to extracellular space. Digitalis appears to act by inhibiting Na⁺-K⁺ activated ATPase in the cell
membrane and thus reducing the energy supply for the sodium pump. An increase in intracellular Na⁺ will force a decrease in
intracellular K⁺, leading to arrhythmias and somehow an increase in delivery of Ca²⁺ in step 2.

cise in clinical bioassay, and additional quantitative measurements in humans are mentioned below.

Pharmacologic Actions
a. Mechanism of Action:
1. Of the therapeutic effect–Studies on the effect of cardiac glycosides on intracellular potentials and ion fluxes have led to the development of plausible and attractive theories to explain the ability of the digitalis compounds to increase the force of myocardial contraction. These theories may, however, be held only tentatively if 2 conditions are imposed: (1) the effect interpreted must be demonstrable in therapeutic (low) rather than only in toxic (high) concentrations of cardiac glycosides, and (2) the effect must be demonstrable in cardiac muscle and not extrapolated from axon or erythrocyte.

The biochemical analysis of digitalis effect showed that the action is not on myocardial energy production, storage, or liberation. Neither does it have a direct action on the contractile protein.

The effect that correlates best with the cardiotonic activity of various compounds, the ability to inhibit the activity of Na^+-K^+ activated ATPase, would reduce the energy available to the sodium pump and lead to an increase in intracellular Na^+ (Fig 15–3) with a resulting increase in availability of intracellular Ca^{2+}.

2. Of the toxic effects–The cardiac arrhythmias that occur as part of digitalis toxicity can be explained as an extension of the effect on membrane ATPase. If intracellular Na^+ is increased, K^+ must be lost to maintain an isosmotic state. The concentrations of potassium involved are smaller than the amounts of Na^+, and an important change in the ratio of K^+ inside to K^+ outside can occur. The intracellular potential would be brought closer to the threshold, and diastolic depolarization would occur. In addition, conduction delay leading to reentry is a common mechanism for the production of arrhythmias.

Potassium depletion clearly favors the development of digitalis-induced arrhythmias. Potassium supplementation has an easily demonstrable effect on digitalis toxicity in the laboratory, but its clinical usefulness is limited once the patient is repleted. Potassium depletion or supplementation is unrelated to the therapeutic effect.

B. Effects:
1. Effects on the myocardium–The heart is not a homogeneous organ with a single function. Some drugs may exert directly opposite effects on the same primary function in different areas of the heart. In the case of digitalis and quinidine, it is particularly important to specify both the effect and the area of the heart in which it is manifested. Each of the essential properties of cardiac muscle—contractility, conduction, refractoriness, and automaticity—are altered by digitalis. However, the effects may be different on atrial muscle, the atrioventricular node, the sinoatrial node, Purkinje tissue, or ventricular muscle.

a. Increased force and velocity of contraction (inotropic action)–Digitalis enables the failing heart to contract more forcefully. The therapeutically important effect of digitalis is due to a direct action on the ventricular muscle and is demonstrable on normal as well as failing hearts (Figs 15–4 and 15–5).

As a result of the increased force of contraction, cardiac output may be increased. The cardiac output at rest of patients with congestive failure may not be greatly different from that of normals, but digitalis restores the ability to elevate output in response to need. Systolic emptying is more complete and diastolic size is decreased.

In recent years many cardiologists have attempted to deemphasize the value of digitalis in the treatment of congestive heart failure in patients who are in sinus rhythm. Acute clinical studies have shown a relatively small increase in cardiac output. However, long-term clinical studies have confirmed a significant value in such patients.

b. Slowed atrioventricular conduction (dromotropic conduction)–Digitalis slows conduction through the specialized tissue connecting the atria and the interventricular septum, ie, through the atrioventricular node. The effect is manifest as a P–R prolongation leading to increasing degrees of heart block in the presence of sinus rhythm and progressive slowing of the ventricular response in atrial fibrillation and atrial flutter. Intraventricular conduction (measured by QRS duration) is not affected (as it is by quinidine). This action is predominantly a direct effect, and is due only in small part to the vagal stimulation mentioned below.

MYOCARDIAL CONTRACTILE FORCE

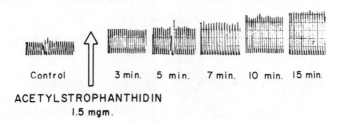

Control   3 min.   5 min.   7 min.   10 min.   15 min.

ACETYLSTROPHANTHIDIN
1.5 mgm.

Figure 15–4. An illustration of the ability of a cardiac glycoside to increase the force of ventricular contraction in a patient not in congestive failure. A strain gauge was applied at the operation to correct an atrial septal defect. (Reproduced, with permission, from Braunwald & others: Studies on digitalis. J Clin Invest 40:52, 1961.)

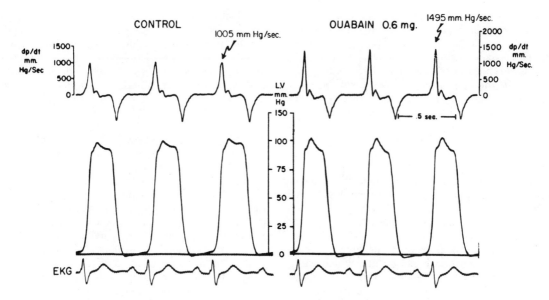

Figure 15 –5. Recordings of left ventricular (LV) pressure and rate of change (dp/dt) before and 30 minutes after ouabain administration. (Reproduced, with permission, from Mason & Braunwald: Studies on digitalis. IV. Effects of ouabain on the nonfailing human heart. J Clin Invest 42:1108, 1963.)

c. Prolonged refractory period of atrioventricular node –The effect of digitalis in prolonging the atrioventricular nodal refractory period will not be clinically apparent so long as a slow atrial rate allows time for recovery of atrioventricular tissue between each beat. In the presence of a normal sinus rhythm, only a great prolongation of atrioventricular node refractory period will add to the effect on conduction to produce atrioventricular block.

However, in the presence of a rapid atrial rate (typically in atrial fibrillation, common in atrial flutter, and least common in atrial tachycardia), the prolongation of the refractory period will reduce the number of atrial impulses activating the atrioventricular node and thereby reduce the number of waves of depolarization reaching the ventricles. Digitalis will therefore slow the rapid ventricular rate associated with an atrial arrhythmia whether it alters the atrial rhythm or not.

For example, in atrial flutter with an atrial rate of 240 and a 2:1 block, the ventricular rate would be 120, the atrioventricular node responding to every second stimulus (Fig 15–6). After digitalis, the atrioventricular node is refractory for the time occupied by 3 cycles subsequent to each response (4:1 block) and the ventricular rate would be 60 (Fig 15–7).

In the presence of atrial tachycardia with 1:1 atrioventricular conduction not due to digitalis toxicity, digitalis therapy will often result in reversion to sinus rhythm. This is the result of atrioventricular nodal conduction delay which interrupts the reentry pathway within the atrioventricular node which is responsible for the tachycardia.

d. Increased ectopic impulse formation –Toxic doses of the digitalis glycosides increase the automaticity of all areas of the heart except the sinoatrial node. (By automaticity is meant the ability to initiate

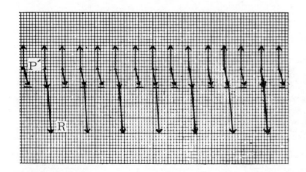

Figure 15 –6. Atrial flutter before digitalis. Atrial rate 240, 2:1 block. Ventricular rate, 120. P′ = atrial depolarizations. R = ventricular depolarizations.

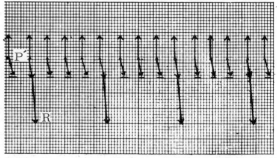

Figure 15 –7. Atrial flutter after digitalis. Atrial rate 240, 4:1 block. Ventricular rate, 60. P′ = atrial depolarizations. R = ventricular depolarizations.

and propagate an impulse.)

If, as is usually the case, the effect is primarily on Purkinje fibers in the ventricles, the sequence (important in understanding the toxic signs) is (1) ventricular ectopic beats when the effect is minimal; (2) bigeminy or coupling if an ectopic beat follows each normal beat; (3) ventricular tachycardia; and (4) ventricular fibrillation terminally.

Atrial tachycardia, usually with 2:1 atrioventricular block, atrioventricular junctional rhythms, atrioventricular block, and combinations of any of the above are common digitalis-induced arrhythmias.

e. Decreased rate of sinoatrial node (chronotropic action)–The rate of the normal pacemaker—ie, the pulse rate if a normal sinus rhythm is present—is depressed by the cardiac glycosides. With smaller doses, this effect is due mostly to vagal stimulation and is reversed by atropine. With larger doses of digitalis, the effect of decreasing sinoatrial rate is direct, ie, it is not blocked by atropine. The effect of reducing the rate of the sinoatrial node appears to be inconsistent with the ability to increase automaticity. However, it is probably not due to an effect on diastolic depolarization but represents conduction failure in atrial muscle with continued rhythmicity of the sinoatrial node. This is the least clinically reliable effect of digitalis and cannot be utilized to evaluate digitalis dosage.

2. Effects secondary to relief of congestive failure–The increased force of cardiac contraction and the resultant increase in cardiac output relieve congestive heart failure to a degree depending upon the severity of the underlying disease. The following secondary changes are then observed: (1) Diuresis occurs, with mobilization of peripheral edema. (The

glycosides have no important direct effect on the renal tubules.) (2) Venous pressure is reduced as extracellular fluid volume is contracted and by a direct effect of digitalis on venous capacitance. (3) The tachycardia that accompanies congestive failure declines—due, probably, to the fall in pressures on the right side of the circulation. (4) Heart size decreases.

3. Resume of effects on rate–The factors that slow cardiac rate can now be summarized: (1) Correction of failure. (2) Reflex vagal stimulation. (3) Depression of sinoatrial node. (4) Prolongation of the refractory period of the atrioventricular node. (5) Slowing of atrioventricular conduction.

Action (4) is important only with a rapid atrial rate, and (5) will cause significant slowing only when atrioventricular block occurs. The vagal factors operate first; the extravagal influences, especially (3), later. Regardless of the rhythm, the slowing of the rate is not essential to the action of digitalis. This has been demonstrated by human studies in which the rate was kept elevated by atropine during digitalis administration; cardiac output increased and symptoms regressed nonetheless.

4. Electrographic effects–The electrophysiologic changes induced by the cardiac glycosides in part explain the mechanisms of the effects just described. In addition to the ECG, records from microelectrodes and surface electrodes are useful.

Microelectrodes can be placed within single cardiac fibers and the effect of cardiac glycosides on the resting and action potential observed. Fig 15–8 illustrates the results of one such experiment in which the recording was from Purkinje tissue. (Similar changes

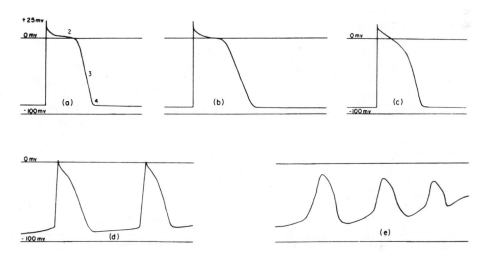

Figure 15–8. Effect of increasing concentrations of ouabain on the action potential of isolated canine Purkinje fibers. The preparation is stimulated at the rate of 30/min. *(a)* Control record. *(b)* Initial prolongation of repolarization. *(c)* Onset of progressive decrease in duration of action potential due to shortening of duration of plateau (refractory period shortened). *(d)* Depolarization during diastole (pacemaker activity) appears. Resting potential decreases. Rate of rise and amplitude of action potential decrease. *(e)* More rapid depolarization between stimuli leads to spontaneous rather than driven activity equivalent to a ventricular rhythm. Resting potential and amplitude of action potential decrease until arrest and inexcitability occur. (Modified and reproduced, with permission, from Hoffman & Singer: Effects of digitalis on electrical activity of cardiac fibers. Prog Cardiovasc Dis 7:236, 1964.)

are seen in ventricular and atrial muscle cells.) The significant features are (1) a shortening of repolarization (mainly phase 2) with resulting ST changes in the ECG; (2) an increase in the slope of phase 4 resulting in automaticity as a factor in arrhythmia production; and (3) reduction in membrane resting potential, leading to conduction delay and reentry as an important mechanism of arrhythmia induction.

Electrodes may be placed on the surface of the myocardium of animals or implanted in appropriate areas. The ECGs so recorded provide information about the origin, pathway, and speed of conduction of the propagated impulse. From such studies it is seen that in addition to causing more rapid recovery of ventricular muscle, digitalis changes the direction of that process—ie, instead of proceeding from epicardium to endocardium, it occurs in the reverse direction.

The electrocardiographic changes to be described at this point can be anticipated from the above facts.

a. Electrocardiographic changes due to changes in ventricular repolarization–The wave of depolarization is rapidly distributed by Purkinje tissue through the subendocardial area. The activation of the ventricular wall proceeds from endocardial to epicardial surfaces. However, repolarization proceeds from epicardial to endocardial surface—ie, the first areas to be depolarized are the last to recover (see Fig 15–9). If the ventricular complex, reflecting depolarization (negative to positive intracellular potentials), is upright, the T wave will also be upright, since the repolarization that it reflects is opposite to activation not only in electrical direction (zero to negative) but also in anatomic direction. After even subtherapeutic amounts of the cardiac glycosides have been given, the repolarization of the ventricle occurs sooner (shortened refractory period), proceeds more rapidly, and deviates from the normal epicardial to endocardial path. If recovery begins before excitation is completed, the overlapping of the 2 processes will displace the RS–T junction and the ST segment and cause ST sagging. The more rapid course will shorten the Q–T interval, and the loss of the ventricular gradient, ie, the change in order of recovery, will lower or invert the T wave.

b. Electrocardiographic signs of digitalis toxicity–Digitalis toxicity is manifested by (1) marked sinus bradycardia (rate under 50 per min); (2) first, second, or third degree atrioventricular block; (3) atrioventricular junctional rhythms; (4) atrial arrhythmias, most commonly atrial tachycardia with 2:1 atrioventricular conduction; (5) ventricular arrhythmias (ectopic beats, bigeminy, tachycardia, fibrillation); and (6) any combination of the above.

The ECG does not provide an index of adequate digitalization. The changes listed in (a) above mean only that the patient has had some digitalis. The later electrocardiographic changes (b) are signs of digitalis toxicity. These changes do not appear in any predictable order, but ectopic beats and undue slowing are common early warning signs.

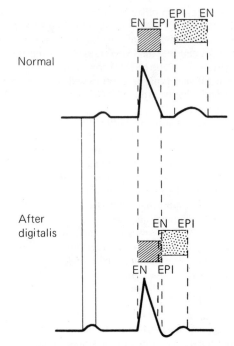

Figure 15–9. Diagram of a recording from an epicardial electrode illustrating the effects of digitalis on the ECG. Order and rate of activation of the ventricular muscle is unchanged by digitalis (cross-lined). Repolarization (stippled) is reversed from the ordinary epicardial to endocardial direction, lowering or inverting the T wave. Repolarization occurs sooner, shortening the Q–T interval or distorting the RS–T junction (J) and the RS–T segment. (Redrawn and reproduced, with permission, from Westlake & others: The effect of digitoxin on the electrocardiogram. Am Heart J 44:7, 1952.)

Among the common precipitating causes of cardiac failure is myocardial infarction. The ST segment and T wave changes that might have been helpful in the cardiographic diagnosis of an infarct can be obscured by similar changes due to digitalis. A preliminary ECG can serve as a base line for the later differentiation of digitalis effect or toxicity and disease.

5. Effects on other systems–

a. Vascular–The cardiac glycosides have a direct constrictor action on vascular smooth muscle. The pressor effect may be marked after the injection of the rapidly acting glycosides. In interpreting reports of the action of digitalis in shock or other hypotensive states, one must consider this direct vascular effect as well as a cardiac action. Digitalis constricts the veins of normal subjects. The venous constriction that occurs in congestive heart failure, however, decreases after treatment with digitalis. The decrease in venous tone and venous pressure follows the improvement in cardiac function and is not entirely related to digitalis action.

b. Gastrointestinal–Nausea and vomiting appear after absorption of toxic doses and are central and reflex in origin. Large doses of the leaf also have a local irritant action.

c. Central nervous system–Visual and psychic toxic symptoms are central in origin. The vagal symptoms responsible for some of the action in slowing the pulse are in part due to a reflex arising in the carotid sinus area and in part to a direct central action.

d. Local–Injections other than intravenous are painful because of the local tissue irritation of the glycosides and the vehicle (alcohol) in the preparation.

6. Effect on the normal heart–Whether the beneficial effect of digitalis occurs in the absence of congestive failure is an important question, because it raises the possibility of prophylactic use of digitalis and because it was long questioned whether digitalis action could be analyzed using normal hearts. Digitalis is the only drug that can increase the contractility of the heart in failure; when given to a normal human, however, it has no appreciable effect on cardiac output. Until recently, many workers had concluded that digitalis acts on a specific defect present only in congestive failure.

Now, however, the effect of digitalis on contractility can be shown on the hearts of animals and of humans without congestive failure, either by attaching a strain gauge to the ventricle or by following the rate of pressure rise within the left ventricle. These types of experiments have already been illustrated in Figs 15–4 and 15–5. Cardiac output does not increase because the rise in systemic vascular resistance offsets the inotropic action of the drug.

It does not follow from this that the prophylactic use of digitalis is necessarily beneficial, since in the absence of congestive failure, basal cardiac output and heart size are unchanged. It does suggest that cardiac performance will not be impaired by digitalis given before cardiac surgery or before the development of overt congestive failure provided that digitalis toxicity is not precipitated by other metabolic or electrolyte derangements.

Absorption, Metabolism, & Excretion

Digoxin and digitoxin are the most commonly used digitalis preparations. Digitalis leaf, commonly used in years past, is rarely used today because of the unreliability of the glycoside content and its unreliable absorption. Strophanthin, ouabain, and lanatoside C are not recommended for oral use.

A. Digoxin: Approximately 75% of orally administered digoxin will be absorbed. This will vary depending on several factors: (1) bioavailability (see below), (2) concomitant use of nonabsorbable drugs or antacids, (3) malabsorptive diseases of the gastrointestinal tract, and (4) thyroid status (decreased in hypothyroidism and increased in hyperthyroidism). Digoxin is mainly excreted by the kidney, and proper dosage is therefore dependent on renal function (creatinine clearance). In the presence of normal renal function, the mean half-life of digoxin is 33 hours. Approximately one-third of the body stores of digoxin are excreted daily (assuming normal renal function). Therefore, a daily dose of digoxin given for 4–5 half-lives (5–7 days) will result in a steady-state of serum

digoxin levels. Digoxin is tightly bound to tissues and is not removed by dialysis or open heart bypass procedures.

B. Digitoxin: This glycoside is completely absorbed after oral administration. Its cardiac effects are identical with those of digoxin, with 2 major differences in its pharmokinetics: (1) The half-life of digitoxin is 4–6 days. Therefore, it will take longer for the drug to be excreted, a fact of clinical significance when toxicity occurs. (2) In contrast to the major renal excretion of digoxin, digitoxin is mainly excreted by the liver. Therefore, liver function is an important determinant of the dose of digitoxin. The digitoxin excreted with bile is reabsorbed from the gut, which in part explains its longer duration of action. Cholestyramine, which interferes with this cycle, has been recommended for the treatment of digitoxin toxicity.

Digitalis Blood Levels

Radioimmunoassay technics are now available for rapid and accurate determinations of digoxin and digitoxin blood levels. Because of the more common use of digoxin, clinical data concerning blood levels of this drug are more widely available. Criteria have been offered for usual therapeutic and toxic serum levels. In general, values of 0.6–2.5 ng/mL are considered therapeutic, and levels above 3 ng/mL are consistent with toxicity. However, it must be appreciated that many other variables enter into the evaluation of digitalis efficacy or toxicity, and the serum level alone does not always make this differential. For example, a patient with a serum level in the "therapeutic range" may be digitalis-toxic clinically (if hypokalemia is present) or may not show any evidence of clinical toxicity with levels in excess of 3 ng/mL (as in atrial fibrillation).

Corresponding serum levels for digitoxin are as follows: Therapeutic, 20–35 ng/mL; toxic, 45+ ng/mL.

Quinidine Effect on Digitalis Kinetics

When quinidine is given to a patient who is receiving digoxin, there will be an acute rise in the serum level of digoxin. The mechanism for this is at least 2-fold: (1) displacement of digoxin-binding sites by quinidine and (2) altered renal clearance of digoxin. This can assume clinical significance and result in digitalis toxicity. Digoxin levels fall when quinidine is withdrawn. Therefore, careful adjustments of both drugs must be made when such combination therapy is indicated or altered.

A similar response has been reported with large doses of aspirin and ibuprofen in animals, but has not as yet been evaluated in humans.

Latent Period & Duration of Action

A. Parenteral Preparations: Digoxin (intravenously) will begin to have effect in 20–30 minutes, have maximal action within 2 hours, with some continuing effect for 1–3 days. Deslanoside has similar speed and duration of activity, and therefore it has no advantage over digoxin. Digitoxin (intravenously) will be effective within 3–8 hours and have a duration up to 14–21 days. Ouabain (intravenously) will be effective within 3–10 minutes. Therefore, its major indication is the rare situation when such rapid effect is desired.

B. Oral Preparations: Digoxin will show some effect within 2 hours, reach peak effect in 4–6 hours, and persist for 2–6 days. Digitoxin (and digitalis leaf) will be effective within 6–8 hours and persist for 14–21 days.

Adverse Reactions

Statistics on the incidence of toxic reactions and mortality are difficult to evaluate, but there is no doubt that digitalis is among the most dangerous as well as most valuable therapeutic agents employed. Because of the narrow therapeutic margin, the usual distinction between side-effects and toxic effects cannot be maintained.

The order of appearance of the toxic effects is unpredictable. A serious arrhythmia may be the first indication of toxicity. Intermittent anorexia and nausea, extrasystoles, and bradycardia are often early signs, and a patient receiving digitalis should be carefully observed for their appearance. The duration of a toxic episode when toxicity is deliberately induced for investigative purposes is usually about 2 days (but may be as long as 2 weeks) after discontinuance of the drug whether the toxicity is precipitated by digitoxin or the theoretically shorter-acting digoxin.

Allergic reactions to digitalis are almost unknown.

It must be appreciated that digitalis toxicity is not only related to the dose of the drug used but also to many other variables: (1) electrolyte imbalance, especially hypokalemia and hypomagnesemia; (2) renal insufficiency (digoxin); (3) hepatic insufficiency (digitoxin); (4) age of patient (decreasing renal function with increasing age); (5) size of patient; (6) severity of the underlying myocardial disease; (7) cor pulmonale; and (8) hypothyroidism.

A. Gastrointestinal: Anorexia, nausea, vomiting, and diarrhea occur. However, visceral congestion as a manifestation of congestive failure can also produce gastrointestinal discomfort.

B. Cardiac: Listed above under electrocardiographic effects.

C. Visual: Yellow or green vision, white halos around objects, snow-covered appearance of objects, and a variety of other visual symptoms are uncommon and usually late toxic signs.

D. Central Nervous System: Central nervous system disturbances allegedly due to digitalis toxicity often turn out to be the result of sodium depletion. However, drowsiness, headache, confusion, and toxic psychosis may be rare and late effects.

Treatment of Digitalis Toxicity

The treatment of digitalis toxicity consists first and most importantly of the discontinuance of the drug. Supplementary potassium may reverse some ar-

rhythmias. Both mercurial and thiazide diuretics (especially the latter) can lead to a depletion of intracellular potassium, and their use should be discontinued temporarily. It has been shown by repeatedly titrating the same patient to the point of toxicity before and after decreasing total body potassium by diuretics that digitalis effects are increased by potassium depletion. Conversely, sensitivity to digitalis is lowered by potassium supplementation. Potassium should be given by mouth as potassium chloride, approximately 2 g every 4 hours to a total of 4–10 g daily. A slow intravenous infusion (20 mEq/h) with constant electrocardiographic control may be used but is rarely required.

The beta-adrenergic blocking drug propranolol (Inderal), discussed in Chapter 11, is useful in the treatment of digitalis-induced arrhythmias in part because of an associated quinidinelike action but is contraindicated in the presence of high degree atrioventricular block. The use of supplemental potassium and the interest in the beta-blockers have decreased interest in other investigative treatments and in older drugs such as quinidine. Phenytoin is also of value in the treatment of digitalis-induced arrhythmias.

Digitalis antibodies have been prepared and have been shown to have clinical efficacy. Their status is investigational.

Clinical Uses

Digitalis is used in the treatment of congestive failure, atrial fibrillation, atrial flutter, and supraventricular tachycardia. The last 3 uses are discussed in the next chapter. (For dosages, see p 145 and Table 15–1.)

Cardiac edema will usually be improved by digitalis if it is due to myocardial insufficiency; digitalis is not effective when the underlying condition is mechanical in origin, as with constrictive pericarditis, congenital heart disease, and most cases of cor pulmonale.

Contraindications & Cautions

All contraindications are relative rather than absolute. There are rare contraindications in the presence of heart failure.

A. Recent Myocardial Infarction: A common cause of death following myocardial infarction is the development of an arrhythmia. Digitalis also causes serious arrhythmias and might increase this tendency. When a series of patients with recent myocardial infarction was divided randomly into treated and untreated groups, digitalization did not increase the mortality or the incidence of arrhythmias. Digitalis does increase the oxygen needs of the myocardium and therefore its use is usually avoided in the presence of "mild" heart failure, which may be treated with diuretics, sodium restriction, or nitrates. However, in the presence of "severe" failure or atrial fibrillation with a rapid ventricular response, digitalis is indicated.

B. Ventricular Tachycardia: If ventricular tachycardia is due to digitalis, the drug should be discontinued. Tachycardia due to other causes might theoretically be converted to ventricular fibrillation by digitalis. However, digitalis has often been used to treat the failure associated with a persistent ventricular tachycardia without difficulty and, at times, with reversion to sinus rhythm.

C. Partial Heart Block: Digitalis may convert partial heart block to complete block. This change may be undesirable, but, if it halts a shifting arrhythmia, it may actually prevent Stokes-Adams attacks. However, electronic pacing is a much more effective and reliable method of treating the latter.

D. Acute Myocardial Insufficiency: Infectious myocarditis and shock following myocardial infarction are not usually benefited by digitalis.

E. Previous Digitalis Therapy: Before beginning digitalization, be absolutely certain that the patient is not already taking "green tablets," small white or pink "pills," "green drops," etc. A digitalized patient has already received approximately one-third of a lethal dose.

F. Calcium Administration: Digitalis and calcium act synergistically under experimental conditions to increase both the therapeutic and toxic effects of digitalis. Sudden deaths have been reported following the rapid intravenous administration of calcium salts to digitalized patients.

G. Potassium Depletion: Potassium depletion due to diuretics or other causes may precipitate digitalis toxicity. Magnesium depletion has a similar effect.

H. Renal and Hepatic Insufficiency: The dose of digoxin must be reduced (or avoided) in relation to the degree of renal insufficiency. Similarly, digitoxin dose must be adjusted to the degree of hepatic insufficiency.

I. Specific Cardiac Diseases:

1. Atrial fibrillation (or flutter) in association with the preexcitation syndrome (Wolff-Parkinson-White syndrome) – In this situation, digitalis favors conduction via the accessory pathway and can precipitate ventricular fibrillation.

2. Obstructive hypertrophic cardiomyopathy (subaortic stenosis) – The inotropic action of digitalis can increase the left ventricular outflow gradient and worsen the clinical status of the patient.

Dosage (Table 15–1)

It has long been taught that, unlike most of the drugs that have been discussed thus far—which have small effects after small doses and greater effects after larger doses—digitalis must be present in the body in a certain "saturating" amount before any effect on congestive failure is noted. The effect then becomes nearly maximal all at once. The initial saturating process is accomplished by giving large initial doses or "digitalizing" doses. If smaller daily doses are given, less of the drug is metabolized each day and digitalization will only be achieved very slowly as the drug accumulates.

Recently it has been shown that small doses of digitalis glycosides do have an effect on contractility of

Table 15–1. Cardiac glycosides: Dosages.*

	Digitalizing Dose		Maintenance (Oral)
	Oral	IV	
Digitalis leaf	1.2–1.5 g	...	0.1 g
Digitoxin	1.2–1.5 mg	1.2 mg	0.1–0.2 mg
Acetyldigitoxin (Acylanid)	1.8 mg	...	0.1–0.2 mg
Gitalin (Gitaligin)	5 mg	...	0.5 mg
Digoxin	1–1.5 mg	0.5–1 mg	0.25–0.75 mg
Lanatoside C (Cedilanid)	6 mg	...	1 mg
Deslanoside (Cedilanid-D)	...	1.2–1.8 mg (6–8 mL)	...
Ouabain	...	0.5 mg	...
Acetylstrophan-thidin	...	0.6 mg	...

*Average doses for adults. May vary considerably, depending on clinical situation.

the failing heart and that the dose-effect relationship is not nearly as "all-or-none" as had been thought. These observations have led to the use of smaller and safer digitalizing doses and more dependence upon accumulation.

After the initial dosages, digitalis must be given in amounts sufficient to replace that which is destroyed or excreted; this need is provided by daily "maintenance" doses. The size of the maintenance dose must be determined for each patient, and a less than optimal dose will not accumulate.

A. Digitalizing Dose: No routine, either rapid or cumulative, guarantees full digitalization or freedom from toxicity. The usual doses may be too large or, what is more likely, additional small doses must be given before the maintenance dose can be started.

1. Cumulative method – If there is no clinical urgency, digoxin can be given in a usual daily "maintenance dose" without a loading dose. This will result in a steady state after 5–7 days. The usual adult dose of digoxin is 0.25 mg/d, but it can vary considerably depending on above-mentioned clinical variables. Digitoxin can be used in a similar fashion with an average adult daily dose of 0.1 mg.

2. Rapid loading method – This is mainly indicated in clinical situations in which there is severe heart failure and usually associated with atrial fibrillation and a rapid ventricular response. Digoxin is the drug of choice. It can be given intravenously (or orally if clinical situation is less urgent) in a dose of 0.5–0.75 mg and repeated at intervals of 2–4 hours until a total of 1.5 mg has been given or the ventricular rate in the presence of atrial fibrillation has been controlled. The usual maintenance dose is then given. Digitoxin is less desirable because of the larger interval for its onset of action.

B. Maintenance Dose: Average daily maintenance dosages are listed in Table 15–1. The most effective use of digitalis requires that an optimal dosage be determined for each patient. If the therapeutic regimen involves only digitalis, diuresis or relief of the symptoms of congestive failure can be used as the end point. If atrial fibrillation is present, the ventricular rate is a good index. But in most patients, especially after they have been under treatment for months or years, the only means of establishing adequate effectiveness of digitalis are careful clinical evaluation of the patient and determination of serum levels. A former recommendation that the dose be increased purposely to produce toxicity and then reduced is only mentioned to be condemned.

Selection of a Digitalis Preparation

The factors determining the choice of cardiac glycoside have all been discussed above. The purified glycosides allow more rapid digitalization. The shorter latent period of digoxin or its equivalent is important in the treatment of atrial arrhythmias when rapid onset of action is desirable. The longer duration of action of digitoxin or digitalis leaf prevents the fluctuation of effect sometimes seen with a rapidly dissipated drug such as digoxin. Theoretically, the toxic reactions that occur following the use of digoxin should be briefer in duration than those precipitated by digitoxin. Actually, no such difference could be demonstrated in one clinical trial.

Recently, different preparations of digoxin, including tablets made at different times by the same manufacturer, were discovered to be different in bioavailability—ie, after the same dose, blood levels varied because of differences in absorption. To correct this defect, FDA has established standards for the dissolution of digoxin tablets, and each batch is now certified by that agency.

The activity of digitalis leaf is due entirely to its digitoxin content.

Ouabain has been credited on the basis of clinical impressions with being relatively more effective in stimulating the left ventricle and relatively less active in its effect on the conducting tissues. Objective studies to verify this impression are equivocal at best. Ouabain can be given only intravenously. Ouabain acts rapidly and is water-soluble and is therefore frequently used in the animal laboratory.

Gitalin has properties intermediate between digitoxin and digoxin but is not, in spite of some claims, qualitatively different from the other glycosides. Acetylstrophanthidin (intravenously) is effective within minutes. It has been advocated to evaluate digitalis efficacy or toxicity. Unless used by a physician who is well trained and experienced in the use of this drug, it is not recommended.

In summary, the choice among the glycosides is not of critical importance except in those situations where an immediate effect is desirable. Most physicians use the one with which they have had the most experience, often the one introduced at a critical time in their training.

● ● ●

References

Balcon R & others: Hemodynamic effects of rapid digitalization following acute myocardial infarction. Br Heart J 30:373, 1968.

Bigger JT Jr: Pharmacologic and clinical control of antiarrhythmic drugs. Am J Med 58:479, 1975.

Bigger JT Jr: The quinidine-digoxin reaction: What do we know about it? N Engl J Med 301:779, 1979.

Braunwald E, Mason DT, Ross J Jr: Studies on the cardiocirculatory actions of digitalis. Medicine 44:233, 1965.

Cagin NA & others: Digitalis: New knowledge about an old drug. Cardiovasc Med 2:183, 1977.

Church G & others: Deliberate digitalis intoxication: A comparison of the toxic effects of four glycoside preparations. Ann Intern Med 57:946, 1962.

Cohn K & others: Variability of hemodynamic responses to acute digitalization in chronic cardiac failure due to cardiomyopathy and coronary artery disease. Am J Cardiol 35:461, 1975.

Doering W: Quinidine-digoxin interaction: Pharmacokinetics, underlying mechanism and clinical implications. N Engl J Med 301:400, 1979.

Doherty JE & others: Clinical pharmokinetics of digitalis glycosides. Prog Cardiovasc Dis 21:141, 1978.

Doherty JE & others: Digoxin-quinidine interaction. Am J Cardiol 45:1196, 1980.

Fisch C: Treatment of arrhythmias due to digitalis. J Indiana State Med Assoc 60:146, 1967.

Fogelman AM & others: Fallibility of plasma-digoxin in differentiating toxic from non-toxic patients. Lancet 2:727, 1971.

Katzung BG, Meyers FH: Excretion of radioactive digitoxin by the dog. J Pharmacol Exp Ther 149:257, 1965.

Langer GA: The intrinsic control of myocardial contraction: Ionic factors. N Engl J Med 285:1065, 1971.

Lee KS, Klaus W: The subcellular basis for the mechanism of inotropic action of cardiac glycosides. Pharmacol Rev 23:193, 1971.

Marcus FI: Current concepts of digoxin therapy. Mod Concepts Cardiovasc Dis 45:77, 1976.

Marcus FI: Digitalis pharmacokinetics and metabolism. Am J Med 58:452, 1975.

Mason DT: Digitalis pharmacology and therapeutics: Recent advances. Ann Intern Med 80:520, 1974.

McMichael J: The heart and digitalis. Br Med J 2:73, 1963.

Mintz GS, Bharadwaja K: Clinical pharmacology of digoxin. Drug Ther (Hosp edition) 1:15, Jan 1976.

Neill CA: The use of digitalis in infants and children. Prog Cardiovasc Dis 7:399, 1965.

Robertson DM, Hollenhorst RW, Callahan JA: Ocular manifestations of digitalis toxicity: Discussion and report of three cases of central scotoma. Arch Ophthalmol 76:640, 1966.

Rutledge DI, Haddad R: Digitalis intoxication: Gastrointestinal manifestations. Med Clin North Am 50:501, 1966.

Smith TW, Haber E: Digitalis. (4 parts.) N Engl J Med 289:945, 1010, 1063, 1125, 1973.

Drug Treatment of Cardiac Arrhythmias | 16

This chapter introduces the pharmacology of quinidine, lidocaine, and other drugs that are able to suppress arrhythmias by a direct action on the membrane of the cardiac cell, allowing restoration of a normal sinus rhythm. However, other methods of treatment (both drug and electrical) are available, and quinidine is not often the treatment of choice for an arrhythmia. Even when indicated, it is rarely used alone. A discussion of the treatment of cardiac arrhythmias will therefore follow the discussion of quinidine and will include references to other drugs.

QUINIDINE

Quinidine is the D-isomer of quinine, and the sources and properties of the 2 naturally occurring alkaloids are similar. The effect of quinine in correcting his atrial fibrillation was noted by a Dutch Colonial who had taken it in Java for malaria. De Senec, in 1749, recommended quinine for "rebellious palpitations." Wenckebach, an Austrian cardiologist, accepted and verified this observation and in 1914 introduced quinine as an antiarrhythmia drug. Quinidine was introduced shortly thereafter. Quinidine and quinine are equipotent in small doses, but when large doses are used, quinidine is more active against arrhythmias.

Quinidine

Pharmacologic Actions
A. Mechanisms of Action: Discussion of the mechanism of action of the quinidinelike drugs in abolishing cardiac arrhythmias still involves many areas of speculation and disagreement. Quinidine, in

concentrations attained in the intact organism, does not have the profound effects on intracellular potentials that were anticipated.

The major difficulty, however, is that the physiologic mechanism underlying the clinically important arrhythmias cannot be established with certainty, and the interpretation of the effects of the antiarrhythmia drugs is conditioned by one's understanding of the origin of the arrhythmias.

A rapid arrhythmia may be due to the rapid firing of an ectopic pacemaker in the atrium or in Purkinje tissue. After toxic doses of digitalis, for example, Purkinje fibers develop oscillatory afterpotentials during phase 3, and it is easy to visualize the development of a rapid rate of repetitive depolarization. If the arrhythmias are conceived of as due to abnormal or ectopic impulse formation, explanation of the action of quinidine will be sought in its ability to decrease the rate of the autonomous pacemaker.

There are, however, some observations and much theory leading to the concept of reentry as an explanation for the rapid rate of firing of the ectopic pacemaker. Owing to a disturbance of conduction, the initially normal wave of depolarization can move in a circular path, continuously reentering the path and continuously depolarizing adjacent tissue at a rapid rate. Once such a process has begun, no discrete pacemaker is required to maintain the abnormal rhythm. (See Fig 16–4.)

If such a mechanism is demonstrated or envisaged, the explanation for the effect of quinidine will be sought in its effect on refractory period or conduction.

Discussion of the mechanism of the arrhythmias should not be emphasized to the neglect of the empiric basis for the effective use of quinidine and related drugs, which will not change when the theory is clarified.

1. Mechanism of atrial arrhythmias–For many years, the circus movement theory of Thomas Lewis was dominant. This theory held that excitation originating in a focus close to the point of entry of the great veins into the atria could not spread uniformly but would be channeled into a circular path. The wave of depolarization could travel this devious path at such a rate that, when it again reached the site of origin, the tissue was no longer refractory and reentry or reexcitation could occur. From the rapidly recurring, circular wave, daughter (secondary) waves would arise and spread throughout the atria. Depending upon the rate of the process, the atria might be able to respond to each impulse (tachycardia, or flutter) or be unable to follow the rapid electrical rate (fibrillation). If a drug could prolong the refractory period, as quinidine was incorrectly alleged to do, the circus movement would be interrupted because the head of the wave would reach the tail while the tissue there was still refractory. Effects on conduction could be similarly invoked.

A circus movement and accompanying atrial arrhythmias can be experimentally produced in animals by crushing an area of the atrial wall of proper size. However, the arrhythmias that occur in humans are better explained by another hypothesis.

The unitary theory of the nature of atrial arrhythmias suggests that the only difference between the arrhythmias is in the rate of firing of the ectopic focus responsible. An ectopic pacemaker with a rate of 160–180 would be described as producing atrial or supraventricular tachycardia. If the ectopic rate were somewhat more rapid—eg, 240—there would be some degree of atrioventricular block and the condition would be clinically described as atrial flutter. If the abnormal rate were raised to 300–500/minute and the atria were unable to follow each electrical stimulus, effective atrial contractions would disappear and atrial fibrillation would result. If an ectopic focus is established by the subepicardial injection of a cholinergic alkaloid—aconitine (to cite one experiment)—and the rate of firing controlled by cooling or with quinidine, each of the predicted arrhythmias can be produced. (Table 16–1 shows an equivalent demonstration in humans.) In the clinical arrhythmias, however, the

Table 16–1. Summary of the atrial arrhythmias, illustrated by portions of the continuous esophageal (E_{35}) ECG of a patient who manifested all the rhythms illustrated within a single 5-minute period.* An ectopic focus in the atrium is responsible for the development of atrial premature contractions, atrial tachycardia, atrial flutter (which can also be called atrial tachycardia with atrioventricular block), and atrial fibrillation. The rate at which this ectopic atrial focus discharges will determine the type of the atrial arrhythmia.

Rate of Discharge of Atrial Ectopic Focus	Arrhythmia
Occasional discharge at a rate slower than the basic sinus rhythm. Atrial premature contractions.	
About 160 to about 220 Atrial tachycardia (with 1:1 conduction).	
About 220 to about 350 Atrial flutter (ie, atrial tachycardia with A–V block).	
Over 350 Atrial fibrillation.	

*Reproduced, with permission, from Goldman MJ: *Principles of Clinical Electrocardiography,* 10th ed. Lange, 1979.

pacemakers responsible for the different atrial arrhythmias are located in different areas of the atrium.

The question of the nature of the arrhythmias as they occur in humans was approached using high-speed motion pictures and electrocardiograms at the time of commissurotomy as well as by esophageal electrocardiographic leads. In such instances, no evidence of a circular pathway or of daughter waves was seen. On the contrary, during flutter, contraction waves and electrical activity—and, during fibrillation, electrical activity—can be seen to originate from a single point.

The unitary theory of the atrial arrhythmias suggests that the ability of a drug to decrease the rate of firing of an abnormal pacemaker would be its important effect.

An explanation for atrial tachycardia and possibly other atrial arrhythmias that utilizes the reentry concept and is not inconsistent with the available data, including that just presented, is atrioventricular reciprocation. The atrioventricular node is visualized as being functionally differentiated into ascending and descending components, with the atria first activating the ventricles and then being themselves activated by a ventricular "echo."

2. Mechanism of ventricular arrhythmias— Since ventricular ectopic beats are often clearly precipitated by the preceding normal beat, the need for a mechanism involving reentry is great. Various possible processes are suggested, each requiring a circular path containing a unidirectional block at one point. One of the suggested variations is shown in Fig 16–4.

3. Effect of quinidine on action potentials–The availability of microelectrode studies showing the effect of quinidine on intracellular potentials has not eliminated controversy about the mechanism of the antiarrhythmia action of quinidine. Reasonable concentrations of quinidine and related drugs acting on normal tissues cause only subtle changes that are limited to a slight decrease in the rate of rise of the upstroke of the action potential (phase 0, Fig 16–1) and a minor prolongation of duration of the action potential.

Isolated cardiac muscle or specialized conducting tissue can be suspended in a bath and stimulated at varying rates or allowed to contract spontaneously while a microelectrode is in place within single units.

Pacemaking fibers such as Purkinje tissue that depolarize spontaneously fire at a slower rate when therapeutic concentrations of quinidine are added. The sinoatrial node is not much affected at the same concentration—ie, an ectopic pacemaker could be slowed to a point at which the sinoatrial node would again be the most rapidly firing area.

With driven (rhythmically stimulated) tissues, the effect is minor at slow rates of stimulation but is much more apparent at rapid rates.

Furthermore, the ability of quinidine to depress excitability and conduction is much greater on ischemic tissues. A major mechanism of action of antiarrhythmia drugs may be to suppress the abnormal electrical activity of ischemic, partially depolarized cells, leaving the electrical activity of normal cardiac tissue virtually unchanged.

When depolarization progresses slowly, the threshold at which complete depolarization abruptly occurs is elevated. The antiarrhythmia activity of quinidine is explained by the decreased rate of depolarization and the associated failure of the impulse to be propagated to adjacent units.

Quinidine in therapeutic concentrations has only a minor effect on the refractory period of normal tissue, as the refractory period is derived from intracellular potential changes. Overshoot is slightly reduced. Resting potential is unchanged.

4. Effect of quinidine on cell membrane–The initial phase of the action potential is generated by a rapid inward sodium current. The transport is visualized as occurring through specialized sodium channels that exist in the membrane together with potassium channels and the sodium pump.

The antiarrhythmia drugs (like the local anesthetics) impede the sodium current by blocking the sodium channel. This effect on sodium conductance is also greater with more rapid rates of depolarization. The recovery (clearing of drug) of sodium conductance

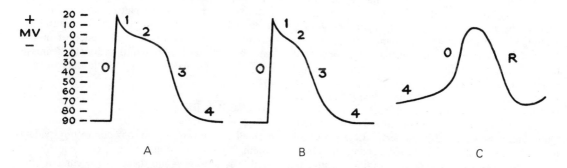

Figure 16–1. Diagrams of action potential curves. *A:* Ventricular muscle cell. *B:* Atrial muscle cell. *C:* Sinoatrial node. 0 = depolarization; 1, 2, 3 = phases of repolarization; 4 = diastolic phase = MRP (membrane resting potential); R = repolarization phase of spontaneously depolarizing tissue not divisible into phases 1, 2, and 3. (Reproduced, with permission, from Goldman MJ: *Principles of Clinical Electrocardiography,* 10th ed. Lange, 1979.)

is slowed in ischemic depolarized tissue and can lead to a prolonged refractory period in damaged if not in normal tissues.

A number of drugs impede the depolarization process without altering the resting potential and are sometimes described together as "membrane stabilizers." The drugs share the chemical pattern described in other chapters for the parasympatholytics, antihistamines, tranquilizers, and local anesthetics and here for quinidinelike drugs—ie, an amine function connected to a bulky cyclic or polycyclic group by a short chain. How the specificity seen in the actions of these drugs arises is conjectural, but all have quinidinelike actions.

B. Pharmacologic Effects:

1. On the myocardium—

a. Rhythmic function is depressed–Regardless of the mechanism, quinidine slows the rate of firing of the normal and of ectopic rhythmic foci. Thus, even before conversion to normal sinus rhythm, the frequency of the f (fibrillation) waves in atrial fibrillation and of the atrial rate in flutter will be slowed.

The conversion of fibrillation is not all-or-none but stepwise, as the unitary theory would predict. The percentage of patients with atrial fibrillation who are seen to pass through atrial flutter en route to a normal sinus rhythm rises as the amount of electrocardiographic surveillance is increased. Examples in which atrial tachycardia occurs as an intermediate step before normal sinus rhythm are also available. Even the normal sinus pacemaker is depressed by quinidine, although—fortunately—it is relatively insensitive. Nevertheless, periods of asystole (usually brief) may on rare occasions be seen at the time of resumption of normal sinus rhythm. In the usual doses, quinidine has little effect on normal sinus rhythm.

b. Conduction velocity–Both intraventricular and atrioventricular conduction velocity is decreased or conduction time is prolonged. On the electrocardiogram, the duration of both the ventricular complex and the P–R interval is increased, but this is evident only with toxic doses.

c. Refractory period–The absolute refractory period as measured by intracellular recordings is not much altered by quinidine. Some older technics appeared to show that quinidine lengthened the refractory period. These methods could not distinguish between a prolongation of refractory period and a failure of the wave of depolarization to be propagated and conducted to a recording electrode. Conduction in cardiac muscle can be decremental rather than all-or-none—ie, a wave of depolarization may initially be propagated or conducted away from the excitable focus at a rapid rate but slow progressively before failing to be propagated. Quinidine exaggerates this property. Lewis himself recognized that what he had called a change in refractory period was actually conduction failure. Unfortunately, he renamed this the **"effective refractory period,"** and the term is now applied to a phase of the action potential.

d. Intracardiac vagal block is the term applied to an atropinelike action of quinidine on vagal efferents reaching the atrioventricular node. There is no accompanying peripheral atropinelike effect. As a result of decreased vagal influence, the atrioventricular refractory period is shortened and, in the presence of a rapid atrial rate, more impulses pass through the node to activate the ventricles. Larger doses of quinidine are required for this effect, and the action may coincide with the conversion of fibrillation to flutter, resulting in a very rapid ventricular rate. To prevent this adverse result, quinidine is given in the presence of a rapid atrial rate only after the administration of adequate doses of digitalis.

e. Ventricular tachycardia–Quinidine may be used in the treatment of ventricular tachycardia. As a toxic effect, however, quinidine may cause ventricular tachycardia. (Ventricular tachycardia does not refer simply to a rapid ventricular rate but to a specific arrhythmia arising from one or more rapidly firing ventricular foci.)

f. Depression of myocardial contractility–In the laboratory animal, quinidine depresses contractility of the myocardium. There is no evidence that this action is measurably present during its clinical use.

2. Extracardiac effects–

a. Vasodilatation–Quinidine has a direct relaxing effect on vascular smooth muscle, and the resulting vasodilatation can lead to hypotension.

b. On skeletal muscle–Quinidine has a very weak curarelike ability to weaken skeletal muscle response. It is used to relieve the muscle hypertonicity present in the rare case of congenital myotonia. Intensification of effect of curare has been noted in postsurgical patients.

Absorption, Metabolism, & Excretion

The bioavailability of orally administered quinidine ranges from 60–80%. The major route of elimination is via hepatic metabolism. Almost 20% of the drug is excreted unchanged in the urine. Thus, the dose does not have to be altered in patients with renal failure. The clearance of quinidine is about 290 mL/kg/h, but there is wide individual variability, and monitoring plasma concentrations can be useful in adjusting doses. However, it is important that a specific assay that can discriminate between quinidine and its metabolites be used. The normal half-life of quinidine is 6–8 hours. The clearance of quinidine can be increased, with a proportionate decrease in half-life, by the induction of hepatic microsomal enzymes.

Adverse Reactions

The dose-related toxic effects of quinidine can be divided into those that may occur in any patient—whether a normal sinus rhythm or some abnormal rhythm is present—and those that occur only in the presence of an abnormal rhythm.

A. Toxic Effects of Quinidine Not Necessarily Associated With an Arrhythmia:

1. Gastrointestinal–Nausea and vomiting, abdominal cramps, and diarrhea are common local irritant effects of quinidine.

2. Cinchonism–Symptoms of quinidine toxicity similar to those caused by other cinchona alkaloids or by salicylates include giddiness, light-headedness, tremulousness, tinnitus, impaired hearing, and blurred or double vision.

3. QRS prolongation–If the effect on intraventricular conduction leads to an increase of more than 25% in the duration of the ventricular complex (or a duration greater than 0.14 seconds), further administration of the drug should be carried out very cautiously. A 50% widening of the QRS complex is often followed by ventricular fibrillation. Q–T prolongation is important in relation to ventricular ectopy.

4. Ventricular tachycardia, if it occurs after the administration of quinidine, is, of course, an indication for discontinuing the drug. Premonitory ventricular premature beats may be observed.

5. Ventricular fibrillation may occur with or without a preceding period of ventricular tachycardia. Brief periods or paroxysms of fibrillation may cause syncope, just as may periods of asystole.

6. Hypotension, which can occur after oral administration but is more common after the parenteral administration of quinidine, may necessitate discontinuance of efforts to convert an arrhythmia.

B. Toxic Effects of Quinidine in the Presence of an Arrhythmia:

1. Rapid ventricular rate–The intracardiac vagal block and consequent decrease in refractory period of the atrioventricular node caused by quinidine may lead to a sudden increase in the number of waves of excitation that reach the ventricles. This may occur with either atrial fibrillation or flutter. To prevent the increase in ventricular rate, digitalis should always be given before quinidine is used in the treatment of an atrial arrhythmia unless electrical conversion is contemplated.

2. Asystole–The normal pacemaker as well as the ectopic sites are depressed by larger doses of quinidine. When a stubborn arrhythmia has finally been suppressed, there may be a delay before the slower pacemaker takes over. This period of asystole may be recognized on the electrocardiogram or may appear as syncope or convulsions due to cerebral ischemia.

C. Allergic Reactions: Fever, urticaria, other skin rashes, asthma, and, rarely, thrombocytopenic purpura may result from acquired sensitivity to quinidine.

D. Idiosyncratic Reactions: Anaphylactic reactions or syncope may occur.

Contraindications & Cautions

In the presence of complete heart block, the effect of quinidine in slowing the ventricular focus could be disastrous. The effect of quinidine on atrioventricular conduction could convert an incomplete block to complete atrioventricular block. Quinidine should not, therefore, be used in the presence of any degree of block other than that usually associated with the atrial arrhythmias. Similarly, in the presence of bundle branch block or intraventricular conduction defects, quinidine should be used with special caution. Active rheumatic fever, infective endocarditis, pregnancy, and untreated thyrotoxicosis are relative contraindications to the use of quinidine.

In the presence of atrial arrhythmias (flutter or fibrillation), digitalis should always be used in optimal amounts before quinidine is given, except when the prompt treatment of an arrhythmia is necessary or when cardioversion is planned in order to prevent the precipitation of a rapid ventricular rate as discussed above. Congestive heart failure should be corrected to the greatest extent possible before quinidine is used.

A test dose should be given if the situation permits (see below).

Dosages

Much larger doses of quinidine are required to convert an arrhythmia than to prevent recurrence or occurrence of an arrhythmia. Dosage is therefore divided into dosage for conversion and dosage for maintenance.

A. Conversion:

1. Oral–Unless the need for treatment is immediate, a test dose of 0.1 or 0.2 g of quinidine is given orally and the patient observed for at least 2 hours to eliminate the rare patient who is allergic to quinidine or unusually sensitive to its toxic effects.

The dosage of quinidine is determined by the therapeutic objective and is reached by a preselected plan. The plan must take into consideration that the disappearance of the drug from the body occurs slowly and that nearly 10% of the dose may remain after 24 hours.

The usual or anticipated dosage varies depending upon the arrhythmia being treated. The treatment of the specific arrhythmias is outlined below.

Quinidine is a hazardous drug and, since other methods of treatment are available, the tendency is to use even greater caution than in the past.

The following 2 schemes or regimens used to attempt the conversion of atrial fibrillation to a normal sinus rhythm are given as examples:

a. One common method that requires hospitalization and close observation is as follows: On the first day, give quinidine, 0.2 g every 2 hours, until therapeutic response to toxicity is noted or until 4–5 doses have been given. The amount of quinidine excreted depends in part upon the amount in the body, and after 4–5 doses on this schedule no further cumulative effect on blood levels is seen. On the second day, give 0.4 g of quinidine every 2 hours for 5 doses. On subsequent days, the dosage may be increased to 0.6 g every 2 hours for 5 doses. There is a residual level in the morning following the above dosages, and electrocardiographic control and clinical observation are necessary before each dose is given.

b. An alternative method is to give a fixed dose—eg, 0.2 g—4 times a day and, in the absence of toxicity or a response, increase the dose every 2–3 days.

2. Intramuscular–The same doses by the intramuscular route can be used if the patient is unable to take the medication orally and the situation is not critical. Quinidine gluconate is available for injection. Absorption is unpredictable, and effects are therefore variable.

3. Intravenous–The intravenous route should be used only when the urgency is great. The onset of action is delayed, since intracellular levels increase only slowly. Lidocaine is more often used when intravenous antiarrhythmia therapy is necessary.

B. Maintenance or Prevention: Doses of 0.1–0.6 g orally every 6 hours are used to prevent recurrence of the arrhythmia. The reliability of the sustained-release preparations available for prolonged action has not been completely confirmed. Adjustment of doses can be based on plasma levels. Therapeutic levels of 3–5 μg/mL are usually effective.

OTHER ANTIARRHYTHMIA DRUGS

What has been said about the cardiac effects of quinidine applies also to the drugs discussed below unless a specific exception is made.

PROCAINAMIDE
(Pronestyl)

The local anesthetics have quinidinelike action in addition to their primary effect. Procaine has been shown to be active in suppressing ventricular arrhythmias, but its action is very brief, since it is an ester and is rapidly hydrolyzed. Procainamide is the amide analog of procaine. It retains the quinidinelike actions of procaine but is not rapidly hydrolyzed, and its action persists long enough so that it is active after oral as well as parenteral administration.

Pharmacologically, procainamide is the equivalent of quinidine. It causes the same toxic effects except that cinchonism does not occur and allergic reactions are more frequent. A series of patients have developed a reversible but potentially damaging form of disseminated lupus erythematosus as a result of long-term procainamide therapy; a larger fraction shows antinuclear antibody without symptoms.

When procainamide was first introduced, its parenteral dosage form was superior to the then available forms of injectable quinidine. It is used for treatment of ventricular arrhythmias. Its use as an equivalent or alternative to quinidine when a parenteral drug was needed in the treatment of ventricular tachycardia has decreased with the advent of electrical treatment and other drugs.

Absorption, Metabolism, & Excretion
About 70–90% of an oral dose of procainamide is absorbed into the systemic circulation. The clearance is about 500 mL/kg/h, but there is much individual variability. The normal half-life is about 3 hours. The volume of distribution is about 2 L/kg. A metabolite of procainamide, N-acetylprocainamide, has pharmacologic activity the clinical significance of which is currently debated. Renal excretion is the major route of elimination for N-acetylprocainamide.

The dose of procainamide must be reduced for patients with renal insufficiency; it is important to monitor plasma levels, clinical response, and toxic effects.

Dosages
For long-term oral administration, the dose is 3–6 g/d divided into 4–8 doses to achieve a plasma level of 4–8 μg/mL. If a rapid effect is required, procainamide is given intravenously at a rate of 50 mg every 5 minutes (maximum rate, 50 mg/min) to a total dose of up to 1000 mg to reach the plasma level of 4–8 μg/mL.

LIDOCAINE
(Xylocaine)

Lidocaine is another local anesthetic used to treat ventricular arrhythmias. In its need to be given by

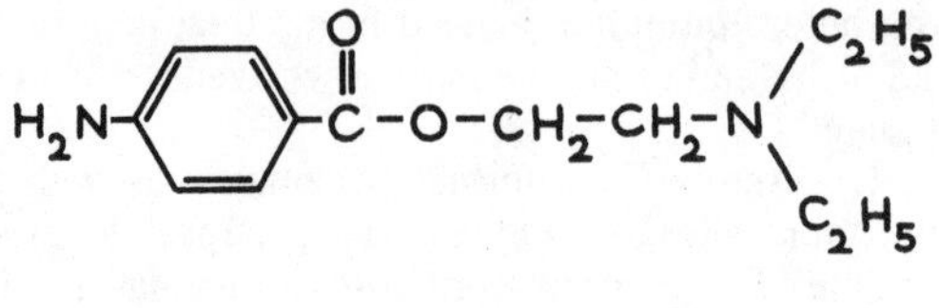

Procaine

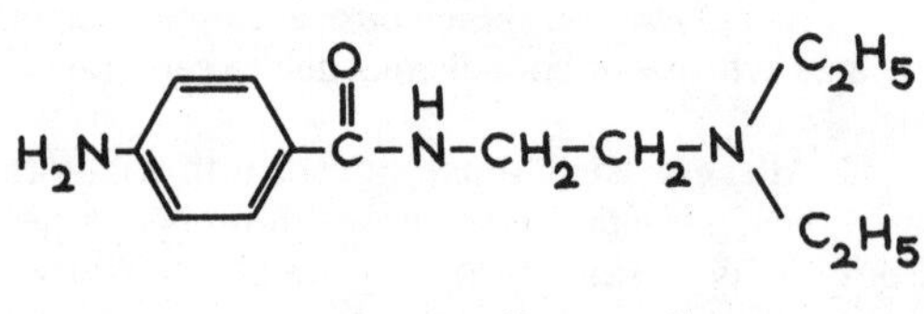

Procainamide (Pronestyl)

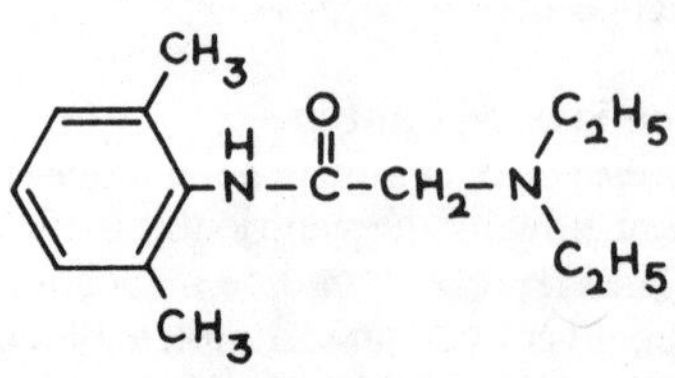

Lidocaine (Xylocaine)

constant intravenous infusion, it resembles procaine more than procainamide. The advantage claimed is that in small doses it causes less hypotension. In the usual doses it causes drowsiness, but toxic concentrations may cause muscle twitching, confusion, and focal or generalized convulsions. Its other effects, including the ability to precipitate as well as to suppress ventricular arrhythmias, are similar to those of procainamide or quinidine.

Lidocaine is currently the most widely used antiarrhythmia drug in intensive care units in patients who are postoperative or who have a recent myocardial infarction. It is used to treat ventricular arrhythmias or to prevent their occurrence either as routine prophylaxis or in the presence of ventricular ectopic beats possibly premonitory of tachycardia. Controlled studies do not verify the superiority claimed for lidocaine in this situation or establish its safety. Reports of the "recurrence" of ventricular arrhythmias during the continued administration of the drug or the progression of an arrhythmia in the face of increasing dose may as easily be interpreted as toxic reactions.

Absorption, Metabolism, & Excretion

Lidocaine is metabolized by the liver, and less than 10% of a dose is excreted unchanged by the kidney. The clearance is about 660 mL/kg/h; but, as with quinidine and procainamide, there is wide individual variability. Because the liver metabolizes lidocaine at a rapid rate, bioavailability when the drug is given orally is low, and it must be administered parenterally. When lidocaine is given intravenously, the onset of action is rapid. However, the initial effect may also disappear quickly, because of rapid redistribution of the drug. For this reason, about 1 mg/kg of lidocaine should be given as a rapid intravenous bolus, followed in 10 minutes by a second bolus of 0.5 mg/kg. The first bolus should be followed by an infusion of 1–4 mg/min. Cardiac failure reduces both the clearance and volume of distribution of lidocaine. As a first approximation, both the loading doses (bolus) and the infusion rate should be halved in patients with heart failure. Patients with liver disease require reduced infusion rates, but the loading dose need not be changed. Monitoring of plasma levels and of the clinical state is imperative. Therapeutic plasma levels range from 1.4 to 6 μg/mL.

Tocainamide and mexitelene are lidocaine analogs that are active when taken orally. They are under investigation.

BETA–ADRENERGIC BLOCKING AGENTS

The beta-receptor blocking agents—eg, propranolol (Inderal)—are discussed in Chapter 11 as one class of drugs that decrease the effect of sympathetic mediators on the heart and other tissues. They happen—coincidentally, and independently of their beta-blocking property—to be quinidinelike.

Because they block the effect of norepinephrine or epinephrine on atrioventricular nodal tissue, nodal refractory time is prolonged. In the presence of a rapid atrial rate—eg, atrial flutter or fibrillation—fewer of the waves of depolarization from above will reach the ventricles after propranolol administration. Propranolol will, like digitalis, slow the ventricular rate even though the rapid atrial rate continues.

The beta blockers also slow the rate of firing of normal sinus and other atrial pacemakers by reducing the sympathetic accelerator influence.

Propranolol can be used in lieu of digitalis to slow the ventricular rate when conversion by DC countershock is planned, since it does not predispose to ventricular arrhythmias as digitalis does.

The beta blockers are more useful than quinidine and its congeners in treating arrhythmias due to digitalis toxicity. The arrhythmias are suppressed, and a normal rhythm is established.

OTHER QUINIDINE EQUIVALENTS

Disopyramide (Norpace) is the tertiary amine analog of isopropamide (Darbid), a synthetic atropine substitute that is a quaternary amine. It thus extends the occurrence of quinidinelike effects through the above spectrum to the parasympatholytic prototype. Its effects are virtually identical to those of quinidine. It is marketed for use against ventricular arrhythmias, but no injectable form is available. Adverse reactions include atropinelike effects, vomiting, diarrhea, confusion, and cardiac effects including ventricular fibrillation (as with quinidine), congestive failure, and shock. Because of a substantial depressant action on myocardial contractility, it should not be used in the presence of heart failure.

Phenytoin (Dilantin), an anticonvulsant, is also able to suppress ventricular arrhythmias both in the experimental animal and clinically. Some investigators, on the basis of laboratory studies open to conflicting interpretations, conclude that it is qualitatively different from quinidine. It does not lower blood pressure or depress cardiac contractility unless given with propylene glycol, the solvent usually supplied. However, after intravenous administration it has demonstrated most of the actions of quinidine, including changes in conduction and the production of fatal ventricular arrhythmias.

The antipsychotic tranquilizers—eg, chlorpromazine or other phenothiazine derivatives, the closely related antidepressants such as imipramine—and many of the antihistamines have antiarrhythmia actions in the laboratory and clinically. These drugs probably act by the same mechanism as does quinidine, but the available data are insufficient to be certain. The slightly greater frequency of sudden, unexplained deaths in patients treated with large doses of tranquilizers and some aspects of the acute toxicity of the antidepressants are apparently related to the quinidinelike cardiac effects.

NEWER DRUGS

VERAPAMIL

The rapid depolarization discussed above and shown in Fig 16–2A depends upon the rapid entry of sodium ion into the cell. In addition, and predominating in some cardiac cells, there is a slow response (Fig 16–2C) mediated by calcium. Abnormal conduction frequently depends upon the slow calcium current.

Verapamil is of great interest, although still at the investigational level, because it blocks the calcium channel. As a result, it has actions similar to those of propranolol, ie, a selective slowing of atrioventricular conduction and an effect in suppressing supraventricular arrhythmias. It also has a prominent depressant effect on contractility and is a vasodilator.

BRETYLIUM
(Bretylol)

Bretylium is available only in an injectable form for trial against persistent or recurring ventricular tachycardia after other treatment (DC countershock, lidocaine) has failed.

It is an adrenergic neuron blocking agent similar to guanethidine. As expected, it causes an initial sympathomimetic effect and a later hypotension, predominantly postural.

OTHER NEW DRUGS

Newer drugs not yet available in the USA include aprindine, amiodarone, ethmozin, and nifedipine. Studies in Europe and in the USA indicate that these drugs have clinical utility, and some of them may soon be available in this country.

TREATMENT OF CARDIAC ARRHYTHMIAS

The treatment of the common cardiac arrhythmias not only involves several drug groups—ie, digitalis, quinidine, beta-adrenergic blockers, and sympathomimetics—but also a physical technic, direct current (DC) countershock. DC countershock (cardioversion) applies a high-voltage direct current of brief duration (2.5 ms) through the chest at the level of the heart. The externally applied charge is sufficient to depolarize the entire heart, and a normal sinus rhythm is often established upon recovery. The shock is electrically triggered by the R wave of the electrocardiogram to avoid the vulnerable period of the myocardium. Quinidine used prior to DC countershock increases the number of successful conversions, and maintenance doses are given to prevent recurrence of the arrhythmia. Digitalis is discontinued for at least 48 hours before cardioversion because it increases the risk of ventricular tachycardia and fibrillation. A beta-adrenergic blocking agent may be used prior to cardioversion in place of digitalis to maintain a slow ventricular rate in the presence of a continued rapid atrial rate.

PAROXYSMAL ATRIAL TACHYCARDIA

The paroxysmal supraventricular tachycardias are usually self-limiting disorders but may be recurrent. Treatment is both immediate (to terminate the paroxysm) and prophylactic in those few patients with frequent recurrences.

Treatment of Acute Episode

Assuming that paroxysmal atrial tachycardia is not due to digitalis toxicity, it will probably occur in an otherwise healthy individual and treatment should involve minimal hazard. Sedation and the removal of precipitating factors (fatigue, tobacco, alcohol) may suffice.

A. Augment Vagal Influences on the Heart: This can be done in various ways: (1) by applying carotid sinus pressure; (2) by immersing the face in water; (3) by the Valsalva maneuver; (4) with pressor drugs; or (5) with digitalis. Methacholine and neostigmine have also been used but cause strong and unpleasant side-effects.

B. Antiarrhythmia Drugs: Oral doses of digitalis, quinidine, or propranolol may be used if needed. Digitalis should not be selected if it has been recently administered and the arrhythmia may be a manifestation of digitalis toxicity.

C. DC Countershock: This procedure is effective but rarely justified except in patients in whom the arrhythmia results in hemodynamic compromise.

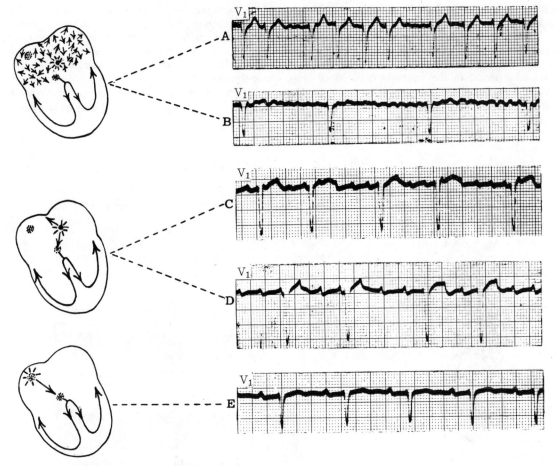

A. Before therapy: Atrial fibrillation; ventricular rate = 120.

B. After digitalization: Atrial fibrillation; ventricular rate = 50.

C. During initial quinidine therapy: Atrial flutter; atrial rate = 300. There is a varying atrioventricular block (3:1 to 5:1), resulting in a ventricular rate of 75.

D. During continued quinidine therapy: Atrial flutter persists, but the atrial rate has been reduced to 210. There is a varying atrioventricular block, resulting in a ventricular rate of 65.

E. Further quinidine therapy: Regular sinus rhythm; rate = 68.

Figure 16-2. Atrial fibrillation: Response to digitalis and quinidine. (Reproduced, with permission, from Goldman MJ: *Principles of Clinical Electrocardiography,* 10th ed. Lange, 1979.)

Prevention of Attacks

Attempt to identify and treat or remove the cause, eg, emotional stress, fatigue, excessive use of alcohol or tobacco, or underlying preexcitation syndrome. Quinidine sulfate, 0.2–0.6 g 3–4 times daily, may be used to prevent frequent and troublesome attacks. Begin with small doses and increase if the attacks are not prevented and toxic effects do not occur.

If quinidine is not effective or not tolerated, full digitalization and maintenance may prevent or decrease the frequency of attacks. Propranolol and verapamil are effective alternatives.

ATRIAL FIBRILLATION

Atrial fibrillation may be due to any of several causes, and the need for treatment and response to treatment are correspondingly diverse. Atrial fibrillation associated with rheumatic mitral valve disease involves the great hazard of repeated emboli arising from thrombi that form on the walls of the noncontracting atrial appendages. If the fibrillation is associated with atherosclerotic heart disease, the hazard of emboli is less. In either case, an increase in cardiac efficiency is attained by conversion of the fibrillation to normal sinus rhythm (especially with exercise) beyond the effect achieved by merely slowing the ventricular rate with digitalis, and the need for conversion is seldom urgent.

Digitalis is the first drug used in the treatment of atrial fibrillation. Digitalis slows the ventricular rate through the additional mechanism of prolonging the refractory period of the atrioventricular node (Fig 16–2). Propranolol will also slow the ventricular rate but will reduce cardiac output and cannot be used if congestive failure is present. If it is then judged advis-able, attempts can be made to correct the atrial fibrilla-tion to a sinus rhythm. DC countershock is now proba-bly most frequently used to accomplish conversion, but quinidine may be used. This not only achieves an increase in cardiac efficiency but also protects against embolization.

Hyperthyroidism diminishes the effectiveness of digitalis, and higher plasma levels may be required to control ventricular rate.

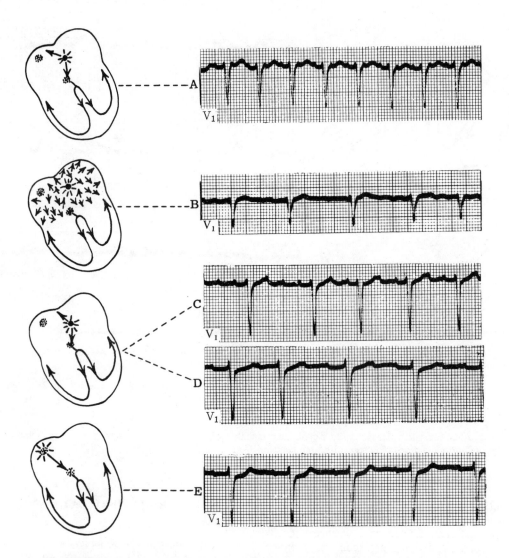

A. Before therapy: Atrial flutter with 2:1 atrioventricular block. Atrial rate = 272; ventricular rate = 136.

B. After digitalization: The rhythm is now atrial fibrillation; the ventricular rate has been slowed to 80.

C. During initial quinidine therapy: Quinidine has changed the atrial fibrillation to atrial flutter. The atrial rate is 272 (as in A), but because of the blocking action of digitalis on the atrioventricular node there is 3:1 and 4:1 atrioventricular block, resulting in a ventricular rate of 85.

D. During continued quinidine therapy: Atrial flutter persists, but the atrial rate has been reduced to 200. There is 2:1 and 3:1 atrioventricular block, resulting in a ventricular rate of 75.

E. Further quinidine therapy: The rhythm has reverted to regular sinus rhythm.

Figure 16–3. Atrial flutter: Response to digitalis and quinidine. (Reproduced, with permission, from Goldman MJ: *Principles of Clinical Electrocardiography,* 10th ed. Lange, 1979.)

ATRIAL FLUTTER

The first (and often the only) drug used in the treatment of atrial flutter is digitalis. Digitalis usually increases the degree of atrioventricular block and thereby slows the ventricular rate and makes the patient comfortable; in addition, in some cases it converts the flutter to atrial fibrillation. Such a recently established atrial fibrillation is not stable and will often convert to a normal sinus rhythm whether digitalis is continued or discontinued and whether quinidine is given or not (Fig 16–3). The dose of digitalis required may be a little larger than that used for congestive heart failure.

DC countershock is effective and convenient in terminating atrial flutter and is usually used in preference to digitalis or quinidine.

If quinidine is used to convert the flutter or a digitalis-induced fibrillation, the patient should be fully digitalized to avoid a sudden increase in ventricular rate.

VENTRICULAR TACHYCARDIA

Ventricular tachycardia constitutes a medical emergency. Treatment is selected from among the following options:

A. Propranolol (Inderal): If the ventricular tachycardia is due to digitalis toxicity, the beta-adrenergic blocking agent propranolol (Inderal) can be used. See Chapter 11 and above.

B. DC Countershock: When the arrhythmia is clearly not due to digitalis toxicity, DC countershock (when available) is rapidly replacing pharmacologic methods of treatment.

C. Lidocaine: Lidocaine is the drug of choice for this arrhythmia.

D. Procainamide:

1. Oral–Give 0.5 g every 4 hours.

2. Intramuscular–Give 0.5–1 g and repeat in 4 hours.

3. Intravenous–Give procainamide hydrochloride (Pronestyl), 1 g *slowly* intravenously (at a

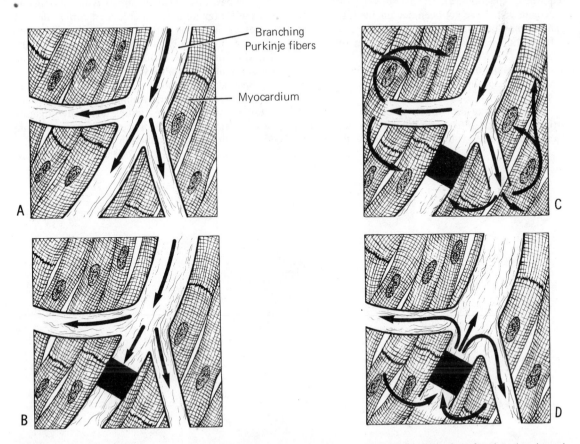

Figure 16–4. Diagrammatic illustration of unidirectional block and reentry. *A:* Normal propagation of an impulse through branching Purkinje fibers with activation of neighboring myocardium. Where wavefronts meet, propagation stops because tissue is refractory. *B:* The hatched area in one Purkinje fiber represents a zone of decremental conduction and unidirectional block. *C:* Propagation through the normally conducting fibers activates the myocardium. *D:* Since the block in the Purkinje fiber is unidirectional, the impulse that has spread through the normally conducting fibers can penetrate the affected fiber in a retrograde direction and reactivate the neighboring Purkinje fibers, producing a second myocardial response (reentry). (Reproduced, with permission, from Goldman MJ: *Principles of Clinical Electrocardiography,* 10th ed. Lange, 1979.)

rate not to exceed 100 mg/min). During the infusion, continuous electrocardiogram or, at least, repeated blood pressure determinations are essential.

E. Quinidine: Give quinidine, 0.4 g orally every 2 hours for 3 doses, if the attack is well tolerated and the patient is not in shock. If the attack continues and there is no toxicity from the quinidine, increase the dose to 0.6 g orally every 2 hours for 3 doses. If the larger oral dosage of quinidine is not successful, give quinidine intramuscularly.

Prevention of Ventricular Arrhythmias

Potentially, the widest and most important use of antiarrhythmia drugs is during the period immediately following a myocardial infarction. This is also the indication that is most controversial and even emotional.

In the minutes and hours following an infarction, ventricular fibrillation is the most common cause of death. Therefore, current practice aims at hospitalization as quickly as possible in a coronary care unit where electrical defibrillation and further treatment as required can be provided. The overall benefits of coronary care units have not been documented, but many patients have been followed who have done well after defibrillation. Efforts to prevent rather than treat fibrillation are of obvious importance.

The results of drug treatment, predominantly in the form of lidocaine infusions, can be summarized in 3 areas.

First, with respect to the effect on ventricular arrhythmias short of fibrillation, lidocaine clearly suppresses premature ventricular contractions that occur late in diastole. The drug is effective against the extrasystoles generally thought to be premonitory of ventricular tachycardia or fibrillation—ie, those that are frequent, multifocal, or appear during the presumed vulnerable period (R on T).

Second, clinical trials have been used to evaluate the ability of drug treatment to reduce the number of episodes of ventricular fibrillation during the crucial period after the myocardial infarction. Since the drug may cause adverse reactions and since observer bias cannot be otherwise excluded, only double-blind studies can be considered. The results are conflicting, but 2 studies have shown efficacy.

Finally, however, none of the studies, with one exception, claim any difference in the eventual number of deaths between treated and untreated groups. Since the only comparison now available fails to show any difference in mortality rates between home and hospital care, it may be that our heroics have no net effect and merely shift burdens among patients, ie, that the number saved and the number who have lethal drug reactions are the same.

Comparisons between antiarrhythmic drugs in this application are not available, and current interest focuses on lidocaine infusions. Procainamide given every 3–6 hours orally, with the dose adjusted on the basis of plasma levels, is the one regimen for which an improvement in mortality figures is claimed.

Beta-adrenergic blocking agents have not proved useful in preventing arrhythmias in the immediate postinfarction period. New drugs under investigation show significant promise for use to control ventricular ectopy, with resulting reduction in mortality rates.

• • •

References

General

Coraboeuf E, Deroubaix E, Hoerter J: Control of ionic permeabilities in normal and ischemic heart. Circ Res 38 (Suppl I):192, 1976.

Hondeghem LM, Katzung BG: Time- and voltage-dependent interactions of antiarrhythmic drugs with cardiac sodium channels. Biochim Biophys Acta 472:373, 1977.

Katzung BG, Gonzalez R, Scheinman MM: Treatment of cardiac arrhythmias. West J Med 131:533, 1979.

Prinzmetal M & others: The nature of spontaneous auricular fibrillation in man. JAMA 157:1175, 1955.

Sokolow M, McIlroy MB: *Clinical Cardiology,* 2nd ed. Lange, 1979.

Quinidine

Bloomfield SS & others: Quinidine for prophylaxis of arrhythmias in acute myocardial infarction. N Engl J Med 285:979, 1971.

Cheng TO: Atrial flutter during quinidine therapy of atrial fibrillation. Am Heart J 52:273, 1956.

Data JL, Wilkinson VR, Nies AS: Interaction of quinidine with anticonvulsant drugs. N Engl J Med 294:699, 1976.

Edwards I, Hancock BW, Saynor R: Correlation between plasma quinidine and cardiac effects. Br J Clin Pharmacol 1:455, 1974.

Kessler KM & others: Quinidine elimination in patients with congestive heart failure or poor renal function. N Engl J Med 290:706, 1974.

Procainamide

Gibson JP & others: Elimination of procainamide in end stage renal failure. Clin Pharmacol Ther 17:321, 1975.

Hoffman BF, Rosen MR, Wit AL: Electrophysiology and pharmacology of cardiac arrhythmias. 7. Cardiac effects of quinidine and procaine amide. Am Heart J 90:117, 1975.

Koch-Weser J, Klein SW: Procainamide dosage schedules, plasma concentrations, and clinical effects. JAMA 215:1454, 1971.

Koch-Weser J & others: Antiarrhythmic prophylaxis with procainamide in acute myocardial infarction. N Engl J Med 281:1253, 1969.

Miller RR & others: Hemodynamic effects of procainamide in patients with acute myocardial infarction and comparison with lidocaine. Am J Med 55:161, 1973.

Lidocaine

Benowitz NL, Meister W: Clinical pharmacokinetics of lidocaine. Clin Pharmacokinetics 3:177, 1978.

Chopra MP & others: Lignocaine therapy for ventricular ectopic activity after acute myocardial infarction: A double-blind trial. Br Med J 3:668, 1971.

Doubts about lignocaine. (Editorial.) Br Med J 1:473, 1975.

Lie KI & others: Lidocaine in the prevention of primary ventricular fibrillation: A double-blind, randomized study of 212 consecutive patients. N Engl J Med 291:1324, 1974.

Miscellaneous

Hagemeijer F: Verapamil in the management of supraventricular tachyarrhythmias occurring after a recent myocardial infarction. Circulation 57:751, 1978.

Heissenbuttel RH, Bigger JT Jr: Bretyllium tosylate: A newly available antiarrhythmic drug for ventricular arrhythmias. Ann Intern Med 91:229, 1979.

Koch-Weser J: Disopyramide. N Engl J Med 300:957, 1979.

Podrid PJ, Schoeneberger A, Lown B: Congestive heart failure caused by oral disopyramide. N Engl J Med 302:614, 1980.

Unger AH, Sklaroff HJ: Fatalities following intravenous use of sodium diphenylhydantoin for cardiac arrhythmias: Report of two cases. JAMA 200:335, 1967.

17 | Diuretics

Congestive heart failure was mentioned in Chapter 15 as a disease process characterized by sodium retention resulting in expanded extracellular fluid volume or edema. The same process of increased renal tubular reabsorption of sodium may accompany cirrhosis of the liver, renal disease, toxemia of pregnancy, the side-effects of drugs, and other states of fluid retention. In all of these situations, treatment directed at the cause is desirable, but treatment of the sodium retention must often also include inhibiting renal tubular function to decrease reabsorption of sodium. It is, therefore, sodium diuresis (natriuresis) rather than merely an increase in urine volume that is the important therapeutic effect of most of the drugs discussed in this chapter.

The following types of compounds and effects are discussed in this chapter:

(1) Thiazide or sulfonamide diuretics: A drug group in wide use for sodium diuresis and in the treatment of hypertension.

(2) Two very potent diuretics: The loop diuretics furosemide and ethacrynic acid.

(3) Potassium-sparing diuretics.

(4) Mercurial diuretics: Potent drugs that are obsolescent because of the availability of orally active thiazides.

(5) Carbonic anhydrase inhibitors: These sulfonamides are unsatisfactory as diuretics but must be discussed because of their use in glaucoma.

(6) Acidifying salts such as ammonium chloride are weak diuretics.

(7) Osmotic diuretics are not used to increase sodium loss but to maintain a high volume of urine or to withdraw water from overhydrated cells.

THIAZIDE DIURETICS

The thiazide diuretics emerged from efforts to synthesize more potent carbonic anhydrase inhibitors. Some disulfonamides (see dichlorphenamide in Fig 17–1) were highly active, but no more useful as diuretics until ring closure involving one of the sulfonamide groups was carried out. The resulting compounds retain a minor ability to inhibit carbonic anhy-

drase. Unexpectedly, however, they have the added effect of marked and persistent natriuresis and of arteriolar dilatation.

Chemistry

The drugs in Table 17–1 are variously called thiazide, benzothiadiazide, or sulfonamide diuretics. The sulfamyl group is essential to their activity. The last 2 compounds in the table, for example, do not contain the thiadiazine ring but are qualitatively similar to the others, which are benzothiazides. Furosemide (Fig 17–1) is a sulfonamide that has a stronger action on the loop of Henle than the thiazides and is discussed separately at the end of this section.

Absorption, Metabolism, & Excretion

All of the thiazides are useful after oral administration, but there are some differences among them in their metabolism. Chlorothiazide (Diuril), the prototype of this group, is less lipid-soluble than the remaining thiazides; it is poorly absorbed and must be given in large doses. Chlorthalidone (Hygroton) is slowly absorbed and, therefore, has a longer apparent duration of action.

All of the thiazides are excreted to at least some extent by the same mechanism responsible for the secretion of uric acid and compete for some of the limited capacity of that system. The excretion of uric acid may therefore be reduced following thiazide administration.

At least some of those thiazides with a substituent on C3 undergo hydrolytic opening of the thiadiazine ring. The resulting disulfamyl metabolites are stronger carbonic anhydrase inhibitors than the parent drug.

Pharmacologic Actions

A. Mechanisms of Action: The mechanisms of the diuretic effect of the thiazides can be partially clarified by outlining the sites in the kidney at which the thiazides and other drugs can act:

1. Proximal tubule–About 75% of the sodium ion filtered at the glomerulus is absorbed by an active process in the proximal convoluted tubule. Ordinarily, bicarbonate is preferentially and completely reabsorbed with sodium at this site. Carbonic anhydrase is required for the process (see Fig 17–2), and, to the minor degree that the sulfonamide diuretics retain

Table 17–1. Chemical structures of thiazide (benzothiadiazide, sulfonamide) and similar diuretics.

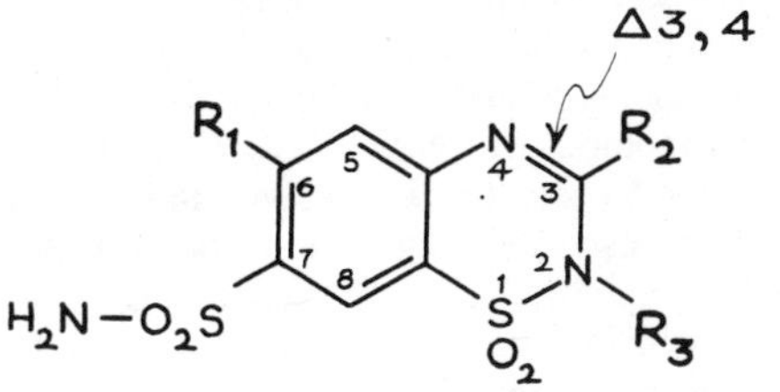

	R_1	$\Delta3=4$	R_2	R_3
Chlorothiazide (Diuril)	Cl–	Yes	–H	–H
Hydrochlorothiazide (Esidrix, Hydrodiuril, Oretic)	Cl–	No	–H	–H
Hydroflumethiazide (Saluron, Diucardin)	F_3C–	No	–H	–H
Methyclothiazide (Enduron)	Cl–	No	$-CH_2-Cl$	$-CH_3$
Trichlormethiazide (Metahydrin, Naqua)	Cl–	No	$-CH-Cl_2$	–H
Benzthiazide (Aquatag, Exna)	Cl–	Yes	$-CH_2-S-CH_2-phenyl$	–H
Bendroflumethiazide (Benuron, Naturetin)	F_3C–	No	$-CH_2-phenyl$	–H
Polythiazide (Renese)	Cl–	No	$-CH_2-S-CH_2-CF_3$	$-CH_3$
Cyclothiazide (Anhydron)	Cl–	No	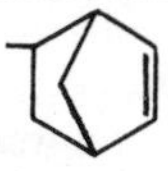	–H
Quinethazone* (Hydromox)	Cl–	No	$-C_2H_5$	–H
Metolazone* (Zaroxolyn)	Cl–	No	$-CH_3$	o-tolyl

*A quinazolinium derivative—ie, at position 1 there is C=O rather than SO_2.

some carbonic anhydrase inhibiting effect, bicarbonate reabsorption is limited and appears in slight excess in the urine, which is therefore more alkaline. Systemically, however, the effect of potassium depletion in causing an alkalosis is prepotent over the tendency toward acidosis caused by bicarbonate loss—ie, administration of the thiazides causes a minor hypokalemic (extracellular) alkalosis.

2. Distal tubule–

a. Cortical portion of thick ascending limb of Henle's loop–The important effect of the thiazides is exerted on this segment, where the active reabsorption of chloride is inhibited, with a corresponding decrease in sodium transport.

b. Aldosterone-governed site–In the distal segment of the distal tubule and in the early collecting duct, sodium is reabsorbed by exchange for potassium and hydrogen ions. The thiazides greatly increase the amount of sodium delivered to the ion exchange site, and more coupled sodium-potassium exchange occurs—ie, potassium loss is greatly increased.

3. Medullary portion of the thick ascending limb of Henle's loop–At this site, a large fraction of the sodium remaining after passage through the proximal tubule is reabsorbed. A diuretic acting on the active transport of chloride from the ascending limb would be potentially very potent.

Several extremely powerful diuretics—eg, furosemide (Lasix) and ethacrynic acid (Edecrin)—clearly do act on the loop of Henle, and it is probable that the thiazides also have some action at that locus at least briefly after large doses.

Sodium reabsorption by the loop of Henle maintains the hyperosmolality of the interstitial fluid in the deep or papillary portion of the medulla. If the osmotic gradient is destroyed by administration of a drug, the ability to finally dilute or concentrate the urine is lost, and a large volume of isotonic urine would be produced. Such an effect is achieved at least briefly with ethacrynic acid.

B. Effects: The thiazides will thus produce a dose-related sodium diuresis. With reasonable doses, only excess sodium will be excreted with appropriate accompanying water loss. With larger doses and with the "loop diuretics," hypovolemia may be induced.

Extrarenal effects—eg, vasodilatation and hyperuricemia—are listed in the sections on uses and adverse reactions.

Clinical Uses

The thiazides are not only the most widely used diuretics but are among the most widely used of all prescription drugs.

A. Essential Hypertension: (See Chapter 12.) A thiazide diuretic is usually the first drug used in the treatment of hypertension. By itself, it causes only a limited (10%) reduction in blood pressure and is suitable for the control of only the mildest cases. However, it potentiates the effect of other hypotensive agents and is almost always the first "layer" of treatment.

The mechanism of the hypotensive effect is not known. The arteriolar dilatation that occurs is not due to sodium or potassium depletion but, presumably, to some undefined ion shift at the wall of the vessel.

B. Fluid Retention States: The thiazides are very useful as part of the treatment of the edema of congestive heart failure. Nephrotic edema is also reduced, but less regularly, and other methods of treatment are available. Patients with edema secondary to cirrhosis react unpredictably and are especially endangered by potassium loss and ammonia retention. Sodium retention due to steroids—whether oral contraceptives, other estrogens, androgens, or endogenous steroids responsible for premenstrual edema—is easily treated with any of the sodium diuretics.

The absorption of oral diuretics is significantly diminished in congestive heart failure. Therefore, in more severe cases, the intravenous route of administration is indicated.

The question of the use of the thiazides during pregnancy is not only controversial but emotional, and few data are available on which to base an opinion. There is no evidence that using thiazides during a normal pregnancy or one complicated by asymptomatic edema reduces the incidence of toxemic states. Nor is it even clear whether volume contraction or expansion is preferable after the toxemic state has developed. There is no question that the thiazide diuretics are useful when congestive heart failure accompanies the pregnancy.

C. Acute Pulmonary Edema: Furosemide, given intravenously, is effective in ameliorating several forms of pulmonary congestion. Most of the experience is with that form of acute pulmonary edema often referred to as acute left ventricular failure. The beneficial effect appears before any diuretic action is apparent and, like the effect on hypertension, is vasomotor (ie, vasodilation) rather than renal in origin.

D. Other Uses: The thiazide diuretics can be used to reduce the volume of urine elaborated by a patient with diabetes insipidus whether of the usual vasopressin-sensitive type or the nephrogenic type. The mechanism is not established.

Furosemide may be used as part of the immediate treatment of elevated calcium levels in blood and urine (see Chapter 36).

Adverse Reactions

A. Side-Effects: Weakness, fatigability, and

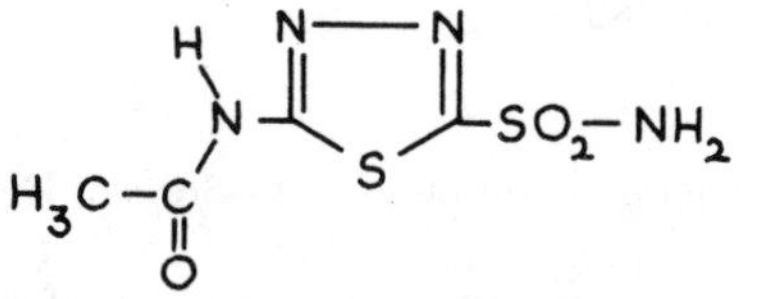

Acetazolamide
(Diamox)

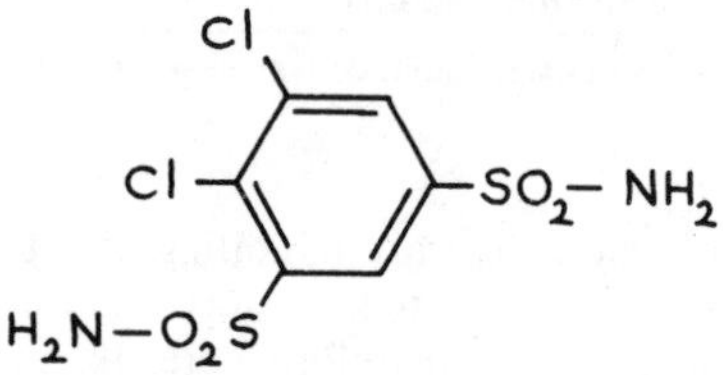

Dichlorphenamide
(Daranide)

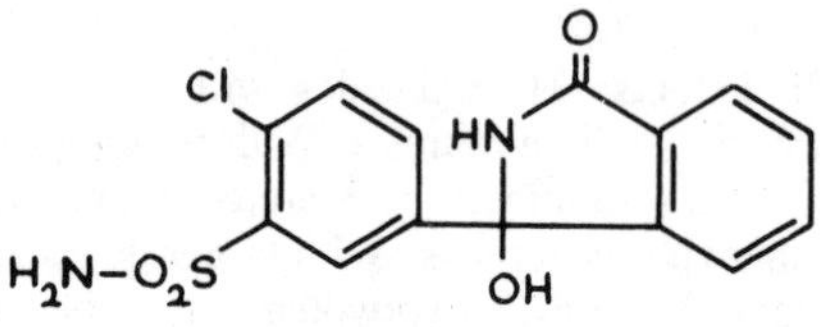

Chlorthalidone
(Hygroton)

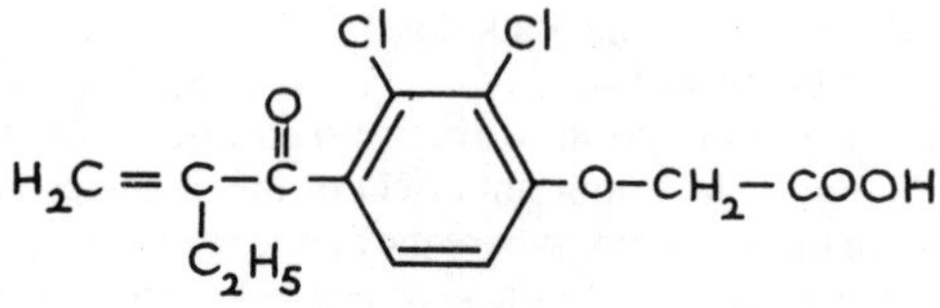

Ethacrynic acid
(Edecrin)

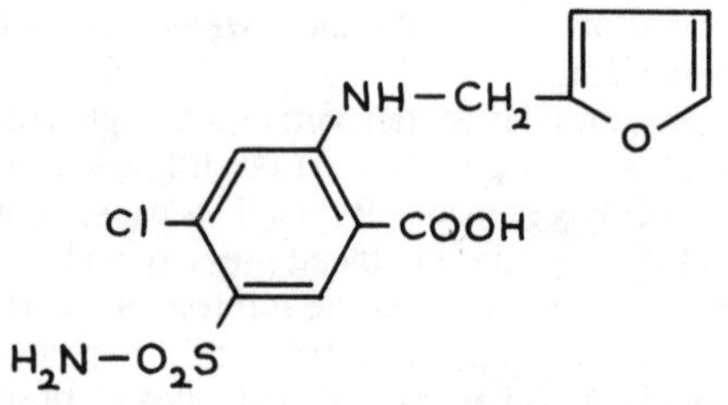

Furosemide
(Lasix)

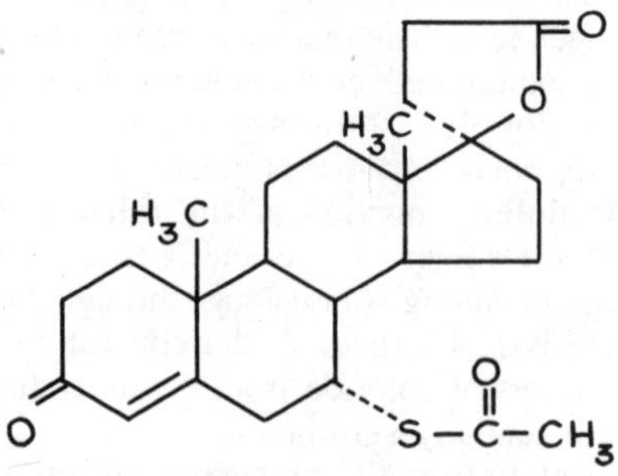

Spironolactone
(Aldactone)

Figure 17–1. Chemical structures of 2 carbonic anhydrase inhibitors and of several diuretics discussed in the text.

paresthesias (as described for the carbonic anhydrase inhibitors) occur. Mild gastrointestinal symptoms — eg, nausea, cramps, and epigastric discomfort — are also common.

B. Dose-Related Toxicity:

1. Potassium depletion–The potassium loss described above may under some conditions progress until signs of potassium depletion appear — eg, anorexia, nausea, weakness, drowsiness, paresthesias, or increased digitalis toxicity. The prediction of these conditions is important in order that potassium supplementation can be provided if necessary but the risk of potassium toxicity avoided if supplementation is not necessary.

In evaluating the degree of potassium depletion, serum potassium levels are of limited usefulness because they do not well reflect changes in total body (exchangeable) potassium until depletion is severe. However, electrocardiography can be helpful because it does reflect the ratio of intracellular to extracellular potassium concentrations.

The potassium loss is most intense early in treatment when diuresis is most profound and when the diet is most likely to be restricted. In patients with uncomplicated hypertension, for example, the loss in exchangeable potassium is rarely greater than 10% and is not progressive. Potassium supplementation can be withheld unless the serum potassium is below 3 mmol/L or the patient is symptomatic.

The following are examples of situations other than clinical signs of depletion when supplementary potassium may be necessary or advisable: (1) when the dietary sources of potassium are inadequate; (2) when diuresis is great and large amounts of excess fluid are mobilized; (3) when the potent loop diuretics — ie, furosemide or ethacrynic acid — are used; (4) when other potassium-losing states are present; and (5) when digitalis is given simultaneously with the diuretic.

Potassium supplementation is not without its own dangers. In one epidemiologic study of therapeutic misadventures, hyperkalemia, sometimes due to potassium-sparing diuretics as well, was the most common cause of lethal reactions. (Hypokalemia and hyperkalemia are further discussed in Chapter 43.)

2. Impaired carbohydrate tolerance–Glucose tolerance is impaired by the thiazides even though certain other sulfonamides are antidiabetic agents. This adverse reaction is unimportant in patients with normal carbohydrate tolerance; but the hyperglycemia of overt diabetes may be intensified, and some patients with abnormal glucose tolerance tests or a family history of diabetes may develop glycosuria when given a thiazide. The effect is dose-related, and continued treatment with smaller doses is often possible. However, a diuretic that does not alter glucose tolerance (eg, triamterene; see below) can be substituted. This toxic effect is rapidly reversible upon discontinuance of the thiazide.

3. Increased blood levels of uric acid–The thiazides, like uric acid, are weak acids secreted by the cells of the proximal tubules and can interfere with the excretion of uric acid. An elevation of plasma uric acid may occur which is unimportant in normal subjects but may precipitate or intensify gout in susceptible patients.

The usual uricosuric agents (see Chapter 40) act at a more distal level of the nephron to block reabsorption — ie, increase urinary excretion — of uric acid. They are still effective during the administration of thiazides.

Ticrynafen, which is structurally similar to ethacrynic acid but in its diuretic action more closely resembles the thiazides (acting on the cortical diluting segment of the distal tubule), has a remarkable uricosuric action, in addition to its natriuretic and kaliuretic actions. This drug was withdrawn because of several reported cases of liver damage.

4. Other toxic effects–The decreased renal excretion of ammonia may be dangerous in the presence of impaired liver function.

One test of thyroid function — protein-bound iodine — will often be decreased to less than normal levels, but ^{131}I uptake is uninfluenced. The size of the iodine pool is probably decreased by the iodide diuresis that accompanies chloride loss.

Enteric-coated tablets that contained both a thiazide and supplemental potassium chloride caused toxic reactions in the past but are no longer available. These preparations released the potassium chloride in the jejunum, and the high local concentration of potassium caused ulceration and subsequent scarring and stenosis in the upper small intestine.

C. Allergic Reactions: Skin rashes are seen occasionally. Serious allergic reactions must be extremely rare considering the wide use of the thiazides. Thrombocytopenic purpura has been reported several times.

Contraindications & Cautions

The thiazide diuretics should be used with caution in the following situations:

(1) Renal insufficiency may be intensified by a contraction of plasma volume.

(2) The arrhythmias of digitalis toxicity are intensified by potassium depletion. Administration of a thiazide may precipitate toxicity in a patient previously stabilized on digitalis.

(3) The reasons have already been given for cautious administration in the presence of diabetes, gout, cirrhosis, and during the administration of corticosteroids or in other potassium-losing states.

The dosage of the thiazides should not be higher than necessary to achieve the desired effect. Intermittent therapy (5 days on and 2 days off) often maintains the therapeutic effect with less hypokalemia.

Dosages & Preparations Available

The preparations listed in Table 17–2 (with the exception of furosemide) differ only in their absolute potency. Chlorthalidone and metolazone are slowly absorbed, and their action is, therefore, more prolonged.

Table 17–2. Thiazides and other diuretics: Dosages.

	Daily Oral Dose	Frequency of Dosage
Bendroflumethiazide (Benuron, Naturetin)	2.5–10 mg	As single dose
Benzthiazide* (Aquatag, Exna)	25–100 mg	In 2 divided doses
Chlorothiazide* (Diuril)	0.5–1 g	In 2 divided doses
Chlorthalidone† (Hygroton)	50–100 mg	As single dose
Cyclothiazide (Anhydron)	1–2 mg	As single dose
Furosemide† (Lasix)	40–80 mg	In 2 divided doses
Hydrochlorothiazide* (Esidrix, Hydrodiuril, Oretic)	25–100 mg	In 2 divided doses
Hydroflumethiazide (Saluron, Diucardin)	25–100 mg	In 2 divided doses
Methyclothiazide (Enduron, Aquatensen)	2.5–10 mg	As single dose
Metolazone† (Zaroxolyn)	2.5–10 mg	As single dose
Polythiazide (Renese)	1–4 mg	As single dose
Quinethazone† (Hydromox)	50–100 mg	As single dose
Trichlormethiazide* (Metahydrin, Naqua)	2–8 mg	As single dose

*Generic preparation available. Trade name included for identification only.
†Not a thiazide but a sulfonamide qualitatively similar to the thiazides.

TWO POTENT DIURETICS

The usual thiazides act predominantly on the cortical portion of the thick ascending limb of the loop of Henle. Furosemide, ethacrynic acid, and an investigative drug, bumetamide, act to block chloride reabsorption along the entire length of the thick portion of the ascending limb.

1. FUROSEMIDE
(Lasix)

This agent is a sulfonamide and retains the properties of the thiazides discussed above. However, it acts on the loop of Henle to a much greater degree, and its potency apppproaches that of ethacrynic acid. It can be contrasted with the usual thiazides in the following ways:

(1) The onset of diuresis and of arteriolar and venous dilatation is rapid, but the effect persists for a shorter period (4 hours).

(2) The generalization—true for reasonable doses of the other thiazides—that only excess sodium will be mobilized does not apply to furosemide, ie, dehydration, potassium depletion, and transient or permanent deafness occurs.

(3) The potency, the rapid onset of action, and the availability of an injectable dosage form have led to the wide use of furosemide as an emergency drug, eg, as a diuretic in the immediate treatment of congestive heart failure and as a vasoactive drug in the treatment of acute pulmonary edema or hypertension.

(4) Furosemide is a more effective diuretic against edema associated with chronic renal failure. The other thiazides are unlikely to be effective when renal function is seriously impaired (80%).

(5) Furosemide combined with a high fluid intake of saline intravenously is very effective in lowering serum Ca^{2+} in the most hypercalcemic patients (see also Chapter 36).

(6) For chronic use, especially in hypertension, any one of the other, longer-acting thiazides (eg, chlorthalidone or metolazone) is demonstrably more effective.

See Table 17–2 for dosage and preparations available. The structure of furosemide is shown in Fig 17–1.

2. ETHACRYNIC ACID
(Edecrin)

Ethacrynic acid is a synthetic drug chemically unrelated to any of the other diuretics so far discussed and remarkable for its potency.

Ethacrynic acid acts to inhibit the active transport of sodium in the proximal tubule and of chloride throughout the loop of Henle. For a brief period after its administration, 40–50% of the sodium and water filtered at the glomerulus escapes reabsorption. In hydropenic subjects, the ability to concentrate tubular urine is lost when ethacrynic acid is given; and in hydrated patients, the urine cannot be as well diluted during its passage through the loop of Henle—ie, the loop loses its ability to dilute or concentrate the urine and its ability to maintain the osmotic gradient in the medulla.

Potassium and hydrogen ion excretion are also increased, presumably because of the increased amount of sodium reaching the distal tubule. Supplementary potassium chloride must be given.

Ethacrynic acid has been used in patients with refractory edema of various causes. There is no doubt about its potency.

However, its toxicity, especially with chronic use, is also greater than that of the thiazides. Most of the toxic reactions are a consequence of its potency—eg, dehydration, hypotension, hypokalemia, alkalosis, deafness—since essential as well as excess sodium may be lost. As would be predicted from its structure (Fig 17–1), ethacrynic acid may cause elevated levels of plasma uric acid. Alterations in glucose tolerance have also been reported. Gastrointestinal bleeding has occurred after its use. The incidence of hepatic damage and agranulocytosis needs to be defined.

The onset of action of ethacrynic acid is rapid. Maximum activity is reached in about 2 hours, and diuresis persists for 6–8 hours.

The initial dose of ethacrynic acid (Edecrin) is 50 mg every 2–3 days. The maximum daily dose is 150–200 mg.

POTASSIUM–SPARING DIURETICS

1. SPIRONOLACTONE
(An Aldosterone Antagonist)

Spironolactone (Aldactone) is a synthetic steroid resembling aldosterone. Its structure is shown in Fig 17–1.

Aldosterone acts on the distal and collecting tubules to enhance the sodium-potassium exchange mechanism—ie, to cause sodium retention and potassium loss. An aldosterone antagonist causes sodium diuresis and potassium retention. The intensity of action of such an antagonist depends upon the amount of aldosterone acting on the kidney—ie, it would not show any diuretic action in an adrenalectomized animal but would be unusually active in those cases in which edema is accompanied by hyperaldosteronism.

Spironolactone is a weak diuretic and is usually given in combination with a thiazide. Its effect develops very slowly, requiring 2–3 days of administration for a maximal effect.

Spironolactone is occasionally used in the treatment of patients with cirrhosis and edema when other diuretics are toxic or ineffective.

Spironolactone frequently causes hyperkalemia; less often, its use leads to elevated blood urea nitrogen levels. Dehydration and gynecomastia may appear with chronic use. Hyperkalemia is often precipitated by the ill-advised use of supplementary potassium. Administration of the potassium may have been suggested by the use of a thiazide in combination with spironolactone. The combination does not usually antagonize the potassium loss caused by the thiazide, nor will it prevent potassium accumulation if a supplement is given.

Spironolactone (Aldactone) is given in a dosage of 25–50 mg 3–4 times daily. The combination with hydrochlorothiazide is called Aldactazide.

2. TRIAMTERENE
(Dyrenium)

Triamterene is a pteridine derivative that has actions (sodium diuresis, potassium retention) similar to those of the aldosterone antagonist. It acts, however, directly on the distal tubule, and its action persists after adrenalectomy. Like spironolactone, it is usually used in combination with a thiazide.

Triamterene produces an elevation in blood urea levels with chronic administration. Other side-effects are minor, and the toxic reactions described for the thiazides do not occur when it is administered as such. It is, however, usually used as a proprietary mixture with a thiazide (Dyazide), in which case the effects of the thiazide predominate and triamterene contributes only a minor reduction in potassium loss.

Initial dosage of triamterene (Dyrenium) may be 100 mg twice daily, but when a response occurs the dosage should be decreased to 100 mg daily or every other day.

Triamterene (Dyrenium)
(2,4,7-triamino-6-phenylpteridine)

MERCURIAL DIURETICS

The diuretic effect of inorganic mercury in the form of calomel (mercurous chloride) was noted 4 centuries ago, but the effective use of mercury as a diuretic was an outgrowth of observations made in 1919 during the treatment of syphilis with an organic mercurial drug. The use of the mercurials increased thereafter as understanding of the role of sodium in the production of edema grew. These drugs came into wide use as potent sodium diuretics that caused few toxic reactions. However, they could be given only by injection, and since 1957 they have been replaced by the orally active thiazides.

Chemistry

Mercuric ion (Hg^{2+}) is essential for the action of these diuretics, but it must be provided in the form of a weakly dissociated organic compound.

The general chemical structure of a mercurial diuretic can be represented as follows:

$$R_1-CH_2-CH(O-CH_3)-CH_2-Hg-R_2$$

R_1 represents a variety of substituents. R_2 represents theophylline or thioglycollate. The organic mercurials dissociate to give only small amounts of mercuric ion. They react only slightly with tissue and plasma protein and reach the renal tubules in high concentration.

Absorption, Route of Administration, & Excretion

The major limitation of the mercurial diuretics is their poor absorption after oral administration and the almost invariable gastrointestinal irritation that they cause. They are, therefore, given by intramuscular injection, following which their action begins in about 2 hours, becomes maximal in 5–6 hours, and is dissipated in less than 24 hours.

The mercurial diuretics are concentrated in the renal cortex, where there is a high concentration of sulfhydryl groups with which they react. The mercury is excreted mostly by the renal tubules. Smaller amounts are excreted into the colon and mouth. Excretion is rapid and is nearly complete in 24 hours.

Pharmacologic Effects

A. Site and Mechanism of Action: The mercurials also act on the cortical segment of the thick ascending limb of Henle's loop to block the reabsorption of chloride and accompanying sodium. The thiazides and mercurials must act on 2 functional sites, since even maximal effects of the 2 drugs are additive—ie, 2 separate functions are saturated.

B. Pattern of Electrolyte Loss: The mercurials have the effect of either enhancing or inhibiting potassium secretion, depending upon the concentration of potassium at some governing site. Thus, potassium depletion is not a problem. An excess of potassium and hydrogen ions over sodium is usually excreted, with a corresponding excess loss of chloride and production of hypochloremic alkalosis. In the presence of such hypochloremic alkalosis, the effect of the mercurials is reduced. Activity after repeated doses is restored, and even the effect of initial doses is increased, by pretreatment with ammonium chloride.

Clinical Uses

Mercurials are now used in only occasional hospitalized patients with edema resistant to other drugs or when the intense action is desirable. They should not be used in the presence of renal failure.

Adverse Reactions

During the period of intensive use of the mercurials, toxic reactions were exceedingly rare. A few deaths from ventricular fibrillation followed intravenous injections, and a rare case of renal tubular necrosis was reported.

Sodium depletion—ie, low plasma concentrations of sodium in the face of continuing edema— occurred following intensive use, especially with the patient taking a restricted diet. Potassium depletion was rare.

Dosages

The dosage is 1–2 mL (usually 2 mL) intramuscu-larly. Mercaptomerin and mercuhydrin can be given subcutaneously.

CARBONIC ANHYDRASE INHIBITORS

Inhibitors of carbonic anhydrase are no longer used as diuretics. However, they are important in the treatment of one form of glaucoma and are discussed at this particular point because of their relation to the thiazide diuretics.

Chemistry

Some of the earlier, unsubstituted bacteriostatic sulfonamides caused a systemic acidosis and, paradoxically, the production of a large volume of alkaline urine. This action was shown to be due to inhibition of carbonic anhydrase activity and a consequent decrease in the ability to acidify the urine. More potent inhibitors have since been synthesized, and all, like the thiazide diuretics, bear a free sulfonamide (sulfamyl) group. The structure of 2 representative carbonic anhydrase inhibitors is shown in Fig 17–1.

Pharmacologic Actions

A. Mechanism of Diuretic Action: The hydration of carbon dioxide takes place very slowly unless accelerated by the enzyme carbonic anhydrase. Carbonic anhydrase is a metalloprotein, and its inhibitors combine with the zinc in the molecule of enzyme to cause a noncompetitive inhibition. The rate of production within cells of hydrogen and bicarbonate ion is greatly reduced and the amount available for active transport into secretions decreased.

$$CO_2 + H_2O \rightleftharpoons H_2CO_3 \rightleftharpoons H^+ + HCO_3^-$$

In the kidney, the consequences of carbonic anhydrase inhibition are apparent at the ion exchange site of the distal tubule. The reactions shown in Fig 17–2 accompany the following changes in the composition of the urine:

1. Reduced reabsorption of sodium–Most of the sodium in the proximal tubular urine is reabsorbed by an active process, and, during this reabsorption, an equivalent amount of easily diffusible anion, chloride, is also reabsorbed. This process is not altered by inhibition of carbonic anhydrase. Sodium that accompanies a less easily diffusible anion, bicarbonate, is reabsorbed only by exchange for hydrogen or potassium ions secreted into the lumen of the tubule by the renal cells. If the amount of available hydrogen ion is reduced, there will be less reabsorption of this small fraction of the total sodium reabsorbed by the kidney.

2. Bicarbonate excretion increased– Ordinarily, the secreted hydrogen ion combines with

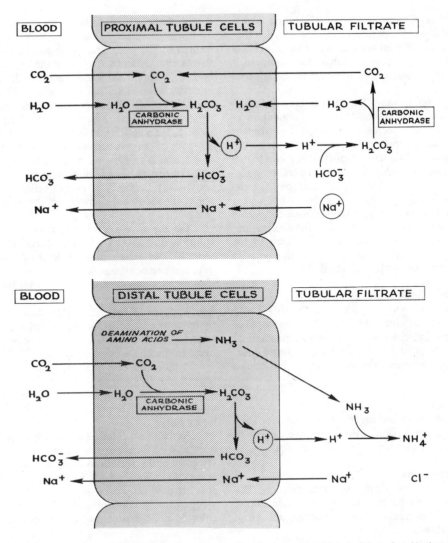

Figure 17 –2. Role of carbonic anhydrase in producing hydrogen ions in the proximal tubule *(above)* and in the production of ammonium ions *(below).* See text for explanation. (Reproduced, with permission, from Harper HA, Rodwell VW, Mayes PA: *Review of Physiological Chemistry,* 17th ed. Lange, 1979.)

bicarbonate ion provided by the glomerular filtrate, and the carbonic acid thus formed is mostly reabsorbed as CO_2. In effect, the bicarbonate ion is normally reabsorbed almost completely. If carbonic anhydrase is inhibited and hydrogen ion is lacking, bicarbonate will remain in its poorly diffusible form and will be excreted in unusually large amounts. The urine will thereupon become alkaline. Plasma bicarbonate will fall, and, as plasma chloride is elevated, a mild systemic acidosis will appear.

3. Increased potassium excretion–Potassium competes with hydrogen ion for the limited capacity of the same transport system. If the amount of H^+ available is reduced, a larger amount of K^+ will be exchanged for Na^+. Carbonic anhydrase inhibitors, therefore, cause a loss of potassium.

4. Ammonia retained–The availability of hydrogen ion normally allows the conversion of am-

monia to ammonium ion, which remains in tubular and bladder urine. After carbonic anhydrase inhibition, uncharged ammonia diffuses back into the renal cells and blood.

B. Limitation of Usefulness as Diuretics: The carbonic anhydrase inhibitors cannot cause a great sodium diuresis because the amount of bicarbonate and, therefore, the amount of sodium reabsorption tied to the excretion of that poorly diffusible ion is small.

More important, even the small sodium diuresis caused by carbonic anhydrase inhibition lasts for only a day or two. As the bicarbonate load presented to the renal tubules decreases—ie, as systemic acidosis develops—sodium excretion is restored to normal.

Even though the natriuretic effect is transient, inhibition of carbonic anhydrase can be maintained for long periods and effects other than sodium diuresis will persist.

C. Other Consequences of Carbonic Anhydrase Inhibition: Many secretory processes other than those in the kidney involve the active transport of H^+ or HCO_3^-. However, carbonic anhydrase inhibition is clinically important only in the case of the aqueous humor.

1. Aqueous humor–The aqueous contains a high concentration of bicarbonate ion, and inhibition of carbonic anhydrase decreases the rate of formation of aqueous, reducing intraocular pressure.

2. Carbon dioxide transport–It is possible that carbonic anhydrase inhibition leads to a transient elevation of tissue P_{CO_2}, but the CO_2 transport mechanisms are generally resistant.

3. Central nervous system–Carbonic anhydrase inhibition decreases the rate of spinal fluid formation. However, the central nervous system effects of the inhibitors—eg, somnolence and an anticonvulsant action—cannot be explained on this basis.

Absorption, Metabolism, & Excretion

All of the carbonic anhydrase inhibitors are well absorbed after oral administration. Effects on the pH of the urine are apparent within 30 minutes, are maximal in 2 hours, and persist for 12 hours after a single dose. Excretion, as for other organic acids, is by tubular secretion.

Clinical Uses

These drugs are no longer used as diuretics. They are used as a supplement to other drugs or surgery in the treatment of glaucoma. (See Chapter 9.)

Adverse Reactions

Paresthesias and drowsiness are common. The low urinary citrate that accompanies the alkaline urine can lead to the precipitation of calcium phosphate crystals or stones.

Dosages & Preparations Available

See Table 17–3.

Table 17–3. Carbonic anhydrase inhibitors used in treatment of glaucoma: Dosages.

	Usual Oral Dose (1–4 Times Daily)
Acetazolamide (Diamox)	250 mg
Dichlorphenamide (Daranide)	50 mg
Ethoxzolamide (Cardrase)	62.5–125 mg
Methazolamide (Neptazane)	50 mg

ACIDIFYING SALTS

Acidifying salts are no longer used as diuretics, but they may still be used to potentiate the mercurial diuretics or for uses unrelated to renal function. Clinical use is extremely rare.

Ammonium chloride is the common acid salt. Following absorption, the ammonium ion is converted to urea by the liver, leading to an excess of chloride that is retained in the plasma at the expense of bicarbonate. In the patient with severe liver disease, metabolism of ammonium ion is impaired. Therefore, administration of ammonium chloride may elevate blood ammonia and cause encephalopathy. Even in a normal subject, the acidosis that follows the administration of 10–15 g of ammonium chloride may cause increased ventilation at rest and exertional dyspnea. In a patient with congestive heart failure, the increased respiratory activity may not only be uncomfortable but may also place an additional demand on the limited cardiac reserve.

On the first day of administration, the excess chloride is excreted with an equivalent amount of sodium. The sodium diuresis decreases after the first day, and compensation is complete in less than 5 days if administration of ammonium chloride is continuous. Of the several mechanisms restricting sodium loss, the most important is the increased production of ammonia by renal tubular cells; the excess chloride is thus excreted as ammonium chloride, and only a negligible osmotic diuretic action persists.

Ammonium chloride may be used to increase or restore sensitivity to mercurial diuretics. In this context, it may be given with potassium chloride. The minimal dose of ammonium chloride is 1–1.5 g 4 times daily.

Ammonium chloride is also an expectorant—ie, it is able to increase the volume and decrease the viscosity of the secretions of the respiratory tract secondary to its local gastric irritant effect. For this purpose, it obviously must not be coated but used as a syrup, usually containing 0.3 g/5 mL. Ammonium chloride as an expectorant is inferior to the iodides.

OSMOTIC DIURETICS

Osmotic diuretics are used to induce water diuresis rather than natriuresis, and their applications are totally different from those of the sodium diuretics so far discussed.

Two concepts or uses included in the term osmotic diuretic are discussed below.

Maintenance of High Urine Volume

If a drug that is not metabolized—eg, mannitol—appears in the glomerular filtrate but is not reabsorbed by the renal tubules, it will hold in the lumen of the tubule enough water to maintain it in an isosmotic solution. Since mannitol and other osmotic diuretics are not reabsorbed in the proximal tubule, a greatly increased volume of isotonic tubular fluid reaches the loop of Henle. The sodium-transporting capacity of the ascending loop is limited, and sodium cannot be reabsorbed rapidly enough to maintain the hyperosmolality of the medullary interstitium—ie, some isotonic fluid diffuses out of the tubule and weakens the countercurrent mechanism by reducing the osmotic gradient along the pyramids. Because of this lesser gradient, less water leaves the collecting ducts and urine volume is increased.

This action is used to maintain a high urine volume but not to extract abnormal amounts of fluid from the body. Thus, the osmotic diuretics can be used to prevent anuria following a hemolytic reaction, extensive surgery, or trauma and hemorrhage; and to maintain a very high urine volume during the treatment of intoxication by barbiturates, salicylates, or other agents excreted in the urine.

In oliguric patients, a test dose of 12.5 g of mannitol is administered intravenously over a period of 3–5 minutes. Unless urine output increases during the next 3 hours to 40–60 mL/h, the condition is probably unresponsive to mannitol. If urine volume does increase, mannitol is given by intravenous infusion to produce a urine flow of about 100 mL/h. If mannitol is used prophylactically or to promote the excretion of a poison, an initial intravenous loading dose of 25 g can be given followed by infusion to maintain the desired urine output.

Dehydrating Action

If a substance that does not enter the cells or does not enter a particular anatomic area such as the brain or anterior chamber of the eye is given as a very strong solution, water will leave the cells or anatomic area to dilute the drug to isotonicity pending its excretion. This "dehydrating" action is used in 2 situations:

A. To Reduce Intracranial Pressure: Increased intracranial pressure (eg, in brain tumor, head injury, brain swelling) may be reduced for 3–10 hours by intravenous administration of urea. Give urea as 30% solution (in 10% invert sugar) in a dosage of about 1 g/kg at a rate of about 60 drops/min. Poor renal function and active intracranial bleeding are contraindications.

B. To Reduce Intraocular Pressure: Three different agents (urea, mannitol, and glycerol) have been used to lower intraocular pressure preoperatively in angle-closure glaucoma. Urea and mannitol are administered intravenously. Glycerol may be given orally. The dosage of all 3 of these osmotic drugs is 1.5 g/kg.

• • •

References

General

Burg M, Stoner L: Renal tubular chloride transport and the mode of action of some diuretics. Annu Rev Physiol 38:37, 1976.

Jacobson HR, Kokko JP: Diuretics: Sites and mechanisms of action. Annu Rev Pharmacol 16:201, 1976.

Lief PD: Diuretics. Am Heart J 96:824, 1978.

Lindheimer MD, Katz AI: Sodium and diuretics in pregnancy. N Engl J Med 288:891, 1973.

Loriaux DL & others: Spironolactone and endocrine dysfunction. Ann Intern Med 85:630, 1976.

Management of refractory oedema. (Editorial.) Br J Med 1:148, 1979.

Sopko JA, Freeman RM: Salt substitutes as a source of potassium. JAMA 238:608, 1977.

Thiazide Derivatives

Boley SJ & others: Potassium-induced lesions of the small bowel. JAMA 193:997, 1965.

Dargie HJ & others: Total body potassium in long-term furosemide therapy: Is potassium supplementation necessary? Br Med J 4:316, 1974.

Dikshit K & others: Renal and extrarenal hemodynamic effects of furosemide in congestive heart failure after acute myocardial infarction. N Engl J Med 288:1087, 1973.

Moser RH: Bibliographies on diseases of medical progress: Modern oral diuretics. Clin Pharmacol Ther 8:755, 1976.

Picking a diuretic. (Editorial.) Br Med J 3:521, 1975.

Schwartz AB, Swartz CD: Dosage of potassium chloride elixir to correct thiazide-induced hypokalemia. JAMA 230:702, 1974.

Wilkinson PR & others: Total body and serum potassium during prolonged thiazide therapy for essential hypertension. Lancet 2:759, 1975.

Mercurials

Levitt MF, Goldstein MH: Mercurial diuretics. Bull NY Acad Med 38:249, 1962.

Others

Fishman RA: Brain edema. N Engl J Med 293:706, 1975.

Flanigan WJ, Ackerman GL: Site of action of ethacrynic acid. Arch Intern Med 118:117, 1966.

Frohlich ED: Ticrynafen: A new thiazide-like but uricosuric antihypertensive diuretic. N Engl J Med 301:1378, 1979.

Galin MA, Davidson R, Shachter N: Ophthalmological use of osmotic therapy. Am J Ophthalmol 62:629, 1966.

Gennari FJ, Kassirer JP: Osmotic diuresis. N Engl J Med 291:714, 1974.

Greenblatt DJ, Koch-Weser J: Adverse reactions to spironolactone. JAMA 225:40, 1973.

Maren TH: Carbonic anhydrase: Chemistry, physiology, and inhibition. Physiol Rev 47:595, 1967.

Russell RP, Lindeman RD, Prescott LF: Metabolic and hypotensive effects of ethacrynic acid: Comparative study with hydrochlorothiazide. JAMA 205:11, 1968.

18 | Antithrombotic Agents

The elaborate mechanisms that enable the blood to clot are of obvious importance, but in view of the easily activated clotting mechanism, the ability of blood to remain fluid within blood vessels is also essential. The formation of thrombi within arteries or veins can have lethal consequences in the form of, for example, myocardial infarctions or pulmonary emboli. In current standard treatment and in important current clinical research, the clotting mechanisms are frequently inhibited by drugs.

The drug classes discussed are (1) inhibitors of prothrombin synthesis; (2) heparin, an antithrombin; (3) aspirin and other inhibitors of platelet function; (4) vitamin K, which is involved in the synthesis of clotting factors physiologically and in relation to drugs; (5) fibrin-clot lysing agents; and (6) a few other enzymes.

INHIBITORS OF PROTHROMBIN SYNTHESIS

Source & Chemistry

The first inhibitor of prothrombin synthesis, bishydroxycoumarin, was originally isolated from fermented clover that was causing hemorrhagic disease in cattle. Drugs of this class are now synthetically prepared and inexpensive compared with a natural product such as heparin. They can be grouped into 2 classes: the coumarin derivatives, and the appreciably more toxic indandiones (Table 18–1 and Fig 18–1).

Warfarin sodium and dicumarol (bishydroxycoumarin), examples of the first class, are the 2 most commonly used prothrombin depressants. Warfarin is the only agent that is soluble in water and available for injection. All drugs of this class are, however, well absorbed after oral administration. Other available derivatives are listed in Table 18–1.

The structure of a vitamin K is shown in Fig 18–1 to suggest a relation between vitamin K and these inhibitors. Salicylates are also weak inhibitors of the liver synthesis of clotting factors and may add to the anticoagulant effect of more potent drugs.

Absorption & Metabolism

Unlike heparin, the prothrombin depressants are active after oral administration.

Following administration of these drugs, there is a latent period; when the drug is discontinued, there is a period of many days before prothrombin concentration returns to normal. The period that elapses until activity is maximal and the period necessary for recovery vary somewhat with the different drugs. However, the latent period is due in part to the need to metabolize prothrombin already present, and the long duration of action reflects the time needed for resynthesis of prothrombin rather than the persistence in the body of the inhibitors of synthesis.

The variation of the maintenance dose between patients is due in part to variations in the rate of biotransformation.

Pharmacologic Actions

A. Clotting Mechanism: In this and subsequent sections, it may be helpful to refer to Fig 18–2, a scheme of the clotting mechanism that includes the presently characterized factors but omits many details of the sequence of events. Most of the coagulation factors exist in an inactive or precursor form so that blood remains fluid until its clotting is initiated by contact with injured tissue or lysed platelets or by contact with a wettable surface such as glass. Phase 1 of clotting results in the formation of active thromboplastin. Three of the factors involved—VII (proconvertin), IX (PTC), and X (Stuart-Prower factor)—are synthesized in the liver, and the synthesis is dependent upon adequate vitamin K. Phase 2 is the conversion of prothrombin to thrombin. Prothrombin is a protein similarly synthesized. Phase 3 is the proteolytic action of thrombin on fibrinogen to form a fibrin unit that can then further polymerize to form the blood clot.

B. Inhibition of Prothrombin Synthesis: Vitamin K is necessary for the synthesis in the liver not only of prothrombin (factor II) itself but also of proconvertin (VII), PTC (IX), and Stuart-Prower (X) factor. Vitamin K is not incorporated into any of these proteins, but their synthesis is defective in the absence of vitamin K or in the presence of any of the coumarin drugs. It is convenient and not greatly misleading to refer to these antagonists as if prothrombin were the

Table 18–1. Prothrombin depressants: Dosages and preparations available.

	Dosage (Oral)*			Approximate Time to Peak Effect	Approximate Duration of Effect
	1st Day	2nd Day	Usual Maintenance Dose and Range		
Coumarin derivatives					
Dicumarol (bishydroxy-coumarin)†	100–200 mg	100–200 mg	75 mg (25–150)	2–3 d	4–5 d
Warfarin (Coumadin, Panwarfin, Athrombin-K)	10–15 mg	10–15 mg	7.5 mg (5–15)	1–2 d	2–3 d
Phenprocoumon (Liquamar)	10 mg	10 mg	3 mg (1.5–6)	1–2 d	4 d
Acenocoumarol (Sintrom)	8–16 mg	8–16 mg	6 mg (2–10)	1–2 d	2 d
Indandione derivatives					
Diphenadione (Dipaxin)	40–60 mg	10–20 mg	7 mg (2.5–10)	2–4 d	10 d
Phenindione (Hedulin)	100–250 mg twice daily	25–75 mg twice daily	50 mg (12.5–75) twice daily	1–2 d	2–4 d
Anisindione (Miradon)	300 mg	200 mg	75 mg (25–250)	1–2 d	4 d

*Only warfarin may be given intravenously. Dosages are single daily doses unless otherwise specified.
†Generic preparation available.

only protein whose synthesis was affected. Carboxylation of glutamic acid residue is catalyzed by vitamin K:

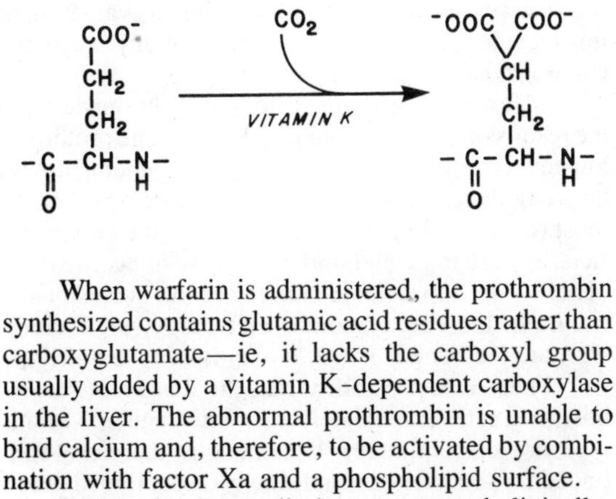

When warfarin is administered, the prothrombin synthesized contains glutamic acid residues rather than carboxyglutamate—ie, it lacks the carboxyl group usually added by a vitamin K–dependent carboxylase in the liver. The abnormal prothrombin is unable to bind calcium and, therefore, to be activated by combination with factor Xa and a phospholipid surface.

Within the dosage limits encountered clinically, the warfarin-vitamin K relationship appears to be competitive—ie, larger doses of one overcome the effects of the other. However, the 2 are not metabolic antagonists, and the noncompetitive relationship is demonstrable in animals. Vitamin K exists in equilibrium with its epoxide, and warfarin probably acts to block the reconversion of the epoxide to the active vitamin.

The lowering of plasma prothrombin concentration will develop slowly following administration of one any of these inhibitors. In part, the length of the delay depends upon the drug used; even with the most rapidly acting drugs, however, time must be allowed for the disappearance of prothrombin already synthesized. Similarly, the duration of action reflects the time

necessary for resynthesis of prothrombin as well as the duration of action of the particular drug used.

It is also obvious that the addition of bishydroxy-coumarin to drawn blood will not prevent clotting, since the action of the drug is on the synthesis of clotting factors in the liver.

Clinical Uses

A. Prevention or Treatment of Venous Thrombosis: Bed rest enforced on elderly patients by an illness such as a myocardial infarction or by surgery such as a hip replacement or nailing a fracture of the femoral neck involves a great hazard of venous thrombosis. Blood flow in the deep veins of the leg or pelvis may be so slow that intravascular clotting occurs, or a vessel wall may have been damaged at operation. The process is noninflammatory, and the clot is not bound to the walls of the veins. The thrombus may grow or be propagated by the accretion of additional material, and either the original clot or an extension that reaches a more rapidly flowing channel may be broken loose. The embolus thus formed will be impacted in a pulmonary vessel, with results depending upon the size of the infarct. The most important use of the oral anticoagulants is (1) to prevent the occurrence of venous thrombosis during a period of unusual risk or (2) to prevent the propagation of a clot once it has been formed and thus to prevent embolization until the clot has been bound to the wall of the vein.

When a venous thrombosis has already occurred, the use of anticoagulants is obligatory. The patient should receive the immediately effective heparin intravenously, and administration of the slower acting oral anticoagulants should be begun at the same time.

The usefulness of routine prophylactic anticoagu-

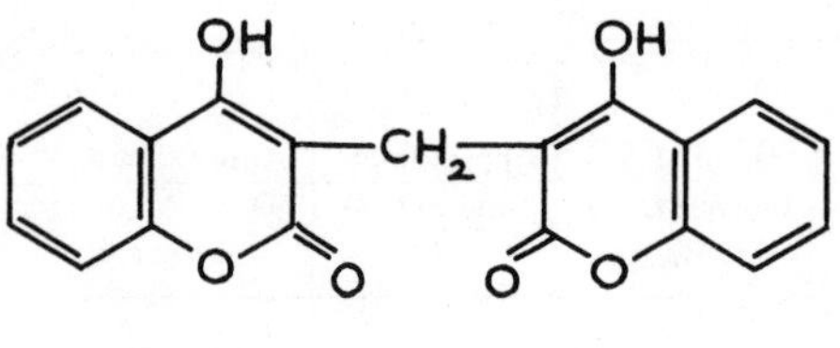

Figure 18–1. Anticoagulant drugs. The structural formulas of the 2 most commonly used coumarin type anticoagulants (dicumarol and warfarin) and a representative of the indandione type (phenindione) are shown. Menadione is a synthetic vitamin K. Salicylic acid also has minor prothrombin depressant effects.

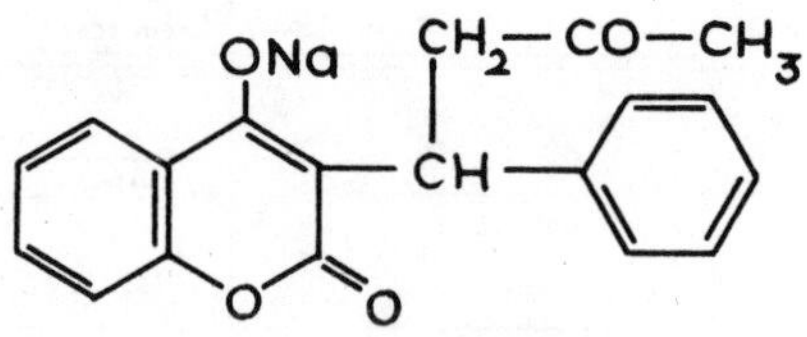

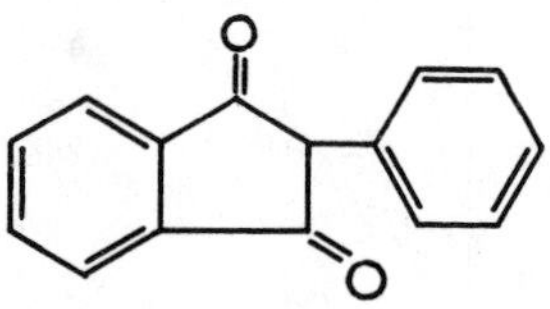

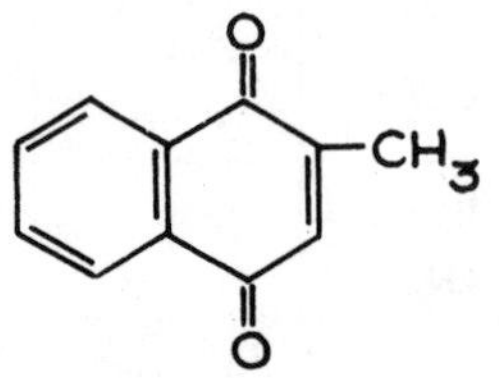

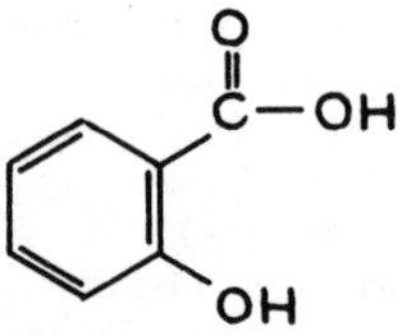

lant therapy has been repeatedly demonstrated in several situations.

For example, pulmonary embolism is still the most common cause of death after fractures of the hip in the elderly. The results of anticoagulant therapy in these aged patients are impressive. In a recent careful study, for example, thromboembolic complications occurred in 22 of 83 control patients and only 7 of 83 treated patients.

In the prevention of postoperative thromboembolic complications, warfarin anticoagulation is the only method whose efficacy is no longer arguable when judged on the basis of clinical outcome (death, emboli) rather than "intermediate" data such as fibrin deposition or phlebography. Yet concern over possible bleeding and problems of dosage and its control have greatly limited the application of coumarin type anticoagulants. Alternate regimens of lesser complexity using heparin or antiplatelet drugs are discussed below.

B. Acute Arterial Occlusion: The effects of acute arterial occlusion (eg, by an embolus) are intensified by thrombosis in the area. Anticoagulation with heparin is initiated at once for its immediate effect, and an inhibitor of prothrombin synthesis is given for its persistent effect.

C. Prevention of Thrombus Formations in Fibrillating Atria: Mural thrombi may form on the noncontracting walls of the atrial appendage during atrial fibrillation. Emboli from the atria are an important complication of rheumatic mitral valve disease. Long-term anticoagulant therapy will prevent the formation of new thrombi and allow old thrombi to become fixed in place as scar tissue develops. Such treatment is usually preparatory to surgical treatment of the mitral valve deformation or conversion of the arrhythmia.

D. Prevention of Coronary Thrombosis: The

atherosclerotic process may gradually occlude a coronary artery. Usually, however, the occlusion is due to formation of a clot on the surface of an atherosclerotic plaque. The question arises whether reducing coagulability by continuous, long-term anticoagulant therapy will prevent or defer the final episode. The answer to this question requires a laborious clinical evaluation of impeccable design. Unfortunately, many available studies must be ignored.

A few cautious conclusions may be made from the results of some acceptable trials: (1) The prothrombin levels often accepted during the general use of anticoagulants are ineffective. (2) Those who benefit most (or, according to some observers, the only beneficiaries) are male and under 60 years of age. (3) The benefit—ie, lower incidence of second occlusions— occurs in the first 6 months of therapy. (4) Patients with angina benefit if the angina is of recent origin.

There is a possibility that the danger of thrombosis is greater immediately after anticoagulants of this type are discontinued. Treatment is therefore continued for several years and slowly discontinued over a period of weeks or months.

Control of Dose

Once production of new clotting factors is blocked, the rate at which depression of clotting factors occurs relates to the half-life of the individual factors. Large initial doses of coumarin drugs do not hasten degradation of the factors involved. Adequate plasma levels of warfarin, for example, can be achieved by administration of 10–15 mg/d until the prothrombin time reaches 1.5–2.5 times the control level. Desired prolongation of the prothrombin time can be achieved in 3–5 days. Prothrombin times should be determined before the first dose and the third dose and daily thereafter until the maintenance dose is established. The maintenance dose is determined for

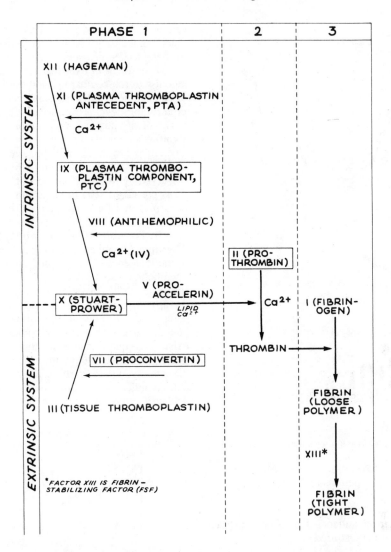

Figure 18–2. The coagulation mechanism (simplified). The conversion of prothrombin to thrombin is accomplished by 2 series of reactions that converge on factor X. The synthesis of coagulation factors shown within the boxes is inhibited by the dicumarol type of anticoagulant. *Phase 1:* The system intrinsic to the blood begins with the activation of factor XII by contact with a proper surface. A cascade of reactions successively converts the factors shown to an active form that acts on the next substance in the sequence until activated factor X is generated. In the extrinsic system, tissue components act on factor X after activation by proconvertin. *Phase 2:* Stuart-Prower factor acting on prothrombin in the presence of calcium produces thrombin. *Phase 3:* Thrombin combines with fibrinogen to form fibrin.

each patient on the basis of prothrombin times. The prothrombin time on a given day will reflect the action of the dose of anticoagulant given 2 days previously except when the more rapidly acting warfarin is used. The prothrombin time is usually maintained at 10–30% of normal for the first few weeks of treatment. What constitutes an adequate level of prothrombin depression thereafter is arguable, but the level is usually allowed to rise to between 30 and 40%, probably with a decrease in therapeutic effectiveness.

The usual (Quick) prothrombin time is sensitive to changes in the concentration of factors VII and X in addition to prothrombin (II). Which of these is important in determining the therapeutic effect or in deter-

mining whether bleeding occurs is not known. The sensitivity or lack of specificity of the prothrombin time is generally regarded as adequate, and the Quick test is the commonly used test. It is, however, not altered by changes in the concentration of IX (PTC), whereas one alternative test (Thrombotest) is sensitive to changes in the concentration of all 4 factors lowered by dicumarol.

In the experience or judgment of some investigators, bleeding may occur early in the use of anticoagulants because factor X is reduced to dangerous levels but prothrombin times are at apparently therapeutic levels.

In judging the results of different clinical trials,

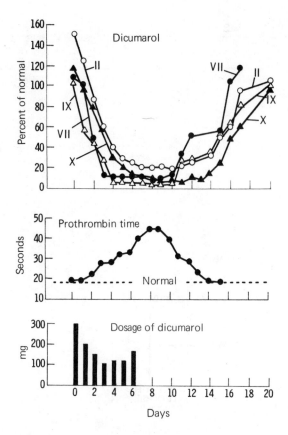

Figure 18 –3. Typical effect of dicumarol on factors VII, IX, X, and II. (Redrawn and reproduced, with permission, from Kazmier & others: Effect of oral anticoagulants on factors VII, IX, X, and II. Arch Intern Med 115:668, 1965.)

the comparison of the anticoagulant effect must take into consideration the test used.

Adverse Reactions

Side-effects are minor, consisting of mild diarrhea or soft stools.

A. Hemorrhage: The important toxicity of the anticoagulants is hemorrhage, which may be significant because of the amount of blood lost or because the bleeding is into a critical area. The occurrence of hemorrhage is not exactly predictable on the basis of prothrombin time determinations. Hemorrhage may occur when prothrombin times are within "safe" limits, and it does not always occur when prothrombin times greatly exceed the desired values. Hemorrhage usually occurs in an area of previous vascular damage; following myocardial infarction, for example, intracardiac bleeding or hemopericardium is a hazard. Bleeding may be renal (hematuria), gastrointestinal, rectal, intracranial, retroperitoneal, into the skin, and in many other sites. The reported incidence of bleeding will depend upon the intensity of therapeutic effect achieved and upon the care with which bleeding is sought. If microscopic hematuria is considered significant bleeding, the complication of bleeding may be

said to be present in as many as one-third of patients receiving the drug. Serious hemorrhage may occur in as many as 2% of patients.

Treatment of overdosage: Vitamin K is the antagonist to the coumarins, and the administration of phytonadione (emulsion of vitamin K_1) will restore the prothrombin level. However, the action even of this most potent vitamin K preparation requires hours for significant clinical effect. When an immediate effect is desired, prothrombin must be given. Prothrombin is available in the form of fresh blood or of plasma preserved by freeze-drying so that prothrombin activity is preserved. The prothrombin complex itself has been prepared for investigative use and shown to be active.

B. Possible Risks of Abrupt Cessation of Therapy: A number of investigators noted an increase in the incidence of myocardial infarction and thromboembolic episodes during the 1- to 3-month period following abrupt cessation of long-term anticoagulant therapy. An increase in the concentration of factor VIII is reported to be present at this time. Not all groups of patients have shown this "rebound" hazard—ie, its existence is questionable, and the differences between groups in reported studies merely reflect differences in the severity of the underlying disease. Another view is that complications deferred by the benefits of anticoagulant therapy appear when therapy is discontinued

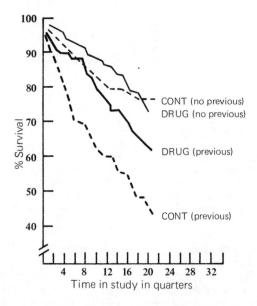

Figure 18 –4. The effect on survival of long-term treatment with dicumarol sufficient to prolong prothrombin time to 2–2½ times normal. The men followed in this collaborative study were separated into a group of those who had had a myocardial infarction prior to the one for which they were hospitalized (80 treated, 72 controls) and a group without a history of infarction (305 treated, 278 controls). (Reproduced, with permission, from Ebert & others: Long-term anticoagulant therapy after myocardial infarction. JAMA 207:2266, 1969.)

too soon. If practice is based on changes in the laboratory tests of coagulability, the drug should be withdrawn over a period of at least 2 months after long-term (but not short-term) treatment.

C. Allergic Reactions to the Indandiones: The indandiones cause frequent and serious allergic toxicity. For example, allergic toxicity occurs in as many as 3% of patients receiving phenindione. It may be manifested as rash, fever, neutropenia or agranulocytosis, and hepatic or renal damage. Since the coumarin derivatives lack this potential, there are few occasions for the use of the indandiones.

Contraindications & Cautions

The contraindications to the use of anticoagulants cannot be reduced to a list satisfactory to every physician and applicable to every patient. Factors to be considered include the following:

A. Bleeding or Potential Bleeding From Any Site: Active peptic ulcer, hematologic disease, possible cerebral hemorrhage, active infective endocarditis, and any other intercurrent disease with a hemorrhagic potential are contraindications to the use of anticoagulants. Any local factor such as a catheter, Wangensteen drainage, or a drain in a wound will increase the danger of bleeding. Anticoagulants are usually discontinued before a major surgical procedure. However, with prothrombin levels of 15–20%, all but central nervous system and eye surgery can be done. Minor procedures can be carried out without great hazard. Many of the procedures in dental surgery, for example, including open and closed extractions, have been performed on patients receiving continuous anticoagulant therapy. Bleeding can be avoided by careful hemostasis and packing to provide optimal mechanical factors for clotting and avoiding cavities in the socket.

Anticoagulant therapy can be initiated soon after obstetric delivery but should not be given close to the time of delivery because such use increases the incidence of hemorrhage in the fetus. Heparin should be substituted for the oral anticoagulants during the first trimester, since the coumarins are very probably teratogenic.

Coumarin anticoagulants should not be used if laboratory facilities for the determination of prothrombin times are unavailable or inadequate.

B. Other Contraindications: The dosage of an anticoagulant should be adjusted with great care in the presence of hepatic or renal disease. Untreated, severe hypertension is a contraindication in the opinion of some physicians, as is advanced age or debility.

C. Interaction With Other Drugs: The anticoagulants are often given for long periods of time, and their very use implies that the patient has a serious primary problem that will require the use of other drugs. Drug interactions are therefore likely to be common, and their consequences may be disastrous.

It is also true that the interactions with other drugs have been widely studied because technics for the determination of plasma levels of coumarin anticoagulants and of their biologic effects (in the form of pro-

thrombin times) are more easily available than is true for most drug groups. Many of the suggested interactions are based on studies in animals or on studies of binding to plasma albumin in glass. Many of the hypothesized reactions have not had their clinical significance established and are not included in the examples below. (See also Chapter 2.)

1. Stimulation of metabolism–The administration of many lipid-soluble drugs in continued dosages can increase the amount and activity of the hydroxylating enzymes contained in liver microsomes. An anticoagulant given after such enzyme induction may be metabolized with unusual rapidity, with a reduction in the anticoagulant effect. More dangerous is the possibility of an increase in anticoagulant effect if the inducing drug is discontinued.

The administration of phenobarbital and other long-acting barbiturates, glutethimide (Doriden), and griseofulvin reduces both plasma levels and the hypoprothrombinemic effect of the coumarin drugs. All barbiturates cause the same effect but must be given at proper intervals if they are short-acting.

With adequate dosage of the inducing drug, all patients will show a change after a week of treatment, but the extent of the change is highly variable. Recovery requires 2–3 weeks. If prothrombin times and dosage adjustment are done at proper intervals, no mishap need occur; in fact, epidemiologic studies (rather than anecdotal evaluations) do not incriminate drug interactions in many bleeding episodes.

2. Displacement from binding sites–The coumarins in plasma are bound to albumin to a large extent (97%) and are protected from metabolic change or excretion until they dissociate to replace the unbound drug that leaves the vascular compartment. Phenylbutazone, sulfinpyrazone, and norethandrolone (Nilevar) displace warfarin and dicumarol from binding sites on plasma protein and increase the amount of anticoagulant delivered to its site of action in the liver. An intensification of anticoagulant effect is maximal after 3–5 days of administration of the second agent.

Displacement from bound to free form also increases the rate of metabolism and excretion; after 1–2 weeks, a new steady state is established during which the original dose will again give the same blood levels and achieve the same anticoagulant effect.

3. Inhibition of metabolism–Allopurinol administration greatly prolongs the half-life of dicumarol, but the effect on prothrombin time is not yet established. Disulfiram (Antabuse) has a similar effect.

4. Others–Clofibrate (Atromid-S) markedly potentiates the effect of anticoagulants, but the mechanism is not clear. Quinidine has a lesser effect.

Cholestyramine interferes with the absorption of the anticoagulants (and many other drugs) unless an interval of several hours elapses between administration of cholestyramine and the other agent.

5. Effects of anticoagulants on other drugs–When dicumarol and, presumably, warfarin are added to the regimen of a patient receiving chlorpropamide, tolbutamide, phenytoin, or phenobarbital, the effect of these drugs is greatly prolonged and intensified by mechanisms that have not yet been established.

HEPARIN

Source & Chemistry

Heparin, together with histamine and serotonin, occurs in the granules of basophils (circulating) or mast cells (in tissue). It is a strongly acidic mucopolysaccharide. The recurring units include uronic acid and N-sulfated glucosamine.

Heparin for drug use is extracted from beef lung and liver. Heparin is a heterogeneous polysaccharide, and different preparations vary in their anticoagulant effects. Most of the activity is in a small fraction of the heparin, and the dosage of heparin is measured in USP units. The bioassay is based on its ability to prevent clotting of sheep plasma under standardized conditions.

Pharmacologic Actions

A. Anticoagulant: Thrombin (factor IIa) is central in the clotting process, and an antithrombin is present in plasma to maintain intravascular fluidity of the blood. Heparin acts by combining with antithrombin; the heparin-antithrombin complex combines with and neutralizes thrombin within seconds rather than in 10–15 minutes. Thrombin is a serine protease, and the inhibition by heparin described for thrombin applies also to factors IXa, XIa, XIIa, and plasmin, which are also serine proteases. Heparin acts as an anticoagulant immediately, both in vivo and in vitro. The duration of the effect is dependent on the dose, but it is brief. After intravenous injection of ordinary doses, the effect is about 50% dissipated in 1 hour and clotting time is again normal in less than 4 hours. Heparin and the coumarin anticoagulants are compared in Table 18–2.

B. Other Effects: Plasma that is turbid from chylomicrons is "cleared" more rapidly if heparin is injected postprandially. The "clearing factor" produced in vivo is increased "lipoprotein lipase" activity. This action is not related to the normal mechanism of chylomicron metabolism, and no therapeutic role for this action of heparin has been demonstrated.

Clinical Uses

A. Acute Anticoagulant Effect: Heparin is used, most commonly as a constant intravenous infusion, to provide an anticoagulant effect during the interval required for the effect of a coumarin compound to develop and stabilize. It is also used when it may become desirable to rapidly terminate the anticoagulant effect, as during cardiac surgery or in the treatment of acute arterial occlusion when surgical treatment may become advisable.

B. Long-Term Anticoagulant Effect: Heparin may be used for an extended period in the same situations listed in the discussion of inhibitors of prothrombin synthesis. Its cost and the need for repeated injection or infusion are important disadvantages.

1. Prevention of venous thrombosis postoperatively–Heparin, when used prophylactically, is used as "low-dose heparin." Heparin, 5000 units subcutaneously, is given prior to surgery before the platelet system is activated by trauma and every 12 hours thereafter. These dosages are not enough to prevent the propagation of an established thrombus after amplification of the clotting process has occurred. However, these doses carry no risk of bleeding, and no laboratory control of dosage is necessary.

It has not been possible to establish the effectiveness of low-dose heparin in protecting patients against thrombi during the period after a myocardial infarct or after operative treatment of femoral neck fractures. In patients undergoing hip replacement, a situation in which the need can be anticipated before the trauma, an influential multicenter trial showed a significant difference in the number of patients dying with pulmonary emboli (16 in the control group compared with 2 among the treated in a total group of 4121). An effect on thrombus formation in calf veins, if not more proximally, has been detected by ^{125}I scanning or phlebographically.

2. During pregnancy–Pregnancy and the need for anticoagulant therapy sometimes coexist. Since the coumarin anticoagulants are very probably teratogenic, heparin should be used if an anticoagulant is needed during the first trimester. Two weeks before delivery, heparin should again be substituted for the oral anticoagulants to avoid fetal bleeding perinatally.

Control of Dose

Except in low-dose heparin prophylaxis, heparin effects should be quantified by a partial thromboplastin time or, more commonly, by a whole blood clotting time. (Clotting time is a specific test, not a general description. The Lee-White tube method is used.) Heparin prolongs prothrombin time and can interfere with the adjustment of dicumarol dosage. During intravenous infusion, when blood free of heparin cannot be drawn, an allowance of 2–4 seconds' prolongation

Table 18–2. Comparison of heparin and coumarin anticoagulants.

	Heparin	Coumarin Derivatives
Onset of action	Immediate	Gradual to peak at 48 hours
Duration	< 4 hours	2–5 days
Route of administration	Parenteral	Oral
Laboratory control of dose	Clotting time	Prothrombin time
Treatment of overdose	Protamine	Fresh blood, plasma, vitamin K
Cost	Expensive (dollars/day)	Inexpensive (pennies/day)
Active in vitro	Yes	No

of the prothrombin time should be made in adjusting the dosage of coumarin anticoagulant.

Adverse Reactions

The important toxic effect of heparin is hemorrhage as discussed in detail in the above section on coumarin derivatives.

According to a recent collaborative study, heparin is responsible for a relatively large number of the drug-related deaths in hospital inpatients.

Patients receiving 15,000 units or more per day of heparin during long-term therapy develop osteoporosis. This effect is also demonstrable in animals. The mechanism of the osteoporosis is unknown but is not related to the anticoagulant properties of heparin.

Treatment of overdosage: Because heparin is so short-acting, it is rarely necessary to neutralize its effect. The most common situation requiring a heparin antagonist is postsurgical management when an extracorporeal pump has been used.

Protamine, a strongly basic protein, will neutralize the acid heparin on approximately a milligram per milligram basis. A 1% solution of protamine sulfate is available for slow intravenous injection.

Contraindications & Cautions

Present or potential bleeding from any site, as listed above for the hypoprothrombinemic agents, is the only contraindication to the use of heparin.

Dosages

Heparin is given only by injection. Sodium heparin solutions for injection contain 1000–40,000 units/mL.

Heparin is most commonly given as a continuous intravenous infusion. After a loading dose, the rate of infusion, usually about 16 units/kg/h, is adjusted to maintain the clotting test at double its usual value. See above for low-dose prophylaxis.

INHIBITORS OF PLATELET AGGREGATION

The platelet phase of clotting, which results in a platelet plug in and around which the fibrin clot develops, can be inhibited by several drugs referred to as antiplatelet drugs or as inhibitors of platelet function or aggregation.

Of the many drugs that can interfere with the platelet phase of clotting, 3 have reached clinical trials in the prevention of thrombi in humans: (1) aspirin, which serves as the type compound for all of the organic acids discussed as nonnarcotic analgesics in Chapter 27; (2) sulfinpyrazone (Anturane), a congener of phenylbutazone (Chapter 27) and the standard uricosuric agent; and (3) dipyridamole (Persantine), a vasodilator (Chapter 13).

General Considerations

A. Platelet Function in Clotting: A platelet ordinarily circulates for 8–10 days without interacting with other platelets or with the vascular endothelium. However, the platelet has a fluffy mucopolysaccharide coat outside of its plasma membrane, and, in the presence of vascular damage, adhesion (attachment to a surface) and aggregation (attachment to other platelets) occur. The resulting platelet plug at a traumatized site or site of venous or arterial endothelial damage is the nidus for a fibrin clot that may stop the bleeding or may occlude a vessel. The sequence of reactions can be diagrammed:

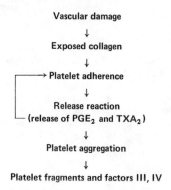

B. Prostaglandin and Thromboxane Synthesis: The prostaglandins are defined and their application as oxytocic drugs is discussed in Chapter 14. They also function as local hormones in modifying the platelet phase of clotting.

Their synthesis is summarized in Fig 18–5. Platelets are able to synthesize thromboxane A_2 (TXA_2) as well as other prostaglandins. TXA_2 is unusually potent in augmenting platelet aggregation and the release reaction, and it, together with the other prostaglandins less active in this effect, is secreted from dense granules during the release reaction.

The prostaglandins are not stored but are synthesized according to need and rapidly metabolized. Aspirin acts to inhibit cyclo-oxygenase; prostaglandins and TXA_2 are then no longer provided by platelets, and the release reaction and platelet aggregation are no longer such intensely self-accelerating processes.

Mechanisms of Action of Inhibitory Drugs

A. Aspirin: Aspirin in low concentrations—ie, single daily doses of 0.3 g—reduces the cyclo-oxygenase activity of platelets by 90%. The enzyme is acetylated, and since platelets are not nucleated, no new enzyme protein is made. The effect, therefore, remains maximal for almost 2 days, and an effect on bleeding time in normal individuals is apparent for 5 days.

B. Dipyridamole: In addition to the prostaglandins mentioned above, adenosine diphosphate (ADP) is secreted from dense granules during the release reaction and causes platelet aggregation. Dipyridamole is a phosphodiesterase inhibitor (see Fig

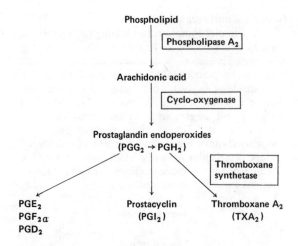

Phospholipid

Phospholipase A₂

Arachidonic acid

Cyclo-oxygenase

Prostaglandin endoperoxides
(PGG₂ → PGH₂)

Thromboxane
synthetase

PGE₂   Prostacyclin   Thromboxane A₂
PGF₂ₐ   (PGI₂)   (TXA₂)
PGD₂

Figure 18–5. Pathways of prostaglandin synthesis. All tissues synthesize prostaglandins. In addition, platelets can synthesize TXA₂, which is potent in accelerating the platelet phase of clotting, ie, in favoring thrombus formation. In the walls of arteries and veins, PGI₂ is synthesized, and it has effects on platelet function opposite to those of TXA₂, ie, it may act to maintain the fluidity of blood in contact with endothelium.

33–2), and its use results in elevated levels of cyclic adenosine monophosphate (cAMP) and less ADP in platelets.

Dipyridamole reduces aggregation and also changes platelet survival time toward normal when survival time is reduced by a process (arterial thrombosis) that consumes platelets.

C. Sulfinpyrazone: The mechanism of action is uncertain. If it is related to prostaglandin synthesis, the inhibitory process is more rapidly reversible than with aspirin.

Clinical Uses

Do the effects of aspirin and related drugs on platelet function make them useful in situations now treated with the more dangerous anticoagulants? Interest is recent and the clinical evaluations are incomplete and conflicting, but the ability to reduce thrombotic problems has been studied in the following situations.

A. Prosthetic Heart Valves: The addition of dipyridamole or aspirin to treatment with warfarin reduces the numbers of thromboembolic complications in patients with an aortic valve prosthesis. Aspirin alone is ineffective.

B. Arteriovenous Shunt: Sulfinpyrazone reduces the incidence of thromboses in arteriovenous shunts constructed to facilitate hemodialysis.

C. Prophylaxis of Venous Thrombosis: Most available studies are flawed by accidents during their execution. One prospective study of patients undergoing hip replacement shows some protection by aspirin in men but not in women. The more favorable results of warfarin use should be noted.

D. Prevention of Strokes: Men (but not women) experiencing episodes of transient cerebral ischemia and not suitable for vascular surgery progressed to stroke and death somewhat less often if treated with aspirin.

E. Prevention of Myocardial Infarction: Large-scale trials of chronic aspirin administration in subjects who had had a previous infarct have not shown any significant effect on mortality rate. A retrospective study did show that aspirin use was significantly lower in a group of patients entering the hospital with an infarct than in controls hospitalized for other reasons. One study showed that with use of sulfinpyrazone there was a significant reduction in the number of sudden deaths in the year following an infarct. Major studies are in progress.

K VITAMINS

Chemistry

The naturally occurring K *(Koagulation)* vitamins are fat-soluble and are not absorbed from the gut lumen unless bile is also present. The important pharmacology of the K vitamins centers about this fact.

Vitamin K₁ is called phytonadione when used as a drug, either orally or as an injectable emulsion. Its structure is shown in Fig 18–6. Menadione is not active as such but is transformed by the liver into active vitamin K₂. Menadione is itself lipid-soluble, but the 2 derivatives shown are water-soluble and have therefore had some use not only as injectable preparations but also as oral agents absorbed in the absence of bile acids, ie, during obstructive jaundice.

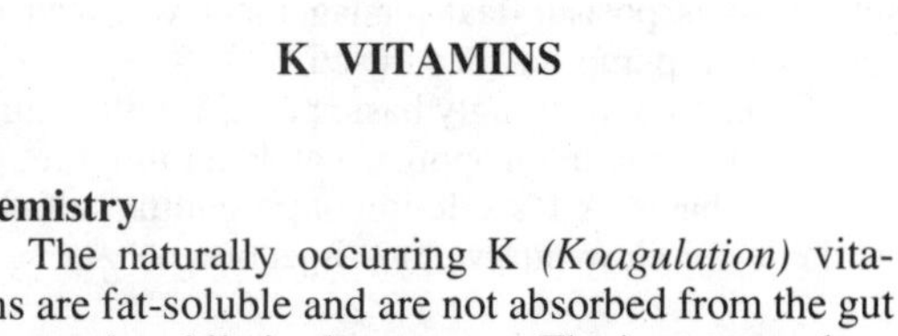

Phytonadione (vitamin K₁)

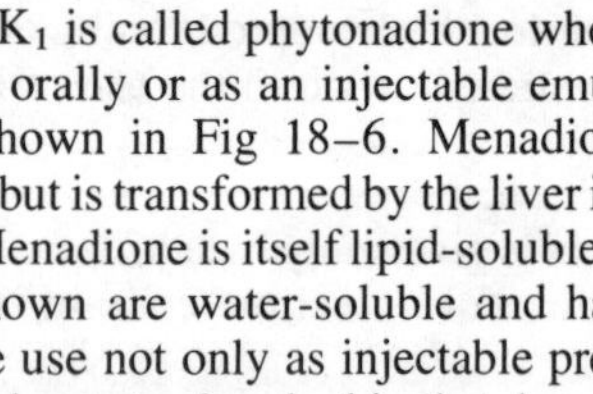

Menadione sodium bisulfite
(Hykinone)

Figure 18–6. Chemical structure of natural vitamin K₁ and of a water-soluble derivative of menadione.

Table 18–3. Vitamin K: Dosages and preparations available.

| | Postnatal | Prenatal | Drug-Induced Hypoprothrombinemia | | Obstructive Jaundice, etc |
			Minor	With Bleeding	
Phytonadione (Mephyton, AquaMephyton, Konakion)	0.5–1 mg IM, IV, or orally	1 mg IM on admission	2.5–10 mg IM or orally	10–50 mg IM or IV	2.5–25 mg IM or orally
Menadione sodium bisulfite (Hykinone)	1 mg IV or IM	. . .	. . .	. . .	5 mg IM or orally daily
Menadiol sodium diphosphate (Synkayvite, Kappadione)	. . .	5 mg IM or IV on admission	. . .	. . .	5 mg IM or orally daily

Pharmacologic Actions

Vitamin K is necessary for the liver synthesis of prothrombin and factors VII, IX, and X. Deficiency, whether dietary, drug-induced, or accompanying liver disease, leads to hypoprothrombinemia and hemorrhage. Disturbances in the absorption of vitamin K from the gastrointestinal tract are common in humans, but dietary deficiency is so rare that the possibility can almost be ignored. No minimum dietary requirements have been established, and it is usually held that synthesis by intestinal bacteria provides a supply of vitamin independent of the diet. Certainly this is true for coprophagous species, but the response of normal and warfarin-treated humans suggests that absorption from the colon does not occur and that the dietary source is the important one. In any case, the wide occurrence of K vitamins makes dietary deficiency states unimportant except possibly in explaining some variability in the response of patients receiving anticoagulants.

Additional aspects of the pharmacology of vitamin K are discussed with the uses of the drug.

Clinical Uses

A. In Obstructive Jaundice: Unlike other fat-soluble vitamins, vitamin K is stored in only small amounts in the body. In the absence of the bile necessary for continued absorption, hypoprothrombinemia will develop in a few days. If bile deficiency is due to obstructive jaundice and not to hepatocellular damage, injected vitamin K will rapidly restore prothrombin levels to normal. Preoperative administration of vitamin K in patients with surgically correctable obstructive jaundice has reduced hemorrhagic complications during the procedure. If the jaundice is due to hepatocellular damage and the hypoprothrombinemia is due not to failure of absorption but to inability of liver cells to synthesize prothrombin, the hemorrhagic tendency cannot be reversed with vitamin K.

B. Possible Prevention of Hemorrhagic Disease of the Newborn: Prothrombin levels are low at birth and fall further during the first few days after birth. The fall during the neonatal period is terminated, it is usually said, when the intestinal tract is contaminated and bacterial synthesis provides vitamin K. There are reasons to question this explanation and to look instead for a dietary explanation. In any case, neonatal hypoprothrombinemia can be minimized by either prenatal administration of vitamin K to the mother or postnatal administration to the newborn. The prothrombin levels certainly are elevated by such treatment, but the routine use of prenatal vitamin K for many years has not resulted in any decrease in the incidence of bleeding during the neonatal period other than postcircumcision bleeding. Because of the risk of kernicterus, the administration of vitamin K to a premature infant should be limited to a single dose of 0.5–1 mg of phytonadione parenterally.

C. Treatment of Anticoagulant Toxicity: The rapid reversal of drug-induced hypoprothrombinemia requires the use of a source of prothrombin such as fresh blood or plasma as discussed above. Vitamin K may be used if the situation is not urgent or as a supplement to one of the immediate sources of prothrombin. Phytonadione acts more rapidly than the water-soluble menadione derivatives, a significant effect developing in 3–6 hours after the intravenous administration of 50–150 mg.

Adverse Reactions

Vitamin K is a nutritional factor but nevertheless has some toxicity when used as a drug.

A. Hyperbilirubinemia: Newborns and, especially, premature infants are unusually susceptible to some toxic effects of drugs because of their immaturity. Rapid hemolysis in the immediate postnatal period leads to an increase in the amount of bilirubin that must be conjugated with glucuronide and excreted into the bile. After needlessly large doses of vitamin K postnatally and even after very large maternal doses of menadione sodium bisulfite in the immediate prenatal period, the elevation of serum bilirubin has been great enough to result in kernicterus. Which of the possible mechanisms that can cause hyperbilirubinemia is responsible in the case of vitamin K is not established.

B. Impaired Liver Function and Hypoprothrombinemia: In a few cases, repeated, large intravenous doses of any of the vitamin K drugs have caused liver damage and hypoprothrombinemia.

C. Hemolytic Anemia: Menadione and its water-soluble analogs are among those drugs that can precipitate hemolysis in patients with a genetically determined deficiency of glucose-6-phosphate dehydrogenase (G6PD).

Contraindications & Cautions

Vitamin K should be used only in the presence of hypoprothrombinemia—not indiscriminately in the presence of all bleeding. As is mentioned above, it should not be used as a substitute for blood or plasma if bleeding occurs after anticoagulant drug administration, and newborns should receive only a single 1-mg dose.

If phytonadione is given intravenously, as it often is, the rate of administration should not exceed 5 or 10 mg/min to prevent hypotensive episodes. The emulsion may be diluted with isotonic saline or glucose solutions.

FIBRINOLYTIC SYSTEMS

PLASMIN (FIBRINOLYSIN) & PLASMIN ACTIVATORS

Agents that could act on thrombi and emboli after their formation—ie, to dissolve them rather than prevent their extension as the anticoagulants do—would be of great usefulness. Efforts to reach this goal have so far stemmed from a study of the natural clot-removing, or fibrinolytic, mechanism.

This mechanism is summarized in Fig 18–7.

Activators or kinases involved in the first step may be found in urine (urokinase) and some tissues in an active form. The physiologically important kinase exists as an inactive proactivator until activated by various stimuli including streptokinase, an enzyme formed during the growth of hemolytic streptococci.

An activated kinase converts plasminogen, a plasma globulin, to plasmin or fibrinolysin, a proteolytic enzyme that acts on fibrin and other proteins at lysine-arginine bonds.

The drugs suggested by studies of the fibrinolytic system for trial as thrombolytic agents are (1) **fibrinolysin,** prepared by the action of streptokinase on human or bovine blood; (2) **bacterial streptokinase,** which would act following administration to increase the concentration of plasmin within a clot; and (3)

urokinase, derived from human urine.

Human fibrinolysin (Thrombolysin) has been available for many years, but its lack of efficacy is now generally acknowledged.

Streptokinase (Streptase), an enzyme of bacterial origin, and **urokinase (Abbokinase, Win-Kase),** which is derived from urine, were recently released (1978) by the FDA for the intravenous treatment of massive pulmonary embolism. Streptokinase is additionally approved for deep vein thrombosis. The enzyme thrombolytic therapy would appear to result in a more rapid resolution of the clot than that occurring with anticoagulant therapy. As might be expected, the agents can cause serious bleeding, particularly in predisposed individuals. The drugs are contraindicated in postsurgical, postpartum, and postcardiovascular accident patients as well as in patients with severe hypertension and certain other conditions. The manufacturers' recommendations for administration and precautions must be followed carefully. The enzymes are costly, and their safety and efficacy have not been fully established.

AMINOCAPROIC ACID
(Inhibitor of Fibrinolysis)

Aminocaproic acid (Amicar, ϵ-aminocaproic acid, $H_2N-C_5H_{10}-COOH$) is a synthetic compound related to lysine. It acts as a competitive antagonist to activators of plasminogen—ie, it prevents the generation of plasmin.

Aminocaproic acid has been used in specific situations when unusually great fibrinolytic activity has been established. Primary hyperfibrinolysis is extremely rare. Secondary hyperfibrinolysis is a compensatory mechanism that follows widespread intravascular clotting—eg, after abruptio placentae or surgical procedures utilizing cardiac bypass. The exact indications for the use of aminocaproic acid in these situations depend upon the response to other therapy—eg, transfusion and heparin.

This drug has also been used when fibrin formation—as in hemophilia—is so deficient that inhibition of even the normal fibrinolytic process may be beneficial.

The systemic toxicity, including the possibility of thrombotic complications, has not been completely evaluated in humans.

The suggested oral and intravenous dose (in the USA) is 5 g initially followed by 1.25 g/h.

OTHER ENZYMES

A number of other enzymes are used as drugs. Some of these—eg, penicillinase, pancreatin, and

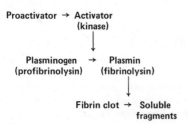

Figure 18 –7. Summary of the fibrinolytic system.

Table 18–4. Proteolytic and other enzymes: Sources and suggested uses.

	Source	Action	Suggested Uses
Chymotrypsin (Chymoral, Zolyse, Avazyme, Orenzyme, Catarase)	Beef pancreas	Proteolytic	Cataract extraction, anti-inflammatory agent, liquefaction of respiratory secretions
Streptokinase-streptodornase (Varidase)	*Streptococcus*	Fibrinolytic Deoxyribonuclease	Anti-inflammatory, topical debridement
Fibrinolysin and deoxyribonuclease (Elase)	Beef blood beef pancreas	Fibrinolytic Deoxyribonuclease	Topical debridement
Plant protease concentrate (bromelains, Ananase)	Pineapple	Proteolytic	Anti-inflammatory
Proteolytic enzymes from *Carica papaya* (Papase)	Papaya	Proteolytic	Anti-inflammatory
Sutilains (Travase)	Bacterial	Proteolytic	Topical debridement

hyaluronidase—are discussed in other chapters. Several proteolytic enzymes, deoxyribonuclease (which depolymerizes DNA), and amylase are suggested for several uses, but only one of these (zonulolysis) is well established. The preparations are listed in Table 18–4.

Intraocular Use of Chymotrypsin

Pancreatic chymotrypsin injected into the posterior chamber dissolves the zonular fibers and facilitates lens extraction in the treatment of cataract.

Anti-inflammatory Uses

Many of these enzymes are suggested for use in hastening the resolution of inflammation due to various forms of trauma. The theory apparently is that the enzymes will (even after oral administration) reach the site of injury and hasten dissolution of fibrin clots. No clinical trials have supported the suggested use. Injected enzymes—eg, chymotrypsin—have caused several deaths from anaphylactic shock.

Topical Debridement

Enzymes can be applied to the skin as solutions or ointments, injected into empyema cavities or other accumulations of exudate, or inhaled as an aerosol to act on the surface of the respiratory tract. They are probably active in some of these situations, but studies to evaluate their efficacy have usually included other forms of treatment also. Only fibrinous clots and exudates of inflammatory cells are liquified. Bone and dead tissues are not affected.

● ● ●

References

Anticoagulants

Assessment of short-term anticoagulant administration after cardiac infarction. Report of the working party on anticoagulant therapy. Br Med J 1:335, 1969.

Behrman SJ, Wright IS: Dental surgery during continuous anticoagulant therapy. JAMA 175:483, 1961.

Chalmers TC & others: Evidence favoring the use of anticoagulants in the hospital phase of acute myocardial infarction. N Engl J Med 297:1091, 1977.

Ebert RV & others: Long-term anticoagulant therapy after myocardial infarction: Final report of the VA cooperative study. JAMA 207:2263, 1969.

Genton E: Guidelines for heparin therapy. Ann Intern Med 80:77, 1974.

Kakkar VV & others: Prevention of fatal postoperative pulmonary embolism by low doses of heparin. Lancet 2:45, 1975. [Or see N Engl J Med 293:300, 1975.]

Koch-Weser J, Sellers EM: Drug interactions with coumarin anticoagulants. (2 parts.) N Engl J Med 285:487, 547, 1971.

Mibashan RS (editor): Hemostasis and thrombosis III. Semin Hematol 15:1, 1978. [Entire issue devoted to heparin, oral anticoagulants, thrombolysis, and platelet-suppressive agents.]

Mitchell JRA: Can we really prevent postoperative pulmonary emboli? Br Med J 2:1523, 1979.

Porter J, Jick H: Drug-related deaths among medical inpatients. JAMA 237:879, 1977.

Rebound thrombosis after stopping anticoagulants. Br Med J 2:1343, 1966.

Salzman EW, Harris WH, DeSanctis RW: Anticoagulation for prevention of thromboembolism following fractures of the hip. N Engl J Med 275:122, 1966.

Sevitt S, Gallagher NG: Prevention of venous thrombosis and pulmonary embolism in injured patients. Lancet 2:981, 1959.

Szklo M & others: Additional data favoring use of anticoagulant therapy in myocardial infarction. JAMA 242:1261, 1979.

Symposium: Molecular basis of heparin action. Fed Proc 36:9, 1977.

Symposium: Vitamin K (and prothrombin synthesis). Fed Proc 37:2599, 1978.

Wessler S, Gitel SN: Heparin: New concepts relevant to clinical use. Blood 53:525, 1979.

Inhibitors of Platelet Function

Canadian Cooperative Study Group: A randomized trial of aspirin and sulfinpyrazone in threatened stroke. N Engl J Med 299:53, 1978.

Harris WH & others: Aspirin prophylaxis of venous thromboembolism after total hip replacement. N Engl J Med 297:1246, 1977.

Jick H, Miettinen OS: Regular aspirin use and myocardial infarction. Br Med J 2:1057, 1976.

Moncada S, Vane JR: Arachidonic acid metabolites and the interactions between platelets and blood-vessel walls. N Engl J Med 300:1142, 1979.

Weiss HJ: Antiplatelet therapy. (2 parts.) N Engl J Med 298:1344, 1403, 1978.

Vitamin K

Ansell JE, Kumar R, Deykin D: The spectrum of vitamin K deficiency. JAMA 238:40, 1977.

Potter EL: Effect on infant mortality of vitamin K administered during labor. Am J Obstet Gynecol 50:235, 1945.

Udall JA: Human sources and absorption of vitamin K in relation to anticoagulation stability. JAMA 194:127, 1965.

Wolf IL, Babior BM: Vitamin K and warfarin: Metabolism, function and interaction. Am J Med 53:261, 1972.

Enzymes

Colman RW: Proteolytic enzymes in clinical medicine. Clin Pharmacol Ther 6:598, 1965.

Elase and other proteolytic enzyme drugs. Med Lett Drugs Ther 9:17, 1967.

Fratantoni JC, Ness P, Simon TL: Thrombolytic therapy: Current status. N Engl J Med 293:1073, 1975.

Pechet L: Fibrinolysis. (2 parts.) N Engl J Med 273:966, 1024, 1965.

Streptokinase and urokinase. Med Lett Drugs Ther 20:37, 1978.

Histamine, Antihistamines, H₂ Antagonists, Serotonin | 19

A great amount of information of physiologic or pathologic significance has originated in the study of substances extracted from the body. Some workers have even introduced the term autopharmacology to describe this research area, postulating that a potent substance that is widely distributed in large amounts in the body will eventually be shown to have a physiologic role. Histamine and serotonin are 2 such substances that are important in a number of pathologic states and in the explanation of the action of other drugs, especially the 2 types of antihistamines.

HISTAMINE

Chemistry, Occurrence, & Metabolism

Histamine is formed by the decarboxylation of histidine. The reaction may occur within the lumen of the intestine (the enzymatic activity deriving from coliform organisms) or within many types of cells. Histamine formed within the intestine or ingested preformed is absorbed, but it is rapidly metabolized by the intestine and liver and probably does not contribute to the histamine stored in the body.

Histamine occurs in at least 3 pools or types of storage sites. One fraction is held in the granules of mast cells and of basophils, the equivalent cells in peripheral blood. In these granules, histamine is bound with heparin and cannot exert an effect or be metabolized. The mast cells are degranulated and the histamine released by the antigen-antibody complex formed as the first step in the anaphylactic type of allergic reaction and by the histamine-liberating chemicals listed below.

Histamine also occurs in the mucosal layer of the gastrointestinal tract, where it is not contained in mast cells and not depleted by histamine liberators. The hypothalamus and area postrema contain histamine that reacts still differently, being depleted by reserpine.

The metabolism of histamine is summarized in Fig 19–1. Its activity is terminated within 5–15 minutes, principally by methylation and subsequent deamination by monoamine oxidase. A second histaminase, diamine oxidase, also acts to deaminate histamine.

Pharmacologic Actions

A. Mechanisms of Action: In humans, at least, the effects of histamine can be summarized as direct stimulation of glands and contraction of nonvascular smooth muscle but relaxation of vascular smooth muscle. The action is directly on the gland or smooth muscle, ie, it is unrelated to innervation. Since specific antagonists are known that block the actions of histamine without blocking the actions of agents such as epinephrine or acetylcholine, it is possible to speak of specific histamine receptors.

These receptors—or these effects of histamine—can be separated into 2 categories. H₁ receptors or effects include vasodilation, increased capillary permeability, and contraction of nonvascular smooth muscle—ie, the effects blocked by the older, H₁ antihistamines. H₂ receptors mediate a minor cardiac stimulating effect and, most importantly, histamine stimulation of gastric acid secretion. These effects can be blocked by an analog of histamine or H₂ antagonist, cimetidine.

In the preceding chapters a number of other drugs that act directly on smooth muscle have been discussed. They are reviewed in Table 19–1.

B. Effects:

1. On blood vessels–Our understanding of the effects of histamine is still incomplete. Histamine acts on the smallest vessels, which are difficult to study. In addition, there are important variations between species in the response to histamine; the rat and rabbit, for example, respond with arteriolar constriction rather than the dilatation seen in humans. In the human,

Table 19–1. Summary of drugs acting directly on smooth muscle. (+ denotes stimulation or constriction; − denotes relaxation or dilatation.)

	Effect On	
	Vascular Smooth Muscle	Other Smooth Muscle
Nitroglycerin Quinidine Papaverine	−	−
Ergot alkaloids Vasopressin	+	+
Histamine Bradykinin	−	+

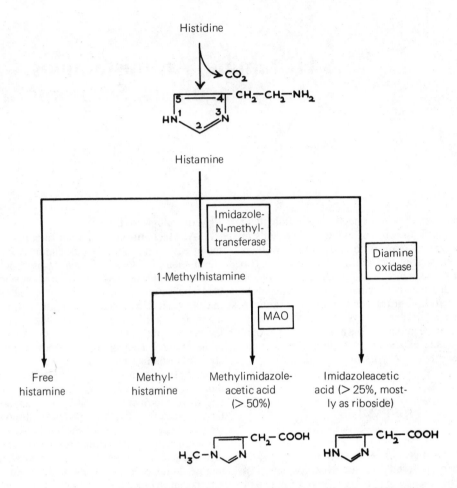

Figure 19–1. Synthesis, metabolism, and common urinary metabolites of histamine.

histamine acts to dilate arterioles, capillaries, and venules. Blood pressure is lowered in part by arteriolar dilatation, but the postural nature of the hypotension and studies of the change in distensibility of veins suggest that venous pooling of blood is a more important mechanism. In addition, the face is flushed, and the subject may experience a throbbing vascular headache, evidence of arteriolar dilation.

The hypotension caused by histamine leads to sympathoadrenal activation and tachycardia. With large doses, the combined venous pooling and arteriolar constriction lead to shock.

2. Capillary Permeability–Permeability of the walls of capillaries and small venules is increased by the action of histamine. If the effect is local and circumscribed, the accumulation of extravascular extracellular fluid is apparent as a wheal (hive, urticarial lesion). A more generalized effect is demonstrated by the abnormal ease with which a large trypan blue molecule leaves the blood vessels and stains tissues and by the hemoconcentration and elevation of the hematocrit. The increased capillary permeability is usually said to be a consequence of capillary and venular dilatation.

3. Contraction of nonvascular smooth muscle–Bronchiolar constriction and increased intestinal motility are the clinically important manifestations of the generalized smooth muscle stimulation caused by histamine.

4. Stimulation of gastric secretion–Histamine causes maximal secretion of acid and pepsin, and is the standard stimulus applied in the study of gastric secretion. It is found in high concentrations in the gastric mucosa and appears in gastric secretions. The ability of the H_2 receptor antagonists to reduce gastric secretion regardless of the nature of the primary stimulus suggests that histamine is the final step in the process leading to acid secretion. The conventional antihistamines decrease histamine-induced hypersecretion only when they are given in doses large enough to have an atropine (acetylcholine-blocking) effect.

Except for an increase in salivation, the action of histamine on other glands is unimportant. The sympathoadrenal discharge initiated by the hypotension resulting from histamine administration will, of course, cause sweating.

5. Local action–If histamine is injected intradermally or is released by trauma, a "triple response" is seen: (1) Capillary dilatation results in a small red area at the site of injection. This area soon becomes slightly bluish or is obscured by blanching due to edema. (2) Arteriolar dilatation causes redness ("flare") over a wider area. The flare is mediated through an axon reflex—ie, the afferent impulse initiated by histamine travels in the expected direction toward the neuronal cell body, and at the same time an antidromic vasodilator impulse travels centrifugally down another branch of the same sensory neuron. (3) A wheal of localized edema forms in the area of capillary dilatation.

These changes are accompanied by transient pain and itching.

Clinical Uses

A. Gastric Analysis: Gastric analysis is necessary to establish or eliminate the existence of achlorhydria (the absence of acid following histamine stimulation). If acid is demonstrated in a fasting sample aspirated through a gastric tube, no stimulus to secretion is necessary. If, however, the fasting specimen contains no acid, histamine, 0.5 mg, is injected subcutaneously and samples are collected for the following hour or until acid is shown to be present.

In the doses needed for stimulation of gastric secretion, histamine often causes flushing, sweating, tachycardia, and hypotension, and sometimes a throbbing headache. Betazole (Histalog), an alternative drug to histamine, also causes maximal stimulation of gastric secretion but without the high incidence of side-effects that occurs with histamine. Betazole is an isomer of histamine, a pyrazole rather than an imidazole derivative. A subcutaneous injection of 50 mg of betazole is equivalent to 0.3 mg of histamine.

An agent that is at least partially replacing betazole in gastric analysis is pentagastrin (Peptavlon). This synthetic peptide represents the active fragment of gastrin and acts through histamine to stimulate acid secretion.

B. Diagnosis of Pheochromocytoma: (See Chapter 11.) When pheochromocytoma is suspected but the patient has a normal blood pressure, histamine will cause the release of catecholamines from the tumor if one is present. Paroxysmal hypertension rather than the usual fall in blood pressure will then follow the administration of histamine.

Adverse Reactions

Even with the small doses (0.01 mg/kg subcutaneously) used in gastric analysis, a flush, headache, and precipitous fall in blood pressure may be seen. The hypotension is predominantly postural and usually requires no treatment other than the recumbent position. If treatment is required, epinephrine (0.3 mg subcutaneously) is an effective physiologic antagonist.

Pain and itching at the injection site are also common.

Contraindications & Cautions

Histamine should not be used in asthmatics or when hypotension may be especially dangerous—eg, in the presence of angina.

Dosages

Histamine is dispensed as solutions of the diphosphate or dihydrochloride salts. However, doses and labeling are expressed in terms of the equivalent amount of free base.

For gastric analysis, the dose is 0.01 mg/kg subcutaneously or intramuscularly. Betazole (Histalog) is given subcutaneously or intramuscularly, either 0.5 mg/kg or as a total dose of 50 mg. In either case the dose is equivalent to about half the standard dose of histamine.

For use in the diagnosis of pheochromocytoma, 0.05 mg histamine is diluted to 5 mL with saline and injected rapidly intravenously (*hazardous!*).

Histamine Liberation by Drugs & Toxins

No function has been established for histamine in any physiologic process other than gastric acid secretion. Many hypotheses have been tested and rejected. Current suggestions are as yet unconvincing.

There are several pathologic processes involving histamine that have a relation to drug therapy. Anaphylaxis and other immediate type I allergic reactions result when basophilic granules disgorge histamine, heparin, serotonin (in some species), kinins, and slow-reacting substance (SRS), a poorly characterized long-acting bronchial constrictor.

In addition, a number of drugs and toxins act to degranulate basophils. Histamine liberation explains some of the effects of a few therapeutic and toxic agents, and histamine liberation can be used to deplete an organism of histamine for investigative purposes.

A. Classes of Histamine Liberators:

1. Compounds that cause general tissue damage–Trypsin, peptone, snake and bee venoms, detergents.

2. Large molecules–Polyvinylpyrrolidone, horse serum, some dextrans.

3. Endotoxins.

4. Bases–Some simple amines (epinephrine, morphine, codeine, meperidine), but especially diamines (stilbamidine, propamidine, D-tubocurarine, dimethyl-tubocurarine, succinylcholine, 1,10-diaminodecane, and 48/80).

The last substance (48/80) is a polymer made up of units of a substituted phenylethylamine connected through methylene groups. It is the agent commonly used in the laboratory to deplete histamine stores in an animal.

B. Effects: Histamine liberators actually release all of the constituents of basophilic granules. The immediate effects are, therefore, comparable to anaphylaxis in the species being studied. The late effects do not involve serotonin or heparin but are due to histamine depletion and exhaustion of those responses due to histamine liberation. For example, repeated small doses of 48/80 can be given to an animal. After the liberated histamine is metabolized, another drug may be given and that part of its action due to histamine release will no longer occur. The histamine contained in the central nervous system is not released by the above compounds but is released by treatment with reserpine.

THE ANTIHISTAMINES
(Classic or H₁ Antagonists)

History

Reasoning from the atropine-acetylcholine type of antagonism, Bovet concluded that there should be compounds with the ability to block the actions of histamine. The first such compound, reported by Bovet and Staub in 1937, was not clinically efficacious, but useful drugs were developed in France during World War II.

Chemistry & Classification

In the discussion of the chemistry of atropine and its congeners (see Chapter 9), the members of a large group of drugs were characterized as chemically similar in being made up of a large blocking group connected by a group of proper length to a tertiary amine function.

The antihistamines, parasympatholytics, and antipsychotics have this chemical configuration and can be expected to share some of the same pharmacologic properties. Nevertheless, it is possible to selectively emphasize one property or another in choosing compounds for a specific therapeutic purpose. Thus, the antihistamines are more potent as histamine antagonists than as acetylcholine antagonists but will retain atropinelike side-effects and cause sedation of the tranquilizer type.

The antihistamines are often classified chemically on the basis of the nature of the connecting group. Examples are given below.

1. Ethers or ethanolamine derivatives–

Diphenhydramine hydrochloride (Benadryl)
or dimenhydrinate chlorotheophyllinate
(Dramamine)

2. Ethylenediamine derivatives–

Tripelennamine (Pyribenzamine)

3. Phenothiazine derivatives–The phenothiazines used as antihistamines and antinauseants are often considered a separate chemical class, but the relation to the other antihistamines is clearer if they are regarded as ethylenediamine derivatives.

Promethazine (Phenergan)

4. Alkylamine derivatives–

Chlorpheniramine (Chlor-Trimeton)

The foregoing provides examples rather than a complete chemical classification. The chemical type is not ordinarily considered in selecting an antihistamine for use in a specific situation. The alkylamines (4) are in widest use because they are effective but less likely to cause depression than other types.

The chemical classification does reemphasize that there is considerable arbitrariness in classifying drugs within the antipsychotic-antihistamine-parasympatholytic group. Diphenhydramine hydrochloride (Benadryl), for example, is classed as an "antihistamine" because of its most common clinical usage, but it has important atropinelike actions and causes sedation like a "tranquilizer." It is also a more potent local anesthetic than procaine and has been used in the treatment of parkinsonism and cardiac arrhythmias. A different salt, the chlorotheophyllinate (Dramamine), is widely used to prevent motion sickness.

Absorption, Metabolism, & Excretion

The antihistamines are well absorbed after oral administration. This action begins as soon as they are absorbed—ie, 10–30 minutes after an oral dose. They are metabolized by both liver and kidney. Most antihistamines act for about 4 hours and are administered 4 times daily. Some antihistamines—eg, promethazine or chlorcyclizine—are transformed more slowly and may be given at 12-hour intervals.

Pharmacologic Actions

A. Mechanisms of Action: The antihistamines have multiple effects and may act through several mechanisms. Their primary effect is competitive antagonism to histamine. The antigen-antibody reaction or other histamine-liberating stimulus is unaltered, but histamine is prevented from acting on the effector organ. The relation is competitive, ie, enough histamine can overcome the blockade of a given amount of antihistamine. In combating an acute allergic reaction (eg, laryngeal edema or bronchiolar constriction), an antihistamine may block any further effect of histamine, but, lacking any effect of its own, it cannot immediately repair the damage. In contrast to this competitive antagonism of histamine is the action of a physiologic antagonist that, by an action of its own that is opposite in direction to that of histamine, can immediately repair the lesion and reverse the clinical course. Epinephrine and other sympathomimetics are physiologic antagonists of histamine.

When dosage is controlled, the histamine-antagonizing effect can be specific—ie, the response of smooth muscle or other effector to histamine is blocked by concentrations of an antihistamine that do not block the action of acetylcholine or other agonists. With larger concentrations, the acetylcholine blocking action interferes and the even greater concentrations possible in laboratory experiments block the reaction of smooth muscle to almost all stimulants.

B. Effects:

1. Histamine antagonism–With the exception of the stimulation of gastric acid secretion, the effects of histamine described above are prevented or reduced when an antihistamine is administered. After pretreatment with an antihistamine, the organism no longer responds to injected histamine (or histamine derived from mast cell disruption) by a fall in blood pressure, bronchiolar constriction, or laryngeal or other edema. In theory, the relation being competitive, the histamine effects could be completely blocked. In practice, the amount of antihistamine that can be administered is limited by side-effects and toxic reactions, and protection may not be absolute.

2. Central nervous system effects–In the usual therapeutic doses, the antihistamines cause the specific kind of depression or sedation described for the antipsychotics (see Chapter 25). Unlike the euphoriant effect of alcohol or other sedative-hypnotics, the behavioral change associated with antihistamine use is generally perceived as unpleasant by the patient.

In a few patients, even therapeutic doses cause restlessness and hyperactivity—evidence that the underlying neurophysiologic change is stimulation rather than depression. With toxic doses, signs of stimulation (including convulsions) accompany the sedation more frequently than is the case with the antipsychotics. Extrapyramidal signs do occur, if only rarely. The central nervous system effects of the antihistamine group of drugs are unrelated to their histamine-antagonizing properties.

3. Other effects–The antihistamines are topically active local anesthetics, atropinelike or parasympatholytics, and have quinidinelike effects that are used investigationally in the treatment of cardiac arrhythmias.

Clinical Uses

A. Some Type I Allergic Reactions:

1. Anaphylaxis–The antihistamines can be useful in the treatment of allergic reactions only when the reaction is mediated by histamine. In type I reactions (anaphylaxis, urticaria, hay fever), the sensitizing exposure to the antigen generates IgE antibodies that are fixed to mast cells. Upon reexposure, the allergen-antibody reaction on the cell surface results in degranulation of the mast cells, with release of histamine and other less dangerous mediators. The signs of the anaphylactic reaction vary among different species depending upon their reaction to histamine and upon the amounts of histamine or serotonin available for release. In humans, histamine and heparin (but not serotonin) are released, and urticaria, bronchial spasm, laryngeal edema, and hypotension are prominent manifestations.

The antihistamines can completely protect experimental animals against anaphylaxis, and anaphylaxis in the human could presumably be prevented or modified by adequate prior doses of an antihistamine. However, the treatment of this emergency is not with antihistamines but with the sympathomimetics that are physiologic antagonists to histamine. The antihistamines could only prevent further histamine effects, but respiratory obstruction and shock would be lethal before the histamine effects already present had dissipated. An acute anaphylactic reaction, therefore, is treated by injection of epinephrine in doses of 0.3–0.6 mg intramuscularly or intravenously. When there is reason to fear that an anaphylactic reaction may occur when medical care is not available, the patient may be provided with isoproterenol to be used sublingually or by inhalation.

2. Urticaria and angioneurotic edema–The swelling, redness, and itching of hives are reduced by the antihistamines. It may be desirable to reinforce these effects with a sympathomimetic such as ephedrine.

3. Hay fever–Acute allergic rhinitis, especially if it is seasonal or otherwise clearly related to a specific antigen, usually responds dramatically to the antihistamines. Chronic nasopharyngeal congestion—eg, chronic sinusitis—is not often allergic in origin and, when it is, an infection secondary to the initial allergic process may also be present; therefore, it is much less likely to respond. A trial of antihistamine treatment may be justified, but the continued use of an antihistamine without evidence of therapeutic response or the routine combination of an antihistamine with a nasal decongestant of the sympathomimetic type is not rational.

4. Other allergic reactions–A rare patient with asthma that is an episodic reaction to a specific antigen is comparable to the patient with hay fever and is benefited by treatment with the antihistamines. In general, asthma is felt to be a contraindication to the use of antihistamines because of the atropinelike effects that cause drying of bronchial secretions.

There is no theoretic or empiric basis for the use of antihistamines in the treatment of allergic reactions of any other type.

The anti-inflammatory steroids will suppress all inflammatory reactions, including both immediate and delayed allergic reactions. The mechanism of this effect (see Chapter 35) is not related to histamine antagonism.

B. Motion Sickness: The parasympatholytic drugs, the antihistamines, and the phenothiazine tranquilizers all have a central depressant action that is useful in preventing or treating motion sickness. The

discussion is placed in this chapter because the agents most commonly used in treatment or prevention are antihistamines or are chemically related to them.

Motion sickness occurs when changes in acceleration continuously stimulate the hair cells of the maculae and, to a lesser extent, the cristae of the semicircular canals. The afferent activity, conditioned by individual and environmental factors, results in malaise, nausea, and vomiting.

The ability of a drug to prevent motion sickness is not correlated with its potency as a peripheral antihistamine or parasympatholytic or with its potency as an antipsychotic tranquilizer. The most widely used drugs, therefore, are selected because they have few atropinelike or sedative side-effects.

Owing to the interest of the armed forces, many field studies and clinical trials evaluating drugs against motion sickness are available. The studies vary in their control of the variables involved, but Fig 19–2 illustrates that, when the principles of bioassay are applied, the data are as precise as in most laboratory evaluations. Unfortunately, such data are available only for scopolamine.

The effectiveness of drugs will vary with individual susceptibility, the intensity and duration of the motion, the interval between medication and onset of

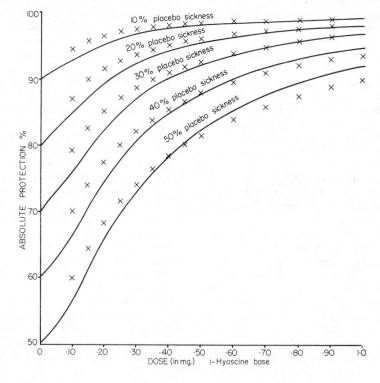

Figure 19–2. Illustration of the protection against motion sickness afforded by the prior administration of scopolamine. This figure also illustrates the great precision achieved in a clinical trial if the principles of bioassay are followed. Data from various published studies utilizing several different situations are combined to provide a dose-effect curve. An objective quantal response is recorded—ie, vomiting or no vomiting. Crosses represent the change in pattern when only the data from trials in small ships are plotted. (Reproduced, with permission, from Brand & Perry: Drugs used in motion sickness. Pharmacol Rev 18:905, 1966.)

Table 19–2. Drugs used to treat motion sickness and vomiting.

	Usual Adult Dose (3–4 Times Daily)
Motion sickness preventives	
Cyclizine (Marezine)	50 mg
Meclizine* (Antivert, Bonine)†	50 mg 1–2 times daily
Dimenhydrinate* (Dramamine)†	25–50 mg
Antiemetics	
Diphenidol (Vontrol)	25–50 mg
Prochlorperazine (Compazine)	5–10 mg
Thiethylperazine (Torecan)	10 mg
Trimethobenzamide (Tigan)	250 mg
Benzquinamide (Emete-con)	IM only

*Generic preparations available.
†Available without prescription.

motion, dosage, and whether effectiveness is measured by a subjective report or the objective occurrence of vomiting. Percentage figures for effectiveness are, therefore, meaningful only if the situation is carefully described. In general, the following drugs are effective:

1. Cyclizine (Marezine), meclizine (Antivert, Bonine), and dimenhydrinate (Dramamine) are generally equivalent, but dimenhydrinate use is associated with a high incidence of sedation (Table 19–2).

2. Promethazine (Phenergan), 25 mg 3 times daily, is effective if the first dose is given 2–4 hours before motion begins.

3. Scopolamine, 0.6–1 mg in 1 dose at onset of motion. In many studies involving motion of brief duration, scopolamine appears most effective. If the dose must be repeated 2–3 times daily—ie, for long-continued motion—it is relatively less effective and causes more side-effects than other available drugs.

4. Amphetamine may be given with any of the above to counteract sedation. In some experimental situations (human centrifuge), it is active by itself.

C. Nausea and Vomiting: Nausea and vomiting may result from many causes other than the excess labyrinthine stimulation that leads to motion sickness, and these other forms must be distinguished from motion sickness because their response to drug treatment is different.

1. Mechanism of vomiting—The laboratory analysis of vomiting can be partially applied to the occurrence of the symptom in humans. There has been identified in the lateral reticular matter of the brain stem a vomiting center that coordinates the act of vomiting when it is sufficiently activated by various afferent stimuli. The act of vomiting involves predominantly striated muscle—relaxation of the fundus and pylorospasm are notable exceptions—but the vomiting center is topographically close to other medullary centers that account for the associated intense vagal activity, salivation, forced inspiration, and jerky respiratory movements.

The afferent activity that reaches the vomiting center (Fig 19–3) originates not only in higher centers and from the viscera but also from another medullary center, the chemoreceptor trigger zone. This structure, located on the floor of the fourth ventricle in or close to the area postrema, is stimulated by circulating substances. Thus, stimuli such as intravenous copper sulfate (in the laboratory), apomorphine and other narcotic analgesics, digitalis, ergot, or uremia act first on the chemoreceptor trigger zone, which in turn stimulates the vomiting center. Other drugs such as iron, aspirin, or tetracyclines and many diseases of the viscera or peritoneum act on peripheral receptors to increase the sensory activity reaching the vomiting center.

Precise application of the above scheme to an explanation of the antiemetic effects of drugs is not yet possible because of the diffuse central nervous system effects of the drugs.

2. Clinical evaluations—Nausea and vomiting occur commonly, but very few controlled studies are available that allow comparison of drugs. Placebo effects are significant, and many trials are needed, since data from one situation cannot necessarily be extended to another type of vomiting. Perhaps only in the *prevention* of postoperative vomiting—a problem of small and decreasing dimensions—do the data approach adequacy.

a. Sedatives—Phenobarbital or other sedative has understandable effectiveness if anxiety is an important factor, but it apparently has a small additional effect. Sedation is still widely used in the treatment of nausea and vomiting of pregnancy because of a fear of the effects of less familiar drugs on the fetus. Cyclizine and meclizine, for example, are teratogenic in animals and, justifiably or not, the labels of their over-the-counter preparations must warn against use during pregnancy.

The use of sedative-hypnotics to treat the vomiting associated with chemotherapy or radiation therapy of cancer is being reintroduced through the vehicle of marihuana and tetrahydrocannabinol (THC). The better results achieved in this way emphasize the limitations of the phenothiazines.

b. Narcotic analgesics—Morphine and related drugs may cause vomiting in single doses or early in the course of their action, but larger or repeated small doses will depress vomiting.

c. Anti-motion-sickness drugs—The antihistamines and scopolamine mentioned above are much less effective in vomiting that is not labyrinthine in origin than they are in motion sickness. They are commonly prescribed, but when the need is great the phenothiazines are more often used.

d. Phenothiazines—In clinical trials the phenothiazines or related antipsychotics have been shown to be more effective than placebo medication in the vomiting that occurs postoperatively, after the use of drugs in cancer chemotherapy, and in radiation sickness. Two phenothiazines (Table 19–2) are advertised as if they had special usefulness in vomiting, but all antipsychotics appear to be effective, and prac-

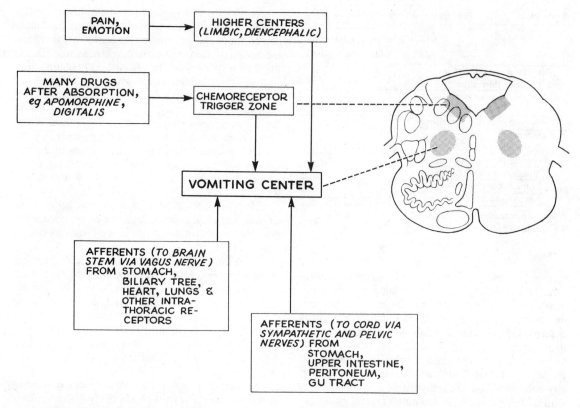

Figure 19–3. The block diagram summarizes the influences that stimulate emesis upon reaching the vomiting center. The locations of the vomiting center and chemoreceptor trigger zone are indicated on the outline of the brain stem above.

titioners can simply use the ones with which they are most familiar, presumably chlorpromazine. (See Chapter 25.)

e. Others–Trimethobenzamide (Tigan) is widely used even though it is the antiemetic whose usefulness has been least well established. It does, of course, cause fewer side-effects than the more active drugs.

Diphenidol (Vontrol) is similar to the parasympatholytics. It has some effectiveness but frequently causes a toxic psychosis (confusion, auditory and visual hallucinations). It can only be used under close and continuous supervision.

Benzquinamide (Emete-con) is a poorly characterized drug suggested for use against nausea and vomiting after anesthesia and surgery. It must be given by injection.

D. Ineffectiveness Against the Common Cold: Though the efficacy of the antihistamines in the treatment of the common cold has never been shown, it is obvious from sales figures of both prescription and nonprescription preparations that it is the advertising agencies rather than the clinical pharmacologist who determine the use of these preparations.

Beginning in 1947, there appeared a series of poorly controlled studies reporting that antihistamines cured the common cold in 85–100% of cases. These trials were not double-blind; assignments to control or treated groups were not random; and the diagnosis was established on the basis of the patient's statements. Subsequent studies that utilized the most elementary controls were unable to verify any action of the antihistamines on the duration, severity, or incidence of colds.

The common preparations are mixtures containing not only the antihistamine but also a sympathomimetic that, depending upon the amine chosen and the dose, may or may not be effective as a nasal decongestant (see Chapter 10). Aspirin or aspirin compound and cough suppressants may also be included in the mixture. The current PDR lists over 60 such preparations as "cold preparations" or "cough-cold preparations," and other mixtures of such "expensive aspirin" are available without prescription.

E. Bedtime Medication: The sedation that is judged unpleasant during the day is not a problem at night. Many physicians prescribe a sedating antihistamine, eg, diphenhydramine, as a bedtime medication rather than a barbiturate or benzodiazepine. Objective trials justify the practice.

Over-the-counter (non-prescription) "sleep aids" contain pyrilamine or doxylamine.

Adverse Reactions

A. Side-Effects: The most common side-effect is "drowsiness" or "sedation." This sedation is similar to that caused by the phenothiazine tranquilizers rather than that caused by the barbiturates or other sedative-hypnotic agents. Depending upon the patient, the antihistamine selected, and the dose or preparation used, the incidence of "drowsiness" may vary from 2–50% of patients. Most patients find the sensation unpleasant and may complain of tiredness or dizziness. This drowsiness may be ignored or may even be advantageous when the medication is given at bedtime or when it is desirable to reduce activity.

Very rarely, a symptom of central nervous system stimulation—eg, nervousness or insomnia—may be reported.

Early in their administration, the antihistamines may rarely cause acute facial dystonias, but parkinsonism has not been reported. Tardive dyskinesia has occurred after prolonged use of a decongestant mixture.

Of the atropinelike side-effects, dry mouth is the most common. Blurred vision, urinary retention, palpitations, and constipation are rare but do occur with higher doses.

Acute (Overdosage) Toxicity: Serious toxicity in the adult is rarely encountered. Children may be attracted to the colorful tablets found in many homes and are more susceptible. A recent review collected 17 fatal cases of antihistamine toxicity, 13 of which were in children. What fraction of the total cases of deaths due to antihistamines this represents is not known.

The expected drowsiness may progress to coma, often with a period of restlessness or excitement at some time. The coma may be preceded by preconvulsant jerks or progress to actual convulsions. Respiratory depression may occur with huge doses. Atropinelike effects are also seen: dilated pupils, tachycardia, and a red, hot, dry skin.

There is no specific treatment, and symptomatic treatment should not be too vigorous. The convulsions are probably not so threatening as the additional depression caused by efforts to control the convulsions with thiopental or similar drugs.

C. Allergic Reactions: These drugs, used in the treatment of allergic reactions, may act as sensitizing agents and cause dermatitis when applied to the skin as creams or ointments. Only isolated reports of serious systemic reactions—eg, agranulocytosis—have appeared.

Contraindications & Cautions

The label of antihistamines sold without a prescription must bear a warning against driving or operating machinery while using the drugs, since they may cause drowsiness. The patient receiving antihistamines by prescription should perhaps receive the same warning. However, many patients using antihistamines chronically do drive and work and there is no epidemiologic evidence that this group is involved in an unusual number of accidents. Anecdotal evidence from individual cases is undependable because of the tendency to use any prescribed drug retrospectively as an excuse for a mishap or as a cover for the effect of alcohol or other clearly dangerous drugs. The effects

Table 19–3. Antihistamines: Dosages.

	Single Adult Dose
Sedation infrequent	
Chlorpheniramine (Chlor-Trimeton, Teldrin)*	4 mg
Dexchlorpheniramine (Polaramine)	2 mg
Brompheniramine (Dimetane)*	4 mg
Azatadine (Optimine)	2 mg
Carbinoxamine (Clistin)	4 mg
Clemastine (Tavist)†	2 mg
Tripolidine (Actidil)*†	2.5 mg
Dimethindene (Forhistal, Triten)	2 mg
Cyproheptadine (Periactin)	4 mg
Sedation often prominent	
Diphenhydramine (Benadryl)*	50 mg
Bromodiphenhydramine (Ambodryl)	25 mg
Doxylamine (Decapryn)*	25 mg
Methdilazine (Tacaryl)	4 mg
Tripelennamine (Pyribenzamine)*	50 mg
Pyrilamine, mepyramine*	50 mg
Promethazine (Phenergan)*†‡	25 mg

*Generic preparation available.
†These longer-acting drugs are given twice daily; the others, 3–4 times daily.
‡Phenothiazine derivative (see also Table 25–1).

of the antihistamines are additive to those of other antipsychotics or other sedative-hypnotics.

If a patient reports undue sedation, the dosage should be reduced or a different antihistamine tried. If necessary, amphetamine or a related sympathomimetic stimulant may be given to combat the sedation.

Preparations & Dosages

A. Therapeutic Classification: (Table 19–3.) The antihistamines can be classified according to the degree of sedation anticipated as a side-effect, their potency, and their duration of action. Patients vary in their reaction to the antihistamines but generally prefer one of the less sedating drugs—eg, chlorpheniramine, the most widely prescribed antihistamine, or a related compound. The advantage of the longer-acting drugs (8 rather than 4 hours) is most apparent when they are given at bedtime.

Chlorpheniramine is available without a prescription.

B. Topical Application: None of the available antihistamine creams or ointments are active when applied to the intact skin. Applied to the denuded skin, they act more because of their local anesthetic effect and the physical properties of the preparation (cream or other base) than because they are antihistamines.

C. Cyproheptadine: Cyproheptadine (Periactin) is promoted as a serotonin antagonist (see below) as well as a histamine antagonist. Several other antihistamines have the same limited antiserotonin property, and there is no evidence that this is related to their therapeutic effects. Unlike chlorpheniramine, the other antihistamine with which it was compared, cyproheptadine does increase appetite and leads to increased weight gain and linear growth in children. Unfortunately, comparison with a phenothiazine is not available.

Azatadine (Optimine) is a congener of cyproheptadine marketed as an antihistamine.

H₂ RECEPTOR ANTAGONISTS
(Cimetidine)

The conventional (classic) antihistamines must be differentiated from the H₂ receptor antagonists, which are drugs that block the effect of histamine on gastric secretion.

Chemistry

The H₂ antagonists can be considered as analogs of histamine with a modified side chain. The only available drug is cimetidine (Tagamet):

Cimetidine (Tagamet)

Pharmacologic Effects

A. Mechanism of Action: The effects of histamine that are antagonized by the antihistamines are described as due to activation of H_1 receptors. These effects include vasodilatation, constriction of other smooth muscle tubes, and production of localized edema.

There are other effects of histamine, mediated by H_2 receptors, that are blocked by cimetidine or other H_2 antagonists. The most important of these effects is the action of histamine in stimulating gastric acid secretion. Two other H_2 effects—cardioacceleration and relaxation of the uterus—are seen in isolated tissue preparations and are useful in the laboratory evaluation of H_2 antagonists. The histamine-H_2 receptor antagonist relationship is competitive.

B. Effects: The H_2 antagonists reduce the volume and acidity of gastric secretion regardless of the nature of the stimulus to secretion or the physiologic state of the subject. That is, in normal subjects and in patients with peptic disease, gastric acid secretion can be stimulated beyond the basal level by insulin (vagally mediated), food, gastrin, parasympathomimetic drugs, caffeine, and histamine. The effect of all of these stimuli is blocked by H_2 antagonists, suggesting that histamine is the final stimulus to parietal cell secretion regardless of the nature of prior steps in the process. Basal or unstimulated secretion, including nocturnal secretion, is also reduced. Both the volume of secretion and the concentration of acid in the secretion are reduced, resulting in an impressive decrease in the secretion of total acid per unit of time.

Cimetidine can reduce acid secretion 85–100% compared with 0–35% with tolerated doses of atropine. The elaboration of pepsin decreases proportionately to the decrease in volume. There is no effect on gastric motility or on pancreatic or biliary secretion.

Pharmacokinetics

Cimetidine is well absorbed after oral administration. Absorption is slowed and the effect prolonged if the drug is taken with food, ie, with or after each meal. Cimetidine is largely (70%) excreted unchanged in the urine. The chemical half-life is nominally 2 hours, but an effect on overnight secretion is apparent for 8 hours.

Clinical Uses

In the USA, the marketer of cimetidine can claim established efficacy only in the treatment of duodenal ulcer and in the rare hypersecretory conditions (Zollinger-Ellison syndrome, mastocytosis, and endocrine adenomatosis). In addition, the manufacturer cannot suggest that the drug be used for longer than 8 weeks, presumably because the regulatory agency fears that unanticipated toxic reactions will appear in the postmarketing period. The individual physician is not necessarily bound by the restriction on the claims that can be made, and the convenience of cimetidine when compared with antacid treatment and its efficacy in treating duodenal ulcers has brought it into very wide use.

A. Duodenal or Prepyloric Peptic Ulcers: The course of peptic disease is cyclic and relapsing, placebo-responsive, and responsive to antacid treatment. In a clinical trial, the presence of an ulcer must be objectively established by x-ray or endoscopy, and the conditions of actual clinical practice that are purportedly simulated must be clearly described.

1. Healing of duodenal ulcer–The results of many carefully controlled trials indicate an incidence of complete healing in 4–6 weeks of no less than 70% in the cimetidine-treated groups; and in some trials, the rate reached 90%. In placebo-treated control groups, the incidence of healing reached 40% in outpatients. However, intensive antacid therapy in patients hospitalized for initiation of treatment yielded results comparable to those produced by cimetidine, 300 mg with each meal.

The group treated with cimetidine experienced more rapid relief of pain and preferred treatment with cimetidine because of the convenience and the absence of changes in the stools.

2. Recurrences–Following discontinuation of either treatment, relapses were the rule. However, the rate of recurrence could be significantly lowered by continued small doses of cimetidine, eg, 400 mg at bedtime or twice each day.

B. Gastric Ulcer: Trials with smaller groups of patients suggest a favorable effect on the healing of gastric ulcers, but such effect remains to be established.

C. Other Uses: Cimetidine is effective (with

other therapy) in the hypersecretory states mentioned (Zollinger-Ellison syndrome, etc). It is being used in the presence of acute upper gastrointestinal bleeding, but no evidence of superiority to antacids is available. In pancreatic insufficiency, it does appear to protect supplementary enzymes from destruction in the stomach (see Chapter 31).

Adverse Reactions

Minor side-effects—diarrhea, headache, tiredness, dizziness, muscle pain, diarrhea, constipation, or rash—are uncommon.

Serum creatinine may be slightly and reversibly elevated.

Transaminases and alkaline phosphatase may be persistently elevated or may return to normal even with continued use of the drug. Centrilobular hepatitis has been established in 2 patients.

Confusion, agitation, delirium, and coma have been reported in isolated cases.

There are clear indications that prolonged administration of cimetidine will result in at least minor endocrine dysfunction in males. Impotence has been reported, and patients receiving protracted therapy for a hypersecretory state have developed gynecomastia with soreness and sometimes galactorrhea. In animals, cimetidine is a weak antiandrogen causing a decrease in the size of the testis and accessory glands. In human volunteers, the sperm count was reduced 43% after 9 weeks of treatment with 1200 mg/d. At the same time, the output of luteinizing hormone after the administration of releasing factor was less.

No acute overdosage toxicity is seen.

Contraindications & Cautions

The effect of warfarin may be increased by the concurrent administration of cimetidine.

Dosage

Cimetidine (Tagamet) is available in tablet form and as a solution in vials. The usual dosage is 300 mg with each meal and at bedtime. Antacids are given as needed for pain or in large amounts, depending upon the physician. The goal of giving only the bedtime dosage for as much as possible of the 8-week period permitted should be pursued only as long as objective evidence of healing is available.

SEROTONIN

Serotonin (5-hydroxytryptamine, 5-HT, enteramine) is not a therapeutic agent but is important in relation to the action of other drugs and several disease states. Important physiologic functions have been suggested for it, but the establishment of any one of these roles awaits additional experimental analysis.

Chemistry

A. Synthesis: Serotonin is synthesized from di-etary tryptophan by hydroxylation and decarboxylation (Fig 19–4). The synthesis occurs at all of the storage sites except the platelets, which take up preformed serotonin.

B. Distribution: The largest fraction (90%) of serotonin in the body is synthesized and stored in the argentaffin or enterochromaffin cells of the mucosa of the gastrointestinal tract. It is also stored in platelets and released by platelet disintegration and is, therefore, found in serum and in the spleen. In some species (but not humans), it is found in the granules of mast cells and liberated concurrently with histamine. Serotonin occurs in some invertebrates and is a chemical mediator in some molluscs. One banana contains several milligrams of serotonin—enough to elevate urinary levels of its metabolite, 5-hydroxyindoleacetic acid (5-HIAA), and interfere with diagnostic tests for carcinoid.

However, the fraction of serotonin that has occasioned most current interest is that in the central nervous system. Here its occurrence parallels that of norepinephrine—ie, concentrations are greatest in the hypothalamus and mesencephalon. However, even here the concentration does not exceed 1 μg/g, compared with 2–15 μg/g in the gastrointestinal tract, 0.1–0.2 μg/mL of blood, and 2 mg/g of carcinoid tissue.

C. Metabolism: Serotonin is oxidatively deaminated to 5-HIAA. No alternate pathway comparable to the methylation of catecholamines is present to cooperate in terminating the action. However, in the pineal gland, N-acetylation and 5-methylation produce melatonin.

Pharmacologic Effects

A. Mechanisms of Action: As is true of many drugs, serotonin has multiple and sometimes conflicting actions. These include the augmentation of afferent activity from chemoreceptors, 2 direct actions on smooth muscle, and an excitatory or stimulant effect on the central nervous system. Serotonin may have multiple mechanisms of action, or these effects may all be due to the demonstrated depolarizing action on cell membranes.

B. Effects:

1. Cardiovascular and respiratory–Serotonin can cause an immediate fall in blood pressure accompanied by bradycardia, a rise in blood pressure accompanied by tachycardia, and a prolonged fall in blood pressure. Which of these effects is predominant depends upon the method of administration (rapid intravenous injection or infusion), dosage, and other factors. The use of blocking agents allows each effect to be demonstrated in each species.

a. Reflexly generated effect–The rapid intravenous injection of serotonin is followed by a fall in blood pressure; a paradoxic bradycardia—ie, slowing rather than the tachycardia expected to accompany a fall in blood pressure; and a complex change in respiration. This combination of changes, often referred to as the Bezold or Bezold-Jarisch triad, was mentioned

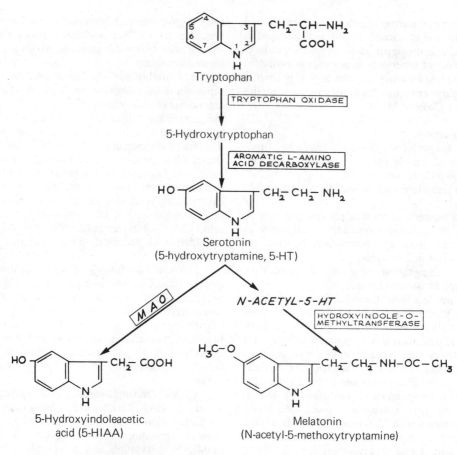

Figure 19–4. Synthesis and metabolism of serotonin. Note that the same enzyme catalyzes the carboxylation of 5-hydroxytryptophan to serotonin and dopa to dopamine.

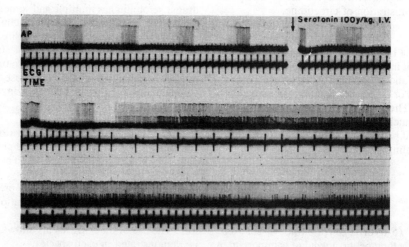

Figure 19–5. Effect of serotonin on action potentials recorded from a single afferent vagal fiber active with inspiration. The record is from a cat maintained with artificial respiration. Time is in seconds. Eight seconds after the intravenous injection of serotonin (at arrow), bradycardia started abruptly. Simultaneously, additional, smaller action potentials of undetermined origin appeared. Nine seconds after the injection of serotonin, a continuous flow of action potentials occurred on pulmonary afferent vagus fibers. As the bradycardia subsided, the smaller spikes disappeared whereas pulmonary afferent fibers still showed a continuous flow of action potentials. (Reproduced, with permission, from Schneider & Yonkman: Action of serotonin [5-hydroxytryptamine] on vagal afferent impulses in the cat. Am J Physiol 174:131, 1953.)

above (Chapter 12) in explaining the action of the veratrum alkaloids. The drug sensitizes peripheral chemo- and pressoreceptors, and the increased afferent activity reaching the brain stem augments vagal and decreases sympathetic tone. In the case of serotonin, 3 areas are sensitized or 3 reflexes initiated. The **coronary chemoreflex** depends upon receptors located in the distribution of the left coronary artery. These receptors are not necessarily within the myocardium but may lie in relation to the pulmonary artery dorsal to the heart. The bradycardia and hypotension are blocked by severing the afferent pathway (by vagal section) or the efferent arm of the reflex by hexamethonium or other ganglion blocking agents. Atropine will block only the bradycrotic effect. A **pulmonary depressor reflex** due to stimulation of chemoreceptors in the pulmonary circulation augments the fall in blood pressure. A **pulmonary respiratory chemoreflex** inhibits respiration, but stimulation of carotid sinus receptors may cause hyperpnea. The change in respiration is thus variable but consists typically of brief apnea followed by an increased respiratory rate.

The receptors adapt rapidly, and the reflex effect is usually followed in a fraction of a minute by a pressor effect.

b. Pressor effect–Following the period of hypotension, or if the above reflex effects are abolished by pretreatment with hexamethonium, serotonin causes an epinephrinelike pressor effect. The rise in blood pressure is accompanied by an increase in heart rate, cardiac output, and blood glucose levels and is prevented by alpha-adrenergic blocking agents. Serotonin is also qualitatively similar to epinephrine in elevating pressures on the right side of the circulation but is relatively more potent. Tachyphylaxis (acute tolerance) to the pressor effect develops after only a few injections.

c. Prolonged fall in blood pressure–A constant intravenous infusion of serotonin, perhaps the experimental situation most closely analogous to release of endogenous serotonin, causes a prolonged fall in blood pressure due to vasodilatation. Cardiac output is increased during the infusion. The exact mechanism is not known.

2. Other smooth muscle–Nonvascular smooth muscle is stimulated by serotonin. The bronchiolar constriction and increased intestinal motility that result are clinically important. The action on other smooth muscle—eg, the uterus—is not important in the intact animal, but the stimulation of isolated tissue provides a basis for assaying this effect of serotonin.

3. Central nervous system–See below.

Relation to Physiologic & Pathologic Processes

A. Possible Chemical Mediation in Central Nervous System: The demonstration that serotonin is found in the hypothalamus and a few other areas of the brain and the finding that the effect of reserpine is accompanied by a decreased concentration of serotonin in those areas led to the plausible hypothesis that serotonin is a mediator of transsynaptic conduction in the central nervous system or, at least, a modulator of transmission.

The concentrations of serotonin and norepinephrine often vary together—eg, after monoamine oxidase (MAO) inhibition or reserpine—and depletion experiments cannot distinguish between the effects of a decrease in the concentration of bound serotonin and the related high local concentration of free amine. Furthermore, much of the research on serotonin was done before the importance of dopamine was recognized. It appears that its overall effect is depressant.

B. Carcinoid Tumors: Neoplasms that arise from argentaffin cells are always "functional" in the sense that they synthesize and store serotonin. The serotonin liberated by the primary carcinoid tumor of the gastrointestinal tract is small in amount and destroyed during its passage through the liver. Primary ileal tumors may metastasize to the liver, and the serotonin from the larger tumor mass enters the hepatic veins rather than the portal bed. In this situation (and in rare cases of bronchial adenoma), the circulating serotonin causes a characteristic syndrome consisting of diarrhea, asthma (bronchiolar constriction), and cutaneous flushing. These signs occur paroxysmally and may be precipitated by eating, emotion, exertion, or pressure on a tumor mass. They can be duplicated by infusions of serotonin. In addition, subendocardial fibrosis leads to pulmonary valve stenosis and tricuspid insufficiency. The diagnosis depends in part upon the demonstration of large amounts of the serotonin metabolite 5-hydroxyindoleacetic acid in the urine.

Bradykinin also produces vasodilatation and a flush; and in some cases of carcinoid, elevated bradykinin levels have been demonstrated during episodes of flushing.

The expectation that this syndrome could be ameliorated pharmacologically has not been realized. Of the serotonin antagonists discussed below, only phenoxybenzamine and chlorpromazine (alpha-adrenergic blockers) are active and are helpful only against the flush. Prednisolone may slow the course of the right-sided heart disease. The debilitating diarrhea can be controlled with atropine or by slowing the synthesis of serotonin by the administration of parachlorphenylalanine.

Parachlorphenylalanine (PCPA, Fenclonine) is an investigative drug and laboratory tool that inhibits tryptophan hydroxylase and interrupts serotonin synthesis by interfering with the rate-limiting step in the reactions shown in Fig 19–4. Parachloramphetamine (PCA) and parachlormethamphetamine (PCMA) are more satisfactory depletors of brain serotonin but have not yet improved the management of patients with carcinoid syndrome or contributed to the analysis of the central nervous system effects of serotonin.

SEROTONIN ANTAGONISTS

An antagonist to serotonin would be potentially as important an analytic tool and therapeutic agent as atropine. This fact has perhaps generated enthusiasm for compounds and hypotheses not yet justified by the data available.

Effects

Serotonin has, as emphasized above, multiple physiologic and pharmacologic effects. In speaking of a serotonin antagonist, it is necessary to specify the serotonin action antagonized; and antagonism of one action does not imply action against all serotonin effects. It is probable that the search should be for multiple types of serotonin antagonists, just as 3 types of antagonists to acetylcholine have been defined.

The indole-ethylamine, serotonin, has some effects comparable to those of a phenylethylamine such as epinephrine. Cardiac stimulation, vasoconstriction, and the contraction of the estrogen pretreated rat uterus are blocked by phenoxybenzamine or other alpha-adrenergic blocking agents whether the stimulus is serotonin or epinephrine. These and a few other isolated tissue responses are the type of actions blocked by serotonin antagonists as currently defined.

Examples

A. Lysergic Acid Diethylamide (LSD): (See also Chapter 7.) LSD was among the first compounds other than known alpha-adrenergic blockers to be used in the laboratory as a serotonin antagonist. This action was related to its ability to cause a toxic psychosis (also called a model psychosis or hallucinatory state), and theories explaining the origin of the psychoses were propounded. However, other ergot derivatives—eg, 2-bromo-LSD—are more potent serotonin antagonists (in vitro) but lack the behavioral effects in humans.

B. Methysergide (Sansert) is discussed with other ergot alkaloids used in the treatment of migraine. It is the most potent antiserotonin of all the ergot derivatives, but is also potent enough as a vasoconstrictor to be effective (and dangerous) in the treatment of migraine.

C. Cyproheptadine (Periactin) is an ordinary antihistamine and, in tests on isolated tissues, an antiserotonin (as are many other antihistamines also). The demonstration that it is a serotonin antagonist in the inact animal is actually a demonstration of the development of tachyphylaxis to repeated injections of serotonin. It is nevertheless wrongly alleged to have special properties owing to its antiserotonin action.

OTHER DERIVATIVES OF TRYPTAMINE

Exogenous serotonin has negligible central nervous system effects because it does not reach the parenchymal cells of the central nervous system. Derivatives of tryptamine that are less polar enter the central nervous system more easily, and several are hallucinogenic.

Tryptamine itself is generally similar to serotonin but is a convulsant.

DMT and **DET** (N,N-dimethyl- and N,N-diethyl-tryptamine) are hallucinogenic if given by injection or smoked. Their action differs from that of LSD in that more sympathomimetic side-effects occur and the duration of action is less than 1 hour.

Psilocybin is derived from psilocine, or 4-hydroxydimethyltryptamine, by phosphorylation of the 4-hydroxyl group. It is isolated from a mushroom, *Psilocybe mexicana*, used by Mexican Indians for its hallucinogenic effect.

Bufotenine or **dimethylserotonin** is isolated from the secretions of toad skin and from the seeds of a plant, *Piptadenia peregrina*, used as snuff by some South American Indians. It is hallucinogenic after injection.

There is no evidence that methoxylation or N-methylation of serotonin occurs in the body to generate a psychotogenic substance.

• • •

References

Histamine

Beaven MA: Histamine. (2 parts.) N Engl J Med 294:30, 320, 1976.

Weiss S, Robb GP, Ellis LB: The systemic effects of histamine in man. Arch Intern Med 49:360, 1932.

West GB: Studies on the mechanism of anaphylaxis: A possible basis for a pharmacologic approach to allergy. Clin Pharmacol Ther 4:749, 1963.

Wolstenholme GEW, O'Connor CM (editors): *Ciba Foundation Symposium on Histamine.* Little, Brown, 1956.

Antihistamines

Bovet D: Introduction to antihistamine agents and Antergan derivatives. Ann NY Acad Sci 50:1089, 1950.

Brand JJ, Perry WLM: Drugs used in motion sickness. Pharmacol Rev 18:895, 1966.

Burrage WS: Antihistamines: Their use and abuse. N Engl J Med 245:532, 1951.

Lavenstein AF & others: Effects of cyproheptadine on asthmatic children: Study of appetite, weight gain and linear growth. JAMA 180:912, 1962.

Lavenstein BL, Cantor FK: Acute dystocia: An unusual reaction to diphenhydramine. JAMA 236:291, 1976.

H₂ Receptor Antagonists

Fordtran JS: Placebos, antacids and cimetidine for duodenal ulcer. (Editorial.) N Engl J Med 298:1081, 1978.

Frost F: Cimetidine in patients with gastric ulcer: A multicenter controlled trial. Br Med J 2:795, 1977.

Gray GR & others: Oral cimetidine in severe duodenal ulceration. Lancet 1:4, 1977.

Gudmand-Hoyer E & others: Prophylactic effect of cimetidine in duodenal ulcer disease. Br Med J 1:1095, 1978.

Scharschmidt B: Cimetidine. West J Med 131:417, 1979.

Symposium: Histamine H₂-receptor antagonists. Fed Proc 35:1923, 1976.

Symposium: Third symposium on histamine H₂-receptor antagonists. Gastroenterology 74:402, 1978.

Van Thiel DH & others: Hypothalamic-pituitary-gonadal dysfunction in men using cimetidine. N Engl J Med 300:1012, 1979.

Serotonin

Keel CA, Armstrong D: *Substances Producing Pain and Itch.* Williams & Wilkins, 1964.

Robson JM, Stacey RS: 5-Hydroxytryptamine. Chap 4, pages 122–155, in: *Recent Advances in Pharmacology,* 3rd ed. Churchill Livingstone, 1962.

Satterlee WG, Serpick A, Bianchine JR: Carcinoid syndrome: Chronic treatment with *p*-chloro-phenylalanine. Ann Intern Med 72:919, 1970.

Sjoerdsma A: Serotonin. (2 parts.) N Engl J Med 261:181, 231, 1959.

Surgical approaches and drug treatment in the carcinoid syndrome. (Leading article.) Br Med J 2:1572, 1978.

Symposium: Pharmacology of serotonin neurones in the central nervous system. Fed Proc 36:2133, 1977.

Part III. Central Nervous System Drugs

20 | General Anesthetics

Surgical anesthesia—abolition of the patient's perception of and reactions to pain—can be produced in 2 ways: **General anesthesia** is accomplished by using the drugs discussed in this chapter to produce unconsciousness; **local, regional,** or **conduction anesthesia** is induced by applying drugs to nerves or nerve roots to block the centripetal conduction of sensation from only a part or region of the body without influencing consciousness.

General anesthesia is further categorized as inhalation or intravenous. **Inhalation anesthesia** (emphasized in this chapter) is produced by administration through the respiratory tract of gases or volatile liquids. **Intravenous anesthetics** such as thiopental are ultrashort-acting barbiturates and are similar to the barbiturates discussed in Chapter 23.

History

Neither alcohol nor opium provides enough analgesia to allow living tissue to be incised and dissected without the most terrible pain terminated only by shock. Before the days of general anesthesia, the encounter between patient and surgeon was a screaming, savage matter limited to desperately necessary procedures.

Humphrey Davy, discoverer of nitrous oxide, inhaled that gas to ease his own dental pain, and in 1800 he suggested that it be used in surgery. Ether was also proposed as an anesthetic by Faraday in 1818, but both these agents were initially used only for amusement.

Following observations at an ether frolic, Crawford W. Long used ether for surgical anesthesia in Georgia in 1842 but did not report his experience and had no influence.

In 1844, a New England dentist, Horace Wells, attended a demonstration of nitrous oxide effects by one "Professor" Colton. He noticed that a friend who had inhaled laughing gas did not notice pain when he gashed his leg on one of the crude plank seats. Wells used nitrous oxide in his dental practice, but a demonstration at Massachusetts General Hospital failed. Wells not only abandoned his trials of anesthesia but became habituated to the disinhibiting vapors of chloroform and died a suicide in 1848.

Wells's former partner in dental practice in Boston, Wm. T.G. Morton, continued a planned effort to develop anesthesia. Complete dentures had until that time been crude devices carved out of hippopotamus tusk with the upper and lower plates joined and held in place by a spring at the back. Morton adopted methods then appearing for making porcelain teeth and, most importantly, for exploiting the new suction cup principle of separate upper and lower plates. Now it was no longer possible to fit dentures over the snags and roots of the remaining teeth, and the pain attending multiple, complete extractions became a matter of concern for Morton in his lucrative practice. In an attempt to find a solution to his problem, he enrolled in the Harvard Medical School, starting on the standard course that required two 4-month "years" of lectures and a year of apprenticeship.

Morton arranged for the unsuccessful demonstration of nitrous oxide by his former partner and then used ether, the complete anesthetic, for extractions in his office. He developed a proper nonrebreathing inhaler and on October 16, 1846, carried out a demonstration at Massachusetts General Hospital during which a subcutaneous tumor was painlessly excised.

Ether and—very soon thereafter—chloroform were rapidly accepted throughout the world. Morton patented his drug and inhaler, as was not unusual for his period, but collected no money and wasted most of his remaining life pressing his claims for compensation by the federal government until his death at age 48. His fame and income were severely limited by the claims of participation in the discovery by others. His primary detractor was a psychotic chemist, Charles Jackson, whom Morton had indeed consulted. Jackson, at other times in his generally admirable career, had claimed credit for the invention of the telegraph and guncotton and had also claimed that St. Martin was his patient rather than Beaumont's.

Chemical Properties

Compounds of many different chemical types can induce general anesthesia. The drugs used as intravenous anesthetics illustrate that the barbiturates and other drugs classed as sedative-hypnotics are general anesthetics. It is usual but slightly misleading to consider the inhalation anesthetics as a separate drug class because of the unusual importance of their physical rather than chemical properties.

Volatile liquids or gases are selected because administration by inhalation permits close control and easy adjustment of the dose and rapid reversibility of effect, since the vapor is eliminated in expired air rather than by metabolism in the body.

The inhalation anesthetics in common use include the following chemical types:

A. Ethers: Eg, diethyl ether or methoxyflurane (Penthrane, $Cl_2HC-CF_2-O-CH_3$).

B. Halogenated Hydrocarbons: Eg, chloroform, trichloroethylene, halothane ($F_3C-CHClBr$). One of the few structure-action generalizations that is possible is that halogenated hydrocarbons are very apt to sensitize the myocardium to the ability of epinephrine to cause ventricular arrhythmias. Such a toxic effect is seen not only with inhalation anesthetics but also with compounds primarily of toxicologic interest—eg, carbon tetrachloride and the chlorinated hydrocarbon type of insecticides.

C. Alicyclic Hydrocarbons: Cyclopropane is the only example.

D. Other Hydrocarbons: Ethylene has been used as an anesthetic. Other aliphatic and aromatic hydrocarbons—eg, gasoline, toluene—are toxic or abused substances.

E. One Inorganic Oxide: The only agent in this group is nitrous oxide (N_2O).

Physical Properties

A. Flammability and Explosiveness: Most of the halogenated compounds—eg, halothane, methoxyflurane, and chloroform—present no hazard in this regard. Ether, cyclopropane, and other less valuable drugs can be dangerous in the presence of the electrocautery or a spark from a static discharge. Mixtures of nitrous oxide and oxygen are not explosive since both are oxidizing agents. Nitrous oxide will, however, support combustion—eg, mixtures of nitrous oxide and ether are potentially explosive and, in an atmosphere of nitrous oxide and oxygen, fires are of explosive intensity.

B. Uptake and Elimination: The initial or induction stages of anesthesia described below may pass rapidly and pleasantly for the patient or may be prolonged and unpleasant. A stormy induction period inherent in an agent to be used as the definitive anesthetic is avoided by heavy premedication or by first using a more suitable agent for induction. Neverthe-

less, consideration of uptake and elimination in terms of induction and recovery is a useful way to outline the physical factors involved in the transport or distribution of inhalation anesthetics.

Intravenous anesthetics establish a maximum blood level immediately upon injection and are carried in large amounts to the brain and other tissues with a high blood flow. Inhalation anesthetics are distributed in several compartments—ie, inspired air, alveolar air, blood, brain, and various other tissues. The equilibration rate between successively traversed compartments depends upon the relative solubility of the agent in the 2 compartments and blood flow through one of the compartments. The rates of equilibration determine how rapidly the partial pressure of the gas in the central nervous system reaches anesthetic levels—ie, equilibrates with anesthetic levels of agent in inspired air. Some physical properties of anesthetics relevant to the following discussion are shown in Table 20–1.

1. In the lung–The transport of anesthetic agent from inspired air to blood during induction or the reverse during recovery will be influenced by the following factors:

a. The blood-air partition coefficient, ie, the solubility in blood compared with the amount present in alveolar air.

b. The concentration of agent in the inspired air.

c. The concentration of agent in alveolar air, which is not necessarily the same as the concentration in inspired air.

d. The concentration in pulmonary arterial blood.

e. The rate and depth of respiration.

f. The cardiac output, ie, the volume of blood that equilibrates with alveolar air.

To illustrate the above factors, induction with ether and cyclopropane can be contrasted.

Ether is distinctive in that it is very soluble in blood. Upon the first inhalation of ether—and assuming some ordinary values for tidal volume (less dead space) and for functional residual volume—the anesthetic will be diluted in the alveoli to half its concentration in inspired air.

Since ether is highly soluble in blood, it will all be removed from alveolar air, providing a limited total amount of ether to be transferred to tissues. The partial pressure of ether in alveolar air falls rapidly to zero, but since the blood can dissolve such a large amount of

Table 20–1. Physical properties of several inhalation anesthetics.

| | Flammable and Explosive | Concentrations for Surgical Anesthesia | | Partition Coefficients | | | Clearance Rate of Blood Passing Lung* (% Alveolar Tension) |
		Inhaled Concentration (Vol%)	Blood Level (mg/dL)	Blood/Air	Brain/Blood	Oil (Fat)/Blood	
Ether	Yes	5–10	130–150	12–15	1.1	5.4	5
Halothane	No	1–3	5–25	2.3	2.6	97	26
Cyclopropane	Yes	10–25	10–20	0.42	1.3	26.7	66
Nitrous oxide	No	80–85	30–50	0.47	1.1	3	63

*Percentage equilibrium between inspired gas tension and tension in pulmonary capillary blood achieved in one passage through the lung during induction.

gas, the partial pressure in blood is elevated by only a small increment of the eventual partial pressure upon equilibration and only small amounts are transferred to tissue.

The alveolar air against which the blood equilibrates during the next inspiration will again contain a low concentration and a small absolute amount of ether. Many respiratory cycles will be needed to provide enough ether to build up the concentration in the brain, and induction will be slow.

An anesthetic such as cyclopropane, on the other hand, has low solubility in blood. With each respiratory cycle, only a small fraction of the cyclopropane in alveolar air will enter the blood; the concentration of drug in the alveolar air will rapidly approach that in inspired air, and arterial blood will also quickly equilibrate with alveolar air.

Apart from explaining the slow induction with ether—which after all is no longer used for induction—the above suggests that when a very soluble agent is used in anesthesia, equilibrium is only slowly achieved and the concentration of agent in inspired air would need to be reduced progressively during a long procedure. It further suggests that the concentration of anesthetic in inspired air is a poor index of anesthetic potency until equilibrium is reached. Blood levels or minimum alveolar concentrations (MAC) provide a better basis for comparing agents and determining the effect of other drugs and alteration in physiologic state. MAC is defined as the alveolar concentration that will block movement of a patient in response to incision (or of an animal in response to a standard stimulus) in half of cases.

2. In the central nervous system–Equilibration between blood and brain is rapid because solubility in the 2 tissues is similar and cerebral blood flow great.

3. In other tissues–Other tissues with a high lipid content would be expected to take up disproportionate amounts of anesthetics with a high lipid solubility—eg, ether or halothane. Accumulation of large amounts of anesthetic in fat does occur, but blood flow through such tissue is low and the process is, therefore, slow. The longer anesthesia is continued with ether or halothane, the greater the amount sequestered in fat. During recovery, this pool of anesthetic will only slowly equilibrate with blood because of the high oil/blood partition coefficient. During induction, however, the high cerebral blood flow carries greater absolute amounts of agent to the brain.

Pharmacologic Effects
A. Mechanisms of Action:
1. Theories–Most of the substances commonly used as general anesthetics (but by no means most of the substances capable of producing general anesthesia) are metabolized to only a limited extent by the body and do not react chemically with any body constituents. Indeed, the inert gas xenon can produce anesthesia. The structural diversity of the agents used as anesthetics and the rapid appearance and reversal of

anesthesia also indicate a biochemical change. Theories attempting to explain the action of anesthetics have, therefore, emphasized physical rather than chemical properties.

An early theory, developed independently by Meyer and Overton, emphasized the close correlation of the lipid solubility of a substance with its anesthetic potency. In their experiments, an atmosphere containing an anesthetic concentration of various agents was equilibrated against olive oil. The tension of the anesthetics in the gas phase varied from 30 atmospheres for nitrogen to 0.5% of 1 atmosphere for chloroform. However, since lipid solubility is greater for the more active agents, the final concentration of all agents in the olive oil varied only slightly in spite of the 6000-fold difference in potency. Using modern technics, most researchers have concluded that anesthesia occurs when a certain number of molecules are dissolved in some crucial hydrophobic site. Whether the action is on the cell membrane and at what functional site and by what mechanism of action it occurs are matters of speculation.

2. Action on reticular activating system–One of the effects of anesthetics, the loss of consciousness, can be explained by their action in depressing conduction within the ascending reticular activating system (RAS) or midbrain reticular formation. As the sensitivity or threshold to stimulation of the reticular activating system is reduced, the ascending activating influence on the cortex is reduced (Fig 20–1). The electrical activity of the cortex and behavior are then both suppressed. (The electroencephalographic consequences of general anesthesia are shown in Fig 20–2.)

General anesthetics produce a generalized, graded depression of all levels of the central nervous system. Only the loss of consciousness is clearly related to an action on the reticular activating system.

B. Pharmacologic Effects Related to Staging of Anesthesia: The importance of controlling the dosage of an anesthetic—ie, the depth of anesthesia—has led to the adoption of a conventionalized scale for describing the degree or stage of anesthetic action. In practice, many of the suggested observations are obscured by the presence of other drugs, but the definitions agreed upon are extremely useful in describing the effects not only of the general anesthetics but also of the sedative-hypnotic drugs and alcohol (see Chapters 23 and 24). This section will describe the effects involved in defining the stages of anesthesia, which is equivalent to describing the primary pharmacologic effects of the drugs. Other effects, more important in defining the differences among the several agents, are described later.

The stages of anesthesia detailed below and in Table 20–2 are as follows:

Stage 1: Analgesia
Stage 2: Excitement
Stage 3: Surgical anesthesia
Stage 4: Medullary paralysis

The details of the conventionalized description or

AROUSAL BY OLFACTORY STIMULATION

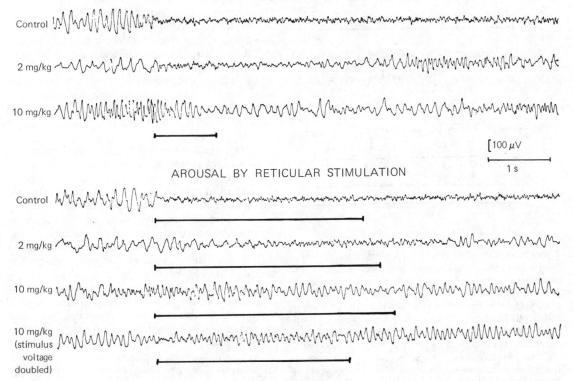

Figure 20–1. The effect of a general anesthetic on the cortical arousal that follows brief afferent stimulation that is projected diffusely to the cortex through the reticular activating system. Electrocorticogram from a curarized rabbit. Stimulation by clove oil *(above)* and direct excitation of brain stem reticular formation *(below)*. Electroencephalographic arousal (lower voltage, higher frequency waves, and desynchronization) follows stimulation in the control records but is reduced by small doses of a general anesthetic. The agent used in this experiment was sodium pentobarbital, but ether and other agents act similarly. (Reproduced, with permission, from Arduini & Arduini: Effect of drugs and metabolic alterations on brain stem arousal mechanism. J Pharmacol Exp Ther 110:77, 1954.)

staging apply to the effects of ether on a patient uninfluenced by premedication or adjuvant drugs, a situation never encountered in this day of balanced (multiple-agent) anesthesia. The following description will vary for different anesthetics and will be modified by adjunctive drugs. It is, nevertheless, a useful organizing device.

The alteration of central nervous system function by anesthetics follows a pattern characterized as a combination of ascending and descending depression that spares the medulla until large doses are used. This means that depression of the caudal segments of the spinal cord and of the cortex occur earliest. With more intense effects, depression spreads upward through the cord and downward through subcortical and midbrain functions until, eventually, actions on the medulla and cervical cord lead to vasomotor collapse and respiratory arrest. This pattern of depression can be applied to several functions:

1. Behavior and state of consciousness–

a. Stage 1 (analgesia)–The patient remains conscious and responsive but, with depression of the highest centers and the beginning of disinhibition, experiences analgesia and euphoria. The analgesia is intense enough to be useful during minor procedures—eg, dental extractions or the second stage of labor.

Nitrous oxide, ether, and other less commonly used agents produce good analgesia. Halothane is a poor analgesic until consciousness is lost. Thiopental provides poor analgesia even during the equivalent of stage 3—ie, the patient continues to react to painful stimuli. Thiopental in small doses is even said to augment the perception of pain, but the exaggerated response to pain probably represents behavior during the excited stage.

In addition to euphoria, the patient may experience a dreamlike state with disordered perceptions that are sometimes described as hallucinations. Dreams or fantasies are probably better terms. A variable degree of amnesia for the events of this stage occurs.

b. Stage 2 (excitement)–With more marked disinhibition—ie, the release of lower centers from the constant inhibitory influence of a higher center—consciousness is lost, and the patient becomes excited and may struggle and shout in a drunken, delirious manner.

Stages 1 and 2 together make up the stage or

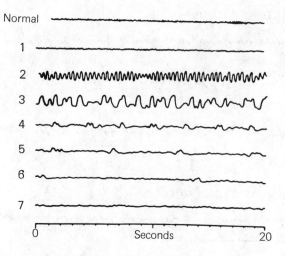

Figure 20–2. Classification of EEG pattern changes during increasing depth of ether-oxygen or nitrous oxide, oxygen, and ether anesthesia of human beings. The first and second patterns occur during induction, the third, fourth, and fifth occurring during light, moderate, and deep surgical anesthesia. The last 2 patterns are seen during excessively deep anesthesia. (Reproduced, with permission, from Faulconer: Correlation of concentrations of ether in arterial blood with electroencephalographic patterns occurring during nitrous oxide, oxygen and ether anesthesia of human surgical patients. Anesthesiology 13:361, 1952.)

process of induction. The amount of excitement that takes place is variable, depending upon (1) the amount of depressant premedication, (2) the anesthetic agent used, and (3) the amount of external stimulation present. Ether, for example, not only has a long induction period, but its irritant, unpleasant vapors further stimulate the patient. A patient may become quite excited during induction near the operating room but will remain quiet in the recovery room after the operation when the same intensity of drug effect is present.

With adequate premedication and the use of separate agents for induction and maintenance, excitement during induction is now rare. Its occurrence is, however, important in classifying and analyzing drug effects.

Beyond stage 2, responses by the anesthetized patient, even if they involve voluntary muscle, are generated by reflex.

2. Voluntary muscle–As the concentration of anesthetic in the body is increased, contraction of voluntary muscle is weakened and then abolished. The drug acts on the spinal cord or, in the case of muscles innervated by cranial nerves, on the brain stem. Polysynaptic reflexes and tonic nervous outflow to muscle are reduced. Monosynaptic reflexes are persistent and of no value in establishing the depth of anesthesia. Ether has a significant curariform activity in addition to its central effect.

Muscle relaxation determines the ease of exposure of deep structures during surgery. In addition, the

pattern of ascending and descending depression of muscle activity is important in describing the changes in respiration with deepening anesthesia. Eye movement—ie, extraocular muscle activity—is also useful in judging the depth of anesthesia.

a. Respiration–

(1) Stage 1–Respiration is not altered during stage 1 unless the agent used is ether or chloroform. These irritant substances may increase the rate and cause some irregularity in pattern, including breathholding.

(2) Stage 2–During the stage of excitement, the activity of the patient and exaggerated respiratory reflexes may cause a rapid, irregular, and rapidly changing pattern of respiration. As is true for all changes during stage 2, premedication reduces this response.

(3) Stage 3–The entry into stage 3 is marked by the onset of a regular pattern of respiration.

Stage 3 is further divided into 4 planes. In planes i and ii, respiration continues full and regular. (The border between planes i and ii is marked by disappearance of eye movements.) As depression ascends, those segments of the thoracic cord innervating the intercostal muscles are affected first. The diaphragm, which is innervated by the phrenic nerve from cervical segments 3 and 4, is not paralyzed until later.

Plane iii is characterized by incomplete intercostal paralysis. Thoracic movement is reduced and lags behind abdominal (diaphragmatic) movement upon inspiration.

Plane iv begins when intercostal paralysis is complete. The purely abdominal (diaphragmatic) breathing is rapid and shallow. Accessory muscles of respiration (scalenes, sternocleidomastoid) are used. The completely inactive intercostal muscles are not only unable to move the thorax; they are also unable to prevent its inward movement with each inspiration. The paradoxic collapse of the chest with each rising of the abdomen results in "rocking" respiration.

(4) Stage 4–Because of medullary as well as cervical cord depression, no respiratory movements occur in stage 4.

Ether is distinctive in its effect on respiration in that its irritant action stimulates respiration and delays the appearance of respiratory depression. Halothane and cyclopropane cause progressive depression of minute volume through stage 3, and their use requires that respiration be assisted to prevent CO_2 retention. Nitrous oxide does not depress respiration.

b. Extraocular muscles–When the extrinsic muscles of the eye are weakened, they no longer act in a coordinated way and the eyes rove—ie, the globes move slowly and not necessarily symmetrically. Movement is marked during stage 2 and decreases progressively during plane i of stage 3. In plane ii or beyond, both eyes are fixed in the same position but there may be slight convergence or divergence.

c. Other muscles–During stage 1, the muscles are under the usual voluntary control. Some ataxia may be present but is not ordinarily observed. Following the uncontrolled activity of stage 2, the extremities are

Table 20–2. Stages and planes of anesthesia. (In = inspiration.)

	Stage 1	Stage 2	Stage 3				Stage 4
			i	ii	iii	iv	
Consciousness							
Excitement							
Respiration — Abdominal / Thoracic							
Eye movement							
Reflexes — Lid or wink							
Reflexes — Vomiting							
Reflexes — Swallowing							
Reflexes — Laryngeal							
Reflexes — Corneal and peritoneal							
Pupil dilatation							
Tachycardia							
Elevated blood pressure							
Lowered blood pressure							

relaxed but the abdominal and other muscles retain normal tone during plane i. Relaxation during plane ii (without the adjunctive use of curariform drugs) is sufficient for some surgical procedures, but the common intra-abdominal procedures require plane iii.

3. Changes secondary to excitement and asphyxia–

a. Pupillary size–During the excitement stage of induction, sympatho-adrenal discharge increases and the pupils dilate. Following excitement, and throughout planes i and ii, the pupils return to their initial size, which may have been influenced by morphine or atropine used as preanesthetic medication. With the appearance of intercostal paralysis (and assuming that respiration is not assisted by the anesthetist), some CO_2 retention occurs, and sympatho-adrenal stimulation again leads to pupillary dilatation.

b. Pulse rate and blood pressure–During the period of excitement, pulse rate and blood pressure are both elevated just as the pupils are dilated. However, the progressive asphyxial changes of deep anesthesia are accompanied by depression of medullary vasomotor centers. Thus, pulse rate rises but blood pressure falls progressively. Respiration ceases before the heart stops, and, if the patient can be artificially ventilated for a few breaths to remove some of the

anesthetic agent, the changes of stage 4 are reversible.

4. Specific reflexes–Several specific reflexes indicate the depth of anesthesia.

a. Lid reflex–The lid ''reflex'' is present when retraction of the closed lid by the anesthetist evokes active closing or a resistance to opening. It disappears at the border between stages 2 and 3 when the tone of the orbicularis muscle is sufficiently reduced.

b. Swallowing and vomiting–The ability to swallow is lost in the upper part of plane i or, during recovery, is regained at that level. During recovery, vomiting does not occur until a slightly lighter stage—the border between stages 2 and 3—is reached. This order of recovery of the protective reflexes makes anesthesia much safer by reducing the problem of aspiration of vomitus.

c. Laryngeal and pharyngeal–Reaction to stimulation of the pharynx—eg, by an airway—disappears and reappears midway in plane i. Reaction to laryngeal stimulation, important when a tracheal tube is present or is to be inserted, marks the border between planes i and ii. Adjuvant drugs such as succinylcholine permit intubation at a lighter level of anesthesia.

d. Peritoneal–The reflex responsiveness of the patient to peritoneal traction or other stimulation persists until deep in plane ii. Anesthesia must be deep enough to abolish cardiovascular and respiratory responses. The corneal reflex (lid closure in response to touching the corneal conjunctiva) behaves similarly, but testing it adds the hazard of corneal abrasion.

Adverse Effects

Since the therapeutic effect of anesthetics is to produce unconsciousness and loss of perception to pain, the other pharmacologic effects are mostly undesirable. An understanding of these effects is necessary so that the adverse results of anesthesia can be minimized and is important in the selection of the anesthetic to be used from among the various agents available.

A. Cardiovascular Effects: During the stage of excitement and whenever respiratory depression with even minor hypercapnia develops, there is increased release of epinephrine from the adrenal medulla and norepinephrine from sympathetic nerve. Furthermore, as anesthesia deepens, there is vasomotor depression. The consequences of these processes—eg, tachycardia, hypertension during excitement and hypotension with deep anesthesia—have already been mentioned. All agents have a direct effect in depressing the myocardium. The impairment is not great under light anesthesia and is greatest with halothane.

1. Blood pressure—Changes in blood pressure should be described as the resultant of changes in cardiac contractility and vasomotor activity. The data needed to allow such a description are not complete or uniformly accepted, especially when mechanisms of action are proposed or the relative importance of several possible factors must be assayed. However, several descriptive statements can be made about the ability of anesthetics to maintain blood pressure or "support the circulation."

Because of the importance of medullary depression, the use of light rather than deep anesthesia is the most important factor in maintenance of blood pressure. Again, the use of a mixture or balance of agents to achieve a satisfactory degree of analgesia and muscular relaxation allows reduction of the dose of any one of the potent agents.

Cyclopropane is unusual in its ability to maintain or even slightly elevate blood pressure. Cardiac output is elevated—ie, there is some peripheral vasodilatation and maintained tissue perfusion.

Halothane is equally distinctive in the production of hypotension by reduced force of cardiac contractility and peripheral vasodilatation.

2. Cardiac arrhythmias—

a. Atrial rhythmicity—During induction or light anesthesia, especially with chloroform, cyclopropane, and halothane, vagal influence on the heart is greatly increased. Bradycardia, wandering atrial pacemaker, and atrioventricular junctional rhythms result. If the bradycardia is quite marked, it may exaggerate any hypotension present. Adequate premedication with atropine and avoidance of high initial concentrations of the anesthetic agent will minimize this action.

b. Ventricular arrhythmias—The production of

ventricular arrhythmias is partially explained by the sensitization of the myocardium to the effects of epinephrine by cyclopropane and halogenated compounds such as halothane and chloroform. Epinephrine release during induction can be avoided by heavy premedication or by using agents that produce induction without excitement.

During deeper anesthesia, ventilation must be assisted when halothane or cyclopropane is used in order to maintain normal P_{CO_2}. Cyclopropane is currently the only agent in wide use that presents a considerable risk of ventricular arrhythmias; if the concentration of cyclopropane is great enough, arrhythmias may appear even without hypercapnia.

B. Hepatotoxicity: Transient impairment of liver function can be demonstrated in 50% of patients receiving general or spinal anesthesia even when the surgical procedure is not intra-abdominal, and is presumably due to hypoxia. The hypoxia, in turn, is probably due to splanchnic vasoconstriction resulting from sympathoadrenal discharge and leading to a great reduction in liver blood flow.

Much more important is the occurrence of fatal hepatic necrosis and the possible risk associated with the use of halothane. When the question of halothane hepatotoxicity was raised, several retrospective studies were done. One massive study concluded that hepatic necrosis within 6 weeks of surgery occurred in one out of every 10,000 administrations (82 out of 856,000) and was unrelated to the anesthetic used. Halothane, especially after repeated administrations, may on rare occasions cause an allergic hepatitis.

C. Effects on Smooth Muscle: In some patients, usually those with a history of asthma, bronchiolar constriction occurs during light anesthesia. Since it is abolished by deeper anesthesia, it is presumed to be reflex in origin.

Uterine contractions during and after delivery are inhibited by light anesthesia with halothane (and chloroform). Other agents have this action only at deeper levels.

Preanesthetic Medication

The pharmacologic preparation of a patient prior to the induction of anesthesia has 2 essential goals: the relief of anxiety and the drying of secretions. In addition, the central nervous system depression caused by preanesthetic medication adds to the effects of anesthetic agents and facilitates induction.

Preanesthetic medication should not be reduced to a ritual. However, a few typical methods of achieving the following goals can be outlined.

A. Relief of Anxiety: At bedtime on the night before the procedure, the patient is given enough of a sedative-hypnotic to ensure a restful night—eg, 100–200 mg of sodium pentobarbital. In the morning, pentobarbital or an equivalent drug may be repeated for its effect in reducing anxiety. Morphine and other narcotic analgesics are regarded by most anesthetists as the best depressants of acute anxiety. About 45 minutes before induction or when the patient is to be moved to the surgical floor, morphine, 8–15 mg subcutaneously, is given in combination with atropine or a similar parasympatholytic drug.

B. Decrease of Secretions: Atropine or scopolamine is an invariable part of preanesthetic medication whatever the agent used. Ether increases secretions of the respiratory tract, but even the normal volume of secretions can be dangerous. A very small amount of secretion (or any other material) can stimulate laryngospasm. Laryngospasm is associated more often with the use of thiopental. It is not a serious threat if the operator is prepared to treat it—if necessary, by giving succinylcholine to relax the larynx.

Premedication with atropine also controls the reflex bradycardia discussed above.

C. Increase of Anesthetic Effect: In the production of balanced anesthesia, the distinction between preanesthetic medication and adjuncts used during anesthesia becomes indistinct—ie, whether heavy premedication with meperidine is given or an intravenous injection of the same narcotic is given following induction, the same goals will be accomplished. These are the production of a deeper level of anesthesia with a mild agent and a reduction in the amount of the inhalation agent required.

ANESTHETIC AGENTS

The objectives of general anesthesia—obliteration of consciousness, blockade of reflex responses to surgical manipulation, and muscular relaxation sufficient for the procedure—are today rarely accomplished with a single agent. The properties of individual agents are discussed below, but they are used in various combinations and with adjunctive drugs to provide "balanced" anesthesia.

For example, induction in a premedicated patient is carried out with thiopental or, less commonly, nitrous oxide. Analgesia is augmented with narcotic analgesics given intravenously. (The availability of narcotic antagonists has made this practice safer.) Muscle relaxation is achieved with curariform or neuromuscular blocking drugs (see Chapter 21). Light anesthesia is maintained with nitrous oxide, or a potent agent—eg, halothane—is added as needed.

Factors influencing the choice of agents and technics include the following:

(1) Patient preference, eg, a bias against regional (spinal) anesthesia and an insistence on rapid induction.

(2) Patient's condition, eg, drugs used preoperatively, presence of shock or hypovolemia.

(3) Nature of the procedure, eg, need for use of electrocautery, degree of muscle relaxation required, intensity of stimulation inherent in the procedure, and estimated duration of the procedure.

Technics of Administering Inhalation Anesthesia

A. Open Drop: A volatile liquid (ethers, chloroform) is administered drop by drop onto the gauze or cloth covering of a wire frame mask applied over the mouth and nose. The inhaled concentration is controlled by the rate of drip.

B. Insufflation: This method consists of blowing anesthetic vapors or gases into the mouth, pharynx, or trachea. Some type of anesthesia machine is required for metering gas flows and vaporizing volatile agents. Insufflation has its greatest usefulness in operations for which a mask cannot be used (eg, tonsillectomy).

C. Nonrebreathing: A nonrebreathing or open technic supplies a continuous fresh supply of anesthetic agent with adequate oxygen through an apparatus which channels each exhalation to the atmosphere.

D. Partial and Total Rebreathing: These methods require anesthesia machines and are named according to the amount of exhalation the patient is required to rebreathe. A means of absorbing the exhaled CO_2 must be provided in all instances except where the rebreathing is minimal.

ETHER

Ether (diethyl ether, $H_5C_2-O-C_2H_5$) is an irritant liquid with an unpleasant odor. For over 100 years, it was the safest and most widely used of the complete anesthetics.

Ether can be administered by simple technics. It is safe because its irritant properties maintain or even stimulate respiration until the deeper planes of anesthesia; because there is a wide margin between the amount needed to provide surgical anesthesia and the amount that produces medullary paralysis; and because it has no special toxic effects on the cardiovascular or other systems although it causes vasodilatation with a warm, flushed skin. It produces good muscle relaxation without adjunctive drugs. When muscle relaxants are used, the dosage—especially that of the nondepolarizing or tubocurarine type—can be reduced.

Induction with ether is slow and unpleasant, but the use of other agents for induction overcomes this disadvantage. However, ether is explosive, and recovery is prolonged and is accompanied by nausea and vomiting somewhat more often than with other agents.

HALOTHANE

Halothane (Fluothane, $F_3C-CHClBr$), a heavy liquid, has become the most widely used inhalation agent because it is not explosive and only rarely causes serious adverse reactions. Postoperative nausea and vomiting is remarkably rare.

Chapter 20. General Anesthetics

The following properties should, however, be recalled from the discussion above:

(1) Blood pressure is not always well maintained by halothane. Vasodilatation occurs, but cardiac output is only slightly decreased, and hypotension is unusual now that the concentration is controlled by adequate technic.

(2) Unlike ether, halothane causes progressive respiratory depression during stage 3.

(3) Arrhythmias occur uncommonly, but respiration should be assisted to maintain normocapnia, since sensitization to epinephrine is demonstrable.

(4) Muscle relaxation is usually not adequate unless another agent is used also.

(5) Halothane on rare occasions—usually after repeated use—causes hepatitis and massive liver necrosis through an allergic mechanism.

It was mentioned above that hepatic necrosis from all causes—shock, infection, preexisting liver disease—occurs in one out of 10,000 cases within 6 weeks of operation. To establish the relationship of a small excess of cases of acute liver atrophy to an anesthetic agent was difficult. Data showing the relationship to repeated exposure have led to general agreement that halothane causes a fatal allergic or autoimmune hepatitis in approximately one out of 800,000 administrations.

Halothane hepatitis is not dose-related. In about 75% of cases, it follows repeated use of halothane, and prior use may have been accompanied by evidence of a reaction—eg, fever occurring after an initially afebrile postoperative period, or jaundice. Deliberate reexposure can induce changes in liver function in sensitized subjects. It is difficult to explain why only 2 of the many anesthetists and others exposed repeatedly to halothane in the operating room have shown reactions.

(6) Malignant hyperpyrexia is a rare complication of halothane anesthesia that may develop slowly during the administration of halothane or appear abruptly following the injection of succinylcholine.

The syndrome, which is fatal in 70% of cases, is characterized by a rapid rise in temperature and other signs of increased muscle metabolism such as elevated blood pressure, tachycardia, and sweating. Muscle rigidity does not occur in the sporadic cases seen in older patients. Rigidity is always present in patients under 20 years of age who have a genetically determined predisposition or subclinical myopathy with elevated resting levels of creatine phosphokinase. The presumed immediate cause is an excess of myoplasmic calcium from an unidentified source. Treatment (generally unsuccessful) is with dantrolene (see Chapter 21).

ENFLURANE

Enflurane (Ethrane, $FClC-CF_2-O-CHF_2$) is an ether with general properties similar to those of halothane but producing, like diethyl ether, better muscular relaxation. The amount of agent metabolized (2%) and the serum fluoride levels seen are less than after the use of methoxyflurane, and renal toxicity has not been a problem. With deeper anesthesia and in the presence of hypocapnia, enflurane causes central nervous system stimulation, shown by a spike and dome pattern on the EEG and by muscle twitching.

METHOXYFLURANE

Methoxyflurane (Penthrane, $Cl_2HC-CF_2-O-CH_3$) is an ether that is a liquid with a comparatively high boiling point. It is the most potent agent available (0.5% concentration will maintain surgical anesthesia), but induction may require 20 minutes. Respiration must be assisted. Cardiovascular effects are less than with halothane, and muscular relaxation is better.

Methoxyflurane is metabolized in the liver, and both inorganic fluoride and nonvolatile organic fluorides are demonstrable in blood and urine after its use. The amounts of inorganic fluoride generated are sufficient to explain the "fluoride diabetes insipidus" seen to some extent in all patients after the use of methoxyflurane. The process is characterized by varying degrees of unresponsiveness to ADH (vasopressin), with polyuria, dehydration, and thirst, hyperosmolality of the plasma, and nitrogen and uric acid retention. Slow recovery usually occurs, but the number of reported fatalities is excessive considering the limited use of the drug.

FLUROXENE

Fluroxene (Fluoromar, $F_3C-CH_2-O-CH=CH_2$) is an ether that must be considered flammable, although the hazard is minor. Induction is rapid and pleasant, and recovery is very rapid. Cardiovascular changes are less than with halothane.

Fluroxene can be administered by all technics and appears to be useful for brief procedures.

CYCLOPROPANE

Cyclopropane $\left(\begin{array}{c} H_2C-CH_2 \\ \backslash / \\ C \\ H_2 \end{array}\right)$ is a gas given by the closed (total rebreathing) method for reasons of safety. The explosive hazard of cyclopropane use is real but can be guarded against, and it perhaps unduly restricted the use of this very good agent during the period when it had to be compared with ether, which is also explosive. Now, of course, it must be compared with nonexplosive halothane.

Induction is extremely rapid, and so also is the progression through the stages of anesthesia. Respiration is progressively depressed. Blood pressure and cardiac output are well maintained during anesthesia, and cyclopropane is still selected for use in patients in shock or in whom shock is impending.

CHLOROFORM

Chloroform ($CHCl_3$) is a volatile liquid that is more potent than ether. It is easily administered, but care is required. Initial concentrations that are too great will cause cardiac arrest by augmenting vagal tone. This effect is avoided by adequate premedication with atropine. (An alternative opinion ascribes accidents during induction to ventricular fibrillation due to sensitization of the myocardium to the effects of epinephrine.) With deep anesthesia, and a degree of hypercapnia, ventricular arrhythmias may occur. Chloroform is also hepatotoxic.

The use of chloroform was a matter of great controversy. Undoubtedly the dangers inherent in its use were exaggerated, but it is at least slightly more dangerous than other potent agents even when used for brief procedures, and alternative drugs are available.

NITROUS OXIDE

Nitrous oxide (N_2O, gas, laughing gas) is an incomplete anesthetic and the one most likely to be used by the general physician or dentist.

Potency & Effects

Nitrous oxide cannot depress the unpremedicated patient beyond stage 2. The greatest concentration of N_2O that can be used continuously without some degree of hypoxia is a 65:35 mixture in oxygen. With this concentration, or even an 80:20 mixture, the patient remains in stage 1 with euphoria and some analgesia. With an 85:15 mixture or a "few" breaths of 100% gas, the patient enters stage 2, with analgesia, euphoria, possibly excitement, giddiness, ringing in the ears, possibly a flushed face, variable amnesia upon recovery, and sometimes a dreamy or fantasizing state occasionally described inaccurately as hallucinatory.

Nitrous oxide does not cause respiratory depression or add to the respiratory depression of more potent agents. A depressant effect on the myocardium is barely measurable.

The euphoriant effect appears after a few breaths, and effects are stable after 2–3 minutes. Unpremedicated patients given a high initial concentration may experience the "rush" of the developing effect as pleasant or alarming, depending upon their prior experience.

Elimination of the gas is equally rapid, large volumes appearing in the expired air in the first 2–3 minutes. Nitrous oxide is not detectable in the blood after 10 minutes.

When a patient is changed from breathing a nitrous oxide mixture to room air, the large amounts of nitrous oxide entering the lung may cause a brief period of diffusion hypoxia. Since little nitrogen is absorbed into the blood from alveolar air, the entrance of N_2O into the alveoli will displace oxygen. A common practice is to prevent the hypoxia by giving the patient a few breaths of 100% oxygen during desaturation from nitrous oxide.

Adverse Reactions

A. Excitement: With greater concentrations of N_2O and in the presence of pain or other stimuli, the patient may become uncooperative.

B. Dreaming: Upon recovery, the patient may not separate fantasy or imagined events from reality and may accuse the practitioner of improper behavior. This is why it is recommended that a third person should be in the room during the administration of nitrous oxide.

C. Nausea: Nausea occurs in less than 1% of patients.

D. Flammability: Nitrous oxide is not explosive, but it can act like oxygen and support intense combustion. The danger is controlled in dental offices, for example, by the installation of proper equipment.

E. Abuse: Nitrous oxide is not generally available for use as a disinhibiting agent, but a startling number of dentists have become habituated. A few of the dentists who had subjected themselves to prolonged exposure developed sensory and motor changes in the legs similar to those seen as a result of the degenerative changes in the posterior and lateral (corticospinal) columns of the spinal cord seen in pernicious anemia. Slow recovery has been the rule, but at least one patient has sustained permanent damage.

Clinical Uses

In medicine, nitrous oxide can be used as an agent for induction after heavy premedication with narcotic analgesics and barbiturates. Its greatest usefulness, however, is as a component of balanced anesthesia. It is also used for production of intermittent analgesia during delivery.

Recent experience in dentistry has demonstrated the usefulness of nitrous oxide for producing continuous sedation during a procedure. A low concentration of N_2O (35–50%) is given through a nose mask. Local anesthesia is added, suggesting that the goal is not analgesia but sedation or the relief of anxiety.

KETAMINE

Ketamine (Ketaject, Ketalar) is an incomplete anesthetic that produces effects slightly more profound than those of N_2O. It can be given intravenously or intramuscularly.

Chemistry

Ketamine (2-chlorophenyl-2-methylaminocyclohexanone) is chemically and pharmacologically related to phencyclidine (phenyl-cyclohexyl-piperidine, PCP, Sernylan), an agent used in veterinary practice to immobilize primates and a drug commonly if illegally used by ingestion or smoking to produce euphoria and a fantasizing state.

Ketamine   Phencyclidine (PCP, Sernylan)

Pharmacologic Effects

Following the administration of ketamine, the patient rapidly passes into a fugue or trance: The eyes remain open, but the patient does not respond. Some movement may continue, and muscle tone and resistance to movement may be markedly increased. Good analgesia is produced, and there is later amnesia for the experience.

Respiration is not depressed except by large or too-rapidly administered doses. Whether laryngeal and pharyngeal reflexes are depressed sufficiently to make aspiration a danger is still arguable. Blood pressure and pulse rate are increased significantly.

The onset of action after intravenous administration is about 1 minute. The useful effect lasts 5–10 minutes after intravenous administration and 10–20 minutes after intramuscular administration. Complete recovery takes much longer.

For longer procedures, the dose can be repeated or the agent given intramuscularly.

Adverse Reactions

During recovery, adults frequently (incidence > 15%) experience vivid dreams that may be unpleasant and accompanied by excitement. Children are much less susceptible. (In considering the similarity of ketamine and nitrous oxide, recall the usual caution that nitrous oxide never be administered unless a third person is in the room to protect the operator from accusations based on dreaming or fantasizing.)

Clinical Uses

Ketamine is used by itself and mostly in children to provide analgesia during painful procedures—eg, burn dressings, cystoscopy.

INTRAVENOUS OR FIXED ANESTHETICS

Thiopental and similar ultrashort-acting barbiturates are shown in Table 23–3 and discussed in that chapter.

•   •   •

• • •

References

Atkinson RS: Trichloroethylene anaesthesia. Anesthesiology 21:67, 1960.

Black GW: A review of the pharmacology of halothane [Fluothane]. Br J Anaesth 37:688, 1965.

Britt BA: Etiology and pathophysiology of malignant hyperthermia. Fed Proc 38:44, 1979.

Bruce DL: What is a "safe" interval between halothane exposures? JAMA 221:1140, 1972.

Cohen EN: Metabolism of the volatile anesthetics. Anesthesiology 35:193, 1971.

Collins VJ: *Principles of Anesthesia,* 2nd ed. Lea & Febiger, 1976.

Cousins MJ, Mazze RI: Methoxyflurane nephrotoxicity: A study of dose response in man. JAMA 225:1611, 1973.

Duncum BM: An outline of the history of anesthesia, 1846–1900. Br Med Bull 4:120, 1946.

Dundee JW: Clinical pharmacology of general anesthetics. Clin Pharmacol Ther 8:91, 1967.

Eastwood DW (editor): *Nitrous Oxide.* Clinical Anesthesia Series. Davis, 1964. [Note chapter on ethylene.]

Eyring H & others: A molecular mechanism of general anesthesia. Anesthesiology 38:415, 1973.

Fairlie CW & others: Metabolic effects of anesthesia in man. 4. A comparison of the effects of certain anesthetic agents on the normal liver. N Engl J Med 244:615, 1951.

Halpren BA & others: Interstitial fibrosis and chronic renal failure following methoxyflurane anesthesia. JAMA 223:1239, 1973.

Inman WHW, Mushin WW: Jaundice after repeated exposure to halothane: A further analysis of reports to the Committee on Safety of Medicines. Br Med J 4:1455, 1978.

Kaufman RD: Biophysical mechanisms of anesthesia action. Anesthesiology 46:49, 1977.

Klatskin G, Kimberg DV: Recurrent hepatitis attributable to halothane sensitization in an anesthetist. N Engl J Med 280:515, 1969.

Koblin DD, Eger EI: Theories of narcosis. N Engl J Med 301:1222, 1979.

Layzer RB: Myeloneuropathy after prolonged exposure to nitrous oxide. Lancet 2:1227, 1978.

McPeek B, Gilbert JP: Onset of postoperative jaundice related to anesthetic history. Br Med J 3:615, 1974.

Ngai SH: Effects of anesthetics on various organs. N Engl J Med 302:564, 1980.

Price HL, Cohen PJ (editors): *Effects of Anesthetics on the Circulation.* Thomas, 1964.

Robinson V: *Victory Over Pain: A History of Anesthesia.* Schuman, 1946.

Thal ER, Montgomery SJ, Atkins JM: Self-administered analgesia with nitrous oxide. JAMA 242:2418, 1979.

Tomlin PJ: Health problems of anaesthetists and their families in the West Midlands. Br Med J 1:779, 1979.

Trey C, Lipworth L, Davidson CS: The clinical syndrome of halothane hepatitis. Anesth Analg 48:1033, 1969.

Vergani D & others: Sensitisation to halothane-altered liver components in severe hepatic necrosis after halothane anaesthesia. Lancet 2:801, 1978.

Wollman H, Greenhow DE (editors): Symposium on recent developments in anesthesia. Surg Clin North Am 55:757, 1975.

Wynne J: Hemodynamic effects of nitrous oxide administered during cardiac catheterization. JAMA 243:1440, 1980.

21 | Curariform or Neuromuscular Blocking Drugs

Drugs that paralyze voluntary muscle are used primarily as adjunctive agents during anesthesia. The pharmacology of these drugs has already been presented by implication in earlier chapters, along with the discussions of other drugs that act by blocking or intensifying the action of acetylcholine. Curare and related synthetic drugs act as competitive antagonists to acetylcholine and share properties with the ganglion blocking agents. In mechanism of action they are comparable to the parasympatholytics. The other large group of neuromuscular blocking drugs is similar to the cholinomimetic drugs (Chapter 8); the initial stimulating (depolarizing) effect is minimized, and the action in preventing repolarization of the motor end-plate is increased.

History

Indians in the farthest reaches of the Amazon and Orinoco Valleys and in the rain forests of Guiana used crude curare as an arrow and dart poison in hunting. They prepared a gummy aqueous extract from huge creeping vines, or "bushropes," (probably *Chondodendron tomentosum* in Ecuador and Peru and *Strychnos lethalis* in the more eastern area). Before the resinous mass was rubbed into the grooves in arrow tips, it was stored in gourds, clay pots, or bamboo tubes—thus the name tubocurarine for the alkaloid finally isolated from tube curare.

During the centuries following the Spanish conquest, many reports on the properties of curare were received in the Old World along with actual samples of tube, pot, and calabash (gourd) curare. One of these samples from the greatest of naturalist explorers, Humboldt, was given to Magendie, characterized in Chapter 1 as the man who first systematically applied the experimental method to physiology. Magendie used curare to immobilize experimental animals and transferred an interest in arrow poisons to his successor, Claude Bernard. Bernard demonstrated that, in an animal poisoned with curare, a muscle could still be directly stimulated even though it would not respond to stimulation of its nerve. This experiment was the first demonstration of the independent excitability of muscle and localized the action of curare at a site between nerve and muscle. He recognized that curare had no central nervous system effect and speculated that the apparently peaceful death it caused might actually be a horrifying experience for "an intelligence finding it-self still living in an unresponsive body."

Not until 1935 were reasonably standardized extracts of curare available, and the introduction of curare into the practice of anesthesia followed the work of Griffith in 1942.

Chemistry

The 2 major groups of curariform drugs—those that prevent depolarization and those that prevent repolarization or maintain depolarization—have certain similarities in chemical structure (Fig 21–1). For both groups, optimal activity is found in compounds that contain 2 quaternary nitrogens separated by a distance of about 1.4 nm, or the distance occupied by 10 intervening atoms. As with other agonists and antagonists discussed earlier, it is helpful to explain the similar structural requirements by using the concepts of affinity and intrinsic activity. A molecule with great affinity for the receptor at some postsynaptic site on the motor end-plate but lacking some additional property essential for initiating depolarization—eg, tubocurarine—will act as a competitive antagonist. A compound that combines affinity for the receptor with great intrinsic activity in initiating a response—eg, succinylcholine—will act like a great excess of the physiologic mediator acetylcholine.

A. Nondepolarizing Agents: Tubocurarine, the semisynthetic derivative dimethyltubocurarine, and gallamine, a synthetic drug, are examples of this group. The curarines are still derived from the plant source, but it is no longer necessary that they pass through the hands of an Indian witch. Agents of this class are also known as pachycurares because of their compact rather than linear molecular configuration; as stabilizing agents because they prevent the depolarizing effect of acetylcholine on the postsynaptic membrane; and as competitive agents because the effect can be overcome by the accumulation of an excess amount of acetylcholine.

B. Depolarizing Agents: Agents of this class that cause persistent depolarization are exemplified by succinylcholine or decamethonium (Fig 21–1). They are also occasionally referred to as leptocurares because of the apparent linear or threadlike configuration of the molecule.

Absorption, Metabolism, & Excretion

The available neuromuscular blocking agents are

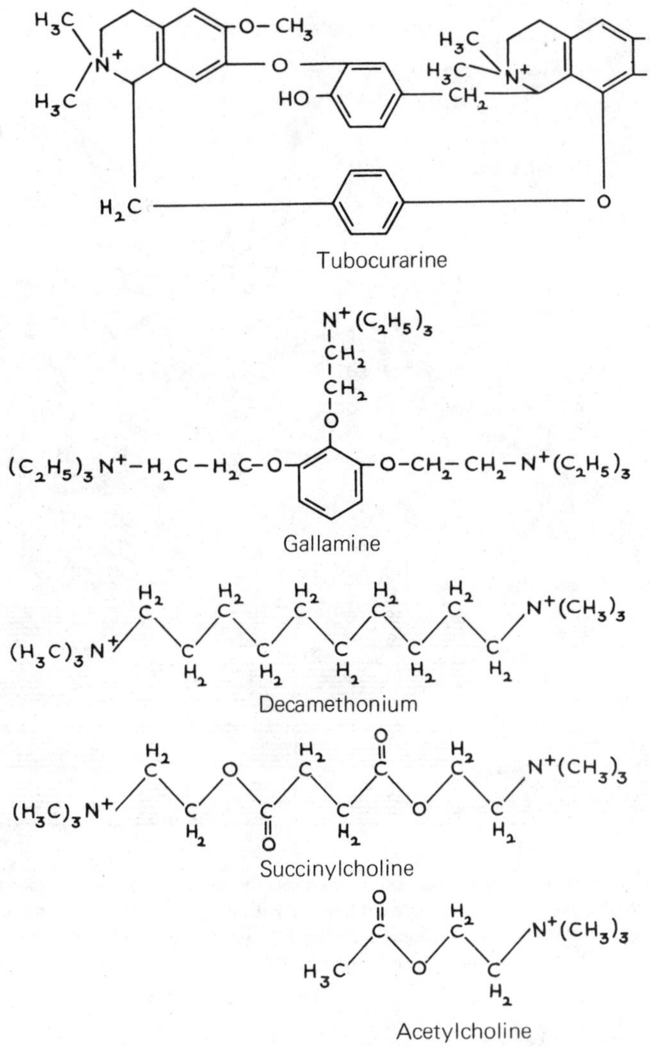

Tubocurarine

Gallamine

Decamethonium

Succinylcholine

Acetylcholine

Figure 21–1. *Above:* The chemical structures of 2 nondepolarizing pachycurares. *Below:* The structures of 2 depolarizing blocking agents are compared with acetylcholine.

all quaternary amines and are not suitable for oral administration. They are well absorbed from all injection sites, but the established uses all specify the intravenous route. None of these quaternary amines cross the placental barrier.

Tubocurarine is rapidly removed from plasma. Its metabolic fate is not known. It appears that the comparatively rapid termination of its action is due to redistribution rather than destruction or excretion.

Succinylcholine is hydrolyzed stepwise to succinylmonocholine and then to succinate and choline. Pseudocholinesterase governs the first step of the hydrolysis.

Pharmacologic Effects

A. Mechanisms of Action: The acetylcholine liberated by somatic nerve does not act diffusely or directly on striated muscle to depolarize it but acts first on the membrane of an intermediate structure, the

motor end-plate. The axon of the motor nerve divides as it approaches its termination on muscle, and variable numbers (5–300) of branches go to each fiber in the motor unit. At the neuromuscular junction, the axonal branch loses its myelin sheath and expands and branches into a folded end-foot with a great surface area (Fig 21–2). The underlying sarcoplasm is thickened and elevates the sarcolemma. The sarcolemma, in this area called the end-plate membrane, is complexly folded and closely applied to the end-foot of the axonal branch. However, an ultramicroscopic cleft separates the 2 structures, and, upon stimulation of the nerve, acetylcholine is liberated into the synaptic cleft to depolarize the end-plate membrane—ie, to generate an end-plate potential. Depolarization of the motor end-plate is propagated to the muscle mass.

1. Nondepolarizing agents–Tubocurarine and analogous compounds act at the motor end-plate in a manner comparable to atropine at parasympathetic

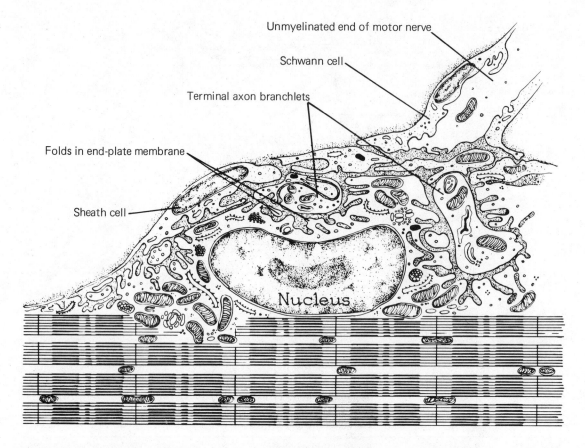

Figure 21–2. Neuromuscular junction. The drawing is based on electron micrographs of tissue from mice. It shows the terminal ends of a motor neuron axon buried in the end-plate cytoplasm, with the much folded end-plate membrane around them. (Modified and redrawn, with permission, from Anderson-Cedegren: Ultrastructure of motor end plate and sarcoplasmic components of skeletal muscle fiber. J Ultrastruct Res, Suppl 1, 1959.)

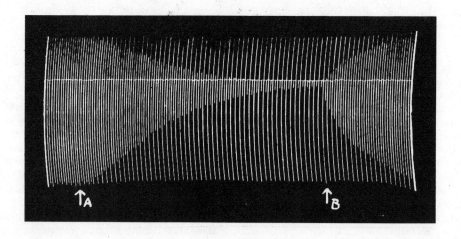

Figure 21–3. The action of tubocurarine on a preparation of rat diaphragm in an isolated tissue bath. Alternate stimuli are applied to the phrenic nerve and directly to the muscle. At *A,* 20 μg of D-tubocurarine chloride were added. Direct stimulation of the muscle continues to cause contraction, but indirect stimulation through the nerve loses its effect until, at *B,* the curare is washed out. (Reproduced, with permission, from Holmes & others: The analysis of the mode of action of curare on neuromuscular transmission. J Pharmacol Exp Ther 103:383, 1951.)

neuroeffector junctions. Acetylcholine is still liberated, but, in the presence of the blocking agent, depolarization of the postsynaptic membrane does not take place. The action is purely one of blockade, and no initial stimulation occurs (Fig 21–3). The relation between tubocurarine and acetylcholine is competitive and can be overcome by the increased amounts of acetylcholine that accumulate following the administration of a cholinesterase inhibitor such as neostigmine. Drugs that have themselves a strong acetylcholinelike action—eg, succinylcholine or other drugs of the depolarizing class discussed next—also antagonize the effects of curare.

2. Depolarizing agents–Succinylcholine and decamethonium act like a great excess of acetylcholine to depolarize the membrane of the motor end-plate and to prevent its repolarization. The initial phase of their activity, therefore, involves a dissolution of the resting potential or the appearance of an action potential and is accompanied by stimulation of muscular contraction prior to the development of a flaccid paralysis. The persistent depolarization involves only the region of the motor end-plate. The adjoining muscle has its usual resting potential but is inexcitable—a familiar if unexplained observation in electrophysiology called cathodal block. At least theoretically, the effect of these drugs is antagonized by blocking agents of the nondepolarizing type.

In the case of both classes of neuromuscular blocking drugs, direct stimulation of muscle causes contraction even though stimulation through the nerve is ineffective.

In the laboratory and evidently in some clinical situations, the above classification does not hold for large doses of succinylcholine or decamethonium. In this special case, the depolarizing effect (phase I) may be followed by a stage (phase II) during which the motor end-plate is repolarized but protected against the effects of acetylcholine, much as if curare had been used. If this second phase of "desensitizing block" is reached, the action of succinylcholine may be prolonged rather than brief.

B. Effects:
1. Skeletal muscle weakness and paralysis–
a. Nondepolarizing agents–After the intravenous injection of tubocurarine or related drugs, muscle weakness or flaccid paralysis, depending upon the dose, begins in less than 2 minutes and a maximal effect is reached within 5 minutes. Muscles of the face, neck, eyes, and pharynx are weakened first—leading, in the conscious patient, to difficulty in speaking, accumulation of secretions in the throat, and diplopia. Other small muscles such as those of the hand and the intercostal muscles are next affected, followed by action on muscles of the limbs, abdomen, chest, and finally, the diaphragm. The ability to maintain a sustained contraction is altered before the strength of a single contraction is weakened. The effect is first apparent upon sustained effort. In the anesthetized patient, the effect is seen after applying both single and rapidly repetitive (tetanizing) stimuli, when the nondepolarizing block is characterized by a decreasing response to repeated, single stimuli (fading) and poorly sustained tetanus.

b. Depolarizing agents–The initial stimulating effect of the depolarizing agents leads to incoordinated contraction of muscles. The stimulating effect causes fasciculations of groups of muscle fibers, apparent as rapid wormlike movements beneath the skin. The contractions may occasionally cause elevation of an arm or arching of the back. The stimulated contractions are equivalent to exercise to which the patient is unaccustomed and are followed during the postoperative period by muscle soreness in the neck, back, or pharynx.

During electrical stimulation, depolarizing block is seen to cause a weakening of contraction to a degree dependent upon dose. Additional fading after single stimuli is not seen, however, and tetanus is sustained but at a reduced level.

2. Other effects–Other pharmacologic effects must be related to the individual compounds rather than to groups of compounds. Tubocurarine, for example, causes some ganglionic blockade and is a weak histamine liberator. It may, therefore, cause a fall in blood pressure and bronchiolar constriction. Gallamine lacks those actions but antagonizes acetylcholine at cardiac vagal endings and may cause tachycardia. Succinylcholine has some cholinergic effects on the heart and may cause bradycardia.

Clinical Uses
A. Augmentation of Muscle Relaxation During Anesthesia: In addition to rendering the patient unconscious and preventing perception of and reaction to painful stimuli, optimal anesthesia provides enough voluntary muscle relaxation to permit the exposure needed (or deemed necessary) by the surgeon. If muscle relaxation is achieved by a curariform drug, less potent anesthetics can be used or smaller amounts of the complete anesthetics are needed during the procedure. Thus, "balanced anesthesia"—eg, thiopental-nitrous oxide-tubocurarine, as defined in the preceding chapter—can be used rather than deep anesthesia with ether. Furthermore, tracheal intubation can be carried out without or before deep anesthesia if the jaws and deeper structures are relaxed with succinylcholine.

This theory is widely accepted and is the basis for the almost invariable use of muscle relaxants. Nevertheless, when the practice was coming into use, study of over half a million anesthesias in 10 separate hospitals suggested an increase in deaths during the interval prior to actual surgery if curare had been used.

B. Modification of Convulsions Due to Electroconvulsive Therapy: The convulsions of electroshock therapy, still advisable for some depressed or schizophrenic patients, can collapse a vertebral body or even break a long bone. The muscular contractions can be weakened or even prevented by muscle relaxants without interfering with the therapeutic effect of the central nervous system discharge. For this purpose, the patient is given a single intravenous dose of succinylcholine after a few inhalations of oxygen. Thiopental anesthesia is usually also provided.

C. Other Suggested Uses: Curariform drugs have also been tried in various spastic and convulsive states, including tetanus. In each case, either the drug is not useful or other better treatments are available.

Contraindications & Cautions

The neuromuscular blocking drugs are ordinarily used by anesthetists who have the requisite experience and equipment. In other applications—eg, prior to electroconvulsive therapy—facilities for intubating and ventilating the patient should be available in the event of apnea.

The dosage of neuromuscular blocking agents is modified by interaction with other drugs and disease states.

A. General Anesthetics: When diethyl ether is used, the dosage of curare type agents is reduced about 65%; halothane and cyclopropane reduce the requirement by 20% or less.

B. Antibiotics: The effect of tubocurarine is intensified in some situations by neomycin, streptomycin, kanamycin, gentamicin, polymyxin B, and colistin.

C. Quinidine and Lidocaine: Isolated reports have appeared of recurarization when antiarrhythmic therapy is given during the postoperative period. The interaction is easily demonstrable in the laboratory.

D. Glaucoma: Succinylcholine, presumably by causing the initial contraction of extraocular muscles, elevates intraocular pressure and could be dangerous in the presence of acute glaucoma or a puncture wound of the globe. The effect can be prevented by the prior administration of a small (3 mg) dose of tubocurarine.

E. Myasthenia Gravis: These patients are very sensitive to nondepolarizing agents and very resistant to the depolarizing type.

Adverse Reactions

Apnea following the use of curariform drugs may extend into the postoperative period and may require assisted ventilation for extended periods. The unexpectedly prolonged action may follow overdosage or, in the case of succinylcholine only, may be due to a defect in the patient's ability to metabolize the drug.

A. Antagonists to Tubocurarine and Related Drugs: The nondepolarizing agents such as tubocurarine, dimethyltubocurarine, and gallamine can be antagonized by cholinesterase inhibitors of the type discussed in Chapter 8.

The cholinesterase inhibitors such as neostigmine and edrophonium (Tensilon) act predominantly by allowing the accumulation of acetylcholine liberated at the neuromuscular junction. They have, however, a direct action in strengthening the force of muscle contraction—ie, an effect that can be demonstrated on muscle following denervation when acetylcholine is not present.

Neostigmine (1–3 mg intravenously) or edrophonium (10–30 mg intravenously) will terminate the action of tubocurarine. They will intensify the action of the depolarizing type of blocking agent. They can be given combined with atropine to minimize parasympathomimetic effects on secretion. The effect of edrophonium lasts for only about 10 minutes.

B. Prolonged Apnea After Succinylcholine: In an occasional patient, the duration of action of succinylcholine following a single intravenous dose or following termination of a continuous infusion will be not the expected 2–4 minutes but 1–4 hours or more. This has not been completely explained. Most patients who experience apnea have adequate plasma cholinesterase levels and probably have developed a nondepolarizing block rather than the initial depolarizing block. The more persistent action may be due to succinylmonocholine, the first metabolic product of the hydrolysis of succinyldicholine.

A few apneic patients may show a deficiency of plasma cholinesterase, or pseudocholinesterase. This enzyme is differentiated from true cholinesterase by its ability to hydrolyze benzoylcholine and the ability of dibucaine to inhibit the reaction. There are few studies using succinylcholine itself as the substrate. Most individuals (96%) are homozygous for the gene determining the activity of this enzyme. At least 2 other genes occur at this locus, and a few individuals (1 in 2800) are homozygous for one of the mutants and are then grossly deficient in benzoylcholinesterase.

Dosages

A. Tubocurarine (D-Tubocurarine): In addition to its neuromuscular blocking action, tubocurarine can act weakly as an acetylcholine antagonist at ganglia and, like many other diamines, can act as a histamine liberator. These effects can cause a fall in blood pressure, and histamine release will on rare occasions lead to bronchiolar constriction.

The effect of tubocurarine, as of all of the drugs of this class, is almost immediate after intravenous injection. About 10 minutes after a single dose, the effect diminishes rapidly, and muscle strength is completely normal after about 40 minutes.

The dosage is variable and not predictable on the basis of weight or other apparent factors. The dose is, therefore, given fractionally or in increments until the desired effect is achieved. The average dose is about 6–9 mg intravenously. Ether anesthesia reduces the amount of curare required to about one-third of the usual dose.

Quinidine, lidocaine, and a number of antibiotics (neomycin, streptomycin, polymyxin B, colistin, kanamycin, and viomycin) may intensify the effects of curare.

B. Dimethyltubocurarine, or Metocurine (Metubine): This preparation is equivalent to tubocurarine but is about 3 times as potent.

C. Gallamine Triethiodide (Flaxedil): Gallamine has cholinolytic actions at the vagal as well as voluntary nerve endings and can cause tachycardia. Its duration of action is somewhat shorter than that of tubocurarine.

D. Pancuronium (Pavulon): In this compound the 2 quaternary ammoniums are separated by the steroid nucleus. It is generally similar to the other nondepolarizing relaxants, but the ganglion blocking and histamine liberating actions of tubocurarine and the consequent hypotension and bronchiolar constriction are virtually absent. The advantage claimed over gallamine is that there is no difficulty in reversing the action of large doses. Pancuronium is 5 times as potent as D-tubocurarine.

E. Succinylcholine (Anectine): In addition to the brief initial stimulation of voluntary muscle mentioned above, succinylcholine has other acetylcholinelike effects. These may result in bradycardia and a fall in blood pressure (parasympathomimetic effect) followed by tachycardia and a rise in blood pressure (sympathomimetic, or nicotinic, effect).

A single injection of about 30 mg intravenously given over a period of 10–20 seconds produces transient apnea. A sustained effect is accomplished by a continuous intravenous infusion of 2–4 mg/min.

F. Decamethonium (Syncurine): This depolarizing agent is now rarely used. It has a more sustained action than succinylcholine. Maximal effect after a single injection persists for 4–8 minutes and is completely dissipated in 20 minutes, when it is excreted into the urine.

DANTROLENE
(Dantrium)

Curare was purified and introduced into modern medicine in the hope that it would meet the great need for a treatment for spasticity—eg, in hemiplegia, paraplegia, or cerebral palsy. However, it causes general rather than specific relaxation and has not been useful. Dantrolene, introduced in 1974, is also a diffuse muscle relaxant. The use of sedatives as depressants of polysynaptic reflexes and as sedatives in the treatment of spasticity is discussed in Chapter 23.

The published literature on this drug is scanty.

Chemistry
Like phenytoin or similar anticonvulsants shown in Table 29–1, dantrolene is a hydantoin derivative.

Dantrolene (Dantrium)

Pharmacologic Action

Dantrolene has no effect on the release of acetylcholine or on membrane behavior, and the muscle itself still responds to electrical stimulation while the drug is acting—ie, the effect is exerted at a site beyond that of curare but proximal to the contractile mechanism in the poorly understood functional area of excitation-contraction coupling. Generalized muscle weakness is produced.

Clinical Use

An effect in relaxing spastic muscles following oral administration is demonstrable but small in degree. A parenteral dosage form is available for the treatment of malignant hyperthermia.

Adverse Reactions

The effect on spastic muscles cannot be intensified by increasing the dosage because of consequent diffuse muscle weakness. Diarrhea and sedation also appear. More importantly, when the drug is given chronically (more than 60 days), chemical evidence of liver damage appears in about 0.5–1% of patients, with fatal hepatitis in one or 2 patients per thousand trials. The risk appears great for the subtle improvement that is seen.

BACLOFEN
(Lioresal)

Baclofen, an analog of the neurotransmitter gamma-aminobutyric acid, was recently (1977) introduced as a muscle relaxant for the relief of spasticity. The drug is believed to act primarily by inhibiting the synaptic reflexes at the spinal level, but the mechanism of action is not known.

The drug has been recommended for the treatment of painful spasticity, clonus, and muscular rigidity of multiple sclerosis and other spinal cord disorders.

The central nervous system depressant properties of the drug may result in sedation with tolerance, postural hypotension, ataxia, and cardiorespiratory depression. Relief of spasticity, therefore, (as in the case of other muscle relaxants) may result in some loss of the patient's mobility. Experience with the drug has been relatively limited, and its long-term clinical usefulness remains to be established.

CYCLOBENZAPRINE
(Flexeril)

Cyclobenzaprine is another muscle relaxant drug pharmacologically similar to the tricyclic antidepressants. The drug has been recommended for relief of painful spasm associated with acute musculoskeletal disorders. Sedation is prominent. Experience with the drug has been too limited to permit critical appraisal.

This drug is discussed also in Chapter 28 as an equivalent to the antidepressants.

●　　●　　●

References

Beecher HK, Todd DP: A study of the deaths associated with anesthesia and surgery. Ann Surg 140:2, 1954.

Dantrolene hepatotoxicity. FDA Drug Bulletin 5:12, 1978.

Eckenhoff JE (editor): A symposium on muscle relaxants. Anesthesiology 20:407, 1959.

Flexeril: A new muscle relaxant. Med Lett Drugs Ther 20:9, 1978.

Foldes FF: The pharmacology of neuromuscular blocking agents in man. Clin Pharmacol Ther 1:345, 1960.

Hunter AR: Suxamethonium apnea. Anaesthesia 21:325, 1966.

Katz RL: Clinical neuromuscular pharmacology of pancuronium. Anesthesiology 34:550, 1971.

McIntyre AR: *Curare: Its History, Nature and Clinical Use.* Univ of Chicago Press, 1947.

Pittinger C, Adamson R: Antibiotic blockade of neuromuscular function. Annu Rev Pharmacol 12:169, 1972.

Rumble L & others: Observations during apnea in conscious human subjects. Anesthesiology 18:419, 1957.

Sachais BA, Logue JN, Carey MS: Baclofen, a new antispastic drug: A controlled multicenter trial in patients with multiple sclerosis. Arch Neurol 34:422, 1977.

Taylor DB, Nedergaard OA: Relation between structure and action of quaternary ammonium neuromuscular blocking agents. Physiol Rev 45:523, 1965.

Various authors: Dantrolene. Arch Phys Med Rehabil 55:331, 1974.

Way WL, Miller RD: Clinical pharmacology of neuromuscular blocking agents. GP 38:100, Dec 1968.

Local Anesthetics | 22

Local anesthetics can block conduction along the axon and can prevent the sense organ from initiating an afferent impulse. They are, therefore, applied to nerve roots or trunks or peripheral nerves or infiltrated into an area of the body to provide regional (or conduction) or local anesthesia—ie, anesthesia of an area without the loss of consciousness that attends general anesthesia. Motor and autonomic fibers are also blocked. Some of the local anesthetics may also act to anesthetize mucous membranes after topical application, and all have potentially dangerous systemic toxic effects after absorption.

History

The application of cocaine as the first local anesthetic grew out of the interest in its central nervous system stimulating effect. The history of such use is discussed together with that of amphetamine in Chapter 28.

Following a period of personal and professional use of cocaine as a euphoriant, Sigmund Freud and his chief, Joseph Breuer, invited a young ophthalmologist, Carl Koller, to collaborate in further study. Freud was primarily interested in the systemic effects of cocaine, but Koller had previously tested many drugs as local anesthetics in the eye without success. Credit is generally accorded Koller (1884) for introducing the concept of local anesthesia, especially since the experiments were done while Freud was away visiting his fiancée. William Halsted probably deserves credit for first defining and using regional anesthesia (1885).

Cocaine is an ester of benzoic acid, and synthetic substitutes that were esters of *p*-aminobenzoic acid soon appeared. In 1904, Fourneau introduced butethamine; but procaine, the compound synthesized by Einhorn, was unchallenged as the standard drug for 40 years. Drugs active after topical application to mucous membranes and some with a duration of action exceeding that of procaine were added. In 1943, lidocaine was introduced following the work of Löfgren and Lundquist and remains the most widely used local anesthetic. Since its introduction in 1973, bupivacaine, a versatile long-acting local anesthetic, has become increasingly popular.

Chemistry

A. Structure-Action Relationships: Certain generalizations about the structural requirements for local anesthetic activity are frequently made. A secondary or tertiary amine is linked through a connecting group of proper length to an aromatic residue (Fig 22–1). The same generalization about structure has been applied to other "membrane stabilizers," and the parasympatholytics, antihistamines, tranquilizers, and quinidinelike drugs generally are potent local anesthetics even though tissue irritation or other effects may preclude their use as local anesthetics. However, the compounds selected for use as local anesthetics do have some specificity in their action—ie, except for quinidinelike actions, they share few properties with the above classes of drugs.

Many substances are local anesthetics even though their chemical structure does not conform to the above generalization.

B. Chemical Classes: The commonly used local anesthetics can be classified on the basis of the connecting group between the amine function and the hydrocarbon residue. Thus, the common local anesthetics may be esters, amides, ethers, or ketones. (See Fig 22–1.) The esters may be further classified on the basis of the acid contributing to ester formation—eg, esters of benzoic acid or of *p*-aminobenzoic acid. An example of the variations and proliferation of compounds possible within just one of the general chemical classes is shown in Table 22–1.

One application of this classification arises in the rare situation of a patient or doctor allergic to a local anesthetic. Since cross-sensitivity to agents of the different classes does not occur, a substitute drug can be selected—eg, for a patient sensitized to procaine or other ester of *p*-aminobenzoic acid, an amide can be substituted.

Note that the suffix "caine" does not identify any one of the chemical groups.

C. Properties as Weak Bases: The local anesthetics (with the exception of a few topically active agents) are amines and are weak bases—ie, acceptors of hydrogen ion. The free base is an oil or amorphous solid, lipid-soluble but insoluble in water. Suspensions of the free base may be used, but the drugs are usually dispensed as crystals or aqueous solutions of a salt, almost always the hydrochloride. Solutions of the salts are acid (pH 4.0–6.0) and stable.

The salt of a weak base $R-NH_2$ and a strong acid hydrolyzes:

$$R-NH_2^+ + Cl^- \rightleftharpoons R-NH_2 + H^+ + Cl^-$$

In an acid solution (greater concentration of H^+), the local anesthetic will be present as the charged, salt form, which is water-soluble and less diffusible. At body pH or if alkali is added—ie, hydronium ions removed—the reaction will move to the right and a larger fraction of the local anesthetic will exist as the lipid-soluble, uncharged free base, which will partition more readily into the lipid material of the cell membrane. The drugs penetrate nerve in the form of the free base but are dispensed as clear solutions of the salt.

D. Pharmacologic Classification: Most of the local anesthetics listed below can be used either by injection or by topical application; a few are suitable only for topical application, and some, notably procaine, act only after injection. This property merely reflects the necessity of dispensing procaine in acid solutions, in which it is stable. In alkaline solutions, the lipid solubility and topical activity of procaine is greater. Cocaine has sympathomimetic properties and a potential for abuse, and it must be considered as a special case.

Absorption & Metabolism

The rate of absorption from the common sites of injection depends upon the vascularity and blood flow to the area and is similar to absorption after other intramuscular or subcutaneous injections. After application of local anesthetics to the mucosa of the pharynx or respiratory tract, blood levels may be almost as high and almost as rapidly attained as after intravenous injection.

Metabolism of the local anesthetics does not take place at the site of application but in the plasma or liver. Reducing blood flow to the site of injection and slowing absorption by the addition of a vasoconstrictor to the local anesthetic solution will, therefore, reduce systemic toxicity. Esters such as procaine are hydrolyzed by pseudocholinesterase of plasma. Amides such as lidocaine are hydrolyzed more slowly in the liver.

Pharmacologic Effects

A. Mechanism of Local Anesthetic Action: The local anesthetics act on all types of nerve fibers to block conduction. (Not all of the many compounds in use have been studied, but the properties of all are similar enough that it seems safe to generalize from the data acquired for procaine and a few other prototypes.)

1. Effects on electrophysiologic events–Conduction in segments of an axon proximal and distal to an area exposed to a local anesthetic is normal. In the segment exposed to concentrations of anesthetic above a certain threshold value, an action potential is not generated—ie, depolarization and propagation of the impulse stops when the wave of excitation reaches that part of the nerve exposed to the anesthetic. The resting potential is practically unchanged.

The changes in the electrical events and in conduction time are graded rather than all-or-none—ie, the earliest changes are a slowing of the rate of depolarization and of conduction, very much like those already described for quinidine.

Local anesthetics reversibly alter the action potential or stabilize the membrane by decreasing the permeability of the cell membrane to Na^+, thus blocking the first event in the generation of an action potential. The effect on K^+ conductance is minor—ie, the refractory period is altered only slightly at a time when the rate of rise of the spike potential is slowed. The effect on Na^+ transport is probably secondary to an effect on Ca^{2+} transport, since the local anesthetic appears to compete with Ca^{2+} for a receptor site on the interior (axoplasmic side) of the membrane.

2. Site of action and active molecular form–The potency of local anesthetics applied topically or to intact nerves is increased in alkaline solutions—ie, with more of the drug in the form of the free base.

Table 22–1. Structures of esters of *p*-aminobenzoic acid.

	R_1	R_2	R_3	R_4	R_5
Procaine				$-C_2H_5$	$-C_2H_5$
Chloroprocaine			$-Cl$	$-C_2H_5$	$-C_2H_5$
Butethamine					$-C_4H_7$
Naepaine					$-C_5H_{11}$
Proparacaine		$-O-C_3H_7$		$-C_2H_5$	$-C_2H_5$
Benoxinate		$-O-C_4H_9$		$-C_2H_5$	$-C_2H_5$
Propoxycaine			$-O-C_3H_7$	$-C_2H_5$	$-C_2H_5$
Tetracaine	$-C_4H_9$			$-CH_3$	$-CH_3$

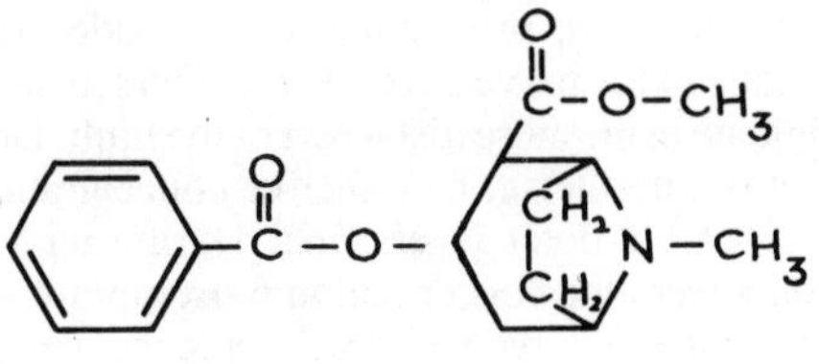

Ester of benzoic acid: cocaine

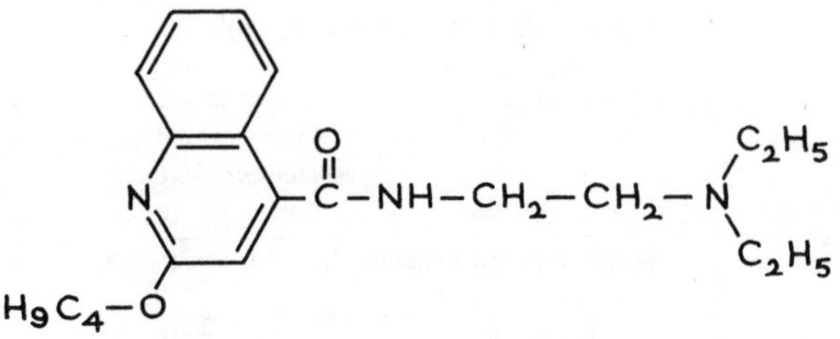

Amide: dibucaine (Nupercaine)

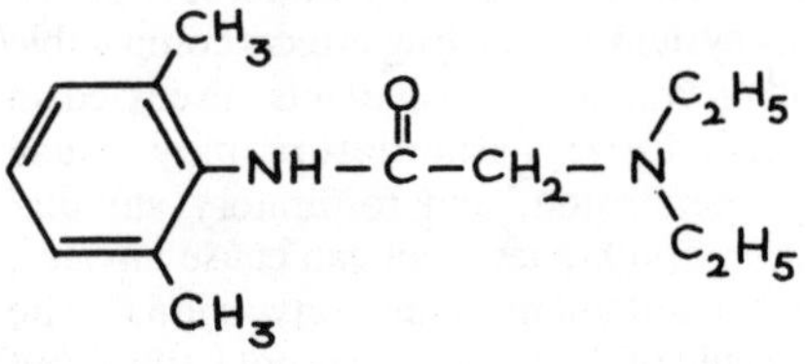

Amide: lidocaine (Xylocaine)

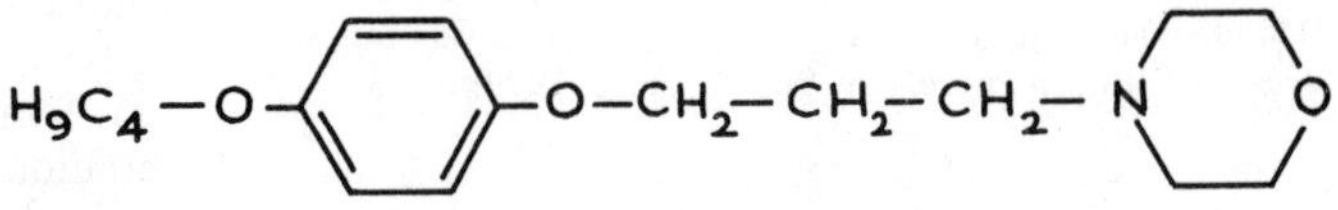

Ether: pramoxine (Tronothane)

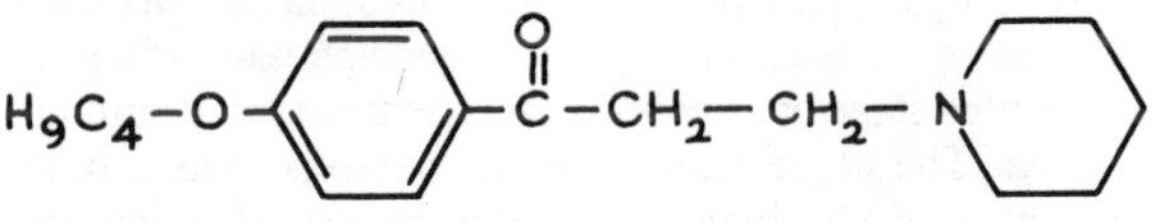

Ketone: dyclonine (Dyclone)

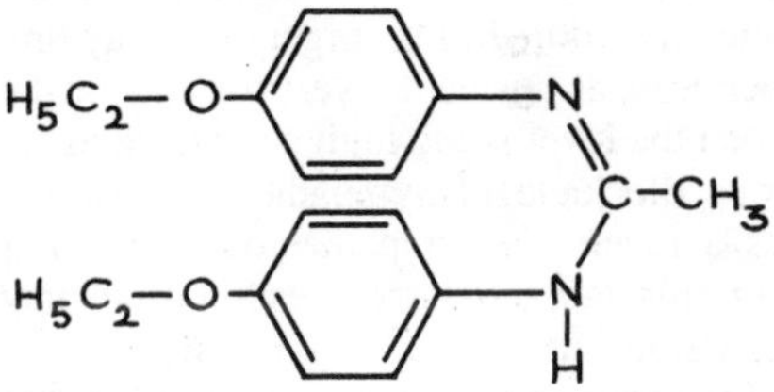

Phenetidin derivative: phenacaine (Holocaine)

Figure 22-1. Chemical classes of local anesthetics.

However, experiments on desheathed nerves suggest that the uncharged form merely diffuses to the axonal membrane more rapidly but that most of the local anesthetics are more active as cations in a neutral solution. Significant amounts of procaine are found in the axoplasm—ie, enter the cell—when the drug is applied to the (large, squid) axon.

A local anesthetic must cross the plasma membrane of the axon before it can act. The thicker a nerve fiber, the greater the concentration of local anesthetic required to block it. In the case of spinal anesthesia, the drug acts on nerve roots, and mixing and diffusion in the spinal fluid rapidly bring the local anesthetic into contact with the neuron. As the nerves course distally, they are surrounded more heavily by connective tissue structures (sheath, epineurium, perineurium) and the perilemma that is continuous with the pia-arachnoid. These structures slow access to the axon even if the local anesthetic is deposited on the nerve. As a result, axons in the outer layers of the nerve, the mantle fibers, are anesthetized before those in the nerve's center (the so-called core fibers). Using a stronger solution of anesthetic will hasten diffusion and the onset of anesthesia and also increase the chance of a toxic reaction. The popularity of some agents—eg, lidocaine—is based on their greater diffusibility and

more rapid onset of action.

All axons are embedded in the cytoplasm of Schwann cells, but the covering is interrupted by a continuous cleft, and in nonmyelinated nerves Schwann cells are not an important barrier to diffusion or to ion transport at the surface of the axon. In myelinated nerves, the Schwann cells have encircled the axon with layers of dense lipid that are barriers to the diffusion of drugs and also to ion transport. Local anesthetics act on myelinated fibers only at the nodes of Ranvier, where the myelin is interrupted. Depolarization also jumps from node to node, and the speed of conduction is greater in myelinated nerves. To be effective, a local anesthetic must be applied for a certain minimum distance along the length of the nerve, requiring a minimum span of 2 or 3 adjacent nodes.

B. Effects:

1. Local effects on neural transmission–The local anesthetics block transmission through all nerve fibers whether they are sensory, motor, or autonomic in function. The effect on specialized sensory receptors is either to prevent their depolarization by stimuli or to produce the equivalent effect by blocking conduction in their axon close to the sense organ.

Since all fiber types may be blocked, regional

Table 22–2. Nerve fiber types in mammalian nerve.*

Fiber Type		Function	Fiber Diameter (μm)	Conduction Velocity (m/s)
A	α	Proprioception; somatic motor	12–20	70–120
	β	Touch, pressure	5–12	30–70
	γ	Motor to muscle spindles	3–6	15–30
	δ	Pain, temperature	2–5	12–30
B		Preganglionic autonomic	< 3	3–15
C	dorsal root	Pain	0.4–1.2	0.5–2
	sympathetic	Postganglionic sympathetics	0.3–1.3	0.7–2.3

*Modified and reproduced, with permission, from Ganong WF: *Review of Medical Physiology,* 9th ed. Lange, 1979.

anesthesia can produce changes other than the primarily desired loss of sensation. The motor paralysis produced may have the desirable effect of producing good muscle relaxation during surgery but may limit patient cooperation, as during delivery; or may be dangerous, as when the level is too high and weakens respiratory efforts. Blockade of sympathetic transmission produces a reversible sympathectomy of a region; but during spinal or epidural anesthesia, it may lead to hypotension.

Local anesthetics may have a differential effect when applied to a mixed nerve because the smaller the fiber (axon), the more sensitive it is to the action of local anesthetics. (Table 22–2 summarizes the fiber types found in nerve. A fibers are myelinated; B fibers are lightly myelinated; C fibers are unmyelinated.) As regional anesthesia develops following the application of a local anesthetic to a nerve or nerve root, the first modalities affected are those mediated by small, nonmyelinated (C) fibers (ie, pain and vasoconstrictors maintained by sympathetic postganglionic activity) and small, myelinated (A δ) fibers (ie, pain and temperature). Other sensation mediated by large A fibers disappears next, and motor function (Aα) is the last to be affected.

The differential effects are most apparent during the development of the block and during recovery, but it is possible to achieve a persistent differential anesthesia—ie, sensory loss without muscle paralysis—by applying a suitably low concentration of the anesthetic.

During recovery, the least sensitive fibers recover first. After motor function returns, sensation returns as the more sensitive, small fibers regain function.

The least sensitive fibers are those with the thickest myelin sheath; however, the differential sensitivity is not related simply to the direct influence of the myelin sheath as a barrier, since the local anesthetics act only at the nodes of Ranvier.

Another differential effect is seen during the appearance and recovery from a nerve block and is related to the distribution of nerve fibers within the nerve

sheath. Block of both motor and sensory function begins proximally and progresses distally because fibers from the more proximal sites are added to the outer mantle of the nerve covering the fibers in the core that originate in the more distal part of the limb. During the onset of anesthesia, an effective concentration of drug reaches the outer layers first. During recovery, diffusion lowers the concentration most rapidly in the same area, so that recovery will proceed from the proximal to the distal part of the limb.

2. Central nervous system stimulation–All of the local anesthetics have, under certain conditions, central nervous system stimulating effects comparable to those of other convulsant stimulants discussed in Chapter 28. Medullary stimulation may cause bradycardia, hypertension, and respiratory stimulation. Stimulation of a higher level can cause anxiety, tremulousness, excitement, and convulsions. The mechanism and site of the last action is not known, but convulsions can still be produced in animals following decerebration.

3. Central nervous system depression–If the central nervous system stimulating effect progresses to convulsions, a period of postictal depression can occur. In addition, however, the local anesthetics have a primary depressant effect on the medulla and on higher centers. The depressed stage may occur without a prior excited stage or after only a transient period of stimulation. The depression of central nervous system function results in hypotension due to loss of vasomotor control, severe respiratory depression, and stupor or coma. The period of depression is more dangerous to the patient than the stimulated state and is intensified by barbiturates or similar drugs.

4. Cardiovascular effects–

a. Hypotension–The local anesthetics can alter blood pressure by several mechanisms. During the period of central nervous system stimulation, blood pressure may be elevated. It is, however, the later profound hypotension that occurs as a toxic effect during the period of central nervous system depression that is more dangerous. The hypotensive effect is intensified by the direct vasodilator effect of all local anesthetics except cocaine and is comparable to that described for quinidine and procainamide. A direct depressant effect on the heart can be demonstrated in the laboratory, although its clinical significance in toxic reactions to local anesthetics is not established.

b. Quinidinelike effects–The local anesthetics possess those cardiac actions described for quinidine and related antiarrhythmia drugs in Chapter 16. Lidocaine is used in the treatment of cardiac arrhythmia, and all local anesthetics are capable of producing the same changes in conduction as those described for quinidine.

5. Additional effects of cocaine–Cocaine has 2 general effects not shared with the other local anesthetics. It can be used by injection or ingestion or as snuff to produce a long-acting central nervous system stimulating effect generally comparable to that of amphetamine. Because of the feeling of euphoria at the time of injection and the stimulation produced, cocaine may be misused.

In addition, cocaine has sympathomimetic properties due to its ability to prevent the reentry into sympathetic nerve of norepinephrine liberated at the nerve ending. Of the norepinephrine liberated by sympathetic nerves as a chemical mediator, about half reenters the terminal portion of the sympathetic nerve. Cocaine's ability to block norepinephrine reuptake results in its sympathomimetic actions. It will potentiate injected sympathomimetics, dilate the pupil, and, most important in relation to its use as a local anesthetic, act as a vasoconstrictor either after injection or when applied topically to a mucous membrane.

6. Other effects–Procaine and related drugs are weak antihistamines and even weaker parasympatholytics. In large doses they possess curarelike activity; however, this action has little clinical significance.

Clinical Uses & Technics of Administration

The choice of the local anesthetic preparation and its potential toxicity are influenced by the anesthetic technic employed.

A. Topical Application: Not even those local anesthetics classified as topically active can penetrate the keratinized surface of the intact skin. It is conceivable that the free base in a proper oily vehicle or solvent could act on the skin, but no useful preparation is now available. The local anesthetics will act on grossly denuded skin, but far more important is their ability to anesthetize mucosal surfaces that are not keratinized. The corneal surface or the mucosa of the mouth, oral and nasal pharynx, larynx, trachea, and urethra are easily anesthetized. The discomfort of an endoscopy or other procedure and pain (eg, the pain of a herpetic lesion) can be reduced.

Absorption of the agent from a mucosal surface is extremely rapid, and the total dose used should be no more than one-quarter the maximum allowed for injection. Premedication with a sedative-hypnotic, eg, diazepam, may reduce the incidence of toxic reactions.

Procaine and closely related compounds are not topically active. Many agents are marketed only for topical use either in the eye or, with little justification, on the skin.

B. Local Infiltration: In all of the remaining technics of administration, the anesthetic agent is injected. The site of injection may be anywhere along the course of the nerve from the peripheral receptor to the entry of the nerve root into the central nervous system.

Infiltration anesthesia is produced by injecting the agent throughout the area to be rendered insensitive. Infiltration along the line of an incision or infiltration of the edges of a laceration to be sutured are the most common examples. As is true for most of the injection technics, this procedure usually begins with the production of a wheal in the overlying skin, using a small needle. A larger needle is then introduced through the insensitive area in the skin. The needle advances along an area of decreased sensitivity provided by injecting the agent through the advancing needle, carefully aspirating for blood before injecting in order to avoid an intravascular injection.

C. Field Block: In producing a field block, the anesthetic agent is injected not into the area to be dissected but into an area surrounding it. Field blocks are applicable to the scalp and anterior abdominal wall where nerves course superficially to reach the area to be anesthetized.

D. Peripheral Nerve Block: Local anesthetics may be deposited close to a mixed nerve or nerves—eg, the palatine, inferior alveolar, pudendal, the brachial plexus, and many others—and the area innervated will become anesthetized.

E. Spinal (Subarachnoid) Anesthesia: The term spinal anesthesia denotes subarachnoid or intrathecal injection of a local anesthetic agent. For the production of spinal anesthesia, a lumbar puncture is done—ie, the point of the needle enters the dural sac lower than the most caudal extension of the spinal cord. A previously prepared solution of the local anesthetic is injected, or the crystalline agent is dissolved in cerebrospinal fluid which is then reinjected. The local anesthetic solution may be made heavier (hyperbaric) by using 10% dextrose or lighter by using sterile water as the solvent.

Following the injection, functions disappear in the order described above, and a level of anesthesia is established. The level must be high enough to permit performance of the desired procedure without pain but should not be needlessly high in order to prevent respiratory weakness or severe hypotension and central nervous system depression (including transient loss of consciousness). The level is controlled by altering the volume of solution injected, the rate of injection, the amount of local anesthetic, and the position of the patient. The anesthetic agent is rapidly removed from the cerebrospinal fluid and fixed in the nerve roots and sensory ganglia, and the height of the level does not vary after about 15 minutes.

Spinal anesthesia produced by tetracaine, probably the currently most commonly used agent, lasts for 1–2 hours. Procaine and lidocaine are shorter-acting agents. The duration of spinal anesthesia can be increased about one-third by the addition of 0.2 mg (0.2 mL of 1:1000) epinephrine.

A variation of spinal anesthesia commonly used for obstetric analgesia is called saddle block. With the patient in a sitting position, a hyperbaric solution is injected and settles to the lowest portion of the dural sac, where it anesthetizes those nerve roots that originate from the most terminal segments of the cord, ie, those that innervate the body segments that would be in contact with a saddle.

F. Epidural Anesthesia: In this technically more difficult procedure, the point of the needle enters the epidural space, which is not fluid-filled and which extends from the foramen magnum to the sacral hiatus. The concentration and total dose of the local anesthetic is very large, and care must be taken to prevent its subarachnoid injection. Since the subarachnoid space is not entered, spinal headaches are less common and patients are less likely to object to the procedure.

In caudal anesthesia, a technically simpler variation of epidural anesthesia, a needle enters the epidural space through the sacral hiatus below the termination of the dural sac. Anesthesia of only the most caudal segments can be achieved, making the method suitable for obstetric analgesia and lower abdominal or superficial lower extremity procedures. A catheter can be inserted through the lumen of the needle and left in place for periodic supplementation of anesthesia (continuous caudal anesthesia).

Adverse Reactions

A confusing variety of reactions can occur just after the injection of a local anesthetic, and they may or may not be related to the effect of the drug used. Conventionalized definitions and terms must be used accurately to minimize confusion. Overdosage toxicity can occur, and one patient may be affected by a smaller dose than another. Such a response should never be described as "hypersensitivity," a term preempted by the immunochemist and denoting true allergy. Allergic reactions to the local anesthetics are extremely rare. Anxiety is very common during the procedure and may culminate in vasovagal syncope. If a vasoconstrictor is added to the anesthetic solution, it may reach toxic levels and thereby produce symptomatic sympathetic stimulation. For these reasons, reactions not directly related to the anesthetic agent as well as direct toxic reactions are discussed separately.

A. Overdosage Toxicity: Dose-related toxic reactions occur when the precautions outlined below are not followed and an excessive amount of drug enters the systemic circulation in a brief time. These incidents occur most often prior to endoscopy when a mucosal surface is flooded with solution, giving poor control of the total amount. Toxic reactions are also seen during obstetric procedures and other situations in which multiple or repeated injections may be given. Dentists are responsible for very little overdosage toxicity, however many vasovagal reactions they may induce.

The reaction may involve transient or persistent central nervous system stimulation followed by central nervous system and cardiovascular depression, or the depressed stage may appear without apparent prior central nervous system stimulation. The initial symptoms consist of generalized sensations of lightheadedness or dizziness and auditory or visual disturbances (eg, tinnitus, blurred vision). Stimulation may first be apparent as excitement, apprehension, slurred speech, shivering, or nausea. At this time, the pulse rate will usually be slightly slowed and blood pressure slightly elevated. Respiration will be increased in rate and depth. The skin will be pale, cool, and moist, and the total picture will resemble an epinephrine effect or severe anxiety. More profound central nervous system stimulation will lead to preconvulsive muscular twitchings and then to convulsions. At this time, blood pressure and pulse rate will be elevated, and even between convulsions the patient may be dyspneic and cyanotic,

with rapid, shallow respirations. Following the period of excitement (or without going through a period of excitement), the patient will be depressed and may lapse into shock due to the mechanisms mentioned above—ie, medullary depression, vasodilatation, and postconvulsant depression. Areflexia and coma, extreme hypotension, and respiratory failure may follow.

Treatment of overdosage: Treatment differs depending upon whether it is given in the early (convulsive) or late (shock) stage. Vigorous treatment of the convulsive stage may intensify the difficulties of the shock stage.

(1) Convulsions: The period of convulsions is so alarming that the patient is likely to be overtreated. The convulsions are self-limited and usually well tolerated if the patient is kept oxygenated and ventilation is assisted if necessary. Oxygen together with masks and bag should be available whenever local anesthesia is given. A patient who is oxygenated between convulsions can be carried through the period of excitation without being subjected to the hazard of receiving central nervous system depressant drugs that add to the postictal depressed state or the primary depression.

A variety of further treatment methods have been suggested to control the convulsions. If an anesthetist is in attendance and prepared to give intravenous medications and to control ventilation, the peripheral manifestations of the convulsant activity may be blocked with succinylcholine. Various intravenous barbiturates or benzodiazepines are suggested, but even the shortest-acting barbiturates may add a hazard to the later course of the patient.

(2) Shock: Treatment of the depressed or shock stage is the same as for any other form of shock, but the prognosis is much less favorable. Because of the respiratory depression, the need for assisted ventilation is greater in this than in other forms of shock. Vasopressors have been used, but the results are unimpressive.

B. Allergic Reactions:

1. Systemic reactions–Anaphylactic reactions following the use of local anesthetics are theoretically possible but are extremely rare. Ester derivatives of p-aminobenzoic acid, eg, procaine and tetracaine, are responsible for most of the suspected allergic reactions attributed to local anesthetics. Dentists occasionally observe facial swelling in their patients several hours after the injection of a local anesthetic. The swelling is not due to hemorrhage and is suggestive of angioneurotic edema.

2. Dermatitis–Topical sensitization to local anesthetics requires frequent contact. It is occasionally seen in dentists who repeatedly get the drug on their fingers.

C. Sequelae of Spinal Anesthesia:

1. Hypotension–Spinal anesthesia may lead to hypotension due to blockade or sympathetic vasoconstrictor fibers. The higher the level of spinal anesthesia, the more intense the hypotension may become. Prophylactic hydration with 500–1000 mL of a balanced salt solution will avoid the hypotension usually associated with spinal anesthesia. Vasopressor drugs—eg, ephedrine or other sympathomimetic amine—may be injected prior to spinal anesthesia when hypotension is anticipated, or they may be given to treat hypotension when it develops.

2. Trauma of lumbar puncture–The anesthetist is generally more skilled in performing a lumbar puncture than most practitioners, but even an anesthetist may traumatize the area, causing a transient backache. Whenever the dural sac is punctured, there is always the risk of postspinal headache due to leakage of cerebrospinal fluid.

3. Neurologic damage–Spinal anesthesia does not differ appreciably from general anesthesia in the incidence of serious complications or less dangerous side-effects. Rare cases of lasting spinal cord or nerve root damage have occurred, but these episodes have been less frequent since the methods of handling and sterilizing the ampules of the drug were changed. The necessary precautions involve not only the physician and pharmacist but also the administrators responsible for drug storage and distribution. The assumption now is that neurologic damage due to spinal or epidural anesthesia is caused by the introduction of chemical or bacterial contaminants with the agent or the use of improper concentrations of the local anesthetic. Such contamination leads to meningitis (aseptic, purulent, or chronic adhesive) with signs varying from a minor cauda equina syndrome to transverse myelitis. Recently, case reports have appeared in the anesthesia literature regarding irreversible nerve damage when high concentrations of procaine were inadvertently injected into the subarachnoid space.

The following precautions should be observed: (1) Ampules containing the local anesthetic should be sterilized by autoclaving either on the spinal tray or in glass tubes from which they can be dumped onto the open spinal tray without introducing contamination or being themselves contaminated in the process. The ampules must not be sterilized by immersing in any germicidal solution, since imperceptible cracks in the glass may admit the irritant solution to the inside of the ampule. (2) Syringes and needles must be rinsed with special care after cleaning so that detergents or other chemical irritants do not adhere. Disposable equipment offers an advantage in this respect. (3) Skin preparation and sterile technic should be carried out with great care. (4) If the lumbar puncture is extremely difficult, plans for the anesthesia should be modified. (5) If paresthesias, indicating contact with nerve tissue, persist after insertion of the needle, it should be repositioned before injection of the local anesthetic.

D. Other Adverse Effects: Prolonged use of any of the local anesthetics in the eye can lead to keratitis comparable to that which occurs following sensory denervation.

Following paracervical block, a significant fetal bradycardia or tachycardia may occur. Studies of concurrent maternal and fetal blood levels suggest that the drug reaches the placenta and fetus by direct entry from the injection site rather than by transfer from maternal to fetal circulations.

E. Reactions Not Due to the Local Anesthetic Agent:

1. Vasovagal syncope–The common faint (sometimes called primary shock or neurogenic fainting) must be differentiated from drug reactions. This type of fainting occurs in patients who react with great anxiety to the impending procedure and especially to the ordeal of the needle. During the period of anxiety, the patient shows the usual signs of epinephrine release. With the sudden release of anxiety when the injection is completed and the needle withdrawn, some additional stimulus initiates an intense vagal surge, with resultant bradycardia and peripheral pooling of blood leading to hypotension, which causes, in turn, cerebral ischemia and fainting. At the moment of fainting, the pulse is slow and bounding, but the patient has the appearance of one in shock, ie, is pale, cool, and sweating. The faint is benign unless the patient is kept erect or has significant cerebral or coronary vascular disease.

2. Reaction to epinephrine–Anesthesia for some procedures requires injection into highly vascular areas, and the duration of anesthesia is often unsatisfactory unless epinephrine is added to the solution. The epinephrine could conceivably precipitate anginal pain in a patient with coronary artery disease.

The dentist is especially sensitive to the possible dangers of added vasoconstrictor because the referring or consulting physician may forbid the use of epinephrine. The 1.8-mL cartridge of local anesthetic typically used in dental practice contains 18 μg of epinephrine. Only if it were injected into a vein as a bolus would such a dose have even a brief effect on cardiac work. (Fig 11–2 shows the effect in the human of the intravenous injection of about that dose over a period of 15 seconds.)

The interprofessional groups that have made recommendations in this area emphasize that the amounts of epinephrine provided are small compared to the amounts endogenously liberated by an anxious patient and especially by a patient experiencing pain due to inadequate anesthesia. Slow injection, the use of the smallest amounts of solution possible, and perhaps premedication to minimize anxiety permit the use of epinephrine-containing solutions, even in patients with angina.

Epinephrine, 1:250,000, gives a maximal effect in prolonging the duration of anesthesia. Commercially prepared local anesthetic solutions containing epinephrine are buffered to a lower pH to minimize oxidation of the vasoconstrictor. As a result, the acid solutions seem to be less effective than the nearly neutral standard local anesthetic solutions.

Contraindications & Cautions

The only absolute contraindication to the use of local anesthetics is injection into an infected area. A number of precautions are important.

A. Control Total Dose: The lowest effective concentration and the smallest effective total volume of a local anesthetic should be used. The need to increase the concentration or volume above accepted levels often suggests inadequate technic.

The package inserts for each local anesthetic preparation establish a maximum total dose for various technics. These assume that there will be no difficulty such as inadvertent intravascular administration. If repeated injections are necessary for extensive procedures or because an initial injection was unsuccessful, an interval of even a few minutes between applications greatly enhances safety.

B. Add Vasoconstrictors to Injected Anesthetics: The addition of epinephrine to all but topically applied anesthetics reduces blood flow through the infiltrated area and slows absorption of the local anesthetic. The duration of the anesthetic effect is prolonged, and, since biotransformation can keep pace with a slower rate of absorption, blood levels do not rise as high and toxicity is decreased.

The addition of epinephrine is especially indicated when injection is into a very vascular area or when more concentrated solutions of the anesthetic are used.

Epinephrine should not be added to solutions to be injected into the fingers, ears, or penis, since vasoconstriction can lead to tissue necrosis.

C. Premedication: In the laboratory, sedation with a barbiturate or benzodiazepine provides protection against convulsions and the immediate toxicity of local anesthetics. The effect on total mortality rates— ie, early and late—is less. Adequate premedication of the human subject with barbiturates would presumably provide similar protection, but the effectiveness of the small doses usually used is probably very limited.

D. Avoid Intravascular Injection: The most important precaution in avoiding intravenous injection is to give the injection slowly so that pressure does not build up locally and force the solution into vessels. Aspirating before injection may draw blood into the syringe if the needle is in a vessel or if a vessel has been opened by the point of the needle—providing the needle is not too small. If blood is aspirated, the needle should be repositioned, but failure to aspirate blood does not protect against intravascular injection as well as does slow injection. Finally, the quality of the field block produced by local infiltration is improved and the possibility of an intravascular injection lessened if the drug is injected while the needle is being withdrawn.

Selection of Drugs

A. How Available Drugs Differ: It has already been emphasized that not all of the marketed local anesthetics are active after topical application and that others, because of local irritative effects or because limited investigative work has been performed, are suitable only for topical application. Those local anesthetics intended for use by injection do differ considerably among themselves. However, the properties of potency, toxicity, and duration of action generally change together; and an advantage gained by altering one property is often lost by a correlated change in another. The evaluation of a compound, therefore, is dependent upon the intended use.

1. Potency and systemic toxicity–Potency can be evaluated in the laboratory in many ways, eg, by determining the concentration necessary to abolish the corneal reflex in rabbits or to block conduction in an isolated nerve trunk. Ultimately, potency is measured as the least concentration required to consistently produce a particular block in humans.

Systemic toxicity in the human is accurately predicted by determinations of median lethal doses in animals. The LD_{50} is not an absolute value but depends upon species, route of administration, concentration of the injected solution, and many other variables. The toxicity of local anesthetics can be compared only if the determinations are made under identical conditions.

In the compounds now available for use, anesthetic potency and systemic toxicity have not been separated, and the more potent drugs are also the more toxic.

2. Duration of action–The duration of action generally correlates well with potency and systemic toxicity. When a longer duration of action is an important consideration in the intended use, a more toxic drug must be selected. Thus, tetracaine is widely used in spinal anesthesia because of its somewhat longer duration of action, but it is uncommonly used for other technics. Dibucaine may be used, even though its greater toxicity virtually contraindicates its use in any other situation except topical application.

3. Onset of action–The interval between deposition of the local anesthetic and appearance of complete anesthesia is a property that is also correlated with the above 3.

4. Diffusibility–Some agents have a latent period that is shorter than would be predicted by their potency. The same drugs appear to produce a good block more dependably than other agents when they are deposited slightly distant from the intended site. This decreased latent period and increased tolerance for minor errors in technic is probably related to the greater diffusibility of the particular drug. This property has been important in establishing the wide use of lidocaine.

B. Injectable Local Anesthetics: Many local anesthetics are available. Those with distinctive properties have already been mentioned. Many are advertised for specific applications—eg, dental anesthesia—without any established superiority over older, unprotected compounds.

A few local anesthetics suggested for use by injection can be categorized as follows:

1. Procaine was the standard drug but has been supplanted by lidocaine. Chloroprocaine (Nesacaine) is more rapidly hydrolyzed than procaine; it acts for a shorter period but is less toxic. Hexylcaine (Cyclaine) is an example of a related drug of intermediate potency and duration of action; in a situation in which procaine produces anesthesia for 1 hour, the action of the intermediate drugs may persist for 1½–2 hours.

2. Lidocaine and related amides have the advantages inherent in their greater diffusibility and intermediate duration of action. Mepivacaine (Carbocaine) is slightly longer acting than lidocaine. Prilocaine (Citanest) has intermediate properties but can produce methemoglobinemia.

3. Tetracaine (Pontocaine), dibucaine (Nupercaine), and bupivacaine (Marcaine) have distinctively long durations of action.

4. Eleven local anesthetics are approved for dental use by the ADA. The 3 amides mentioned above (lidocaine, mepivacaine, and prilocaine) have replaced procaine in use. Propoxycaine (Blockain and in the mixture Ravocaine) and tetracaine are more toxic. The others (isobucaine, meprylcaine, metabutethamine, butethamine, and pyrrocaine) offer no advantages over lidocaine.

C. Topical Anesthetics:

1. Cocaine–Of the topically active agents, cocaine is distinctive in its ability to cause vasoconstriction when applied to mucous membranes. Its use is now limited to application to the mucosa of the nose and pharynx. In other applications, it has been replaced by less irritant and more easily dispensed drugs.

2. Benzocaine–Benzocaine (ethyl aminobenzoate) is a substance with very low solubility in water that is present in proprietary sprays, powders, and creams. It acts briefly—ie, only for as long as it is in contact with a mucosal surface.

●　　●　　●

References

Adriani J: Reactions to local anesthetics. JAMA 196:405, 1966.

Adriani J, Zepernick R: Clinical effectiveness of drugs used for topical anesthesia. JAMA 188:711, 1964. [Or Clin Pharmacol Ther 5:49, 1964.]

American Dental Association and American Heart Association: Management of dental problems in patients with cardiovascular disease: Report of a joint conference. J Am Dent Assoc 68:333, 1964.

Covino BG: Local anesthesia. (2 parts.) N Engl J Med 286:975, 1035, 1972.

Covino BG & others: Prolonged sensory/motor deficits following inadvertent spinal anesthesia. Anesth Analg (Cleve) 59:399, 1980.

De Jong RH: *Physiology and Pharmacology of Local Anesthesia,* 2nd ed. Thomas, 1977.

Johnson HA: Infiltration with epinephrine and local anesthetic mixture in the hand. JAMA 200:990, 1967.

Keesling GR, Hinds EC: Optimal concentrations of epinephrine in lidocaine solutions. J Am Dent Assoc 66:337, 1963.

Kennedy BR, Duthie AM, Parbrook GD: Intravenous regional analgesia: An appraisal. Br Med J 1:954, 1965.

Lee AG: A consumer's guide to models of local anesthetic action. Anesthesiology 54:64, 1979.

Moore DC & others: Bupivicaine: A review of 11,080 cases. Anesth Analg (Cleve) 57:42, 1978.

Park WK & others: Effects of patient age, pH of cerebrospinal fluid, and vasopressors on onset and duration of spinal anesthesia. Anesth Analg (Cleve) 54:455, 1975.

Phillips OC & others: Neurologic complications following spinal anesthesia with lidocaine: Prospective review of 10,440 cases. Anesthesiology 30:284, 1969.

Sharpey-Schafer EP, Hayter CJ, Barlow ED: Mechanism of acute hypotension from fear or nausea. Br Med J 2:878, 1958.

Smith BE, Hehre FW, Hess OW: Convulsions associated with anesthetic agents during labor and delivery. Anesth Analg (Cleve) 43:476, 1964.

Vandam LD, Dripps RD: Long-term follow-up of patients who received 10,098 spinal anesthetics. 4. Neurologic disease incidental to traumatic lumbar puncture during spinal anesthesia. JAMA 172:1483, 1960.

23 | Sedative–Hypnotics

The sedative-hypnotic drugs have pharmacologic properties that are quite similar to those of the general anesthetics. When large doses are used, as in a suicidal attempt or when a barbiturate such as thiopental is used to induce general anesthesia, the difference between a sedative-hypnotic and a general anesthetic disappears. General anesthetics are gases or volatile liquids selected from among the general central nervous system depressants because their physical properties allow rapid onset and ready reversibility of action. The sedative-hypnotics are solid or liquid substances that cause generalized depression of the central nervous system for a longer period than do the rapidly exhaled gases. They are thus more conveniently compounded and more suitable for oral administration for the induction of sleep or the relief of anxiety.

These 2 uses—the induction of sleep and the symptomatic relief of anxiety—represent a huge need and market, and the proliferation of compounds is correspondingly great. Loose application of the term "tranquilizer" has led to additional confusion. Before the many individual compounds in this general class of drugs are identified, a preliminary discussion of the classification of drugs is required.

Classification of Drugs
(See Table 23–1)

It is not necessary or feasible for individual physicians to evaluate separately each of the many drugs

available and suggested for use in practice. The more recently introduced and vigorously promoted drugs provide the greatest challenge to the confidence of a physician. Genuinely new drug effects are in fact discovered at intervals of several years, usually with great impact on medicine; but most new drugs are selected for marketing not because they are essentially different from other drugs but because they are similar to drugs that have already been marketed successfully. It is, therefore, usually possible and efficient to study the effects of a large group of drugs or of a prototype drug and then look for smaller variations within the group. Classifications in general break down at the borders between categories, but this is not usually true for drugs because they are usually selected prior to marketing to conform to the classification. This chapter will emphasize data that justify including the many drugs listed in the broad class of sedative-hypnotics.

A Further Note on Terminology

These preliminary cautions are necessary because it has been difficult to integrate the new antipsychotic tranquilizers and a large number of recently marketed sedatives into medical practice.

The sedative class of drugs, exemplified by the barbiturates, has been used for the relief of anxiety and the induction of sleep since about 1903. After 1950, the antipsychotic tranquilizers were recognized as a separate class of drugs, and their use revolutionized the institutional practice of psychiatry. Physicians in noninstitutional practice, dealing regularly with anxious rather than psychotic patients, believed that this important advance should have an impact on private practice also. However, when the tranquilizers were used in the treatment of anxiety, the results were disappointing. At this point, the physicians should have concluded that a drug of the sedative-hypnotic class rather than of the antipsychotic class was indicated (as in the past) for this group of patients. But what was offered was a series of sedative drugs advertised as "tranquilizers," "minor tranquilizers," "successors to the tranquilizers," etc. Physicians then adopted one of these mislabeled sedatives, concluding that it was "the only tranquilizer that worked." Recognition of the fact that meprobamate was merely an expensive variant of an intermediate-acting sedative required 10 years. The influence of advertising and

Table 23–1. Chemical classification of sedative-hypnotics.

Compounds	Example
Monoureides	Carbromal
Diureides	Barbiturates
Piperidinedione derivatives	Glutethimide (Doriden)
Carbamates	Ethinamate (Valmid)
Dicarbamates	Meprobamate (Miltown)
Benzodiazepines	Chlordiazepoxide (Librium)
Quinazolones	Methaqualone (Quaalude)
Alcohols	Ethanol, chloral hydrate
Tertiary alcohols	Ethchlorvynol (Placidyl)
Bromides	Sodium bromide
Ethers, cyclic	Paraldehyde
Antihistamines	Promethazine (Phenergan)
Parasympatholytics	Scopolamine
Miscellaneous	Hydrocarbons, esters, ketones

References

Sedative-Hypnotics

Ayd FJ Jr: Benzodiazepines: Dependency and withdrawal. (Editorial.) JAMA 242:1401, 1979.

Bloomer HA: Limited usefulness of alkaline diuresis and peritoneal dialysis in pentobarbital intoxication. N Engl J Med 272:1309, 1965.

Bunn HF, Lubash GD: A controlled study of induced diuresis in barbiturate intoxication. Ann Intern Med 62:246, 1965.

Bush MT, Berry G, Hume A: Ultra-short acting barbiturates as oral hypnotic agents in man. Clin Pharmacol Ther 7:373, 1966.

Costa E, Guidotti A: Molecular mechanisms in the receptor action of the benzodiazepines. Annu Rev Pharmacol Toxicol 19:531, 1979.

Dalen JE & others: The hemodynamic and respiratory effects of diazepam (Valium). Anesthesiology 30:259, 1969.

Finkle BS, McCloskey KL, Goodman L: Diazepam and drug-associated deaths: A survey in the US and Canada. JAMA 242:429, 1979.

Gillin JC & others: The neuropharmacology of sleep and wakefulness. Annu Rev Pharmacol Toxicol 18:563, 1978.

Greenblatt DJ, Shader RS: Prazepam and lorazepam, two new benzodiazepines. N Engl J Med 299:1342, 1979.

Greenblatt DJ, Allen MD, Shader RI: Toxicity of high-dose flurazepam in the elderly. Clin Pharmacol Ther 21:355, 1977.

Hollister L: *Clinical Pharmacology of Psychotherapeutic Drugs.* Churchill Livingstone, 1978.

Kales A: Chronic hypnotic-drug use: Ineffectiveness, drug-withdrawal insomnia, and dependence. JAMA 227:513, 1974.

Kales A, Kales JD: Sleep disorders: Recent findings in the diagnosis and treatment of disturbed sleep. N Engl J Med 290:487, 1974.

Kales A & others: Rebound insomnia: A potential hazard following withdrawal of certain benzodiazepines. JAMA 241:1692, 1979.

Mellin GW, Katzenstein M: The saga of thalidomide. (2 parts.) N Engl J Med 267:1184, 1238, 1962.

Mellinger GD & others: Psychic distress, life crisis and use of psychotherapeutic medications. National household survey data. Arch Gen Psychiatry 35:1045, 1978.

Oswald I, Priest RG: Five weeks to escape the sleeping-pill habit. Br Med J 2:1093, 1965.

Price HL & others: The uptake of thiopental by body tissues and its relation to the duration of narcosis. Clin Pharmacol Ther 1:16, 1960.

Proudfoot AT, Park J: Changing pattern of drugs used for self-poisoning. Br Med J 1:90, 1978.

Richards CD: On the mechanism of barbiturate anesthesia. J Physiol 227:749, 1972.

Setter JG, Maher JF, Schreiner GE: Barbiturate intoxication: Evaluation of therapy including dialysis in a large series selectively referred because of severity. Arch Intern Med 117:224, 1966.

Smith AL: Barbiturate protection in cerebral hypoxia. Anesthesiology 47:286, 1977.

Solomon F & others: Sleeping pills, insomnia and medical practice. N Engl J Med 300:803, 1979.

Weise CE, Price SF: *The Benzodiazepines –Patterns of Use: An Annotated Bibliography.* Addiction Research Foundation of Ontario, 1975.

Spinal Cord Depressants

Balter MB, Levine J, Manheimer DI: Cross national study of the extent of anti-anxiety and sedative drug use. N Engl J Med 290:769, 1974.

Lasagna L: The role of benzodiazepines in non-psychiatric medical practice. Am J Psychiat 134:656, 1977.

Laurence DR, Webster RA: Pathologic physiology, pharmacology, and therapeutics of tetanus. Clin Pharmacol Ther 4:36, 1963.

Payne RW & others: Diazepam, meprobamate, and placebo in musculoskeletal disorders. JAMA 188:229, 1964.

Preskorn SH, Denner LJ: Benzodiazepines and withdrawal psychosis. JAMA 237:36, 1977.

Update on sedative hypnotics: IOM report on use of sleeping pills. FDA Drug Bull 9:16, 1979.

24 | Alcohols

ETHYL ALCOHOL
(Ethanol)

The pharmacologic effects of ethyl alcohol and a few other alcohols of toxicologic interest are very similar to those of the sedative-hypnotics discussed in the preceding chapter. Alcohol is discussed separately because its wide use and abuse leads to more behavioral and organic toxicity than does any other agent. The social and therapeutic problems thus generated are an unavoidable concern of every practitioner.

Source & Chemistry

The growth of a ubiquitous yeast in a sugar-containing medium forms alcohol and CO_2. Since Paleolithic times, in one culture or another, virtually every fruit juice, plant sap, tuber, honey, and grain has been fermented in order to produce an alcoholic drink. If grain is used as the source of carbohydrate, the simpler sugars must be made available for utilization by the yeast. This is accomplished by first adding malt, a powder made from sprouted barley that contains diastase. Yeast ceases its growth when the concentration of ethanol in the medium reaches 14–16%. Stronger liquors can then be obtained by distilling the wine or distiller's beer formed from fruit juice or grain.

In addition to ethanol, fermentation produces higher alcohols and a variety of aldehydes, acids, esters, and ketones. Most of these ''congeners'' are volatile and appear in the distilled beverage as well as in wine. The higher alcohols, mostly isoamyl alcohol, are referred to as fusel oil. Isoamyl alcohol and ethyl acetate, the congeners present in greatest concentrations, are long-acting depressants and may add to the effects of alcoholic beverages.

Beer ordinarily contains no more than 2–4% alcohol, although some beers may contain up to 6%. Wines contain approximately 12% alcohol. Fortified wines (sherry or port) are prepared by adding brandy to wine, and their alcohol content may be in excess of 20%. Variations of the fortified wines are the sweet wines popular among the alcoholics in the skid rows of most cities. In the preparation of these sweet wines, fermentation is halted by the addition of concentrated alcohol before much of the sugar has been consumed. These strong, sweet wines provide a large number of calories but no other nutritive factors. In the lives of some people, they may almost completely take the place of food. Whisky, brandy, rum, gin, and other distilled liquors contain 35–50% alcohol.

Absorption

The discussion of the absorption and metabolism of alcohol has special importance because of the need to define, for legal purposes, the degree of intoxication of an individual. The judgment must usually be made retrospectively, after the subject has been arrested for some offense.

Alcohol requires no digestion or dissolution and is a small, neutral, water-soluble molecule. It is, therefore, rapidly absorbed by simple diffusion over the entire gastrointestinal tract. Absorption from the stomach occurs promptly but at a rate slower than that in the upper small intestine. In the fasting state, about 20% of a single dose of alcohol is absorbed from the stomach; the remainder is absorbed from the small intestine as rapidly as it leaves the stomach. After a single dose of alcohol, absorption is 90% complete in 1 hour, the peak blood level being reached in approximately 40 minutes. The blood alcohol level returns to zero in 8–10 hours. (Fig 24–1.)

Food in the stomach slows the absorption of alcohol by prolonging the emptying time and, since it covers some of the mucosal surface, by slowing diffusion. Dilute alcoholic solutions—eg, beer or tall drinks—are absorbed more slowly than moderately concentrated (30%) solutions such as cocktails.

Distribution

The distribution of alcohol throughout the body is in proportion to the water content of the various tissues.

Small amounts of alcohol (2–4% of the total dose) are lost into the urine and into the alveolar air by diffusion. The alcohol in alveolar air is in equilibrium with the alcohol in the blood passing through the lungs; a determination of the alcohol concentration in respiratory air can therefore be used to estimate blood concentrations for medicolegal purposes. The concentration of alcohol in the urine is less precisely proportionate to the average blood concentration during the period of urine collection. Urine specimens are, therefore, less useful for legal purposes.

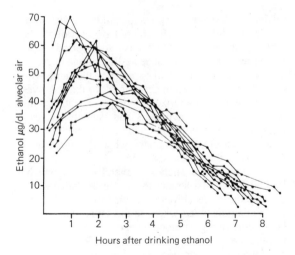

Figure 24 –1. The rate of absorption and metabolism of ethanol, 0.5 mL/lb body weight, in 10 tests on the same subject over a 2-month period. The level of alcohol in alveolar air reflects the blood level. (Reproduced, with permission, from Freund & O'Hollaren: Acetaldehyde concentrations in alveolar air following a standard dose of ethanol in man. J Lipid Res 6:473, 1965.)

Metabolism

A. Steps in Oxidation: Ethanol is converted in the liver to acetaldehyde, which is oxidized to acetate or acetyl-CoA, which in turn enters the tricarboxylic acid (TCA) cycle for further oxidation to CO_2 and water.

The first step occurs, practically speaking, only in the liver.

$$H_3C-CH_2-OH \xrightarrow[\quad NAD^+ \quad NADH+H^+\quad]{\boxed{\text{ALCOHOL DEHYDROGENASE}}} H_3C-\overset{\overset{\displaystyle H}{|}}{C}=O$$

The second step, the oxidation of acetaldehyde, occurs in the liver and other tissues that contain aldehyde dehydrogenase. The first reaction takes place more slowly than does the oxidation of acetaldehyde—ie, the hepatic conversion of alcohol to acetaldehyde is the rate-limiting step. Thus, alcohol and acetaldehyde levels rise together, but acetaldehyde levels are only 1/1000 those of alcohol. When aldehyde dehydrogenase and, therefore, the metabolism of acetaldehyde are inhibited by the prior administration of disulfiram, acetaldehyde blood levels are higher and symptoms of acetaldehyde toxicity occur. (Fig 24–2.)

The above pathway accounts for 90–95% of ingested labeled (^{14}C) alcohol.

B. Maximal Rate of Metabolism: The rate of conversion of alcohol to acetaldehyde in the liver reaches a maximum when the dehydrogenase system is saturated. This occurs with blood levels of about 0.1%. The maximum rate is fairly constant for a given individual. Variation between individuals and among experimenters is greater, but one common generalization is that the typical 70-kg human can metabolize 10 mL (8 g) of alcohol per hour, or about 20 mL of 100-proof (50%) whisky per hour. Other estimates are closer to 30 mL of whisky per hour. Since ethanol provides 7 kcal/g (5.6 kcal/mL), a persistent drinker can derive 1800 kcal/d from alcohol.

C. Alteration of Rate of Metabolism: Insofar as the practical goal of hastening the treatment of acute intoxication is concerned, it can be said that there is no way of increasing the rate of metabolism of alcohol. The administration of fructose in the investigative situation does have such an effect both in animals and in humans.

Pharmacologic Effects

A. Mechanism of Action: The mechanisms of action of alcohol, like its effect in general, are similar to those of the short-acting barbiturates discussed in the previous chapter. Alcohol diffusely depresses the central nervous system, but the mechanism of this effect is as obscure as it is in the case of the sedative-hypnotics. The loss of consciousness eventually in-

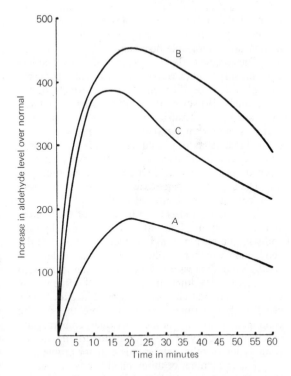

Figure 24 –2. The effect of pretreatment with disulfiram on acetaldehyde blood levels (μg/dL). *A:* Levels after 0.5 mL/kg of 45% alcohol in 10 patients. *B:* Levels after the same dose of alcohol in 44 patients pretreated with disulfiram. *C:* Levels after half the previous dose of alcohol in 29 pretreated patients. (Reproduced, with permission, from Hine & others: Human pharmacology of Antabuse-alcohol reactions. J Clin Invest 31:319, 1952.)

duced is caused by depression of the reticular activating system.

Alcohol does have effects on organ systems other than the central nervous system, and these actions are not present in the other sedative-hypnotics. The vasodilating, local, and nutritional effects of alcohol are discussed below.

B. Effects:
1. Central nervous system depression–
a. Behavioral-Alcohol is simply one example of a short-acting sedative-hypnotic, and the description of the central nervous system effects of the sedatives presented in Chapter 23 is entirely applicable to alcohol and need not be repeated here in detail. The actions of the sedatives were, in turn, related to the stages of general anesthesia, and the distinctiveness of alcohol is most easily made clear by reference to these stages. Useful general anesthetics quickly carry the patient through stages 1 and 2 (induction) and cause a prolonged stage 3, ie, there is a wide margin between the anesthetic dose and the lethal, or stage 4, dose. The dose-effect relation for alcohol is such that stages 1 and 2 are prolonged, but once anesthesia is achieved, only a small additional amount can lead to the stage of medullary paralysis.

Small amounts of alcohol lead to sedation and the relief of anxiety. Larger amounts cause more pronounced disinhibition, with ataxia, impaired psychomotor performance, faulty judgment, and uninhibited or irresponsible behavior.

The manifest effects of the ingestion of alcohol in amounts sufficient to cause drunkenness may appear at first glance to be different from the effects of the barbiturates. However, if barbiturates or other sedatives are taken in sufficient amounts in a situation where stimulation persists, the same excited or disinhibited behavior is seen. Alcohol is a social drug and is taken not at bedtime with the expectation of sleep but in a setting that requires continued functioning. The apparently paradoxic excitement is therefore more commonly seen after alcohol.

The manifest effects on behavior of the depression caused by alcohol will vary with the individual and with the setting. The individual reaction will depend upon whether alcohol unmasks an underlying ebullience or depression. Whether alcohol is ingested at a party or at bedtime in the home will influence the kind of behavioral change it causes. Since alcohol is usually taken at times and in situations that require continued functioning of the individual, embarrassing or criminal behavior—eg, drunken driving or the commission of other crimes—is a major problem.

The excitement or uninhibited behavior that occurs after the use of alcohol is a manifestation of depression, not stimulation. This distinction between the manifest behavioral change and the underlying pharmacologic mechanism must always be made especially since alcohol is still often called a stimulant.

It is, of course, possible to drink to the point of unconsciousness, or anesthesia. It is also possible to ingest a lethal amount of alcohol, although this is difficult unless other depressant drugs are also used.

b. Withdrawal–The compulsive user of alcohol who ingests large amounts for extended periods, when forced by some circumstance to discontinue or reduce alcohol consumption, will experience the same withdrawal state described in Chapter 23 for the sedatives. This state is characterized by hyperexcitability that may progress to convulsions and, sometimes, by a toxic psychosis with hallucinatory behavior. This state, called delirium tremens when the agent is alcohol, is further discussed below.

c. Tolerance–There are several ways in which a limited degree of tolerance to the effects of alcohol can develop during its chronic use. One form of tolerance can be demonstrated when, in the same individual, a larger dose or higher blood level of alcohol is required to produce the same pharmacologic effect following continued administration. This kind of tolerance can be established, but, as is also true of the barbiturates, it is small in degree. Only small changes in the metabolism of alcohol occur during the development of this form of tolerance, and it is presumed to be an adaptation of the central nervous system to the effect of alcohol.

A quantitatively more significant form of tolerance can be demonstrated by comparing the effects of alcohol on experienced and inexperienced drinkers. In this case, the presumption is that tolerance is due to a behavioral adaptation, ie, users learn to control their manifest behavior following repeated experience of the depressant or disinhibiting effect.

2. Vasodilatation–
The primary cardiovascular effect of alcohol administration is vasodilatation. The cardiovascular effects are best understood in comparison with the actions of other direct smooth muscle relaxants such as nitroglycerin. The vasodilating action of alcohol is often said to be secondary to central depression, but this conclusion is based largely on the difficulty of demonstrating a vasodilating action of alcohol in isolated preparations. Central depression of comparable degree induced by other depressant drugs does not cause the same amount of vasodilatation, and it appears quite likely that the vasodilatation ascribed to alcohol is in fact due to the action of the active metabolite, acetaldehyde, an extremely potent vasodilator. Since the blood levels of alcohol and acetaldehyde rise and fall almost synchronously, it is impossible to separate their effects in the intact organism. Infusions of acetaldehyde or the accumulation of endogenous acetaldehyde following the administration of disulfiram lead to vasodilatation and other effects ordinarily described as due to alcohol. Similarly, the bradycardia and fall in blood pressure mentioned below may be due in part to the depletion of norepinephrine from its stores within the body, and this effect also is brought about by acetaldehyde administration.

The vasodilatation causes a warm, flushed skin and a subjective feeling of warmth. Loss of heat from the body is increased. Cerebral blood flow is not changed. Anginal pain is sometimes relieved, but, since the relief of pain is not accompanied by electrocardiographic evidence of a decrease in myocardial ischemia, the effect is usually explained as analgesia due to central depression. For reasons elaborated in the discussion of the treatment of angina, it now seems probable that alcohol ingestion relieves anginal pain because it is a generalized vasodilator and reduces cardiac work.

The effects on heart rate and blood pressure are secondary to the decrease in peripheral resistance or to the reflex sympathetic activation caused by the vasodilatation and aborted fall in blood pressure. Heart rate and stroke volume may increase, and only with huge doses is bradycardia seen. The change in blood pressure varies widely with the dose of alcohol. With small or extremely large doses, a decrease in blood pressure is usual. Moderate doses may actually increase blood pressure.

3. Respiration–Very large doses of alcohol cause the respiratory depression predictable on the basis of the central depressant effect. Small or moderate amounts of alcohol cause stimulation of respiration. This action is also more easily explained as due to acetaldehyde.

4. Gastrointestinal–The central nervous system depressant effect of alcohol and the accompanying relief of anxiety or euphoriant effect can increase the appetite. The bitter taste of sherry or other alcoholic beverages is also said, on less substantial grounds, to be useful in this regard.

Gastric acid secretion is increased by the ingestion of alcohol in all but the most concentrated forms. A local effect on the antrum to release gastrin explains at least a fraction of the hypersecretion, but an action on the upper small intestine is also present. Alcohol obviously should be avoided by the patient with an active peptic ulcer, and either avoided or used only with the protection of antacids and atropine by the ulcer patient wishing to avoid recurrences.

Alcohol ingested in a concentrated form even in the presence of food will cause gastric irritation with hyperemia, prolonged emptying time due to pylorospasm and decreased gastric motility, increased mucus and decreased acid secretion, and, eventually, vomiting and bleeding.

Chronic atrophic gastritis occurs in a small fraction of chronic alcoholics.

5. Diuresis–Initially, alcohol suppresses the action of antidiuretic hormone (ADH) and causes diuresis independent of the volume of fluid taken in as a beverage. Later, urine volume generally reflects fluid intake, but some sodium retention occurs.

Clinical Uses

A. Sedative: Alcohol used as a sedative has the same disadvantages as any other short-acting sedative, ie, patients quickly associate the production of euphoria with the medication and, noting also the brief duration of the effect, may, personality and situation permitting, assume control of the dose themselves. For continuous sedation, a longer-acting compound is preferable. Whether the physician prohibits or sug-

gests alcohol in the form of a social beverage usually depends upon personal habits and attitudes.

B. Antiseptic: Ethyl alcohol is germicidal. In order to achieve a germicidal effect on dried surfaces or matter, its concentration should be close to 70%. It, or the equivalent (but nontaxed and nonpotable) isopropyl alcohol, is still used to prepare the skin at the site of an injection or for similar purposes. In this application the cleansing properties are probably more useful than the germicidal effect. Alcohol is not active against spores and viruses. Hexachlorophene or quaternary ammonium chlorides have replaced alcohol to a large extent for skin preparation or wet sterilization.

Adverse Reactions

In 1976 in the USA, alcohol consumption amounted to 2.54 gallons of hard liquor for every person over 14 plus 3 billion gallons of beer and 250 million gallons of wine. The cost at retail of these social drugs was 20 billion dollars. Approximately 70% of American adults drink, but half of the production is consumed by less than 10% (perhaps as few as 6%) of the adult population. The consequent toxicity dwarfs all but a few other problems of public and individual health.

A. Acute Behavioral Changes:

1. Acute alcoholic intoxication–In small doses the disinhibiting effect of alcohol relieves anxiety and facilitates social behavior. It is suitable and accepted as a social or recreational drug.

Alcohol also impairs measurable psychomotor performance, and impairs judgment by reducing conscious self-control during the period of disinhibition. The drinker is the person least able to judge the degree of impairment and continues to drive cars and interact with other individuals without appreciating the disability.

The duration of action of alcohol, especially in the face of continued absorption, is long enough so that the intoxicated individual becomes responsible for a significant fraction of the total of antisocial and criminal acts. For example, when special studies rather than routine accident reports are considered, it is established that approximately 3 out of 5 fatally injured drivers had been drinking and that 60% of these had blood alcohol concentrations above 0.1% (100 mg/dL).

The physician is not often called upon to treat acute alcoholic states but occasionally will be asked to quiet an excited drunk. For this purpose, chlorpromazine, 25–50 mg intramuscularly or orally, is often used. If a sedative is used instead of a major tranquilizer, it should be a long-acting one such as phenobarbital or chlordiazepoxide. Short-acting sedatives act exactly as alcohol does. They may be effective for a time, but the patient will soon return to the excited level.

2. Quantitative measures of intoxication–The relation between blood alcohol concentration and pharmacologic effect is variable in different individuals, and the effect of the same level is greater when the level is rising than during recovery. The following generalizations can be made:

50 mg/dL: (The level produced by 60 mL of whisky in 2 hours.) Euphoria and minor motor disturbances.

60 mg/dL: Nystagmus. More errors on simple tests.

80 mg/dL: (90 mL whisky.) Impaired driving ability. First electroencephalographic changes.

100–150 mg/dL: Gross motor incoordination.

200–300 mg/dL: Amnesia for the experience.

300–350 mg/dL: Coma.

355–600 mg/dL: May cause or contribute to death.

Robbery is defined and punished as a crime whether the individual was intoxicated at the time of the act or not. On the other hand, whether it is a "crime" to drive a car or cause an accident may depend on whether the individual is under the influence of alcohol or not. The measurement of blood alcohol levels and the study of the relation between blood levels and behavior have consequently been emphasized in this context. No absolute definition of the degree of intoxication that constitutes drunk driving is acceptable to all groups at this time. Impairment of performance of real or simulated driving provides an index acceptable to most investigators and is the basis for the British definition of drunk driving as driving with a blood alcohol concentration of 80 mg/dL or more, ie, after drinking 3 or more 30-mL (1-oz) whiskies within an hour. However, some laboratory tests of motor performance are not impaired until higher blood alcohol concentrations are reached and provide a basis for setting a higher level—eg, the ridiculously high level of 150 mg/dL defended in courts in the USA by some experts. Still another group argues persuasively that judgment is impaired before psychomotor tests are impaired, and blood levels of 50 mg/dL are penalized in some countries.

In most states in the USA, there is no statutory definition of the blood alcohol concentration defining drunkenness, and in each case the analysis must be interpreted for the court by an expert witness. Some states have defined drunk driving by law—eg, in California, a blood level over 100 mg/dL. In Britain it is an offense to drive with a blood alcohol concentration of 80 mg/dL or above.

In some jurisdictions—eg, California, New York, Britain—an "implied consent" law is in effect. In accepting a license to drive, the citizen consents to the collection of blood or other specimen for alcohol determination if detained by the police; if permission to take the sample is withheld, the arrestee's license to drive can be taken away.

3. Alcoholic coma–Acute overdosage toxicity may, under special circumstances, progress to a state of anesthesia. This usually requires that someone already quite drunk take in an additional huge increment of alcohol over a short period of time.

The problem and the treatment are similar to those of barbiturate overdosage. However, the margin between the anesthetic dose and the lethal dose is narrower in the case of alcohol than with the barbiturates, and the differential diagnosis is more difficult because of the greater likelihood that some disorder such as head injury or pneumonia may be superimposed on a comparatively minor toxic state.

Treatment is as described for barbiturate intoxication (see p 234) except that neither alkaline or osmotic diuresis is used.

4. Hangover–The occurrence of hangover is more common after alcohol ingestion than after use of the other short-acting sedative-hypnotics discussed in Chapter 23, in part because of the metabolic effects of alcohol but also because so many more doses of alcohol are consumed. Hangover is in part simply a manifestation of withdrawal less completely developed than the severe state described below. Using sleep patterns as an index, it can be established that the first half of a night's rest after alcohol may be deeper than usual, but that after 4 hours a disturbed sleep pattern reflecting increased excitability is seen. Nondrug factors are certainly involved in the production of alcoholic hangover—eg, remorse or at least regret, loss of sleep, unaccustomed activity, and anxiety—but some of the symptoms are demonstrable under conditions that control these factors.

The signs and symptoms of hangover include tremors, fatigue, vertigo, throbbing headache, labile blood pressure, gastritis with nausea and vomiting that is partly local and partly central in origin, acidosis, weakness, and dehydration with persistent thirst.

Treatment logically begins the night before, with restraint. Failing this, prophylactic measures can be carried out at bedtime. Emesis can be induced, usually with no difficulty, to get rid of some of the unabsorbed alcohol. Fluids, aspirin, and sodium bicarbonate can be taken at this time to anticipate the dehydration, malaise, and acidosis.

The quickest and most effective treatment for alcoholic hangover is to terminate the acute withdrawal state with alcohol, but the danger of this in establishing or maintaining a pattern of drinking is apparent.

Other methods of treatment include fluids, aspirin, a systemic alkali such as sodium bicarbonate for the systemic acidosis, and a nonabsorbed antacid if gastritis is prominent. The amphetamines are widely used by those to whom they are available; there is no reason to doubt that they make people feel better.

B. Withdrawal State; Delirium Tremens: The "DTs," or shakes of alcohol withdrawal, are closely comparable to the withdrawal syndrome described for the sedative-hypnotics, but the alcohol withdrawal syndrome is both more common and more severe and occurs in patients with generally poor health.

After a binge of 2 weeks or more, the drinker may choose or be forced to stop drinking or taper off and may then ask a physician for treatment when the symptoms are still minor. The subsequent course will vary in severity depending upon how heavy the drinking bout has been and the abruptness of withdrawal. In mild cases, symptoms may last for only 2 days; in other instances, symptoms may increase in severity for several days and culminate in a period of delirium lasting 3–4 days. Symptoms of hyperexcitability may progress to a typical toxic psychosis characterized by marked alterations in perception with auditory, visual and tactile hallucinations.

Specific signs and symptoms may include anxiety, tremors, restlessness, agitation, insomnia, irritability, sweating, nausea and vomiting, exaggerated reflexes, tachycardia, slight elevation of temperature in moderately severe cases (< 38 C), convulsions (often before delirium), delusions, hallucinations, and, in severe cases, temperature > 38 C. The mortality rate in various recent series ranges from 1% to 37%.

Treatment. Patients usually need fluids, but not necessarily parenterally. Vitamins are probably needed in most cases, but they are not required immediately and repeated administration is not necessary.

Even when most seriously disturbed, these patients are responding in a distorted way to stimuli that are truly present. Explanation, lighted rooms, and attendants with supportive attitudes will minimize the reaction. Jail or other threatening environments will usually intensify the excitement and paranoia.

Replacing the short-acting sedative alcohol with a long-acting sedative makes slow withdrawal possible. This policy has come into widespread use because of interest in chlordiazepoxide (Librium), but phenobarbital in large doses is just as satisfactory. Short-acting sedatives—barbiturates, chloral hydrate, or the traditional paraldehyde— usually need be given only once at the beginning of treatment. Major tranquilizers such as chlorpromazine have been used instead of the sedatives; they are probably equally satisfactory in mild cases and may even return the patient to a normal status more quickly. However, antipsychotic tranquilizers increase the likelihood of convulsions, and the mortality rate is higher if they are used. Phenytoin prevents convulsions during withdrawal in patients who have demonstrated a predisposition to seizures.

C. Nutritional Toxicity: Alcohol is easily available for chronic use and is ingested in large absolute amounts—ie, in doses of many grams as compared with the milligram doses of other abused drugs. When such large amounts of alcohol are ingested, it is not added to the diet but replaces a part or most of the normal diet. The calories derived from alcohol are unaccompanied by vitamins or protein, and one or more of the following deficiencies or disease states may result:

1. Folic acid and iron deficiency.

2. Pellagra, or at least the dermatitis characteristic of that disease.

3. Nutritional polyneuropathy–Peripheral nerve degeneration with muscle wasting is only slowly reversible, and the specific deficiency has not been identified.

4. Cardiac beriberi–High-output cardiac failure due specifically to thiamine deficiency is a rare occurrence.

5. Wernicke's syndrome–Wernicke's encephalopathy (ataxia, oculomotor palsy, confusion) is an acute disorder due to thiamine deficiency.

6. Korsakoff's psychosis–Following Wernicke's encephalopathy or other signs of acute thiamine deficiency, there may occur a chronic degenerative change characterized by poor memory for recent events often covered by confabulation.

D. Hepatotoxicity: There is a clear correlation between the amount of alcohol consumed and the death rate from portal cirrhosis in a community or group. The relative importance of nutritional factors and of a direct toxic effect in causing the sequence of hepatotoxic events described below was argued for many years. The process was described only in humans, and the lack of an animal model made separation of the causal factors difficult. The same changes have now been produced in baboons by the isocaloric substitution of alcohol for carbohydrate in an otherwise adequate diet. The definite hepatotoxicity of alcohol may still be modified by nutritional factors.

1. Alcoholic fatty liver–The rapid accumulation of triglyceride within liver cells following the ingestion of alcohol in humans or animals is clearly not nutritional in origin.

The deposition of dietary or other fat in the hepatocyte is often explained as being due to the generation of unusual amounts of NADH as alcohol is oxidized in the liver cell. (See reaction on p 243.) The increased NADH/NAD ratio raises the concentration of glycerophosphate, causes trapping of fatty acid, and promotes fatty acid synthesis. The decrease in the amount of NAD depresses the citric acid cycle, and ethanol supplants fatty acid as an energy source for the liver.

The fatty changes are reversible, but they may progress to hepatitis, the link to cirrhosis, in the face of a continued alcohol effect.

2. Alcoholic hepatitis–Hepatocellular injury or necrosis occurs with inflammation, possibly jaundice, characteristic cytoplasmic inclusions, and centrilobular fibrosis.

3. Portal cirrhosis–Whether the fibrosis spreads to the portal tracts and cirrhosis develops depends upon the duration of alcohol use and the total amount consumed.

E. Fetal Alcohol Syndrome: Excessive alcohol intake by the mother clearly impairs prenatal growth. In addition, a teratogenic effect is said—on the basis of incomplete epidemiologic studies—to cause a "fetal alcohol syndrome" characterized by pre- and postnatal growth deficiency, short palpebral fissures, and other defects including microcephaly and mental retardation.

Safe levels of alcohol during pregnancy have not been determined, but it would appear prudent to counsel pregnant women to limit alcohol intake.

CHRONIC ALCOHOLISM

The magnitude of the problem of alcohol misuse requires that it be discussed as a separate entity. It is, however, a variation of the general problem of drug abuse discussed in Chapter 7 and should be considered in the same general terms of drug, individual, and social factors.

The importance of individual susceptibility and the spectrum of misuse is more apparent with alcohol than with other drugs because it is used openly. Many individuals, perhaps 30%, actively avoid the experience of drinking. Others accept it when the social situation suggests or almost imposes it. A large group uses alcohol intemperately but episodically, and a few find that its use has become a compulsion dominating their entire lives. Estimates of the incidence of chronic alcoholism vary depending upon where along this continuum a division is made. It is probable that a million people in the USA are drug-driven, chronic alcoholics by everyone's definition and 4–6 million qualify as problem drinkers. Most definitions of chronic alcoholism emphasize the compulsive nature of the behavior—often, however, using another term or description. Sociologic factors involved in the problem of alcoholism are most apparent in the general approval of the use, possession, and sale of alcohol. The compulsive alcoholic will, like other compulsive drug users, subordinate all other activities to maintain a supply of the drug. In addition, however, the acute effects of the drug prevent the drinker from functioning effectively, and alcohol has significant chronic toxicity. Society is damaged not only by the dependency of the individual but also by irresponsible acts performed by persons who have been drinking.

The fact that only some individuals compulsively misuse alcohol has led some investigators to search for a biochemical rather than a personality defect. The several suggestions for individual need or intolerance for alcohol have transiently influenced treatment but have no basis. Emphasis on the importance of the first drink reflects the danger of disinhibition by alcohol, which encourages further intake, and the traditional proscription against the first drink acknowledges the vulnerability of the compulsive user.

Treatment

The general approach to the treatment of alcoholism is the same as for other problems of drug misuse. The penal or punitive approach is not effective and lacks public support. The psychotherapeutic approach (including variations provided by the churches and by Alcoholics Anonymous) is effective in those individuals who acknowledge that they are sick and themselves solicit help. The percentage of a randomly selected group of alcoholics assigned to any treatment program that are helped is small until the patient accepts the need to change. Group therapy with major responsibility assigned to former users is then perhaps most profitable.

Disulfiram
(Antabuse, tetraethylthiuram disulfide)

In the face of general social approval and widening individual use, no efforts at abatement by education are likely to be effective, especially since such efforts are in competition with the proselytizing efforts of a huge advertising outlay.

A. Pharmacologic Blockade With Disulfiram: Disulfiram (Antabuse, and generic) is used industrially in the vulcanization of rubber. It was studied as an anthelmintic, and its ability to produce alcohol intolerance was observed fortuitously.

1. Pharmacologic action–Disulfiram acts by inhibiting aldehyde dehydrogenase. Alcohol is then oxidized at the usual rate to acetaldehyde, which accumulates and causes toxic effects that render the patient extremely uncomfortable (Fig 24–2).

Disulfiram thus has few effects unless the patient ingests alcohol; then warmth, a flush, a throbbing headache, nausea and vomiting, drowsiness, and a hangover are experienced. The blood pressure falls to a degree determined mostly by posture. The reaction is reproduced by acetaldehyde infusions in humans.

2. Technic of administration–The patient must agree to accept the drug daily and must understand that drinking will lead to a most unpleasant experience. The drug must not be administered surreptitiously.

Disulfiram (at first, 0.5 g, and later 0.25 g) is given daily. After a few days, the patient is given a test dose of alcohol by the physician (½ oz whisky followed in 30 minutes, if necessary, by an additional ½ oz) and experiences a didactic reaction. The test experience may be repeated at a later date or may be deferred or foregone.

The fear of the reaction is the deterrent to drinking, and the drug must be taken indefinitely. If possible, the prescribed drug is dispensed to a member of the family or other person who can witness its ingestion each day.

At least 12 hours are required for the effect of disulfiram to develop. The patient cannot drink for 3–10 days after discontinuing the medication. The reaction occurs within 20 minutes after the ingestion of alcohol and lasts for 30–120 minutes. Nonbeverage alcohol—eg, inhaled after-shave lotion—has caused mild reactions.

3. Adverse reactions–Disulfiram itself causes drowsiness, nausea, headache, cramps, fatigability, and a metallic taste in some patients. The most serious reaction, uncommon with the doses now used, is a confusional state.

Giving up the use of alcohol may lead to indirect adverse results such as anxiety, hostility, and experimentation with other drugs.

The acetaldehyde reaction itself has not been dangerous. One case has been reported of myocardial infarction developing during the reaction. The reaction is treated by recumbency and ephedrine.

4. Contraindications–Disulfiram is contraindicated in serious cardiovascular disease, epilepsy, and cirrhosis. The drug should not be given if the subject has been drinking or taking paraldehyde.

5. Effectiveness–Disulfiram was introduced at a time when drug treatment was unfashionable in psychiatry and when the lowering of blood pressure with drugs was a frightening novelty. Some adverse judgments were not based on experience. On the other hand, few controlled evaluations are available. The more carefully selected the patient group and the shorter the follow-up, the better the results. Nevertheless, some workers report complete success in 50% of their group.

B. Related Compounds: A few individuals who have taken some therapeutic agents have experienced disulfiramlike reactions after the ingestion of alcohol. The conditions of dosage and other factors associated with the reaction are poorly defined. These agents include tolbutamide, chloramphenicol, griseofulvin, furazolidone (Furazone), and possibly metronidazole (Flagyl).

OTHER TOXIC ALCOHOLS

A number of alcohols—eg, trichloroethanol, phenaglycodol (Ultran), and others listed in Chapter 23—are more potent than ethanol and are used as sedatives.

Other monols are used industrially and are occasionally inhaled or mistakenly ingested. Most of these have the same acute toxicity as ethanol—ie, they are general anesthetics. In general, the potency of the alcohols increases as the length of the carbon chain increases. Unsaturation or chlorine substitution adjacent to the hydroxyl group also increases activity.

Methanol must be discussed separately because it has specific toxic effects in addition to the expected central nervous system depressant action. Isopropyl alcohol is widely available and is occasionally used as an ethanol substitute. It is in part oxidized to acetone and causes some reversible impairment of renal function.

1. METHYL ALCOHOL
(Methanol)

Methanol (wood alcohol, $H_3C–OH$) is encountered as duplicating machine fluid, as an adulterant in illegal liquor, in canned heat, and as an industrial solvent. It is ingested mistakenly or in desperation by individuals who want ethanol. The lethal dose of methanol is 2–8 oz.

Methanol is metabolized, in large part to formic acid, only at one-fifth the rate of ethanol, and its effects are, therefore, long-lasting and cumulative. More of a given dose appears in the urine and expired air than in the case of ethanol. Methanol is much less active as a central depressant than ethanol, but it produces a severe acidosis only partially explicable by the amount of formic acid generated. The human optic nerve is especially vulnerable to the acidosis, the formic acid, or some metabolite unique to the human.

Following ingestion of methanol, the individual becomes drunk. Six to 36 hours later (an interval allowing the ingestion of more methanol), headache, dizziness, nausea, blindness, excitement, coma, and acidosis appear. Blindness or impaired vision may persist if the patient recovers.

Treatment

Treatment, other than supportive, includes the following:

A. Ethanol: Simultaneously administered alcohols compete for the limited capacity of the organism to metabolize alcohols. Ethanol is metabolized preferentially over methanol, and the conversion of methanol to formic acid is delayed. Give 50% alcohol or equivalent beverage, 1 mL/kg orally, followed by 0.5 mL/kg every 2 hours for 4 days.

B. Sodium Bicarbonate: Give sodium bicarbonate orally or intravenously in amounts large enough to restore normal plasma bicarbonate or maintain an alkaline urine.

C. Dialysis: Dialysis, preferably hemodialysis, should be considered early if it is available.

2. GLYCOLS

Ethylene glycol ($HOH_2C–CH_2OH$) is a component of antifreeze and an industrial solvent. It is a central nervous system depressant, but chronic exposure also causes renal tubular necrosis. It is oxidized to oxalate, crystals of which are deposited in the kidney. As little as 100 mL has been fatal.

Diethylene glycol ($HOH_2C–H_2C–O–CH_2–CH_2OH$) is similar to ethylene glycol but less toxic. It can cause hepatic necrosis in addition to renal damage.

Propylene glycol ($H_3C–CHOH–CH_2OH$) and **polyethylene glycols** ($HOH_2C[H_2C–O–CH_2]_x–CH_2OH$) are much less toxic and may be used in oral and injectable drug preparations and in cosmetics.

• • •

References

Ethanol

Clarren SK, Smith DW: The fetal alcohol syndrome. N Engl J Med 298:1063, 1978.

Davis VE & others: Alteration of endogenous catecholamine metabolism by ethanol ingestion. Proc Soc Exp Biol Med 125:1140, 1967.

Gillespie JA: Vasodilator properties of alcohol. Br Med J 2:274, 1967.

Jacob MS, Sellers EM: The role of drugs in chronic alcoholism. Drug Ther 8:53, Jan 1978.

Jones KS & others: Patterns of malformation in offspring of chronic alcoholic women. Lancet 1:1267, 1973.

Knott DH, Beard JD, Fink RD: Guidelines for diagnosis and alcohol detoxification. Drug Ther 8:35, Jan 1978.

Lieber CS: Alcohol and malnutrition in the pathogenesis of liver disease. JAMA 233:1077, 1975. [Also in N Engl J Med 298:888, 1978.]

Lowenstein LM & others: Effect of fructose on alcohol concentrations in the blood in man. JAMA 213:1899, 1970.

Mardones J: The alcohols. Pages 99–183 in: *Physiological Pharmacology.* Vol 1. Root WS, Hofmann FG (editors). Academic Press, 1963.

Murphree HB, Greenberg LA, Carroll R: Neuropharmacological effects of substances other than ethanol in alcoholic beverages. Fed Proc 26:1468, 1967.

Ouellette EM & others: Adverse effects on offspring of maternal alcohol abuse during pregnancy. N Engl J Med 297:528, 1977.

Roueche B: *The Neutral Spirit: A Portrait of Alcohol.* Little, Brown, 1960.

Rubin E, Lieber CS: Fatty liver, alcoholic hepatitis and cirrhosis produced by alcohol in primates. N Engl J Med 290:128, 1974. [Also in Science 182:712, 1973.]

Rubin E, Smuckler EA (editors): The biology of alcohol and alcoholism. Fed Proc 34:2038, 1975.

Sampliner R, Iber FL: Diphenylhydantoin control of alcohol withdrawal seizures. JAMA 230:1430, 1974.

Seixas FA: Alcohol and its drug interactions. Ann Intern Med 83:86, 1975.

Sellers EM, Kalant H: Alcohol intoxication and withdrawal. N Engl J Med 294:757, 1976.

Waller JA: Chronic medical conditions and traffic safety: Review of the California experience. N Engl J Med 273:1413, 1965.

Waller JA: Use and misuse of alcoholic beverages as factors in motor vehicle accidents. Public Health Rep 81:591, 1966.

Whitfield CL & others: Detoxification of 1,024 alcoholic patients without psychoactive drugs. JAMA 239:1409, 1978.

Yules RB, Lippman ME, Freedman DX: Alcohol administration prior to sleep: The effect on EEG sleep stages. Arch Gen Psychiatry 16:94, 1967.

Other Alcohols

Bennett IL Jr & others: Acute methyl alcohol poisoning: A review based on experiences in an outbreak of 323 cases. Medicine 32:431, 1953.

Keyvan-Larijarni H, Tannenberg AM: Methanol intoxication. Arch Intern Med 134:293, 1974.

Parry MF, Wallach R: Ethylene glycol poisoning. Am J Med 57:143, 1974.

Antipsychotic Tranquilizers | 25

All of the drugs listed in Chapter 23 as sedative-hypnotics are useful in the treatment of anxiety. The sedative-hypnotics cannot, however, alter the course of a psychotic episode and cannot dependably quiet a manic patient without inducing a state of anesthesia. In contrast, the antipsychotics are not effective against anxiety but can suppress schizophrenic ideation and behavior. Even after huge doses have been given the patient can still be aroused, but the possibility of extrapyramidal toxic effects is very great.

Terminology in this area of study has caused much confusion. "Neuroleptic," the term originally applied to this drug group, is still used in Europe and is useful because it is not applied to any other drug group or effect.

The term "tranquilizer," which implies a pleasant effect, still causes confusion. The effect of the antipsychotic drugs is actually subjectively unpleasant. Furthermore, in common as well as in medical usage the term is also applied to sedatives that do cause euphoria, often with the intent of obscuring the similarity of some new drugs to the older sedatives and in this way suggesting a relationship to the nonabused antipsychotics. Confusion can be avoided by calling drugs of this class antipsychotics even though they have additional effects and uses. The term tranquilizer should always be qualified—eg, "antipsychotic tranquilizer" or "phenothiazine type tranquilizer."

History

The drug effect that we now attribute to the antipsychotics, which has certainly revolutionized the institutional practice of psychiatry and perhaps psychiatry in general, had been described for other drug classes, but its distinctiveness from that of the sedatives and its wide usefulness were first clearly described by Laborit in 1951. Substituted phenothiazines were available years before, and promethazine (Phenergan) was marketed as an antihistamine in 1945. A large number of additional phenothiazines were synthesized by a French drug company, Rhône-Poulenc, and their potency as depressants was reported by Charpentier in 1950. Henri Laborit, a French naval surgeon, had been studying shock for 7 years and had concluded that shock was dangerous because of hyperactivity of the sympathetic nervous system. In 1951, he and Huguenard intro-

duced what might now be called the treatment of shock with vasodilators. Vasoconstriction was blocked with a "lytic cocktail" of chlorpromazine, promethazine, and meperidine, which also produced deep sedation and hypothermia ("artificial hibernation"). In addition to modifying the treatment of shock and reintroducing hypothermic anesthesia, these workers also suggested that the phenothiazines would be useful in the treatment of psychotic patients, and in 1952 Delay and Deniker described their application in a psychiatric hospital.

At about the same time, the second general group of tranquilizers, the *Rauwolfia* alkaloids, especially reserpine, came into use. They are still used in the treatment of hypertension, but rarely as antipsychotics.

Chemistry

The antipsychotic tranquilizers most widely used are phenothiazine derivatives. There are, however, 4 general groups:

A. Reserpine and Other Central Sympathoplegics: Reserpine affects behavior as other antipsychotic tranquilizers do, and the drug was used briefly in the treatment of psychotic states. However, it is now regarded as an antihypertensive drug, and the behavioral depression is regarded as a side-effect. Reserpine is discussed in Chapter 12. The effects on amine depletion and storage described for reserpine do not occur with the phenothiazine tranquilizers.

Other drugs that also cause the distinctive kind of sedation seen with the antipsychotics include the dihydroergots (Hydergine), alpha methyldopa (Aldomet), and the beta-adrenergic blocking agent propranolol (Inderal).

B. Phenothiazine Tranquilizers: The phenothiazines may be classified according to the nature of the side chain that bears the tertiary amine function (Table 25–1). The piperazinylpropyl class causes less sedation and more extrapyramidal side-effects than the other subclasses, and the members of this class are sometimes referred to as "stimulant" tranquilizers.

All are bases (some with 2 amine functions) and are dispensed as salts of a variety of acids. The few cases where the nature of the salt is of interest are discussed under Selection of Drug.

Table 25—1. Chemical structures of antipsychotic tranquilizers.

	R_1	R_2	Names
Dimethylaminopropyl derivatives			
	$-Cl$		Chlorpromazine (Thorazine)
	$-H$		Promazine (Sparine)
	$-CF_3$		Triflupromazine (Vesprin)
Dimethylaminoisopropyl derivatives			
	$-H$		Promethazine (Phenergan)
	$-\overset{\displaystyle O}{\overset{\|}{C}}-C_2H_5$		Propiomazine (Largon)
Piperazinylpropyl derivatives			
	$-Cl$	$-CH_3$	Prochlorperazine (Compazine)
	$-CF_3$	$-CH_3$	Trifluoperazine (Stelazine)
	$-S-C_2H_5$	$-CH_3$	Thiethylperazine (Torecan)
	$-Cl$	$-CH_2-CH_2-OH$	Perphenazine (Trilafon)
	$-CF_3$	$-CH_2-CH_2-OH$	Fluphenazine (Prolixin, Permitil)
	$-\overset{\displaystyle O}{\overset{\|}{C}}-CH_3$	$-CH_2-CH_2-OH$	Acetophenazine (Tindal)
	$-\overset{\displaystyle O}{\overset{\|}{C}}-C_2H_5$	$-CH_2-CH_2-OH$	Carphenazine (Proketazine)
	$-\overset{\displaystyle O}{\overset{\|}{C}}-C_3H_7$	$-CH_3$	Butaperazine (Repoise)
Piperidyl derivatives			
	$-S-CH_3$		Thioridazine (Mellaril)
	$-\overset{}{\underset{\displaystyle O}{\overset{\displaystyle S}{-}}}-CH_3$		Mesoridazine (Serentil)
	$-\overset{\displaystyle O}{\overset{\|}{C}}-CH_3$	$-CH_2-N\big\rangle-C_2H_4OH$	Piperacetazine (Quide)
Thioxanthene derivatives			
	$-Cl$	$-N(CH_3)_2$	Chlorprothixene (Taractan)
	$-SO_2-N(CH_3)_2$	$-N\big\rangle N-CH_3$	Thiothixene (Navane)

C. Nonphenothiazine Tranquilizers: The phenothiazine part of the tranquilizer molecule is not essential and may be replaced by some other bulky chemical group. Chlorprothixene (Taractan), shown in Table 25–1, loxapine (Loxitane), and the antidepressant drugs shown in Table 28–1 are not substituted phenothiazines but contain an equivalent tricyclic moiety. Their pharmacologic effects are similar to those of chlorpromazine.

Haloperidol (Haldol), shown in Fig 25–4, is a butyrophenone derivative, and molindone (Moban) is chemically unrelated to any of the above, but both are comparable to the stimulant type of phenothiazine tranquilizer.

Others, eg, hydroxyzine (Atarax, Vistaril), are qualitatively similar to the phenothiazine tranquilizers but are less potent in the sense that the atropinelike side-effects limit the size of the dose that can be used. Several nonphenothiazine tranquilizers are characterized below in the section on Selection of Drug.

D. Related Drug Groups: The antihistamines, including those characterized as antiemetics in Chapter 19 and the parasympatholytic drugs, have central nervous system effects comparable to those of the tranquilizers. Conversely, the tranquilizers have parasympatholytic and histamine-blocking properties similar to the other drugs.

Pharmacologic Effects

A. Mechanism of Action: The mechanism of action of these drugs that can attenuate schizophrenic symptoms is of special interest not so much because of what it would teach about rational drug use as because of what it might teach about the mediation or perhaps even the cause of schizophrenia. The search is complicated by the fact that the drugs have multiple effects and, it appears, multiple mechanisms of action. The wealth of biochemical and physiologic data that have been accumulated cannot yet be organized into a unified concept.

At the biochemical level, at least 3 theories are still considered. The most prevalent is based on the unquestioned observation that many of the antipsychotics increase the rate of dopamine turnover in many areas of the central nervous system. (Turnover is the rate of synthesis and destruction and differs from tissue levels or content discussed in relation to reserpine.) The theory holds that dopamine-mediated transmission is blocked by antipsychotics and that the increased turnover is compensatory to the continued release of transmitter from dopaminergic neurons. Parkinsonism (see Chapter 30) is related to a nigrostriatal deficiency in dopamine, and the theory is a plausible explanation for the extrapyramidal side-effects of the antipsychotics.

The behavioral effects of chlorpromazine are reversed by cholinesterase inhibitors that can reach the central nervous system (physostigmine), suggesting that a central cholinolytic effect may be important.

Chlorpromazine and several related antipsychotics and antidepressants inhibit the effect of guanethidine by blocking its uptake into adrenergic neurons. This is the same path that mediates norepinephrine reuptake, suggesting the possibility of a central effect on catecholamine action.

At the physiologic level, the behavioral or manifest effect of the tranquilizers is depression in the sense of reduced activity and attentiveness, but the neurophysiologic mechanism of action appears—to the extent that it is understood—to be stimulation. As larger and larger doses are given, signs of stimulation culminating in convulsions may appear. Electrographic studies show the limbic system to be the most sensitive electrically. The seizures caused by very large doses begin here and spread to cortical structures.

Lower levels of the central nervous system are depressed, presumably as a result of increased inhibitory influences from above. The diencephalon is inhibited in its function. Hypothalamic control of the anterior pituitary is reduced, temperature regulation is altered, and sham rage is reduced.

Chlorpromazine does not block the response to stimulation of the reticular activating system (RAS); in fact, it increases the response to peripheral nerve or thalamic stimulation. The mechanism of action may therefore be an increased filtering of afferent activity by the RAS due to a facilitating rather than a blocking effect, an action comparable to adaptation to a continuing stimulus.

B. Effects:

1. Behavioral–The antipsychotics and related drugs, whether given as antipsychotics, as antinauseants, as hypotensive agents, or as antihistamines, cause a kind of sedation distinct from that seen after the use of sedatives. Even with the huge doses used in the treatment of psychotic patients, this sedation does not progress to anesthesia. The patient experiences a state of indifference or apathy, with a drowsy feeling and motor retardation, but can be aroused even after large doses by ordinary stimuli. Euphoria is not present, and subjectively the type of sedation is not pleasant. Excitement is unusual but may occur early in the course of treatment. Some tolerance to the sedative (and most other) effects develops with continued treatment. Thus, small initial dosages can be progressively increased without the patient's being disabled by depression and hypotension as would occur with a large initial dose. Nevertheless, a patient receiving, for example, 2 g of chlorpromazine a day may remain immobile throughout most of the day.

It is understandable that this tranquilizing effect can reduce the activity of a grossly disturbed patient without inducing anesthesia and thus merely converting the patient into another kind of nursing problem as the sedatives would do. However, the tranquilizers also act on the disturbed thinking of schizophrenics who are not excited. Whether this represents a specific antipsychotic effect or is merely an extension of the sedative action is one of the controversial but crucial questions related to this drug group.

2. Autonomic–

a. Parasympatholytic effect–The synthetic

tranquilizers (but not reserpine) have atropinelike properties that become very prominent because of the large doses used. Dry mouth, failure of accommodation for near vision, constipation, and urinary retention are manifestations of this effect. The expected pupillary dilatation and tachycardia may or may not appear; in fact, the opposite effect—bradycardia and pupillary constriction—may be seen.

b. Beta-adrenergic effects–The phenothiazines and related synthetics (but not reserpine) cause an extremely marked vasodilatation and postural hypotension.

An alpha-adrenergic blocking effect is often invoked to explain these signs of decreased sympathetic effect. The effect of epinephrine on blood pressure does appear to be blocked, but the blockade cannot be demonstrated against norepinephrine (which was available only with difficulty when the phenothiazines were first studied). With the availability of beta-adrenergic blocking agents, it became apparent that the blockade of epinephrine and intensification of the effects of isoproterenol are prevented by beta-adrenergic blocking agents, ie, they are apparently beta-adrenergic effects. The phenothiazines, therefore, intensify the vasodilating and other beta-adrenergic effects of epinephrine or sympathetic nerve stimulation. Patients may, therefore, show signs of vasodilatation with postural hypotension but nevertheless respond to norepinephrine. Infusion of epinephrine (or isoproterenol) would lower the blood pressure even more.

With continued use even of very large doses, chlorpromazine and related tranquilizers and antidepressants cause only a moderate and easily tolerated degree of postural hypotension. Early in the use of these drugs and especially after parenteral administration, postural hypotension may be prominent and lead to faintness and syncope. Even when blood pressure has fallen to very low levels, the skin is warm and dry and cardiac output not dangerously reduced, ie, hypotension is present but shock is not. Chlorpromazine was first used in the treatment of shock, and its effectiveness was presumably due to its vasodilating or isoproterenollike effect.

c. Central sympathoplegic effect–The tranquilizers cause changes that cannot be explained on the basis of parasympatholytic or beta-adrenergic effects—eg, pulse rate may be slowed, pupillary constriction may be seen instead of dilatation, and failure of ejaculation may be a prominent complaint. These sympathoplegic effects of the tranquilizers must be presumed to be central in origin.

3. Temperature regulation–The phenothiazine antipsychotics cause a minor fall in body temperature in conscious patients except in the extremities, where vasodilatation leads to a rise in superficial temperature. Chlorpromazine and its congeners not only cause vasodilatation but suppress shivering as well, and are therefore useful when it is desirable to induce hypothermia by lowering the ambient temperature as in hypothermic anesthesia.

4. Endocrine effects–As the hypothalamus is depressed, the amounts of the several releasing factors that reach the anterior pituitary are decreased. Gonadotropin liberation is decreased, as shown by assays of urinary excretion and by disturbances of the menstrual cycle or even, with large doses, amenorrhea. Another common side-effect is nonpuerperal lactation due to decreased production of hypothalamic prolactin inhibitory factor with the resultant increase of lactogenic hormone.

5. Extrapyramidal effects–See Adverse Reactions.

6. Convulsant effect–Huge doses of any tranquilizer may cause convulsions, although this is rare clinically. Epileptics are far more susceptible.

7. Quinidinelike effect–The antipsychotics and the antidepressants that are closely related have effects on the heart similar to those of quinidine. The ECG may show T wave changes, P–R and QRS prolongation reflecting slowed conduction, and ventricular ectopic pacemaker activity. In addition, ventricular fibrillation and sudden death may be precipitated. It is probable that thioridazine (Mellaril) offers a special hazard in this regard.

8. Effects not present–Habituation to the antipsychotics does not occur, and physical dependence or abuse does not develop. A withdrawal state does not occur. Supposed withdrawal symptoms must be distinguished from reemergence of a psychosis following discontinuance of the drug.

Pharmacokinetics

The absorption of those tranquilizers that have been studied is slow and either is incomplete or the long residence time in the intestine allows them to be degraded and absorbed as inactive metabolites. The effect after intramuscular or intravenous injection is immediate; after oral administration the maximum effect does not develop for several hours but then persists for about 24 hours. Fig 25–1 demonstrates the more complete absorption of both intramuscular and liquid preparations compared with ordinary tablets and especially with a "prolonged release" capsule.

The principal metabolic pathways involve oxidation to a sulfoxide and hydroxylation of the rings at several sites. The metabolites can be demonstrated in the urine by simple color tests for phenols. No one of the metabolites has been shown to be active in humans.

The first step in oxidation to the sulfoxide involves formation of a free radical that may participate in the abnormal pigment deposition discussed below (see Adverse Reactions).

Methods for determining chlorpromazine in blood are just now coming into wide use. It appears that the variability in the dosages of those drugs that are needed and some of the variability in therapeutic effectiveness are due to a correspondingly great variation in serum levels that occurs as a result of irregular absorption.

Clinical Uses

A. Treatment of Schizophrenic Reaction: The

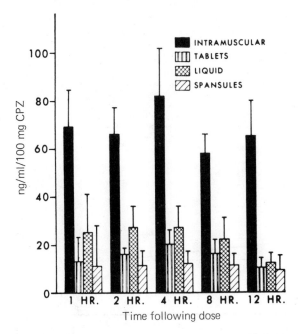

Figure 25–1. Plasma levels following the administration of chlorpromazine in 4 dosage forms. Patients had been receiving the same dosage form prior to the test dose, but initial plasma levels were low. Levels are adjusted to reflect the difference in dosage between the 13 subjects and the smaller (50–100 mg) intramuscular dose. (Reproduced, with permission, from Hollister LE & others: Studies of delayed action medication. Clin Pharmacol Ther 11:54, 1970.)

phenothiazines can reduce excitement and control hostile and aggressive behavior in psychotic patients. This effect has had a tremendous impact on the practice of psychiatry by reducing the amount of restraint needed and even the need for hospitalization.

Further than this, however, the tranquilizers suppress symptoms, particularly psychotic ideation, in a manner that cannot be explained easily by the mere behavioral depressant effect of the drugs. To some observers—especially those who tend to accept the hypothesis that schizophrenia is due to some biochemical abnormality—the normalization of behavior suggests that the phenothiazines exert a specific antipsychotic effect. Others point out that patients are anything but normal while taking the large doses of phenothiazines required and that even though they may be able to remain in the community on maintenance doses, they may not be undamaged by the medication.

Therefore, the clinical evaluation of the antipsychotic drugs must consider more than the usual trials that establish an effect on a symptom and allow comparison of available drugs. One must also consider the effect that the availability of these drugs will have on the type and amount of treatment that is offered—and even ask whether the drugs are always given for the benefit of the patient or whether the motive for controlling these patients is societal gain or the convenience of family and treating personnel.

It has been repeatedly demonstrated that the phenothiazines decreased the duration of hospitalization required for severe psychosis and even prevented hospitalization in many cases. The number of patients in mental hospitals in the USA increased steadily from the end of World War II to a maximum of 555,000 in 1955. The number decreased by 100,000 during the next decade as tranquilizers came into wide use. The additional halving of the number of patients in state and federal institutions in the decade 1963–1972 was possible because the phenothiazines rendered patients tractable enough for the growth of the concept (if not the execution) of community mental health programs. Fig 25–2 shows the improvement in release rates since the availability of the tranquilizers in one selected group: male Caucasian patients age 25–44 admitted to California state hospitals for the first time with a diagnosis of schizophrenic reaction.

However, factors other than the introduction of tranquilizers could have caused the changes since 1950—eg, increased funds for institutional care or the trend toward community-centered care. Only controlled studies can establish the efficacy of the drugs and permit comparison with other available drugs. One well-designed study from the same California hospitals permits correlation of short-term drug effects with the eventual gain described in Fig 25–2. This investigation utilized patients age 20–50 who had been hospitalized in a large state institution for 2–10 years before treatment. In a double-blind manner, they were given one of 4 phenothiazines, and the dosages were gradually increased to the optimal level over a period of 30 days. One group received an inactive placebo, but another control group received an active placebo of atropine and phenobarbital to mimic in part the side-effects of the phenothiazines and maintain a more truly blind situation. The active drugs used and the mean modal doses of each were as follows:

> Chlorpromazine, 1800 mg
> Perphenazine, 182 mg
> Prochlorperazine, 338 mg
> Triflupromazine, 621 mg

Fig 25–3 shows the degree of improvement as measured by a rating scale. The apparent lag in the effect of one phenothiazine is probably due to masking of improvement by side-effects. The meaning of this improvement in scores is shown by the fact that at the end of the treatment period only 5 out of 96 patients who received placebos were ready for discharge, whereas 70 of 192 treated patients were ready to leave the institution.

One collaborative study utilized 409 newly admitted patients from psychiatric hospitals of several types. Three phenothiazines and a placebo were given in a double-blind manner for 6 weeks. Symptoms were rated and the overall state and degree of improvement judged. On a 7-point scale of severity of mental illness, for example, drug-treated patients were judged to have changed from markedly or severely ill ("5.5") to

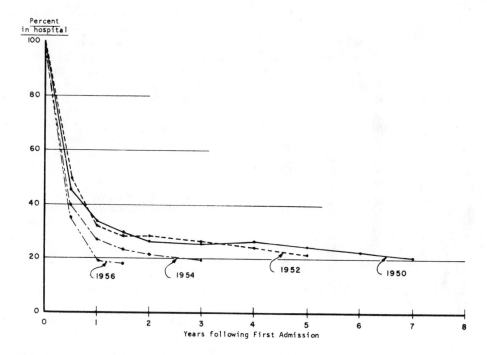

Figure 25–2. Retention curves for first-admission male patients with the diagnosis of schizophrenic reaction, demonstrating the shorter periods of hospitalization as antipsychotic tranquilizers came into wider use. (Reproduced, with permission, from Epstein & Morgan: Trends in release rates of schizophrenic patients. Compr Psychiatry 2:199, 1961.)

mildly ill ("3"). The mean of the placebo group changed to moderately or markedly ill ("4.5").

This kind of evaluation has its limitations but permits some conclusions. The 3 active drugs—chlorpromazine (600 mg average daily dose), fluphenazine (6 mg/d), and thioridazine (700 mg/d)—did not differ in therapeutic effectiveness. Fluphenazine, of the piperazinylpropyl group, caused more extrapyramidal side-effects but less drowsiness. Thioridazine caused less muscle rigidity but appreciably more vomiting.

Drugs that appear equivalent when tested on groups of patients (as above) might have different effectiveness if tested on patients further segregated by symptoms, ie, different tranquilizers might be selectively more effective against paranoia, motor retardation, or the behavior patterns. Such is probably the case, but only fragmentary data are available even in patients with depression.

Concurrent use of more than one antipsychotic drug is rarely, if ever, indicated for the treatment of schizophrenia.

B. Depression: The present discussion will conform to a questionable and changing convention that classifies and separately discusses certain drugs as antidepressants even though differentiation from tranquilizers is not possible pharmacologically (see Chapter 28). Both tranquilizers and the drugs listed in Table 28–1 are effective in the treatment of the major endogenous depressions. When an antidepressant or a tranquilizer is used in treating depression, the dosage is not progressively increased to an effective level as in the

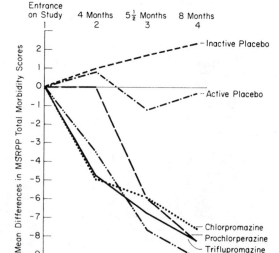

Figure 25–3. Effectiveness of antipsychotic tranquilizers. Groups of 48 hospitalized psychotic patients were studied on each of 6 treatments. The initial score on a rating scale is plotted at zero; a decrease in total morbidity score indicates improvement. (Reproduced, with permission, from Adelson & Epstein: A study of phenothiazines with male and female chronically ill schizophrenic patients. J Nerv Ment Dis 134:547, 1962.)

Table 25—2. Antipsychotic tranquilizers: Dosages and preparations available.

	Equivalent Adult Daily Oral Dose (CPZ = 100 mg)	Preparations Available
Tranquilizers with moderate stimulant effects		
Chlorpromazine* (Thorazine)	75—400 mg	Tablets, 10, 25, 50, 100, and 200 mg Concentrate, 30 mg/mL, 120 mL and 1 gal Syrup, 10 mg/5 mL Suppositories, 25 and 100 mg Injectable (IM, IV†), 25 mg/mL; 1- and 2-mL ampules and 10-mL vials
Promazine (Sparine)	10—200 mg	Tablets, 10, 25, 50, 100, and 200 mg Concentrate, 30 mg/mL, 120 mL; 100 mg/mL, 30 mL Syrup, 10 mg/5 mL, 120 mL Injectable (IM, IV†), 50 mg/mL, 1- and 2-mL ampules; 25 and 50 mg/mL, 10-mL vials; 25 and 50 mg/mL, 1- and 2-mL Tubex
Triflupromazine (Vesprin)	15—20 mg	Tablets, 10, 25, and 50 mg Suspension, 10 mg/mL, 120 mL Injectable (IM, IV†), 10 mg/mL, 10-mL vials; 20 mg/mL, 1-mL ampules
Thioridazine (Mellaril)	50—100 mg	Tablets, 10, 25, 50, 100, and 200 mg Concentrate, 30 mg/mL, 120 mL
Mesoridazine (Serentil)	30—150 mg	Tablets, 10, 25, 50, and 100 mg Injectable (IM), 25 mg/mL, 1-mL ampules
Chlorprothixene (Taractan)	25—50 mg 3—4 times daily	Tablets, 10, 25, 50, and 100 mg Concentrate, 100 mg/5 mL, 16 oz Injectable (IM), 25 mg in 2-mL ampules
Tranquilizers with prominent stimulant effects		
Trifluoperazine (Stelazine)	8 mg	Tablets, 1, 2, 5, and 10 mg Concentrate, 10 mg/mL, 60 mL Injectable (IM), 2 mg/mL, 10-mL vials
Perphenazine (Trilafon)	8—16 mg 2—4 times daily	Tablets, 2, 4, 8, and 16 mg Concentrate, 16 mg/5 mL, 120 mL Injectable (IM, IV), 5 mg/mL, 1-mL ampules and 10-mL vials
Fluphenazine (Permitil Hydrochloride)	1—5 mg	Tablets, 0.25, 1, 2.5, 5, and 10 mg Concentrate, 5 mg/mL, 120 mL
(Prolixin Hydrochloride)	2 mg	Tablets, 1, 2.5, and 5 mg Elixir, 0.5 mg/mL, 60 and 480 mL Injectable (IM), 2.5 mg/mL, 10-mL vials
(Prolixin Enanthate)	. . .	Injectable (subcut, IM), 25 mg/mL (in sesame oil), 5-mL vials
(Prolixin Decanoate)	. . .	Injectable (subcut, IM), 25 mg/mL (in oil), 1- and 5-mL vials
Acetophenazine (Tindal)	40—80 mg	Tablets, 20 mg
Butaperazine (Repoise)	10 mg	Tablets, 5, 10, and 25 mg
Piperacetazine (Quide)	20 mg	Tablets, 10 and 25 mg
Carphenazine (Proketazine)	12.5—25 mg	Tablets, 12.5, 25, and 50 mg Concentrate, 50 mg/mL, 120 mL
Thiothixene (Navane)	4 mg	Capsules, 1, 2, 5, and 10 mg Concentrate, 5 mg/mL Injectable (IM), 2 mg/mL in 2-mL ampules
Haloperidol (Haldol)	2—4 mg	Tablets, 0.5, 1, 2, and 5 mg Concentrate, 2 mg/mL, 15 and 120 mL Injectable (IM), 5 mg/mL
Loxapine (Loxitane)	. . .	Tablets, 10, 25, and 50 mg
Molindone (Moban)	5—225 mg	Tablets, 5, 10, and 25 mg
Tranquilizers with prominent sedative effects		
Promethazine* (Phenergan, Remsed)	25 mg	Tablets, 12.5, 25, and 50 mg Syrup, 6.25 mg/5 mL and 25 mg/5 mL, 480 mL Suppositories, 25 and 50 mg Injectable (IM, IV), 25 and 50 mg/mL, 1-mL ampules and 10-mL vials

*Generic preparations available. Trade name included for identification only.

†All intravenous injections should be given with great caution because of the possibility of precipitous hypotension.

treatment of other psychoses, but a ceiling dose is observed.

C. Other Psychiatric Problems: Emotional instability and odd behavior in aged patients with "chronic brain syndrome" may be controlled with phenothiazines. Usefulness in other situations cannot be assumed. Disturbed mentally retarded patients, for example, are not improved by phenothiazine treatment.

D. Pruritus: Itching associated with an allergic reaction of the immediate type—eg, urticaria—may be relieved by antihistamines, some of which are phenothiazines. The antihistamines are not usually effective in other pruritic states, and, if they are, it is not because of their antihistaminic effects. Tranquilizers have only limited usefulness against itching in general. Some studies fail to show any superiority over a placebo, which gives the expected 40% favorable response. Some studies do show a superiority over a placebo but not over a sedative. Tranquilizers may be preferable in this condition to sedatives in children because of the lower incidence of excitement due to disinhibition, which sometimes follows the administration of sedatives. Selective antipruritus action is claimed without good basis for 2 phenothiazines. One is trimeprazine (Temaril), which, however, causes sleepiness in the usual dose of 2.5 mg 4 times a day. The sleepiness is not objectionable at bedtime, and a larger dose may be used; but the other phenothiazines are equivalent to trimeprazine. Methdilazine (Tacaryl) is another phenothiazine, often classed as an antihistamine, suggested for this special use.

E. Antiemetic: See Chapter 19.

F. Preprocedural Medications in Combination With Narcotic Analgesics: Narcotic analgesics and tranquilizers both cause sedation, but the effect of injecting a mixture of the 2 is more than additive. Such mixtures—eg, meperidine and promethazine—are therefore used as preoperative medication. The potentiating effects on sedation do not extend to the analgesic action in the opinion of some investigators, but this conclusion is still uncertain. For additional discussion, see Chapter 26.

G. Analgesia: Methotrimeprazine (Levoprome, Nozinan) is a phenothiazine similar in structure and effects to the other tranquilizers. However, the analgesic properties that are present to a negligible degree in chlorpromazine are greatly increased in this compound. When given by injection, it is nearly as potent as morphine. Huge doses must be given orally, but this compound is of great interest because it is the most potent nonaddicting analgesic so far studied. This drug is not available in the USA.

Adverse Reactions

In those situations in which a few small doses of an antipsychotic are used, it might be possible to differentiate side-effects and overdosage toxicity. However, because these drugs are most commonly used in large doses for prolonged periods, this differentiation is usually not possible.

A. Dose-Related Toxicity:

1. Behavioral—

a. Somnolence—Again it must be emphasized that taking an antipsychotic tranquilizer is not a subjectively pleasant experience. The feelings of lassitude and fatigability are unpleasant. With continued administration, patients become somewhat tolerant or accustomed to this effect, but it limits their function to some extent and decreases the dependability with which they will take their medication without supervision—ie, as an outpatient. The incidence of suicide is greater among psychotics receiving drug therapy than in groups receiving only institutional care. The greater freedom of activity permitted the patient controlled by drugs is probably a factor, but so probably is the behavioral depression caused by the tranquilizers.

b. Others—A few patients may experience feelings of excitement and restlessness. These feelings are more common early in treatment and after the administration of those piperazine or piperazinylpropyl derivatives characterized as "stimulant" tranquilizers.

With all of the antipsychotics, less time is spent in deep sleep and more in REM sleep. The increased amount of dreaming is often perceived and reported by the patient as the appearance of nightmares.

Early in treatment, a patient depressed by a tranquilizer may at the same time develop a toxic psychosis with confusion and hallucinations. Such a reaction is more common with those drugs that resemble the antihistamines and atropine substitutes.

2. Extrapyramidal effects—Disturbances of the extrapyramidal motor system appear in 4 general patterns.

a. Parkinsonism equivalent—As the phenothiazines are given to schizophrenic patients—ie, to therapeutic response or the maximum tolerated dose—parkinsonism is among the most frequent side-effects. It consists of akinesia, muscular rigidity, and fine resting tremors and may vary in severity from slight impairment of facial mobility to completely disabling rigidity.

To minimize the development of muscular rigidity, many physicians administer an antiparkinsonism drug—eg, benztropine (Cogentin)—when large doses of a phenothiazine tranquilizer are being used. The advisability of this practice had been questioned by some clinicians on the basis of observations that it is better to give the antiparkinsonism agent only after the signs appear. Now that chlorpromazine blood levels are available, it appears that chlorpromazine absorption and blood levels are decreased by benztropine administration—ie, any benefit is at the expense of efficacy.

b. Dystonias—Dystonias are most commonly seen in children and young adults either early in treatment or immediately following the injection of a phenothiazine or the accidental ingestion of a single large dose. The muscles of the shoulder girdle and jaws are most likely to be involved. Violent dystonias with movements of the arms and head that can be mistaken for convulsions may occur, or there may be athetoid movements or persistent oculogyrate movements. Since they occur in a depressed, unresponsive patient, these reactions may be misdiagnosed and therefore overtreated and overstudied.

This toxic reaction is well tolerated and should be treated conservatively. Of the drugs that may relieve the dystonia, diphenhydramine (Benadryl) is apparently most useful.

c. Akathisia–Akathisia is a feeling of restlessness or of compelling need for movement. Patients may walk about impatiently, tap their feet incessantly, or complain of "restless legs."

d. Tardive dyskinesia–The drug-induced extrapyramidal states described above are completely reversible upon discontinuation or reduced dosage of the tranquilizer. Tardive dyskinesia, however, is not only irreversible; it is usually intensified when the phenothiazine is withdrawn.

The late dyskinesia occurs, usually in patients above 40 years of age and more commonly in women, after exposure to large doses of tranquilizers for periods of 6 months to 2 years or longer. In contrast to the acute dystonias, the onset is insidious and the movements are rhythmic and coordinated rather than spasmodic. The tongue, lips, face, and jaws are most commonly involved, resulting in a picture suggestive of Huntington's chorea or the toxic effect of levodopa. The state may be suppressed with high doses of tranquilizer, presumably with additional risk. Other treatments—eg, amantadine or reasonable doses of reserpine—are being evaluated. Estimates of the incidence of this toxic effect vary—peculiarly—from a denial of its existence to 50% of certain groups of patients; as high as 50% in some groups followed for long periods; 3% in the general population of patients receiving the drug; and 40–50% in the elderly groups.

3. Convulsions–Precipitation of convulsions is possible but quite rare during the use of the antipsychotic tranquilizers unless some additional factor is present—eg, if the patient is an epileptic or if another convulsant drug is being used.

4. Atropinelike effects–Parasympatholytic side-effects may be quite prominent. They include dry mouth, blurred vision, and constipation or even paralytic ileus. The expected tachycardia and pupillary dilatation may appear, especially with large doses, but these measurements may be little changed or bradycardia and pupillary constriction may be observed. This variability in the response of the heart rate and pupillary size suggests that a central sympatholytic effect is also present.

5. Postural hypotension–The intensification of the beta-agonist effects (vasodilatation) of the sympathomimetic amines was described above as the basis for the fall in blood pressure. This side-effect is especially troublesome after injection of the tranquilizer and early in treatment. It may be intense enough to cause dizziness or fainting.

6. Metabolic and endocrinologic changes–Weight gain is a common side-effect of prolonged administration of chlorpromazine and reserpine but not of all of the antipsychotics. The increase in caloric intake cannot be explained by changes in the behavioral state—ie, it does not merely reflect an elevation of mood, as is true for the similar effect of antidepressant drugs.

The endocrinologic side-effects are due to hypothalamic depression and consequent decrease in some of the tropic hormones of the anterior pituitary. Decrease in gonadotropin liberation leads to menstrual irregularities that usually become less with continued treatment. Lactation may occur for the reasons discussed above. Serum levels of growth hormone are decreased in acromegalics.

7. Oculocutaneous pigmentation–For some patients, the continued use of large doses of a phenothiazine is the only alternative to grossly disturbed behavior or recurrent hospitalization. In some patients, especially women, the exposed parts of the skin (face, neck, back of hands) take on a mauve or slate color after years of therapy with chlorpromazine. Pigment deposits in the anterior lens capsule and posterior surface of the cornea can be seen by slitlamp examination in a third or half of some groups receiving prolonged chlorpromazine therapy. Visual acuity is not reduced, but some blurring of vision may be reported. At autopsy, the pigment is also seen in macrophages throughout the body.

Thus far, chlorpromazine and thioridazine are the only phenothiazines that have caused this state. The daily dosage of chlorpromazine must exceed 500 mg/d. Experimentally, a single large dose followed by exposure to ultraviolet or visible light causes an unusual degree of erythema, but in clinical practice this occurs only after treatment for 3 years or longer. Women are far more susceptible.

The dense granules that accumulate are not identical with melanin or unchanged chlorpromazine ultramicroscopically, but they may be a combination of melanin and a photo-oxidation product of chlorpromazine.

The process is very slowly reversible over a period of several months. Treatment consists of protection from light and substitution of a phenothiazine that requires a smaller absolute dose or of a combination of chlorpromazine with such an agent.

8. Pigmentary retinopathy–Deposition of pigment in the retina with impaired vision occurs rarely and by a process separate from the more common oculocutaneous pigmentation. Smaller doses and brief periods are involved. Thioridazine (Mellaril) has caused most of the few reported cases.

9. Ventricular dysrhythmias–The hazard of the quinidinelike action of the antipsychotics is discussed above.

B. Acute Intoxication: The acute overdosage toxicity of the tranquilizers is very low in adults, and the possibility of a fatal outcome following attempted suicidal or accidental ingestion is negligible unless a second depressant drug is also involved.

These drugs are only slightly more dangerous in children; however, children are especially susceptible to the dystonic state described above, and such states are occasionally seen following accidental ingestion of one of the drugs or its therapeutic use in the treatment of vomiting.

C. Allergic Reactions:

1. Cholestatic jaundice–Chlorpromazine and a few other drugs such as methyltestosterone and erythromycin estolate can cause jaundice or less marked degrees of liver dysfunction by causing intrahepatic biliary obstruction rather than by direct liver cell damage. The obstruction is at the level of the smallest biliary radicles, and initially the usual clinical laboratory tests give results consistent with obstructive jaundice. As in other forms of jaundice, the laboratory tests may later give evidence of hepatocellular damage, but the process is benign and completely reversible although many weeks may be required. In the early days of chlorpromazine use, the incidence of this adverse reaction was very high, perhaps 3–5%. The number of cases then decreased rapidly, and for the past few years chlorpromazine jaundice has been rare. The reaction was apparently due to an unidentified impurity that was removed as methods of preparing the drug were improved. The reaction is often assumed, without immunochemical evidence, to have been allergic in origin. Prior sensitization is not a factor, since the jaundice appeared in almost every case within the first 6 weeks of treatment.

2. Other allergic reactions–The rare occurrence of agranulocytosis appears to reflect the extent of use of the individual drugs except in the case of promazine, which is unusually hazardous in this regard. Contact dermatitis can occur when the situation permits, as in nurses who handle the drug. Other cutaneous reactions also occur, including a photosensitivity reaction that resembles eczema.

Contraindications & Cautions

The antipsychotic tranquilizers should not be used in comatose patients and should be given with care and in reduced doses if central nervous system depressant drugs have been taken. These include alcohol as well as the barbiturates and narcotics.

With chronic administration—even of large doses—the problem of drug interactions is reduced; there is, for example, no apparent change in the response of institutionalized patients to general anesthesia. The effect of the hypotensive agent guanethidine is blocked by chlorpromazine and presumably by the other antipsychotics.

Selection of Drug

From the discussion above, the following ideas should be repeated: (1) The antipsychotic tranquilizers are not effective antianxiety drugs. (2) In the treatment of schizophrenia, no differences in effectiveness among the potent drugs have yet been established. (3) Most psychotic patients will require maintenance doses of tranquilizers after discharge from the hospital. The dosage required may be very large and should not be arbitrarily reduced by the physician in the commu-

nity. The drug can be discontinued when the illness has run its course—a time that can be defined only by trials at intervals. (4) The duration of action of the major tranquilizers is such that administration once or twice daily provides a sustained effect. (5) Liquid preparations were introduced for convenience in institutional practice and to prevent the hoarding of tablets by patients, but they also provide for more complete absorption.

The available drugs, whether phenothiazines or not, can now be discussed using the classification suggested in the section on the chemistry of the phenothiazines: (1) chlorpromazine and similar drugs; (2) the "stimulant" tranquilizers, which cause less somnolence but more extrapyramidal side-effects; (3) those that cause more sedation; (4) those with limited potency; and (5) those suggested for special application against vomiting and itching.

A. Chlorpromazine and Comparable Agents: Chlorpromazine no longer causes jaundice with the distressing frequency that it once did, and the consensus would clearly name it as the standard drug of the tranquilizer class. It is also less expensive than other antipsychotics. In the treatment of psychotics, it is often combined with one of the piperazinylpropyl compounds such as trifluoperazine (Stelazine) because of the unquantitated impression that a balance of sedation and stimulation is thus achieved.

Promazine (Sparine) has caused a high incidence of agranulocytosis. With so many alternative drugs available, there is no need to use it.

Thioridazine (Mellaril) is favored by some physicians because it probably causes less parkinsonism. However, it is also more likely to cause vomiting, retinopathy, and ventricular dysrhythmias.

B. "Stimulant" Tranquilizers: There is little basis for differentiating among the piperazinylpropyl derivatives shown in Table 25–1.

Haloperidol (Haldol) is not a phenothiazine but one of a group of butyrophenones. It causes many extrapyramidal reactions but little sedation and perhaps fewer autonomic side-effects. Droperidol (Inapsine) is also a butyrophenone chemically and pharmacologically similar to haloperidol. Rarely used by itself, this long-acting drug is encountered as a component of Innovar, in which it is combined with a short-acting narcotic.

Fluphenazine (Prolixin) is provided in the form of 2 salts that are relatively insoluble and therefore slowly absorbed after injection. The injections need be given only at intervals of 2 weeks in the case of the enanthate, or perhaps even longer if the decanoate is used. The advantage claimed is less dependence upon the daily cooperation of patients on oral medication.

C. Tranquilizers That Cause More Somnolence: Promethazine (Phenergan) is not used in the treatment of psychotic patients because of the sedation that it causes.

Propiomazine (Largon) is similar to promethazine and offers no advantage over the more widely used compounds. It is available only in an injectable

Table 25–3. Nonphenothiazine (antihistamine) tranquilizers with limited potency: Dosages.

	Adult Oral Dose (3–4 Times/Day)
Tranquilizers of limited potency	
Hydroxyzine	
hydrochloride (Atarax, Vistaril)	
pamoate (Vistaril)	25–50 mg
Antipruritics	
Methdilazine (Tacaryl)	8 mg
Trimeprazine (Temaril)	2.5 mg

dosage form, and experience has been limited to adjunctive uses in anesthesia.

D. Less Potent Tranquilizers: (Table 25–3.) Nonphenothiazine compounds may be potent and useful tranquilizers—eg, haloperidol or chlorprothixene. However, the nonphenothiazine tranquilizers listed below are much less useful. They are often called "diphenylmethane derivatives"; they resemble the chemically similar antihistamines and synthetic substitutes for atropine, and their dosages and effectiveness are limited by their atropinelike side-effects. They are listed here for identification only and are not suggested for any of the uses discussed above. These "minor tranquilizers" should not be used specifically in the treatment of anxiety.

Hydroxyzine (Atarax, Vistaril) is closely related chemically to the familiar antihistamines and antinauseants. It is used in allergic dermatoses (eg, urticaria), especially when an additional mild sedative effect is desired.

Benactyzine differs from one of the earliest synthetic atropines, adiphenine (Trasentine), only in the hydroxyl group on the benzilic acid moiety. It is not used much by itself (as Suavitil), but is present in Deprol in combination with meprobamate.

• • •

LITHIUM

Lithium ion, administered in the form of lithium carbonate, is used as an alternative or supplement to the major tranquilizers in the control of the manic stage of manic-depressive illness.

Pharmacologic Effects

Therapeutic doses of lithium do not have gross effects comparable to those of either the tranquilizers or the sedatives, and its mechanism of action is not known. Lithium is distributed more evenly between intra- and extracellular spaces than is sodium or potassium—ie, lithium ion behaves at the cell membrane somewhat like both sodium and potassium. How this property relates to the mechanism of action is as yet undefined.

The onset of action is delayed for several days after the drug is started, and 6–10 days elapse before the peak effect is reached.

Absorption, Metabolism, & Excretion

The drug is well absorbed after oral administration. It is excreted by the kidneys and at therapeutic dosages has a half-life of 24 hours. Of the lithium in glomerular filtrate, about 80% is reabsorbed by the tubules; this percentage is not influenced by diuretic drugs.

Clinical Uses

A. Control of Manic Episodes: Lithium is considered to be the drug of choice for treating the mania of manic-depressive disorders. Patients entering the manic phase of their illness are more likely to be hypomanic than violent, and a delay of a few days is often not critical if they can be protected against the consequences of their destructive behavior. Lithium is the preferable drug at such times, because it is usually effective and causes less impairment of function than other antipsychotic agents. If possible, lithium carbon-

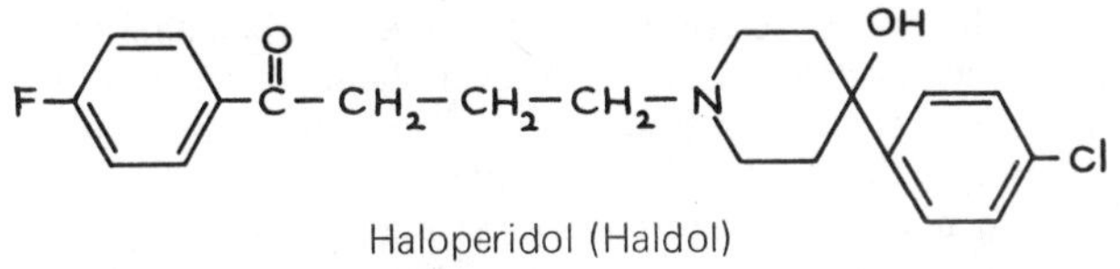

Haloperidol (Haldol)

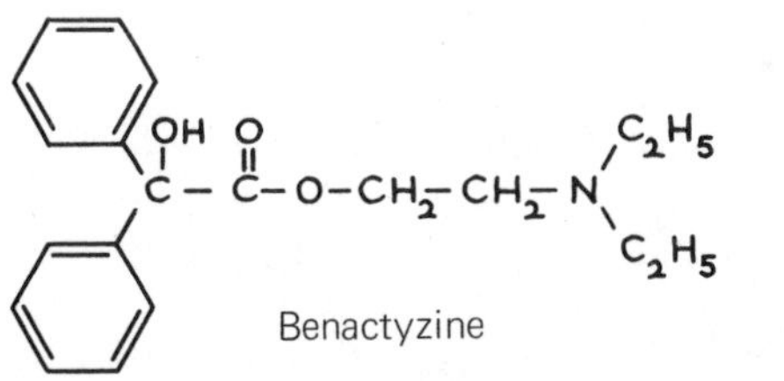

Benactyzine

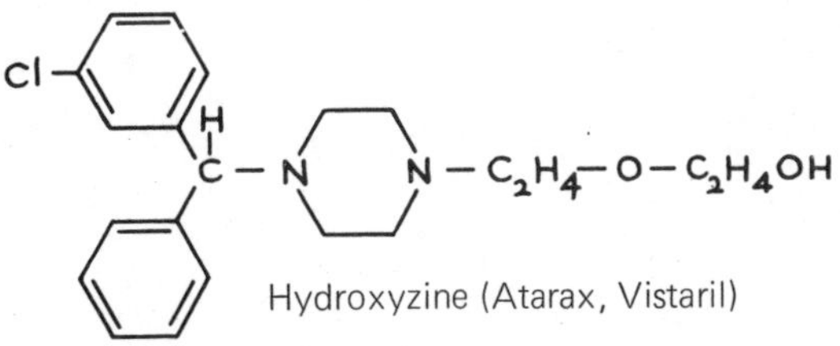

Hydroxyzine (Atarax, Vistaril)

Figure 25–4. Chemical structures of some nonphenothiazine tranquilizers.

ate should be started promptly during the hypomanic period, since it takes about 3–6 days for the salt to produce blood levels in the therapeutic range (1.0–1.3 mEq/L). The latent period for full effect may be even longer during frank mania.

If the patient is violently manic, it is necessary to use antipsychotic drugs such as the phenothiazines or haloperidol as an adjunct to lithium. When the acute mania subsides, the antipsychotic drugs should be gradually withdrawn and lithium continued as the sole drug.

Long-term maintenance therapy with lithium modifies the frequency and intensity of the episodes rather than obliterating them entirely. A few patients have no recurrences, but failure rates up to 55% have been reported. Patients must be followed carefully, both clinically and with serum lithium levels, adjusting lithium dosage according to fluctuations inherent in the illness as well as contributing physiologic changes.

B. Prophylaxis Against Affective Illness: Lithium is clearly not effective in the treatment of an established depression, but it has been claimed that it can prevent cyclic changes in mood and thus prevent not only manic attacks but also the development of depression and of the depressed stage of the manic-depressive syndrome. Some of these reports have been quite enthusiastic, and it may be that this use will ultimately be justified by adequately controlled double-blind studies. At present, however, the consensus is that the value of lithium in the prevention of depression is unestablished. If the effect is present, it requires 6–12 months for its appearance.

Lithium carbonate is approved for marketing in the USA only for use in the control of mania; its use in the prophylaxis of unipolar endogenous depression is investigational. The use of lithium in schizo-affective disorders, hyperkinetic disorders of children, behavioral disorders in adults, chronic alcoholism, cluster headaches, and other conditions has not been established.

Adverse Reactions

Toxic effects during chronic administration are predicted by serum levels, which must be determined during treatment with lithium. Side-effects are generally mild if the serum level is kept below 1.5 mEq/L. When serum levels exceed 2 mEq/L, dosage should be decreased or the drug withheld temporarily. Serum lithium decreases by half every 24 hours.

Acute toxic effects may be graded as follows:

A. Mild: Nausea that passes after a few days. A fine tremor of the hands or jaw may interfere with the patient's function and is not relieved by antiparkinson agents.

B. Moderate: Anorexia, vomiting, diarrhea, thirst and polyuria, coarse tremor, muscle weakness and twitching, sedation, and ataxia.

C. Severe: Chorea, athetosis, confusion, stupor, and convulsions.

D. Terminal: Coma.

Chronic administration often leads to the development of a goiter that can be reduced by treatment with thyroid substance. Only in isolated cases has hypothyroidism developed. T-wave depression is seen but with no accompanying evidence of cardiac dysfunction. Polyuria may occur. Excessive urine volume and thirst may be unpleasant but are not due to renal damage. The action of ADH is probably antagonized by lithium.

Contraindications & Cautions

Lithium should not be used in the presence of impaired renal function or cardiovascular disease or in any other situation that involves a restricted diet or diuretic drugs, since sodium restriction or increased loss leads to lithium retention. Excessive loss of fluid or inadequate intake also leads to higher than expected lithium levels.

Lithium given in the first trimester of pregnancy can increase the incidence of fetal cardiovascular malformations. It should therefore be withheld during that period unless its effect is absolutely essential. Changes in renal clearance must be anticipated during pregnancy and after delivery, and the babies of treated mothers should not be breast-fed. It should not be used when facilities for the determination of serum lithium levels are not available.

Dosages

Dosage is controlled by the regular determination of lithium levels in serum drawn 8–12 hours after the last dose.

Manic patients are given initial doses of 600 mg of lithium carbonate 3 times each day, but the serum level should not exceed 1.5 mEq/L. As excitement subsides, the maintenance dose should give serum levels of 0.5–1 mEq/L. The usual maintenance dose is 300 mg 3 times each day. A single daily dose is satisfactory once a stable serum level is established.

• • •

References

General

Anderson WH & others: Rapid treatment of acute psychosis. Am J Psychiatry 133:1076, 1976.

Appleton WS: Third psychoactive usage guide. Dis Nerv Syst 37:39, 1976.

Ayd FJ Jr: The depot fluphenazines: A reappraisal after 10 years' clinical experience. Am J Psychiatry 132:491, 1975.

Ayd FJ Jr: Haloperidol: Twenty years' clinical experience. J Clin Psychiatry 39:807, 1978.

Baldessarini RJ: Schizophrenia. N Engl J Med 297:988, 1977.

Bunney WE: Drug therapy and psychologic research advances in the psychoses in the past decade. Am J Psychiatry (Suppl) 135:8, 1978.

Carlsson A: Antipsychotic drugs, neurotransmitters and schizophrenia. Am J Psychiatry 135:164, 1978.

Davis JM, Casper R: Antipsychotic drugs: Clinical pharmacology and therapeutic use. Drugs 14:260, 1977.

Gokhale SD, Gulati OD, Parikh HM: An investigation of the adrenergic blocking action of chlorpromazine. Br J Pharmacol 23:508, 1964.

Hirsch SR & others: Outpatient maintenance of chronic schizophrenic patients with long-acting fluphenazine: Double-blind placebo trial. Br Med J 1:633, 1973.

Hollister L: *Clinical Pharmacology of Psychotherapeutic Drugs.* Churchill Livingstone, 1978.

Hollister LE & others: Specific indications for different classes of phenothiazines. Arch Gen Psychiatry 30:94, 1974.

Jarvik ME (editor): *Psychopharmacology in the Practice of Medicine.* Appleton-Century-Crofts, 1977.

Matthysse S: Antipsychotic drug actions. Fed Proc 32:200, 1973.

National Institute of Mental Health Collaborative Study Group: Differences in clinical effects of three phenothiazines in "acute" schizophrenia. Dis Nerv Syst 28:369, 1967.

National Institute of Mental Health Collaborative Study Group: Effectiveness of phenothiazine treatment of acute schizophrenic psychoses. Arch Gen Psychiatry 10:246, 1964.

Rifkin A & others: Are prophylactic antiparkinson drugs necessary? Arch Gen Psychiatry 35:483, 1978.

Adverse Reactions

American College of Neuropsychopharmacology-FDA Task Force: Neurologic syndromes associated with antipsychotic drug use. N Engl J Med 289:20, 1973.

Chlorpromazine melanosis. (Leading article.) Br Med J 2:630, 1967.

Crane GE: High doses of trifluoperazine and tardive dyskinesia. Arch Neurol 22:176, 1970.

Crane GE, Naranjo ER: Motor disorders induced by neuroleptics. Arch Gen Psychiatry 24:179, 1971.

Klawans HL: The pharmacology of tardive dyskinesias. Am J Psychiatry 130:82, 1976.

Kobayashi RM: Tardive dyskinesia. N Engl J Med 296:257, 1977.

Mathalone MBR: Eye and skin changes in psychiatric patients treated with chlorpromazine. Br J Ophthalmol 51:86, 1967.

Pisciotta AV: Agranulocytosis induced by certain phenothiazine derivatives. JAMA 208:1862, 1969.

Rivera-Calimlim L, Castañeda L, Lasagna L: Effects of mode of management on plasma chlorpromazine in psychiatric patients. Clin Pharmacol Ther 14:978, 1973.

Satanove A, McIntosh JS: Phototoxic reactions induced by high doses of chlorpromazine and thioridazine. JAMA 200:209, 1967.

Methotrimeprazine

Beaver WT & others: A comparison of the analgesic effects of methotrimeprazine and morphine in patients with cancer. Clin Pharmacol Ther 7:436, 1966.

De Kornfeld TJ, Pearson JW, Lasagna L: Methotrimeprazine in the treatment of labor pain. N Engl J Med 270:391, 1964.

Lithium

Baldessarini RJ, Lipinski JF: Lithium salts: 1970–1975. Ann Intern Med 83:527, 1975.

Goodwin FK: Lithium ion: Impact on treatment and research. Arch Gen Psychiatry 36:833, 1979.

Maletzky BM, Shore JH: Lithium treatment for psychiatric disorders. West J Med 128:488, 1978.

Miller PD & others: Central, renal and adrenal effects of lithium in man. Am J Med 66:797, 1979.

Prien RF & others: Comparison of lithium carbonate and chlorpromazine in treatment of mania. Arch Gen Psychiatry 26:146, 1972.

Prien RF & others: Lithium carbonate and imipramine in prevention of affective episodes. Arch Gen Psychiatry 29:420, 1973.

Rosenbaum AH, Maruta T, Richelson E: Drugs that alter mood. 2. Lithium. Mayo Clin Proc 54:401, 1979.

Schou M: Pharmacology and toxicology of lithium. Annu Rev Pharmacol Toxicol 16:231, 1976.

Singer I, Rotenberg D: Mechanisms of lithium action. N Engl J Med 289:254, 1973.

Warick LH: Lithium poisoning: Report of a case with neurologic, cardiac and hepatic sequelae. West J Med 130:259, 1979.

Weinstein MR, Goldfield MD: Cardiovascular malformations with lithium use during pregnancy. Am J Psychiatry 132:529, 1975.

Wykert J: Warning: Lithium pushers are dangerous to your health. New York Magazine, p 52, Dec 8, 1975.

26 | Narcotic Analgesics & Narcotic Antagonists

NARCOTIC ANALGESICS

Ideally, drugs should relieve pain by acting on a specific pathologic state. If specific drug therapy is not available—or during the interval between the start of therapy and effective control—it is often necessary to give drugs for the pain itself rather than for the underlying disease.

In this section are discussed the narcotic analgesics or narcotics—ie, morphine, codeine, and other alkaloids derived from opium and some equivalent synthetic analogs. In therapeutic doses these drugs relieve pain without causing general central nervous system depression as the general anesthetics do. In larger doses the narcotics are more general depressants, and all are subject to misuse or addiction. The nonnarcotic or antipyretic analgesics such as aspirin are discussed in the next chapter.

History

The opium poppy is indigenous to Asia Minor, and awareness of the euphoriant effect of some part of the poppy plant is implicit in the Sumerian records of 4000 BC. Clear accounts exist of its use in the Egyptian, Greek, and Roman cultures. Paracelsus was aware of its usefulness and prepared the first tincture of opium (laudanum), subsequently simplified by Sydenham.

Friedrich Sertürner (1783–1841) isolated morphine from opium and demonstrated for the first time that a single purified chemical substance could account for the pharmacologic effects of a natural product. Sertürner, a reluctant apprentice to a pharmacist in Prussia, was disturbed by the variable potency of available opium preparations and set out to purify and standardize it. Working at a time when neither experimental pharmacology nor the chemistry of natural products were recognized fields of endeavor, Sertürner succeeded in isolating morphine from opium. Using a bioassay in dogs, he established that morphine, as he named the alkaline substance, was the somnifacient principle of opium. His early reports (1803) were either rejected by editors or ignored after publication. He eventually tested his purified preparation on himself and 3 friends, administering 3 doses of 30 mg in 45 minutes and observing the vomiting, flush, and near

coma. This work was finally published in 1817 and attracted the interest of the influential French chemist Gay-Lussac. The work of Sertürner influenced Pelletier and Caventou, and in the same year other pure principles from plant sources were successfully isolated.

The addicting properties of opium have also been important in its history. In China, opium was used only for the treatment of dysentery until the mid-1700s. The English, Portuguese, and Dutch built up a large trade supplying opium to China, and addiction had become so much of a problem by the early 1800s that the Chinese government acted to bar the importation of opium and reduce the amount of opium smoking. These acts precipitated a 3-year war terminated by the Treaty of Nanking (1842), which gave England Hong Kong, opened 5 ports to British traders, and specifically authorized continued trade in opium.

The risk of addiction was probably underestimated in the West for some time thereafter. Opium and morphine were widely prescribed and easily available in many patent medicines. Misuse was common until about 1920, but the predominant pattern was one of oral use. Since the laws were changed at that time, the number of people involved has become comparatively small but the narcotic is injected. The compulsion based on the experience at the time of injection is very difficult to treat, and associated criminal activity has greatly increased.

Source & Chemistry

A. Source: Morphine and other naturally occurring narcotics are isolated from opium. Opium is collected from only one variety of poppy, *Papaver somniferum*. A few days after the petals fall, the unripe, still succulent seed pod is lightly incised. A day later the sticky brown gum that has collected is scraped from the surface of the pod. As much as 25% of this crude opium may be made up of alkaloids. The content of morphine varies from 9 to 14% and is adjusted to 10% in the standardized preparations.

The legal production of opium is regulated by the United Nations. India, Turkey, and Russia are the largest producers of opium from which morphine and other alkaloids are isolated. Morphine is used as such; however, a larger amount is converted chemically into codeine, which occurs in opium in amounts insufficient to meet the needs of medicine.

The illegal production of opium is huge. The large amounts of opium still used in the Orient are produced mostly in Southeast Asia. For many years, the illegal heroin that reached the USA originated as opium in Turkey. Mexican opium is now the primary source of heroin, with smaller contributions from the Orient and Iran.

The naturally occurring narcotic analgesics—eg, morphine and codeine—may be used as such or may be modified chemically to form the many semisynthetic opiates listed in Table 26–1. In addition, purely synthetic compounds have been prepared that have pharmacologic properties similar to those of the naturally occurring drugs.

B. Chemical Classification of Narcotic Analgesics: The chemical classification serves to identify the large number of drugs available prior to a discussion of their biologic effects. The chemical classification does not correlate well with the more useful pharmacologic classification based on the intensity of the pain that can be relieved by the narcotic, which ability is closely correlated with addiction liability. Thus, the first class listed below (the opiate alkaloids)

includes morphine, a potent and strongly habituating analgesic, and codeine, which will not relieve severe pain but has much less potential for misuse. In the second group are methadone, which has potent analgesic properties, and propoxyphene (Darvon), a compound that is not classified as a narcotic.

Chemists have not only modified the natural opiates but have isolated smaller fragments of the opiate molecule that retain narcotic effects. The outline below will identify most of the available analgesics (agonists), antagonists, and compounds that have mixed agonist-antagonist effects.

1. Natural and semisynthetic opiates–The alkaloids that occur in opium are placed in 2 general chemical classes: benzylisoquinoline alkaloids and phenanthrene derivatives.

The benzylisoquinoline alkaloids are not narcotics or analgesics, nor are the legal controls as strict as for other opiates. Papaverine (see Chapter 13) is a smooth muscle relaxant or vasodilator. Noscapine is similar to papaverine but is suggested for use in the control of cough.

The analgesic alkaloids are called phenanthrene derivatives because of the tricyclic system they con-

Table 26–1. The naturally occurring opium alkaloids and some semisynthetic opiates.

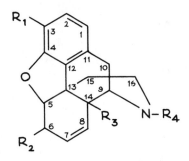

	R_1	R_2	$\Delta 7,8$	R_3	R_4
Morphine	—OH	—OH	Present	—H	—CH$_3$
Oxymorphone (dihydrohydroxy-morphinone, Numorphan)	—OH	=O	Absent	—OH	—CH$_3$
Hydromorphone (dihydromorphi-none, Dilaudid)	—OH	=O	Absent	—H	—CH$_3$
Codeine (methylmorphine)	—O–CH$_3$	—OH	Present	—H	—CH$_3$
Dihydrocodeine (Paracodin)	—O–CH$_3$	—OH	Absent	—H	—CH$_3$
Hydrocodone (dihydrocodeinone, in Hycodan)	—O–CH$_3$	=O	Absent	—H	—CH$_3$
Oxycodone (dihydrohydroxy-codeinone, in Percodan)	—O–CH$_3$	=O	Absent	—OH	—CH$_3$
Heroin (diacetylmorphine)	O ‖ —O–C–CH$_3$	O ‖ —O–C–CH$_3$	Present	—H	—CH$_3$
Nalbuphine (Nubain)*	—OH	—OH	Absent	—OH	cyclobutylmethyl
Naloxone (Narcan)†	—OH	=O	Absent	—OH	allyl
Thebaine	—O–CH$_3$	—O–CH$_3$	‡	—H	—CH$_3$

*A mixed agonist-antagonist.

†An antagonist.

‡Double bonds between C6 and C7 and between C8 and C14.

tain. The general structure is shown in Table 26–1, and the critical changes occur at R_1 and R_2. In morphine, hydroxyl groups are present at both R_1 (phenolic) and R_2 (alcoholic).

Methylmorphine (codeine) contains a methyl ether or methoxy group at R_1. All such methylmorphine derivatives are named as codeine derivatives even though some—eg, oxycodone—may be more potent pharmacologically than codeine. If the free phenolic hydroxyl remains, the compound is named as a derivative of morphine.

The alcoholic hydroxyl at R_2 can be oxidized to a keto group, with subsequent saturation of the double bond between C7 and C8. Such derivatives are named morphones or codones.

Heroin (diacetylmorphine) is rapidly hydrolyzed in the brain and liver to morphine.

As is true for all of the compounds discussed in this chapter, the opiate alkaloids are dispensed as the water-soluble salts.

2. Methadone–A large number of synthetic compounds have been tested in an effort to improve on the properties of the natural alkaloids of opium and especially to separate the analgesic and addicting properties. Whether any of these drugs offer advantages over the older alkaloids is questionable, but some have come into wide use and are of theoretical importance and promise.

Methadone was not the first synthetic narcotic to be prepared, but it will be listed first, since reference to Fig 26–1 will show that the phenylheptylamines represent the simplest of the chemical classes.

Methadone is distinct from morphine in that it is well absorbed from the intestine and has a slightly

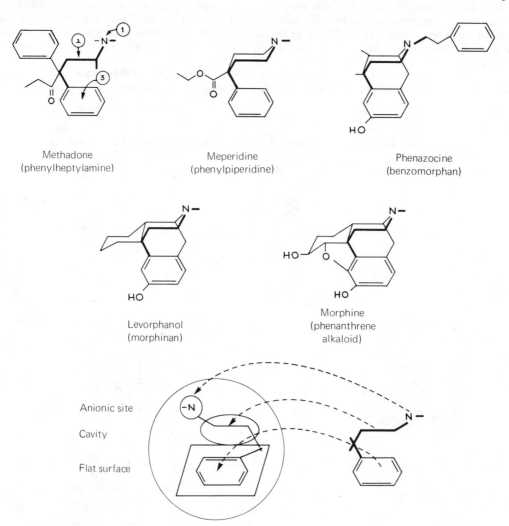

Figure 26–1. *Above:* The chemical structures of an opium alkaloid and 4 examples of synthetic narcotic analgesics written to emphasize the structure common to all: (1) a tertiary nitrogen; (2) a short hydrocarbon chain held in a plane perpendicular to the page; (3) a flat aryl group held in the plane of the page. *Below:* The skeleton structure is shown next to a hypothetical receptor surface (Beckett and Casy) that can accept the narcotic agent but not its mirror image isomer. Narcotic antagonists can attach to the receptor, but the N-substituent reduces their potency as agonists.

longer duration of action. The withdrawal state following methadone administration is more prolonged but of lesser intensity than that following withdrawal from other narcotics, and methadone may be substituted for heroin prior to withdrawal. Propoxyphene (Darvon) is generally regarded as an analog of methadone even though it is an ester rather than a ketone (Fig 26–2).

The analgesic and euphoriant properties of methadone, as is true also in the case of other narcotics, are in the levorotatory form, although the drug is dispensed as a racemic mixture. In the case of dextropropoxyphene, it is claimed that the dextro isomer possesses analgesic potency comparable to that of codeine without measurable addiction liability. This doubtful claim is discussed below (see p 277).

3. Meperidine and other phenylpiperidines–Meperidine (Demerol), the first of the synthetic analgesics to be prepared, was synthesized in the belief that it would have atropinelike properties. Reference to Fig 26–1 will show how it can be considered as resulting from ring closure (piperidine ring formation) of the alkylamine of methadone. The belief that meperidine is nonaddicting and parasympatholytic has been difficult to discredit. It and the analogs listed in Table 26–2 have effects that are qualitatively identical with those of the other narcotic analgesics, and their potency and potential for abuse are much greater than those of codeine.

Diphenoxylate is a weaker analog of meperidine available only in a proprietary mixture with atropine (Lomotil) for the treatment of diarrhea. In this form it is exempt from some of the regulations governing prescriptions of narcotics. Ethoheptazine (Zactane) contains a 7-membered ring in place of the piperidine ring and is virtually inactive.

4. Morphinans–The morphinans (Table 26–3) can be considered as derived from the natural alkaloids by the removal of the oxygen or of one ring—ie, they are tetracyclic rather than pentacyclic. However, they are prepared synthetically. Levorphanol (Levo-Dromoran) is a drug of this class that is equivalent to morphine. Methorphan can be considered as related to levorphan in the same way codeine is related to morphine. Its dextro isomer, dextromethorphan, is devoid of analgesic or habituating abilities but is widely used in proprietary cough medicines.

5. Benzomorphans–(Table 26–4.) One member of this group (phenazocine [Prinadol]) was formerly available as a morphine substitute. The most widely used member of the class today is pentazocine (Talwin), a drug with mixed agonist (analgesic) and antagonist properties. It is an analgesic with limited potential for abuse.

6. Narcotic antagonists–An allyl group $(-CH_2-CH=CH_2)$ is substituted for the methyl group attached to the basic nitrogen of morphine, levor-

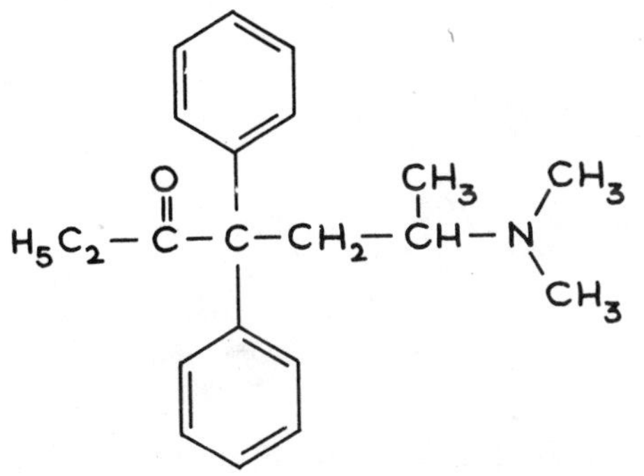

Methadone

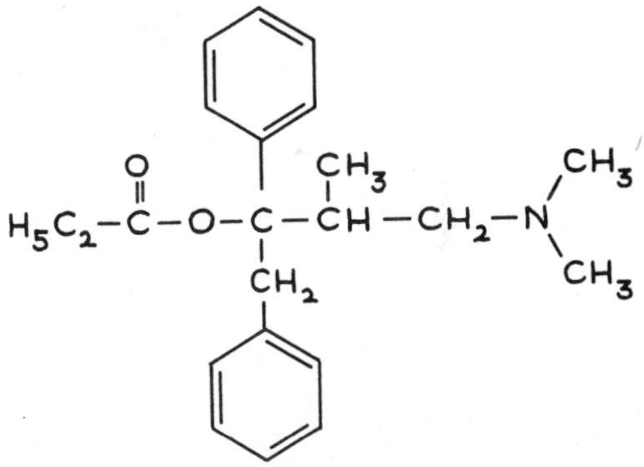

Propoxyphene
(Darvon)

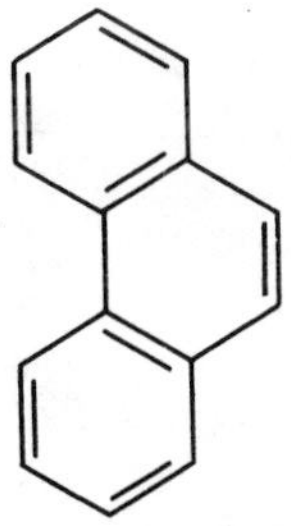

Phenanthrene

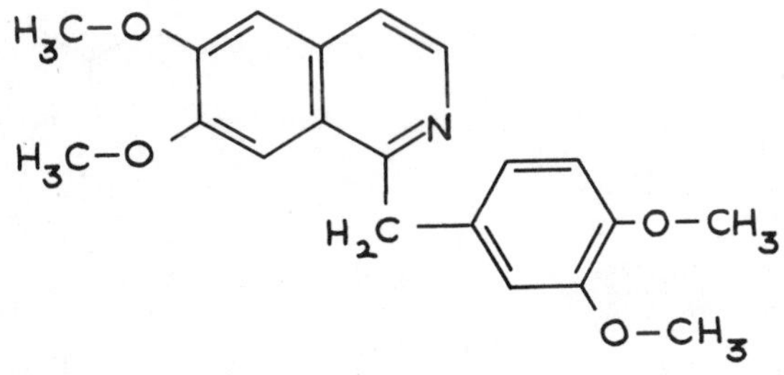

Papaverine (a benzyliso-
quinoline alkaloid)

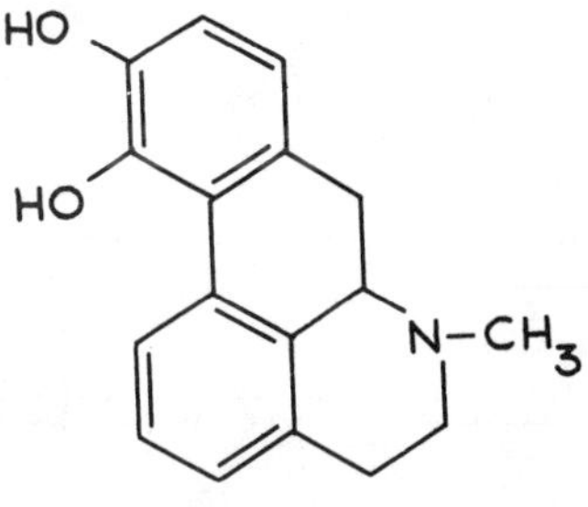

Apomorphine

Figure 26–2. The chemical structures of several compounds not included in the tables above and mentioned in the text.

Table 26—2. Meperidine and related synthetic analgesics of the phenylpiperidine type.

	R_1	R_2
Meperidine (Demerol)*	—H	—CH$_3$
Alphaprodine (Nisentil)	—CH$_3$	—CH$_3$
Anileridine (Leritine)	—H	—CH$_2$—CH$_2$—⬡—NH$_2$
Piminodine (Alvodine)	—H	—CH$_2$—CH$_2$—CH$_2$—NH—⬡
Diphenoxylate (in Lomotil)	—H	—CH$_2$—CH$_2$—C—C≡N (with two phenyl groups)

*Generic preparation available.

Table 26—3. Synthetic analogs of the opiates that are morphinan derivatives.

	R_1	R_2
Levorphanol (Levo-Dromoran)	—OH	—CH$_3$
Methorphan	—O—CH$_3$	—CH$_3$
Levallorphan (Lorfan)*	—OH	—CH$_2$—CH=CH$_2$ (allyl)
Butorphanol (Stadol)†	—OH	cyclobutylmethyl

*An antagonist.
†A mixed agonist-antagonist.

Table 26—4. A mixed agonist-antagonist (pentazocine) that is a benzomorphan derivative.

	R_1
Pentazocine (Talwin)*	—CH$_2$—CH=C with CH$_3$ / and CH$_3$ \

*A mixed agonist-antagonist.

phanol, or oxymorphone to form N-allyl-normorphine (nalorphine, Nalline), levallorphan (Lorfan), and naloxone (Narcan). These specific antagonists are able to reverse all of the depressant effects of all of the narcotics, natural and synthetic, mentioned in this chapter. Nalorphine and levallorphan retain weak morphinelike effects; naloxone is a pure antagonist. In pentazocine (Talwin), the mixed agonist-antagonist, the larger (5-carbon) substituent confers weak antagonistic properties and a significant agonistic (analgesic) effect is retained.

Pharmacologic Effects

The qualitative differences among the many narcotic analgesics are minor. If the narcotic antagonists and the dextro isomers of some of the compounds are excluded, the actions of all of the drugs listed above can be described together. Important differences between the drugs are summarized below when the choice of a preparation is discussed.

A. Mechanism of Action: The effects of morphine and related drugs are due to a mixture of depression of some specific central nervous system functions and stimulation of others and a mixture of sympathomimetic and parasympathomimetic influences. Some specific mechanisms—eg, cholinesterase inhibition or histamine liberation—have been established. In general, studies on mechanism of action are currently inconclusive; however, 2 promising areas of research exist.

1. The opiate receptor–The opiates exert their effects after binding to receptor sites on the cell membrane of the neuron, smooth muscle cell, or other effector. The existence and characteristics of the receptor are shown by the characteristics of the binding.

As shown in Fig 26–1, the binding is, first of all, highly specific in that not only is a specific molecular configuration required, but it must be the levo isomer. The binding is specific also in that the ^{3}H-labeled opiate cannot easily be washed out of the tissue after combining with it. The receptor can be saturated, ie, only a certain amount of agonist can be firmly held in combination. The opiate agonist can be displaced from combination with the receptor by opiate antagonists; and, finally, the ability to bind to the receptor substance parallels the pharmacologic potency of the agent.

Opiate receptors are widely distributed but are present in highest concentrations in areas of the brain and spinal cord associated with the perception of pain.

These receptors, present in all vertebrates, can hardly have evolved in anticipation of the use of opiates. The question of why they should be present has led to the search for endogenous ligands and the discovery of the newest of the peptides of the brain.

2. Endogenous morphinomimetic peptides–

a. Endorphins–The study of the endorphins (endogenous morphines) actually began with the isolation from the pars intermedia of the pituitary gland of beta-lipotropin, a molecule of 91 amino acid residues.

Beta-lipotropin is a prohormone that splits into melanocyte-stimulating hormone (MSH) and beta-endorphin (beta-lipotropin 61-91). This endorphin (there are 2 others) occurs in the pituitary and gut and, in much smaller amounts, in the brain. Applied on isolated tissue preparations or given by injection into the cerebral ventricles, it reacts with the opiate receptor exactly as described above. On a molar basis, beta-endorphin produces an analgesic effect 5–10 times as potent as that of morphine, and the effect lasts for 3–4 hours. Given peripherally (intravenously), it has no morphinelike effects.

b. Enkephalins–Five related peptides with 5 residues have been isolated, differing only in the terminal amino acid, eg, methionine enkephalin and leucine enkephalin. The enkephalin amino acid sequence is found in the endorphin molecules; however, the evidence suggests that they are not metabolites of endorphins but that the 2 categories have a common precursor.

The enkephalins are not found in the same neurons as the endorphins, but their distribution parallels that of the opiate receptors and that of monoamine concentration. They also occur in the gastrointestinal tract.

Their effect is evanescent (consistent with a suggested function as neurotransmitter), and analgesia is not demonstrable with the naturally occurring enkephalins.

There is, of course, much speculation about the role of these substances in normal function and in disease. It appears very important to note the absence of effect on normal and abnormal behavior of doses of the specific antagonist sufficient to saturate the opiate receptor. Their potential as therapeutic agents is limited by their inability to reach the neurons of the central nervous system.

B. Effects:

1. Analgesia–The essential pharmacologic effect of the strong analgesics is to relieve pain following the administration of doses so small that they do not cause general central nervous system depression with sedation, respiratory depression, or other disabling results.

Pain is not the result of a precise neurophysiologic process but is the highly subjective interpretation of certain sensory stimuli by a specific individual in a given situation. Pain is usually said to involve 2 components: the sensation reaching the central nervous system and the perception of the stimulus—ie, the individual ("psychic") processing and reaction. Morphine alters the second of these processes, so that the patient may report that the pain is still present but is less distressing.

The subjective nature of pain introduces intricate problems in the evaluation of the effectiveness of analgesic drugs. The evaluation, discussed in more detail below, can be carried out only in humans enduring real—ie, pathologic or spontaneously occurring—pain, and not in any laboratory preparation nor even in humans undergoing experimentally induced pain.

The narcotic analgesics relieve pain almost regardless of its origin or intensity. In fact, the more intense the pain, the easier it is to demonstrate the effectiveness of the drug.

2. On behavior–The opiates are commonly said to produce euphoria, but this is an oversimplification. When given to a subject who has not previously experienced the effects of the drug and who is not in pain, morphine and codeine will more commonly produce a subjectively unpleasant reaction. A barbiturate and, even more dependably, amphetamine will evoke euphoric responses in the same subject under double-blind conditions. In the presence of pain or fear, the reaction of a patient to an opiate may be much less dysphoric, and, in some people, the relief from anxiety and aggressive feelings may be pleasurable enough to provoke a desire for repetition of the experience.

In therapeutic doses, the sedative effects are minimal, the patient being quiet but responsive and functional. After increasingly larger doses, the subject will become drowsy, inattentive, and inefficient and fall into a sleep from which arousal is still easy. Very large doses induce coma.

Excitement rather than depression is rarely seen in humans unless a combination of drugs is used—eg, morphine and scopolamine in obstetric analgesia. The various members of this drug group vary in their ability to cause excitement, however. Toxic doses of codeine, meperidine, or propoxyphene may do so and may finally cause convulsions that are suprasegmental in origin. Some species, notably the cat and the horse, respond regularly with excitement.

3. On respiration–The sensitivity of medullary centers to CO_2 is reduced and respiration correspondingly depressed. After therapeutic doses, the decrease in rate and volume may be no more than that which can be explained by the decreased activity. However, even after such therapeutic doses, a decreased responsiveness to increased concentrations of CO_2 in the inspired air is demonstrable. With larger doses, respiratory rate falls progressively and finally becomes not only slow but shallow and irregular in pattern.

The respiratory depression and CO_2 retention have 2 further important consequences. Intracranial vessels are dilated by the elevated level of CO_2. Cerebral blood flow and intracranial blood volume increase, and intracranial pressure is thereby elevated. The asphyxial changes also cause hyperglycemia, which in humans is usually minor. The hyperglycemia can be prevented by controlling the respiration or, in animals, by adrenalectomy, establishing that it results from the sympathoadrenal discharge caused by asphyxia.

While medullary sensitivity to CO_2 is reduced, the sensitivity of the chemoreceptors in the carotid sinus and aortic arch areas is increased and the respiratory center is still able to respond to the stimulus of hypoxia. Increasing the concentration of oxygen in the inspired air may reduce this stimulus and further depress respiration.

4. On other areas of the central nervous system–Nausea and vomiting are caused by a stimulating action of morphine on the chemoreceptor trigger zone of the medulla. However, movement intensifies and recumbency reduces the emetic effect, suggesting that vestibular factors are also involved. Following the initial stimulation, the vomiting center is depressed, so that vomiting does not result from closely spaced doses.

Coughing is suppressed by the narcotic analgesics, and this is the one action that can be separated from the analgesic potency of these drugs.

Morphine stimulates the release of growth hormone and prolactin but depresses the titer of LH and FSH. With chronic use, these effects of morphine are manifested by an altered menstrual pattern. The opiates have antidiuretic actions.

5. On the cardiovascular system–The skin is warm and flushed. The heart rate is slowed only by large doses. Postural hypotension severe enough to cause dizziness or fainting can occur even after therapeutic doses of narcotics if the patient arises suddenly or is studied on a tilt table. The hypotensive effect is intensified by the simultaneous administration of phenothiazine tranquilizers or atropinelike drugs.

The cause of the hypotension is not clear but is probably central in origin—ie, due to medullary vasomotor depression. Many of the strong analgesics have been shown to be histamine liberators of significant potency. Such action adequately explains the itching and urticaria that appear after the administration of these drugs. However, the hypotension is longer lasting and probably too intense to be explained by this mechanism.

6. On the gastrointestinal tract–The important observation is that the net effect of the opiates or their surrogates is constipating. Constipation is a frequent side-effect of repeated doses, and diarrhea can be effectively treated with narcotics.

The explanations for this fact introduce confusion and some conflict. Most laboratory investigators have concluded that these drugs increase intestinal contraction to such an extent that propulsive or effective activity is decreased. They have, however, used very large doses in animals and have made their observations only for a short period after administration; furthermore, their technic of measurement has often added the stimulating effect of distending the intestine. Clinical investigators using roentgenologic technics and those laboratory investigators who have used smaller doses and followed their animals for extended periods have described a phase of markedly inhibited activity following the transient stimulation. An exception to this generalization is the occurrence of a persistent pylorospasm that prolongs gastric emptying time. Despite the various interpretations, there is no argument with the observation that the ultimate effect is one of constipation.

7. On the biliary tract–The smooth muscle of the biliary tract, including the sphincter of Oddi, is stimulated—at least acutely. This is true for all of the narcotics studied, including meperidine. One of these drugs may nevertheless be used to relieve the pain of biliary colic.

The impaired drainage from the common duct into the intestine has several metabolic consequences. Serum amylase and lipase levels are elevated by the administration of morphine whether pancreatitis is present or not. SGOT and alkaline phosphatase levels are unchanged following the administration of morphine if a functioning gallbladder is present. In the presence of biliary tract disease or following cholecystectomy, the levels may rise—due, presumably, to contraction of the sphincter of Oddi with reflux.

8. On pupillary size–The decrease in pupillary size is of considerable practical importance in recognizing narcotic intoxication and is also the basis for a test for drug misuse described below. The miosis is replaced by pupillary dilatation when epinephrine liberation is provoked either by excitement or by respiratory depression and asphyxia.

9. Tolerance and physical dependence–These problems are discussed in detail below in relation to drug misuse or dependence. However, they do occur during the therapeutic use of narcotic analgesics and should be defined here. As **tolerance** develops, larger and larger doses of the drug must be administered in order to achieve the same effect. **Physical dependence** exists when drug administration must be continued to maintain normal function—ie, to prevent the withdrawal state.

Absorption, Metabolism, & Excretion

All of the opiates and synthetic equivalents are well absorbed from injection sites, but their suitability for oral administration varies between compounds. Morphine has a greatly delayed onset of action after oral administration, and the oral dose must be several times the injected dose. It appears that absorption is complete, although variable in rate, and that rapid conjugation, either in the liver or the intestinal wall, occurs. Many alternative drugs (see Table 26–5) are preferable to morphine for oral administration.

Morphine is inactivated for the most part by conversion to the 3-monoglucuronide in the liver. A small amount is demethylated to normorphine. Both free and conjugated morphine are excreted into the urine. A small fraction (10%) is excreted in the feces following excretion into bile.

The conversion of all injected heroin and a small fraction of a dose of codeine to morphine is discussed in relation to those drugs below.

Clinical Uses

A. Relief of Pain: Morphine or one of its less potent surrogates can be used to relieve pain almost regardless of its nature. Isolated, sharp pains—eg, those generated by movement or touching a sensitive area—are probably less effectively suppressed than constant pain. The pain of trauma, myocardial infarction, biliary or ureteral colic, inflammation, infiltration or pressure by a neoplasm, etc are examples of

situations in which a narcotic analgesic is used.

Contraindications to the use of narcotics are listed below, and the hazard of addiction precludes the use of all but the least potent agents in chronic or recurrent pain that threatens to be of long duration—eg, arthritis, migraine, or trigeminal neuralgia. However, the narcotic analgesics should be used as a general rule to relieve pain for which the antipyretic analgesics such as aspirin are ineffective or until specific treatment becomes effective.

B. Problems of Clinical Evaluation: Relief of pain is the prototype of a subjective response to a drug whose clinical evaluation is difficult. There is no question about the effectiveness of the familiar agents, but the problem of clinical evaluation becomes important and difficult when comparisons must be made between available drugs; when new compounds must be evaluated; when precise information about dose is required; or when the nature of pain is studied.

The subjective nature of pain emphasized above becomes even more apparent when the action of drugs on pain is studied. The nature of the pain associated with a particular disease can be quite accurately described (quality, radiation, etc), and the stimulus and afferent pathways can be defined. None of these factors nor the threshold for perception of a particular stimulus, however, constitute an adequate definition of pain, since they do not consider those subjective factors that alter the individual reaction. Pain originates not only from the original sensation but also from the meaning that the individual attaches to the stimulus. The significance of this "meaning of the stimulus" is shown by studies comparing the amount of analgesic drug needed by patients sustaining roughly comparable injuries in 2 different situations. The civilian threatened by the consequences of an accident suffers more pain and requires more morphine than the soldier whose almost identical injury may promise relief from combat duty. The narcotic analgesics alter the anxiety engendered by the anticipation of pain and other factors constituting the "psychic processing" of the original sensation.

Because of the subjective nature of pain, it is unlikely that any available experimentally induced pain in laboratory animals or in humans has significant value in the clinical evaluation of analgesics. The common technics for measuring the alteration of response to pain in animals involve measuring the intensity of a reflex response initiated by a stimulus presumed to be painful. For example, a source of heat may be focused on the tail of a rodent (blackened to absorb heat) and the time until the response (tail flick) measured. This response is a spinal reflex that can still be modified by drugs in the cord-sectioned animal.

Experimental pain may be produced in humans by stimulation with heat, pressure, electricity, or ischemia. This is equivalent to measuring the pain threshold, which is not only not constant in different subjects or at different times in the same subject but also bears no dependable relation to the clinical actions of analgesics.

Consequently, the consensus today is that pain can be studied and analgesic drugs assayed only in the human experiencing pathologic or spontaneously arising pain—ie, nonexperimentally induced pain. The group of patients available in sufficient numbers and experiencing generally comparable pain are those suffering postoperative or incisional pain. The responses of these patients to drugs is studied following the general pattern described for an acceptable clinical trial in Chapter 3. A comparison of the drug under study with either a placebo or a standard analgesic must be included, and the patients must be randomly assigned to groups or the order of drug administration randomly determined. The double-blind technic must, of course, be employed. At intervals before and after the administration of the drug, the patient is queried by a disinterested technician or other observer about the intensity of pain and the presence of side-effects. When these subjective responses are converted to an arbitrary descriptive scale and the data properly organized, remarkably fine discrimination and reproducibility are possible. There is no question of the applicability to the clinical situation, since the assay situation is simply the clinical situation organized to permit quantitative, controlled observations.

C. Sedation or Relief of Anxiety: Sedative-hypnotics of the barbiturate type produce a disinhibited, euphoric state more dependably than the narcotics and are clearly more suitable for the treatment of most anxiety states. However, the more potent narcotic analgesics alter the reaction of the patient to stimuli other than pain and relieve anxiety in the most acute and distressing situations—eg, bereavement.

This property is relevant to the problem of selecting a preanesthetic or preprocedural medication. As has been discussed in Chapter 20, some anesthetists have argued that in a patient free of pain the barbiturates are a more rational drug for the relief of anxiety preoperatively. However, morphine or another potent narcotic, especially when combined with other depressant drugs, is generally regarded as more dependable for producing indifference to the impending events.

D. Acute Pulmonary Edema: Morphine is the drug of first choice in the treatment of acute pulmonary edema, and its effectiveness is such that it is often described as a "specific" treatment. Furosemide and oxygen may also be administered. The mechanism by which morphine brings about relief is not clear. Its effectiveness is one of several pieces of data suggesting that acute pulmonary edema, which occurs in association with other than cardiac disease, should not be thought of as a consequence of acute left ventricular failure but as a reflexly generated state that can be interrupted by this central depressant.

E. Cough: The narcotics depress the cough reflex, and this action can be separated from the analgesic effect. For example, the dextrorotatory isomer of some compounds is devoid of analgesic effects but may be used to suppress coughing.

For control of coughing, the ordinary narcotics can be given by mouth in doses approximately half the analgesic doses listed in Table 26–5. The least potent agent that is effective should be used—ie, codeine in most cases.

Table 26–5. Narcotic analgesics: Dosages.

	Dose	
	Subcut*	Oral
Most potent		
Morphine	8–15 mg	50 mg
Heroin	. . .	. . .
Hydromorphone (dihydromorphinone, Dilaudid)	2 mg	2 mg
Oxymorphone (Numorphan)	1.5 mg	. . .
Levorphanol (Levo-Dromoran)	2 mg	2 mg
Phenazocine (Prinadol)	2 mg (IM)	. . .
Methadone (Dolophine, various others)	5 mg	5 mg
Intermediate potency		
Meperidine (Demerol, various others)	75–150 mg (IM)	75–100 mg
Alphaprodine (Nisentil)	40–60 mg	. . .
Anileridine (Leritine)	25–50 mg	25–50 mg
Piminodine (Alvodine)	10–20 mg	25–50 mg
Dihydrocodeinone (in Hycodan)	. . .	. . .
Oxycodone (in Percodan)	. . .	. . .
Butorphanol (Stadol)†	2 mg	. . .
Nalbuphine (Nubain)†	10 mg	. . .
Pentazocine (Talwin)	30 mg	50 mg
Least potent		
Codeine	30–65 mg	30–65 mg
Dihydrocodeine	65 mg	65 mg

*Recommended single dose. Give subcutaneously except as noted. Most preparations can also be given intravenously in emergencies.
†Mixed agonist-antagonist.

F. Diarrhea: The constipating effects of the narcotics, ordinarily a troublesome side-effect, may be used in the symptomatic treatment of acute diarrhea. The traditional preparation often selected for this application is paregoric (camphorated opium tincture), which acts because of the morphine that it contains. All narcotics possess constipating activity in proportion to other analgesic effect. Codeine (15 mg orally 3 times daily) and diphenoxylate with atropine (Lomotil) are the most common alternatives to paregoric.

Adverse Reactions
 A. Side-Effects: One or more of the side-effects listed below occur in most patients receiving narcotics in therapeutic doses. The potent drugs cause more intense side-effects, but the weaker analgesics such as codeine given chronically lead to side-effects with equal or greater frequency.
 1. Behavioral–Even in the presence of pain, the subjective reaction is not invariably pleasant. Feelings of anxiety, lethargy, or confusion may make the experience unpleasant. Agents such as codeine or propoxyphene that possess the excitant properties to a greater extent may cause restlessness, tremulousness, and hyperactivity.
 2. Nausea and vomiting–This action has been discussed under Pharmacologic Effects.
 3. Constipation–The ability of the narcotic analgesic to decrease propulsive activity in the intestine can lead to a constipating effect that may outlast the analgesic effect by a day or more. The same effect of morphine or a similar agent given preoperatively contributes to the development of paralytic ileus or a delayed return of intestinal activity postoperatively. All patients are distended by air swallowed during general anesthesia, as can be shown by simple measurements of their girth pre- and postoperatively, and preoperative narcotics prolong the effect of this distention.
 4. Urinary retention–The incidence of postoperative urinary retention is similarly increased by narcotics.
 5. Itching, urticaria–The histamine-liberating abilities of the narcotic analgesics, apparent after injection more commonly than after oral administration, may lead to itching, especially in the skin about the nose, or even to the appearance of wheals.
 6. Cardiovascular–The acute postural hypotension already described is most often seen when a patient quickly arises while the drug is acting, when dizziness, faintness, or even syncope may occur.
 7. Respiratory–Therapeutic doses of the narcotics do not usually cause alarming respiratory depression unless other depressant drugs are also acting. General anesthesia is, of course, the common situation in which their use is combined with the use of other respiratory depressant drugs. Postoperatively, the depression of respiration, the depression of cough reflexes, and the suppression of the occasional deep breath that is part of the normal pattern of respiration can predispose to atelectasis.

B. Acute Toxicity: Acute opiate toxicity is seen following suicidal or accidental ingestion of prescribed medication and after therapeutic accidents, but drug users provide most of the cases seen. The diagnosis depends upon the history or evidence (such as needle marks) of narcotic misuse. The comatose patient will have slow, shallow, irregular respiration. The decrease in rate is usually more marked than is the case after barbiturate intoxication. The pupils may be constricted, but asphyxial changes obscure this change more often than not. Blood pressure may be slightly reduced. The pulse rate is also slowed until the tachycardia of shock supervenes.

The treatment of acute opiate intoxication depends upon the use of narcotic antagonists. These drugs (discussed in detail below) are competitive antagonists to all of the natural and synthetic narcotics and rapidly reverse all of the depressant effects of the narcotics. Nalorphine (Nalline), levallorphan (Lorfan), and naloxone (Narcan) are examples of narcotic antagonists. They can also be used to reverse unexpected reactions to therapeutic doses.

C. Habituation and Misuse: The problem of the abuse of central depressant and central stimulant drugs involves not merely the pharmacologic properties of the drug but psychiatric and sociologic factors as well. Misuse of the opiates should not be set off as a separate problem but should be considered as part of a general medical problem involving several drug types (see Chapter 7).
 1. Tolerance–Tolerance to the effects of the narcotics develops more quickly and to a much greater degree than tolerance to other drugs subject to abuse. Animals given repeated and progressively larger doses and humans who have access to large amounts of heroin or other narcotics are soon able to tolerate many multiples of the usual lethal doses. Tolerance develops to all of the depressant effects listed above except constipation and pupillary constriction. Tolerance can thus be defined as a state when larger doses are required to elicit the same effect or when a fixed dose exerts a decreasing effect.

The rate at which tolerance develops depends upon several factors, including especially the interval between doses and the amount of drug provided. The development of tolerance in heroin addicts today is limited by the difficulty and expense involved in obtaining the drug, and many are able to continue more or less indefinitely on a fixed dose, continuing to experience the "rush" at the time of injection but showing little depression later. In the therapeutic situation, if constant and severe pain forces the administration of potent narcotics at 4- to 6-hour intervals, the analgesic effect may decrease within a few days. If the interval between therapeutic doses can be lengthened well beyond the duration of action of the drug—ie, given 2 times per day—tolerance may not be apparent after several weeks.
 2. Physical dependence and withdrawal–Parallel to the development of tolerance and independent of any psychologic dependence, the organism

develops a need for the continued administration of the narcotic in the sense that continued administration is necessary to prevent the development of the physiologic disturbances known as the abstinence (withdrawal) syndrome. Or, to restate the definition in the same terms used in the discussion of alcohol and barbiturates, if narcotic administration is abruptly discontinued following the administration of the drug for an adequate period, a withdrawal state is seen.

The onset of the withdrawal state follows the last dose after an interval that varies with the amount of narcotic used and with the specific compound used. In the case of morphine or heroin, symptoms appear 8–16 hours or more following the final dose and increase in intensity for 48–72 hours, after which they slowly subside. The most persistent symptom, insomnia, may last 4 weeks or longer. The figures are somewhat smaller in the case of the shorter-acting meperidine, and the duration is prolonged after the administration of methadone.

The mechanism or mechanisms underlying tolerance and the abstinence syndrome are not known. The signs and symptoms can be remembered by considering that the body adapts to the continued presence of a depressant drug by activating excitatory systems whose activity persists after the drug is withdrawn. The abstinence syndrome will thus bear close similarity to the effects of large doses of amphetamines.

The signs and symptoms can be organized as follows: (1) **Autonomic hyperactivity:** Sympathetic effects are lacrimation, rhinorrhea, sweating, piloerection ("gooseflesh" or "cold turkey"), dilated pupils, elevated blood pressure and pulse rate, and hyperpyrexia. Parasympathetic hyperactivity causes emesis, abdominal pain, and diarrhea. (2) **Behavioral hyperexcitability:** Anxiety, restlessness, yawning, tremor, insomnia. In the most severe states (unusual at this time), the hyperexcitability may progress to convulsions or a toxic psychosis. (3) **Muscle and joint pains.** (4) **Anxiety** beyond that due to physical withdrawal but which occurs because the compulsive act is no longer performed. This anxiety is the therapeutically important problem in treating heroin abuse as well as cigarette smoking, overeating, or other compulsion.

In the therapeutic situation, especially if the narcotics are used only as required, withdrawal is mild and not usually related by the patient to the analgesic. The person who uses illegal opiates experiences and recognizes the withdrawal state whenever the routine of use usually maintained is interrupted. Dangerously severe withdrawal states are uncommon in the compulsive heroin user today because of the restraint placed upon the amounts available by the cost and the dilution of the illegal drug. The actual discomfort and the fear of the physical effects of withdrawal is, nevertheless, an important initial barrier to the treatment of heroin users and presents a situation during which they deserve support by drugs and other means.

Withdrawal is, however, the least difficult part of treatment of this compulsion. Typical heroin users withdraw and return to the drug many times during their careers, demonstrating that factors other than "junk sickness" are operating.

3. Patterns and effects of misuse–Narcotics, whether injected, swallowed, or smoked, are subject to varying degrees of misuse. One individual may use single doses sporadically and another may use them compulsively 4 or more times a day regardless of the consequences. The damage to the individual is variable but may be quite minor. The sporadic user may be unaffected in general social behavior, but the compulsive user usually loses interest in everything but the need to maintain the habit, which inevitably forces the individual into criminal activity. It is this associated criminal activity rather than any inherent action of the drug that is damaging to society and to the individual.

4. Treatment–Some general ideas apply to the treatment of drug misuse regardless of the specific agent involved (see Chapter 7). The individual may be handled as a criminal; therapy in various forms may be provided; or the drug may be provided under controlled conditions. Only 2 special aspects of treatment are discussed here.

a. Withdrawal–Withdrawal is not often supervised by a physician but occurs in the room of the user or in jail. In theory, humane and safe withdrawal is best accomplished by substituting methadone for heroin, the dosage depending upon the degree of tolerance and dependence. The dosage of methadone can then be slowly reduced, with only a mild withdrawal state. The dosage of methadone required can be reduced by sedation and autonomic blocking agents. In practice, methadone substitution and withdrawal are not often successful and without other efforts at treatment become part of a "revolving door" style of treatment.

The use of methadone is restricted to formal programs, and the general physician would have to use other drugs in any case, since the law forbids the use of narcotics in the treatment of addiction. These other drugs include mecamylamine (Inversine) for autonomic hyperactivity, a "nonnarcotic" such as propoxyphene phenobarbital or other daytime sedation, and a hypnotic at bedtime. Clonidine is currently being evaluated as a central sympatholytic especially useful during withdrawal.

b. Methadone maintenance–Rather than provide the individual with heroin for intravenous use, a current treatment concept is to offer large oral daily doses of methadone—large so that the effect will last for the 24 hours until the next daily dose. As tolerance occurs to the large doses of methadone used (40–120 mg/d), the individual can no longer achieve any effect from reasonable amounts of heroin. Since oral methadone does not provide an experience equivalent to intravenous heroin, the programs provide blockade rather than maintenance. In theory, the patient is freed of the need to engage in criminal activity and can separate from the drug culture. In practice, heroin is often used irregularly, and, in an effort to relieve the nervousness that results from having given up the compulsive act, the patient abuses many depressant and stimulant drugs. Alcoholism is a major problem among patients in methadone programs. Moreover, the patient on methadone is not free of narcotic effects—ie, tolerance is not absolute.

Perhaps methadone programs have resulted in some gain to society and, less clearly, have benefited some individual patients. However, it appears that disillusionment about the ultimate effectiveness of methadone programs is growing among patients and therapists.

Methadone is subject to strict regulation by federal and state authorities. It may be shipped only to programs approved by federal and state agencies for use in maintenance or withdrawal or to hospital pharmacies for use as an analgesic or for inpatient withdrawal. The patient selected for maintenance treatment must be 18 years of age or older; must have a verified history of heroin abuse for at least 2 years; and must show evidence from urinalysis of current use. Initially, the patient must appear daily at the clinic to receive the allocation of the drug; later, "take-home doses" may be allowed, and the patient need appear only twice weekly. Methadone must be dissolved in juice so that it cannot be injected. Weekly urinalysis to detect morphine (the metabolite of heroin) is required.

An investigative drug, L-acetyl-alpha-methadol (LAAM, LAM, or "long-acting methadone"), is currently being evaluated in large-scale clinical trials as a substitute for methadone. It can be dispensed every second day, reducing the program cost.

Contraindications & Cautions

Morphine and the other more potent narcotic analgesics are potentially very dangerous drugs in some patients. Nevertheless, the contraindications are, in general, relative rather than absolute, calling for a great reduction in dose or the use of a less potent agent such as codeine rather than a more depressant drug of this group. Obviously, opiates should not be used unless there is an indication for their use—eg, a patient in traumatic shock may be apathetic rather than complaining of pain, and the use of analgesics should then be deferred. The following precautions should be observed.

A. Increased Intracranial Pressure From Head Injury or Other Cause: If administration of a narcotic causes even a minor degree of respiratory depression, the CO_2 retention can cause dilatation of intracranial vessels and a further increase in intracranial pressure. The increase can be controlled during anesthesia by assisting the respiration.

B. Chronic Pain: Some types of chronic pain—eg, that associated with the terminal stages of malignancy—require the chronic use of narcotics. The smallest amount of the least potent agent is used, with the longest interval possible between doses, in order to minimize side-effects and tolerance and to maintain the benefit to the patient—but not because of any legal concern about habituation. Pain such as that of migraine or arthritis that recurs over a period of many

years should be treated with narcotics with great caution. Codeine is virtually free of addiction liability in a situation of this kind unless the patient has had experience with more potent narcotics, in which case codeine may be used to maintain a habituation established primarily with another agent.

C. Asthma: Morphine and meperidine have been effective in interrupting an otherwise resistant attack of asthma. However, it appears that bronchiolar smooth muscle, like other smooth muscle, may respond in 2 ways to morphine. A very rare patient, instead of responding with bronchiolar dilatation, may show greatly increased respiratory distress and die suddenly after the administration of morphine or meperidine. The narcotics are not essential in the treatment of asthma and should not be used.

D. Other Pulmonary Disease: In the presence of cor pulmonale, emphysema, kyphoscoliosis, or other conditions in which no reserve of respiratory function exists, the slightest additional depression may lead to respiratory decompensation.

E. When Narcotics Might Delay or Obscure Diagnosis: This caution is perhaps more theoretic than real. It may be necessary to use morphine in the presence of acute abdominal pain, and even when pancreatitis is suspected (in which case the narcotic may elevate the serum enzyme levels that are useful in diagnosis).

F. Grossly Impaired Liver Function: As would be predicted from other tests of the metabolic function of the liver, the response to morphine is not altered until liver function is greatly decreased. However, in the presence of cirrhosis accompanied by encephalopathy, jaundice, or ascites, the risk of coma is increased by the administration of an opiate. The mechanism by which coma is precipitated is not known.

G. Hypothyroid State: Myxedematous patients are said, on the basis of clinical observations, to be unusually sensitive to narcotics.

H. Combination With Other Drugs: The effects (especially the respiratory depressant effects) of the sedative-hypnotics—whether barbiturates, alcohol, or other—are additive to those of a narcotic. When a narcotic and an antipsychotic are combined, the sedation is greatly intensified without much increase in respiratory depression.

Dosages & Selection of Drug

A. Differences Among Drugs of This Class:

1. Potency–The potency of the various members of this drug group should not be defined by the number of milligrams used but in terms of the intensity of the pain that can be relieved. Very intense pain, such as that occurring early in the course of a myocardial infarction or the pain of ureteral colic, may not be relieved by codeine no matter how much is used but responds well to morphine. It has not yet been possible to separate potency from the addiction liability inherent in the narcotic. Therefore, the more important and most useful classification of narcotics is the one that places them in 3 groups depending upon their ability to relieve pain (see Table 26–5). Morphine and its congeners relieve the most severe pain but are also most potent in causing euphoria. Codeine will not relieve all types of pain, but the hazard of primary addiction is negligible. Meperidine and its analogs form an intermediate class somewhat below morphine but far more potent and addicting than codeine.

2. Other qualitative differences–The narcotics can differ in the balance between sedative and excitant effects that each causes. This difference is most apparent in the side-effects that occur. Morphine rarely causes excitement; codeine only rarely causes sedation.

3. Duration of action–Methadone has a duration of action perhaps 25% longer and meperidine about 25% shorter than that of morphine.

4. Prescription regulations–See Chapter 4.

B. Most Potent Narcotics: Drugs of this class relieve the most severe pain but have a correspondingly high addiction liability and cause a high incidence of the more uncomfortable side-effects.

1. Morphine is the most important drug in this category. It is most often given subcutaneously. The technics described in the section on clinical evaluation are sufficiently sensitive to permit accurate determination of the relation of dosage to effectiveness, duration of action, and incidence of side-effects. The optimal subcutaneous dose is 10 mg. An increase to 15 mg provides a minor increase in duration of effect but a significant increase in the number of side-effects and degree of respiratory depression.

Morphine, 4–8 mg, may be given intravenously in situations of great urgency (acute pulmonary edema or severe pain) or when the interference with blood levels of muscle enzymes by the trauma of other injection would give falsely high serum enzyme levels and result in diagnostic uncertainty. Slow intravenous infusion also permits very accurate titration of the minimal dose. Morphine is less dependable by mouth than by other routes of administration.

2. Paregoric (camphorated tincture of opium) is an antidiarrheal preparation containing 1.6 mg of morphine in each 4 mL of an unpleasantly flavored vehicle. More pleasant solutions of morphine alone could be prepared, but paregoric is an official preparation and its standard concentration causes less confusion. The now official name "paregoric" minimizes the possibility of confusion with the much stronger tincture of opium (laudanum), which is practically never used.

3. Heroin is slightly more potent than morphine and is preferred as a smuggled commodity. Drug users can differentiate it from morphine after intravenous administration and prefer heroin because of its more intense immediate effect—ie, the orgasmlike sensation that accompanies injection. Heroin is deacetylated stepwise and excreted as morphine. 6-Monacetylmorphine enters the brain rapidly. Because of the problem of heroin misuse, the drug has been outlawed as a therapeutic agent in many countries.

4. Methadone has been mentioned above because of its use in withdrawing patients from other narcotics and in the blockade of heroin effect in the treatment of heroin users. It is also available for use as an analgesic. The effects of therapeutic doses persist for 6 hours. With doses larger than 20 mg—eg, the 40–120 mg dosage used in the methadone maintenance treatment of heroin abuse—the effects last for 24 hours or longer.

5. Hydromorphone (Dilaudid) has a slightly shorter duration of effect than morphine but is much better absorbed.

6. Oxymorphone (Numorphan) is more potent than morphine but causes more euphoria and more nausea and vomiting.

7. Levorphanol (Levo-Dromoran) is a well absorbed synthetic.

C. Narcotics of Intermediate Potency:

1. Meperidine (pethidine BP; Demerol) is the prototype of this group of analgesics that are more potent than codeine but less effective than morphine. Meperidine is like codeine in that its excitant properties are prominent. Its duration of action is shorter than that of morphine (approximately 3 rather than 4 hours), an advantage for brief procedures or when used prior to delivery. It is injected intramuscularly rather than subcutaneously because of its irritant properties. It is well absorbed from the gastrointestinal tract.

Early claims were that meperidine had low or even no addicting properties. Perhaps because of this claim and because of factors of availability, it soon became and has remained the narcotic which doctors and nurses are most likely to misuse.

Meperidine was originally synthesized as an atropine substitute and was marketed with claims that, in contrast to morphine, it relaxed smooth muscle. Whenever meperidine has been compared with morphine for its effects on intestine, biliary tract, bronchioles, etc, no difference has been demonstrated when equipotent doses were used. The original claim has been difficult to dispel.

2. Alphaprodine (Nisentil), anileridine (Leritine), and piminodine (Alvodine) are equivalent to meperidine, although their duration of action may be even briefer.

3. Oxycodone has been used in proprietary mixtures, especially Percodan. The suggestive similarity of the name of this mixture to codeine was allowed to suggest to many a therapeutic equivalence with codeine. It is actually more potent and more addicting.

D. Least Potent Narcotics:

1. Codeine is the most commonly used narcotic analgesic, and whenever possible, when narcotics are necessary, treatment should begin with and be limited to this weak analgesic. Primary addiction to codeine—ie, misuse without prior experience with a more potent drug—is virtually unheard of. Side-effects are common but minor in nature compared with morphine or meperidine. Sedation is unusual. Excitement may occur, and large doses may even cause

convulsions in children. Respiratory depression is negligible.

Codeine is demethylated to form small amounts of morphine and normorphine. These substances probably have no role in producing the effects of codeine.

Codeine is given orally in doses of 30 or 65 mg (½ or 1 grain). If it is dispensed in combination with another active drug—eg, aspirin or aspirin compound (APC)—fewer legal restraints on prescribing exist (see Chapter 4). In such mixtures it is the codeine that determines the analgesic effectiveness of the mixture.

2. Dihydrocodeine is given in smaller doses than codeine but is otherwise equivalent.

3. Ethylmorphine (Dionin) is not used as an analgesic. It is identified because of occasional references to its use as a corneal irritant.

4. Diphenoxylate is contained in a proprietary mixture (Lomotil) used in the treatment of diarrhea. The presence of another ingredient (atropine) exempts the mixture from some of the rules governing narcotic prescriptions, but the mixture is not superior to codeine, 15 mg 3–4 times each day, and is more toxic.

5. Dextromethorphan is the dextro isomer of a derivative of levorphanol (Table 26–3). It is almost completely free of analgesic and respiratory depressant properties and is a component of many over-the-counter and prescription medications for cough.

6. Thebaine (Table 26–1) has no therapeutic applications but is of theoretic interest because it possesses the excitatory but none of the depressant properties of morphine. It causes excitement and convulsions. The convulsions are at first suprasegmental in origin but, with larger doses, originate in the spinal cord and are comparable to those that occur after toxic doses of strychnine.

7. Apomorphine (Fig 26–2) is prepared by heating morphine with strong acid. It very dependably induces emesis by stimulating the chemoreceptor trigger zone of the medulla. It is a depressant like morphine, and its action is terminated by the narcotic antagonists. Its use in acute intoxications as an emetic agent is discussed in Chapter 64.

E. Propoxyphene (Dextropropoxyphene, Darvon, Darvon-N): It has been impossible to demonstrate a significant analgesic effect for propoxyphene; nevertheless, for a number of years it (alone and in combination with aspirin compound) has been the drug most often prescribed in the USA. If it is virtually inactive for its primary purpose, it is still an important cause of suicidal and accidental deaths. It is at best a feeble narcotic, but it is suggested for use in treating heroin withdrawal symptoms and even as a substitute for methadone in maintaining compulsive heroin abusers. This paradox can be resolved, and the use of the drug made rational, by viewing it as a central stimulant comparable to thebaine.

1. Chemistry—Propoxyphene is the D-isomer of a compound related to methadone. It was first dispensed as the hydrochloride, and propoxyphene hydrochloride (with or without aspirin compound) remains the most economical way of prescribing the drug. When the patent expired and generic preparations of the hydrochloride became available, advantages were claimed for the less soluble napsylate (Darvon-N). However, no differences between the absorption, metabolism, or effects of the 2 salts have been shown in humans. Because of the difference in molecular weights, 100 mg of the napsylate are equivalent to 65 mg of the hydrochloride.

2. Analgesic effectiveness–The claim that propoxyphene is equivalent in potency to codeine has not been substantiated in clinical trials. Obviously, Darvon Compound must be compared with aspirin compound as well as with codeine with aspirin to establish its relative potency. The analgesic effect of 32 mg of propoxyphene is not greater than that of aspirin compound. Propoxyphene in doses of 65 mg may have an effect somewhat greater than that of the aspirin compound with which it is mixed, but the effect is quantitatively so small that not all trials can establish it. The favorable subjective response of some patients, with or without pain, may be due to the mild euphoria associated with the central nervous system stimulant effect.

3. Side-effects and toxicity–Tremulousness, restlessness ("speeding"), and mild euphoria should probably be considered as part of the primary effect of the agent rather than as side-effects. These feelings, together with side-effects such as nausea and dizziness or light-headedness, occur frequently.

The acute toxic effects that follow accidental or suicidal overdose by mouth differ from those of the usual narcotic in that the course is rapid, leading to convulsions and, later, respiratory depression and coma. Deaths are surprisingly common—probably several hundred each year.

The narcotic antagonists alter the toxicity of propoxyphene to only a limited degree by preventing convulsions—ie, the propoxyphene-antagonist relationship is not comparable to that between narcotic agonists and antagonists described below.

4. Addiction liability–Viewed as a narcotic, it is feeble even in comparison with codeine if it has any narcotic activity at all. Misuse may nevertheless occur because the central nervous system stimulant effect is pleasurable to some people. Misuse is commonly seen when propoxyphene is used in drug abuse treatment programs. The wide prescription use of an agent inactive for its primary purpose must also be presumed to present a situation comparable to the wide use of diet pills.

Reasonable dosages of propoxyphene combined with other symptomatic medication appear to be useful in relieving the narcotic withdrawal state, just as strychnine was in the past.

NARCOTIC ANTAGONISTS

Some references to the narcotic antagonists have already been made. Their properties are discussed in this section, with repetition of some material.

Chemistry

The narcotic analgesics are N-substituted — usually N-methyl — derivatives of the common pattern described above. The narcotic antagonists are prepared by altering the N-substituent. Naloxone, nalorphine, and levallorphan are the N-allyl ($-CH_2-CH=CH_2$) derivatives of oxymorphone, morphine, and levorphanol.

Pharmacologic Effects

A. Mechanism of Action: If any one of the narcotic analgesics, natural or synthetic, is acting, the antagonists will immediately terminate the effect. The relation is competitive, and the action is most commonly explained by the displacement of the agonist from the receptor.

B. Effects:

1. Morphinelike–By themselves, nalorphine and levallorphan produce all of the effects described above for the potent analgesics. With small doses, euphoria may be experienced, but misuse is not a problem because larger doses lead to subjectively unpleasant feelings or to a toxic psychosis. In the case of nalorphine and levallorphan, not even large doses cause the same degree of respiratory depression and analgesia as morphine. Pentazocine, however, can be used to produce anesthesia comparable to that following the use of morphine. Naloxone lacks any morphinelike action.

2. Narcotic antagonism–All of the depressant effects of the opiates are immediately reversed, but the stimulant effects (excitement, convulsions) are not modified. Not only are respiratory and other depressant effects antagonized, but, in a tolerant subject, the withdrawal state is promptly induced.

Clinical Uses

A. Treatment of Acute Poisoning Due to Narcotics: Acute poisoning of major or minor degree induced in the course of the therapeutic or other use of the narcotics can be dramatically treated with the narcotic antagonists. However, a beneficial effect appears only if the depression is due to a morphinelike drug.

Naloxone (Narcan) is a pure antagonist — ie, unlike nalorphine or levallorphan, it has no morphinelike, agonist effects. It would not add to the respiratory depression caused by a barbiturate or other depressant and should replace the older drugs. It should be given in 0.4 mg dosage increments, intravenously if possible but intramuscularly if veins cannot be easily located and entered.

An abstinence syndrome or withdrawal reaction can be precipitated in an addict intoxicated by an overdose. The necessary dose of the antagonist should be reached by increments even in the very depressed subject, since the sudden precipitation of withdrawal symptoms by a large dose can be dangerous.

A special situation is the use of narcotic antagonists in the mother who has been given narcotics during delivery and whose degree of respiratory depression predicts a depressed infant. The *mother* should be given naloxone 10–15 minutes before delivery. If the neonate shows dangerous respiratory depression due to narcotic administration to the mother, the antagonist can be given into the umbilical vein. The dosage for naloxone in this application has not yet been established.

B. As a Nonaddicting Analgesic: Theoretically, a proper balancing of agonist-antagonist effects should result in a compound that is an effective analgesic at low doses but produces dysphoria with larger doses. The early antagonists could not be used as analgesics because the dysphoria and alterations of perception were common and intense.

Pentazocine (Talwin) is an analgesic of intermediate potency and also a very weak narcotic antagonist. Given to a heroin-dependent patient within 12 hours after the last dose of the narcotic, it may precipitate mild discomfort. Thereafter it will partially relieve the withdrawal state. Its continued use may lead to a mild withdrawal state when it is discontinued. Examples of misuse, especially by people with prior experience with narcotics, are now common.

During its therapeutic use, pentazocine may cause side-effects similar to those of other narcotic analgesics. It may also cause dizziness, distortion of visual perception, and hallucinations, especially if the dosage is rapidly increased.

C. Detection of Narcotic Use: Testing for narcotic use is often made a condition of parole or probation. In the past, the "Nalline test" was used. Under controlled conditions of lighting, a standard dose of nalorphine was given subcutaneously. More than minimal pupillary dilation was an indication that withdrawal had been precipitated — ie, the subject had been using heroin. The test was counterproductive in that a mild narcotic effect was experienced, the subject was brought into contact with a group of drug users, and the physician was placed in the role of agent of the state rather than therapist.

Urinalysis has replaced the Nalline test in this police or social function. The chromatographic methods now used can demonstrate morphine in the urine for about 3 days after heroin use, and other abused drugs can also be detected.

Today, the precipitation of withdrawal by an antagonist is either a therapeutic mishap or an investigational use of the antagonist to establish that a new compound is or is not a narcotic. Signs and symptoms of withdrawal appear in 5–15 minutes, peak in 30–45 minutes, and last only a few hours but are intense.

Doctors worry, perhaps unduly, about being victimized by narcotics users. In the presence of pain or trauma, any error in prescribing narcotics should be on the permissive side.

D. Treatment of Narcotic Abuse: If an antagonist free of side-effects could be given in such a way as to exert a constant effect, the heroin user so treated would find it pointless to inject heroin, since no effects would be felt. One investigative drug, nal-

trexone (N-cyclopropylmethyl-nor-oxymorphone), is orally active, has a long duration of action, and does not cause dysphoria or other side-effects. It is being evaluated in treatment but, as might have been predicted, is acceptable to only a few patients.

●   ●   ●

References

General

Bonica JJ (editor): Symposium on pain. Arch Surg 112:749, 1977.

Clovet DH (editor): *Narcotic Drugs: Biochemical Pharmacology.* Plenum Press, 1971.

Reynolds AK, Randall LO: *Morphine and Allied Drugs.* Univ of Toronto Press, 1957.

Snyder SH: Opiate receptors in the brain. N Engl J Med 296:266, 1977.

Vandam LD: Analgetic drugs: The potent analgetics. N Engl J Med 286:249, 1972.

Clinical Effects & Evaluation

Beaver WT & others: A comparison of the analgesic effects of pentazocine and morphine in patients with cancer. Clin Pharmacol Ther 7:740, 1966.

Beecher HK: *Measurement of Subjective Responses: Quantitative Effects of Drugs.* Oxford Univ Press (New York), 1959.

Gold MS: Opiate withdrawal using clonidine. JAMA 243:343, 1980.

Katz KH, Chandler HL: Morphine hypersensitivity in kyphoscoliosis. N Engl J Med 238:322, 1948.

Keats AS, Mithoefer JC: The mechanism of increased intracranial pressure induced by morphine. N Engl J Med 252:1110, 1955.

Laidlaw J, Read AE, Sherlock S: Morphine tolerance in hepatic cirrhosis. Gastroenterology 40:389, 1961.

Lasagna L: The clinical evaluation of morphine and its substitutes as analgesics. Pharmacol Rev 16:47, 1964.

Lasagna L, Beecher HK: The optimal dose of morphine. JAMA 156:230, 1954.

Mezzak B: The Brompton mixture versus morphine solution given orally. Can Med Assoc J 120:435, 1979.

Miller RR, Feingold A, Paxinos J: Propoxyphene hydrochloride: A critical review. JAMA 213:996, 1970.

Mossberg SM & others: Serum enzyme activities following morphine: A study of transaminase and alkaline phosphatase levels in normal persons and those with gallbladder disease. Arch Intern Med 109:429, 1962.

Rutter PC, Murphy F, Dudley HAF: Morphine: Controlled trial of different methods of administration for postoperative pain relief. Br Med J 1:12, 1980.

Sturner WQ, Garriott JC: Deaths involving propoxyphene: A study of 41 cases over a two-year period. JAMA 223:1125, 1973.

Vandam L: Butorphanol. N Engl J Med 302:381, 1980.

Wolen RL, Ziege EA, Gruber CM Jr: Determination of propoxyphene and norpropoxyphene by chemical ionization mass fragmentography. Clin Pharmacol Ther 17:15, 1975.

Zelis R & others: Cardiovascular effects of morphine. J Clin Invest 54:1247, 1974.

Zelson C, Lee SJ, Casalino M: Neonatal narcotic addiction: Comparative effects of maternal intake of heroin and methadone. N Engl J Med 289:1216, 1973.

Abuse (See Chapter 7.)

Antagonists

Evans JM & others: Degree and duration of reversal by naloxone of effects of morphine in conscious subjects. Br Med J 2:589, 1974.

Evans LEJ & others: Treatment of drug overdosage with naloxone, a specific narcotic antagonist. Lancet 1:452, 1973.

Foldes FF: Human pharmacology and clinical use of narcotic antagonists. Med Clin North Am 48:421, 1964.

Michaelis LL & others: Ventricular irritability associated with the use of naloxone hydrochloride: Two case reports and laboratory assessment of the effect of the drug on cardiac excitability. Ann Thorac Surg 18:608, 1974.

27 | Antipyretic Anti-inflammatory Analgesics

with Martin A. Shearn, MD

Aspirin and the other drugs of this class are usually designated antipyretic or nonnarcotic analgesics to separate them from the more potent narcotic analgesics, but they are also highly effective anti-inflammatory agents. They relieve mild pain of diverse causes, including some of the most common complaints—tension headache, joint and muscle pain, the malaise of viral infections, etc. They lower an elevated body temperature and reduce the inflammation of rheumatoid arthritis and rheumatic fever.

Aspirin is by far the most important and most commonly used drug of the group. Other antipyretic analgesics offer an advantage over aspirin in a few situations, but most are far more toxic. Many are available without a prescription, and a large number of combinations and preparations are advertised.

Drugs of this class are often referred to as nonsteroidal anti-inflammatory drugs (NSAID). Other anti-inflammatory drugs used in testing rheumatic diseases are discussed at the end of this chapter.

Classification of Antipyretic Analgesics

A. Salicylates: Aspirin and sodium salicylate.

B. Other Organic Acids: A number of derivatives of organic acids other than salicylic acid have recently been introduced as possible substitutes for aspirin. New drugs in this group include ibuprofen (Motrin), naproxen (Naprosyn), and fenoprofen (Nalfon), which are propionic acid derivatives and tolmetin (Tolectin), an acetic acid derivative.

C. Para-aminophenol Derivatives: Phenacetin and acetaminophen. These aniline derivatives are equivalent to the salicylates except that they are not anti-inflammatory and acetaminophen is not quite as safe as the salicylates for chronic use; however, these drugs cause less acute gastric irritation.

D. Pyrazolone Derivatives: Aminopyrine, phenylbutazone, etc. The use of the older drugs of this group has declined because of their serious allergic toxicity. The newer compounds also have much greater acute and chronic toxicity than the salicylates.

E. Quinoline Derivatives: Quinine was the first antipyretic analgesic, but it is no longer used as such.

Martin A. Shearn is Clinical Professor, University of California School of Medicine (San Francisco); Director of Medical Education, Kaiser-Permanente Medical Center (Oakland).

History

Cinchona bark and the quinine and quinidine therein are the oldest of the drugs known to lower an elevated body temperature and relieve mild pain. The same action is exhibited by willow bark, which was shown in 1829 to contain salicin, a glucoside of salicyl alcohol. Because quinine also has a specific effect on the fever of malaria and because of confusion in the taxonomy of fevers, these old folk remedies were actually of little importance in the development of that most essential of modern remedies, aspirin.

A German chemist, Kolbe, proposed in 1873 that salicylic acid be used to treat infections because it obviously would liberate free phenol and therefore prove bactericidal. At about the time that the initially favorable reports were being modified, a Swiss physician, Carl Buss, noted its antipyretic effect and retrospectively related it to the salicylate (salicin) in willow bark. The antirheumatic effect was described soon after. The antirheumatic effect of pure salicin was independently reported at about the same time, but this discovery was not essential to the development of the salicylates.

A second class of antipyretics was defined when another German chemist (Knorr, 1883) attempted the synthesis of a part of the quinine molecule. He discovered the effect of antipyrine, and only later clarified the structure and realized that no relation to quinine existed.

In 1886, 2 students of the internist Kussmaul gave a patient acetanilid from a bottle with a deteriorated label, thinking that it was the naphthalene that they had been told to test as a parasiticide. Fortunately, the patient had a fever and the beneficial effect was noted.

The last error suggested to the Bayer organization that they might dispose of a huge surplus of para-aminophenol by converting it to some analog of acetanilid, and in this way ethoxyacetanilide, or phenacetin, was prepared. The same laboratory, looking for an alternative to sodium salicylate, restudied acetylsalicylic acid (*a*cetyl *Spir*säure; hence the name aspirin) and demonstrated the superiority of aspirin as an antipyretic in 1899.

Finally, in 1900, the analgesic effect of these agents was established. Both the mistakes and the advances in research have been minor since that time.

ASPIRIN & OTHER SALICYLATES

SALICYLATES

Salicylates are effective anti-inflammatory agents in high dosage, whereas in lower doses they are utilized for their antipyretic and analgesic properties. Aspirin is available without prescription in various preparations and combinations. Aspirin is so widely and often so indiscriminately used that it lacks some of the magic of prescription drugs. It is, however, the standard against which all other anti-inflammatory agents are measured.

Chemistry

Aspirin (acetylsalicylic acid, ASA) has a pharmacologic action of its own, but it is rapidly metabolized to salicylic acid (Fig 27–1). Salicylate may be given directly as sodium salicylate, but this preparation causes more gastric irritation and is less effective. The strongly acidic properties of aspirin and salicylic acid predict many of its properties.

Salicylamide, a weak and short-acting analgesic usually discussed with the salicylates, is not converted to salicylate but acts (feebly) as the amide and is rapidly excreted as such.

Salicylic acid used as such rather than sodium salicylate should be thought of as a topical keratolytic agent and not as a systemic drug. Methyl salicylate (oil of wintergreen) should also be considered separately as a counterirritant or liniment; it is much more toxic when taken systemically than the familiar salicylates.

Aspirin is the most potent agent in this group. Sodium salicylate causes less gastric irritation but also possesses less anti-inflammatory properties.

Absorption, Metabolism, & Excretion

The salicylates are rapidly absorbed from the stomach and upper small intestine, yielding a peak plasma salicylate level within 2 hours. Providing a more acid medium in the stomach keeps a larger fraction of the salicylate in the nonionized form and promotes absorption. However, in the acid milieu of the stomach, salicylate, with its pKa of 3.5, can readily enter the mucosal cell and damage the normal mucosal barrier. The resulting back-diffusion of hydrogen ions may damage capillaries and cause bleeding. Blood loss associated with aspirin ingestion is dose-related. The amount of blood loss is usually minimal, but overt bleeding may occasionally result. Raising the gastric pH to 3.5 or higher by a suitable buffer minimizes gastric irritation. Aspirin is absorbed as such and hydrolized to acetic acid and salicylate by esterases in tissue and blood. Salicylate is bound to albumin, but, as serum concentrations of salicylate increase, a greater proportion is unbound and thus available to tissues. Ingested salicylate or that generated by the hydrolysis of aspirin may be excreted as such, but most is converted to water-soluble conjugates that are rapidly cleared by the kidney (Fig 27–1). The pathway for

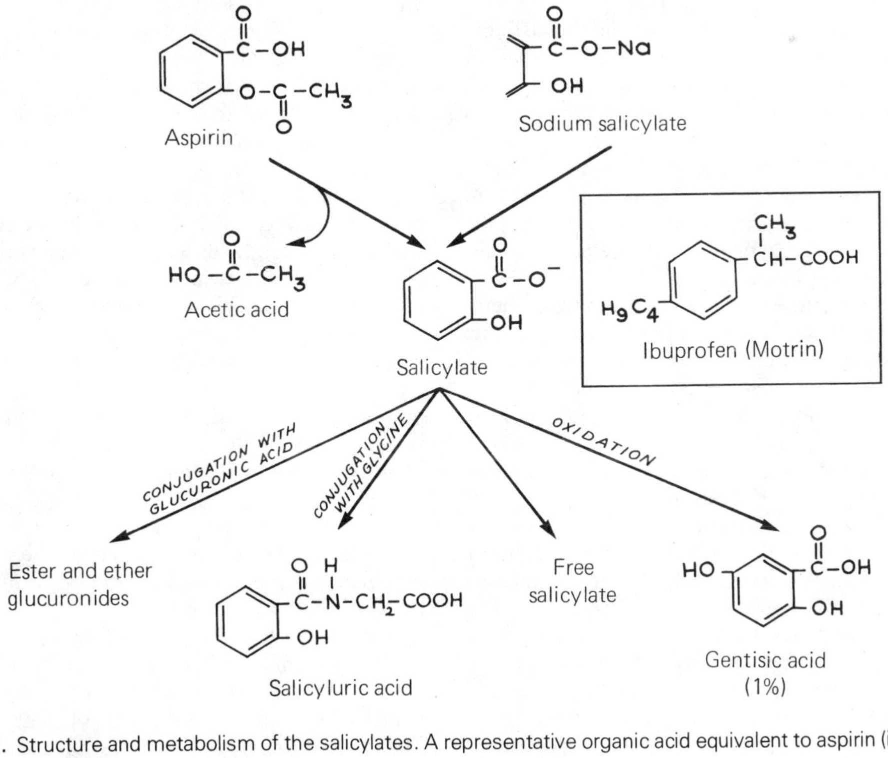

Figure 27–1. Structure and metabolism of the salicylates. A representative organic acid equivalent to aspirin (ibuprofen) is shown for comparison.

conjugation can become saturated, and a small increase in dose will then result in a large increase in plasma levels. Alkalinization of the urine increases the rate of excretion of the free salicylate. When aspirin is used in low concentrations (650 mg), elimination is in accordance with first-order kinetics, and serum half-life is about 3–5 hours. However, with higher doses, zero-order kinetics prevail, and, at dosages of 4–5 g/d, the half-life increases to 15 hours or more. This effect takes about a week to occur and is related to saturation of hepatic enzymes that catalyze the formation of salicylate conversion compounds, salicylglucuronide and gentisic acid.

Pharmacologic Effects & Mechanisms of Action

The nonnarcotic or antipyretic analgesics (most of what is said about aspirin applies to the other classes also) have multiple pharmacologic effects and presumably also have multiple mechanisms of action.

A. Anti-inflammatory Effects: Prostaglandins of the E and F series are released and intensify the effects of the primary mediation of inflammation, and the effectiveness of the salicylates is mainly due to their ability to inhibit the enzyme cyclo-oxygenase (prostaglandin synthetase), which is essential to prostaglandin synthesis (see Chapters 14 and 18). Aspirin is the most potent agent in this group. Salicylate metabolites appear to be weak inhibitors of prostaglandins. Salicylates also inhibit the migration of polymorphonuclear leukocytes and macrophages into the site of inflammation and seem to inhibit granulocyte adherence. Vasodilatation induced by aspirin may play a role in reducing inflammation.

B. Analgesic Effects: Pain of many different types is relieved. It may be of muscular, vascular, or inflammatory (whether traumatic or irritative) origin. Pain associated with tension or other types of headache, arthritis, bursitis, the postpartum state, incisions, dental extractions, cancer, and a host of other causes is often responsive to treatment with aspirin. The point of this extended list is to emphasize that the intensity rather than the nature of the pain determines whether aspirin will be effective.

C. Antipyretic Effects: Normal body temperature is only slightly affected, but fever is reduced. The fall in temperature is due to dilatation of superficial blood vessels, with increased dissipation of heat rather than decreased heat production. The fall may be precipitous and accompanied by profuse sweating. The cooling due to evaporation of the perspiration is not essential to the action of these antipyretics, the effect persisting even if sweating is prevented by the administration of atropine. Aspirin also lowers experimentally elevated temperature in animals with hypothalamic lesions that abolish the sweating response to heat. The antipyretic effect thus is mediated by vasodilatation following a "resetting" of a hypothalamic temperature control center. The antipyretic effect can be assayed and analyzed in animals following the production of fever by the injection of bacterial endotoxin or other pyrogen.

D. Central Nervous System Stimulation:

1. Respiration–In large amounts, the salicylates (but not the other drugs discussed in this chapter) markedly increase the rate and depth of respiration. With even larger doses or late in the course of an intoxication, respiration is depressed. The initial respiratory alkalosis is followed later in the period of intoxication by a metabolic acidosis, and the acidosis is intensified by respiratory depression.

2. Behavioral–Toxic doses may cause excitement, confusion, coma, convulsions, and, rarely, toxic psychosis.

3. Nausea and vomiting–Aspirin can have an irritant effect on the gastric mucosa, causing epigastric discomfort and sometimes nausea, but severe nausea and actual vomiting are usually due to central nervous system stimulation by the drug after absorption.

E. Metabolic and Endocrine Effects:

1. ACTH release–In animals, the adrenal cortex is stimulated by the administration of aspirin. The effect is blocked by a hypothalamic (median eminence) lesion as well as by hypophysectomy. The drug must then be acting through the hypothalamus to stimulate the liberation of ACTH. In humans, however, not even large doses of aspirin lead to evidence of adrenocortical hyperfunction, and the anti-inflammatory action is not mediated by the corticosteroids.

2. Hypoprothrombinemia–The salicylates are weak inhibitors of prothrombin synthesis. The decrease in prothrombin concentration is not great enough to explain any bleeding episode associated with the administration of aspirin alone.

3. Platelet dysfunction–Aspirin does have an effect on hemostasis. Single doses of aspirin will produce a small prolongation of bleeding time, and a doubling if administration is continued for a week. The change is explained by the inhibition of platelet aggregation.

Hemostasis (and possibly arterial thrombosis) begins with the formation of a platelet plug at the site of vascular damage, with subsequent deposition of fibrin through the processes described in Chapter 18. Platelets first adhere to collagen fibers or other surfaces and then undergo the release reaction. Their shape is altered (providing platelet factor 3 for the clotting process), and the contents of intracellular granules are extruded. Among the substances released is adenosine diphosphate (ADP), which acts on the platelets to increase their adhesiveness and leads to aggregation.

The prior administration of aspirin inhibits prostaglandin synthesis. Since prostaglandin in most sites accelerates aggregation, the effect of aspirin is to inhibit platelet aggregation.

No relation has been established between platelet dysfunction and gastrointestinal bleeding, nor is the hazard of bleeding at surgery increased unless the patient has an inherited disorder of platelet function. The interest is not so much in possible toxicity as in the possibility that prolonged suppression of platelet aggregation might provide an antithrombotic technic superior to the use of inhibitors of prothrombin synthesis. The widespread use of aspirin to prevent arterial and venous thrombosis is discussed in Chapter 18.

The effect of aspirin on platelet aggregation lasts for 8 days—ie, until new platelets are formed. Aspirin has a longer duration of effect and is evidently more potent than the many other compounds that inhibit platelet aggregation—eg, clofibrate, pyrazolone analgesics, dipyridamole, tranquilizers, antidepressants, and others.

4. Other—Like other organic acids that use the same pathway, the salicylates may interfere with both the excretion and the reabsorption of uric acid by the renal tubules. The uricosuric effect of the salicylates appears only after large doses; smaller doses may have an opposite effect by interfering with uric acid secretion (excretion) by the tubule. The salicylates have been replaced as uricosuric agents by other more dependable drugs.

Glucose tolerance is slightly impaired, but ordinary doses can be used in diabetic patients without interference with the action of oral antidiabetic drugs or change in insulin requirement.

Clinical Uses

A. Pain: Salicylates have a potency comparable in some kinds of pain to small doses of narcotics, and they should be tried in most cases where analgesia is necessary. In general, visceral cramping pain would not be expected to respond, but some types—eg, dysmenorrhea—may in fact respond to aspirin.

B. Fever: Obviously, antipyretic drugs should not replace specific therapy, but there is no reason they should not be used while the effect of the specific drug is developing or when no specific therapy is available—eg, in the case of influenza. Not only is temperature lowered, but malaise and muscular discomfort are reduced.

C. Specific Inflammatory States: These drugs are used in the treatment of rheumatoid arthritis, acute rheumatic fever, and other diseases with inflammatory components.

Adverse Reactions

A. Side-Effects: The side-effects of aspirin are usually limited to epigastric discomfort, heartburn, or nausea. When larger doses must be employed, as in rheumatoid arthritis, or in a few of the most sensitive individuals, tinnitus or other symptoms of salicylism may appear.

1. Gastric irritation—The mechanism by which aspirin causes gastric irritation and bleeding is important because it also relates to other drugs and possibly even to the pathogenesis of peptic ulcer.

The gastric mucosa is ordinarily an impervious barrier that is not damaged by acid, enzymes, and irritant drugs within the lumen. For hydrogen ions themselves to enter and damage the mucosa, the concentration of hydrochloric acid must reach 3 times that of undiluted gastric secretion.

However, if both acid and aspirin are present, the aspirin will exist in part as the lipid-soluble free acid and be absorbed. As the salicylates are absorbed, they damage the mucosal cells and disrupt the tight junctions between those cells. Acid as well as salicylate can then damage the underlying tissues, and epithelial cells, red blood cells, plasma proteins, and ions enter the gastric contents. Other substances that act like aspirin in the presence of acid (in the dog, at least) are alcohol and detergents—including bile salts, which can reach the stomach if the pyloric sphincter does not act as an efficient barrier to reflux from the duodenum.

2. Gastrointestinal bleeding—Not only do side-effects indicative of gastric irritation occur, but the amount of occult bleeding into the gastrointestinal tract is increased following the administration of aspirin. Blood loss is measured by labeling the red blood cells of the subject and measuring the radioactivity recovered in the feces following the administration of the drug. Normally, less than 1 mL of blood is lost in the stools each day. This figure is increased to perhaps 4 mL/d following the use of ordinary aspirin in the usual doses, but it may reach 10 mL or even 30 mL in an occasional patient.

The buffered preparations described below have been developed in an effort to avoid the effect of aspirin in the presence of stomach acid. The interest is a valid one but has been overemphasized by proponents of various buffered or soluble aspirin preparations.

Aspirin is a comparatively strong acid, having a carboxyl group with a pKa of 3.5—ie, in a solution with pH 3.5, half of the substance exists in the form of the free acid and half as the ionized salt form. Therefore, administration of aspirin in combination with an alkali would decrease the rate of absorption of the drug from the stomach by increasing the fraction of aspirin present as the charged, poorly absorbed salt (Fig 2–2). Adequately buffered preparations would reduce gastric irritation, and the brief delay in absorption is not important. Cimetidine, a histamine (H-2 receptor) antagonist, when given with aspirin, appears to protect gastric mucosa.

In evaluating the special preparations, it should be recalled that gastric irritation is only occasionally troublesome; that the gastric mucosa rapidly replaces and repairs itself; and that few of the preparations contain significant amounts of alkali. No one of the special preparations is superior to aspirin administered with a full glass of water. Presumably, the more rapid passage of the aspirin into the intestine and its greater dilution are responsible for the beneficial effect of the additional fluid.

The effect of aspirin on the stomach would become extremely important if a correlation could be demonstrated between chronic administration of aspirin and anemia or an increased incidence of peptic ulcer or gastrointestinal bleeding. Only the last has been suggested, and that has been by retrospective studies difficult to interpret.

3. Increased bleeding tendency—Aspirin increases the bleeding tendency in a wide variety of hematologic disorders (eg, von Willebrand's disease, anticoagulant therapy). Platelet aggregation is inhibited by aspirin, and massive doses of aspirin can cause hypoprothrombinemia.

4. Hepatic and renal impairment–Liver and kidney parenchymal impairment have both been recognized as a complication of aspirin therapy. The injury is reversible upon withdrawal of the drug, but caution is warranted in using large doses of aspirin in patients with preexisting hepatic or renal disease.

5. Ototoxicity–See below.

B. Overdosage Toxicity: Aspirin is the most common household drug, and its ingestion out of curiosity or imitativeness makes it the most common cause of poisoning in very young children. As a general rule, one may expect serious intoxication if the amount ingested exceeds 150–175 mg/kg.

1. Salicylism–High-pitched tinnitus, vertigo, and deafness may occur at times with therapeutic doses as well as after toxic amounts. These effects are reversible.

2. Hyperthermia–In contrast to the effect of therapeutic doses, toxic doses—due to an uncharacterized central nervous system effect—will greatly elevate body temperature.

3. Behavioral–Central nervous system stimulation is followed by depression. Agitation and confusion or even convulsions are followed by stupor and coma. Rarely, a toxic psychosis with paranoid and hallucinatory behavior will appear. Asterixis can be demonstrated as in hepatic failure.

4. Initial respiratory alkalosis due to respiratory stimulation.

5. Compensated respiratory alkalosis–If urine volume is maintained, renal excretion of bicarbonate, sodium, and potassium will increase, lowering plasma bicarbonate and returning pH to normal.

6. Respiratory and metabolic acidosis–If respiratory depression follows the initial respiratory stimulation, CO_2 retention will occur, with a bicarbonate level already lowered by the previous compensation. Whether or not this respiratory acidosis develops, metabolic acidosis will appear. This acidosis is due in small part to the salicylic acid, to a larger extent to decreased renal function with retention of acid metabolites, and to the largest extent to the production of large amounts of organic acids (pyruvic, lactic, acetoacetic) due to unexplained effect of salicylate on carbohydrate metabolism.

C. Treatment of Overdosage Toxicity: If the patient is seen soon enough and if the amount taken is unknown or if it is known to exceed the arbitrary guide of 150–175 mg/kg, gastric lavage should be performed. Hyperthermia should be treated as vigorously as necessary with tepid water or alcohol sponges or with ice packs. Urine volume should be maintained at a high level (500 mL/h). When urine volume or direct measurements establish that a compensated alkalosis or acidosis has developed, bicarbonate should be administered and the fluid should

contain potassium. If the renal tubular urine is kept alkaline, the salicylate will exist in the salt (ionized) form and be less readily reabsorbed than the free acid—ie, excretion of salicylate will be hastened. If the usual treatment maintains a large volume of alkaline urine, dialysis or other radical treatment will rarely be needed. Acetazolamide (Diamox) may also be used to alkalinize the urine.

D. Allergic Reactions: Considering the large amounts involved and the varied patterns of salicylate use, it is amazing that allergic reactions are so uncommon.

E. Analgesic-Induced Asthma Syndrome: Single small doses of aspirin may cause rhinorrhea, bronchiolar constriction, and shock—symptoms superficially suggestive of an allergic reaction but actually lacking an immunochemical basis. In this situation, patients with a history of asthma with onset in young adulthood react unpredictably to aspirin. The reaction may be limited to profuse rhinorrhea, often with nasal polyps; it may include asthma that is difficult to treat and that may be accompanied by urticaria; and, in a few cases, the bronchoconstriction is followed by shock and the possibility of a fatal outcome.

In a series of 1200 asthmatics, 24 were made worse by the administration of aspirin, but the estimate of the incidence would have been higher if forced expiratory volumes had been measured.

Susceptible patients may respond to a number of drugs, too varied to show cross-sensitivity, either by the development of asthma or by a reduction in forced expiratory volume. These agents include aspirin (but not other salicylates), indomethacin, acetaminophen, propoxyphene, pentazocine, and, in a few cases, tartrazine, a common yellow food coloring agent.

Contraindications & Cautions

Most aspirin is sold and used without a prescription, and the important caution should be directed to families with children: aspirin—indeed, all medicines—should be kept out of reach of children. Aspirin is the agent most often responsible for poisonings in children under age 5 years. It should be kept in the child-resistant vial in which it is dispensed. Colorful, flavored, and liquid preparations should be treated with special care.

Aspirin should be given with great care to patients with a history of peptic ulcer or of bleeding or asthma at a prior administration. Aspirin is contraindicated for patients with hypersensitivity or hemophilia. Magnesium salicylate is contraindicated in patients with chronic renal failure.

Drug Interactions

Drugs that enhance salicylate intoxication include acetazolamide and ammonium chloride, whereas alcohol increases gastrointestinal bleeding produced by salicylates. Aspirin displaces a number of drugs from plasma protein binding sites. These include tolbutamide, chlorpropamide, nonsteroidal anti-inflammatory agents such as naproxen and phenyl-butazone, methotrexate, phenytoin, and probenecid. Corticosteroids may decrease salicylate concentration. Aspirin reduces the pharmacologic activity of spironolactone, antagonizes the effect of heparin, competes with penicillin G for renal tubular secretion, and inhibits the uricosuric effect of sulfinpyrazone.

Dosage

The optimal analgesic or antipyretic dose of aspirin is less than the 0.6 g commonly used. Larger doses may prolong the effect but will not increase its intensity. The usual dose may be repeated every 4 hours and smaller doses (0.3 g) every 3 hours.

The familiar rule that children should receive 65 mg per year of age is a safe and useful guide to pediatric dosage.

When aspirin is employed as an anti-inflammatory agent, higher dosages are necessary than when it is used for simple analgesia. The average-sized adult can usually tolerate 4–6 g daily when required. Dosage must be reduced if ototoxic manifestations occur. The total daily dose of aspirin is a more critical factor in determining steady state salicylate levels than the timing and size or fraction of the daily dose. Differences in the patient's body weight must also be taken into consideration. Blood levels of 15–30 mg/dL are associated with anti-inflammatory effects. Because of the long half-life (±14 hours) of aspirin, frequent dosing is not necessary when doses of 4 g or more are used. A convenient method is to give the total amount divided into 3 doses, which are given after each meal.

Preparations Available

A. Standard Aspirin Tablets: The official preparation of aspirin is available from many different manufacturers. These do not vary in the content of aspirin but may vary in the way in which the tablets are pressed and in the binder used. They may vary in their appearance and in the texture of the surface, but a disintegration test is part of the official standard and there is no evidence that differences among tablets are clinically significant.

B. Nominally Buffered Aspirin: The most popular buffered aspirins (Bufferin and others) do not contain enough alkali to modify the irritative process described above. Repeated studies have shown that blood levels, clinical effectiveness, and incidence of side-effects do not differ when this kind of buffered aspirin is compared with standard aspirin.

C. True Buffered Aspirin: The effervescent preparations of aspirin (Alka-Seltzer and others) contain enough alkali to solubilize the aspirin and to elevate the pH of the gastric contents. Since they are systemic antacids, they are not suitable for chronic administration.

An adequately buffered aspirin preparation or alkali separately administered in amounts sufficient to alkalinize the urine would increase renal excretion and give lower plasma levels and a lesser effect.

D. Aspirin Compound (APC): Aspirin com-

Table 27–1. Antipyretic analgesics and dosages.

	Usual Oral Dose
Salicylates	
Aspirin	Adult: 0.3–1 g
	Pediatric: 60 mg/kg/d in 4–6 doses
Aspirin compound	1–2 tablets every 4–6 hours
Sodium salicylate	0.3–1 g every 4–6 hours
Salicylamide	Adult: 0.3–1 g
	Pediatric: 60 mg/kg/d in 6 doses
Other Organic Acids	
Indomethacin (Indocin)	25–50 mg 3 times daily
Ibuprofen (Brufen, Motrin)	300–600 mg 3–4 times daily
Mefenamic acid (Ponstel)	See text.
Naproxen (Naprosyn)	250–375 mg 2 times daily
Fenoprofen (Nalfon)	300–900 mg 4 times daily
Solindac (Clinoril)	200 mg 2 times daily
Tolmetin (Tolectin)	400 mg 3–4 times daily
Para-aminophenols	
Phenacetin	300 mg every 4 hours
Acetaminophen	Adult: 0.3–1 g
	Pediatric: 60 mg/kg/d in 4–6 doses

pound is an official preparation of standard composition containing aspirin, phenacetin, and caffeine (Table 27–1).

Many popular proprietary combinations were originally similar to aspirin compound, but their composition changed following the recent recognition of the chronic toxicity of phenacetin.

E. Enteric-Coated and Sustained-Release Preparations: In sensitive patients or when prolonged high dosage is required, gastric irritation can be reduced by coating the tablets with a substance that dissolves only after they have entered the small intestine. The properties of such coatings are variable, as is the rate of passage of the tablet through the stomach. With the possible exception of one preparation (Ecotrin), absorption of aspirin from enteric-coated preparations appears to be incomplete. The cost is considerably more than that of aspirin.

Sustained-release preparations of aspirin do not give the significant prolongation of effect claimed for them.

OTHER ORGANIC ACIDS

The side-effects of aspirin can become troublesome or even dangerous when the chronic administration of large doses is necessary, as in the management of rheumatoid arthritis. Furthermore, aspirin in the common chronic rheumatic states is ordinarily not completely satisfactory. Because a less toxic or more efficacious alternative to aspirin would be important, many derivatives of organic acids other than salicylic acid have recently been tested; 7 are now marketed in the USA, and more than 50 are in investigational use.

These new drugs have so far been either exactly

equivalent to aspirin or, if more efficacious than aspirin, also more toxic. They are often referred to, especially in advertisements, as nonsteroidal anti-inflammatory drugs (NSAID), a perfectly satisfactory description so long as it is recognized that it applies equally well to aspirin.

Many aryl-alkyl carboxylic acids are active. The marketed drugs include derivatives of phenylpropionic acid (Fig 27–1), anthranilic acid, and aryl acetic acid.

There are differences among the several NSAIDs, but before these are discussed, it can be said that most of the properties described above for aspirin are present in the new drugs. All are, to varying degrees, inhibitors of prothrombin synthesis, and are analgesic, anti-inflammatory, and antipyretic and inhibit platelet aggregation. They are gastric and intestinal irritants.

They are efficacious in the same situations as aspirin. Since they are newly marketed drugs, their purveyors can claim efficacy only for indications for which acceptable clinical trials have been completed. Thus, a new claim, eg, usefulness in relieving dysmenorrhea, does not represent a new concept but is merely one way in which the new drug is "catching up" with aspirin. Certainly the nonspecific effects of treatment with these prescription drugs exceed those of aspirin, but the prescriber should recall that the impressive placebo effects already mentioned apply to one or 2 doses of an analgesic medication and not to chronic use. The cost of the newer acids ($20–30 per month) is not a negligible factor when compared to the cost of a few cents for generic over-the-counter aspirin.

Except as noted below for mefenamic acid and indomethacin, these drugs differ from aspirin in minor ways. Some patients tolerate a new analgesic better than aspirin, but in others the opposite is true.

Ibuprofen (Brufen, Motrin)

Ibuprofen is a simple derivative of phenylpropionic acid. In doses of 2200–2400 mg/d, ibuprofen is equivalent to aspirin in anti-inflammatory effect. The drug is usually prescribed at much lower doses, where it may be analgesic but inferior as an anti-inflammatory agent. Gastrointestinal irritation and bleeding occur, though somewhat less frequently than with aspirin. Ibuprofen interacts with coumarin and augments its effect. The use of ibuprofen concomitantly with aspirin may decrease the net anti-inflammatory effect. The drug is contraindicated in individuals with the syndrome of nasal polyps, angioedema, and bronchospastic reactivity to aspirin. Side-effects are dose-related. In addition to gastrointestinal symptoms, which can be modified by administration with meals or milk, rash, pruritus, tinnitus, dizziness, headache, anxiety, and fluid retention also occur. The analgesic dose is 400 mg 3–4 times daily; for rheumatoid arthritis, 2200–2400 mg daily.

Naproxen (Naprosyn)

Naproxen is a naphthyl propionic acid that binds to plasma protein. As a result, it has a long half-life (13

hours) and need be taken only twice each day. Antacids may delay the absorption of naproxen. Like ibuprofen, naproxen competes with aspirin for plasma protein binding sites. In addition, it displaces the coumarin type anticoagulants from binding sites on plasma proteins, which results in an increase in anticoagulant effect.

Fenoprofen (Nalfon)

Fenoprofen is another derivative of propionic acid that apparently does cause less gastrointestinal distress, but there also appears to be greater variability in the therapeutic response.

Sulindac (Clinoril)

Sulindac, like tolmetin and indomethacin, is a complexly substituted acetic acid. The form in which it is administered, a sulfoxide, is inactive but is converted by liver cytochrome to the sulfide, an active metabolite. The sulfide is excreted in the bile and reabsorbed from the intestine. The enterohepatic cycling prolongs the duration of action, so that the drug need be given only twice daily.

Mefenamic Acid (Ponstel)

Mefenamic acid is probably less effective than aspirin and is clearly more toxic. It is marketed with the condition that it not be used for longer than 1 week and that it not be used for children.

Indomethacin (Indocin)

Indomethacin is distinctive in that it is certainly more toxic and probably more effective than aspirin or any of the substitutes suggested above. In the laboratory, it is the most potent of the inhibitors of prostaglandin synthesis.

Indomethacin (Indocin)

A. Clinical Uses: Indomethacin, like phenylbutazone, is not suggested for general use as a simple analgesic but for use only in a few special situations and after safer drugs have not given a desired effect. The doubtful justification for using it in these special situations is that indomethacin causes fewer serious toxic reactions than phenylbutazone, although the total number of all adverse reactions may be larger.

The special situations are acute gouty arthritis,

rheumatoid (ankylosing) spondylitis, and osteoarthritis of the hip.

Indomethacin is also used in rheumatoid arthritis, but it is no more effective than aspirin and certainly causes more toxic reactions and side-effects. Some of the earlier studies that claimed to establish its usefulness are unacceptable or used doses that led to a prohibitive number of side-effects and toxic reactions.

B. Adverse Reactions: Indomethacin also causes frequent adverse reactions. Morning headache or migrainous daytime headaches (20%), vertigo, confusion, depression, or somnolence are common, although they may decrease with continued use or dose reduction. Nausea, blurred vision indicative of retinal damage, epigastric pain, diarrhea, activation of peptic ulcers, bleeding from any level of the gastrointestinal tract, and other reactions almost too numerous to list have been reported. Caution should be used in administering indomethacin with oral anticoagulants and with beta blocking agents. Probenecid blocks secretion of indomethacin and thus raises its blood levels. The drug also competes with penicillin G for renal tubular secretion. When indomethacin is used with furosemide, impaired response to both drugs may be seen. Aspirin and antacids inhibit gastrointestinal absorption. Avoid the use of indomethacin in patients with nasal polyps and angioedema who react to other nonsteroidal anti-inflammatory drugs and in those who show hypersensitivity to the drug.

C. Dosage & Preparations: See Table 27–1. Indomethacin is for adult use only, at least 3 sudden deaths having occurred in children. It should be taken with food or immediately after a meal.

PHENACETIN & OTHER PARA–AMINOPHENOL DERIVATIVES

Chemistry & Metabolism

There are 2 analgesic drugs in this class: (1) Phenacetin (Fig 27–2) (acetophenetidin) is deethylated to form acetaminophen, which is actually the form of the drug responsible for the analgesic effect. (2) Acetaminophen, the active metabolite, may be administered as such. The acetaminophen formed or ingested is conjugated and excreted in the urine. A third compound, acetanilid, is no longer used as an analgesic. It is not a phenol as administered but is hydroxylated by the liver to acetaminophen.

Small amounts of acetanilid and phenacetin are converted to aniline and ethoxyaniline and can, therefore, cause methemoglobinemia. Acetanilid was more active in this regard.

Pharmacologic Effects

These drugs have the same analgesic and antipyretic effects as were described for aspirin. However, they are not anti-inflammatory, uricosuric, or platelet inhibiting, do not cause gastrointestinal tract irritation, and do not have the same effect on carbohydrate metabolism or respiration as aspirin.

Phenacetin has been said to cause drowsiness and slight euphoria after small doses in humans, and there is indirect evidence of a sedative effect in animals. The effect must be minor, but analgesics containing phenacetin have been compulsively misused by people who believe that they relieve anxiety.

Clinical Uses

A. Aspirin Equivalent: The usefulness of the

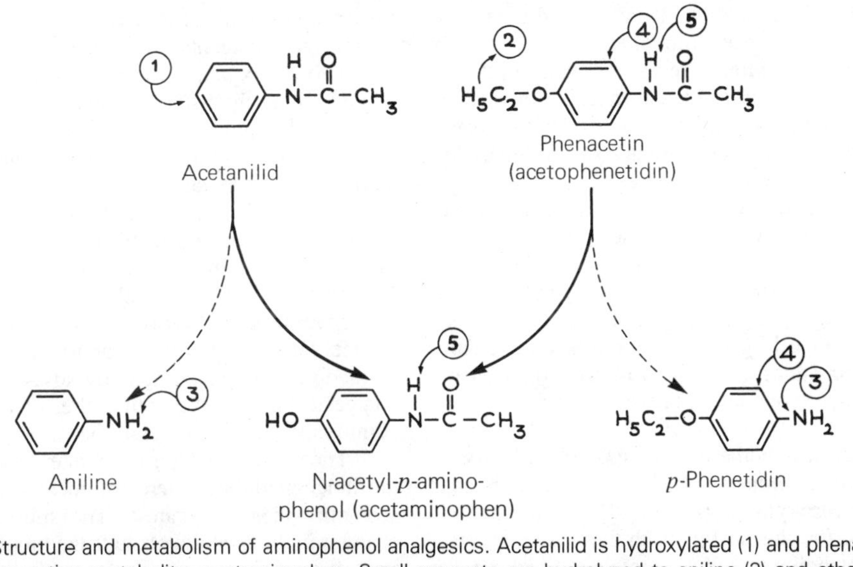

Figure 27–2. Structure and metabolism of aminophenol analgesics. Acetanilid is hydroxylated (1) and phenacetin deethylated (2) to the active metabolite, acetaminophen. Small amounts are hydrolyzed to aniline (3) and ethoxyaniline (3). Phenacetin may also be hydroxylated (4) to form 2-hydroxyphenacetin and 2-hydroxyphenetidin. N-Hydroxylation can occur at (5) in phenacetin and is assumed to occur in acetaminophen and cause hepatotoxicity.

aminophenol derivatives in acute rheumatic fever has not been established, and their use in chronic conditions such as rheumatoid arthritis would seem to be inadvisable because of the toxicity discussed below. Phenacetin is generally used only in analgesic mixtures. As the toxicity of phenacetin is recognized, acetaminophen is used more and more by itself and in proprietary combinations. A liquid preparation is popular in pediatric practice. The effectiveness is neither greater nor less than that of aspirin, and they may be used when the gastric irritation of aspirin is a problem.

B. In Analgesic Mixtures: The most common of these mixtures is the official aspirin compound or APC tablets and equivalent proprietary mixtures. These contain aspirin, phenacetin, and caffeine. No advantage of these mixtures as analgesics has been definitely established. The effectiveness of the 2 analgesics is merely additive.

Adverse Reactions

Phenacetin is rapidly converted to acetaminophen, but the 2 drugs have different toxic effects: Phenacetin has lethal chronic toxicity not seen with acetaminophen; acetaminophen, unlike phenacetin, causes acute hepatic necrosis as an acute toxic effect. The toxic effects, then, must be due to minor metabolites.

A. Side-Effects: In contrast to aspirin, the side-effects of the usual doses are negligible.

B. Acute Overdosage Toxicity:

1. Phenacetin—The acute toxicity of phenacetin is less than that of aspirin, and it is less likely to be available for accidental or suicidal ingestion. When one of the mixtures is involved, the toxic effects of the salicylate usually predominate. Large doses of phenacetin may cause dizziness, excitement, and a toxic psychosis. Methemoglobinemia and acute hemolytic episodes can occur after phenacetin and even after huge single doses of acetaminophen.

2. Acetaminophen—Acetaminophen in large acute doses—eg, after accidental ingestion in a child or a suicide attempt in an adult—can cause hepatocellular damage, progressing in some cases to lethal hepatic necrosis.

Diagnosis and management can be difficult because of the slow evolution of the clinical picture. Ingestion of 10 g or more in a single dose causes liver damage within the first 12 hours, but symptoms and signs of damage may not appear for 24–48 hours. Doses greater than 15 g are often fatal. Severe hepatic centrilobular necrosis may result in death. Acetaminophen blood levels provide a guide to treatment.

The present hypothesis to explain the toxicity is based on the assumption that acetaminophen can undergo N-hydroxylation (see Fig 27–2), a reaction demonstrated for phenacetin. With therapeutic doses, the toxic metabolite would be conjugated and detoxified by glutathione. After large doses, the sulfhydryl-bearing compounds of the liver would be exhausted, and the toxic action would then appear.

Treatment, then, would consist of providing sulfhydryl groups to neutralize the toxic metabolite. Glutathione does not enter cells, and the experience now centers about acetylcysteine. The evidence for its effectiveness when given intravenously in humans is tentatively convincing. In the USA, it is given by mouth, utilizing a preparation (Mucomyst) available as a mucolytic agent. Evaluation of efficacy of acetylcysteine continues (see Rumack reference).

C. Toxicity Due to Chronic Use:

1. Methemoglobinemia and other pigmentation—Methemoglobinemia with a dusky skin color and signs of anemia may follow the chronic use of phenacetin in some susceptible individuals, possibly those with a reduced ability to transform phenacetin to acetaminophen. Larger amounts of 2-hydroxyphenacetin and 2-hydroxyphenetidin are then formed (Fig 27–2). Metabolites of the aniline derivatives cause methemoglobinemia. In addition, the skin may assume a gray appearance that is often said to be due to sulfhemoglobinemia; but the chemical evidence for this change is not conclusive, and some alternative explanation, perhaps one including pigments derived from the chronic hemolysis, is probable.

2. Hemolytic anemia—The aminophenols have a dose-related effect of decreasing erythrocyte survival time and may cause chronic hemolytic anemia. "Primaquine-sensitive" individuals whose erythrocytes are deficient in the enzyme glucose-6-phosphate dehydrogenase are unusually susceptible to hemolysis by phenacetin, but the hemolytic anemias also occur in patients with normal enzyme levels.

3. Interstitial nephritis and renal papillary necrosis—(Fig 27–3.) The recent epidemic of renal papillary necrosis associated with the habitual misuse of phenacetin is probably receding. The episode nevertheless demonstrates the difficulty of anticipating toxic effects of agents even when they have been in use for many years and also emphasizes the caution that should attend the use of phenacetin.

Renal papillary necrosis was a rare disease until recently. Beginning in 1953, it began to appear in startling numbers and without the usual association with diabetes. The cases occurred in clusters and were associated with the habitual, prolonged use of phenacetin-containing mixtures. Factory workers in Europe were provided with the analgesic mixtures, which were taken in an effort to increase efficiency and reduce fatigue. In other countries, patients either learned or were encouraged by advertisement to take analgesics habitually for the relief of anxiety or, less commonly, to relieve headache or other minor pain.

The primary lesion is an interstitial nephritis in the inner medulla, where the local concentration of acetaminophen is greatest. The subsequent fibrotic changes in the medulla occlude the tubular vessels and compromise the blood supply to the renal papillae, which become necrotic and slough into the renal pelvis. Infection is not a necessary factor, although py-

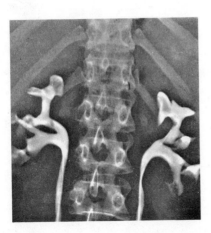
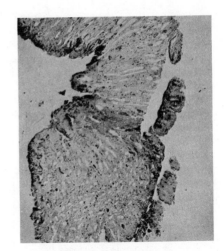

Figure 27–3. Renal papillary necrosis. *Left:* Retrograde urogram. Calcyes appear enlarged because of absence of papillae. In the medial and lowest calyces on the left, the contrast medium is less dense ("negative" shadows) because of retained sloughed papillae. *Right:* Papilla passed in urine. (Reproduced, with permission, from Smith DR: *General Urology,* 9th ed. Lange, 1978.)

elonephritis commonly follows.

The diagnosis is suggested by the history and by renal insufficiency with loss of concentrating ability but minor changes in urine sediment. Excretory urograms and renal biopsy can establish the diagnosis.

Phenacetin (but not aspirin) is the ingredient common to all of the mixtures that have caused serious toxicity. The compulsive self-administration of 6–8 APC tablets per day can cause lethal changes in 3–20 years. Larger daily doses shorten the latent period. The manufacturers of several of the proprietary mixtures responsible for many cases have now removed the phenacetin from their product. In the USA, phenacetin-containing drugs must now be labeled with a warning against chronic use.

It is difficult to argue a priori that acetaminophen should be less toxic than phenacetin. However, the anticipated nephrotoxicity has not yet appeared.

4. Carcinogenesis–In one population in which phenacetin (but not aspirin) has been misused for a long period, carcinomas of the renal pelvis have appeared in association with renal papillary necrosis. Other aminophenols can cause bladder cancer, and the presumption is that the phenacetin nephropathy makes the renal pelvis more susceptible.

PHENYLBUTAZONE & OTHER PYRAZOLONE DERIVATIVES

Analgesics of this class are longer-acting and probably more potent for acute rheumatic disorders than aspirin, but they are also more toxic. Antipyrine, the oldest and least toxic of the group, is the least used; the more toxic and more heavily advertised phenylbutazone is the most commonly used.

Chemistry

The pyrazolone derivatives are identified in Table 27–2. Aminopyrine and its sulfonate are more potent allergens than antipyrine. Phenylbutazone is hydroxylated in the body to oxyphenbutazone, and this metabolite is also available as a drug.

Antipyrine is slowly metabolized by hydroxylation at liver microsomes, with a half-life of about 8 hours. Phenylbutazone and oxyphenbutazone are even more slowly metabolized and are well reabsorbed by the renal tubules, resulting in a half-life in excess of 2 days.

Sulfinpyrazone (Anturane), the metabolite of a compound closely related to phenylbutazone, is a useful uricosuric agent.

Pharmacologic Effects

The therapeutic effects are similar to those of aspirin—ie, these drugs are analgesic, antipyretic, and anti-inflammatory.

Clinical Uses & Dosages

The pyrazolone drugs exert an antipyretic effect in some situations in which aspirin is not completely effective—eg, Hodgkin's disease with fever unresponsive to salicylates or chemotherapy. They are probably also more potent as analgesics and anti-inflammatory agents in arthritis, bursitis, and thrombophlebitis. There is no justification for the use of aminopyrine or dipyrone.

A. Antipyrine: Antipyrine can be used orally, 0.3–0.6 g every 4–6 hours, as an alternative to aspirin. The volume of distribution of antipyrine or its metabolite, N-acetyl-4-aminoantipyrine, may also be used to measure total body water.

B. Phenylbutazone (Butazolidin) and Oxyphenbutazone (Tandearil): Butazolidin, Tandearil, and Butazolidin Alka are among the 200 drugs

Table 27–2. Pyrazolone analgesics.

	R_1	R_2	R_3
Antipyrine	$-CH_3$	$-CH_3$	$-H$
Aminopyrine (amidopyrine)	$-CH_3$	$-CH_3$	$-N{<}^{CH_3}_{CH_3}$
Dipyrone (aminopyrinesulfonate, methampyrone)	$-CH_3$	$-CH_3$	$-N{<}^{CH_3}_{CH_2-SO_3Na}$
Phenylbutazone (Butazolidin)	$-$phenyl	$-OH$	$-C_4H_9$
Oxyphenbutazone (Tandearil)	$-p$-hydroxyphenyl	$-OH$	$-C_4H_9$
Sulfinpyrazone (Anturane)*	$-$phenyl	$-OH$	$-C_2H_4-SO-$phenyl

*Uricosuric agent discussed in Chapter 40.

most commonly prescribed by physicians in the USA, suggesting that they are often used as first treatment drugs rather than as alternatives to aspirin. Yet the restrictions on their use and the contraindications and cautions made a part of the labeling by the manufacturer are so stringent and comprehensive that responsibility for any adverse result of therapy would probably devolve on the physician. The drugs should not be used without reference to the package insert.

The use of these drugs is suggested or permitted in acute rheumatoid arthritis or spondylitis, osteoarthritis, psoriatic arthritis, "painful shoulder," acute superficial thrombophlebitis, and acute gouty arthritis.

The daily dose is stated to be 300–600 mg by the labeling. A more conservative position limits the daily dose to 200 mg. These drugs should be discontinued if no improvement is observed in 4–5 days.

Adverse Reactions

The toxicity of the pyrazolone analgesics restricts their use.

A. Antipyrine: Antipyrine causes fewer side-effects than aspirin. Unlike aminopyrine, it has rarely been associated with agranulocytosis. It has caused an

Table 27–3. Pyrazolone derivatives and dosages.

	Usual Adult Dose
Aminopyrine*	300–600 mg/d
Antipyrine	300–600 mg every 4 hours
Dipyrone (Pyriligin, Narone)*	325–650 mg every 4–6 hours
Phenylbutazone (Butazolidin)	100 mg 3–4 times daily
Oxyphenbutazone (Tandearil)	100 mg 3–4 times daily

*Not recommended for any use. See text.

allergic erythematous rash, often about the mouth, that leaves pigmented areas when it resolves.

B. Agranulocytosis From Aminopyrine and Dipyrone: The unusually high risk of agranulocytosis following the use of these 2 analgesics is generally acknowledged. As is true for many therapeutic agents, the quantification of the risk is difficult, and the drugs continue to be used in some countries. Dipyrone was probably not recognized by physicians as a derivative of aminopyrine, emphasizing the need to think of drugs in terms of general classes rather than individual compounds. The use of drugs under their trade names and the prescribing of proprietary mixtures without first identifying the ingredients undoubtedly also led to the misuse.

In the USA, any preparation or mixture containing aminopyrine or dipyrone must now bear a label warning that the drug may cause agranulocytosis and that it should be used only when specifically indicated and when less toxic drugs—eg, salicylates—have proved ineffective or are not tolerated.

The characteristics of agranulocytosis are discussed in Chapter 6. The reaction is allergic in origin rather than dose-related and is due to the sudden peripheral destruction of granulocytes.

C. Phenylbutazone: Phenylbutazone and its metabolite, oxyphenbutazone, frequently cause side-effects, and serious toxic reactions are frequent enough that their use should be greatly restricted. Dose-related toxic effects include sodium retention and edema, dry mouth, nausea and vomiting, peptic ulceration and hemorrhage, and rare cases of renal tubular necrosis and liver necrosis. Allergic reactions include dermatitis, which may rarely progress to exfoliative dermatitis, and agranulocytosis. The drug may impair platelet function. Hemolytic and aplastic anemia may occur. Phenylbutazone may cause a reversible leukemoid reaction; of greater concern, however, is the possibility (not yet well established) that its chronic use may be associated with a high incidence of acute leukemia. Phenylbutazone also causes erythema nodosum and erythema multiforme, fever, nephrotic syndrome, hypertension, optic neuritis, hearing loss, and abnormalities in thyroid function.

Administration of phenylbutazone increases the effects of tolbutamide and warfarin. Phenylbutazone affects renal clearance of methotrexate and prolongs the half-life of acetohexamide. It displaces phenytoin and salicylates from protein binding sites and interacts with levodopa. Barbiturates stimulate the metabolism of the drug.

Patients with blood dyscrasias and with renal, hepatic, and cardiac disease should be given phenylbutazone with great caution, and the drug should not be given to patients receiving long-term anticoagulant therapy. The drug is contraindicated in children under 14 years of age, and great care should be exercised in phenylbutazone treatment of elderly patients.

The usual dose is 200–400 mg/d. Because of its serious toxicity, phenylbutazone should be restricted to periods of about 1 week. Whenever possible, other nonsteroidal anti-inflammatory agents with lower toxicity should be used.

ADDITIONAL AGENTS USED IN RHEUMATOID ARTHRITIS

Slow-Acting Anti-inflammatory Agents

A. Antimalarial Drugs (Chloroquine, Hydroxychloroquine): The pharmacology of the 4-aminoquinoline derivatives is fully discussed in Chapter 62. Chloroquine and hydroxychloroquine have been used in the treatment of rheumatoid arthritis and systemic lupus erythematosus since the 1950s, and their efficacy has been confirmed in carefully controlled studies. Rheumatoid factor declined after prolonged chloroquine use. There was no evidence, however, that chloroquine decreased the progression of erosive bone lesions over that of controls.

The mechanism of action of chloroquine and hydroxychloroquine in rheumatic disorders is unclear, but some of the following effects may be partly responsible for their anti-inflammatory action. The 4-aminoquinolines suppress the responsiveness of T lymphocytes to mitogens, interfere with the replication of viruses, decrease leukocyte chemotaxis, stabilize lysosomal membranes, inhibit DNA and RNA synthesis, and trap free radicals. Although exerting an anti-inflammatory effect in rheumatoid arthritis somewhat less potent than that of gold, the action of chloroquine—like that of gold and penicillamine—is not apparent until after a latent period of 4–12 weeks. The drug is often useful as an adjunct to treatment with

nonsteroidal anti-inflammatory agents, has no adverse interaction with other antirheumatic agents, and increases its anti-inflammatory action with time.

1. Side-Effects–Chloroquine enjoyed widespread popularity until pigmentary retinopathy, with blindness in some cases, was recognized as an adverse effect of the drug (see p 626). Because of the potential severity of the retinal toxicity, it is advisable to recommend that patients receive low-dose therapy (1 or 2 chloroquine or hydroxychloroquine tablets daily), have periodic eye examinations, and wear dark glasses out of doors to reduce light transmission to the retina.

2. Indications–Antimalarials are often administered to patients with early rheumatoid arthritis who have not responded optimally to salicylates, but they may also be employed in more advanced stages of the disease. In addition to rheumatoid arthritis, antimalarials have been used successfully for their anti-inflammatory effect in juvenile rheumatoid arthritis, Sjögren's syndrome, and systemic lupus erythematosus. In the latter disease, they have a beneficial effect on both joint and skin findings. These drugs should not be used in psoriatic arthritis, because of the possible development of exfoliative dermatitis.

3. Method of therapy–Hydroxychloroquine (Plaquenil) in tablets of 200 mg (155 mg base) is the preferable drug. Treatment can be started with a dosage of 2 tablets daily, and when clinical improvement occurs, the maintenance dose may be reduced to 1 tablet a day. Approximately 70% of patients respond favorably.

B. Gold: Gold compounds, shown by Robert Koch to have antituberculosis properties, were introduced in the treatment of rheumatoid arthritis in the mistaken belief that chronic arthritis might have a tuberculous origin. Although favorable results were reported in the 1920s, it was not until 1960, following a report of the double-blind trial by the Empire Rheumatism Council, that the efficacy of gold salts in the management of rheumatoid arthritis was clearly established. Subsequent controlled studies have confirmed the value of gold salts and have also demonstrated that these agents retard the progression rate of bone and articular destruction determined roentgenographically. In this regard, gold salts are unique among most other agents used to treat rheumatoid arthritis. Further impetus to the popularity of gold salts has been the demonstration that they may be continued for years, allaying earlier fears of toxicity from accumulation.

1. Chemistry–The 2 most commonly administered gold preparations are gold sodium thiomalate (Myochrysine) and aurothioglucose (Solganal). They are administered intramuscularly as water-soluble gold salts containing 50% elemental gold. An oral gold preparation (Auranofin), which appears to be better tolerated yet as effective as intramuscular gold, is presently being tested.

2. Absorption, metabolism, and excretion–Gold salts are largely protein bound, with approximately 95% bound to albumin, and transported by the blood. Although they tend to concentrate in the synovial membrane, gold salts are also distributed in considerable concentration in the liver, kidney, spleen, adrenal glands, lymph nodes, and bone marrow. The reticular endothelial system displays an avidity for gold. Following intramuscular injection, peak levels are reached in 2–6 hours and fall gradually over the next week. After a standard injection of gold, 40% is excreted within a week, about two-thirds in the urine and one-third in the feces. One month after a 50-mg intramuscular injection, approximately 75–80% of the drug has been eliminated. Certain tissue compartments such as the epithelial cells of the renal tubules, which have a particular affinity for gold, show the presence of gold many years after therapy has ceased. Most studies have failed to show a correlation between serum gold concentration and either therapeutic effect or toxicity.

3. Pharmacologic action–The precise manner in which gold salts produce their beneficial effects in patients with rheumatoid arthritis and allied disorders is unknown.

4. Indications–Gold is usually reserved for patients who have been given an adequate trial of therapy with nonsteroidal anti-inflammatory agents for a period of 3–4 months and continue to show active synovitis. Patients with rheumatoid arthritis in the presence of Sjögren's syndrome and individuals with juvenile rheumatoid arthritis may also be considered for gold therapy. The usefulness in the treatment of psoriatic arthritis is less clear. The major contraindication to gold is a confirmed history of toxicity to the drug. It is inadvisable to initiate gold therapy during pregnancy, and considerable caution should be exercised with gold therapy in the presence of serious impairment of liver or renal function and in patients with blood dyscrasias. Gold is not contraindicated in conjunction with other antirheumatic medication, although caution is required when it is used concomitantly with phenylbutazone or other agents that, like gold, may produce bone marrow suppression.

5. Adverse effects–Approximately one-third of patients receiving gold salts experience some form of toxicity. Dermatitis (usually pruritic) is the most common side-effect, occurring in 15–20% of patients. It often involves the periorbital areas, hands, and trunk. The rash may take a variety of forms, the most serious of which is exfoliative dermatitis. Eosinophilia may precede or be associated with cutaneous lesions. Hematologic abnormalities, including thrombocytopenia, leukopenia, and pancytopenia, occur in 1–2% of patients. Aplastic anemia, although rare, may be fatal. About 8–10% of patients develop proteinuria, which may progress to nephrotic syndrome in a small minority of cases. Other side-effects include stomatitis, a metallic taste in the mouth, skin pigmentation, enterocolitis, cholestatic jaundice, peripheral neuropathy, pulmonary infiltrates, and corneal deposition of gold. Transient aggravation of arthritic symptoms may occur after injections of gold.

6. Method of administration–Presently, gold salts are administered at weekly intervals by the intramuscular route. See other texts for details.

Gold toxicity may appear at any time during treatment. Penicillamine and dimercaprol, which increase the excretion rate of gold, have been used to treat severe toxicity with varying success. Improvement may be expected in 60–70% of those patients who tolerate the drug.

C. Penicillamine: Penicillamine (Cuprimine), a metabolite of penicillin, is an analog of cysteine (see p 694). The drug's ability to dissociate macroglobulins in vitro and thereby decrease the titer of rheumatoid factor led to its introduction in the treatment of rheumatoid disease. As expected, rheumatoid factor titers decreased in patients receiving the agent; however, clinical improvement also occurred.

1. Absorption, metabolism, and excretion– See p 685.

2. Mechanism of action–Penicillamine is not only an effective chelator of metals; it also has antiviral properties and may inhibit lymphocyte transformation in vitro. The drug has been shown to dissociate lymphocyte membrane receptors. Penicillamine suppresses arthropathy in experimental animal models. Rheumatoid factor titer falls following administration of the drug, probably reflecting disruption of disulfide bonds of macroglobulins, but it is perhaps also a basic action of the drug on the immune system. The mechanism of penicillamine's action in rheumatoid arthritis is unclear. Penicillamine is neither cytotoxic nor immunosuppressive.

3. Indications–The clinical use of penicillamine is similar to that of gold in its period of latency (about 3 months) and its overall efficacy. Penicillamine is reserved for patients who have active, progressive erosive rheumatoid disease not controlled by more conservative therapy. At present, the use of penicillamine is restricted to patients with rheumatoid arthritis, and the drug is not useful in seronegative arthropathies or juvenile rheumatoid arthritis. Penicillamine should not be administered at the same time as other medications because it tends to impede absorption of many drugs.

4. Adverse reactions–See p 685.

5. Preparations and dosages–See p 686.

Experimental Antirheumatic Agents

A. Levamisole: See Antihelmintic Drugs, pp 525 and 658.

B. Immunosuppressive Drugs: (See Chapter 46.) The immunosuppressive agents have been employed for over 2 decades in the therapy of rheumatic diseases. The drugs are still considered experimental, and their current use is largely restricted to certain life-threatening disorders. Because of their toxic potential, they should be employed only by those completely familiar with their actions. Reliable methods of selecting one drug instead of another are not available, and acceptable controlled studies demonstrating efficacy in humans are lacking.

Drugs for which there is adequate experience include the alkylators, mechlorethamine, cyclophosphamide, and chlorambucil; the purine antagonist azathioprine; and the folate antagonist methotrexate.

Immunosuppressive agents have been shown to be effective in some patients with vasculitis syndromes, especially Wegener's granulomatosis, lupus nephritis, and rheumatoid arthritis, and occasionally in those with other rheumatic diseases. Because these agents are still experimental and because of the severity of their side-effects—especially the oncogenic effects and bone-marrow depression—immunosuppressive drugs should be given only by physicians thoroughly experienced in their use.

C. Glucocorticoid Agents: The corticosteroids have the following effects on inflammation: (1) Peripheral lymphocytes are fewer in number, circulating lymphocytes are returned to bone marrow, there is a preferential decrease in the number of T cells, and the interaction of helper T cells and B cells is impaired. (2) Macrophages are prevented from leaving bone marrow, migrating to tissues, and acting as phagocytes. (3) Neutrophils leave bone marrow in increased numbers, but neutrophil migration to tissues is reduced. (4) There is decreased clearance of immune complexes.

•　•　•

References

General

Roe RL: Drug therapy in rheumatic diseases. Med Clin North Am 61:405, 1977.

Simon LS, Mills JA: Drug therapy: Nonsteroidal anti-inflammatory drugs. (2 parts.) N Engl J Med 320:1179, 1237, 1980.

Salicylates

Anderson RJ & others: Unrecognized adult salicylate intoxication. Ann Intern Med 85:745, 1976.

Champion GD & others: Salicylates in rheumatoid arthritis. Bull Rheum Dis 1:245, 1975.

Cohen LS: Clinical pharmacology of acetylsalicylic acid. Semin Thromb Hemostas 2:146, 1976.

Davenport HW: Salicylate damage to the gastric mucosal barrier. N Engl J Med 276:1307, 1967. [See also editorial, N Engl J Med 288:316, 1973.]

Gabow PA & others: Acid-base disturbances in the salicylate-intoxicated adult. Arch Intern Med 138:1343, 1978.

Genton E & others: Platelet-inhibiting drugs in the prevention of clinical thrombotic disease. (3 parts.) N Engl J Med 293:1173, 1236, 1296, 1975.

Hill JB: Salicylate intoxication. N Engl J Med 288:1110, 1973.

Hunter J: Study of antipyretic therapy in current use. Arch Dis Child 48:313, 1973.

Kimberly RP, Plotz PH: Aspirin-induced depression of renal function. N Engl J Med 296:418, 1977.

Leist ER, Banwell JG: Products containing aspirin. N Engl J Med 291:710, 1974.

Levy G, Tsuchiya T: Salicylate accumulation kinetics in man. N Engl J Med 287, 430, 1972.

Silvoso GR & others: Incidence of gastric lesions in patients with rheumatic disease on chronic aspirin therapy. Ann Intern Med 91:517, 1979.

Vane JR: The mode of action of aspirin and similar compounds. Hosp Formulary 10:618, 1976.

Willkens RF: The use of nonsteroidal anti-inflammatory agents. JAMA 240:1632, 1978.

Zimmerman HJ: Aspirin-induced hepatic injury. Ann Intern Med 80:103, 1974.

Phenacetin & Acetaminophen

Ameer B, Greenblatt DJ: Acetaminophen. Ann Intern Med 87:202, 1977.

Barker JD, de Carle DJ, Anuras S: Chronic excessive acetaminophen use and liver damage. Ann Intern Med 87:299, 1977.

Kingsley DPE & others: Analgesic nephropathy. Br Med J 4:656, 1972.

Koch-Weser J: Acetaminophen. N Engl J Med 295:1297, 1976.

Murray RM: Analgesic nephropathy: Removal of phenacetin from proprietary analgesics. Br Med J 4:131, 1972.

Peterson RG, Rumack BH: Treating acute acetaminophen poisoning with acetylcysteine. JAMA 237:2406, 1977.

Phenacetin and bladder cancer. Leading article. Br Med J 4:701, 1969.

Rumack BH, Peterson RG: Acetaminophen overdose: Incidence, diagnosis, and management in 416 patients. Pediatrics 62 (Suppl):898, 1978.

Other Nonsteroidal Drugs

American Rheumatism Association, Cooperating Clinics Committee: A three-month trial of indomethacin in rheumatoid arthritis, with special reference to analysis and inference. Clin Pharmacol Ther 8:11, 1967.

Bowers DE: Naproxen in rheumatoid arthritis: A controlled trial. Ann Intern Med 83:470, 1975.

Bunch TW, O'Duffy JD: Disease-modifying drugs for progressive rheumatoid arthritis. Mayo Clin Proc 55:161, 1980.

Donnelly P, Lloyd K, Campbell H: Indomethacin in rheumatoid arthritis: An evaluation of its anti-inflammatory and side effects. Br Med J 1:69, 1967.

Huguley CM Jr: Agranulocytosis induced by dipyrone, a hazardous antipyretic and analgesic. JAMA 189:938, 1964.

Kantor TG: Ibuprofen. Ann Intern Med 91:877, 1979.

Leavesley GM & others: Phenylbutazone and leukemia. Med J Aust 2:963, 1969.

Miscellaneous Antirheumatic Drugs

Bluhm GB: The treatment of rheumatoid arthritis with gold. Semin Arthritis Rheum 5:147, 1975.

Dwosh IL & others: Azathioprine in early rheumatoid arthritis: Comparison with gold and chloroquine. Arthritis Rheum 20:685, 1977.

Fauci AS & others: Cyclophosphamide therapy of severe systemic necrotizing vasculitis. N Engl J Med 301:235, 1979.

Kean WF, Anastassiades TP: Long term chrysotherapy: Incidence of toxicity and efficacy during sequential time periods. Arthritis Rheum 22:495, 1979.

Lyle WH: Penicillamine. Clin Rheum Dis 5:569, 1979.

Mackenzie AH: An appraisal of chloroquine. Arthritis Rheum 13:280, 1970.

Stein HB & others: Adverse effects of D-penicillamine in rheumatoid arthritis. Ann Intern Med 92:24, 1980.

Symoens J, Schuermans Y: Levamisole. Clin Rheum Dis 5:603, 1979.

Wolff SM & others: Wegener's granulomatosis. Ann Intern Med 81:513, 1974.

Zvaifler NJ: Antimalarials in the treatment of rheumatoid arthritis. Mod Treat 8:769, 1971.

The central nervous system stimulants and antidepressants and the therapeutic problems related to these drugs are discussed together for reasons of practicality and common usage. Any confusion generated by the grouping of several diverse classes of drugs can be minimized by emphasizing 2 preliminary ideas. First, the drugs considered here as central nervous system stimulants may have other important pharmacologic effects and may have been discussed in part in other chapters. Second—and this is the major source of confusion—one drug group is included because it is widely used in the treatment of major depressions but is actually not distinct from the group of antipsychotic tranquilizers already discussed.

In this chapter, therefore, the pharmacology and use of each class of central nervous system stimulants or antidepressants will be reviewed or introduced. The treatment of depression is discussed as an application of the antidepressants that resemble tranquilizers.

Types of Central Nervous System Stimulants & Antidepressants

A. Antidepressants That Resemble Tranquilizers: Drugs of the amitriptyline (Elavil) or imipramine (Tofranil) type are widely used antidepressants. However, their properties are similar to those of the antipsychotic tranquilizers.

B. Sympathomimetic Amines: Amphetamine and related drugs are sympathomimetics comparable to ephedrine, and their autonomic effects are discussed in Chapter 10.

C. Monoamine Oxidase (MAO) Inhibitors: The monoamine oxidase inhibitors are no longer widely used in the treatment of depression, but great interest in their mechanism of action remains. They have central nervous system stimulant properties that are qualitatively similar to amphetamine and also sympathomimetic and sympathoplegic effects.

D. Miscellaneous Convulsant Stimulants: These drugs, exemplified by pentylenetetrazol (Metrazol), are often called medullary stimulants but their action culminates in convulsions. It is doubtful whether any indication for their use remains.

E. Xanthines: Caffeine, aminophylline, and other xanthines are discussed in Chapter 13. The xanthines contained in beverages such as coffee or tea have a minor stimulant effect that is manifested as

relief of fatigue or as wakefulness. The central nervous system stimulant effect of the xanthines cannot be increased to a therapeutically useful degree because of the appearance of cardiovascular side-effects. The specific effect of aminophylline in abolishing Cheyne-Stokes respiration is due to its content of ethylenediamine.

ANTIDEPRESSANT DRUGS RESEMBLING ANTIPSYCHOTICS

Before attempting to treat the patient having symptoms of depression—fatigue, inactivity, apathy, despondency, insomnia, loss of appetite, vague somatic complaints, weight loss, and decreased libido—it is important to distinguish between the 3 major types of depressive disorders:

(1) Reactive or secondary depression of varying degree is exceedingly common, is due to recognizable causes (eg, anxiety, grief, alcohol, drugs), and is of relatively short duration. This type of depression usually responds to emotional support, psychotherapy, and the judicious use of sedative drugs. Antidepressant drugs are not ordinarily indicated.

(2) Endogenous depression is usually more severe and more prolonged, may arise without significant aggravating cause, responds poorly to psychotherapy, tends to recur, and is perhaps due to a genetically determined biochemical abnormality. Tricyclic antidepressant drugs are usually quite effective in endogenous depression; MAO inhibitors are usually less so.

(3) The depressive phase of manic-depressive disorders is often indistinguishable from straight endogenous depression except that there is a longitudinal history of attacks of manic behavior. This disorder is also probably due to a genetically determined biochemical abnormality. Lithium is the preferred treatment.

When the antipsychotic tranquilizers were first evaluated, a few investigators reported a beneficial effect on patients with severe depressions—especially early in treatment, before the dosage had reached high levels. However, the use of the antipsychotics in depressed patients was generally held to be contraindicated. Imipramine, a compound synthesized as a possible analog of the antipsychotic tranquilizers, was reported in 1958 to be effective in treating endogenous depressions. For a few years, imipramine and related compounds were generally described as a drug class distinct from the tranquilizers. Pharmacologically there was no basis for this distinction, and a few clinicians soon began to substitute mixtures of a phenothiazine tranquilizer and imipramine in treating depressions. Many antipsychotic tranquilizers have now been shown to be not only effective in certain types of depression but even preferable to the newer antidepressants. Discussion of these drugs can, therefore, be shortened by reference to the properties of the antipsychotic tranquilizers already discussed.

Chemistry

The drugs in this category are shown in Table 28–1. The evidence of the similarity between antipsychotics and antidepressants begins with their chemical structure. Imipramine and amitriptyline differ from the tranquilizers promazine (Sparine) and chlorprothixene

(Taractan) in that a bridge of 2 methylene groups has been substituted for the sulfur of the older drugs and the chlorine present in chlorprothixene is not present in amitriptyline.

When it became apparent that the antidepressants had properties similar to those of the tranquilizers, it was claimed that the demethylated metabolites were active as stimulants and that this explained the difference from the phenothiazines. The active metabolites are now available and are used, but there are no differences in effects between the parent compounds and the metabolites.

These drugs are also called imidodibenzyl, dibenzazepine, and tricyclic antidepressants. The phenothiazine tranquilizers are also tricyclic compounds.

Absorption, Metabolism, & Excretion

The pharmacokinetics of these antidepressants are similar to those described for the major tranquilizers, ie, plasma levels rise slowly after oral administration and the chemical half-life is more than 12 hours after the administration of single doses. There is a lag

Table 28–1. Antidepressants: Formulas, dosages.

	R	Maximum Usual Starting Dose	Daily Dose
Imipramine* (Tofranil)			
	—CH₃	25 mg 3 times daily	200 mg
Desipramine (Pertofrane, Norpramin)			
	—H	25 mg 3 times daily	200 mg
Trimipramine (Surmontil) (Methyl at site shown by arrow)			
	—CH₃	25 mg 3 times daily	200 mg
Amitriptyline*† (Elavil, Endep)			
	—CH₃	25 mg 3 times daily	150 mg
Nortriptyline (Aventyl, Pamelor)			
	—H	10 mg 3 times daily	100 mg
Doxepin (Adapin, Sinequan) (Oxygen at site shown by arrow)			
	—CH₃	25 mg 3 times daily	300 mg
Protriptyline (Vivactil)			
		5–10 mg 3 times daily	60 mg

*Generic preparation available.

†Cyclobenzaprine (Flexeril) differs from amitriptyline in that it has a double bond at the position shown by the arrow.

of several hours between ingestion and the appearance of pharmacologic effects; this must not be confused with a latent period of as long as 3 weeks before a therapeutic effect on the psychotically depressed patient develops.

The drugs are well absorbed. Demethylation of the dimethyl compounds does occur and the metabolites are active, but no new properties are conferred by the change, nor does their effect appear any sooner when the demethylated derivatives are used.

Plasma level determinations are now generally available, but, except for detecting patient noncompliance, their use remains a research area. Preliminary results verify the clinical observation that there is not only an ineffectively low level but a level high enough to destroy the therapeutic effect—ie, that the drugs must be used with a ceiling on the dose to achieve a level within the "therapeutic window."

Pharmacologic Effects

The section on the pharmacologic effects of the tranquilizers in Chapter 25 can be applied without modification to the antidepressants.

The sedation induced is unpleasant, and the antidepressants must not be called stimulants or mood elevators. The antidepressants may interrupt a major depression, but, during the latent period before they act or when used on the ubiquitous neurotically anxious patient, they will cause a further depression of mood. Parasympatholytic and quinidinelike properties are relatively prominent even with the usual doses, and extrapyramidal effects are less frequent.

The ability of imipramine and its relatives to prevent the uptake of norepinephrine by sympathetic nerves is currently being emphasized as a possible explanation for its mechanism of action. This action has also been demonstrated for chlorpromazine and is not distinctive for the antidepressants.

The animal laboratory provides no basis for separating the 2 groups even though a large volume of work is available.

Clinical Uses

A. Treatment of Depressive Reactions:

1. Problems in evaluation of therapy–The usual factors that require a controlled evaluation operate prominently during the drug treatment of depressions. The major depressions are variable in their course and are often rapidly self-limiting, so that almost any treatment may appear to be effective if it is started early.

In addition, the inadequate diagnostic differentiation of depressions can result in confusion. Depression may be a symptom—a description of mood that may be applied to different groups of patients whose depression originates from several causes and who are not comparable in their response to drugs—but depression is also a specific disease entity or category of dysfunction. One cannot assume that reactive (situational) depression, the depression that is symptomatic of neurotic anxiety, and major endogenous depres-

sions will all respond similarly to drugs. Patients have not been carefully categorized in some of the available trials. Experience with severely ill, institutionalized populations is not interchangeable with experience in office practice, in which much of the depression that is seen is symptomatic of anxiety. At this time, the antidepressants that resemble the antipsychotics are being widely misused in anxious patients, often with the misapprehension that an "antidepressant" will elevate mood as an amphetamine does.

2. Alternative treatments–

a. Amphetamine–Amphetamine and related sympathomimetic amines are generally said to be useful antidepressants only if the depression is mild, but there is little evidence for or against that conclusion. Tranylcypromine (Parnate), which is similar to amphetamine, is still used. Part of the resistance to the use of amphetamine is based on a fear that its therapeutic use will lead to unsupervised abuse. The danger is certainly present but must be small when the drug is taken by mouth.

b. Sedatives–The older sedatives (eg, phenobarbital) have long been used in the treatment of patients whose manifest depression is symptomatic of anxiety rather than of an endogenous depression. Recently, chlordiazepoxide (Librium), another long-acting sedative, has gained a reputation as an antidepressant. The sedatives are effective in relieving anxiety, but their use should not be extended to all categories of depression.

c. Antidepressants related to tranquilizers– The usefulness of the antidepressants as an alternative to electroconvulsive therapy in the treatment of severe endogenous depressions in hospitalized patients is established by controlled studies. Electroconvulsive therapy is effective, and results are quickly apparent, but it is usually done only during hospitalization and is an unpleasant experience.

The response to drugs is slower, occurring usually after a latent period as long as 3 weeks. As after electroshock therapy, the response is not a graded improvement but a relatively sudden interruption of the depression. The antidepressant drugs, in this one area of established usefulness, have the advantages that continued or maintenance treatment is possible, that they are less expensive, and that they evoke fewer objections from patients. Drug and electroconvulsive therapy treatments can be combined.

A more precise statement of the results in the treatment of depression is difficult to formulate. Serious depressions are often episodic and self-limiting regardless of treatment. Assignment of depressed patients to diagnostic categories is difficult, and the use of drugs has not improved the criteria by differentiating subtypes more or less apt to respond favorably to different drugs. Because of variations in diagnostic criteria, control groups are essential for every new evaluation. The criteria of improvement also vary— eg, duration of hospitalization, a test score, or a subjective estimate of the degree of depression.

d. Antipsychotic tranquilizers–(See discussion

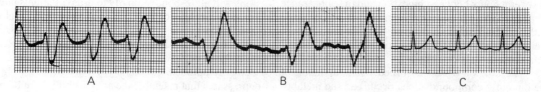

A   B   C

Figure 28 –1. Amitriptyline toxicity. Quinidinelike cardiotoxicity shown in lead II of the electrocardiogram following ingestion of about 2 g of amitriptyline. *A:* **On admission:** Patient comatose and hypotensive. Idioventricular rhythm with wide ventricular complexes. *B:* **One hour later:** Atrial fibrillation probably now present. AV block and wide QRS complexes persist. *C:* **Six hours after admission:** Normal sinus rhythm with normal intraventricular conduction time, but the $Q-T_c$ is still prolonged. (Reproduced, with permission, from Goldman MJ: *Principles of Clinical Electrocardiography,* 10th ed. Lange, 1979.)

on p 295.) Combinations of an antipsychotic and an antidepressant combined in a single tablet or capsule are also in wide use.

The necessary corollary of the above ideas—that the antidepressants act like the antipsychotics in schizophrenics—has also been demonstrated.

e. MAO inhibitors–These drugs, discussed below, are of limited therapeutic importance.

B. Enuresis: The antidepressants, like the antipsychotics, alter the sleep pattern by decreasing the fraction of sleep time spent in deep sleep, the phase during which bedwetting occurs. The effectiveness of imipramine and amitriptyline in enuresis is established by careful trials, but these potent drugs should not be used to the exclusion of other attempts to deal with the problem.

C. Other: Cyclobenzaprine (Flexeril) is an analog of amitriptyline marketed for the relief of acute voluntary muscle spasm. Claims of efficacy are based on limited data. (See the discussion of the treatment of tetanus in Chapter 23 for a theoretic basis for the use in that context.)

Adverse Reactions

A. Side-Effects: Side-effects are similar to those seen after the administration of the tranquilizers. After the usual doses, atropinelike effects and postural hypotension are relatively prominent.

1. Behavioral–The distinctive kind of sedation that occurs after the administration of tranquilizers also appears after imipramine and similar antidepressants. The patient may complain of weakness, drowsiness, or additional depression of mood. Increased tension, tremulousness, visual hallucinations, and agitation are sometimes induced.

2. Autonomic–Dry mouth and constipation are common atropinelike effects; blurred vision and tachycardia are uncommon. Postural hypotension occurs frequently and is the side-effect that most commonly limits the comfortable dose of these drugs.

3. Other–Extrapyramidal signs are rare with the doses usually employed. Weight gain, prolonged atrioventricular conduction time, and ventricular arrhythmias occur.

B. Overdose Toxicity: The acute toxicity of the antidepressants appears at first glance to be greater

than that of the antipsychotics in that accidental deaths and suicides are more frequently recorded. The greater apparent toxicity arises in part from the fact that the drugs are prescribed for depression and for enuresis and are thus available to adults with suicidal ideas and to exploring children.

The clinical picture includes sedation, excitement, convulsions, coma, hypotension, disturbances of cardiac conduction, and ventricular arrhythmias, including fibrillation.

The central nervous system signs of toxicity are antagonized by intravenous injections of physostigmine (eserine), a cholinesterase inhibitor that is a tertiary amine and reaches the central nervous system. There is no credible evidence that the serious cardiac effects are antagonized. The occurrence of the dangerous ventricular arrhythmias may be delayed for a day, and the poisoned individual should not be released from surveillance even if the clinical picture does not appear threatening.

C. Allergic Reactions: Isolated reports of cholestatic jaundice have appeared.

D. Drug Reactions: The effects of alcohol and other depressants are additive to the sedation caused by these "antidepressants." It is generally recommended that up to 14 days elapse between the administration of an MAO inhibitor and the initiation of treatment with these drugs to avoid episodes of hypertension or excitement with convulsions. Even so, drugs of the 2 classes have often been given together without difficulty.

Dosages

Treatment with each of the drugs is started at a low dosage level (Table 28–1). The dosage is increased at intervals of several days until a response occurs or the maximum daily dose is reached. Most patients will improve within 3 weeks of starting therapy if they are going to improve at all. The usual maximum daily dose may be exceeded in hospitalized patients. Aged patients are usually more sensitive to these drugs.

When a favorable response is achieved, the dose is slowly decreased to a maintenance level at or below the usual starting dosage. A single daily dose at bedtime is effective and convenient. Treatment is continued for at least 3 months and the drug is gradually withdrawn.

AMPHETAMINE & RELATED SYMPATHOMIMETIC STIMULANTS

The drugs in this category are variants of the ephedrine class of sympathomimetics selected because they exhibit relatively more potent central stimulant effects and relatively less potent cardiovascular effects.

Chemistry

The structures of the sympathomimetic stimulants are shown in Table 28–2 to suggest that, like the other indirect-acting sympathomimetics, they are phenylisopropylamines or are isosteric with phenylisopropylamine.

Pharmacologic Actions

A. Mechanism of Action: As has been explained in the case of ephedrine, the amphetamines do not act directly on the effectors to bring about their peripheral sympathomimetic effects such as tachycardia or elevated blood pressure. They act indirectly through the catecholamines of the organism in part by liberating the amines and in part by a second undefined mechanism which allows their action to persist after depletion of norepinephrine with reserpine.

That the central nervous system–stimulating effects are also mediated through catecholamines is suggested by the ability of α-methyl-p-tyrosine to block the central effects of amphetamine in animals and in humans. This amino acid is an inhibitor of tyrosine hydroxylase and is assumed to deplete the brain of some specific pool of either dopamine or norepinephrine that is necessary for the action of amphetamine.

B. Effects: Refer to the discussion in Chapter 10. The duration of action of amphetamine and methamphetamine is much longer than that of ephedrine, the central effects persisting for more than 12–24 hours.

Clinical Uses

A. Obesity: The great interest in the anorexigenic effect of the sympathomimetics is based on more than the vanity of the patient; obesity increases susceptibility to a number of diseases, and life expectancy is reduced by even a minor increase in weight above an ideal weight based on insurance statistics.

The ability of ephedrine, amphetamine, and the other phenylisopropylamines to decrease appetite parallels their potency as central nervous system stimulants. An intense anorexigenic action can be demonstrated on animals in the laboratory, and a specific central nervous system effect is therefore assumed to be important rather than a change in mood, distraction,

or increased activity. The amphetamines act in mentally deficient as well as normal humans.

When any of the drugs related to amphetamine is tested in obese patients under controlled conditions and is given in adequate dosage, it exerts an anorexigenic effect that is clearly beyond that of the placebo. However, after a few weeks (4–6 weeks maximum), the weight loss ceases and the patient usually resumes previous eating and gaining habits unless other forms of treatment have been more successful. All of the controlled studies utilize a fixed dosage throughout the period of study, since a progressive increase in dosage to overcome whatever process is leading to tolerance would presumably add the risk of drug misuse or habituation. Periods of treatment with amphetamines for 2 weeks alternating with equal periods without treatment are as effective as continuous treatment.

Various regulatory agencies project an attitude of disapproval toward physicians' prescribing of the amphetamines in almost any circumstance. At the same time, regulations are formulated encouraging the over-the-counter sale for weight control of a combination of caffeine and phenylpropanolamine, a not very potent ephedrine congener.

B. As Euphoriant and Antidepressant: Controlled tests show that amphetamines produce euphoria more consistently in normal humans than either morphine or pentobarbital. This action partly explains the misuse of the amphetamines and their use in mild (usually situational or reactive) depressions. Since the amphetamines are only transiently effective in treating obesity in careful trials and probably even less effective in general use, it must be concluded that most of the 5 billion doses of diet pills made in the USA each year are actually used as euphoriants.

C. To Improve Performance: Amphetamine and its congeners are used, perhaps ill-advisedly but nevertheless effectively, to improve psychomotor performance. The deterioration of performance with fatigue can be in part prevented or reversed and a state of wakefulness maintained. This generalization applies to comparatively simple psychomotor tests; concentration in complex learning situations and judgment are not necessarily improved.

Without suggesting that the practice is anything but pernicious, it must be acknowledged that the administration of amphetamine 90 minutes before a test situation improves athletic performance (swimming, running, weight throwing) to a degree that would be highly significant in competition.

D. In Treatment of Drug Depression: The amphetamines are no longer used in the treatment of barbiturate intoxication. They are often given to patients receiving antipsychotics or anticonvulsant medication to minimize sedation.

E. Hyperkinetic State in Children: The use of stimulant and other drugs is clearly effective in controlling some children with major behavioral and learning problems associated with brain damage or with the objectively demonstrable dysfunction associated with

Table 28–2. Formulas of amphetamine and related anorexigenic and stimulant amines.

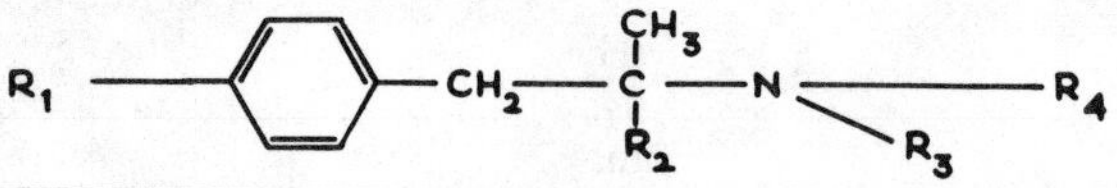

$$R_1 - \text{[ring]} - CH_2 - \overset{CH_3}{\underset{R_2}{C}} - N \overset{}{\underset{R_3}{}} - R_4$$

	R_1	R_2	R_3	R_4
Amphetamine*				
Methamphetamine*			$-CH_3$	
Phentermine* (Wilpo; Ionamin, a complex with a resin)		$-CH_3$		
Chlorphentermine* (Pre-Sate)	$Cl-$	$-CH_3$		
Clortermine (Voranil)	$Cl-$†	$-CH_3$		
Fenfluramine (Pondimin)	F_3C-‡		$-C_2H_5$	
Benzphetamine (Didrex)			$-CH_3$	$-CH_2-$⬡ 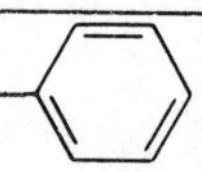

Phenmetrazine (Preludin)

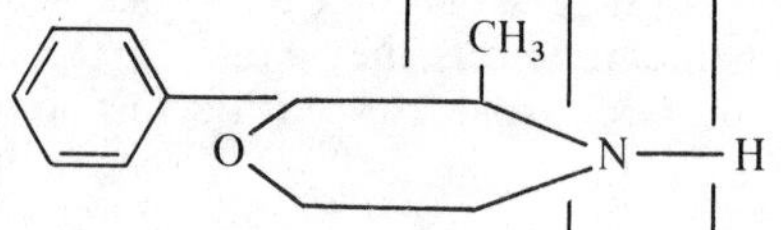

[structure: phenyl–morpholine-type ring with O, CH_3, and $N-H$]

Phendimetrazine* (Plegine)

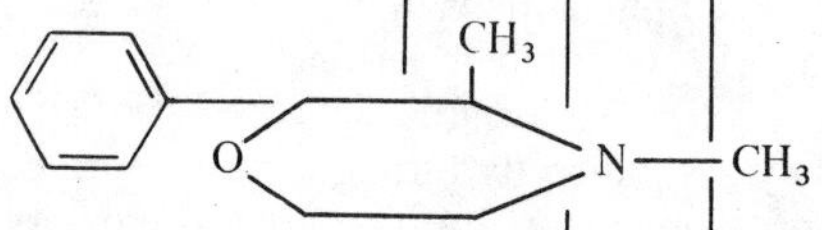

[structure: phenyl–morpholine-type ring with O, CH_3, and $N-CH_3$]

Diethylpropion* (Tenuate, Tepanil)

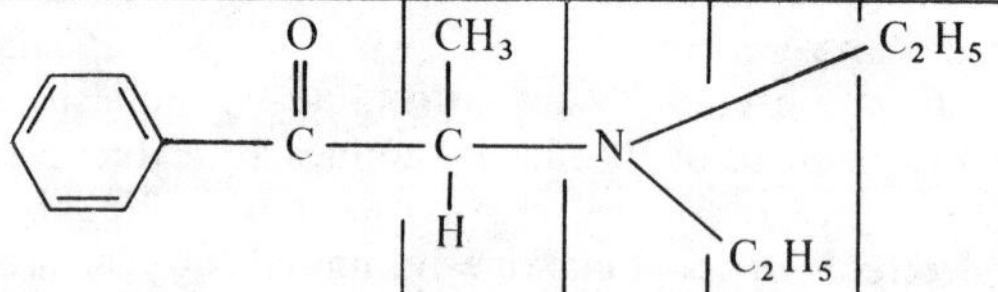

[structure: phenyl$-\overset{O}{C}-\overset{CH_3}{\underset{H}{C}}-N(\,C_2H_5\,)(\,C_2H_5\,)$]

Methylphenidate* (Ritalin)

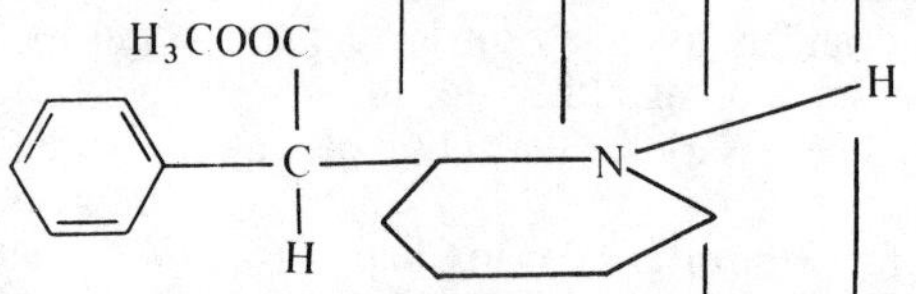

[structure: phenyl$-\overset{H_3COOC}{\underset{H}{C}}-$piperidine ring with $N-H$]

Pemoline (Cylert)

[structure: phenyl attached to ring containing O, $=O$, $N-H$, N]

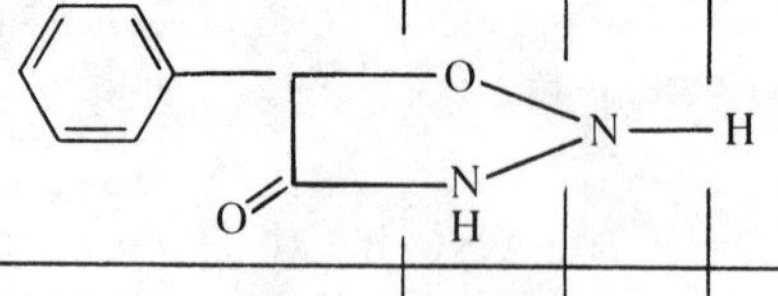

Tranylcypromine (Parnate)

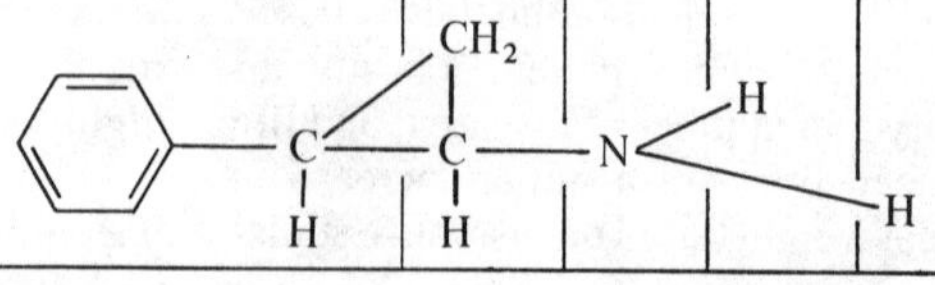

[structure: phenyl$-\overset{}{\underset{H}{C}}\overset{CH_2}{\underset{H}{C}}-N(H)(H)$ cyclopropane ring]

*Generic preparations available.
†In ortho position.
‡In meta position.

epilepsy. There is in addition a controversial and emotion-laden indication for the amphetamines that was originally defined in terms of minimal brain **damage** but has now shifted to minimal brain **dysfunction.** The hyperkinetic or minimal brain damaged child would show one or more symptoms such as hyperactivity, aggressiveness, perseveration, poor performance in school, or specific learning defect. The wide variation in the number of children treated in different neighborhoods suggests that the indications for drug treatment vary with the enthusiasm of the physician. Treatment is often based on the complaint of the parent or teacher rather than on examination of the child.

Controlled studies to evaluate the usefulness of amphetamine (or methylphenidate) in these loosely defined groups of troublesome children are few. Short-term observations do show that behavior and performance are improved. The improvement in hyperactive children is often said to be a paradoxic quieting effect of the stimulant, but the results are very much as described above for normal subjects — euphoria and improved psychomotor performance.

Are these short-term gains extended into long-term benefits? The few controlled studies show no benefit from amphetamine use. Uncontrolled observations of treated groups show the subjects still in trouble in school and society after years of treatment.

The adult doses of amphetamine used in these children cause comparatively minor side-effects — less sleep, irritability, euphoria, loss of appetite — but there may be major long-term hazards. Weight gain and growth in stature were reduced during a 2-year period, presumably because of the appetite suppression but also because of the demonstrated effect of amphetamine in reducing the level of growth hormone. At about the junior high school age, problems of abuse appear. Probably most importantly, the use of drugs replaces other treatment (psychiatric and educational) and offers parents and teachers a simple means of divesting themselves of responsibility.

F. Convulsant States: In specific situations (petit mal), amphetamines are used in the management of convulsive states. (See Chapter 29.)

G. Narcolepsy: Narcolepsy is a rare condition characterized by lapses into normal sleep during periods of monotony or inactivity such as working at repetitive jobs or driving. Amphetamine prevents these lapses. A single morning dose of 10–15 mg may be adequate, or larger doses several times a day may be necessary. Cataplexy — ie, sudden loss of muscle tone without loss of consciousness at the time of an emotional expression — is often associated with narcolepsy but is not altered favorably by treatment with amphetamine.

Adverse Reactions

This discussion applies to all of the amphetamine congeners as well as to ephedrine and related drugs. Because some of the drugs are given only in small doses or have not become widely used, all of the reactions listed below may not yet actually have been encountered in practice.

A. Side-Effects: Common side-effects may include tremulousness, anxiety, awareness of heart action, dry mouth, and alteration of sleep habits such as insomnia or light sleep. The side-effects are usually not troublesome after a few days of continued use, but some patients are unable to tolerate the stimulation of any amphetamine.

B. Toxicity Due to Overdosage:

1. Acute toxicity – The acute toxicity of the amphetamines is low. Reported fatalities are due to a complicating coexistent disease or to the result of treatment. The lethal dose of dextroamphetamine is probably several grams. Restlessness or toxic psychosis, hypertension, and tachycardia may be prominent. Treatment consists of sedation unless excitement or psychotic behavior is prominent, when an antipsychotic should be used. Maintaining a high volume of acid urine should increase the rate of excretion of the drug. In acid urine this weak base is converted to the salt form, and renal tubular reabsorption of the charged form is less and urinary excretion greater. Fig 28–2 shows such an effect. The value of acidifying the urine in acute intoxication has not actually been demonstrated. It is possible that the metabolic path is merely shifted from urinary excretion to chemical change.

2. Chronic toxicity – Continued use of large doses of amphetamines may lead to long periods of wakefulness and weight loss. Various depressants (especially barbiturates, marihuana, heroin, and alcohol) are often taken by chronic users of amphetamines to "turn off" the effect.

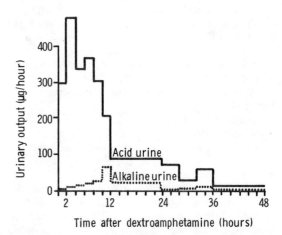

Figure 28–2. Mean excretion of amphetamine by 3 normal subjects after injection of 10 mg of dextroamphetamine sulfate. pH range of acid urine, 4.5–5.6; pH range of alkaline urine, 7.1–8.0. In an acid urine, amphetamine exists in the salt (charged) form and renal tubular reabsorption is decreased, ie, excretion is facilitated. The urine was acidified by the ingestion of ammonium chloride. (Reproduced, with permission, from Asatoor & others: The excretion of dexamphetamine and its derivatives. Br J Pharmacol 24:295, 1965.)

3. Toxic psychosis–Behavior is not usually greatly altered by chronic oral use of these stimulants. The subject complains of depression if deprived of the drug but does not acknowledge any euphoria when it is supplied. In large and repeated doses—especially intravenously—the drug becomes a psychotomimetic agent. Intense anxiety, restlessness, feelings of depersonalization, and altered perception may progress to a state similar to paranoid schizophrenia. As in other toxic psychoses, auditory and visual hallucinations are prominent, but the patient usually continues to recognize the relation between altered perception and the drug. If paranoia or delirium is prominent, a small dose of chlorpromazine or other antipsychotic may be useful, but sedation with a barbiturate is usually adequate treatment.

C. Misuse and Abuse: The amphetamines, like other drugs with a potential for misuse, are abused by different individuals to different degrees, and the several patterns may vary in their hazards from minimal, as in the occasional use of a diet pill, to a totally destructive pattern, as is the case when large amounts are injected intravenously.

Cocaine is the prototype of a major central nervous system stimulant liable to be abused, and the history of its use parallels the recent history of methamphetamine use.

1. History of stimulant usage–When the Spanish conquistadors reached the Andean highlands, they observed the use by some of the residents of leaves from the coca plant *(Erythroxylon coca)*. Leaves from the small tree or shrub were chewed, together with some alkali (lime or ashes) that liberated the free base for rapid absorption across the mucosa. At that time, coca leaves were used as a ritual drug only by the elite Incas and not by the administrators and peasants of the Inca nation. The Spaniards destroyed the structure of the society, diffused the use of coca leaves widely, and encouraged their compulsive use. The enslaved people were then able to work continuously for more than a day without food or sleep even at high altitudes.

Leaves of the Peruvian plant reached Göttingen and the laboratory of Wöhler, the first chemist to synthesize an organic compound. His student, Nieman, isolated cocaine in 1860 and noted the anesthetic effect on his tongue.

After the American Civil War, cocaine was described by some American physicians as a specific treatment for morphine addiction. Sigmund Freud was among those who used and recommended to others the use of cocaine as a euphoriant. Thus, when a colleague who had become addicted to morphine because of the pain of neuromas in an amputation stump consulted Freud, continuous use of cocaine (and cocaine addiction) was substituted for continuous use of morphine. Breuer interested Köller in the drug, and this led to application of the local anesthetic effect.

Cocaine is still used today by the South American Indians and, after years of only limited use in Western countries, it has recently become very popular.

Following the isolation of ephedrine, Gordon Alles studied many amines in the search for an agent superior to ephedrine in the treatment of asthma. When he restudied phenylisopropylamine (amphetamine), he described its central nervous system-stimulating effects (1933). It was promptly misused, but to a limited extent, until after World War II. Even when abuse became worldwide, the drug continued to be taken by mouth.

However, in 1957–60, several physicians repeated the error made earlier with cocaine and introduced heroin users to the intravenous use of methamphetamine. The drug was inexpensive, and many heroin users switched to methamphetamine ("speed," "crystal"), to their short-term benefit inasmuch as the new preparation was easier to obtain.

Later (1967), a new group of younger drug users discovered methamphetamine and used huge and frequent injections of it. For about 2 years, methamphetamine was by far the most widely used "hard drug." Heroin is now once again the favored injected drug among both former speed users and new compulsive users.

2. Patterns of amphetamine use–

a. Oral–Amphetamines may be used episodically as "spree" drugs to improve performance, defer fatigue, or prolong an alcoholic binge. They may be used intermittently over a long period but in moderate doses for their euphoriant or antidepressant effect.

A few people become compulsive users of one or another of the amphetamines taken by mouth. Considering the huge amounts prescribed or otherwise made available, compulsive oral use must develop in only a tiny fraction of those people who have contact with amphetamine.

b. Intravenous–The hazard of developing a compulsive pattern of use is much greater when an amphetamine is injected because of the orgasmlike "rush" at the time of injection. Following the large doses of methamphetamine ("speed") used during the recent "epidemic," the individual did not function well because of anxiety and suspiciousness. As a result, the use of speed was associated with a high frequency of violence, most of it directed toward other users.

c. Dependence and tolerance–Physical dependence manifested as withdrawal signs is difficult to establish. A depression maximal on the fourth day appears, and electroencephalographic changes and altered sleep patterns persist for days after the drug is discontinued.

The development of tolerance is also not easy to prove, although side-effects become less prominent with continued use.

An isomer of phenylpropanolamine (D-norpseudoephedrine) is contained in a plant, kat, grown in Ethiopia and habitually chewed by almost the entire population in one isolated area, Aden and Yemen.

3. Patterns of cocaine abuse–Cocaine is not an amphetamine, but it is a sympathomimetic stimulant whose patterns of abuse can be conveniently interpolated here. Its properties are similar to those of amphetamine, but its duration of action is comparatively brief.

Used intravenously, as was the case in the past, it gives a "rush," and the danger of compulsion formation is extremely great. Inhaled or swallowed, it provides a euphoria of rapid onset but brief duration. Converted to the free base and smoked, it is appreciably more dangerous—ie, closer to the intravenous experience.

Contraindications & Cautions

Amphetamine should not be used in the presence of hypertension, angina pectoris, hyperthyroidism, or agitation. It will greatly intensify the effects of other sympathomimetic drugs and central stimulants of the amine oxidase inhibitor type.

Preparations & Dosages

If the drugs listed in Table 28–2 are given in equipotent doses, they are generally equivalent in therapeutic effectiveness and, with the exception of chlorphentermine and fenfluramine, in toxicity. A few have not yet been used in doses sufficient to cause toxic psychosis, but other side-effects are similar.

Dextroamphetamine is the standard drug of the group. It is often given in doses of 5 mg 3 times daily before meals. Taking the drug before meals may serve as a reminder to the patient that self-discipline is necessary, but 15 mg of this long-acting drug as a single morning dose is equally effective. Some disturbance of sleep habits will be apparent 24 hours after a single dose—an observation important in interpreting the claims made for sustained-release dosage forms.

Racemic DL-amphetamine (Benzedrine) causes more cardiovascular side-effects for the same amount of central stimulation.

Methamphetamine is about twice as potent as dextroamphetamine, but there are no other differences.

Of the other available preparations, only chlorphentermine and fenfluramine show any qualitative differences from amphetamine. Chlorphentermine (Pre-Sate) causes the same restlessness as amphetamine but, depending upon the dosage and the individual, may cause an as yet poorly defined kind of sedation or behavioral depression. Amphetamine sometimes causes a similar side-effect, but the sedation is often interpreted as after-depression. Clortermine (Voranil) is simply the hydroxy isomer of chlorphentermine.

In the case of fenfluramine (Pondimin), only the depressant effect is seen and the blood pressure is not elevated by the drug. Side-effects—drowsiness, depression, increased dreaming, and gastrointestinal irritation—occur more frequently than after the administration of other anorexigenic agents. With larger doses, euphoria and feelings of depersonalization may appear, and a few cases of abuse of the drug have been reported. A withdrawal state has been demonstrated.

Mazindol (Sanorex) is chemically dissimilar to all of the phenylisopropylamines discussed above but is pharmacologically similar to the amphetamines.

Mazindol (Sanorex)

Tranylcypromine (Parnate) is chemically and pharmacologically similar to amphetamine. It is suggested for the treatment of depression rather than obesity and is given in comparatively large doses. It is a more potent amine oxidase (MAO) inhibitor than amphetamine, and is further discussed with those drugs.

Pemoline (Cylert) is chemically similar to phenmetrazine, but its sympathomimetic and central nervous system stimulant effects are extremely limited. Repeated efforts over many years failed to establish any indications for its use other than as a very weak amphetamine. It was recently approved for marketing for use in the treatment of "minimal brain dysfunction." Clinical testing in the area of minimal brain dysfunction is difficult and evokes much skepticism; however, it can be said that the data establishing its minimal efficacy also establish the greater efficacy of amphetamine.

AMINE OXIDASE INHIBITORS

Inhibitors of monoamine oxidase (MAO) are no longer widely used in therapy. Much of the remaining interest in these drugs and much of their overenthusiastic use in the past is based on an interest in mechanism of action.

Chemistry & Classification

The drugs usually classified as MAO inhibitors are listed in Table 28–3. Iproniazid is no longer available for human use because of the liver damage that it caused, but it is still widely used in laboratory investigation because of its potency. Iproniazid and one of the other drugs still suggested for use as antidepressants are hydrazides—ie, acyl-substituted hydrazines or amides. Another is a hydrazine rather than a hydrazide. Pargyline (Eutonyl) is an amine or "nonhydrazine" MAO inhibitor already mentioned because of its use in treating hypertension (see Chapter 12).

Table 28–3. Monoamine oxidase (MAO) inhibitors: Drugs and dosages.

Drugs	Initial and Maintenance Doses (per day)
Hydrazides (R_1—CO—HN—NH—R_2)	
Iproniazid (Marsilid)	. . .
Isocarboxazid (Marplan)	20–30 mg, then 10 mg (maximum)
Hydrazines (R_1—HN—NH—R_2)	
Phenelzine (Nardil)	30–45 mg, then 5–20 mg
Amines	
Pargyline (Eutonyl)	25–50 mg, then 10–100 mg
Tranylcypromine (Parnate)	20 mg, then 10–20 mg

Tranylcypromine is closely related to amphetamine. The ephedrine or amphetamine type of sympathomimetic drugs are MAO inhibitors, as are many other amines.

Pharmacologic Actions

A. Mechanisms of Action: The MAO inhibitors cause a long-lasting inhibition (irreversible or nonequilibrium blockade) of MAO. The action is demonstrable in humans by changes in the excretion products of amines and by actual assay of enzyme activity in biopsy specimens from the jejunum. However, it is not clear which of the pharmacologic effects are due to MAO inhibition and which are independent of enzyme inhibition.

1. Function of MAO–MAO governs the oxidative deamination of many simple primary and secondary amines. Typical reactions involving the catecholamines and serotonin have been shown in Chapters 10 and 19.

The general reaction is as follows:

$$R-CH_2-NH_2 + H_2O + O_2 \longrightarrow$$

$$R - \overset{O}{\overset{\|}{C}}H + NH_3 + H_2O_2$$

The aldehyde formed is usually oxidized to an acid, but smaller amounts are reduced to the corresponding alcohol.

Whether MAO is important in relation to any of its possible substrates depends upon the existence of alternate metabolic pathways for that substrate and the accessibility of substrate to enzyme. The action of norepinephrine that is injected or liberated by nerve activity, for example, can be terminated by reentry of the norepinephrine into nerve or by its O-methylation. Inhibition of MAO does not, therefore, prolong or intensify the peripheral actions of norepinephrine. The metabolism of tyramine depends entirely upon MAO, and its pressor and central nervous system stimulant effects are tremendously increased by prior administration of MAO inhibitor because its effect of liberating norepinephrine continues for a longer time.

Norepinephrine and serotonin in the central nervous system (and the norepinephrine of peripheral nerves in the stable pool) are metabolized by MAO. These amines are deaminated by the intracellular (mitochondrial) MAO before they can leave the cell body. MAO inhibition may, therefore, have greater importance in the central than in the peripheral effects of the MAO inhibitors.

The sympathomimetic actions described below are not related to MAO inhibition. The central nervous system stimulant action probably is a direct result of MAO inhibition.

2. Biochemical effects–MAO inhibition develops over a period of several days following therapeutic doses of these drugs. The inhibition is a nonequilibrium or noncompetitive block and persists for about 2 weeks. Reversible, brief-acting MAO inhibitors—eg, the alkaloid harmine—are available as investigative agents.

During the period of MAO inhibition, the concentration of norepinephrine, dopamine, and serotonin rises in the central nervous system and heart because destruction is slowed. The activity of the precursors of these amines—dopa and 5-hydroxytryptophan—is greatly augmented. An increased central nervous system action of the amines themselves cannot be demonstrated, since they do not enter the central nervous system after systemic administration.

B. Effects:

1. Central nervous system stimulation–The MAO inhibitors produce a series of changes similar to those described for amphetamine: wakefulness, euphoria, respiratory stimulation, excitement, and, after large doses, a toxic psychosis. Convulsions are rare, and the drugs are anticonvulsants in the laboratory and clinically. An increase in appetite is much more often seen than anorexia.

2. Sympathoplegic effects–The mechanism by which a decrease in sympathetic influence on the tissues is brought about is not understood. The action is slow in onset, and acute animal studies are therefore not relevant. The effects are similar to those of the postganglionic blocking agents. Postural hypotension occurs, and cardiac output is reduced; venous dilatation is therefore present.

3. Sympathomimetic effects–Drugs of this class differ in the intensity of their sympathomimetic effects, but all can produce hypertension, tachycardia, and smooth muscle relaxation after large doses.

Absorption, Metabolism, & Excretion

All of the drugs of this group are given by mouth. They are rapidly metabolized and excreted. However, their MAO-inhibiting effect persists long after elimination or discontinuation of the medication.

Clinical Uses

A. Treatment of Depression: The MAO inhibitors have been almost completely superseded by the antidepressants related to the tranquilizers. In retrospect, it is doubtful whether even iproniazid had significant usefulness in major depressions. Indeed, there are many studies that question whether the hydrazines are superior to placebos.

B. Hypertension: The use of pargyline is discussed in Chapter 12.

C. Angina: The hydrazines in which the sympathoplegic or vasodilating properties predominate were investigated for possible usefulness in the prevention of anginal attacks. Clinical trials testing their effectiveness gave conflicting results, but some of the skepticism is based on objections to the use of a general vasodilator rather than a coronary dilator—a probable fallacy discussed in Chapter 13.

Adverse Reactions

A. Side-Effects: A given action of the MAO inhibitors—eg, hypotension or psychomotor stimulation—may be an undesirable side-effect or the therapeutic action, depending upon the application of the drug.

1. Sympathoplegic effects–Postural hypotension with complaints of dizziness or fainting is common. Vasodilatation may also cause a flush and a feeling of warmth or may precipitate a vascular headache. Decreased sweating may be noted, but the sympathomimetic action may cause increased sweating, especially of the upper parts of the body. Edema may occur, as it does during the use of other postural hypotensive agents that lower cardiac output.

2. Sympathomimetic effects–These are usually limited to constipation, urinary hesitancy, and dry mouth. Hypertension may occur, but is dangerous only in the case of tranylcypromine (Parnate) or when dietary tyramine or other sympathomimetic drugs are ingested concurrently.

3. Central nervous system effects–These include euphoria, insomnia, restlessness, and, usually, increased appetite, although the anorexia that would be expected on the basis of experience with sympathomimetic stimulants occasionally occurs. Appetite may also increase because depression is relieved.

B. Overdosage Toxicity:

1. Central nervous system effects–Euphoria may be replaced by excitement or a toxic psychosis. After large single doses, the patient may become stuporous and unresponsive. Convulsions are rare, but fibrillary muscle jerks are common.

2. Hypertensive crises–After toxic doses, the mixture of sympathomimetic and sympathoplegic actions usually persists. Hypotension may be present but can be controlled by keeping the patient recumbent.

Serious hypertensive crises may occur if the patient ingests tyramine-containing foods during a period when MAO activity is depressed. The absorbed tyramine is not destroyed at the usual rapid rate and so releases norepinephrine from stores augmented by administration of the MAO inhibitor. Signs of intense sympathomimetic action result, and fatal reactions due to intracranial hemorrhage have occurred. Reactions have been most often recorded during treatment with tranylcypromine (Parnate) but may occur during the use of the other MAO inhibitors also.

Reactions are extremely rare, but patients should avoid some fermented foods (cheddar cheese, Chianti wine) and the pods (but not the seeds) of broad beans.

3. Hepatotoxicity–Iproniazid caused hepatocellular injury with such frequency that it was removed from the market. The diffuse cellular necrosis and inflammatory changes were comparable to those seen during infectious hepatitis, but a fatal outcome was more frequent. The occurrence of jaundice is unpredictable but is a direct toxic effect and not an allergic reaction. The MAO inhibitors still available have also caused hepatic damage. Perhaps the incidence of hepatocellular damage is less, but the fewer cases reported may only reflect the now decreased use of these drugs.

Contraindications & Cautions

Explain to the patient the possible hypertensive reactions to dietary tyramine discussed above and caution against the use of other sympathomimetic drugs, including over-the-counter cold tablets or capsules. In addition, the MAO inhibitors potentiate the effect of narcotic analgesics, tranquilizers, and sedatives such as alcohol and barbiturates. The mechanism of this potentiation is not known, but drugs of these classes should be used in smaller dosages. Both the antidepressants similar to the tranquilizers and the MAO inhibitors were likely to be tried in a patient with a depression, and frequent reactions occurred unless an interval of at least 2 weeks separated the administration of the MAO inhibitor and the antidepressant in either order.

Impaired liver function is a contraindication to the use of these drugs, and liver function tests should be done during the period of treatment.

Dosages

Whether there are still any indications for the clinical use of MAO inhibitors is questionable. If they are used, they are given in an initial dosage (Table 28–3) that is continued for 2–6 weeks or until a response is noted. The dosage is then slowly reduced to the maintenance doses listed.

Excluding pargyline (the hypotensive agent) and tranylcypromine, there is no basis for preferring one or the other of these drugs. Tranylcypromine (Parnate) is a special case. Its return to the market after the serious and lethal hypertensive episodes described above was permitted only with special restrictive labeling. It can be used only in those depressions that have failed to respond to other (not further defined) therapy. The package insert should be read by anyone contemplating the use of tranylcypromine because it is by law part of the labeling and places the responsibility for any poor result on the physician.

MEDULLARY OR CONVULSANT STIMULANTS

The central nervous system stimulants discussed thus far—amphetamine, caffeine, and MAO inhibitors—cause awakening and mood elevation as early effects. They are, therefore, often referred to as cortical or cerebral stimulants even though it is probable that they act on the brain stem (RAS) and only indirectly activate the cortex. The drugs listed below act on the brain stem selectively to augment its descending influences and are often called medullary stimulants. If they are called convulsant stimulants, an important limiting property is suggested. Although they were widely used in the past, no established use for these drugs remains.

The group of medullary stimulants includes drugs of varied chemical types. Their common properties will be discussed first, and the differences between the compounds will be mentioned in the discussion of each drug.

Pharmacologic Effects

Stimulation of the respiratory, vasomotor, and vagal centers of the medulla leads to increased respiratory minute volume, a rise in blood pressure, a slowing of the pulse, and nausea and vomiting. Doses only slightly larger than those required to stimulate depressed respiration cause convulsions comparable to a grand mal seizure. The convulsions can still be precipitated in animals after decerebration. Awakening and spinal cord stimulation appear only with larger doses. Hyperthermia and cardiac arrhythmias are important toxic effects.

Suggested Uses

The treatment of severe depression due to barbiturate or other sedative-hypnotic drug has been discussed (see Chapter 23). The success of the conservative or physiologic method of treating drug depression depends in part upon abandoning the use of convulsant stimulants. The action on respiration of these stimulants is brief compared to the duration of the treatment problem. The margin between the respiratory stimulant and the convulsant dose is narrow, and postconvulsant depression is disastrous. Hyperthermia, cardiac arrhythmias, and, in the awakening patient, toxic psychosis are other dangerous reactions.

Preparations

A. Pentylenetetrazol (Metrazol): Pentylenetetrazol is of historical interest because of its use in convulsant therapy before electroshock therapy. It is used in the laboratory evaluation of anticonvulsant drugs. It is active after oral administration and is suggested, without adequate basis, for the treatment of senile confusion or memory loss.

B. Nikethamide (Coramine): Diethylnicotinamide is a weak stimulant that is converted, in part, to nicotinamide in the body.

C. Doxapram (Dopram): This drug is the agent most recently suggested for use in the postanesthetic period. It is presented as if it were in general comparable with the drugs listed in this section but with a wider range between the dose needed to stimulate respiration and the convulsant dose. It is certainly not a potent convulsant, but it causes many sympathomimetic effects and acts on the reticular activating system much as amphetamine does. Chemically, it is somewhat similar to methylphenidate (Ritalin). It thus appears to be a sympathomimetic stimulant with a very brief duration (2–5 minutes) of action.

D. Camphor and Thujone: Characterization of these old drugs is difficult. Camphor is certainly a convulsant, but it is possible that the locus of convulsant action is cortical rather than pontile. Thujone, chemically closely related to camphor, was the constituent responsible for the habituating properties of absinthe liqueur and must, therefore, have had properties different from the medullary stimulants. Present-day absinthe is flavored with anise and offers no advantage over any other 40% solution of alcohol.

E. Others: The following drugs are no longer used but may be encountered in the older literature.

Picrotoxin is the "bitter poison" found in the berries of an Indonesian plant and used originally to poison fish and allow them to be gathered. It was in the past used like pentylenetetrazol in the treatment of barbiturate intoxication.

Ethamivan (Emivan) is an analog of nikethamide no longer used.

Flurothyl (hexafluorodiethyl ether, Indoklon) is a convulsant inhalation agent used briefly as an alternative to electroshock therapy.

•   •   •

References

Amphetamine

Barkley RA: A review of stimulant drug research with hyperactive children. J Child Psychol Psychiatry 18:137, 1977.

Chandler JV, Blair SN: The effect of amphetamines on selected physiological components related to athletic success. Med Sci Sports Exercise 12:65, 1980.

Costa E, Garattini S (editors): *International Symposium on Amphetamine and Related Compounds*. Raven Press, 1970.

Jönsson L-E, Anggaro E, Gunne L-M: Blockade of intravenous amphetamine euphoria in man. Clin Pharmacol Ther 12:889, 1971.

Krager JM, Safer DM: Type and prevalence of medication used in the treatment of hyperactive children. N Engl J Med 291:118, 1974.

Lewis SA, Oswald I, Dunleavy DLF: Chronic fenfluramine administration: Some cerebral effects. Br Med J 3:67, 1971.

Safer D, Allen R, Barr E: Depression of growth in hyperactive children on stimulant drugs. N Engl J Med 287:217, 1972.

Stunkard A, Rickels K, Hesbacher P: Fenfluramine in the treatment of obesity. Lancet 1:503, 1973.

Sulzbacher SI: The learning-disabled or hyperactive child. JAMA 234:938, 1975.

Swanson JM, Kinsbourne M: Stimulant-related state-dependent learning in hyperactive children. Science 192:1754, 1976.

Tecce JJ, Cole JO: Amphetamine effects in man: Paradoxical drowsiness and lowered electrical brain activity. Science 185:451, 1974.

Update on amphetamine abuse and labelling. FDA Drug Bull 9:24, 1979.

Antidepressants

Ballin JC: Toxicity of tricyclic antidepressants. JAMA 231:1369, 1975.

Bielski RJ, Friedel RO: Prediction of tricyclic antidepressant response: A critical review. Arch Gen Psychiatry 33:1479, 1976.

Bielski RJ, Friedel RO: Subtypes of depression: Diagnosis and medical management. West J Med 126:347, 1977.

Bigger JT & others: Is physostigmine effective for cardiac toxicity of tricyclic antidepressant drugs? JAMA 237:1311, 1977.

Crimson C: Chlorpromazine and imipramine: Parallel studies in animals. Psychopharmacol Bull 4(2):1, 1967.

Cronin AJ, Khalil R, Little TM: Poisoning with tricyclic antidepressants: An avoidable cause of childhood deaths. Br Med J 1:722, 1979. [And editorial in same issue.]

Ericksen SE: Recent advances in antidepressant drug treatment. West J Med 131:104, 1979.

Goel KM, Shanks RA: Amitriptyline and imipramine poisoning in children. Br Med J 1:261, 1974.

Gottlieb RM, Nappi T, Strain JJ: The physician's knowledge of psychotropic drugs: Preliminary results. Am J Psychiatry 135:29, 1978.

Herr F, Stewart J, Charest M-P: Tranquilizers and antidepressants: A pharmacological comparison. Arch Int Pharmacodyn Ther 134:328, 1961.

Hollister LE: *Clinical Pharmacology of Psychotherapeutic Drugs*. Churchill Livingstone, 1978.

Hollister LE: Treatment of depression with drugs. Ann Intern Med 89:78, 1978.

Hollister LE: Tricyclic antidepressants. (2 parts.) N Engl J Med 299:1106, 1168, 1978.

Klerman GL, Hirschfeld RMA: The use of antidepressants in clinical practice. JAMA 240:1403, 1978.

Maletzky BM, Shore JH: Lithium treatment for psychiatric disorders. West J Med 128:488, 1978.

Maxwell MD, Seldrup J: Imipramine in the treatment of childhood enuresis. Practitioner 207:809, 1971.

Overall JE & others: Nosology of depression and differential response to drugs. JAMA 195:946, 1966.

Ravaris CL & others: Use of MAOI antidepressants. Am Fam Pract 18:105, 1978.

Rickels K & others: Drug treatment in depression: Antidepressant or tranquilizer? JAMA 201:675, 1967.

Robinson DS, Barker E: Tricyclic depressant cardiotoxicity. JAMA 236:2089, 1976.

Other Drugs

Atkinson RM, Ditman KS: Tranylcypromine: A review. Clin Pharmacol Ther 6:631, 1965.

Goldberg LI: Monoamine oxidase inhibitors: Adverse reactions and possible mechanisms. JAMA 190:456, 1964.

Hahn F: Analeptics. Pharmacol Rev 12:447, 1960.

29 | Anticonvulsant Drugs

The anticonvulsant drugs are used primarily in the treatment of epilepsy but are also effective in controlling convulsions due to other causes—eg, intracranial tumor or trauma or uremia. The types of seizures will be defined below after the properties of the several classes of anticonvulsant drugs have been discussed. Because most patients who are treated for epileptic states receive more than one drug and because treatment is continuous for many years, the chronic toxicity of the anticonvulsant drugs is of particular importance.

The anticonvulsant drugs are classified as follows: (1) long-acting barbiturates; (2) phenytoin (diphenylhydantoin) and related hydantoin derivatives; (3) trimethadione, succinimides, and sodium valproate, all used in the treatment of petit mal (absence) states; (4) phenacemide, a drug both unusually effective and unusually toxic; and (5) adjunctive drugs.

LONG–ACTING BARBITURATES

All of the drugs defined in Chapter 23 as sedative-hypnotics are anticonvulsant drugs and may be used acutely to terminate a convulsive state. Large doses are required, however, and for chronic administration only the long-acting sedatives are satisfactory. Phenobarbital and related barbiturates are the standard drugs, but other long-acting sedatives—eg, chlordiazepoxide (Librium)—are efficacious. Intermediate-acting sedatives such as meprobamate and diazepam (Valium) have been used, but the rapidly changing level of activity of the short- and intermediate-acting sedatives makes them less suitable for continued use.

Chemistry & Metabolism

Phenobarbital was characterized in the discussion of sedative-hypnotics as the standard long-acting sedative. It is also the most commonly used anticonvulsant barbiturate.

Table 23–3 shows the structures of 3 other compounds that are occasionally used as anticonvulsants. Mephobarbital (Mebaral) is demethylated rapidly to phenobarbital, and metharbital (Gemonil) is demeth-

ylated to barbital, a long-acting barbiturate that has been replaced in therapeutic use by phenobarbital.

Primidone (Mysoline) is 2-desoxyphenobarbital and is oxidized to phenobarbital, so that after 4 days of treatment, phenobarbital blood levels are as high as those seen after the usual anticonvulsant doses of phenobarbital. Primidone is also metabolized to phenylethylmalonamide (PEMA), which has anticonvulsant effects in the animal laboratory.

Blood levels of unchanged primidone and of PEMA are about a third those of phenobarbital, and it is possible that primidone has an action somewhat different from that of phenobarbital. The blood levels of phenobarbital that follow ingestion of each of these 3 compounds are adequate to explain their toxic effects.

Pharmacologic Effects

A. Mechanisms of Action: Unlike the short-acting barbiturates, phenobarbital and related compounds are anticonvulsant in doses that are not anesthetic or even markedly sedative. One point of view holds that this establishes a specific anticonvulsant action for phenobarbital. Another view, however, is that the usefulness of these drugs derives from their sustained, constant level of effect. The basis for the anticonvulsant action of these general central nervous system depressants remains conjectural. It can be said, however, that the well-established effect of the sedatives on the ascending reticular activating system is not related to their anticonvulsant activity, since amphetamine, which facilitates transmission within the reticular activating system, can be used to counteract the sedation without abolishing the anticonvulsant action.

B. Effects: The effects of phenobarbital have been discussed in Chapter 23.

Clinical Uses

Phenobarbital and similar drugs are useful in grand mal epilepsy and in the control of symptomatic convulsions. They are less often effective in psychomotor epilepsy, petit mal epilepsy, and other clinical types of seizures.

Adverse Reactions

A. Side-Effects: The most common adverse reactions to the sedatives during antiepileptic treatment are those related to sedation and disinhibition—ie, drowsiness, dizziness, ataxia, diplopia (with or without nystagmus), and behavioral (personality) changes. These effects are minimized by using combinations of anticonvulsant drugs, each in less than disturbing doses. Phenobarbital is usually well tolerated.

B. Withdrawal: Epileptic patients are unusually susceptible to the hyperexcitable state induced by withdrawal or too rapid reduction of dosage not only of sedatives but of other anticonvulsants also. To avoid precipitating convulsions, the dosage should be reduced by small decrements, with, if possible, intervals of several weeks between adjustments. If toxicity specific for one compound appears—eg, drug rash or other allergic reaction—another anticonvulsant drug in equipotent dosage should be substituted.

C. Effects of Chronic Treatment: Long-continued treatment with phenobarbital is not dangerous, and habituation is not a problem. The learning and intelligence of epileptic children are not impaired by chronic treatment with the usual doses, but prolonged treatment with combinations of anticonvulsant drugs may be damaging.

Primidone, like phenytoin, can interfere with folic acid absorption and cause macrocytosis. A similar but weaker effect is demonstrable with phenobarbital.

Dosages

A. Phenobarbital: The usual adult dose is 100–200 mg daily. Doses as large as 400 mg daily may sometimes be necessary and are often well tolerated. The long-acting sedatives are usually given in 3–4 divided doses daily, but there is no need to do so. Larger doses can be divided into 2 daily doses, and the smaller doses usually required are often given as a single dose each day. In children, the initial dosage can be based either on weight or on age, but the tolerated dose may be more than predicted by weight or age and is determined by the response and tolerance of each patient.

B. Mephobarbital (Mebaral): The daily dose is twice that of phenobarbital given in divided doses—ie, 200–400 mg daily.

C. Metharbital (Gemonil): The usual dose is 100 mg 2–3 times daily.

D. Primidone (Mysoline): Dizziness and sedation are sometimes severe at the beginning of treatment with primidone. The initial small doses—50 mg 3 times daily—can be increased to 250 or even 500 mg 3 times daily.

PHENYTOIN & CONGENERS

The generic name of this substance in the USA was recently changed. Phenytoin was known for 40 years as diphenylhydantoin (DPH, Dilantin). The older name must be remembered so that the older medical literature and indexes can be used.

Chemistry

The chemical structures of phenytoin (Dilantin) and 2 related hydantoin derivatives are shown in Table 29–1. The hydantoins can be considered as ureides and are related to the barbiturates. Nevertheless, phenytoin is a specific rather than a general depressant—ie, it is able to control convulsions without causing general sedation. It was suggested for clinical trial because of its ability to modify electroshock convulsions in the laboratory.

Pharmacologic Effects

A. Mechanisms of Action:

1. Origin of convulsions–Any speculation about the site of action of an anticonvulsant drug must be based on information about the site of origin of the convulsion. Phenytoin (and, even more clearly, phenobarbital) acts on many levels of the central nervous system, and not all actions are necessarily related to the anticonvulsant effect. The action of phenytoin on the brain stem or cerebellum, for example, is relevant only if convulsions originate at these levels. Unfortunately, the site of origin and mechanism of action of most convulsions are not clear. Jacksonian or focal convulsions clearly originate in the cortex, and an experimental analog can be produced by an irritative lesion in the cortex. But most convulsions begin with a loss of consciousness, and the abnormality is diffuse rather than focal. They are subcortical in origin, but the site cannot be more exactly defined. Many experimentally induced convulsions, including the pentylenetetrazol convulsions used to screen potential anticonvulsant drugs, appear even after precollicular section of the neuraxis.

2. Possible mechanisms–It is customary to assume that—whatever the level of origin—convulsions are due to the spread of activity from a focus of abnormal function into normal neural tissue. Anticonvulsant drugs could then act by suppressing the seizure focus or by preventing the spread of the impulse through normal tissue.

Phenytoin does not suppress the discharge from an experimentally produced focus, nor does it necessarily alter the electroencephalographic evidence of focal discharge in humans. Diffuse electroencephalo-

Table 29–1. Anticonvulsant drugs: Structures and dosages.

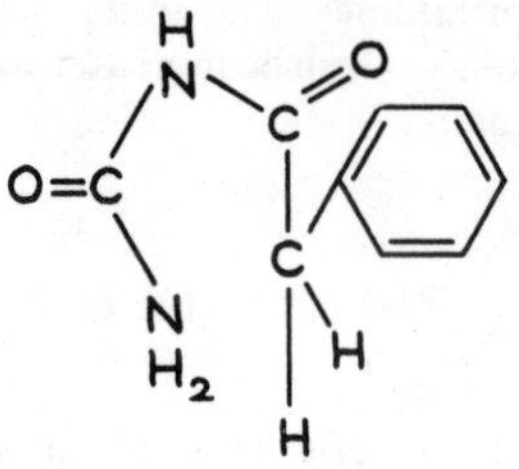

Phenylacetylurea

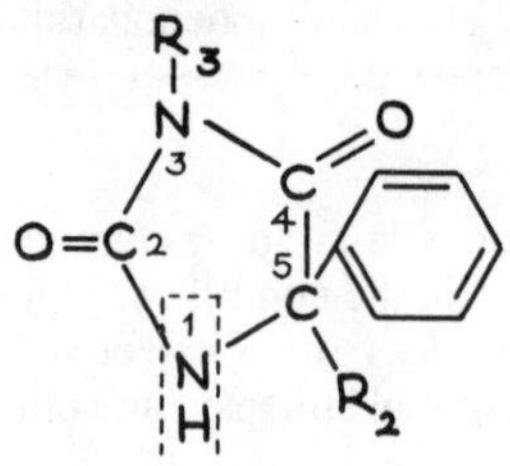

Hydantoin derivatives

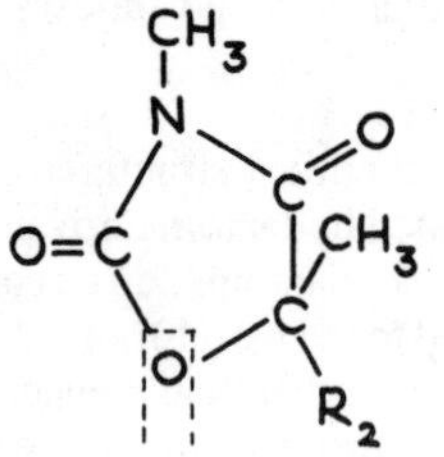

Oxazolidinediones

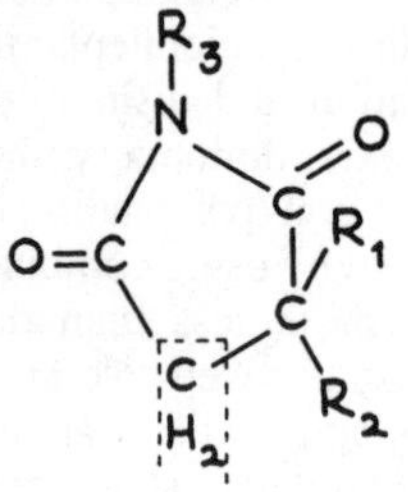

Succinimides

	R_1	R_2	R_3	Usual Adult Dose (Oral)
Phenylacetylurea				
Phenacemide (Phenurone)*				1 g 2–3 times/d
Hydantoin derivatives				
Phenytoin (diphenylhy- dantoin, Dilantin)*		—phenyl	—H	100–300 mg 1–2 times/d
Mephenytoin (Mesantoin)		—C_2H_5	—CH_3	100–300 mg 2 times/d
Ethotoin (Peganone)		—H	—C_2H_5	0.5–1 g 2–3 times/d
Oxazolidinediones				
Trimethadione (Tridione)		—CH_3		300 mg 1–4 times/d
Paramethadione (Paradione)		—C_2H_5		300 mg 1–4 times/d
Succinimides				
Ethosuximide (Zarontin)	—C_2H_5	—CH_3	—H	250–500 mg 2 times/d
Methsuximide (Celontin)	—phenyl	—CH_3	—CH_3	0.3–0.6 g 2 times/d
Phensuximide (Milontin)	—phenyl	—H	—CH_3	0.5–1 g 2 times/d

*Trade names included only for identification. These drugs are available from many suppliers under their generic names.

graphic abnormalities may be decreased. The best explanation for the action of phenytoin is, therefore, that it prevents the spread of abnormal electrical activity. Various explanations have been offered for the stabilization of neurons: reduction of post-tetanic potentiation, prolonged refractory period, elevation of synaptic threshold, and augmentation of some chemical inhibitory influence. The action may be on all neurons rather than on a precise area of the central nervous system, since one diffuse process—hypocalcemic tetany—may also be suppressed by phenytoin.

B. Effects: Effects of these drugs other than their anticonvulsant action are listed under Adverse Reactions, below.

Absorption, Metabolism, & Excretion

The maximum blood level is not reached until 8 hours after oral administration of phenytoin. The drug is metabolized by hydroxylation of the phenyl ring, a reaction governed by hepatic microsomal enzymes, and is then conjugated and excreted as a glucuronide. Metabolism is slow; the half-life of phenytoin in the plasma following discontinuance of chronic medication averages 22 hours. When the drug is given chronically, a stable blood level is reached only after administration of a fixed dose for a period of a week, at which time excretion matches absorption.

Administration once daily will maintain constant blood levels. However, large doses of the alkaline drug may be divided between the morning and evening mealtimes to minimize gastrointestinal irritation.

Absorption from intramuscular injection sites is also slow, and the drug must be given intravenously when a rapid effect is needed.

Phenytoin blood levels are easily done by gas-liquid chromatography and are valuable in studying the unresponsive patient or one with toxicity at unexpectedly low dosages. The most common cause of low levels is the failure of the patient to take his medication; some metabolize the drug at an unusually high rate and a few may absorb it poorly.

Clinical Uses

A. As Anticonvulsant: Phenytoin (alone or in combination with phenobarbital) is used in the treatment of grand mal epilepsy, symptomatic convulsions, and psychomotor epilepsy. It may intensify the petit mal attacks in mixed epilepsy.

B. Trigeminal Neuralgia and Atypical Facial Pain: See carbamazepine (Tegretol) below.

C. Cardiac Arrhythmias: Phenytoin has electrocardiographic and other effects comparable to those of quinidine. It has been used as an investigative drug to treat cardiac arrhythmias.

Adverse Reactions

A. Phenytoin:

1. Side-effects–

a. Central nervous system–The most common side-effects are vestibulocerebellar in origin—ie, ataxia, nystagmus, and slurred speech. These may be accompanied in some patients by tremors and nervousness and in others by drowsiness and fatigue.

b. Gingival hypertrophy–Hypertrophy of the gums is a frequent (20%) side-effect. It may be cosmetically displeasing but causes no other difficulty beyond minor bleeding. It is both more common and more severe in younger patients.

The mechanism underlying the proliferation of the gingival stroma is not known. It has been noted that hypertrophy does not occur in edentulous patients and that phenytoin appears in the saliva whether the drug is given by mouth or parenterally.

Brushing the teeth regularly and vigorously may be of some value in minimizing gingival hypertrophy, but excision of the hypertrophied gingivas by a dental surgeon may be necessary. Neither antihistamines nor ascorbic acid are helpful in spite of isolated claims to the contrary. The hyperplastic tissue does not regress when the drug is discontinued.

c. Folate deficiency–Prolonged administration of phenytoin may lead to macrocytosis or megaloblastic anemia due to folic acid deficiency. Dietary folic acid occurs in the form of polyglutamates, which must be hydrolyzed to folate monoglutamate before absorption can occur (see Chapter 44 for chemical structure). Phenytoin and, to a lesser extent, phenobarbital and primidone inhibit the deconjugation in the ileum and reduce absorption. The changes in the red cells can be prevented or treated by small oral doses of folic acid or vitamin B_{12}.

It has also been suggested that prolonged folate deficiency and the demonstrated decrease in cerebrospinal fluid levels of tetrahydrofolate may lead to a deterioration of the mental state of youthful epileptics.

Controlled studies using supplementary folate fail to show any improvement in behavior as was originally claimed. However, cerebrospinal fluid tetrahydrofolate levels do not rise during trials of this kind. The possibility of chronic behavioral toxicity and the suggestion that mixtures of anticonvulsant drugs interfere with the reduction of folate require further study.

d. Vitamin D deficiency–In a population of epileptics, those who have received large, chronic doses of primidone, phenytoin, barbiturates, or combinations thereof have lowered serum calcium, increased alkaline phosphatase levels, decreased bone mass, and decreased serum levels of 25-hydroxycalciferol compared with patients on the same adequate diet not receiving those drugs. A few patients after many years of treatment show adult rickets—ie, osteomalacia with pathologic fractures and muscle weakness. The chemical findings are reversed by vitamin D, and supplements of vitamin D should be given to patients on these antiepileptic drugs.

A younger population of retarded patients with seizures requiring years of therapy develop thickening of the calvarium and coarsening of the facies due to enlargement of the lips and nose. Alkaline phosphatase is elevated. In one study it was objectively established by comparison of old and new photos (Fig 29–1) and by impartial evaluation of skull films that this dose-related state affected two-thirds of the patients.

Each of the drugs implicated is a known inducer of liver microsomal enzymes, and the obvious hypothesis is that a larger fraction of cholecalciferol (D_3) is hydroxylated to polar, inactive metabolites excreted into the bile and less is available for hydroxylation by the liver and kidney to forms active in tissues. Induction of microsomal enzyme activity would also be expected to favor the conversion of cholecalciferol to 25-cholecalciferol, the first step in its activation.

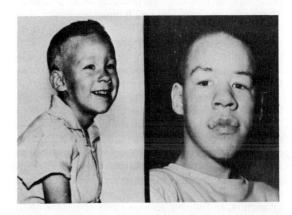

Figure 29–1. Facial coarsening and calvarial thickening in an epileptic boy shown at age 4 *(left)* and at age 16 after 15 years of anticonvulsant therapy. (Reprinted, with permission, from Lefebvre EB, Haining RG, Labbé RE: Coarse facies, calvarial thickening, and hyperphosphatasia associated with long-term anticonvulsant therapy. N Engl J Med 286:1302, 1972.)

e. Teratogenesis–Retrospective studies appear to establish that the risk of having a child with a congenital defect is increased 3-fold if the mother receives treatment for epilepsy during the first trimester of her pregnancy. The increased risk is preponderantly due to an increase in the occurrence of cleft lip and palate.

Many factors could confound an epidemiologic study correlating drug use and the occurrence of congenital defects. However, at least 2 studies have adequate numbers of patients combining an epileptic state and pregnancy and can compare infants born to epileptic mothers with and without drug treatment. None of the studies permit identification of phenytoin as the single agent responsible in the several combinations used, although such must be the case. A majority of neurologists accept the teratogenicity of phenytoin but nevertheless feel compelled to continue its use into pregnancy.

f. Others–Phenytoin is dispensed as the sodium salt and as such is very alkaline. The resultant nausea and epigastric pain can be minimized by giving the drug with or after meals.

Tests of thyroid function are falsely low, since this diphenylmethane compound (like others) displaces thyroxine from protein-binding sites. Thyroid function, however, is not altered.

Hirsutism of the extremities occurs in girls with no demonstrable endocrinopathy.

Rare toxic effects include toxic psychosis, hepatitis, and systemic lupus erythematosus.

2. Overdosage toxicity–The ingestion of large doses of phenytoin results in intensification of the cerebellar signs listed above and in excitement and confusion followed by depression. The acute toxicity is very low.

3. Allergic reactions–A morbilliform rash occurs in 2–10% (reports vary) of patients receiving phenytoin. In some cases the rash may be accompanied by pyrexia, eosinophilia, and lymphadenopathy. The reaction has been mistaken for measles, infectious mononucleosis, and, in at least one case, lymphosarcoma even after biopsy. A few cases of agranulocytosis, thrombocytopenia, and exfoliative dermatitis have been reported.

B. Mephenytoin (Mesantoin): This drug has anticonvulsant properties similar to those of phenytoin but has sedative rather than excitant effects. It is metabolized by demethylation to phenylethylhydantoin, a sedative that (as Nirvanol) was abandoned in 1920 because of its bone marrow toxicity. Perhaps predictably, mephenytoin is also very toxic. Rash and neutropenia occur frequently and pancytopenia, aplastic anemia, and hepatic damage rarely (but more often than with phenytoin). Mephenytoin causes much less gingival hyperplasia and other side-effects but more drowsiness than does phenytoin.

C. Ethotoin (Peganone): This hydantoin also causes less gingival hyperplasia and hirsutism than phenytoin, but it is less effective.

CARBAMAZEPINE (TEGRETOL) & TRIGEMINAL NEURALGIA

Carbamazepine (Tegretol) is generally equivalent to phenytoin in its pharmacologic effects but is superior to phenytoin in preventing the paroxysms of terrible pain in trigeminal neuralgia. In chemical structure it is superficially similar to imipramine.

Carbamazepine
(Tegretol)

Uses

A. Trigeminal Neuralgia: Patients with classic tic douloureux treated with phenytoin or carbamazepine will respond well enough in at least three-fourths of cases to avoid injection of the ganglion or surgical treatment. Carbamazepine is significantly more effective, but treatment is still often started with phenytoin rather than the newer drug. If necessary for the relief of pain, the 2 drugs can be used concurrently.

B. Anticonvulsant: As an anticonvulsant, carbamazepine is undoubtedly equivalent to phenytoin, but no advantages have been established. It is suggested for use in grand mal and psychomotor epilepsy in which the usual combinations give less than optimal benefits or in which side-effects limit dosage.

C. Behavioral: Especially in institutional practice, carbamazepine is used to normalize behavior in retarded patients, often in the absence of convulsions. Such controlled studies as show a beneficial effect are often discounted as demonstrating the value of general anticonvulsant treatment or the value of discontinuing antipsychotic medication.

Adverse Reactions

Side-effects are common and include ataxia, dizziness, and nausea and vomiting. As might be anticipated from its similarity to the antidepressant imipramine, carbamazepine causes anticholinergic effects—eg, blurred vision, dry mouth, and urinary retention—and unpleasant sedation.

During the early period of its use, carbamazepine was associated with a small number of cases of aplastic anemia, thrombocytopenia, and agranulocytosis. Reports of serious toxic reactions have not appeared recently, but in the package insert (see PDR) the manufacturer places a considerable responsibility on the prescriber. For this reason there are lingering doubts about the toxicity of carbamazepine and about the reporting of all adverse reactions that might have occurred.

Dosages

Initial dosage is 400 mg/d orally, increasing to 800–1200 mg/d, divided into 4 doses, if necessary.

TRIMETHADIONE

Trimethadione (Tridione) is still widely used in the treatment of petit mal epilepsy, although the succinimides are more popular. Paramethadione (Paradione) is a related oxazolidinedione compound that is both less toxic and less effective (Table 29–1).

Pharmacologic Effects

A. Mechanisms of Action: Trimethadione is useful in reducing the number of petit mal attacks whether they are of the typical pattern or one of the variants with associated motor signs. Patients subject to these attacks have characteristic abnormal electroencephalographic patterns more or less continuously rather than only during the clinical episode, as is usually the case in grand mal epilepsy. The abnormal pattern of petit mal is diffuse and symmetric and usually characterized by a 3/s spike-and-dome pattern. Trimethadione restores the EEG toward normal. In patients who respond well, the 3/s pattern no longer appears even after hyperventilation. Since the electroencephalographic abnormality is diffuse, it does not follow that trimethadione is suppressing an irritable focus.

B. Effects: Large doses of trimethadione given to animals cause sedation and respiratory depression. The drug has only a minor sedative effect in humans even when given in large doses. Its analgesic property is now clinically unimportant but led to the original trials of the drug.

Absorption, Metabolism, & Excretion

Trimethadione is rapidly and completely absorbed. The N-demethylated derivative, dimethadione, is only slowly excreted and accumulates in the body during therapy. It is an active metabolite.

Clinical Uses

An oxazolidinedione is used in the treatment of petit mal epilepsy and variants showing the spike-and-dome or other bilaterally synchronous or symmetric electroencephalographic pattern. It may be combined with phenobarbital. Trimethadione may increase the number of major seizures in patients with seizures of mixed types by suppressing the minor seizures, and should in these cases be combined with phenytoin. There may be a transitory increase in the number of petit mal episodes at the beginning of treatment.

Adverse Reactions

A. Trimethadione:

1. Side-effects–Sedation is uncommon and usually decreases with continued administration. A daily dose of amphetamine can be given to minimize sedation. Amphetamine so used will not antagonize and may even intensify the anticonvulsant effect.

A common side-effect, especially in adults, is a glary, blurred, or snowy appearance of objects in bright light (hemeralopia). The effect is due to an action on the retina but is reversible and controlled by reduced dosage or by wearing dark glasses. As described by the patient, it is different from photophobia, or general intolerance to light.

Most patients (80%) receiving trimethadione show a reduction in the number of neutrophils. This graded or controlled neutropenia can be followed by blood counts at intervals of 3 months. It is not dangerous but is mentioned to distinguish it from agranulocytosis.

Exacerbation of grand mal epilepsy is mentioned above. Reversible nephrosis has occurred. Hepatitis and acneiform dermatitis are apparently rare side-effects.

2. Overdosage toxicity–The acute (large or deliberate overdosage) toxicity of trimethadione is very low.

3. Allergic reactions–In contrast to the controlled neutropenia described above, agranulocytosis or pancytopenia may appear suddenly. If a morbilliform rash appears, the drug should be at least temporarily discontinued, since cases of exfoliative dermatitis have been reported.

B. Paramethadione: The toxicity of paramethadione is similar to that of trimethadione, but reports of serious toxic reactions are fewer. Paramethadione may be substituted for trimethadione in an effort to reduce adverse reactions. However, if an allergic reaction to trimethadione has occurred, paramethadione should be used cautiously, since cross-sensitivity may exist.

Contraindications & Cautions

When any of the anticonvulsant drugs are used, a responsible member of the patient's family should be asked to record the number of attacks and report signs of serious toxicity—bleeding or bruising, sore throat (accompanying agranulocytosis), fever, rash, pallor, behavioral changes, etc. Urinalysis and blood counts should be done monthly at first and then at intervals of about 3 months.

Because of the remote possibility of causing or aggravating hepatic or renal damage, trimethadione should be avoided or used with particular care in the presence of liver or kidney disease.

Trimethadione in combination with mephenytoin (Mesantoin) has been associated with aplastic anemia in several instances, and this combination should therefore not be given.

SUCCINIMIDES

Many neurologists now characterize trimethadione as obsolescent and regard ethosuximide (Zarontin) as the drug of first choice in the treatment of petit mal epilepsy. They argue that it is at least as effective as trimethadione and that toxic reactions are no more frequent and are of less serious types.

Ethosuximide has recently been implicated in isolated cases of agranulocytosis and pancytopenia, and evaluation of its toxicity is difficult. Side-effects during its use are certainly no greater than those of trimethadione, especially if, as is true for all anticonvulsants, the dose is slowly increased. Side-effects include signs of gastrointestinal irritation, drowsiness or depression, ataxia, hiccup, and insomnia or agitation after larger doses.

Experience with methsuximide (Celontin) is too limited to permit confident recommendations for its use. Phensuximide (Milontin) is less effective.

VALPROATE SODIUM
(Valproic Acid)

Valproic acid and its sodium salt have been marketed in many European countries for more than a decade without satisfactory definitions of their usefulness or toxicity. Some groups in the USA decided that it was a wonder drug being withheld from use by an ineffectual regulatory agency. The agency demonstrated its responsiveness by directing the manufacturer to proceed with what appears at this time to be premature marketing.

Chemistry & Pharmacokinetics

Valproic acid (Depakene) is dipropylacetic acid ($[C_3H_7]_2CHCOOH$), a branched chain, liquid fatty acid. It is rapidly absorbed after oral administration and metabolized by hepatic microsomal systems to hydroxy and keto acids.

Nothing is known of its mechanism of action, ie, there is no evidence for any of the assumptions made.

Clinical Uses

Only a few controlled studies are available, and they involve small numbers of subjects. Valproic acid was usually added to an existing regimen—a complicating factor, since the effect of simultaneously administered phenobarbital is increased.

The drug is marketed in the USA for the control of absences (petit mal and mixed seizure types with absences), and it does seem efficacious in this application. It is not useful for other types of seizures.

Adverse Reactions

Gastrointestinal disturbances (nausea, vomiting, diarrhea) occur in about a third of patients early in treatment. Transient loss of hair and a long list of isolated or infrequent reactions have been reported.

The precise incidence and the seriousness of 3 toxic reactions have not been clarified: fatal hepatitis has occurred in 7 reported cases, the second phase of platelet aggregation is interfered with, and petechiae and epistaxis are seen. Finally, the significance of the lenticular opacities observed has not been established.

Drug Interactions

When valproic acid is given to a patient already receiving phenobarbital, the serum level of the phenobarbital is increased by approximately one-quarter. Whether the effect is due to an action of valproate on protein binding or metabolism of phenobarbital is not known.

The keto acids mentioned above interfere with urine tests for ketone bodies.

Dosages

Valproic acid is usually used in children, and dosage should be based on weight. An initial dose of 15 mg/kg/d can be increased to a maximum of 30 mg/kg/d, divided into 3 doses. The effect may develop over a period of 2 weeks.

PHENACEMIDE
(Phenurone)

Phenacemide is a monoureide and is thus chemically related to one class of sedative-hypnotic drugs. It is the most effective (and most toxic) of the anticonvulsants, and reference to Table 29–1 suggests that the other anticonvulsants can be regarded as closed chain derivatives of phenacemide.

Phenacemide is effective in the treatment of all types of epilepsy, but because of its toxicity it is used only in rare cases of psychomotor epilepsy which cannot be controlled with other drugs. It causes only mild sedation, but personality changes are frequent (20%). Hepatitis accounted for 4 deaths among the first 1500 patients treated. Proteinuria, exfoliative dermatitis, and aplastic anemia are also reported.

OTHER ANTICONVULSANT DRUGS

A number of drugs not primarily classified as anticonvulsants may be used in the control of some convulsive states.

Amphetamine

Dextroamphetamine or one of the related sympathomimetic stimulants (see Chapter 28) may be used to counteract the sedation induced by some anticonvulsant drugs. In addition, amphetamine probably has a minor anticonvulsant action. It modifies experimental convulsions in animals. Its awakening effect may perhaps also prevent seizures that occur during deep sleep or during drowsiness.

Sedatives & Tranquilizers

Sedatives other than the long-acting barbiturates have been used in the treatment of epilepsy. Some of these—meprobamate (Equanil, Miltown), chlordiazepoxide (Librium), and diazepam (Valium)—are often referred to as tranquilizers. Therefore, it must be emphasized again that the antipsychotic tranquilizers—the phenothiazines and reserpine—are convulsant agents and should not be given to patients with epilepsy. Psychomotor epilepsy with an accompanying psychosis may be an unavoidable exception requiring the use of antipsychotics.

The use of chlordiazepoxide as an anticonvulsant is still investigational. The parenteral use of diazepam, 2–10 mg intramuscularly or intravenously, in the control of status epilepticus or the use of oral diazepam in combination with other agents is established rather than investigational—ie, the FDA has approved marketing and advertising for this purpose.

Clonazepam (Clonopin), like chlordiazepoxide, is a long-acting sedative of the benzodiazepine type (see Table 23–5). Unlike phenobarbital or chlordiazepoxide, which are generally more effective against grand mal convulsions, clonazepam is marketed for use in patients with petit mal who are unresponsive to the succinimides and in akinetic and myoclonic seizures. In addition to the expected risk of sedation, respiratory depression, withdrawal, and other signs of sedative effect, this nitro-substituted benzodiazepine has caused a great variety of other unexpected toxic effects.

Acetazolamide & Other Diuretics

The carbonic anhydrase inhibitors are diuretics (see Chapter 17) that produce a mild acidosis as well as a loss of sodium and potassium. The clinical efficacy of acetazolamide (Diamox) is difficult to evaluate, but it is used in the treatment of petit mal states. The same drug or a thiazide type of diuretic may be used in patients who tend to have grand mal seizures at the time of their menstrual periods.

Quinacrine

Quinacrine (Atabrine) is an antimalarial drug (see Chapter 62) that may be tried in patients with petit mal who do not respond to other drugs. The mechanism of its anticonvulsant effect is not known.

Corticosteroids & Corticotropin

Corticosteroids and corticotropin are used in the treatment of hypsarrhythmia or myoclonic spasms of infancy.

Salicylates

In children susceptible to febrile convulsions, prompt lowering of an elevated temperature by aspirin or other antipyretic analgesics may prevent the seizures.

SUMMARY OF USES OF ANTICONVULSANTS BY SEIZURE TYPES

Problems in Clinical Evaluation

There is no question that the treatment of epilepsy with the standard drugs is effective. However, the comparison of drugs within the general classes—and the evaluation of new agents—is extremely difficult. The imprecise and sometimes unsatisfactory statements often made about the usefulness of alternative drugs reflect the difficulty.

A satisfactory regimen for a patient with seizures must be highly individualized and may involve multiple drugs, especially for the one-third of patients who experience seizures of more than one type. Modification of a regimen of proved value not only may give less satisfactory results but may precipitate great difficulty. New drugs are often tried, therefore, in patients who are poorly controlled with older drugs. This technic appears to be a stringent test of the newer agent, but only if the old drug was optimally used. The interest in the new drug often results in greater care with dosage and other factors in treatment. It may be that some sort of double-blind substitution test is needed.

Another problem is statistical. If the standard drug has already reduced the incidence of seizures to a low level, the difference between old and new drugs cannot be great, and a large number of patients and a long period of observation would be necessary to establish a significant difference between groups of patients.

Laboratory Evaluation

Perhaps because clinical evaluation is so difficult, the laboratory evaluation of potential anticonvulsant drugs has attracted great interest. The influence of and interest in laboratory evaluation seem disproportionately great when one considers that intensive study has not led to the introduction of drugs of a new or unexpected chemical type.

Convulsions can be induced in experimental animals by electrical or chemical stimulation.

A. Electroshock: In this method an alternating current passes diffusely through the brain from surface electrodes. The threshold—ie, the minimum current that produces a convulsion—can be determined before and after the administration of a drug. This method does not predict the clinical usefulness of anticonvulsant drugs other than the sedatives, which do elevate the threshold.

A preferable technic is to produce a convulsion of predictable pattern by a maximal electroshock. Such convulsions are modified by the hydantoins, phenacemide, and the sedatives—ie, by drugs that are of established usefulness in the treatment of major or grand mal convulsions. In humans, these drugs prevent rather than modify the convulsions.

B. Chemoshock or Pentylenetetrazol Convulsions: The convulsions caused by pentylenetetrazol

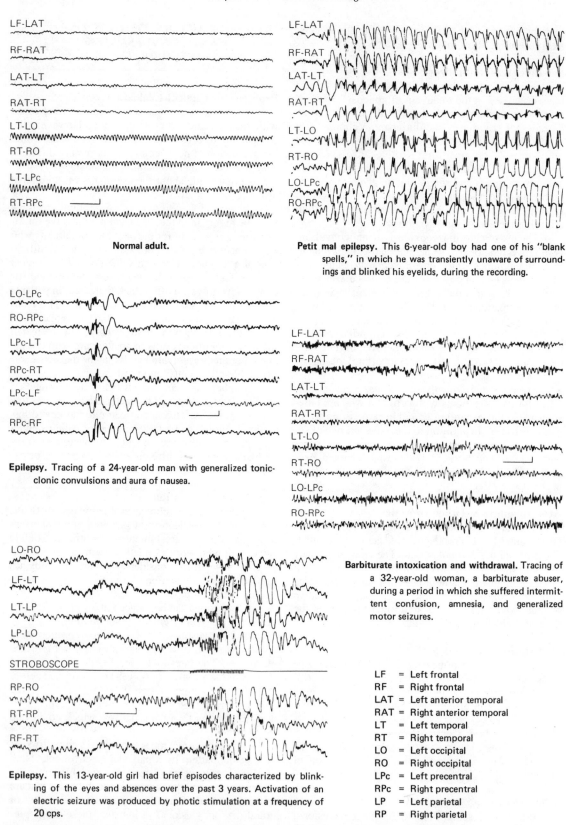

Normal adult.

Petit mal epilepsy. This 6-year-old boy had one of his "blank spells," in which he was transiently unaware of surroundings and blinked his eyelids, during the recording.

Epilepsy. Tracing of a 24-year-old man with generalized tonic-clonic convulsions and aura of nausea.

Barbiturate intoxication and withdrawal. Tracing of a 32-year-old woman, a barbiturate abuser, during a period in which she suffered intermittent confusion, amnesia, and generalized motor seizures.

Epilepsy. This 13-year-old girl had brief episodes characterized by blinking of the eyes and absences over the past 3 years. Activation of an electric seizure was produced by photic stimulation at a frequency of 20 cps.

LF	= Left frontal
RF	= Right frontal
LAT	= Left anterior temporal
RAT	= Right anterior temporal
LT	= Left temporal
RT	= Right temporal
LO	= Left occipital
RO	= Right occipital
LPc	= Left precentral
RPc	= Right precentral
LP	= Left parietal
RP	= Right parietal

Figure 29–2. Representative electroencephalograms. *Calibration:* 50 μV (vertical) and 1 s (horizontal). (Reproduced, with permission, from Chusid JG: *Correlative Neuroanatomy & Functional Neurology,* 17th ed. Lange, 1979.)

(Cardiazol, Metrazol) are prevented or modified by trimethadione and other agents useful in the treatment of petit mal epilepsy.

Seizure Types

No single formal classification of the types of convulsions is uniformly satisfactory or accepted by all neurologists. The following common grouping permits some generalizations about treatment. The first important distinction is between symptomatic convulsions, which may have a reversible underlying organic cause, and idiopathic epilepsy.

A. Epilepsy:

1. Grand mal–A major motor seizure begins in a majority of patients with some premonitory sensory or motor change (aura) if they are awake. Following the aura, consciousness is lost and the patient falls, as all muscles are tonically contracted. As the intensity of the attack wanes, clonic movements occur, consciousness slowly returns, and a period of confusion and depression follows. These attacks may occur during sleep and may be evidenced only by incontinence or injury occurring during the clonic phase.

Phenobarbital and phenytoin are the standard drugs used in the treatment of grand mal epilepsy and are generally effective, but there is some variation in the order of their use. Some physicians argue that treatment should begin with and, if possible, be restricted to phenobarbital, the least toxic drug, especially in children. Others believe that phenytoin alone should be used in order to avoid the sedative effect of the barbiturate drug. It is probable that most patients ultimately receive both drugs, either because the combination is thought to cause fewer side-effects or because both drugs are required for optimal control.

2. Petit mal group–Petit mal epilepsy, or generalized seizure with absences, in contrast to grand mal, is associated with distinctive electroencephalographic abnormality, which is present or easily induced by hyperventilation or photic stimulation between attacks. The electroencephalographic changes (Fig 29–2) are diffuse and symmetric and are reduced by trimethadione. Brief lapses of consciousness— apparent as gaps in speech or as immobility for a few seconds—may occur scores of times each day or less frequently. There are 2 motor variants of petit mal that may accompany the absence or occur without interruption of consciousness. The myoclonic variant shows isolated muscle jerks comparable to those experienced by normal persons as sleep begins. The treatment is the same as that for petit mal. The akinetic variant involves a sudden, complete loss of muscle tone. It must generally be treated like grand mal.

Phenobarbital is often tried initially in the treatment of petit mal, but the more toxic trimethadione or ethosuximide must almost always be added. If major motor attacks also occur in the same patient, phenytoin is also used. A mixed pattern is common, and petit mal attacks in children may be completely replaced by grand mal episodes after puberty.

3. Psychomotor epilepsy–The definition and diagnosis of psychomotor attacks, or complex partial seizures, is a matter of controversy. The usual description is of amnesic periods during which automatisms—ie, senseless or antisocial motor acts—are carried out. The electroencephalogram shows spiking activity in the anterior temporal areas even between attacks; the abnormality spreads during an attack; and the electroencephalographic changes may be activated by light sleep.

The usual treatment is with phenytoin with or without phenobarbital. The results of treatment are inconsistent, and many drugs including even phenacemide have been tried. As is true whenever a diffuse synchronous electroencephalographic abnormality is present, trimethadione may be tried.

B. Symptomatic Convulsions: The treatment of symptomatic convulsions obviously depends upon the cause. The term is most often used to include the convulsions associated with intracranial tumor, scar, or vascular change. These seizures may be grand mal or focal in type, and the treatment is as discussed for grand mal epilepsy.

Convulsions due to many causes require treatment other than the anticonvulsant drugs. The treatment of hypoglycemia, hypocalcemia, isoniazid toxicity, lead poisoning, etc is discussed in other sections of this book. Convulsions caused by therapeutic agents—eg, phenothiazine tranquilizers (Chapter 25) or local anesthetics (Chapter 22)—are often less dangerous than the additional depression caused by improperly used anticonvulsant medication. Strychnine and tetanus toxin (Chapter 23) act predominantly on the spinal cord and are antagonized by barbiturates or phenothiazine type antipsychotics.

C. Status Epilepticus: Status epilepticus is a period during which seizures recur at short intervals so that the patient is threatened with exhaustion, hyperpyrexia, and even death. The basis of treatment is best established by noting that control may ultimately be achieved by inducing general anesthesia with the safeguards provided by the presence of an anesthesiologist and appropriate equipment. Short of that measure, a sedative-hypnotic is given intravenously or intramuscularly in incremental dosage, with the aim of stopping the convulsions without reaching a dangerous level of anesthesia. Diazepam (Valium), 10 mg intravenously slowly, repeated 2 or 3 times in 30–60 minutes as necessary, is currently the drug most often used. Amobarbital and phenobarbital are also used.

•   •   •

References

Bogan J, Smith H: Relation between primidone and phenobarbital blood levels. J Pharm Pharmacol 20:64, 1968.

Dalby MA: Behavioral effects of carbamazepine. Adv Neurol 11:331, 1975.

Hahn TJ & others: Serum 25-hydroxycalciferol levels and bone mass in children on chronic anticonvulsant therapy. N Engl J Med 292:550, 1975. [See also editorial, p 587, in same issue.]

Kutt H, McDowell F: Management of epilepsy with diphenylhydantoin sodium: Dosage regulation for problem patients. JAMA 203:969, 1968.

Lefebvre EB, Haining RG, Labbé RF: Coarse facies, calvarial thickening and hyperphosphatasia associated with long-term anticonvulsant therapy. N Engl J Med 286:1301, 1972.

Livingston S, Berman W, Pauli LL: Anticonvulsant drug blood levels. JAMA 232:60, 1975.

Mattson RH & others: Folate therapy in epilepsy: A controlled study. Arch Neurol 29:78, 1973.

Monson RR & others: Diphenylhydantoin and selected congenital malformations. N Engl J Med 289:1049, 1973. [See also editorial, p 1089, in same issue.]

Nicol CF: Status epilepticus. JAMA 234:419, 1975.

Rockliff BW, Davis EH: Controlled sequential trials of carbamazepine (Tegretol) in trigeminal neuralgia. Arch Neurol 15:129, 1966.

Silver J & others: Prevalence and treatment of vitamin D deficiency in children on anticonvulsant drugs. Arch Dis Child 49:344, 1974.

Sodium valproate: A new anticonvulsant. Med Lett Drugs Ther 19:93, 1977.

Suchy FJ & others: Acute hepatic failure associated with the use of sodium valproate. N Engl J Med 300:962, 1979.

Wapner I, Thurston DL, Holowach J: Phenobarbital: Its effect on learning in epileptic children. JAMA 182:937, 1962.

Wilder BJ, Serrano EE, Ramsay RE: Plasma diphenylhydantoin levels after loading and maintenance doses. Clin Pharmacol Ther 14:797, 1973.

Woodbury DM, Penry JK, Schmidt RP (editors): *Antiepileptic Drugs*. Raven Press, 1972.

Drug Treatment of Parkinsonism | 30

Parkinsonism (paralysis agitans) is associated with lesions in the substantia nigra and globus pallidus that result in increased but improper modulation of motor activity by the extrapyramidal system. The manifestations of parkinsonism can be placed in 3 groups for purposes of evaluating drug therapy: (1) Akinesia: A paucity of or difficulty in initiating movement beyond that enforced by rigidity. (2) Rigidity: A rigidity that is mild and plastic ("waxy")—ie, it is easily overcome, and the limb stays in the new position forced on it. (3) Tremor: A fine, repetitive tremor may be present at rest.

Levodopa (L-dopa), through its metabolite dopamine, acts on the biochemical defect of parkinsonism and, together with other dopamine agonists such as bromocriptine, provides the most effective treatment of this disease. Atropinelike drugs and sympathomimetic stimulants are less effective but can be given in combination with levodopa.

Chemistry

Dopa is a precursor of dopamine and of norepinephrine (Fig 30–1). Its biotransformation is further discussed below.

Pharmacologic Effects

A. Mechanisms of Action: The distribution of dopamine within the central nervous system parallels that of its metabolite norepinephrine. In addition, the dopamine content of the caudate nuclei and putamen is also high even though these areas contain no norepinephrine.

The idea that supplementary dopamine might be therapeutically useful was first suggested by the study of reserpine. Reserpine depletes the central nervous system of dopamine and causes a state of extrapyramidal rigidity that is relieved by the use of dopa but not by the administration of hydroxytryptophan, the corresponding precursor of serotonin.

Studies using fluorescence microscopy and differential centrifugation show that the dopamine is concentrated in nerve endings in the caudate nucleus and adjacent striatal areas. These fibers appear to arise from cell bodies in the substantia nigra and are assumed to be dopaminergic—ie, to act by releasing dopamine as a mediator.

In autopsy material from patients with parkin-

sonism, the dopamine content of the caudate nucleus and putamen is low. The primary histopathologic change in parkinsonism is a decrease in the number of pigmented neurons in the substantia nigra. These ob-

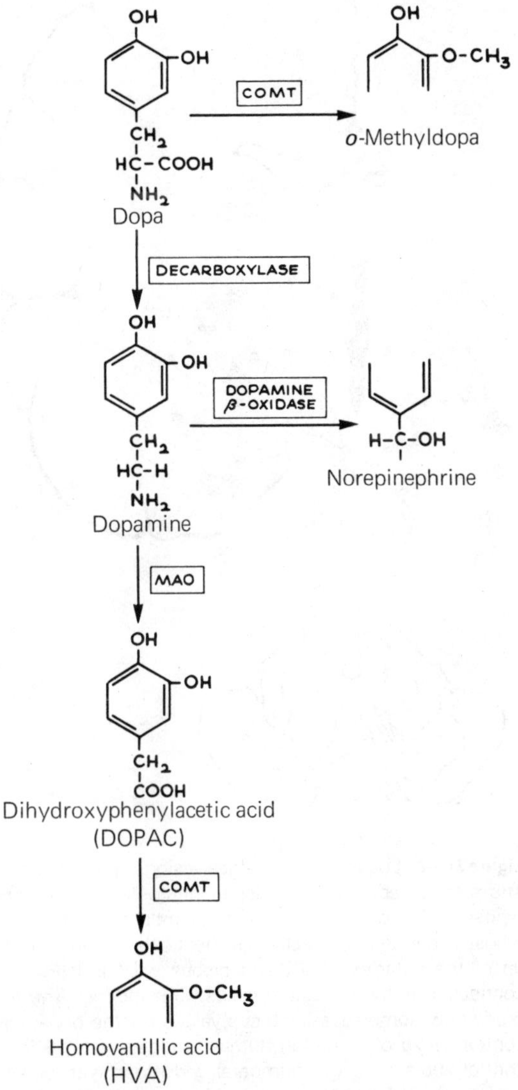

Figure 30–1. Metabolism of dopa and dopamine.

319

servations also suggested that restoring dopamine levels toward normal might ameliorate the signs of parkinsonism.

The first trials of levodopa gave equivocal results, but its usefulness became apparent when chronic treatment with large oral dosages was tried.

The mechanism of action as currently formulated is that levodopa administration leads to a repair of the dopamine deficiency responsible for parkinsonism. The nigrostriatal fibers that undergo degeneration are dopaminergic and inhibitory on the next neuron. Symptoms then would be due to uninhibited activity of striatofugal fibers beyond the lesion. The neuron released from dopamine inhibition is further assumed to be cholinergic and to be the site of action of the parasympatholytic drugs discussed below. It must be assumed that the degenerated nigrostriatal fibers are still able to accumulate dopamine if large amounts of levodopa are provided. If dopamine acts on receptors in cells beyond the nigrostriatal lesion, it is difficult to explain the slow onset of action in the face of the rapid conversion of dopa to dopamine. It is also difficult to reconcile the above formulation with the observation that dopa is still effective after the postulated pathways have been interrupted by previous destructive lesions in the ventrolateral thalamus.

B. Effects:

1. Central nervous system–The accumulation of dopamine reduces the intensity of parkinsonism but has no effect on extrapyramidal functions in normal subjects. Other central nervous system effects reflect a stimulant action comparable to that of the sympathomimetic stimulants.

2. Peripheral–Dopamine is a beta-sympathomimetic agonist, although with large doses an alpha-agonist (vasoconstricting) effect appears. The pupils are dilated, the force of cardiac contraction is increased, and cardiac arrhythmias may be produced. Pupillary dilatation is prevented by the use of guanethidine, suggesting that that sympathomimetic effect at least is not due to a direct action of dopamine on receptors but to a release of norepinephrine. Large doses of dopamine may cause an elevation of blood pressure, but levodopa is more likely to cause postural hypotension through a mechanism as yet unclarified.

Absorption, Metabolism, & Excretion

Levodopa is rapidly and completely absorbed after oral administration, and, even though its effect is slow in onset and prolonged in duration, it is rapidly metabolized, with two-thirds of an oral dose appearing in the urine as metabolites within 8 hours.

The metabolism of levodopa is predominantly by decarboxylation to dopamine. Dopamine does not enter the brain, and only that small fraction (perhaps 1–5%) of levodopa that is decarboxylated to dopamine after reaching the central nervous system can contribute to the therapeutic effect. Decarboxylation also occurs in the lumen of the intestine and in the liver and other organs, and a significant fraction of ingested levodopa is inactivated by conversion to o-methyldopa before decarboxylation.

Levodopa must, therefore, be given in large amounts to exert its beneficial effects on the central nervous system because most of it is wasted by metabolism in the periphery. Decarboxylase inhibitors that do not enter the central nervous system slow the peripheral destruction of levodopa and increase the amount available for entry into the central nervous system. If an inhibitor is added, the dosage of levodopa

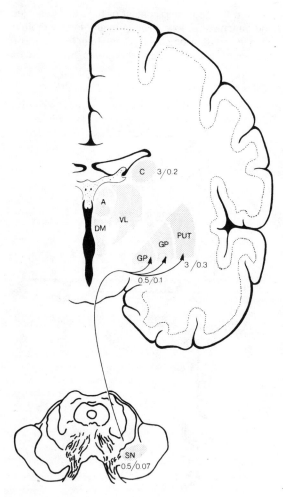

Figure 30–2. Locus of the chemical lesion in parkinsonism. The arrows represent the dopamine-containing neurons whose cell bodies are in the substantia nigra (SN) and whose axons course directly to the lenticular nucleus, made up of the putamen (PUT) and globus pallidus (GP). The connection to the caudate nucleus (C) is indirect. The figures show some representative values for the dopamine content (μg/g of tissue) in human autopsy material from control subjects (larger numbers) and those with parkinsonism. A, DM, and VL are the anterior, dorsomedial, and ventrolateral nuclei of the thalamus.

may be only one-fourth of the original dose.

The available decarboxylase inhibitor, carbidopa, is a hydrazine derivative of methyldopa:

$$HO-\overset{HO}{\underset{}{\bigcirc}}-CH_2-\underset{\underset{NH-NH_2}{|}}{\overset{\overset{CH_3}{|}}{C}}-COOH$$

It is marketed only as a combination with levodopa in fixed proportion (Sinemet) but has proved useful in some patients in whom nausea and vomiting are prominent side-effects.

Monoamine oxidase (MAO) inhibitors might also be expected to intensify the levodopa effect by decreasing the metabolism of dopamine, but they must not be used, since their administration results in hypertensive episodes due to augmented peripheral effects.

Dopamine is oxidatively deaminated to phenylacetic acid derivatives and o-methylated. Of the 25–30 urinary metabolites, homovanillic acid (Fig 30–1) is predominant, accounting for 40% of a single dose. Only a minute amount of the remaining dopamine is converted to norepinephrine.

Clinical Use

The effectiveness of levodopa in the treatment of idiopathic parkinsonism has been established by double-blind studies and by studies using objective evaluations of motor function. Levodopa is clearly superior to the parasympatholytic type of drug and to amantadine, but it can be combined with those drugs for added benefit.

Akinesia is most improved—ie, the patient is more active even if rigidity and tremor persist. Rigidity usually is relieved. Tremor may subside only after a long period of treatment or may be uninfluenced. Only about one out of 4 patients fails to benefit significantly or cannot tolerate levodopa.

Improvement may not be maximal until treatment has been continued for 2–6 months. The beneficial effect persists for more than 3 weeks after the administration of levodopa is discontinued. Patients with idiopathic parkinsonism may slowly deteriorate as a result of progression of their disease. However, it also appears that, with continued treatment, there is decreased responsiveness to the medication and more trouble with side-effects.

Patients with postencephalitic parkinsonism—a small group now since the epidemic peaked in 1917—tolerate only small doses of levodopa and experience more side-effects, especially choreiform movements. Parkinsonism that results from damage due to manganese, hypoxia, or trauma also responds.

An interesting result of the availability of effective therapy is that drug sales became an indication of the incidence of the disease, which now appears to be much lower than previously estimated.

Adverse Reactions

As levodopa is used—in gradually increasing doses—side-effects invariably occur, and the distinction between side-effects and overdosage toxicity disappears. Adverse reactions force discontinuance of therapy in only about 5% of cases, although they limit dosage in a much larger percentage of patients.

A. Gastrointestinal: Nausea and anorexia (often with vomiting) occur in virtually all patients. The symptoms are partially local in origin and to that extent can be controlled by dividing the dose and giving the drug with food or antacids. However, vomiting also occurs after the injection of levodopa.

Those antiemetics that are phenothiazines and major tranquilizers are said by some investigators to be contraindicated because they will counteract the levodopa effect; other investigators report that they are useful.

B. Cardiovascular:

1. Cardiac arrhythmias–The sympathomimetic effect of the dopamine generated outside of the central nervous system can cause tachycardia, ventricular extrasystoles, and, rarely, atrial fibrillation.

2. Hypotension–The hypertension that would be predicted as a dopamine effect does occur, but only after huge doses of levodopa or in the presence of MAO inhibitors or other sympathomimetics. However, postural hypotension is always demonstrable and may cause faintness. The hypotension tends to become less severe with continued treatment.

C. Neurologic:

1. Behavioral–Levodopa has some effects comparable to those of a sympathomimetic stimulant such as amphetamine. These result in euphoria, anxiety, and insomnia and may progress to a toxic psychosis or acute brain syndrome with delusions and hallucinations and paranoid behavior.

On the other hand, depression and somnolence may also appear.

2. Dyskinetic–Patients with parkinsonism may develop abnormal, involuntary movements during treatment with levodopa—ie, in large doses the drug may precipitate some extrapyramidal signs as it is relieving others. The choreiform movements may involve the head and limbs but are often faciolingual. The grimacing and chewing movements, together with uncontrolled movement of the tongue, can be socially disabling and force a reduction in dosage even if this also reduces the therapeutic effect. The state resembles tardive dyskinesia but is reversible.

A fine tremor that is not extrapyramidal in origin may also appear.

D. Other: Patients receiving large daily dosages of levodopa may show sudden "oscillations in performance" or rapid exacerbation of the parkinsonism combined with profound weakness. These attacks develop within minutes and last for 1–3 hours. The cyclic change, or "on-off phenomenon," usually appears at the same time each day and is probably due to an excessive levodopa level due to unusually rapid absorption.

Prolonged (more than 1 year) administration of dopa may also lead to elevated serum levels of growth hormone, decreased glucose tolerance, and augmented response to insulin. The changes have so far been confined to the laboratory findings; no related clinical problems have occurred in patients treated for as long as 7 years.

The Coombs test may become positive during treatment with levodopa but without the hemolytic episodes seen during methyldopa administration.

Contraindications & Cautions

Levodopa should not be given to patients with recent myocardial infarction, to those with a cardiac dysrhythmia, or to excited or paranoid psychotics.

Levodopa should be used only with caution and careful observation of the patient in the presence of depression.

Interaction With Other Drugs

Levodopa should be combined with the anticholinergic type of antiparkinson drugs and has been combined with amantadine and amphetamine without difficulty. The efforts to increase the effects of levodopa by giving it in combination with an inhibitor of decarboxylase are mentioned above.

A. Pyridoxine: The administration of pyridoxine even in the form of the ordinary vitamin preparations is equivalent to a reduction in the dosage of levodopa. The antagonism is presumably due to an increase in the activity of decarboxylases outside of the central nervous system for which pyridoxine is a cofactor.

B. MAO Inhibitors: MAO inhibition augments the peripheral effects of dopamine and may cause hypertension and tachycardia.

C. Major Tranquilizers: Reserpine, which depletes the basal ganglia of dopamine, should not be given with levodopa. The phenothiazine type of antipsychotic tranquilizer may also cause a parkinsonismlike state in toxic dosage, but there is no evidence—although this has often been suggested—that smaller (antiemetic) doses interfere with the action of dopa. Antidepressants of the imipramine type are pharmacologically indistinguishable from the phenothiazines but are actually recommended for use. Methyldopa, an antihypertensive drug with side-effects similar to the tranquilizers, has been described as both useful and deleterious when combined with dopa.

Dosages

Levodopa is given in gradually increasing dosage until the maximal therapeutic response is achieved, until side-effects severe enough to limit the dosage appear, or until a dosage of 8 g/d is reached. The usual requirement is 4–6 g/d.

The initial dosage is usually 0.5-1 g/d divided into 2 doses with food. The daily amount is increased by 150–500 mg/d every 2–3 days. Extending the interval over which the final dosage is reached does not decrease the incidence of side-effects or change the max-

imal tolerated dose. By the time maximal dosage is reached, the drug should be given 3–6 times daily with food.

OTHER DOPAMINE AGONISTS

Dopamine and dopaminergic nerves are involved in the genesis and treatment of parkinsonism. Experience with other drug groups suggests that dopamine agonists other than dopamine itself could be identified and that such alternatives to levodopa might have advantages of selectivity—ie, fewer norepinephrine effects—and longer duration of action. The actions of any dopamine agonist are expanded by the fact that dopamine is either the prolactin inhibitory factor or closely related to it. Some derivatives of apomorphine are dopamine agonists, but the most promising such drug is bromocriptine.

Bromocriptine (Parlodel)

A. Chemistry and Metabolism: Table 14–1 shows the structure of ergotamine, a naturally occurring amino acid ergot alkaloid. Bromocriptine is the 2–bromo derivative of a very similar alkaloid. It is metabolized in the liver and excreted into the bile. Its half-life is 6–8 hours, much longer than that of levodopa.

B. Pharmacologic Effects: Bromocriptine is a dopamine agonist, ie, like dopamine, it acts on the postsynaptic receptors of a responsive cell to activate it. Its action in the presence of parkinsonism, its other central nervous system effects, and the results of its peripheral sympathomimetic activity are as described above for levodopa.

In addition, bromocriptine acts more dependably than levodopa to reduce high levels of prolactin (lactogenic hormone). The hypothalamic and anterior pituitary hormones are discussed in detail in Chapter 39. In summary, dopaminergic neurons terminate on the portal blood vessels of the infundibulum and release dopamine as prolactin inhibitory factor (PIF). Unlike other hypothalamic hormones that are releasing factors, PIF tonically inhibits the secretion of prolactin; thus, dopaminergic agents reduce prolactin release and plasma prolactin levels. Since prolactin stimulates milk production in the breast that has been prepared for this by other hormones, lowering the prolactin level with PIF will stop lactation.

The high concentration of growth hormone in acromegaly is also lowered by bromocriptine.

C. Clinical Uses:

1. Suppression of lactation–Only small doses of bromocriptine are required to reduce the amount of prolactin secreted and thus suppress lactation in the immediate postpartum period and prevent painful breast engorgement when the infant is not to be nursed. Other (nonpuerperal) lactation associated with high luteinizing hormone levels and amenorrhea can also be treated.

2. Parkinsonism–Bromocriptine in large doses (50–100 mg/d) gives improvement comparable to that seen with levodopa. If treatment with levodopa is not successful, treatment with bromocriptine will also fail. Bromocriptine can be combined with levodopa to minimize the usual decline in effectiveness after long continued treatment (several years) and is also useful when levodopa causes "on-off" responses or dyskinesia.

3. Other uses–The amenorrhea-galactorrhea syndrome due to elevated prolactin levels will respond to treatment with bromocriptine, but infertility in general is not an indication for the drug because its efficacy in this situation and safety during pregnancy are not established. The suggested effects of bromocriptine on gonadal function and sexuality require more study (see Prolactin in Chapter 39).

D. Adverse Reactions: Side-effects similar to those outlined above for levodopa occur—ie, nausea and vomiting, dizziness, nasal congestion, constipation, diarrhea, orthostatic hypotension, dyskinesia, distorted perception, and toxic psychosis. With the large doses of bromocriptine used in the treatment of parkinsonism, the psychotic behavior may include violent and delusional behavior that may not be rapidly reversible upon termination of the drug. Some vasospasm has been noted but without serious ischemic changes.

The present high cost of bromocriptine is a factor limiting its use.

ATROPINELIKE DRUGS

Chemistry & Classification

The central anticholinergic drugs used in the treatment of parkinsonism are selected from or related to drug classes already discussed.

A. Parasympatholytic or Cholinolytic: The belladonna alkaloids were the first drugs used to relieve the rigidity of extrapyramidal states. Scopolamine (hyoscine) is still used infrequently, but the natural alkaloids have been largely replaced by synthetic drugs related to the synthetic substitutes for atropine. (See Fig 30–3 and Table 30–1.)

B. Antihistamines: The structure and pharmacology of diphenhydramine (Benadryl) is given in Chapter 19. Orphenadrine and chlorphenoxamine (Table 30–1) are methyl- and chloro- derivatives.

C. Phenothiazine Tranquilizer: Ethopropazine is a phenothiazine derivative, the diethyl analog of the antipsychotic tranquilizer promethazine (Table 25–1).

Pharmacologic Effects

A. Mechanisms of Action: The central anticholinergic action of these drugs is established by the observation that physostigmine (a cholinesterase inhibitor that enters the central nervous system) exacerbates the signs of parkinsonism and that this action is blocked by tertiary amine but not by quaternary amine atropinelike drugs.

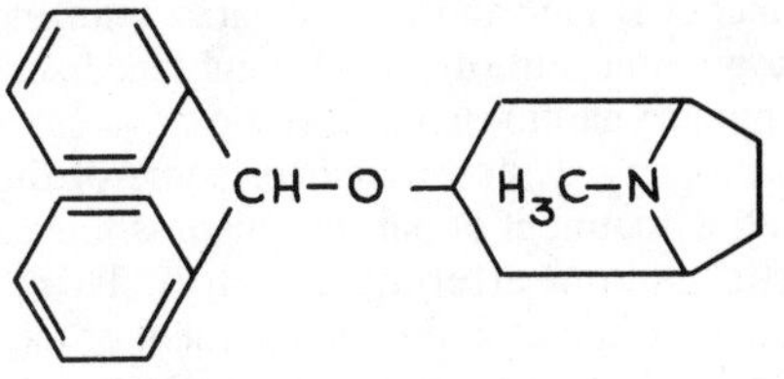

Benztropine (Cogentin)

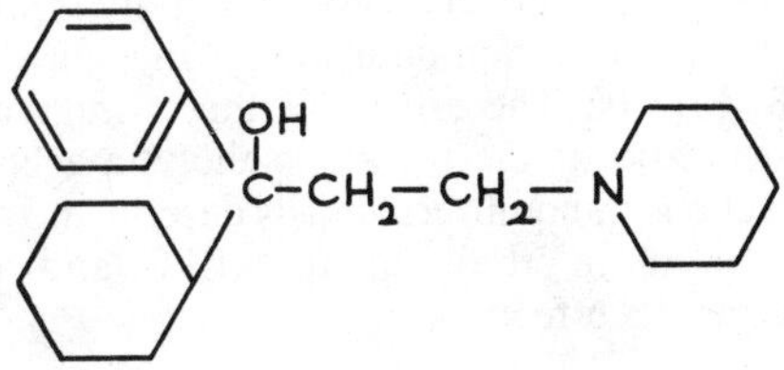

Trihexyphenidyl (Artane)

Figure 30–3. Chemical structure of representative drugs that resemble the synthetic substitutes for atropine and the antihistamines and are used in the treatment of parkinsonism.

The most common suggestion is that the site of action is a cholinergic neuron immediately distal to the dopaminergic fiber that courses from the substantia nigra to the caudate nucleus. In parkinsonism, the cholinergic system is relieved of the constant inhibitory effect of dopamine following degeneration of the fibers from the substantia nigra. It is assumed that the resulting signs of parkinsonism are due to increased activity of the cholinergic system and are blocked by acetylcholine antagonists. The primary pathologic change is undoubtedly in the basal ganglia, but drugs may act at any of several levels to modify the resulting process. The rigidity of parkinsonism is due to persistent activity in both the agonist and antagonist muscles

Table 30–1. Atropinelike drugs used in the treatment of parkinsonism.

	Usual Adult Dosage (3–4 Times Daily)
Parasympatholytics	
Trihexyphenidyl (Artane, Pipanol, Tremin)*	1–5 mg
Procyclidine (Kemadrin)	2–5 mg
Cycrimine (Pagitane)	1.25–5 mg
Biperiden (Akineton)	1–2 mg
Benztropine (Cogentin)	0.5–2.5 mg (twice daily)
Antihistamines	
Diphenhydramine (Benadryl)*	50 mg
Orphenadrine (Disipal, Norflex)	50 mg
Chlorphenoxamine (Phenoxene)	50 mg
Phenothiazine	
Ethopropazine (Parsidol)	25–50 mg

*Generic preparation available.

of a functional pair and is associated with increased gamma-efferent outflow and a heightened sensitivity of the monosynaptic (tendon) reflexes.

A property demonstrated for some of the drugs used in the treatment of parkinsonism is the ability to suppress gamma-efferent activity. This effect, discussed in Chapter 23 in the treatment of tetanus, is most clearly demonstrated for chlorpromazine. Chlorpromazine and related tranquilizers relieve parkinsonism when given in small doses and precipitate it in larger doses. The effect on cord reactivity is probably secondary to an action on a suprasegmental site.

B. Effects: The effects of these drugs are the same as those of the parasympatholytic agents and antipsychotic tranquilizers already described. They are less potent in their atropinelike and chlorpromazinelike effects.

Use in Parkinsonism

The effectiveness of these drugs by themselves is usually not very great. Some amelioration of the rigidity is the expected response. However, combined with levodopa, the atropinelike drugs help control hypersalivation and add to the effectiveness of levodopa, although the incidence of dystonias is increased.

Adverse Reactions

All of these drugs cause atropinelike effects—eg, blurred vision, dry mouth, constipation—as well as drowsiness, dizziness, and a subjectively unpleasant feeling of sedation.

Contraindications & Cautions

These atropinelike drugs can be used in the presence of glaucoma if glaucoma treatment is continued and the intraocular pressure is determined periodically.

Preparations & Dosages (Table 30–1)

There are no sound clinical studies to permit accurate comparison of agents or to suggest one regimen or another.

Treatment should be started with small doses and the amount slowly increased to tolerance or the maximum recommended dose. Abrupt changes in drug or dosage should not be made, since this may intensify the symptoms.

OTHER DRUGS USED IN THE TREATMENT OF PARKINSONISM

In the past, dextroamphetamine was often used to minimize the tranquilizing effect of the anticholinergics. It also was said to increase mobility and prevent the oculogyric crises of postencephalitic parkinsonism.

Amantadine (Symmetrel) is another amine used in the treatment of parkinsonism. Its chemical structure is shown in Chapter 57, where amantadine is discussed as an antiviral drug. Amantadine has limited efficacy when used alone, but it can be combined with levodopa. In large doses, it has central stimulant and hallucinatory effects. It tends to lose effectiveness with continued administration.

● ● ●

References

Birket-Smith E: Abnormal involuntary movements in relation to anticholinergics and levodopa therapy. Acta Neurol Scand 50:801, 1974.
Claveria LE, Calne DB, Allen JG: "On-off" phenomena related to high plasma levodopa. Br Med J 2:641, 1973.
Friedman AH, Everett GM: Pharmacological aspects of parkinsonism. Adv Pharmacol 3:83, 1964.
Godwin-Austen RB, Frears CC, Bergman S: Incidence of side-effects from levodopa during the introduction of treatment. Br Med J 1:267, 1971.
Hornykiewicz O: Parkinson's disease: From brain homogenate to treatment. Fed Proc 32:183, 1973.
Hughes RC & others: Levodopa in parkinsonism: The effects of withdrawal of anticholinergic drugs. Br Med J 2:487, 1971.
Marsden CD, Parkes JD, Rees JE: A year's comparison of treatment of patients with Parkinson's disease with levodopa combined with carbidopa versus treatment with levodopa alone. Lancet 2:1459, 1973.
Parkes D: Bromocriptine. N Engl J Med 301:873, 1979.
Pearce I, Pearce JMS: Bromocriptine in parkinsonism. Br Med J 1:1402, 1978.
Rushworth G: Some aspects of the pathophysiology of spasticity and rigidity. Clin Pharmacol Ther 5:828, 1964.
Schwab RS & others: Amantadine in Parkinson's disease. JAMA 222:792, 1972.
Sweet RD, McDowell FH: Five years' treatment of Parkinson's disease with levodopa. Ann Intern Med 83:456, 1975.
Walker JE & others: Amantadine and levodopa in the treatment of Parkinson's disease. Clin Pharmacol Ther 13:28, 1972.
Wass JAH & others: Long term treatment of acromegaly with bromocriptine. Br Med J 1:875, 1977.
Wright CS, Steele SJ, Jacobs HS: Value of bromocriptine in unexplained primary infertility: A double-blind controlled study. Br Med J 1:1037, 1979.

Gastrointestinal Drugs | 31

Some of the drugs that act on the gastrointestinal tract have already been discussed. The parasympatholytic drugs and narcotic analgesics decrease intestinal motility, and the parasympathomimetic drugs augment motility. The present chapter considers those drugs that are primarily used for the treatment of the digestive disorders. A number of less commonly applied gastrointestinal drug actions are also defined.

ANTACIDS

Gastric antacids are weak bases that partially neutralize the acid gastric secretion. If they elevate the pH above 4.0–4.5, they also inhibit the activity of pepsin.

Antacids are divided into 2 classes. **Systemic antacids,** of which sodium bicarbonate is the only common example, can be absorbed and cause systemic alkalosis. The more commonly used **nonsystemic antacids** either form insoluble products in the small intestine or contain a nonabsorbable cation.

Pharmacologic Effects

A. Systemic Antacids: Sodium bicarbonate (baking soda) is the only systemic antacid that need be considered. A fraction of the sodium bicarbonate reacts with hydrochloric acid to liberate carbon dioxide:

$$HCO_3^- + H^+ \rightarrow H_2O + CO_2$$

Ingesting sodium bicarbonate is equivalent to ingesting additional sodium without additional chloride. Bicarbonate in the intestine is increased either (1) by that ingested and not neutralized in the stomach, or (2) by the sparing of the bicarbonate of intestinal secretions that would otherwise be used to neutralize the acid mixture reaching the small intestine. Since it is easily absorbed, the sodium bicarbonate is, in effect, added to extracellular fluid. An alkaline urine is excreted until the excess sodium is disposed of.

The rapid action, the apparently beneficial effect of the gaseous distention, the subjective relief afforded by the belching induced, and its availability in most households probably account for the popularity of "soda" as a nonprescription medication. The systemic alkalosis is usually mild in degree even after repeated doses of bicarbonate. Sodium content and the occurrence of rebound hypersecretion are the significant objections to its use.

Freely soluble sodium bicarbonate acts rapidly and is able to neutralize enough acid to raise the pH in the antrum and to cause the release of gastrin. Therefore, it greatly increases gastric secretion shortly after its administration, and the hypersecretion may outlast the presence of bicarbonate in the gastric contents.

B. Nonsystemic Antacids:

1. Action as antacids–Nonsystemic antacids react to remove hydrogen ions from solution at the acid pH of the gastric contents. However, in the alkaline medium of the small intestine, hydrogen ion is again released, and the antacid is either restored to its original insoluble state or, as in the case of magnesium compounds, the products of the reaction are not absorbed even if they are slightly soluble.

For example, aluminum (or magnesium) hydroxide reacts as follows:

$$Al(OH)_3 + 3HCl \underset{\text{In intestine}}{\overset{\text{In stomach}}{\rightleftharpoons}} AlCl_3 + 3H_2O$$

Magnesium trisilicate ($2MgO \cdot 3SiO_2{}^{2-} xH_2O$) reacts thus:

$$Mg_2Si_3O_8 + 4H^+ \rightarrow 2Mg^{2+} + 3SiO_2 + 2H_2O$$

The trisilicate is not regenerated, but the reaction is, in effect, reversible, since at the alkaline pH of the intestine magnesium carbonate is formed and chloride made available for reabsorption.

Another nonsystemic antacid and perhaps the most effective agent in use is calcium carbonate, which reacts in the stomach as does sodium bicarbonate:

$$CaCO_3 + 2H^+ \rightarrow Ca^{2+} + H_2O + CO_2$$

but which at pH 8.0 in the intestine is precipitated again as $CaCO_3$. Calcium carbonate is absorbed enough to cause a minor degree of hypercalcemia. It acts slowly and causes some rebound hypersecretion due to an increase in gastrin liberation. Prolonged use can cause nephrolithiasis.

A final example is magnesium oxide, a powder, which in suspension is hydrated to magnesium hydroxide or milk of magnesia.

2. Other properties–The insoluble nonsystemic antacids such as aluminum hydroxide or calcium carbonate are constipating. The nonabsorbable but slightly soluble magnesium salts have a laxative effect.

The colloidal suspensions formed by the aluminum preparations or by magnesium hydroxide or magnesium trisilicate are adsorbent, but there is no reason to relate this property to their effectiveness as antacids.

Clinical Uses

A. Treatment of Peptic Ulcer: The treatment of peptic ulcer provides a good example of the need for controlled clinical trials in all areas of therapy, whether by means of drugs or other modalities. It is impossible to present more than an intuitive evaluation of many of the diverse and strongly held opinions about treatment of this very common problem. Therapeutic trials of the drugs used in the treatment of peptic ulcer must separately evaluate the rate of healing of an ulcer, the number of recurrences and the intervals between recurrences, and the relief of pain during acute episodes. It is apparently true that treatment does relieve the pain of peptic ulcer, but it has not been established that highly restricted diets, parasympatholytic drugs, or antacids as ordinarily used have a favorable effect on healing or recurrence of ulcers. That the technic of the controlled clinical trial is valid is shown by the recent experience with cimetidine, an agent that does hasten the healing of peptic ulcer.

Components of the treatment regimen for ulcer, discussed in this chapter or earlier, include the following:

1. Nonspecific treatment–Explanation and reassurance, often in the form of hospitalization, and assistance with the problem of learning to live with stressful factors in the environment are not the least of the treatment resources the physician can offer ulcer patients. Sedatives may be given for daytime anxiety and hypnotics for sleep.

2. Antacids–When antacids are used, the suggestions listed below (see Selection of Antacid) should be followed. Gastric emptying usually limits the duration of antacid effect to 30–60 minutes. Liquid antacids should be given at hourly intervals. Tablets are inferior to liquid antacids, since neutralizing ability depends upon very small particle size. Only if large amounts of antacid are used can any effect on the rate of healing of duodenal (but not gastric) ulcer be demonstrated.

3. Diet–Food, in the context of this discussion, is both an antacid and a stimulus to acid secretion. Food containing protein may neutralize acid for a few minutes and reduce motility, but will then increase gastric secretion and perhaps pain.

Regularity of meals is important. Interval feedings or frequent small feedings are ineffective in buffering the stomach acid. It has been shown that food, regardless of content or consistency, markedly increases gastric acidity. Certain commonsense dietary restrictions (eg, all foods known by the patient to cause distress) are an important part of management.

4. Parasympatholytics–In the discussion of the use of atropine and its congeners, it was emphasized that the acute effects of large single doses cannot be extrapolated to predict the effects of doses that are tolerated when the drugs are chronically administered. Many explanations have been offered for the possible beneficial effects of atropine—eg, that by decreasing motility it holds the antacid in the stomach for a longer period—but the beneficial effect in the chronic rather than the acute situation has yet to be demonstrated.

Acutely, the parasympatholytic drugs do appear to reduce that fraction of discomfort associated with hypermotility or pylorospasm.

5. Cimetidine (Tagamet)–The H_2-receptor antagonists reduce basal and stimulated gastric secretion. They are used to hasten the healing of peptic ulcers and can be used to prevent recurrences, although such application is more difficult. They are discussed in detail in Chapter 19.

6. Other drugs–The deleterious effects of coffee, alcohol, tobacco, aspirin, phenylbutazone, and corticosteroids on the course of some patients with a peptic ulcer have been mentioned in other chapters. These drugs should be avoided in the ulcer patient, but if avoidance is not possible, their ill effects can be minimized in some cases by simultaneous administration of an antacid.

7. Investigative drugs–Carbenoxolone (Biogastrone) is an anti-inflammatory agent related to glycyrrhizinic acid and isolated from licorice. It has a demonstrated beneficial effect on gastric but not duodenal ulcers. Side-effects are frequent owing to its aldosteronelike actions. It is still an investigational drug in the USA.

B. Other Uses: Many functional gastroduodenal upsets (heartburn, pylorospasm, etc) are treated with antacids, with good symptomatic relief. Antacids in these as in other situations are often self-prescribed and purchased without a prescription.

Hiatal hernias are treated with drugs as are peptic ulcers.

Aluminum hydroxide gel is sometimes used in large doses to reduce phosphate absorption in uremia.

Adverse Reactions

Considering the frequency with which large amounts of antacids are chronically used, they must be regarded as almost innocuous agents.

A. Change in Bowel Habits: Some patients do not find the continuous use of a single antacid acceptable, since all of them have disadvantages. Calcium carbonate is constipating; the hydrated aluminum salts are partially dried in the large intestine and result in powdery and difficult stools; and the magnesium salts by themselves may cause frequent or liquid movements. As a result, preparations that are mixtures of several antacids are more satisfactory.

Table 31–1. Some representative antacids.

	Usual Adult Dose
Aluminum hydroxide gel or tablets (Amphojel and other proprietary preparations)	1–2 tsp in ½ glass water or 1–2 tablets chewed and swallowed with ½ glass water
Aluminum hydroxide with magnesium trisilicate (Gelusil and others)	2 tablets or 1–2 tsp
Aluminum and magnesium hydroxide (Aludrox, Bidrox, Creamalin, Kolantyl, Maalox, Mylanta II, Wingel, and others)	1–2 tablets or 5–10 mL
Calcium carbonate	1–4 g of powder suspended in water or tablets chewed and swallowed

B. Alkalosis: Sodium bicarbonate used chronically will cause metabolic alkalosis.

C. Milk-Alkali Syndrome: A few cases have been reported in which systemic alkalosis from soluble antacids and a high calcium intake from milk also used in the treatment of ulcers has led to hypercalcemia and metastatic calcification, especially in the kidneys, and stone formation.

Selection of Antacid

A. Time and Frequency of Administration: The ability of an antacid to neutralize gastric acid and the duration of its effect—ie, its duration in the stomach—have been studied by gastroscopic examination and by aspirating a series of samples through a gastric tube. Most studies show a duration of action of no more than 1 hour, although it is probable that if the antacid is given within 1 hour after a meal, it may be slowly carried out of the stomach and the effect will persist for as long as 3 hours. When the treatment problem is acute, antacids are usually given hourly until the response allows a lengthening of the interval between doses.

B. Potency: No antacid exceeds calcium carbonate in its acid-neutralizing ability. Magnesium trisilicate is less potent as an antacid, but differences in potency among the various preparations are not otherwise great. The suggested doses of the common antacids (2 tsp or 2 tablets) are minimal doses.

C. Patient Acceptance: Patient preference then becomes a major factor in the choice of an antacid. Antacids are available without prescription, and most patients try several and soon develop a preference for liquid or tablet or for a preparation with a particular texture or flavor. More important, they react to the changes in bowel habits. The physician and pharmacist should cooperate in finding a preparation that does not cause an intolerable change in consistency or frequency of bowel movements or should teach the patient to use more than one preparation.

LAXATIVES

Purgation was at one time just as popular and probably just as dangerous a form of treatment as bleeding. Physicians have stopped prescribing or advising the use of purgatives, but the laity are only slowly and reluctantly giving up the idea that laxatives and enemas are an important part of general treatment for virtually all illnesses. These drugs were classified during the older period according to the intensity of their effect, and several terms persist—laxative, aperient, cathartic, purgative, "drastic"—depending upon whether the agent is mild in its action or is able to cause more frequent and liquid movements. It is probably better to avoid the old terms and to classify laxatives according to their mechanism of action. The mechanism may be simply to stimulate motility and cause defecation. However, drugs may also be given to increase the bulk of the stool or to soften it.

Pharmacologic Effects

A. Irritant or Stimulant Laxatives:

1. Castor oil–Castor oil has a distinctive and unpleasant taste. When it is hydrolyzed like other fats in the upper small intestine, irritating ricinoleic acid is liberated and acts locally to increase intestinal motility. The action of castor oil is thus prompt and is eventually exerted along the entire length of the gastrointestinal tract. By stimulating motility, it hastens its own excretion with the feces, but until this occurs it is a vigorous laxative, causing repeated movements, often with cramping.

A number of other powerful irritants such as croton oil or calomel were once used as "drastics" but are now obsolete.

2. Anthraquinone or emodin alkaloids– Cascara, senna, rhubarb, and aloes contain emodin alkaloids in the inactive form of glycosides. The active alkaloid is liberated from the glycoside after absorption, and it is then excreted into the colon. After a period of 6–8 hours (the time required for absorption and excretion), these drugs act locally on the colon to stimulate peristalsis.

3. Phenolphthalein is also a powerful stimulant of the large bowel. Some of it is absorbed, excreted through the bile, and absorbed again, and this enterohepatic cycle prolongs its activity. It is present in proprietaries and can cause a fixed drug eruption.

Bisacodyl (Dulcolax) is a synthetic compound chemically similar to phenolphthalein and similarly absorbed and excreted.

B. Bulk Laxatives: Distention is a powerful stimulus to intestinal activity, and bulk and bulk-producing substances or solutions may therefore be used to augment intestinal activity. Furthermore, what some patients refer to as constipation is actually a subjective feeling of dissatisfaction with their bowel habits; this may be relieved by increasing the bulk of the movements rather than their frequency.

1. Hydrophilic colloids–The indigestible parts

of fruits and vegetables are the obvious natural source of this material, and a diet that contains adequate amounts of these items serves the same purpose as the prepared products. Bran, agar, psyllium seed, and methylcellulose are examples of substances that form gels within the large intestine and accomplish the dual purpose of distending the colon and satisfying a need of the patient.

2. Saline cathartics or nonabsorbable salts– The volume of the intestinal contents can be kept large by the ingestion of a nonabsorbable salt. The salt will hold water in the intestine in amounts sufficient to maintain its isotonic concentration, and soft or liquid bowel movements will follow when the saline solution is carried to the terminal part of the colon. Examples of this class are magnesium sulfate (Epsom salts), magnesium citrate, and magnesium hydroxide (milk of magnesia).

C. Fecal Softeners: Here again, factors other than the number of bowel movements are involved. During illness with immobilization and dietary change, the contents of the distal colon may become desiccated, hard, or even impacted. It may be desirable to maintain a soft stool to minimize the discomfort or actual work involved in defecation. For this purpose, agents that mix with the fecal material or act as emulsifying agents are used.

Mineral oil is a commonly used example of this class. It is often referred to as a lubricant, but it softens the fecal material by becoming emulsified with it rather than acting as a lubricant in the mechanical sense. If a slight excess of mineral oil is given, some may pass the anal sphincter and soil the skin or clothing. The concern that the chronic administration of mineral oil might dissolve significant amounts of fat-soluble vitamins and prevent their absorption is entirely theoretic.

Other examples of this class are glycerin suppositories, soapy or mineral oil enemas, and detergents such as dioctyl sodium sulfosuccinate, an anionic surface active agent marketed under many names.

Clinical Uses

A. Treatment of Constipation: These drugs may be ordered by the physician to treat constipation in specific situations of brief duration—eg, they may be used to relieve the constipation that follows the use of opiate drugs or to keep the feces soft during the period following hemorrhoidectomy.

However, most of the huge amount of these drugs consumed is self-prescribed for the treatment of what the individual considers to be constipation. Some people feel that there is a normal frequency of bowel movements that must be maintained; others still feel, perhaps as a carry-over of the concept of autointoxication, that they must clean themselves out at intervals to maintain good health; and many people have a neurotic preoccupation with their bowel habits that is not concerned solely with the number of movements.

Constipation is more common among older people, in part because of restricted activity and di-

Table 31–2. Some representative laxatives.

	Usual Adult Dose
Irritant or stimulant	
Castor oil	15 mL
Emulsified castor oil (Neoloid)	2–4 tbsp
Cascara sagrada, aromatic fluid-extract	2 mL
Cascara tablets	300 mg
Bisacodyl (Dulcolax)	10–15 mg at bedtime
Bulk producers	
Milk of magnesia	15–30 mL
Sodium phosphate	4–8 g before breakfast with water
Methylcellulose	1–4 g/d
Sodium carboxymethylcellulose	3–6 g/d
Fecal softeners	
Mineral oil	15–30 mL daily
Dioctyl sodium sulfosuccinate (Colace, Doxinate, and others)	50–240 mg/d

etary factors or failure to drink enough water. However, they also tend to use more laxatives because their attitudes were formed during a period when "regular bowel habits" were felt to be important to general well-being. Explanation is undoubtedly the preferred treatment, but it is rarely accepted and laxatives are freely available without prescription.

The objection to the use of laxatives is that they may reinforce a neurotic preoccupation with bowel habits. Furthermore, the use of laxatives may become habitual, since there must be an interval following an evacuation induced by a laxative before the next movement (while the content of the colon is replenished from above). If this interval seems too long, the individual may repeat the laxative rather than wait for an unstimulated movement. This again defers the unstimulated movement and again suggests the use of a laxative, and the cycle can be repeated indefinitely.

B. Other Uses: Castor oil and cleansing enemas are frequently used in preparation for x-ray studies. The colon must be emptied prior to outlining it with a contrast medium. Gas and fecal material that might otherwise cast interfering shadows are also removed by castor oil or other laxatives prior to gallbladder studies, intravenous and retrograde urograms, and other diagnostic procedures.

Adverse Reactions

The possibility that the use of laxatives may reinforce the patient's concept of constipation as a health hazard or may establish the laxative habit has been mentioned. Cramping pain is the only other common side-effect of these drugs. The continued use of cathartics has on very rare occasions led to reversible hypokalemia or to a persistent diarrhea and hypokalemia due to damage to the colon.

Ingestion of laxatives containing oxyphenisatin, an irritant laxative related to phenolphthalein, has been associated with hepatocellular damage (chronic active hepatitis) as a hypersensitivity reaction. Oxyphenisatin has been removed from the market in the USA.

Contraindications & Cautions

Laxatives should not be used in the presence of undiagnosed abdominal pain or when the constipation is due to obstruction, including fecal impaction. Magnesium salts should not be used if renal insufficiency is present, and all but the mildest agents should be avoided during the later stages of pregnancy. The emodin alkaloids are transmitted by the nursing mother to the child.

ANTIPERISTALTIC OR ANTIDIARRHEAL DRUGS

Codeine

See Chapter 26.

Diphenoxylate

Diphenoxylate is contained in a proprietary mixture (Lomotil) used in the treatment of diarrhea. The drug is a weaker analog of meperidine and is a schedule V controlled substance. The presence of another drug (atropine) exempts the mixture from some of the rules governing narcotic prescriptions, but the mixture is not superior to codeine. The drug should be used with caution when diarrhea is caused by invasive bacteria or antibiotics and should be avoided in inflammatory bowel disease of the ulcerative type because of the possibility of inducing toxic dilatation of the colon.

Loperamide

Loperamide (Imodium), another phenylpiperidine drug, was recently introduced for the treatment of acute and chronic diarrhea. Like diphenoxylate, it is a weaker analog of meperidine and is a schedule V controlled drug. It does not contain atropine. The advantages of this drug over earlier agents, if any, remain to be determined.

A FEW ADDITIONAL DEFINITIONS

Demulcents are substances with physical properties that allow them to coat and protect and soothe a surface. Antipruritic preparations applied to the skin and cough syrups are examples. Among the gastrointestinal drugs, bismuth carbonate, bismuth subacetate, and bismuth subgallate were at one time used to coat the irritated or ulcerated gastric mucosa. They are now rarely used.

Adsorbents are colloidal substances (charcoal, clays such as kaolin, and gels such as pectin) able to adsorb undesired constituents from solution. They are used in proprietary antidiarrheal mixtures because of their presumed ability to adsorb preformed toxins responsible for some types of food poisoning.

Bitters are preparations of alkaloids or other plant products given before meals to increase appetite.

Hydrochloric acid was formerly used as replacement therapy in a few patients with achlorhydria and symptoms thought to be related thereto. The consensus now is that there is no real indication for the use of this acid.

Glutamic acid hydrochloride, which releases hydrochloric acid in the stomach, was also used in the past, but it has been withdrawn from the market.

A **carminative** is a volatile oil (in drug, liqueur, or candy) that is able to relieve the feeling of discomfort and distention after eating by aiding in eructation or the movement of gas from the stomach. Some patients with serious diseases do have their food intake limited by discomfort of this kind, and some physicians still prescribe a few drops of oil of peppermint in a small glass of warm water. Studies on the response of the gastroesophageal sphincter provide some objective basis for the practice.

A **cholagogue** is a drug or procedure that causes the gallbladder to contract and empty. The fatty meal used after the gallbladder is filled with a contrast medium to demonstrate that it empties or "functions" is an example—as is, of course, the average meal, which causes the release of 8 g of bile salts into the intestine. Magnesium sulfate was instilled into the duodenum in the past and the duodenal contents subsequently aspirated for study.

Choleretics are drugs that increase the total flow of bile, with a decrease in viscosity of the bile. Salts of bile acids (hog and ox bile extracts) do have this effect, but indications for their use have not been established. When they are used, **dehydrocholic acid** is preferred. It has a bitter taste and does have established use in measuring arm-to-tongue circulation time. In this application, 5 mL of a 20% solution of **sodium dehydrocholate (Decholin Sodium** and other names) are rapidly injected into an antecubital vein. Normally, the subject will report a bitter taste within 10–16 seconds. **Florantyrone (Zanchol)** is a synthetic drug structurally unrelated to the bile salts, but it is also a choleretic.

CHENODEOXYCHOLIC ACID
(Chenic Acid)

Chenodeoxycholic acid (chenic acid, CDCA) offers the prospect of nonsurgical treatment for one type of cholelithiasis. It is one of the 3 common bile acids in humans. (The structure of cholic acid is shown in Fig 15–2. Chenic acid lacks the hydroxyl on C12.)

Cholesterol is held in suspension in the bile by micelles of bile acids and lecithin. In patients with cholesterol stones or a genetic predisposition to stone formation, there is a reduction in the amount of bile salts that appear in the bile each day and a reduction in the ratio of bile salts and lecithin to cholesterol in bile recovered from the duodenum. Chenic acid appears in the bile after oral administration and corrects the disordered ratio. Given for periods of 6 months or longer, it has dissolved or reduced the size of small (multiple) radiolucent gallstones in patients in whom bile reaches the gallbladder—ie, those in whom the gallbladder can be seen on x-ray.

In a population known to be susceptible to gallstone formation, chenic acid alters the properties of "lithogenic" bile and will prevent the precipitation of cholesterol from its supersaturated solution in bile.

The supply of chenic acid is limited, and it remains an investigational drug.

PANCREATIN

Lipolytic and proteolytic enzymes must be given as replacement therapy to patients with pancreatic (exocrine) insufficiency.

Pancreatin is an alcoholic extract of hog pancreas standardized for amylase and trypsin activity. No assay for lipase is established, and the activity of the official preparation is variable.

Pancrelipase (Cotazym), a lipase-enriched pancreatin, and Viokase, which consists of desiccated gland rather than an extract, are more active than the official preparation. Problems of standardization, size

and frequency of dose, and inactivation by gastric acid persist. The most favorable effects on lipid and nitrogen absorption have been achieved when gastric acid secretion is reduced by cimetidine.

LACTULOSE (CEPHULAC)

Lactulose is a synthetic disaccharide (galactose-fructose) that is not digested and absorbed as, for example, lactose (galactose-glucose) is.

It is used to lower blood ammonia levels during chronic hepatic failure. The ammonia formed by bacterial metabolism in the colon ordinarily enters the portal circulation and is converted by the liver to ammonia. In the presence of portal obstruction by cirrhosis, portal blood and ammonia enter the systemic circulation and cause symptoms (portosystemic encephalopathy).

Lactulose is degraded by bacteria in the colon to lactic, acetic, and other acids. It is assumed that in the resulting acid medium, ammonia is converted to nonabsorbed ammonium ion. However, the effect on colon transport of the osmotic cathartic may be the important effect, or the bacterial flora may be modified.

Lactulose is as effective as neomycin and can be combined with it.

• • •

References

Antacids

Brown P & others: Double-blind trial of carbenoxolone sodium capsules in duodenal ulcer therapy, based on endoscopic diagnosis and follow-up. Br Med J 3:661, 1972.

Cutler P, Welch RW: Ulcer therapy: Goodbye to tradition. Curr Prescribing 3:84, 1977.

Feldman M & others: Effect of low-dose propantheline on food-stimulated acid secretion. N Engl J Med 297:1427, 1977.

Fordtran JS: Acid secretion and peptic ulcer. In: *Gastrointestinal Disease: Pathophysiology-Diagnosis-Management*. Sleisinger MH, Fordtran JS (editors). Saunders, 1973.

Fordtran JS: Placebos, antacids and cimetidine for duodenal ulcer. N Engl J Med 298:1081, 1978.

Fordtran JS & others: In vivo and in vitro evaluation of liquid antacids. N Engl J Med 288:923, 1973.

Hastings PR & others: Antacid prophylaxis of bleeding in the critically ill. N Engl J Med 298:1041, 1978.

Hollander D, Harlan J: Antacids vs placebos in peptic ulcer therapy. JAMA 226:1181, 1973.

Kaehny WD, Hegg AP, Alfrey AC: Gastrointestinal absorption of aluminum from aluminum-containing antacids. N Engl J Med 296:1389, 1977.

Kirsner JB: Symposium: Clinical drug evaluation. Part XIII. Problems in the evaluation of gastrointestinal drugs. Clin Pharmacol Ther 3:510, 1962.

McMillan DE, Freeman RB: The milk-alkali syndrome: A study of the acute disorder with comments on the development of the chronic condition. Medicine 44:485, 1965.

Peterson WL & others: Healing of duodenal ulcer with an antacid regimen. N Engl J Med 297:341, 1977.

Laxatives

Binder HJ, Donowitz M: A new look at laxative action. Gastroenterology 69:1001, 1975.

Davidson M, Kugler MM, Bauer CH: Diagnosis and management in children with severe and protracted constipation and obstipation. J Pediatr 62:261, 1963.

Rawson MD: Cathartic colon. Lancet 1:1121, 1966.

Reynolds TB, Peters RL, Yamada S: Chronic active and lupoid hepatitis caused by a laxative, oxyphenisatin. N Engl J Med 285:813, 1971.

Smith B: Effect of irritant purgatives on the myenteric plexus in man and the mouse. Gut 9:139, 1968.

Others

Chenic acid for gall stones. (Leading article.) Br Med J 2:847, 1978.

Conn HO & others: Comparison of lactulose and neomycin in the treatment of chronic portal-systemic encephalopathy. Gastroenterology 72:573, 1977.

DiMagno EP & others: Fate of orally ingested enzymes in pancreatic insufficiency. N Engl J Med 296:1318, 1977.

Fordtran JS, Grossman MI: Third symposium on histamine H_2-receptor antagonists: Clinical results with cimetidine. Gastroenterology 74:338, 1978.

Graham DY: Enzyme replacement therapy of exocrine pancreatic insufficiency in man. N Engl J Med 296:1314, 1977.

Iser JH: Chenodeoxycholic acid treatment of gallstones. N Engl J Med 293:378, 1975.

Loperamide for diarrhea. Med Lett Drugs Ther 19:73, 1977.

Maudgal DP & others: Low-cholesterol diet: Enhancement of effect of CDCA in patients with gall stones. Br Med J 2:851, 1978.

Meyer JH: The ins and outs of oral pancreatic enzymes. N Engl J Med 296:1347, 1977.

Regan PT & others: Comparative effects of antacids, cimetidine and enteric coating on the therapeutic response to oral enzymes in severe pancreatic insufficiency. N Engl J Med 297:854, 1977.

Sigmund CJ, McNally EF: The action of a carminative on the lower esophageal sphincter. Gastroenterology 56:13, 1969.

Sollmann T: *A Manual of Pharmacology*, 8th ed. Saunders, 1957.

32 | Respiratory Drugs

Many drugs that act either primarily or incidentally on the respiratory tract or on tissue respiration are discussed in other chapters, where their inclusion is determined by their mechanism of action (eg, the bronchodilators are discussed with the sympathomimetic agents). A few therapeutic agents that escape other classification are included in this chapter—ie, oxygen, expectorants, and nonnarcotic cough remedies.

OXYGEN THERAPY & ASSISTED VENTILATION

In practice, the consideration of oxygen as a therapeutic agent should not be dissociated from methods for maintaining adequate ventilation. Ventilatory assistance is needed when neural drive, muscle power, or thoracic mechanics are inadequate. Many of these situations will require the simultaneous application of mechanical assistance and oxygen administration—eg, central respiratory depression due to drugs, severe shock, and acute and chronic pulmonary disease. The use of oxygen requires an adequate airway—maintained, if necessary, by tracheal intubation or tracheostomy—and a positive pressure device that can send pulses of oxygen to the tube or mask if necessary.

Technic of Administration
The method of administering oxygen is selected from among the following depending upon the concentration desired and the need for ventilatory assistance.

Oxygen should always be administered by bubbling through water before it is delivered to the patient's airway.

A. Tent: Concentrations of 25–50% oxygen can be reached, depending upon the rate of inflow of oxygen and the permeability of the material of the tent.

B. Head Tents or Hoods: (50–80% oxygen concentration.) These are smaller than tents and can be made of less permeable material.

C. Nasal Catheter or Cannula (Prongs): (40–60% oxygen concentration.) This technic is adequate

for most purposes and is more readily accepted by the patient than the tent or mask.

D. Mask: (80–100% concentration.) Orofacial or oronasal masks can be used with a positive pressure device. Venturi masks, which permit the controlled admixture of room air to the oxygen stream, allow the adjustment of oxygen content over a wide range.

E. Endotracheal Tube: 80–100% concentrations can be delivered by this method.

F. Hyperbaric Oxygen: When the necessary equipment is available, oxygen can be given under pressures greater than 1 atmosphere. This special technic is discussed separately below.

Mechanism of Action
The question is not how oxygen acts but how can concentrations greater than that in air exert a beneficial effect. Room air contains 20.9% oxygen, which exerts a partial pressure of 159 mm Hg in inspired air. The P_{O_2} in the alveoli is about 100 mm Hg, and there is a small (6 mm Hg) gradient across the alveolar membrane, so that the P_{O_2} in arterial blood is about 90 mm Hg. Under this usual condition, hemoglobin is almost completely (96%) saturated with oxygen. How oxygen can exert a beneficial effect will depend upon the cause of the hypoxia. When hemoglobin is already nearly saturated—ie, except in anoxic anoxia—it can act only through the increase of dissolved oxygen from 0.3 to 2 mL/dL.

Clinical Uses
A. Anoxic Anoxia:

1. Inadequate ventilation–When respiratory mechanics are inadequate and arterial blood is not completely saturated during its course through the pulmonary circulation, increasing the concentration of oxygen in the ambient air can increase the P_{O_2} in the alveoli and increase the hemoglobin saturation in arterial blood. The use of oxygen will not reduce the P_{CO_2}; in fact, the respiratory depressant effect of oxygen may increase it slightly. Thus, ventilatory assistance, even if with room air, may be much more rational.

2. Interference with diffusion–States that interfere with the transfer of oxygen across the alveolar membrane result in incomplete saturation of arterial blood. Increasing the concentration of oxygen in the inspired air will increase the alveolar P_{O_2} and increase the gradient across the alveolar membrane. Changing from room air to 100% oxygen, for example, will change the P_{O_2} in the alveoli from 100 mm Hg to 670 mm Hg.

3. Right-to-left shunts–When desaturated blood is shunted into the arterial side of the circulation, respiration is maintained or stimulated. Because the fraction of the blood flow that goes through the lungs is already well oxygenated, little is gained by the use of oxygen. However, the small increase in oxygen in solution may be useful.

4. Ventilation-perfusion abnormalities–In some conditions, of which asthma is the most common example, ventilation of the alveoli is not uniform throughout the lung. The blood that continues to perfuse the nonventilated alveoli will not be oxygenated, and, in effect, a right-to-left shunt is established. This type of shunt is benefited by oxygen use.

B. Anemic Anoxia: Anoxia due to a decrease in the amount of hemoglobin available to transport oxygen is not often treated with oxygen. An exception is intoxication with carbon monoxide, which forms carboxyhemoglobin that cannot transport oxygen. The benefits of oxygen use are due to the increase in the amount of dissolved oxygen and to the dissociation of carboxyhemoglobin brought about by the increased oxygen tension.

C. Stagnant Anoxia: Local circulatory changes can lead to a decrease in the absolute amount of oxygen available to an area. High concentrations of oxygen (but not those achieved in tents) have a demonstrable effect on the pain of myocardial infarction. Severe shock is probably also benefited.

D. Histotoxic Anoxia: Theoretically, increasing the partial pressure of oxygen in the blood—and presumably at the cristae of the mitochondria, where oxygen reduction takes place—should have no effect on the poisoned cellular functions. Actually, oxygen is clearly useful in the treatment of poisoning by cyanide, which exerts its lethal effect by the inactivation of cytochrome oxidase it causes.

Adverse Reactions

A. Respiratory Depression: After a long period of respiratory insufficiency with chronic hypercarbia and hypoxia, respiration may be maintained by the stimulus of hypoxia on peripheral chemoreceptors rather than by the effect of CO_2. Unless ventilation is assisted, administration of oxygen to a patient in this situation could lead to respiratory depression with further accumulation of CO_2.

When respiratory failure is being treated with oxygen, sedatives and narcotics should not be used unless a means of ventilating the patient is available.

B. Respiratory Tract Irritation: The use of oxygen can lead to irritation of the nose, pharynx, and trachea, with a slight cough and substernal soreness. Occurrence of the symptoms depends upon the concentration of oxygen and the duration of exposure. For example, 100% oxygen at a pressure of 1 atmosphere will produce symptoms in less than a day. If the concentration is kept below 60%, the reaction does not occur.

With the above respiratory tract irritation, a decrease in vital capacity may be seen, but no other signs of pulmonary damage have been established.

C. Retrolental Fibroplasia: An epidemic of retrolental fibroplasia occurred between 1946 and 1954 coincident with the increased use in nurseries of oxygen in high concentrations. This condition of bilateral, destructive retinal proliferation affects premature infants. During this period, 77% of the cases of blindness in preschool children in California were due to retrolental fibroplasia.

To avoid all but sporadic cases, oxygen should be used only if needed and the concentration should not exceed 40% except for brief periods as necessary. In premature nurseries, the concentration should actually be determined rather than calculated from flow rates.

Preparations

Medical or USP oxygen is available in cylinders that by convention are painted green. Commercial or welding oxygen is equally pure and may be used if necessary.

Hyperbaric Oxygen

Oxygen can be provided under pressures as high as 3 atmospheres if an appropriate chamber is available. The patient (and preferably the physician or attendant also) is placed in a chamber that can be pressurized with oxygen itself or can be pressurized with air and the subject given oxygen at high pressure by mask.

At 3 atmospheres pressure and 100% oxygen, enough oxygen is dissolved in the blood (6 mL/dL) to meet the needs of the tissues without any desaturating of hemoglobin.

Oxygen toxicity is, of course, increased at the higher pressures, and exposure times must be limited to protect the lungs, retinas, and central nervous system. Fifty percent of subjects exposed to oxygen at 2 atmospheres pressure will show a decrease in vital capacity after 4 hours. Continued exposure can lead to pulmonary consolidation. Vasoconstriction is marked, and the oxygen supply to many tissues is reduced. At pressures above 3 atmospheres, convulsions occur.

Oxygen at high pressure is effective in the treatment of carbon monoxide posioning and of gas gangrene if it is of a diffuse type with spreading muscle necroses uncontrollable by penicillin. Other suggested applications are still being evaluated, including shock, anaerobic infections, and chronic osteomyelitis.

ANTITUSSIVE DRUGS

Coughing is a reflex that may be initiated by irritation occurring from the pharynx to the deepest level of the respiratory tract. It may be initiated by increased secretion or irritation due to trivial or serious disease. Coughing is useful to the extent that it clears the respiratory tract of accumulated secretions or protects it from a noxious environment. In most cases, however, it can be suppressed without danger to the patient, and cough suppressant drugs are widely used to decrease discomfort and provide rest.

Treatment designed to provide symptomatic relief utilizes not only cough suppressants but also expectorants—ie, drugs that increase and liquefy bronchial secretions—and bronchodilators, usually dispensed in a demulcent vehicle that is itself active.

The antitussive drugs or cough suppressants act, with one possible exception, on the central connections of the cough reflex in the brain stem. These agents can be divided into the narcotic drugs and some nonnarcotic agents of lesser potency.

Problems of Clinical Evaluation

It is not possible to present an evaluation of the clinical efficacy of antitussive drugs that will be accepted as a consensus even by the few investigators who have worked in the area.

The drugs have been evaluated in animals on cough generated by mechanical or electrical stimulation or by chemical irritation achieved by adding ammonia or acid to inhaled air. The drugs listed below are active in this form of testing; however, in the absence of correlation with clinical effectiveness, the results are of doubtful significance.

The same conclusion applies to testing on experimental cough in humans. The significance of drug effects on cough stimulated by inhalation of aerosols containing citric acid or ammonia is vitiated by the results of trials in humans with cough due to some disease process.

Such trials have in some cases objectified the effect of antitussive drugs by recording the number and intensity of the coughs and have also collected patient evaluations for comparison with objective measurements or the records of observers.

The results of clinical trials are conflicting. It appears, however, that cough, like pain and many other symptoms, has a subjective component. Patient evaluation of an antitussive drug may be more favorable than would be predicted by the objective effects. The narcotic drugs are probably effective both in reducing cough and in altering the patient's reaction to it. The effectiveness of the nonnarcotic drugs is debatable but at best limited.

Narcotics as Cough Suppressants

The effectiveness of the narcotics as cough suppressants generally parallels their potency as analgesics and their potential for misuse. Codeine, in doses of 7.5 or 15 mg, is usually adequate, and the danger of abuse is minimal. Side-effects, especially constipation, do occur. Dextromethorphan (see Chapter 26) is a very weak analgesic not subject to the prescription regulations governing narcotics; in fact, it

is sold without prescription as an ingredient of many cough medicines. It is probably active but much less so than codeine.

Nonnarcotic Antitussives

The nonnarcotic cough suppressants are a diverse group pharmacologically. The following list ignores a few drugs that have practically, if not legally, disappeared from the market.

A. Peripherally Acting: Benzonatate (Tessalon) is a local anesthetic of the amide type related to tetracaine (see Chapter 22). In animals given the drug parenterally, it has been shown to reduce activity from pulmonary stretch receptors, and its antitussive activity is therefore assumed to be due to a peripheral rather than a central action. The clinical studies available do not permit an evaluation of its usefulness. The usual dosage is 100 mg as often as 6 times daily.

B. Centrally Acting: It is claimed that the following drugs are active by themselves, and they are available as such. Their wide use, however, is due to their incorporation into a number of popular prescription and nonprescription proprietary mixtures.

1. Caramiphen is the ethanedisulfonate salt of the drug also dispensed as an antiparkinson agent as the hydrochloride (Panparnit). Atropinelike side-effects may occur.

2. Carbetapentane is also anticholinergic. Like other synthetic substitutes for atropine, it is a potent local anesthetic.

3. Noscapine or narcotine is a benzylisoquinoline alkaloid isolated from opium and comparable to papaverine (Fig 26–2). It is not a narcotic in any sense. When used by itself, the usual dose is 15–30 mg.

EXPECTORANTS

Expectorants are drugs (or procedures) that increase the amount of and liquefy bronchial secretions. They thus make it easier for the patient to move secretions toward the mouth and dispose of them. In asthma or other obstructive pulmonary disease, they are useful to the extent that obstruction is due to secretions rather than to bronchiolar obstruction.

In the past, a complex classification of expectorants was used. Cough suppressants were included, and some of the terminology was confusing. These terms can now be ignored.

Water, in the form of moisture in a closed room or in the form of inhaled steam or aerosol, dilutes and liquefies respiratory tract secretions. It has the great advantage of acting rapidly. Adequate hydration—ie, adequate intake—is also useful. Some clinicians feel that water is an excellent expectorant, particularly in bronchial asthma, where large amounts of water are lost by the labored breathing. Water, 300–500 mL per hour, may be advisable when fluid loss is great and the sputum is very viscous.

The common drugs used as expectorants all act reflexly by acting as gastric irritants.

Potassium Iodide

The actions of iodide related to thyroid function are discussed in Chapter 34.

In animal and human studies, potassium iodide is active in increasing the volume and decreasing the viscosity not only of the secretion of the bronchial glands but also of salivary, nasal, and lacrimal secretions. The action is due at least in part to reflex secretion generated by gastric irritation. Such irritation can be effective even though frank nausea does not occur.

Even though iodides have been shown to act through the gastric reflex, they either have an additional effect or act after absorption, since they do not lose their effectiveness when given as enteric-coated tablets.

The use of potassium iodide can lead to an unpleasant awareness of hypersecretion in the eyes, nose, and mouth. Sneezing and conjunctival irritation may lead to a condition closely resembling the common cold. A brassy taste may be noted. Parotid swelling may occur, and an acneiform skin rash may appear. These actions are dose-related rather than allergic. Treatment consists of discontinuing use of the drug. Potassium iodide, unlike the bromides, is rapidly excreted.

The dosage of potassium iodide is 0.3 g 3–4 times daily. It may be made up as saturated solutions (SSKI) and dispensed in a dosage of 10 drops 3 times daily.

Ammonium Chloride

Ammonium chloride and other ammonium salts are demonstrably active as expectorants, but less so than potassium iodide. Ammonium chloride, like potassium iodide, acts by causing gastric irritation. Unlike potassium iodide, however, when it is used as an expectorant it must not be given as an enteric-coated tablet. (Such a preparation is available and was used in conjunction with diuretics.)

An ammonium chloride syrup is available, but the drug is most often used in mixtures.

Syrup of Ipecac

Ipecac is undoubtedly effective as an expectorant, but nausea is a common side-effect. It is included in some cough mixtures. If it is used—eg, by an asthmatic who cannot tolerate potassium iodide—the dose of the syrup is 0.5 mL 4 times daily.

Guaifenesin (Glyceryl Guaiacolate)

Guaifenesin is not used by itself but is incorporated into many cough syrups. It is much less effective than any of the above.

DRUG TREATMENT OF ASTHMA

Asthma can be subdivided on etiologic grounds into 2 types. "Extrinsic asthma" is precipitated by inhalant allergens that cause a histamine release from mast cells following their combination with specific IgE. The etiologic basis of "intrinsic asthma" is not known, but a state of hyperreactive airways is a feature of this type of asthma. The pathophysiologic sequence of events is common to both types of asthma and can be summarized as follows: the afferent arc of the vagal bronchoconstrictor reflex arises in the rapidly adapting bronchiolar irritant receptors. The efferent vagal innervation terminates in the bronchial muscle and submucosal glands. Early in the asthmatic attack, the important factor is bronchoconstriction; with time, inspissated mucus plugs and inflammatory cellular infiltrates assume greater importance.

Therapy of asthma is directed at the pathophysiologic factors listed above. Beta-adrenergic agonists and theophylline and its derivatives are bronchodilators and are used to reverse the acute early bronchospasm. Corticosteroids are used to reverse the inflammatory response that follows if the initial bronchoconstriction is not reversed.

Beta-Adrenergic Agonists

Metaproterenol is effective in dosages of 10–20 mg every 6 hours. It reaches its peak effect within 1 hour, and the duration of action is 4–6 hours. Another effective drug is terbutaline, with a recommended dose of 5 mg every 6 hours. Peak activity is reached within 1 hour and lasts 4–6 hours. Albuterol is a very effective beta-adrenergic agonist not yet available in the USA. At the recommended dose of 2–6 mg, a clinical effect is evident in 15 minutes, the peak effect in 1 hour, and the duration of action is 4–6 hours. The major side-effect of these drugs is tremor, which can be controlled by reduction of the dosage.

An alternative method of delivery of the beta-adrenergic agonists for treatment of asthma is in the aerosolized form. Isoproterenol, 250 μg; isoetharine, 640 μg; metaproterenol, 1300 μg; or albuterol (not available in the USA), 100–200 μg—all at 4-hour intervals—are very effective at reversing the acute bronchospastic episode.

Theophylline drugs in dosages of 400–800 mg of anhydrous equivalent may also be used as primary bronchodilator drugs. The optimal plasma level of theophylline is 10–20 μg/mL. The earliest side-effects of theophylline intoxication are nausea and vomiting. Higher plasma levels can precipitate cardiac arrhythmias and seizures. Therefore, close monitoring of theophylline plasma levels, especially when the drug is administered by the intravenous route, is mandatory. Beta-adrenergic agonists act synergistically with aminophylline and may be used to supplement aminophylline.

Corticosteroids

When the bronchospastic episode has progressed to the inflammatory stage and secretion of thick mucus causes inspissation of mucus plugs in the bronchioles, sympathomimetic drugs no longer can reverse the process. Addition of corticosteroids then becomes necessary. The route, dosages, and regimen of drug administration depend on the severity of the disease and will be discussed below.

CROMOLYN SODIUM

Chemistry

Cromolyn (disodium cromoglycate, Aarane, Intal) is a bis-chromone, a synthetic substance related to khellin, a chromone plant product that is a smooth muscle relaxant in the laboratory but was not useful clinically.

Pharmacokinetics

Cromolyn is a water-soluble substance that is effective in animals after injection but is given to humans only by inhalation or by topical application to the nasal mucosa. After inhalation, about 5% of the dose is absorbed and excreted unchanged in the urine. The balance is deposited on mucous membranes and swallowed and appears in the feces. The chemical half-life is about 1 hour, but some of the biologic effects seem to persist for several weeks.

Pharmacologic Actions

A. Mechanism of Action: The effect of cromolyn that is assumed to underlie its action in the treatment of asthma is its ability to prevent mast cell degranulation and the release of the mediators (histamine, slow-reacting substance, and, in some animals, serotonin) of the anaphylactic type of immediate allergic reactions. Neither the fixation of antibody (both IgE and IgA) to the cell surface nor the antibody-antigen combination is prevented. Histamine release by direct liberators such as dextran or compound 48/80 is also prevented, and passive cutaneous anaphylaxis is inhibited.

B. Effects: The effects of cromolyn are limited to those just described. The drug is not an antihistamine, and no effects on isolated smooth muscle are seen.

Clinical Uses

A. Adjunct in Prevention of Asthmatic Attacks: The only clinical use of this drug is in prevention of asthmatic episodes. Therefore, only patients who are clinically stable and free of wheezing will benefit from it. A few patients with asthma that is clearly extrinsic receive benefit from cromolyn alone, but the effect of the drug used alone is generally small and inconsistent. Cromolyn is used if control of asthma is inadequate with other drugs—ie, it is usually added to theophylline and steroids. Effectiveness can be

measured by symptomatic improvement or a reduction in the amounts of corticosteroid required. Objective measurements—eg, forced expiratory volumes—do not always improve as much. The current generalization is that 50% of adults and as many as 85% of children will benefit from the addition of cromolyn to their regimen. The chances of benefiting from cromolyn are the same with extrinsic asthma—ie, clear hypersensitivity to an identifiable or seasonal allergen—and with intrinsic asthma.

B. Other Uses: If cromolyn acts through the suggested mechanism, it should have wider usefulness. A powder for nasal insufflation in the treatment of allergic rhinitis is marketed in Great Britain, but the evidence for its usefulness is scant.

Adverse Reactions

Inhalation of the fine powder occasionally causes increased bronchospasm and throat irritation.

Dosages

The initial dosage is a capsule 4 times each day. Chronic use is very expensive (each capsule currently costs 17 cents at wholesale).

MANAGEMENT OF ASTHMA

Mild Asthma

This type of asthma can be managed by either oral beta-adrenergic agonists (metaproterenol, terbutaline, albuterol) or aerosolized beta-adrenergic agonists (isoproterenol, metaproterenol, isoetharine, albuterol). Theophylline can serve as a primary drug in the management of mild asthma, or it can be used as a back-up drug if beta-adrenergic agonists fail to reverse the bronchospasm. Sometimes a combination of a beta-adrenergic agonist and theophylline may become necessary.

Moderate Chronic Asthma

Management is with oral beta-adrenergic agonists, either alone or in combination with theophylline. Occasionally, when symptoms cannot be controlled with the combination of oral beta-adrenergic agonists and theophylline, short courses of corticosteroids may have to be added. A typical regimen is prednisone, 50 mg daily, or an equivalent dose of another corticosteroid (eg, hydrocortisone) for 3–4 days, followed by rapid tapering and discontinuation in 5–7 days.

Severe Chronic Asthma

If a combination of oral beta-adrenergic agonists and theophylline fails to control the symptoms, long-term corticosteroid therapy is indicated. The initial dose can range up to 80 mg of prednisone (or its equivalent) and should be tapered cautiously to the lowest possible dose. It has been suggested that the criteria for dosage of corticosteroids should be suppression of total eosinophil count below $50/\mu L$ and stabilization of normal pulmonary function. In order to minimize suppression of the hypothalamic-pituitary-adrenal axis, an attempt should be made to switch to alternate-day therapy. This can be accomplished by doubling the daily dose and administering the drug on alternative mornings, between 7 and 8 AM.

Corticosteroids can also be given in aerosol form, but only after the patient has been stabilized and the oral corticosteroid has been tapered to its lowest effective dose. Use of aerosolized corticosteroids will reduce the required dose of oral agents, and in many cases it may even completely replace them in the therapeutic regimen. A typical daily dose of beclomethasone dipropionate is 1200 μg. The major adverse effect of this drug is localized oropharyngeal infection *(Candida albicans, Aspergillus niger)*, which can be minimized by thoroughly rinsing the mouth after each administration.

Acute Asthma

Parenteral treatment is required. An aqueous 1:1000 solution of epinephrine, 0.3 mL, is given subcutaneously or intramuscularly. This can be repeated at intervals of 30–60 minutes. *Epinephrine should not be employed in adults over 50 years of age.* A sub-cutaneous injection of 0.2 mL of Sus-Phrine—a micronized suspension of epinephrine—can be given every 6 hours. Terbutaline can also be given subcutaneously in a dosage of 0.25 mg every 4 hours.

If no relief of bronchospasm occurs within 30–60 minutes or if the patient's bronchospasm is severe, intravenous aminophylline is started. The loading dose is 5.6 mg/kg, followed by continuous infusion of 0.5–0.9 mg/kg/h. A "safe" rate of infusion is 180 mg/6 h in a 60-kg adult who is otherwise normal. However, in patients with congestive heart failure, liver disease, or pulmonary emphysema, the maintenance dose should be halved, since metabolism of the drug is impaired. On the other hand, cigarette smokers require higher maintenance doses because of enhanced metabolism. In any event, close monitoring of theophylline plasma levels is mandatory.

If intravenous aminophylline fails to reverse the course of the disease, intravenous corticosteroids should be given. A typical regimen is 100–200 mg of hydrocortisone every 4–6 hours or 20–40 mg of methylprednisolone every 4–6 hours. With clinical improvement, intravenous corticosteroids should be tapered, switched to the oral drug, and then cautiously tapered as described above to the lowest dose that maintains good pulmonary function.

● ● ●

References

Oxygen

Pontoppidan HB & others: Acute respiratory failure in the adult. (3 parts.) N Engl J Med 287:690, 743, 799, 1972.

Springer RR, Vazquez G, Stevens PM: The effects of continuous positive pressure breathing on survival of patients with refractory hypoxemia. Am Rev Respir Dis 113:156, 1976.

Thomas HM & others: The oxyhemoglobin dissociation curve in health and disease. Am J Med 57:331, 1974.

Antitussive Agents

Bickerman HA: Clinical pharmacology of antitussive agents. Clin Pharmacol Ther 3:353, 1962.

Expectorants

Beckman H: Expectorants. JAMA 167:1638, 1958.

Asthma

Bergner RK, Bergner A: Rational asthma therapy for the outpatient. JAMA 235:288, 1976.

Intravenous aminophylline: A cautionary note. (Editorial.) Lancet 1:746, 1980.

Webb-Johnson DC, Andrews JL Jr: Drug therapy: Bronchodilator therapy. (2 parts.) N Engl J Med 297:758, 1977.

Cromolyn

Bernstein IL & others: A controlled study of cromolyn sodium sponsored by the Drug Committee of the American Academy of Allergy. J Allergy Clin Immunol 50:4, 1972.

Hyde JS, Isenberg PD, Floro LD: Short- and long-term prophylaxis with cromolyn sodium in chronic asthma. Chest 63:875, 1973.

Sodium cromoglycate in chronic asthma: Northern General Hospital, Brampton Hospital, and Medical Research Council collaborative trial. Br Med J 1:361, 1976.

Part V. Endocrine Drugs

33 | The Hormones

This section of the book deals with a chemically, physiologically, and therapeutically diverse group of compounds called hormones. They are the biologically active agents of a single organ system, the natural products of the glands of internal secretion released directly into the circulation to act at distant sites. Along with the nervous system, they are responsible for the integration of the many different processes that allow a complicated organism to function as a unit. They are similar to catalysts in that they are not destroyed in the process of affecting cellular function and serve to control the rate at which functions occur. Furthermore, their presence in proper amounts is required for normal function.

Hormones are used to replace a deficiency of those produced endogenously or to otherwise modify endocrine and metabolic abnormalities. They are also employed in tests of endocrine function or to evaluate the response to hormones. Therefore, a somewhat more detailed description of the normal (physiologic) role of hormones as well as of the disease states produced by a deficiency or by an excess of hormones is required in order to provide an understanding of hormonal therapy.

The greatest use of some of these agents, however, is as therapeutic agents in the treatment of nonendocrine disorders by taking advantage of special physiologic or pharmacologic effects.

A large number of compounds with properties identical or similar to the native hormones have been synthesized. In many instances these compounds differ sufficiently from the human product to provide special advantage in any given patient if the differences are appreciated.

Excessive amounts of a hormone may lead to serious disturbances. Such disorders may be the result of the therapeutic use of the hormone or may result from endogenous overproduction due to glandular hypertrophy, hyperplasia, or hormone-producing tumors. The naturally occurring states are often treated surgically by excision of glandular tissue or tumors producing the hormones. However, an increasing number of medicinal compounds are becoming available for the treatment of such disturbances. Some are competitive inhibitors of the hormones and interfere with their action at the target cell; others interfere with their synthesis or release.

MECHANISMS OF ACTION

The means by which hormones exert their effects are the subject of intensive research. Several important kinds of effects have been found at the cellular and subcellular level. Some of these effects or actions are common to several hormones, and some hormones, if not all, act through more than one of the known mechanisms. In many instances, the specificity of hormone action depends upon where rather than how the hormone acts.

Steroid Hormones

Steroid hormones such as corticosteroids, estrogens, androgens, progesterone, and vitamin D enter the cell from the circulation. It is not known whether this is by passive diffusion or active transport. Once in the cell, the steroids bind to specific protein molecules called hormone receptors. This binding forms an active complex that is translocated to the nucleus, where it binds to the genome of the cell and is then able to regulate transcription of specific genes. The target cell responds by increasing the synthesis of specific messenger RNA. The messenger RNA thus formed leaves the nucleus, enters the cytoplasm, and stimulates protein synthesis. A few examples are given in Table 33–1, and the process is summarized in Fig 33–1.

Steroid hormones have also been shown to have effects that are not mediated by this pathway but that result from direct effects on cell membranes or cytoplasmic processes.

Thyroid Hormones

Thyroid hormones also act on the genome. The receptors mediating this affect are found in the nucleus. Thyroid hormone readily enters the cell and reaches the nucleus to bind to these receptors, forming

Table 33–1. Specific proteins induced by steroid hormones.

Hormone	Tissue	Protein
Estrogen	Rat pituitary	Prolactin
Progesterone	Rabbit uterus	Uteroglobin
Androgen	Rat liver	Alpha$_2$-globulin
Glucocorticoids	Rat liver	Tyrosine aminotransferase

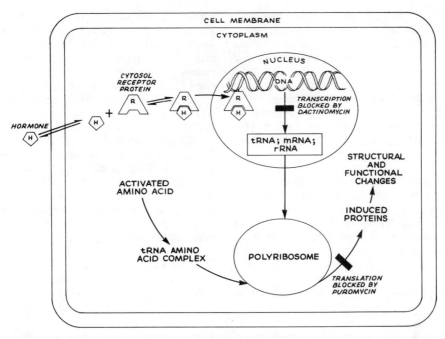

Figure 33 –1. Mechanism of steroid hormone action on protein synthesis. The hormone enters the cell and combines with a receptor in the cytoplasm to generate an active complex that enters the nucleus and interacts with the chromatin to increase messenger RNA (mRNA) and ribosomal RNA (rRNA) (transcription), which in turn leads to the induction of protein synthesis (translation).

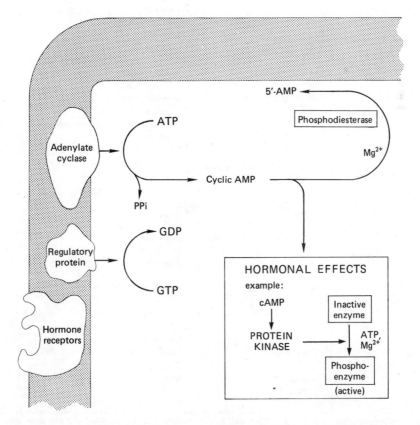

Figure 33 –2. A mechanism of action of hormones that activate adenylate cyclase.

a complex which then binds to chromatin. This reaction is followed by the appearance of specific messenger RNAs, indicating that the nuclear action of the complex is similar to that described above for steroid hormones.

Extranuclear binding to membrane, cytoplasmic and mitochondrial fractions, and the effects on amino acid transport not dependent on protein synthesis all suggest that there are other mechanisms of action of the thyroid hormones not mediated by the nuclear receptors.

Catecholamine & Peptide Hormone Receptors

The receptors for catecholamines and the peptide hormones are mainly protein, but they may contain carbohydrate and lipid components. They are found on the cell surface in the cell membrane. Binding of the hormone to the receptor initiates a series of events that result in the changes in cellular activity produced by the hormone.

Many of these hormones initiate their effects on the cell by activating the enzyme adenylate cyclase. This enzyme is commonly called a "second messenger" (Table 33–2). When these hormones bind to their specific receptors, another protein linked to guanosine triphosphate (GTP) then couples the activated receptor to adenylate cyclase (Fig 33–2).

Adenylate cyclase stimulates the conversion of ATP to cAMP (Fig 33–2). In many tissues, cAMP activates protein kinases, which in turn catalyze the transfer of phosphate from ATP to enzymes and other proteins whose activity is altered by phosphorylation.

Cyclic AMP is degraded by the action of the enzyme phosphodiesterase. Some of the hormones inhibit this enzyme in their target tissues. Phosphodiesterase is also inhibited by theophylline and its derivatives (see p 124), and the effects of these hormones are enhanced by such compounds.

Transport Effects

Several hormones have been shown to affect their target cells in such a way as to increase the transfer of

Table 33–2. Some hormonal influences on cAMP levels in various tissues and the consequences of the alteration. Only the prominent or most thoroughly studied effects of the hormones on their target tissues are listed.[*]

Hormone	Tissue	Effect
Increased cAMP levels		
Adrenocorticotropic hormone	Adrenal cortex	↑ Steroidogenesis
	Fat (rat)	↑ Lipolysis
Luteinizing hormone	Corpus luteum, ovary, testis	↑ Steroidogenesis
	Fat	↑ Lipolysis
Catecholamines	Fat	↑ Lipolysis
	Liver	↑ Glycogenolysis, ↑ gluconeogenesis
	Skeletal muscle	↑ Glycogenolysis
	Heart	↑ Inotropic effect
	Salivary gland	↑ Amylase secretion
	Uterus	Relaxation
Glucagon	Liver	↑ Glycogenolysis, ↑ gluconeogenesis, ↑ induction of enzymes
	Fat	↑ Lipolysis
	Pancreatic β-cells	↑ Insulin release
	Heart	↑ Inotropic effect
Thyroid-stimulating hormone	Thyroid	↑ Thyroid hormone release
	Fat	↑ Lipolysis
Melanocyte-stimulating hormone	Dorsal frog skin	↑ Darkening
Parathyroid hormone	Kidney	↑ Phosphaturia
	Bone	↑ Ca^{2+} resorption
Vasopressin	Toad bladder, renal medulla	↑ Permeability
Hypothalmic releasing factors	Adenohypophysis	↑ Release of trophic hormones
Prostaglandins	Platelets	↑ Aggregation
	Thyroid	↑ Thyroid hormone release
	Adenohypophysis	↑ Release of trophic hormones
Decreased cAMP levels		
Insulin	Fat	↓ Lipolysis
	Liver	↓ Glycogenolysis, ↓ gluconeogenesis
Prostaglandins	Fat	↓ Lipolysis
	Toad bladder	↓ Permeability
Catecholamines (a-adrenergic stimuli)	Frog skin	↓ Darkening
	Pancreas	↓ Insulin release
	Platelets	↓ Aggregation
Melatonin	Frog skin	↓ Darkening

*Reproduced, with permission, from Butcher RW, Robison GA, Sutherland EW: Cyclic AMP and hormone action. Chapter 2 in: *Biochemical Actions of Hormones.* Vol 2. Litwack G (editor). Academic Press, 1972.

substrates into the cell. In some instances, this appears to be a membrane effect and active transport does not seem to be involved. An example of this kind of effect is that of insulin on the rate of glucose and amino acid entry into muscle or fat cells. In the case of the enhancement of iodide uptake by thyrotropin, a gradient must be overcome, and alterations of membrane permeability alone could not explain the effect.

Role of Calcium Ion

The effects of most protein hormones are inhibited in the absence of calcium. Calcium may be derived from the extracellular fluid or intracellular stores. Protein hormones acting on the membrane increase the uptake of calcium ion by the cell.

The effects or actions of the hormones are controlled or modulated by changes in their rates of synthesis and secretion, the nature of the transport system in plasma, conversion to other active forms, and the rates of degradation and excretion. Secretory rates are subject to feedback regulation. The specific receptors at the target tissue are also subject to feedback regulation and control by other hormones.

•   •   •

References

Baxter JD, Funder JW: Hormone receptors. N Engl J Med 301:1149, 1979.

Chan L, O'Malley BW: Steroid hormone action: Recent advances. Ann Intern Med 89:694, 1978.

Edelman IS: Mechanism of action of steroid hormones. J Steroid Biochem 6:147, 1975.

Insel PA: Membrane-active hormones: Receptors and receptor regulation. Pages 1–43 in: *Biochemistry and Mode of Action of Hormones II*. Rickenberg HV (editor). University Park Press, 1978.

O'Malley BW, Birnbaumer L (editors): *Receptors and Hormone Action*. Academic Press, 1978.

Rasmussen H, Goodman DBP: Calcium and cAMP as interrelated intracellular messengers. Ann NY Acad Sci 253:789, 1975.

Sutherland EW: Studies on the mechanism of hormone action. Science 177:401, 1972.

Williams RH (editor): *Textbook of Endocrinology*, 5th ed. Saunders, 1974.

Winegrad A & others (editors): *Endocrinology*. 3 vols. Grune & Stratton, 1979.

34 | Thyroid & Antithyroid Drugs

THYROID

The thyroid gland is responsible for the synthesis and release of thyroxine (T_4) and triiodothyronine (T_3) (Fig 34–1). Both are iodine-containing amino acid analogs that regulate the rate of cellular oxidative processes. Calcitonin, a hormone produced by the parafollicular cells of the thyroid gland, is discussed in Chapter 36.

Metabolism of Thyroid Hormones

The major steps in the biosynthesis, secretion, and degradation of the active thyroid hormones are summarized in Fig 34–2.

Dietary iodine is absorbed and circulates as iodide in the blood in low concentration (0.2–0.4 μg/dL). It is actively removed from the blood by the cells of the thyroid gland, where it is concentrated 10–200 times or more depending upon the degree of stimulation of the concentrating mechanism by thyrotropin (TSH). The details of the iodine "trapping mechanism" in the thyroid are not completely understood, but the mecha-

nism is known to require intact, actively respiring thyroid cells and may be coupled to potassium transport into these cells. This reaction is of interest also because it is the site of action of a number of ions, such as perchlorate and thiocyanate, that inhibit the production of T_4 and T_3 by interfering with thyroidal iodide transport. About 90% of total body iodine is in the thyroid, most of it in organic form. About 1% of stored iodine is released daily as T_3 and T_4.

The activity of the concentrating mechanism is stimulated by TSH or by depletion of iodine stores within the gland. Iodine-concentrating mechanisms similar to that in the thyroid gland are found in the salivary and mammary glands, gastric mucosa, placenta, and skin. These differ in that they are not significantly influenced by changes in thyrotropin concentration.

Once in the gland, thyroidal iodide is oxidized to iodine. This conversion, thought to be due to the action of a peroxidase, leaves the iodine in a highly activated form.

T_3 & T_4 Synthesis

The activated iodine rapidly combines with

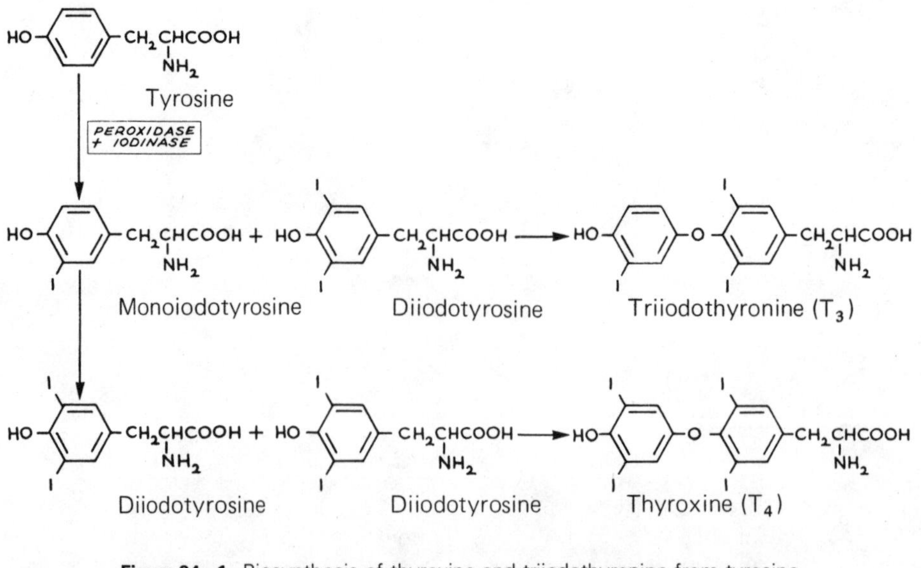

Figure 34–1. Biosynthesis of thyroxine and triiodothyronine from tyrosine.

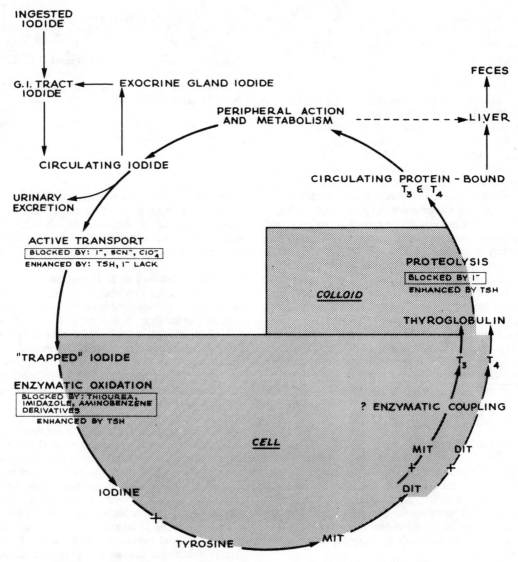

Figure 34–2. Pathways of biosynthesis, secretion, and degradation of thyroid hormones.

tyrosine groups on thyroglobulin near the apical border of the cell. Thyroglobulin is a large glycoprotein with a molecular weight of about 650,000. It contains 110–115 tyrosyl groups, of which about 26 are iodinated. Monoiodotyrosine (MIT) and diiodotyrosine (DIT) are thus formed in situ on thyroglobulin. Appropriately situated MIT and DIT residues are then coupled, perhaps enzymatically, to form T_4 (DIT + DIT) and T_3 (MIT + DIT) (Fig 34–1). Small amounts of 3,3',5'-triiodothyronine (reverse T_3) are also formed. A higher proportion of MIT occurs when the diet is deficient in iodine or when oxidation is blocked. The higher proportion of MIT favors the formation of T_3; however, if DIT is deficient (because of extreme iodine deficiency), the rate of formation of both thyronines is impaired. In most species, about 25% of thyroidal iodine is in the form of T_4; a similar amount is present in MIT; 30–50% is present as DIT; and only 1–2% is present as T_3.

Secretion & Transport

The hormones, bound to thyroglobulin, are stored in the follicles of the thyroid gland as colloid. The normal gland stores a 2-month supply of T_4. Droplets of thyroglobulin are taken up by pinocytosis at the villous border under the influence of TSH. Secretion of these hormones (T_3 and T_4) follows their release from thyroglobulin by a proteolytic enzyme. Each molecule yields 2–5 molecules of T_4, which are released into the capillaries by the cells of the gland. The MIT and DIT are also products of the proteolysis, but they are degraded in situ by iodotyrosine dehalogenase, and the iodide released becomes available for hormone synthesis.

It has been estimated that about 75 μg of thyroxine (containing 50 μg of iodine) and 25 μg of triiodothyronine (15 μg of iodine) are released into the circulation daily. These figures indicate that the biologic activity is rather evenly shared by these compounds. Although the thyroxine is secreted by the thyroid gland, 80% of the circulating triiodothyronine is derived from thyroxine that has been deiodinated in peripheral tissues.

Control of Secretion

The activity of the thyroid gland is normally controlled by thyrotropin (TSH) released by the anterior pituitary. In the absence of TSH (eg, after hypophysectomy), thyroid function is depressed and the gland becomes atrophic. Under the influence of TSH, the cells hypertrophy, iodine uptake increases, thyroxine synthesis is stimulated, blood flow through the gland increases, and more hormone is released into the circulation. Under stable environmental conditions in the normal individual, the rate of secretion is self-regulating, since thyroid hormones act on the anterior pituitary to decrease TSH release. Disturbances of this feedback mechanism are present in several clinical disorders of thyroid function. TSH secretion is also influenced by hypothalamic neurohumor secretion. The median eminence of the hypothalamus produces a thyrotropin-releasing hormone (TRH) that is carried to the anterior pituitary, where it stimulates the release of TSH (see p 430). Alterations of the environmental temperature affect thyroid function through hypothalamic centers. The depression of glandular activity observed in a variety of stressful situations and illnesses and during food deprivation is also thought to be mediated via the hypothalamus.

Circulating Hormones

Thyroxine and triiodothyronine are largely bound to plasma proteins in the circulation. However, only the small amount that is free can enter the cells and exert biologic activity, including regulation of the pituitary feedback mechanism. Therefore, there is in the plasma a very large pool of bound hormone that is in dynamic equilibrium with the hormone reaching the target cells.

Thyroxine-binding globulin (TBG), a monomeric acid glycoprotein (MW about 50,000), has the highest affinity for thyroid hormone. About 85% of T_4 and 70% of T_3 are bound to TBG. When fully saturated, TBG, at its normal concentration of 1–2 mg/dL, can carry approximately 20 μg/dL of T_4. Thyroxine-binding prealbumin (TBPA) is present at 20 times the concentration of TBG (25 mg/dL). However, it binds less T_4 and little T_3 because of its lower affinity for these substances. These hormones also bind to serum albumin, which, although it has the lowest affinity for T_4 and T_3, binds significant amounts because of its relatively high concentration (3–4 g/dL). The serum concentrations of total and free circulating T_3 and T_4 are shown in Table 34–1.

High levels of circulating estrogen, such as are seen during pregnancy and in women taking oral contraceptives, increase the thyroxine-binding globulin (TBG) levels, and this in turn increases the binding of thyroxine and triiodothyronine and therefore increases the blood levels of these hormones. The concentration

Table 34–1. Thyroid hormone kinetics.

	T_4	T_3
Total serum concentration	4–11 μg/dL	80–180 ng/dL
amount free (%)	0.03	0.3
concentration of free	1.5–3 ng/dL	0.2–0.6 ng/dL
Amount produced per 24 h (μg)	80	30
Amount stored in body (μg)	800	50
Volume of distribution (L)	10	38
Metabolic clearance rate (L/d)	1	22
Half-life (days)	8	1

of TBG is reduced by androgens and by loss into urine in patients with nephrotic syndromes. The binding of thyroid hormone can be competitively inhibited by related compounds and by a variety of unrelated chemicals such as phenytoin, aspirin, and dinitrophenol.

Peripheral Metabolism & Excretion

Tracer studies with labeled thyroxine indicate that about 30% of the secreted hormone is in the circulation, 30% in the liver, 30% in the ECF, and 10% in the cells of the body. It is removed from the body slowly. Triiodothyronine is cleared from the circulation more rapidly than thyroxine and normally constitutes little more than 5% of hormonal iodide. Its intracellular distribution differs from thyroxine in that much less is found in liver and more in the kidneys, muscle, and skin. A comparison of the metabolism of these hormones is presented in Table 34–1. The rate of removal of these hormones is decreased when the metabolic rate is reduced, as in hypothyroidism (when production is decreased), or when there is increased binding to plasma proteins, as in pregnancy. Turnover is increased in hyperthyroidism, in the presence of hypoproteinemia (eg, nephrotic syndrome, cirrhosis), and when binding is inhibited by drugs (see above).

The thyroid hormones are deiodinated and the alanine side chain degraded to pyruvate, lactate, or acetate derivatives (Table 34–2). This occurs at the mitochondria, predominantly in liver and kidney. In liver and to a small extent in the kidney, the phenolic hydroxyl group is conjugated to glucuronide or sulfate esters. Very small amounts of free T_3 and T_4 are excreted into the urine.

Effects of Thyroid Hormones

The thyroid hormones are general metabolic stimulants affecting almost all tissues of the body. Although in vitro studies have shown that the oxygen consumption of the pituitary is suppressed and that of some tissues (including testes, spleen, lymph nodes, and brain) is unaffected, heat production and oxygen consumption are increased in the intact animal under the influence of thyroxine. These general effects are accompanied by widespread metabolic and physiologic changes. These include increased metabolism of carbohydrate, fat, and protein as well as increased cholesterol synthesis. Cardiac output is increased, as is gastrointestinal motility and bone turnover. Nervous system irritability is increased and enhanced sympathetic activity occurs. The latter may be mediated by an increase in tissue adrenergic receptors.

Thyroid hormone–induced thermogenesis can be largely accounted for by increased activity of the sodium pump, which maintains intracellular potassium ion concentrations. The large amount of energy required makes this process a principal source of heat.

Thyroxine has been shown to alter the activity of more than 30 enzymes in vitro and twice as many in vivo. It also increases the incorporation of amino acids into protein in stimulated tissues.

Thyroid hormones are essential for normal growth and development in many species, including humans. The sensitivity of this response is illustrated by the observation in thyroidectomized rats that growth can be restored to normal by one-tenth the amount of thyroxine required to restore the normal rate of metabolism.

Thyroid hormones are also important for normal fetal development. Their presence is required for normal growth and particularly for neural and skeletal development. Therefore, intrauterine deficiency of thyroid hormone leads to cretinism, which is characterized by mental retardation and dwarfism. The fetus is dependent on its own hormone, since there is very little transfer of T_3 or T_4 to the fetus from the mother.

The thyroid hormones have chronotropic and inotropic effects on the heart and also appear to regulate the effects of catecholamines. Increased thyroid function produces excessive sensitivity to catecholamines by increasing the concentration of beta-adrenergic receptors in the heart. Thyroid hormones are also necessary for the normal control of respiration.

Mechanisms of Action of Thyroid Hormones

Thyroid hormones enter target cells and are taken up by a specific protein in the nucleus. Cytosol-binding proteins have been reported in some tissues but are not required for transport of hormone to the nuclear binding site. Interaction of the hormone with its receptor leads to induction of RNA polymerase and increased synthesis of specific classes of RNA, including messenger RNA. This leads to synthesis of new protein (enzymes and structural proteins). Direct effects on mitochondrial metabolism and synthetic processes may also occur (see Chapter 33).

Structure-Activity Relationships

Several metabolites of thyroxine and triiodothyronine have been found in tissues and possess hormonal activity (Table 34–2). These include the thyroacetic, thyropropionic, and thyrolactic acid products of deamination. In addition, the activity of many other iodinated synthetic derivatives of thyronine has been investigated. Studies of these compounds indicate that 2 aromatic rings joined by an ether or thioether linkage and having a side chain containing a carboxyl group on the first ring and a phenolic hydroxyl group in the para position of the second ring are required for biologic activity. Although the specific steric arrangement of the 2 rings (perpendicular to each other) appears to be more important than the nature of the substituent groups, maximal activity requires the presence of iodine at the 3 and 5 positions. Iodine is less critical on the phenolic ring. It has been suggested that the phenylalanine ring with the 2 iodines is concerned with binding to the receptor site. An understanding of structure-function relationships has led to the development of competitive inhibitors such as 2′,6′-diiodothyronine, 3,5-diiodo-4-hydroxybenzoic acid, and 3,3′5′-triiodothyronine.

It is of interest that the biologic activities of the analogs of thyroxine and triiodothyronine are not always parallel in their effects on oxygen consumption, pituitary secretion of TSH cholesterol metabolism, and the induction of growth and metamorphosis in the tadpole (Table 34–2).

Table 34–2. Relative potencies of thyroxine derivatives.* All of these compounds except D-thyroxine are probably formed in the body. Note that in each column the potency of the derivatives is stated relative to an arbitrary value of 100 for thyroxine.

Name	Synonyms	Relative Potency			
		^{131}I†	Goiter Prevention‡	BMR§	Cholesterol Lowering
L-3,5,3′,5′-Tetraiodothyronine	L-Thyroxine; T_4	100	100	100	100
D-3,5,3′,5′-Tetraiodothyronine	D-Thyroxine; D-T_4	30	...	...	500
L-3,5,3′-Triiodothyronine	Triiodothyronine; TIT; T_3	300	800	800	...
3,3′,5′-Triiodothyronine (D, L tested)	Reverse T_3	75	<1	<1	...
3,5,3′,5′-Tetraiodothyropropionic acid	T_4 PROP	60	14	6	...
3,5,3′-Triiodothyropropionic acid	T_3 PROP	60	28	10	...
3,5,3′,5′-Tetraiodothyroacetic acid	TETRAC	75	63	9	250
3,5,3′-Triiodothyroacetic acid	TRIAC	75	51	21	...

*Data mostly from Money & others: Comparative effects of thyroxine analogues in experimental animals. Ann NY Acad Sci 86:512, 1960.

†Inhibition of radioactive iodine uptake.

‡Prevention of goiter in propylthiouracil-treated animals (pituitary-inhibiting effect).

§Calorigenic effect.

CLINICAL DISORDERS OF THYROID FUNCTION

The clinical disorders of thyroid function in humans result from a deficient or excessive production of thyroid hormones, mechanical disturbances produced by enlargement of the gland, neoplastic changes, or combinations of these factors.

Hypothyroidism

Hypothyroidism may result from a variety of congenital disorders such as athyrotic cretinism (failure of the gland to develop) and defects in hormone metabolism, eg, synthesis and release. Acquired hypothyroidism may be secondary to the failure of thyrotropin secretion by the pituitary or may be the sequel to thyroidectomy, thyroiditis, antithyroid drugs, or autoimmune disease.

When thyroid deficiency is present at birth, it produces cretinism. Although not usually recognized at birth, a characteristic syndrome may develop consisting of a puffy, expressionless face with large tongue and thick lips, yellowish skin, short extremities, poor appetite, umbilical hernia, and a reduction of body temperature and pulse rate. Replacement therapy, to be fully effective, must be started before these advanced changes occur. When the deficiency occurs later in childhood, it is associated with a reduction in the rate of growth and development.

In the adult, severe thyroid deficiency produces myxedema, characterized by marked retardation of mental and physical activity; hoarseness; dry, pale, coarse skin; dry sparse hair; thickening of the skin and subcutaneous tissues (myxedema); constipation; cold intolerance; anemia; and other changes. However, hypothyroidism is usually recognized before it has progressed to this point.

Hyperthyroidism

Hyperthyroidism results from the excessive production of thyroid hormone. Although it is occasionally due to a neoplastic process, the disorder most commonly responsible is thyrotoxic goiter (Graves' disease). The cause of Graves' disease is not established, but hyperfunction of the gland is usually associated with the presence of thyroid-stimulating immunoglobulins such as LATS (long-acting thyroid stimulating substance), LATS protector, and human thyroid stimulator (HTS). Patients with hyperthyroidism also have an increased incidence of autoimmune disorders.

Hereditary factors seem to be involved, as evidenced by the high incidence of the disorder in the families of patients. It has also been observed that some members of the patient's family who do not manifest the disorder fail to show suppression of thyroid hormone synthesis and release when given thyroid hormone, as do normal individuals. It has been suggested that they inherit a specific defect in suppressor T lymphocytes.

The clinical manifestations of hyperthyroidism include the signs and symptoms of hypermetabolism such as weight loss, increased appetite, heat intolerance, perspiration, and flushing. There is overactivity of the heart, with tachycardia and bounding pulses, and neuromuscular irritability. Anxiety is a prominent complaint. Muscle wasting and weakness are sometimes striking.

THYROID HORMONE PREPARATIONS
(Table 34–3.)

Thyroid USP (Desiccated Thyroid; Thyroid Extract)

The USP thyroid preparation is powdered, acetone-dried, and defatted thyroid tissue obtained from hogs, cattle, or sheep in the slaughterhouse. It is normally assayed by its iodine content, which must be

Table 34–3. Thyroid hormone preparations.

	$T_4:T_3$ Ratio (weight)	Onset of Activity	Effect on Some Tests in Patients on Replacement Therapy		Dosage Equivalent
			PBI or Serum T_4	T_3 Resin Uptake	
Thyroid USP (many preparations)	Beef, 4:1 Hog, 2.5:1	Intermediate	Normal or slightly lower	Normal or low	60 mg (1 grain)
Thyroglobulin (Proloid, Thyrar)	2–2.5:1	Intermediate	Normal or slightly lower	Normal or low	60 mg (1 grain)
Sodium levothyroxine (tetraiodothyronine) (Levothroid, L-T-S, Noroxine, Synthroid. Outside USA: Eltroxin, Levaxin, Thyratabs, Thyrex.)	Synthetic, pure T_4	Slow	Slightly higher	High	100 µg
Sodium liothyronine (L-triiodothyronine) (Cytomel, Liomel. Outside USA: Cynomel, Thybon, Tertroxin, Trithyron.)	Synthetic, pure T_3	Rapid	Low	Normal	25 µg
Liotrix (sodium levothyroxine with sodium liothyronine) (Euthroid, Thyrolar. Outside USA: Combithyrex, Cynoplus, Novotrial,	4:1	Intermediate	Normal	Normal	50 µg T_4 + 12.5 µg T_3

between 0.17 and 0.23%. Tablets are made from the compressed powder and are not always assayed for their content of thyroxine or triiodothyronine. The variations in preparations of these substances contribute to a lack of uniformity from one product to another and probably explain why the porcine product is more calorigenic than that derived from beef or sheep. Different proportions of T_3 and T_4 will also result in different T_4 levels for a given therapeutic effect. In spite of these variations, the official preparation is well absorbed and, in general, a satisfactory preparation for clinical use.

Synthetic iodinated proteins are quite active and have been used primarily in animal experimentation.

Thyroglobulin

Thyroglobulin, extracted from animal thyroid glands, is also available in tablet form. This preparation contains thyroxine and triiodothyronine and is standardized both by iodine content and bioassay.

Thyroxine

This preparation is widely used, since it contains only one substance. The sodium salt of the natural isomer of thyroxine is employed because it is more reliably absorbed, although as much as 50% can sometimes be found in the stool. Absorption of thyroxine is significantly higher when it is taken in the fasting state than when ingested with meals. It is dispensed in the form of tablets and is also available in an injectable form suitable for use in the treatment of myxedema coma. Synthetic L-thyroxine (levothyroxine) is now generally accepted as the preferred preparation for the treatment of hypothyroidism and the suppression of nontoxic goiter. Treatment with this preparation results in constant serum levels of T_4 and T_3, since the T_3 found is the result of peripheral deiodination of the administered T_4. It provides a smooth clinical effect as compared to preparations containing T_3, such as thyroid extract or liotrix. The plasma concentration of T_4 will be slightly higher with this preparation than with those containing T_3.

Triiodothyronine

This hormone produces effects that are qualitatively similar to those of thyroxine. However, it has special properties that make it useful under certain circumstances. Triiodothyronine is useful when a rapid onset of action is vital, such as in myxedema coma; but its brief effect makes it less useful for prolonged maintenance therapy in hypothyroidism. When used chronically, it is equivalent to 3 times the amount of thyroxine and should be given in divided doses. It is almost completely absorbed when taken orally.

When T_3 is administered, circulating levels of T_4 are very low. This preparation is therefore useful for testing the suppressibility of endogenous thyroxine production (see below).

Liotrix

Liotrix is a combination of thyroxine and triiodo-thyronine in a 4:1 ratio. It is designed to mimic the natural secretion of the thyroid gland.

Its use is similar to that of thyroid USP, which also contains a mixture of T_3 and T_4. However, it is more expensive, and there is little practical reason for its use.

DIMIT

3,5-Dimethyl-3′-isopropylthyronine (DIMIT) is a thyroxine analog with the unique property of freely passing through the placenta. It has proved useful in experimental studies and is potentially useful in the treatment of congenital hypothyroidism during gestation.

THERAPEUTIC USES OF THYROID HORMONES

The 2 specific indications for the use of thyroid hormones are replacement therapy in thyroid deficiency and therapeutic or diagnostic suppression of pituitary TSH production.

Although all of the preparations in Table 34–3 can be used for replacement therapy, thyroxine is favored by many endocrinologists because its bioavailability and biologic activity are more constant and predictable. The dosage of hormone used to initiate replacement therapy will depend on the patient's age, on the severity and duration of the deficiency, and on the presence of other disorders (eg, heart disease, adrenal insufficiency).

Hypothyroidism is frequently diagnosed in elderly patients, in whom coronary insufficiency or a decrease in cardiac reserve is common. Full replacement of doses of thyroxine may precipitate angina or congestive heart failure. Doses of 0.025–0.05 mg daily should be given during the first few weeks and then slowly increased. If doses adequate to control hypothyroidism cannot be administered without inducing angina, the combination of thyroxine and propranolol may be helpful.

Because of the recent institution of neonatal screening programs, the diagnosis of hypothyroidism is more commonly being made during the first weeks of life. Early detection and treatment prevent the mental retardation that occurs when treatment is delayed for months. Treatment may be instituted by the intramuscular injection of 0.1 mg of levothyroxine for 2 or 3 days, followed by maintenance doses of 0.05–0.1 mg orally daily for the first year. The dose is gradually increased thereafter until adult levels are reached. When hypothyroidism is diagnosed in older children, it is usually safe to start treatment with 0.2 mg of thyroxine. The dose must be carefully adjusted to obtain optimal growth.

During pregnancy, it is particularly important to maintain optimal replacement of thyroid hormone. Inadequate treatment is reported to be associated with a marked increase in abnormalities in fetal development.

Myxedema coma is a medical emergency requiring prompt treatment of the hypothyroidism as well as careful attention to the diseases or factors precipitating its onset. Treatment requires the intravenous administration of thyroid hormone and has been facilitated by the availability of parenteral levothyroxine. Triiodothyronine is also useful; it is prepared by dissolving in 0.1 N sodium hydroxide and diluting with saline to bring the sodium hydroxide to one-tenth of its initial concentration. Treatment is initiated with an initial intravenous dose of 200–400 μg of thyroxine and maintained with 100 μg/d. The onset of action is within 24 hours. Large doses of hydrocortisone are also administered, starting with 100 mg intravenously every 6 hours. Sedatives, narcotics, and overhydration must be avoided, and body temperature must be maintained by the use of blankets and heat as necessary. Supportive measures may be required to maintain adequate pulmonary and cardiac function.

Overtreatment with thyroid hormones is characterized by nervousness, tremor, tachycardia or arrhythmias, hypermetabolism, and hypertension. In patients with heart disease, congestive heart failure or coronary insufficiency may be provoked by the injudicious use of these hormones.

Thyroid hormones, by suppressing TSH production, will cause a reduction in the size of a simple goiter such as is present when defective hormone synthesis occurs. In endemic or iodine deficiency goiter, a prompt response is usually observed unless the gland has become nodular. The maximal response may require many months of treatment.

These hormones have also been used for the treatment of functioning single nodules of thyroid tissue. If these do not regress with full replacement therapy, surgical removal is advocated.

A variety of analogs of thyroxine, particularly D-thyroxine, have been studied for use in the treatment of hypercholesterolemia, since they increase the degradation of cholesterol more than its synthesis, leading to a reduction in serum cholesterol levels (see p 451).

Nonspecific Therapy

Thyroid hormones have been used in the treatment of gynecologic conditions, including amenorrhea, anovulatory cycles, hypermenorrhea, habitual abortion, and infertility with no discernible cause. Oligospermia in the male, obesity, and metabolic insufficiency have also been reported to respond favorably to thyroxine or triiodothyronine. Although many physicians have had successful experiences with thyroid treatment of the above symptoms in the absence of diagnosable hypothyroidism, there is no evidence that the success rate is greater than that achieved by the use of placebos.

DINITROPHENOL

Dinitrophenol in a dose of 3–5 mg/kg increases the metabolic rate more than 20% for 24–48 hours. If given chronically, a 50% elevation can be maintained. Dinitrophenol has none of the hormonal effects of thyroxine. It increases the rate of oxidation by uncoupling oxidation from the formation of high-energy phosphates and leads to the generation of heat.

Dinitrophenol is a yellow dye that is rapidly absorbed from the intestine and is secreted both unchanged and in a reduced form (2-amino-4-nitrophenol). In the past it was used for the treatment of obesity; but serious side-effects, including cataracts, neuritis, anemia, agranulocytosis, purpura, and liver and kidney damage, led to its withdrawal from use.

ANTITHYROID AGENTS

Reduction of thyroid activity or the effects of thyroid hormones can be accomplished by the use of drugs that interfere with the production of the thyroid hormones; by drugs that modify the actions of the hormone in the tissues; and by the destruction of part or all of the gland, either surgically or by the use of ionizing radiation.

INHIBITORS OF HORMONE BIOSYNTHESIS

The commonly used antithyroid drugs in this group are the thiocarbamides (thionamides) such as propylthiouracil and methimazole (Fig 34–3). These compounds interfere with the binding, into organic form, of the iodide accumulated by the thyroid gland. They are thought to act by inhibiting the oxidation of iodide to iodine. They also appear to interfere with the coupling of iodotyrosines (Fig 34–2).

Propylthiouracil is rapidly absorbed into the circulation. Peak plasma concentrations are reached in 2 hours. It is distributed in a space that is somewhat less than total body water. It is concentrated in the thyroid to the same degree as iodide. It is rapidly removed from the body through the kidneys, and its rapid turnover makes frequent administration advisable: a dose of propylthiouracil as large as 500 mg will completely inhibit the thyroid gland for 6–8 hours. Methimazole is more slowly absorbed, reaching a peak in the plasma at about 8 hours. It has a more prolonged effect, and a single dose of 30 mg continues to exert an inhibitory effect after 24 hours. Carbimazole is a derivative of methimazole and is converted to methimazole in the body.

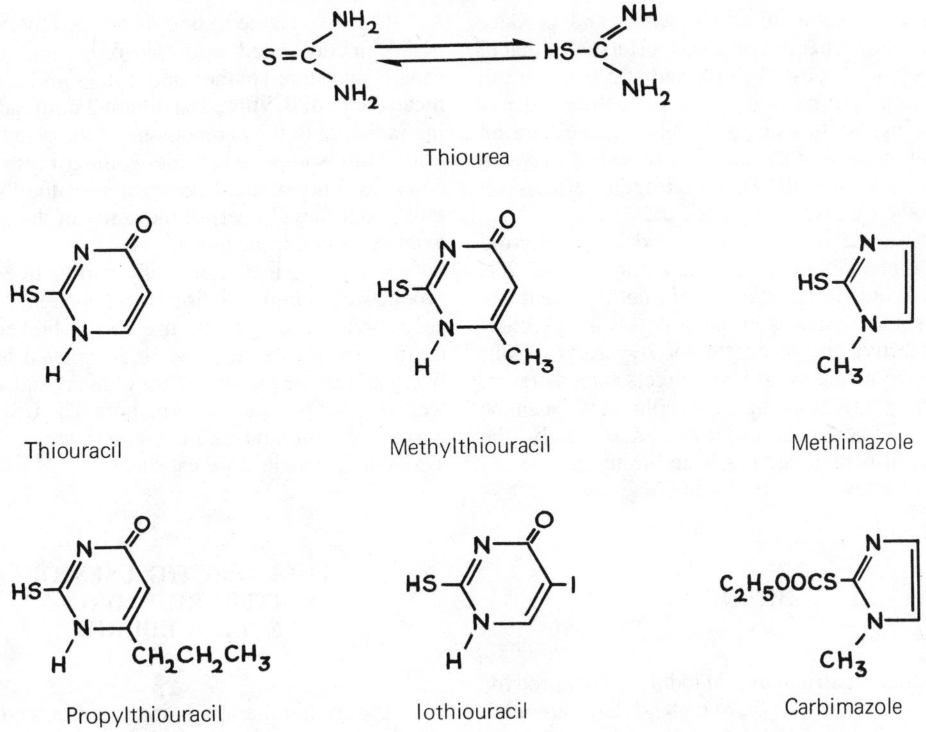

Figure 34–3. Antithyroid drugs.

The thiocarbamides readily cross the placenta of pregnant women, and, when large doses are administered, a goiter may be produced in the fetus. Doses of propylthiouracil less than 150 mg/d (or equivalent) seldom have this effect. These drugs are also secreted into the milk in lactating women and may produce goiters in nursing infants.

Propylthiouracil and methimazole appear to have fewer toxic effects than some of the others used. The most common of them are a pruritic papular rash and joint pain and stiffness that may disappear with continued use; however, the arthritic manifestations may require discontinuation of the drug. These or mild gastrointestinal symptoms occur in 3% of patients receiving propylthiouracil and 7% of those taking methimazole. The incidence of agranulocytosis is less than 0.5%, and jaundice rarely occurs. When one of the drugs causes adverse effects, another may be tried.

The thiocarbamides interfere with the feedback inhibition of pituitary TSH secretion by reducing the amount of circulating thyroxine and triiodothyronine. The increase in TSH stimulates the thyroid and leads to enlargement of the gland, or goiter. This property is shared by a large number of chemically unrelated substances. Such compounds are referred to as goitrogens.

Vegetables of the Brassicaceae family such as turnips and rutabagas have been known to produce thyroid enlargement. This has been found to be due to their content of a substance (progoitrin) that can be converted to goitrin (Fig 34–4) by a heat-labile activator found in the plants or by substances in the gastrointestinal tract. Goitrin has a potency similar to that of propylthiouracil. In addition to this naturally occurring inhibitor, a variety of useful drugs and chemicals have been shown to have low degrees of goitrogenic activity by virtue of their interference with thyroid hormone synthesis. This group includes lithium, sulfanilamide, phenylbutazone, *p*-aminobenzoic acid, cyanocobalamin, amphenone B, barbiturates, phentolamine, metahexamide, and carbutamide.

IONIC INHIBITORS

A group of monovalent hydrated anions, including thiocyanate (SCN^-), perchlorate (ClO_4^-), and ni-

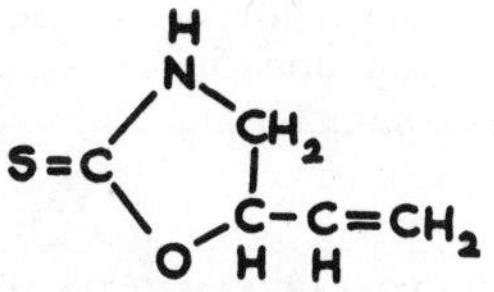

Goitrin
(L-5-vinyl-2-thio-oxazolidone)

Figure 34–4. The naturally occurring goitrogen in vegetables of the family Brassicaceae.

trate (NO_3^-), inhibit thyroid function and produce goiters. Their mechanism of action differs from that of the compounds discussed above and appears to result from competitive inhibition of the iodine-concentrating mechanism of the gland. They are all capable of abolishing the gradient of iodide between plasma and thyroid cells. Their goitrogenic effects can be overcome by thyroxine or iodide.

Thiocyanate is not concentrated in the thyroid gland, as is perchlorate, and is one-tenth as active. It is widely distributed in food and is normally present to a small extent in plasma. Sodium or potassium perchlorate is effective in the control of hyperthyroidism. Although the incidence of toxic effects such as fever, rash, enteric irritation, and agranulocytosis can be minimized by administering less than 1 g daily, the usefulness of perchlorate has been limited by the occurrence of a few cases of aplastic anemia.

IODIDE

Although small amounts of iodide are required for hormone synthesis by the thyroid gland, large amounts may produce goiter and hypothyroidism when given to normal individuals for prolonged periods. Iodide can be rapidly effective in ameliorating hyperthyroidism. Maximal effects are seen in about 2 weeks and include improvement in signs and symptoms and reduction in the size and vascularity of the gland. Unfortunately, it is not often possible to achieve a complete remission or to maintain the degree of control achieved for more than a few weeks.

Iodide administration seems to inhibit many aspects of thyroid function, including the organic binding of iodine and, in the toxic gland, the release of T_3 and T_4 from thyroglobulin. Its use in hyperthyroidism is at present limited to the preparation for thyroid surgery, although in some instances the disease has been treated with iodide alone.

The effects of a high intake of iodide are complex. Stimulation of hormone production leading to thyrotoxicosis occurs, particularly in patients with goiters who live in geographic areas where natural iodine supplies are deficient.

Saturated solution of potassium iodide is available as such. In areas of endemic goiter, iodized poppyseed oil has been useful when iodized salt could not be used. Lugol's solution (5% iodine and 10% potassium iodide) is commonly used.

RADIOACTIVE IODINE

^{131}Iodine (half-life 8 days) is the most commonly employed isotope of iodine. ^{130}I (half-life 12.3 hours) and ^{125}I (half-life 60 days) have also been used for experimental purposes.

^{131}I, like stable iodine, is trapped by the thyroid gland, incorporated into thyroxine and triiodothyronine, and stored in the colloid. It emits beta rays to a mean depth of 0.5 mm (maximum 2 mm), administering radiation to the parenchyma of the gland and little else. This isotope also emits gamma rays. They account for only a small percentage of the therapeutic effect, but they do permit the study of the isotope by external counting technics.

^{131}I is obtained essentially carrier-free from the products of uranium fission. It is supplied in low concentrations for diagnostic use and in higher concentrations for therapeutic use. It is assayed before delivery and labeled to show time of assay and activity as well as other pertinent information. The USP solution is prepared for oral or intravenous use. ^{131}I is also available in single dose capsules.

THERAPEUTIC USES OF ANTITHYROID DRUGS & PROCEDURES

Antithyroid therapy is indicated in the treatment of hyperthyroidism and occasionally in euthyroid individuals with intractable angina pectoris.

Hyperthyroidism may be treated in several ways, depending in part upon the specific problem the patient presents and in part upon the experience and preferences of the physician.

Radioiodine Therapy

In general, radioiodine therapy is reserved for individuals over 30 years of age and is specifically contraindicated in pregnancy. The average dose is 4–5 mCi and can be calculated on the basis of the estimated gland weight and iodine uptake to provide 7–10 thousand rads/g of tissue. Ten to 15% of patients fail to respond to the first dose. The symptoms subside gradually over a period of months, and several doses may be required. Radioiodine may be used in conjunction with other drugs to obtain more rapid control of symptoms (see below). It has become apparent with time that an increasing number of patients treated with radioiodine become hypothyroid. The incidence of this complication is estimated to be 70% after 10 years. A similar phenomenon is observed following subtotal thyroidectomy, although the incidence is less than 50%. Since hypothyroidism can be insidious in its appearance and very disabling, the institution of thyroid hormone replacement shortly after radioiodine or surgical treatment may be advisable.

Although x-ray treatment of the head, neck, and chest areas in infants and children increases the incidence of thyroid neoplasms, careful follow-up of many thousands of patients treated with these doses of radioiodine failed to disclose any increase in the incidence of thyroid neoplasms or leukemia.

When large doses (25–75 mCi) are used to destroy normal tissue in patients with intractable angina pectoris, thyroiditis may occur, and acute hyperthyroidism secondary to the loss of stored hormone from the damaged gland has been observed. Studies in patients receiving ^{131}I indicate that this treatment can produce abnormal chromosomes.

Antithyroid Drug Therapy

Antithyroid drugs may be used to control hyperthyroidism until a remission is achieved by radiotherapy (as noted above), in preparation for subtotal thyroidectomy, or as definitive treatment. Treatment is started with large doses of the drug (eg, 100–150 mg of propylthiouracil every 6 hours) in order to achieve maximal inhibition of hormone synthesis. Improvement begins rapidly, although its onset is slower after pretreatment with iodine or in the presence of a large gland with much stored hormone. When single dose therapy is indicated, methimazole in a dose of 80–100 mg daily can produce a similar effect. When a euthyroid state is achieved, the dose can be reduced to a maintenance level of 5–10 mg of methimazole or 100–150 mg of propylthiouracil in divided doses. When continued for a year, about 50% of patients will be in a lasting remission. In 25% of cases, symptoms return upon cessation of therapy. The recurrence can be predicted if the normal suppressibility of thyroid function does not return in the posttreatment period. This can be monitored by maintaining the patient on triiodothyronine and measuring the thyroxine in the plasma. The latter will increase if the gland does not remain suppressed by exogenous hormone. Patients in whom the thyroid gland is not greatly enlarged and whose disease is of short duration are more likely to respond favorably. Reduction in the size of the gland during therapy and return of normal suppressibility of thyroid function are favorable prognostic signs. The frequency of remissions is reduced by a high iodine content in the diet. This treatment is frequently used in children and young adults and in others in whom surgery and ^{131}I are contraindicated. The disadvantages of this treatment are the prolonged period of active therapy required, the toxic effects of the drugs, and the uncertainty of a lasting remission. Its advantages are the avoidance of surgery and anesthesia and the attendant risks of hypoparathyroidism and recurrent laryngeal nerve injury. Antithyroid drug therapy also avoids the risk of hypoparathyroidism associated with ablative therapy.

Propylthiouracil and methimazole are most commonly used in divided doses; however, single-dose therapy has been reported to be effective in most patients. The starting doses are 300 mg of propylthiouracil or 30 mg of methimazole. If clinical or chemical improvement does not occur, the dose may be doubled. In patients with severe hyperthyroidism, antithyroid drugs are the treatment of choice during pregnancy. Treatment may be initiated in the same way as in nonpregnant patients; however, it is important to reduce the dose to less than 150 mg of propylthiouracil or 15 mg of methimazole daily during the last trimester of pregnancy. As noted above, neonatal hypothyroidism and goiter are rare when doses can be kept below this range.

When antithyroid drugs are used in preparation for surgery, they are administered in the same fashion. When the patient is euthyroid, iodides are given for 10 days in order to reduce the vascularity of the gland. Such treatment has reduced the surgical risk to negligible levels in the hands of an experienced thyroid surgeon. Preliminary studies suggest that the combination of potassium iodide and propranolol may be useful in the preparation of patients with Graves' disease for thyroid surgery.

Antithyroid drugs can be used in conjunction with ^{131}I therapy. These agents can be used to control thyrotoxicosis. The treatment is then stopped for 3–5 days and the ^{131}I administered. Therapy is resumed in 1 week.

The observation that many signs and symptoms of hyperthyroidism resemble the effects of catecholamines suggested the use of drugs such as reserpine, guanethidine, and propranolol to control the manifestations. The first 2 drugs have been disappointing in this application, and simple sedation with agents such as phenobarbital is just as effective. Propranolol (see p 98) is effective in controlling many symptoms of thyrotoxicosis and does not affect the uptake of [131]I. In doses of 40 mg every 6 hours there is a rapid response. Much higher doses are sometimes required and the response is not complete. This drug can be used to control severe tachycardia if present as well as to ameliorate symptoms prior to and during the early part of antithyroid therapy if such a control is required. The safety of this drug during pregnancy has not been established.

References

Becker DV: Current status of radioactive iodine treatment of hyperthyroidism. Thyroid Today 2:7, 1979.

Bernal J, Refetoff S: The action of thyroid hormone. Clin Endocrinol 6:227, 1977.

DeGroot LV, Stanbury JB: *The Thyroid and Its Diseases.* Wiley, 1975.

Edelman I: Thyroid thermogenesis. N Engl J Med 290:1303, 1974.

Feek CM & others: Combination of potassium iodide and propranolol in preparation of patients with Graves' disease for thyroid surgery. N Engl J Med 302:883, 1980.

Greer MA: Antithyroid drugs in the treatment of thyrotoxicosis. Thyroid Today 3:1, 1980.

Greer MA, Kammer H, Bouma DJ: Short-term antithyroid drug therapy for the thyrotoxicosis of Graves's disease. N Engl J Med 297:173, 1977.

Greer MA, Solomon DH (editors): *Handbook of Physiology.* Section 7, vol 3. *Thyroid.* American Physiological Society, 1974.

Harrison MT: The prevention and treatment of thyroid storm. Pharmacol Physicians 2:1, 1968.

Ingbar SH: Management of emergencies. 9. Thyroid storm. N Engl J Med 274:1252, 1966.

Liberti P, Stanbury JB: The pharmacology of substances affecting the thyroid gland. Annu Rev Pharmacol 11:113, 1971.

Nofal MM, Beierwaltes WH, Paton ME: Treatment of hyperthyroidism with sodium iodide I^{131}. JAMA 197:605, 1966.

Oppenheimer JH & others: Nuclear receptors and the initiation of thyroid hormone action. Recent Prog Horm Res 32:529, 1976.

Oppenheimer JH & others: Nuclear receptors and thyroid hormone action: A progress report. Fed Proc 38:2154, 1979.

Sterling K: *Diagnosis and Treatment of Thyroid Diseases.* Chemical Rubber Company Press, 1975.

Sterling K: Thyroid hormone action at the cell level. (2 parts.) N Engl J Med 300:117, 173, 1979.

Stock JM, Surks IM, Oppenheimer JH: Replacement dosage of L-Thyroxine in hypothyroidism. N Engl J Med 290:529, 1974.

Werner SC (editor): *The Thyroid: A Fundamental and Clinical Text,* 3rd ed. Hoeber, 1971.

The Adrenocortical Steroids | 35

The natural adrenocortical hormones are steroid molecules produced and released by the adrenal cortex. The secretory process is controlled by the pituitary release of corticotropin (ACTH). Secretion of the salt-retaining hormone aldosterone is also under the influence of angiotensin. Corticotropin has some actions that do not depend upon its effect on adrenocortical secretion. However, its pharmacologic value as an anti-inflammatory agent and its use in testing adrenal function depend on its trophic action. Therefore, its pharmacology will be discussed with the adrenocortical hormones.

This group of hormones has been employed in the diagnosis and treatment of a variety of disorders of adrenal function and as anti-inflammatory agents.

ADRENOCORTICOSTEROIDS

The adrenal cortex releases a large number of steroids into the circulation. Some have minimal biologic activity and function primarily as precursors, and there are some for which no function has been established. The hormonal steroids may be classified as those having important effects on intermediary metabolism (glucocorticoids), those having principally salt-retaining activity (mineralocorticoids), and those having androgenic or estrogenic activity (see Chapter 38). In humans, the major glucocorticoid is cortisol and the most important mineralocorticoid is aldosterone. Quantitatively, dehydroepiandrosterone (DHEA) is the major androgen, since about 20 mg are secreted daily, partly as the sulfate. However, both DHEA and androstenedione are very weak androgens. A small amount of testosterone is secreted by the adrenal and may be of greater importance as an androgen. Little is known about the estrogens secreted by the adrenal. However, it has been shown that the adrenal androgens such as testosterone and androstenedione can be converted to estrone in small amounts by nonendocrine tissues and that they constitute the major endogenous source of estrogen in women after menopause.

THE NATURALLY OCCURRING GLUCOCORTICOIDS; CORTISOL
(Hydrocortisone, Compound F)

Chemistry & Metabolism

The major glucocorticoid in humans is cortisol, a colorless, crystalline steroid with a molecular weight of 362.5 and a melting point of 217–220 C. It is slightly soluble in water (0.28 mg/mL). It is synthesized from cholesterol (as shown in Fig 35–1) by the cells of the zona fasciculata and zona reticularis and released into the circulation under the influence of ACTH. The mechanisms controlling its secretion are discussed in Chapter 39.

In the normal adult in the absence of stress, about 20 mg of cortisol are secreted daily. The rate of secretion changes in a circadian rhythm (Fig 35–2). In plasma, cortisol is bound to plasma proteins. Corticosteroid-binding globulin (CBG), an alpha$_2$ globulin synthesized by the liver, binds 95% of the circulating hormone under normal circumstances. The remaining 5% is the metabolically active fraction. When plasma cortisol levels exceed 20–30 μg/dL, CBG is saturated and most of the excess is loosely bound to albumin.

The half-life of cortisol in the circulation is normally about 90–110 minutes; it may be increased when large amounts are present or in hypothyroidism. Cortisol is removed from the circulation in the liver, where it is reduced and conjugated to form water-soluble compounds that are excreted into the urine (Fig 35–3). The side chain (C20 and 21) is removed from about 5–10% of the cortisol, and the resulting compounds are further metabolized and excreted into the urine as 11-oxy 17-ketosteroids.

In some species (eg, the rat), corticosterone is the major glucocorticoid. It is less firmly bound to protein and therefore metabolized more rapidly. The pathways of its degradation are similar to those of cortisol.

Physiologic & Pharmacologic Effects

The glucocorticoids have widespread effects because they influence the function of most cells in the body. Although many of the effects are dose-related and become magnified when large amounts are administered for therapeutic purposes, there are also

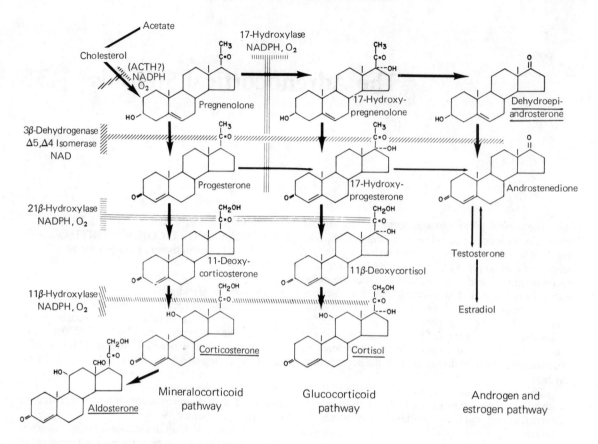

Figure 35–1. Outline of major pathways in adrenocortical hormone biosynthesis. The major secretory products are underlined. Pregnenolone is the major precursor of corticosterone and aldosterone, and 17-hydroxypregnenolone is the major precursor of cortisol. The enzymes and cofactors for the reactions progressing down each column are shown on the left and from the first to the second column at the top of the figure. When a particular enzyme is deficient, hormone production is blocked at the points indicated by the shaded bars. (Modified after Welikey, Mulrow, & others; reproduced, with permission, from Ganong WF: *Review of Medical Physiology,* 9th ed. Lange, 1979.)

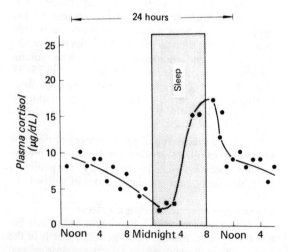

Figure 35–2. Circadian rhythm of plasma cortisol (free and protein bound). (After Liddle, 1966.)

"permissive effects." In other words, many normal reactions that take place at a significant rate only in the presence of corticoids are not further stimulated in the presence of large amounts of corticoids.

These hormones have important effects on intermediary metabolism. They stimulate the production of glucose (gluconeogenesis) from proteins. The increase in circulating glucose stimulates the production of insulin and leads to the deposition of fat, particularly in the trunk, face, and mesentery. Cortisol has an anti-insulin effect and also decreases the utilization of amino acids in muscle and adipose tissue.

Cortisol or another glucocorticoid is required for maintenance of the normal alpha rhythm in the electroencephalogram. Experimentally, glucocorticoids lower the threshold to electrically induced convulsions. These compounds also inhibit the secretion of ACTH (see Chapter 39). Their presence is required for the normal function of both smooth and striated muscle. Large doses of glucocorticoids stimulate excessive

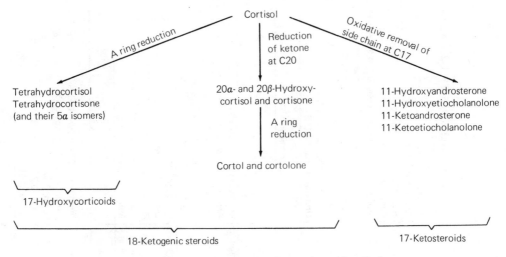

Figure 35–3. Primary excretion products of cortisol.

production of acid and pepsin in the stomach and may cause peptic ulcer. They facilitate fat absorption and appear to antagonize the effect of vitamin D on calcium absorption. The glucocorticoids also have important effects on the hematopoietic system, decreasing the number of lymphocytes, eosinophils, and basophils while increasing the number of neutrophils, platelets, and red blood cells.

In the absence of physiologic amounts of cortisol, renal function (particularly glomerular filtration) is impaired and there is an inability to excrete a water load.

Natural and synthetic glucocorticoids and anti-inflammatory steroids have been found to bind to specific intracellular receptors upon entering target tissues. The macromolecular complex thus formed is transported into the nucleus, where it interacts with chromosomal constituents to alter gene expression. These hormones alter the regulation of many cellular processes, including enzyme synthesis and activity, membrane permeability, transport processes, and structure (see Chapter 33).

SYNTHETIC ADRENOCORTICOSTEROIDS

ACTH and steroids having glucocorticoid activity have become important agents for use in the treatment of many inflammatory and allergic disorders. This has stimulated the search for and development of many steroids with anti-inflammatory activity.

Source & Chemistry

Although the natural corticosteroids can be obtained from animal adrenals, they are usually synthesized from cholic acid (obtained from cattle) or steroid sapogenins, diosgenin in particular, found in plants of the Liliaceae and Dioscoreaceae families. Further

modifications of these steroids at the 1, 2, 6, 9, 16, and other positions have led to the marketing of a large group of synthetic steroids with special characteristics that are pharmacologically and therapeutically important (Table 35–1).

Metabolism

The metabolism of the naturally occurring adrenal steroids has been discussed above. The synthetic corticosteroids for oral use (Table 35–1) are in most cases rapidly and completely absorbed when given by mouth. Although they are transported and metabolized in a fashion similar to the endogenous steroids, important differences exist.

Alterations in the molecule influence the degree of protein binding, side chain stability, rate of reduction, and end products. Halogenation at the 9 position, unsaturation of the Δ1-2 bond of the A ring, and methylation at the 2 or 16 position will prolong the half-life by more than 50%. The 11-hydroxyl group also appears to inhibit destruction, since the half-life of 11-deoxycortisol is half that of cortisol. The Δ1 compounds are excreted in the free form.

The mechanism of action of the synthetic steroids is similar to that of cortisol (see above). They have been found to bind to the specific intracellular receptor protein.

Pharmacologic Effects

The corticosteroids have the capacity to dramatically relieve the manifestations of inflammation, allergic reactions, and some immunologic phenomena. The mechanisms by which these processes are altered are not clearly understood. However, the following effects of corticosteroids have been reported:

Corticosteroids alter the vascular response to injury by limiting the capillary dilatation and increased permeability that normally occur. Thus, fewer polymorphonuclear leukocytes and macrophages leave the vessels at the site of injury. The corticoste-

Table 35–1. Commonly used natural and synthetic corticosteroids.

Agent	Activity Anti-inflammatory	Activity Topical	Activity Salt Retaining	Equiv. Oral Dose (mg)	Preparations Available Oral	Injectables*	Topical
Short-acting glucocorticoids							
Hydrocortisone (cortisol) (11β,17,21-trihydroxy-4-pregnene-3,20-dione)	1	1	1	20	Tablets, 5, 10, 20, and 25 mg; Syrup, 2 mg/mL; Oral paste, 0.5%	25, 50, and 125 mg/mL	Ointments, 0.125, 0.5, 1, and 2.5%; Creams, lotions, 0.125, 0.25, 0.5, 1, 2, and 2.5%; Talc, 0.1%; Aerosol, 0.5 and 1%; Rectal foam, 1 and 10%; Retention enema, 100 mg; Suppositories, 10, 15, and 25 mg; Otic solutions and suspensions, 0.2, 0.25, and 1%; Ophthalmic suspension, 25 mg/mL; Ophthalmic ointments, 0.5, 1, and 1.5%; Scalp lotions, 0.25 and 1%; Scalp aerosols, 0.25 and 0.3%; Urethral inserts, 1% (1.3 mg)
Cortisone (17,21-dihydroxy-4-pregnene-3,11,20-trione)	0.8	0	0.8	25	Tablets, 5, 10, and 25 mg	25 and 50 mg/mL	Ophthalmic drops, 0.5 and 1%†
Prednisone (17,21-dihydroxy-1,4-pregnadiene-3,11,20-trione)	4	0	0.3	5	Tablets, 1, 2.5, 5, 10, 20, and 50 mg; Capsules, 1.25 mg		Ophthalmic ointment, 1%†
Prednisolone (11β,17,21-trihydroxy-1,4-pregnadiene-3,20-dione)	5	4	0.3	5	Tablets, 5 mg	20, 25, 40, 50, and 100 mg/mL; Powder, 50 mg/vial	Creams, ointments, 0.5%; Aerosol, 0.5 mg/3-second spray; Ophthalmic ointment, 0.25%; Ophthalmic solutions and suspensions, 0.1, 0.2, 0.25, 0.5, and 1%
Fluocortolone (6α-fluoro-11β,21-dihydroxy-16α-methyl-1,4-pregnadiene-3,20-dione)†				5	Tablets, 5, 20, and 50 mg		Cream, 0.2 and 0.5%; Lotion, ointment, spray, 0.5%; Plaster, 0.025 mg/cm²
Methylprednisolone (6α-methyl-prednisolone)	5	5	0	4	Tablets, 2, 4, and 16 mg; Medules, 2 and 4 mg	20, 40, 62.5, and 80 mg/mL; Powder, 500 and 1000 mg/vial	Cream, ointment, 0.1, 0.25, and 1%; Retention enema, 40 mg
Meprednisone (16β-methylprednisone)	5	0	0	4	Tablets, 4 mg	40 mg/mL†	
Intermediate-acting glucocorticoids							
Triamcinolone (acetonide) (9α-fluoro-16α-hydroxyprednisolone) (16,17-acetonide)	5	5‡	0	4	Tablets, 1, 2, 4, 8, and 16 mg; Syrup, 0.4 and 0.8 mg/mL; Dental paste, 0.1%	5, 10, 20, 25, and 40 mg/mL	Ointment, 0.025, 0.1, and 0.5%; Lotion, 0.025, 0.05, and 0.1%; Foam, 0.1%; Spray, 0.2 mg/3-second spray; Cream, 0.01, 0.025, 0.05, 0.1, and 0.5%
Paramethasone (6α-fluoro-16α-methylprednisolone)	10	0	0	2	Tablets, 1, 2, and 6 mg	5 and 20 mg/mL†	
Fluprednisolone (6α-fluoroprednisolone)	15	7	0	1.5	Tablets, 0.75 and 1.5		

				Oral	Parenteral	Topical
Long-acting glucocorticoids						
Betamethasone (9α-fluoro-16β-methylprednisolone)	25–40	10	0	0.6	Tablets, 0.5 and 0.6 mg Syrup, 0.12 mg/mL Pellets, 0.1 mg (for aphthous ulcers)	4 and 6 mg/mL	Cream, 0.01, 0.025, 0.05, 0.1, and 0.2% Gel, 0.025% Aerosol, 0.15% Lotion, ointment, 0.05 and 0.1% Ear, eye, or nose drops, 0.1% Enema, 5 mg/unit Suppositories, 0.5 mg
Dexamethasone (9α-fluoro-16α-methylprednisolone)	30	10	0	0.75	Tablets, 0.25, 0.5, 0.75, 1, 1.5, and 4 mg Elixir, 0.05 and 0.1 mg/mL	1, 2, 4, 5, and 8 mg/mL	Ear, eye ointment, 0.05% Ear, eye solution, 0.1% Aerosol, 0.023 and 0.084 mg/spray Cream, 0.1 and 0.25% Gel, 0.1% Ointment, 0.2%
Mineralocorticoids						
Fludrocortisone (9α-fluorohydrocortisone)	10	10	250	2	Tablets, 0.1 mg	3 mg/mL	Otic suspension, 0.1% Ointment, 0.1%
Desoxycorticosterone (11-deoxycorticosterone)	0	0	20	0	Linguets, 1 and 5 mg	Pellets, 125 mg, 10 and 25 mg/mL (In oil, 5, 10, and 50 mg/mL)	

*Solutions usually as sodium succinate or 21-phosphate for intramuscular or intravenous injection.
†Outside USA.
‡Acetonide: Up to 100.

roids also appear to stabilize lysosomal membranes in these cells, preventing the release of vasoactive kinins and destructive enzymes. The growth of new capillaries into sites of injury is inhibited.

The corticosteroids generally do not interfere with the development of acquired immunity. Experimentally, however, large doses given with the stimulus can inhibit the normal antibody response. Delayed hypersensitivity can be inhibited. The corticosteroids markedly inhibit homograft rejection reactions and are employed for this purpose in the treatment of patients receiving organ transplants. They may work by reducing the amount of antigen liberated by the grafted tissue; by delaying revascularization; and by interfering with the sensitization of antibody-forming cells.

Clinical Uses

A. Diagnosis and Treatment of Disturbed Adrenal Function:

1. Adrenocortical insufficiency (Addison's disease)–Chronic adrenocortical insufficiency (addisonism) is characterized by hyperpigmentation, weakness, fatigue, weight loss, hypotension, and inability to maintain the blood glucose level with fasting. In such individuals, minor noxious, traumatic, or infectious stimuli may produce acute adrenal insufficiency with shock and finally death.

In adrenal insufficiency, whether primary or following adrenalectomy, about 20–30 mg of cortisol must be given daily, with increased amounts during periods of stress. This must be supplemented by an appropriate amount of salt-retaining hormone such as desoxycorticosterone (DOC) or fludrocortisone. It is for this reason that glucocorticoids devoid of salt-retaining activity are not indicated for these patients.

Aldosterone is not used for replacement therapy, since the supply is too small. However, desoxycorticosterone pivalate (trimethylacetate) given in monthly injections and fludrocortisone given orally are excellent preparations for this purpose.

When a rapidly acting intravenous preparation is needed for the management of acute adrenal insufficiency (or to prevent adrenal insufficiency during major stress such as surgery), the water-soluble hemisuccinate of cortisol is ideal. Intramuscular administration of cortisol or cortisone or their acetates is not satisfactory because the rate of absorption is unpredictable and the onset of effect is too slow for emergency use.

2. Adrenocortical hyperfunction–

a. Congenital adrenal hyperplasia–This group of disorders is characterized by specific defects in the synthesis of cortisol. The most common is a decrease in or lack of 21-hydroxylase activity. As can be seen in Fig 35–1, this would lead to a reduction in cortisol synthesis and produce a compensatory increase in ACTH release. If sufficient enzyme activity is present, a normal amount of cortisol will be produced in response to the increased level of ACTH, but the gland will become hyperplastic and produce abnormally

large amounts of precursors such as 17-hydroxyprogesterone that can be diverted to the androgen pathway, leading to virilization. Metabolism of this compound in the liver leads to pregnanetriol, which is characteristically excreted into the urine in large amounts in this disorder.

If the defect is in 11-hydroxylation, hypertension is prominent. When 17-hydroxylation is defective in the adrenals and gonads, hypogonadism will be present. However, increased amounts of 11-deoxycorticosterone (DOC) (see p 364) are formed and the signs and symptoms associated with mineralocorticoid excess—such as hypertension and hypokalemia—are found.

Cortisol and cortisone have been used in the treatment of congenital adrenal hyperplasia. Since ACTH suppression is an important objective of therapy, slowly absorbed parenteral preparations can be given in smaller amounts than the oral preparations, which are rapidly absorbed and metabolized and must be given in divided doses. When treating these patients, larger doses of cortisone (25–100 mg daily intramuscularly, depending upon age) can be given for 5–10 days to achieve adequate suppression of adrenal secretion. The dose is then reduced to 4–6 mg/d and adjusted to maintain a low urinary ketosteroid excretion. Treatment with orally administered hydrocortisone in a dose of 25 mg/d/m^2 of body surface or less can be used as the basis of therapy. Undesirable effects are minimized by giving the larger part of the dose in the morning. The dose must also be adjusted over the long course of therapy to permit normal growth, since excessive amounts of glucocorticoids inhibit linear growth in children. In some infants, salt-retaining hormone therapy is also required.

b. Cushing's syndrome–Cushing's syndrome is usually the result of bilateral adrenal hyperplasia but occasionally is due to tumors of the gland. The manifestations are those associated with the presence of excessive glucocorticoids. When changes are marked, a rounded, plethoric face and trunk obesity are striking in appearance. In general, the manifestations of protein loss are severe and include muscle wasting, thinning of the skin, striae, easy bruisability, poor wound healing, and osteoporosis. Other serious disturbances include mental disorders, hypertension, and diabetes. This disorder is treated by surgical removal of the tumor producing the hormone, irradiation or removal of a pituitary microadenoma producing ACTH, or resection of hyperplastic adrenals. These patients must receive large doses of cortisol during and following the surgical procedure. Doses of 300 mg of soluble hydrocortisone are given as a continuous intravenous infusion on the day of surgery. The dose must be reduced slowly to normal replacement levels, since rapid reduction in dose may produce symptoms including fever and joint pain. If adrenalectomy has been performed, long-term maintenance is similar to that outlined above for adrenal insufficiency (see p 358).

c. Hyperaldosteronism–Primary hyperaldosteronism usually results from the excessive production of aldosterone by an adrenal adenoma. It may result from abnormal secretion of hyperplastic glands or from a malignant tumor. The clinical findings of hypertension, polyuria, polydipsia, weakness, and tetany are related to the continued renal loss of potassium, which leads to hypokalemia, alkalosis, and hypernatremia.

In contrast to patients with secondary hyperaldosteronism (see below), these patients have low (suppressed) levels of plasma renin activity and angiotensin II. When treated with desoxycorticosterone acetate (20 mg intramuscularly daily for 3 days), they fail to retain sodium and their secretion of aldosterone is not significantly reduced. They are generally improved when treated with spironolactone, and their response to this agent is of diagnostic value (see p 366).

3. Use of glucocorticoids for diagnostic purposes–It is sometimes necessary to suppress the production of ACTH in order to identify the source of a particular hormone or to establish whether or not its production is influenced by the secretion of ACTH. In these circumstances, it is advantageous to employ a very potent substance such as dexamethasone or betamethasone. Although these preparations are no more effective, the use of small quantities reduces the possibility of confusion in the interpretation of hormone assays in blood or urine. For example, if complete suppression is achieved by the use of 50 mg of cortisol, the urinary 17-hydroxycorticoids will be 15–18 mg/24 h, since one-third of the dose is recovered in urine, as 17-hydroxycorticoid. If 1.5 mg of dexamethasone are employed, the excretion will be only 0.5 mg/24 h.

In an individual with normal adrenal function, 2 mg/d of dexamethasone or betamethasone are adequate to achieve suppression in the absence of stress. In patients with Cushing's syndrome, 8 mg/d are usually effective if the excessive cortisol is produced by hyperplastic adrenals but will not suppress hormones secreted by an adenoma or carcinoma of the adrenal.

Suppression of the adrenal with glucocorticoids and of the ovary with estrogens can be useful in locating the source of androgen production in a hirsute woman if the effect on testosterone levels in blood can be measured before and during hormone administration.

B. Adrenocorticosteroids and Stimulation of Lung Maturation in the Fetus: Lung maturation in the fetus is regulated by the fetal secretion of cortisol. Treatment of the mother with large doses of glucocorticoid reduces the incidence of respiratory distress syndrome in infants delivered prematurely. When delivery is anticipated before 34 weeks of gestation, betamethasone, 12 mg, followed by an additional dose of 12 mg 18–24 hours later, is commonly used. Protein binding of this corticosteroid is less than that of cortisol, allowing increased transfer across the placenta to the fetus. Corticosteroid levels achieved in the fetus are equivalent to those observed when the fetus is stressed. The safety of this treatment in patients with severe preeclampsia or hypertension—or diabetes with renal complications—has not been established.

C. Adrenocorticosteroids and Nonadrenal Disorders: Cortisol and its synthetic analogs have been found to be useful in the treatment of a diverse group of diseases unrelated to any known disturbance of adrenal function. The usefulness of corticosteroids in these disorders is a function of their ability to suppress inflammatory and immune responses as described above. In disorders in which host response is the cause of the major manifestations of the disease, these agents are useful. In instances where the inflammatory or immune response is important in controlling the pathologic process, therapy with corticosteroids may be dangerous and is used in conjunction with specific therapy for the disease process to prevent irreparable damage from an inflammatory response.

Since the corticosteroids are not usually curative, the pathologic process may progress while clinical manifestations are suppressed. Therefore, systemic therapy with these drugs should be undertaken with great care and only when the seriousness of the disorder warrants their use and less hazardous measures have been exhausted.

In general, attempts should be made to bring the disease process under control using short-acting agents as well as all ancillary measures possible to keep the dose low. Where possible, alternate-day therapy should be utilized (see p 363). Therapy should not be decreased or stopped abruptly. When prolonged therapy is anticipated, it is helpful to obtain chest films and a tuberculin test. The presence of diabetes, peptic ulcer, osteoporosis, and psychologic disturbances should be excluded, and cardiovascular function should be assessed.

The following supplemental measures should be considered: The diet should be rich in potassium and low in sodium to prevent electrolyte disturbances. Caloric management to prevent obesity should be instituted. High protein intake is required to compensate for the loss due to the increased breakdown of protein from gluconeogenesis. Antacids should be used 3–4 times daily in patients prone to epigastric distress. Where osteoporosis is of concern, the use of physical therapy, fluorides, androgens, and vitamin D (with careful monitoring of serum calcium levels) has been recommended.

1. Some therapeutic indications for glucocorticoids in nonadrenal disorders–

Allergic disorders (angioneurotic edema, asthma, bee stings, contact dermatitis, drug reactions, hay fever, serum sickness, urticaria)

Arthritis, bursitis, and tenosynovitis

Collagen vascular disorders (giant cell arteritis, lupus erythematosus, mixed connective tissue syndromes, polymyositis, polymyalgia rheumatica, rheumatoid arthritis, temporal arteritis)

Hematologic disorders (acquired hemolytic anemia, acute allergic purpura, leukemia, autoimmune hemolytic anemia, idiopathic

Table 35–2. Synthetic corticosteroids for topical use.

	Double Bond at 1-2 (Δ^1)	R (11)	Substituents at Carbons					16-17 Acetonide	Preparations Available
			6	9	16	17	21		
Flurandrenolide (fludroxycortide) (6α-fluoro-16α-hydroxyhydrocortisone-16,17-acetonide)	−	−OH	α-fluoro		α-OH			+	Lotion, 0.05% Cream, ointment, 0.025 and 0.05% Tape, 4 μg/cm²
Flunisolide (6α-fluoro-16α-hydroxyprednisolone-16,17-acetonide)	+	−OH	α-fluoro		α-OH			+	?
Fluperolone acetate (9α-fluoro-21-methylprednisolone acetate)	+	−OH		α-fluoro			methyl and acetate	−	Ointment, 0.1%
Fluprednidene (9α-fluoro-16-methylene-prednisolone)	+	−OH		α-fluoro	methylene (=CH₂)			−	Aerosol, cream, lotion, ointment, 0.1%
Fluorometholone (6α-methyl-9α-fluoro-21-deoxy-prednisolone)	+	−OH	α-methyl	α-fluoro			deoxy	−	Cream, spray, 0.025% Ointment, 0.05% Ophthalmic suspension, 0.1%
Fluocinolone acetonide (6α,9α-difluoro-16α-hydroxyprednisolone-16,17-acetonide)	+	−OH	α-fluoro	α-fluoro	α-OH			+	Cream, 0.01, 0.025, and 0.2% Gel, ointment, 0.025% Lotion, 0.01 and 0.025%
Fluocinonide (21-acetate ester of fluocinolone acetonide)	+	−OH	α-fluoro	α-fluoro	α-OH		acetate	+	Cream, 0.01 and 0.05% Gel, 0.05% Lotion, 0.025% Ointment, 0.01, 0.025 and 0.05%
Flumethasone (6α-fluoro-dexamethasone)	+	−OH	α-fluoro	α-fluoro	α-methyl			−	Cream, 0.02 and 0.03% Ointment, spray, 0.02%
Desoxymethasone (17-deoxy-dexamethasone)	+	−OH		α-fluoro	α-methyl	deoxy			Cream, ointment, 0.25%
Descinolone acetonide (9α-fluoro-16α-hydroxy-prednisolone-16,17-acetonide)	+	−OH		α-fluoro	α-OH			+	?
Desonide (16α-hydroxyprednisolone-16,17-acetonide)	+	−OH			α-OH			+	Cream, ointment, 0.05 and 0.1% Lotion, 0.05%
Chloroprednisone (6α-chloroprednisone)	+	=O	α-chloro					−	?
Halcinonide (21-chloro-21-deoxy-9α-fluoro-16α-hydroxyhydrocortisone-16,17-acetonide)	−	−OH		α-fluoro	α-OH		deoxy and chloro	+	Cream, 0.1%

Beclomethasone (9α-chloro-16β-methylpred-nisolone)	+	–OH		α-chloro	β-methyl			–	Spray for inhalation, 50 μg/spray; Cream, lotion, ointment, 0.025%
Clobetasol (21-chloro-21-deoxybetamethasone-17-propionate)	+	–OH		α-fluoro	β-methyl	propi-onate	deoxy and chloro	–	Cream, ointment, 0.05%
Clocortolone (9α-chloro-paramethasone)	+	–OH	α-fluoro	α-chloro	α-methyl			–	?
Flucloronide (9α,11β-dichloro-6α-fluoro-16α,17α-21-trihydroxy-1,4-pregnadiene-3,20-dione-16,17-acetonide)	+	β-chloro	α-fluoro	α-chloro	α-OH			+	Cream, ointment, 0.025%
Tralonide (9β,11β-dichloro-6α,21-difluoro-16α,17α-dihydroxy-1,4-pregnadiene-3,20-dione-16,17-acetonide)	+	β-chloro	α-fluoro	β-chloro	α-OH		deoxy and fluoro	+	?

thrombocytopenic purpura, lymphoblastic leukemia, multiple myeloma)

Eye diseases (acute uveitis, allergic conjunctivitis, choroiditis, optic neuritis)

Gastrointestinal diseases (inflammatory bowel disease, nontropical sprue, regional enteritis, subacute hepatic necrosis, ulcerative colitis)

Hypercalcemia (immunosuppression [transplants], carcinoma, sarcoidosis)

Malignant exophthalmos and subacute thyroiditis

Neurologic diseases

Pulmonary diseases (aspiration pneumonia, bronchial asthma, prevention of infant respiratory distress syndrome, sarcoidosis)

Renal diseases (certain nephrotic syndromes)

Infection (gram-negative septicemia, shock; occasionally helpful to suppress excessive inflammation)

Skin disorders (atopic dermatitis, dermatoses [see above], lichen simplex chronicus [localized neurodermatitis], mycosis fungoides, pemphigus, seborrheic dermatitis, xerosis)

2. Adverse reactions–The benefits obtained from the use of these compounds vary considerably. They must be carefully weighed in each patient against the widespread effects on every part of the organism. The major undesirable effects of the glucocorticoids are not toxic effects but exaggerations of their hormonal actions (see above) and lead to the clinical picture of iatrogenic Cushing's syndrome.

When the glucocorticoids are used for short periods (less than 1 week), it is unusual to see serious side-effects even with moderately large doses. However, behavioral changes and acute peptic ulcers are occasionally observed.

a. Adrenal suppression–When corticosteroids are administered for a period of months or years, adrenal suppression occurs and the patient should be given supplementary therapy at times of severe stress such as accidental trauma or surgery. The degree of adrenal unresponsiveness is a function of the dose and the length of time the patient has been treated. The dose is a less important variable when the threshold for suppression has been exceeded. With very rare exceptions, recovery occurs when the drug is withdrawn; however, after prolonged suppression, a state of relative insufficiency may persist for 6–9 months or longer.

Treatment with ACTH does not significantly reduce the suppression of pituitary-adrenal function. The problem can be approached by treating the patient with an amount of steroid that is slightly less than the replacement dose. This will not prevent the return of adrenal function but will provide support for the patient in the interim. The dose can be augmented during periods of acute stress.

b. Metabolic effects–Most patients who are given daily doses of 100 mg of cortisol or more (or the equivalent amount of synthetic steroid) for longer than 2 weeks undergo a series of changes that have been termed iatrogenic Cushing's syndrome. The rate of development is a function of the dose. The appearance of the face is altered by rounding, puffiness, and plethora. Fat tends to be redistributed from the extremities to the trunk and face. There is an increased growth of fine hair over the thighs and trunk and sometimes the face. Acne may increase or appear, and insomnia and increased appetite are noted. In the treatment of dangerous or disabling disorders, these changes may not require cessation of therapy. However, the underlying metabolic changes accompanying them can be very serious by the time they become obvious. The continuing breakdown of protein and diversion of amino acids to glucose production increase the need for insulin and over a period of time result in **weight gain;** fat deposition; muscle wasting; thinning of the skin, with striae and bruising; hyperglycemia; and eventually the development of **osteoporosis** and **diabetes.** When diabetes occurs, it is treated by diet and insulin. These patients are often resistant to insulin but rarely develop ketoacidosis. In general, patients treated with corticosteroids should be on high-protein diets, and increased potassium and anabolic steroids should be used when required.

3. Other complications–Other serious complications include the development of peptic ulcers and their complications. The clinical findings associated with other disorders, particularly bacterial and mycotic infections, may be masked by the corticosteroids, and patients must be carefully watched to avoid serious mishap when large doses are used. Some patients develop a myopathy the nature of which is unknown. The frequency of myopathy is greater in patients treated with triamcinolone. The administration of this drug as well as of methylprednisolone has been associated with nausea, dizziness, and weight loss in some patients. It is treated by changing drugs, reducing dosage, and increasing the potassium and protein intake.

Psychosis may occur, particularly in patients receiving large doses of corticosteroids. Long-term therapy is associated with the development of posterior subcapsular **cataracts.** Increased intraocular pressure is common, and **glaucoma** may be induced. **Benign intracranial hypertension** also occurs. In doses of 45 mg/m^2/d or more, **growth retardation** occurs in children.

When given in greater than physiologic amounts, steroids such as cortisone and hydrocortisone, which have mineralocorticoid effects in addition to glucocorticoid effects, cause some sodium and fluid retention and loss of potassium. In patients with normal cardiovascular and renal function, this leads to a **hypokalemic, hypochloremic alkalosis** and eventually a rise in blood pressure. In patients with hypoproteinemia, renal disease, or liver disease, edema may also occur. In patients with heart disease, even small degrees of sodium retention may lead to congestive heart failure. These effects can be minimized by sodium restriction and judicious use of potassium supplements. Many of the synthetic steroids have so little mineralocorticoid effect that these problems can be avoided. However, for the same reason, such compounds are not indicated for replacement therapy in adrenal insufficiency.

Children with asthma treated for prolonged periods with these steroids have been reported to develop cataracts with increased frequency. Periodic slit-lamp examination is indicated in such patients.

Contraindications & Cautions

A. Special Precautions: Patients receiving these drugs must be observed carefully for the development of hyperglycemia, glycosuria, sodium retention with edema or hypertension, hypokalemia, peptic ulcer, osteoporosis, and hidden infections. In order to minimize undesirable effects, periodic clinical examination with determination of plasma glucose and serum potassium is useful. A high-protein diet and adequate calcium intake are necessary. In patients with limited cardiac reserve, sodium restriction may be required. When more than physiologic amounts of steroids have been used, sudden cessation of therapy should be avoided in order to prevent an acute exacerbation of the disease process or symptoms of adrenal insufficiency.

The dosage should be kept as low as possible and intermittent dosage (eg, alternate-day) employed when satisfactory therapeutic results can be obtained on this schedule. In patients being maintained on relatively low doses of corticosteroids, supplementary therapy may be required at times of stress such as when surgical procedures are performed or accidents occur.

B. Contraindications: These agents must be used with the greatest of caution in patients with the following disorders:

1. Peptic ulcer–In the presence of active peptic ulcer disease, these steroids may cause hemorrhage or perforation. In patients with previous ulceration, activation is likely. Careful dietary control and antacids should be used when corticosteroids must be given to these patients. Cimetidine may be useful.

2. Heart disease or hypertension with congestive heart failure–Measures to avoid the accumulation of extracellular fluid should be utilized. The concomitant use of potassium-wasting diuretics may create serious problems in patients receiving digitalis.

3. Infections–Since natural indicators of and defenses against infection are attenuated, great care is required even when antibiotics are used. Antituberculosis therapy may be required even in patients with inactive tuberculosis. Ophthalmic herpes simplex is particularly dangerous in the presence of corticosteroids (see Herpes simplex).

4. Psychoses–Serious behavioral disturbances may occur in patients on steroid therapy, and prior disturbances are thought to predispose patients to acute psychoses.

5. Diabetes–Since these agents increase glucose production, more insulin may be required. However, the corticosteroids rarely cause acidosis or coma unless complications (such as an infection) occur.

6. Osteoporosis.

7. Glaucoma may be made worse by corticosteroid therapy.

8. Herpes simplex involving the cornea is particularly destructive in patients receiving corticosteroid therapy.

Selection of Drug & Dosage Schedule

Since these preparations differ with respect to relative anti-inflammatory and mineralocorticoid effect (Table 35–1), duration of action, cost, and dosage forms available, these factors should be taken into account in selecting the drug to be used.

A. ACTH Versus Adrenocortical Steroids: In patients with normal adrenals, ACTH has been used to induce the endogenous production of cortisol to obtain similar effects. However, when exogenous ACTH is given, the total amount of cortisol released by the adrenal can only be measured in retrospect. Furthermore, following ACTH administration the adrenal also increases its output of other hormones, including the androgens, which may not be desirable. Therefore, except when the increase in androgens is desirable, the use of ACTH as a therapeutic agent is probably unjustified. Instances in which ACTH has been claimed to be more effective than glucocorticoids are probably due to the administration of smaller amounts of corticoids than were produced by the dosage of ACTH.

B. Dosage: In determining the dose to be used, the physician must consider the seriousness of the disease, the amount of drug likely to be required to obtain the desired effect, and the duration of therapy. In some diseases, the amount required for maintenance of the desired therapeutic effect is less than the dose needed to obtain the initial effect, and the lowest possible dose for the needed effect should be determined by gradually lowering the dose until an increase in signs or symptoms is noted.

Many types of dosage schedules have been used in administering glucocorticoids. When it is necessary to maintain continuously elevated plasma corticosteroid levels in order to suppress ACTH, a slowly absorbed parenteral preparation or small doses at frequent intervals are required. In order to maintain the same level throughout the day, a much larger dose would be required and very high plasma levels would be present for a short period of time. The opposite situation exists with respect to the use of corticosteroids in the treatment of inflammatory and allergic disorders. The same total quantity given in a few doses may be more effective than when given in many smaller doses or in a slowly absorbed parenteral form. In addition, the other less desirable effects of the hormone may be less marked because there is a recovery period between each dose. The intermittent use of large doses of shorter-acting corticosteroids has been very helpful in the chronic treatment of disorders such as asthma and the nephrotic syndrome. When used in this manner, very large amounts (eg, 100 mg prednisone daily) can sometimes be administered with only minimal side-effects. The transition to an alternate-day schedule can be made after the disease process is under control. It should be done gradually and with additional supportive measures between doses. A typical

schedule for a patient maintained on 50 mg of prednisone daily would be as follows:

Day 1: 50 mg
       2: 40 mg
       3: 60 mg
       4: 30 mg
       5: 70 mg
       6: 10 mg
       7: 75 mg
       8: 5 mg
       9: 70 mg
      10: 5 mg
      11: 65 mg
      12: 5 mg
          etc

When selecting a drug for use in large doses, a
shorter-acting synthetic steroid with little mineralocorticoid effect is advisable. If possible, it should be given
as a single AM dose.

C. Special Dosage Forms: The use of local
therapy such as topical preparations for skin disease,
ophthalmic forms for eye disease, intra-articular injections for joint disease, and hydrocortisone enemas for
ulcerative colitis provides a means of delivering large
amounts of steroid to the diseased tissue without serious systemic effects.

Beclomethasone dipropionate administered as an
aerosol containing a microcrystalline suspension in
doses of 400 μg daily has been found to be effective in
the treatment of asthma. In this dose, endogenous
adrenal function is not significantly depressed and
systemic effects are minimal. This agent and its
metabolites are excreted mainly in the feces. The transfer from therapy with systemic glucocorticoids to
aerosol therapy with beclomethasone must be undertaken with caution, since adrenal insufficiency will
occur if adrenal function is suppressed. In such patients, a slow, graded reduction of systemic therapy
should accompany the institution of aerosol administration. During an acute attack, the aerosol is not a
dependable route of administration. The possibility of
local atrophic changes with long-term use has not been
excluded. Mycotic infections occur in 5–10% of patients, and most patients have positive oral cultures for
Candida albicans.

Topical application of these agents is of value in
the treatment of chronic lesions found in atopic dermatitis, seborrhea, psoriasis, eczema, and pruritus ani. In
their more severe forms, the lesions may be susceptible
to the application of preparations with occlusion of the
surface by a plastic film or medicated tape. About 1%
of the steroid is ordinarily absorbed through the skin.
However, approximately 10% may be taken up if it is
applied with occlusion.

Side-effects are unusual. However, clinical evidence of excessive absorption has been observed with
the more potent preparations. The most common manifestation is adrenal suppression. Local changes—
including striae, ectasia, atrophy, exacerbation of

acne, telangiectasia, and purpura—can occur with the
more potent preparations, and hydrocortisone preparations are preferred on the face. It is safer and less
expensive to use the lowest effective concentration
available. Allergic reactions to the base or vehicles
used in the preparations have been reported.

Combinations of anti-inflammatory steroids with
antibacterial agents have not been found to be of value.
The addition of antifungal agents may be useful.

MINERALOCORTICOIDS
(Aldosterone, Deoxycorticosterone, Fludrocortisone)

The most important mineralocorticoid in humans
is aldosterone. However, small amounts of deoxycorticosterone (DOC) are also formed and released. Although the amounts are normally insignificant, DOC is
of some importance therapeutically. Its actions, effects, and metabolism are similar to those described
below for aldosterone. Fludrocortisone, a synthetic
corticosteroid, is the most commonly used salt-
retaining hormone.

1. ALDOSTERONE

Aldosterone is synthesized mainly in the zona
glomerulosa of the adrenal cortex. Its structure and
synthesis are illustrated in Fig 35–1.

The rate of aldosterone secretion is subject to
several influences. ACTH produces a moderate stimulation of its release, but this effect is not sustained for
more than a few days in the normal individual. Although aldosterone is no less than one-third as effective as cortisol in suppressing ACTH, the minute quantities of aldosterone produced by the adrenal cortex
prevent it from participating in any feedback relationship in the control of ACTH secretion.

After hypophysectomy, aldosterone secretion
gradually falls to about half the normal rate, which
means that other factors are able to maintain and
perhaps regulate its secretion. Independent variations
between cortisol and aldosterone secretion can also be
demonstrated by means of lesions in the nervous system such as decerebration, which decreases the secretion of hydrocortisone while increasing the secretion of
aldosterone.

One of the important stimuli of aldosterone secretion is a reduction in blood volume, whether due to
hemorrhage, dietary sodium restriction, or sodium loss
following administration of diuretics (Fig 35–4).
These stimuli lead to a decrease in mean renal arterial
pressure that is associated with an increase in the
release of renin by the cells of the juxtaglomerular
apparatus. The enzyme renin then acts upon a circulat-

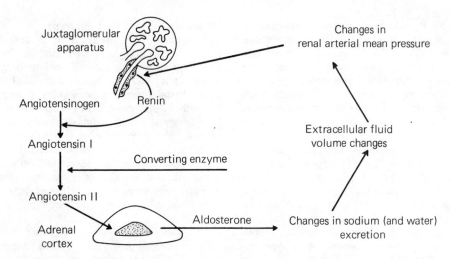

Figure 35–4. A postulated feedback mechanism regulating aldosterone secretion. (Reproduced, with permission, from Ganong WF: *Review of Medical Physiology,* 9th ed. Lange, 1979.)

ing alpha$_2$ globulin (renin substrate), releasing angiotensin I, which is then converted to angiotensin II. Angiotensin is a powerful stimulant of aldosterone production, only a few micrograms being required to show an effect in humans (see p 132). A metabolite of angiotensin II, the heptapeptide formed by the removal of asparagine from the N-terminal, is also a potent stimulator of aldosterone production.

Physiologic & Pharmacologic Effects

Aldosterone and other steroids with mineralocorticoid properties induce the reabsorption of sodium from urine by the distal renal tubules in exchange for potassium and hydrogen ion. Sodium reabsorption in the sweat and salivary glands, gastrointestinal mucosa, and across cell membranes in general is also increased. Excessive levels of aldosterone produced by tumors or overdosage with other mineralocorticoids lead to hypernatremia, hypokalemia, metabolic alkalosis, increased plasma volume, and hypertension.

Aldosterone has a delayed action on sodium transport. Recent experiments indicate that its action is dependent upon the synthesis of an enzyme required by the transport mechanism. The hormone appears to stimulate the formation of nuclear RNA, which in turn serves the induction of enzyme synthesis.

Metabolism

Aldosterone is secreted at the rate of 100–200 μg/d in normal individuals with a moderate dietary salt intake. The plasma level in males (resting supine) is about 0.007 μg/dL. The half-life of aldosterone injected in tracer quantities is 15–20 minutes, and it does not appear to be firmly bound to serum proteins.

The metabolism of aldosterone is similar to that of cortisol, about 50 μg/24 h appearing in the urine as conjugated tetrahydroaldosterone. Approximately 5–15 μg/24 h are excreted free or as the 3-oxo glucuronide.

2. DESOXYCORTICOSTERONE (DOC)

DOC, which also serves as a precursor of aldosterone (Fig 35–1), is normally secreted in amounts of about 200 μg/d. Its half-life when injected into the human circulation is about 70 minutes. Preliminary estimates of its concentration in plasma are approximately 0.03 μg/dL. The control of its secretion differs from that of aldosterone in that the secretion of DOC is primarily under the control of ACTH. Although the response to ACTH is enhanced by dietary sodium restriction, a low-salt diet does not increase DOC secretion.

3. FLUDROCORTISONE

This compound, a potent glucocorticoid and mineralocorticoid, has become the most widely used mineralocorticoid. Doses too small to have important anti-inflammatory effects have potent salt-retaining activity and are used in the treatment of adrenocortical insufficiency.

The clinical uses of fludrocortisone are discussed in the section on adrenocortical insufficiency. The available preparations are listed in Table 35–1.

ALDOSTERONE ANTAGONISTS

In addition to agents that interfere with aldosterone synthesis such as amphenone B (see below), there are steroids that compete with aldosterone for binding sites and decrease its effect peripherally. Progesterone is mildly active in this respect. However, it has been found that substitution of a 17-spironolactone group for the C20-21 side chain of deoxycorticosterone results in a compound capable of blocking the sodium-retaining effect of aldosterone.

Spironolactone (Aldactone) is a 7α-acetylthiospironolactone. Little is known about its metabolism. The onset of activity is slow, and the effects last for 2–3 days after the drug is discontinued. It is used in the treatment of primary hyperaldosteronism in doses of 50–100 mg/d in divided doses. This agent will reverse many of the findings of hyperaldosteronism. It has been useful in establishing the diagnosis in some patients and in ameliorating the signs and symptoms when surgical removal of an adenoma is delayed. When used diagnostically for the detection of hyperaldosteronism in hypokalemic patients with hypertension, doses of 400–500 mg/d for 4–8 days—with an adequate intake of sodium and potassium—will restore potassium levels to or toward normal. This agent is also useful in preparing these patients for surgery. Doses of 300–400 mg/d for 2 weeks are used for this purpose and may reduce the incidence of cardiac arrhythmias.

Spironolactone
(Aldactone; 3-[3-oxo-7α-acetylthio-17β-hydroxy-4-androsten-17α-yl] propionic acid γ-lactone)

Spironolactone finds limited use as a diuretic in patients with secondary hyperaldosteronism who are resistant to other diuretics (see Chapter 17).

Occasional sedative effects, headache, gastrointestinal symptoms, and skin rashes are the only reported adverse reactions.

ADRENOCORTICAL ANTAGONISTS

It has been possible to partially separate the mineralocorticoid and glucocorticoid effects by structural modifications of corticosteroids. However, it has not been possible to develop a compound that strongly inhibits ACTH production without having glucocorticoid activity.

Mitotane (*o,p'*-DDD, Lysodren)

Attempts to suppress adrenal steroidogenesis using derivatives of DDT have met with limited success. One compound, 2,2-bis(*o*-chlorophenyl-*p*-chlorophenyl)-1,1-dichloroethane—*o,p'*-DDD—will produce adrenal atrophy in dogs and will interfere with biosynthetic pathways. Doses of up to 10 g daily have been administered to patients with carcinoma of the adrenal. The production of corticosteroids was reduced, and in a few patients some reduction in tumor size was noted. However, severe toxic effects, including central nervous system depression, tremors, and skin and gastrointestinal disturbances, limit the effective use of this experimental compound.

Amphenone B

Amphenone B is a more potent inhibitor of synthesis, blocking hydroxylation at the 11, 17, and 21 positions. It does not have a destructive effect on the tissue, and the synthetic block leads to increased production of ACTH and hyperplasia of the gland. Amphenone also causes central nervous system depression and gastrointestinal tract and skin disorders, and impairs liver and thyroid function.

Metyrapone

Metyrapone (Metopirone) has a more selective effect at low doses. It inhibits 11-hydroxylation, interfering with cortisol and corticosterone synthesis and leading to the secretion of 11-deoxycortisol. In the presence of a normal pituitary gland, there is a compensatory increase in 11-deoxycortisol production. This response is a measure of the capacity of the anterior pituitary to produce ACTH and has been adapted for clinical use. Although the toxicity of metyrapone is much lower than that of the above agents, it does produce transient dizziness and gastrointestinal disturbances. This agent has not been widely used for the treatment of Cushing's syndrome. However, in doses of 0.25 g twice daily to 1 g 4 times daily, metyrapone can reduce cortisol production to normal levels in some patients with adrenal tumors, ectopic ACTH syndromes, and hyperplasia. It may be useful in the management of severe manifestations of cortisol excess while the cause is being determined or in conjunction with radiation or surgical treatment. The major side-effects observed are salt and water retention and hirsutism resulting from diversion of precursor to DOC and androgen synthesis.

Metyrapone is most commonly used in tests of adrenal function. The blood levels of 11-deoxycortisol and the urinary excretion of 17-hydroxycorticoids are measured before and after administration of the compound. Normally, there is a 2-fold or greater increase in the urinary 17-hydroxycorticoid excretion. A dosage of 300–500 mg every 4 hours for 6 doses is commonly used, and urine collections are made on the day before and the day after treatment. In patients with Cushing's syndrome, a normal response to metyrapone indicates that the cortisol excess is not the result of adrenal carcinoma or autonomous adenoma,

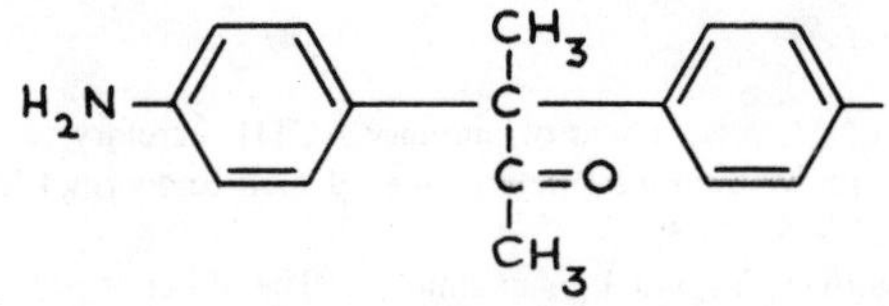

Amphenone B

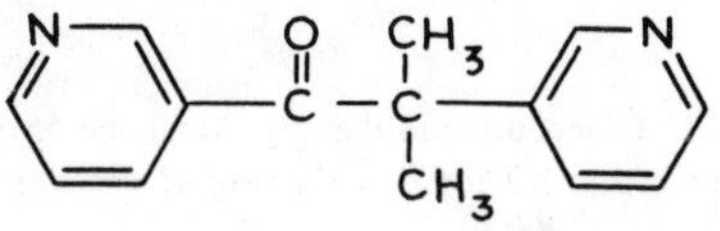

Metyrapone (Su 4885, Metopirone)

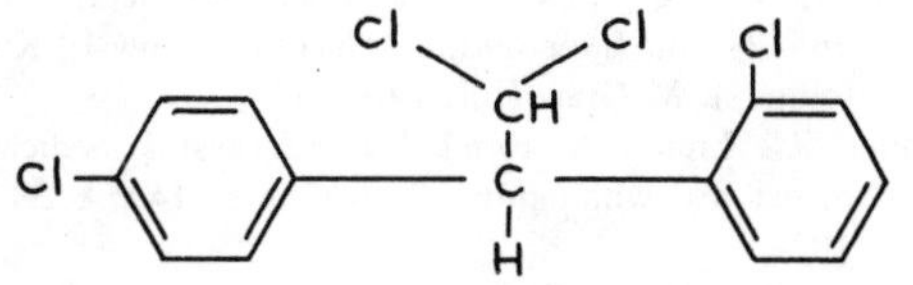

Mitotane (*o,p'*-DDD; dichloro-diphenyldichloroethane; Lysodren)

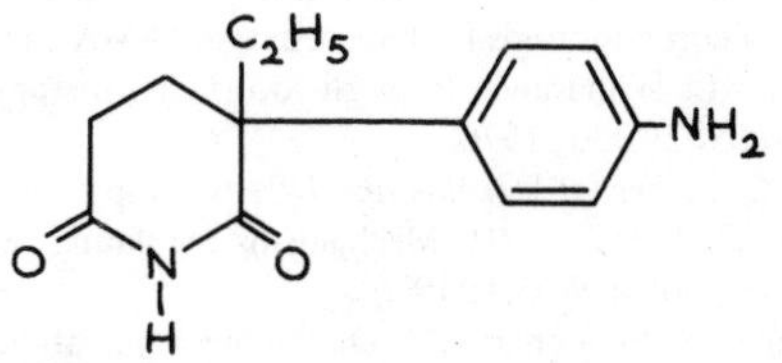

Aminoglutethimide (Elipten)

Figure 35–5. Adrenocortical antagonists.

since secretion by such tumors produces suppression of ACTH and atrophy of normal adrenal cortex.

Adrenal function may also be tested by administering metyrapone, 2–3 g orally at midnight, and measuring the level of ACTH or 11-deoxycortisol in blood drawn at 8:00 AM, or by comparing the excretion of 17-hydroxycorticosteroids in the urine during the 24-hour periods preceding and following administration of the drug.

In patients with suspected or known lesions of the pituitary, this procedure is a means of estimating the ability of the gland to produce ACTH.

Aminoglutethimide

Aminoglutethimide blocks the conversion of cholesterol to pregnenolone and causes a reduction in the synthesis of all hormonally active steroids (Fig 35–1). It has been used in conjunction with dexamethasone to reduce or eliminate estrogen and androgen production in patients with carcinoma of the breast. In doses of 1 g daily it was well tolerated; however, with higher doses, lethargy was a common effect. This drug may prove to be useful in reducing steroid secretion in patients with adrenocortical malignancy. It has been shown to enhance the metabolism of dexamethasone. During treatment, the half-life of ^{3}H-dexamethasone was reduced from 264 to 120 minutes.

Other Adrenocortical Antagonists

A number of other agents have been used in experimental work, including Su 9055, which inhibits 17-hydroxylation. Studies of the toxicity of these compounds have been sufficient to discourage extensive trials in humans.

• • •

References

Axelrod L: Glucocorticoid therapy. Medicine 55:39, 1976.

Bartter FC (editor): *The Clinical Use of Aldosterone Antagonists*. Thomas, 1960.

Bethune JE: *The Adrenal Cortex*. (A Scope Monograph.) Upjohn, 1974.

Bongiovanni AM, Root AW: The adrenogenital syndrome. (3 parts.) N Engl J Med 268:1283, 1342, 1391, 1963.

Brook CGD & others: Experience with long-term therapy in congenital adrenal hyperplasia. J Pediatr 85:12, 1974.

Burdick KH, Poulsen B, Place VA: Extemporaneous formulation of corticosteroids for topical usage. JAMA 211:462, 1970.

Byyny RL: Withdrawal from glucocorticoid therapy. N Engl J Med 295:30, 1976.

Cope CL: *Adrenal Steroids and Disease*. Lippincott, 1972.

Davis JO, Freeman RH: Mechanisms regulating renin release. Physiol Rev 56:1, 1976.

Edelman IS, Fimognari GM: On the biochemical mechanism of action of aldosterone. Recent Progr Horm Res 24:1, 1968.

Hutter AM Jr, Kayhoe DE: Adrenal cortical carcinoma: Results of treatment with o,p'DDD in 138 patients. Am J Med 41:581, 1966.

Jeffcoate WJ & others: Metyrapone in long-term management of Cushing's disease. Br Med J 2:215, 1977.

Jubiz W & others: Plasma metyrapone, adrenocorticotropic hormone, cortisol, and deoxycortisol levels: Sequential changes during oral and intravenous metyrapone administration. Arch Intern Med 125:468, 1970.

Kaplan NM: Assessment of pituitary ACTH secretory capacity with Metopirone [metyrapone]. J Clin Endocrinol Metab 23:945, 1963.

Morimoto Y, Yagura T, Yamamura Y: The effect of prolonged administration of beclomethasone dipropionate inhaler on adrenocortical functions in bronchial asthma. J Med 8:1, 1977.

Myles AB, Daly JR: *Corticosteroid and ACTH Treatment*. Williams & Wilkins, 1974.

Reid IA, Ganong WF: Control of aldosterone secretion. Pages 265–292 in: *Hypertension*. Genest J, Koiw E, Kuchel O (editors). McGraw-Hill, 1976.

Santen RJ, Lipton A, Kendall J: Successful medical adrenalectomy with amino-glutethimide. JAMA 230:1661, 1974.

Scoggins RB, Kliman B: Percutaneous absorption of corticosteroids: Systemic effects. N Engl J Med 273:831, 1965.

Slaunwhite W Jr, Sandberg A: Transcortin: A corticosteroid-binding protein of plasma. J Clin Invest 38:384, 1959.

Thorn GW: Clinical considerations in the use of corticosteroids. N Engl J Med 274:775, 1966.

Thorn GW, Lauler DP: Clinical therapeutics of adrenal disorders. Am J Med 53:673, 1972.

Zachmann M & others: Effect of aminoglutethimide on urinary cortisol and cortisol metabolites in adolescents with Cushing's syndrome. Clin Endocrinol 7:63, 1977.

CALCIUM METABOLISM

Calcium is the fifth most abundant element in the body. More than 98% of it is found in bone, largely as hydroxyapatite, but the small amounts found in the extracellular fluid and in the soft tissues have vitally important functions.

Plasma calcium exists in several forms. The normal distribution of the element in plasma is shown in Fig 36–1. However, the amount bound to protein is a function of the protein concentration and may vary accordingly in the presence of a normal level of ionized

calcium. The concentrations of these moieties and the proportions in which they are found have varied slightly depending on analytic methods. Since it is the ionized calcium that is physiologically active in plasma, none of the pathologic changes associated with hypo- or hypercalcemia are found in pathologic states of plasma protein concentrations.

The calcium in bone exchanges with extracellular fluid (Fig 36–2). The concentration of calcium ion in plasma and extracellular fluid is the resultant of several factors, including the relative rates of bone formation and dissolution, absorption from the bowel, and excretion into the bowel and by the kidney. Physiologic

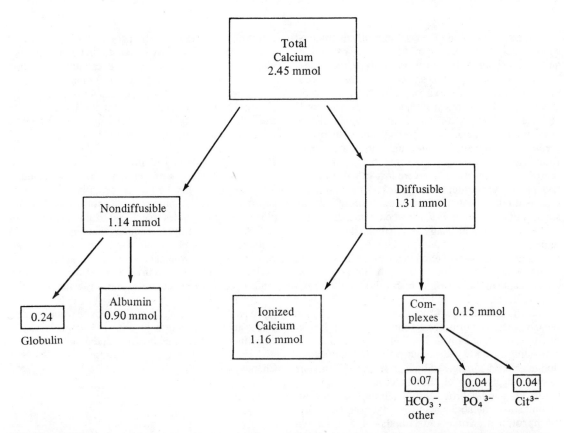

Figure 36–1. Distribution of the calcium in 1 liter of plasma. (Reproduced, with permission, from Neuman & Neuman: *The Chemical Dynamics of Bone Mineral.* University of Chicago Press, 1958. Copyright by the University of Chicago.)

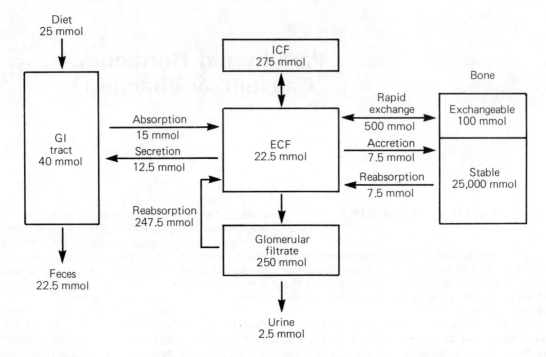

Figure 36–2. Calcium metabolism in an adult human ingesting 1000 mg (25 mmol) of calcium per day. (Modified from Rasmussen H: Parathyroid hormone, calcitonin and calciferols. In: *Textbook of Endocrinology,* 5th ed. Williams RH [editor]. Saunders, 1974.)

concentrations of calcium ion are normally maintained by the interplay of parathyroid hormone, calcitonin, and vitamin D and their effects on the above processes.

Calcium absorption is an active transport process that takes place in the proximal part of the small bowel. It is increased by parathyroid hormone and vitamin D and possibly by lactose and amino acids. Calcium absorption is decreased by cortisol and also by the presence of phytate, oxalate, and phosphate, which form insoluble salts or complexes with calcium. In the presence of steatorrhea, a severe loss of calcium may take place; the amount may be in excess of that in the diet. Not only is calcium lost in the form of calcium soaps, but less vitamin D is absorbed, which increases the loss of calcium normally secreted into the intestinal lumen.

Calcium is also excreted in the urine. It is present in the glomerular filtrate, and, of the portion of calcium retained, about 70% is reabsorbed in the proximal tubule, about 20% in the loop of Henle, and about 10% in the distal tubule. Calcium is not secreted by the renal tubules. The urinary excretion of calcium is relatively constant on a given diet, but it can be enhanced by loading the body with sodium salts. Calcium excretion may also be increased by high levels of diffusible calcium, deprivation of phosphate, high levels of vitamin D, adrenocorticosteroid administration, immobilization, metabolic acidosis, glycosuria, and hyperthyroidism. Some individuals—for unknown reasons—excrete large amounts of calcium. Urinary excretion of calcium is decreased when the glomerular filtration rate is reduced, by parathyroid hormone, by vitamin D deficiency, by increased dietary phosphate, and in the presence of increased calcium utilization during growth, pregnancy, and lactation.

The rate at which calcium leaves and enters the circulation from the readily exchangeable portion of the bone pool is controlled largely by parathyroid hormone and calcitonin (see below).

Physiologic Role of Calcium

In addition to its role in bone formation, calcium ion is necessary for the normal coagulation of blood; substances that combine with it to form soluble complexes or precipitates (such as oxalate, citrate, or EDTA) can be used as anticoagulants in vitro. In conjunction with potassium and magnesium ion, calcium regulates cardiac and skeletal muscle and nerve excitability. The effect is inversely proportionate to the ionized calcium concentration in these tissues. (For example, reduction of serum calcium concentration increases excitability.) The opposite relationship exists at the myoneural junction. Calcium is also a constituent of the intercellular cement substance.

For a more detailed discussion of calcium, see Chapter 43.

PARATHYROID HORMONE
(Parathormone, Parathyrin)

Source & Chemistry

Parathyroid hormone is secreted by 4 small glands located bilaterally at the upper and lower poles of the thyroid gland. (The number and positions may vary at times.)

Parathyroid hormone is a polypeptide consisting of 84 amino acids (Fig 36–3). It is synthesized in the chief cells as a large precursor molecule that is then cleaved to a smaller prohormone with a molecular weight of approximately 12,000. Proparathyroid hormone is not a major secretory product and has low biologic activity. This molecule is cleaved to form parathyroid hormone, which is then packaged into secretory granules that are stored within the gland or released by exocytosis. The biosynthesis of parathyroid hormone is not directly linked to secretion.

Synthetic peptides containing the first 34 N-terminal amino acids are less active but qualitatively identical to the large polypeptide. Precursor and degradation products are also found in plasma and have biologic activity.

Polypeptides with parathyroid hormone activity are also formed by malignant tumors of other tissues, including the ovaries, kidneys, and lungs.

Secretion & Metabolism

Parathyroid hormone secretion appears to be under the control of a negative feedback mechanism mediated by the direct effect of the plasma calcium ion perfusing the parathyroid gland. Hypertrophy of the gland can be induced by hypocalcemia, and involution by hypercalcemia. The hormone is not stored in appreciable amounts, constituting only about 0.04% of the glands by weight; synthesis as well as secretion can

change on a minute-to-minute basis. Parathyroid hormone released into the circulation disappears with a half-life of 15–20 minutes. The kidney removes and excretes approximately 20% of the hormone presented to it. The remainder undergoes cleavage in the liver into fragments. The N-terminal fragments have a very short half-life, whereas C-terminal fragments persist for longer periods of time. Both are excreted by the kidney.

Although the primary control of parathyroid hormone secretion is exerted by the level of plasma ionized calcium, its secretion is stimulated by low concentrations of magnesium ion, beta-adrenergic agonists, and prostaglandin E. Parathyroid hormone secretion is inhibited by high levels of calcium ion, beta-adrenergic antagonists, and severe magnesium depletion and may also be reduced during the neonatal period in premature infants.

A radioimmunoassay for parathyroid hormone has been developed. Values reported for immunoreactive parathyroid hormone are different in different laboratories, because the antisera used in the assay are heterogeneous. Levels reported are about 1 ng/mL and are inversely related to the serum calcium level.

Physiologic & Pharmacologic Considerations

A. Effects of Deficiency or Excess: Serious disturbances occur when the plasma ionized calcium level deviates from normal (see Disorders of Parathyroid Function, below). When the parathyroid glands are removed, the plasma calcium falls from its normal level of about 4.5–5.5 mEq/L to 3.5 mEq/L or less, resulting in tetany. This fall occurs within hours in the rat, but it may take several days in humans. Fall in plasma calcium is associated with an increase in serum inorganic phosphate. When parathyroid hormone is injected, the reverse occurs.

The above changes are mediated largely via the

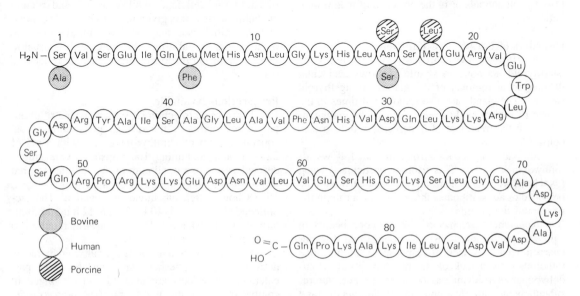

Figure 36–3. Comparison of amino acid sequences of human, porcine, and bovine parathyroid hormones.

effect of the hormone on bone metabolism and renal function. Bone is the major reservoir of calcium in the body, and parathyroid hormone acts directly on bone to release calcium, along with hydroxyproline, into the extracellular fluid by stimulating osteoclastic resorption of bone. Crude parathyroid extracts have been shown to increase the proximal renal tubular reabsorption of calcium, but studies with highly purified preparations do not seem to have this property consistently.

In addition to the effects on calcium, parathyroid hormone inhibits the renal reabsorption of phosphate at the proximal convoluted tubule and increases the excretion of cAMP.

The effect of parathyroid hormone on bone requires vitamin D, whereas the effect on renal phosphate excretion does not.

B. Mechanisms of Action: Parathyroid hormone activates adenylate cyclase in renal and bone cells. It has been postulated that this leads to increased formation of cAMP, which promotes the synthesis and release of specific lysosomal enzymes that break down the organic matrix of bone and release calcium. The calcium release may be aided by the increase in plasma citrate concentration, which is also produced by parathyroid hormone. Parathyroid hormone stimulates the uptake of ionic calcium in bone and kidney cells. In the absence of calcium, parathyroid hormone still increases cAMP but does not stimulate osteoclastic activity or bone resorption. Circulating phosphate ion can inhibit the action of parathyroid hormone at the cell. It has been shown that large amounts of purified parathyroid hormone will stimulate the oxidation and phosphate uptake of actinomycin-inhibited mitochondria. The physiologic significance of this action, if any, is not known. Parathyroid hormone in the presence of vitamin D will also stimulate the release of calcium from mitochondria under certain conditions. The response to this hormone is diminished in vitamin D-deficient animals or in the presence of magnesium deficiency.

Disorders of Parathyroid Function

A. Hypoparathyroidism: A deficiency of parathyroid hormone most often follows accidental damage to or removal of the glands during thyroid surgery. The glands are also removed at times in the course of radical neck surgery for various malignancies or in the treatment of hyperparathyroidism (see below).

Idiopathic hypoparathyroidism also follows atrophy of these glands. This disorder, particularly when associated with adrenal atrophy, is associated with the presence of autoantibodies that may play a role in the genesis of the disorder.

Apparent deficiency of the hormone occurs in "pseudohypoparathyroidism," a congenital disorder characterized by a lack of response to the hormone rather than by a lack of the hormone itself. Pseudohypoparathyroidism is associated with short stature, subcutaneous calcification, mental deficiency, and dental and skeletal abnormalities. This constellation of

congenital abnormalities also occurs with normal tissue responsiveness to parathyroid hormone (pseudopseudohypoparathyroidism).

These disorders (except for pseudopseudohypoparathyroidism) produce the symptoms of hypocalcemia (see p 377).

B. Hyperparathyroidism: Excessive production of parathyroid hormone may result from its overproduction by tissues not responsive to feedback control, such as is seen with adenomas, carcinoma, or hyperplasia of the parathyroid glands (primary hyperparathyroidism). The symptoms are due to hypercalcemia, renal calculi produced by the hypercalciuria, and skeletal lesions, including osteoclastic tumor and bone dissolution. The symptoms of hypercalcemia are discussed below. Fortunately, the measurement of serum calcium levels as a screening procedure allows diagnosis of this disorder before serious problems arise. Polypeptides with parathyroid hormone activity are also produced by tumors of other tissue and may cause hyperparathyroidism.

Excessive production of parathyroid hormone also occurs as a compensatory mechanism when chronic hypocalcemia is present, such as with intestinal malabsorption, with vitamin D lack, and with renal insufficiency (secondary hyperparathyroidism). Under these circumstances, hypercalcemia is not present and bone lesions may be prominent.

Clinical Uses

The usefulness of parathyroid extract is quite limited. Although it has been given as replacement therapy to maintain plasma calcium in hypoparathyroidism for prolonged periods of time, a combination of vitamin D preparations and calcium is much more useful.

Parathyroid extract has been used most extensively for the control of hypocalcemic manifestations of parathyroid deficiency while vitamin D and calcium are being started. It is given in doses of 50–150 units, and the initial dose may be given intravenously to obtain a more rapid effect. In any case, it is usual to give calcium intravenously for immediate relief (see below).

Preparations Available

Parathyroid injection USP (parathyroid solution, parathyroid extract), the official preparation, is an aqueous extract of parathyroid glands with a pH of 2.5–3.0 and containing 100 units/mL. One unit is defined as one one-hundredth of the amount required to raise the blood calcium of an intact dog 1 mg/dL 15–18 hours after subcutaneous injection. The recommended dose is 20–40 USP units/12 h intramuscularly or subcutaneously for 5–6 days as required to maintain serum calcium levels.

Since it is protein in nature, parathyroid extract is destroyed in the intestines and must be given parenterally. Its effects are delayed and prolonged in comparison with the highly purified preparations. When given subcutaneously in large doses, the peak effect occurs within 18 hours and may last for 38 hours. Some effect may be demonstrated as early as 4 hours after injection. If large doses are to be given, sensitivity of a patient to this protein can be tested by injecting a small amount subcutaneously or instilling it into the conjunctival sac. When used chronically, these preparations lose activity because antibodies to them develop.

CALCITONIN
(Thyrocalcitonin)

Source & Chemistry

Calcitonin is a polypeptide synthesized and secreted by cells derived embryologically from the last 2 pharyngeal pouches of the primitive foregut. In lower species, these cells are the major constituent of the ultimobranchial body. In humans and other mammals, they are distributed throughout the thyroid gland. Parafollicular cells are probably of neural crest origin and migrate to this and many other areas during embryogenesis.

Calcitonin has been isolated and purified and its structure determined. There are marked species differences. However, all of the known calcitonins contain 32 amino acids and a cystine bridge between amino acids 1 and 7. The entire structure seems to be necessary for full activity, although some activity has been observed in preparations containing the first 25 amino acids. Calcitonins derived from humans, other mammals, and lower vertebrates have been studied. Although their biologic activity is similar, there are important differences among them in amino acid sequence and potency (Fig 36–5). However, it has been difficult to relate the structure of the various molecules to their biologic activity. Salmon calcitonin has the greatest biologic activity; it is less susceptible to degradation by serum factors and has a greater affinity for receptors in bone and kidney.

Metabolism

As with other polypeptide hormones, calcitonin may be synthesized as a prohormone. Two proteins having 2 and 4 times the molecular weight of calcitonin have been identified that cross-react immunologically with calcitonin antibodies. Its secretion is controlled by the concentration of calcium in the blood perfusing the secretory tissue. A rise in serum calcium causes a prompt increase in the release of the hormone into the circulation. In normal human plasma, immunoreactive calcitonin concentrations are less than 100 pg/mL. These levels rise severalfold following intravenous infusion of calcium ion. The levels appear to be higher in men than women.

It has been proposed that a major physiologic role of calcitonin is to prevent hypercalcemia following calcium ingestion. Plasma levels of calcitonin can be increased by administration of calcium, pentagastrin, and glucagon in animals and in patients with tumors composed of calcitonin-secreting cells (eg, medullary carcinoma of the thyroid). It has also been shown that other substances increasing the intracellular cAMP levels can augment the secretion of calcitonin or its production in vitro.

The estimated half-life is 5–15 minutes. It is estimated that in humans the secretion of calcitonin may be as high as 0.4 mg/d. In contrast to parathyroid hormone, the reserve of calcitonin is large. It is found in highest concentrations in the liver and kidney. The kidney is thought to be the major site of degradation.

Physiologic Considerations

Calcitonin appears to act by inhibiting bone resorption. It has been shown to inhibit or antagonize the bone resorption induced by parathyroid hormone or vitamin D. In the rat, human calcitonin lowers serum phosphate and magnesium. Chronic administration of active extracts leads to increased bone mass, which can be accounted for entirely by the inhibition of bone resorption. However, other effects have been reported. Calcitonin augments the urinary excretion of sodium, potassium, calcium, magnesium, and phosphate. It

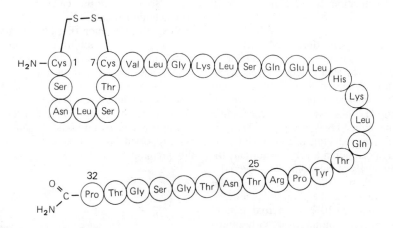

Figure 36–4. Chemical structure of synthetic salmon calcitonin.

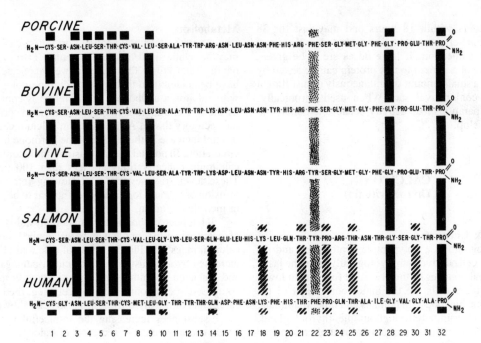

Figure 36–5. Amino acid sequences of the calcitonins.

has also been shown to inhibit calcium absorption and gastric acid secretion, and it augments the secretion of water and electrolytes in the jejunum.

Calcitonin binds to receptors on cell membranes and activates adenylate cyclase. These receptors have been found in bone, kidney, and white blood cells. Calcitonin has been shown to reduce the release of citrate into the medium when bone is cultured in vitro. Inhibitors of phosphodiesterase such as theophylline block the hypocalcemic effect of calcitonin. This observation has led to the hypothesis that calcitonin may inhibit bone resorption by increasing the rate of destruction of cAMP.

Although the physiologic role of calcitonin in the human body has not been established, studies in young animals, as noted above, suggest that it may function to decrease the mobilization of calcium from bone when calcium is ingested.

Disorders of Calcitonin Secretion

Since calcitonin inhibits the resorption of bone, it would not be expected to alter calcium levels when bone turnover is slow. When calcitonin is injected into normal adults, little change is observed. However, more marked changes are observed in the presence of a hypercalcemic state. When bone turnover is elevated, as in Paget's disease, the reduction of calcium levels is marked even though calcitonin levels are normal. Increased circulating levels of calcitonin have been detected in patients with medullary carcinoma of the thyroid, a tumor arising from the parafollicular cells. These tumors constitute 5–10% of thyroid tumors and are often found in conjunction with pheochromocytomas, chief cell adenomas (multiple endo-

crine neoplasia, type 2), or pheochromocytomas and mucosal neuromas (multiple endocrine neoplasia, type 3). These syndromes have a high familial occurrence. The detection of increased levels of calcitonin has been useful in the diagnosis of these disorders.

Preparations

Several preparations of calcitonin have been studied for use in humans. The most potent of these is salmon ultimobranchial calcitonin, which has detectable effects in doses as low as 0.3 μg (one-tenth the dose of synthetic human calcitonin and one one-hundredth the amount of porcine calcitonin required for comparable effects).

Preliminary studies indicate that calcitonin can produce remissions in patients with Paget's disease. It will also lower serum calcium levels in some hypercalcemic patients.

Synthetic salmon (Fig 36–4) calcitonin is available as a sterile lyophilized powder containing 400 MRC units per vial with gelatin. It is reconstituted with diluent and injected intravenously or intramuscularly in doses of 100 MRC units daily. Careful monitoring of serum calcium levels is required. It is approved for use in Paget's disease. Allergic reactions may occur. The appearance of antibodies to salmon calcitonin has been reported in some patients under treatment with this preparation.

VITAMIN D

A major physiologic regulator of mineral metabolism in humans, 1,25-dihydroxyvitamin D, is produced from vitamin D precursors in response to alterations in calcium and phosphate metabolism by the enzyme 1α-hydroxylase. The primary stimulus to the activity of this enzyme appears to be low serum phosphate and low serum calcium. Although low phosphate may act directly at the kidney, the low calcium signal probably is transmitted by stimulation of parathyroid hormone release from the parathyroid gland, which then acts on the kidney. There is evidence that 1,25-dihydroxyvitamin D also exerts feedback regulation on its own formation. When levels of this hormone are enhanced in the blood, calcium and phosphate are mobilized from intestine and bone, correcting the original stimulus. When calcium alone is deficient in the plasma, the parathyroid hormone that is secreted causes a loss of phosphate in the urine, allowing individual modulation of calcium and phosphorus levels.

Source & Chemistry

The D vitamins are sterols formed from precursors (provitamins) derived from plant and animal sources. The structures and synthetic pathways in humans are shown in Fig 36–6. Ergosterol, which is derived from plants, and 7-dehydrocholesterol, from animal sources, are converted to ergocalciferol (vitamin D_2) and cholecalciferol (vitamin D_3), respectively, by ultraviolet radiation in the skin. Cholecalciferol appears to be a major storage form of vitamin D.

The skin contains 3–4% 7-dehydrocholesterol in adults, and infants may have twice as much. Skin also contains 3.2 μg/g—17 IU/cm²—of cholecalciferol, and more than 200 IU are formed daily with exposure to the sun. The cholecalciferol formed enters the circulation and is bound to a specific carrier globulin.

Ergocalciferol and cholecalciferol and their precursors are well absorbed through the skin, the gastrointestinal tract, and when given parenterally. However, when steatorrhea is present or mineral oil is given, intestinal absorption is poor. When radioactive cholecalciferol is given by mouth to normal subjects, about 80% is absorbed and the remainder is recovered from the feces unchanged. The radioactive sterol initially appears in the chylomicron fraction of plasma and is gradually transferred to a carrier globulin.

Ergocalciferol and cholecalciferol are converted to their 25-hydroxyl derivatives in the liver. 25-Hydroxycholecalciferol and 25-hydroxyergocalciferol appear to be equally active, and both bind to the cytosol acceptor proteins in the kidney. They constitute the major fraction of circulating vitamin D (Table 36–1) but are relatively inactive. In the kidney, 25-hydroxycholecalciferol is converted to either 1,25- or 24,25-dihydroxycholecalciferol. The former substance is the most active form of vitamin D known (Table 36–1); the latter has little activity. Conversion to the active form, 1,25-dihydroxycholecalciferol, by the kidney, is stimulated by parathyroid hormone. This mechanism may serve in the feedback regulation of circulating vitamin D activity.

Further information on the metabolism and excretion of these sterols is not available. Less than 3% of an oral or intravenous dose is recovered in urine in 48–72 hours, and most of this material is in the form of biologically inactive water-soluble conjugates.

Physiologic Considerations

Vitamin D is one of several factors required for normal calcium and phosphorus metabolism. As noted above (see p 372), it may be required for the normal activity of parathyroid hormone. The D vitamins and related sterols increase the gastrointestinal absorption of ingested calcium and phosphorus. Administration of this vitamin increases the citrate content of bone, heart, kidneys, and blood of experimental animals.

The mechanism of action of vitamin D leading to the dissolution of bone is not well understood. However, its effects on the gastrointestinal absorption of calcium have been extensively studied. Vitamin D enhances the transfer of calcium across the intestine in both directions. It increases the uptake and release of this ion and induces the formation of a calcium-binding protein responsible for the transfer. The normal lack of permeability of the intestine to calcium is an active process requiring an expenditure of energy to be maintained. Vitamin D also stimulates a phosphate transport system separate from the calcium transport system.

A. Vitamin D Deficiency: A deficiency in vitamin D leads to inadequate absorption of calcium and phosphorus. In order to maintain plasma calcium levels, parathyroid hormone is secreted, leading to the mobilization of calcium and phosphorus from bone. In children, the resulting demineralization produces rickets; in adults, osteomalacia.

Table 36–1. Plasma concentration, turnover, and comparative effects of various sterols.

Substance	Plasma Level (in USA)	Gut	Activity Bone	Kidney	Half-Life
Cholecalciferol	8–45 ng/mL	+	−	−	19–25 h
25-Hydroxyergocalciferol (25-HEC) and	7–50 ng/mL	++	+	+	29 d
25-Hydroxycholecalciferol (25-HCC)					
1,25-Dihydroxycholecalciferol (1,25-DHCC)	25–40 pg/mL	++++	++++	−	−

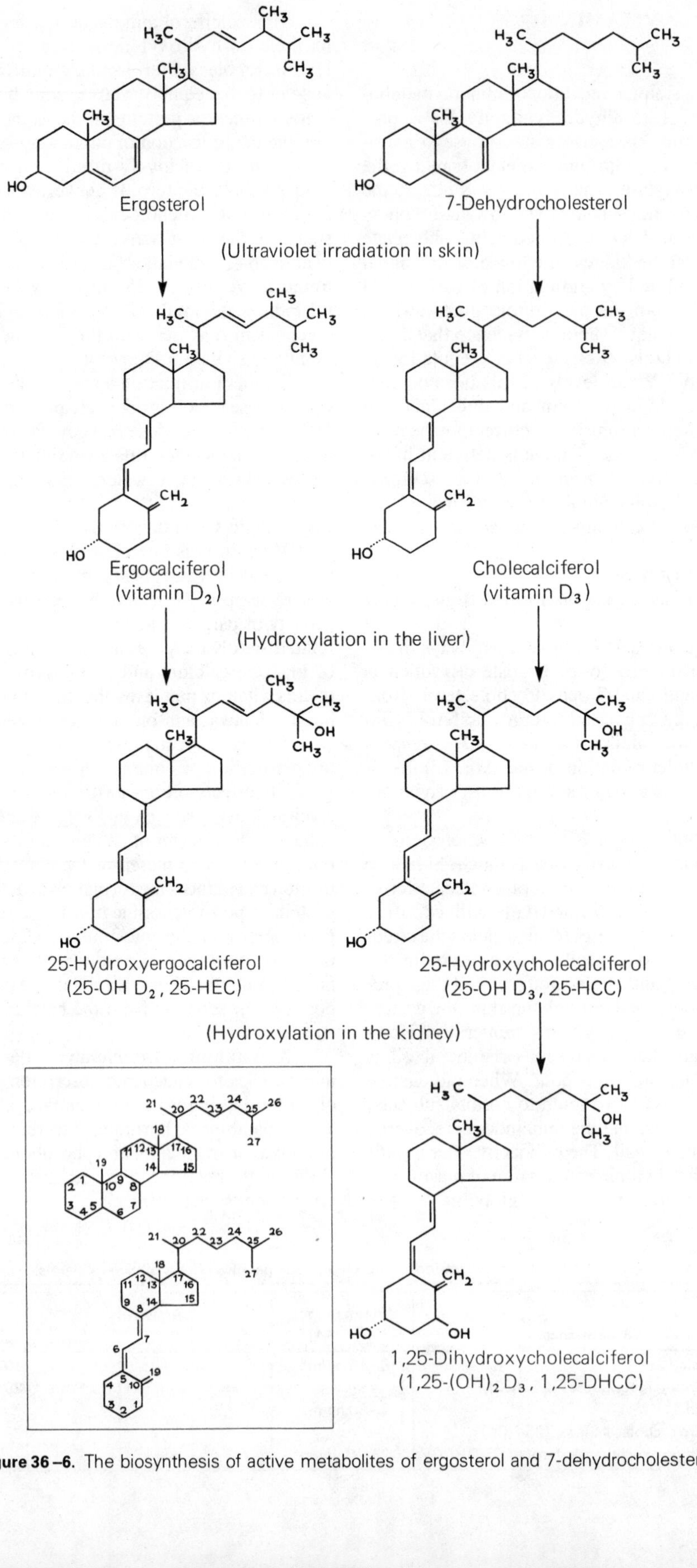

Ergosterol

7-Dehydrocholesterol

(Ultraviolet irradiation in skin)

Ergocalciferol
(vitamin D_2)

Cholecalciferol
(vitamin D_3)

(Hydroxylation in the liver)

25-Hydroxyergocalciferol
(25-OH D_2, 25-HEC)

25-Hydroxycholecalciferol
(25-OH D_3, 25-HCC)

(Hydroxylation in the kidney)

1,25-Dihydroxycholecalciferol
(1,25-$(OH)_2 D_3$, 1,25-DHCC)

Figure 36–6. The biosynthesis of active metabolites of ergosterol and 7-dehydrocholesterol.

Recent studies indicate that patients with vitamin D-resistant rickets have abnormal vitamin D metabolism marked by a decreased rate of conversion of vitamin D to its active metabolites. Patients with renal osteodystrophy also show defective conversion.

B. Vitamin D Excess: Hypervitaminosis D results from the chronic ingestion of large doses (150,000 units/d) of the vitamin. This is a serious disorder in which the usual signs, symptoms, and sequelae of hypercalcemia are produced (see below). Metastatic calcification of soft tissues is common.

Clinical Uses

Vitamin D_2 is most commonly used (with calcium) to supplement the diet of infants in order to prevent rickets. With rare exceptions, an intake of about 400 units daily provides optimal concentrations of vitamin D.

When a deficiency has become established, large doses may shorten the recovery time. Doses of 3000–4000 units daily may be administered for several weeks. In vitamin D-resistant rickets, as much as 500,000 units may be required daily.

In preliminary studies, hydroxycholecalciferol (D_3), in doses of 15 mg 1–3 times weekly, or 25-hydroxy D_3, 1α-hydroxy D_3, and 1,25-dihydroxy D_3 in microgram doses daily have been found to inhibit or reverse the development of renal osteodystrophy in patients with severe kidney disease.

Vitamin D and dihydrotachysterol (see below) are useful in the treatment of hypocalcemia due to hypoparathyroidism. Ergocalciferol in doses of 50–250 thousand units daily is frequently given with supplemental calcium salts, the dose being determined by the effects on the serum calcium level.

Vitamin D in large doses has been used in the treatment of other diseases such as rheumatoid arthritis and psoriasis. There is no convincing evidence that it is effective in controlling these disorders, and the incidence of serious toxicity makes its use inadvisable.

Vitamin D metabolites such as 25-hydroxycholecalciferol (calcifediol) and 1,25-dihydroxycholecalciferol are under study for clinical use. Dihydrotachysterol and 1,25-dihydroxycholecalciferol may be useful when renal damage is sufficiently

Dihydrotachysterol$_2$

marked to interfere with hydroxylation at the 1 position.

1α-Hydroxycholecalciferol has also been used as a potent vitamin D analog that can bypass the inability of the kidney to perform the 1α hydroxylation. This compound is converted by the liver to 1,25-dihydroxyvitamin D.

TREATMENT OF HYPOCALCEMIA

Hypocalcemia is characterized by neuromuscular excitability, tetanic muscular contractions, and positive Chvostek's and Trousseau's signs. When chronic, it is commonly associated with cataracts, papilledema, skin disorders, and calcification of the basal ganglia. It is most often seen following removal of the parathyroid glands, in malabsorption syndromes, and in chronic renal failure.

When manifestations of hypocalcemia are severe, they are relieved by the slow intravenous administration of 5–20 mL of 5% calcium chloride or 10% calcium gluconate. A large variety of preparations are available for oral use when symptoms are mild. In the treatment of hypoparathyroidism, these preparations are given with vitamin D, the dose being adjusted to maintain serum calcium at normal concentrations.

TREATMENT OF HYPERCALCEMIA

Hypercalcemia is seen in a variety of circumstances including malignant tumors of the breast and other tissues, hyperparathyroidism, vitamin D intoxication, milk-alkali syndrome, hyperthyroidism, idiopathic hypercalcemia of infants, and others. Regardless of the cause, serious complications may follow if there is calcium deposition in the kidney or if the serum calcium is markedly elevated. The cause of the disorder must be ascertained and treated in order to maintain control over the process.

The treatment of hypercalcemia should include general supportive measures, nonspecific measures to reduce serum calcium levels, and specific therapy of the underlying disorder. Supportive measures include the correction of dehydration by the administration of large quantities of fluid (parenterally if necessary). This will serve to dilute serum calcium and promote its loss in the urine by increasing glomerular filtration and urine volume. Associated electrolyte disturbances can be corrected at the same time. In patients with heart disease, consideration must be given to adjustments in digitalis dosage and the treatment of arrhythmias.

When serum calcium levels are markedly elevated or when signs and symptoms of hypercalcemia are present (eg, weakness, polyuria, thirst, anorexia, nausea, somnolence, azotemia, or stupor), it is urgent that measures to reduce calcium levels be instituted. Since calcium excretion parallels that of sodium excretion (except with thiazide administration) and since patients are usually dehydrated, initial therapy consists of giving large volumes of saline along with furosemide to promote natriuresis. Sodium sulfate orally (5–10 g/d) or intravenously (200 mEq/L) will enhance the loss of calcium. The careful measurement and replacement of other substances lost (water, potassium, magnesium, etc) may be required.

Calcitonin in doses of approximately 4 MRC units/kg intramuscularly every 12 hours will produce a rapid fall in serum calcium concentrations in about 6 hours in about 80% of patients. Salmon calcitonin is the most potent and has the longest duration of action. Reductions of the serum calcium concentration of more than 0.7 mmol/L (3 mg/dL) are unusual, and in severe hypercalcemia this treatment requires supplementation with other measures.

Sodium phytate (Rencal), a drug currently being studied, administered in doses of 3 g 3 times daily by mouth, will reduce calcium absorption. Disodium ethylenediaminetetraacetate (EDTA) has been used to chelate calcium ion, but the rapid reduction of calcium levels that may occur is dangerous and this form of therapy is rarely used.

When renal failure is present, hemodialysis may be useful. In patients with heart failure, the enhancement of digitalis toxicity should be kept in mind.

Glucocorticoids such as prednisone (30–50 mg/d) will usually reduce hypercalcemia in patients with sarcoidosis and malignancies, but this rarely happens in patients with hyperparathyroidism. Once the level is lowered, the improvement can usually be maintained by lower doses of the steroid and the elimination of milk and dairy products from the diet.

When these measures fail, mithramycin and inorganic phosphate may be used, although they are potentially very toxic. A fall in serum calcium is produced by phosphate, but much of the calcium is deposited in the body rather than excreted in the urine. This may lead to metastatic calcification as well as deposition in bone. This form of therapy may be more useful when phosphate depletion and hypophosphatemia accompany hypercalcemia, as is the case in patients with renal transplants or primary hyperparathyroidism.

• • •

References

Anast C & others: Thyrocalcitonin and the response to parathyroid hormone. J Clin Invest 46:57, 1967.

Aurbach GD & others: Polypeptide hormones and calcium metabolism. Ann Intern Med 70:1243, 1969.

Chakmakjian ZH, Bethune JE: Sodium sulfate treatment of hypercalcemia. N Engl J Med 275:862, 1966.

Copp DH: Endocrine control of calcium homeostasis. J Endocrinol 43:137, 1969.

DeLuca HF: Vitamin D metabolism and function. Arch Intern Med 138:836, 1978.

Eisman JA & others: Modulation of plasma 1,25-dihydroxyvitamin D in man by stimulation and suppression tests. Lancet 2:931, 1979.

F. Raymond Keating Jr Memorial Symposium: Hyperparathyroidism, 1970. Am J Med 50:557, 1971.

Forscher BK, Arnaud CD (editors): Third Raymond Keating Jr Memorial Symposium: Parathyroid hormone, calcitonin, and vitamin D. Medicine 56:73, 1974.

Habener JF, Potts JT Jr: Biosynthesis of parathyroid hormone. N Engl J Med 299:580, 1978.

Haussler MR, McCain TA: Basic and clinical concepts related to vitamin D metabolism and action. (2 parts.) N Engl J Med 297:104, 974, 1977.

Hirsch PF, Munson PL: Thyrocalcitonin. Physiol Rev 49:548, 1969.

Howard JE, Thomas WC: Clinical disorders of calcium homeostasis. Medicine 42:25, 1963.

Martin KJ & others: The peripheral metabolism of parathyroid hormone. N Engl J Med 301:1092, 1979.

Medalle R, Waterhouse C, Hahn TJ: Vitamin D resistance in mangesium deficiency. Am J Clin Nutr 19:296, 1976.

Nordin BCE (editor): *Calcium, Phosphate and Magnesium Metabolism: Clinical Physiology and Diagnostic Procedures.* Churchill Livingstone, 1976.

Norman AW: Vitamin D metabolism and calcium absorption. Am J Med 67:989, 1979.

Nusynowitz ML, Frame B, Kolb FO: The spectrum of hypoparathyroid states based on physiologic principles. Medicine 55:105, 1976.

Potts JT Jr, Aurbach GD, Sherwood LM: Parathyroid hormone: Chemical properties and structural requirements for biological and immunological activity. Recent Progr Horm Res 22:101, 1966.

Queener SF, Bell NH: Calcitonin: A general survey. Metabolism 24:555, 1975.

Singer FR & others: Mithramycin treatment of intractable hypercalcemia due to parathyroid carcinoma. N Engl J Med 283:634, 1970.

Steichen JJ & others: Vitamin D homeostasis in the perinatal period: 1,25-Dihydroxyvitamin D in maternal, cord and neonatal blood. N Engl J Med 302:315, 1980.

Talmage RM, Munson PL (editors): *Calcium, Parathyroid Hormone and the Calcitonins.* Excerpta Medica, 1972.

Wallach S & others: Effect of salmon calcitonin on skeletal mass in osteoporosis. Curr Ther Res 22:556, 1977.

Wisneski LA & others: Salmon calcitonin in hypercalcemia. Clin Pharmacol Ther 24:219, 1978.

Insulin, Glucagon, Oral Antidiabetic Drugs, & Hyperglycemic Agents | 37

The pancreatic islet cell hormones, including insulin and glucagon, are secreted by the islets of Langerhans. These islets comprise 2–3% of the pancreas, with a total weight of 1–2 g in the adult human. There are approximately 1 million islets, and when extracted they are found to contain approximately 8 mg of insulin. At least 4 types of cells have been identified in these islets, and they are shown in Table 37–1 with their secretory products. The cell types are not evenly distributed through the human pancreas. In some islets in the posterior portion of the head of the pancreas, there are lobules in which PP cells make up as much as 80% of the cells and A cells less than 1%.

INSULIN

Chemistry

Insulin is a small protein with a molecular weight of approximately 6000. It contains 51 amino acids arranged in 2 chains (A and B) linked by disulfide bridges, and there are species differences in the amino acids of both chains (Fig 37–1). Insulin is synthesized in the pancreas by the B cells of the islets of Langerhans, from which it can be extracted for pharmaceutical purposes. It is usually obtained from beef or pork pancreas. When purified, it crystallizes in the presence of zinc as an odorless white powder that is insoluble at neutral pH but soluble in dilute mineral acids or alkali.

Table 37–1. Distribution of cell types in the pancreatic islets.

Cell	Approximate Percent of Islet Cells	Secretory Products
Alpha or A	20	Glucagon, proglucagon
Beta or B	75	Insulin, proinsulin, C-peptide
Delta or D	24	Somatostatin
PP or F	1	Pancreatic polypeptide*

*Pancreatic polypeptide has been isolated and characterized; however, its physiologic role is undefined.

Structural modifications found to destroy biologic activity include esterification of the carboxyl groups; oxidation or reduction of the disulfide groups; degradation by chymotrypsin, pepsin, or papain and removal of the C-terminal group of the A chain; modification of the free amino groups or aliphatic hydroxyl groups; and reduction with thioglycolate and removal of the C-terminal alanine from the B chain. Although limited proteolysis with carboxypeptidase or trypsin will not destroy the biologic activity of the insulin molecule, destruction by the proteolytic activity in the digestive tract prevents its oral use.

Physiologic & Pharmacologic Considerations

A. Biosynthesis and Metabolism: Insulin synthesis in the B cell of the pancreatic islets begins with the synthesis of a long single-chain peptide molecule within the rough endoplasmic reticulum. This peptide, called preproinsulin, has a molecular weight of 12,000. It is converted to proinsulin and transported to the Golgi apparatus to be packaged into granules. Proteolysis occurs in the granules by cleavage of the polypeptide connecting the amino terminal of the A chain to the carboxy terminal of the B chain (Fig 37–2). The amino acids shown with dashed borders are removed, leaving insulin and the 31-amino-acid connecting or C-peptide. During the process of secretion, the insulin-containing granules move to the cell membrane, attach to the microtubular-microfilament system, and are released by emeiocytosis in response to appropriate stimuli. It is estimated that approximately 2 mg (50 units) are released into the portal vein daily. Along with the insulin, proinsulin—its precursor—which constitutes about 5% of the immunoreactive insulin extracted from the human pancreas, is also released. Proinsulin is biologically inactive, and, since it is not removed by the liver, it has a longer half-life than insulin and accumulates in the blood. In fasting plasma, proinsulin represents 10–20% of circulating immunoreactive insulin (17 pmol/L). The C-peptide, which is also biologically inactive, is released in equimolar ratio to each insulin molecule. It has a slightly longer half-life than insulin. The average fasting plasma level is 1000 pmol/L.

The concentration of insulin in the fasting human is, on the average, 70 pmol/L (0.4 ng/mL, 10 mU/mL). After meals, there is a slow rise in peripheral

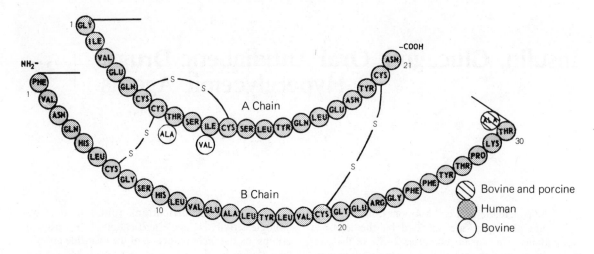

Figure 37–1. Structure of human insulin, with differences in amino acid sequences of porcine and bovine insulin.

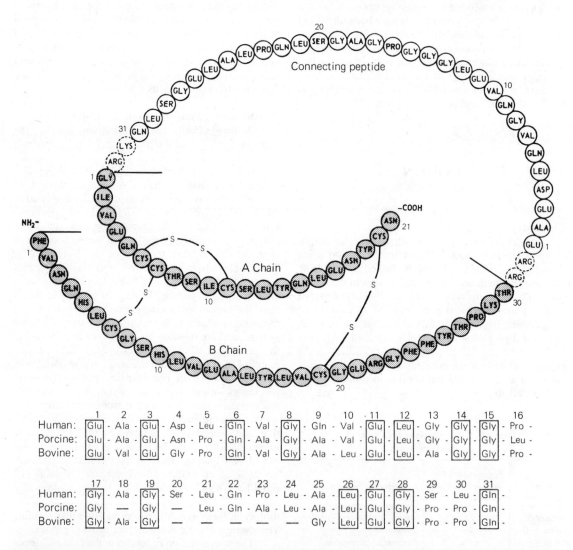

	1	2	3	4	5	6	7	8	9	10	11	12	13	14	15	16
Human:	Glu	Ala	Glu	Asp	Leu	Gln	Val	Gly	Gln	Val	Glu	Leu	Gly	Gly	Gly	Pro -
Porcine:	Glu	Ala	Glu	Asn	Pro	Gln	Ala	Gly	Ala	Val	Glu	Leu	Gly	Gly	Gly	Leu -
Bovine:	Glu	Val	Glu	Gly	Pro	Gln	Val	Gly	Ala	Leu	Glu	Leu	Ala	Gly	Gly	Pro -

	17	18	19	20	21	22	23	24	25	26	27	28	29	30	31
Human:	Gly	Ala	Gly	Ser	Leu	Gln	Pro	Leu	Ala	Leu	Glu	Gly	Ser	Leu	Gln -
Porcine:	Gly	—	Gly	—	Leu	Gln	Ala	Leu	Ala	Leu	Glu	Gly	Pro	Pro	Gln -
Bovine:	Gly	Ala	Gly	—	—	—	—	—	Gly	Leu	Glu	Gly	Pro	Pro	Gln -

Figure 37–2. Structure of human proinsulin. Comparisons of human, porcine, and bovine C-peptides are shown in the accompanying diagram. Identical residues are shown in boxes.

levels of insulin beginning about 10 minutes after food ingestion and reaching a peak in 30–45 minutes. Levels seldom exceed 700 pmol/L (100 mU/mL). Normally, the release of insulin is controlled by the concentration of glucose in the plasma perfusing the gland. Glucose directly stimulates the release of stored insulin within 30–60 seconds. This initial phase of insulin secretion is blocked by dinitrophenyl but not by puromycin, which inhibits insulin synthesis. If levels of glucose perfusing the gland remain elevated, glucose also stimulates insulin synthesis. It is not known whether glucose itself or a metabolite provides the signal for secretion or synthesis. The stimulation of insulin secretion by glucose can be blocked by mannoheptulose, glucosamine, and 2-deoxyglucose. Some agents such as amino acids and fatty acids can stimulate insulin release but only in the presence of glucose. This suggests a mechanism requiring more than one site of activation. Mannose—and fructose to a lesser extent—will also stimulate insulin release, whereas nonmetabolizable sugars (eg, galactose, ribose, and xylose) will not.

Other stimuli are known to affect the rate of secretion. It is increased by secretory products of the gastrointestinal tract such as secretin, gastrin, pancreozymin, and a glucagonlike factor and by some of the oral hypoglycemic agents (see below). Gastric inhibitory peptide (GIP), although not a B cell stimulant at normal blood sugar levels, promotes insulin release at plasma glucose levels of about 100 mg/dL and becomes more effective as the sugar level rises. Secretion is inhibited by epinephrine and related compounds with alpha-adrenergic activity by activation of the alpha-adrenergic receptor. Blocking of the alpha receptor by phentolamine results in the stimulation of insulin release by epinephrine by activation of the beta-adrenergic receptor. Stimulation of the vagus increases insulin release. Other hormones such as growth hormone and glucocorticoids also increase levels of circulating insulin in the intact animal. However, this may not be a direct effect on the pancreas.

When secreted, insulin may be bound in part to the serum globulins, but the specificity of this binding in persons not treated with insulin has not been established. Once insulin has entered the circulation, it is taken up by the tissues or metabolized rapidly, as indicated by a half-life of about 10 minutes. A large proportion of the secreted hormone is taken up by the liver. In spite of the rapid rate of clearance from the circulation, its effects may be manifest for hours. In the fasting or postabsorptive state, the concentration of insulin is about 25 μU/mL plasma by immunoassay, and the concentration may rise to as much as 5 times that level after a glucose load. Plasma concentrations of insulinlike activity (ILA), when determined by in vitro bioassay utilizing changes in glucose uptake by rat diaphragm or epididymal fat pad, appear to be much higher, and the excess is largely due to circulating somatomedins (see Growth Hormone, p 418).

The breakdown of insulin is the result of the action of glutathione insulin transhydrogenase on the A and B chains that have been separated by reductive cleavage of the disulfide linkages. After the reductive cleavage, further degradation by proteolysis occurs. These changes take place mainly in the liver. However, kidney, placenta, muscle, and, to a lesser extent, plasma exhibit the ability to degrade insulin.

The uptake by tissue and rate of destruction may be inhibited by the binding of insulin to antibodies and other proteins under abnormal circumstances (eg, diabetes mellitus).

B. Effects of Insulin: Insulin influences the metabolism of a wide variety of tissues. It plays a key role in the intermediary metabolism of muscle and adipose tissue and has important effects in the liver.

Insulin is taken up by most tissues studied, except for red blood cells and portions of the brain. It is bound to receptors on the cell membrane and exerts many of its effects at that site. Insulin receptors—specific molecules with a high specificity and affinity for insulin—are present on the surface membranes of almost all cells in the body. Their concentration is decreased by exposure to high levels of insulin; consequently, they are present in reduced concentrations in obesity, hyperinsulinemia, and diabetes and in the presence of excess growth hormone. The decrease in concentration is associated with a decrease in the insulin response. Glucocorticoids cause resistance to insulin by decreasing the receptor's affinity for insulin. The affinity for insulin is increased in states of insulin sensitivity produced by glucocorticoid or growth hormone deficiency or by exercise. Insulin may also enter the cell and actuate some processes by binding to intracellular receptors. The means by which membrane-bound insulin stimulates intracellular processes and membrane transport is unknown.

In muscle and adipose tissue, insulin increases the cellular uptake of amino acids, nucleotides, glucose, and other monosaccharides along with potassium and phosphate ions. (Similar effects occur in connective tissue and leukocytes but not in brain, kidney, or red blood cells.)

In muscle and adipose tissue, the uptake of glucose is a rate-limiting step in the subsequent metabolism of this sugar. The uptake of nonmetabolizable sugars is also increased, indicating that the further metabolism of glucose is not required for this action of insulin. The transport effects of insulin occur in minutes and are not inhibited by actinomycin, suggesting that the synthesis of new proteins is not required. Insulin appears to activate glycogen synthetase and hexokinase, although the effect has not been proved to be directly on the enzyme.

In adipose tissue, insulin inhibits the lipase that breaks down triglycerides to glycerol and fatty acids, and it promotes the production of glycerophosphate from glucose, leading to the resynthesis of triglycerides from fatty acids.

In the liver, the intracellular glucose concentration is dependent upon the concentration of glucose in the perfusing plasma and is not directly altered by insulin. However, insulin decreases the output of glu-

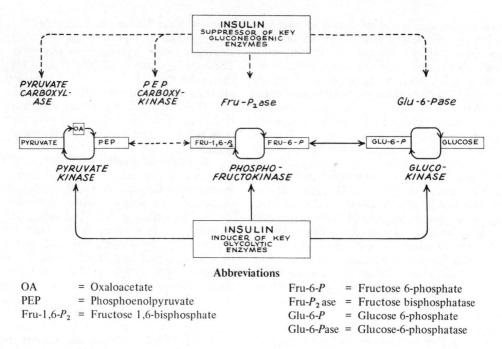

Figure 37–3. Suppressor and inducer function of insulin on key liver enzymes. (Reproduced, with permission, from Harper HA, Rodwell VW, Mayes PA: *Review of Physiological Chemistry*, 17th ed. Lange, 1979.)

cose and urea by the liver and increases the uptake of potassium and phosphate by this organ. Insulin stimulates glycolysis and inhibits gluconeogenesis by inducing the formation of enzymes controlling the former process and repressing those promoting the latter process (Fig 37–3). These changes may also be secondary to other metabolic alterations rather than direct effects of insulin.

C. Abnormalities of Insulin Action: A deficiency of insulin effect occurs most commonly in diabetes mellitus, a complex group of disorders that includes rare instances of abnormal insulin production, anti-insulin receptor antibodies, toxic destruction of the pancreatic islets by pesticides containing alloxan (see p 391), pancreatectomy, and Cushing's syndrome, or that may occur following glucocorticoid therapy or in the presence of growth hormone excess. Most commonly, diabetes appears to be the result of one or more inherited defects, destruction of the pancreatic islets by viral infections or an autoimmune process, or a combination of these factors.

Clinical Uses

A. Diabetes Mellitus: Two important aspects of diabetes mellitus are the deficiency in insulin effect and the basement membrane thickening found in small blood vessels. These are the earliest detectable findings, and their relationship to each other is not known. The characteristic symptoms of the disorder are the consequence of the relative or complete lack of insulin on intermediary metabolism, whereas many of the complications result from disease of the blood vessels. Unfortunately, even properly treated and well-controlled diabetes (from the metabolic standpoint) may progress to serious vascular complications. The symptoms of diabetes result from decreased utilization of glucose in peripheral tissues such as muscle and adipose tissue and increased release of glucose (gluconeogenesis) into the circulation by the liver.

The clinical disorder is not detectable in its earliest stages. As the severity increases, the above-mentioned defect in insulin action can be identified. This is followed by an alteration in carbohydrate metabolism characterized by a reduction in the rate at which glucose is removed from the circulation (impaired glucose tolerance). The disorder progresses until blood glucose levels are sufficiently high to permit the loss of this sugar in the urine. When insulin deficiency is marked, as in early onset or "juvenile" diabetes, large amounts of glucose appear in the urine, and the ensuing osmotic diuresis and loss of carbohydrate leads to the full-blown syndrome of polyphagia, polydipsia, polyuria, and weight loss.

The increased utilization of fat from adipose tissue stores as a source of energy and the conversion of protein to glucose—much of which is lost in the urine—leads to weight loss in spite of increased food intake.

Fat that is mobilized as free fatty acids is partly converted to triglyceride in the liver and partly oxidized in the liver and other tissues. An excess of acetylcoenzyme A is formed in the liver and converted to ketones, some of which are organic acids. When ketone production exceeds the rate of utilization, organic acids accumulate in the body and cause metabolic acidosis. This in turn leads to the loss of fixed

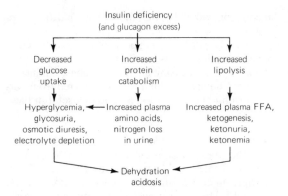

Figure 37–4. Effects of insulin deficiency. (Courtesy of RJ Havel. Reproduced, with permission, from Ganong WF: *Review of Medical Physiology,* 9th ed. Lange, 1979.)

base (sodium and potassium). The metabolic changes in diabetes are summarized in Fig 37–4. These changes can be prevented or corrected by the administration of insulin and a proper diet. However, if not checked by the institution of an appropriate therapeutic program, the loss of water and electrolytes and the accumulation of hydrogen ion lead to diabetic acidosis and coma, which may be fatal.

The dose and type of insulin must be determined for each patient by clinical trial. In a given patient, the amount required will depend upon the amount of endogenous insulin available, the diet, and exercise (which tends to decrease the need for insulin). The management of the patient therefore requires coordinated control of diet, exercise, and insulin dosage and distribution. In diabetic as well as in nondiabetic individuals, blood sugar rises after each feeding. Degree and duration of the increase is proportionate to the amount of carbohydrate ingested, and the duration of the peak depends as well on the rate of absorption. The use of intermittent injections of short-acting insulin (prior to meals) or the use of 1 or 2 injections of a longer-acting preparation—or a mixture of short- and longer-acting insulin (eg, regular and NPH)—serves to reduce blood sugar increase after meals. When large doses of long-acting insulin are administered and circulating insulin levels are continuously elevated, it is useful to have the patient ingest small amounts of food at frequent intervals. Insulin therapy must be adapted to the patient's habits in order to prevent excessive hypoglycemia or hyperglycemia if the patient is unable to conform to a set pattern of activity and eating.

Insulin requirements rise with increased metabolic activity due to fever, thyrotoxicosis, and pregnancy, and also during periods of stress such as surgery, traumatic injuries, infections, and diabetic acidosis. Increased insulin requirements may be associated with the presence of high titers of insulin-binding antibodies.

B. Insulin Tolerance Test: The insulin tolerance test consists of the intravenous injection of crystalline insulin in a dose of 0.1 unit/kg body weight and the

measurement of blood glucose at frequent intervals thereafter (eg, 0, 15, 30, 45, and 60 minutes; or 0, 20, 30, 40, and 60 minutes). A normal individual, after an overnight fast, will have a fall in blood glucose of about 50–70% in 20–40 minutes and a return to normal in 60–90 minutes. A decrease in the hypoglycemic effect of insulin is found in acromegaly (excessive growth hormone production), Cushing's syndrome, and diabetes mellitus. Patients with pituitary or adrenocortical insufficiency are highly sensitive to insulin, and the test should not be administered to such patients.

Insulin-induced hypoglycemia also increases the plasma levels of growth hormone as measured by immunoassay and is used to test the reserve of this hormone. Arginine infusions will provoke a similar rise in growth hormone levels; in patients suspected of having a deficiency of growth hormone, arginine is safer than insulin for this purpose.

Adverse Reactions

A. Hyperinsulinism: The toxicity of insulin is essentially confined to the effects of overdosage (hyperinsulinism), usually the result of unanticipated changes in the insulin requirements of diabetic patients.* This often occurs because of the omission of meals or increased exercise. It may also occur as a result of errors in filling syringes and failure to understand the physician's directions, particularly when more than one preparation of insulin is employed.

The predominant symptoms vary with the type of insulin—probably a reflection of the rate at which the blood glucose falls. Although symptoms do not usually occur unless the blood glucose falls to levels below 50 mg/dL, a rapid fall from very high to slightly elevated or normal levels will sometimes provoke characteristic symptoms. The signs and symptoms stem primarily from alterations in the nervous system, which under these circumstances is deprived of its major substrate. The changes affect first the cerebral cortex and then the lower centers.

Hypoglycemic reactions following the administration of regular insulin usually start with a feeling of hunger and weakness followed by light-headedness, sweating, tachycardia, anxiety, numbness, a tingling sensation, and tremor. These symptoms are largely due to sympathoadrenal activation. When produced by a long-acting insulin, the above-mentioned symptoms may not be present, and headache and mental, motor, and emotional disturbances are more prominent. The intermediate-acting preparations produce a mixture of these symptoms. If severe, the reactions may lead to convulsions, coma, and death.

A variety of mechanisms designed to restore the blood glucose to normal come into play during a hypoglycemic reaction. These include the release of epi-

---

*Excessive insulin leading to hypoglycemia may be due to islet cell tumors of the pancreas and perhaps to malignancies of other organs. Functional hyperinsulinism also occurs, and it is common in prediabetic individuals.

Table 37–2. A comparison of some conditions found in hypoglycemic reactions and ketoacidosis.

	Hypoglycemic Reactions	Ketoacidosis
Respiration	Normal or snoring, irregular	Regular, deep (Kussmaul)
Acetone breath	Absent or faint	Strong
Skin	Moist, pale; normal elasticity	Dry, often reddened; reduced elasticity
Sweat	Increased	Absent
Pupils	Dilated	Normal or constricted
Tremor	Present	Absent
Babinski sign	Often positive both sides	Negative
Blood pressure	Normal to elevated	Decreasing
Pulse	Full, bounding	Weak, rapid
Urine		
Sugar	None to slight	Much
Acetone	Seldom present	Much
Blood		
Sugar	Usually < 60 mg/dL or falling quickly	Usually > 400 mg/dL
Alkali reserve	Normal	Reduced
Leukocytes	Normal	Increased
Reaction to administration of carbohydrates	Prompt improvement	No improvement

nephrine and glucagon, which mobilize glucose from glycogen stores in the liver, and glucocorticoids, which increase gluconeogenesis. Stimulation of sympathetic nerve fibers to adipose tissue and growth hormone released by the pituitary increase the amount of free fatty acids available to meet energy requirements of many tissues.

Treatment consists of giving 50% glucose solution, by vein if necessary, to restore consciousness. Glucagon has also been used to increase blood glucose (see below).

In severely obtunded or comatose diabetic patients, hypoglycemia must be distinguished from severe ketoacidosis. In the absence of antecedent information, the findings in these conditions (Table 37–2) will facilitate the correct diagnosis.

B. Allergic Reactions: About 25% of diabetics under treatment with insulin will, at some time, show an allergy to insulin. The reactions are usually mild and transient and consist of localized itching, swelling, and erythema at the site of injection. A few patients develop generalized urticaria, particularly after the intermittent use of insulin. Demonstrable IgE antibodies are present in these patients. Patients sensitive to beef and pork insulin can be managed with insulin derived from another species (sheep, fish) if necessary. Antihistamines are also useful in the treatment of mild allergies. These agents may be injected with insulin or administered orally. When the allergy is more severe, treatment with corticosteroids, desensitization to insulin, or, in certain maturity-onset cases, treatment with an oral hypoglycemic agent may be required. Allergic reactions are becoming increasingly

uncommon with the newer, more highly purified preparations.

Highly purified (monocomponent, single component) insulin may be used in some sensitized individuals without causing allergic reactions. An insulin similar to human insulin has been prepared from porcine insulin and may also prove to be useful in these patients.

Preparations Available

The types of insulin currently used in the USA are listed in Table 37–3. They are dispensed in 10-mL multiple injection vials in a concentration of 100 units/mL. These are used with a 1-mL syringe or a 0.5-mL syringe for smaller doses. More highly purified preparations of insulin have been marketed recently containing only minute amounts of proinsulin and glucagon.

The international unit of insulin is defined as the amount required to lower the blood glucose of a fasting, 2-kg rabbit from 120 to 45 mg/dL. The international reference material has an activity of 22 units/mg.

Although the above assay is used for pharmaceutical purposes, exquisitely sensitive methods are needed and have been developed for studies of insulin secretion and metabolism in intact animals. These include immunochemical assays and in vitro bioassays involving changes in the metabolism of muscle or adipose tissue.

A. Crystalline Zinc Insulin (Regular Insulin): This preparation is used for a brief effect with rapid onset, often in combination with long-acting preparations. It is the only preparation that can be given intravenously and is so used in the treatment of diabetic acidosis. It is also used for testing purposes (see above) and in insulin coma therapy for psychiatric disorders.

Table 37–3. Insulin: Sources and activity.

Type of Preparations	Animal Source*	Activity (Hours)	
		Peak	Duration†
Rapid-acting			
Insulin injection USP (regular, crystalline zinc)	Beef, pork, or mixture	½–3	5–7
Insulin zinc suspension USP (prompt, semilente)	Beef, pork, or mixture	1–4	12–16
Intermediate-acting			
Globin zinc insulin injection USP	Beef	6–10	12–18
Isophane insulin suspension USP (NPH insulin)	Beef, pork, or mixture	8–12	18–24
Insulin zinc suspension USP (lente)	Beef, pork, or mixture	8–12	18–24
Long-acting			
Protamine zinc insulin suspension USP (PZI)	Beef, pork, or mixture	8–16	24–36
Insulin zinc suspension extended USP (ultra-lente)	Beef, pork, or mixture	8–16	24–36

*Fish insulin is available commercially in Japan but not in the USA; sheep insulin is an investigational drug in the USA.

†The duration of action is increased with increasing doses.

It is a clear solution with a pH of approximately 3.0 that contains 0.02–0.04 mg of zinc per 100 units.

B. Globin Insulin: Globin insulin, a clear solution with a pH of 3.7, contains 3.8 mg of erythrocyte globin and 0.3 mg of zinc per 100 units of crystalline insulin. When injected, the solution is neutralized in the tissues and the insulin-protein complex precipitates. The action of insulin in this form is not sufficiently prolonged to be generally useful for single dose administration of the 24-hour requirement.

C. Protamine Zinc Insulin (PZI): PZI is a preparation in which crystalline insulin is combined with an excess of protamine in phosphate buffer at pH 7.2 to form a fine precipitate containing 1.25 mg of protamine per 100 units insulin. The preparation is stabilized by the addition of 0.2 mg of zinc per 100 units. The insulin is released from the protein by proteolytic enzymes, resulting in a steady prolonged effect. Since there is an excess of protamine, this preparation is given in a separate syringe when used in conjunction with regular insulin in order to prevent binding of the regular insulin. Free protamine also combines with prothrombin and may cause local plugging of the lymphatics and irregular absorption.

D. Isophane (Neutral-Protamine-Hagedorn, NPH) Insulin: NPH insulin is a suspension of crystals of protamine zinc insulin (0.4 mg protamine per 100 units insulin) in neutral phosphate buffer (pH 7.2) containing just enough protamine to bind the insulin. Its action is intermediate between that of PZI and regular insulin. It may be mixed with regular insulin without altering either preparation. It is frequently useful in a single dose per 24 hours, alone or in combination with regular insulin. When insulin requirements are very high, it can be administered in divided doses (two-thirds in the morning and one-third in the late afternoon).

E. Insulin Zinc Suspensions: These preparations are made by substituting acetate for phosphate buffer, making the insulin insoluble at pH 7.2. This process may result in the formation of small amorphous particles or larger crystals. The amorphous preparation is called prompt insulin zinc suspension USP (semi-lente) and has an action similar to that of regular insulin. The crystalline form is more slowly absorbed, having an action slightly more prolonged than PZI, and is called extended insulin zinc suspension USP (ultra-lente). An intermediate preparation, insulin zinc suspension USP (lente), is a mixture consisting of 30% semi-lente and 70% ultra-lente.

ORAL HYPOGLYCEMIC AGENTS

A wide variety of compounds are capable of causing a reduction in blood glucose. These include sul-

Synthalin A
(decamethylene diguanidine)

Hypoglycin A
(a-Amino-β-[2-methylenecyclopropyl] propionic acid)

fonamides, salicylates, and a variety of plant substances as well as the compounds discussed more fully below. Although insulin is a practical and satisfactory agent for the treatment of diabetes, it has the disadvantage of requiring parenteral administration one or more times daily. The search continues for a means of controlling hyperglycemia in diabetes by the use of oral preparations of insulin or therapeutic agents other than insulin. Early attempts to treat patients with guanidine derivatives (Synthalin) and hypoglycin (a West Indian plant derivative) met with failure because of the toxicity of these agents. At present, 2 classes of compounds, the sulfonylureas and the biguanides, have provided clinically useful preparations.

SULFONYLUREAS

Many sulfonylurea compounds have been studied. Some members of this class in current use are shown in Table 37–4. Their mechanism of action is thought to be the same, but they differ in their metabolism sufficiently to produce important and possibly useful differences in potency and duration of action.

Metabolism

The sulfonylureas are promptly and completely absorbed from the intestine after oral administration. They are distributed throughout the extracellular fluid compartment. In the plasma, they are partially bound to serum protein. The rate and means of degradation of these drugs vary.

Tolbutamide, the shortest acting drug, is readily converted in the liver to hydroxy- and carboxytolbutamide, which are rapidly excreted by the kidney. Its half-life in the body is 4–6 hours. Carbutamide is acetylated in the liver and excreted in the urine. Almost all of it is removed from the body in 36 hours. The peak hypoglycemic effect occurs in about 5 hours.

Acetohexamide has a very short half-life in the

Table 37—4. Sulfonylureas.

Sulfonylurea	Chemical Structure	Daily Dose	Duration of Action (Hours)
Tolbutamide (Orinase)	H_3C—⟨⟩—SO_2—NH—$\overset{O}{\overset{\|}{C}}$—NH—$(CH_2)_3$—$CH_3$	0.5–3 g in divided doses	6–12
Tolazamide (Tolinase)	H_3C—⟨⟩—SO_2—NH—$\overset{O}{\overset{\|}{C}}$—NH—N⟨⟩	0.1–0.5 g as single dose or in divided doses	10–14
Tolcyclamide [Glycyclamide]* (Diaboral, Tolhexamide)*	H_3C—⟨⟩—SO_2—NH—$\overset{O}{\overset{\|}{C}}$—NH—⟨⟩	0.25–1 g	...
Glibornuridum* [Glibornuride]* (Glutril)*	H_3C—⟨⟩—SO_2—NH—$\overset{O}{\overset{\|}{C}}$—NH—⟨⟩ (HO, CH_3, H_3C-C-CH_3)	0.01–0.05 g	...
Acetohexamide (Dymelor)	H_3C—$\overset{O}{\overset{\|}{C}}$—⟨⟩—$SO_2$—NH—$\overset{O}{\overset{\|}{C}}$—NH—⟨⟩	0.25–1.5 g as single dose or in divided doses	12–24
Chlorpropamide (Diabinese)	Cl—⟨⟩—SO_2—NH—$\overset{O}{\overset{\|}{C}}$—NH—$(CH_2)_2$—$CH_3$	0.1–0.5 g as single dose	Up to 60
Carbutamide* (many products)	H_2N—⟨⟩—SO_2—NH—$\overset{O}{\overset{\|}{C}}$—NH—$(CH_2)_3$—$CH_3$	0.5–3 g	Up to 60
Glyburide* [Glibenclamide]* (many products)	Cl, $\overset{O}{\overset{\|}{C}}$-NH-$(CH_2)_2$—⟨⟩—$SO_2$—NH—$\overset{O}{\overset{\|}{C}}$-NH—⟨⟩, OCH_3	0.0025–0.02 g	10–24
Glipizide* [Glydiazinamide]* (Glibenese, Minidab, Minodiab)*	N⟨⟩, $\overset{O}{\overset{\|}{C}}$-NH-$(CH_2)_2$—⟨⟩—$SO_2$—NH—$\overset{O}{\overset{\|}{C}}$-NH—⟨⟩, H_3C—N	0.0025–0.02 g	3–8

*Outside USA.

circulation (½–2 hours). However, it is metabolized to 1-hydroxyhexamide, which is even more potent than its precursor. The combined half-life of acetohexamide and its reduced compound is 5–7 hours, so that the action of the drug has a time course slower than that of tolbutamide. It also differs from tolbutamide in that about 10% of the metabolites are excreted in the bile and appear in the stool.

Tolazamide is more slowly absorbed than the other sulfonylureas, and its effects on blood glucose are not apparent for several hours. Its half-life is about 7 hours. It is metabolized to *p*-carboxytolazamide, 4-hydroxymethyltolazamide, and other compounds, some of which have potent hypoglycemic effects.

The half-life of chlorpropamide in the circulation is 36 hours, so that its effects last for several days. Most of this drug is slowly excreted by the kidney without significant alteration. It is bound to plasma albumin, and a maximum blood level is not reached until after 4 days of therapy. Since a plateau is not reached for some time, the dose should not be increased sooner than 7–10 days after starting treatment with any given dose. Weeks may be required for elimi-

nation from the body. The peak hypoglycemic effect is reached 10 hours after ingestion.

Glyburide (Glibenclamide), an oral sulfonylurea derivative available outside the USA, appears to be suitable for use in the treatment of patients with diabetes. It is a very active compound, and patients can be maintained on as little as 2.5 mg daily. When administered orally, peak concentrations occur in 4 hours. More than 95% is removed from the circulation in 24 hours. After a single oral dose of 5 mg, the plasma glucose levels remain lower than control levels for more than 15 hours. Experience has not been sufficient to evaluate toxicity with prolonged use. This compound has a rapid onset of action and may cause hypoglycemia unless it is given immediately before eating.

Glipizide, another sulfonylurea, is rapidly absorbed from the gastrointestinal tract. It is bound to one or more plasma proteins and disappears with a half-life of 2–4 hours. Its metabolites are rapidly excreted by the kidney.

Although the rate of metabolism of these drugs tends to increase as treatment progresses, in the presence of hepatic dysfunction and, particularly, with impaired renal function, marked reduction in the clearance of these drugs leading to serious reactions has been observed.

Sodium glymidine (glidiazine, glycodiazine), although not a sulfonylurea derivative, is closely related to this group of compounds. It is a sulfapyrimidine without antibacterial activity, and its mechanism of action is similar to that of the sulfonylureas. It is marketed in Europe under the following trade names: Glycanol, Glyconormal, Lycanol, Gondafon, and Redul. It is used in doses of 0.5–2 g/d. It has a half-life of 4 hours and is generally well tolerated. There appears to be no cross-allergy with sulfonylureas, and this agent may be useful in patients sensitive to sulfonylurea preparations.

Sodium glymidine

Pharmacologic Effects

The hypoglycemic effect of the sulfonylureas is thought to be due to their ability to cause the release of insulin from the pancreas. The administration of one of these agents is attended by an increase in plasma insulin level and by a decrease in the insulin content of the pancreas. In the dosages usually employed, these compounds do not produce hypoglycemia in the absence of the pancreas; larger doses appear to have a direct effect on the liver production of glucose.

The peripheral metabolic events following the administration of this class of compounds are similar to but not exactly the same as the effects of parenterally administered insulin. These differences are thought to be due to the fact that the insulin is released for a prolonged period in small amounts and passes through the liver before entering the general circulation. A comparison of the effects of the sulfonylureas to insulin and biguanide is shown in Table 37–5.

Clinical Uses

A. Diabetes Mellitus: These drugs find their greatest use in the treatment of maturity-onset diabetes in the patient whose pancreas still has the capacity to produce insulin. They are usually ineffective even in this group when more than 25–35 units of insulin are required for maintenance. Experience with oral hypoglycemic agents in diabetes mellitus is now extensive. In one large study (The University Group Diabetes Program [UGDP]) in which 12 clinics participated, the effects of insulin, tolbutamide, phenformin (see p 389), and a lactose placebo were studied. In this study, a significant increase was found in the number of cardiovascular deaths (12.7%) after 8 years in the group treated with tolbutamide as compared with placebo-treated controls (4.9%). The use of phenformin in this study was also discontinued because of increased mortality (see below).

Although the reasons for the deaths are not clear and other studies have not confirmed these findings, the fact that a comparable degree of restoration of glucose tolerance and control of hyperglycemia can be achieved by weight reduction alone must not be overlooked by the physician. Every attempt must be made to achieve weight reduction before or during the course of therapy with oral hypoglycemic agents. These agents should be reserved for elderly patients and those for whom the use of insulin or diet control is particularly difficult. When patients maintained on oral hypoglycemic agents develop infections or other complications that increase insulin requirements, they often require treatment with parenteral insulin.

When a decision is made to use sulfonylureas because levels of fasting blood sugars remain over

Table 37–5. Comparisons of some actions of insulin, sulfonylureas, and phenethylbiguanide.*

	Insulin	Sulfonylureas	Phenethylbiguanide
Major action	Increased glucose transfer into cells	Increased insulin secretion	Increased anaerobiosis
Some subsidiary effects			
Insulin secretion	Decreased	Increased†	Decreased
Glucose uptake by peripheral tissues	Increased	Increased	Increased
Hepatic glucogenesis	Decreased	Decreased	Decreased
Gluconeogenesis	Decreased	Decreased	Decreased
Liver glycogen	Increased	Increased	Decreased
Oxidative phosphorylation	Increased	Increased	Decreased
Blood sugar-lowering effect			
Normal subjects	Marked	Moderate	None
Depancreatized subjects	Marked	None	Slight
Marked hypoglycemia	Common	Rare	None
Lactate utilization	Increased	Increased	Decreased
Irreversible side-effects	Present	Rare	None

*Reproduced, with permission, from Williams RH (editor): *Textbook of Endocrinology,* 5th ed. Saunders, 1974.

†Plasma ILA is lowered after 2 weeks of therapy with chlorpropamide.

180–200 mg/dL despite adherence to the prescribed diet, the patient can be started on the dose expected to be required for maintenance. The choice of agent and dose prescribed will depend on the physician's preference and experience. Using chlorpropamide as an example, treatment can be started with 100 mg daily, increasing the dose every few days until acceptable fasting and postprandial blood sugar levels are achieved. Chlorpropamide, because of its short duration of action, is given in a single dose daily; other preparations may require multiple-dose schedules.

The failure of therapy after a period of treatment may be related to an alteration in metabolism of the drug. It has been found that some patients, in whom the rate of degradation of tolbutamide may be increased, will respond to chlorpropamide. If therapy cannot be maintained with 0.5 g chlorpropamide, 2 g tolbutamide, 1.25 g acetohexamide, or 0.75 g tolazamide daily, larger doses should not be used. The effects of these drugs are additive when combined with insulin and phenformin, and they may be used in combination.

The effectiveness of these drugs varies with time. There may be an increased effect during the first 4–6 weeks of treatment or a secondary failure of the drug after 6–12 months of treatment. Lack of continued medical supervision may therefore lead to death from hypoglycemia or ketoacidosis.

The effects of these drugs can be altered by interactions with other agents. Large doses of corticosteroids, thyroid hormone, oral contraceptives, and furosemide and thiazide diuretics antagonize the hypoglycemic agents. Large doses of nicotinic acid also have this effect.

Potentiation of these drugs also occurs by a variety of mechanisms. Agents such as alcohol and salicylates have hypoglycemic effects of their own that are additive. Phenylbutazone prolongs the biologic half-life of tolbutamide by inhibiting its oxidation and interferes with the urinary excretion of hydroxyhexamide, a hypoglycemic metabolite of an acetohexamide. Dicumarol and sulfafenazole also prolong the biologic half-life of tolbutamide by inhibiting its oxidation. Aspirin interferes with the urinary excretion of chlorpropamide and increases the blood level of this drug. These actions are probably not important with the salicylate levels achieved after doses used for headache and minor pain.

B. Diagnostic Tests: The response to tolbutamide is also used for testing purposes. In most patients with insulinomas (insulin-producing tumors of the pancreas), 1 g of sodium tolbutamide in 20 mL saline, given intravenously in 2 minutes, will produce a profound and prolonged hypoglycemia. A similar test has been used to determine whether or not a diabetic patient would be a suitable candidate for sulfonylurea therapy. However, therapeutic trial is more reliable.

Tolbutamide is also useful for testing patients with borderline abnormalities in the glucose tolerance test or postprandial blood glucose levels. The oral administration of 2 g of tolbutamide with 2 g of sodium bicarbonate produces a fall in blood glucose levels to 78% of the control value or less in more than 90% of normal subjects even in the presence of obesity, liver disease, hyperthyroidism, and other abnormalities affecting carbohydrate tolerance.

C. Chlorpropamide in Diabetes Insipidus: Chlorpropamide has been found to have an antidiuretic effect in patients with diabetes insipidus. This effect appears to be similar to that produced by vasopressin. It causes a reduction of free water clearance without reducing glomerular filtration or osmolal clearance. This property is not shared by other sulfonylureas. It has been used in doses of 0.25–0.5 g/d or more in the treatment of patients with diabetes insipidus. It may act by enhancing the effects of low concentrations of vasopressin on the kidney.

Adverse Reactions

The undesirable side-effects of these drugs are due to their toxicity; allergic reactions are rare. All of the sulfonylureas cause similar toxic reactions, but the frequency of untoward reactions does vary. It is usually possible to reduce the dose or substitute another drug when toxic reactions occur.

The incidence of undesirable effects is estimated to be about 5% for this group of drugs—somewhat lower for tolbutamide than for carbutamide and the longer-acting agents. The increased gastric secretion produced by these drugs may lead to heartburn, nausea, abdominal pain, and diarrhea. These effects are dose-related and are treated by reduction of dose, administration of antacids, and use of a bland diet. Central nervous system effects such as confusion, vertigo, ataxia, and weakness have been observed with the use of large doses of chlorpropamide. Flushing reactions to alcohol, also dose-related, occur most frequently with carbutamide and chlorpropamide. The sulfonylureas have also been reported to produce hypothyroidism.

The antidiuretic effect of chlorpropamide (see above), while useful in the treatment of diabetes insipidus, represents a hazard in diabetes mellitus. Several patients have been reported to develop severe hyponatremia and water intoxication.

The more serious toxic effects, granulocytopenia and cholestatic jaundice, are frequently preceded by fever, malaise, and skin eruptions or photosensitivity. These tend to occur in the first 1–2 months of therapy. They are more frequent with large doses of chlorpropamide. Exacerbation of hemolytic anemia has been reported in the presence of red blood cell enzyme deficiency.

The most serious acute problems connected with the use of these agents are profound and prolonged hypoglycemia (especially with chlorpropamide) and diabetic acidosis. The long-term problems have been mentioned above (see p 387).

Table 37–6. Biguanides.

Biguanide	$R-\underset{\underset{NH}{\|\|}}{C}\;\underset{\underset{NH}{\|\|}}{\overset{\overset{H}{\underset{N}{\|}}}{C}}-NH_2$	Daily Dose	Duration of Action (Hours)
Phenformin (DBI, Meltrol)	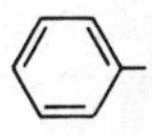 ⬡$-(CH_2)_2-NH-$	0.025–0.15 g as single dose or in divided doses	4–6 8–14
Buformin*	$CH_3-(CH_2)_3-NH-$	0.05–0.3 g in divided doses	...
Metformin*	$(CH_3)_2-N-$	1–3 g in divided doses	...

*In clinical use outside USA.

BIGUANIDES

Although guanidine and many of its derivatives can produce hypoglycemia, only phenethylbiguanide (phenformin) is in use at the present time in the USA. It is a white crystalline powder with the structure shown in Table 37–6. Although it has been found to have the effects noted in Table 37–5 in various experimental studies, its hypoglycemic effect in patients with diabetes is not well understood. It is of interest that the compound does not cause a reduction in blood glucose in normal human subjects. It has been shown to potentiate the effects of insulin in vivo and in vitro and may antagonize anti-insulin factors. It has been shown to decrease glucose absorption from the gut and increase glucose uptake in peripheral tissues.

Phenformin is bound to plasma protein when incubated at 37 C. It disappears from the circulation with a half-life of 11 hours. About one-third of the drug is excreted unchanged into the urine over a period of several days after a single oral dose of 100 mg.

Phenformin (DBI) is dispensed as rapidly disintegrating 25-mg tablets or as slow-release 50-mg capsules (DBI-TD) designed to release one-third of the drug during the first hour, two-thirds by the fourth hour, and the remainder within 8 hours. The slow-release capsules are easier to use in most patients. Half to two-thirds of the dose can be given in the morning and the rest with the evening meal.

The average dose is slightly less than 0.5 mg/kg body weight. The symptoms of an excessive dose include nausea, anorexia, foul breath, vomiting, diarrhea, and abdominal cramps. A metallic taste may be noted as well as malaise. These symptoms are less common with doses of 100 mg/d or less and can be controlled by reduction of the dose or cessation of therapy. Lactic acidosis has been noted, particularly in patients with severe hepatic, renal, or cardiac disease and when other symptoms of toxicity have been present for several days.

Phenformin has been reported by some investigators to lead to a slow but consistent weight loss. This observation has not been confirmed by carefully controlled studies. However, this agent lowers blood sugar without promoting insulin release. Therefore, in addition to reducing the postprandial need for insulin

from the pancreas, it might reduce the deposition of fat.

Phenformin has been used in combination with sulfonylureas or insulin. About half of patients taking sulfonylureas alone will become unresponsive to therapy within 4 years, and the majority of these can be controlled for a variable period by the addition of phenformin. In patients in whom diabetes is difficult to control, even with large doses of insulin, the addition of phenformin to the therapeutic regimen has improved blood sugar control.

In the UGDP study, phenformin given in a dosage of 100 mg/d showed no favorable effects in comparison with the control group of patients. Its use was accompanied by increased blood pressure and heart rate as well as an increase in fatal and nonfatal events. These observations indicate that the use of biguanides is of doubtful value in the mild diabetic.

It has become apparent that phenformin-associated lactic acidosis occurs with a higher incidence than had been appreciated. The incidence is currently estimated to be 0.25–4 cases per 1000 users per year, with a death rate of 50%. It has also become apparent that lactic acidosis can occur even in patients taking doses of 100 mg or less who have none of the underlying risk factors noted above. It is recommended, therefore, that phenformin use be limited to a small group of maturity-onset nonketotic diabetics in whom the use of insulin poses special problems. These include patients who are symptomatic but cannot be controlled by diet and sulfonylureas alone; who cannot take sulfonylureas because of allergies and have none of the underlying risk factors that contraindicate the use of phenformin; whose symptoms are controlled by phenformin but who cannot take insulin because of serious mental or physical disability; or whose occupation is such that the risk of hypoglycemia from insulin would threaten job performance or be a hazard to others.

HYPERGLYCEMIC AGENTS

Blood glucose levels can be increased by several means. Therapeutically, the usual method is to give glucose orally or, in unconscious patients, intravenously in concentrated solutions. Glucagon or epinephrine is occasionally used to achieve a rapid rise in blood glucose concentrations from glycogen stores. More prolonged effects (for experimental or therapeutic purposes) can be achieved by pancreatectomy, by destruction of the islets with drugs such as alloxan and streptozocin; and, under certain circumstances, by hormones such as the glucocorticoids and growth hormone or drugs such as diazoxide.

Table 37–7. Factors affecting glucagon secretion.*

Stimulators	Inhibitors
Amino acids (particularly the glucogenic amino acids: alanine, serine, glycine, cysteine, and threonine)	Glucose
	Secretin
	FFA
CCK, gastrin	Ketones
β-Adrenergic stimulators	Phenytoin
Theophylline	α-Adrenergic stimulators
Cortisol	Somatostatin
Exercise	
Infections	
Other stresses	

*Reproduced, with permission, from Ganong WF: *Review of Medical Physiology,* 9th ed. Lange, 1979.

GLUCAGON

Chemistry & Metabolism

Glucagon is produced by the A cells of the islets of Langerhans, and a "glucagonlike" hormone is produced by cells in the gastric and duodenal mucosa. Glucagon is a polypeptide composed of a single chain of 29 amino acids (Fig 37–5) and has a molecular weight of 3485. When isolated, it is a white crystalline material soluble in acid and alkali but relatively insoluble in the range of pH 4.0–9.0.

Glucagon has been measured by immunoassay procedures and found to be present in serum in a concentration of about 100 pg/mL. In the circulation, it does not appear to be bound to a specific protein.

The control of glucagon secretion is complex, and many factors have been shown to influence the process (see Table 37–7). In the presence of insulin, the secretion of glucagon is stimulated by a fall in blood sugar or an increase in amino acids. Exercise, infection, and other stresses increase its secretion—possibly via a β-adrenergic mechanism. During a fasting period, glucagon secretion rises and reaches a peak by the third day. As gluconeogenesis declines and more fatty acids and ketones are utilized, the rate of secretion falls. The

observation that somatostatin inhibits glucagon release is of special interest and is potentially useful in the treatment of diabetes (see p 382). However, a physiologic role for this hormone in the regulation of insulin secretion has not been established. Cholecystokinin-pancreozymin (CCK) and gastrin increase glucagon secretion. It is inhibited by secretin.

"Gut Glucagon"

A glucagonlike material has been extracted from the stomach and intestine, consisting of 2 active fractions (MW 3500 and 6000–10,000). It stimulates the secretion of insulin and was thought to mediate the early rise of insulin seen after oral administration of glucose. This effect is now known to be due to gastric inhibitory peptide (GIP), and the role of "gut glucagon" is unknown.

Little is known about the degradation of glucagon in vivo. Beef liver contains an enzyme that hydrolyzes glucagon at the peptide bond between serine and glutamine, removing the first 2 amino acids.

Pharmacologic Effects

Glucagon stimulates the formation of cAMP from ATP in the liver. This leads to the activation of phosphorylase, the rate-limiting enzyme in the conversion of glycogen to glucose. It has been shown to increase gluconeogenesis from amino acids and lactic acid in the perfused liver. However, the rise in blood glucose produced by this hormone is primarily the result of glycogenolysis. In adipose tissue, it causes lipolysis and increases circulating free fatty acids. Glycogenolysis is increased in the heart but not in skeletal muscle.

Glucagon increases the release of epinephrine by the adrenal medulla, insulin by the pancreas, growth hormone and ACTH by the anterior pituitary, and calcitonin in patients with medullary carcinoma of the thyroid. The physiologic significance of some of these observations is unclear.

Although no clinical syndrome due to a deficiency of glucagon has been established, glucagon-secreting tumors have been found. A patient with a glucagon-producing A cell carcinoma of the pancreas

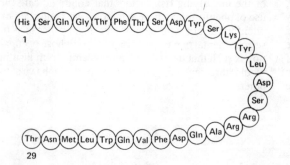

Figure 37 –5. Amino acid sequence of glucagon polypeptide.

has been described. He was found to be diabetic. An abnormal increase in glucagon secretion may be an important factor in postprandial hyperglycemia in patients with diabetes.

Clinical Uses

Glucagon is used as an adjunct to glucose for the treatment of acute hypoglycemic reactions. It is particularly useful when oral and intravenous administration of glucose is not possible. It is effective in doses of 0.5–1 mg subcutaneously, intramuscularly, or intravenously. In managing a labile diabetic, the patient's family, when instructed by the physician, can administer glucagon to a person with a severe hypoglycemic reaction while awaiting the physician's arrival.

The response may occur as early as 5 minutes after administration of glucagon, but more commonly it takes 10–25 minutes. If no response occurs in 25 minutes, a second dose may be administered. Glucagon and glucose may be administered concomitantly, and glucose should be used if there is no response to glucagon.

Recent studies indicate that glucagon has an important inotropic effect on the heart which resembles that produced by the catecholamines. It is not prevented by propranolol. The observation that it does not seem to increase the tendency toward arrhythmias in the failing or damaged heart indicates that it may be of therapeutic value clinically. Under some circumstances, it has been useful in the treatment of cardiogenic shock and congestive heart failure.

Glucagon is useful as a diagnostic agent. The intravenous injection of 0.5–1 mg of glucagon will usually provoke a paroxysm in more than 90% of patients with pheochromocytomas. It appears to be as reliable as histamine, and its injection is not accompanied by the unpleasant flush and headache produced by the injection of histamine.

Glucagon in 1-mg doses will also increase the release of growth hormone and ACTH by the pituitary and can be used to test pituitary function. It has also been used to provoke insulin release by the pancreatic B cells for testing purposes. The ability of glucagon to stimulate calcitonin release may be of value in the recognition of medullary carcinoma of the thyroid.

Adverse Reactions

Except for occasional episodes of nausea and vomiting, particularly with large doses, the administration of glucagon has not caused serious side-effects. Hypotensive reactions due to glucagon sensitivity have been reported following intravenous administration.

Contraindications & Cautions

There are no established contraindications to the use of glucagon. The greatest danger in its use is the possibility of overlooking coma due to other causes in the mistaken belief that the unconscious patient is having an insulin reaction.

DIAZOXIDE

Diazoxide is chemically related to the thiazide diuretics. It was first studied because of its antihypertensive properties but has proved to be useful in the treatment of hypoglycemia.

Diazoxide

Diazoxide can increase blood glucose by several mechanisms. In large doses, it leads to the adrenal medullary release of epinephrine. It also inhibits the release of insulin. However, in the presence of adequate glycogen stores, it can produce an increase in plasma glucose and free fatty acid (FFA) levels in pancreatectomized and adrenalectomized animals. In the intact animal, diazoxide increases hepatic release of glucose, inhibits glucose utilization in the periphery, and increases the rate of mobilization of FFA. Little is known about its metabolism.

Diazoxide has been used experimentally in several hypoglycemic states, including idiopathic hypoglycemia and von Gierke's disease. Its most important potential use at present is in the management of insulin-producing tumors that are not amenable to or have not responded to surgery or irradiation. Doses as high as 200 mg every 6 hours have been used in patients with islet cell tumors. However, at doses this high and at even lower doses, persistent nausea and vomiting, edema, and excessive hair growth occur. Hypogammaglobulinemia has also been reported in patients under treatment with this drug. In order to minimize its undesirable effects, diazoxide has been used in combination with other agents such as growth hormone, glucocorticoids, and benzothiadiazines.

OTHER HYPERGLYCEMIC AGENTS

Many compounds such as uric acid, dehydroascorbic acid, quinolones, and alloxan have been reported to selectively destroy the insulin-secreting cells of the pancreas. Alloxan has been used exten-

Alloxan

sively. It has proved to be a convenient means of producing insulin deficiency in laboratory animals. Attempts to use this compound in the treatment of insulin-secreting tumors have not been successful.

Streptozocin, an antibiotic derived from *Streptomyces achromogenes,* causes a highly specific and irreversible destruction of the activity of pancreatic B cells when given in doses of 50–100 mg/kg to rats. At doses of 65 mg/kg, there is a prompt initial rise in plasma glucose, reaching a peak in 2 hours. This is followed in 2 hours by marked hypoglycemia. In 24 hours, a marked and permanent hyperglycemia is present. This agent has been used to treat insulin-producing islet cell tumors with some success. However, its usefulness is limited by severe renal and hepatic toxicity.

Streptozocin

• • •

References

Alkalay D & others: Pharmacokinetics of phenformin in man. J Clin Pharmacol 15:446, 1975.

Arieff AI, Carroll HJ: Non-ketotic hyperosmolar coma with hyperglycemia. Medicine 51:73, 1972.

Balodimos MC, Camerini-Dávalos RA, Marble A: Nine years' experience with tolbutamide in the treatment of diabetes. Metabolism 15:957, 1966.

Berson SA, Yalow RS (editors): *Peptide Hormones.* Vol 2B: *Non-Pituitary Hormones.* American Elsevier, 1973.

Bond VP (moderator): Symposium on insulin. Am J Med 40:651, 1966.

Bressler R, Corredor C, Brendel K: Hypoglycin and hypoglycin-like compounds. Pharmacol Rev 21:105, 1969.

Brown JC, Otte SC: Gastrointestinal hormones and the control of insulin secretion. Diabetes 27:782, 1978.

Earley LE: Chlorpropamide antidiuresis. N Engl J Med 284:103, 1971.

Ellenberg M, Rifkin H (editors): *Diabetes Mellitus: Theory and Practice.* McGraw-Hill, 1970.

Gerich JE, Charles MA, Grodsky GM: Regulation of pancreatic and insulin and glucagon secretion. Annu Rev Physiol 38:353, 1976.

Gerich JE & others: Adrenergic modulation of pancreatic glucagon secretion in man. J Clin Invest 53:1441, 1974.

Graber AL, Porte D Jr, Williams RH: Clinical use of diazoxide [Hyperstat] and mechanism for its hyperglycemic effects. Diabetes 15:143, 1966.

Jaspan JB, Rubenstein AH: Circulating glucagon. Diabetes 26:887, 1977.

Junod A & others: Diabetogenic action of streptozotocin: Relationship of dose to metabolic response. J Clin Invest 48:2129, 1969.

Kahn CR: The role of insulin receptors and receptor antibodies in states of altered insulin action. Proc Soc Exp Biol Med 162:13, 1979.

Kilo C, Miller PJ, Williamson JR: The Achilles heel of the University Group Diabetes Program. JAMA 243:450, 1980.

Kitabchi AE: Proinsulin and C-peptide: A review. Metabolism 26:547, 1977.

Kreisberg RA: Diabetic ketoacidosis: New concepts and trends in pathogenesis and treatment. Ann Intern Med 88:681, 1978.

Lefebvre PJ: Glucagon and diabetes: A reappraisal. Diabetologia 16:347, 1979.

Lukens FD: The rediscovery of regular insulin. N Engl J Med 272:130, 1965.

Martin HE, Smith K, Wilson ML: The fluid and electrolyte therapy of severe diabetic acidosis and ketosis: A study of 29 episodes (26 patients). Am J Med 24:376, 1958.

Mereu TR, Kassoff A, Goodman AD: Diazoxide in the treatment of infantile hypoglycemia. N Engl J Med 275:1455, 1966.

Parmley WW: The role of glucagon as a cardiovascular drug. Drug Ther, June 1972 (p 16).

Rosenbloom AL, Smith DW, Cohan RC: Zinc glucagon in idiopathic hypoglycemia of infancy. Am J Dis Child 112:107, 1966.

Ross SA, Brown JC, Dupre J: Hypersecretion of gastric inhibitory polypeptide following oral glucose in diabetes mellitus. Diabetes 26:525, 1977.

Roth H & others: Zinc glucagon in the management of refractory hypoglycemia due to insulin-producing tumors. N Engl J Med 274:493, 1966.

Rubenstein AH, Spitz I: Role of the kidney in insulin metabolism and excretion. Diabetes 17:161, 1968.

Seltzer HS: A summary of criticisms of the findings and conclusions of the University Group Diabetes Program (UGDP). Diabetes 21:976, 1972.

Shen SW, Bressler R: Clinical pharmacology of oral antidiabetic agents. (2 parts.) N Engl J Med 296:493, 787, 1977.

Symposium on diabetes mellitus. Arch Intern Med 123:219, 1969.

Turkington RW: Encephalopathy induced by oral hypoglycemic drugs. Arch Intern Med 137:1082, 1977.

The University Group Diabetes Program: A study of the effects of hypoglycemic agents on vascular complications in patients with adult-onset diabetes. Diabetes 19 (Suppl 2):747, 1970; 24 (Suppl 1):65, 1975.

Weaver DC & others: Molecular requirements for recognition at a glucoreceptor for insulin release. Mol Pharmacol 16:361, 1979.

THE OVARY
(Estrogens, Progestins, Other Ovarian Hormones, Oral Contraceptives, Other Uses of Estrogens & Progestins, & Ovulation-Inducing Agents)

The ovary has important gametogenic functions that are integrated with its complex hormonal activity. Our present understanding of these functions, their interrelationships, and the differences from one species to another is incomplete. In the human female,

the gonad is relatively quiescent during the period of rapid growth and maturation. At puberty the ovary begins a 30- to 40-year period of cyclic function called the menstrual cycle because of the regular episodes of bleeding that are its most obvious manifestation. It then fails to respond to gonadotropins secreted by the anterior pituitary gland, and the cessation of cyclic bleeding that occurs is called the menopause.

The nature of the mechanism responsible for the onset of ovarian function at the time of puberty is thought to be neural in origin because the immature gonad can be stimulated by gonadotropins already

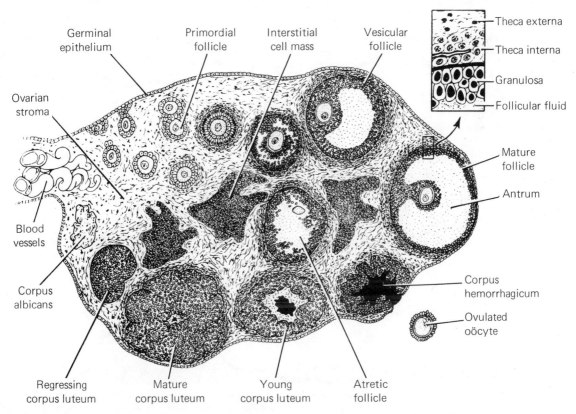

Figure 38–1. Diagram of a mammalian ovary, showing the sequential development of a follicle, formation of a corpus luteum, and, in the center, follicular atresia. A section of the wall of a mature follicle is enlarged at the upper right. The interstitial cell mass is not prominent in primates. (After Patten & Eakin. Reproduced, with permission, from Gorbman & Bern: *Textbook of Comparative Endocrinology.* Wiley, 1962.)

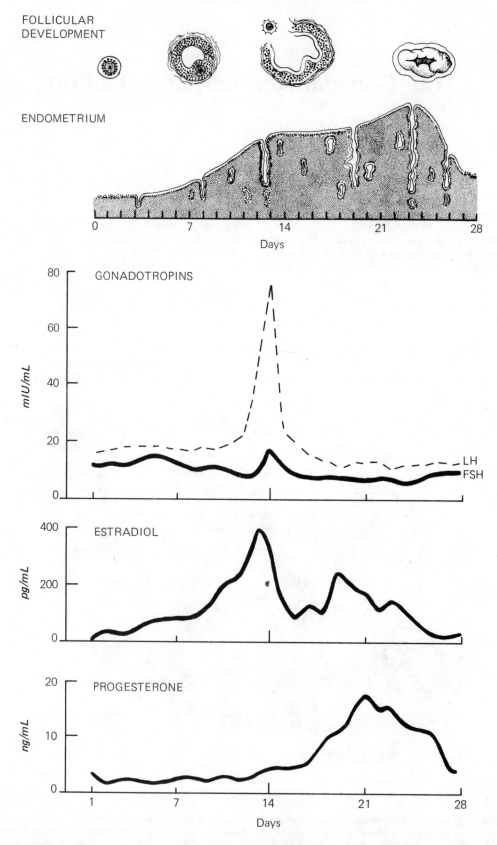

Figure 38 –2. The menstrual cycle, showing pituitary and ovarian hormones and histologic changes.

present in the hypothalamus and because the pituitary is responsive to hypothalamic gonadotropin-releasing hormones. The maturation of centers such as the amygdala in the brain may release an inhibition of the cells in the median eminence of the hypothalamus, allowing them to produce gonadotropin-releasing hormone, which stimulates the release of follicle-stimulating hormone (FSH) and luteinizing hormone (LH) (see Chapter 39). These latter 2 hormones are carried to the anterior pituitary, where they stimulate the secretion of FSH and LH. At first, small amounts of these hormones are released and the limited quantities of estrogens secreted cause breast development, alterations in fat distribution, and a growth spurt associated with epiphyseal closure in the long bones. The small amounts of androgens produced by the ovary and adrenal contribute to the appearance of axillary and pubic hair at this time.

After a year or two, sufficient estrogen is produced to induce endometrial changes and periodic bleeding. After the first few cycles, which may be anovulatory, normal cyclic function is established.

At the beginning of each cycle a variable number of follicles, each containing an ovum, begin to enlarge in response to FSH. After 5 or 6 days, one of the follicles begins to develop more rapidly. The granulosa cells of this follicle multiply and, under the influence of LH, synthesize estrogens and release them at an increasing rate. The estrogens appear to inhibit FSH release, which may lead to the regression of the smaller, less mature follicles and produces local stimulation of the maturing follicle. The ovum undergoes meiotic reduction division at this time. This structure is called the ovarian follicle and consists of an ovum surrounded by a fluid-filled antrum lined by granulosa and theca cells (Fig 38–1). The estrogen secretion reaches a peak just before midcycle and stimulates the brief surge in LH and FSH release that precedes (and causes) ovulation. At the time of ovulation, the granulosa cells are beginning to secrete progesterone. When the follicle ruptures, the ovum is released into the abdominal cavity near the uterine tube.

Following the above events, the cavity of the ruptured follicle fills with blood and the luteinized theca and granulosa cells proliferate and replace the blood to form the corpus luteum. The cells of this structure produce estrogens and progesterone for the remainder of the cycle, or longer if pregnancy occurs. The maintenance of a functioning corpus luteum requires the elaboration of prolactin in the rodent. However, in the human female the structure is supported by the presence of LH. Its life can be prolonged by chorionic gonadotropin, and, when the ovum is fertilized and implants in the endometrium, it produces sufficient amounts of chorionic gonadotropin to maintain the corpus luteum for a prolonged period of time.

If pregnancy does not occur, the corpus luteum begins to degenerate and ceases hormone production. The cause of luteolysis is unknown. Most other hormonal events occurring during the normal ovarian cycle can be explained on the basis of feedback regulation. The endometrium, which proliferated during the follicular phase and developed its glandular structure during the luteal phase, is shed in the process of menstruation. These events are summarized in Fig 38–2.

The ovary normally ceases its gametogenic and endocrine function with time. This change is accompanied by a cessation in uterine bleeding (menopause) and occurs at a mean age of 52 years in the USA. Although the ovary ceases to secrete estrogen, many women maintain significant levels of estrogen by converting adrenal steroids such as androstenedione to estrone and estradiol in nonendocrine tissues.

Disturbances in Ovarian Function

The control of ovarian function is complex. It involves several parts of the brain, including the hypothalamus and the limbic system. Chemical transmitters produced by the ventral hypothalamus appear to regulate the production of the gonadotropic hormones by the pituitary; these hormones in turn control follicular development, ovulation, and hormone production in the ovary. Disturbances of cyclic function are common even during the peak years of reproduction. A minority of these result from inflammatory or neoplastic processes that destroy the uterus, ovaries, or pituitary, but the causes of most menstrual problems are poorly understood. Many of the minor disturbances leading to periods of amenorrhea or anovulatory cycles are functional in nature and self-limited. They are often associated with emotional or environmental changes and are thought to represent temporary disorders in the centers in the brain that control the secretion of the hypothalamic releasing factors. Amenorrhea is at times associated with inappropriate lactation, indicating a loss of the inhibitory influence of the hypothalamus on the pituitary secretion of prolactin. This disturbance occurs commonly in women who have used hormonal contraceptives. Pituitary adenomas are not uncommon in patients with galactorrhea. In some patients, the biosynthesis of estrogens is deranged in a fashion that allows increased amounts of androgens, including testosterone, to be secreted by the ovary. This produces hirsutism in association with menstrual disturbances. Normal ovarian function can be modified by androgens produced by the adrenal cortex or tumors arising from it. The ovary also gives rise to androgen-producing neoplasms such as arrhenoblastomas and Leydig cell tumors.

THE ESTROGENS

Estrogenic activity is shared by a large number of chemical substances. In addition to the variety of steroidal estrogens derived from animal sources, nonsteroidal estrogens have been synthesized. Many phenols are estrogenic, and estrogenic activity has been identified in such diverse forms of life as those found in the sediments of the seas and certain species of clover.

The Natural Estrogens

The major estrogens produced by women are estradiol, estrone, and estriol (Fig 38–5). Estradiol appears to be the major secretory product of the ovary. Although some estrone is produced in the ovary, most of it (and estriol) is formed in the liver from estradiol or formed in peripheral tissues from androstenedione and other androgens. As noted above, during the first part of the menstrual cycle estrogens are produced in the ovarian follicle by the theca cells. After ovulation, the estrogens as well as progesterone are synthesized by the granulosa cells of the corpus luteum, and the pathways of biosynthesis are slightly different. The biosynthetic pathways during both of these phases are illustrated in Fig 38–3.

During pregnancy, a large amount of estrogen is synthesized by the fetoplacental unit. Neither the placenta nor the fetal adrenal contains all the enzymes necessary for this synthesis, and there is a remarkable coordination of activity leading to the production of this hormone. The pathways involved and the locations of the enzymes are shown in Fig 38–4. The estriol synthesized by the fetoplacental unit is released into the maternal circulation and excreted into the urine. Repeated assay of maternal urinary estriol excretion has been useful in the assessment of fetal well-being.

One of the most prolific natural sources of estrogenic substances is the stallion, which liberates more of this hormone than the pregnant mare or pregnant human woman. The equine estrogens—equilenin and equilin—and their congeners are unsaturated in the B as well as the A ring and are excreted in large quantities in urine, from which they are recovered and used for medicinal purposes.

In normal women, estradiol is produced at a rate that varies from 50 to 350 μg/d during the cycle. Plasma levels of estrogen vary during the menstrual cycle (Fig 38–2). The values range from a low of 50 pg/mL to as high as 350–850 pg/mL at the time of the preovulatory peak. There is very little precise information about the binding of natural estrogens to plasma proteins and what role this might play in their function and metabolism. However, the initial half-life of tracer amounts of estradiol infused into the circulation is approximately 50 minutes. Estradiol is converted by the liver and other tissues to estrone and estriol (and many other metabolites), which are found in the urine as the water-soluble sulfates and glucuronides (Fig 38–3). Estrogens are also excreted in the breast milk of nursing mothers.

Synthetic Estrogens

A variety of chemical alterations have been produced in the natural estrogens. The most important effect of these alterations has been to increase the effectiveness of the estrogens when administered

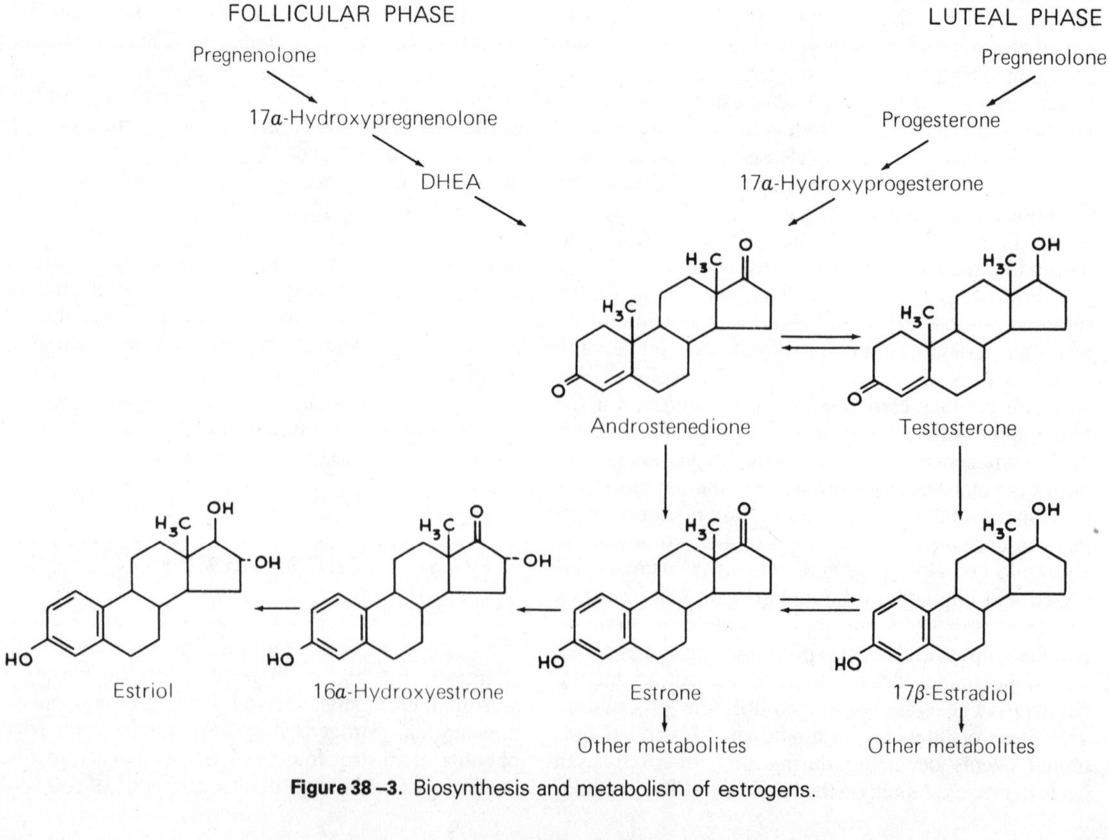

Figure 38 –3. Biosynthesis and metabolism of estrogens.

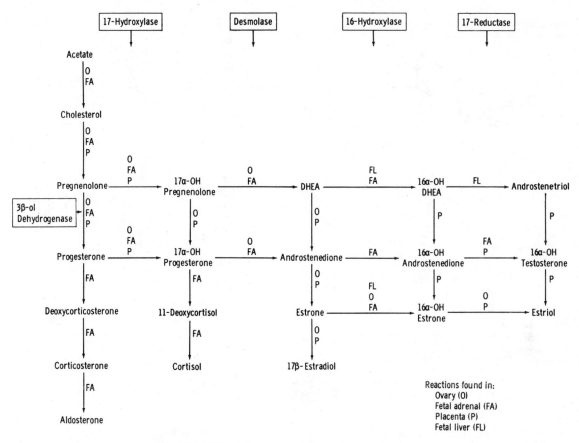

Figure 38–4. Steroid biosynthesis in the fetus and placenta.

orally. Those with pharmaceutical use are listed in Table 38–1.

In addition to the steroidal estrogens, a variety of nonsteroidal compounds with estrogenic activity have been synthesized and used clinically. These include dienestrol, benzestrol, hexestrol, methestrol, methallenestril, and chlorotrianisene.

Physiologic Effects

The estrogens are required for the normal maturation of the female. They stimulate the development of the vagina, uterus, and uterine tubes as well as the secondary sex characteristics. They stimulate stromal development and ductal growth in the breast and are responsible for the accelerated growth phase and the closing of the epiphyses of the long bones that occurs at puberty. They contribute to the growth of the axillary and pubic hair and alter the distribution of body fat so as to produce typical female body contours, including some accumulation of body fat around the hips and breasts. Larger quantities also stimulate development of pigmentation in the skin, most prominent in the region of the nipples and areola and in the genital region.

In addition to its growth effects on the uterine muscle, estrogen also plays an important role in the development of the endometrial lining. Continuous exposure to estrogens for prolonged periods leads to an abnormal hyperplasia of the endometrium that is usually associated with abnormal bleeding patterns. When the estrogen production is properly coordinated with the production of progesterone during the normal human menstrual cycle, regular periodic bleeding and shedding of the endometrial lining occur.

Estrogens have a number of important metabolic effects. They seem to be partially responsible for the maintenance of the normal structure of the skin and blood vessels in women. Estrogens decrease the rate of resorption of bone by antagonizing the effect of parathyroid hormone on bone but do not stimulate bone formation. Estrogens may have important effects on intestinal absorption because they reduce the motility of the bowel. In addition to stimulating the synthesis of enzymes leading to uterine growth, they alter the production and activity of many other enzymes in the body. In the liver, metabolism of α_2 globulin is altered, so that there is a higher circulating level of this group of proteins (Table 38–2). This results in an increase in thyroxine, estrogen, testosterone, iron, copper, and other transport proteins.

Estrogens enhance the coagulability of blood. Many changes in factors influencing coagulation have been reported, including increased circulating levels of factors II, VII, IX, and X. Increased plasminogen

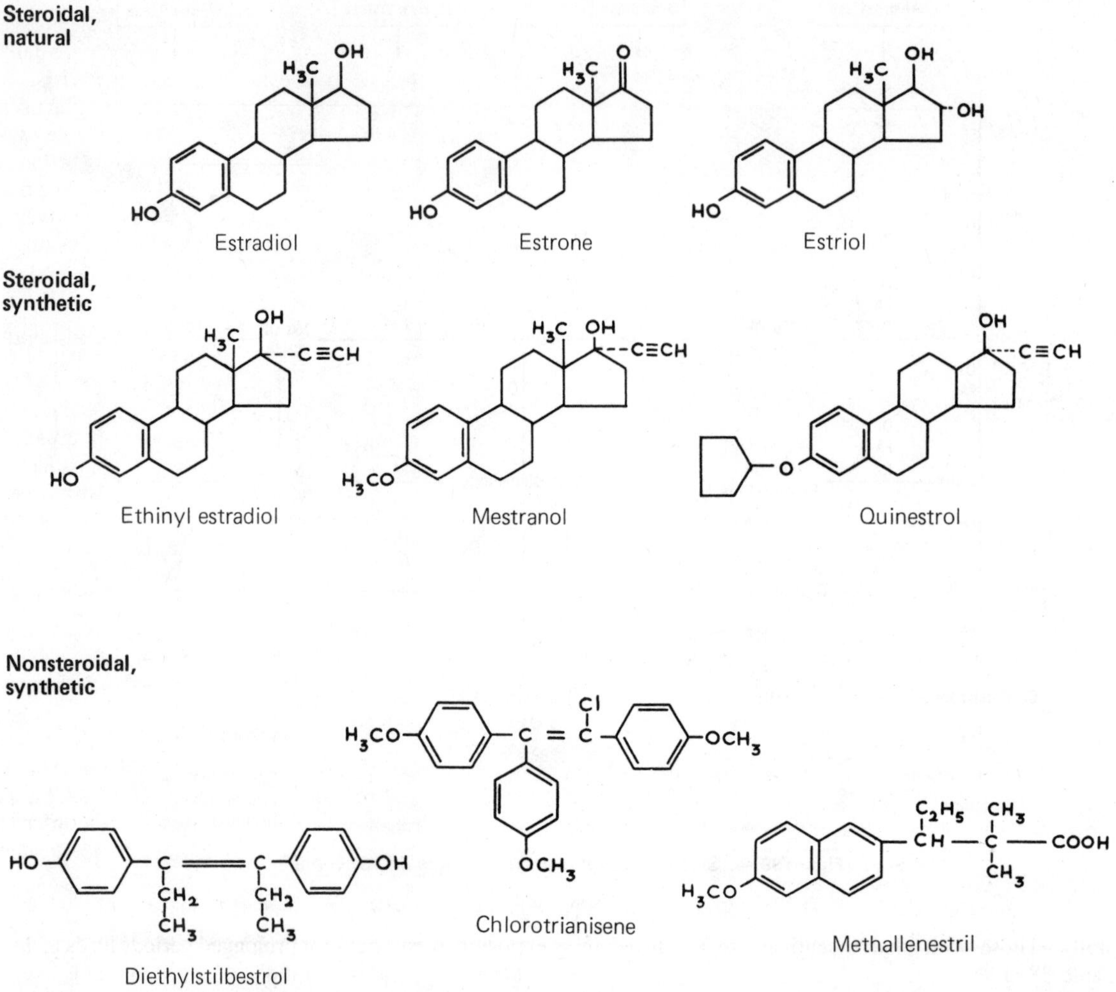

Steroidal, natural

Estradiol   Estrone   Estriol

Steroidal, synthetic

Ethinyl estradiol   Mestranol   Quinestrol

Nonsteroidal, synthetic

Diethylstilbestrol   Chlorotrianisene   Methallenestril

Figure 38–5. Compounds with estrogenic activity. First 3 rows: steroidal compounds; lower 4 rows: nonsteroidal compounds.

levels and decreased platelet adhesiveness have been found.

Alterations in the composition of the plasma lipids caused by estrogens are characterized by an increase in the alpha lipoproteins, a slight reduction in the beta lipoproteins, and a reduction in plasma cholesterol levels. Plasma triglyceride levels are increased (Table 38–3).

Estrogens have many other effects. They are responsible for estrous behavior in animals and influence libido in humans. They facilitate the loss of intravascular fluid into the extracellular space, producing edema. The resulting decrease in plasma volume causes a compensatory retention of sodium and water by the kidney. Estrogens also modulate sympathetic nervous system control of smooth muscle function.

Therapeutic Uses

Estrogens have been used extensively for replacement therapy in estrogen-deficient patients. The estrogen deficiency may be due to primary failure of development of the ovaries, castration, or menopause. When used for this purpose, small doses are usually adequate. Since prolonged unopposed estrogen therapy usually leads to endometrial hyperplasia, estrogens are administered cyclically and, preferably, in conjunction with a progestin, unless the uterus has been removed. A typical regimen consists of giving the medication daily for 21 days, followed by 1 week without therapy. A more regular cycle can usually be obtained by the addition of a progestational agent for the last 5 days of each cycle. It has been found that 5–10 μg of ethinyl estradiol daily are sufficient to reduce the elevated gonadotropin levels in menopausal patients.

Estrogens are widely used in the menopause. The need for and response to estrogen are quite variable, and many symptoms and disorders in menopausal women are probably unrelated to its deficiency. Hot flushes, sweating, and atrophic vaginitis are generally

Table 38–1. Commonly used estrogens.

	Average Replacement Dose
Ethinyl estradiol	0.01–0.05 mg/d
Micronized estradiol	1–2 mg/d
Estradiol	0.2–0.5 mg/d
Estradiol cypionate	2–5 mg every 3–4 weeks
Estradiol valerate	2–20 mg every other week
Piperazine estrone sulfate	1.25–5 mg/d
Conjugated, esterified, or mixed estrogenic substances:	
Oral	0.3–2.5 mg/d
Injectable	0.2–20 mg/d
Topical	. . .
Diethylstilbestrol	0.1–0.5 mg/d
Quinestrol	0.1–0.2 mg/week
Dienestrol	. . .
Chlorotrianisene	12–25 mg/d
Methallenestril	3–9 mg/d

relieved by estrogens, and many patients experience some increased sense of well-being, but depression and other psychopathologic states are seldom improved.

The role of estrogens in the prevention and treatment of osteoporosis has been carefully studied. The amount of bone present is maximal in the young active adult and begins to decline in middle age in men and women. The development of osteoporosis depends on the amount of bone present at the start of this process as well as activity. Since estrogen opposes the resorption caused by parathyroid hormone, bone loss is accelerated at the time of the menopause (artificial or natural). Estrogen therapy has been shown to reduce this loss. However, estrogens do not increase bone formation and cannot repair the process by increasing bone formation. Factors other than change in estrogen secre-

tion are important in the development of osteoporosis. The equivalent of 0.6 mg of conjugated estrogens daily may be sufficient to prevent or treat osteoporisis.

Estrogens combined with progestins can be used to suppress ovulation in patients with intractable dysmenorrhea or when suppression of ovarian function is used in the treatment of hirsutism and amenorrhea due to excessive secretion of androgens by the ovary. Under these circumstances, marked suppression is needed, and oral contraceptives containing $80–100\ \mu g$ of estrogen are usually recommended (Table 38–5).

Estrogens have been used to stop excessive uterine bleeding due to endometrial hyperplasia. Repeated doses of $20\ \mu g$ of ethinyl estradiol every few hours or the administration of 20 mg of conjugated estrogens intravenously have been useful in arresting blood loss temporarily.

Adverse Effects

A large number of adverse effects of variable severity have been reported with the therapeutic use of estrogens. Many other effects reported in conjunction with hormonal contraceptives may be related to their estrogen content. These are discussed on pp 407–410.

Estrogen therapy has now become the major cause of postmenopausal bleeding. Unfortunately, vaginal bleeding at this time of life may be due to carcinoma of the endometrium, and a large number of women have been and will be subjected to dilatation and curettage of the uterus unnecessarily. In order to avoid this complication, patients should be treated with the smallest amount of estrogen possible. It should be given cyclically so that bleeding, when it occurs, will be more likely to occur during the withdrawal period. Endometrial hyperplasia that leads to this bleeding can be prevented by administration of a

Table 38–2. The effects of testosterone, progesterone, estradiol, and pregnancy on plasma proteins.* (↑ = increased, ↓ = decreased, − = unchanged.)

Measurement	Testosterone	Progesterone	Estradiol	Pregnancy
Serum proteins	0	0	−	−
TBPA†	+	0	−	−
Albumin	0	0	−	−
Orosomucoid		0	−	−
TBG‡	−	0	+	+
Trypsin inhibitor	0	0	+	+
CBG§	−	0	+	+
Transferrin	−	0	0	+
Ceruloplasmin	0	0	+	+
Haptoglobin	0	0	−	0
Immunoglobulins	0	0	0	0
Plasminogen	0	0	+	+
Fibrinogen	−	0	+	+
Renin substrate		0	↑	↑
Plasma amino acids	↑	↓	↑	

*Reproduced, with permission, from Salhanick HA, Kipnis DM, Vande Wiele RL (editors): *Metabolic Effects of Gonadal Hormones and Contraceptive Steroids.* Plenum Press, 1969.
†Thyroxine-binding prealbumin.
‡Thyroxine-binding globulin.
§Corticosteroid-binding globulin.

Table 38–3. Some effects of oral contraceptives on plasma lipids (Dec 1968).*

	Estrogen	Progestin	Cholesterol	Phospholipid	Triglyceride
	All	...	↓	↑	↑
	...	All	0	0	0
Provest	Ethinyl estradiol	Medroxyprogesterone	0	↑	↑
Volidan	Ethinyl estradiol	Megestrol	0	↑	↑
Anovlar	Ethinyl estradiol	Norethisterone	↓	sl↓	?↑
Enovid	Mestranol	Norethynodrel	0	...	↑
Ovulen	Mestranol	Ethynodiol	0	↑	↑

*Reproduced, with permission, from Salhanick HA, Kipnis DM, Vande Wiele RL (editors): *Metabolic Effects of Gonadal Hormones and Contraceptive Steroids.* Plenum Press, 1969.

progestational agent for several days with the last doses of estrogen in each cycle. For example, the patient may take 0.3–0.6 mg of conjugated estrogens for the first 20 days of each month, and 10 mg of medroxyprogesterone can be added on days 18, 19, and 20. This will usually produce regular and predictable withdrawal bleeding. Endometrial hyperplasia and consequent bleeding can also be minimized by combining the estrogen with an androgen such as methyltestosterone in doses of 5 mg daily. The long-term metabolic effects of androgens in postmenopausal women have not been adequately assessed.

Nausea and breast tenderness are common and can be minimized by using the smallest effective dose of estrogen. They may be more marked at the beginning of therapy. The presence of cystic mastitis or fibroids that increase in size during treatment may also interfere with the use of estrogen. Hyperpigmentation also occurs. Estrogen therapy is associated with an increase in frequency of migraine headaches as well as cholestasis, hypertension, and gallbladder disease. The relationship of estrogen therapy to cancer continues to be the subject of intensive investigation.

Although it has not been possible to establish that there is an increased risk in the incidence of breast cancer, it is not clear that it is safe to use these agents in patients considered to be at high risk for this tumor. Many studies have been published showing an increased risk of endometrial carcinoma in patients taking estrogens. The risk seems to vary with the dose and duration of treatment: 15 times as great in patients taking large doses of estrogen for 5 or more years, in contrast with 2–4 times greater in patients receiving lower doses for short periods. Several recent studies indicate that the concomitant use of a progestin not only prevents this increased risk but actually reduces the incidence of endometrial cancer below that in the general population.

A number of papers have appeared reporting the occurrence of adenocarcinoma of the vagina in young women whose mothers were treated with large doses of diethylstilbestrol early in pregnancy. There is no good indication for its use at that time, and it should be avoided. It is not known whether other estrogens have a similar effect or whether this is peculiar to diethylstilbestrol. This agent should be limited to use in the treatment of cancer (eg, prostate) or to use as a "morning after" contraceptive (see p 403).

Cautions

Since the risks of estrogen therapy cannot be accurately assessed at present, these agents should be used with caution in postmenopausal women with symptoms. Both physician and patient should be alert to the manifestations of thrombophlebitis and cerebral and retinal thrombosis. If these occur or are suspected, estrogens should be discontinued. They should be used with caution in patients with epilepsy, migraine, asthma, recurrent depression, and cardiac and renal failure. Estrogens can cause exacerbation of symptoms in patients with porphyria. They may activate endometriosis.

Estrogens may influence tests of endocrine and liver function (see Hormonal Contraception).

The vaginal route of administration should not be considered to have only local effects, since the hormone is well absorbed by this route.

Contraindications

Estrogens should not be used in patients with estrogen-dependent neoplasms such as carcinoma of the endometrium or in patients with known or suspected carcinoma of the breast. They should be avoided in patients with undiagnosed genital bleeding, liver disease, or a history of thromboembolic disorder.

Preparations & Dosages

The commonly used natural and synthetic preparations and equivalent dosages are given in Table 38–1.

THE PROGESTINS

1. PROGESTERONE

Progesterone is the most important progestin in humans. In addition to having important hormonal effects, it serves as a precursor to the estrogens, androgens, and adrenocortical steroids. It is synthesized in

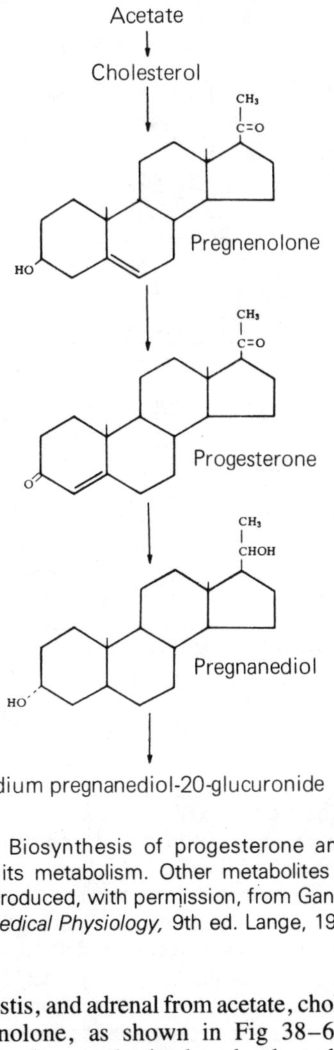

Acetate

↓

Cholesterol

Pregnenolone

Progesterone

Pregnanediol

↓

Sodium pregnanediol-20-glucuronide

Figure 38 –6. Biosynthesis of progesterone and major pathway for its metabolism. Other metabolites are also formed. (Reproduced, with permission, from Ganong WF: *Review of Medical Physiology,* 9th ed. Lange, 1979.)

the ovary, testis, and adrenal from acetate, cholesterol, and pregnenolone, as shown in Fig 38–6. Large amounts are also synthesized and released by the placenta during pregnancy (Fig 38–4).

In the ovary, progesterone is produced primarily by the corpus luteum and secreted in amounts of 20–30 mg/d during the luteal phase. Normal males appear to secrete 1–5 mg of progesterone daily, resulting in plasma levels of about 0.03 μg/dL. The level is only slightly higher in the female during the follicular phase of the cycle, when only a few milligrams per day of progesterone are secreted. During the luteal phase, 20–30 mg/d are released into the circulation and the plasma levels range from 0.5 to more than 2 μg/dL (Fig 38–2).

Progesterone is rapidly absorbed following administration by any route. Its half-life in the plasma is approximately 5 minutes, and small amounts are stored temporarily in body fat. It is almost completely metabolized in one passage through the liver, and for that reason it is quite ineffective when administered orally.

In the liver, progesterone is metabolized to pregnanediol and conjugated to glucuronic acid. It is excreted into the urine as pregnanediol glucuronide

(Fig 38–6). The amount of pregnanediol in the urine has been used as an index of progesterone secretion. It has been very useful in spite of the fact that the proportion of secreted progesterone converted to this compound varies from day to day and from individual to individual. Although a variety of biologic assays have been used for the measurement of progesterone in the past, several excellent methods including double-isotope derivative technics, gas chromatographic technics, and ligand-binding assays are now available.

In addition to progesterone, 20α- and 20β-hydroxyprogesterone (20α- or 20β-hydroxy-4-pregnene-3-one) are also found. These compounds have about one-fifth the progestational activity of progesterone in humans and other species. Little is known of the role of these compounds, but 20α-hydroxyprogesterone is produced in large amounts in some species and may be of some importance biologically.

The effects of progesterone on lipid and protein metabolism are summarized in Tables 38–2 and 38–3. Progesterone has important effects on carbohydrate metabolism. A dose of 50 mg intramuscularly daily can reproduce the increased insulin levels and decreased response of blood glucose levels to insulin observed in normal pregnancy.

Progesterone can compete with aldosterone at the renal tubule, causing a decrease in Na$^+$ reabsorption. This leads to an increased secretion of aldosterone by the adrenal cortex (eg, in pregnancy). Progesterone increases the body temperature in humans. The mechanism of this effect is not known, but an alteration of the temperature-regulating centers in the hypothalamus has been suggested. Progesterone also alters the function of the respiratory centers. The ventilatory response to CO_2 is increased (synthetic progestins with an ethinyl group do not have respiratory effects). This leads to a measurable reduction in arterial and alveolar P_{CO_2} during pregnancy and in the luteal phase of the menstrual cycle. Progesterone and related steroids also have hypnotic effects on the brain.

Progesterone is responsible for the alveolobular development of the secretory apparatus in the breast. It also causes the maturation and secretory changes in the endometrium that are seen following ovulation (Fig 38–2).

Progesterone decreases the plasma levels of many amino acids and leads to increased urinary nitrogen excretion. It has been found to induce changes in the smooth endoplasmic reticulum and its functions in experimental animals.

Other effects are noted in the section on oral contraceptives, below.

2. SYNTHETIC PROGESTATIONAL AGENTS

A variety of progestational compounds have now been synthesized. Some of these are active when given

Table 38–4. Activities of progestational agents.

		Activities*				
	Duration of Action	Estrogenic	Androgenic	Anti-estrogenic	Anti-androgenic	Anabolic
Progesterone and derivatives						
Progesterone	· 1 d	−	−	+	−	−
Dydrogesterone	1–3 d	−	−	+	−	−
Hydroxyprogesterone caproate	8–14 d	sl	sl	−	−	−
Medroxyprogesterone acetate	Tablets: 1–3 d	−	+	+	−	−
	Injectable: 4–12 weeks					
Chlormadinone acetate	. . .	−	−	+	+	−
Megestrol acetate	1–3 d	−	−	+	+	−
17a-Ethinyl testosterone derivatives						
Testosterone derivatives						
Dimethisterone	1–3 d	−	−	sl	−	−
19-Nortestosterone derivatives						
Norethynodrel†	1–3 d	+	−	−	−	−
Lynestrenol	1–3 d	+	+	−	−	+
(Not available in USA)						
Norethindrone†	1–3 d	sl	+	+	−	+
Norethindrone acetate†	1–3 d	sl	+	+	−	+
Ethynodiol diacetate†	1–3 d	sl	+	+	−	−
dl-Norgestrel†	1–3 d	−	+	+	−	+

*Interpretation: + = active; − = inactive; sl = slight activity. Activities have been reported in various species using various end points and may not apply to humans.
†See Table 38–5.

by mouth. They are not a uniform group of compounds, and all of them differ from progesterone in one or more respects. Table 38–4 lists many of these compounds.

In general, the compounds related to progesterone can produce a secretory endometrium and maintain pregnancy in animals. They antagonize aldosterone-induced sodium retention (see above) and have no androgenic or estrogenic effects. The remaining compounds produce a decidual change in the endometrial stroma, do not support pregnancy in test animals, are more effective gonadotropin inhibitors, and may have minimal estrogenic and androgenic or anabolic activity.

Therapeutic Uses

The major use of progestational hormones is for hormonal contraception (see below). However, they are useful in producing long-term ovarian suppression for other purposes. When used alone in large doses parenterally (eg, medroxyprogesterone acetate, 150 mg intramuscularly every 90 days), prolonged anovulation and amenorrhea are produced. This procedure has been employed in the treatment of dysmenorrhea, endometriosis, hirsutism, and bleeding disorders when estrogens are contraindicated. The major problem with this regimen is the prolonged time required for ovulatory function to return after cessation of therapy in some patients. It should not be used for patients planning a pregnancy in the near future.

Progestins do not appear to have any place in the therapy of threatened or habitual abortion. Early re-

ports of the usefulness of these agents resulted from the unwarranted assumption that after several abortions the likelihood of repeated abortions was over 90%. When progestational agents were administered to patients with previous abortions, a salvage rate of 80% was obtained. It is now recognized that similar patients abort only 20% of the time even when untreated.

In some patients with "threatened" abortion, it has been noted that progesterone production is decreased. It is likely that the decrease in progesterone reflects damage to the placenta or fetus and is another result of the events leading to abortion rather than the cause of the abortion. The administration of progesterone in these circumstances does not appear to be useful and may result in delaying recognition of an abortion that has occurred. In addition, progesterone and progestational agents administered early in pregnancy have been incriminated in the masculinization of the external genitalia in the female fetus and induction of congenital anomalies. Prolonged postpartum bleeding has been reported in some patients treated with repository medroxyprogesterone or hydroxyprogesterone caproate and, when used in women with "threatened" abortion, may cause a delay in the expulsion of a dead fetus.

Progesterone and medroxyprogesterone have been used in the treatment of women who have difficulty in conceiving and who demonstrate a slow rise in basal body temperature. Some investigators believe that these patients suffer from a relative luteal insufficiency, and progesterone or related compounds are given to replace the deficiency. There is no convincing evidence that this treatment is effective. The successes reported are impossible to distinguish from placebo effects in the absence of satisfactory controls.

Diagnostic Uses

Progesterone can also be used as a test of estrogen secretion. The administration of progesterone, 150 mg/d, or medroxyprogesterone, 10 mg/d for 5–7 days, is followed by withdrawal bleeding in amenorrheic patients only when the endometrium has been stimulated by estrogens. A combination of estrogen and progestin can be given to test the responsiveness of the endometrium in patients with amenorrhea.

Contraindications, Cautions, & Adverse Effects

See Hormonal Contraception, below.

3. COMBINATIONS OF ESTROGENS & PROGESTINS

Since estrogens and progestins are often used in combination with one another, a variety of combined preparations are available. Most of them have been designed for use as oral contraceptives, and their properties as a class of drugs will be discussed below (see Hormonal Contraception).

OTHER OVARIAN HORMONES

The normal ovary produces small amounts of androgens, including testosterone, androstenedione, and dehydroepiandrosterone. Only testosterone has a significant amount of biologic activity, although androstenedione can be converted to estrone in peripheral tissues. The normal woman produces a total of less than 200 μg of testosterone in 24 hours, and about one-third of this is probably formed in the ovary directly. The physiologic significance of these small amounts of androgens is not established, but they may be partly responsible for normal hair growth at puberty and may have other important metabolic effects. The androgen production by the ovary may be markedly increased in some abnormal states, usually in association with amenorrhea as noted above.

The ovary also produces one or more substances similar to the inhibin produced by the testis that decreases the pituitary release of FSH.

Relaxin

Relaxin is a polypeptide that has been extracted from the ovary. In certain animal species, it appears to play an important role at the time of parturition. It causes relaxation of the pelvic ligaments and softening of the uterine cervix.

In women, relaxin has been measured by immunoassay. Levels were highest immediately after the LH surge and during menstruation. A physiologic role for this hormone has not been established.

Clinical trials with relaxin have been carried out in patients with dysmenorrhea. Relaxin has also been administered to patients in premature labor and during prolonged labor. The therapeutic value of this hormone has not been established.

HORMONAL CONTRACEPTION (Oral Contraceptives)

A large number of oral contraceptives containing estrogens or progestins (or both) are now available for clinical use. These preparations vary chemically and, as might be expected, have many properties in common, but they exhibit definite differences. Experience with some of the drugs has been much greater than with others, and more differences may emerge as further experience accumulates.

Three types of preparations have been used for oral contraception: (1) combinations of estrogens and progestins; (2) the sequential use of estrogens followed by combined estrogens and progestins; and (3) continuous progestin therapy without concomitant administration of estrogens.

The preparations for oral use are all well absorbed, and the metabolism of the drugs is not known to be profoundly altered by simultaneous administration. Little information is available concerning the turnover time and excretion of some of these compounds.

Pharmacologic Effects

A. Mechanism of Contraceptive Action: The combinations of estrogens and progestins and the sequential agents appear to exert their effect largely through inhibition of ovulation. The combination agents containing estrogens and progestins also produce a change in the cervical mucus, in the uterine endometrium, and in the motility and secretion in the uterine tubes, all of which decrease the likelihood of conception and implantation. The continuous use of progestins alone does not inhibit ovulation. The other factors mentioned, therefore, play a major role in the prevention of pregnancy when these agents are used.

B. General Effects: Chronic use of combination or sequential agents appears to depress ovarian function. The gross appearance of the ovary is that of relative inactivity; there is a minimum of follicular development; and corpora lutea, larger follicles, stromal edema, and other morphologic features normally seen in ovulating women are absent. In general, the amounts of the endogenous estrogens excreted in the urine are less than those observed in normal menstruating women, and pregnanediol excretion is not usually increased in the latter phase of the cycle. It

Table 38–5. Oral contraceptive agents in use. The estrogen-containing compounds are arranged in order of increasing content of estrogen (ethinyl estradiol and mestranol have similar potencies). The relative progestational potencies are shown in the last column.

	Estrogen (mg)		Progestin (mg)		PP*
Combination tablets					
Loestrin 1/20 Zorane 1/20	Ethinyl estradiol	0.02	Norethindrone acetate	1.0	4
Loestrin 1.5/30 Zorane 1.5/30	Ethinyl estradiol	0.03	Norethindrone acetate	1.5	6
Ovcon 35	Ethinyl estradiol	0.035	Norethindrone	0.4	0.8
Brevicon Modicon	Ethinyl estradiol	0.035	Norethindrone	0.5	1
Lo/Ovral	Ethinyl estradiol	0.03	dl-Norgestrel	0.3	18
Ovral	Ethinyl estradiol	0.05	dl-Norgestrel	0.5	30
Norlestrin 1/50 Zorane 1/50	Ethinyl estradiol	0.05	Norethindrone acetate	1.0	4
Norlestrin 2.5/50	Ethinyl estradiol	0.05	Norethindrone acetate	2.5	10
Demulen	Ethinyl estradiol	0.05	Ethynodiol diacetate	1.0	30
Ovcon 50	Ethinyl estradiol	0.05	Norethindrone	1.0	2
Norinyl 1/50 Ortho-Novum 1/50	Mestranol	0.05	Norethindrone	1.0	2
Norinyl 1/80 Ortho-Novum 1/80	Mestranol	0.8	Norethindrone	1.0	2
Norinyl-2 Ortho-Novum-2	Mestranol	0.1	Norethindrone	2.0	4
Ovulen	Mestranol	0.1	Ethynodiol diacetate	1.0	30
Enovid 5	Mestranol	0.075	Norethynodrel	5.0	11
Enovid E	Mestranol	0.1	Norethynodrel	2.5	6
Daily progestin tablets					
Micronor Nor-QD	. . .		Norethindrone	0.35	0.7
Ovrette	. . .		dl-Norgestrel	0.075	3

*Progestational potency.

is not known whether the few instances in which pregnanediol excretion is elevated are due to escape ovulation in these patients or whether corpora lutea have been formed without ovulation. Although cystic follicles have been described in patients being treated with oral contraceptives, the ovaries usually become smaller even when enlarged before therapy.

The great majority of patients return to normal menstrual patterns when therapy is terminated. About 75% will ovulate in the first posttreatment cycle, and 97% by the third posttreatment cycle. Patients with a history of irregular cycles seem more liable to the development of amenorrhea following cessation of therapy.

About 2% of patients remain amenorrheic for periods of up to several years after therapy has been concluded, and the prevalence of amenorrhea, often with galactorrhea, is higher in women who have used this form of contraception.

These preparations have important effects on the genital tract. The cytologic findings on vaginal smears vary depending on the preparation used. For example, with the use of sequential regimens a high maturation index—ie, cornified epithelium—is noted until the progestational drug is added during the last 5 days. With almost all of the combined drugs, a low maturation index is found because of the presence of progestational agents.

These agents have important effects on the uterus. After prolonged use, the cervix may show some hypertrophy and polyp formation. There are also important effects on the cervical mucus. Normally, through the menstrual cycle, there is an increasing amount of clear liquefied mucus that is altered by the secretion of progesterone following ovulation. At that time it becomes thick and less copious and contains much cellular debris. This sequence is not much altered by the sequential preparations; however, the combined products as well as continuous progesterone therapy produce the expected changes in the mucus.

Initially there is some stimulation of the uterine muscle, resulting in some softening and increase in size. This effect is neither common nor marked and is due to the estrogens. The endometrial changes vary markedly with the preparation. With sequential agents the sequence of changes does not vary greatly from normal. During the last 5 days, progressive progestational effects on the glandular tissues are observed. In contrast to this, agents containing both estrogens and progestins produce a stromal deciduation toward the end of the cycle. The agents containing the 19-nor compounds—particularly those with the smaller amounts of estrogen—tend to produce more glandular atrophy and usually less bleeding, whereas combination agents containing progestins that produce more physiologic changes in the endometrium (eg, medroxyprogesterone) are associated with spotting between periods and more bleeding at the time of menses. The flow during menses tends to be slightly heavier than or similar to that prior to therapy when sequential regimens are used.

Although studies in rodents suggest that the development of the blastocyst and the endometrium must be very precisely matched for implantation to occur, pregnancies occur in some patients who omit a few tablets or when the medication was begun too late in a given cycle to prevent ovulation.

Although studies in humans are not available, animal experiments indicate that alterations in the transport of the gamete through the uterine tube are produced by estrogens and progestins. The effect on germ cell transport is thought by some to be an important mechanism for the impairment of fertility, particularly with the use of low-dosage continuous progestin therapy as noted above.

Stimulation of the breasts occurs in most patients receiving estrogen-containing agents. Some enlargement is generally noted. The administration of estrogens and combinations of estrogens and progestins tends to suppress lactation. When the doses are small, the effects on breast feeding are not appreciable. However, when postpartum mothers are examined, milk is found in the breasts of fewer patients taking oral contraceptives than in untreated mothers. Preliminary studies of the transport of the oral contraceptives into the breast milk suggest that only small amounts of these compounds are found, and they have not been considered to be of importance.

C. Extragenital Effects of the Oral Contraceptives: The state of knowledge about these effects is incomplete at present, even though they reflect effects of either estrogens or progestins that have been used for many years. The possible consequences of these compounds have been brought to our attention more forcefully because of the large and growing number of normal individuals using them. In some cases the effects are known to be secondary to the estrogens and in other cases to the progestins. However, in many instances the agent responsible for the effects is not known. Various effects may be more pronounced with one of the preparations than with others.

1. Central nervous system effects–The central nervous system effects of the oral contraceptives have not been well studied in humans. A variety of effects of estrogen and progesterone have been noted in animals. Estrogens tend to lower the threshold of excitability in the brain, whereas progesterone tends to increase it. The thermogenic action of progesterone and some of the synthetic progestins is also thought to be in the central nervous system. The suppression of ovarian function that results from inhibition of gonadotropin secretion is also thought to be due to an influence on the hypothalamus or other parts of the nervous system.

It is very difficult to evaluate any behavioral or emotional effects of these compounds. Although the incidence of pronounced changes in mood, affect, and behavior reported in most studies is low, milder changes are common. These changes are variable and therefore difficult to evaluate in relation to the pharmacologic effects of the drug. They may be psychologically induced by the act of using contraception or the circumstances surrounding it. However, it is possible that the changes in neuronal activity and thresholds produced by these drugs may lead to changes conditioned by other factors.

2. Effects on endocrine function–The effects on the endocrine system are not well understood at present. The inhibition of pituitary gonadotropin secretion has been mentioned. Estrogens are known to alter adrenal structure and function. In humans, a few changes are of note. Estrogens increase the plasma concentration of the α_2 globulin that binds hydrocortisone (cortisol-binding protein). This does not appear to lead to any chronic alteration in the rate of secretion of cortisol, but plasma concentrations may be more than double the levels found in untreated individuals. It has also been observed that the ACTH response to the administration of metyrapone (see Chapter 39) is

attenuated by estrogens and the oral contraceptives.

These preparations cause alterations in the angiotensin-aldosterone system. Plasma renin activity has been found to increase, and there is an increase in aldosterone secretion. The relationship between these alterations and the hypertension that occurs in some patients taking oral contraceptives is not clear.

Thyroxine-binding globulin is increased. As a result, the plasma protein-bound iodine (PBI) and butanol-extractable iodine (BEI) levels are increased to those commonly seen during pregnancy. Since more of the thyroxine is bound, red cell T_3 uptake of radioactive iodine is not altered. The free thyroxine level in these patients is also normal.

3. Hematologic effects–Serious thromboembolic phenomena occurring in women taking oral contraceptives have stimulated a great many studies of the effects of these compounds on blood coagulation. A clear picture of such effects has not yet emerged. The oral contraceptives do not consistently alter bleeding or clotting time. Many studies have been reported of the effects of this group of agents on the clotting factors. A great deal of conflicting information has arisen from these studies. Preliminary indications are that the changes observed are similar to those reported in pregnancy. There is an increase in factors VII, VIII, IX, and X. Increased amounts of coumarin derivatives are required to produce a reduction in prothrombin time in patients taking oral contraceptives. Vitamin K-dependent clotting activity is increased in vitro only after the storage of blood for 16 hours in plastic tubes.

In addition to the changes in clotting factors, there are important changes in serum proteins. There is an increase in the α_2 globulins that affects the concentrations of hormones and other serum constituents that are protein-bound (Table 38–2). There is an increase in serum iron and total iron-binding capacity similar to that reported in patients with hepatitis.

Significant alterations in the cellular components of blood have not been reported with any consistency. However, the platelet aggregation response to catecholamines is increased. A number of patients have been reported to develop folic acid deficiency anemias. Preliminary studies indicate that the oral contraceptives inhibit the conversion of polyglutamic folate (found in food) to the monoglutamic folate that can be absorbed in the gastrointestinal tract. This can be reversed by supplementary folic acid or cessation of oral contraceptives.

4. Hepatic effects–The liver plays an important role in the inactivation and conversion to water-soluble conjugates of the estrogens and progestins used in oral contraceptives. These hormones have profound effects on the function of the liver in other respects. Some of these effects are deleterious and will be considered below under Adverse Reactions.

The effects on serum proteins noted above result from the effects of the estrogens on the synthesis of the various α_2 globulins and fibrinogen. Serum haptoglobins that also arise from the liver are depressed rather than increased by estrogen.

Some of the effects on carbohydrate and lipid metabolism are probably influenced by changes in liver metabolism. However, detailed studies of these changes have not been reported.

Important alterations in drug excretion and metabolism are also found in the liver. Estrogens in the amounts seen during pregnancy or used in oral contraceptive agents delay the clearance of Bromsulphalein (BSP) and reduce bile flow. These alterations result from impairment of the transfer of cholephilic substances from hepatic cells into the bile. Some of these effects of estrogens and progestins may be indirectly induced or due to metabolites of the hormones rather than the hormones themselves. These changes may cause the observed increase in cholelithiasis associated with use of these agents.

These agents increase the saturation of cholesterol in bile. The proportion of cholic acid in bile acids is increased while the proportion of chenodeoxycholic acid is decreased.

5. Effects on lipid metabolism–(Table 38–3.) The effects on lipid metabolism are potentially important in evaluating the long-term use of these compounds. There are conflicting reports about the effects of the oral contraceptive drugs containing mixtures of estrogens and progestins.

The available studies indicate that estrogens increase serum triglycerides and free and esterified cholesterol. Phospholipids are also increased, as are high-density lipoproteins. Low-density lipoproteins usually decrease. Although the effects are marked with doses of 100 mg of mestranol or ethinyl estradiol, doses of 50 mg or less have minimal effects. The progestins (particularly the 19-nortestosterone derivatives) tend to antagonize the effects of estrogen. Preparations containing small amounts of estrogen and a progestin may slightly decrease triglycerides and high-density lipoproteins.

6. Effects on carbohydrate metabolism–The administration of oral contraceptives produces alterations in carbohydrate metabolism similar to those observed in pregnancy. There is a reduction in the rate of absorption of carbohydrates from the gastrointestinal tract. Many individuals exhibit decreases in glucose tolerance; others, although their glucose tolerance has not been altered, have been shown to secrete increased amounts of insulin following the ingestion or injection of glucose. In general, these changes have been more marked in patients with a family history of diabetes. Since estrogens are known to enhance the secretion of growth hormone by the pituitary, it has been suggested that this may be responsible for some of the observed effects. Studies in experimental animals indicate that estrogens stimulate islet cell function and increase the ability of the pancreas to secrete insulin. Progesterone, on the other hand, clearly interferes with insulin action. Preliminary observations indicate that both effects occur in women. Although the changes in glucose tolerance are reversible on discontinuing medication, the implications of long-term treatment in patients who inherit the trait for diabetes is not known.

7. Cardiovascular effects–These agents cause small increases in cardiac output associated with higher systolic and diastolic blood pressure and heart rate. Pathologic increases in blood pressure have been reported in a small number of patients. This may be related to the enhancement of plasma renin activity as a result of oral contraceptive drugs. The pressure slowly returns to normal when treatment is terminated. Although the magnitude of the pressure change is small in many patients, it is marked in others. It is important that blood pressure be followed in each patient. An increase in blood pressure has been reported to occur in postmenopausal women treated with estrogens alone.

Although not found consistently, venous engorgement has been reported in some patients. Changes in the connective tissue in the arteries of rodents have been reported, but the significance of these changes is not known. Plasma from women taking oral contraceptives stimulates growth of arterial smooth muscle in tissue culture. It is postulated that this effect enhances the atherosclerotic process.

8. Effects on the skin–The oral contraceptives have been noted to increase pigmentation of the skin of patients (chloasma). This effect seems to be enhanced in women who have dark complexions and by exposure to ultraviolet light. Some of the androgenlike progestins may increase the production of sebum. The sequential oral contraceptive preparations as well as estrogens often decrease sebum production. This may be due to suppression of the ovarian production of androgens. Estrogens also decrease pore size and lead to acne in some patients.

Clinical Uses

The most important use of the estrogens and progestins is for oral contraception. A large number of preparations are available for this specific purpose. They are specially packaged to provide for ease of administration. In general, they are very effective; when these agents are taken according to directions, the risk of conception is extremely small. The pregnancy rate is estimated to be about 0.5–1 per 100 woman years at risk with combination agents; the pregnancy rate is slightly higher for the sequential preparations.

Progestins and estrogens are also useful in the treatment of endometriosis. When severe dysmenorrhea is the major symptom, the suppression of ovulation with estrogen may be followed by painless periods. However, in most patients this approach to therapy is inadequate. The long-term administration of large doses of progestins or combinations of progestins and estrogens prevents the periodic breakdown of the endometrial tissue and in some cases will lead to endometrial fibrosis and prevent the reactivation of implants for prolonged periods.

When these agents are not taken as directed and one or more doses are missed, there appears to be a significantly higher pregnancy rate in patients taking the formerly available sequential agents than when the combinations are employed.

As is true with most hormonal preparations, many of the side-effects are physiologic or pharmacologic effects of the drugs that are objectionable only because they are not pertinent to the situation for which they are being used. Therefore, the product containing the smallest amounts of hormones should be selected for use.

The differences between preparations can be used to advantage in selecting a preparation for an individual patient when special needs arise. These differences reflect differences in the amounts of estrogen, the amounts of progestin, and the type of progestin. Preparations containing larger amounts of estrogen tend to produce more withdrawal bleeding, nausea, and mastalgia. Preparations containing 19-nortestosterone derivatives tend to reduce the amount of withdrawal bleeding and have more anabolic or androgenic effects.

Adverse Reactions

The incidence of serious known side-effects associated with the use of these drugs is low. There are a number of reversible changes in intermediary metabolism. However, the long-term effects of such changes as an increase in plasma triglycerides or decrease in glucose tolerance cannot be assessed as yet. Minor side-effects are frequent, but most are mild and many are transient. Although it is not often necessary to discontinue medication for these, as many as one-third of all patients started on oral contraception with combined or sequential agents discontinue therapy for reasons other than a desire to become pregnant.

It is difficult to evaluate the significance of some of the complaints. The great variability of side-effects in different patients taking the same preparation suggests that they are not directly or entirely due to the hormones. This does not mean that they can be ignored in the context of the oral contraceptive administration, however, and each case must be evaluated individually. Common minor problems may respond to simple changes in pill formulation. A brief summary of some symptoms and suggested changes is as follows:

(1) Nausea, breast tenderness, edema, chloasma: Decrease estrogen content.

(2) Early and midcycle spotting, decreased flow or amenorrhea: Increase estrogen content or decrease progestin content (or both).

(3) Weight gain, hair growth, depression, tiredness: Decrease progestin content.

(4) Excessive bleeding, late cycle spotting: Increase progestin content or decrease estrogen content (or both).

A. Mild Side-Effects:

1. Nausea, mastalgia, breakthrough bleeding, and edema are related to the amount of estrogen in the preparation. They were more common with the sequential preparations because of the larger amounts of estrogen present and can often be alleviated by a shift to a combination agent or to a preparation containing smaller amounts of estrogen or to agents containing progestational compounds with androgenlike effects.

2. Changes in serum proteins and other effects on endocrine function (see above) must be taken into account when thyroid, adrenal, or pituitary function is being evaluated. Increases in sedimentation rate are thought to be due to increased levels of fibrinogen.

3. Psychologic changes are often transient and are not predictable with any of the preparations. In general, most patients "feel better" because they are relieved of anxiety about becoming pregnant. Some patients experience premenstrual-like symptoms of irritability and depression throughout the cycle.

4. Headache is mild and often transient. Migraine is often made worse and has been reported to be associated with an increased frequency of cerebrovascular accidents. When this occurs, or when migraine has its onset during therapy with these agents, treatment should be discontinued.

5. Libido is increased or decreased in a few patients and unchanged in the majority. Similar changes have been observed with placebo therapy.

6. Withdrawal bleeding sometimes fails to occur—most often with combination preparations—and may cause confusion with regard to pregnancy. If this is disturbing to the patient, a different preparation may be tried or other methods of contraception used.

B. More Annoying Side-Effects: Any of the following may require discontinuation of oral contraceptives:

1. Breakthrough bleeding is the most common problem in using progestational agents alone for contraception. It occurs in as many as 25% of patients. It is more frequently encountered in patients taking low-dose preparations than in those taking combination pills with higher levels of progestin and estrogen.

2. Weight gain is more common with the combination agents containing androgenlike progestins. It can usually be controlled by shifting preparations with less progestin effect or by dieting.

3. Increased skin pigmentation may be distressing in dark-skinned women. It tends to increase with time, the incidence being about 5% at the end of the first year and about 40% after 8 years. It is thought to be exacerbated by vitamin B deficiency. It is often reversible upon discontinuance of medication, but in occasional cases the pigmentation disappears very slowly.

4. Acne may be exacerbated by agents containing androgenlike progestins, whereas agents containing large amounts of estrogen frequently cause marked improvement in acne.

5. Hirsutism may also be aggravated by the 19-nortestosterone derivatives, and the combination containing nonandrogenic progestins is preferred.

6. Ureteral dilatation similar to that observed in pregnancy has been reported, and bacteriuria is more frequent.

7. Vaginal infections are more common and more difficult to treat in patients who are receiving oral contraceptives.

8. Amenorrhea after discontinuation–Following cessation of administration of oral contraceptives,

95% of patients with normal menstrual histories resume normal periods and all but a few resume normal cycles during the next few months. However, some patients remain amenorrheic for several years. Many of these patients also have galactorrhea. Patients who have had menstrual irregularities before taking oral contraceptives are particularly susceptible to prolonged amenorrhea when the agents are discontinued.

C. Severe Side-Effects:

1. Vascular disorders–The most serious thromboembolic disorders observed in association with the use of oral contraceptives are thrombophlebitis, pulmonary embolization, and cerebrovascular thrombosis. The results of most studies indicate a 5- to 10-fold increase in the incidence of thromboembolic disorders in women taking oral contraceptives. The underlying changes leading to thrombophlebitis in these patients have not been identified. Although the risk is small, the seriousness of the consequences is so great that many clinicians are of the opinion that women who can satisfactorily and successfully use other forms of contraception should be advised to do so. There appear to be fewer untoward vascular complications in patients with blood group O as compared with A, B, or AB.

Recent studies also indicate that the risk of myocardial infarction is greater in women taking oral contraceptives. The risks seem to increase with age and are particularly high in the presence of other risk factors such as hypertension, hypercholesterolemia, and cigarette smoking.

The risk of cardiovascular death increases with age, and this form of contraception is not recommended for women over 35 or those who smoke except in circumstances where other methods are not feasible.

Severe hypertension develops in some women during therapy and may become malignant in a few.

2. Gastrointestinal disorders–Many cases of cholestatic jaundice have been reported in patients taking progestin-containing drugs. The differences in incidence of these disorders from one population to another suggest that genetic factors may be involved.

The jaundice caused by these agents is similar to that produced by other 17-alkyl–substituted steroids. It is most often observed in the first 3 cycles and is particularly common in women with a history of cholestatic jaundice during pregnancy. Liver biopsies taken from such women show bile thrombi in the canaliculi and occasional focal necrosis. Serum alkaline phosphatase and SGPT are increased. The BSP retention and serum enzyme changes observed in some patients may indicate liver damage.

Jaundice and pruritus disappear 1–8 weeks after the drug is discontinued.

These agents have also been found to increase the incidence of symptomatic gallbladder disease, including cholecystitis and cholangitis. This is probably the result of the alterations in bile described above.

It also appears that the incidence of hepatic adenomas is increased in women taking oral contraceptives. Ischemic bowel disease secondary to thrombosis

of the celiac and superior and inferior mesenteric arteries and veins has also been reported in women using these drugs.

3. Depression–Depression of sufficient degree to require cessation of therapy occurs in about 6% of patients treated with some preparations.

In addition to the above effects, a number of other adverse reactions have been reported for which a causal relationship has not been established. These include alopecia, erythema multiforme, erythema nodosum, and other skin disorders.

Contraindications & Cautions

These drugs are contraindicated in patients with thrombophlebitis, thromboembolic phenomena, and cerebrovascular disorders or a past history of these conditions. They should not be used to treat vaginal bleeding when the cause is unknown. They should be avoided in patients known or suspected to have a tumor of the breast or other estrogen-dependent neoplasm.

Since these preparations have caused aggravation of preexisting disorders, they should be avoided or used with caution in patients with liver disease, asthma, eczema, migraine, diabetes, hypertension, optic neuritis, retrobulbar neuritis, or convulsive disorders.

Since these compounds may produce edema, they should be used with great caution in patients in congestive failure or in whom edema is otherwise undesirable or dangerous.

Estrogens may increase the rate of growth of fibroids. Therefore, for women with these tumors, agents with the smallest amounts of estrogen and the most androgenic progestins should be selected. The use of progestational agents alone for contraception might be especially useful in such patients (see below).

At present these agents are contraindicated in adolescents in whom epiphyseal closure has not yet been completed.

Since the long-term consequences of the changes in lipid and carbohydrate metabolism are unknown, and since estrogens are such potent carcinogens in some mammals, the precise risks involved in the prolonged use of these doses of estrogenic and progestational agents cannot be accurately assessed. This fact (and the known risks) should be explained to all patients for whom these drugs are prescribed.

Contraception with progestins or estrogens alone. Small doses of progestins administered orally can be used for contraception. They are particularly suited for use in patients for whom estrogen administration is undesirable. They are about as effective as intrauterine devices or combination pills containing 20–30 μg of ethinyl estradiol. There is a high incidence of abnormal bleeding. The use of infrequent injections of long-acting progestins (see above) such as medroxyprogesterone acetate has also found limited usefulness. The use of large doses of oral progestins at the time of intercourse is under study.

Diethylstilbestrol in doses of 25 mg twice a day

for 5 days, beginning preferably within 24 hours and not later than 72 hours after exposure, is effective in preventing pregnancy. However, this form of contraception should not be used routinely or frequently, since serious questions about the teratogenic potency of this compound have been raised. Because of the possibility that diethylstilbestrol may cause vaginal cancer in the offspring of mothers treated later in pregnancy, the voluntary termination of pregnancy should be considered when conception occurs in these patients. Side-effects include nausea, vomiting, headache, dizziness, breast tenderness, and abdominal and leg cramps.

ANTIESTROGENS

Tamoxifen

Tamoxifen is a competitive inhibitor of estradiol at the receptor and is being used in the palliative treatment of advanced breast cancer in post-menopausal women. It is a nonsteroidal agent which is given orally. Peak plasma levels are reached in a few hours. It has an initial half-life of 7–14 hours in the circulation and is predominantly excreted by the liver. It is dispensed as the citrate in the form of tablets containing the equivalent of 10 mg tamoxifen. It is used in doses of 10–20 mg twice daily. Hot flashes and nausea and vomiting occur in 25% of patients, and many other adverse effects are observed.

Clomiphene

Clomiphene citrate is a weak estrogen that also acts as a competitive inhibitor of endogenous estrogens. It has found use as an ovulation-inducing agent (see below).

OVULATION–INDUCING AGENTS

1. CLOMIPHENE CITRATE
(Clomid)

Interest in the discovery of antiestrogenic compounds has been stimulated by the increasing need for antifertility compounds. Several of the synthetic estrogens have been shown to have significant antiestrogen properties. They are able to successfully compete for binding sites, yet have weaker hormonal properties. Clomiphene citrate is one such compound. It is closely related to other pharmacologically active compounds such as the estrogen chlorotrianisene (Fig 38–5) and the cholesterol inhibitor triparanol.

This compound is active when taken orally, since it is readily absorbed. Very little is known about its metabolism, but available studies indicate that about half of the compound is excreted into the stools within 5 days after administration. Studies of the metabolism of clomiphene have been more extensive in animals. In monkeys the half-life of clomiphene citrate, when given intravenously, is approximately 48 hours. When 90% of the dose has been eliminated from the body, the liver, gallbladder, and bile have the highest concentrations of the remaining compound. It has been suggested that clomiphene is slowly excreted from an enterohepatic pool.

Pharmacologic Effects
A. Mechanisms of Action: Clomiphene citrate is a weak estrogen. The estrogenic effects are best demonstrated in animals with marked gonadal deficiency. Clomiphene has also been shown to effectively inhibit the action of stronger estrogens. In humans it leads to an increase in the secretion of gonadotropins and estrogens.

B. Effects: The pharmacologic importance of this compound rests on its ability to stimulate ovulation in women with amenorrhea and other ovulatory disorders. The mechanism by which ovulation is produced is not known. It has been suggested that it blocks an inhibitory influence of estrogens on the hypothalamus and increases the production of gonadotropins. Clomiphene will not work in the absence of a pituitary gland capable of producing gonadotropins. It has been shown in the rat that crystals of this compound implanted in the pituitary have no effect, whereas those implanted in parts of the median eminence are able to induce ovulation. The observation that this compound can induce ovulation in patients with very low estrogen levels does not support the hypothesis that it works by breaking a feedback inhibition. However, it does stimulate gonadotropin production by the pituitary by an action on the hypothalamus.

Clinical Uses
Clomiphene citrate is used for the treatment of disorders of ovulation in patients wishing to become

$(C_2H_5)_2 NCH_2 CH_2 O$ —⟨ ⟩— $C = C$ —⟨ ⟩— $\cdot\ C_6H_8O_7$

Clomiphene citrate

pregnant. In general, a single ovulation is induced by a single course of therapy, and the patient must be treated repeatedly until pregnancy is achieved, since normal ovulatory function does not usually resume. The compound is of no use in patients with ovarian or pituitary failure.

Standardized procedures for the use of clomiphene as a testing substance have not been established. This substance can serve as a useful test of the ability of the pituitary gland to secrete gonadotropins.

When clomiphene is administered in doses of 100 mg daily for 5 days, a rise in plasma LH and FSH is observed several days after starting. In patients who ovulate, the initial rise is followed by a second rise of gonadotropin levels just prior to ovulation.

Adverse Reactions

The most common side-effects in patients treated with this drug are hot flushes, which resemble those experienced by menopausal patients. They tend to be mild and disappear when the drug is discontinued. There have been occasional reports of eye symptoms due to intensification and prolongation of afterimages. These are generally of short duration. Headache, constipation, allergic skin reactions, and reversible hair loss have been reported occasionally.

The effective use of clomiphene is associated with some stimulation of the ovaries and usually with ovarian enlargement. The degree of enlargement tends to be greater and its incidence higher in patients who have enlarged ovaries at the beginning of therapy.

A variety of other symptoms such as nausea and vomiting, increased nervous tension, depression, fatigue, breast soreness, weight gain, urinary frequency, and heavy menses have also been reported. However, these appear to be due to the hormonal changes associated with an ovulatory menstrual cycle rather than a result of the medication. The incidence of multiple pregnancy is approximately 10%.

Clomiphene has not been shown to have an adverse effect in human pregnancy. However, since the only current indication for clomiphene therapy is to achieve pregnancy, existing pregnancy is a contraindication to its use.

Contraindications & Cautions

Special precautions should be observed in patients with enlarged ovaries. These women are thought to be more sensitive to this drug and should receive small doses. Any patient who complains of abdominal symptoms should be carefully examined. The maximum ovarian enlargement occurs after the 5-day course has been completed, and many patients can be shown to have a palpable increase in ovarian size by the seventh to tenth days.

Special precautions must also be taken in patients who have visual symptoms associated with clomiphene therapy, since these symptoms may make activities such as driving more hazardous.

Dosages

The recommended dose of clomiphene citrate (Clomid) at the beginning of therapy is 50 mg/d for 5 days. If ovulation occurs, this same course may be repeated until pregnancy is achieved. If ovulation does not occur, the dose is doubled to 100 mg/d for 5 days. If ovulation and menses occur, the next course can be started on the fifth day of the cycle. Experience to date suggests that patients who do not ovulate after 3 courses of 100 mg/d of clomiphene are not likely to respond to continued therapy. However, such patients occasionally respond to slightly larger doses or more prolonged treatment schedules.

About 80% of patients with anovulatory disorders or amenorrhea can be expected to respond by having ovulatory cycles. Approximately half of these patients will become pregnant. In the patients in whom pregnancy is achieved, the incidence of early abortion seems to be slightly increased. Although a variety of congenital defects have been described in the children resulting from these pregnancies, the incidence does not appear to be greater than occurs spontaneously. Clomiphene has also been used in combination with menotropins to reduce the amount of the latter required to induce ovulation.

2. HUMAN MENOPAUSAL GONADOTROPIN (HMG, Menotropins)

Because of antibody formation and species differences in response, animal preparations of FSH have not been very useful in humans. Studies are currently in progress utilizing partially purified extracts of human pituitary glands or pooled urine obtained from postmenopausal women that contains both FSH and LH activity. The LH content is estimated by observing changes in the weight of the ventral prostate in hypophysectomized immature rats or depletion of ascorbic acid from the ovaries of immature rats. An ovarian augmentation assay is available for measuring FSH content. The pituitary extracts are available in only a few laboratories, but HMG is now more widely available.

Clinical Uses

HMG—in conjunction with human chorionic gonadotropin (HCG); see p 427—is used to stimulate ovulation in patients who do not ovulate but have potentially functional ovarian tissue. It has been successful in the induction of ovulation in patients with hypopituitarism and other defects in gonadotropin secretion. It has also been used in patients with amenorrhea or anovulatory cycles and in patients in whom ovulatory disturbances are associated with galactorrhea or hirsutism. Ovarian failure should be excluded in patients considered for therapy. Since therapy is difficult and expensive, it is useful to look for the existence of other factors such as obstruction of the uterine tubes or abnormalities in sperm production by the husband. The acceptability of multiple birth by the patient must be considered.

Preparations of human menopausal gonadotropin can stimulate spermatogenesis in males with isolated gonadotropin deficiency. Using HMG in conjunction with HCG (see Chapter 39), endocrine and gametogenic function has been restored in a few of these patients.

Contraindications & Cautions

HMG is a potentially dangerous agent and should be administered only after thorough acquaintance with its use and by physicians experienced in dealing with endocrine disturbances and problems of reproductive function. Careful selection of patients is required.

This preparation should not be used in early pregnancy (which may be difficult to diagnose in patients with irregular cycles), or in patients with ovarian failure except as a diagnostic procedure. In patients with pituitary and other intracranial tumors, the primary disease process should be treated before undertaking therapy with HMG. HMG should not be used in patients with other causes of infertility than lack of ovulation.

Adverse Reactions

The most common problem encountered is excessive ovarian stimulation. Ovarian enlargement is common. When marked (hyperstimulation syndrome), it may be accompanied by pain, ascites, and pleural effusion. Arterial thromboembolism has been reported in 2 patients. Occasional patients experience swelling and fever along with discomfort at the injection site. Undesirable results of therapy include the high incidence of multiple pregnancy and abortion (Table 38–6). The frequency of birth defects has not been elevated in the offspring of patients who have succeeded in carrying their pregnancies to term.

The typical outcome of therapy in suitably selected patients treated by experienced physicians is shown in Table 38–6.

It is clear that this mode of therapy is complicated, time-consuming, and expensive. It should not be undertaken lightly but can be very helpful to the proper patient after simpler therapeutic methods have failed.

Dosages

Human menopausal gonadotropins (menotropins, Pergonal) are supplied in lyophilized form in ampules containing 75 IU each of FSH and LH and 10

Table 38–6. Results of treatment with HMG.

Pregnancy Achieved	Multiple Pregnancy		Aborting	Hyper-stimulation Syndrome
	Twins	Triplets, Etc		
25–40%	10–20%	5–10%	20–30%	0.5–1.5%

mg of lactose. The usual dosage is 1 or more ampules intramuscularly daily until estrogen production is optimal (plasma levels of 600–1000 pg/mL). HCG (see Chapter 39) in doses of 5000–10,000 IU intramuscularly is then administered on one or more occasions; if estrogen production becomes excessive, HCG should be withheld. Patients must be examined frequently for 2 weeks following the last injection (daily or on alternate days) to detect signs of overstimulation. Frequent intercourse near the time of expected ovulation is advisable.

THE TESTIS
(Androgens & Anabolic Steroids)

The testis, like the ovary, has both gametogenic and endocrine functions. The gametogenic function of the testes is controlled largely by the secretion of FSH by the pituitary. High concentrations of androgens locally are also required for sperm production in the seminiferous tubules. The Sertoli cells in the seminiferous tubules may be the source of the estrogens produced in the testes. The androgens are produced in the interstitial or Leydig cells found in the spaces between the seminiferous tubules.

In humans the most important androgen secreted by the testis is testosterone. The pathways of synthesis of testosterone in the testes are similar to those previously described in the ovary and the adrenal except that the hormone and its precursors are the primary secretory products of the gland (Fig 38–7).

In the male, about 8 mg of testosterone, almost all of which is derived from the testes, are secreted daily. Plasma levels of testosterone in males are about 0.6 μg/dL after puberty and do not appear to vary significantly with age. Testosterone is also present in the plasma of women in concentrations of approximately 0.03 μg/dL and is derived in approximately equal parts from the ovaries, the adrenals, and by the peripheral conversion of other hormones.

About 65% of circulating testosterone is bound to a plasma protein. This protein has been shown to be specific, and, as is the case with many other hormone-binding proteins, its concentration is increased by estrogens and is elevated during pregnancy.

Metabolism

In many target tissues, testosterone is converted to dihydrotestosterone by the enzyme 5α-reductase. In these tissues, dihydrotestosterone is the major androgen. The conversion of testosterone to estradiol also occurs in some tissues, including the hypothalamus, and may be of importance in regulating gonadal function.

The major pathway for the degradation of testosterone in humans is illustrated in Fig 38–8. In the liver,

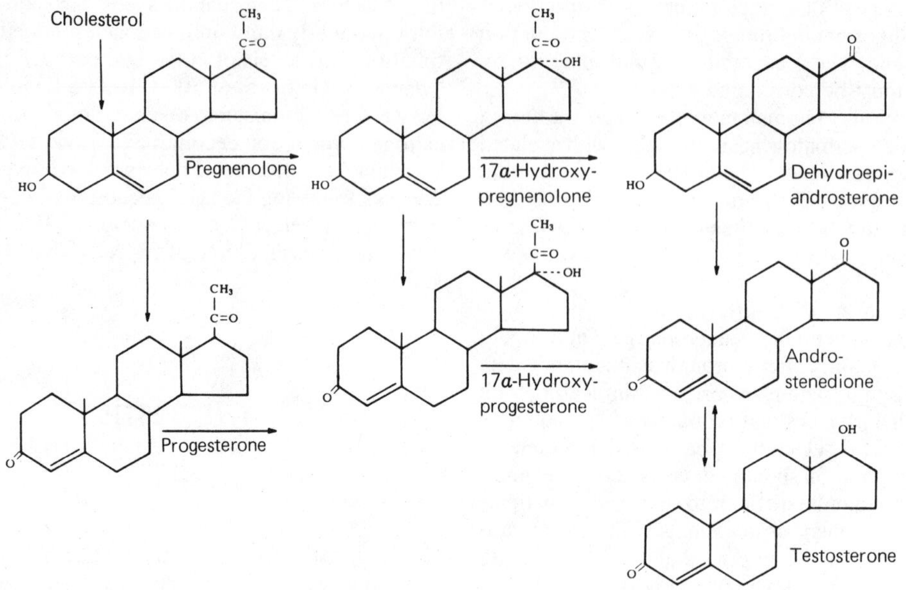

Figure 38 –7. Biosynthesis of testosterone. (Reproduced, with permission, from Ganong WF: *Review of Medical Physiology,* 8th ed. Lange, 1977.)

the reduction of the double bond and ketone in the A ring, as is seen in other steroids with a Δ^4-ketone configuration in the A ring, leads to the production of inactive substances such as androsterone and etiocholanolone that are then conjugated and excreted into the urine.

Androstenedione and dehydroepiandrosterone (Fig 38–7) are also produced in significant amounts in humans, although largely in the adrenal rather than in the testes. These compounds do not have significant androgenic activity, but they are to a large extent metabolized in the same fashion as testosterone. Both compounds—but particularly androstenedione—can be converted by peripheral tissues to estrone in very small amounts (1–5%).

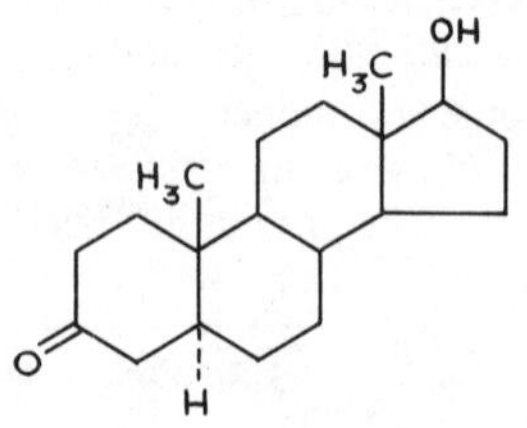

5α-Dihydrotestosterone
(androstanolone, stanolone, DHT)

Control of Secretion

The production of testosterone by the testes is controlled by the pituitary release of LH, which in turn is controlled by luteinizing hormone–releasing factor (LHRF), produced in the median eminence of the hypothalamus. The administration of testosterone not only suppresses LH but in large doses can reduce the secretion of FSH by the pituitary. It is thought that the physiologic control of FSH secretion is influenced by estrogens or other substances produced in the testes rather than being entirely the result of a negative feedback effect of testosterone.

Physiologic Effects

In the normal male, testosterone is responsible for the many changes that occur in puberty. In addition to the general growth-promoting properties of androgens on the body tissues, these hormones are responsible for penile and scrotal growth. Changes in the skin include the appearance of pubic hair, axillary hair, and beard hair. The sebaceous glands become more active, and the skin tends to become thicker and oilier. The larynx grows and the vocal cords become thicker, leading to a lower pitched voice. Skeletal growth is stimulated and epiphyseal closure accelerated. Other effects include growth of the prostate and seminal vesicles, darkening of the skin, and increased skin circulation. Psychologic and behavioral changes also occur.

Synthetic Steroids With Androgenic & Anabolic Action

Testosterone, when administered by mouth, is rapidly absorbed. However, it is largely converted to inactive metabolites, and only about one-sixth of the hormone is available in active form. Testosterone can be administered parenterally, but it has a more prolonged absorption time and greater activity when esterified. Methyltestosterone and fluoxymesterone are active when given by mouth.

Testosterone and its derivatives have been used for their anabolic effects as well as for the replacement of testosterone deficiency. Although testosterone and

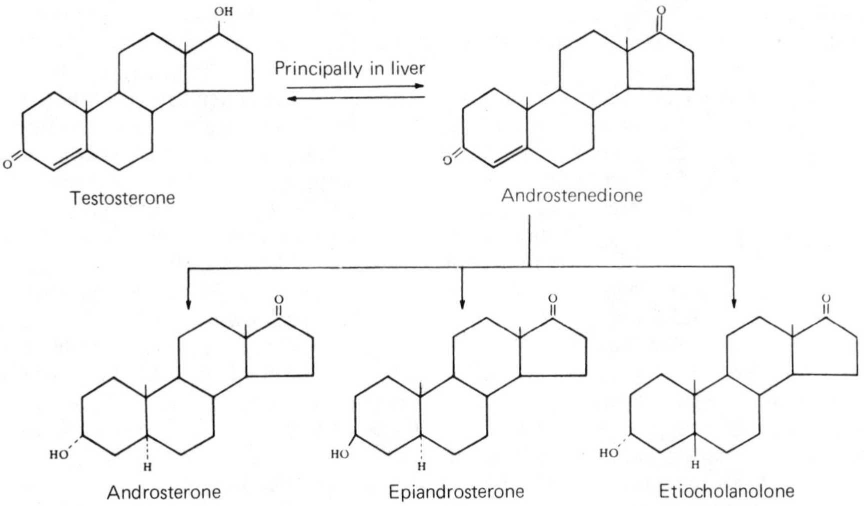

Figure 38–8. Metabolism of testosterone. (Reproduced, with permission, from Ganong WF: *Review of Medical Physiology,* 8th ed. Lange, 1977.)

other known active steroids can be isolated in pure form and measured by weight, biologic assays are still used in the investigation of new compounds. In some of these studies in animals, the anabolic effects of the compound—as measured by trophic effects on muscles or the reduction of nitrogen excretion—may be dissociated from the other androgenic effects. This has led to the marketing of a substantial group of compounds that are supposed to have marked anabolic activity associated with only weak androgenic effects. This dissociation does not appear to be complete, and in humans it is less marked than in the animals used for testing. Though they may be less virilizing than equivalent doses of testosterone, doses of these drugs large enough to promote nitrogen retention can also produce unwanted androgenic effects.

Pharmacologic Effects

A. Mechanisms of Action: In target cells, testosterone appears to bind to a specific cytosol receptor or in some tissues to be converted to 5α-dihydrotestosterone that binds to the cytosol receptor. As is the case with other steroid hormones (see Chapter 33), it is transported to the nucleus and interacts with chromatin to stimulate the production of RNA and protein. A variety of enzymes, particularly in the liver, are known to be influenced by androgens. In the rat, testosterone is converted to dihydrotestosterone in the nucleus; the latter compound appears to be more firmly bound to the receptor protein than testosterone itself and is probably the most active form of the hormone.

B. Effects: In the male at puberty, androgens cause development of the secondary sex characteristics (see above). In the adult male, large doses of testosterone or its derivatives suppress the secretion of gonadotropins and result in some atrophy of the interstitial tissue and the tubules of the testes. Since fairly large doses of androgens are required to suppress

gonadotropic secretion, it has been postulated that estrogens produced in the testis (either in combination with androgens or instead of androgens) are responsible for the feedback control of secretion. In women, androgens are capable of producing changes similar to those observed in the prepubertal male. These include growth of facial hair and body hair, deepening of the voice, enlargement of the clitoris, frontal baldness, and prominent musculature. The natural androgens stimulate red cell production.

The administration of androgens reduces the excretion of nitrogen into the urine, indicating an increase in protein synthesis or decrease in protein breakdown within the body. This effect is much more pronounced in women and children than in normal men.

Clinical Uses

A. Androgen Replacement Therapy in Men: The most important indication for androgen therapy is for replacement of androgen deficiency in men with hypogonadism or hypopituitarism. When therapy is begun in patients with hypogonadism that occurs after maturation, 1–2 injections of 50 mg of testosterone propionate weekly are usually sufficient. It is often more convenient to use a long-acting preparation in doses of 200–300 mg/month. Oral preparations, eg, methyltestosterone or fluoxymesterone, may also be used. When treating patients in whom deficiency occurred before maturation, larger doses of testosterone must be used, and even then full masculinization may not be achieved. In younger people, one can start with smaller doses to allow the gradual development of the changes as they naturally occur in puberty. However, for a period of 2–3 years, therapy must be pursued with relatively large doses of androgen. In patients with hypopituitarism, androgens are not added to the treatment regimen until puberty, at which time they are instituted in gradually increasing doses to achieve the growth spurt and the development of secondary sex characteristics.

B. Gynecologic Disorders: Androgens are used occasionally in the treatment of certain gynecologic disorders, but the undesirable effects in women are such that they must be used with great caution. Androgens have been used to reduce breast engorgement during the postpartum period, usually in conjunction with estrogens. For example, 4 mL of a preparation containing 90 mg/mL of testosterone enanthate and 4 mg/mL of estradiol are useful for this purpose when given at the onset of the second stage of labor.

Androgens are sometimes given in combination with estrogens for replacement therapy in the postmenopausal period in an attempt to eliminate the endometrial bleeding that may occur when only estrogens are used. They are also used for the chemotherapy of breast tumors in premenopausal women.

C. Use as Protein Anabolic Agents: Androgens and anabolic steroids have been used in conjunction with dietary measures and exercises in an attempt to reverse protein loss after trauma, surgery, or prolonged immobilization and in patients with debilitating diseases.

D. Anemia: Large doses of androgens have been employed in the treatment of refractory anemias and have resulted in some increase in reticulocytosis and hemoglobin levels. The large amounts required prevent this from being a useful method of therapy in women.

E. Osteoporosis: Androgens and anabolic agents have been used in the treatment of osteoporosis, either alone or in conjunction with estrogens. The benefits of androgens in these patients have not been substantiated by careful studies.

F. Use as Metabolic Stimulators: These agents have been used to stimulate growth in prepubertal boys. If the drugs are used carefully, these children will probably achieve their expected adult height (and sooner than normal). If treatment is too vigorous, the patient may grow rapidly at first but will not achieve full stature because of the accelerated epiphyseal closure that occurs. It is difficult to control this type of therapy adequately even with frequent x-ray examination of the epiphyses, since the action of the hormones on epiphyseal centers may continue for many months after therapy is discontinued.

G. Contraceptive in Males: Danazol in combination with testosterone is an effective suppressant of spermatogenesis in the male. Its use as a reversible male contraceptive is under study.

Danazol is a very weak androgen that effectively inhibits gonadotropin release by the anterior pituitary. It is neither estrogenic nor progestational. It therefore has antigonadal effects in men and women. As noted above, it has been studied in men for use as a contraceptive agent. However, it causes loss of libido and must be given in combination with testosterone. In women it may produce flushing, sweating, and vaginal dryness by suppressing estrogen production, as well as

a reduction in breast size, acne, mild hirsutism, and, rarely, other signs of androgen excess.

This agent is indicated for the treatment of endometriosis in patients requiring hormonal therapy but in whom other agents are ineffective or contraindicated. It is dispensed in capsules containing 200 mg. The recommended dose is 400 mg twice daily.

The amenorrhea that is produced is usually followed by a return of menses in 60–90 days following cessation of therapy. Fluid retention has been reported, and the drug should be used cautiously in conditions that might be adversely affected. Central nervous system effects may occur, ie, headaches, loss of libido, dizziness, tremor, paresthesias, sleep disorders, and appetite changes. Nausea and vomiting, cramps, hair loss, and rashes have also been reported.

Adverse Reactions

The adverse effects of these compounds are due largely to their masculinizing actions and are most noticeable in women and prepubertal children. In women, the administration of more than 200–300 mg of testosterone per month is usually associated with hirsutism, acne, depression of menses, clitoral enlargement, and deepening of the voice. These effects may occur on even smaller doses in some women. Some of the androgenic steroids exert progestational activity leading to endometrial bleeding. These hormones also alter serum lipids and could conceivably increase susceptibility to atherosclerotic disease of the vessels in women. Except under the most unusual circumstances, androgens should not be used in infants. Recent studies in animals suggest that administration of androgens in early life may have profound effects on maturation of central nervous system centers governing sexual development, particularly in the female. Administration of these drugs to pregnant females may lead to masculinization of the external genitalia in the infant. Although the above-mentioned effects may be less marked with the anabolic agents, they do occur.

Sodium retention and edema are not common but must be carefully watched for in patients with heart and kidney disease.

Most of the synthetic androgens and anabolic agents are 17-alkyl–substituted steroids. Administration of drugs with this structure is associated with increase in BSP retention and SGOT levels. Alkaline phosphatase values are also elevated. These changes usually occur early in the course of treatment, and the degree is proportionate to the dose. Bilirubin levels occasionally increase until clinical jaundice is apparent. The cholestatic jaundice is reversible upon cessation of therapy, and permanent changes do not occur.

Contraindications & Cautions

The use of androgenic steroids is contraindicated in pregnant women or women who may become pregnant during the course of therapy.

Androgens should not be administered to male patients with carcinoma of the prostate or breast.

Table 38—7. Androgens: Preparations available and relative androgen/anabolic activity.

	Androgenic/Anabolic Activity
Testosterone	1:1
Testosterone cypionate	1:1
Testosterone enanthate	1:1
Testosterone propionate	1:1
Methyltestosterone	1:1
Methandriol	1:2
Methandriol dipropionate	1:2
Fluoxymesterone	1:2
Methandrostenolone (metandienone)	1:3
Oxymetholone	1:3
Ethylestrenol	1:4—1:8
Oxandrolone	1:3—1:13
Nandrolone phenpropionate	1:3—1:6
Nandrolone decanoate	1:2.5—1:4
Stanozolol	1:3—1:6
Dromostanolone propionate	1:3—1:4

Until more is known about the effects of these hormones on the central nervous system in developing children, they should be avoided in infants and young children.

Special caution is required in giving these drugs to children to produce a growth spurt.

Care should be exercised in the administration of these drugs to patients with renal or cardiac disease predisposed to edema. If sodium and water retention occurs, it will respond to diuretic therapy.

Methyltestosterone therapy is associated with creatinuria, but the significance of this finding is not known.

Caution: Several cases of hepatocellular carcinoma have been reported in patients with aplastic anemia treated with androgen anabolic therapy.

ANTIANDROGENS

The potential usefulness of antiandrogens for the treatment of patients producing excessive amounts of testosterone has led to the search for effective drugs that can be used for this purpose. Two approaches to the problem have met with limited success experimentally.

Several compounds have been developed that inhibit the 17-hydroxylation of progesterone or pregnenolone, thereby preventing the action of the side chain–splitting enzyme and the further transformation of these steroid precursors to active androgens. A few of these compounds have been tested clinically but have been too toxic for prolonged use.

Another approach has been the development of steroids that are chemically similar and act as competitive inhibitors. A few of these have been tried in patients on a limited basis.

Cyproterone and cyproterone acetate are effective antiandrogens that inhibit the action of the androgens at the target organ. The acetate form has a marked progestational effect that suppresses the feedback enhancement of LH and FSH, leading to a more effective antiandrogen effect. These compounds have been used to decrease excessive sexual drive and are being studied in other conditions in which the reduction of androgenic effects would be useful.

•   •   •

References

Androgens II and antiandrogens. Vol 35, part 2, in: *Handbook of Experimental Pharmacology*. (New series.) Springer, 1974.

Antunes CMF & others: Endometrial cancer and estrogen use. N Engl J Med 300:9, 1979.

Beck P: Contraceptive steroids: Modifications of carbohydrate and lipid metabolism. Metabolism 22:841, 1973.

Bibbo M & others: Follow-up study of male and female offspring of DES-exposed mothers. Obstet Gynecol 49:1, 1977.

Bingel AS, Benoit PS: Oral contraceptives: Therapeutics versus adverse reactions, with an outlook for the future. (2 parts.) J Pharm Sci 62:179, 349, 1973.

Bradley BD & others: Serum high-density-lipoprotein cholesterol in women using oral contraceptives, estrogen and progestins. N Engl J Med 299:17, 1978.

Carter DE & others: Effect of oral contraceptives on drug metabolism. Clin Pharmacol Ther 15:22, 1974.

Cohen H: Relaxin: Studies dealing with the isolation, purification, and characterization. Trans NY Acad Sci 25:313, 1963.

Collaborative Group for the Study of Stroke in Young Women: Oral contraception and increased risk of cerebral ischemia or thrombosis. N Engl J Med 288:871, 1973.

Dmowski WP: Endocrine properties and clinical application of danazol. Fertil Steril 31:237, 1979.

Franchimont P & others: Effects of oral testosterone undecanoate in hypogonadal male patients. Clin Endocrinol 9:313, 1978.

Garattini S, Berendes HW: *Pharmacology of Steroid Contraceptive Drugs*. Raven Press, 1977.

Goldzieher JW, Dozier TS, de la Pena A: Plasma levels and pharmacokinetics of ethynyl estrogens in various populations. 1. Ethynylestradiol. Contraception 21:1, 1980.

Griffin JE, Wilson JD: The syndromes of androgen resistance. N Engl J Med 302:198, 1980.

Gusberg SB: Current concepts in cancer: The changing nature of endometrial cancer. N Engl J Med 302:729, 1980.

Hahn HB Jr, Hayles AB, Albert A: Medroxyprogesterone [Provera] and constitutional precocious puberty. Mayo Clin Proc 39:182, 1964.

Haller J: *Hormonal Contraception*. Geron-X, 1972. [Translated by H Gottfried.]

Hertz R: Physiologic effects of androgens and estrogens in man. Am J Med 21:671, 1956.

Howard RP & others: Testicular deficiency: A clinical and pathologic study. J Clin Endocrinol Metab 10:121, 1950.

Huggins GR, Guintoli RL: Oral contraceptives and neoplasia. Fertil Steril 32:1, 1979.

Jeppsson S, Johansson EDB: Medroxyprogesterone acetate, estradiol, FSH and LH in peripheral blood after intramuscular administration of Depo-Provera to women. Contraception 14:461, 1976.

Jick H, Dinan B, Rothman KJ: Non-contraceptive estrogens and non-fatal myocardial infarction. JAMA 239:1406, 1978.

Jick H, Dinan B, Rothman KJ: Oral contraceptives and non-fatal myocardial infarction. JAMA 239:1403, 1978.

Jick H & others: Myocardial infarction and other vascular diseases in young women: Role of estrogens and other factors. JAMA 240:2548, 1978.

Jick H & others: Replacement estrogens and endometrial cancer. N Engl J Med 300:218, 1979.

Johnson FL & others: Association of androgenic-anabolic steroid therapy with development of hepatocellular carcinoma. Lancet 2:1273, 1972.

Mann JI, Inman WHW: Oral contraceptives and death from myocardial infarction. Br Med J 2:245, 1975.

Mann JI & others: Myocardial infarction in young women with special reference to oral contraceptive practice. Br Med J 2:241, 1975.

Nachtigall LE & others: Estrogen replacement therapy. 1. A ten year prospective study in the relationship to osteoporosis. Obstet Gynecol 53:277, 1979.

Neumann F: Pharmacology and potential use of cyproterone acetate. Horm Metabol Res 9:1, 1977.

Nora JJ & others: Exogenous progestogein and estrogen implicated in birth defects. JAMA 240:837, 1978.

Progesterone, progestational drugs and antifertility agents. Section 48 in: *International Encyclopedia of Pharmacology and Therapeutics*. Tausk M (editor). Permagon Press, vol 1, 1971; vol 2, 1972.

Rigberg SV, Brodsky I: Potential roles of androgens and the anabolic steroids in the treatment of cancer: A review. J Med 6:271, 1975.

Robboy SJ, Bradley R: Changing trends and prognostic features in endometrial cancer associated with exogenous estrogen therapy. Obstet Gynecol 54:269, 1979.

Rosemberg E (editor): *Gonadotropin Therapy in Female Infertility*. International Congress Series No. 266. Excerpta Medica, 1973.

Royal College of General Practitioners: *Oral Contraceptives and Health*. Pitman, 1974.

Salhanick HA, Kipnis DM, Vande Wiele RL (editors): *Metabolic Effects of Gonadal Hormones and Contraceptive Steroids*. Plenum Press, 1969.

Schwartz NB, Channing CP: Evidence for ovarian "inhibin": Suppression of the secondary rise in serum follicle stimulating hormone levels in proestrus rats by injection of porcine follicular fluid. Proc Natl Acad Sci USA 74:5721, 1977.

Shapiro AG, Thomas T, Epstein M: Management of hyperstimulation syndrome. Fertil Steril 28:237, 1977.

Shapiro S & others: Oral-contraceptive use in relation to myocardial infarction. Lancet 1:743, 1979.

Smith DC & others: Association of exogenous estrogen and endometrial carcinoma. N Engl J Med 293:1164, 1975.

Spellacy WN, Buhi WC, Birk SA: Effect of estrogen treatment for one year on carbohydrate and lipid metabolism in women with normal and abnormal glucose tolerance test results. Am J Obstet Gynecol 131:87, 1978.

Van Keep PA, Lauritzen C (editors): *Ageing and Estrogens*. Frontiers of Hormone Research, vol 2. Karger, 1973.

Weiss G & others: Distribution of relaxin in women during pregnancy. Obstet Gynecol 52:569, 1978.

Weiss NS, Sayvetz TA: Incidence of endometrial cancer in relation to the use of oral contraceptives. N Engl J Med 302:551, 1980.

Wise AJ, Gross MA, Schalch DS: Quantitative relationships of the pituitary-gonadal axis in postmenopausal women. J Lab Clin Med 81:28, 1973.

Wolstenholme GEW, O'Connor M (editors): Endocrinology of the testis. Ciba Found Colloq Endocrinol 16:1, 1967.

Ziel HK, Finkle WD: Increased risk of endometrial carcinoma among users of conjugated estrogens. N Engl J Med 293:1167, 1975.

Hypothalamic & Pituitary Hormones | 39

The pituitary gland is a remarkable structure consisting of an anterior lobe (adenohypophysis), intermediate lobe, and posterior lobe (neurohypophysis). This organ is known to produce or release 10 hormones and may produce others (Table 39–1). Since the secretion of these hormones is regulated by chemical mediators or hormones released by the hypothalamus, the 2 organs are considered together.

THE ANTERIOR PITUITARY & ITS HORMONES

The anterior lobe of the pituitary gland constitutes two-thirds of the organ and is derived from the ventral portion of Rathke's pouch (an outpocketing of oral ectoderm). It is made up of several types of cells that have been classified in several ways on the basis of morphologic and staining characteristics. In humans, about half of the cells appear agranular and are called chromophobes. It is thought that these cells differentiate into cells with granules that readily accept acidic or basic dyes. Approximately two-thirds of the chromophilic cells are acidophils and the rest basophils. The cellular origin of some of the pituitary hormones in humans is shown in Table 39–1.

The secretion of the known hormones of the anterior lobe is regulated by chemical mediators formed in the median eminence of the hypothalamus (Fig 39–1) and carried to the adenohypophysis by a portal system of blood vessels that traverse the pituitary stalk and form sinusoids in the anterior pituitary.

In contrast to the complex nature of the proteins and glycoproteins produced by the adenohypophysis, the hypothalamic hormones that have been identified chemically are smaller molecules. They can be synthesized economically, and analogs can be produced that might act as inhibitors or otherwise differ from the native hormone. It can be anticipated that the therapeutic and diagnostic use of these compounds will increase more rapidly than the use of the hormones they stimulate or inhibit. It appears that the secretion of the hypothalamic hormones is regulated in part by neurons releasing dopamine, norepinephrine, or serotonin.

Table 39–1. Pituitary hormones.*

Name and Source	Principal Actions
Anterior lobe	
Thyroid-stimulating hormone (TSH, thyrotropin)	Stimulates thyroid secretion and growth
Adrenocorticotropic hormone (ACTH, corticotropin)	Stimulates adrenocortical secretion and growth
Growth hormone (GH, somatotropin, STH)	Accelerates body growth
Follicle-stimulating hormone (FSH)	Stimulates ovarian follicle growth in female and spermatogenesis in male
Luteinizing hormone (LH, interstitial cell stimulating hormone, ICSH)	Stimulates ovulation and luteinization of ovarian follicles in female and testosterone secretion in male
Prolactin (luteotropic hormone, LTH, luteotropin, lactogenic hormone, mammotropin)	Stimulates secretion of milk and maternal behavior; maintains corpus luteum in female rodents but apparently not in other species
β-lipotropin (β-LPH)	?
Intermediate lobe	
a- and β-Melanocyte-stimulating hormones (a- and β-MSH; referred to collectively as melanotropin or intermedin)	Expand melanophores
Posterior lobe	
Vasopressin (antidiuretic hormone, ADH)	Promotes water retention
Oxytocin	Causes milk ejection

*Reproduced, with permission, from Ganong WF: *Review of Medical Physiology,* 9th ed. Lange, 1979.

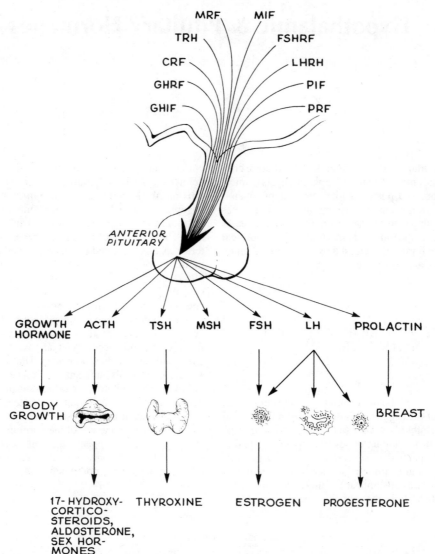

Figure 39–1. Hypothalamic releasing factors and actions of anterior pituitary hormones. GHRF, growth hormone–releasing factor; GHIF (somatostatin); CRF, corticotropin-releasing factor; TRH, thyrotropin-releasing factor; MRF, melanocyte-releasing factor; MIF, melanocyte-inhibiting factor; FSHRF, follicle-stimulating hormone–releasing factor; LHRH, luteinizing hormone–releasing factor; PIF, prolactin-inhibiting factor; and PRF, prolactin-releasing factor.

GROWTH HORMONE
(GH, Somatotropin, STH)

Growth hormone is synthesized in the anterior pituitary gland. It has been prepared in highly purified form from a variety of animal sources including humans and monkeys. The structure varies considerably from one species to another. Human growth hormone (Fig 39–2) contains 190 amino acids in a chain and has 2 disulfide bridges. The molecular weight is 21,500. Growth hormone prepared from the rhesus monkey has a molecular weight of 25,400 and 4 disulfide bridges. In contrast to this, the cattle hormone contains about 400 amino acids, has a molecular weight of 46,000, and has a branched Y type structure. The relationships between structure and activity have not been clearly established. Preliminary studies indicate that the entire molecule is not required for activity. The smallest active fragment of human growth hormone has not been identified, but preparations smaller than the natural hormone have been found to be active.

The marked structural variation may account for the fact that growth hormone from one species may not be active in another (Table 39–2). This phenomenon, called species specificity, was first well characterized in the study of this substance.

This hormone comprises about 10% of the weight

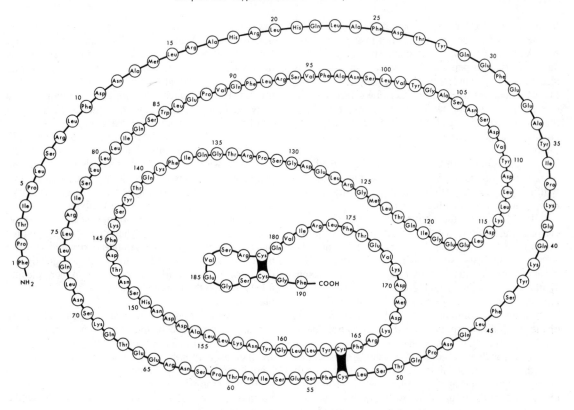

Figure 39–2. Human growth hormone. (Courtesy of CH Li.)

of the anterior pituitary, and its activity is relatively stable with chemical manipulation. Even the most highly purified preparations can be separated into several active components by various technics such as starch gel electrophoresis and gel filtration with Sephadex or other forms of chromatography. Relatively simple procedures are successful in extracting almost half of the material in the gland in clinically useful form.

Table 39–2. Activity of growth hormones in other species.* + = active; − = inactive.

Growth Hormone From	Stimulates Growth In				
	Fish	Birds	Rats	Monkeys	Humans
Fish			−		
Reptiles			+		
Amphibia			+		
Birds			+		
Cows	+	−†	+	−	−‡
Sheep	+		+	−	−
Pigs	+	−†	+	−	−‡
Whales			+		−
Monkeys	+		+		+
Humans	+		+	+	

*Reproduced, with permission, from Ganong WF: *Review of Medical Physiology,* 9th ed. Lange, 1979.
†Probable diabetogenic effect.
‡Slight diabetogenic effect.

Growth hormone is destroyed in the gastrointestinal tract and must be administered parenterally. Very little is known about its transport, metabolism, and excretion in humans.

Growth hormone has many important effects in the body. It stimulates protein synthesis and growth in almost all tissues of the body including bone, skin, muscle, collagen, and visceral organs. These effects of the hormone cannot be shown in vitro and have been found to be due to substances induced in vivo when growth hormone is secreted.

Somatomedins

Growth hormone has been known to induce bone growth by inducing an intermediary substance that, in contrast to growth hormone is active in vitro. It has been called sulfation factor. When given in vivo or incubated with cartilage in vitro, it causes an increase in the tissue uptake of substances such as leucine, uridine, thymidine, and sulfate ion and converts proline to hydroxyproline.

Attempts to isolate this factor have led to the identification and isolation of a group of compounds that have been named somatomedins. They appear to be produced in liver, kidney, muscle, and other tissues and are increased by growth hormone administration or secretion and are weakly stimulated by prolactin. They are also influenced by nutritional factors such as dietary protein.

Somatomedins are small peptides that circulate in

the body bound to larger carrier proteins. The peptides isolated thus far resemble proinsulin in that they have both A and B chains with intrachain sulfhydryl bridges and a connecting peptide. The tertiary structure may also be similar. The molecular weights are approximately 7000, but a few are larger. Two forms of the carrier protein having molecular weights of approximately 70,000 and 120,000, have been identified. However, a biologic role has not been established for them.

These compounds can be assayed biologically or by radioreceptor assay. They appear in the circulation within hours after growth hormone administration and disappear with a half-life of 12 hours.

In addition to the above-mentioned effects on cartilage, these compounds have an insulinlike effect on adipose tissue, causing increased lipid synthesis, decreased lipolysis, and a decrease in adenylate cyclase activity. In muscle, they cause increased protein synthesis, amino acid and glucose uptake, and decreased adenylate cyclase activity. These findings suggest that the somatomedins may account for most of the insulinlike activity in plasma that is not due to insulin (plasma ILA; see p 381).

The growth effects of this hormone are associated with the retention of mineral substances such as calcium, sodium, potassium, and phosphate in proportion to the amount of tissue added to the body.

The importance of these compounds clinically has not been fully explored. However, there appears to be a form of dwarfism in which growth hormone does not induce normal amounts of somatomedin. It has also been found that pygmies respond poorly to these compounds.

In addition to the effects on carbohydrate and fat metabolism noted above, growth hormone has actions mediated through a separate mechanism. When administered to intact animals or humans, the available preparations of growth hormone rapidly produce a brief fall in blood glucose and fatty acids followed by a slow rise over a period of several hours in the free fatty acids in plasma.

Growth hormone also has important effects on carbohydrate metabolism. When injected over a prolonged period, it can lead to the development of diabetes mellitus in animals and impairment of glucose tolerance in humans. In muscle, growth hormone influences several steps in the metabolism of glucose, impairing glycolysis and glucose transport. It is not known whether these are direct effects of growth hormone or secondary to the mobilization of free fatty acids from adipose tissue. Hyperglycemia, which can be produced by growth hormone, results from a combination of the above effects associated with increased hepatic gluconeogenesis.

Metabolism

In humans, growth hormone is secreted at the rate of about 4 mg/d. Little is known about its transport or degradation. However, it is rapidly removed from the circulation. The half-life is estimated to be 20–30

minutes. The circulating levels of growth hormone in humans have been measured by an immunoassay. Under basal conditions, levels are low—usually less than 5 ng/mL. In adult women with normal ovarian function or under treatment with estrogen, the circulating levels may reach 15 ng/mL even with normal activity. Levels are somewhat higher in very young children. They gradually decrease until age 4–5.

Growth hormone can be measured by bioassay as well as immunologically. The bioassay involving the growth in width of the tibial epiphysis is an excellent measure of the growth-promoting activities of this hormone. The immunoassay is a more rapid, sensitive, and simple technic that has markedly increased our understanding of growth hormone secretion. However, it is not entirely clear whether all of the activities that are associated with preparations extracted from the pituitary are represented by the immunologically active hormone under all circumstances. In men, plasma levels of growth hormone range from 0 to 5 ng/mL of plasma.

Growth hormone is at least in part regulated by substances produced in the median eminence of the hypothalamus (Fig 39–1). Levels of growth hormone are increased rapidly by a wide variety of stresses, including exercise; by hypoglycemia; and by amino acids such as arginine. The release of this hormone can be inhibited by glucose and by hydrocortisonelike compounds. The hypothalamic regulators of growth hormone release are described below.

Disorders of Growth Hormone Production

Excessive production of growth hormone occurs in the presence of adenomas of the pituitary (eosinophilic) that produce this substance. When this occurs before puberty, excessive growth (gigantism) occurs. After fusion of epiphyseal plates of the long bones, acromegaly is produced. This disorder is accompanied by an overgrowth of the soft tissues, mandible, sinuses, and visceral organs, leading to an easily recognizable characteristic appearance.

Growth hormone may be congenitally absent or defective, leading to dwarfism. Deficiency may also result from partial or complete destruction of the anterior pituitary gland. Such patients fail to grow and may have episodes of hypoglycemia. They often have symptoms due to the deficiency of other tropic hormones.

The ability of the pituitary to produce growth hormone can be tested in several ways. The basal levels can be measured as well as the responses to several stimuli. Among those for which standardized procedures have been developed are the responses to insulin-induced hypoglycemia, intravenous infusions of arginine monochloride, and the injection of glucagon. The injection of vasopressin or production of fever with pyrogen have also been used to test growth hormone reserve.

Clinical Uses

No preparations of human growth hormone are

commercially available for clinical use. However, small amounts have been made available to investigators for the treatment of patients with growth hormone deficiency. A small number of patients have been treated for growth failures secondary to hypopituitarism. The majority have shown a significant improvement in growth rate, although a few have failed to respond. Antibodies have been found in some of these patients after prolonged treatment but as a rule have not been associated with diminished response. Growth failures for reasons other than growth hormone deficiency have not responded well to treatment with this substance. The undesirable side-effects associated with treatment have been discomfort, pain and swelling associated with frequent injections, and occasional allergic reactions. It has not been possible to assess the long-term effects on carbohydrate metabolism, although the hormone has been observed to make diabetes mellitus worse.

Growth hormone is conceivably useful in a variety of other circumstances because of its fat-mobilizing and protein anabolic effects. It is not likely that these will be thoroughly investigated until a more abundant supply of active material is available. Although larger amounts of growth hormone derived from nonhuman sources have been available (Table 39–2), these preparations are not fully active in humans. There is a specifity of action that is probably related to the structural differences of hormones from various species.

The placenta produces a substance that has chemical and biologic properties similar to those exhibited by human growth hormone. (See Human Chorionic Somatomammotropin, below.)

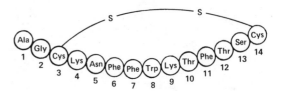

Figure 39–3. Amino acid sequence of somatostatin.

substance has been shown to inhibit growth hormone release in response to a wide variety of stimuli in normal individuals. It produces a decrease in circulating insulin and glucose levels and interferes with the ability of thyrotropin-releasing hormone to cause thyrotropin release.

Exogenously administered somatostatin is rapidly cleared from the circulation, with an initial half-life of 1–3 minutes. The kidney appears to play an important role in its metabolism and excretion.

Somatostatin can effectively inhibit growth hormone release in patients with acromegaly. However, its usefulness in the treatment of this disorder has not been adequately studied.

Somatostatin has also been identified in the pancreas and other sites in the gastrointestinal tract. It has been shown to inhibit the release of glucagon, insulin, and gastrin. These effects are blocked or reversed by calcium ion, and the ability of somatostatin to decrease glucagon secretion can be inhibited by alpha-adrenergic stimulation.

Peptides have been synthesized with some dissociation of the properties of somatostatin, and a 7-aminoheptanoic acid derivative containing only 4 of the 14 amino acids of somatostatin has been found to block the effect of somatostatin.

GROWTH HORMONE–RELEASING HORMONE
(GHRH, GRF, Somatotropin-Releasing Factor)

Growth hormone secretion is stimulated by a polypeptide produced in the median eminence of the hypothalamus. It has a molecular weight of approximately 2000, and its secretion is under the control of adrenergic neurons in the median eminence. Its release is increased by norepinephrine and blocked by alpha blockers.

SOMATOSTATIN
(Growth Hormone–Inhibiting Hormone, GIF, Somatotropin-Releasing–Inhibiting Factor)

Somatostatin, a tetradecapeptide, has been isolated from the hypothalamus and other parts of the central nervous system. Its structure has been determined, and it has been synthesized (Fig 39–3). This

PROLACTIN
(Luteotropic Hormone, LTH; Luteotropin, Lactogenic Hormone, Mammotropin)

Although preparations of highly purified prolactin have been obtained from ovine sources (Fig 39–4), the most active substances in the human pituitary promoting lactation thus far are found in preparations of growth hormone. The inability to separate these activities completely suggests that the 2 substances are chemically and structurally similar. The comparative effects of prolactin are remarkably diverse and include the stimulation of milk production in mammals, the maintenance of corpus luteum function (luteotropic action) in some rodents, and important behavioral effects in lower vertebrates.

In women, prolactin is the hormone primarily responsible for lactation. The role of prolactin in breast development is less certain. In tissue culture, prolactin, estrogen, progesterone, and insulin are required for growth and differentiation. Once breast develop-

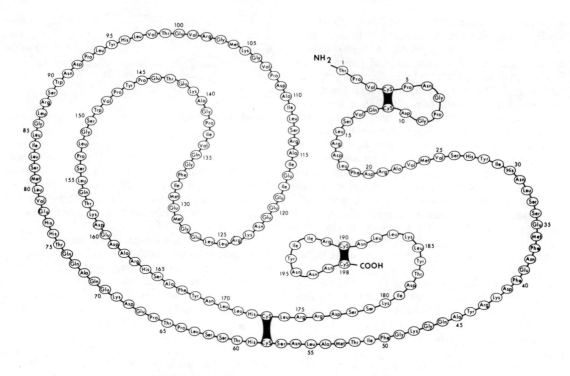

Figure 39–4. Ovine prolactin. (Courtesy of CH Li.)

ment occurs, prolactin, insulin, and cortisol are required to maintain milk secretion. Estrogen antagonizes the stimulation of milk production by prolactin. Although high prolactin levels may be accompanied by anovulation, the relationship between prolactin and gonadotropin secretion is not understood. Other possible actions of prolactin have not been adequately studied.

The availability of sensitive bioassay and immunoassay technics for the estimation of prolactin levels in the body is providing some understanding of the control of its secretion in humans. Prolactin is secreted during fetal life and circulates in high concentrations at birth. The level gradually falls and remains at low levels in men. In women, levels increase at puberty in response to rising estrogen levels and decline at the menopause. Plasma concentrations of prolactin rise during sleep and fall by morning. The secretion appears to be pulsatile.

In normal women, the mean plasma level is about 10 ng/mL. During pregnancy, levels increase to 200 ng/mL.

Prolactin secretion is tonically inhibited by dopamine-releasing neurons. Destruction or inhibition of these neurons results in augmented prolactin secretion. Prolactin is also secreted in response to physical or emotional distress or by suckling. Secretion of prolactin can be stimulated by estrogens, phenothiazines and other tranquilizers, dopamine, and thyrotropin-releasing hormone (see p 430), and inhibited by ergot derivatives. Preparations of growth hormone with high prolactin activity have been administered successfully

in an attempt to improve milk production in lactating women.

Elevated levels of prolactin are also seen in patients with prolactin-secreting tumors of the pituitary. Patients with such tumors often present with amenorrhea and galactorrhea. Even very small tumors can be identified by careful tomographic radiologic studies of the pituitary gland.

BROMOCRIPTINE

Bromocriptine (2-brom-ergocryptine methanesulfonate) is an ergot derivative with agonist activity at the dopamine receptor but little effect on the alpha-adrenergic receptors of the uterus and peripheral blood vessels. Bromocriptine has an effect similar to that of dopamine in inhibiting the release of prolactin from the pituitary, but the effect is more prolonged. It causes a brief rise in plasma growth hormone levels in normal individuals but a sustained fall in plasma growth hormone levels in patients with acromegaly.

Clinical Uses

Bromocriptine in doses of 2.5 mg 2 or 3 times a day reduces postpartum prolactin levels to normal. It prevents breast tenderness and engorgement and inhibits lactation. It is generally well tolerated, and in these doses it does not usually cause motor disorders. Ovarian function and fertility are usually restored ear-

Bromocriptine

lier (4 weeks after delivery) than in patients treated with large doses of estrogens or those who breast feed.

In addition to suppressing physiologic lactation, bromocriptine is effective in the treatment of amenorrhea and galactorrhea associated with hyperprolactinemia. In these patients, 2.5–5 mg 2–3 times daily will stop milk production in 90% of patients and restore ovulatory cycles in about two-thirds of patients. Patients with prolactin-secreting adenomas have also been treated with this agent. Preliminary studies indicate that doses of 2.5–10 mg 3–4 times daily will produce immediate suppression of prolactin and restoration of fertility in many of these patients. Reduction in the size of some of these tumors has been reported; however, the natural history of prolactinomas is not known. It is felt by many investigators that pregnancy should be avoided in patients with tumors, since rapid expansion of tumors may occur during pregnancy. It is also recommended that patients with amenorrhea treated with bromocriptine avoid pregnancy. Contraception other than estrogen-containing oral contraceptives should be utilized.

As noted above, bromocriptine in doses of 5–20 mg 3 times daily causes a sustained reduction in growth hormone levels in patients with acromegaly. Most patients will show a reduction in growth hormone levels after several weeks of treatment, although normal levels are seldom reached. Variable improvement will occur clinically and can be maintained for several years. Complete remission occurs in a minority of patients and may not be proportionate to the fall in plasma growth hormone levels. Since it does not cause a reduction in the size of tumors, bromocriptine should be considered to be an adjunct to rather than a replacement for surgery or radiation therapy.

Bromocriptine has also been used to treat Parkinson's disease. Large doses are required, sometimes up to 200 mg daily. It appears to be somewhat less potent than levodopa for this purpose. At the doses used, side-effects are similar to those produced by levodopa (see p 321).

Metabolism

Bromocriptine is rapidly and completely absorbed from the gastrointestinal tract. Peak plasma levels are reached in 2–3 hours, and effects last hours to days. It is metabolized to a large number of excretory products that are eliminated predominantly in the bile. About 5–10% is excreted unchanged or as metabolites in the urine.

Adverse Reactions

The most common side-effect is nausea; however, postural hypotension, dizziness, headaches, vomiting, and constipation have been reported. These effects may respond to temporary dose reduction. Cold-induced vasospasm of the fingers has also been observed.

HUMAN CHORIONIC SOMATOMAMMOTROPIN (HCS, Chorionic Prolactin, HPL)

The human placenta also produces a protein hormone with growth hormone-like and prolactinlike activities. This material, called human chorionic somatomammotropin (HCS), is produced in large amounts throughout pregnancy and has a specific activity much lower than that of the pituitary hormones (see above). As much as 5 g of this protein are released by the placenta into the maternal circulation. It has been studied as an indicator of placental function and, along with urinary estriol excretion, has found limited use for this purpose (see Chapter 38). Its structure is closely related to that of human growth hormone, and it has growth hormone-like activity.

CORTICOTROPIN (Adrenocorticotropic Hormone, ACTH)

Source & Chemistry

Corticotropin is a polypeptide that in humans contains 39 amino acids in the sequence illustrated in Fig 39–5. In other species, the isolated polypeptide shows minor variations in amino acids 25–33. The molecular weights of these preparations are between 4500 and 4600.

Clinical preparations of corticotropin are derived largely from bovine, porcine, and ovine pituitary glands. Since it is rapidly destroyed by proteolytic enzymes, corticotropin cannot be administered orally. However, corticotropin is readily absorbed when given by intramuscular injection or as an intravenous infusion.

Corticotropin is assayed biologically by its ability to cause an increase in adrenocortical steroid production or ascorbic acid depletion—or sometimes by its ability to maintain adrenal weight in the hypophysectomized animal. It is now possible to measure small amounts of corticotropin in the circulation by means of an immunoassay.

		Human	Bovine	Porcine	Ovine
Pro 24	25	Asp	Asp	Asp	Ala
Tyr 23	26	Ala	Gly	Gly	Gly
Val 22	27	Gly	Glu	Ala	Glu
Lys 21	28	Glu	Ala	Glu	Asp
Val 20	29	Asp	Glu	Asp	Asp
Pro 19	30	Gln	Asp	Gln	Glu
Arg 18	31	Ser	Ser	Leu	Ala
Arg 17	32	Ala	Ala	Ala	Ser
Lys 16	33	Glu	Gln	Glu	Glu
Lys 15	34	Ala			
Gly 14	35	Phe			
Val 13	36	Pro			
Pro 12	37	Leu			
Lys 11	38	Glu			
Gly 10	39	Phe			
Trp 9					
Arg 8					
Phe 7		Amino acid sequence			
His 6		in common with α-MSH			
Glu 5					
Met 4					
Ser 3					
Tyr 2					
Ser 1	--(N-terminal)				

Figure 39–5. Amino acid sequences of human, bovine, porcine, and ovine corticotropin.

Pure corticotropin has a biologic activity of 150–200 units/mL. (One USP unit is the activity contained in 1 mg of the international standard.) It is a white powder, soluble in water and 70% alcohol or acetone, and has an isoelectric point of about 4.7. It is stable in neutral or slightly acidic solutions but labile in alkaline solutions.

Studies with fragments of this polypeptide and with synthetic polypeptides indicate that the entire molecule is not required for biologic activity. Synthetic polypeptides having as few as 19 or 23 amino acids have essentially complete activity.

It has been found that structural changes can independently alter the biologic and immunologic properties of this hormone. Modification of the N-terminal amino acid can reduce or eliminate biologic activity without materially altering its immunologic activity. The reverse is true when alterations are confined to the C-terminal amino acid.

Biosynthesis & Secretion

ACTH is synthesized as part of a large precursor molecule containing 260 amino acids (MW 31,000).

This molecule is of special interest because it contains ACTH and a 91-amino-acid sequence called lipotropin. Lipotropin contains a 30-amino-acid sequence with the structure of beta-endorphin as well as sequences with the structure of beta-MSH and metenkephalin. Endorphins and enkephalins bind to receptors in the nervous system which mediate the effects of opiates. They are thought to play an important role in endogenous pain control and other aspects of behavior. During stress, these substances are released into the circulation with ACTH (see p 269).

Metabolism

Corticotropin has a half-life of less than 20 minutes. At rest, the plasma level is 0.3–0.88 mU/dL (21–63 pg/mL); with activity or stress, the level may increase to as high as 2.8 mU/dL (200 pg/mL). The human anterior pituitary contains 5–10 mg of corticotropin per gram of tissue and releases a fraction of a milligram per day at rest. In the circulation it is associated with plasma proteins (Cohn fractions II and III) and is concentrated in several tissues, including the adrenal cortex, kidneys, and placenta. Some appears in the urine.

Mechanism of Action

Corticotropin increases the production of cortisol and its precursors primarily in the zona fasciculata and zona reticularis and of aldosterone in the zona glomerulosa of the adrenal cortex (see Chapter 35). Many of the precursors are common to both pathways; however, the enzymes involved may be specific for each pathway (Fig 35–1).

The rate-limiting step in synthesis stimulated by corticotropin appears to be the conversion of cholesterol to pregnenolone. The precise mechanism of action involved in the stimulation of the adrenal cortex is not known, but a number of associated molecular events have been described. These include an increase in the cellular uptake of glucose and amino acids and production of cAMP (cyclic 3′,5′-adenosine monophosphate). The latter substance activates dephosphorylase kinase, which produces an increase in active phosphorylase in the zona fasciculata. It has been shown that cAMP is capable of markedly stimulating steroidogenesis, probably as the result of increased production of energy substrate and dihydronicotinamide adenine dinucleotide phosphate (NADPH), which can increase corticosteroid production in vitro. A number of structural changes in the adrenal involving the mitochondria are observed to follow corticotropin stimulation.

Physiologic & Pharmacologic Effects

Corticotropin stimulates the growth of the adrenal gland and the production and release of hormonal steroids by the adrenal cortex; to some extent, it also increases the flow of blood through the gland.

In addition to controlling adrenocortical secretion, corticotropin has some direct effects. Its melanocyte-stimulating activity is probably related to the fact that it is structurally related to melanocyte-stimulating hormone (MSH). α-MSH of beef origin has a sequence of 13 amino acids in common with corticotropin (Fig 39–5). Corticotropin mobilizes lipids from adipose tissue in the form of free fatty acids (FFA). The FFA are in part converted to neutral lipids and ketones by the liver. The remaining FFA are oxidized or reesterified into triglycerides in muscle and other tissues. The effect on adipose tissue is probably mediated by stimulation of a hormone-sensitive lipase. Corticotropin has been shown to have additional effects in adrenalectomized animals. It causes a reduction of the rate of disappearance of plasma glucose and a reduction in the level of glucose and amino acids, and it inhibits the degradation of the corticosteroids. It also has a minor positive inotropic effect on the heart. It is doubtful whether any of these effects are of more than minor importance physiologically.

Regulation of Secretion

The control of corticotropin secretion is dual in nature and appears to be mediated by the hypothalamic secretion of a substance called corticotropin-releasing factor (CRF; Fig 39–1). Increased circulating cortisol levels depress corticotropin release; decreased cortisol levels increase the rate of its secretion. This phenomenon is referred to as negative feedback control. Corticotropin also decreases the further release of corticotropin by inhibiting the secretion of corticotropin-releasing factor (CRF; Fig 39–1)—an example of "short loop" feedback inhibition of pituitary hormones.

A second mechanism, activated by stress, involves other parts of the brain. Stimulation of portions of the anterior median eminence of the hypothalamus, the limbic system, and the amygdaloid complex and removal of the cerebral cortex also increase corticotropin secretion. Lesions in the anterior median eminence and transection of the midbrain interfere with the normal increase observed in response to stress.

In the absence of stress and in the presence of intact feedback regulation, the rate of corticotropin secretion varies throughout the day, reaching its maximum in the morning hours and being low during the evening. This variation can be blocked by morphine and does not occur in patients with diseases of the nervous system associated with extensive brain destruction. It therefore appears that the level at which feedback regulation occurs is determined by a center in the brain. It is not known whether this center is related to or identical with those controlling circadian rhythms of other bodily processes such as temperature and renal function.

Noxious stimuli can overcome feedback inhibition unless there is severe atrophy of the biochemical mechanism involved in the formation and release of corticotropin and adrenocortical steroids. Atrophy of this degree is seen after prolonged administration of corticotropin or one of the glucocorticoids or following the removal of a cortisol-producing tumor.

The pituitary reserve can be tested by utilizing both pathways. The feedback response can be provoked by the 11-hydroxylase inhibitor metyrapone (see Chapter 35). Increased ACTH release can also be provoked by hypoglycemia, lysine vasopressin, or pyrogen.

Clinical Uses

A. Therapeutic Uses: The most obvious use for corticotropin is in the replacement of a deficiency of endogenous corticotropin such as might be found when the anterior pituitary is destroyed by a tumor, thrombosis of its vascular supply, or other injury. However, it has been found to be more convenient, comfortable, and accurate (as well as less expensive) to replace the adrenocortical hormones whose production is stimulated by corticotropin directly, since corticotropin must be given parenterally (see Chapter 35).

Corticotropin is occasionally used in the treatment of allergic inflammatory disorders that are favorably influenced by glucocorticoids. It has been proposed that the tropic effect on the adrenal cortex might prevent or minimize the occurrence of iatrogenic adrenal insufficiency (produced by prolonged suppression of endogenous adrenocortical secretion). However, careful studies of pituitary and adrenal function following prolonged treatment with large doses of glucocorticoids or corticotropin indicate that the response to stress is inhibited to a similar degree in patients receiving both preparations.

B. Diagnostic Uses: Corticotropin is widely used in the study of adrenocortical function. In the patient suffering from adrenocortical insufficiency, the increase in production of cortisol and other corticosteroids following administration of corticotropin will be absent if the disorder resides in the adrenal. When the deficiency is due to a reduction in corticotropin, the adrenal response will be present—albeit sluggish if the deficiency is severe and of long duration.

The patient who is able to produce a normal amount of corticosteroid at rest but is unable to increase the rate of secretion during periods of stress can be identified by a failure to respond to corticotropin even though the resting levels of secretion are normal.

The infusion of corticotropin may be helpful as an adjunct to suppression tests in the differential diagnosis of Cushing's syndrome. In patients with bilateral adrenal hyperplasia, the steroidogenic response to corticotropin is marked. When the source of the excessive hormone production is carcinoma of the adrenal, this hyperactive response is usually absent. Benign adenomas producing adrenocortical steroids vary in their response to corticotropin.

Corticotropin tests can be performed in several ways. When possible, the intravenous infusion of synthetic corticotropin is preferred because the responses are more reproducible and because the source of material can be immediately removed if an allergic reaction occurs.

When synthetic corticotropin (0.25 mg) is injected intravenously in a few milliliters of saline, peak plasma cortisol levels are reached in 45–60 minutes.

The levels are sufficiently elevated in 30 minutes to yield reliable results in most patients. When the same amount is infused over 8 hours in saline or glucose, the increase in plasma cortisol or urinary 17-hydroxycorticoid excretion can be measured as an index of adrenal response.

C. Preparations Available: Corticotropin is available in preparations suitable for intravenous or intramuscular use. The latter consist of corticotropin in gelatin solution or adsorbed to zinc hydroxide to prolong the action of the drug.

The corticotropin in these preparations is derived from animal pituitary glands, since synthetic materials have not been made available for commercial use until recently. The potency is determined by bioassay. The USP unit is equivalent to the activity contained in one-fifth of an ampule (1 mg) of the Third International Standard for Corticotropin using the adrenal ascorbic acid depletion assay.

A synthetic preparation of corticotropin (cosyntropin) is now available for clinical use. It contains the first 24 amino acids of β-corticotropin. A dose of 0.25 mg is equivalent to 25 IU. This preparation appears to be free of allergic reactions and, in contrast to others, can be given as reliably by the intramuscular as by the intravenous route. It will cause a 2- to 3-fold elevation of plasma corticosteroids in 60–70 minutes in normal subjects.

Since the half-life is less than 20 minutes, the effects of intravenously administered corticotropin do not persist for a long period following injection; when larger doses are given (eg, more than 10 mg), the steroidogenic effect is directly related to the duration of the infusion. When corticotropin is given by the intramuscular route, the effects are not greatly prolonged unless gelatin is added or the drug is adsorbed to zinc hydroxide.

Contraindications & Cautions

The major contraindication to the administration of corticotropin is a history of a previous hypersensitivity reaction. Most patients exhibiting such responses will tolerate synthetic corticotropin. However, a few reactions have occurred, and an intradermal test should be done even with this preparation.

GONADOTROPINS

The pituitary hormones regulating ovarian and testicular function are known as gonadotropins. The control of ovarian function varies from one species to another. Three hormones are known to have gonadotropic activity in some species. They are luteinizing hormone (LH), follicle-stimulating hormone (FSH), and prolactin (see above). The function of the latter is well established in the rodent, but its activity in controlling ovarian function in the human female has not been established. FSH and LH appear to be important

in all species studied. In addition to these hormones produced by the anterior pituitary, human placenta produces chorionic gonadotropin (HCG), which is related and will be considered below.

Preparations of LH and HCG have been used experimentally to stimulate the production of androgens by the testes or by the ovary for the purpose of testing endocrine function. They are also used in conjunction with FSH, human menopausal urine gonadotropin preparations, and clomiphene (Clomid) to produce ovulation in women with abnormal menstrual function (see Chapter 38).

The gonadotropins—LH, FSH, and HCG—and thyrotropin are glycoproteins. They have each been shown to consist of 2 chains designated α and β. The α chains are quite similar to each other and can be interchanged without altering biologic activity (Table 39–3). The β chains confer biologic specificity.

Gonadotropin-Releasing Hormone (GnRH, LH, FSH-RH)

The regulation of FSH and LH secretion from the pituitary is complex. It involves feedback regulation by the gonadal hormones at the hypothalamus and pituitary level and direct feedback effects of the gonadotropins on the secretion of hypothalamic releasing factors or hormones. A polypeptide with FSH and LH releasing activity has been isolated and its structure determined, and it has been synthesized (Fig 39–6). This material (FSH-RH/LH-RH) can increase LH levels in 15 minutes when 1 μg is injected intravenously. About 3 μg will induce a comparable increase in serum FSH. Studies of the metabolism of this hormone indicate that it is rapidly removed from the circulation, with an initial half-life of 8 minutes.

This agent can be used to distinguish hy-

Table 39–3. Properties of the pituitary glycoprotein subunits.*

	ICSH-α	TSH-α	FSH-α
Hexose (%)	8.3	7.3	2.8
Hexosamine (%)	8.6	13.3	2.3
Sialic acid (%)	...	...	0.8
N-terminal	Phe	Phe	Phe
C-terminal	Ser	Ser	Ser
Partial amino acid content†			
Lysine	10	10	10.5
Arginine	3	3	4.5
Proline	7	7	5.6
Half-cystine	10	10	4.9
Methionine	4	4	0.3
Leucine	2	2	9.0
Tyrosine	5	5	2.7

*Reproduced, with permission, from Papkoff H: Gen Comp Endocrinol (Suppl 3):609, 1972.

†Values for ICSH-α and TSH-α are residues per molecule determined by structure analysis; values for FSH-α are expressed as residues/100 residues determined by amino acid analysis.

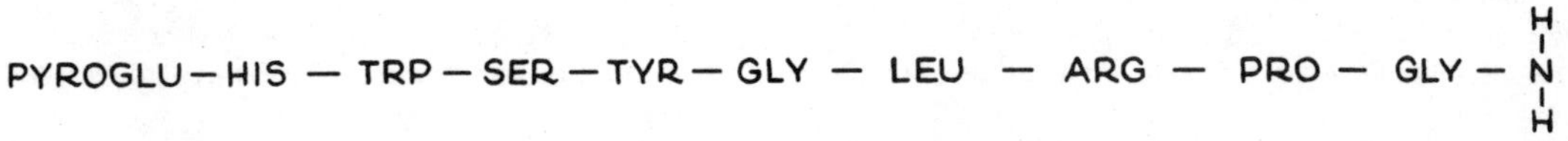

PYROGLU — HIS — TRP — SER — TYR — GLY — LEU — ARG — PRO — GLY — $\overset{\overset{\text{H}}{|}}{\underset{\overset{|}{\text{H}}}{\text{N}}}$

Figure 39–6. The molecular structure of porcine FSH- and LH-releasing hormone (gonadorelin) (FSH-RH/LH-RH).

pothalamic from pituitary deficiency as the cause of hypogonadism in patients with responsive ovaries and low levels of circulating gonadotropins. Its potential uses for inducing ovulation and otherwise altering the menstrual cycle or spermatogenesis and fertility are being explored. Ovulation can be induced in some amenorrheic women with daily injections of 500 μg daily subcutaneously.

1. FOLLICLE–STIMULATING HORMONE (FSH)

FSH is a glycoprotein composed of 2 polypeptide chains. The α chain, as noted above, is similar to that of LH (Fig 39–7). It has a molecular weight of approximately 32,000 and a carbohydrate content of 18%. Its high solubility, acidity, and resistance to inactivation by proteolytic enzymes have served to facilitate its separation. It is inactivated by neuraminidase, with the release of sialic acid.

FSH appears to be responsible for the stimulation of the growth of and possibly the secretion of estrogen by the graafian follicle. In the male, this hormone stimulates the development of the germinal elements leading to the production of sperm cells.

Very few studies of the metabolism of FSH have been reported. Preliminary studies indicate that the premenopausal production rate in women is in the range of 200–300 IU/d and that it may be 10–15 times as high in postmenopausal women. The initial half-life is approximately 10 minutes. Studies of the blood level of this hormone throughout the menstrual cycle in women have been performed by several methods utilizing both immunoassay and bioassay procedures. Recent studies utilizing immunoassay procedures indicate that there is an increase in plasma FSH concentration early in the cycle as well as a peak coincident with the peak in LH secretion at midcycle (Fig 38–2). These peaks appear to precede ovulation by about 16 hours.

Little is known about the metabolism of FSH except that an estimated 10–20% of the amount secreted can be identified in the urine by immunoassay or bioassay.

2. LUTEINIZING HORMONE (LH; Interstitial Cell-Stimulating Hormone, ICSH; Ovulating Hormone)

The structure of LH is shown in Fig 39–7. It is similar to those of FSH and thyrotropin.

Good preparations have been obtained from the pituitary glands of several species, including humans. However, only small amounts of the latter preparation have been available.

LH is produced at about 2–4 times the rate of FSH in normal menstruating women. However, it is not secreted at a constant rate. The rate of secretion is somewhat higher in the first half of the cycle than in the second, but there is a high peak that seems to be associated with (and may be the cause of) ovulation in humans and other species. Its half-life in humans appears to be about 20–25 minutes. Plasma levels of LH during the menstrual cycle are plotted in Fig 38–2.

Little is known about the metabolism of LH except that a portion is excreted into the urine in a biologically active form detectable by immunoassay.

LH is responsible for the stimulation of the Leydig cells in the testes, leading to the production of testosterone. In the female it is thought also to stimulate the interstitial cells in the ovary, leading to the production of some androgens; and it has also been shown to stimulate the production of estrogen by the follicle and progesterone by the cells of the corpus luteum obtained from the human ovary. Although the actual site of LH action in the production of progesterone in the corpus luteum is unknown, experimental evidence suggests that it accelerates the conversion of acetate to squalene and of cholesterol to 20α-hydroxycholesterol. LH has been shown to increase the production of cAMP, leading to an increase in the activation of phosphorylase. This enzyme, by its effects on carbohydrate metabolism, provides NADPH, which is required for the conversion of cholesterol to progesterone in the corpus luteum.

Although no preparations of LH are available for clinical use, HCG is commonly used to obtain this activity.

3. CHORIONIC GONADOTROPIN (Human Chorionic Gonadotropin, HCG)

Human chorionic gonadotropin is a water-soluble glycoprotein resembling the above compounds except

Alpha chain:

H-Phe-Pro-Asp-Gly-Glu-Phe-Thr-Met-Gln-Gly-Cys-Pro-Glu-Cys-Lys-Leu-Lys-Glu-Asn-Lys-Tyr-Phe-Ser-Lys-Pro-Asp-Ala-
                                    10   20

Pro-Ile-Tyr-Gln-Cys-Met-Gly-Cys-Cys-Phe-Ser-Arg-Ala-Tyr-Pro-Thr-Pro-Ala-Arg-Ser-Lys-Lys-Thr-Met-Leu-Val-Pro-Lys-
                    30   40   50

                CHO   CHO
                 | |
Asn-Ile-Thr-Ser-Glu-Ala-Thr-Cys-Cys-Val-Ala-Lys-Ala-Phe-Thr-Lys-Ala-Thr-Val-Met-Gly-Asn-Val-Arg-Val-Glx-Asn-His-
                    60   70   80

Thr-Glu-Cys-His-Ser-Cys-Thr-Cys-Tyr-Tyr-His-Lys-Ser-OH
                    90

Beta chain:

H-Ser-Arg-Gly-Pro-Leu-Arg-Pro-Leu-Cys-Glu-Pro-Ile-Asn-Ala-Ile-Leu-Ala-Ala-Glu-Lys-Glu-Gly-Cys-Pro-Val-Cys-Ile-Thr-
                                10   20

Phe-Thr-Thr-Ser-Ile-Cys-Ala-Gly-Tyr-Cys-Pro-Ser-Met-Lys-Arg-Val-Leu-Pro-Val-Ile-Leu-Pro-Pro-Met-Pro-Gln-Arg-Val-
                30   40   50

Cys-Thr-Tyr-His-Gln-Leu-Arg-Phe-Ala-Ser-Val-Arg-Leu-Pro-Gly-Cys-Pro-Pro-Gly-Val-Asp-Pro-Met-Val-Ser-Phe-Pro-Val-
                60   70   80

Ala-Leu-Ser-Cys-His-Cys-Gly-Pro-Cys-Arg-Leu-Ser-Ser-Thr-Asp-Cys-Gly-Pro-Gly-Arg-Thr-Glu-Pro-Leu-Ala-Cys-Asp-His-
                    90   100   110

Pro-Pro-Leu-Pro-Asp-Ile-Leu-OH
                    119

Figure 39–7. Amino acid sequence of ovine luteinizing hormone.

that it is more highly acidic. The study of highly purified preparations indicates that the hormone may be composed of 2 polypeptide chains. Amino acid analyses of these preparations suggest a molecular weight of about 27,000. However, other technics have suggested a larger molecule. The nature of the carbohydrate chains indicates that the structure is highly complex. The specific activity of the hormone is about 12,000 IU/mg. It sufficiently resembles LH that an antiserum prepared from HCG will cross-react with LH extracted from human pituitary glands. Its biologic activities are similar to those of LH, but little is known of its metabolism. HCG is produced in detectable amounts by trophoblast of the placenta shortly after implantation of the blastocyst. Its production is greatest 6–8 weeks later, and levels remain high until

parturition. It disappears from the circulation slowly (over a period of days) at the termination of pregnancy. It is obtained for clinical use by extraction from the urine of pregnant women. Removal of the sialic acid residues from this molecule markedly decreases its biologic activity in vivo but not in vitro. It has been suggested that the carbohydrate moiety inhibits its rapid destruction in the body.

Clinical Uses

HCG is used in conjunction with FSH for the induction of ovulation (see Chapter 38). It is also used for diagnostic purposes in order to determine the ability of the gonads to produce gonadal steroids. Doses of 5000–10,000 IU daily for several days are required to produce a marked effect.

HCG is used to produce ovulation in patients treated with human menopausal gonadotropin and occasionally in conjunction with clomiphene citrate therapy (see Chapter 38).

HCG has also been used in conjunction with a 600-calorie diet to produce weight loss. It is said to reduce the appetite and aid in adherence to the stringent diet. Although the regimen can be effective, there is no evidence that the HCG contributes by a pharmacologic or metabolic action. A combination of the expense and the biweekly visit to the physician may be an important incentive for the patient to remain on the diet. However, in controlled studies HCG is no more effective than a placebo injection.

THYROID–STIMULATING HORMONE (TSH, Thyrotropin)

TSH, the pituitary hormone responsible for the regulation of thyroid gland activity, is a glycoprotein.

Chemistry

TSH has not been completely purified and characterized, although some aspects of its structure are known. TSH is composed of 2 polypeptide chains. The alpha chain is similar to LH and FSH-α, and the beta subunit is quite active when combined with LH or FSH-α. TSH contains glucosamine and galactosamine and has a molecular weight of approximately 28,000. The structural differences in TSH derived from different species are thought to be small, since the preparations are active in species other than the one from which they are derived. It has been shown, however, that antibodies may form under these circumstances, limiting the time during which the hormone will be effective in other species. These observations indicate that the determinants of biologic and immunologic activity differ, as was noted with corticotropin.

Assay

TSH can be assayed by its effects on the thyroid gland. Thyroid weight, hormone synthesis, iodine or phosphorus uptake, and morphologic changes (follicular cell height) have been employed. More recently, radioimmunoassay and fluorescent staining procedures have been used.

Effects

TSH has an important effect in the regulation of most processes leading to the synthesis and release of thyroxine and triiodothyronine. Its administration is followed by the biologic effects of these hormones. TSH stimulates the accumulation of iodine, glucose, and amino acids by the cells of the thyroid and increases oxidative metabolism, proteolysis of colloid, and release of hormone.

The molecular mechanisms involved in these actions have not been defined. TSH enhances the metabolism of glucose via the hexose monophosphate shunt pathway. This leads to an increase in available NADPH. TSH has been reported to increase cAMP, but its known actions do not appear to be dependent upon protein synthesis.

Control of Secretion

The release of TSH by the pituitary is regulated in part by negative feedback control that involves the inhibition of release by thyroxine and triiodothyronine acting both at the pituitary and at hypothalamic centers that secrete a thyrotropin-releasing factor or hormone (TRF, TRH, see below).

Metabolism

When released into the circulation, TSH is rapidly cleared by the kidney. Its half-life is about 35 minutes in the normal individual but is increased in patients with hypothyroidism and decreased in patients with hyperthyroidism.

Plasma levels, as determined by the most sensitive assay available, have been found to range from 3 to 10 ng/mL in normal subjects. Plasma TSH can be suppressed by the administration of thyroid hormone and is usually markedly elevated in the presence of thyroid deficiency.

Disorders of Thyrotropin Secretion

A deficiency of thyrotropin production is caused by destructive lesions of the anterior pituitary gland or hypothalamus. Hyperfunction of the thyroid is not ordinarily produced by TSH (see Hyperthyroidism, p 346).

Clinical Uses

A. Therapeutic Uses: TSH (as thyrotropin; Thytropar) is not used for the replacement of endogenous deficiencies of the hormone because it is less satisfactory than administering thyroid hormone orally. In addition, bovine TSH is active for only a short time in humans because of antibody formation.

TSH has been successfully used to stimulate the iodine uptake of toxic adenomatous goiters and in the treatment of metastatic thyroid disease in patients with thyroid cancer to enhance the effectiveness of therapy with radioactive iodine (^{131}I). It can be given in 3 or more daily doses of 10 units intramuscularly for several days until an adequate response is obtained.

B. Diagnostic Uses: TSH has also been used for diagnostic purposes. Hypothyroidism due to disturbances of the thyroid gland can be distinguished from that secondary to pituitary deficiency of TSH production. In addition, it is possible to distinguish primary hypothyroidism from iatrogenic suppression of thyroid function in patients who have been treated with thyroid hormone for prolonged periods. When used for these purposes, 10 units of TSH given for 1–3 days will cause an increase in the serum thyroxine and an increase in the ^{131}I uptake by the thyroid gland in the presence of normal thyroid tissue. When available, the measurement of TSH provides similar information.

C. Available Forms: Thyrotropin (Thytropar), derived from beef pituitaries, is available for intramuscular administration in ampules as a partially lyophilized powder devoid of significant amounts of corticotropin, gonadotropin, somatotropin, oxytocin, and vasopressin.

Contraindications & Cautions

TSH should not be given to patients in whom an increase in thyroid function might be harmful. This would include patients with angina pectoris, recent myocardial infarction, or congestive heart failure. It should be used with caution in patients with hypopituitarism or adrenal insufficiency.

TSH may produce temporary swelling of the thyroid; arrhythmias, including atrial fibrillation and tachycardias; fever; and nausea and vomiting.

In addition to the problems caused by the hormonal effects, anaphylactic reactions have occurred. Other allergic reactions including urticaria, fever, and transient hypotension have been reported and can usually be prevented by prior administration of antihistamines.

THYROTROPIN–RELEASING HORMONE (TRH)

TRH has been isolated, purified, and characterized. It appears to be a tripeptide with the structure illustrated below. Its release is controlled by thyroxine, as mentioned above, and directly by higher centers in the nervous system in response to environmental changes.

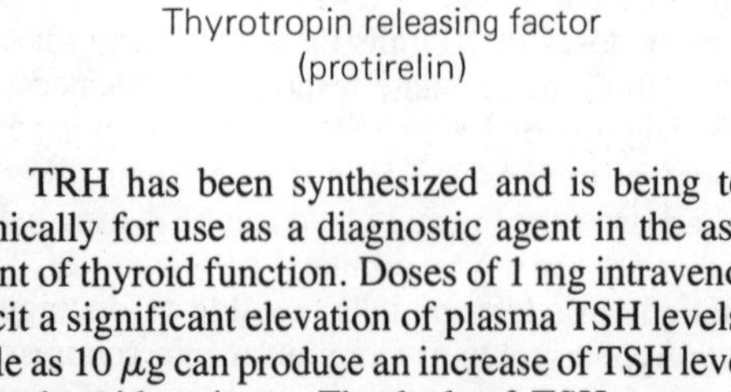

Thyrotropin releasing factor
(protirelin)

TRH has been synthesized and is being tested clinically for use as a diagnostic agent in the assessment of thyroid function. Doses of 1 mg intravenously elicit a significant elevation of plasma TSH levels. As little as 10 μg can produce an increase of TSH levels in hypothyroid patients. The lack of TSH response to TRH, even in mild hyperthyroidism, suggests that TRH may be useful in the diagnosis of borderline hyperthyroidism. The hormone is orally active, but larger doses are required. Potential therapeutic uses of the agent are being explored. Possible applications include the stimulation of ^{131}I uptake for increased

efficacy of ^{131}I therapy of thyrotoxicosis and thyroid carcinoma. Thus far, only minimal side-effects such as transient nausea have been observed.

TRH also stimulates the release of prolactin in humans and will augment lactation (see page 422). It has been suggested that it acts as a mediator or alters norepinephrine turnover in other parts of the brain (or both), since it is widely distributed outside the hypothalamus. This hypothesis is also suggested by its antidepressant effects. TRH also increases the plasma levels of prolactin and can be used to determine the ability of the pituitary to increase prolactin release.

INTERMEDIATE LOBE OF THE PITUITARY

The intermediate lobe of the pituitary is formed from the dorsal part of Rathke's pouch and is separated from the anterior lobe by the residual of the pocket formed by that structure. This part of the gland is less well developed in humans than in other species. Two polypeptides have been isolated from the cells of this lobe that disperse melanin granules in pigment cells. They have been named α- and β-melanocyte-stimulating hormone (MSH). Their structures have a number of amino acids in a sequence found in corticotropin (Table 39–4). Corticotropin has "MSH-like" activity but is much less potent than α- or β-MSH. Preliminary studies of changes in plasma MSH levels, as measured by immunoassay, indicate that, in humans, the secretion of this hormone follows that of corticotropin and is not related to alterations in pigmentation other than those produced by changes in adrenocortical function.

In fish, amphibia, and reptiles, MSH appears to play a role in the control of skin coloration. MSH secretion causes darkening of the skin in these species, and its secretion is under the control of neural centers and regulated by photoreceptors. Its source in the human is the anterior lobe, and its function is not established.

An MSH inhibitory factor (MIF) has been isolated from the hypothalamus and has been reported to have effects on behavior in emotionally disturbed patients.

THE POSTERIOR PITUITARY (NEUROHYPOPHYSIS)

The posterior lobe of the pituitary is an extension of the nervous system derived from the floor of the

Table 39–4. The relationship between the structure of the MSHs and amino acids 1–19 of the 39 amino acids in ACTH.*

		Ser-	Tyr-	Ser-	Met-Glu-His-Phe-Arg-Trp-Gly-	Lys-	Pro-	Val-	
ACTH (pig, sheep, beef)		1	2	3	4 5 6 7 8 9 10	11	12	13	Gly-Lys-Lys-Arg-Arg-Pro 14 15 16 17 18 19
α MSH (pig, beef, horse)	CH₃CO-	Ser- 1	Tyr- 2	Ser- 3	Met-Glu-His-Phe-Arg-Trp-Gly- 4 5 6 7 8 9 10	Lys- 11	Pro- 12	Val- 13	NH₂
β MSH (pig)	Asp-Glu-Gly-Pro- 1 2 3 4	Tyr- 5	Lys- 6		Met-Glu-His-Phe-Arg-Trp-Gly- 7 8 9 10 11 12 13	Ser- 14	Pro- 15	Pro- 16	Lys-Asp 17 18
β MSH (beef)	Asp-Ser-Gly-Pro- 1 2 3 4	Tyr- 5	Lys- 6		Met-Glu-His-Phe-Arg-Trp-Gly- 7 8 9 10 11 12 13	Ser- 14	Pro- 15	Pro- 16	Lys-Asp 17 18
β MSH (horse)	Asp-Glu-Gly-Pro- 1 2 3 4	Tyr- 5	Lys- 6		Met-Glu-His-Phe-Arg-Trp-Gly- 7 8 9 10 11 12 13	Ser- 14	Pro- 15	Arg- 16	Lys-Asp 17 18
β MSH (human)	Ala-Glu-Lys-Lys-Asp-Glu-Gly-Pro- 1 2 3 4 5 6 7 8	Tyr- 9	Arg- 10		Met-Glu-His-Phe-Arg-Trp-Gly- 11 12 13 14 15 16 17	Ser- 18	Pro- 19	Pro- 20	Lys-Asp 21 22

*Reproduced, with permission, from Li CH: Some aspects of the relation of peptide structure to activity in pituitary hormones. Vitam Horm 19:313, 1961.

thalamic portion of the brain. It contains neuroglial cells, pituicytes, and the axons of neurons in the supraoptic and paraventricular nuclei of the hypothalamus.

Although vasopressin and oxytocin have been extracted from the posterior pituitary, it is now known that they are neurosecretory products of neurons of the supraoptic and paraventricular nuclei. The structures of these hormones are illustrated in Table 39–6, and some of the species differences which have been documented are noted in Table 39–7.

VASOPRESSIN
(Antidiuretic Hormone, ADH)

Although methods are available for the measurement of vasopressin, the lack of agreement in results from different laboratories leaves us with little information about the rates of secretion, plasma levels, and metabolism of this substance. When vasopressin is injected intravenously or secreted into the bloodstream, it behaves as though it were cleared by a single passage through the liver and kidney. When relatively large amounts are injected, the half-life is less than 20 minutes. When it is given intramuscularly or subcutaneously, its effects may persist for several hours, and its activity can be further prolonged by injecting it as vasopressin tannate in oil.

Vasopressin has now been synthesized and is available for use in a highly purified form.

The mechanism of action of vasopressin in the kidneys is under study. It binds firmly to renal tissue, and its action can be inhibited by agents that block the sulfhydryl group. It is known that vasopressin activates the enzyme that increases concentrations of cAMP in the kidney; and cAMP is able to duplicate many of the actions of vasopressin in this tissue.

Control of Secretion

Vasopressin is produced by the nerve cells in the supraoptic and paraventricular nuclei of the hypothalamus. It appears to then be transported along the nerve fibers to the pituicytes of the posterior lobe of the pituitary. In the pituitary gland, it is bound to a specific group of proteins called neurophysin, which contains 3 polypeptide binding sites per molecule. It can be discharged from this area by electrical stimulation or acetylcholine. Vasopressin release is mediated in part through osmoreceptors, which are thought to be located in the region of the hypothalamic nuclei; and an increase in plasma osmolality resulting from water withdrawal or dehydration leads to increased release of the hormone. Hydration, on the other hand, reduces the secretion to a level that cannot be detected in the plasma or urine. The secretion of vasopressin can also be modified by changes in volume. In addition to these homeostatic mechanisms, the secretion of vasopressin can be increased by emotional and physical stress as well as by drugs such as nicotine and morphine. Vasopressin secretion can be altered by alcohol and other drugs (Table 39–5).

Effects of Deficiency or Excess

The absence of vasopressin causes diabetes insipidus, a disorder characterized by severe polyuria.

An excess of vasopressin results in water retention and dilutional hyponatremia. This disorder occurs under a variety of circumstances, particularly in the presence of pulmonary disease. Tumors have also been reported that appear to produce vasopressin or a similar substance.

Clinical Uses

The major therapeutic use of vasopressin is in the treatment of diabetes insipidus due to a deficiency of this hormone. Since the half-life of vasopressin is short, aqueous solutions are not convenient for chronic control and vasopressin tannate in oil is used instead. A dose of 0.25–1 unit or more may be required daily, and a few patients can be maintained on injections at greater intervals.

Table 39–5. The effects of drugs on vasopressin and oxytocin.*

	Vasopressin	Oxytocin
Release		
Stimulation	Chlorpropamide	Prostaglandin E_2
	Clofibrate	Prostaglandin $F_{2\alpha}$
	Acetylcholine	
	Nicotine	
	Alpha agonists	
	Anesthetics	
Inhibition	Ethanol	Ethanol
	Atropine	
	Alpha blockers	
	Beta agonists	
	Corticosteroids	
	Phenytoin	
Peripheral action		
Potentiation	p-Chlorobenzenesul-	Procaine
	fonyl-3-propylurea	D-N-Isopropyl-n-
	(chlorpropamide)	nitrophenyl-
	p-Chlorobenzenesul-	ethanolamine
	phonylurea	
	p-Chlorobenzenesul-	
	phonamide	
Inhibition	Lithium	Propranolol
	Alpha agonists	Guancydine
		4-Leucine-arginine
		vasotocin
		n-Carbamoyl-2-O-
		methyl-tyrosine
		oxytocin

*Adapted from Edwards & others: See references.

Vasopressin deficiency may not be the only cause of diabetes insipidus, since some individuals with renal tubular defects fail to respond to the hormone. Although vasopressin is not useful in these patients, it can be used as a diagnostic test—keeping in mind that after prolonged polyuria even the normal renal tubule will not immediately respond to vasopressin.

In addition to the intramuscular preparations, vasopressin can be given as nasal snuff, 30–60 mg 2–3 times a day; this is the least expensive form of treatment, but it may be quite irritating and absorption is uncertain.

Desmopressin (1-desamino-8-D-arginine vasopressin, DDAVP), a synthetic analog of vasopressin, has a much higher antidiuretic-to-pressor activity ratio (400:1) than arginine vasopressin. It has a prolonged action, and, when administered intranasally, doses of 5–20 μg result in a maximal antidiuresis for 8–20 hours in patients with severe central diabetes insipidus. Few adverse reactions have been reported. High doses occasionally produce headaches, nasal congestion, cramps, and slight elevations of blood pressure.

For patients who are allergic to animal vasopressin, a synthetic substitute, lysine-8 vasopressin, is available as a nasal spray. This preparation is free of local side-effects, and water intoxication, which is not unusual with vasopressin tannate in oil, does not occur.

Large doses of vasopressin produce a reduction in portal blood pressure and blood flow and have been used along with other measures in the treatment of esophageal bleeding. With the large doses used (10–20 units), a moderate rise in arterial blood pressure is observed.

Lysine vasopressin given in doses of 5 units intravenously has been used to stimulate growth hormone and ACTH secretion in order to test pituitary function. Atropine can be given to minimize gastrointestinal disturbances without affecting the test. Since normal individuals may fail to respond, it has been used in conjunction with other stimuli such as insulin and pyrogen.

Chlorpropamide has also been used in the treatment of mild diabetes insipidus (see Chapter 37).

Adverse Reactions

When large doses of vasopressin are injected, vasoconstriction occurs, leading to some increase in blood pressure and pallor of the skin. There is also an increase in intestinal activity that may result in nausea and cramping. Women occasionally experience uterine cramps. Coronary vessels may also constrict, resulting in anginal attacks in patients with coronary atherosclerosis. These attacks may be precipitated by very small amounts, and vasopressin must be used with the greatest of care and only if absolutely necessary in such individuals.

Preparations Available

See Table 39–7.

OXYTOCIN

Oxytocin was the first polypeptide hormone to be synthesized. As shown in Table 39–6, it is a cyclic polypeptide containing 8 amino acids and having a molecular weight of about 1000. This hormone also contains a disulfide bond and in other respects is quite similar to vasopressin. Analogs of these hormones have been produced by substitution of various groups. Desamino oxytocin, which lacks a free primary amino group in the terminal cystine residue, has 5 times the antidiuretic activity of oxytocin. Other modifications of biologic activity have been produced by changes in structure.

Oxytocin stimulates uterine smooth muscle, resulting in contraction of the uterus; it also stimulates smooth muscle of the mammary gland, causing the ejection of milk. The action of oxytocin on the uterus is conditioned by the levels of estrogens and progesterone present as well as by concentrations of ions such as calcium, magnesium, and potassium. The sensitivity of the human uterus to oxytocin increases gradually during pregnancy. It is not known whether oxytocin plays a physiologic role in stimulating the onset of labor. However, stimulation of the nipple by suckling

Table 39–6. Structure and activity of posterior pituitary hormones.

Variations From Amino Acid Sequence of Vasopressin										Activity		
										Pressor	Anti-diuretic	Oxy-tocic
1	2	3	4	5	6	7	8	9				
Cys	Tyr	Phe	Glu	Asp	Cys	Pro	Arg	Gly	Vasopressin	+	+	sl*
Des-amino							D-Arg		DDAVP†	–	++	–
							Lys		Lypressin‡	+	+	sl
							Orn		Ornipressin	++	sl	–
	Phe						Lys		Felypressin	+	sl	–
		Ile					Leu		Oxytocin	–	–	+
		Ile							Vasotocin	sl	sl	+

*Sl = slight.
†DDAVP = desmopressin, 1-desamino-8-D-arginine vasopressin.
‡Synthetic lypressin has no oxytocic activity.

leads to the reflex release of oxytocin that causes contraction of the smooth muscle of the mammary gland, leading to the reflex ejection of milk. If large amounts are administered, oxytocin appears to have a transient relaxing effect on the smooth muscle, resulting in a decrease in systolic and diastolic blood pressure, flushing, and increased brain blood flow. Reflex tachycardia may also occur. The chicken, a species in which this response is particularly marked, has been used to assay oxytocin.

Oxytocin has also been observed to have an insulinlike effect when incubated with the epididymal fat pad of the rat. Nothing is known of its metabolic actions in humans. As is true of vasopressin also, oxytocin is destroyed when given by mouth.

Vasopressin is destroyed by trypsin, whereas oxytocin is resistant to trypsin but is inactivated by chymotrypsin. It can be given by any parenteral route, including intranasal application. Once in the body, it is rapidly removed, having a half-life of less than 15 minutes. It is thought to be removed primarily by the kidney. During pregnancy, an enzyme (aminopeptidase) appears that is capable of rapidly destroying this hormone. The concentration of this enzyme increases throughout pregnancy, reaching a maximum at the time of parturition.

Clinical Uses

Oxytocin is employed in the induction of labor in pregnant women. In general, larger amounts are re-

Table 39–7. Posterior pituitary hormones: Preparations and sources.

	Preparations Available	Source or Physiologic Distribution
Vasopressin (AVP, arginine vasopressin, Argipressine)	Injectables, 20 units/mL, and in oil, 5 units/mL	Most mammals
Desmopressin acetate (DDAVP, 1-des-amino-8-D-arginine vasopressin)	Nasal solution,* 0.1 mg/mL (400 units)	Synthetic
Lypressin (LVP, lysine vasopressin)	Nasal spray, 50 units/mL (0.185 mg/mL) Nasal solution,* 100 units/mL Injectable,* 10 and 20 units/mL	Pig, hippopotamus, peccary, and synthetic
Ornipressin (ornithine vasopressin)	(For local hemostasis.)* 5 units/mL	Synthetic
Felypressin (phenylalanine vasopressin)	No longer available	Synthetic
Oxytocin (argiprestocin)	Buccal tablets, 100 and 200 units Lingual tablets,* 10 units Nasal solution,* 100 units/mL Nasal spray, 40 units/mL Injectable, 2 units/mL	Many vertebrates and synthetic
Vasotocin	None available	Nonmammalian vertebrates (reported to be present in the human fetus)

*Outside USA.

quired earlier in pregnancy. The administration of small amounts of oxytocin is capable of stimulating apparently normal labor; however, when large amounts are given, tetanic contractions of the uterus occur.

Oxytocin is most safely administered in the form of a dilute intravenous solution containing about 10 units/L of 5% dextrose. The solution is administered at a very slow rate that can be gradually increased until effective contractions occur. This procedure should be carried out under the supervision of a physician, with careful attention to the frequency and intensity of contractions and the effects of these contractions on the fetal heart tones. When oxytocin is used in combination with amniotomy, it is possible to induce labor in almost any patient at or near the end of pregnancy.

Oxytocin is also used after delivery to facilitate recovery of the placenta. It may also be given to enhance uterine contractions for the purpose of reduc-

ing the amount of bleeding. However, it is not usually employed in this way, since the ergot derivatives (see Chapter 14) produce a rapid and long-lasting response with low toxicity.

Contraindications & Cautions

The major adverse reaction is related to the production of tetanic contractions of the uterus. However, lack of care and control of infusions occasionally leads to the administration of large amounts of water and the production of hyponatremia.

Labor should not be induced by oxytocin if there are any abnormalities of the uterus or if the patient has had previous uterine surgery, or if the pelvic structures are too small to allow passage of the baby through the birth canal.

Preparations Available

See Table 39–7.

•   •   •

References

Bahl OP: Human chorionic gonadotropin. 1. Purification and physicochemical properties. 2. Nature of the carbohydrate units. J Biol Chem 244:567, 575, 1969.

Calne DB & others: Long-term treatment of parkinsonism with bromocriptine. Lancet 1:735, 1978.

Carroll BJ, Pearson JM, Martin FIR: Evaluation of three acute tests of hypothalamic-pituitary-adrenal function. Metabolism 18:476, 1969.

Catt KJ & others: Hormonal regulation of peptide receptors and target cell responses. Nature 280:109, 1979.

Cobb WE & others: Neurogenic diabetes insipidus: Management with DDAVP. Ann Intern Med 88:183, 1978.

Coulan CB & others: Pituitary adenoma and oral contraceptives: A case control study. Fertil Steril 31:25, 1979.

Crowley WF Jr & others: The biologic activity of a potent analog of gonadotropin-releasing hormone in normal and hypogonadotropic men. N Engl J Med 302:1052, 1980.

Cuellar FJ: Bromocriptine mesylate (Parlodel) in the management of amenorrhea/galactorrhea associated with hyperprolactinemia. Obstet Gynecol 55:278, 1980.

Daughaday WH, Herrington AC, Phillips LS: The regulation of growth by endocrines. Ann Rev Physiol 37:211, 1975.

Del Pozo E & others: Clinical and hormonal response to bromocriptine (CB-154) in the galactorrhea syndromes. J Clin Endocrinol Metab 39:18, 1974.

Deutsch S, Mescon H: Melanin pigmentation and its endocrine control. (2 parts.) N Engl J Med 257:222, 268, 1957.

Douglas RG, Kramer EE, Bonsnes R: Oxytocin: Newer knowledge and present clinical usage. Am J Obstet Gynecol 73:1206, 1957.

Edwards CW, Martin M, Besser M: Drugs and the posterior pituitary. In: *Endocrine-Metabolic Drugs.* McMahon FG (editor). Futura, 1974.

Frantz AG: Prolactin. N Engl J Med 298:201, 1978.

Growth Hormone. Excerpta Medica, International Congress Series No. 158. Excerpta Medica Foundation, 1968.

Hollenberg MD, Hope DB: The isolation of the native hormone-binding proteins from bovine pituitary posterior lobes: Crystallization of neurophysin-I and -II as complexes with (8-arginine)-vasopressin. Biochem J 106:557, 1968.

Kleeman CR, Fichman MP: The clinical physiology of water metabolism. N Engl J Med 277:1300, 1967.

Knobil E, Hotchkiss J: Growth hormone. Annu Rev Physiol 26:47, 1964.

Krejs GJ & others: Somatostatinoma syndrome: Biochemical, morphologic and clinical features. N Engl J Med 301:285, 1979.

Lerner AA, Case JD: Melatonin. Fed Proc 19:590, 1960.

Malarkey WB: Recently discovered hypothalamic-pituitary hormones. Clin Chem 22:5, 1976.

March CM & others: Galactorrhea and pituitary tumors in post-pill and non-post-pill secondary amenorrhea. (2 parts.) Am J Obstet Gynecol 134:45, 1979.

Martini L, Ganong WF (editors): *Neuroendocrinology.* 2 vols. Academic Press, 1967.

McGregor AM & others: Effects of bromocriptine on pituitary tumor size. Br Med J 2:700, 1979.

Milner RDG & others: Experience with human growth hormone in Great Britain: The report of the MRS working party. Clin Endocrinol 11:15, 1979.

Moses AM, Miller M, Stretin DHP: Pathophysiologic and pharmacologic alterations in the release and action of ADH. Metabolism 26:697, 1976.

Mroveh AM, Siler-Khodr TM: Bromocryptine therapy in cases of amenorrhea-galactorrhea. Am J Obstet Gynecol 127:291, 1977.

Parkes D: Drug therapy: Bromocriptine. N Engl J Med 301:873, 1979.

Peake GT & others: Ultrastructural, histologic and hormonal characterization of a prolactin-rich human pituitary tumor. J Clin Endocrinol Metab 29:1383, 1969.

Phillips LS, Vassilopoulou-Sellin R: Somatomedins. (2 parts.) N Engl J Med 302:371, 438, 1980.

Pittman JA: Thyrotropin-releasing hormone. Adv Intern Med 19:303, 1974.

Prader A & others: The metabolic effect of a small uniform dose of human growth hormone in hypopituitary dwarfs and in control children. 1. Nitrogen, α-amino-N, creatine-creatinine and calcium excretion and serum urea-N, α-amino-N, inorganic phosphorus and alkaline phosphatase. 2. Blood glucose response to insulin-induced hypoglycaemia. Acta Endocrinol (Kbh) 57:115, 129, 1968.

Robinson AG: DDAVP in the treatment of central diabetes insipidus. N Engl J Med 294:507, 1976.

Sairam MR, Li CH: Human pituitary lutropin: Isolation, properties, and the complete amino acid sequence of the β-subunit. Biochim Biophys Acta 412:70, 1975.

Sairam MR, Papkoff H, Li CH: Human pituitary interstitial cell stimulating hormone: Primary structure of the α subunit. Biochem Biophys Res Commun 48:530, 1972.

Sheppard M & others: Metabolic clearance and plasma half disappearance time of exogenous somatostatin in man. JCEM 48:50, 1979.

Tolis G, Franks S (editors): *Physiology and Pathology of Prolactin Secretion. Clinical Neuroendocrinology: A Pathophysiologic Approach.* Raven Press, 1979.

Treatment of abnormal height in children. Med Lett Drugs Ther 11:13, 1969.

Van Wyk JJ, Underwood LE: Relation between growth hormone and somatomedin. Annu Rev Med 26:427, 1975.

Wiebe RH, Hammond CB, Handwerger S: Treatment of functional amenorrhea-galactorrhea with 2-bromoergocryptine. Fertil Steril 28:426, 1977.

Yen SSC: Gonadotropin-releasing hormone. Annu Rev Med 26:403, 1975.

Yen SSC & others: The operating characteristics of the hypothalamic-pituitary system during the menstrual cycle and observations of biological action of somatostatin. Recent Prog Horm Res 31:321, 1975.

Part VI. Agents Used in the Treatment of Nutritional & Metabolic Derangements

40 | Drugs Used in the Treatment of Gout

Unlike most other mammals, humans are unable to convert poorly soluble uric acid to allantoin because they do not possess the enzyme uricase. Uric acid is a major end product of exogenous and endogenous purine metabolism (and thus indirectly of amino acid metabolism), and normal plasma and urinary uric acid levels are near the saturation point. A moderate increase in uric acid production can lead to the deposition of sodium urate microcrystals in and around the joints and in the kidneys and other tissues, and uric acid stones may form in the lumen of the urinary tract. These are the features of gout.

The treatment of gout may be aimed at (1) relieving an acute attack of gouty arthritis or (2) reducing the serum urate concentration by increasing excretion or blocking production in order to prevent recurrent attacks of inflammatory arthritis or to lead to resorption of urate deposits. In this chapter we will discuss, correspondingly, (1) colchicine, indomethacin, and other drugs used in treating an acute attack of gout; (2) urate diuretics such as probenecid and sulfinpyrazone; and (3) allopurinol, an inhibitor of uric acid synthesis.

COLCHICINE

Chemistry

Colchicine is an alkaloid isolated from the autumn crocus, *Colchicum autumnale*.

Pharmacologic Effects

Colchicine can dramatically relieve pain and bring about a decrease in the inflammatory changes of

Colchicine

gout in 12–24 hours. Yet it does not alter the metabolism or excretion of urates and has no generalized analgesic or anti-inflammatory action. The explanation of the effect of colchicine involves its reaction with microtubules and the mechanism of gouty inflammation.

Microtubules are the organelles responsible for intracellular motion, eg, the separation of chromosome pairs during mitosis, ameboid movements, and, presumably, the movements of phagocytosis. Microtubules are assembled by the polymerization of tubulin, a protein similar to actin. Colchicine, together with the vinca alkaloids discussed in Chapter 45, combines with tubulin to prevent its polymerization. As a result, colchicine is able, in the intact organism and in cultures, to arrest mitosis at metaphase. It is thus used to facilitate studies on the morphology of chromosomes and the rate of mitotic activity. It has been superseded by newer agents in cancer chemotherapy.

Gouty inflammation is initiated by urate crystals within tissue or joint space. The deposited crystals are ingested by neutrophils, but the crystals disrupt the phagolysosome formed, with the release of enzymes and the destruction of the cell. Not only is the crystal released to restart the cycle, but chemotactic factors are released that attract more neutrophils. Colchicine acts to prevent phagocytosis and also to prevent the release of chemotactic factors and the response of neutrophils to them. Definitive proof that the action of colchicine on phagocytosis is due to its action on microtubules is not yet available.

Clinical Uses

Colchicine is still the drug most often used to reduce the pain and inflammation of an attack of acute gouty arthritis, and it may also be given on a long-term basis to prevent or reduce the frequency of attacks. The specificity of the response to colchicine provides diagnostic information, but diarrhea is a common and disturbing side-effect. Phenylbutazone and indomethacin are as satisfactory as colchicine for the brief treatment of an acute attack, but colchicine is preferable for prolonged prophylactic use because of the greater toxicity of the nonspecific analgesics.

With the availability of drugs effective in lowering serum urate concentrations, the prolonged use of colchicine is now uncommon. Colchicine should be given concurrently with the hypouricemic agents early in treatment, since the patient is vulnerable to acute attacks when the urate deposits are mobilized.

Colchicine is almost specific for gout, acting on other inflammatory arthritis only rarely. By some undefined mechanism, it also prevents episodes of familial Mediterranean fever.

Adverse Reactions
A. Side-Effects: The important toxic effect that limits the patient's tolerance is diarrhea accompanied by nausea and vomiting and abdominal pain. These effects are systemic rather than local in origin and also follow parenteral administration.

The effect of colchicine in inhibiting mitosis is not a source of toxicity in this application.

B. Overdosage Toxicity: Acute intoxication following ingestion of large (nontherapeutic) doses of the alkaloid or its plant source is characterized by burning throat pain, bloody diarrhea, shock, hematuria and oliguria, and ascending central nervous system depression.

Dosages
For terminating an attack, the dosage is usually 1 or 1.2 mg orally initially followed by 0.5 or 0.6 mg every hour until the pain is relieved or nausea and diarrhea appear. When the need or tolerance of the patient has been previously established (usually 4–8 mg), the initial dose should be 1 mg less. If necessary, the drug may be given intravenously.

The prophylactic dose of colchicine is 0.5 mg 3 times daily.

OTHER DRUGS USED FOR ACUTE ATTACKS OF GOUT

Indomethacin (Indocin) & Congeners
The anti-inflammatory nonnarcotic analgesics (see Chapter 27) may be used either as initial treatment or when treatment with colchicine is unsuccessful or causes too much discomfort. Indomethacin is the analgesic most often used and may actually be nearly as popular as colchicine.

Phenylbutazone (Butazolidin) is also effective and has a slight uricosuric effect in addition to its anti-inflammatory action.

Corticotropin or Corticosteroids
Prednisone or other anti-inflammatory steroid or ACTH will terminate an acute attack of gout. However, the effect is a nonspecific suppression of the inflammatory reaction, which reappears when the drug is discontinued. Since colchicine or phenylbutazone will probably have to be used ultimately, treatment should be started with one of these drugs and the steroid added only if necessary.

URICOSURIC AGENTS
(Sulfinpyrazone & Probenecid)

Two drug effects can be used to control serum urate concentrations for indefinite periods in order to prevent arthritis and renal damage. The first is the increase of urinary excretion of uric acid by interference with renal tubular reabsorption. The second is the decrease of uric acid synthesis by allopurinol.

Chemistry
Uricosuric agents or urate diuretics compete with uric acid at the anionic transport sites of the renal tubule. To do this they must be organic acids. The structures of the 2 most commonly used uricosuric drugs, sulfinpyrazone and probenecid, are shown above together with that of uric acid. Sulfinpyrazone is a metabolite of an analog of phenylbutazone (Table 27–3).

Absorption, Metabolism, & Excretion
Probenecid is completely reabsorbed by the renal

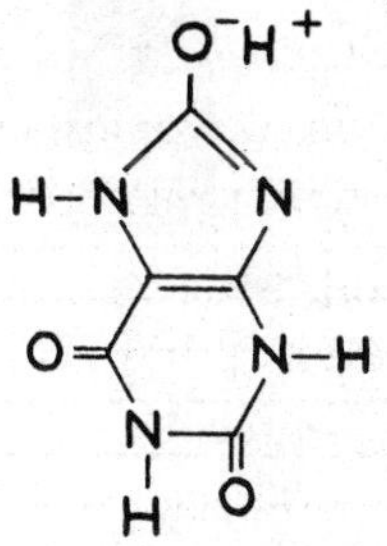

Uric acid

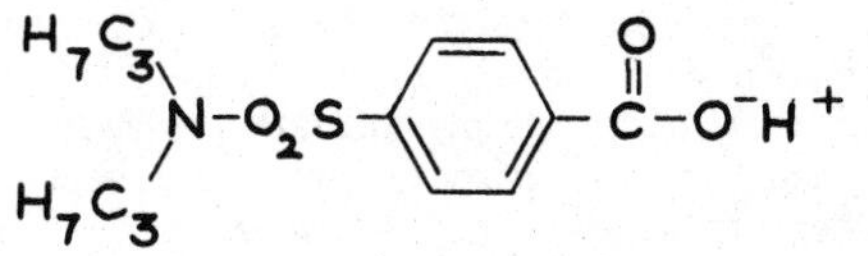

Probenecid
(Benemid)

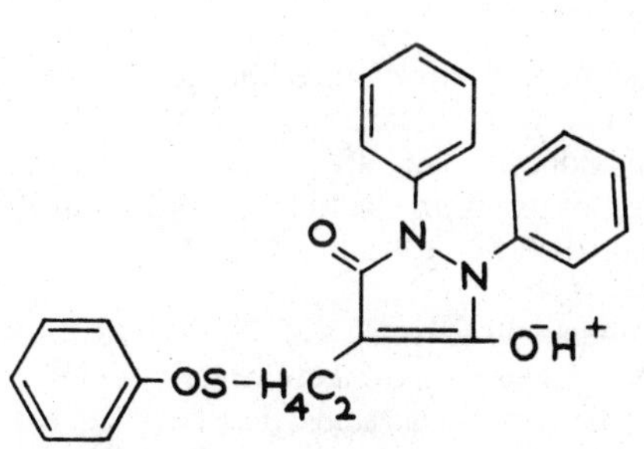

Sulfinpyrazone
(Anturane)
(enol form)

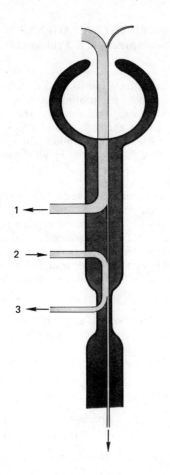

carrier presumed to be involved in the tubular transport mechanism could preempt the capacity (tubular maximum) at either the reabsorbing or the secreting sites.

Small doses of uricosuric agents may preferentially reduce secretion and have a uric acid retaining effect, but therapeutic doses block reabsorption and greatly increase the urinary output of uric acid. (The salicylates are unsatisfactory because large doses are required to reach a uricosuric effect; smaller doses cause a net retention of uric acid. They should not be used even as analgesics in patients with gout.)

The secretion of other organic acids—eg, PSP and penicillin—is reduced by uricosuric agents. Probenecid was developed as an agent to prolong penicillin blood levels.

The reabsorption of phosphate anion is also reduced.

B. Effects: As the urinary excretion of uric acid increases, the plasma level may not be greatly reduced but the size of the urate pool decreases. In patients who respond favorably, tophaceous deposits of urate will be resorbed, with relief of arthritis and remineralization of bone. With the ensuing increase in uric acid excretion, the predisposition to the formation of renal stones is augmented rather than decreased; therefore, the urine volume should be maintained at a high level and, at least early in treatment, the urine pH kept above 6.0 by the administration of alkali.

Clinical Uses

The effectiveness of probenecid and sulfinpyrazone is established not only by increased urinary excretion and somewhat lower plasma levels of uric acid but also by decreased frequency of acute arthritic attacks and by x-ray and gross observations of the depletion of urate deposits in the tissues.

Therapy should be initiated when acute attacks have occurred, when physical or x-ray evidence of tophi appears, or when plasma levels of uric acid are so high (> 8 mg/dL) that tissue damage is almost inevitable. Therapy should not be started until 2–3 weeks after an acute attack.

Probenecid was used in the past to block the renal tubular secretion of penicillin and reduce penicillin excretion to that amount provided by glomerular filtration. It is now more practical merely to increase the dosage of penicillin.

Adverse Reactions

Side-effects do not provide a basis for preferring one or the other of the uricosuric agents. Both of these organic acids cause gastrointestinal irritation, but sulfinpyrazone is more active in this regard and should be administered with food. Probenecid is more likely to cause allergic dermatitis, but a rash may appear after the use of either compound.

Contraindications & Cautions

The essential caution is to maintain a large urine volume to minimize the possibility of stone formation.

Figure 40 –1. Renal handling of uric acid and sites of action of drugs. At the glomerulus, all but the protein-bound urate (5%) is filtered into tubular urine. *1:* In the proximal tubule, virtually all urate is actively reabsorbed. Uricosuric agents—sulfinpyrazone, probenecid, and large doses of aspirin—act preferentially at this site to increase the amount of urate that remains in tubular urine. *2:* In the anion secretion site of the proximal tubule, approximately half of the amount of urate originally filtered and reabsorbed is secreted into tubular urine. The usual doses of aspirin and very small doses of the uricosuric agents reduce urate secretion at this site. *3:* Of the secreted urate, about 80% is actively reabsorbed at a more distant site.

tubules and very slowly metabolized. Sulfinpyrazone or its active hydroxylated derivative is rapidly excreted by the kidneys. Yet, after oral administration, the duration of its effect is almost as long as that of probenecid. (See Fig 40–1.)

Pharmacologic Effects

A. Mechanisms of Action: Uric acid, like many other anions of weak acids, is freely filtered at the glomerulus. It is completely reabsorbed in the proximal convolution and then secreted by another system for the transport of organic acids in the proximal tubule. Another anion with a greater affinity for the

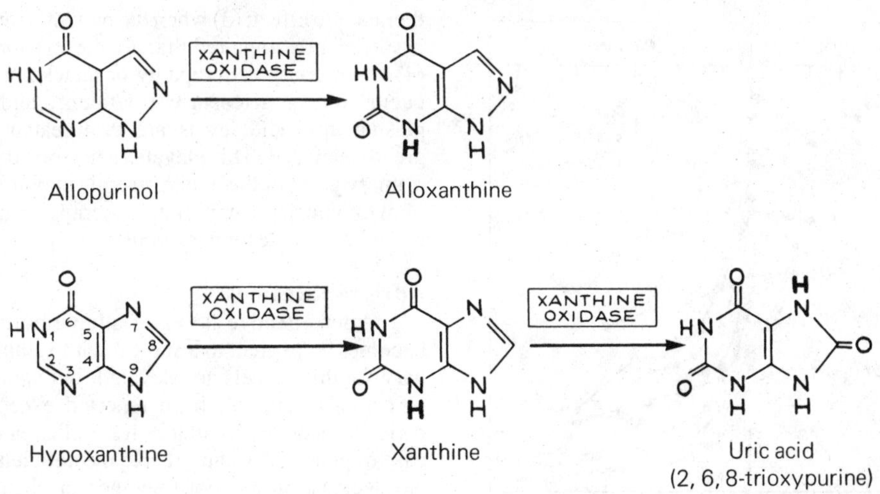

Figure 40–2. Inhibition of uric acid synthesis by allopurinol. Hypoxanthine (from inosine) or xanthine (from guanine) is converted to uric acid by aerobic oxidation. Xanthine oxidase is inhibited by allopurinol and its metabolite alloxanthine.

The urine of patients with gout tends to be acid— perhaps, as one hypothesis suggests, because the synthesis of ammonia from glutamine is reduced. If urine volume can be maintained at 2 L or more per day, the addition of alkali is not essential but is advisable early in treatment.

Initiation of treatment with the urate diuretics is believed by some physicians to be associated with an increased risk of acute arthritic attacks. This impression may be carried over from experience with the salicylates. Some physicians give colchicine (0.5 mg 3 times a day) for some weeks when beginning therapy with probenecid or sulfinpyrazone. Salicylates should not be used in combination with these drugs, since some of the uricosuric effect will be lost.

Sulfinpyrazone also inhibits the renal secretion of penicillin G and accentuates the action of coumarin type anticoagulants. It potentiates the action of sulfonamides and the hypoglycemia caused by sulfonurea agents and insulin. It is contraindicated in active peptic ulcer.

Probenecid may decrease renal elimination of a number of drugs including rifampin, indomethacin, sulfonamides, allopurinol, aminosalicylic acid, cephalosporins, dapsone, furosemide, and nalidixic acid. It should not be given to patients receiving methotrexate.

Dosages

The dosage of probenecid is 0.25 g twice daily for 1 week and 0.5 g twice daily thereafter. If necessary (and tolerated), the dosage may be increased in 0.5-g increments to 2 g/d.

Begin sulfinpyrazone (Anturane) with 50 mg 4 times daily with meals and at bedtime with milk, increasing to 400 mg/d (divided as above) within 1 week. If necessary (and tolerated), dosage may be increased to 800 mg/d.

Urinary output should be maintained at 2 L or more to prevent precipitation of uric acid in the urinary tract. In early treatment, maintain urine pH above 6.0 by administration of alkalinizing agents.

ALLOPURINOL
(Inhibitor of Uric Acid Synthesis)

An alternative increasing uric acid excretion in the treatment of gout is to reduce its synthesis by inhibiting xanthine oxidase with allopurinol.

Chemistry

The structure of allopurinol, an isomer of hypoxanthine, is shown in Fig 40–2.

Metabolism

Allopurinol is itself acted upon by xanthine oxidase. The resulting compound, alloxanthine, retains the ability to inhibit xanthine oxidase and has a long enough duration of action so that allopurinol need be given only once daily.

Pharmacologic Effects

A. Mechanisms of Action: Dietary purines are a comparatively unimportant source of uric acid. The quantitatively important fractions of purines are formed from amino acids, formate, and CO_2 in the body. Those purine ribonucleotides not incorporated into nucleic acids and those derived from the degradation of nucleic acids are converted to xanthine or hypoxanthine and oxidized to uric acid. When this last step is inhibited by allopurinol, there is a fall in the plasma urate level and a decrease in the size of the urate pool (Fig 40–3).

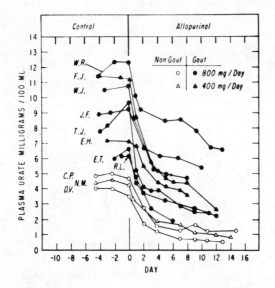

Figure 40–3. The effect of allopurinol on the concentration of urate in plasma of gouty and normal subjects. (Reproduced, with permission, from Klinenberg & others: The effectiveness of the xanthine oxidase inhibitor allopurinol in the treatment of gout. Ann Intern Med 62:643, 1965.)

B. Effects: The only pharmacologic effects of allopurinol are those that result from inhibition of uric acid synthesis. Serum uric acid levels begin to fall immediately, and normal or subnormal levels are reached in 7–10 days. Resorption of tophaceous deposits is gradual, but is usually impressive within 6–12 months.

Clinical Uses

Treatment with allopurinol, as with the uricosuric agents, is begun with the expectation that it will be continued for many years if not for life. One of the indications or predictors of damage listed above should be present before treatment is initiated. It is not indicated for treatment of asymptomatic hyperuricemia, ie, of a patient with no history of gout or urate lithiasis.

Whether allopurinol or one of the uricosuric agents is selected is a matter of individual preference. Both are effective and relatively safe. Allopurinol is a newer agent, and some investigators continue to express concern about the possible toxicity of an agent that causes such interesting biochemical changes.

Allopurinol clearly would be preferable (1) when probenecid or sulfinpyrazone cannot be used because of side-effects or allergic reactions; (2) when the uricosuric agents are providing a less than optimal therapeutic effect; (3) when the patient's renal function is sufficiently impaired that urate excretion is limited; (4) when gouty nephropathy or attacks of renal colic occur during uricosuric treatment; and (5) when plasma uric acid levels are or threaten to become greatly elevated. This elevation may occur with severe primary gout, or the hyperuricemia may follow the use of cytotoxic drugs or radiation therapy in the treatment of leukemias (secondary gout).

Adverse Reactions

After effective doses of allopurinol, the patient becomes equivalent to a subject with xanthinuria. Urinary xanthine levels are elevated, but xanthine stones or crystals have not been reported except in a few patients receiving treatment for leukemia or in a rare case of genetically caused enzyme deficiency disease. No decrease in alcohol tolerance or changes in iron metabolism have been reported, although these could conceivably have followed xanthine oxidase inhibition.

A. Side-Effects: Acute attacks of gouty arthritis occur early in treatment with allopurinol when urate crystals are being withdrawn from the tissues and plasma levels are below normal. To prevent acute attacks, colchicine should be given during the initial period of therapy with allopurinol unless allopurinol is being used in combination with probenecid or sulfinpyrazone. Gastrointestinal intolerance, including nausea and vomiting and diarrhea, may occur. Peripheral neuritis and necrotizing vasculitis, depression of bone marrow elements, and, rarely, aplastic anemia may also occur.

B. Allergic Reactions: As many as 3% of patients develop a pruritic maculopapular rash. A type of allergic reaction similar to drug fever occurs less commonly. Isolated cases of exfoliative dermatitis have been reported.

C. Interactions and Contraindications: The dose of mercaptopurines given concomitantly must be reduced by about 25%. Allopurinol may also increase the effect of cyclophosphamide. Allopurinol inhibits the metabolism of probenecid and oral anticoagulants and may increase hepatic iron concentration. The drug is contraindicated in children, nursing mothers, and individuals known to be hypersensitive to the drug.

Dosages

The initial dose of allopurinol (Zyloprim) is 100 mg daily. A daily dose of 300 mg is reached in 3 weeks and is adequate for most patients.

Colchicine, 0.5 mg twice daily, should be given also during the first weeks of therapy.

● ● ●

References

Boss GR, Seegmiller JE: Hyperuricemia and gout: Classification, complications and management. N Engl J Med 300:1459, 1979.

Goldfinger SE: Drug therapy: Treatment of gout. N Engl J Med 285:1303, 1971.

Krakoff IH: Clinical pharmacology of drugs which influence uric acid production and excretion. Clin Pharmacol Ther 8:124, 1967.

Landgrebe AR, Nyhan WL, Coleman M: Urinary-tract stones resulting from the excretion of oxypurinol. N Engl J Med 292:626, 1975.

Muggia FM, Ball TJ Jr, Ultmann JE: Allopurinol in the treatment of neoplastic disease complicated by hyperuricemia. Arch Intern Med 120:12, 1967.

Rodnan GP & others: Allopurinol and gouty hyperuricemia: Efficacy of a single daily dose. JAMA 231:1143, 1975.

Schweitz MC, Nashel DJ, Alepa P: Ibuprofen in the treatment of acute gouty arthritis. JAMA 239:34, 1978.

Scott JT: Symposium on allopurinol. Ann Rheum Dis 25:599, 1966.

Velayos EE, Smyth CJ: Urate diuretic therapy in chronic gout: A comparative study of probenecid and sulfinpyrazone. Arch Intern Med 116:212, 1965.

Wilson GM Jr, Huffman ER, Smyth CJ: Oral phenylbutazone in the treatment of acute gouty arthritis. Am J Med 21:232, 1956.

Wilson L & others: Interaction of drugs with microtubule proteins. Fed Proc 33:158, 1974.

Wright DG & others: Efficacy of intermittent colchicine therapy in familial Mediterranean fever. Ann Intern Med 86:165, 1977.

Yü TF: Milestones in the treatment of gout. Am J Med 56:676, 1974.

41 | Vitamins & Other Therapeutic Nutritional Agents

This chapter will discuss vitamins as therapeutic agents and the reduction of atherosclerosis, a metabolic disease treated by diet as well as by hypolipidemic drugs.

THE VITAMINS

The skeptical and negative attitude with which many people now approach the discussion of vitamins as therapeutic agents suggests to others either that they do not appreciate the importance of vitamins or that they are callously forgetting that not all populations are overfed. Let us begin, therefore, by acknowledging the biochemical importance of the vitamins and the great contribution to human welfare that has been made by those who have elucidated the role of vitamins in nutrition.

However, the function of this section is not to review the biochemistry of vitamins but to discuss vitamins as drugs used in humans. Several vitamins with specific, well-understood therapeutic functions are discussed elsewhere in this book— cyanocobalamin (vitamin B_{12}), folic acid, the K vitamins, and vitamin D. The problem with the therapeutic applications of the remaining vitamins is that the need is mostly to argue against their use except in the form of natural foodstuffs. The important exceptions of infants, some pregnant women, and those rare individuals suffering from vitamin deficiencies will not be ignored, but the burden of this discussion is to evaluate the promiscuous and unestablished uses of vitamins. The intention is not to deprecate nutritional studies. On the contrary, preoccupation with the vitamins has probably delayed our understanding of other areas of nutritional therapy—eg, the treatment of atherosclerosis.

For each vitamin, certain information is needed to judge the advisability or necessity of its supplementation in the diet. The most important of these factors is the daily requirement. The data on a representative water-soluble vitamin and a representative fat-soluble vitamin will be examined in detail in order to provide information against which certain suggested minimum daily requirements can be measured.

I. FAT–SOLUBLE VITAMINS*

VITAMIN A

The fat-soluble vitamins, of which vitamin A is a convenient example, have several characteristics in common. They may occur in plant tissues either as the vitamin or as a provitamin, but in animals they are concentrated in a few tissues. Their absorption parallels that of other fats, and deficiencies may occur during interference with fat absorption—eg, the deficiency of vitamin K with hypoprothrombinemia that occurs during obstructive jaundice. Fat-soluble vitamins are stored in the liver and to a lesser extent in other fatty tissues. The stores are large, and utilization or excretion extremely slow.

Source & Chemistry

Vitamin A is provided by butterfat, eggs, liver, and, to a lesser extent, by other meats. Precursors of vitamin A, the carotenoid pigments, are present in large amounts in colored vegetables and fruits and are converted, although inefficiently, to vitamin A in the intestinal mucosa.

Human Requirement

Early in World War II, the governments of the USA and Great Britain became concerned with possible nutritional deficiency in the civilian population and attempted to establish minimum daily requirements. In the USA, the effort was made by a committee of the National Research Council (NRC). Although the report of the committee was labeled as conjectural, the high allowances it reported provided an authoritative basis for the exploitation of fears of undernutrition. In

*For fat-soluble vitamins D and K, see Chapters 36 and 18, respectively.

1955, presumably because of misuse of the recommendations, the Food & Nutrition Board decided to withhold further printing of the report. However, a revised report with essentially the same allowances was recently published.

The British effort involved the collection of new data, and this experience will be discussed here and in the section on vitamin C to show that the theoretic allowances are unreasonably high. Twenty-three conscientious objectors were isolated and placed on a diet lacking butter, whole milk, liver, fat, fish, and all colored vegetables. The trial was continued for 14 months, at which time only 3 of the volunteers showed changes in dark adaptation greater than the seasonal variation seen in control subjects on a diet adequate in vitamin A. This minor change was effectively treated with 1300 units of vitamin A per day—ie, the therapeutic dose appears to be 1300 units or less per day even though the NRC maintenance allowance has been placed at 5000 units per day. Plasma carotenoids disappeared within a few weeks on the above diet, but the mean plasma vitamin A content fell less than 30% during the 14 months. Thus, vitamin A stores in the body are adequate to meet the needs of humans for extended periods without supplementary vitamins.

Vitamin A deficiency does occur in malnourished children in tropical countries of Southeast Asia, Latin America, Africa, and the Middle East. In very young children, the corneal epithelium may be irreversibly damaged (xerophthalmia), and an associated susceptibility to infection leads to many deaths.

Toxicity

The indiscriminate use of vitamin A, unlike the use of most vitamins, cannot be justified on the basis that it at least does no harm. Toxic reactions have occurred in children given large amounts of high-potency oils by their mothers and in adults who have taken unusually large amounts because of the alleged anti-infective action of an excess of the vitamin or some other faddist concept. In studies of possible pharmacologic actions of vitamin A, toxicity has been therapeutically induced. In children, the important toxicity consists of cortical (subperiosteal) hyperostosis and interference with bone growth. In adults, changes include dry, itching, scaling skin, hyperkeratosis, fatigue, hepatomegaly, and cirrhosis but no bone changes or alterations in calcium dynamics.

VITAMIN D
(See Chapter 36.)

VITAMIN E

A variety of heavy oils, the tocopherols, possess vitamin E activity. α-Tocopherol, the synthetic form used as a dietary supplement, is given in the form of the stable acetate which is converted in the body to the free alcohol that is the active form of the vitamin. The richest sources of tocopherols are vegetable oils, especially wheat germ oil, but they are so widely distributed in common foods that a dietary deficiency is probably impossible except transiently in the newborn. However, defects in absorption are possible.

Deficiency State in Humans

The effect of vitamin E deficiency in animals varies widely with the species studied. In the adult human, studies of the deficiency state are difficult because a vitamin E-deficient diet is so difficult to prepare. In the only feeding experiment available, 19 adults were placed on a diet containing one-third the amount of vitamin E found in the typical American diet and compared with a control group. The experiment continued for 8 years. Blood levels of α-tocopherol declined to 20% of control levels, but there was no apparent impairment beyond a minor decrease in erythrocyte survival time.

In a few premature infants (birth weight less than 1500 g), vitamin E deficiency has occurred, resulting in hemolytic anemia and edema. These episodes occurred in association with the use of commercial formulas that combined a high content of polyunsaturated fats with a low content of vitamin E. Polyunsaturated fats increase the requirement for vitamin E but ordinarily are correspondingly rich sources of the vitamin. The vitamin E content of infant formula is now regulated. Iron supplementation also favors the development of the deficiency.

Vitamin E also protects the adult erythrocyte against peroxide-induced hemolysis. If erythrocytes from deficient animals or humans are exposed to hydrogen peroxide, the cell membrane is altered and hemolysis occurs in a larger fraction of the cells than in a sample from a normal subject. Vitamin E, either fed or added in vitro, protects against the hemolysis. In the presence of steatorrhea, depletion of tocopherol can be demonstrated and the red cells of a fraction of these patients will be unusually susceptible to peroxide hemolysis.

Human Requirement

The nominal human requirements are based on the amounts of vitamin E found in an adequate diet and not on any dietary or therapeutic trials. In the presence of impaired fat absorption, the absorption of vitamin E will also be decreased and the dietary requirement will be more than the 15 IU/d of α-tocopherol usually said to be the daily requirement. (An international unit is the activity of 1 mg of DL-α-tocopherol acetate.)

Toxicity

Vitamin E is much more widely used than would be predicted from the above data. The uses derive from the misapplication of data from animal studies and from clinical trials that could never be replicated. Demonstrated toxicity has been limited to a single reported case of creatinuria. A few uncontrolled observations suggest that malaise may follow the use of large doses.

II. WATER–SOLUBLE VITAMINS

ASCORBIC ACID
(Vitamin C)

Ascorbic acid and the B vitamins are water-soluble. Interference with the absorption of the water-soluble vitamins is not a problem, but rediffusion into the intestinal lumen (as may occur during diarrhea) and excretion by the kidney can remove significant amounts. The water-soluble vitamins are distributed more uniformly throughout the tissues, and there are no large depots such as that of vitamin A in the liver. The water-soluble vitamins are therefore more rapidly depleted than the fat-soluble vitamins. The rapidity of the process and the amount of supplementation required are probably less than is generally stated.

Source & Chemistry
Vitamin C is present in significant amounts in all fruits and vegetables. Foods of animal origin, with the exception of milk, are not important sources of vitamin C. Ascorbic acid is stable only when in acid solution and protected from air; it is destroyed by heating in contact with oxygen. Fruits maintain their vitamin C content. Vegetables lose their vitamin C content during storage unless they are "living foods" such as potatoes or bananas—ie, plants whose cells continue metabolic activity during storage. Frozen and canned vegetables vary in their content of ascorbic acid but usually contain useful amounts.

Human Requirements
A. In Infants: Scurvy can occur at any age, but the needs of the very young will be considered separately, since there is no disagreement about the need for vitamin C supplementation. The extremely rare cases of scurvy seen today occur most often between the ages of 7 months and 2 years.

Breast milk contains vitamin C in adequate amounts. Commercial (powdered) formulas contain added vitamin C, but the amount preserved or destroyed depends upon the extent of heating during preparation. It is, therefore, standard practice to add supplementary ascorbate to the diet until the infant is eating fresh or commercially canned or frozen fruits or vegetables and "living foods" such as bananas. A solution of ascorbic acid or a preparation containing several other vitamins may be added by dropper to the formula *after* sterilization, or multivitamin drops may be given orally.

B. In Adults: Scurvy does occur in adult pri-

mates, but the decision about when supplementation is indicated should be based on information on how long a period of deprivation is required to produce scurvy and what the minimum daily requirement is. The NRC allowance of 60 mg may be compared with the figure derived from a human experiment. Under double-blind conditions, volunteers (conscientious objectors) were placed in several groups. All received a diet that contained no more than 1 mg/d of ascorbic acid.

One group of 7 subjects received a supplement of 10 mg/d of vitamin C and showed no abnormalities after 160 days, and 4 of these were continued on the trial for 14 months without the appearance of abnormal signs.

A group of 10 subjects received no vitamin C supplementation. The subjects in this group developed hyperkeratosis and enlargement of the hair follicles after 17–21 weeks of deprivation. After 26–34 weeks, perifollicular hemorrhages were seen; after 30–38 weeks, swelling and bleeding from the gums occurred. The effect on wound healing was assayed by observing the healing of standardized incisions made on the thigh down to the fascia lata. Only after 7 months on the experimental diet did old scars become livid and new scars heal poorly. The other expected or classic signs of scurvy were not demonstrated. It should be noted that 100 days elapsed between the disappearance of vitamin C from the plasma and the appearance of symptoms—ie, biochemical and clinical criteria of deficiency are not the same. All of the changes regressed in 1–2 weeks in response to 10 mg/d of ascorbic acid with the exception of the gum changes, which required 10–14 weeks.

Both the maintenance and the therapeutic dose of ascorbic acid appear to be less than 10 mg/d rather than the much larger amounts suggested by the NRC.

Pharmacologic Effects
Pharmacologic amounts of vitamin C—ie, doses too large to relate to the nutritional effects of a vitamin—were claimed on the basis of the intuition of an eminent scientist to prevent and cure the common cold.

None of the controlled studies done subsequent to the introduction of large dosages of ascorbate into wide use suggest that vitamin C has any effect in preventing colds or undifferentiated upper respiratory infections. There are, however, trials that suggest that ascorbic acid, 0.5–2 g/d, will slightly reduce the number of days of morbidity associated with each attack. There are fewer symptomatic days per infection because of less cough and runny nose and, possibly, less malaise.

The question whether one should at this time recommend taking ascorbic acid every day in an attempt to prevent or modify the effects of colds is one the physician should be prepared to answer. The clinical trials do involve difficult problems of design, and important questions of diagnosis, dosage, and age and sex of responsive patients remain unanswered. Furthermore, not all studies have given results concordant with the above summary. Toxicity has been limited to signs of gastrointestinal irritation and the potential danger of a chronically acid urine, but experience with large doses of ascorbate is limited. The possible benefits are comparatively small, and it would seem reasonable therefore to await the results of additional careful studies before recommending widespread use of vitamin C for this purpose. The same must be said of the practice of taking large doses of ascorbate at the onset of symptoms—no data are available to validate the many anecdotal claims of benefit in terminating the infectious process early.

The usefulness of supplementary ascorbic acid in other situations has not been established. Two qualifications must be added pending further information: (1) It is possible that supplementary ascorbic acid may favorably influence bacterial pharyngitis and tonsillitis; and (2) the requirement for ascorbate is increased postoperatively, especially if inflammation is prominent, and amounts as large as 300 mg/d may be necessary to establish biochemical repair. However, no relationship between the biochemical defect—ie, decreased levels of ascorbate—and defective wound healing has been established, although the adverse effect of true ascorbic acid deficiency on wound healing is well established. The role of vitamin C in wound healing is presumably related to the importance of the vitamin in collagen formation; vitamin C is essential for the conversion of proline to hydroxyproline in a protein precursor of collagen.

Not only are there no data to justify the use of vitamin C in patients with cancer—there are controlled trials demonstrating the absence of any benefit for any purpose except demonstrated deficiency resulting in clinical signs of scurvy.

OTHER WATER–SOLUBLE VITAMINS

1. THIAMINE
(Vitamin B₁)

Thiamine deficiency occurs in 2 widely different situations. It may occur in populations subjected to real nutritional deficiency, or in groups that still use polished rice as a staple food—ie, discard all but the starch-containing portion—to the exclusion of other foods. (The daily requirement of thiamine is proportionate to the amount of carbohydrate metabolized.)

It may also occur in an occasional chronic alcoholic patient who derives most caloric needs from alcohol and the sugar in fortified wine. These patients may develop cardiac (wet) beriberi with high output congestive failure, Wernicke's encephalopathy (cerebral beriberi), or Korsakoff's psychosis due to thiamine deficiency. The peripheral neuropathy also seen (dry beriberi) is less clearly related to thiamine deficiency.

Vitamin deficiencies are often multiple in the above situations, and treatment should provide supplements of more than just thiamine.

2. NIACIN
(Nicotinic Acid)

Nicotinic acid is converted to nicotinic acid amide in the body or may be ingested as the amide. Nicotinic acid amide is incorporated into nicotinamide adenine dinucleotide (NAD, DPN). Niacin and niacinamide are the official names in the USA.

The deficiency state associated with niacin is pellagra. Niacin can be synthesized in the body from tryptophan. Epidemic pellagra, now controlled, therefore occurred only in the southern USA and a few other areas (Egypt, South Africa) where corn, which is virtually free of tryptophan, was a staple in the diet. Sporadic pellagra is extremely rare; dietary sources of tryptophan or niacin are abundant; in fact, in many countries several times the minimum daily requirement is present in the beans and coffee consumed.

Secondary pellagra, with dermatitis (but not necessarily the expected triad including diarrhea and dementia), has been reported rarely in association with isoniazid therapy, carcinoid syndrome, and Hartnup's disease.

Niacin and niacinamide have been used for nonnutritional or pharmacologic effects in 3 situations without demonstrated efficacy in any of them:

(1) Nicotinic acid (but not the amide) is a vasodilator. Except when large doses are given intravenously, its action is limited to the skin, causing a flush and an intense feeling of warmth. No beneficial action on the cerebral or peripheral circulation has been shown.

(2) The action of nicotinic acid in lowering blood lipid levels and its toxicity are discussed below.

(3) Niacinamide or NAD has been used in the treatment of schizophrenia and drug-induced hallucinatory states, and nicotinic acid is used in the treatment of alcoholism. The effectiveness claimed initially has not been verified by controlled studies.

3. PYRIDOXINE
(Vitamin B₆)

Dietary Deficiency

The pyridoxine deficiency state cannot ordinarily be produced by dietary restriction, its demonstration requiring the use of a competitive antagonist, deoxypyridoxine, or depletion with an amine as described below. In one incident or brief epidemic, infants maintained on a proprietary formula lacking pyridoxine (and perhaps because of the particular fat

Table 41–1. Vitamins essential or probably essential to human nutrition.

Vitamin*	Action	Deficiency Symptoms	Sources	RDA†
Vitamin A (A_1 and A_2)	Constituents of visual pigments; maintain epithelia	Night blindness, hyper-keratosis	Colored vegetables and fruit	5000 IU
B complex				
Thiamine (B_1)	Coenzyme for pyruvate decarboxylation and in hexose monophosphate shunt	Beriberi, neuritis	Liver, unrefined cereal grains	1.5 mg
Riboflavin (B_2)	Constituent of riboflavin adenine dinucleotide (FAD)	Glossitis	Liver, milk	1.7 mg
Niacin	Constituent of NAD	Pellagra	Yeast, lean meat, liver	20 mg
Pyridoxine (B_6)	Forms prosthetic group of decarboxylases and transaminases. Converted in body to pyridoxal phosphate and pyridoxamine phosphate.	Convulsions, hyperirri-tability	Yeast, wheat, corn, liver	2 mg
Pantothenic acid	Constituent of CoA	Burning feet syndrome in humans (?)		10 mg
Biotin	Catalyzes CO_2 "fixation" (in fatty acid synthesis, etc)	Dermatitis, enteritis in animals	Egg yolk, liver, tomatoes	0.3 mg
Vitamin C	Role in collagen synthesis and other unknown actions	Scurvy	Fruits and vegetables	60 mg
Vitamin E		Hemolytic anemia in humans	Milk, eggs, meat, leafy vegetables, wheat germ	30 IU

*Cyanocobalamin (Vitamin B_{12}) and folic acid are discussed in Chapter 44; vitamin K in Chapter 18; and the D vitamins in Chapter 36.

†Recommended Daily Allowances for adult men, Food and Nutrition Board, NAS-NRC.

added) exhibited irritability and even convulsions relieved by supplemental pyridoxine.

Pyridoxine Depletion by Isoniazid

When this vitamin is used as a drug, it is administered in the form of pyridoxine, an alcohol (Table 41–1). It is converted in the body to pyridoxal and functions as a coenzyme in the form of pyridoxal phosphate. Aldehydes such as pyridoxal can react with compounds that are amines to form Schiff bases, which may be stable. (See reaction below.)

$$R_1-\overset{\overset{\displaystyle H}{|}}{C}=O + H_2N-R_2 \rightleftharpoons R_1-\overset{\overset{\displaystyle H}{|}}{C}=N-R_2 + H_2O$$

Isoniazid (isonicotinic acid hydrazide) given chronically can deplete the organism of pyridoxal by increasing its excretion, presumably by the reaction shown above. Peripheral or even optic neuritis can result. If more than 5 mg/kg/d of isoniazid is administered, pyridoxine, 50 or 100 mg daily, should be given.

Pyridoxine-Responsive Anemias

These rare anemias are hypochromic microcytic anemias accompanied by hyperferremia and hemosiderosis. Large doses of pyridoxine or, preferably, pyridoxine phosphate (50–200 mg intramuscularly daily) elevate hemoglobin to normal. No other signs of pyridoxine deficiency appear.

4. FLAVONOIDS

The flavonoids or vitamin P are of interest in relation to the question of how drug efficacy is evaluated rather than because of any nutritional effect. These compounds are yellow plant pigments with a distribution similar to that of vitamin C. From animal experiments, it was concluded that in scurvy they are able to correct capillary fragility more effectively than vitamin C alone. This tentative conclusion was extended to provide indications for their use in many forms of vascular disease and bleeding and in the prevention of colds. When the reevaluation of the efficacy of drugs first marketed in the USA between 1938 and 1962 was begun by the Food & Drug Administration and its outside advisors, these were the first drugs to be ordered withdrawn from the market. At the time, more than 200 prescription and over-the-counter preparations were in use.

GENERAL CONSIDERATIONS IN THE USE OF VITAMINS

"Subclinical Deficiencies"

Recognizable vitamin deficiencies are extremely rare. However, it is conceivable that persistent slight deficiencies might impair bodily functions before the overt signs of deficiency appear, and the claim is constantly made that routine vitamin supplementation is beneficial to health. If these claims are justified, it should be possible to support them by objective evidence under controlled experimental conditions—ie, the criteria of effectiveness should be the same as for any other drug. The fact is that no beneficial effects from multivitamin supplementation have been shown in trials that include placebo control groups. Groups of senile patients in a rest home and groups of steel workers, to select very diverse examples, have been used in trials of this kind. In the latter case, the work records, absenteeism, subjective reports, and slitlamp examination of the eyes did not show any difference between vitamin-supplemented and placebo control groups.

Trials with groups of older patients show that the usual "stimgas" of vitamin deficiency cannot be accepted as evidence of deficiency unless control groups receiving adequate nutrition are shown not to develop the same signs as a result of aging or other causes. Thickening of the bulbar conjunctivas, cheilosis, corneal vascularization, sublingual purpura, and glossodynia are examples of signs that occur independently of the nutritional status and are not altered by treatment with vitamins.

A Biochemical Fallacy

Chemical determinations and nutritional surveys can contribute to the impression that subclinical vitamin deficiencies are a widespread health problem if clinical defects are not used as one criterion of deficiency. If plasma levels of a vitamin, values for excretion products, or even calculated dietary intakes are tabulated for a specific group, the values will be normally distributed and reflect the normal dietary pattern established by cultural and economic factors acting on the group; however, they do not establish minimal or optimal standards. Subjects falling outside of the usual range of variation may be labeled as vitamin deficient, but this does not establish that a deficiency important to the individual exists unless verified by clinical data.

Effects of Real Dietary Deprivation

From the foregoing, it may be inferred that most of the vitamins prescribed in our overfed culture are wasted. This conclusion is reinforced by the observation that even when dietary restriction is extreme, vitamin deficiency is only a minor nutritional problem. Consider, for example, an incident in western Holland at the end of World War II. This population, conditioned by wartime restrictions, was isolated for 6–10 months between the German embargo and the Allied occupation. The diet was 1000 kcal/d (500 if the individual was unable to forage). Five percent of the population developed serious malnutrition, as evidenced by the fact that 10% of the patients admitted to hospitals died. These emaciated, exhausted people showed no signs of vitamin deficiency except, occasionally, redness and tenderness of the tip of the tongue possibly

due to nicotinic acid deficiency. Even more unexpectedly, the mental abilities of those exposed in utero to the deprivation were not impaired when they were tested at age 19.

Prisoners of war repatriated from the Far East did show signs of vitamin deficiency after their long imprisonment, but even in these cases much of the "beriberi" was unresponsive to thiamine and represented protein deficiency.

The results of dietary deprivation in the very young also emphasize the greater importance of protein and total calories rather than vitamins. Undernutrition—ie, deficiency of total calories—in an infant leads to marasmus. The child shows terrible atrophy of muscular and subcutaneous tissues, and growth stops; but organ structure and function and even behavior are less affected.

Protein deficiency in the growing child, usually with some caloric restriction, is seen in many tropical countries beset by poverty and ignorance of nutrition. It is most often called kwashiorkor. Growth and nutrition are arrested; the child is apathetic and anorexic; decreased plasma protein and edema are present; the skin is atrophic and shows hyperkeratosis and pigmentation not distributed in such a way as to suggest pellagra; and the liver is fatty. Vitamin A deficiency may coexist, but no vitamin deficiency is of importance compared to the deficiency of essential amino acids.

When Are Vitamins Indicated?

The ordinary diet in our western culture is more than adequate in quality and amount, and supplementary vitamins have already been added to many staple foods—especially milk, bread, and cereals. Deficiency states will occur only in the presence of a specific disease, during the use of some specific drug, or when alcoholism or other aberrant behavior has led, as it sometimes does, to a deficient diet. Vitamins should be used as other drugs are used—when specific indications are present—and should not be used as tonics or placebos. The danger of indiscriminate use of vitamins does not lie in the extremely rare toxic effect nor even the expense involved, but in the manner in which they may delay or prevent the understanding and treatment of the complaint of the patient. For example, in the treatment of fatigability or other symptoms of neurotic anxiety, the use of vitamins as a "tonic" or simply to provide some positive action may reinforce the patient's conviction that some organic problem is present.

Vitamin Supplementation in Pregnant & Lactating Women

Vitamin supplements have been almost routinely provided as part of prenatal care, but no evidence has accumulated to suggest that they have a favorable effect on the health of the mother or the newborn. For reasons discussed below, the only routine dietary supplements required are iron, calcium, and perhaps, in some communities, folic acid.

Staple foods and infant foods are now enriched with iodine (a most important nutritional factor during pregnancy), vitamins, and even iron. It is customary to justify supplementary vitamins by reasoning that they at least do no harm. However, there is evidence that hypercalcemia and permanent damage may be induced in a few infants by the amounts of vitamin D provided in fortified foods, and less substantial evidence connects excessive intake of vitamin D during pregnancy with congenital heart defects. The British government has acted to reduce the potency of vitamin D supplements. Drastic vitamin deficiencies, often induced with antimetabolites rather than by dietary means, can cause congenital defects in laboratory animals, but there is no epidemiologic evidence associating any diet pattern with the incidence of congenital defects in humans.

The definition of "quality" in the diets of pregnant women is incomplete, but protein content is probably more important than vitamins.

Preparations Available

Preparations of single vitamins are available, and there are indications for the use of a few of them—eg, ascorbic acid in infants, pyridoxine during isoniazid therapy, and perhaps thiamine early in the treatment of malnutrition associated with chronic alcoholism. Usually, however, a preparation containing many vitamins is preferable. Official preparations based on the recommended maintenance and therapeutic allowances are established, and there are many equivalent preparations. Specific preparations or retailers may be suggested, but there is no need to prescribe in the usual way, since even the preparations of single vitamins are available without prescription and are less expensive when so ordered. A prescription is required for those preparations that contain in a single dose more than 10,000 IU of vitamin A or more than 400 IU of vitamin D.

Vitamin A is not given by itself. Vitamin D is discussed in Chapter 36.

III. THE PSEUDOVITAMINS

Laetrile, a substance derived from pulverized apricot pits, has been widely promoted for the prevention, treatment, and cure of cancer. The claim that the drug is a vitamin (B_{17}) has *not* been borne out by any scientific investigation. The major component of laetrile is amygdalin, a cyanide-containin glycoside capable of causing serious and even fatal poisoning. The weight of responsible evidence suggests that the drug has no place in the treatment of cancer.

Pangamic acid (vitamin B_{15}) is a nonvitamin substance introduced by the same individual who created laetrile. At one time it contained dichloroacetate, but it is now dimethylglycine and is claimed to increase athletic performance. It is marketed as a food supplement in health food stores and thus escapes regulation as a drug.

TREATMENT OF HYPERLIPIDEMIA & ATHEROSCLEROSIS

The intense interest in hyperlipidemia and in methods for lowering the concentration of lipids in the plasma is due to the overwhelming importance of atherosclerotic arterial disease as a cause of mortality and morbidity.

Atherosclerosis is a disease of arteries rather than of arterioles (as in hypertension) and can lead to occlusion of coronary, cerebral, and other peripheral arteries. Atherosclerotic lesions develop from the intimal and subintimal deposition of lipid material. Initially the composition of the lipids deposited resembles that of plasma lipids, and it is generally held that lipids are deposited in atherosclerotic plaques by filtration from plasma.

The distribution of the lesions is patchy rather than uniform, and the process shows a predilection for areas of tortuosity and turbulent flow—eg, the sharply branching coronary arteries. The mechanical factors are mentioned as a reminder that hypertension accelerates the progression of atherosclerosis. Restoration of a normal blood pressure in a hypertensive patient (see Chapter 12) is an important factor in controlling atherosclerosis.

As the atherosclerotic plaque ages, the composition of the included lipids changes and fibrosis and calcification occur. However, the process is more or less reversible even late in its course—ie, there is a hopeful basis for treatment.

The Predictive Value of Hyperlipidemia

Many large-scale prospective studies, some lasting for as long as 20 years, have shown a strong positive correlation between the plasma level of cholesterol and excess mortality and morbidity due to coronary artery disease. The relationship is graded—ie, as levels rise progressively from 200 mg/dL, the risk doubles at 250 mg/dL and is fourfold at 280 mg/dL.

The Hyperlipidemias

Serum cholesterol and triglyceride determinations are inexpensive and suitable for following the results of treatment, especially in large studies such as those mentioned above. However, these water-insoluble substances are not transported in the plasma as such but as components of different lipoproteins. These lipoproteins may be described on the basis of

Table 41–2. Major clinical features of primary hyperlipidemias.

Hyperlipidemia Phenotype	Elevated Plasma Component	Incidence	Plasma Cholesterol	Plasma Triglycerides	Accelerated Atherosclerosis	Treatment
I	Chylomicrons	Rare	N/↑	↑	No	Diet: Low-fat.
II	LDL VLDL (less)	Common	↑	N/↑	Yes	Diet: Low in saturated fats and cholesterol. Increased unsaturated fats. Cholestyramine Nicotinic acid
III	Abnormal VLDL	Uncommon	↑	↑	Yes	Weight reduction Diet: Low in saturated fats and carbohydrate. Clofibrate
IV	VLDL	Common	N/↑	↑	Yes	Weight reduction Diet: Increased unsaturated fats, decreased carbohydrates.
V	Chylomicrons	Uncommon	↑	↑	Not known	Weight reduction Diet: Low-fat, low-carbohydrate

↑ = Elevated
N/↑ = Elevated or normal but not diagnostic

LDL = Low-density lipoprotein (β)
VLDL = Very low density lipoprotein (pre-β)

their behavior in the ultracentrifuge or their electrophoretic mobility, or they may be chemically analyzed.

The discussion will refer to (1) VLDL—very low density lipoproteins, pre-β-lipoproteins, rich in triglycerides; and (2) LDL—low-density lipoproteins, β-lipoproteins, cholesterol-rich lipoproteins.

The hyperlipidemias may be a primary entity or may occur secondary to some other pathologic state. Plasma lipids may be elevated secondary to the altered lipid metabolism of diabetic ketosis, hypothyroidism, the nephrotic syndrome, biliary obstruction, or acute alcoholism. Treatment of these secondary hyperlipidemias is aimed at the underlying disease, but drugs may be used—eg, cholestyramine in biliary obstruction.

The major clinical features of the primary hyperlipidemias are summarized in Table 41–2.

The balance of this discussion (except as otherwise noted) refers to type IV, the common endogenous hyperlipemia.

DRUG TREATMENT

1. CLOFIBRATE
(Atromid-S)

Drugs may be used to supplement the benefits of caloric restriction, exercise, and control of hypertension and smoking. The long-term benefits of the chemical changes induced by hypocholesterolemic drugs must be small compared to those resulting from the control of other risk factors. The most widely used drug is clofibrate, selected as the most promising agent

some years ago on the mistaken premise that it was an inhibitor of cholesterol synthesis.

Chemistry

Clofibrate (ethylchlorophenoxyisobutyrate) and its congener probucol (Lorelco) are the only 2 of a large number of comparable compounds yet available for use.

Clofibrate (Atromid-S)

Absorption & Metabolism

Clofibrate is well absorbed after oral administration. After absorption, it is rapidly hydrolyzed to the free acid, bound to plasma albumin, and distributed to extracellular sites. Excreted in the urine as the glucuronide, it is comparatively long-acting, with a chemical half-life of 12 hours, but is nevertheless given 4 times daily.

Pharmacologic Effects

A. Mechanisms of Action: The mechanism by which clofibrate reduces the plasma levels of triglyceride-rich VLDL and, to a lesser extent, the level of cholesterol-rich LDL is not known. It decreases the synthesis of VLDL or perhaps of the protein component of that lipoprotein and also increases its catabolism.

B. Effects: In a population with some initial elevation of plasma lipid levels, clofibrate will reduce the levels of VLDL (pre-β, triglyceride-rich); of LDL (β-lipoprotein, cholesterol-rich) to a lesser extent; and of free fatty acids. As a result, triglyceride levels decrease 30–40% and cholesterol levels 10–20%. The higher the initial levels, the greater the decrease. The effect has been maintained for more than 6 years in individual patients and in groups of patients.

Clofibrate also corrects abnormal platelet adhesiveness, decreases fibrinogen levels, and increases fibrinolysis. Since the therapeutic effects discussed below do not correlate with the lipid-lowering action of clofibrate, these other less completely studied mechanisms may be very important.

Clinical Uses

There are 2 indications for the use of clofibrate as a supplement to other treatment. The first (and less controversial use) is in the treatment of a hyperlipidemia that is symptomatic—eg, with xanthomas or abdominal pain—and that cannot be treated with diet alone. Clofibrate may even be used in a patient with secondary hyperlipemia—eg, a diabetic with lipemic retinopathy. In these situations, the fall in plasma lipid levels reflects a decrease in tissue stores.

The other use, still unestablished, is in asymptomatic patients with the common endogenous hyperlipemia to defer or prevent coronary occlusions, and presumably, other atherosclerotic disease.

Clofibrate can decrease the level of cholesterol and β-lipoproteins, the best predictors of coronary artery disease, although it is more active in lowering triglyceride levels. Whether such lowering will decrease morbidity must be established by adequately controlled clinical trial.

A collaborative study in hospitals of Scotland and England used patients with preexisting atherosclerotic heart disease. This more vulnerable group of 1214 patients was given clofibrate or a placebo for as long as 6 years. Fatal myocardial infarctions occurred in 13% of the controls and 10% of the treated subjects. If patients with angina are excluded, there was little difference in total infarctions in the 2 groups. Surprisingly, patients with angina, who would seem to have less reversible lesions, benefited more than those without angina, and the overall effect did not correlate well with the lipid-lowering effect. These results are in contrast to the effect of dietary treatment, which has no demonstrable benefit when coronary artery disease is already manifest, and they bring into question the relationship between any benefits and an effect on cholesterol.

Clofibrate was also included in the agents studied by the Coronary Drug Project, a large collaborative analysis of the effects of various drug treatments on the course of 8341 men who had already experienced myocardial infarcts. Clofibrate persistently lowered cholesterol and triglyceride levels during the 5–8 years but did not significantly alter the mortality rate.

A WHO study, also prospective and collaborative, used men without previous myocardial infarctions and followed groups of 5000 for 13 years. Plasma cholesterol fell 9% overall (subjects were not stratified into responders and treatment failures), and there was a 20% reduction in the number of nonfatal infarcts in the group with an initially elevated cholesterol level. However, no overall effect on the mortality rate associated with cardiovascular disease was noted.

Adverse Effects

Side-effects of clofibrate have been infrequent. Nausea is common (5%) but usually disappears with continued treatment. Liver function tests (SGOT) are depressed early in treatment. Brittle hair is noted by some women patients, and isolated cases of alopecia have been reported. Male patients report decreased libido and breast tenderness.

Gallbladder disease is slightly more common in patients receiving clofibrate. Clofibrate is carcinogenic in rodents, and the labeling thus suggests that it be used only in patients in whom dietary intervention has failed.

Contraindications & Cautions

In many (but not all) patients, administration of clofibrate leads to intensification of the effect of anticoagulants of the warfarin type, requiring a reduction in the dosage of the inhibitor of 30–50%. Like other drugs that are acids, clofibrate displaces warfarin from the albumin to which it is bound in the plasma. However, plasma levels of warfarin rise rather than fall as they would if displacement were the only mechanism acting; this suggests that clofibrate interferes with the metabolism of warfarin.

Dosages

The dosage of clofibrate (Atromid-S) is 500 mg 4 times a day.

Congeners

Of the many other drugs that interfere with cholesterol synthesis, only probucol (Lorelco) has been marketed. In its effects, it is generally similar to clofibrate, but studies of its long-term efficacy are not available. Cardiotoxicity has been demonstrated in dogs (sensitization to epinephrine) and monkeys (QT prolongation).

2. BILE ACID–BINDING RESINS

Cholestyramine (Questran) and colestipol (Colestid) are basic anion exchange resins, quaternary ammonium chlorides able to exchange chloride for the cholate ion. They are not absorbed after oral administration but appear in the feces together with the bile salts bound to them.

Bile acids—eg, cholic acid or, in the alkaline medium of the small intestine, the bile salt, cholate—are metabolites of cholesterol. They are usually reabsorbed from the intestine and undergo repeated enterohepatic cycling. If they are bound by a resin, their daily excretion is greatly increased, with 2 consequences: (1) In the presence of partial biliary obstruction and jaundice, itching due to the accumulation of bile salts may be relieved; and (2) cholesterol may be depleted as cholic acid synthesis is stimulated. The drugs are useful in type II hyperlipoproteinemia as an adjunct to dietary therapy.

Adverse Reactions

Both of these alkaline resins cause gastrointestinal irritation (nausea, heartburn, and diarrhea) and irritation of the tongue or perianal region. They may cause depletion of vitamins A and D, and there have been rare reports of depletion of vitamin K. They may also combine with other drugs and interfere with their absorption.

Contraindications & Cautions

Consider the need for supplementary vitamins A, D, and K. Give other drugs 1 hour before giving the resin. They should be given suspended in an adequate volume of fluid.

3. OTHER DRUGS

Nicotinic Acid

Given the large doses required, nicotinic acid or niacin (but not the related nicotinic acid amide or niacinamide) causes a reduction in VLDL and LDL. Fat is stored in adipose tissue as triglycerides but is released from fat cells for transport as free fatty acids. It is assumed that the demonstrated ability of nicotinic acid to partially block the release of free fatty acids explains its effect on blood lipids. No effect on the clinical course of atherosclerotic disease has been established.

In the dosage necessary, nicotinic acid almost invariably causes side-effects. Nicotinic acid is a vasodilator of cutaneous vessels and causes a cutaneous flush with itching and feelings of warmth. Gastrointestinal irritation is apparent as nausea, heartburn, and diarrhea. The skin may become dry, and brown pigmentation may appear.

Tests of liver function are depressed. Jaundice may occur. Hyperuricemia is common.

Treatment should begin with low dosage—eg, 250 mg 4 times daily—which is increased over a period of 2–3 weeks to 3 g/d.

Dextrothyroxine (Choloxin)

Endogenous or exogenously induced hyperthyroidism leads to a decrease in cholesterol levels by increasing the rate of excretion and metabolism of cholesterol more than it increases its rate of synthesis. Laboratory studies suggest that some thyroxine analogs can achieve the effect on cholesterol catabolism without increasing the metabolic rate and perhaps precipitating anginal pain in susceptible individuals. The margin between the effective and toxic doses of the one compound used, dextrothyroxine, is narrow. The Coronary Drug Project discontinued the use of dextrothyroxine in the study because of an excessive number of deaths in the treatment group.

Estrogens

Premenopausal women are much less susceptible to atherosclerosis than men of the same age. The administration of estrogens to men produces a female pattern of plasma lipids—eg, total cholesterol is not decreased but occurs more as α-lipoproteins and less as the β-lipoproteins presumed to be associated with the development of atherosclerosis. Feminizing effects occur with the dosage necessary, and an effect is not demonstrable with synthetic estrogens. In the Coronary Drug Project, both dosage levels of conjugated estrogens have been discontinued because of a lack of therapeutic effect and an excessive number of deaths due to thrombotic episodes in the treated group.

Triparanol

Cholesterol present in the organism is derived in part from dietary sources, but synthesis in the liver is more important because it can increase to compensate for changes in the diet. Inhibition of hepatic synthesis would lower plasma cholesterol.

Triparanol (MER/29), a drug no longer marketed, blocked the synthesis of cholesterol at the last step in the series of reactions. The immediate precursor of cholesterol, desmosterol or 24-dehydrocholesterol, accumulated in the organism. After the drug had been marketed for 18 months, an association with the development of cataracts and other less serious adverse reactions was established. It was also established that the manufacturer and 3 scientists had withheld data from animal toxicity testing that anticipated the human toxicity.

Cholesterol is synthesized from acetate. One of the first reactions in the complex sequence is the production of mevalonic acid, and it is this early reaction that is blocked in isolated tissues by clofibrate. Thus, even if the inhibition of cholesterol synthesis should be a property of clofibrate, the triparanol type of toxicity would not be anticipated.

Sitosterols

The sitosterols are plant sterols that are chemically very similar to cholesterol. They are not absorbed following oral administration and decrease the absorption of dietary cholesterol and the enterohepatic cycling of endogenous cholesterol and bile acids. The resulting reduction in plasma cholesterol and LDL is small even when very large doses of this expensive drug are given.

TOTAL PARENTERAL NUTRITION

It is now feasible to administer all required nutritional substrates by parenteral means. Total parenteral nutrition may be successfully employed for extended periods when adequate enteral intake is impossible, improbable, inadvisable, or hazardous. This has proved to be effective and even lifesaving in severe alimentary disturbances and a wide variety of conditions such as extensive trauma or burns, acute and chronic renal failure, and overwhelming infection.

The basic nutrient solution for the average adult consists of 24–80% dextrose, 4–5% synthetic amino acid solution (Freamine, Aminosyn, Travamin), electrolytes, and vitamins. Anabolic requirements of electrolytes include approximately 40 mEq potassium, 20 mEq phosphorus, 35 mEq calcium, 8 mEq magnesium, and sodium as needed per 1000 kcal. The basic solution must be modified for specific individual requirements. A lipid soybean emulsion (Intralipid), a 10% solution containing essential fatty acids and 1.1 kcal/mL, is given twice weekly to prevent fatty acid deficiency. Vitamins and trace elements are added as needed.

The nutrient solution is usually infused into a subclavian vein via catheter. Complications of total parenteral nutrition include physical injuries to structures adjacent to the catheter, local and sytemic infection, and metabolic disturbances.

• • •

References

Vitamins

Babb RR, Kieraldo JH: Cirrhosis due to hypervitamin A. West J Med 128:244, 1978.

Coulehan JL & others: Vitamin C and acute illness in Navajo schoolchildren. N Engl J Med 295:973, 1976.

Cox EV & others: The anemia of scurvy. Am J Med 42:220, 1967.

Crandon JH & others: Ascorbic acid economy in surgical patients as indicated by blood ascorbic acid levels. N Engl J Med 258:105, 1958.

Creagan ET & others: Failure of high-dose vitamin C therapy to benefit patients with advanced cancer. N Engl J Med 301:687, 1979.

Dykes MHM, Meier P: Ascorbic acid and the common cold: Evaluation of its efficacy and toxicity. JAMA 231:1073, 1975.

Goodman DS & others: Vitamin A and retinoids: Recent advances. Fed Proc 38:2501, 1979.

Goldsmith GA: Niacin: Antipellagra factor, hypocholesterolemic agent. JAMA 194:167, 1965.

Horwitt MK: Vitamin E: A reexamination. Am J Clin Nutr 29:569, 1976.

Horwitt MK, Century B, Zeman A: Erythrocyte survival time and reticulocyte level after tocopherol depletion in man. Am J Clin Nutr 12:99, 1963.

Karlowski TR & others: Ascorbic acid for the common cold: A prophylactic and therapeutic trial. JAMA 231:1038, 1975.

Lane M, Alfrey CP Jr: The anemia of human riboflavin deficiency. Blood 25:432, 1965.

Levy JV, Bach-y-Rita P: *Vitamins, Their Use and Abuse.* Liveright, 1976.

Lewis J: Laetril. West J Med 127:55, 1977.

Mason DY, Emerson PM: Primary acquired sideroblastic anaemia: Response to treatment with pyridoxal-5-phosphate. Br Med J 1:389, 1973.

Miller JZ & others: Therapeutic effect of vitamin C: A co-twin control study. JAMA 237:248, 1977.

Muenter MD & others: Chronic vitamin A intoxication in adults. Am J Med 50:129, 1971.

Russell RM & others: Hepatic injury from chronic hypervitaminosis A resulting in portal hypertension and ascites. N Engl J Med 291:435, 1974.

Scriver CR: Pyridoxine deficiency and dependency. Am J Dis Child 113:109, 1967.

Silverman S Jr, Eisenberg E, Renstrup G: A study of the effects of high doses of vitamin A on oral leukoplakia, including toxicity, liver function and skeletal metabolism. J Oral Ther Pharmacol 2:9, 1965.

Tyrrell DAJ: A trial of ascorbic acid in the treatment of the common cold. Br J Prev Soc Med 31:189, 1977.

Vaisrub S: Vitamin abuse. JAMA 238:1782, 1977.

Vitamin-C requirement of human adults: Experimental study of vitamin-C deprivation in man. Medical Research Council. Lancet 1:853, 1948.

Undernutrition

György P: Protein-calorie and vitamin A malnutrition in Southeast Asia. Fed Proc 27:949, 1968.

Keys A, Sinclair H: Real nutritional deficiency. Br Med Bull 8:262, 1952.

Scrimshaw NS, Béhar M: Malnutrition in under-developed countries. (2 parts.) N Engl J Med 272:137, 193, 1965.

Stein Z & others: Nutrition and mental performance. Science 178:708, 1972.

Waterlow JC: Some aspects of childhood malnutrition as a public health problem. Br Med J 4:88, 1974.

Williams ML & others: Role of dietary iron and fat on vitamin E deficiency anemia of infancy. N Engl J Med 292:887, 1975.

Hypolipidemic Agents

Bilheimer DW: Needed: New therapy for hypercholesterolemia. N Engl J Med 296:508, 1977.

Coronary Drug Project Research Group: Clofibrate and niacin. JAMA 231:360, 1975.

Coronary Drug Project Research Group: Estrogen. JAMA 226:652, 1973.

Levy RI: Drug therapy of hyperlipoproteinemia. JAMA 235:2334, 1976.

Levy RI & others: Cholestyramine in type II hyperlipoproteinemia: A double-blind trial. Ann Intern Med 79:51, 1973.

Oliver MF: Cholesterol, coronaries, clofibrate and death. N Engl J Med 299:1360, 1978. [See also: Committee of Principal Investigators: A cooperative trial in the primary prevention of ischaemic heart disease using clofibrate. Br Heart J 40:1069, 1978; Lees RS: Clofibrate and atherosclerosis. N Engl J Med 300:491, 1979.]

Various authors: Clofibrate in ischemic heart disease. Br Med J 4:765, 1971.

Total Parenteral Nutrition

Dudrick SJ, Long JM III: Applications and hazards of intravenous hyperalimentation. Annu Rev Med 28:317, 1977.

Law DH: Current concepts in nutrition: Total parenteral nutrition. N Engl J Med 297:1104, 1977.

42 | Specific Ions: Iron, Fluoride

Ions with osmotic as well as specific chemical effects are discussed as components of parenteral fluids in Chapter 43. Many metals are discussed as toxic agents (Chapter 65), and other ions—eg, calcium, lithium, iodide, or ammonium—are discussed in appropriate places elsewhere in this book.

IRON

Absorption

There are 2 mechanisms for the absorption of ferrous iron. The physiologically important mechanism involves active transport and is able to alter the absorption of iron as need changes. The second mechanism, diffusion across the mucosal barrier, is important after administration of large doses.

The first, or physiologic, process occurs in the duodenum and adjacent jejunum. Of the ferrous iron that enters the mucosal cell, a fraction is transported to the blood but some is converted to ferric iron, held within the protein apoferritin, and stored in the mucosal cells as ferritin. The iron in ferritin is lost into the feces as the mucosal cells are shed at the end of their 5-day life cycle. When an excess of iron is available and stores of ferritin are large, absorption of iron is limited—ie, a "mucosal block" is established.

The large amounts of iron administered therapeutically can partially bypass the above mechanism. However, the control mechanisms must still operate, since administration of an initial dose of ferrous sulfate decreases the amount absorbed from a second dose given 6 hours later, and chronic toxic effects from the prolonged administration of iron are extremely rare.

The presence or absence of gastric acid has little effect on the absorption of iron in the ferrous form. The absorption of dietary iron or ferric salts is greatly enhanced by gastric acid, which favors conversion of iron to the ferrous form and perhaps also favors the formation of chelates with ascorbate and other dietary components. Such chelates remain soluble in the alkaline intestinal contents. The absorption of iron is decreased by gastrectomy (subtotal). The concurrent administration of antacids decreases absorption, as does the combination of iron with phosphate and other

components of food also.

Supplemental iron is best absorbed when given in the fasting state but is nevertheless given with meals to reduce local irritation.

Metabolism & Pharmacologic Effects

Following absorption, iron (as the ferrous ion) combines with CO_2 and a globulin, transferrin, and is carried to several sites. A small fraction (3 mg) functions in metallo-enzymes; about 200 mg are incorporated into myoglobin; and the largest fraction (2500 mg) is incorporated into hemoglobin within red blood cells. About 1 g of iron is stored as ferritin in marrow, liver, and spleen and is available for the synthesis of hemoglobin should blood be lost from the body. Ordinarily, of course, erythrocytes are destroyed and replaced without the loss of any component.

The daily loss of iron in desquamated cells is as low as 1 mg/d. Women may lose an additional 20–30 mg/month, and pregnancy requires replacement of about 500 mg. With the exception of the toxic effect of large doses of iron on the gastrointestinal tract, the pharmacologic action of iron is the same as its action as a dietary factor—ie, to maintain iron stores and hemoglobin synthesis.

Clinical Uses

The only use of systemically administered iron salts is to correct or prevent iron deficiency anemias. Only about half of the iron in food is available for absorption, and the dietary supply is not much above the need. Consequently, a slight increase in blood loss rapidly leads to depletion of the iron stores. Anemia—ie, depletion of hemoglobin iron—follows, and with severe deficiencies tissue iron is also depleted. Until the last stage, the symptoms of iron deficiency are entirely those of anemia.

In addition to blood loss (including that of menstruation), there are other situations that may precipitate iron deficiency and anemia.

Pregnancy places an additional demand on iron stores, which are often marginal at the beginning of pregnancy. Supplementary iron during the later months of pregnancy can maintain hemoglobin to some extent and hasten its resynthesis after the blood loss of delivery. However, most of the anemia of pregnancy is dilutional, as the increase in plasma vol-

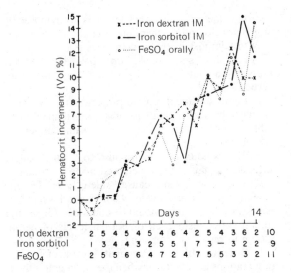

Iron dextran	2	5	4	5	4	5	4	6	4	2	5	4	3	6	2	10
Iron sorbitol	1	3	4	4	3	2	5	5	1	7	3	–	3	2	2	9
$FeSO_4$	2	5	5	6	6	4	7	2	4	7	5	5	3	3	2	11

Figure 42–1. Comparison of the similar rates at which 2 parenteral iron preparations and oral ferrous sulfate correct an iron deficiency anemia. The figures at the bottom are the number of patients included at each point on the graph. (Reproduced, with permission, from McCurdy: Oral and parenteral iron therapy. JAMA 191:861, 1965.)

ume is accompanied by a smaller increase in red cell mass.

Iron deficiency anemia is also common in infants during their first year, and supplementary iron may be needed. The iron stores of full-term infants (but not prematures) are large enough for the needs of the first few months even if the mother was deficient in iron. Rapid growth takes place at a time when dietary iron may be scant, since cow's milk, including the evaporated milk from which the most economical formula is made, contains very little iron. Some prepared formulas and the cereals prepared for infant feeding contain added iron, but these are least likely to be used in the families where they are most needed. In all prematures and in the children of economically marginal families, supplementary iron (as drops providing 1–2 mg/kg in each daily dose) should be supplied during the first year.

Following subtotal gastrectomy, iron absorption is reduced and the need for supplementary iron should be anticipated.

Since the dietary supply of iron is so marginal, supplementary iron (together with thiamine, riboflavin, and niacin) has been added to "enriched" flour since World War II. The resulting breads make up to about two-thirds of those consumed in the USA. There has never been any evidence that the added iron is absorbed in significant amounts when the bread is part of an ordinary meal rather than a simple test meal, and the 2 epidemiologic studies that might have assayed the effect of added iron gave conflicting results. In spite of the dubious state of the evidence, a doubling of the amount of added iron is still proposed. This action is questioned by some hematologists and consumers,

who doubt its effectiveness and fear that toxicity might result in susceptible groups—eg, males with hemochromatosis or a genetic predisposition to that disease and those with sickle cell anemia or cirrhosis.

Adverse Reactions

A. Side-Effects: Gastrointestinal side-effects—eg, gastric discomfort, cramps, and diarrhea—are very common (20% or more of patients) but are usually mild. The patient should be warned to expect black stools.

Side-effects are minimized by taking iron after meals.

B. Overdosage Toxicity: Acute toxicity in young children who accidentally ingest iron tablets is a common occurrence because iron is frequently prescribed for the mother and left about the house in some easily accessible place. As few as 10–30 tablets have been fatal in very young children.

The large amounts of iron involved cause a necrotizing gastroenteritis with bleeding and transudation into the lumen. Shock occurs either because of the loss of fluid or because of some more subtle change—eg, the vasodilating effect of large amounts of ferritin or the action of bacterial toxins that can cross the damaged intestinal wall. Metabolic acidosis and liver damage occur late in the course.

The course of the intoxication is conveniently but only approximately divided into phases. For the first 1–6 hours, the manifestations are those of gastroenteritis and shock—eg, vomiting and diarrhea of bloody material, shock, dyspnea, lethargy. Thereafter, the patient may recover or, after a transient period (6–24 hours) of improvement, develop a metabolic acidosis followed by coma and appearance of liver damage. A third phase that must be quite rare is recovery with scarring leading to pyloric stenosis.

Treatment. If the victim is not vomiting, eggs, milk, or water should be given and emesis induced. If the history justifies it, gastric lavage should then be carried out using a lavage solution that contains phosphate ion to combine with dissolved iron. Following lavage or induced emesis, a volume of phosphate solution appropriate to the size of the child should be left in the stomach to decrease the solubility of iron remaining in the lumen. A proper solution of buffered phosphate is most conveniently prepared by diluting a disposable enema 1:1.

Specific treatment depends upon the use of chelating agents (see Chapter 65), which complex with metal ions, removing them from solution and incorporating them into a less toxic chelate.

Deferoxamine (Desferal; see Fig 65–2) forms a nontoxic complex with iron with such avidity that it is able to extract iron from transferrin and ferritin. If signs of systemic iron toxicity appear, deferoxamine should be given either intramuscularly or by slow intravenous infusion.

Deferoxamine can cause a precipitous hypotension and should not be used unless an accurate history, the appearance of systemic signs of iron toxicity (shock), or the demonstration of an excess of serum iron over iron-binding capacity is present. It should not be used in the presence of anuria or severe renal disease. Deferoxamine (Desferal) is supplied as ampules containing 500 mg of the lyophilized deferoxamine mesylate.

Calcium disodium edetate (Calcium Disodium Versenate) should be used if deferoxamine is not available. Following lavage or emesis, 35–45 mg/kg may be placed in the stomach. Intravenous infusions of the same dose can be given daily if needed.

C. Chronic Toxicity: Hemochromatosis—ie, the deposition of hemosiderin in the parenchyma of the heart, liver, and other organs—has occurred in a few patients given iron for many years. Hemochromatosis also occurs as an inherited disease and following multiple transfusions. Removal of excess iron by treatment with deferoxamine is possible if allowance is made for the short half-life (30 minutes) of the chelator. Patients with thalassemia major, whose survival requires multiple transfusions, are effectively treated with continuous subcutaneous infusions.

Preparations & Dosages

A. Oral: The iron salts and chelates suggested for use can differ in their acute toxicity and in the incidence of side-effects that accompany their use. Both of these properties, like the therapeutic effect, depend upon the amount of iron contained in a dose; and in comparing available preparations, equivalent amounts of iron rather than equal doses of the salt must be compared. If this caution is accepted and if the studies are controlled as in other clinical trials, no superiority over ferrous sulfate can be demonstrated for any of the available preparations.

Ferrous sulfate is the standard drug. If side-effects interfere when it is used, the dose can be decreased or less iron given by substituting ferrous gluconate.

Several preparations are inferior to the sulfate.

Ferroglycine sulfate is a chelate that is decomposed by stomach acid and is, therefore, merely an expensive way to administer ferrous sulfate. A polysaccharide-iron complex can be made into a palatable pediatric preparation, but little if any of the iron can be absorbed.

Some sustained release preparations have been shown to provide less iron for absorption than ordinary tablets; another delivers exactly the same amount of iron as the inexpensive tablet.

The rapidity of the response to ferrous sulfate increases as the dose is increased up to 2 g/d. Such dosage almost always causes side-effects. Dosage should be started at a low level and increased slowly if necessary. Treatment should be continued for several months after restoration of normal levels of hemoglobin to replenish iron stores.

B. Injectable Iron Preparations: Injectable iron preparations are available when the parenteral route is indicated. It is generally thought that such indications are uncommon—eg, intolerance or failure of response to orally administered iron. Parenteral iron should not be used in patients with anemias other than iron deficiency—eg, hemolytic anemias—since iron overload will result. The response to intramuscularly administered iron is no more rapid than that after oral administration. The development of fibrosarcomas in animals after the injection of iron-dextran is well established, and the appearance of malignancies at the injection site has now been reported in 4 patients.

1. Iron-dextran injection (Imferon)–The iron-dextran complex contains 5% iron—ie, 50 mg of iron per mL of solution. Give 1 mL (50 mg iron) intramuscularly on the first day and then 2–5 mL daily or at longer intervals until the calculated dose has been given. Give 250 mg for each gram of hemoglobin below normal. Follow the directions for deep intramuscular injection to avoid discoloring the skin. Anaphylactic reactions have been reported.

2. Iron sorbitex (Jectofer) is an iron-sorbitol

Table 42–1. Iron for oral administration: Dosages and preparations available.*

	Iron Content	Usual Adult Dose (3–4 Times Daily)	Iron/ Dose	Examples of Preparations Available
Ferrous sulfate	20%	300 mg	60 mg	Tablets (plain, coated, or enteric-coated), 200, 300, and 325 mg Controlled release tablets, 525 mg Syrup or elixir, 125 mg/1 mL, 150 mg/5 mL, and 220 mg/5 mL Drops, 75 mg/0.6 mL
Ferrous sulfate, exsiccated (eg, Feosol)†	30%	200 mg	60 mg	Tablets and capsules, 200 mg Sustained release capsules, 150 mg
Ferrous gluconate (eg, Fergon)†	12%	300 mg	36 mg	Tablets (plain, coated, or enteric-coated), 325 mg Elixir, 300 mg/5 mL
Ferrous fumarate (eg, Toleron, Ircon)†	33%	200 mg	66 mg	Tablets (plain, coated, or chewable), 200, 225, 250, and 325 mg Suspension, 100 mg/5 mL

*Ferroglycine sulfate (eg, Ferronord), ferrocholinate (iron choline citrate; eg, Ferrolip, Chel-Iron), and polysaccharide-iron complex (eg, Niferex) are not recommended for use. See text. All preparations listed in the table are available without prescription.
†Available as generic preparations. Protected names shown only for identification.

complex comparable to iron-dextran complex (Imferon). It also contains 50 mg of iron per mL and is supplied as 2-mL ampules.

Ions Adjunctive to Iron

A number of ions—eg, copper, molybdenum, zinc—have been given with iron salts without evidence of usefulness. Cobalt, as cobaltous chloride, while no longer marketed, was active and perhaps useful. Cobalt stimulates the production of erythropoietin, leading in animals to polyeythemia and in humans to improvement in anemias associated with infection and uremia (for example). Unfortunately, its chronic use may lead to thyroid enlargement and hypothyroidism.

FLUORIDE

This discussion relates to fluoride ion—ie, to compounds that release fluoride ion upon ionization or decomposition but not to fluorine contained in organic compounds. The incidence of dental caries is much reduced by the ingestion of adequate amounts of fluoride.

Absorption, Metabolism, & Excretion

Soluble fluorides—eg, sodium fluoride—are rapidly absorbed following oral ingestion. Less soluble salts are only slowly absorbed. Thus the formation of calcium fluoride by the administration of calcium ions in the antidotal treatment of fluoride toxicity delays but does not prevent absorption of fluoride.

Once absorbed, fluoride is initially distributed much as chloride is—ie, it remains extracellular to a large extent. It is slightly less well reabsorbed by the renal tubules than is chloride and is consequently rapidly excreted into the urine. Unlike chloride, however, it is also concentrated in bone. Because of the prompt excretion and deposition, fluoride levels in plasma are only transiently elevated following an oral dose.

At a given dietary level of fluoride, the deposition and release of fluoride from bone are equal. If an increased amount of fluoride is given, half of each dose will be deposited in bone until a new state of equilibrium is reached. It is this increased amount of fluoride in bone and teeth that is important in the action of supplementary fluoride.

Mechanism of Action

A. In Tooth Enamel: The surface layer of enamel contains a higher concentration of fluoride than deeper layers of enamel or dentine, suggesting that enamel takes up fluoride from the surrounding fluid. Enamel with a higher fluoride content is more resistant to erosion by acid—ie, to dental decay. Enamel (and bone) is composed of apatite, a form of crystalline calcium phosphate that contains hydroxyl groups in its crystal lattice. The most probable explanation for the

effect of fluoride on the teeth is that the fluoride exchanges for hydroxyl in the crystal structure.

B. In Bone: In bone, hydroxyapatite is similarly converted to fluorapatite. However, to explain the osteosclerosis that larger doses of fluoride cause, some as yet unclarified additional mechanisms must be present—eg, stimulation of osteoblastic activity.

Clinical Uses

A. Prevention of Dental Caries: Dental decay, which is probably the most widespread of all diseases, follows localized erosion of the enamel of a tooth. Progressively deeper destruction leads to pain, abscess formation, and loss of the tooth. The process is due to the growth of acid-producing bacteria that require carbohydrate for their growth. Control of decay can in part be accomplished by brushing the teeth or rinsing the mouth to remove bacteria and their substrate and by restricting sugar-containing snacks between meals. However, by far the most effective prophylactic measure that is applicable to whole populations is to increase the resistance of the enamel by providing fluoride for incorporation into apatite.

1. Fluoridation of water supplies–Studies of communities in which there was a high incidence of mottling of the teeth showed an association with a high level of fluoride in the communal water supply and also a low incidence of dental decay. Further epidemiologic studies established that protection against caries could be provided by adding fluoride to drinking water in amounts that did not cause mottling or dental fluorosis.

The addition of fluoride to the water supplies of communities receiving less than optimal amounts of fluoride began on a trial basis in 1945. Large-scale evaluations of the effect of added fluoride for periods of 10 and 15 years are now available, and there is no question that fluoridation is effective. In general, the numbers of decayed, missing, or filled teeth are reduced 50–60% in children at age 14–16. The benefits are most striking when the fluoridated water (or other supplemental fluoride) is supplied from infancy. Not only are the permanent teeth better protected, but the benefits of preserving deciduous teeth are added.

Fluoride, usually as sodium silicofluoride, is added to the water supply to a final fluoride concentration of about 1 ppm or 1 mg/L, although the concentration is varied with the climate—ie, with the predicted intake of water. This amount of fluoride has no toxic effects; does not affect the taste or odor of water; and usually costs 5–15 cents a year per individual, a negligible cost compared to the savings in the cost of restorative dentistry.

Nevertheless, objections to fluoridation persist, and voters in a number of cities have rejected proposals to fluoridate. Some of the objections are unjustified, since the possibility of toxic effects has been carefully studied. The one basis for argument is the philosophic one that the individual is being medicated against his or her will. However, it is no more difficult for an individual to remove fluoride from a household water supply than for the majority of householders to add it on an individual basis.

About half of the population of the USA is now supplied with water that contains supplemental or natural fluoride in protective amounts. If the communal water supply is not fluoridated, each child should receive fluoride supplements from infancy through age 12. Deciduous teeth are calcified during the first year, and the beneficial effect of fluoride on the permanent teeth is also limited if fluoride supplementation is delayed until the time when children ordinarily first visit a dentist. Actually, preliminary work suggests great benefit to children whose mothers were given fluoride when pregnant. The physician or the family must, therefore, initiate early supplementation if the water supply is not fluoridated. The amount of supplement depends upon the fluoride content of the available water, and the total intake should approximate 1 mg/d.

2. Topical application of fluorides–Topical application of a fluoride salt will supplement the effect of systemic fluoride in producing acid-resistant tooth structures. If caries is a clinical problem, topical application by a dentist is indicated.

When solutions of sodium fluoride or stannous fluoride are painted on the dry tooth, fluoride is not immediately incorporated into apatite. A depot of calcium fluoride is first formed on the surface of the tooth from which fluoride is released.

Toothpastes containing stannous fluoride or sodium monofluorophosphate are a less effective way of applying fluoride topically. Their regular and frequent use adds a modest gain to the benefits of regular frequent brushing with any tooth cleanser.

No claim can be made that fluoride is effective against any dental disease other than decay. There are hints from epidemiologic studies that periodontal disease is influenced by added fluoride, but no completed studies are available.

B. Investigative Use in Osteoporosis: The progressive loss of bone in osteoporosis has for many years been treated with estrogens or other anabolic steroids on the assumption that the basic process is a loss of protein matrix with secondary loss of calcium. Use of the steroids has not resulted in demonstrable recalcification, and there is current interest in developing other methods of treatment. In the present context, the possible role of fluoride in maintaining normal bone density should be mentioned. In the epidemiologic studies of communities with varying fluoride levels in the drinking water, it was reported that 10–15% of the inhabitants receiving enough fluoride to develop mottled enamel also had coarsened trabeculae and increased density of bone. Even more striking was the higher incidence of osteoporosis in the residents of one city with very little fluoride in the water.

In patients who have osteoporosis, the administration of sodium fluoride does cause increased osteoblastic activity, but the new bone is poorly calcified. Given in combination with vitamin D and supplementary calcium, sodium fluoride does increase skeletal mass, but it will be some years before the extent of clinical improvement can be accurately described.

Other investigative studies of large amounts of sodium fluoride on otosclerosis, multiple myeloma, and Paget's disease appear to establish that recalcification can be accomplished.

Because fluoride is concentrated at areas of rapid remolding of bone, a scan done after the administration of $Na^{18}F$ can be used to identify early bony metastases.

Adverse Reactions

Fluoride in large doses is, as opponents of fluoridation emphasize, dangerously toxic. In the range of milligrams per day it causes only dental fluorosis. The adverse effects of high fluoride intake from natural sources and the possible adverse effects of supplementary fluoride have been investigated on larger samples and with far more care than is expended on other therapeutic agents. No cause for concern has been found.

It must be emphasized that in areas where fluoridation of water is public policy, the daily intake is about 1 mg/d. The acute ingestion of 250 mg leads only to nausea and vomiting.

A. Dental Fluorosis: Excess fluoride during the first 8 years of life leads to areas of irregular and hypoplastic enamel formation. These may be apparent as chalky or paper-white areas. In more advanced form, they may appear as yellowish-brown pits and ridges. These areas are resistant to the development of caries. If they are cosmetically disturbing, the brownish color can be bleached with 30% hydrogen peroxide.

Significant mottling is rare when less than 2 mg/d of fluoride are ingested. It is detectable but cosmetically negligible in almost half of children who received 1.7 ppm of fluoride in drinking water. With 4–6 ppm of fluoride—ie, 4–6 mg/d—mottling is invariable and may be disfiguring.

In communities suffering from endemic mottling, fluoride is removed from the water.

B. Skeletal Fluorosis: Ingestion of fluoride in amounts of 8–20 mg/d for years can lead to increased osteoblastic activity and increased density of bone. Signs include osteosclerosis or thickeneed, more dense trabeculae, periosteal hyperostoses, and calcification of soft tissues attached to bone.

With large doses (20–80 mg/d for 10–20 years), the changes may become crippling. Osteoporosis may replace osteosclerosis after a long period.

A more acute form of osteosclerosis can follow industrial exposure to larger amounts of fluoride.

C. Acute Toxicity: Acute fluoride intoxication does not result from exposure to therapeutic fluoride. An entire tube of fluoride toothpaste does not contain a dangerous amount of fluoride. Sodium fluoride is prescribed so that no more than 200 mg are in the home at any time.

Acute fluoride toxicity usually results from ingestion of an insecticide. Fluoride in these large amounts reacts with calcium and depresses the activity of many enzymes. Initial symptoms are due to gastrointestinal irritation—ie, nausea, vomiting, cramping pain, and diarrhea. Convulsions can occur, and blood pressure and respiration are progressively depressed. Hypoglycemia and hypocalcemia may be prominent findings.

Treatment consists of the following: (1) Lavage with a calcium salt—eg, lime water or calcium chloride—or the induction of emesis following ingestion of the same solution. After lavage or emesis, give calcium salts by mouth. (2) Begin an intravenous infusion of glucose in water or saline, in part to treat hypoglycemia but also so that a calcium salt can be injected intravenously to prevent tetany and ventricular fibrillation.

The fluoride salts used as agricultural chemicals are rapidly absorbed, and treatment must be prompt. Reported lethal doses are as small as 0.5 g in a child, but doses many times that size have not been fatal.

Preparations Available

Bottled water containing added fluoride and sodium fluoride tablets and solutions are available for use in communities without fluoridation of the water supply. The amount of fluoride in the untreated water supply is variable, and information about dosage should be solicited from local public health officals.

• • •

References

Iron

Benz EJ Jr: Molecular pathology of the β-thalessemia syndromes. Page 884 in: Thalassemia major: Molecular and clinical aspects. Nienhuis AW (moderator). Ann Intern Med 91:883, 1979.

Callender ST: Quick- and slow-release iron: A double-blind trial with a single daily dose regimen. Br Med J 4:531, 1969.

Committee on Nutrition of the American Academy of Pediatrics: Iron-fortified formulas. Pediatrics 47:786, 1971.

Cook JD, Finch CA: Iron nutrition. West J Med 122:474, 1975.

Crosby WH: The safety of iron-fortified food. JAMA 239:2026, 1978.

Fairbanks VF, Fahey JL, Beutler E: *Clinical Disorders of Iron Metabolism*, 2nd ed. Grune & Stratton, 1971.

Fischer DS, Parkman R, Finch SC: Acute iron poisoning in children: The problem of appropriate therapy. JAMA 218:1179, 1971.

Marchasin S, Wallerstein RO: The treatment of iron-deficiency anemia with intravenous iron dextran. Blood 23:354, 1964.

Middleton EJ, Nagy E, Morrison AB: Studies on the absorption of orally administered iron from sustained-release preparations. N Engl J Med 274:136, 1966.

Olsson KS & others: Preclinical hemochromatosis in a population on a high-iron-fortified diet. JAMA 239:1999, 1978. [See also editorial in same issue.]

Pritchard JA: Hemoglobin regeneration in iron-deficiency anemia. JAMA 195:717, 1966.

Ross JD: Failure of iron-deficient infants to respond to an orally administered iron-carbohydrate complex. N Engl J Med 269:399, 1963.

Weinbren K, Salm R, Greenberg G: Intramuscular injections of iron compounds and oncogenesis in man. Br Med J 1:683, 1978.

Fluorides

Erickson JD: Mortality in selected cities with fluoridated and non-fluoridated water supplies. N Engl J Med 298:1112, 1978.

Hodge HC, Smith FA: Fluorides and man. Annu Rev Pharmacol 8:395, 1968.

Jowsey J: Effect of combined therapy with sodium fluoride, vitamin D and calcium in osteoporosis. Am J Med 53:43, 1972.

Kyle RA & others: Multiple myeloma bone disease: The comparative effect of sodium fluoride and calcium carbonate vs placebo. N Engl J Med 293:1334, 1975.

Management of osteoporosis. (Editorial.) Br Med J 4:307, 1975.

Margolis FJ: Fluoride: Ten-year prospective study of deciduous and permanent dentition. Am J Dis Child 129:794, 1975. [See also editorial in JAMA 234:312, 1975.]

Sapolsky HM: Science, voters, and the fluoridation controversy. Science 162:427, 1968.

Shambaugh GE, Petrovic A: Effects of sodium fluoride on bone: Application to otosclerosis and other decalcifying bone diseases. JAMA 204:969, 1968.

43 | Fluids & Electrolytes

Marcus A. Krupp, MD

Water and solute made of electrolyte and nonionized organic molecules constitute the body fluids, which vary somewhat in composition in individual organs and compartments.

The body fluids support homeostasis by virtue of 3 closely related factors: volume, concentration, and pharmacologic activity.

Water Volume

(1) Extracellular (plasma, interstitial fluid) and transcellular (cerebrospinal fluid, intraluminal intestinal fluid, ocular fluid).

(2) Intracellular.

Concentration

(1) Osmolality (total solute concentration).

(2) Concentration of individual electrolytes.

Pharmacologic Activity

(1) Concentration of hydrogen ion (pH).

(2) Concentration of electrolytes which exert pharmacologic actions.

WATER VOLUME

"Volume" and "water" are substantially interchangeable in the context of this discussion. Volume of body water is maintained by a balance between intake and excretion. Water as such, in foods and as a product of combustion, is excreted by the kidneys, skin, and lungs. Electrolytes important in maintaining volume and distribution include the cations sodium for extracellular fluid and potassium and magnesium for intracellular fluid, and the anions chloride and bicarbonate for extracellular fluid and organic phosphate and protein for intracellular fluid.

Loss of water or excess of water results in corresponding change in volume in both extra- and intra-

Marcus A. Krupp is Clinical Professor of Medicine Emeritus, Stanford University School of Medicine, Palo Alto, California; Director, Palo Alto Medical Research Foundation, Palo Alto, California.

Table 43–1. Body water distribution in an average normal young adult male.*

	mL/kg† Body Weight	% of Total Body Water
Total extracellular fluid	270	45
Plasma	45	7.5
Interstitial fluid	120	20
Connective tissue and bone	90	15
Transcellular fluid	15	2.5
Total intracellular fluid	330	55
Total body water	600	100

*Modified from Edelman & Liebman: Anatomy of water and electrolytes. Am J Med 27:256, 1959.

$\dagger \dfrac{mL/kg}{10} = \%$, eg, 45 mL/kg = 4.5%

cellular compartments. Loss of sodium (with accompanying anion) or excess of sodium results in decrease or increase, respectively, of the volume of extracellular fluid, with water moving out of the extracellular compartment with sodium loss and into the extracellular compartment with sodium retention.

In response to changes in volume, appropriate servo or feedback mechanisms come into play. The principal elements in regulation are antidiuretic hor-

Table 43–2. Molar and milliequivalent weights.*

	Valence	Molar Weights (g)	Milliequivalent Weights (mg)
Cations			
Na^+	1	23	23
K^+	1	39	39
Ca^{2+}	2	40	20
Mg^{2+}	2	24	12
Anions			
Cl^-	1	35.5	35.5
HCO_3^-	1	61	61
$H_2PO_4^-$	$\left\{ 1 \right.$		
HPO_4^{2-}	$\left. 2 \right\}$	31 (as P)	
SO_4^{2-}	2	96	48

*Reproduced, with permission, from Krupp MA, Chatton MJ (editors): *Current Medical Diagnosis & Treatment 1980.* Lange, 1980.

mone for water, aldosterone and other steroids for sodium (and potassium), and vascular responses affecting glomerular filtration rate for water and sodium.

The average adult requires at least 800–1300 mL of water per day to cover obligatory water needs. A normal adult on an ordinary diet requires 500 mL of water for renal excretion of solute in a maximally concentrated urine plus an additional amount of water to replace that lost via the skin and respiratory tract.

Fluid losses most often include electrolyte as well as water. Sweat, gastrointestinal fluids, urine, and fluid escaping from wounds contain significant quantities of electrolyte. In order to ascertain deficits of water and electrolytes, one must consider the history, change in body weight, clinical state, and appropriate determinations in plasma of concentration of each of the electrolytes, osmolality, protein, and pH. Assessment of renal function is required before repair and maintenance requirements can be determined and prescribed.

WATER DEFICIT

Water deficit results in a decrease in volume of both extracellular and intracellular fluids with a corresponding increase in concentration of both extracellular and intracellular solute in these fluids. In the blood, the loss of body water is reflected in an increased plasma osmolality as concentrations of plasma electrolyte and protein rise. With decreased blood volume, renal blood flow is reduced and excretion of urea falls, resulting in an elevation of urea in body fluids. Antidiuretic hormone secretion is stimulated, providing some protection from water loss by the kidney.

Water deficit results from reduced intake or unusual losses. Reduced intake is likely when the patient is unconscious, disabled, unable to ingest water because of esophageal or pyloric obstruction, or receives inadequate fluids to meet maintenance and replacement needs. Fever or a hot environment increases loss from the lungs and skin. The kidney fails to conserve water when there is inadequate ADH (diabetes insipidus) or insensitivity to ADH (nephrogenic diabetes insipidus), osmotic diuresis in diabetes mellitus, inadequate tubule function due to renal disease, or impaired capacity to reabsorb water secondary to potassium depletion, hypercalcemia, correction of obstructive uropathy, or from intensive diuretic therapy.

Water deficit is characterized by thirst, flushed skin, "dehydrated" appearance, dry mucous membranes, tachycardia, and oliguria. As dehydration increases, hallucinations and delirium, hyperpnea, and coma ensue.

Treatment
Water may be provided with or without electrolyte. If water alone is needed, 2.5–5% dextrose solution may be given intravenously; the dextrose is oxidized to yield water.

In the presence of normal renal function, 2000–3000 mL of water per day (1500 mL/m^2 of body surface) will provide a liberal maintenance ration. If dehydration is present with increased serum sodium concentration and osmolality, extra water replacement can be estimated on the basis of restoring normal osmolality for the total body fluid volume. The need for intracellular water is reflected in the extracellular fluid with which it is in osmotic equilibrium; therefore, any correction of deviation in osmolality must be considered on the basis of the total volume of body water.

The water requirement is increased in the presence of fever as a result of increased loss via skin and lungs.

WATER EXCESS

Water excess (overhydration, dilution syndrome) results in expansion of volume of body fluid and decreased concentration (dilution) of plasma electrolyte and protein, a reduced osmolality of plasma. Similar dilutions occur intracellularly. Normally, ADH secretion is inhibited, enabling the kidneys to excrete the excess water. Water excess results from intake in excess of capacity for excretion, usually from too large a water ration during parenteral administration; or from impaired excretory capacity resulting from acute or chronic renal insufficiency, renal functional changes (lowered glomerular filtration and increased water reabsorption) accompanying heart failure, liver disease with ascites, or administration of ADH or inappropriate secretion of "ADH-like" substance by neoplasms or in complex endocrine disturbances.

Water excess, particularly if it is severe or if it develops acutely, produces the syndrome of water intoxication, characterized by headache, nausea, vomiting, abdominal cramps, weakness, stupor, coma, and convulsions.

Treatment
The basic treatment consists of water restriction. If a real deficit of sodium exists as well, saline solutions should be employed. In the presence of severe water intoxication, administration of hypertonic saline solution may be useful to promote movement of excess intracellular water to the extracellular space, ie, to increase osmolality and diminish intracellular water volume. *Caution:* Overexpansion of extracellular volume may precipitate acute congestive heart failure and pulmonary edema.

CONCENTRATION

The total concentration of solute (osmolality) is apparently the same in intracellular and extracellular water. In the intracellular compartment, protein concentration plays a more important osmolal role than in the plasma. The protein content of interstitial fluid is small, and osmolal effects are therefore negligible. The most accessible and best index of osmolality is the measurement of the solute concentration in the plasma by ascertaining the depression of the freezing point. An indirect and useful measurement is that of plasma sodium concentration, provided due attention is paid to hyperglycemia and high urea concentrations, which cause a significant increase in osmolality; and lipemia and hyperproteinemia, which provide a nonaqueous addition to plasma volume. In the latter situations, sodium concentration determinations yield low values which must be interpreted with consideration of the concentration of the other constituents, ie, in terms of plasma or serum water rather than of the plasma specimen per se.

HYPEROSMOLAR STATES

Hyperosmolar concentrations of solute in body fluids are harmful because of shifts of water out of cells which ensue from increased concentration of solutes excluded from the intracellular space.

Transient or asymptomatic shifts in water occur along with substances that readily cross cell membranes. Urea may be administered to draw water out of cells (ie, in the treatment of cerebral edema), but the effect is brief. Similarly, alcohol equilibrates across cell membranes, adding 22 mOsm/L for every 100 mg/dL concentration.

Hyperosmolarity accompanied by shifts in water from cells to the extracellular spaces is due to increased concentration of solutes which do not readily enter cells; sodium and glucose are commonly involved.

Hypernatremia usually follows loss of water in excess of sodium and thus is usually characterized by hypovolemia as well. Hyperosmolarity due to water deficit and hypernatremia follows use of high-protein formulas or amino acid solutions with inadequate water for excretion of the resultant urea load (osmotic diuresis). Other causes of hypernatremia and hypovolemia include inability to obtain or to ingest water, diabetes insipidus with inadequate access to hypernatremia, and hypothalamic and other central nervous system lesions. Inadvertent infusion of hypertonic saline may produce hypernatremia and expanded extracellular fluid volume. Treatment is directed toward replacement of water deficit with 5% or 2.5% dextrose in water, adding appropriate electrolyte later as indicated clinically and by measurements of electrolyte concentrations in serum.

Hyperglycemia is accompanied by a shift of water from cells. The osmotic diuresis thus induced results in loss of water and Na^+ with resultant dehydration and hypovolemia. This is particularly characteristic of nonketotic hyperglycemic coma. Replacement of water and Na^+ to restore total body water and extracellular fluid volume must be accompanied by appropriate insulin therapy, correction of acidosis, and replacement of other electrolytes, especially K^+ and phosphate.

HYPONATREMIA

A decreased concentration of sodium in extracellular fluid may result from loss of sodium or from dilution by retention of water. Sodium loss occurs with adrenocortical insufficiency, vigorous diuretic therapy, unusual losses of gastrointestinal secretions, renal insufficiency, and unusual sweating. When the deficit of water is replaced with inadequate sodium replacement, hyponatremia ensues. Increased body water volume may follow excessive water intake or inappropriate ADH secretion. The latter may be stimulated by a variety of drugs (narcotics, tricyclic antidepressants, barbiturates, chlorpropamide, thiazides, clofibrate, cyclophosphamide, vincristine), lung abscess, pulmonary tuberculosis, some central nervous system diseases, and some malignant tumors (lung, pancreas, thymus, prostate). In edematous states such as congestive heart failure, hepatic cirrhosis, and nephrotic syndrome, decreased circulating blood volume stimulates ADH secretion.

Treatment

If there is a deficit of sodium, sodium chloride with or without sodium bicarbonate may be used for replacement. For replacement of moderate deficits, 0.9% sodium chloride (155 mEq of Na^+ and Cl^-/L), or Ringer's solution with or without lactate, may be employed. For severe sodium deficit, 3% sodium chloride (513 mEq/L) or 5% sodium chloride (855 mEq/L) may be used with caution. More comprehensive texts on water and electrolyte metabolism must be consulted for specific information on treatment.

Dilutional hyponatremia from water retention should be treated by restriction of intake of water. Since total body sodium is usually elevated or normal, sodium should not be administered.

The concentrations of other electrolytes in extracellular fluids have insignificant osmolar effects.

PHARMACOLOGIC ACTIVITY OF FLUIDS & ELECTROLYTES

HYDROGEN ION CONCENTRATION

The hydrogen ion concentration ($[H^+]$) of body fluids is closely regulated with intracellular concentrations of 10^{-7} molar (pH 7.0) and extracellular fluid concentrations of 4×10^{-8} molar (pH 7.4). In spite of accumulation or loss of H^+, these concentrations are maintained at nearly normal by buffer substances which remove or release H^+. The capacity of buffers is limited, however, and regulation is accomplished principally by the lungs and kidneys. The principal buffer substances include proteins, the oxyhemoglobin-reduced hemoglobin system, primary and secondary phosphate ions, some intracellular phosphate esters, and the carbonic acid–sodium bicarbonate systems.

Most of the food used for energy is completely utilized, with production of water, CO_2, and urea. Sulfate and, to a limited extent, phosphate endproducts are strong acid anions which must be "neutralized" by cations such as sodium. In the utilization of fat and carbohydrate, intermediate products include the strong acids acetoacetic acid and lactic acid. Buffers provide cation and remove H^+, which is utimately excreted by the kidney as acid or as ammonium ion and by the lung as CO_2 and H_2O, equivalent to carbonic acid. The anions of strong acids with cations such as sodium and ammonium are eliminated by the kidney.

The role of the lung and kidney in removal of H^+ and in regulation of H^+ concentration can be viewed as

$$\frac{[H^+]\ [HCO_3^-]}{[B^+]\ [HCO_3^-]} \rightleftarrows P_{CO_2} \quad \frac{\text{lung}}{\text{kidney}}$$

Respiratory control of the partial pressure of CO_2 (P_{CO_2}) in the pulmonary alveoli and therefore in the arterial plasma determines the H_2CO_3 concentration in body fluids:

$$CO_2 + H_2O \rightleftarrows H_2CO_3$$

The elimination of CO_2 via the lung in effect removes carbonic acid. The kidney is responsible for $BHCO_3$ concentration in body fluids, which, with H_2CO_3, constitutes one of the buffer systems for regulation of pH.

The kidney produces carbonic acid from metabolic CO_2 and water by the following reaction:

$$CO_2 + H_2O \xrightarrow{\boxed{\text{Carbonic anhydrase}}} H_2CO_3$$

The carbonic acid serves as a source of H^+ which can be exchanged for Na^+ in the tubular urine so that H^+ is excreted and Na^+ reabsorbed. The exchange affects anions of weak acids:

$$Na^+ + HCO_3^- + H^+ \rightarrow H_2CO_3 \rightarrow CO_2 + H_2O$$

with Na^+ reabsorbed. Although the pH of urine cannot be lowered below pH 4.5, additional H^+ can be excreted by combination with NH_3, generated principally from glutamine within the tubule cell. NH_3 diffuses from the tubule cell into the urine within the tubule where it combines with $H^+ \rightarrow NH_4^+$, providing cations for excretion with anions of strong acids with no increase in H^+ concentration (no lowering of pH). These exchanges in the renal tubule involve active transport systems capable of maintaining a gradient in concentration of extracellular fluid H^+ of 4×10^{-8} molar (pH 7.4) against a tubular urine H^+ of 32×10^{-6} molar (pH 4.5), an 800-fold increase in H^+ concentration.

CLINICAL STATES OF ALTERED H^+ CONCENTRATION

The clinical term **acidosis** signifies a decrease in pH (increase in H^+) of extracellular fluid; the term **alkalosis** signifies an increase in pH (decrease in H^+) of extracellular fluid. The change in H^+ concentration may be the result of metabolic or respiratory abnormalities.

1. RESPIRATORY ACIDOSIS

Respiratory acidosis follows ventilatory abnormalities resulting in CO_2 retention and elevation of P_{CO_2} in alveoli and arterial blood (hypercapnia). Inadequate ventilation during anesthesia, following suppression of the respiratory center by central nervous system disease or drugs, or resulting from respiratory muscle weakness or paralysis, produces CO_2 retention. Changes in anatomic structure of the lung (emphysema) or pulmonary circulation, or abnormal thoracic structure (kyphoscoliosis) may alter alveolar-capillary blood exchange or diminish effective ventilation to prevent CO_2 excretion. Associated with impaired CO_2 excretion, there may be impaired O_2 exchange with low alveolar and arterial P_{O_2} (hypoxemia). In the presence of CO_2 retention and the resultant increase in H_2CO_3 concentration, compensatory reabsorption of HCO_3^- by the kidney provides buffer to reduce H^+ concentration, but this protection cannot be accomplished rapidly and is effectively available only in chronic situations that develop slowly.

Treatment

Treatment is directed toward improving ventilation with mechanical aids, bronchodilators, restoring circulation, correction of heart failure, and antidotes for anesthetics or drugs suppressing the respiratory center. Close monitoring of P_{CO_2}, P_{O_2}, and pH of arterial blood is essential. The respiratory center is readily rendered unresponsive by high P_{CO_2} (hypercapnia), and recovery may be very slow. In the presence of hypercapnia, relief of hypoxemia with oxygen therapy may deprive the patient of the only remaining stimulus to the respiratory center and produce more severe hypoventilation with resultant CO_2 narcosis and death. Assistance with respiration is required until the respiratory center becomes normally responsive to altered CO_2 concentrations.

2. RESPIRATORY ALKALOSIS

Respiratory alkalosis is a result of hyperventilation which produces lowered P_{CO_2} and elevated pH of extracellular fluid. Anxiety is the usual cause. Hyperventilation during anesthesia or from incorrectly used mechanical respiratory aids occurs more commonly than is generally appreciated. Renal compensation by excretion of HCO_3^- (with Na^+ predominantly) is too slow a response to be effective, and elevation of pH may reach a point at which asterixis, tetany, and increased neuromuscular irritability appear.

Treatment

Treatment of spontaneous hyperventilation consists of reducing anxiety by drugs or psychotherapy. Tetany may be alleviated by rebreathing exhaled air, which will increase P_{CO_2} and lower blood pH. Regulation of devices used in assisting with respiration should be determined by measurement of the P_{CO_2} and pH of arterial blood.

3. METABOLIC ACIDOSIS

Metabolic acidosis occurs with starvation, uncontrolled diabetes mellitus with ketosis, lactic acidosis, electrolyte (including bicarbonate) and water loss with diarrhea or enteric fistulas, and renal insufficiency or tubular defect producing inadequate H^+ excretion. Cation loss (Na^+, K^+, Ca^{2+}) and organic acid anion retention occur with starvation and uncontrolled diabetes mellitus. In the presence of renal insufficiency, phosphate and sulfate are retained and cation (especially Na^+) is lost because of limited H^+ secretion for exchange with cation in the renal tubule. Respiratory compensation for metabolic acidosis by hyperventilation provides reduction of P_{CO_2} and thereby reduction of H_2CO_3 in extracellular fluid.

Treatment

Treatment is directed toward correcting the metabolic defect (eg, insulin for control of diabetes) and replenishment of water and of deficits of Na^+, K^+, HCO_3^-, and other electrolytes. Renal insufficiency requires careful replacement of water and electrolyte deficit and closely controlled rations of water, sodium, potassium, calcium, chloride, and bicarbonate to maintain normal extracellular fluid concentrations; the elevated serum phosphate may be lowered by interfering with phosphate absorption from the gut by oral administration of aluminum hydroxide preparations. In the presence of renal insufficiency, elevated extracellular K^+ concentrations may be reduced by either oral administration of ion exchange resins which bind K^+, either ingested or secreted, and prevent absorption in the intestine (see Hyperkalemia, below), or by hemodialysis or peritoneal dialysis.

4. METABOLIC ALKALOSIS

Metabolic alkalosis results from loss of gastric juice rich in HCl or from excessive sodium bicarbonate ingestion, and occurs also in association with K^+ deficit, which is characteristically accompanied by increased urinary excretion of H^+. All of these result in renal retention of HCO_3^-, producing elevated extracellular fluid bicarbonate. Respiratory compensation by hypoventilation produces an elevation in P_{CO_2}, increasing the H_2CO_3 fraction of the bicarbonate buffer system.

Treatment

Treatment consists of replacing Cl^- and K^+ as well as any deficit of water and other electrolyte.

POTASSIUM

Potassium is one of the major intracellular cations, occupying a role that is parallel to that of sodium in extracellular fluid. Physiologic actions of potassium are related primarily to concentration of the cation in extracellular fluid, although the intracellular concentration may have some influence. Potassium plays an important part in muscular contraction, conduction of nerve impulses, enzyme action, and cell membrane function.

Cardiac muscle excitability, conduction, and rhythm are markedly affected by changes in concentration of K^+ in extracellular fluid. Both an increase and a decrease of extracellular K^+ concentration diminish excitability and conduction rate. Higher than normal concentrations produce a marked depression of conductivity with cardiac arrest in diastole; in the presence of very low concentrations, cardiac arrest occurs in systole. The effects of abnormal K$^+$ concentrations in extracellular fluid upon cell membrane potential of cardiac muscle and upon depolarization and repolarization are manifested in the ECG.

Membrane potential and excitability of skeletal and smooth muscle are profoundly affected by the concentrations of K$^+$, Ca^{2+}, and Mg^{2+}, with H$^+$ and Na$^+$ also involved. Conduction across the myoneural junction is under the influence of these cations as well. At both extremes of abnormal concentration of K$^+$ in extracellular fluid, muscle contractility is impaired and flaccid paralysis ensues.

Potassium concentration of extracellular fluid is closely regulated between 3.5–5 mmol/L. Excretion of the 35–100 mmol of potassium contained in the daily diet of the average adult is predominantly via the kidney. There is good evidence that the potassium in glomerular filtrate is reabsorbed in the proximal tubule and that active secretion of potassium into the tubular fluid occurs in the distal portion of the tubule.

1. HYPERKALEMIA

Causes of increased extracellular K$^+$ concentration include failure of the kidney to excrete ingested potassium (acute and chronic renal failure, severe oliguria due to severe dehydration or trauma); unusual release of intracellular potassium in burns, crush injuries, rhabdomyolysis, or severe infections; adrenal insufficiency; and overtreatment with potassium salts. In metabolic acidosis, extracellular K$^+$ concentration is increased, as K$^+$ shifts from cells.

The elevated K$^+$ concentration interferes with normal neuromuscular function to produce weakness and paralysis; abdominal distention and diarrhea may occur. As extracellular concentration of K$^+$ increases, the ECG reflects impaired conduction by peaked T waves of increased amplitude, atrial arrest, spread in the QRS, biphasic QRS–T complexes, and finally ventricular fibrillation and cardiac arrest.

Treatment
Treatment consists of withholding potassium and employing cation exchange resins by mouth or enema. Kayexalate, a sodium cycle sulfonic polystyrene exchange resin, 40–80 g/d in divided doses, is usually effective. In an emergency, insulin may be employed to deposit K$^+$ with glycogen in the liver, and Ca^{2+} may be given intravenously as an antagonist ion. Sodium bicarbonate can be given intravenously as an emergency measure in severe hyperkalemia; the increase in pH so induced results in a shift of K$^+$ into cells. Hemodialysis or peritoneal dialysis may be required to remove K$^+$ in the presence of protracted renal insufficiency.

2. HYPOKALEMIA

Potassium deficit may or may not be accompanied by lowered extracellular fluid K$^+$ concentration; however, when hypokalemia is present, total potassium deficit is usually profound. Exceptions to this common circumstance include the hypokalemia of alkalosis and that following administration of insulin. Causes of potassium deficit include reduced intake due to starvation or upper gastrointestinal obstruction; poor absorption in steatorrhea, short bowel syndrome, and regional enteritis; loss via the gastrointestinal tract due to emesis, diarrhea, and suction; loss via the kidney due to congenital tubule malfunction, diuresis resulting from diabetes or diuretics, accompanying metabolic alkalosis, and following excessive treatment with saline solutions containing little or no potassium; loss of interstitial fluid with burns or freezing; loss of K$^+$ due to adrenocortical hormone (cortisol or aldosterone) excess; and intracellular shift in bouts of familial periodic paralysis. A low concentration of K$^+$ in extracellular fluid results in impaired neuromuscular function with profound weakness of skeletal muscle, leading to impaired ventilation, and of smooth muscle, producing ileus. The ECG shows decreased amplitude and broadening of T waves, prominent U waves, sagging S–T segments, atrioventricular block, and, finally, cardiac arrest. Metabolic alkalosis with elevated plasma pH and bicarbonate concentration develops as a result of potassium deficit which is accompanied by renal excretion of H$^+$ and reabsorption of bicarbonate and by movement of Na$^+$ and H$^+$ from extracellular fluid into cells as K$^+$ is lost. A defect of water reabsorption by the renal tubule also occurs, producing polyuria and hyposthenuria; this is only slowly ameliorated following treatment.

Treatment
Treatment requires replacement of potassium orally or parenterally. Because of the toxicity of potassium, it must be administered cautiously to prevent hyperkalemia. Furthermore, confirmation of adequate renal function is important when potassium is administered since the principal route of excretion is via the kidney. KCl in a total dose of 1–3 mmol/kg/24 h may be given parenterally in glucose or saline solutions (or both) at a rate that will not produce hyperkalemia. Cl$^-$ is almost always needed to relieve the hypochloremia that is associated with the accompanying metabolic alkalosis.

CALCIUM

Calcium constitutes about 2% of body weight, but only about 1% of the total body calcium is in solution in body fluid. In the plasma, calcium is present as a nondiffusible complex with protein (33%); as a diffusible but undissociated complex with anions such as citrate, bicarbonate, and phosphate (12%); and as Ca^{2+}(55%). The normal total plasma (or serum) calcium concentration is 2.1–2.6 mmol/L (8.5–10.5 mg/dL). Bone serves as a reservoir of calcium available to body fluids. Excretion of Ca^{2+} is via the kidney.

Calcium functions as an essential ion for many enzymes. It is an important constituent of mucoproteins and mucopolysaccharides, and it is essential in blood coagulation.

Calcium along with other cations exerts an important effect on cell membrane potential and permeability manifested prominently in neuromuscular function. It plays a central role in muscle contraction as it is released from the sarcolemma to enter into the ATP-ADP reaction. During muscle relaxation, the calcium is actively transferred back to the sarcolemma and sarcoplasmic reticulum.

Neural function is sensitive to Ca^{2+} concentration of interstitial fluid. Excitability is diminished by high Ca^{2+} concentration and increased by low concentration. Signs of elevated Ca^{2+} concentration include dulling of consciousness and stupor and muscular flaccidity and weakness. Low Ca^{2+} concentration increases excitability to produce hyperirritability of muscle, tetany, and convulsions.

Cardiac muscle responds to elevated Ca^{2+} concentration with increased contractility, ventricular extrasystoles, and idioventricular rhythm. These responses are accentuated in the presence of digitalis. With severe calcium toxicity, cardiac arrest in systole may occur. Low concentration of Ca^{2+} produces diminished contractility of the heart and a lengthening of the Q–T interval of the ECG by prolonging the S–T segment.

1. HYPERCALCEMIA

Hypercalcemia results from hyperparathyroidism, invasion of bone by neoplasm (lung, breast, kidney, thyroid), production of a parathyroidlike hormone by isolated neoplasms (ovary, kidney, lung), sarcoidosis, multiple myeloma, milk-alkali syndrome, and vitamin D intoxication.

Hypercalcemia per se affects neuromuscular function to produce weakness, and produces polyuria, thirst, anorexia, vomiting, and constipation. Stupor, coma, and azotemia ensue.

Treatment

Treatment consists of control of the primary disease. Symptomatic hypercalcemia is associated with a high mortality rate; treatment must be promptly instituted. Until the primary disease can be brought under control, renal excretion of calcium with resultant decrease in serum Ca^{2+} concentration can be promoted with a variety of agents. Excretion of Na^+ is accompanied by excretion of Ca^{2+}; therefore, inducing na-

triuresis by giving Na^+ salts intravenously and by adjunctive use of diuretics is the emergency treatment of choice. Sodium chloride or sodium sulfate in large quantities (70–80 mmol/h) with or without diuretics (furosemide) for 12–48 hours may be required. Replacement of water and of K^+ and Mg^{2+} is usually necessary. The use of phosphate is hazardous and should be reserved for unusual cases refractory to saline therapy. When elevated Ca^{2+} concentrations result from sarcoidosis or neoplasm, corticosteroids such as prednisone may be effective. Mithramycin is useful if elevated Ca^{2+} is the result of neoplasm metastatic to bone.

2. HYPOCALCEMIA

Hypocalcemia results from hypoparathyroidism (idiopathic or postoperative), chronic renal insufficiency, rickets and osteomalacia, and malabsorption syndromes.

Hypocalcemia affects neuromuscular function to produce muscle cramps and tetany, convulsions, stridor and dyspnea, diplopia, abdominal cramps, and urinary frequency. Personality changes may occur. In chronic hypoparathyroidism and pseudo-hypoparathyroidism, cataracts may appear and calcification of basal ganglia of the brain may occur. Mental retardation and stunted growth are common in childhood.

Treatment

Treatment depends on the primary disease. Treatment of hypoparathyroidism with vitamin D and calcium is discussed in Chapter 36. For tetany due to hypocalcemia, calcium gluconate, 1–2 g, may be given intravenously. A continuous infusion to sustain plasma calcium concentration may be required. Oral medication with the chloride, gluconate, levulinate, lactate, or carbonate salts of calcium will usually control milder symptoms or latent tetany. The low serum Ca^{2+} associated with low serum albumin concentration is physiologic and does not require calcium replacement.

MAGNESIUM

About 50% of total body magnesium exists in the insoluble state in bone. Only 5% is present as extracellular cation; the remaining 45% is contained in cells as intracellular cation. The normal plasma concentration is 1.8–3 mg/dL (0.8–1.3 mmol/L), with about one-third bound to protein and two-thirds as free cation. Excretion of magnesium ion is via the kidney, with no evidence of active tubule secretion.

Magnesium is an important prosthetic or activator

ion participating in the function of many enzymes involved in phosphate transfer reactions, including those requiring ATP or other nucleotide triphosphate as coenzymes.

Magnesium exerts physiologic effects on the nervous system resembling those of calcium. Elevated Mg^{2+} concentration of interstitial fluid produces sedation and central and peripheral nervous system depression. Low concentrations produce increased irritability, disorientation, and convulsions.

Magnesium acts directly upon the myoneural junction. Elevated levels produce blockade by decreasing acetylcholine release, reducing the effect of acetylcholine on depolarization, and diminishing excitability of the muscle cell. Calcium ion exerts an antagonistic action. Low levels of magnesium increase neuromuscular irritability and contractility, partly by increasing acetylcholine release. Tetany and convulsions may occur.

Cardiac muscle is affected by large increases in magnesium concentration in the range of 10–15 mEq/L. Conduction time is increased, with lengthened duration of P–R and QRS components of the ECG. As the concentration of Mg^{2+} increases further, cardiac arrest in diastole occurs.

Elevated magnesium concentrations produce vasodilatation and a drop in blood pressure by blockade of sympathetic ganglia as well as a direct effect on smooth muscle.

1. HYPERMAGNESEMIA

Magnesium excess is almost always the result of renal insufficiency and inability to excrete what has been absorbed from food or infused. Occasionally, with the use of magnesium sulfate as a cathartic, enough magnesium is absorbed to produce toxicity, particularly in the presence of impaired renal function. Manifestations of hypermagnesemia include muscle weakness, fall in blood pressure, and sedation and confusion. The ECG shows increased P–R interval, broadened QRS complexes, and elevated T waves. Death usually results from respiratory muscle paralysis.

Treatment
Treatment is directed toward alleviating renal insufficiency. Calcium acts as an antagonist to Mg^{2+} and may be employed parenterally for temporary benefit. Extracorporeal or peritoneal dialysis may be indicated.

2. HYPOMAGNESEMIA

Magnesium deficit occurs with diminished absorption associated with malabsorption, gastrointestinal suction, small bowel bypass, malnutrition, and alcoholism; increased loss due to diabetic ketoacidosis, diuretic therapy, diarrhea, hyperaldosteronism, hypercalciuria, and renal wasting of magnesium; and unexplained causes such as hyperparathyroidism or postparathyroidectomy with high-dose vitamin D therapy.

Magnesium deficit is characterized by neuromuscular and central nervous system hyperirritability with athetoid movements; jerking, coarse, and flapping tremor; positive Babinski response, nystagmus, tachycardia, hypertension, and vasomotor changes. Confusion, disorientation, and restlessness are prominent.

Treatment
Treatment consists of the use of parenteral fluids containing magnesium as chloride or sulfate, 5–20 mmol/d during the period of severe deficit followed by 5 mmol/d for maintenance. Magnesium sulfate may also be given intramuscularly, 16–66 mmol daily in 4 divided doses. Serum levels must be monitored to prevent the concentration from rising above 2.5 mmol/L.

PHOSPHATE

Phosphorus is present as inorganic phosphate in bone and teeth and in the extracellular fluid. Organic phosphate is widely distributed within cells in combination with proteins, lipids, and carbohydrates.

Phosphate compounds are involved in energy transfer and in most metabolic processes. In the erythrocyte, 2,3-diphosphoglycerate and ATP are associated with transport of oxygen. In acid-base homeostasis, phosphate serves as the principal urinary buffer (HPO_4^{2-}, $H_2PO_4^{-}$), constituting most of the titratable acidity.

Phosphorus metabolism is under influence of parathyroid hormone, calcitonin, calcium metabolism, sodium intake, glucocorticoids, and growth hormone.

1. HYPERPHOSPHATEMIA

Hyperphosphatemia is most commonly encountered in the setting of renal failure. It also occurs with acromegaly (excessive growth hormone), hypoparathyroidism, unusual tissue destruction, excessive intake of phosphate, and hypervitaminosis D. The accompanying decrease in serum calcium will often be symptomatic.

Symptoms and treatment are those of the primary disease.

Table 43–3. Composition of solutions for parenteral infusion.*

	Ionic Concentration in mmol/L							
	Na$^+$	K$^+$	Ca^{2+}	Mg^{2+}	NH$_4^+$	Cl$^-$	HCO$_3^-$ Equiv	PO$_4^{3-}$
Isotonic saline (0.9%)	155					155		
Sodium chloride (5%)	855					855		
Ringer's solution	147	4	2			155		
Ringer's lactate (Hartmann's)	130	4	1.5			109	28	
M/6 sodium lactate	167						167	
Darrow's solution (KNL)	121	35				103	53	
Potassium chloride								
0.2% in dextrose 5%		27	2.5	1.5		27		
0.3% in dextrose 5%		40				40		
"Modified duodenal solution" with dextrose, 10%	80	36	5	3		64	60	
"Gastric solution" with dextrose, 10%	63	17			70	150		
Ammonium chloride, 0.9%					170	170		
Examples of "maintenance solutions":								
Pediatric electrolyte "No. 48" with dextrose 5%	25	20		1.5		22	23	1
Maintenance electrolyte "No. 75" with dextrose 5%	40	35				40	20	5
Levulose and dextrose with electrolyte (Butler's II)	57	25		2.5		49	25	4.3
Dextrose in 0.2% saline	34					34		
Dextrose in 0.45% saline	77					77		

Ampules (note directions with ampule). Contents per ampule.†

	Na$^+$	K$^+$	Ca^{2+}	Mg^{2+}	NH$_4^+$	Cl$^-$	HCO$_3^-$ Equiv	PO$_4^{3-}$
Potassium phosphate‡, 20 mL		40						40
Potassium chloride‡, 40 mEq		40				40		
KMC‡		25	5	5		45		
Calcium gluconate, 10%, 10 mL			4.5				4.5	
Sodium bicarbonate§, 7.5%, 50 mL	45						45	
Sodium lactate§, molar, 40 mL	40						40	
Ammonium chloride, 100 mEq					100	100		

*Modified and reproduced, with permission, from Krupp MA & others: *Physician's Handbook,* 19th ed. Lange, 1979.
†Many other types of solutions are commercially available and may be used.
‡Dilute to 1 L.
§Dilute as indicated by manufacturer.

Table 43–4. Oral electrolyte preparations.*

Preparation	Supplied as	Electrolyte Content†					
		Na$^+$	K$^+$	NH$_4^+$	Ca^{2+}	Cl$^-$	HCO$_3^-$ (or equivalent)
NaCl	Salt	17				17	
NaHCO$_3$	Salt	12					12
KCl	Salt		14			14	
K-triplex	Elixir		15 mmol/5 mL				15
K gluconate (Kaon)	Elixir		7 mmol/5 mL				7
Ca gluconate	Salt				2.25		
Ca lactate	Salt				5		
NH$_4$Cl (acidifying salt)	Salt			19‡		19	
Kayexalate (ion-exchange resins)	Salt	3§	§				

*Reproduced, with permission, from Krupp MA, Chatton MJ (editors): *Current Medical Diagnosis & Treatment 1980.* Lange, 1980.
†mmol/g unless otherwise specified.
‡NH$_4^+$ is converted to H$^+$ in the body, mmol for mmol.
§1 g resin removes 1 mmol K$^+$ and contributes 3 mmol Na$^+$ to patient.

2. HYPOPHOSPHATEMIA & PHOSPHORUS DEFICIENCY

Hypophosphatemia may occur even though phosphate stores are normal. Serious depletion of body phosphate may exist with low, normal, or high serum phosphorus.

Phosphate depletion results from diminished intake in starvation, parenteral alimentation with inadequate phosphate content, malabsorption syndrome, vitamin D deficiency, and vitamin D-resistant osteomalacia. Increased loss occurs with hyperparathyroidism, defects of renal tubular reabsorption, and inadequately controlled diabetes mellitus.

Hypophosphatemia may follow depletion or accompany hypercalcemia, hypomagnesemia, and respiratory alkalosis.

Clinically significant hypophosphatemia occurs as a result of unusual loss followed by inadequate repletion, as in diabetes mellitus with acidosis, recovery from starvation, hyperalimentation with inadequate ration of phosphate, chronic alcoholism during restoration of normal nutrition (often associated with hypomagnesemia), and recovery from severe burns.

Severe hypophosphatemia may be life-threatening. Chronic depletion may be manifested by anorexia, muscle and bone pain, and fractures. With serum phosphorus levels of 1 mg/dL or lower, there may be serious hemolytic anemia with increased fragility of erythrocytes, impaired oxygen delivery to tissues, increased susceptibility to infection from impaired chemotaxis of leukocytes, platelet dysfunction with petechial hemorrhages, rhabdomyolysis, and central nervous system manifestations of encephalopathy including irritability, weakness, paresthesias, dysarthria, confusion, convulsive seizures, and coma.

Treatment is best directed toward prophylaxis by including phosphate in repletion and maintenance fluids. For intravenous use, phosphate concentrate (a mixture of KH_2PO_4 and K_2HPO_4) may be included. For parenteral alimentation to promote anabolism, 20 mmol of phosphorus are required for 1000 nonprotein kcal to maintain phosphate balance. A daily ration for parenteral fluid maintenance is 20–40 mmol phosphorus. A commercially available KH_2PO_4/K_2HPO_4 mixture (pH 6.5) provides 4.4 mEq of potassium and 3 mmol of phosphorus per mL. In administering phosphate-containing solutions, renal function must be assessed and serum calcium closely monitored. For oral use, phosphate is available in skimmed milk (approximately 33 mmol/L), tablets of mixtures of sodium and potassium phosphate (K-Phos, K-Phos Neutral, containing 3 and 8 mmol of phosphorus, respectively), and capsules (Neutraphos and Neutraphos K, containing 8 mmol phosphorus). Give 16–32 mmol (0.5–1 g) phosphorus daily.

Contraindications to therapy with phosphate salts include hypoparathyroidism, renal insufficiency, tissue damage and necrosis, and hypercalcemia.

MAINTENANCE & REPLACEMENT THERAPY

The range of tolerance for water and electrolytes (homeostatic limits) permits reasonable latitude in therapy provided normal renal function exists to accomplish the final regulation of volume and concentration (Table 43–5).

Deficits should be restored within 24–48 hours, during which time maintenance requirements must also be met. Continuing unusual losses from the gastrointestinal tract, kidney, burns, etc must also be replaced as they are incurred.

In administering fluids parenterally to those who cannot take fluids orally, the total daily ration should be administered continuously over the 24-hour period in order to assure the best utilization by the patient. This is particularly true when losses are large and the total daily infusion is large. With modern technics for continuous intravenous infusions, around-the-clock administration produces little discomfort or hardship.

Table 43–5. Daily maintenance rations for patients requiring parenteral fluids.

	Per m² Body Surface	Average Adult (60–100 kg)
Glucose	60–75 g	100–200 g
Na⁺	50–70 mmol	80–120 mmol
K⁺	50–70 mmol	80–120 mmol
Water	1500 mL	2500 mL

Table 43–6. Equivalent values of salts used for therapy.*

Salt	g	mmol of Cation per Amount Stated
IV or Oral		
NaCl	9	155
NaCl	5.8	100
NaCl	1	17
NaHCO₃	8.4	100
Na lactate	11.2	100
KCl	1.8	25
K acetate	2.5	25
K₂HPO₄ KH₂PO₄	1.35 1.27	25
CaCl₂	1	7
Ca gluconate	4	9
MgSO₄	1	4
Oral		
K citrate	3	25
K tartrate	5	27

*Reproduced, with permission, from Krupp MA & others: *Physician's Handbook*, 19th ed. Lange, 1979.

• • •

References

General

Brenner BM, Rector FC Jr (editors): *The Kidney*. Vol 1. Saunders, 1976.

Fisch C: Relation of electrolyte disturbances to cardiac arrhythmias. Circulation 47:408, 1973.

Maxwell M, Kleeman CR (editors): *Clinical Disorders of Fluid and Electrolyte Metabolism*, 3rd ed. McGraw-Hill, 1979.

Pitts RF: *Physiology of the Kidney and Body Fluids*, 3rd ed. Year Book, 1974.

Schrier RW (editor): *Renal and Electrolyte Disorders*. Little, Brown, 1976.

Fluid Volume & Sodium

Cannon PJ: The kidney in heart failure. N Engl J Med 296:26, 1977.

Feig PU, McCurdy DK: The hypertonic state. N Engl J Med 297:1444, 1977.

Forrest JN & others: Superiority of demeclocycline over lithium in the treatment of chronic syndrome of inappropriate secretion of antidiuretic hormone. N Engl J Med 298:173, 1978. [See also editorial, p 214.]

Hantman D & others: Rapid correction of hyponatremia in the syndrome of inappropriate secretion of antidiuretic hormone. Ann Intern Med 78:870, 1973.

Harrington JT, Cohen JJ: Clinical disorders of urine concentration and dilution. Arch Intern Med 131:810, 1973.

Kleeman CR: Hypo-osmolar syndromes secondary to impaired water excretion. Annu Rev Med 21:259, 1970.

Kokko JP: The role of the renal concentrating mechanisms in the regulation of serum sodium concentration. Am J Med 62:165, 1977.

Schrier RW, Berl T: Non-osmolar factors affecting renal water excretion. (2 parts.) N Engl J Med 292:81, 141, 1975.

Hydrogen Ion

Davenport HW: *The ABC of Acid-Base Chemistry*, 2nd ed. Univ of Chicago Press, 1974.

Filley GF: *Acid-Base and Blood Gas Regulation*. Lea & Febiger, 1971.

Kassirer JP: Serious acid-base disorders. N Engl J Med 291:773, 1974.

Lubowitz H & others: Lactic acidosis. Arch Intern Med 134:148, 1974.

Pitts RF: The role of ammonia production and excretion in the regulation of acid-base balance. N Engl J Med 284:32, 1971.

Sebastian A, Morris RC Jr: Renal tubular acidosis. Clin Nephrol 7:216, 1977.

Simpson DP: Control of hydrogen ion homeostasis and renal acidosis. Medicine 50:503, 1971.

Potassium

Chung EK: Drug-associated EKG changes: Hyperkalemia. Drug Ther 6:129, May 1976.

Katsikas JL & others: Disorders of potassium metabolism. Med Clin North Am 55:503, 1971.

Rovner DR: Use of pharmacologic agents in the treatment of hypokalemia and hyperkalemia. Ration Drug Ther 6:1, Feb 1972.

Calcium

Coburn JW, Hartenbower DL, Norman AW: Metabolism and action of the hormone vitamin D and its relation to calcium homeostasis. West J Med 121:22, 1974.

Deftos LJ, Neer R: Medical management of the hypercalcemia of malignancy. Annu Rev Med 25:323, 1974.

Massry SG, Friedler RM, Coburn JW: The physiology of the renal excretion of phosphate and calcium and its relation to clinical medicine. Arch Intern Med 131:828, 1973.

Rasmussen H: Ionic and hormonal control of calcium homeostasis. Am J Med 50:567, 1971.

Schneider AB, Sherwood LM: Pathogenesis and management of hypoparathyroidism and other hypocalcemic disorders. Metabolism 24:871, 1975.

Singer FR & others: Mithramycin treatment of intractable hypercalcemia due to parathyroid carcinoma. N Engl J Med 283:634, 1970.

Suki WN & others: Acute treatment of hypercalcemia with furosemide. N Engl J Med 283:836, 1970.

Magnesium

Alfrey AC & others: Evaluation of body magnesium stores. J Lab Clin Med 84:153, 1974.

Flink EB, Jones JE (editors): The pathogenesis and clinical significance of magnesium deficiency. Ann NY Acad Sci 162:707–978, 1969. [Entire issue.]

Gitelman HJ, Welt LG: Magnesium deficiency. Annu Rev Med 20:233, 1969.

Hall RCW, Joffe JR: Hypomagnesemia: Physical and psychiatric symptoms. JAMA 224:1749, 1973.

Iseri LT, Freed J, Bures AR: Magnesium deficiency and cardiac disorders. Am J Med 58:837, 1975.

Phosphorus

Hypophosphatemia: Medical Staff Conference, Univ of Calif San Francisco. West J Med 122:482, 1975.

Knochel JP: The pathophysiology and clinical characteristics of severe hypophosphatemia. Arch Intern Med 137:203, 1977.

Scriver CR: Rickets and the pathogenesis of impaired tubular transport of phosphate and other solutes. Am J Med 57:43, 1974.

Folic acid and vitamin B_{12} (cyanocobalamin) are chemically unrelated essential food factors that can be conveniently considered together because a deficiency of either produces a morphologically similar arrest of bone marrow maturation and megaloblastic anemia. This is not surprising, since both compounds are essential for the normal synthesis of deoxyribonucleic acid (DNA) and a deficiency of either interferes with normal mitosis. Other systems characterized by rapid cell division—eg, the gastrointestinal epithelium and the myeloid cells—are also affected by a deficiency state.

Folic acid and vitamin B_{12} are involved in widely differing metabolic reactions, but the pathways are linked at some points and a deficiency of either factor can be at least partially corrected by administration of the other factor. However, the neurologic lesions resulting from cobalamin deficiency are not corrected by folic acid administration.

FOLIC ACID

Source & Chemistry

Folic acid (pteroylmonoglutamic acid, folacin) consists of a pteridine nucleus, p-aminobenzoic acid, and glutamic acid. Sources of folic acid are widespread in foods of both animal and vegetable origin, the highest contents occurring in yeast, liver, and green vegetables such as spinach, asparagus, lettuce, and endive. The term "folate content" is often used to include folic acid (folate monoglutamate) and also conjugates that contain more than one glutamic acid residue. The

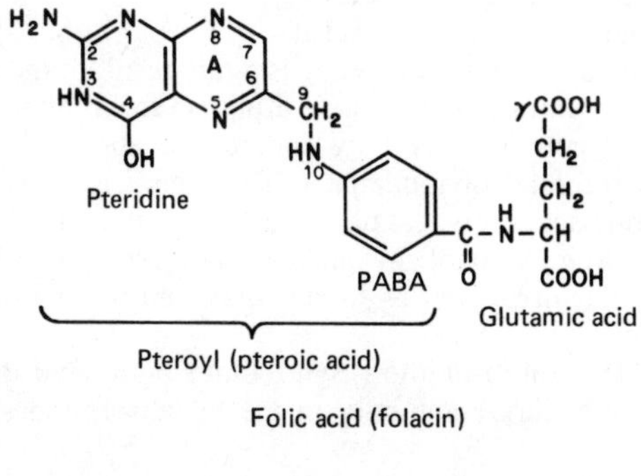

Pteridine

PABA

Glutamic acid

Pteroyl (pteroic acid)

Folic acid (folacin)

degree of absorption and utilization of folate may vary depending on the degree of liberation of folic acid by conjugase enzymes present in the jejunum. Folic acid is destroyed only by prolonged boiling, and the presence of reducing agents such as ascorbic acid reduces the loss.

Absorption, Distribution, & Excretion

Folic acid is readily and completely absorbed by the proximal third of the small intestine. Low concentrations probably utilize an active transport mechanism, but at high concentrations folic acid is probably also absorbed by diffusion. Absorption of orally administered supplemental folic acid is usually satisfactory even in the presence of disorders of the small bowel that have produced a deficiency state. Conjugated folate in food is less readily absorbed, and dietary correction of the deficiency is usually impractical in the presence of intestinal disease. Folic acid is widely distributed to all tissues and concentrated in the cerebrospinal fluid. Only small amounts of folic acid appear in the urine of subjects on normal diets, but excretion by this route is high following large doses.

Requirements & Stores of Folic Acid

The dietary intake of folate in the USA varies widely between 50 and 2000 μg. The availability of the vitamin probably also varies with the type of glutamate conjugate. Stores of folic acid are low compared with stores of vitamin B_{12}, being exhausted in 1–3 months depending upon the previous nutritional status and the rate of utilization.

The minimum daily intake required by a healthy adult is probably about 50 μg daily. Experimental folate deficiency, manifested by slight anemia and megaloblastic changes in the bone marrow, has been produced in humans by administration of a diet containing only 5 μg folate daily for 4½ months. Dietary requirements of an individual subject vary with both physiologic and disease states. Pregnancy can precipitate clinical deficiency in women receiving inadequate diets.

Folate deficiency can be diagnosed on clinical grounds—ie, the appearance of macrocytosis or an overt megaloblastic anemia—or by one of several laboratory procedures. Serum folate levels can be measured by a microbiologic assay or by measurement of the urinary excretion of formiminoglutamic acid (FIGLU) following the administration of histidine. Histidine is enzymatically converted to FIGLU and reacts with tetrahydrofolic acid to form formiminotetrahydrofolic acid and glutamic acid. In folic acid deficiency, this reaction cannot occur and excess FIGLU accumulates and is excreted in the urine. Both the FIGLU test and serum folate levels have proved to be unreliable in some cases of undisputed folic acid deficiency occurring in pregnancy.

Mechanisms of Action

Folic acid is the inactive precursor of several coenzymes, and the main step in their formation is reduction to tetrahydrofolic acid by the enzyme folate reductase. Several derivatives of tetrahydrofolic acid accept and donate single carbon atom units. Formyl, formate, or hydroxymethyl derivatives are formed at the N_{10} (or N_5 and N_{10}) positions. Folinic acid (5-formyltetrahydrofolic acid) is widely regarded as an active form of the coenzyme. This is not strictly true, because conversion to the 10-formyl or 5,10-formyl derivative is required before the compound can be utilized, and this is accomplished by the enzyme tetrahydrofolic acid isomerase. Deficiency of folic acid is not uncommonly associated with deficiency of ascorbic acid, and it has been suggested that ascorbic acid is required for the reduction of folic acid to the tetrahydro derivative. Recent work suggests that this is unlikely, and dietary deficiency of both vitamins appears to be a more reasonable explanation.

Single carbon units are utilized in several reactions, of which the most important are the following:

(1) Purine synthesis entirely from single carbon units via inosinic acid.

(2) Pyrimidine nucleotide synthesis, with the methylation of deoxyuridylic acid to thymidylic acid. It is suggested that deficiency of folic acid coenzymes limits DNA production at this stage.

(3) Amino acid interconversions, including conversion of homocysteine to methionine, a reaction also requiring vitamin B_{12}.

The biologic aspects of the disordered metabolism resulting from folic acid deficiency are related chiefly to disordered growth secondary to defective synthesis of purine and pyrimidine nucleotides. Failure to produce new DNA impairs mitosis, and the biologic effects of this are readily seen in all tissues that contain rapidly dividing cells. Erythropoiesis changes from a normoblastic to megaloblastic appearance. The megaloblast is a large cell with an increased ratio of cytoplasmic to nuclear material. The chromatin is fine-grained, suggesting relative immaturity of the nucleus. The total DNA content of the large cell is normal or slightly increased, whereas the ribonucleic acid (RNA) is markedly increased. The cytoplasmic development continues largely unimpaired, later resulting in hemoglobin production, whereas nuclear changes lag behind. Thymine will reverse the megaloblastic changes produced by folic acid defi-

ciency (but not those secondary to vitamin B_{12} deficiency), suggesting that failure of thymidylate synthesis is the chief limiting factor in this case.

Clinical Uses

In the presence of a megaloblastic anemia, the differentiation between deficiency of folate and vitamin B_{12} must be made and the nature of the process causing a deficiency then clarified.

Deficiency of folic acid may be due to dietary deficiency, although this is rare unless there are increased requirements, as during pregnancy; to decreased utilization due to the use of drugs that are folic acid antagonists; or to interference with absorption.

Supplementary folic acid may, therefore, be used to correct the following states:

A. Dietary Deficiency: Dietary deficiency of folic acid, previously thought to be rare because of the ubiquitous nature of the vitamin, is now more commonly reported. In alcoholics the diet is often deficient in vegetable and animal products, and elderly people may live on restricted diets either for socioeconomic reasons or out of apathy. A recent study of regional ileitis showed that folic acid deficiency was only partly due to defective absorption. Defective intake associated with anorexia was also an important factor. The main treatment in all of these cases consists of correction of the diet, but folic acid, 100–200 μg daily orally, quickly corrects the deficiency.

B. Increased Requirement During Pregnancy: The chief condition precipitating megaloblastic anemia secondary to increased utilization of folic acid is pregnancy. A degree of dietary deficiency also plays a part. The megaloblastic anemia of pregnancy occurs predominantly in poor, multiparous women; it is now uncommon in Western society but still occurs in underdeveloped communities. The greater incidence in twin pregnancies and during the third trimester emphasizes the importance of increased fetal requirements. Folic acid in a dose of 0.5–1 mg daily orally is usually curative. Antenatal care in poor socioeconomic areas frequently includes prophylactic administration of folic acid, 100–300 μg daily orally, often in a preparation that also includes iron. This greatly reduces the incidence of macrocytosis and anemia.

C. Interference with Utilization by Other Drugs: Megaloblastic anemia occurs in many patients receiving the anticonvulsant phenytoin (Dilantin), and also in some patients receiving primidone (Mysoline), carbamazepine (Tegretol), or mephobarbital (Mebaral). Folate deficiency is a rare result of the use of oral contraceptives. These drugs act to inhibit intestinal deconjugase activity and reduce absorption of dietary folate polyglutamates. The anemia is corrected by folic acid or, where practical, by stopping the causative drug. Alcoholism appears to interfere with folate metabolism as well as to encourage nutritional deficiency.

D. Malabsorption Syndrome: Folic acid deficiency occurs commonly in the malabsorption syndrome, due usually to disease of the small intestine but sometimes following partial gastrectomy. Malabsorption syndrome secondary to atrophy of the intestinal villi is seen classically in celiac disease, adult idiopathic steatorrhea, and tropical sprue. The first 2 conditions are often due to intolerance to gluten, and dramatic clinical responses often follow treatment with gluten-free diets. Folic acid supplements are often needed, however, especially in adults.

The cause of tropical sprue is less well understood, and folic acid deficiency probably results from poor intake, poor absorption, and perhaps the increased requirements caused by associated infection. The clinical manifestations often respond quickly to folic acid treatment, though broad-spectrum antibiotics also are sometimes needed for several months.

Folic acid deficiency may also be produced by malabsorption syndromes secondary to gross structural disease of the small intestines—eg, regional ileitis, intestinal tuberculosis, infiltrations by reticuloses and Whipple's disease, intestinal amyloidosis, multiple diverticula, blind loops, extensive surgical resections, and radiation damage.

For many years the therapeutic dose of folic acid has been 10–20 mg daily orally. This is unnecessarily high, and 0.5–1 mg daily is probably sufficient. Even this dose can produce a therapeutic response in anemia due to vitamin B_{12} deficiency, and evidence of vitamin B_{12} deficiency should be sought before treatment with folic acid is begun, particularly if the terminal ileum is diseased or has been surgically removed. If doubt exists regarding the ability of the intestine to absorb folic acid, intramuscular injection is practical for a short period.

Contraindications & Cautions

Because folic acid is generally held to be free of toxic effects, it is frequently given in unnecessarily large doses and sometimes in the absence of a clear indication for its use. An observation that 15 mg/d for as short a period as 1 month may cause behavioral changes has not yet been repeated, but some caution is advisable until the possible toxicity is studied.

Folic acid alone must not be administered to patients with pernicious anemia. Correction of the anemia may occur, but progression of neurologic complications frequently follows.

To treat or mask the development of an anemia due to vitamin B_{12} deficiency requires doses of folic acid that are large compared to the amounts needed for the prevention of folate deficiency. To prevent the masking of the anemia and the development of peripheral nerve and spinal cord changes from vitamin B_{12} deficiency in patients not recognized to have pernicious anemia, multivitamin preparations that may be sold without a prescription are not permitted to contain more than 0.1 mg of folate per daily dose. Preparations sold only upon prescription may contain up to 1 mg per tablet.

FOLINIC ACID
(Citrovorum Factor, Leucovorin)

A folic acid deficiency is produced during therapy with the folic acid analogs aminopterin and amethopterin (methotrexate) used as antineoplastic agents and with the chemotherapeutic agent pyrimethamine. These agents competitively inhibit the conversion of folic acid to folinic acid, but their affinity for the enzyme (folate reductase) is so much greater than that of folic acid that not even large doses of folic acid will correct the drug-induced deficiency. In the event of a severe toxic reaction to the folic acid antagonist, the already reduced form, folinic acid, can be given, since it can be used to form new coenzyme.

Folinic acid is supplied (as calcium leucovorin) for intravenous or intramuscular injection as 1-mL ampules containing 3 mg/mL.

VITAMIN B_{12}
(Cyanocobalamin)

Sources & Chemistry

Several related compounds are able to correct vitamin B_{12} deficiency. Cyanocobalamin was the first member of the group to be isolated, and it is still widely used therapeutically, although it is not found in the bodies of animals. Composed of 2 main groups, the planar group consists of 4 reduced pyrrole rings holding a central cobalt atom. Below the planar group and linked between the central cobalt atom and pyrrole ring IV is a "nucleotide" not found in the usual nucleic acids but composed of ribose and the base 5,6-dimethylbenzimidazole. Above the planar group, there is a cyanide radical linked to the cobalt atom. This cyanide group can be replaced, without loss of biologic activity, by several other substituents: a hydroxyl group, giving hydroxocobalamin; and an adenosyl substitution, forming coenzyme B_{12} (or cobamide), found in highest concentrations of the 3 cobamides.

The ultimate source of the vitamin is synthesis by microorganisms, and it is found only in foodstuffs of animal origin. Liver, kidney, and shellfish have the highest content; muscle, fish, and some cheeses contain moderate amounts. It does not occur in plant products except when they contain symbiotic bacteria (as is the case with legumes).

Bacteria in the human colon synthesize cobalamins, and the patients who used to die of pernicious anemia had fecal excretions of the vitamin far greater than their needs. Vitamin B_{12} in food sources is usually bound to protein and peptides, which are removed before recombination of the vitamin with intrinsic factor in the gut prior to absorption.

The commercially available B_{12} is prepared by fermentation using *Streptomyces griseus*.

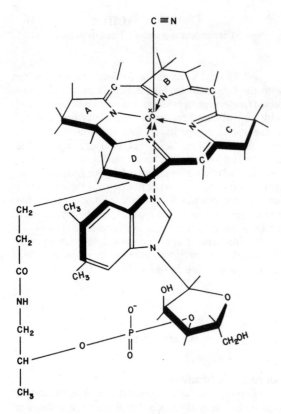

Figure 44 –1. Structure of cyanocobalamin (vitamin B_{12}). (Reproduced, with permission, from Harper HA, Rodwell VW, Mayes PA: *Review of Physiological Chemistry*, 17th ed. Lange, 1979.)

Absorption, Distribution, & Excretion

There are 2 mechanisms for the absorption of vitamin B_{12}. The more important of the 2 is applicable to the small amounts of the vitamin present in the diet. In the stomach, vitamin B_{12} is released from associated peptides and proteins and combines preferentially with intrinsic factor, a glycoprotein (MW 50,000) secreted by the parietal cells of the fundus and body of the stomach. Absorption of vitamin B_{12} then takes place in the lower ileum by a highly specific transport system that requires calcium ions and a pH above 5.7. It is the loss of intrinsic factor and subsequent failure of absorption of vitamin B_{12} that is the cause of pernicious anemia. When large quantities of vitamin B_{12} are given orally, a small percentage is absorbed by diffusion, and this process is independent of the intrinsic factor mechanism. This type of absorption is of therapeutic importance only when patients with pernicious anemia refuse parenteral vitamin B_{12} therapy and are treated with 1000 μg of vitamin B_{12} daily by mouth.

In theory, pernicious anemia could be treated by the combined oral administration of cyanocobalamin and hog intrinsic factor—ie, liver-stomach preparations. However, a refractory state quickly develops.

Isotopically labeled vitamin B_{12} appears to re-

main in the wall of the lower ileum for several hours before entering the blood. In the plasma the vitamin is carried by 2 proteins, an α_1-globulin and a β-globulin, to its storage site in the liver. Intramuscular administration of cyanocobalamin produces a rapid rise in blood level, with saturation of the binding sites on plasma proteins. A large fraction of the injected vitamin (up to 98%) may then be excreted in the urine. Hydroxocobalamin, however, is more completely bound to proteins; a lower fraction of an intramuscular dose is excreted in the urine; and plasma levels following a single injection are maintained 2–3 times as long.

In healthy subjects, excretion of vitamin B_{12} is negligible. Most of the loss occurs as a result of biliary excretion, the vitamin appearing in the feces together with that produced by colonic bacteria. Only a small proportion of vitamin B_{12} excreted in the bile appears in the feces because most is reabsorbed by the terminal ileum.

Requirements & Stores of Cobalamins

The adult human requires about 1 μg of vitamin B_{12} daily to replace the loss that occurs chiefly in the bile and feces. This amount maintains the stores and makes vitamin B_{12} the most potent known vitamin. Dietary intake varies from 1 to 85 μg daily. The total vitamin B_{12} store for an adult human averages 5 mg, most of this being in the liver. It follows that serious deficiency does not usually appear for 3–6 years even in the absence of dietary intake or complete failure of absorption.

Mechanisms of Action

The methylation of homocysteine to methionine requires methyl B_{12}, which receives the methyl group from N^5-methyltetrahydrofolic acid and subsequently transfers it to homocysteine. In the absence of methyl B_{12}, N^5-methyltetrahydrofolic acid cannot be utilized and is trapped, resulting in a situation similar in end result to folic acid deficiency. Experiments performed on microorganisms suggest that vitamin B_{12} may be required for the synthesis of deoxyribose; if this work also applies to mammalian cells, deficiency of the vitamin could limit production of DNA without affecting RNA synthesis. Propionic acid can be metabolized via methylmalonate to succinate, and the last reaction requires coenzyme B_{12}. This reaction, together with the regeneration of methionine, associates vitamin B_{12} with lipid metabolism, and tenuous suggestions have attempted to link these biochemical findings with the defective formation of myelin seen in the nervous system in vitamin B_{12} deficiency. The widespread disturbance of DNA production resulting in the changes seen in cells of the hematopoietic system and most epithelial cells—and which have been previously described for folic acid deficiency—is more easily understood than the lesions of the nervous tissue.

Clinical Uses

Vitamin B_{12}, because of its relative cheapness and lack of toxic effects, is widely used as a placebo and "tonic." This practice should be deplored. Administration should be confined to cases of established deficiency, and, since replacement therapy is usually required for life, a complete investigation of the case should be performed. The degree of deficiency and the underlying cause of the deficiency should then be recorded and the healthy skepticism of successive physicians allayed without the need for repeated studies.

A. Pernicious Anemia: By far the most common justified use of vitamin B_{12} is in the treatment of pernicious anemia (addisonian anemia), a conditional deficiency due to failure of absorption. The primary lesion in pernicious anemia is atrophy of the gastric mucosa, with achlorhydria and failure to secrete intrinsic factor. As a result, dietary vitamin B_{12} is not absorbed by the terminal ileum and is excreted in the feces together with that produced by colonic bacteria. The initial treatment of pernicious anemia consists of parenteral cyanocobalamin or hydroxocobalamin. Doses as high as 1000 μg intramuscularly on alternate days for 10–15 days and as low as 30 μg daily intramuscularly for 5–10 days have been suggested. The tendency has been to use unnecessarily high doses, most of the vitamin appearing in the urine, but the use of hydroxocobalamin reduces the urinary loss. Higher dosages are probably advisable when neurologic changes are present. Within hours of commencing treatment with the vitamin, mental symptoms such as lassitude often improve dramatically and the mild fever that is frequently present may subside. The megaloblastic changes in the marrow disappear in 2–3 days. The reticulocyte response begins in about 3 days, reaching a peak in about 1 week. The hemoglobin and erythrocyte count return to normal in 4–6 weeks. The rate of rise of hemoglobin and the height of the reticulocyte count are greater in cases of greater severity.

The reliability of the response of pernicious anemia to vitamin B_{12} and the insidious fall of hemoglobin that allows cardiovascular compensation largely obviate the need for the transfusion of packed red cells. The response of the neurologic syndrome is slower and less certain than the anemia. Peripheral neuropathy is usually corrected. The subacute combined degeneration of the cord is arrested by vitamin B_{12}, but improvement, if it occurs, is slow. Changes of short duration carry a much better prognosis than a long-standing condition.

Maintenance therapy must be continued for life. Unless the patient understands the disease, the basis for its diagnosis, and the need for repeated treatment, relapses and repeated diagnostic studies are probable. Cyanocobalamin, 100 μg intramuscularly monthly, is effective. Hydroxocobalamin, which is stored in the body for a slightly longer period, may be used instead of cyanocobalamin.

Large amounts of cyanocobalamin by mouth (1000 $\mu g/d$) are effective but less reliable than parenteral vitamin B_{12}. Injectable liver preparations are now standardized in terms of their vitamin B_{12} content and there is no reason to use them. Folic acid will correct the anemia of vitamin B_{12} deficiency but allows the neurologic damage to progress.

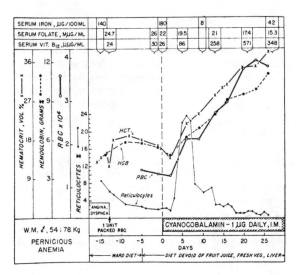

Figure 44 –2. Response to 1 μg of vitamin B_{12} daily in a patient with pernicious anemia. (Reproduced, with permission, from Herbert V: Megaloblastic anemia. N Engl J Med 268:370, 1963.)

B. Investigation of B_{12} Absorption: The cause of suspected vitamin B_{12} deficiency can be investigated by oral administration of a small amount of vitamin B_{12} labeled with radioactive cobalt (^{57}Co). Radioactivity only appears in the urine if the isotopically labeled vitamin is absorbed from the gut. An intramuscular injection of 1000 μg of nonradioactive vitamin B_{12} precedes the oral vitamin and saturates the depleted stores, increasing urinary excretion of the labeled vitamin (Schilling test). Failure of absorption can be further investigated by repeating the test but giving intrinsic factor in addition to isotopically labeled vitamin B_{12}. If absorption of vitamin B_{12} follows this procedure, then deficiency of intrinsic factor is the likely cause; but failure of absorption probably indicates disease of the terminal ileum. Continued and severe deficiency of vitamin B_{12} from any cause produces the classic clinical picture of macrocytic megaloblastic anemia, with mild hemolytic features together with glossitis and weight loss. Varying degrees of peripheral neuropathy, subacute combined degeneration of the spinal cord, retrobulbar neuritis, and mental changes occur and may be present when anemia is absent and megaloblastic changes are slight.

C. Other Uses: All patients who have had a total gastrectomy develop vitamin B_{12} deficiency if they live long enough to exhaust their stores of the vitamin. The deficiency in these cases should be anticipated and parenteral maintenance therapy given. Some patients with partial gastrectomy subsequently develop deficiency of vitamin B_{12}, possibly due to atrophy in the remaining stomach. The treatment is identical to that described for pernicious anemia. Following both total and subtotal gastrectomy, an iron deficiency anemia is likely to develop before the macrocytic anemia.

Dietary deficiency of vitamin B_{12} is extremely rare and has been reported only in association with strict vegetarian diets excluding all meat, eggs, and dairy products. The high intake of folic acid usually prevents any marked hematologic changes. If vitamin B_{12} deficiency is suspected, it can be adequately treated by cyanocobalamin, 5 μg daily orally. The origin of the material from S griseus can be stressed to avoid any conflict.

It has been claimed that the form of retrobulbar neuritis seen in heavy smokers (tobacco amblyopia) is due to the combination of smoking and vitamin B_{12} deficiency. Correction of the deficiency with cyanocobalamin has produced improvement of vision in some cases.

Disorders of the ileum sometimes lead to defective absorption of vitamin B_{12}. Patients with regional ileitis (Crohn's disease), in which the terminal ileum is either diseased or removed, are most prone to this deficiency. All patients with surgical resections, strictures, and bypass operations involving the ileum should be observed periodically for vitamin B_{12} deficiency. Occasionally the generalized mucosal diseases—celiac disease, idiopathic steatorrhea, and tropical sprue—produce vitamin B_{12} deficiency, but this is rare in comparison with the incidence of folic acid deficiency in these cases. Vitamin B_{12} deficiency is not uncommon in association with the blind loop syndrome, possibly because of bacterial competition for the vitamin. Another esoteric cause of deficiency is infestation with the tapeworm Diphyllobothrium latum, which occurs predominantly in people eating uncooked fish from the Baltic Sea.

•   •   •

References

Vitamin B_{12}

Castle WB: Treatment of pernicious anemia: Historical aspects. Clin Pharmacol Ther 7:147, 1966.

Herbert V: Megaloblastic anemia. (2 parts.) N Engl J Med 268:201, 368, 1963.

Herbert V (editor): Vitamin B_{12} and folate. Am J Med 48:539, 1970.

Higginbottom MC, Sweetman L, Nyhan WL: A syndrome of methylmalonic aciduria, homocystinuria, megaloblastic anemia and neurologic abnormalities in a vitamin B_{12}-deficient breast-fed infant of a strict vegetarian. N Engl J Med 299:317, 1978.

Folate

Baldwin JM, Dalessio DJ: Folic acid therapy and spinal cord degeneration in pernicious anemia. N Engl J Med 264:1339, 1961.

Conley CL, Krevans JR: Development of neurologic manifestations of pernicious anemia during multivitamin therapy. N Engl J Med 245:529, 1951.

Gough KR, Thirkettle JL, Read AE: Folic acid deficiency in patients after gastric resection. Q J Med 34:1, 1965.

Herbert V: Folic acid. Annu Rev Med 16:359, 1965.

Lawrence C, Klipstein FA: Megaloblastic anemia of pregnancy in New York City. Ann Intern Med 66:25, 1967.

Rosenberg IH: Folate absorption and malabsorption. N Engl J Med 293:1303, 1975.

Streiff RR: Folate deficiency and oral contraceptives. JAMA 214:105, 1970.

Willoughby MLN, Jewell FG: Folate status throughout pregnancy and in the postpartum period. Br Med J 4:356, 1968.

Part VII. Chemotherapeutic Agents

Cancer Chemotherapy | 45

Sydney E. Salmon, MD

Cancer is a group of neoplastic diseases that occur in humans in all age groups and in all races as well as in animal species. The incidence, geographic distribution, and behavior of specific types of cancer are related to multiple factors including sex, age, race, genetic predisposition, and exposure to environmental carcinogens. Of these various factors, exposure to environmental carcinogens is probably the most important. Chemical carcinogens (particularly those in tobacco smoke), azo dyes, aflatoxins, and other agents have clearly been related to cancer induction in humans as well as in animals. Identification of potential carcinogens in the environment has been greatly simplified with the widespread use of the "Ames test" for mutagenic agents. Ninety percent of carcinogens can be shown to be mutagenic on the basis of this assay. Certain herpes group DNA viruses and type C RNA viruses have also been implicated as causative agents in animal cancers and might be responsible for some human malignancies as well. Oncogenic RNA viruses all appear to contain a "reverse transcriptase" enzyme that permits translation of the RNA message of the tumor virus into the DNA code of the infected cell. Thus, the information governing transformation can become a stable part of the genetics of the host cell. Expression of virus-induced neoplasia probably also depends on additional host and environmental factors that modulate the transformation process.

Whatever the cause, cancer is basically a disease of cells characterized by a shift in control mechanisms that govern cell proliferation and differentiation. Cells that have undergone neoplastic transformation usually express cell surface antigens that appear to be of normal fetal type and also have other signs of apparent "immaturity," including a relative shift to anaerobic metabolism for energy production. Such cells proliferate excessively and form local tumors that can compress or invade adjacent normal structures. A small subpopulation of cells within the tumor can be described as **"tumor stem cells."** They retain the ability to undergo repeated cycles of proliferation as well as migrating to distant sites in the body to colonize various organs in the process called **metastasis.** Such

Sydney E. Salmon is Professor of Medicine and Director of the Cancer Center, University of Arizona College of Medicine, Tucson.

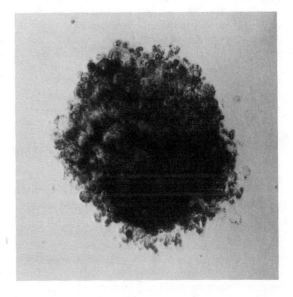

Figure 45–1. Human colon tumor "stem cell" colony in soft agar grown from clonogenic cells from a biopsy of a previously untreated patient. Such tumor-colony-forming cells can be tested with standard and new anticancer drugs with respect to inhibition of clonogenicity.

tumor stem cells thus can express **clonogenic** or colony-forming capability. Maintenance of the clonogenic potential of tumor stem cells can be demonstrated in animals or in vitro by recovering tumor colonies and reseeding the cells that comprise them, thus showing that the cells can renew themselves and give rise to secondary colonies. Fig 45–1 depicts a typical human tumor colony cloned from a tumor stem cell in vitro. Tumor stem cells often have chromosome abnormalities reflecting their genetic instability, which leads to progressive selection of subclones that can survive more readily in the multicellular environment of the host. Quantitative abnormalities in nucleic acid metabolism accompany this process. The invasive and metastatic processes as well as a series of metabolic abnormalities resulting from the cancer cause illness and eventual death of the patient unless the neoplasm can be eradicated with treatment.

Next to heart disease, cancer is the major cause of

death in the USA, causing about 400,000 fatalities
annually. With present methods of treatment, one-
third of patients are cured with local measures (surgery
or radiation therapy), which are quite effective when
the tumor has not metastasized by the time of treatment. Earlier diagnosis might lead to cure of 50% of
patients with such local treatment; however, in the
remaining cases, early micrometastasis is a characteristic feature of the neoplasm, indicating that a systemic approach such as can be attained with
chemotherapy will be required (often along with
surgery or radiation) for effective cancer management.

Cancer chemotherapy as currently employed can
be curative in increasing numbers of disseminated
neoplasms that have undergone either gross or microscopic spread by the time of diagnosis. These include testicular cancer, diffuse histiocytic lymphoma,
Hodgkin's disease, and choriocarcinoma as well as
childhood tumors such as acute lymphoblastic leukemia, Burkitt's lymphoma, Wilms's tumor and embry-
onal rhabdomyosarcoma. Of major importance are the
recent demonstrations that use of chemotherapy along
with initial surgery can increase the cure rate in relatively early stage breast cancer and osteogenic sarcoma. Common carcinomas of the lung and colon are
usually refractory to currently available treatment and
have usually disseminated by the time of diagnosis.

Except for skin cancers (which remain localized),
most cancers in the USA are carcinomas (derived from
epithelium); and the rest are sarcomas (derived from
mesothelium). The 8 most common cancers account
for over 70% of cancer incidence and most of the
fatalities. Lung cancer in smokers is now the most
common lethal cancer in the USA. At first observed
mostly in men, the incidence in women has increased
dramatically with their increased smoking habits. The
current annual USA case incidence of the most common cancers are as follows: lung carcinoma (117,000),
colon and rectal cancer (114,000), female breast
cancer (109,000), uterine carcinoma (54,000), prostate cancer (66,000), bladder and kidney cancer
(52,000), lymphoma (30,100), and leukemia
(22,000). Recent statistics have shown falling mortality rates in Hodgkin's disease, testicular cancer, acute
leukemia, and breast cancer—reflecting advances in
chemotherapy in these disorders.

At present, chemotherapy provides palliative
rather than curative therapy for many forms of disseminated cancer. Effective palliation results in temporary
clearing of the symptoms and signs of cancer and
prolongation of useful life. In the past decade, advances in cancer chemotherapy have also begun to
provide evidence that chemical control of neoplasia
may become a reality for many forms of cancer during
the 1980s. This will probably be achieved first through
combined modality therapy in which optimal combinations of surgery, radiotherapy, and chemotherapy are
used to eradicate both the primary and its occult micrometastases before gross spread can be detected on
physical or x-ray examinations.

In principle, drug research may provide the ulti-

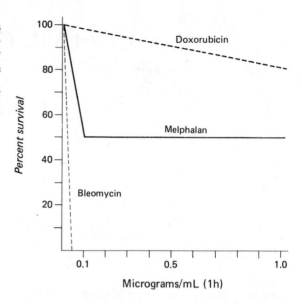

Figure 45 –2. Example of an in vitro sensitivity assay with
pharmacologically achievable doses of cytotoxic anticancer
drugs tested against tumor-colony-forming stem cells from
a patient's tumor biopsy sample. The cells were incubated
in various concentrations of the drugs for 1 hour prior to
plating in soft agar and then cultured for 1 week prior to
counting the survival of tumor-colony-forming units. The
results demonstrate sensitivity to bleomycin, resistance to
doxorubicin, and heterogeneity in response to melphalan.
Fifty percent of the colony-forming cells showed sensitivity
to melphalan at the lowest dose tested, while the remaining
50% were resistant to the highest dose.

mate cure for cancer, although many of the currently
available agents fall short of this goal. A major effort to
develop anticancer drugs through both empiric screening and rational design of new compounds has now
been under way for 2½ decades. This program has
employed testing in a few well-characterized trans-
plantable animal tumor systems. The recent development of a simple in vitro colony assay for measuring
drug sensitivity of human tumor stem cells may augment and shorten the testing program in the near future. An example of such an in vitro assay for standard
anticancer drugs appears in Fig 45–2. Once new drugs
with potential anticancer activity are identified, they
are subjected to preclinical studies of toxicology and
limited pharmacologic studies in animals. Promising
agents that do not have excessive toxicity are then
advanced to phase I clinical trials wherein their pharmacologic and toxic effects are tested in patients with
advanced cancer. Phase II clinical trials are then used
to establish the tumor types for which the drug is
useful, followed by phase III trials to compare the new
agent with the best standard therapy. Subsequently,
the drug may be licensed by the FDA for use in practice. This development program for a single new drug
frequently requires 10 years of testing at the various
steps before a drug is ready for general use.

Ideal anticancer drugs would theoretically be

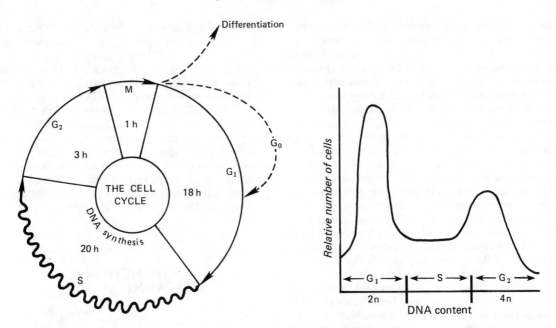

Figure 45–3. The cell cycle and cancer. The illustration at left is a conceptual depiction of the cell cycle phases all cells—normal or neoplastic—must traverse prior to cell division. The relative durations of the various phases of the cycle are typical for a malignant cell population; however, the duration of G_1 can potentially be shortened markedly. At right is a histogram of DNA content of an unperturbed population of tumor cells as determined by flow microfluorimetry (FMF), a technic that permits quantitation of the proportion of cells in the major metabolic phases of the cell cycle. Many of the effective anticancer drugs exert their action on cells traversing the cell cycle and are called cell cycle-specific (CCS) drugs (Table 45–1). A second grouping of agents called cell cycle-nonspecific (CCNS) drugs can sterilize tumor cells irrespective of whether they are cycling or resting in the G_0 compartment. G_1 is the initial phase of the cell cycle of a cell committed to proliferation and is associated with synthesis of enzymes required for DNA synthesis. The S (synthesis) phase is the time during which the DNA code is replicated for the various genes on specific chromosomes. The G_2 phase is associated with synthesis of RNA and proteins required for the mitotic spindle apparatus followed by the brief M (mitotic) phase of cell division. CCNS drugs are capable of killing both G_0 and cycling cells (although cycling cells are more sensitive). The damage induced by CCNS drugs is often manifested as a lengthening of the S phase and an irreversible G_2 block. An FMF curve of cells treated with a CCNS drug would be reduced in size in comparison to that seen above, and with a shift of DNA content of intact cells to a 4n accumulation.

those that eradicate cancer cells without harming normal tissues. Unfortunately, few currently available agents meet this criterion, and a therapeutic index must be determined wherein benefit outweighs toxicity.

Information on cell and population kinetics of cancer cells in part explains the limited effectiveness of most available anticancer drugs. A schematic summary of cell cycle kinetics appears in Fig 45–3. This information is relevant to the mode of action, indications, and scheduling of cell cycle-specific (CCS) and cell cycle-nonspecific (CCNS) drugs. Agents falling in these 2 major classes are summarized in Table 45–1. Two other classes of drugs have recently also entered development: "differentiators," intended to force dividing cells into the differentiation pathway; and "biologic response modifiers," which alter tumor-host metabolic and immunologic relationships. Patients with widespread cancer (eg, acute leukemia) may have 10^{12} (1 trillion) tumor cells throughout the body at the time of diagnosis. If tolerable dosing of an effective drug is capable of killing 99.9% of clonogenic tumor cells, this would induce a clinical remis-

sion of the neoplasm associated with symptomatic improvement. However, there would still be many logs of tumor stem cells remaining in the body, including some that may be inherently resistant to the drug (and could "clone out" despite drug therapy), while others might reside in pharmacologic sanctuaries (eg,

Table 45–1. Mechanism of action of major classes of drugs: Cell cycle relationships.

Cell Cycle – Specific (CCS) Agents	Cell Cycle – Nonspecific (CCNS) Agents
Antimetabolites (azacytidine, cytarabine, fluorouracil, mercaptopurine, methotrexate, PALA, thioguanine)	Alkylating agents (busulfan, cyclophosphamide, mechlorethamine, melphalan, thiotepa)
Bleomycin peptide antibiotics	Antibiotics (dactinomycin,
Podophyllin alkaloids (VP16-213, VM26)	daunorubicin, doxorubicin, mithramycin, mitomycin)
Vinca alkaloids (vincristine, vinblastine, vindesine)	Cisplatin
	Nitrosoureas (BCNU, CCNU, methyl-CCNU)

the central nervous system) where effective drug concentrations may be difficult to achieve. When CCS drugs are used, the tumor stem cells must also be in the sensitive phase of the cell cycle (and not in G_0), so scheduling of these agents is of particular importance. In common bacterial infections, a 3 log reduction in microorganisms might be curative, because host resistance factors can eliminate residual bacteria through immunologic and microbicidal mechanism; however, host mechanisms for eliminating moderate numbers of cancer cells appear to be generally ineffective. To overcome the limited "log kill" of anticancer drugs, rational combinations of agents with differing toxicities and mechanisms of action have been employed. If the drugs do not have too much overlap in toxicity, at least additive cytotoxic effects can be achieved with combination chemotherapy, and subclones resistant to only one of the agents can potentially be eradicated. Additionally, some combinations of anticancer drugs appear to exert true synergism wherein the effect of the 2 drugs is greater than additive. The efficacy of combination chemotherapy has now been validated in many forms of human cancer, and the scientific rationale delineated above appears to be sound. As a result, combination chemotherapy is now the standard approach to curative treatment of testicular cancer and lymphomas and improved palliative treatment of many other tumor types.

Applications of these kinetic concepts to cancer chemotherapy are illustrated in Fig 45–4. It must be emphasized that the exact "phase" of the cell cycle in which cycle-specific agents act is still somewhat uncertain. In general, CCS drugs have proved most effective in hematologic malignancies and other tumors with a relatively large proportion of the cells proliferating or in the **growth fraction.** CCNS drugs (many of which bind to DNA) are useful in low-growth-fraction "solid tumors" as well as high-growth-fraction tumors. In all instances, effective agents sterilize or inactivate tumor stem cells, which are often only a small fraction of the cells within a tumor. Non-stem cells (eg, those that have irreversibly differentiated) are considered sterile by definition and are not a significant component of the cancer problem.

POLYFUNCTIONAL ALKYLATING AGENTS

History

This group of agents was developed from the sulfur mustard vesicant gas dichloroethyl sulfide used in World War I. During World War II, the nitrogen mustards were developed for use as chemical warfare agents. In addition to their vesicant effect upon the skin, these compounds produced atrophy of lymphoid

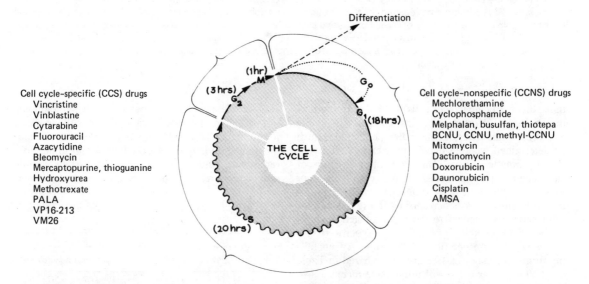

Figure 45–4. The cell cycle and cancer chemotherapeutic agents of cell cycle-specific (CCS) and cell cycle-nonspecific (CCNS) mechanisms of action. Many of the effective cancer chemotherapeutic drugs appear to exert their action on cancer cells going through the cell cycle. G_1 is the phase prior to DNA synthesis during which various enzymes, including those necessary for DNA synthesis, are synthesized; the S phase is the actual period of commitment to division during which DNA is replicated for the various chromosomes; G_2 is a phase of specialized protein and RNA synthesis and manufacture of the mitotic spindle apparatus, followed by the brief M phase of mitosis. G_0 refers to a long resting state in which cells are not cycling and therefore are not affected by CCS drugs. CCNS drugs are capable of killing both G_0 and cycling cells (although cycling cells are more sensitive). The damage induced by CCNS drugs is often manifest as a slowing of the S phase and an irreversible G_2 block rendering the cells incapable of division.

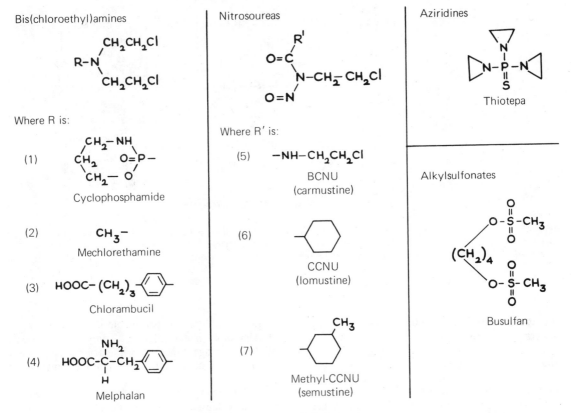

Figure 45–5. Types of alkylating drugs.

tissue and bone marrow. Because of these latter effects, they were introduced for the treatment of malignant lymphomas and leukemias and were later found to be effective against bronchogenic carcinoma and carcinoma of the ovary as well. Since the introduction of the parent nitrogen mustard "HN2"—methyl-bis(β-chloroethyl)amine, mechlorethamine, Mustargen—new and more stable polyfunctional alkylating drugs have been developed in the search for more effective and less toxic agents. It is now recognized that different alkylating agents have some specificity for selected neoplasms.

Chemistry

The major clinically useful alkylating agents (Fig 45–5) have a structure containing a bis(chloroethyl)-amine, ethyleneimine, or nitrosourea moiety. Among the bis(chloroethyl)amines, cyclophosphamide, mechlorethamine, melphalan, and chlorambucil have the greatest utility. The aziridine thiotepa and the alkylsulfonate busulfan are used for specialized purposes for ovarian cancer and chronic myeloid leukemia, respectively. The major nitrosoureas are BCNU (carmustine) and CCNU (lomustine); a related agent, methyl-CCNU (semustine), remains investigational. A variety of investigational alkylating agents have been synthesized that link various hormones or sugar moieties to the alkylating radical. As a class, the alkylating agents act by exerting cytotoxic effects via

alkylation (transfer of their alkyl groups) to various cellular constituents. Alkylations of DNA within the nucleus probably represent the major interactions that lead to cellular lethality. However, these drugs react chemically with sulfhydryl, amino, carboxyl, and phosphate groups as well. The general mechanism of action of these drugs includes formation of carbonium ion, which is then transferred to a cellular constituent as an alkyl group. In addition to alkylation, a secondary mechanism that occurs with nitrosoureas involves carbamoylation of substrates through formation of isocyanate radicals. The major substitute for alkylation within DNA is the N^7 position of the guanine base (Fig 45–6). This interaction can be either on the single strand or cross-link DNA, as the major alkylating agents are all bifunctional with 2 reactive chlorethyl radicals. Alkylation of guanine can result in formation of an abnormal base pair (with thymine), cross-linking of guanines, cleavage of their imidazole rings, or depurination of DNA. Lethal events that result from alkylation are probably due to cellular DNA repair mechanisms that "cut and patch" DNA enzymatically. While single strand alkylations can be excised and repaired by reading the opposite strand, cross-linked alkylations lead to cutting both strands, which fragments the DNA helix of the chromosomes irreparably. As might be anticipated, mispairing of bases and numerous repairs can lead to various "frame shift" or other mutations; therefore, it is not surprising

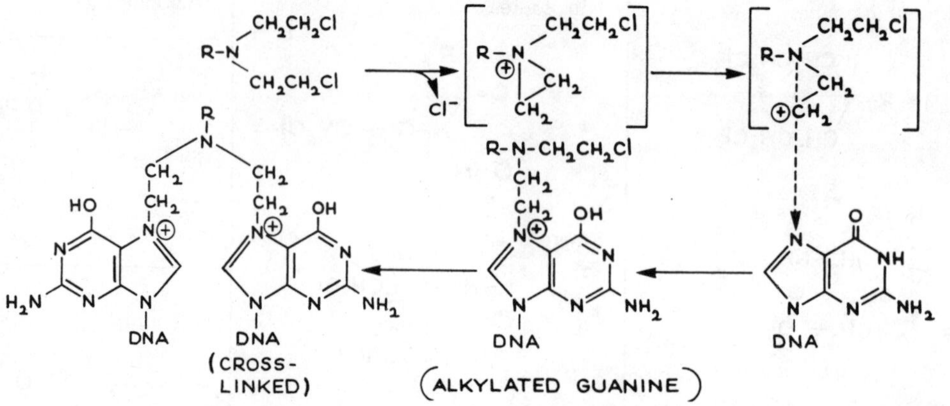

Figure 45–6. Effect of alkylating agents on DNA purines. A bis(chloroethyl)amine forms an ethyleneammonium ion, which opens to form a carbonium ion. The carbonium ion reacts with a base such as N^7 of guanine in DNA, producing an alkylated purine. The alkylated purine, through the illustrated mechanisms of cross-linking DNA strands, leads to cell death.

that these agents have both mutagenic and carcinogenic side-effects.

Pharmacologic Effects

Active alkylating agents have direct vesicant effects and can damage tissues at the site of injection as well as having systemic toxicity. Toxicities are generally dose-related, particularly on the bone marrow, the gastrointestinal tract, and the gonads. After intravenous injection, nausea and vomiting usually occur within 30–60 minutes with mechlorethamine, cyclophosphamide, or BCNU. The emetic effects are of central nervous system origin and can be reduced by pretreatment with phenothiazines or cannabinoids (tetrahydrocannibinol, nabilone). Subcutaneous injection of mechlorethamine or BCNU leads to tissue necrosis and sloughing. Cyclophosphamide is not active as administered and therefore does not have direct vesicant effects; it must be activated by microsomal enzymes in the liver (Fig 45–7). The major toxicity of these agents is on the bone marrow and results in dose-related suppression of myelopoiesis. The white blood count and absolute granulocyte count reach their low point 10–12 days after injection of mechlorethamine or cyclophosphamide, with subsequent recovery within 21 days (cyclophosphamide) to 42 days (mechlorethamine). The white count nadir with nitrosoureas is delayed to 28 days, with recovery by 42 days. Effects on megakaryocytes and platelets parallel those on granulocytes. Because of the long life span of the erythrocyte, effects on erythropoiesis are masked, and the red cell count is usually only mildly reduced. Side-effects on the bone marrow may be more severe when an alkylating agent is given along with other myelosuppressive drugs or radiation therapy, and dose reductions are often required in such circumstances to avoid excessive toxicity.

Following hematopoietic recovery, the agent may be given again on an intermittent dosing schedule at sufficient intervals to permit blood count recovery. Ovarian or testicular failure is a common late sequela of alkylating agent therapy, while acute leukemia is a relatively rare complication of use of these mutagenic agents.

Oral dosing forms of alkylating agents have been of great value and have been developed using more stable alkylators. Oral administration of cyclophosphamide, melphalan, chlorambucil, busulfan, and CCNU represents the most common route of administration of these agents and produces effects simi-

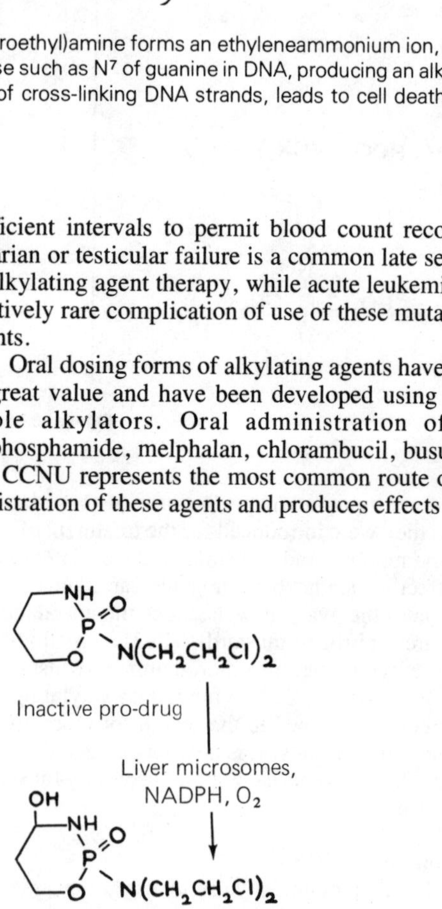

Figure 45–7. Cyclophosphamide metabolism in humans.

lar to those served with parenteral administration. In general, if a tumor is resistant to one alkylating agent, it will be relatively resistant to other agents of this class (although not necessarily to nitrosoureas); however, there are distinct exceptions to this rule for specific tumor types wherein differing transport or resistance mechanisms may be involved. Overall, cyclophosphamide is the most useful alkylating agent currently available. The oral drug busulfan has a surprising degree of specificity for the granulocyte series and therefore has particular value in therapy of chronic myelogenous leukemia. Busulfan does not cause nausea or vomiting despite uniform absorption. Increased skin pigmentation is common with this drug, and rarer syndromes of pulmonary fibrosis or adrenal insufficiency or wasting have also been reported often enough so that they can be attributed to busulfan. With all oral alkylating agents, some degree of leukopenia is desirable to provide evidence that the drug has been absorbed adequately. Repeated blood counts are essential during administration of these agents, as the development of severe leukopenia or thrombocytopenia necessitates interruption of therapy.

ESTRAMUSTINE

Estramustine phosphate (Estracyt) is currently an investigational agent in the USA, although it is commercially available in several European countries. It is a chemical compound of estradiol-17β and the alkylating agent mechlorethamine linked to the C$_3$ of the steroid. Both parts of the estramustine molecule appear to retain biologic activity, since the drug has selective cytotoxic and weak estrogenic effects. In animal tumor systems, estramustine is active in chemically induced mammary carcinoma. In humans it appears to have particular efficacy in carcinoma of the prostate. About 75% of an orally administered dose is absorbed from the gut as estramustine after enzymatic removal of the phosphate group.

Estramustine phosphate (Estracyt)

Estramustine does not have generalized cytotoxic effects and does not cause bone marrow depression. The major toxicities observed with this agent have been occasional nausea and vomiting and mild gynecomastia. Recent investigative work suggests that estramustine is taken up by prostatic tissue and is

hydrolyzed to estradiol and normechlorethamine.

Estramustine has been used clinically in Sweden for the treatment of prostatic carcinoma for over 10 years. A useful dose schedule is 600 mg/m^2/d orally. Treatment has been continued for over 3 years in responsive patients. Recent studies in the USA showed objective evidence of tumor shrinkage in 24% of patients with hormone-resistant, advanced prostatic carcinoma and subjective benefits (pain relief) in an additional 19% of patients. The drug stands as a prototype for a selective anticancer drug targeted toward a specific malignant tissue and is therefore also important from the theoretic standpoint.

NITROSOUREAS

Carmustine (BCNU), lomustine (CCNU), and semustine (methyl-CCNU) are important new drugs which appear to be non-cross-reactive with regard to tumor resistance to other alkylating agents; all probably require biotransformation for antitumor activity, although this can occur by nonenzymatic decomposition. They are highly lipid-soluble and cross the blood-brain barrier. With respect to lomustine, by 1 hour, the plasma metabolites account for virtually all the administered drug and are 33% the cis 4-hydroxy and 62% the trans 4-hydroxy derivatives. The nitrosoureas appear to alkylate the base-pairing regions of the cytosine bases of DNA and RNA. The drugs appear to be more effective against resting than cycling cells, although within a cycling cell population the drugs appear to slow cell progression through the DNA synthetic phase. After oral administration of lomustine or semustine, peak plasma levels of metabolites appear within 1–4 hours, with prompt central nervous system appearance of 30–40% of the activity present in the plasma. While the initial plasma t½ is in the range of 6 hours, a second t½ is in the range of 1–2 days, and 15–20% of the metabolites are still in the body at 5 days. Urinary excretion appears to be the major route of elimination from the body. One naturally occurring sugar-containing nitrosourea, streptozocin, is interesting because it has minimal bone marrow toxicity but is frequently effective in the treatment of insulin-secreting islet cell carcinoma of the pancreas and occasionally in non-Hodgkin lymphomas. Chlorozotocin, a related synthetic nitrosourea, which also lacks marrow toxicity, is now in the stage of early clinical investigation.

RELATED AGENTS WITH POSSIBLE ALKYLATING ACTIVITY

Several compounds have mechanisms of action that may involve special forms of alkylation (eg, in some instances by providing a free CH_3^+). These include procarbazine, dacarbazine, hexamethylmelamine, and cisplatin.

1. PROCARBAZINE

The oral agent procarbazine (N-methylhydrazine, Matulane) is a methylhydrazine derivative with chemotherapeutic activity (particularly in Hodgkin's disease) as a cytotoxic agent. The drug is also leukemogenic and has teratogenic and mutagenic properties.

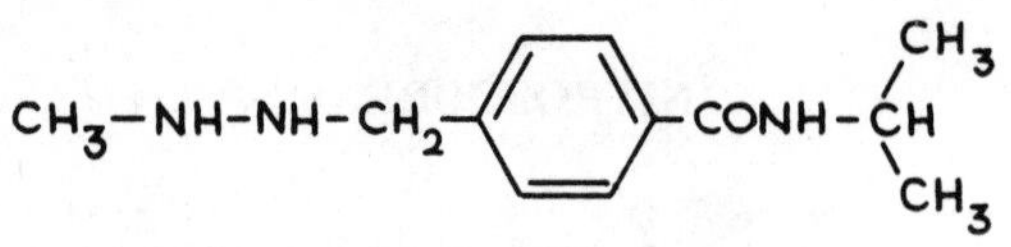

N-Isopropyl-*a*-(2-methylhydrazino)-
p-toluamide (procarbazine, Matulane)

The mechanism of action of procarbazine is uncertain; however, the N-methyl group of procarbazine is labile in vivo. Oxidative breakdown of this drug by microsomal enzymes can generate H_2O_2, hydroxyl radicals, and various metabolites of the drug that may be cytotoxic. One metabolite is a monoamine oxidase inhibitor, and adverse side-effects can occur when procarbazine is given with other MAO inhibitors. In addition to predictable nausea, vomiting, and myelosuppression, hemolytic anemia, pulmonary reactions and adverse responses with alcohol (disulfiramlike) have also been reported, as have skin rashes when procarbazine is given with phenytoin.

Procarbazine has had major use in combination chemotherapy of Hodgkin's disease, as it is not cross-resistant with *Vinca* alkaloids or conventional alkylating agents. However, its leukemogenic properties may eventually lead to its replacement with drugs that have lesser carcinogenic potential.

2. DACARBAZINE

Dacarbazine is a synthetic compound with an obscure mechanism of action that may relate to alkyla-

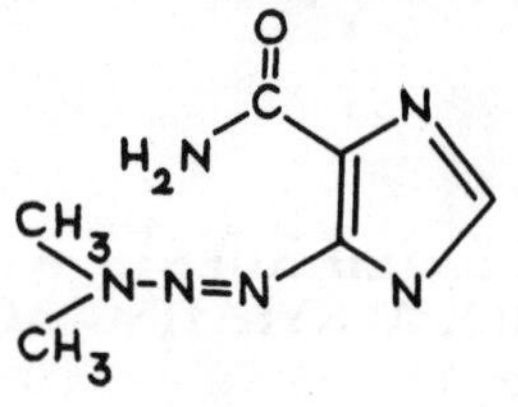

Dacarbazine
(dimethyl imidazole carboxamide)

tion or activity as a structural analog. It is administered parenterally and is not schedule-dependent. As administered, it is relatively inactive, but it is bioactivated by liver microsomes. Dacarbazine produces marked nausea, vomiting, and myelosuppression. Its major applications are in melanoma, Hodgkin's disease, and some soft tissue sarcomas. In the latter 2 tumors, its activity is potentiated by doxorubicin.

3. HEXAMETHYLMELAMINE

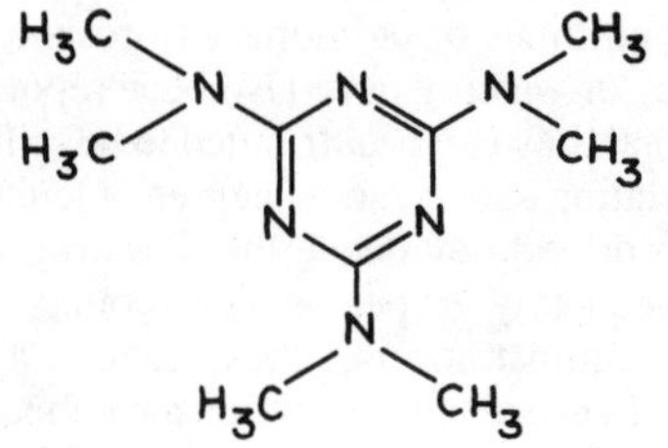

Hexamethylmelamine

Hexamethylmelamine (hexamine) is a melamine tentatively classed as an alkylating agent. It is relatively insoluble and available only in oral form. A related compound, pentamethylmelamine, is more soluble and is now in clinical trial in an intravenous form. Both agents are probably biotransformed to active intermediaries and may act by release of formaldehyde intracellularly. These agents cause nausea, vomiting, and central nervous system and peripheral neuropathies but relatively mild myelosuppression. They are currently classed as investigational. Hexamethylmelamine is useful in alkylating agent-resistant ovarian carcinoma and will probably be approved by the FDA for use in that disorder in the near future.

4. CISPLATIN

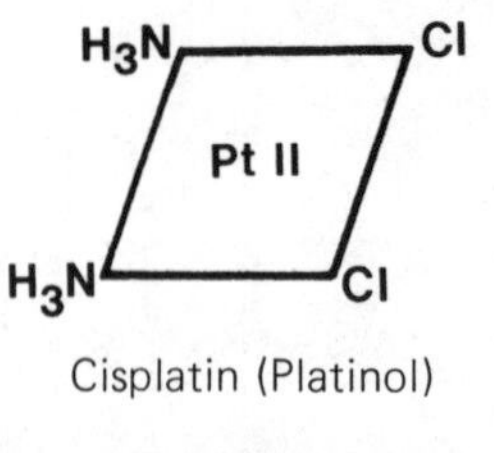

Cisplatin (Platinol)

Cisplatin (cis-dichlorodiammineplatinum II, Platinol) is an organic metal complex recently approved by the FDA for use in cancer chemotherapy. The antitumor activity of platinum coordination complexes was first discovered by Rosenberg after he made the serendipitous observation that bacteria do not proliferate on a platinum electrode. A whole series of platinum analogs have been synthesized, but cisplatin is the only one in clinical use. While the precise mechanism of action of cisplatin is still to be defined, it is thought to act analogously to alkylating agents in its interaction with DNA. Although neutral in plasma, the platinum complex becomes aquated intracellularly to form a positively charged platinum species that is likely to interact with nucleophilic sites. The purine and pyrimidine bases of DNA possess such sites and account for the majority of biologically effective intracellular platinum binding. Possible platinum complex-DNA reactions include bifunctional binding or chelation to one base and intrastrand and interstrand cross-linking. The platinum complexes appear to synergize with certain other anticancer drugs. After intravenous administration, the major acute toxicity is nausea and vomiting. Cisplatin has relatively little effect on the bone marrow, but it can induce significant renal dysfunction and occasional acoustic nerve dysfunction. Hydration with saline infusion—alone or with mannitol or other diuretics— appears to minimize nephrotoxicity.

Cisplatin has major antitumor activity in genitourinary cancers, particularly testicular, ovarian, and bladder cancer. Its use along with vinblastine and bleomycin has been a major advance in the development of curative therapy for nonseminomatous testicular cancers.

CLINICAL USES OF POLYFUNCTIONAL ALKYLATING AGENTS

The alkylating agents are used in the treatment of a wide variety of hematologic malignancies and solid tumors, generally as components of combination chemotherapy. These are summarized in Table 45–2 and discussed under various specific tumors.

ADVERSE REACTIONS TO POLYFUNCTIONAL ALKYLATING AGENTS

Nausea and vomiting are almost universally reported with intravenously administered mechlorethamine, cyclophosphamide, and carmustine and occur with moderate frequency with oral cyclophosphamide.

The important toxic effect of therapeutic doses of virtually all the alkylating drugs is depression of bone marrow and subsequent leukopenia and thrombocytopenia. Severe infections and septicemia may result, with granulocytopenia, below 600 PMNs/μL. Platelet depression below 40,000/μL may be accom-

Table 45–2. Polyfunctional alkylating agents and probable alkylating agents: Dosages and toxicity.

Alkylator	Single Agent Dose	Acute Toxicity	Delayed Toxicity
Nitrogen mustard (HN2, mechlorethamine, Mustargen)	0.4 mg/kg IV in single or divided doses	Nausea and vomiting	Moderate depression of peripheral blood count. Excessive doses produce severe bone marrow depression with leukopenia, thrombocytopenia, and bleeding. Alopecia and hemorrhagic cystitis occasionally occur with cyclophosphamide. Cystitis can be prevented with adequate hydration.
Chlorambucil (Leukeran)	0.1–0.2 mg/kg/d orally; 6–12 mg/d	None	
Cyclophosphamide (Cytoxan)	3.5–5 mg/kg/d orally for 10 days; 1 g/m^2 IV as single dose	Nausea and vomiting	
Melphalan (Alkeran)	0.25 mg/kg/d orally for 4 days every 4–6 weeks	None	
Thiotepa (triethylenethiophosphoramide)	0.2 mg/kg IV for 5 days	None	
Busulfan (Myleran)	2–8 mg/d orally; 150–250 mg/course	None	
Carmustine (BCNU)	200 mg/m^2 IV every 6 weeks	Nausea and vomiting	Leukopenia and thrombocytopenia. Rarely hepatitis.
Lomustine (CCNU)	150 mg/m^2 orally every 6 weeks	Nausea and vomiting	
Semustine (methyl-CCNU)	150 mg/m^2 orally every 6 weeks	Nausea and vomiting	
Hexamethylmelamine	10 mg/kg/d for 21 days	Nausea and vomiting	Leukopenia, thrombocytopenia, and peripheral neuropathy.
Procarbazine	50–200 mg/d orally	Nausea and vomiting	Bone marrow depression, central nervous system depression.
Dacarbazine	300 mg/m^2 daily IV for 5 days	Nausea and vomiting	Bone marrow depression.
Estramustine (Estracyt)	600 mg/m^2/d orally	Occasional nausea	Occasional gynecomastia.
Cisplatin (Platinol)	20 mg/m^2/d IV for 5 days or 50–70 mg/m^2 as single dose every 3 weeks	Nausea and vomiting	Renal dysfunction. Acoustic nerve dysfunction.

panied by induced hemorrhagic phenomena. Cyclophosphamide may produce slight to severe alopecia in up to 30% of patients. It may also cause hemorrhagic cystitis. The cystitis can often be averted with adequate hydration.

The hematopoietic effects of toxic doses of alkylating drugs are treated by discontinuing the agent. Red cell and platelet transfusions and antibiotics to control infections are employed as needed until the marrow has regenerated.

ANTIMETABOLITES
(Structural Analogs)

The development of drugs with actions in intermediary metabolism of proliferating cells has been important both clinically and conceptually. While unique biochemical pathways have yet to be discovered within cancer cells, they do have a number of quantitative differences in metabolism from normal cells that render them more susceptible to a number of antimetabolites or structural analogs. Most of these agents have been rationally designed and synthesized, based on knowledge of cellular enzymology, although a few have been discovered as antibiotics. While the antimetabolites differ greatly in structure, they all share the property of having been designed to inhibit specific enzymes either competitively or noncompetitively and are structurally similar to normal metabolites. The prototype antimetabolite drugs for inhibiting bacterial growth are the sulfonamides; the prototype

for inhibiting malignant growth is the folic acid antagonist methotrexate, which acts directly as a substitute for a normal metabolite.

Biochemical Mechanisms

Antimetabolites or their active products (after biotransformation) can work by any of a number of different mechanisms that inhibit cell proliferation. For example, the antimetabolite may be metabolized instead of the normal substrate for a metabolic pathway, so that the antimetabolite is incorporated into a key molecule which then cannot function properly. A second mechanism involves competition with a normal metabolite that normally acts at either the catalytic site of an enzyme or at an allosteric (regulatory) site. Binding to either of these sites on the enzyme may be reversible or irreversible depending on the specific structure and function of the antimetabolite. One form of antimetabolite that binds to the catalytic site of an enzyme will strongly inhibit it when the enzyme is in a transition state with respect to the substrate. In some instances, inhibition of an enzyme will cause cell death by causing a toxic product to accumulate; however, this mechanism appears to be relatively uncommon.

The biochemical pathways that have thus far proved to be most exploitable with antimetabolites have been those relating to nucleotide and nucleic acid synthesis. In a number of instances, when an enzyme is known to have a major effect in steps leading to cell replication, inhibitors of the step it catalyzes have proved to be useful anticancer drugs. A summary of sites of action of some of the antimetabolites affecting DNA synthesis is depicted in Fig 45–8.

These drugs and their doses and toxicities are shown in Table 45–3. The principal drugs are discussed below.

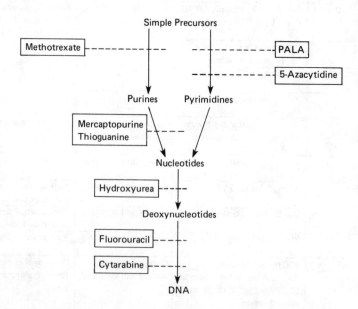

Figure 45 –8. Sites of action of antimetabolites on the DNA synthetic pathway.

Table 45–3. Structural analogs: Dosages and toxicity.

Chemotherapeutic Agent	Single Agent Dose	Delayed Toxicity*
Methotrexate (amethopterin, MTX)	2.5–5 mg/d orally; 10 mg intrathecally 1–2 times weekly	Oral and gastrointestinal tract ulceration, bone marrow depression, leukopenia, thrombocytopenia.
Mercaptopurine (Purinethol, 6-MP)	2.5 mg/kg/d orally	Usually well tolerated. Larger dosages may cause bone marrow depression.
Thioguanine (6-TG)	2 mg/kg/d orally	Usually well tolerated. Larger dosages may cause bone marrow depression.
Fluorouracil (5-FU)	15 mg/kg/d IV for 5 days by 24-hour infusion; 15 mg/kg weekly IV	Nausea, oral and gastrointestinal ulceration, bone marrow depression.
Cytarabine (Ara-C, Cytosar)	100 mg/m² /d for 5–10 days, either by continuous IV infusion or subcutaneously every 8 hours	Nausea and vomiting, bone marrow depression, megaloblastosis, leukopenia, thrombocytopenia.
5-Azacytidine	200 mg/m² /d IV for 5 days	Nausea and vomiting, diarrhea, fever, hypotension, prolonged marrow hypoplasia.

Supportive Agent With All Drugs	Dose	Delayed Toxicity
Allopurinol (Zyloprim)	300–800 mg/d orally for prevention or relief of hyperuricemia	Usually none. Enhances effects and toxicity of 6-MP when used in combination.

*These drugs do not cause acute toxicity.

METHOTREXATE

Methotrexate (4-amino-N^{10}-methylpteroylglutamate, MTX) is a folic acid antagonist that binds tightly to the active catalytic site of dehydrofolate reductase (DHFR), inactivating the essential enzyme required to synthesize the active form of folic acid (tetrahydrofolic acid). Lack of this cofactor interrupts the synthesis of purine precursors and inhibits all growth through interference with DNA synthesis, but it also affects synthesis of RNA and various coenzymes. Tumor cell resistance to methotrexate has been attributed to (1) limited drug uptake and (2) synthesis of increased levels of dehydrofolate reductase. DNA hybridization studies of animal tumor cell lines with acquired resistance to methotrexate have shown that in some instances, the increased synthesis of DHFR results from a marked increase in the number of gene copies that code for this enzyme. It remains to be established whether this genetic resistance mechanism is relevant for other drugs or for resistant tumors in patients receiving methotrexate.

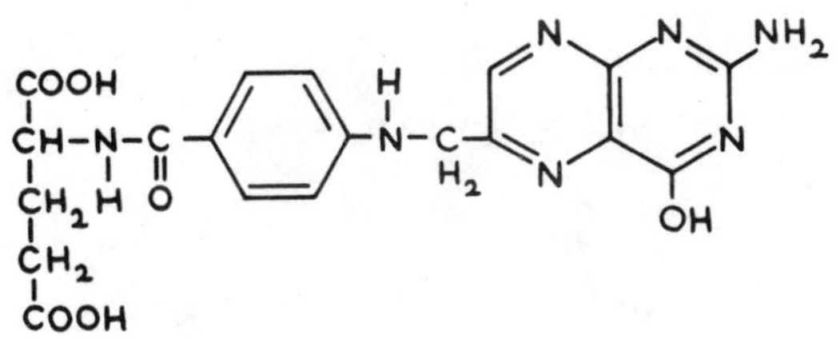

Methotrexate is administered clinically by the intravenous or oral route. Up to 90% of an oral dose is excreted in the urine within 12 hours. The drug is not subject to metabolism, and serum levels are therefore proportionate to dose as long as renal function and hydration status are adequate. Toxic side-effects to proliferating tissues are usually observed on the bone marrow and to a lesser extent the skin and gastrointestinal mucosa. The effects of methotrexate can be reversed by administration of folinic acid (citrovorum factor) or large doses of thymidine. Citrovorum factor "rescue" has been used with accidental overdose or experimentally along with high-dose methotrexate therapy in a protocol intended to recue normal cells while still leaving the tumor cells subject to its cytotoxic action.

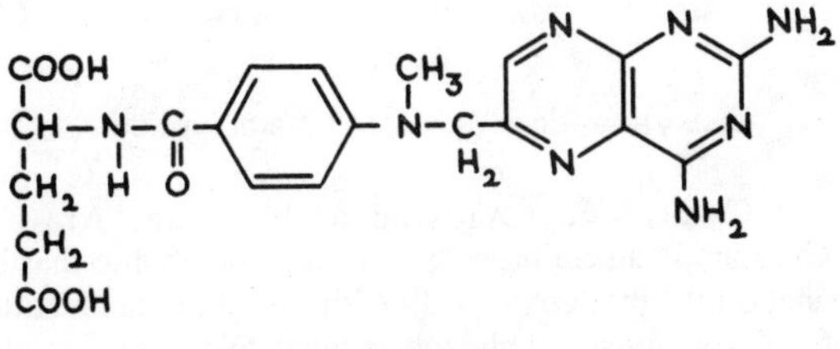

Folic acid

Methotrexate

PURINE ANTAGONISTS

Mercaptopurine (purinethol, 6-MP) was the first of the thiopurine series found useful as an anticancer drug. Like other thiopurines, it must be anabolized to the nucleotide form (6-thioinosinic acid), which in turn inhibits a number of the enzymes of purine interconversion. Significant amounts of thioguanylic acid and 6-methylmercaptopurine ribotide (MMPR) also are formed from 6-MP. These metabolites may also contribute to the action of 6-MP. For example, MMPR potently inhibits de novo purine synthesis. 6-MP is used primarily in the treatment of childhood acute leukemia, although a closely related analog, azathioprine, is used as an immunosuppressive agent (Chapter 46).

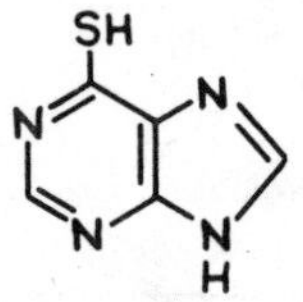

6-Mercapto-
purine

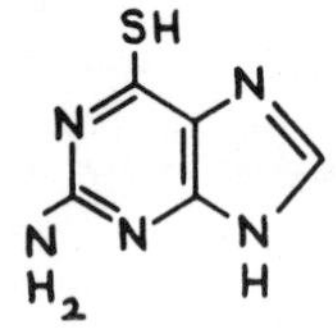

6-Thioguanine

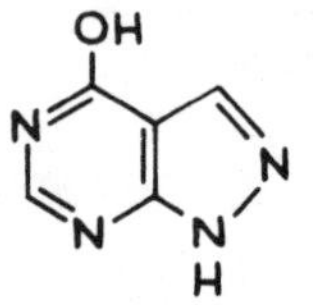

Allopurinol

Thioguanine (6-TG) inhibits several enzymes in the purine pathway, resulting in inhibition of formation of guanine nucleotides. Additionally, a significant fraction of 6-TG is incorporated into DNA instead of the normal guanine component, thus producing altered polynucleotides. This latter mechanism may account for its major cytotoxic action. Thioguanine has a synergistic action when used together with cytarabine in the treatment of adult acute leukemia.

Mercaptopurine and thioguanine are both absorbed rapidly from the gut and excreted mainly in the urine. However, 6-MP is converted to an inactive metabolite (6-thiouric acid) by an oxidation catalyzed by xanthine oxidase, whereas 6-TG is not metabolized by this enzyme. This factor is important because the thiopurine allopurinol (Zyloprim), a potent xanthine oxidase inhibitor, is frequently used along with chemotherapy in hematologic malignancies. Simultaneous therapy with allopurinol and 6-MP will result in excessive mercaptopurine toxicity unless the dose of mercaptopurine is reduced to 25–30% of the usual level. This effect is not relevant for thioguanine, which can be used at full doses despite administration of allopurinol. Allopurinol plays an important supportive role in chemotherapy of the leukemias and lymphomas. Even though it is noncytotoxic, it facilitates the purine loads associated with tumor lysis to be excreted as hypoxanthine rather than uric acid. Nephrotoxicity and acute gout are thereby prevented, because hypoxanthine is highly soluble in comparison to uric acid.

PYRIMIDINE ANTAGONISTS

1. FLUOROURACIL

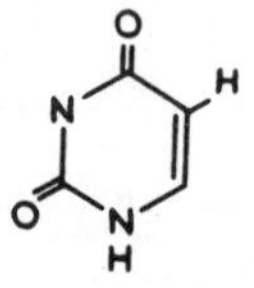

Uracil 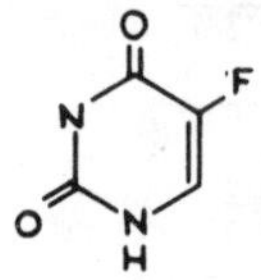   5-FU 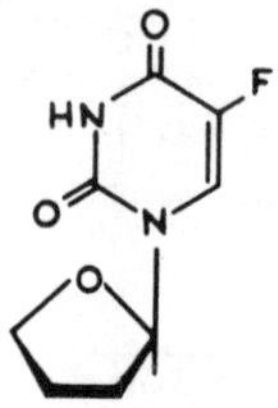   Ftorafur

Fluorouracil (5-FU) undergoes biotransformation into ribosyl and deoxyribosyl metabolites; however, its primary action is on DNA synthesis. Its conversion into fluorodeoxyuridine 5-phosphate inhibits the enzyme thymidylate synthetase from catalyzing the conversion of deoxyuridine into deoxythymidine. Thymidine is essential for DNA synthesis, and without it cell proliferation halts.

5-FU is normally given intravenously and has a short metabolic half-life. Although it is active when given orally, its bioavailability is erratic by that route of administration. Floxuridine (5-fluorodeoxyuridine, FUDR) has an action similar to that of 5-FU and is used for hepatic artery infusions. A cream incorporating 5-FU (Effudex) is used topically for treating skin cancers. A related investigational drug, ftorafur, appears to release 5-FU slowly after it is injected. However, this new agent has neurotoxicity that may limit its utility. Fluorouracil is used systemically in the treatment of a variety of adenocarcinomas. Its major toxicities are myelosuppression and mucositis.

2. CYTARABINE

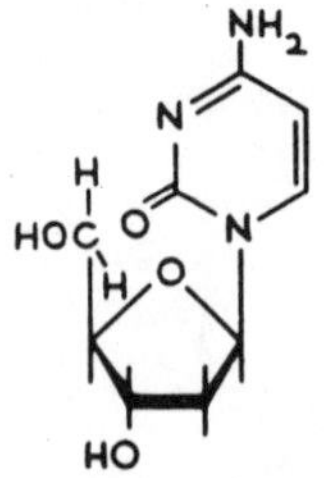

Cytosine
deoxyriboside

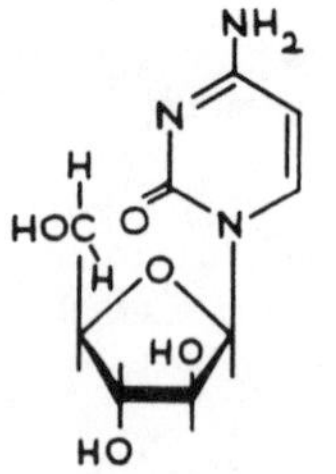

Cytosine
arabinoside

Cytarabine (cytosine arabinoside, Ara-C, Cytosar) is an S phase-specific antimetabolite that is anabolized by deoxycytidine kinase to the nucleotide form and must be phosphorylated to the nucleotide triphosphate (ARA-CTP) before it becomes inhibitory. Cytarabine is known to inhibit the DNA polymerase responsible for replicative DNA synthesis; it also inhibits the conversion of cytidine nucleotide to deoxycytidine nucleotide and its incorporation into DNA. The cellular retention time for ARA-CTP appears to correlate with its lethality to malignant cells.

After intravenous administration, the drug is cleared rapidly, with most of it being deaminated to an inactive form. In view of Ara-C's S phase specificity, the drug is highly schedule-dependent, and it must be given either by continuous infusion or every 8–12 hours for 5–7 days. Its activity is limited almost entirely to treatment of acute myelogenous leukemia, for which it is a major drug. Side-effects include nausea, severe myelosuppression, and varying degrees of stomatitis or alopecia.

3. AZACYTIDINE

Cytidine   5-Azacytidine

Azacytidine was first synthesized by an organic chemist and later also isolated as an antibiotic. Azacytidine is anabolized to a phosphorylated nucleotide that appears to be the active form. Its exact mode of action on DNA is still somewhat uncertain; however, it is known to inhibit orotidylic decarboxylase in a fashion similar to that achieved with the related antimetabolite 6-azaciridine. Azacytidine also is incorporated into RNA; however, its main mode of action appears to be on DNA.

Azacytidine is administered intravenously and must be shielded from light and kept at slightly acid pH, as it is unstable and can undergo ring opening. Nausea and fever are observed during drug administration. The half-life is 3–4 hours, with most of the drug excreted either unchanged or in deaminated form.

Azacytidine is currently an investigational agent in the USA, but it is a recognized "second line agent" in the treatment of acute leukemia. Optimal dosage schedules have yet to be developed. It can produce profound myelosuppressive toxicity of long duration.

4. PHOSPHONACETYL/L–ASPARTATE

PALA

N-(Phosphonacetyl)-L-aspartate (PALA) is an extremely potent transition state inhibitor of the enzyme L-aspartate transcarbamoylase (ATCase). ATCase is the enzyme responsible for one of the first steps in pyrimidine biosynthesis, wherein carbamoyl phosphate is combined with L-aspartic acid to initiate formation of the pyrimidine ring. The drug has significant activity against a variety of animal tumors. Intracellular concentrations of the enzyme ATCase appear to be low in tumors sensitive to this drug. In vitro studies have indicated that tumor inhibition requires continuous prolonged exposure to concentrations of the drug exceeding 10^{-5} M. Tolerable single intravenous doses of PALA maintain drug levels above 10^{-6} M for 24 hours, but continuous infusions might be required.

The drug only recently entered clinical evaluation. Phase I clinical trials have indicated that the dose-limiting toxicities are cutaneous and gastrointestinal; bone marrow toxicity has not been observed. Studies of antitumor activity have only recently been initiated, but some activity in colorectal cancer has been observed. The combination of PALA with fluorouracil is also of interest based on animal studies, and the fact that these 2 agents have specificity for different steps in the pyrimidine pathway and the fact of blockade of pyrimidine synthesis with PALA should increase the utilization of preformed pyrimidines such as fluorouracil. It remains to be determined if this will have a synergistic antitumor effect. PALA is an extremely interesting new agent that, if it proves to be significantly active in human cancers, may have a major role in combination chemotherapy in view of its lack of myelosuppressive toxicity.

PLANT ALKALOIDS

VINBLASTINE

Vinblastine (Velban) is an alkaloid derived from *Vinca rosea*, the periwinkle plant (see below). Its mechanism of action is not completely understood, but

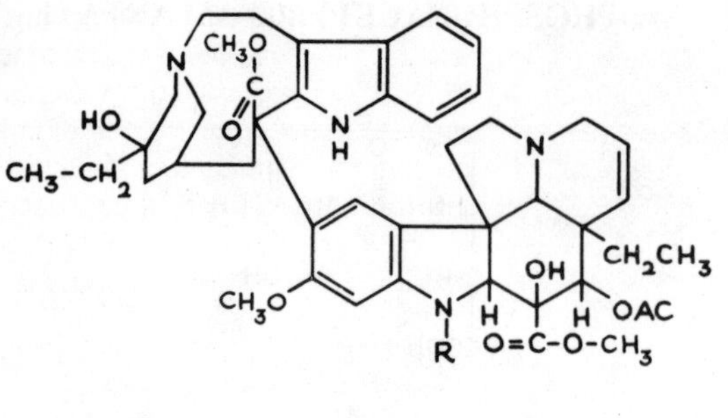

R is O=C–H

Vincristine
(Oncovin)

R is CH₃

Vinblastine
(Velban)

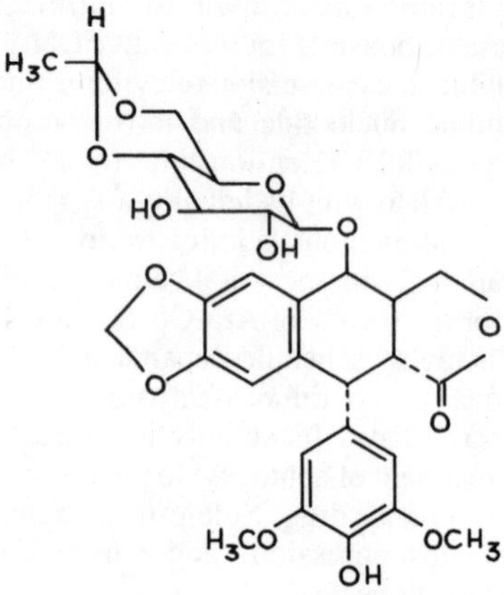

VP16-213, Etoposide
(4^1-demethyl-epipodophyllotoxin-
β-D-ethylidene glucoside)

it binds to the microtubular protein of the mitotic spindle, inactivating it, and causes arrest of mitosis at the metaphase. It produces nausea and vomiting and marrow depression as well as alopecia. It has value in the treatment of systemic Hodgkin's disease and other lymphomas. See clinical section below and Table 45-6. A related agent, desacetylvinblastine (Vindesine), recently entered clinical trial as an investigational drug.

VINCRISTINE

Vincristine (Oncovin) is also an alkaloid derivative of *Vinca rosea*, and is closely related to vinblastine. It also appears to be a "spindle poison" and causes arrest of the mitotic cycle. Despite its marked structural similarity to vinblastine, it has a strikingly different spectrum of activity and qualitatively different toxicities.

Vincristine has been used with considerable success in combination with prednisone for remission induction in childhood acute leukemia. It is also useful in certain other rapidly proliferating neoplasms. It causes a significant incidence of neurotoxicity, which limits its use to short courses. The principal serious toxic effects are areflexia, peripheral neuritis, and paralytic ileus. It occasionally produces bone marrow depression.

PODOPHYLLOTOXINS

Two compounds, VP16 and a related drug, VM26, are promising semisynthetic derivatives of podophyllotoxin, which is extracted from the root of the May apple or mandrake *(Podophyllum peltatum)*. Both drugs are currently on clinical trial in the USA and Europe. VP16 and VM26 are quite similar both chemically and clinically. The mode of action is felt to involve (1) mitotic arrest at metaphase, (2) prevention

of cells from entering mitosis, possibly by inhibition of DNA synthesis, and (3) covalent alkylation of nucleic acids and proteins by the lactane ring portion of the drug. The drugs are water-insoluble and require a lipid solvent vehicle for the clinical formulation. They are protein-bound and evenly distributed throughout the body except for the brain. Excretion is predominantly in the bile, with a lesser amount excreted in the urine. In addition to nausea, vomiting, and alopecia, significant toxicity is limited to the hematopoietic and lymphoid systems. Thus far, VP16 has shown activity in monocytic leukemia and oat cell carcinomas of the lung, and VM26 has activity in various lymphomas. The activity of VP16 in oat cell carcinoma is significant and clinically useful.

ANTIBIOTICS

Screening of microbial products has led to the discovery of a number of growth inhibitors that have proved to be clinically useful in cancer chemotherapy. Many of the antibiotics bind to DNA or fit into the helical lattice (intercalate) between specific bases and block the transcription of new RNA or DNA and cell replication. All of the clinically useful antibiotics are products of various strains of the soil fungus *Streptomyces*. These include the anthracyclines, actinomycin, bleomycin, mitomycin, and mithramycin.

ANTHRACYCLINES

The anthracycline antibiotics, which have been isolated from *Streptomyces peucetius* var *caesius*, are among the most useful cytotoxic anticancer drugs. Two congeners—doxorubicin (Adriamycin) and daunorubicin (Cerubidine)—are FDA-approved and in general use. Their structures are shown below.

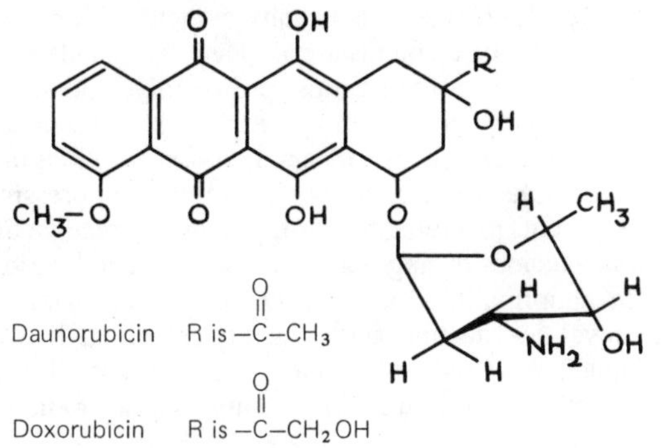

Daunorubicin   R is —C—CH$_3$ (with O double bond)

Doxorubicin   R is —C—CH$_2$OH (with O double bond)

Other anthracyclines are currently being developed, including semisynthetic agents. Daunorubicin (the first agent in this class to be isolated) is used in the treatment of acute leukemia. Doxorubicin has a broad spectrum of potent activity against many different types of carcinomas.

Mechanism of Action

Biochemical and structural studies suggest that the ring portion of the anthracyclines intercalates between nucleotide pairs. The amino sugar binds tightly to DNA, and it has been proposed that the drug has a second mode of binding involving bioreductive alkylation—making it a "two-hit" agent. The binding of the drug to DNA may be stabilized by the sugar moiety. After binding to DNA, these drugs block DNA-directed RNA synthesis and DNA transcription. The anthracyclines are probably active in all cell cycle phases and therefore are classified as CCNS agents.

Absorption, Metabolism, & Excretion

Clinically used anthracyclines are administered only by the intravenous route. Peak concentration halves within the first 30 minutes after injection, but significant levels persist for up to 20 hours. The anthracyclines are metabolized by the liver, with reduction or hydrolysis of the ring substituents. An alcohol form is an active metabolite, whereas the aglycone is inactive. Most of the drug and its metabolites are excreted in bile; about one-sixth in urine. Some metabolites retain antitumor activity. The biliary route of excretion includes enterohepatic recirculation of cytotoxic moieties. Therefore, the initial dose of anthracyclines must be reduced by 75% in patients with significant elevations of serum bilirubin (greater than 2.5 mg/dL).

Clinical Uses

Doxorubicin is one of the most important anticancer drugs, with major clinical application in patients with carcinomas of the breast, endometrium, ovary, testicle, thyroid, and lung and in the treatment of many sarcomas, including neuroblastoma, Ewing's sarcoma, osteosarcoma, and rhabdomyosarcoma. Doxorubicin is useful also in hematologic malignancies, including acute leukemia, multiple myeloma, Hodgkin's disease, and the diffuse non-Hodgkin's lymphomas. Doxorubicin is used in adjuvant therapy in the treatment of osteogenic sarcoma and breast cancer. It is generally used in combination with other agents (eg, cyclophosphamide, cisplatin, and nitrosoureas), with which it often synergizes, yielding longer remissions than are observed when it is used as a single agent. This approach can also minimize some of the toxicities that would otherwise be associated with use of higher dosages of doxorubicin. The major use of daunorubicin is in acute leukemia, and for this purpose the drug may have slightly greater activity than doxorubicin. However, daunorubicin appears to have a far narrower spectrum of utility, as its efficacy in solid tumors appears to be limited.

A series of new anthracycline analogs have recently entered clinical trial as investigational agents. These include aclacynomycin (Japan), 4-epiadriamycin (Italy), karminomycin (USSR), and trifluoroacetyl adriamycin (AD-32) (USA). These new agents may have differing spectrums of action and somewhat less toxicity. For example, initial reports indicate that aclacynomycin causes far less alopecia or cardiac toxicity than other anthracyclines. Antitumor activity is only now being defined for this new agent, although it appears to have activity in a variety of neoplasms.

Adverse Reactions

In common with many other cytotoxic drugs, the anthracyclines cause bone marrow depression, which is of short duration with rapid recovery. Toxicities more pronounced with anthracyclines (doxorubicin and daunorubicin) than with other agents include a potentially irreversible dose-related cardiac toxicity. This is rarely seen at doxorubicin dosages below 500 mg/m^2. Tachycardia is a common clinical sign; however, abnormalities in cardiac scintiscans and results of these studies appear to correlate closely with myocardial fibrosis on endomyocardial biopsies. Other noninvasive tests (echocardiography) appear to be less sensitive. Such studies should probably be obtained on all patients for whom administration of more than 400 mg/m^2 is contemplated. Patients with prior thoracic irradiation (including the heart), significant hypertension, or other intrinsic cardiovascular disease or increased age (over 70) are thought to be at greater risk of anthracycline-induced cardiac toxicity at lower total dosages.

A second toxicity of doxorubicin and daunomycin is the almost universal occurrence of severe or total alopecia at standard dosages. A technic recently devised to minimize doxorubicin-induced alopecia is local application of scalp hypothermia with cold packs (ice or other coolants) 10 minutes prior to intravenous drug administration and maintained for at least an additional 30 minutes. This procedure is not recommended for patients with circulating tumor stem cells (eg, acute leukemia) but appears to be quite satisfactory for a variety of other neoplasms. Hypothermia limits circulation of the drug to the scalp as well as energy-dependent uptake of the drug by the hair follicles.

DACTINOMYCIN

Dactinomycin (actinomycin D, Cosmegen) is a high-molecular-weight antitumor antibiotic isolated from *Streptomyces parvullus*. The drug is comprised of 2 peptide loops linked to a 3-ring aromatic chromophoric member. A number of analogs have been devised, but most have not been tested carefully.

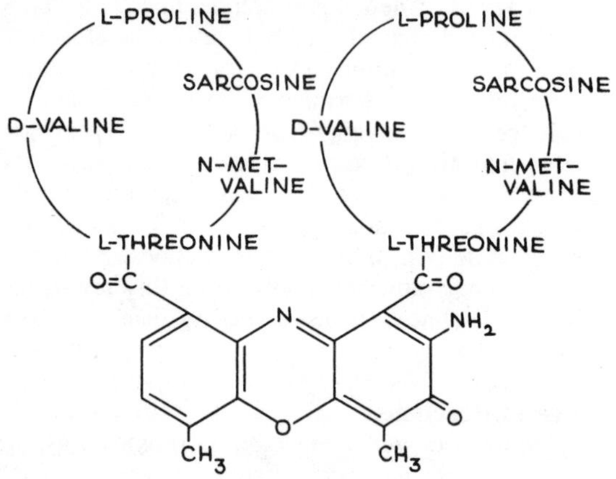

Dactinomycin

Mechanism of Action

Dactinomycin binds to DNA by becoming anchored into or around a purine-pyrimidine (DNA) base pair by intercalation or adlineation. Dactinomycin inhibits messenger RNA synthesis and other forms of DNA-dependent RNA synthesis, including the synthesis of ribosomal RNA in the nucleolus. While maximal cell kill is noted in G_1, the drug is still thought to be primarily a CCNS agent.

Absorption, Metabolism, & Excretion

Approximately half of the intravenous dose of dactinomycin remains unmetabolized and is excreted in the bile; a small amount is lost by urinary excretion. The plasma half-life is short. Because the drug is irritating to tissues, it is usually administered with caution to avoid extravasation and with "flushing" with normal saline to wash out the vein.

Clinical Uses

Dactinomycin is used in combination with surgery and vincristine (with or without radiotherapy) in the adjuvant treatment of Wilms's tumor. It is also used along with methotrexate to provide potentially curative treatment for patients with localized or disseminated gestational choriocarcinoma.

Adverse Reactions

Bone marrow depression, the usual dose-limiting toxicity of this agent, is usually evident within 7–10 days. All blood elements are affected, but platelets and leukocytes are affected most profoundly, and severe thrombocytopenia is sometimes seen. Nausea and vomiting, diarrhea, oral ulcers, and skin eruptions may also be noted. The agent is also immunosuppressive, and patients receiving this drug should not receive live virus vaccines during that time. Alopecia and various skin abnormalities occur occasionally. As with anthracyclines, dactinomycin can interact with radiation, producing a "radiation recall" skin abnormality associated with inflammation at sites of prior radiation therapy.

MITHRAMYCIN

Mithramycin (Mithracin) is one of the chromomycin antibiotics isolated from *Streptomyces plicatus*. It has a high molecular weight and a complex structure that includes a polycyclic chromophoric group with 2 attached sugar chains. The mechanism of action of mithramycin appears to be similar to that of dactinomycin and is thought to involve binding of the drug outside the DNA molecule (by ionic forces) through the process of adlineation, thereby interrupting DNA-directed RNA synthesis. Some intercalation of the agent into DNA is also probable. Additionally, the drug causes a calcium-lowering effect, apparently through an action on osteoclasts that is independent of its action on tumor cells. The drug has some usefulness in testicular cancers refractory to standard treatment, but it is of greater utility in reversing severe hypercalcemia associated with malignant disease.

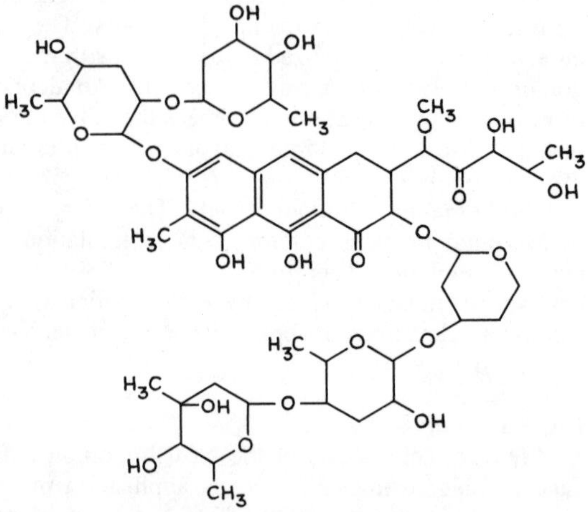

Mithramycin

Toxic side-effects of mithramycin include nausea and vomiting, thrombocytopenia, leukopenia, hypocalcemia, bleeding disorders, and liver toxicity. Aside from its use in management of hypercalcemia, mithramycin currently has few other indications.

Other chromomycin antibiotics (eg, toyomycin) have also been studied in Japan but appear to be of limited utility.

MITOMYCIN

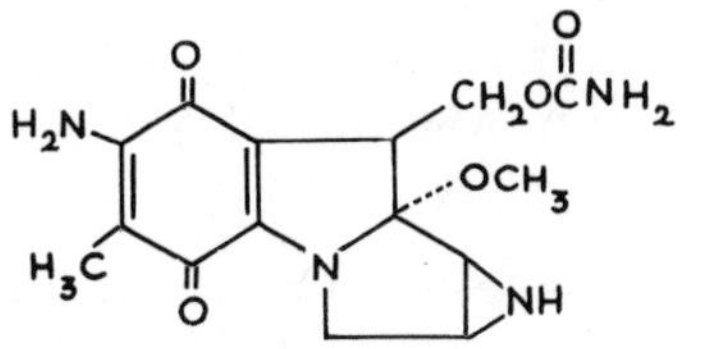

Mitomycin

Mitomycin (mitomycin-C, Mutamycin) is a purple antibiotic isolated from *Streptomyces caespitosus*. It contains quinone, urethane, and aziridine groups, all of which may have activity. The drug undergoes a type of metabolic transformation in vivo and is thought to be a "bioreductive" alkylating agent—and may improve the oxygenation status of tumors thought to be hypoxic and thus increase its own effectiveness. Mitomycin is thought to be a CCNS alkylating agent. While this agent is one of the more toxic drugs available for clinical use, it appears to have increasing usefulness in combination chemotherapy (with bleomycin and vincristine) for squamous cell carcinoma of the cervix and for adenocarcinomas of the stomach, pancreas, and lung (along with doxorubicin and fluorouracil). The drug also has some usefulness as a second line agent for metastatic colon cancer. A special application of the use of mitomycin has been in topical intravesical treatment of small bladder papillomas. Topical instillations of the agent in distilled water are usually held in the bladder for 3 hours, and the procedure is repeated over a course of weeks. Very little of the agent is absorbed systemically, and it can be quite effective at reducing the frequency of such bladder tumors.

Mitomycin is administered intravenously, is cleared rapidly from the vascular compartment, and appears to be eliminated primarily by liver metabolism. Mitomycin causes severe myelosuppression with relatively late toxicity against all 3 formed elements from the bone marrow, with increasingly profound toxicity after repeated doses. This late form of toxicity suggests an action on hematopoietic stem cells as opposed to later progenitors. Nausea, vomiting, and anorexia commonly occur shortly after injection, and occasional instances of renal toxicity and interstitial pneumonitis have also been reported.

BLEOMYCIN

The bleomycins are a series of different antineoplastic antibiotics produced by *Streptomyces verticillus*. Thirteen glycopeptide fractions have been isolated, with the major component being bleomycin A_2. Bleomycin appears to act through scission of DNA strands and interference with DNA polymerase 1. Mitotic arrest is often a consequence of this lethal event. The drug appears to act on both single-stranded and double-stranded DNA and initially binds to DNA, causing strand splitting and inhibition of replication by DNA polymerase. RNA and protein synthesis are inhibited to a lesser extent. Bleomycin is a CCS drug having effects in G_2 and mitosis as well as the S phase. It appears to be schedule-dependent, and chronic low-dose administration by repeated injection or continuous infusion appears to be the most effective

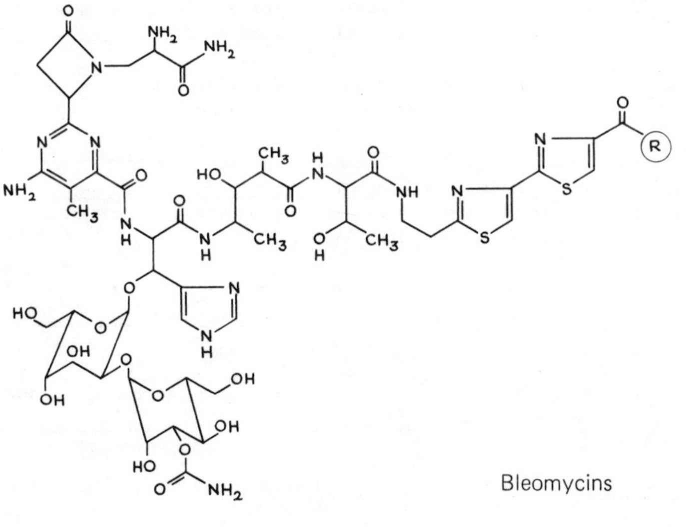

Bleomycin components:

A_1:	$NH_2 \cdot CH_2 \cdot CH_2 \cdot CH_2 \cdot SO \cdot CH_3$
$DM \cdot A_2$:	$NH_2 \cdot CH_2 \cdot CH_2 \cdot CH_2 \cdot S \cdot CH_3$
A_2:	$NH_2 \cdot CH_2 \cdot CH_2 \cdot CH_2 \cdot S^+(CH_3)_2$
$A_2' \cdot a$:	$NH_2 \cdot CH_2 \cdot CH_2 \cdot CH_2 \cdot CH_2 \cdot NH_2$
$A_2' \cdot b$:	$NH_2 \cdot CH_2 \cdot CH_2 \cdot CH_2 \cdot NH_2$
B_2:	$NH_2 \cdot CH_2 \cdot CH_2 \cdot CH_2 \cdot CH_2 \cdot NH \cdot \underset{\parallel NH}{C} \cdot NH_2$
B_4:	$NH_2 \cdot (CH_2)_4 \cdot NH \cdot \underset{\parallel NH}{C} \cdot NH \cdot (CH_2)_4 \cdot NH \cdot \underset{\parallel NH}{C} \cdot NH_2$
A_5:	$NH_2 \cdot (CH_2)_3 \cdot NH \cdot (CH_2)_4 \cdot NH_2$
A_6:	$NH_2 \cdot (CH_2)_3 \cdot NH \cdot (CH_2)_4 \cdot NH \cdot (CH_2)_3 \cdot NH_2$

Bleomycins

schedule. The drug synergizes with other drugs such as vinblastine and cisplatin, thus comprising one-third of the curative regimen used for testicular cancers. It is also used in squamous cell carcinomas of the head and neck, cervix, skin, penis, and rectum, and has utility in combination chemotherapy for the lymphomas. A special use has been for intracavitary therapy of malignant effusions in ovarian and breast cancer. Its efficacy in this latter setting may be associated with intrinsic sensitivity of the tumor stem cells in these effusions, as opposed to a nonspecific vesicant effect. The drug can be given subcutaneously, intramuscularly, or intravenously as well as by the intracavitary route. Peak blood levels of bleomycin after intramuscular injection appear within 30–60 minutes. Intravenous injection of similar dosages yields higher peak concentrations and a terminal half-life of about 2½ hours. Although there is some metabolism of this agent, approximately 50% can be recovered as the active drug in the urine within 24 hours.

A number of toxic side-effects have been described, including lethal anaphylactoid reactions and a high incidence of fever, with or without chills, particularly in patients with lymphoma. Fever may result in dehydration and hypotension in susceptible patients, and small test doses of the drug are commonly used to identify this potentially serious toxicity. More common toxic side-effects include blistering and hyperkeratosis of the palms and anorexia. A form of pulmonary fibrosis is an uncommon but sometimes fatal adverse effect seen particularly in older patients who have received a total dose over 200 mg/m^2 and develop a reduced diffusion capacity for oxygen. Patients receiving large doses should undergo serial pulmonary function studies so that the drug can be

discontinued before severe pulmonary toxicity develops. Cough and pulmonary infiltrates are additional indications for discontinuing bleomycin and initiating therapy with antibiotics and corticosteroids. The drug does not have significant myelosuppressive effects, which means that it may be incorporated into a number of different combination chemotherapy programs with no significant addition to bone marrow toxicity.

MISCELLANEOUS AGENTS

ASPARAGINASE

Asparaginase (L-asparagine amidohydrolase) is an enzyme that can be isolated from various bacteria (eg, E coli and Erwinia caratovora). The active enzyme has a high molecular weight (139,000) and contains a subunit structure thought to have 4 active sites per molecule. The drug recently gained FDA approval for use in childhood acute leukemia. Asparaginase acts indirectly to inhibit the protein synthesis of certain tumor cells, whereas normal cells generally are capable of synthesizing asparagine, thus being less susceptible to its action. The administration of asparaginase hydrolases serum asparagine to aspartic acid and ammonia, thus depriving tumor cells of a required amino acid. Blood glutamine levels are also reduced. Synthesis of those proteins requiring asparagine within tumor cells is thus interrupted, blocking cell proliferation

Table 45—4. Natural product cancer chemotherapy drugs: Dosages and toxicity.

Drug	Single Agent Dose	Acute Toxicity	Delayed Toxicity
Vinblastine (Velban)	0.1–0.2 mg/kg IV weekly	Nausea and vomiting	Alopecia, loss of reflexes, bone marrow depression.
Vincristine (Oncovin)	1.5 mg/m^2 IV (maximum: 2 mg weekly)	None	Areflexia, muscle weakness, peripheral neuritis, paralytic ileus, mild bone marrow depression, alopecia.
Dactinomycin (actinomycin D, Cosmegen)	0.04 mg/kg IV weekly	Nausea and vomiting	Stomatitis, gastrointestinal tract upset, alopecia, bone marrow depression.
Daunorubicin (daunomycin)	30–60 mg/m^2 daily IV for 3 days, or 30–60 mg/m^2 IV weekly	Nausea, fever, red urine (not hematuria)	Cardiotoxicity, bone marrow depression, alopecia.
Doxorubicin (Adriamycin)	60 mg/m^2 IV every 3 weeks to a maximum total dose of 550 mg/ m^2	Nausea, red urine (not hematuria)	Cardiotoxicity, alopecia, bone marrow depression, stomatitis.
Mithramycin (Mithracin)	25–50 µg/kg IV every other day for up to 8 doses	Nausea and vomiting	Thrombocytopenia, hepatotoxicity.
Mitomycin (Mutamycin)	20 mg/m^2 every 6 weeks	Nausea	Thrombocytopenia, leukopenia.
Bleomycin (Blenoxane)	Up to 15 mg/m^2 twice weekly to a total dose of 200 mg/m^2	Allergic reactions, fever, hypotension	Edema of hands, pulmonary fibrosis, stomatitis, alopecia.
Asparaginase	20,000 IU/m^2 daily IV for 5–10 days	Nausea and fever	Hepatotoxicity, mental depression, pancreatitis.

with delayed DNA and RNA synthesis. The enzyme preparation used is a foreign bacterial protein and thus can lead to immunologic inactivation. Toxic effects of the enzyme preparations have included fever, chills, nausea, and hepatic dysfunction as well as mental depression.

STEROID HORMONES

Sex hormones and adrenocortical hormones are employed in the management of several types of neoplastic disease. The sex hormones are concerned with the stimulation and control of proliferation and function of certain tissues, including the mammary and prostate glands. Cancer arising from and retaining properties of these tissues may be inhibited or stimulated by appropriate changes in hormone balance. Cancer of the breast and cancer of the prostate have been effectually palliated with sex hormone therapy or ablation of certain endocrine organs. Recently, antiestrogens have assumed an important role in breast cancer. While such agents are nonsteroidal, they are best discussed in the context of steroid hormones.

The adrenal corticosteroids (particularly the glucocorticoid analogs) have been useful in the treatment of acute leukemia, lymphomas, myeloma, and other hematologic malignancies as well as in advanced breast cancer, and as supportive therapy in the management of hypercalcemia resulting from many types of cancer. These steroids produce dissolution of lymphocytes, regression of lymph nodes, and inhibition of growth of certain mesenchymal tissues.

The most useful steroid hormones are as follows:

(1) Androgens: Testosterone propionate, fluoxymesterone.

(2) Estrogens: Diethylstilbestrol, ethinyl estradiol.

(3) Antiestrogens: Tamoxifen, nafoxidine.

(4) Progestins: Hydroxyprogesterone caproate, medroxyprogesterone, megestrol acetate.

(5) Adrenocortical compounds: Hydrocortisone acetate, prednisone, prednisolone, dexamethasone.

Absorption, Metabolism, & Excretion

With the exception of testosterone propionate and hydroxyprogesterone caproate, the corticosteroids are administered orally and are readily absorbed. Testosterone and hydroxyprogesterone are oil-soluble and must be administered intramuscularly. The mechanisms of their metabolism and excretion are described in Chapter 38.

Pharmacologic Effects

The mechanism of action of steroid hormones on lymphoid, mammary, or prostatic cancer has been clarified. Recent observations indicate that steroid hormones must bind to noncatalytic receptor proteins at the periphery of cancer cells in order for their anti-cancer effects to be exerted. Highly specific receptor proteins have been identified for estradiol, 11β-hydroxycortisol, dexamethasone, and androstenolone. Some data indicate that steroid hormones form a mobile steroid-receptor complex which binds directly to DNA in the nucleus and alters the transcription of structural or regulatory genes. Other data indicate that the lethal event is a steroid-induced rise in free fatty acids at the cancer cell nuclear membrane, which causes dissolution of that membrane and cell death.

Most importantly, while prednisone-sensitive lymphomas and estrogen-sensitive breast and prostatic cancers contain, respectively, specific receptors for prednisone, estrogens, and androgens; most steroid-sensitive cancers have these specific receptors. It is now possible to assay biopsy specimens for steroid receptor content and to predict which individual patients are likely to benefit from steroid therapy. Measurement of the estrogen receptor (ER) protein in breast cancer tissue is now a standard clinical test (Fig 45–9). ER positivity does predict responsiveness to endocrine ablation or additive therapy, whereas patients whose tumors are ER-negative fail to respond to such treatment. Similar observations have recently been reported in prostatic carcinoma. On the basis of

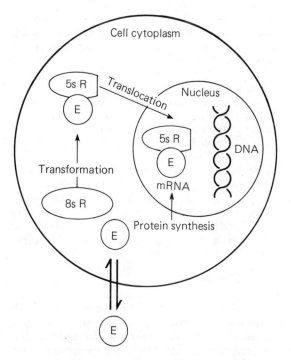

Figure 45–9. Prototype cancer cell that is estrogen receptor "positive." Estrogen (E) binds to a 200,000-MW receptor (R), which then undergoes 2 metabolic transformations, with reduction in molecular weight, after which it is translocated to the cell's nucleus. The complex is then bound to chromatin, and RNA synthesis and protein synthesis are initiated. A similar process appears to apply for progesterone or androgen receptors. Cells bearing such steroid hormone receptors often respond to endocrine therapy.

Table 45–5. Steroid hormones and antagonists: Dosages and toxicity.

	Usual Adult Dose	Acute Toxicity	Delayed Toxicity
Androgens			
Testosterone propionate	100 mg IM 3 times weekly	None	Fluid retention, masculinization.
Fluoxymesterone (Halotestin)	10–20 mg/d orally	None	Cholestatic jaundice in some patients receiving fluoxymesterone.
Calusterone	200 mg/d orally in divided doses	None	None.
Estrogens			
Diethylstilbestrol	1–5 mg 3 times a day orally	Occasional nausea and vomiting	Fluid retention, feminization, uterine bleeding.
Ethinyl estradiol (Estinyl)	3 mg/d orally		
Antiestrogen			
Tamoxifen (Nolvadex)	10 mg twice daily orally	None	None.
Progestins			
Hydroxyprogesterone caproate (Delalutin)	1 g IM twice weekly	None	None.
Medroxyprogesterone (Provera)	100–200 mg/d orally; 200–600 mg orally twice weekly	None	None.
Megestrol acetate (Megace)	40 mg 4 times daily orally	None	Fluid retention.
Adrenocorticosteroids			
Hydrocortisone	50–200 mg/d orally	None	Fluid retention, hypertension, diabetes, increased susceptibility to infection, "moon facies."
Prednisone	20–100 mg/d orally or, when effective, 50–100 mg every other day orally as single dose	None	

animal studies, it appears likely that conversion of a tumor from steroid sensitivity to steroid resistance is associated with loss of the specific receptor protein production, presumably as a result of selection.

Clinical Uses

The sex hormones are employed in cancer of the female and male breast, cancer of the prostate, and cancer of the endometrium of the uterus.

The relationship between hormones and hormone-dependent tumors was initially demonstrated by Beatson in 1896 when it was shown that oophorectomy produced improvement in women with advanced breast cancer. Extensive studies with the androgenic, estrogenic, and progestational sex hormones have demonstrated their value in advanced inoperable mammary cancer, cancer of the prostate, and cancer of the endometrium (see pp 498 and 505–508).

Adverse Reactions

Androgens, estrogens, and adrenocortical hormones all can produce fluid retention through their sodium-retaining effect. Prolonged use of androgens and estrogens will cause masculinization and feminization, respectively. Extended use of the adrenocortical steroids may result in hypertension, diabetes, increased susceptibility to infection, and the development of cushingoid appearance ("moon facies") (see Chapter 35 and Table 45–5).

ANTIESTROGEN

The antiestrogenic compound tamoxifen has proved to be extremely useful for the treatment of breast cancer. As an antiestrogen, it inhibits estrogen-stimulated rises in uterine wet weight and vaginal cornification. Tamoxifen functions as a competitive inhibitor of estrogen and binds to the cytoplasmic estrogen receptor (ER) protein of estrogen-sensitive tissues and tumors. Translocation of the receptor complex to the nucleus appears to occur normally, suggesting that the antiestrogen acts at a nuclear level. Studies in tissue culture have shown that in the absence of estrogen, tamoxifen is cytotoxic to ER-positive breast cancer cells. This provides evidence that the antiestrogen has a potent direct effect even in the absence of the pituitary. However, tamoxifen has a 100- to 1000-fold lower affinity constant for ER than does estradiol, indicating the importance of ablation of endogenous estrogen for optimal antiestrogen effect.

Excellent plasma levels of the drug are obtained after oral administration, and the agent has a much longer biologic half-life than estradiol. The usual dosages in breast cancer treatment are in the range of 10 mg twice daily, although doses up to 100 mg/m^2 have been administered without major toxicity.

Side-effects in the usual dose range are quite mild. Hot flashes are the most frequent side-effect. Nausea is observed occasionally, as is fluid retention and mild hematologic toxicity. Occasional "flares" of breast cancer are observed, but it is uncertain if this is a side-effect or a manifestation of preexisting rapid tumor growth.

Tamoxifen has recently proved to have significant antitumor activity in estrogen-resistant prostatic cancer and progesterone-resistant endometrial cancer. A lesser degree of activity has also been observed in metastatic melanoma, and a variety of tumor types are now being studied for their content of estrogen receptor to determine whether they might also be amenable to growth inhibition with tamoxifen.

Tamoxifen (Nolvadex)

In advanced breast cancer, clinical improvement is observed in 40–50% of patients who receive tamoxifen. Patients who show objective benefit with treatment are largely those who (1) lack endogenous estrogens (oopherectomy or postmenopausal state) and (2) have breast cancers which have the cytoplasmic ER protein demonstrable on radioreceptor assay. Thus, it is unreasonable to use tamoxifen in patients who are known to be ER-negative or have endogenous estrogen production. Thus, oophorectomy is often indicated in premenopausal women whose tumors are ER-positive, as this procedure enhances the utility of tamoxifen.

OTHER
ANTICANCER DRUGS

Hydroxyurea

Hydroxyurea is an analog of urea and is of low molecular weight (76). The exact mechanism of action is still uncertain, although it causes immediate inhibition of DNA synthesis without altering RNA or protein synthesis. It is thought to exert its lethal effect on cells in S phase by inhibiting ribonucleotide reductase and appears to be a CCS agent. The drug is administered orally and is available in capsules (0.5 g). Its major uses are in melanoma and chronic myelogenous leukemia; however, it plays a secondary role in both of these circumstances. Its role in combination

chemotherapy has yet to be defined. The major side-effect of this agent is bone marrow depression. At high dosages (greater than 40 mg/kg/d) megaloblastosis unresponsive to vitamin B_{12} or folic acid may appear. Gastrointestinal symptoms, including nausea, vomiting, and diarrhea, are common in patients receiving high dosages of the drug. Less common reactions include skin reactions and mucositis and occasional renal dysfunction or central nervous system abnormality.

Mitotane (*o,p'*-DDD, Lysodren)

This drug (1,1-dichloro-2-[*o*-chlorophenyl]-2-[*p*-chlorophenyl]-ethane) is a DDT congener that was first found to be adrenolytic in dogs. Subsequently, it was found to be of use in the treatment of adrenal carcinoma. The drug produces tumor regression and relief of the excessive adrenal steroid secretion that often occurs with this malignancy. Toxicities include skin eruptions, diarrhea, and mental depression.

About 40% of an oral dose is absorbed, and 60% is excreted in stool. Of the amount reaching the tissues, most is stored in fat for several weeks. About 25% of an absorbed dose is excreted as a urinary metabolite. It produces anorexia, nausea, somnolence, and dermatitis.

The utility of mitotane appears to be limited to adrenal carcinoma, and it is marketed for that one indication.

Quinacrine

This antimalarial drug has been found to be of occasional use in the control of malignant pleural, pericardial, and abdominal effusions. It is instilled directly into the fluid-containing cavity. Although its exact mechanism of action is uncertain, it is a local irritant and leads to the production of local fibrous adhesions.

INVESTIGATIONAL AGENTS

Several of the drugs mentioned in the text remain in an investigational status in the USA until their efficacy and safety for cancer chemotherapy can be established. In specific instances where treatment with one of these agents seems warranted, it usually can be arranged through a university hospital or cancer center

Table 45–6. Miscellaneous anticancer drugs: Dosages and toxicity.

Drug	Usual Dose	Acute Toxicity	Delayed Toxicity
Hydroxyurea	300 mg/m² orally for 5 days	Nausea and vomiting	Bone marrow depression.
Cisplatin	50–75 mg/m² IV every 3 weeks	Nausea and vomiting	Nephrotoxicity, mild otic and bone marrow toxicity.
Mitotane	6–15 g/d orally	Nausea and vomiting	Dermatitis, diarrhea, mental depression.
Quinacrine	100–300 mg/d by intracavitary injection for 5 days	Local pain and fever	None.

Table 45—7. Malignancies responsive to chemotherapy.*

Diagnosis	Current Treatment of Choice	Other Valuable Agents
Acute lymphocytic leukemia	Induction: vincristine plus prednisone. Remission maintenance: mercaptopurine, methotrexate, and cyclophosphamide in various combinations.	Asparaginase, daunorubicin, carmustine, doxorubicin, cytarabine, allopurinol,‡ craniospinal radiation therapy
Acute myelocytic and myelomonocytic leukemia	Combination chemotherapy: doxorubicin, vincristine, cytarabine, prednisone or thioguanine, cytarabine, and daunorubicin	Methotrexate, thioguanine, mercaptopurine, allopurinol,‡ BCG,† azacytidine,† ribidazone,† AMSA†
Chronic myelocytic leukemia	Busulfan	Vincristine, mercaptopurine, hydroxyurea, melphalan, cytarabine, allopurinol‡
Chronic lymphocytic leukemia	Chlorambucil and prednisone (if indicated)	Vincristine, androgens,‡ allopurinol,‡ doxorubicin
Hodgkin's disease (stages III and IV)	Combination chemotherapy: mechlorethamine, vincristine, procarbazine, prednisone ("MOPP")	Vinblastine, doxorubicin, lomustine, dacarbazine, VM-26,† bleomycin
Non-Hodgkin's lymphomas	Combination chemotherapy: cyclophosphamide, doxorubicin, vincristine, prednisone	Bleomycin, lomustine, carmustine, VM-26,† BCG,† AMSA†
Multiple myeloma	Melphalan plus prednisone	Cyclophosphamide, vincristine, carmustine, doxorubicin, androgens‡
Macroglobulinemia	Chlorambucil	Melphalan
Polycythemia vera	Busulfan, chlorambucil, or cyclophosphamide	
Carcinoma of lung	Cyclophosphamide plus doxorubicin, methotrexate, and lomustine	Cisplatin, quinacrine,‡ hexamethylmelamine,† vincristine, BCG,† VP-16†
"Head and neck" carcinomas	Methotrexate, bleomycin, and cisplatin	Hydroxyurea, fluorouracil, doxorubicin, vinblastine
Carcinoma of endometrium	Doxorubicin plus cyclophosphamide	Progestins, fluorouracil
Carcinoma of ovary	Doxorubicin, cyclophosphamide, and cisplatin	Melphalan, fluorouracil, vincristine, hexamethylmelamine,† bleomycin, BCG†
Carcinoma of the cervix	Mitomycin plus bleomycin and vincristine	Lomustine, cyclophosphamide, doxorubicin, methotrexate
Breast carcinoma	(1) Combination chemotherapy (see text) if lymph nodes are positive at mastectomy. (2) Combination chemotherapy ("D/C" or "CMF"); hormonal manipulation for late recurrence (eg, tamoxifen).	Cyclophosphamide, doxorubicin, vincristine, methotrexate, fluorouracil, quinacrine,‡ prednisone,‡ megestrol, and androgens
Choriocarcinoma (trophoblastic neoplasms)	Methotrexate, alone or in combination with vincristine, dactinomycin, and cyclophosphamide	Vinblastine, mercaptopurine, chlorambucil, doxorubicin
Carcinoma of testis	Combination therapy: cisplatin, vinblastine, bleomycin	Methotrexate, dactinomycin, mithramycin, doxorubicin, cyclophosphamide
Carcinoma of prostate	Estrogens	Doxorubicin plus cyclophosphamide, prednisone,‡ estramustine,† fluorouracil, progestins
Wilms's tumor (children)	Vincristine plus dactinomycin after surgery and radiation therapy	Methotrexate, cyclophosphamide, doxorubicin
Neuroblastoma	Cyclophosphamide plus doxorubicin and vincristine	Dactinomycin, daunorubicin
Carcinoma of thyroid	Radioiodine (^{131}I), doxorubicin	Bleomycin, fluorouracil, melphalan
Carcinoma of adrenal	Mitotane	Doxorubicin
Carcinoma of stomach or pancreas	Fluorouracil plus doxorubicin and mitomycin	Hydroxyurea, lomustine
Carcinoma of colon	Fluorouracil plus semustine	Cyclophosphamide, mitomycin
Carcinoid	Doxorubicin plus cyclophosphamide	Dactinomycin, methysergide,‡ streptozocin
Insulinoma	Streptozocin	Doxorubicin, fluorouracil, mitomycin
Osteogenic sarcoma	Doxorubicin, or methotrexate with citrovorum rescue initiated after amputation	Cyclophosphamide, dacarbazine
Miscellaneous sarcomas	Doxorubicin plus dacarbazine	Methotrexate, dactinomycin, cyclophosphamide, vincristine, vinblastine, AMSA†
Melanoma	Dacarbazine, dactinomycin, and BCG†	Lomustine, hydroxyurea, mitomycin, AMSA†

*Modified and reproduced, with permission, from Krupp MA, Chatton MJ (editors): *Current Medical Diagnosis & Treatment 1980.* Lange, 1980.

†Investigational agent. Treatment available through qualified investigators and centers authorized by National Cancer Institute and Cooperative Oncology Groups.

‡Supportive agent, not oncolytic.

or by contacting the Division of Cancer Treatment of the National Cancer Institute, which can provide further information and identify investigators who are authorized to administer these drugs.

This status applies to rubidazone, deoxycoformycin, and AMSA, useful in acute leukemia; and streptozocin, active in insulinoma. Chemical compounds and other natural products to which this designation also applies include semustine, estramustine, dihydroxyanthracenedione, hexamethylmelamine, azacytidine, ftorafur, desacetylvinblastine, AMSA, and epipodophyllotoxins (VM26, VP16). All of these drugs have substantial toxicities. Until their pharmacology is more completely understood and their net effects have proved to be beneficial, their use will be restricted to clinical research. New inhibitors of various stages in nucleoside and nucleic acid synthesis include phosphonacetyl-L-aspartate (PALA), thymidine in high doses, and the adenosine deaminase inhibitor deoxycoformycin. Of the biologic response modifiers, 13-*cis* retinoic acid (a vitamin A analog) and human interferon appear to be particularly promising. It appears likely that semustine, VP16, AMSA, estramustine, interferon, and hexamethylmelamine will have major uses in cancer chemotherapy and will be added to the practicing oncologist's list of effective anticancer drugs.

CLINICAL APPLICATIONS OF CANCER CHEMOTHERAPEUTIC DRUGS
(See Table 45–7)

Knowledge of the kinetics of tumor cell proliferation and total body tumor cell number, as well as information on the pharmacology and mechanism of action of cancer chemotherapeutic agents, has become important in designing optimal chemotherapeutic regimens for patients with advanced cancer. The strategy for developing drug regimens requires a knowledge of the particular characteristics of specific tumors—eg, Is there a high growth fraction? Is there a high spontaneous cell death rate? Are most of the cells in G_0? Are their normal counterparts under hormonal control? Similarly, knowledge of the pharmacology of specific drugs is equally important—eg, Does the drug have a particular affinity for uptake by the tumor cells (streptozocin)? Are the tumor cells sensitive to the drug? Is the drug cycle-phase specific?

Probable sites of action of various drugs are illustrated in Fig 45–4 and are shown in reference to the cell cycle. It has only recently been recognized that drugs that affect cycling cells can often be used most effectively after treatment with a cycle-nonspecific agent (eg, alkylating agents); this principle has been tested in only a few human tumors, but with increasing success.

Similarly, recognition of true drug synergism (tumor cell kill due to the drug combination greater than the additive effects of the individual drugs) or antagonism is important in the design of combination chemotherapeutic programs. The combination of cytarabine with 6-thioguanine in the treatment of acute myelogenous leukemia, the use of doxorubicin and cyclophosphamide in breast cancer, and the use of vinblastine, cisplatin, and bleomycin in testicular tumors are probably the best examples of true drug synergism against cancer cells but not against normal tissues.

In general, it is preferable to use cytotoxic chemotherapeutic agents in intensive "pulse" courses every 3–4 weeks rather than to give continuous daily dosage schedules. This allows for complete hematologic and immunologic recovery between courses rather than leaving the patient continuously suppressed with cytotoxic therapy. This approach reduces side-effects and does not reduce therapeutic efficacy.

The application of these principles is well illustrated in the current approach to the treatment of acute leukemia, lymphomas, Wilms's tumor, and testicular neoplasms.

ADJUVANT CHEMOTHERAPY FOR MICROMETASTASES: MULTIMODALITY THERAPY

The most important role for effective cancer chemotherapy is undoubtedly as an "adjuvant" to initial or "primary field" treatment with other methods of treatment such as surgery or radiation therapy. Failures with primary field therapy are due principally to occult micrometastases outside the primary field. With the currently available treatment modalities, this form of multimodality therapy appears to offer the greatest chance of curing the largest percentage of patients with solid tumors.

Distant micrometastases are usually present in patients with one or more positive lymph nodes at the time of surgery (eg, in breast cancer) and in patients with tumors having a known propensity for early hematogenous spread (eg, osteogenic sarcoma, Wilms's tumor). The risk of recurrent or metastatic disease in such patients can be extremely high (80%). Only systemic therapy can adequately attack micrometastases. Chemotherapy regimens that are at least moderately effective against advanced cancer may have curative potential (at the right dosage and schedule) when combined with primary therapy such as surgery. Recent studies show prolongation of disease-free survival in patients with osteogenic sarcoma, rhabdomyosarcoma, or breast cancer who receive adjuvant chemotherapy. In osteogenic sarcoma, methotrexate with citrovorum (folinic acid) rescue, doxorubicin alone, and doxorubicin in combination with other drugs have proved effective. Similar comments apply to the use of 3 cycles of combination chemotherapy (MOPP) prior to total nodal radiation in stage IIB Hodgkin's disease.

In breast cancer, women with positive lymph nodes at the time of mastectomy have benefited from combination chemotherapy or single agent chemotherapy with melphalan. Useful combination chemotherapy regimens for adjuvant therapy for breast cancer include CMF (cyclophosphamide-methotrexate-fluorouracil) or the same combination plus vincristine and prednisone (CMFVP), and D/C (doxorubicin-cyclophosphamide). The end results obtained with combination chemotherapy have already proved superior to results obtained with single agents, because combination chemotherapy has a greater tumor cell log kill. Results with CMF appeared best in premenopausal women; however, most post-menopausal women in the CMF trial appear to have received an inadequate dose of drugs (which were given in lower dosage than in premenopausal women). Endocrine studies in premenopausal patients receiving melphalan or CMF have shown a progressive rise in FSH along with falling estrogens but maintenance of normal adrenal function, indicating that ovarian ablation does constitute part of the action of these drug regimens. However, much evidence now indicates that the major effect of adjuvant chemotherapy in breast cancer is its direct cytotoxic effect rather than endocrine ablation. The D/C and CMFVP regimens appear to be effective in both pre- and postmenopausal women, perhaps because of the greater potency of these combinations against breast cancer. Adjuvant chemotherapy should definitely be considered as part of standard and indicated therapy in the patient groups discussed above. Other areas of current investigation include adjuvant chemotherapy for "Dukes C" colon cancer (fluorouracil in combination with semustine or BCG) and in testicular (vinblastine, bleomycin, and cisplatin), head and neck, and gynecologic neoplasms (various drugs). Thus, adjuvant chemotherapy (with curative intent) should now be given serious consideration for patients who undergo primary surgical staging and therapy and are found to have a stage and histologic type of cancer known to be associated with a high risk of micrometastasis. This policy is particularly germane to those tumor types for which palliative chemotherapy has already been developed and been shown to include complete remissions in advanced stages of the disease.

ACUTE LEUKEMIA

Acute leukemia is a general term for a group of malignant disorders of blood leukocytes. Age at onset of disease and certain morphologic characteristics have significant implications for patient survival and responsiveness to chemotherapy. With current agents, childhood acute leukemia is more treatable than that which occurs later in life. In all leukemic patients, major emphasis must be given to intensive support of the patient with necessary red cell and platelet transfusions, and prevention of hyperuricemia and infection.

A useful distinction can be drawn between **remission induction** and **maintenance** chemotherapy because the therapeutic agents used, dosage schedules, and objectives are somewhat different. Remission induction is in general a more intensive type of chemotherapy and often uses multiple agents administered simultaneously. The objective of induction therapy is to clear the body of all detectable leukemic leukocytes, ie, to reduce the leukemic cell number by many logs. This objective can sometimes be obtained using drugs that would have prohibitive toxicities if used on a chronic basis. The objective of maintenance therapy is to keep the population of residual leukemic cells in check so that they do not repopulate the blood and bone marrow and lead to the return of symptoms. In general, drugs used for remission maintenance are those which have relatively little delayed or cumulative toxicity and can be taken for months or years on an outpatient basis. Current schemes of chemotherapy often use courses of "reinduction" medications between remission treatments even though the patient has remained in complete remission. This is intended to further reduce the body's burden of leukemic cells. Thus, the objective today is not remission maintenance but complete cure of acute leukemia.

Leukemia of Childhood

Acute lymphoblastic leukemia (ALL) is the predominant form of leukemia in childhood and the most common form of cancer in children. The usual cell of origin appears to be a "null" lymphocyte. These children now have a relatively good prognosis. A subset of patients with a poor prognosis have neoplastic lymphocytes expressing surface antigenic features of T lymphocytes (see Chapter 46). A cytoplasmic enzyme expressed by normal thymocytes, terminal deoxycytidyl transferase (terminal transferase), is also expressed in many cases of ALL. T cell ALLs also express high levels of the enzyme adenosine deaminase (ADA). (This had led to interest in the use of the ADA-inhibitor deoxycoformycin for treatment of such T cell cases.) Until 1948, the median survival in ALL was 3 months. With the advent of the folic acid antagonists, a major increase in survival was attained. Subsequently, corticosteroids, mercaptopurine, cyclophosphamide, vincristine, daunorubicin, and asparaginase were all found to have activity in this disease. In general, current practice is to employ a combination of vincristine and prednisone for initial induction of remission. Over 85% of children enter complete remission with this therapy, with only minimal toxicity. Because circulating tumor stem cells often lodge in the brain, such cells are not killed by these drugs, as they do not cross the blood-brain barrier. The value of "prophylactic" intrathecal methotrexate therapy for prevention of central nervous

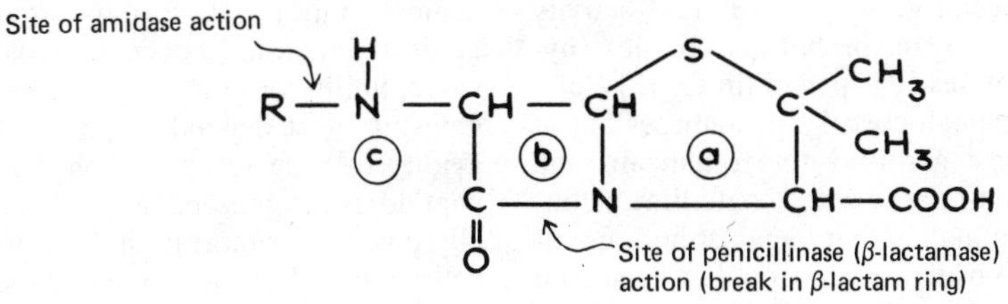

Site of amidase action

6-Aminopenicillanic acid

Site of penicillinase (β-lactamase) action (break in β-lactam ring)

The following structures can each be substituted at R to produce a new penicillin.

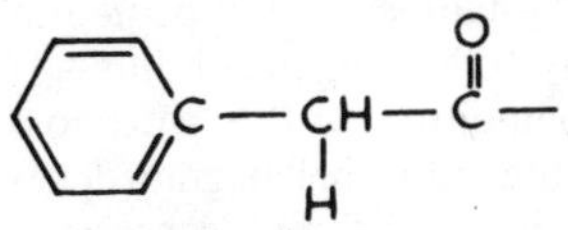

Penicillin G (benzylpenicillin):
High activity against gram-positive bacteria. Low activity against gram-negative bacteria. Acid-labile. Destroyed by β-lactamase; 60% protein bound.

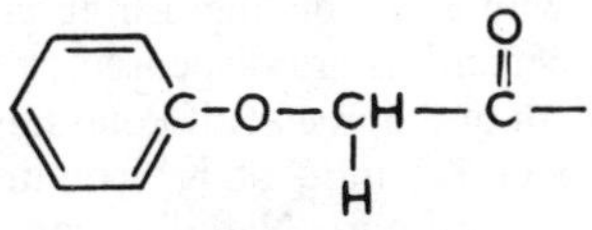

Penicillin V (phenoxymethyl penicillin):
Similar to penicillin G but relatively acid-resistant.

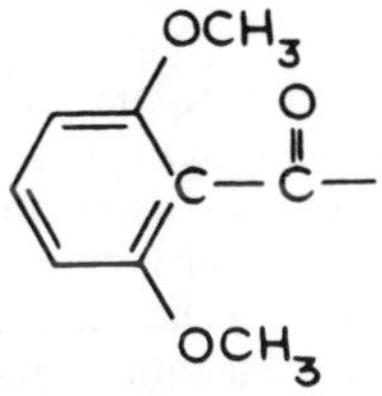

Methicillin (dimethoxyphenylpenicillin):
Lower activity than penicillin G but resistant to β-lactamase. Acid-labile. 40% protein bound.

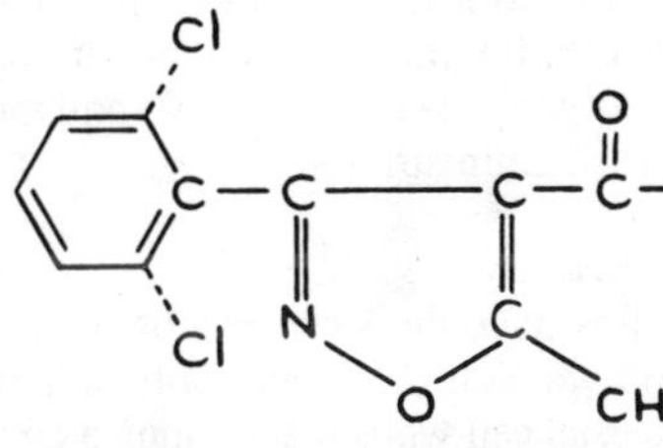

Oxacillin; cloxacillin (one Cl in structure); dicloxacillin (2 Cls in structure); flucloxacillin (one Cl and one F in structure) (isoxazolyl penicillines): Similar to methicillin in β-lactamase resistance, but acid-stable. Highly protein bound (95—98%).

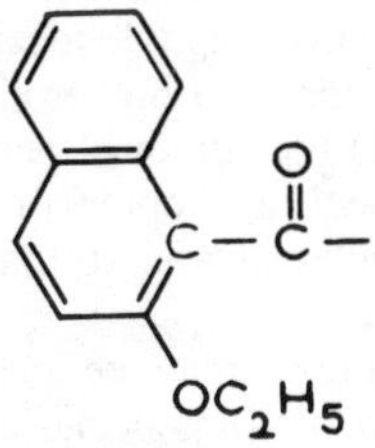

Nafcillin (ethoxynaphthamidopenicillin):
Similar to isoxazolyl penicillins; less strongly protein bound (90%).

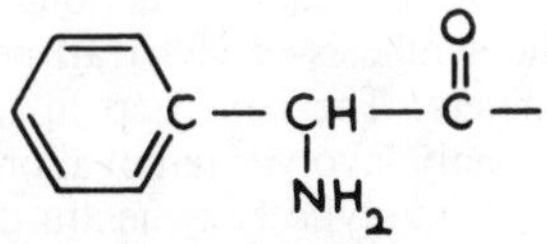

Ampicillin (alpha-aminobenzylpenicillin):
Similar to penicillin G (destroyed by β-lactamase) but acid-stable and more active against gram-negative bacteria. Carbenicillin has —COONa instead of —NH₂ group.

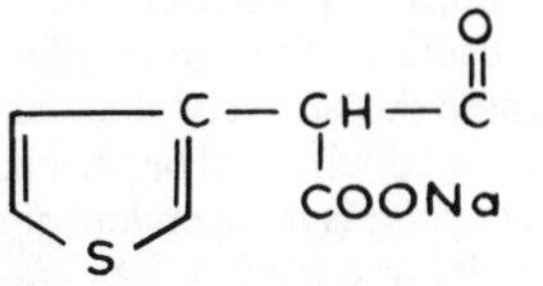

Ticarcillin:
Similar to carbenicillin but gives higher blood levels.

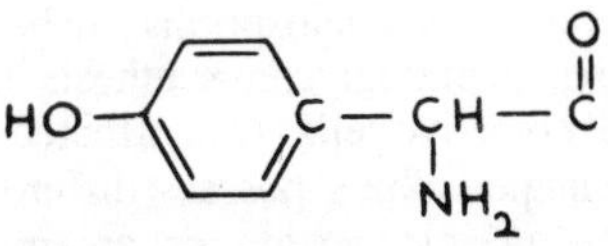

Amoxicillin:
Similar to ampicillin but better absorbed, gives higher blood levels.

Figure 49 –1. Structures of the penicillins.

in 1980 fall into several groups: (1) Highest activity against gram-positive organisms but susceptible to hydrolysis by β-lactamases, eg, penicillin G. (2) Relatively resistant to staphylococcal β-lactamases but of lower activity against gram-positive organisms and inactive against gram-negatives, eg, nafcillin, methicillin. (3) Relatively high activity against both gram-negative and gram-positive organisms but destroyed by β-lactamases, eg, ampicillin, carbenicillin, ticarcillin. (4) Relatively stable to gastric acid and suitable for oral administration, eg, penicillin V, cloxacillin.

Some representatives of each group are shown in Fig 49–1, with a few distinguishing characteristics.

Most penicillins are dispensed as the sodium or potassium salt of the free acid. Potassium penicillin G contains about 1.7 mEq of K^+ per million units of penicillin (2.8 mEq/g). Nafcillin contains Na^+, 2.8 mEq/g. Procaine salts (procaine penicillin) and benzathine salts (benzathine penicillin; Bicillin) are employed to provide repository forms for intramuscular injection.

In dry crystalline form, penicillin salts are stable for long periods (eg, for years at 4 C). Solutions lose their activity rapidly (eg, 24 hours at 20 C) and must be prepared fresh for administration.

Antimicrobial Activity

All penicillins have the same mechanism of antibacterial action. Penicillins specifically inhibit the synthesis of bacterial cell walls that contain a complex "mucopeptide" consisting of polysaccharides and a highly cross-linked polypeptide known as peptidoglycan (murein).

The initial step in penicillin action consists of binding of the drug to cell receptors. At least some of these receptor proteins are transpeptidation enzymes. After attachment of the drug, penicillins and cephalosporins inhibit the activity of various transpeptidation enzymes, and transpeptidation reactions are blocked. As a result, the synthesis of cell wall peptidoglycan remains incomplete. The next step in the action of these drugs probably involves removal or inactivation of an inhibitor of autolytic enzymes in the cell wall. This activates the lytic enzymes and may result in lysis of the organism if the environment is isotonic. In a markedly hypertonic environment (eg, 20% sucrose), the cells change to protoplasts, covered only by the fragile cell membrane. In such protoplasts, the synthesis of proteins and nucleic acids may continue for some time.

Penicillins and cephalosporins can be bactericidal only if active peptidoglycan synthesis takes place. Metabolically inactive cells are unaffected (see p 533).

Different penicillins possess different quantitative activity against certain organisms. Whereas 0.002–0.5 μg/mL of penicillin G is lethal for a majority of susceptible gram-positive bacteria, nafcillin and other β-lactamase–resistant penicillins are 10–100 times less active against the same organisms. While ampicillin, 0.01–0.5 μg/mL, is active against most organisms susceptible to penicillin G, it is also active against gram-negative non–lactamase-producing organisms in similar concentrations. The difference in susceptibility of gram-positive and gram-negative organisms must depend in part on the frequency and avidity of drug receptors; on the relative amount of peptidoglycan present (gram-positive organisms usually possess far more); on the amount of lipids in the cell wall; and on other chemical differences that determine binding, penetration, and resistance to lysis or rupture. The gram-negative neisseriae are as susceptible to penicillin G as many gram-positive organisms.

The activity of penicillin G was originally defined in units. Crystalline sodium penicillin G contains approximately 1600 units/mg (1 unit = 0.6 μg; 1 million units of penicillin = 0.6 g). Most semisynthetic penicillins are prescribed in gram doses only. Different penicillins have different activities per microgram against susceptible microorganisms. The susceptibility of microorganisms is in part generic and in part a characteristic of individual strains.

Resistance

Resistance to penicillins falls into several distinct categories.

A. Certain bacteria (eg, many *Staphylococcus aureus*, some *Haemophilus influenzae* and gonococci, most gram-negative enteric rods) produce β-lactamases (penicillinases), enzymes that inactivate some penicillins by breaking the β-lactam ring. The genetic control of β-lactamase production—there are about 50 different such enzymes—resides in transmissible plasmids (see Chapter 47). Other penicillins (eg, nafcillin) are β-lactamase–resistant because the β-lactam ring is protected by parts of the R- side chain. Such penicillins are active against β-lactamase–producing organisms, especially staphylococci.

B. Other bacteria do not produce β-lactamases but are resistant to the action of penicillins either because they lack specific receptors or because of lack of permeability of outer layers, so that the drug cannot reach the receptor.

C. Some bacteria may be insusceptible to the killing action of penicillins because the autolytic enzymes in the cell wall are not activated. Such "tolerant" organisms (staphylococci, *Listeria*) are inhibited but not killed.

D. Organisms that lack cell walls (*Mycoplasma*, L forms) or are metabolically inactive are insusceptible to penicillins and other cell wall inhibitors because they do not synthesize peptidoglycans.

E. Some bacteria (eg, *Staphylococcus albus*) may be resistant to the action of β-lactamase–resistant penicillins, eg, methicillin. The mechanism of this resistance is unclear; it is independent of any lactamase production, and its frequency varies greatly with time and place.

Absorption, Metabolism, & Excretion

After parenteral administration, absorption of most penicillins is complete and rapid. Because of the irritation and consequent local pain produced by the intramuscular injection of large doses, administration by the intravenous route (intermittent bolus addition to a continuous drip) is often preferred. After oral administration, only a portion of the dose is absorbed—from 1/20 to 1/3, depending upon acid stability, binding to foods, and the presence of buffers. In order to minimize binding to foods, oral penicillins should not be preceded or followed by food for at least 1 hour.

After absorption, penicillins are widely distributed in body fluids and tissues. This varies to some extent with the degree of protein binding exhibited by different penicillins. Penicillin G, methicillin, and ampicillin are moderately protein bound (depending upon the method of measurement, 40–60%), whereas the isoxazolyl penicillins are highly protein bound (95–98%). While the importance of serum binding is far from clear, it is probable that intensive protein binding diminishes the amount of drug available for antibacterial action in vivo and thus delays a therapeutic response. With parenteral doses of 3–6 g (5–10 million units) of penicillin G, injected in divided doses into a continuous infusion or by intramuscular injections, average serum levels of the drug reach 1–10 units (0.6–6 μg)/mL. A rough relationship of 6 g given parenterally per day yielding serum levels of 1–6 μg/mL also applies to other penicillins. Naturally, the highly serum bound isoxazolyl penicillins yield, on the average, lower levels of free drug than less strongly bound penicillins.

Special dosage forms of penicillin have been designed for delayed absorption to yield low blood and tissue levels for long periods. The outstanding example is benzathine penicillin G. After a single intramuscular injection of 1.5 g (2.4 million units), serum levels in excess of 0.03 unit/mL are maintained for 10 days and levels in excess of 0.005 unit/mL for 3 weeks. The latter is sufficient to protect against β-hemolytic streptococcal infection; the former to treat an established infection with these organisms. Procaine penicillin also has delayed absorption, yielding levels for 24 hours.

In many tissues, penicillin concentrations are equal to those in serum. Lower levels are found in the eye and the central nervous system. However, with active inflammation of the meninges, as in bacterial meningitis, penicillin levels in the cerebrospinal fluid exceed 0.2 μg/mL with a daily parenteral dose of 12 g. Thus, pneumococcal and meningococcal meningitis may be treated with systemic penicillin and there is no need for intrathecal injection. It is probable that high levels of penicillins in the cerebrospinal fluid in meningitis are due to (1) increased permeability of meninges, (2) inhibition of active transport of penicillin from the cerebrospinal fluid, which occurs normally, or (3) some binding of penicillin to cerebrospinal fluid proteins.

Most of the absorbed penicillin is rapidly excreted by the kidneys into the urine; small amounts are excreted by other channels. About 10% of renal excretion is by glomerular filtration and 90% by tubular secretion, to a maximum of about 2 g/h in an adult. Ampicil-

lin is secreted more slowly than penicillin G. Nafcillin is excreted 80% into the biliary tract and only 20% by tubular secretion; therefore, it is little affected by renal failure. Tubular secretion can be partially blocked by probenecid (Benemid) to achieve higher systemic and cerebrospinal fluid levels. Renal clearance is less efficient in the newborn, so that proportionately smaller doses result in higher systemic levels that are maintained longer than in the adult. Individuals with impaired renal function likewise tend to maintain higher penicillin levels longer.

Renal excretion of penicillin results in very high levels in the urine. Thus, systemic daily doses of 6 g of penicillin may yield urine levels of 500–3000 μg/mL—enough to suppress not only gram-positive but also many gram-negative bacteria in the urine (provided they produce little β-lactamase).

Penicillin is also excreted into sputum and milk to levels of 3–15% of those present in the serum. This is the case in both humans and cattle. The presence of penicillin in the milk of cows treated for mastitis presents a problem in allergy.

Clinical Uses

Penicillins are by far the most effective and the most widely used antibiotics. All oral penicillins should be given away from meal times (1 hour before or 1–2 hours after), to reduce binding and acid inactivation. Oxacillin is most strongly food bound (ie, protein bound), dicloxacillin somewhat less so. Blood levels of all penicillins can be raised by simultaneous administration of probenecid, 0.5 g every 6 hours orally (10 mg/kg every 6 hours), which impairs tubular secretion.

A. Penicillin G is the drug of choice for infections caused by pneumococci, streptococci, meningococci, non-β-lactamase-producing staphylococci and gonococci, *Treponema pallidum* and many other spirochetes, *Bacillus anthracis* and other gram-positive rods, clostridia, and some *Listeria* and *Bacteroides* (except *Bacteroides fragilis*). Most of these infections respond to daily doses of penicillin G, 0.6–5 million units (0.36–3 g). Intermittent intramuscular injection is the usual method of administration. Much larger amounts (6–120 g daily) can be given by injection during a 20-minute period every 4–6 hours into an intravenous infusion. Such a procedure is useful in serious or complicated infections due to these organisms. Oral administration of **penicillin V** is indicated only in minor infections—eg, of the respiratory tract or its associated structures, especially in children (pharyngitis, otitis, sinusitis)—in a daily dose of 1–4 g. Oral administration is subject to so many variables that it should not be relied upon in seriously ill patients. Many non-β-lactamase-producing gonococci have developed partial resistance to penicillin, requiring 1–3 units/mL for inhibition. Treatment of such gonorrhea now requires procaine penicillin, 4.8 million units once, with probenecid, 1 g orally. In gonococcal prostatitis, arthritis, salpingitis, or other closed lesions, 10 million units must be given daily for

4–14 days, combined with drainage when needed. When β-lactamase-producing gonococci are present, alternative drugs, eg, spectinomycin or tetracycline, must be used.

Penicillin G is inhibitory for enterococci (*Streptococcus faecalis*), but the simultaneous administration of an aminoglycoside is often necessary for bactericidal effects, eg, in enterococcal endocarditis. In urinary tract infections, large doses of penicillin G (eg, 1–10 million units intramuscularly) may provide sufficiently high levels in the urine to inhibit relatively resistant gram-negative coliform bacteria and, in particular, *Proteus mirabilis*. However, such treatment is likely to fail in the presence of large numbers of bacteria producing large amounts of β-lactamase.

B. Benzathine penicillin G is a salt of very low water solubility for intramuscular injection that yields low but prolonged drug levels. A single injection of 1.2 million units intramuscularly is satisfactory for treatment of beta-hemolytic streptococcal pharyngitis. A similar injection given intramuscularly once every 3–4 weeks provides satisfactory prophylaxis against reinfection with beta-hemolytic streptococci. Benzathine penicillin G (2.4 million units intramuscularly once a week for 3 weeks) is effective in the treatment of early or latent syphilis. This drug should never be given by mouth.

C. Ampicillin, Amoxicillin, Carbenicillin, Ticarcillin: These drugs differ from penicillin G in having greater activity against gram-negative bacteria, but they are inactivated by β-lactamases.

Ampicillin, 500 mg orally every 6–8 hours, is used to treat common urinary tract infections with gram-negative coliform bacteria or mixed secondary bacterial infections of the respiratory tract (sinusitis, otitis, bronchitis). Ampicillin, 300 mg/kg/d intravenously, is a current choice for bacterial meningitis in children, especially if the disease is caused by *H influenzae*. However, in some locations, β-lactamase-producing *H influenzae* are emerging, which means that ampicillin is ineffective and chloramphenicol must be used.

Ampicillin is ineffective against *Enterobacter, Pseudomonas,* and indole-positive *Proteus* infections. In invasive *Salmonella* infections (eg, typhoid), ampicillin, 6–12 g/d intravenously, can suppress signs and symptoms and eliminate organisms from some carriers. In typhoid and paratyphoid fevers, ampicillin is an alternative to chloramphenicol or trimethoprim/sulfamethoxazole (co-trimoxazole). However, it is not beneficial in noninvasive *Salmonella* gastroenteritis and may even prolong carriage and shedding. An exception may be salmonellosis in severely malnourished children. In enterococcal sepsis or endocarditis, ampicillin may be more active than penicillin G when combined with an aminoglycoside.

Amoxicillin is similar to ampicillin but is somewhat better absorbed from the gut. The 2 drugs are comparable in spectrum, activity, and side-effects.

Carbenicillin resembles ampicillin but has more activity against *Pseudomonas* and *Proteus,* although *Klebsiella* is usually resistant. In susceptible populations of *Pseudomonas,* resistance to carbenicillin may emerge rapidly. Therefore, in *Pseudomonas* sepsis (eg, burns, leukemia), carbenicillin, 12–30 g/d intravenously (300–500 mg/kg/d), is usually combined with an aminoglycoside, eg, gentamicin, 5–7 mg/kg/d intramuscularly, to delay emergence of resistance and perhaps to obtain synergistic effects. Carbenicillin contains Na^+, 4.7 mEq/g. Carbenicillin indanyl sodium is acid-stable and can be given orally in urinary tract infections.

Ticarcillin resembles carbenicillin in single and combined activity, but the dose may be lower, eg, 200–300 mg/kg/d intravenously. Hetacillin is converted to ampicillin and should not be used.

D. Lactamase-Resistant Penicillins: Methicillin, nafcillin, the isoxazolyl penicillins (oxacillin, cloxacillin, dicloxacillin), and others are relatively resistant to destruction by staphylococcal β-lactamases. The sole indication for use of these drugs is infection by β-lactamase-producing staphylococci.

Oxacillin, cloxacillin, dicloxacillin, or nafcillin, 0.25–0.5 g every 4–6 hours by mouth, is suitable for treatment of mild localized staphylococcal infections (50–100 mg/kg/d for children). All of these drugs are relatively acid-stable and reasonably well-absorbed from the gut. They are all highly protein bound (95–98%). Food interferes with absorption for this reason, and the drugs must be administered 1 hour away from meals.

For serious systemic staphylococcal infections, nafcillin, 8–12 g/d, is administered intravenously, usually by introducing 1–2 g during 20–30 minutes every 2–3 hours into a continuous infusion of 5% dextrose in water or physiologic saline solution. Methicillin is employed similarly but at present is believed to be more nephrotoxic than nafcillin and therefore employed less often. The dose for children is nafcillin or methicillin, 50–100 mg/kg/d.

These antistaphylococcal drugs are not indicated in streptococcal pharyngitis when lactamase-producing staphylococci are also cultured from the throat.

Adverse Reactions

The penicillins undoubtedly possess less direct toxicity than any other antibiotics. Most of the serious side-effects are due to hypersensitivity.

A. Allergy: All penicillins are cross-sensitizing and cross-reacting. Any preparation containing penicillin may induce sensitization, including foods or cosmetics. In general, sensitization occurs in direct proportion to the duration and total dose of penicillin received in the past. The responsible antigenic determinants appear to be degradation products of penicillins, particularly penicilloic acid and products of alkaline hydrolysis bound to host protein. Skin tests with penicilloylpolylysine, with alkaline hydrolysis products, and with undegraded penicillin will identify many hypersensitive individuals. Among positive reactors to skin tests, the incidence of subsequent penicillin reactions is high. Although many persons develop IgG antibodies to antigenic determinants of penicillin, the presence of such antibodies does not appear to be correlated with allergic reactivity (except rare hemolytic anemia), and serologic tests have little predictive value. A history of a penicillin reaction in the past is not reliable; about 5–8% of people claim such a history in the USA. However, in such cases, penicillin should be administered with caution or a substitute drug given.

About 10–15% of persons with a past history of a penicillin reaction have an allergic reaction when given penicillin again. Less than 1% of persons who previously received penicillin without incident will have an allergic reaction when given penicillin again. The incidence of allergic reactions in small children is negligible.

Allergic reactions may occur as typical anaphylactic shock (very rare—0.05% of recipients), typical serum sickness type reactions (urticaria, fever, joint swelling, angioneurotic edema, intense pruritus, and respiratory embarrassment occurring 7–12 days after exposure), and a variety of skin rashes, oral lesions, fever, interstitial nephritis (caused by antibodies to a penicilloyl-basement membrane complex antigen), eosinophilia, hemolytic anemia and other hematologic disturbances, and vasculitis. LE cells are sometimes found.

At times, individuals known to be hypersensitive to penicillin can tolerate the drug during corticosteroid administration. "Desensitization" with gradually increasing doses of penicillin is also occasionally attempted but is not without hazard. Anaphylactic reactions are more rare after oral penicillin administration than after parenteral administration.

B. Toxicity: Since the action of penicillin is directed against a unique bacterial structure, the cell wall, it is virtually without effect on animal cells. The toxic effects of penicillin G are due to the direct irritation caused by intramuscular or intravenous injection of exceedingly high concentrations (eg, 1 g/mL). Such concentrations may cause local pain, induration, thrombophlebitis, or degeneration of an accidentally injected nerve. All penicillins are irritating to the central nervous system and greatly increase the excitability of neurons. For that reason, no more than 20,000 units can be given intrathecally on any one day, but there is little indication for intrathecal administration at present. In rare cases, a patient receiving more than 50 g of penicillin G daily parenterally has exhibited signs of cerebrocortical irritation as a result of the passage of unusually large amounts of penicillin into the central nervous system. With doses of this magnitude, direct cation toxicity (Na^+, K^+) can also occur (see Chemistry, above), particularly in patients with renal failure.

Large doses of penicillins given orally may lead to gastrointestinal upset, particularly nausea, vomiting, and diarrhea. This is more pronounced with the broad-spectrum forms (ampicillin, amoxicillin) than with other penicillins. Oral therapy may also be accompanied by luxuriant overgrowth of staphylococci, *Pseudomonas, Proteus,* or yeasts, which may occasionally cause enteritis. Superinfections in other organ systems may occur with penicillins as with any antibiotic therapy. Methicillin, nafcillin, and isoxazolyl penicillins have occasionally caused granulocytopenia, especially in children. Methicillin causes nephritis more commonly than does nafcillin. The tubular basement membrane protein serves to bind penicillin, and antibody to the carrier-hapten antigen forms a complex, with binding of complement. Carbenicillin can cause hypokalemic alkalosis and transaminase elevation in serum. It can also induce hemostatic defects leading to bleeding tendency. Ampicillin frequently causes skin rashes, some of which are not allergic in nature.

Problems Relating to the Use of the Penicillins

The penicillins are by far the most widely used antibiotics. Several hundred tons of these drugs have been administered to humans during the past 20 years. Therefore, penicillins have been responsible for some of the most drastic consequences of antibiotic misuse.

A significant proportion of the population of many countries (perhaps 1–5%) have become hypersensitive. In many cases, there is no doubt that sensitization has occurred when penicillin was administered without proper indication. It would be desirable to have penicillin-hypersensitive individuals definitely identified, but hypersensitivity may be temporary.

The saturation of certain environments (eg, hospitals) with penicillin has produced a selection pressure against penicillin-sensitive microorganisms and resulted in greater numbers of penicillin-resistant organisms. Hospital environments consequently have become filled with β-lactamase–producing staphylococci. In some instances, these organisms were endowed with enhanced ability to disseminate and produce infection. "Hospital staphylococci" were responsible for outbreaks of lethal disease in newborn nurseries and surgical units in the 1960s.

The suppression of normal flora creates a partial void that is regularly filled with drug-resistant, prevalent organisms. Penicillins are administered to a high proportion of patients in hospitals. These patients are made selectively susceptible to superinfections with microorganisms derived from the hospital environment (*Proteus, Pseudomonas, Enterobacter, Serratia,* yeasts, staphylococci, etc). Such organisms become established in organ systems where the normal flora has been suppressed (eg, the respiratory tract, gut, skin) and can cause disease processes there.

The drastic restriction of penicillin abuse in certain hospitals has illustrated the ability of humans to control the harmful changes in the microflora of the environment. Restricted use of penicillin has led to a return of penicillin-sensitive microorganisms to the environment and reduction of the harmful effects of drug-resistant bacteria.

Plasmids that control β-lactamase production are

being distributed with increasing frequency among different genera of microorganisms. *Neisseria gonorrhoeae* has recently acquired such plasmids, probably by conjugation with *Haemophilus* or enteric organisms. If lactamase-producing gonococci become prevalent, venereal disease control will become even more complex.

7-Aminocephalosporanic acid

CEPHALOSPORINS

Fungi of *Cephalosporium* species yielded several antibiotics that resembled penicillins but were resistant to β-lactamase and were active against both gram-positive and gram-negative bacteria. Methods were eventually developed for the large-scale production of the common nucleus, 7-aminocephalosporanic acid, and these advances made possible the synthesis of many derivatives, the cephalosporins. A bewildering array of semisynthetic cephalosporins has been developed, making it difficult for the physician to choose an appropriate drug. In addition to the synthetics derived from cephalosporanic acid, the cephamycins (fermentation products of *Streptomyces*) may be considered under the same heading because of their very similar properties.

Chemistry

The nucleus of the cephalosporins, 7-aminocephalosporanic acid, bears a close resemblance to the nucleus of the penicillins, 6-aminopenicillanic acid, and also to the nucleus of the cephamycin antibiotics. The intrinsic antimicrobial activity of natural cephalosporins is low, but the attachment of various R_1 and R_2 groups has yielded drugs of good therapeutic activity and low toxicity.

The cephalosporins have molecular weights of 400–450. They are cream-colored solids, freely soluble in water, and relatively stable to pH and temperature changes. They vary in resistance to β-lactamases (penicillinases and cephalosporinases). The sodium salt of cephalothin contains 55 mg Na^+ per gram. Fusidic acid and helvolic acid are related to cephalosporins and have been used in Britain as antistaphylococcal drugs.

Antimicrobial Activity

In vitro, cephalosporins in concentrations of 1–20 μg/mL are active against a variety of gram-positive bacteria, with the exception of *S faecalis*. Among gram-negative organisms, many strains of *Escherichia coli*, *Klebsiella*, and *P mirabilis* are susceptible to 5–30 μg/mL, whereas *B fragilis*, *Enterobacter*, *Serratia*, *Pseudomonas*, most *Proteus*, *Acinetobacter*, and *Providencia* are resistant. Cefamandole and cefoxitin have somewhat greater activity against the latter aerobic and anaerobic gram-negative organisms. There is extensive cross-resistance between cephalosporins and β-lactamase-resistant penicillins.

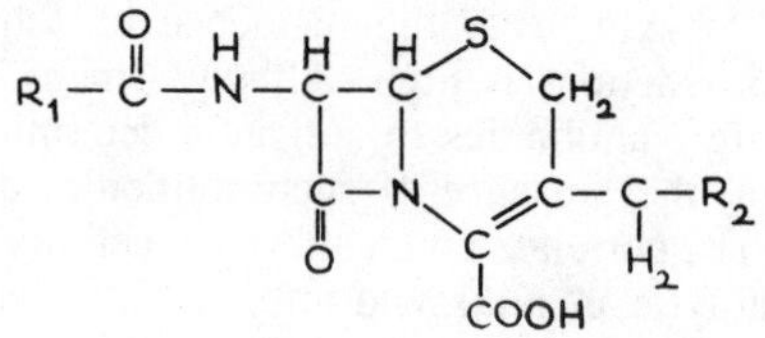

Cephalothin

Cephalexin

Cefazolin

Cephradine

Cephapirin

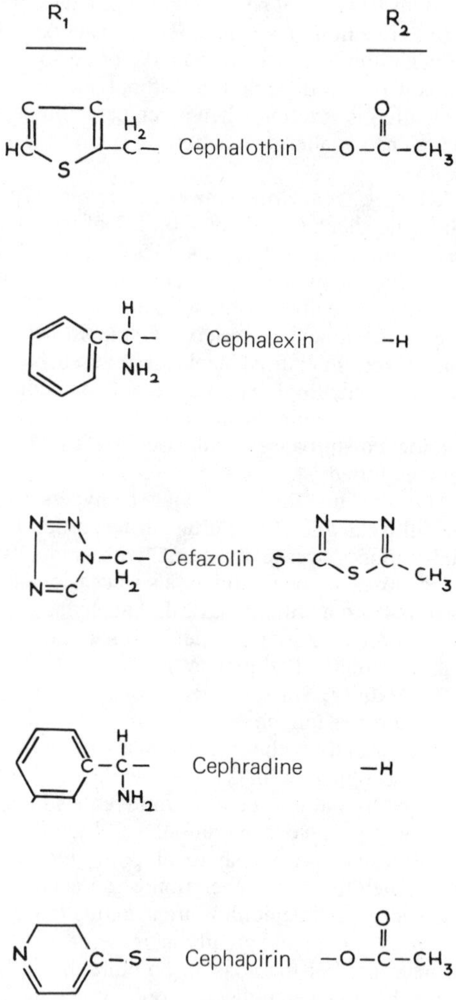

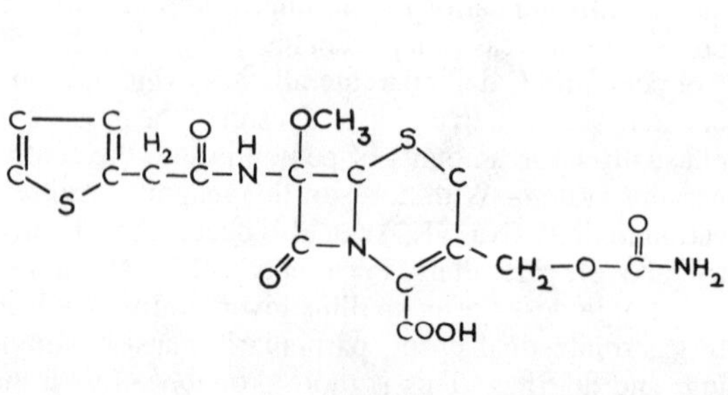

Cefoxitin
(a cephamycin)

Cephalosporins are bactericidal for susceptible bacteria because they block terminal transpeptidation of cell wall mucopeptides in a manner analogous to the action of penicillins.

Absorption, Distribution, & Excretion

Cephalothin, cefazolin, cephapirin, and cefamandole are not adequately absorbed from the gastrointestinal tract and must be given parenterally for systemic therapy. Cephalothin, 6–12 g daily, is usually given as an intravenous bolus at 2- to 4-hour intervals into an intravenous drip to give average serum levels of 5–20 μg/mL, with a protein binding of 60–70% and a serum half-life of 0.8 hour. Cefazolin, 1 g every 4 hours (100 mg/kg/d for children), can be given intravenously or intramuscularly to give serum levels of 20–50 μg/mL, but with 75–85% protein binding and a serum half-life of 120 minutes. Cefamandole given as a 2-g bolus intravenously every 6 hours reaches serum levels of 50–100 μg/mL, with a serum half-life of 1 hour. The values for cephapirin resemble those of cephalothin.

Cefoxitin (a cephamycin drug) has indications and dosage regimens similar to those of cefamandole.

All parenterally administered cephalosporins are widely distributed in tissues and body fluids, including the eye and synovial fluids, but concentration in the central nervous system and cerebrospinal fluid is negligible. Cephalosporins are *not* suitable for treatment of central nervous system infections and meningitis.

Cephalexin and cephradine are well absorbed from the gut; after oral doses of 0.5 g, the serum level reaches 10 μg/mL. About 20% of each of these drugs is protein-bound; serum half-life is 120 minutes, and levels in urine may reach 50–500 μg/mL. Cefaclor is very similar to cephalexin, with a –Cl substituting for the –CH$_3$ group. It has a similar pattern of activity to that of cephalexin except that some *H influenzae* strains are much more susceptible to cefaclor. It has similar activity in vivo and has been recommended for otitis media in children where *Haemophilus* may play a major role. Its side-effects are not yet clearly established.

Cephalosporins are excreted mainly by glomerular filtration and tubular secretion into the urine, where levels may reach 200–2000 μg/mL. Tubular blocking agents (eg, probenecid) may increase serum levels substantially. Those cephalosporins containing acetyl groups in the R$_2$ position (cephalothin, cephapirin) are deacetylated in the liver; the metabolic product is less biologically active. In renal failure, the excretion of cephalosporins may be markedly impaired, and high fluid and tissue levels may exert toxic effects. Levels of cephalosporins in bile are similar to those in serum.

Clinical Uses

Cephalosporins can be considered for the following major applications:

(1) Gram-positive infections in penicillin-sensitive patients–Cephalosporins tend to be resistant to staphylococcal penicillinase; cross-reactions in true penicillin allergy occur in 6–16% of cases. Cephalosporins should never be used as substitutes in persons who have had anaphylactic reactions to penicillin. Cephalosporins themselves induce allergic reactions (fever, skin rashes, eosinophilia) in 2–5% of cases.

(2) Infections due to *Klebsiella*, coliforms, *Proteus*–Cephalosporins continue to be active against many strains of these organisms.

(3) Mixed infections–Cephalosporins can be used for the treatment of cellulitis or skin ulcers in diabetics.

(4) Suspected bacteremia and sepsis due to an unknown organism (most probably a *Staphylococcus* or gram-negative bacteria)–Cephalosporin is given together with an aminoglycoside. (Nephrotoxicity may in some cases be enhanced.)

(5) Selected "surgical prophylaxis" for 2–6 hours before and 12–24 hours after a surgical procedure that has more than a 5% risk of infection.

A. Oral Administration: Cephalexin and cephradine seem virtually identical in terms of absorption, levels in blood (10 μg/mL after 0.5 g every 6 hours), protein binding (20%), antimicrobial activity, and excretion in urine. Use is limited to infections of the urinary tract (levels in urine may reach 500 μg/mL) or to minor infections of the respiratory tract (otitis, sinusitis, tracheobronchitis) caused by susceptible organisms.

B. Parenteral Administration:

1. Intramuscular–Cefazolin, 0.5 g every 4 hours or 1 g every 6 hours, is the present choice (100 mg/kg/d for children). It has replaced cephaloridine, which is too nephrotoxic and less resistant to staphylococcal penicillinase.

2. Intravenous–Cefazolin, 1 g every 4–6 hours added as a bolus to a continuous infusion, is a preferred drug in 1980. It is 85% protein-bound and gives serum levels of 20–50 μg/mL. Cephalothin has been used for the longest time. It or cephapirin is given as a 1- or 2-g bolus every 4 hours into a continuous infusion (50 mg/kg/d). The protein binding is 50–65%, and serum levels of 2–20 μg/mL are achieved. In 1979, the cost of parenteral cephapirin was lower than that of other equivalent cephalosporins. Cefamandole or cefoxitin, 1–2 g into an infusion every 4–6 hours (50–150 mg/kg/d), gives serum levels of 20–40 μg/mL with 60–70% protein binding. *None* of these cephalosporins or cephamycins should be used in meningitis or other central nervous system infections.

Adverse Reactions

A. Toxicity: Local irritation can produce severe pain after intramuscular injection and thrombophlebitis after repeated intravenous injection. Other toxic reactions include anaphylaxis, urticaria, skin rashes, fever, eosinophilia, granulocytopenia, and hemolytic anemia. Some of these are probably hypersensitivity reactions (see below). Renal toxicity producing tubular necrosis has been demonstrated for several cephalosporins. For this reason, cephaloridine has been abandoned.

The oral cephalosporins also produce diarrhea, nausea, vomiting, and SGOT elevation.

B. Allergy: Cephalosporins can be sensitizing, and specific hypersensitivity reactions, including anaphylaxis, can occur. Because of the difference in the chemical structure of the drug nucleus, the antigenicity of cephalosporins differs from that of penicillins. Consequently, many individuals who are hypersensitive to penicillins can tolerate cephalosporins. The degree of cross-allergenicity between penicillins and cephalosporins remains controversial (6–16%). Some cross-antigenicity can be demonstrated in vitro.

●   ●   ●

References

Barret FF & others: Methicillin-resistant *Staphylococcus aureus* at Boston City Hospital. N Engl J Med 279:441, 1968.

Barza M: Antimicrobial spectrum, pharmacology and therapeutic use of penicillins. Am J Hosp Pharm 34:57, 1977.

Border WA & others: Antitubular basement membrane antibodies in methicillin-associated interstitial nephritis. N Engl J Med 291:381, 1974.

Brown CH & others: The hemostatic defect produced by carbenicillin. N Engl J Med 291:265, 1974.

Buchanan CE, Strominger JL: Altered penicillin-binding components in penicillin-resistant mutants of *Bacillus subtilis*. Proc Natl Acad Sci USA 73:1816, 1976.

Collaborative Study Group: Prospective study of ampicillin rash. Br Med J 1:7, 1973.

Grose WE & others: Some pharmacologic features of cefamandole. Clin Pharmacol Ther 20:579, 1976.

Heseltine PN & others: Cefoxitin: Clinical evaluation in thirty-eight patients. Antimicrob Agents Chemother 11:427, 1977.

Kancir LM & others: Adverse reactions to methicillin and nafcillin during treatment of serious *Staphylococcus aureus* infections. Arch Intern Med 138:909, 1978.

Love LJ & others: Randomized trial of empiric antibiotic therapy with ticarcillin in combination with gentamicin, amikacin, or netilmicin in febrile patients with granulocytopenic and cancer. Am J Med 66:603, 1979.

Mangi RJ & others: Development of meningitis during cephalothin therapy. Ann Intern Med 78:347, 1973.

Mitsuhashi S & others: Mechanism of action and development of resistance to a new amidinopenicillin. J Bacteriol 117:578, 1974.

Moellering RC Jr, Swartz MN: The newer cephalosporins. N Engl J Med 294:24, 1976.

Neu HC: Comparative studies of cefoxitin and cephalothin: An overview. Rev Infect Dis 1:144, 1979.

Parker CW: Drug allergy. (3 parts.) N Engl J Med 292:511, 732, 957, 1975.

Parry MF & others: Nafcillin nephritis. JAMA 225:178, 1973.

Petz LD: Immunologic cross reactivity between penicillins and cephalosporins: A review. J Infect Dis 137 (Suppl):S74, 1978.

Phillips JA & others: Ampicillin-associated diarrhea. Pediatrics 58:869, 1976.

Reyes MP & others: Granulocytopenia associated with carbenicillin. Am J Med 54:413, 1973.

Rolinson GN: 6-APA and the development of the beta-lactam antibiotics. J Antimicrob Chemother 5:7, 1979.

Rudolph AH, Price EV: Penicillin reactions among patients in venereal disease clinics. JAMA 223:499, 1973.

Scheifele DW & others: Evaluation of rapid β-lactamase test for detecting ampicillin-resistant strains of *Hemophilus influenzae* type b. Pediatrics 58:382, 1976.

Spector R, Lorenzo AV: Inhibition of penicillin transport from the cerebrospinal fluid after intracisternal inoculation of bacteria. J Clin Invest 54:316, 1974.

Tipper DJ: Mode of action of beta-lactam antibiotics. Rev Infect Dis 1:39, 1979.

CHLORAMPHENICOL

Chloramphenicol was first isolated from cultures of *Streptomyces venezuelae* in 1947 and was synthesized in 1949. It is the only available representative of its chemical type and the only completely synthetic antibiotic of importance to be produced commercially.

Chemistry

Crystalline chloramphenicol is a neutral, stable compound with the following structure:

Chloramphenicol

It consists of colorless crystals with an intensely bitter taste. It is highly soluble in alcohol and poorly soluble in water. Saturated aqueous solutions (0.25%) keep their activity for many months at refrigerator or room temperature if protected from light. Chloramphenicol succinate is highly soluble in water and is hydrolyzed in tissues with the liberation of free chloramphenicol; it is used for parenteral injection.

Antimicrobial Activity

Chloramphenicol is a potent inhibitor of protein synthesis and has little effect on other metabolic functions. It acts on the 50S unit of bacterial ribosomes and interferes markedly with the incorporation of amino acids into newly formed peptides by blocking the action of peptidyl transferase (see Chapter 47). Chloramphenicol also inhibits mitochondrial protein synthesis of mammalian bone marrow cells but does not greatly affect other intact cells.

Chloramphenicol is bacteriostatic for many bacteria and for rickettsiae but is ineffective against chlamydiae. Its action is reversible by removal of the drug. Most gram-positive bacteria are inhibited by chloramphenicol in concentrations of 1–10 μg/mL, and many gram-negative bacteria are inhibited by concentrations of 0.2–5 μg/mL. *Haemophilus influenzae*

and most *Bacteroides* species are often highly susceptible. Some salmonellae are susceptible, but plasmid-mediated resistance to chloramphenicol has appeared with increasing frequency.

Resistance

In most bacterial species, large populations of chloramphenicol-susceptible cells contain occasional resistant mutants. These mutants are usually only 2–4 times more resistant than the parent populations; consequently, they emerge slowly in treated individuals. There is no cross-resistance between chloramphenicol and other drugs, but plasmids (resistance transfer factors, RTF) may transmit multiple drug resistance (chloramphenicol, tetracycline, streptomycin, etc) from one bacterium or species to another by conjugation (see Chapter 47). Such plasmid-mediated resistance to chloramphenicol results from the production of chloramphenicol acetyltransferase, a bacterial enzyme that destroys the drug.

Absorption, Metabolism, & Excretion

After oral administration, crystalline chloramphenicol is rapidly and completely absorbed. With daily doses of 2 g orally, blood levels usually reach 8 μg/mL. Chloramphenicol palmitate, administered to children in doses up to 50 mg/kg/d orally, is hydrolyzed in the intestine to yield free chloramphenicol, but the usual blood levels rarely exceed 10 μg/mL. For parenteral injection, chloramphenicol succinate, 25–50 mg/kg/d intravenously, yields free chloramphenicol by hydrolysis, giving blood levels somewhat lower than those achieved with the orally administered drug.

After absorption, chloramphenicol is widely distributed to virtually all tissues and body fluids, including the central nervous system and cerebrospinal fluid. About 50% is bound to serum protein. An enzymatic assay for chloramphenicol, using acetyltransferase, has been developed. Chloramphenicol penetrates cells readily. Most of the drug is inactivated in the body either by conjugation with glucuronic acid (principally in the liver) or by reduction to inactive aryl amines. Excretion of active chloramphenicol (about 10% of the total dose administered) and of inactive degradation products (about 90% of the total) occurs into the urine. It may be that the active drug is cleared mainly by glomerular filtration and the inactive products mainly by tubular secretion. Only small amounts of active drug are excreted into bile or feces.

Clinical Uses

Chloramphenicol is a possible drug of choice in only a few types of infections: (1) Symptomatic *Salmonella* infection. (*Note:* Since 1972, *Salmonella typhi* in Central America has often been resistant to chloramphenicol, ampicillin, or both.) (2) *Haemophilus influenzae* meningitis, laryngotracheitis, or pneumonia not responding to ampicillin. (3) Occasional bacteremia caused by gram-negative bacteria expected (on the basis of experience) to be resistant to other drugs. (4) Infection with *Bacteroides* and other anaerobes. (5) Meningococcal infection in patients hypersensitive to penicillin. (6) Severe rickettsial infections.

Chloramphenicol is occasionally used topically in the treatment of eye infections.

A. For *Salmonella* infections (eg, typhoid or paratyphoid fever), adults should receive chloramphenicol, 2–3 g daily orally for 14–21 days, and children 30–50 mg/kg/d orally for 14–21 days. Prolonged treatment tends to reduce the frequency of relapses. A similar program may be followed in severe rickettsial infections (eg, scrub typhus or Rocky Mountain spotted fever).

B. For *H influenzae* meningitis or laryngotracheitis (in small children) or pneumonia (in the elderly), chloramphenicol, 50 mg/kg/d orally, has been given for 8–14 days, depending upon clinical response and cerebrospinal fluid changes. However, ampicillin is the drug of first choice at present unless ampicillin-resistant *Haemophilus* strains have been encountered in the community. It has also been recommended that initial treatment for *Haemophilus* meningitis should consist of both chloramphenicol and ampicillin until it can be shown that the organism does not produce β-lactamase. On the other hand, chloramphenicol-resistant *Haemophilus* strains have also appeared.

C. Other Uses: In life-threatening sepsis probably originating in the lower bowel, chloramphenicol, 2 g/d, is sometimes combined with an aminoglycoside (eg, amikacin, 15 mg/kg/d). Because of the excellent penetration of chloramphenicol into all parts of the central nervous system, it is sometimes used in cerebritis or meningitis of ill-defined origin.

In ophthalmology, topical application of chloramphenicol to the eye has been employed because of the wide antibacterial spectrum of the drug and its penetration of ocular tissues and into the aqueous humor. Sepsis caused by some species of *Bacteroides* and severe melioidosis may respond to chloramphenicol.

Adverse Reactions

A. Gastrointestinal Disturbances: Adults taking chloramphenicol, 1.5–2.5 g daily, occasionally develop nausea, vomiting, and diarrhea in 2–5 days. This is rare in children. After 5–10 days, the results of microbial flora alteration may become apparent, with prominent candidiasis of mucous membranes (especially of the mouth and vagina).

B. Bone Marrow Disturbances: Adults taking chloramphenicol in excess of 50 mg/kg/d regularly exhibit disturbances in red cell maturation after 1–2 weeks of blood levels above 25–30 μg/mL. These are characterized by the appearance of markedly vacuolated nucleated red cells in the marrow, anemia, and reticulocytopenia. These anomalies usually disappear when chloramphenicol is discontinued. The disturbance appears to be a maturation arrest associated with a rise in serum iron concentration and a depression of serum phenylalanine levels and is not related to the rare occurrence of aplastic anemia.

Aplastic anemia is a rare consequence of chloramphenicol administration. It probably represents a specific genetically determined idiosyncrasy of the individual. It is not related to dose or time of intake but is seen more frequently with prolonged use. It tends to be irreversible and fatal. The precise incidence of fatal aplastic anemia as a toxic reaction to chloramphenicol administration is not known, but the disease is estimated to occur 13 times more frequently after the use of the drug than it does spontaneously. Leukemia may follow the development of hypoplastic anemia.

C. Toxicity for Newborn Infants: Newborn infants lack an effective glucuronic acid conjugation mechanism for the degradation and detoxification of chloramphenicol. Consequently, when infants are given doses of 75 mg/kg/d or more, the drug may accumulate, resulting in the "gray syndrome," with vomiting, flaccidity, hypothermia, gray color, shock, and collapse. To avoid this toxic effect, chloramphenicol should be used with caution in infants and the dosage should be limited to 50 mg/kg/d or less in full-term infants and 30 mg/kg/d or less in prematures.

D. Interaction With Other Drugs: Chloramphenicol may prolong the action and raise the blood concentration of phenytoin or tolbutamide. It may precipitate a variety of other drugs from solutions.

Medical & Social Implications of Overuse

Because of its "broad spectrum" and its apparent lack of toxicity, chloramphenicol was used indiscriminately between 1948 and 1951 without specific indications. It has been estimated that more than 8 million people received the drug for minor complaints, respiratory (usually viral) illnesses, etc. This inappropriate use was followed by a wave of cases of aplastic anemia which, in turn, almost resulted in the complete abandonment of an effective drug.

TETRACYCLINES

The tetracyclines are a large group of drugs with a common basic structure and activity. Chlortetracycline, isolated from *Streptomyces aureofaciens*, was introduced in 1948. Oxytetracycline, derived from *Streptomyces rimosus*, was introduced in 1950. Tetracycline (many trade names), obtained by catalytic dehalogenation of chlortetracycline, has been available since 1953. Demethylchlortetracycline (demeclocycline) is obtained by demethylation of chlortetracycline.

Chemistry

All of the tetracyclines have the basic structure shown below.

Free tetracyclines are crystalline amphoteric substances of low solubility. They are available as hydrochlorides, which are more soluble (about 10% in water). Such solutions are acid and, with the exception of chlortetracycline, fairly stable. Chlortetracycline is very unstable in vitro, losing much of its activity in a few hours; for this reason, it is not widely used clinically at present. Tetracyclines combine firmly with divalent metal ions, and this chelation can interfere with absorption and activity of the molecule. Tetracyclines fluoresce bright yellow in ultraviolet light of 360 nm.

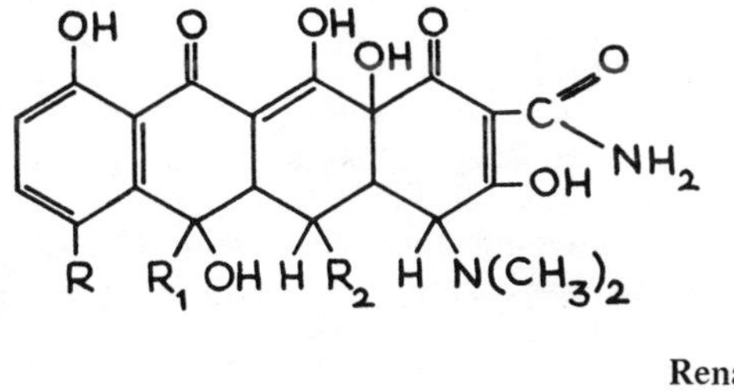

	R	R_1	R_2	Renal Clearance (mL/min)
Chlortetracycline	$-Cl$	$-CH_3$	$-H$	35
Oxytetracycline	$-H$	$-CH_3$	$-OH$	90
Tetracycline	$-H$	$-CH_3$	$-H$	65
Demeclocycline	$-Cl$	$-H$	$-H$	35
Methacycline	$-H$	$=CH_2$ *	$-OH$	31
Doxycycline	$-H$	$-CH_3$ *	$-OH$	16
Minocycline	$-N(CH_3)_2$	$-H$	$-H$	10

*There is no $-OH$ at position 6 on methacycline and doxycycline.

Antimicrobial Activity

Tetracyclines are bacteriostatic for many gram-positive and gram-negative bacteria, including some anaerobes, and strongly inhibitory for the growth of rickettsiae, mycoplasmas, L forms, chlamydiae, and some protozoa, eg, amebas. A 5-day course of tetracycline is effective in eliminating penicillinase-producing gonococci. Equal amounts of all tetracyclines in serum or tissues have approximately equal antimicrobial activity. Minocycline may have greater lipophilic properties than other tetracyclines. Other differences in activity as may be claimed for individual tetracycline drugs are of small magnitude and little practical importance. However, great differences exist in the susceptibility of different strains of a given species of microorganism to tetracyclines, and laboratory tests are therefore important in determining their usefulness in a given patient.

Tetracyclines are inhibitors of protein synthesis, which is the basis of their chemotherapeutic efficacy. Tetracyclines inhibit the binding of aminoacyl-tRNA to 30S units of ribosomes. The basis of their selective action on different organisms may be differences in permeability and concentration of drug by the cell. Susceptible cells have an active transport mechanism for the drug and thus concentrate tetracyclines to a level several times greater than can be found in the cell's environment.

Resistance

Susceptible microbial populations contain small numbers of mutants resistant to tetracyclines. Resistant mutants lack an active transport mechanism across cell membranes and thus do not concentrate tetracycline in their cells. The degree of resistance is variable, usually only 2–6 times higher than that of the parent population. Among gram-negative bacterial species (especially *Pseudomonas, Proteus*, and coliforms), the selection of highly resistant types has already occurred, and tetracyclines have therefore lost some of their usefulness. Tetracycline resistance can be transmitted from one gram-negative species to another by plasmids (RTF). Resistance is increasing even among what were at first highly susceptible bacterial species (eg, pneumococci, *Haemophilus*, streptococci, *Bacteroides*). This is a consequence of the intense selection pressure exerted on microbial populations by the widespread use of tetracycline drugs. The incorporation of tetracyclines in animal feeds enhances the rate of growth and weight gain in animals but also results in spread of tetracycline-resistant microorganisms among farm personnel and others.

Plasmids controlling resistance may be transmitted by transduction or by conjugation. The genes for tetracycline resistance are closely associated with those for other drugs, eg, aminoglycosides, sulfonamides, and chloramphenicol. Plasmids therefore usually transmit resistance to multiple drugs rather than to tetracyclines alone.

Absorption, Metabolism, & Excretion

Tetracyclines are absorbed somewhat irregularly from the gastrointestinal tract. Absorption is limited by the low solubility of the drugs, especially at alkaline pH and by chelation with Ca^{2+} or Fe^{2+}. A large portion of an orally administered dose of tetracycline remains in the gut lumen, modifies intestinal flora, and is excreted in the feces. Citrates and phosphates have been added to tetracyclines to enhance intestinal absorption. Specially buffered tetracycline solutions can be administered intramuscularly or intravenously.

In the bloodstream, 40–70% of absorbed tetracycline is protein-bound. With full systemic doses (2 g/d), the levels of antimicrobially active tetracycline in serum reach 5–8 $\mu g/mL$. The drugs are distributed widely in tissues and body fluids, but the levels in the central nervous system, cerebrospinal fluid, and joint fluids are only 3–10% of serum levels.

Tetracyclines are specifically deposited in growing bones and teeth as a result of chelation with calcium.

Absorbed tetracyclines are excreted mainly in bile and urine. Concentrations in bile are 10 times higher than in serum; some of the drug excreted in bile is probably reabsorbed from the intestine and contributes to maintenance of serum levels. Up to 20% of the oral dose may be excreted in urine, probably by glomerular filtration, resulting in urine levels of 5–50 μg/mL or more. Up to 80% of the oral dose is excreted with feces.

Certain tetracyclines (demeclocycline, methacycline, minocycline) are more slowly excreted than others and therefore can lead to higher blood levels with comparable doses and even to accumulation to toxic levels. Doxycycline is excreted slowly but does not accumulate in renal failure. Minocycline is somewhat better absorbed than other tetracyclines and slowly excreted. It is the only tetracycline to reach appreciable concentration in saliva and nasopharyngeal secretions. Minocycline also has other unusual activity (eg, against *Nocardia*) and toxicity (vestibular).

Clinical Uses

Tetracyclines are the most typical "broad-spectrum" antibiotics. They are effective against a variety of microorganisms and are thus used indiscriminately. There is no convincing evidence that any of the many formulations of tetracycline are therapeutically superior to tetracycline hydrochloride, although the slowly excreted members of the group may require less frequent administration and thus be more convenient.

Tetracyclines are the drugs of choice in cholera and in infections with *Mycoplasma pneumoniae*, chlamydiae, and rickettsiae. They are useful in mixed bacterial infections related to the respiratory tract, especially sinusitis and bronchitis. They may be employed in many gram-positive and gram-negative bacterial infections, including *Bacteroides*, provided the organism is susceptible. Tetracyclines given in full doses for 5 days can eradicate acute infections with penicillin-resistant gonococci. They have been used in pneumonias and in urinary tract and skin infections, particularly acne. It is claimed that 2.5 g of tetracycline hydrochloride as a single oral dose is effective in enteritis caused by both susceptible and resistant shigellae. A single dose of doxycycline, 200 mg, may be as effective in cholera as multiple doses. However, tetracycline resistance has appeared during cholera epidemics.

Minocycline, 200 mg orally daily for 5 days—or rifampin—can eradicate the meningococcal carrier state.

A. Oral Dosage: The minimal effective oral dose for rapidly excreted tetracyclines, equivalent to tetra-cycline hydrochloride, is 0.25 g 4 times daily for adults and 20 mg/kg/d for children. For severe systemic infections, a dose 2–3 times larger for at least 3–5 days is indicated.

Some slowly excreted tetracyclines are less reliably absorbed, produce lower levels, and should probably not be employed in severe infections. The minimal effective daily dose is 600 mg for demeclocycline or methacycline, 100 mg for doxycycline, and 200 mg for minocycline. Tetracyclines chelate with divalent cations, (eg, Ca^{2+}, Mg^{2+}) or with Al^{3+} (eg, aluminum hydroxide) and should therefore not be given with antacids or foods containing them or with ferrous sulfate.

Tetracycline hydrochloride, 250 mg daily, is commonly taken for many months to suppress acne, especially in adolescents and young adults. This low dose presumably suppresses lipase activity of propionibacteria and inhibits inflammatory reactions.

B. Parenteral Dosage: Several tetracyclines are available for intramuscular or intravenous injection in doses of 0.1–0.5 g every 6–12 hours (10–15 mg/kg/d in children).

Adverse Reactions

Hypersensitivity reactions (drug fever, skin rashes) to tetracyclines appear to be uncommon. Most side-effects are due to direct toxicity of the drug or to alteration of microbial flora.

A. Gastrointestinal Side-Effects: Nausea, vomiting, and diarrhea are the commonest reasons for discontinuing tetracycline medication. During the first few days of administration, they appear to be attributable to direct local irritation of the intestinal tract.

After a few days of oral use, tetracyclines tend to modify the normal flora. Although some coliform organisms are suppressed, *Pseudomonas, Proteus*, staphylococci, resistant coliforms, and *Candida* become prominent. This can result in intestinal functional disturbances, anal pruritus, vaginal or oral candidiasis, or even enterocolitis with shock and death. (Clostridial toxins may play a role.)

Nausea, anorexia, and diarrhea can usually be controlled by administering the drug with food or carboxymethylcellulose, reducing drug dosage, or discontinuing the drug.

B. Bony Structures and Teeth: Tetracyclines are readily bound to calcium deposited in newly formed bone or teeth in young children. When the drug is given during pregnancy, it can be deposited in the fetal teeth, leading to fluorescence, discoloration, and enamel dysplasia; it can also be deposited in bone, where it may cause deformity or growth inhibition. If the drug is given to children under 6 years of age for long periods, similar changes can result. Oxytetracyclines are least harmful in this regard.

C. Liver Toxicity: Tetracyclines can probably impair hepatic function, especially during pregnancy, in patients with preexisting hepatic insufficiency, and when high doses are given intravenously. Hepatic necrosis has been reported with daily doses of 4 g intravenously or more.

D. Kidney Toxicity: Renal tubular acidosis and other forms of renal injury resulting in nitrogen retention have been attributed to the administration of outdated tetracycline preparations. This has not been documented for fresh preparations.

Tetracyclines given together with diuretics may produce nitrogen retention. Long-acting tetracyclines, except doxycycline, may cumulate to toxic levels in renal failure.

E. Local Tissue Toxicity: Intravenous injection can lead to venous thrombosis. Intramuscular injection produces painful local irritation which can lead to infiltration.

F. Photosensitization: Systemic tetracycline administration, especially of demeclocycline, can induce sensitivity to sunlight or ultraviolet light, particularly in blonds.

G. Vestibular Reactions: Dizziness, vertigo, nausea, and vomiting have been particularly noted with minocycline. After doses of 200–400 mg/d of minocycline, 35–70% of patients exhibited such reactions.

Medical & Social Implications of Overuse

The widespread use of tetracyclines for minor illnesses has led to the emergence of resistance even among highly susceptible species, eg, pneumococci and group A streptococci. The large-scale use of these drugs in hospitals has resulted in the selection of tetracycline-resistant organisms, particularly staphylococci and *Pseudomonas*, as superinfecting agents. In some measure, the tetracyclines (among other antibiotics) must be blamed for the rising incidence of mycotic infection in hospitalized, severely ill patients.

On the other hand, tetracyclines have been of great benefit not only for the control of existing infection but also for chemoprophylaxis in chronic bronchitis and bronchiectasis, keeping many persons well and at work.

● ● ●

References

Chloramphenicol

Chloramphenicol-induced bone marrow suppression. (Editorial.) JAMA 213:1183, 1970.

Daigneault R, Guitard M: An enzymatic assay for chloramphenicol with purified chloramphenicol acetyltransferase. J Infect Dis 133:515, 1976.

DuPont HL & others: Evaluation of chloramphenicol acid succinate therapy of induced typhoid fever or Rocky Mountain spotted fever. N Engl J Med 282:53, 1970.

Schulkind ML & others: A comparison of ampicillin and chloramphenicol therapy in *Haemophilus influenzae* meningitis. Pediatrics 48:411, 1971.

Scott JL & others: A controlled double-blind study of the hematologic toxicity of chloramphenicol. N Engl J Med 272:1137, 1965.

Snyder MJ & others: Comparative efficacy of chloramphenicol, ampicillin, and co-trimoxazole in the treatment of typhoid fever. Lancet 2:1155, 1976.

Wallerstein RO & others: Statewide study of chloramphenicol therapy and fatal aplastic anemia. JAMA 208:2045, 1969.

Tetracyclines

Allen JC: Drugs five years later: Minocycline. Ann Intern Med 85:482, 1976.

Barza M, Schiefe RT: Antimicrobial spectrum, pharmacology and therapeutic use of antibiotics. 1. Tetracyclines. Am J Hosp Pharm 34:49, 1977.

Chopra I, Howe TGB: Bacterial resistance to tetracyclines. Microbiol Rev 42:707, 1978.

Chow AW & others: Comparative susceptibility of anaerobic bacteria to minocycline, doxycycline, and tetracycline. Antimicrob Agents Chemother 7:46, 1975.

Colwell EJ & others: Tetracycline treatment of chloroquine-resistant falciparum malaria. JAMA 220:684, 1972.

Cunliffe WJ & others: Tetracycline and acne vulgaris: A clinical and laboratory investigation. Br Med J 4:332, 1973.

Devine LF & others: Efficacy of regimen using minocycline and rifampin sequentially for the elimination of meningococci from healthy carriers. Am J Epidemiol 97:394, 1973.

Drew TM & others: Minocycline for prophylaxis of infection with *Neisseria meningitidis*: High rate of side effects in recipients. J Infect Dis 133:194, 1976.

Hoshiwara I & others: Doxycycline treatment of chronic trachoma. JAMA 224:220, 1973.

Levy SB & others: Changes in intestinal flora of farm personnel after introduction of tetracycline-supplemented feed on a farm. N Engl J Med 295:583, 1976.

Mhalu FS & others: Rapid emergence of El Tor *Vibrio cholerae* resistant to antimicrobials during first six months of fourth cholera epidemic in Tanzania. Lancet 1:345, 1979.

Pickering LK & others: Single dose tetracycline therapy for shigellosis in adults. JAMA 239:853, 1978.

Sack DA & others: Single-dose doxycycline for cholera. Antimicrob Agents Chemother 14:462, 1978.

Sauer GC: Safety of long-term tetracycline therapy for acne. Arch Dermatol 112:1603, 1976.

Siegel D: Tetracyclines: New look at old antibiotic. (2 parts.) NY State J Med 78:950, 1115, 1978.

51 | Aminoglycosides & Polymyxins

AMINOGLYCOSIDES

Aminoglycosides are a group of drugs sharing chemical, antimicrobial, pharmacologic, and toxic characteristics. The group includes streptomycin, neomycin, kanamycin, amikacin, viomycin, gentamicin, tobramycin, sisomicin, netilmicin, and others. Streptomycin is the oldest of the aminoglycosides, and its properties and functions are well established. Neomycin is now limited to topical use, and kanamycin is used mainly in small children. Among the newer members, gentamicin and amikacin are now most widely used, whereas the others are not as well established. Because of the marked similarities of the aminoglycosides, a summary of important properties is presented before each drug is taken up individually.

General Properties of Aminoglycosides

A. Physical and Chemical Properties: Aminoglycosides are water-soluble, stable in solution, and more active at alkaline than at acid pH. They are aminocyclitols that have either a streptidine or deoxystreptamine base. They can form complexes with beta-lactam antibiotics when mixed in solution and thus lose some activity.

B. Mechanism of Action: Aminoglycosides are bactericidal for susceptible organisms by virtue of irreversible inhibition of protein synthesis. They attach to the 30S subunit of microbial ribosomes and inhibit their function in several ways: (1) interference with the "initiation complex" of peptide formation, (2) misreading of the mRNA genetic code, and (3) breaking of polysomes into nonfunctional monosomes.

C. Mechanisms of Resistance: Three principal mechanisms have been established: (1) Alteration in the cell surface which interferes with the permeability or active transport of aminoglycoside into the cell. This may be chromosomal or plasmid-controlled, eg, in enterococci, *Pseudomonas*. (2) The receptor (protein) on the 30S ribosomal subunit may be deleted or altered as a result of chromosomal mutation. (3) The microorganism acquires the ability to produce enzymes that destroy the aminoglycoside activity by adenylation, acetylation, or phosphorylation. This is usually plasmid-controlled and is a prominent form of resistance among gram-negative enteric bacteria. This

transmissible resistance is of great clinical and epidemiologic concern. (4) Anaerobic bacteria or facultative organisms growing under anaerobic conditions are usually resistant to aminoglycosides, because transport of these drugs into the cell is an energy-requiring process that is oxygen-dependent.

D. Absorption, Distribution, Metabolism, and Excretion: Aminoglycosides are well absorbed after intramuscular or intravenous injection but are not absorbed from the gut after oral intake. They are distributed widely in tissues and in pleural, ascitic, and synovial fluid in the presence of inflammation, but they diffuse poorly into prostate, eye, or bile. After parenteral administration, there is only minimal penetration into the central nervous system or cerebrospinal fluid. Intrathecal or intraventricular injection is required to achieve central nervous system levels in adults. Protein binding of most aminoglycosides is less than 10%, but that of streptomycin is 35%. There is no significant metabolic breakdown. The half-life in serum is 2–3 hours. Excretion is mainly by glomerular filtration and is greatly reduced in impairment of renal function. Aminoglycosides are partly and irregularly removed by hemodialysis and even less effectively by peritoneal dialysis.

In persons with impaired renal function, there is danger of drug accumulation and toxic effects. Therefore, either the dose of drug is kept constant and the interval between doses is increased, or the interval is kept constant and the dose is reduced. Nomograms and formulas have been constructed relating serum creatinine levels to adjustments in treatment regimens. However, there is considerable variation in aminoglycoside serum levels in different patients with similar serum creatinine values. Therefore, it is highly desirable to monitor drug levels in blood in order to avoid severe toxicity when renal functional capacity changes rapidly. Peak levels should be obtained at 1 hour after infusion; trough levels should be obtained just prior to the next infusion.

E. Adverse Effects: Hypersensitivity occurs infrequently. All aminoglycosides can cause varying degrees of ototoxicity and nephrotoxicity. The ototoxicity can manifest itself either as hearing loss (cochlear damage) noted first with high-frequency tones or as vestibular damage evident by vertigo, ataxia, and loss of balance. Nephrotoxicity results in rising serum creatinine levels or reduced creatinine clearance. In very high doses, aminoglycosides can be neurotoxic, producing a curarelike effect with neuromuscular blockade that results in respiratory paralysis. Neostigmine can be an antidote to this neurotoxic action.

F. Clinical Uses: Aminoglycosides are used most widely against gram-negative enteric bacteria or when there is suspicion of sepsis. In the treatment of bacteremia or endocarditis caused by fecal streptococci or some gram-negative bacteria, the aminoglycoside is given together with a penicillin that enhances permeability and facilitates the entry of the aminoglycoside. Aminoglycosides are selected according to recent susceptibility patterns in a given area or hospital until susceptibility tests become available on a specific isolate. All positively charged aminoglycosides and polymyxins are inhibited in blood cultures by sodium polyanethol sulfonate and other polyanionic detergents. Some aminoglycosides (especially streptomycin and viomycin) are useful as antimycobacterial drugs.

STREPTOMYCINS

Streptomycin was isolated from a strain of *Streptomyces griseus* by Waksman and his associates in 1944. Dihydrostreptomycin can be produced by catalytic reduction of streptomycin trihydrochloride and has also been isolated from strains of *Streptomyces humidus*. Both streptomycin compounds have similar chemical and identical antimicrobial properties. However, dihydrostreptomycin is significantly more ototoxic than streptomycin and has been abandoned.

Streptomycin is a triacidic base with the empirical formula $C_{21}H_{39}N_7O_{12}$. It consists of streptidine, streptose, and N-methyl-L-glucosamine. The latter 2 components are referred to as streptobiosamine (see formula below).

Streptomycin sulfate is a white powder, quite soluble in water and insoluble in alcohol. Neutral solutions are stable for weeks at temperatures below 25 C. Streptomycin is more active at alkaline pH. It can be inactivated by hydroxylamine or cysteine.

The antimicrobial activity of streptomycin is typical of that of other aminoglycosides, as are the mechanisms of resistance. Resistant microorganisms have emerged in most species, severely limiting the current usefulness of streptomycin, with the exceptions listed below. Streptomycin-dependent bacteria require the drug for growth.

The emergence of resistance in an apparently susceptible isolate tends to be rapid, so that treatment with streptomycin as the sole drug is usually limited to 5 days.

Streptomycin is not significantly absorbed from the gut. After intramuscular injection of 0.5 g, peak serum concentrations of 20 μg/mL are reached in 1–2 hours. Streptomycin is widely distributed in tissues except the central nervous system. It does not readily penetrate into the interior of phagocytic cells. Renal excretion results in urine levels 5–50 times higher than those in serum. Adjustment of dosage is required in renal failure.

Clinical Uses

A. Tuberculosis and Other Mycobacterial Infections: In pulmonary and other nondisseminated forms of tuberculosis, streptomycin, 1 g, is injected intramuscularly twice weekly or daily, as part of combined therapy. (When used in the treatment of tuberculosis, streptomycin is always combined with isoniazid, 5–10 mg/kg/d, or other drugs, for many months.) In acute tuberculous pneumonia, miliary dissemination, or meningitis in children, up to 60 mg/kg/d intramuscularly should be administered initially in combination with isoniazid or other drugs. In meningitis, streptomycin, 25 mg dissolved in 10 mL saline, may be injected intrathecally.

B. Nontuberculous Infections: In systemic infections (eg, plague, tularemia), streptomycin, 2–4 g daily intramuscularly, is given in divided doses every 4–8 hours. A second drug may be added (see below).

C. Combined Treatment: In certain infections, penicillin plus an aminoglycoside may be required for eradication of organisms even though in vitro the bacteria appear to be resistant to serum levels of the aminoglycoside alone. For example, in enterococcal endocarditis, streptomycin, 1–2 g intramuscularly daily, may be given in addition to penicillin, 12–60 g intravenously daily (or ampicillin, 4–12 g intravenously daily), to achieve bactericidal levels in serum and clinical cure.

Streptomycin

In *Streptococcus viridans* endocarditis, the addition of an aminoglycoside may also enhance the bactericidal action of a penicillin. In tularemia and plague, streptomycin may be combined with tetracyclines.

Adverse Reactions

A. Allergy: Fever, skin rashes, and other allergic manifestations may result from hypersensitivity to streptomycin. This occurs most frequently upon prolonged contact with the drug, either in patients who receive a prolonged course of treatment (eg, for tuberculosis) or in medical personnel who handle the drug. (Nurses preparing solutions should wear gloves.) Desensitization is occasionally successful.

B. Toxicity: Pain at the injection site is common but usually not severe; it can be relieved by injecting the drug with a local anesthetic (eg, procaine hydrochloride). The most serious toxic effect is disturbance of vestibular function—vertigo and loss of balance. The frequency and severity of this disturbance are proportionate to the age of the patient, the blood levels of the drug, and the duration of administration. Vestibular dysfunction may follow a few weeks of unusually high blood levels (eg, in individuals with impaired renal function) or months of relatively low blood levels. After the drug is discontinued, partial recovery frequently occurs. Because streptomycin can impair semicircular canal function, it has been used to treat Meniere's disease (2–3 g/d for 1–4 weeks).

With streptomycin, hearing loss is less frequent than vestibular impairment. With dihydrostreptomycin, auditory impairment is frequent, severe, and irreversible; for this reason, dihydrostreptomycin has been abandoned. The concurrent or sequential use of other aminoglycosides with streptomycin should be avoided to reduce the likelihood of ototoxicity. Streptomycin given during pregnancy can cause deafness in the newborn.

General Medical Problems Resulting from Overuse

Streptomycin-resistant bacteria have become prevalent as a result of widespread use of the drug, often in unnecessary combination with penicillin. Multiple drug resistance is frequent among bacteria in urinary tract infections, and the hospital transmission of such organisms aggravates treatment problems. Primary infection with streptomycin-resistant tubercle bacilli occurs in up to 15% of cases of pulmonary tuberculosis in children studied in the USA.

KANAMYCIN & NEOMYCIN

These drugs constitute a chemically and biologically closely related group which combines a broad spectrum of antibacterial activity with significant nephrotoxicity and ototoxicity. **Neomycin** was isolated by Waksman in 1949 from *Streptomyces fradiae*; **kanamycin** was isolated by Umezawa in 1957 from *Streptomyces kanamyceticus*. Other members of the group are **framycetin** and **paromomycin.** All have very similar properties.

Chemistry

Each member of this group consists of several components in which amino sugars are coupled by means of glycoside linkages. Kanamycin, the more widely used member of the group, has the formula $C_{18}H_{36}N_4O_{11}$ and consists of 3-D-glucosamine and 6-D-glucosamine linked to deoxystreptamine.

Commercial neomycin is a mixture of 2 related compounds, neomycin B and C. (Neomycin A is not used.) Each contains diaminohexose linked to deoxystreptamine and D-ribose. Paromomycin consists of glucosamine and a disaccharide linked to an inositol derivative.

Kanamycin A

Antimicrobial Activity

Drugs of the neomycin group are bactericidal in concentrations of 1–10 $\mu g/mL$ for many gram-positive and gram-negative bacteria and mycobacteria. *Proteus* organisms are often susceptible, but *Pseudomonas* and streptococci are generally resistant. The mechanism of antibacterial action of the neomycin group is typical of the aminoglycosides, and they can substitute for streptomycin in streptomycin-dependent organisms.

Resistance

Resistance mechanisms are the same as with other aminoglycosides. The widespread use of neomycin-kanamycin in bowel preparation for elective surgery of the colon has led to the selection of resistant organisms in some hospitals and outbreaks of enterocolitis. While cross-resistance between neomycin and kanamycin is complete, there is limited cross-resistance with other aminoglycosides.

Absorption, Metabolism, & Excretion

Drugs of the neomycin group are not significantly absorbed from the gastrointestinal tract. After oral administration, the intestinal flora is suppressed or modified and the drug is excreted in the feces.

After parenteral injection (0.5 g intramuscularly every 6–12 hours), serum levels reach 5–15 $\mu g/mL$. The drugs are fairly widely distributed, but they do not reach significant levels in the cerebrospinal fluid or joint or pleural fluid unless they are injected locally.

Excretion is mainly through glomerular filtration into the urine, where levels of 10–50 μg/mL may be reached. Some excretion also occurs in the bile. In the presence of renal insufficiency, the dose or the frequency of injection of these drugs must be greatly reduced.

Clinical Uses

At present, kanamycin is the preferred drug of this group for parenteral administration because it is slightly less toxic than neomycin. The other members of the group are used only topically or orally.

A. Topical: Solutions containing 1–5 mg/mL are used on infected surfaces or injected into joints, the pleural cavity, tissue spaces, or abscess cavities where infection is present. The total amount of drug given in this fashion must be restricted because much of it can be absorbed, giving rise to systemic toxicity. Ointments containing 1–5 mg/g are applied to infected skin lesions or in the nares for suppression of staphylococci. Some ointments contain polymyxin and bacitracin in addition to neomycin.

B. Oral: For preoperative reduction of gut flora, 1 g every 4–6 hours is given for 2–3 days before surgery. This is sometimes combined with oral erythromycin base. In hepatic coma, the coliform flora can be suppressed for prolonged periods by giving 1 g every 6–8 hours, together with reduced protein intake, thus reducing ammonia intoxication. Paromomycin (Humatin), 1 g every 6 hours orally for 2 weeks, has been effective in intestinal amebiasis. Kanamycin or neomycin can suppress intestinal infection with enteropathogenic *Escherichia coli* and other bacteria, but they are not effective in the treatment of *Shigella* or *Salmonella* infections.

C. Parenteral: Kanamycin, 0.5 g every 6–12 hours intramuscularly (15 mg/kg/d), may be effective in the treatment of bacteremia caused by gram-negative enteric organisms. It is sometimes combined with clindamycin in penetrating abdominal wounds. The use of kanamycin systemically is often limited to infants and children.

Adverse Reactions

All members of the neomycin group have nephrotoxic and ototoxic side-effects. Kanamycin is the preferred drug at present because it is somewhat better tolerated. However, ototoxicity resulting in deafness without premonitory signs has given kanamycin a dubious reputation. Deafness occurred especially in adults with impaired renal function and prolonged elevated drug levels.

The sudden absorption of postoperatively instilled kanamycin from the peritoneal cavity (3–5 g) has resulted in respiratory arrest.

While hypersensitivity is not common, prolonged application of neomycin-containing ointments to skin and eyes has resulted in severe allergic dermatitis.

AMIKACIN

Amikacin is a semisynthetic derivative of kanamycin. It is relatively resistant to several of the enzymes that inactivate gentamicin and tobramycin, and it therefore can be employed against some microorganisms resistant to the latter drugs. However, bacterial resistance due to impermeability to amikacin is increasing. Many gram-negative enteric bacteria, including many strains of *Proteus, Pseudomonas,* enterobacteria, and *Serratia*, are inhibited by 1–20 μg/mL amikacin in vitro. After the injection of 500 mg amikacin every 12 hours (15 mg/kg/d) intramuscularly, peak levels in serum are 10–30 μg/mL. Some infections caused by gram-negative bacteria resistant to gentamicin respond to amikacin. Central nervous system infections require intrathecal or intraventricular injection of 1–10 mg daily.

Like all aminoglycosides, amikacin is nephro- and ototoxic (particularly for the auditory portion of the eighth nerve). Its levels should be monitored in patients with renal failure. Avoid concurrent use with diuretics, eg, furosemide, ethacrynic acid.

GENTAMICIN

Gentamicin is an aminoglycoside antibiotic complex isolated from *Micromonospora purpurea*. It is effective against both gram-positive and gram-negative organisms, and many of its properties resemble those of other aminoglycosides. Sisomicin is very similar to the C_{1a} component of gentamicin.

Chemistry

The 3 active antibiotic components of gentamicin C have molecular weights of 450–475 and differ principally in methyl group content. The proposed structural formula is shown below. The sulfate is used for intramuscular injection; it is soluble in water, and such solutions are stable for weeks. The antibacterial activity of the drug is much greater at alkaline than at acid pH.

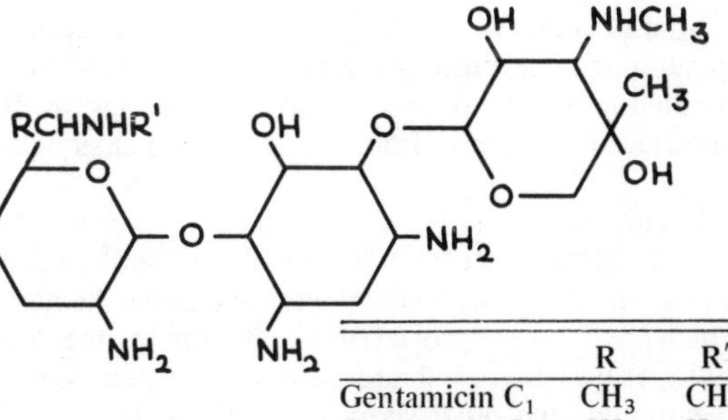

	R	R'
Gentamicin C_1	CH_3	CH_3
Gentamicin C_2	CH_3	H
Gentamicin C_{1a}	H	H

Antimicrobial Activity

In concentrations of 0.5–5 μg/mL, gentamicin is rapidly bactericidal for many gram-positive and gram-negative bacteria. Gentamicin sulfate, 10 μg/mL, inhibits in vitro many strains of staphylococci, coliform organisms (*Escherichia coli*, *Klebsiella*, *Enterobacter*), *Pseudomonas aeruginosa*, *Proteus*, and *Serratia*. Bactericidal action is due to inhibition of protein synthesis such as is postulated for other aminoglycosides.

The simultaneous use of carbenicillin or ticarcillin and gentamicin may result in synergistic enhancement and activity against some strains of *P aeruginosa* and may permit use of smaller doses of gentamicin. However, a penicillin and gentamicin cannot be mixed in vitro.

Resistance

Most streptococci are resistant to gentamicin but can be killed by synergistic mixtures of a cell wall-inhibitory drug (eg, penicillin) with gentamicin. This resistance is based on lack of transport of gentamicin into the cell. Among gram-negative bacteria, resistance to gentamicin is increasing somewhat in proportion to the amount of drug used in a given hospital environment. This resistance is most commonly attributable to the spread of plasmids that govern gentamicin-destroying enzymes. Organisms resistant to gentamicin are often resistant to kanamycin and sometimes to tobramycin but infrequently (as yet) to amikacin.

Absorption, Metabolism, & Excretion

The drug is not significantly absorbed after oral administration. After intramuscular injection, gentamicin is rapidly absorbed and widely distributed in tissues. About 25% of the drug in plasma is protein-bound. With the usual doses, serum levels reach 3–7 μg/mL in persons with normal renal function, although serum levels vary widely. Assay of concentrations in serum is possible using microbiologic or radioimmune methods. The drug is excreted largely by glomerular filtration through the kidneys into the urine. Concentrations in urine may be 10–100 times higher than in serum. There can be marked cumulation of drug in the presence of azotemia. Gentamicin does not penetrate well into the central nervous system or the cerebrospinal fluid, and intrathecal or intraventricular injection is necessary to achieve high cerebrospinal fluid concentration. Gentamicin may have to be instilled into joints or abscess cavities, because diffusion into these spaces from the serum is inadequate.

Clinical Uses

A. Intramuscular: Gentamicin is employed in severe infections caused by gram-negative bacteria which are likely (or proved) to be resistant to other less toxic drugs. Included are sepsis, infected burns, pneumonia, and other serious infections due to coliform organisms, *Klebsiella-Enterobacter*, *Proteus*, *Pseudomonas*, and *Serratia*. In these disorders, gentamicin is employed in full systemic doses: 5–7 mg/kg/d intramuscularly (or, rarely, intravenously) in 3 equal doses for 7–10 days. Renal, auditory, and vestibular functions should be monitored, particularly in patients with preexisting nitrogen retentioon. In renal failure, the dose must be reduced, or the interval between doses must be lengthened. Direct enzymatic or radioimmunoassays of gentamicin concentration in serum exist (see Chapter 48).

In urinary tract infections caused by these organisms, 0.8–1.2 mg/kg/d is injected intramuscularly in 2 or 3 equal divided doses for 10 days or more. Gentamicin may be employed together with a penicillin for enhanced (synergistic) action against streptococcal endocarditis or gram-negative sepsis.

B. Topical: Creams, ointments, or solutions containing 0.1–0.3% gentamicin sulfate have been used for the treatment of infected burns, wounds, or skin lesions and the prevention of intravenous catheter infections. Topical gentamicin is partly inactivated by purulent exudates. Ten mg can be injected subconjunctivally.

C. Intrathecal: Meningitis caused by gram-negative bacteria has been treated by the intrathecal injection of 1–10 mg gentamicin sulfate per day. Epidural abscess has been instilled with gentamicin, 20 mg/d for 10 days.

Adverse Reactions

These are analogous to the side-effects of other aminoglycosides. Nephrotoxicity requires adjustment of regimens, especially in diminished renal function. Whenever possible, gentamicin serum levels should serve as a guide in difficult clinical situations. Ototoxicity manifests itself mainly as vestibular dysfunction, perhaps due to destruction of hair cells by prolonged elevated drug levels (more than 12 μg/mL). Loss of hearing can occur and has occasionally been extensive and irreversible. The incidence of hypersensitivity reactions to gentamicin is insufficiently defined.

TOBRAMYCIN

This aminoglycoside antibiotic, available since 1975, has an antibacterial spectrum similar to that of gentamicin but is more active than the latter against *Pseudomonas* sp. While there is some cross-resistance between gentamicin and tobramycin, it is unpredictable in individual strains. Separate laboratory susceptibility tests are therefore necessary.

The pharmacologic properties of tobramycin are virtually identical to those of gentamicin. The daily dose of tobramycin is 3–5 mg/kg/d intramuscularly divided in 3 equal amounts and given every 8 hours. Such dosage produces blood levels of 2–5 μg/mL in the presence of normal renal function. About 80% of the drug is excreted by glomerular filtration into the urine within 24 hours of administration. In uremia, the drug dosage must be reduced. A formula for such dosage is 1 mg/kg every (6 × serum creatinine level) hours. However, monitoring blood levels in renal insufficiency is desirable. Tobramycin can be cleared somewhat during peritoneal dialysis.

Like other aminoglycosides, tobramycin is ototoxic and nephrotoxic. Nephrotoxicity of tobramycin may be less than that of gentamicin. It should not be used concurrently with other drugs having similar adverse effects or with diuretics, which tend to enhance aminoglycoside tissue concentrations.

SPECTINOMYCIN

Spectinomycin is an aminocyclitol antibiotic (related to aminoglycosides) dispensed as the dihydrochloride pentahydrate for intramuscular injection. While active in vitro against many gram-positive and gram-negative organisms, spectinomycin is proposed only as an alternative treatment for gonorrhea in patients who might be hypersensitive to penicillin or whose gonococci are resistant to penicillin. Most gonococci are inhibited by 6 μg/mL of spectinomycin. About 10% of gonococci may be resistant to spectinomycin, but there is no cross-resistance with other drugs used in gonorrhea.

Spectinomycin is rapidly absorbed after intramuscular injection. A dose of 2 g injected intramuscularly once results in serum levels of 100 μg/mL and is said to result in 85–90% cure of gonorrhea. There is pain at the injection site and occasionally fever and nausea. Nephrotoxicity and anemia have been observed rarely.

THE POLYMYXIN GROUP

The polymyxins are a group of basic polypeptides selectively active against gram-negative bacilli. Polymyxins A, B, C, D, and E were derived from a spore-forming gram-positive bacillus *(Bacillus polymyxa, B aerosporus)* in 1947. All but polymyxins B and E have been discarded because of excessive nephrotoxicity. Colistin, introduced in 1950, is identical with polymyxin E.

Chemistry

All polymyxins are cationic, basic polypeptides with molecular weights of about 1400. All contain the fatty acid D-6-methyloctan-1-oic acid and the amino acids L-threonine and L-diaminobutyric acid. In addition, polymyxins B and E contain L-leucine; B contains D-phenylalanine; and E contains D-leucine. The sulfates of polymyxins are freely soluble in water and very stable. Methanesulfonate (sulfo-methyl) complexes can be prepared which slowly release the active peptide. One microgram of pure polymyxin B sulfate equals 10 units. The relationship between mg and units appears to be variable in the case of methanesulfonate complexes. The positively charged polymyxins are inhibited in vitro by polyanionic detergents, eg, sodium polyanethol sulfonate in blood culture media.

Antimicrobial Activity

The activity of polymyxin B sulfate is identical with that of polymyxin E (colistin) sulfate. Similarly, the methanesulfonate complexes of polymyxins B and E have the same activity. However, it is misleading to compare quantitatively the activity of the sulfate of one polymyxin with the methanesulfonate of another. Sulfates are used in disk tests and do not reflect methanesulfonate activity.

Polymyxins are active mainly against gramnegative bacilli, particularly *Pseudomonas* and coliform organisms. They are strongly bactericidal in concentrations of 1–5 μg/mL. They act by attaching to the cell membranes of bacteria and other membranes rich in phosphatidylethanolamine and disrupting the osmotic properties and transport mechanisms of the membrane. This results in leakage of macromolecules and death of the cell. This action is inhibited by cations. The action of polymyxins is markedly inhibited by purulent exudates.

Resistance

Proteus species, gram-positive organisms, and neisseriae are highly resistant. This is probably due to the impermeability of the outer cell wall structures to polymyxins. In susceptible bacterial populations, resistant mutants are rare. There is complete cross-resistance between polymyxin B and polymyxin E (colistin).

Absorption, Metabolism, & Excretion

Polymyxins are not absorbed from the gastrointestinal tract.

With parenterally injected polymyxins (2.5 mg/kg/d), blood levels rarely exceed 1–4 μg/mL. Tissue concentrations are even lower. Polymyxins pass the placenta but do not reach the central nervous system or cerebrospinal fluid unless injected intrathecally. They do not reach joint fluids or ocular tissues unless injected locally. Polymyxins are strongly bound by cell debris, acid phospholipids, and purulent exudates. They do not penetrate into cells, and phagocytized or intracellular bacteria are therefore unaffected.

Excretion is mainly in the urine, where concentrations of 25–300 μg/mL may be reached during prolonged administration. Excretion is impaired in renal insufficiency.

Clinical Uses

Polymyxins were drugs of choice for the treatment of infections caused by *Pseudomonas* or coliform bacteria resistant to other antimicrobial drugs. Polymyxin treatment is limited by the restricted distribution and penetration of the drug, by its toxicity, and by its binding to many tissue components.

A. Topical: Solutions containing 1 mg/mL of polymyxin B or E sulfate can be applied to wounds, burns, sinuses, and other surfaces infected with *P aeruginosa* or other resistant microorganisms. Similar solutions (up to a total dose of 2.5 mg/kg/d) can be injected intrapleurally or intraperitoneally. Solutions of 1–10 mg/mL are inhaled as aerosols in *Pseudomonas* infections of the bronchi and lungs. Up to 20 mg of polymyxin B sulfate may be injected subconjunctivally in *Pseudomonas* infections of the eye. Ointments containing 0.5 mg/g of polymyxin B sulfate in mixture with bacitracin or neomycin (or both) are commonly applied to infected skin lesions. Solutions containing polymyxin B, 20 mg/L, and neomycin, 40 mg/L, can be employed as antiseptic for continuous irrigation of the urinary bladder through a 3-way catheter in a closed sterile system. This can delay bacterial contamination of the drainage system.

B. Intrathecal: In *Pseudomonas* meningitis, the intrathecal injection of polymyxin B or E sulfate, 2–10 mg in saline daily for 2–3 days, and then every other day for 2–3 weeks, can be curative. Polymyxin methanesulfonates should never be given intrathecally.

C. Intramuscular: The intramuscular injection of polymyxin sulfates is painful and requires the simultaneous administration of a local anesthetic. For this reason, the methanesulfonate complex, which sometimes includes a local anesthetic and slowly releases active drug after intramuscular injection, is preferred. The total systemic dose can be 2.5–5 mg/kg/d. It can be used in urinary tract infections with *Pseudomonas, Enterobacter*, or other coliforms resistant to less toxic drugs. *Salmonella* infections do not respond to polymyxins in spite of in vitro susceptibility.

D. Intravenous: In serious, rapidly progressive infection, the intravenous injection of polymyxin B sulfate is preferable. The intravenous injection by slow drip of 2.5 mg/kg/d of polymyxin B sulfate in 5% dextrose in water is indicated in *Pseudomonas* bacteremia or peritonitis (eg, after peritoneal dialysis). When renal function is impaired, the drug may be administered in full doses once every 3–5 days. Hemodialysis does not remove polymyxins rapidly.

E. Oral: Polymyxins are not absorbed from the gut but have been used to suppress gram-negative members of the intestinal flora in immunosuppressed persons.

Adverse Reactions

The general toxicity of polymyxins limits both the dose and the duration of therapy. The sulfates produce intense local pain on intramuscular injection and are rapidly absorbed, whereas the methanesulfonates produce (with little pain) a local depot from which absorption proceeds more slowly. The principal side-effects are neurotoxicity and nephrotoxicity. Hypersensitivity appears to be very rare. Very high blood levels (> 30 μg/mL) of any polymyxin can cause respiratory arrest. Respiratory paralysis caused by polymyxins can be reversed by calcium gluconate.

A. Neurotoxic Effects: Adequate systemic concentrations of any polymyxin can cause paresthesias (circumoral and stocking or glove distribution), dizziness, flushing, and incoordination. All of these disappear promptly when the drug has been discontinued and excreted. With very high levels, paralysis may occur.

B. Nephrotoxic Effects: Some degree of proteinuria, hematuria, or cylindruria commonly accompanies the administration of polymyxin B or E and is evidence of tubular injury. These urinary signs usually disappear soon after the drug is discontinued. Nitrogen retention may occur, particularly with doses in excess of 2 mg/kg/d. In individuals with preexisting renal disease, nitrogen retention must be monitored and the dose of polymyxin adjusted. Accidental overdosage may result in renal failure, neuromuscular paralysis, and even death.

Laboratory

The large molecules of the polymyxins diffuse poorly through agar. Consequently, disk tests reveal very narrow zones of inhibition even with fully susceptible microorganisms. Colistin disks contain sulfate, not methanesulfonate.

Medical Aspects of Overuse

Polymyxins are again becoming important because of the increasing numbers of patients infected with *Pseudomonas* and *Enterobacter* resistant to other drugs. These are often hospitalized patients with immunosuppression and impaired renal function who require careful adjustments of a polymyxin regimen.

•   •   •

References

Bennett WM & others: A guide to drug therapy in renal failure. JAMA 230:1544, 1974.

Brynan LE & others: Mechanism of aminoglycoside antibiotic resistance in anaerobic bacteria. Antimicrob Agents Chemother 15:7, 1979.

Chan RA & others: Gentamicin therapy in renal failure: A dosage nomogram. Ann Intern Med 76:773, 1972.

Egan EA & others: Prospective controlled trial of oral kanamycin in prevention of neonatal necrotizing enterocolitis. J Pediatr 89:467, 1976.

Finitzohieber T & others: Ototoxicity in neonates treated with gentamicin and kanamycin. Results of a 4-year controlled follow-up study. Pediatrics 63:443, 1979.

Hoeprich PH: The polymyxins. Med Clin North Am 54:1257, 1970.

Hollifield JW, Kaiser AB, McGee ZA: Gram-negative bacillary meningitis therapy: Polyradiculitis following intralumbar aminoglycoside administration. JAMA 236:1264, 1976.

Kaiser AB, McGee ZA: Aminoglycoside therapy of gram-negative bacillary meningitis. N Engl J Med 293:1215, 1975.

Khan AJ & others: Amikacin pharmacokinetics in therapy of childhood urinary tract infection. Pediatrics 58:873, 1976.

Klastersky J & others: Comparative clinical study of tobramycin and gentamicin. Antimicrob Agents Chemother 5:133, 1974.

Krogstad DJ & others: Plasmid-mediated resistance to antibiotic synergism in enterococci. J Clin Invest 61:1645, 1978.

Love LJ & others: Randomized trial of empiric antibiotic therapy with ticarcillin in combination with gentamicin, amikacin or netilmicin in febrile patients with granulocytopenia and cancer. Am J Med 66:603, 1979.

McCormack WM, Finland M: Spectinomycin. Ann Intern Med 84:712, 1976.

McCracken GH: Clinical pharmacology of gentamicin in infants. Am J Dis Child 124:884, 1972.

Meyers BR & others: Pharmacokinetic parameters of sisomicin. Antimicrob Agents Chemother 10:25, 1976.

Moellering RC & others: Experience with tobramycin therapy of infections due to gentamicin-resistant organisms. J Infect Dis 134 (Suppl):S40, 1976.

Murillo J & others: Gentamicin and ticarcillin serum levels. JAMA 241:2401, 1979.

Neu HC: Tobramycin: An overview. J Infect Dis 134 (Suppl):S3, 1976.

Panwalker AP & others: Netilmicin: Clinical efficacy, tolerance and toxicity. Antimicrob Agents Chemother 13:170, 1978.

Riff LJ, Jackson GG: Conditions for gentamicin inactivation by carbenicillin. Arch Intern Med 130:887, 1972.

Sarubbi FA, Hull JH: Amikacin serum concentrations: Prediction of levels and dosage guidelines. Ann Intern Med 89:612, 1978.

Smith AL, Smith DH: Gentamicin adenine mononucleotide transferase. J Infect Dis 129:391, 1974.

Young LS: The aminoglycosides. J Surg Practice, March–April, 1978.

52 | Antituberculosis Drugs

Streptomycin was the first antimicrobial drug to exhibit striking action against tubercle bacilli. It remains an important agent in the management of severe tuberculosis and has also found a place in other forms of antibiotic therapy (see Table 48–1 and discussion in Chapter 51). Other important antituberculosis drugs in use at present—isoniazid and ethambutol—are of importance only in tuberculosis. Several agents which are drugs of second choice in the treatment of tuberculosis are mentioned here only briefly.

Singular problems exist in the treatment of tuberculosis and related mycobacterial infections. The infections tend to be exceedingly chronic, but may also give rise to hyperacute, lethal complications. The organisms are frequently intracellular, exhibit long periods of metabolic inactivity, and tend to develop resistance to any one drug. All these points contribute to the complexity of antituberculosis therapy.

In extensive pulmonary or other organ tuberculosis, miliary tuberculosis, and tuberculous meningitis, treatment is usually started with 3 drugs (isoniazid + streptomycin + either ethambutol or rifampin). With improvement, parenteral streptomycin can be omitted and treatment continued with the oral drugs for a total of 18–24 months or longer. Most patients become noninfectious within 2–4 weeks (or even sooner) after starting therapy with effective drugs. Short courses (9–12 months) have been proposed (see p 568).

STREPTOMYCIN

The pharmacologic features of streptomycin have been discussed on p 557. It is assumed that the mechanism of action of streptomycin against mycobacteria is the same as that against other microorganisms. Most tubercle bacilli are inhibited, and may be killed, by streptomycin, 1–10 μg/mL, in vitro. Most "atypical" mycobacteria are resistant to streptomycin in pharmacologic concentrations. All large populations of tubercle bacilli contain some streptomycin-resistant mutants. On the average, 1 in 10^8 to 1 in 10^{10} tubercle bacilli can be expected to be resistant to streptomycin at serum levels of 10–100 μg/mL. Certain of these mutants tend to survive the in vivo exposure to therapeutic concentrations of streptomycin. This results in "treatment resistance" of clinical tuberculosis and may induce primary streptomycin-resistant new infections in contacts. Such a sequence may occur within 2–4 months of treatment with streptomycin alone. This is a prime reason for employing streptomycin in combination with another drug effective against tubercle bacilli. Combined treatment can markedly delay the emergence of streptomycin-resistant mutants. It is estimated that among primary infections in children in 1970, about 15% were caused by streptomycin-resistant *Mycobacterium tuberculosis*.

Streptomycin exerts its action mainly on extracellular tubercle bacilli. Only about 10% of the drug penetrates into cells which harbor intracellular organisms. Thus, even if the entire microbial population were streptomycin-susceptible, at any one moment a large percentage of the tubercle bacilli would be unaffected by streptomycin. Treatment for many months is therefore required.

Streptomycin remains an important drug in the treatment of tuberculosis. It is employed principally in individuals with severe, possibly life-threatening forms of tuberculosis, particularly tuberculous meningitis, miliary dissemination, and extensive, active pulmonary or renal involvement. The usual dosage is 1 g intramuscularly daily for adults (20 mg/kg/d for children) for weeks, followed by 1 g intramuscularly 2–3 times weekly for several months. Other drugs are always given simultaneously.

Intrathecal injection of streptomycin in tuberculous meningitis has been largely abandoned.

The toxicity for the eighth nerve of streptomycin injected intramuscularly for many weeks manifests itself principally as dysfunction of the labyrinth, resulting in inability to maintain equilibrium and in deafness. The latter is often permanent, but some compensation for the former often occurs. Dihydrostreptomycin produces irreversible deafness more frequently. Therefore, its use has been abandoned.

ISONIAZID (INH)

Isoniazid, introduced in 1952, is the most active tuberculostatic drug.

Chemistry
Isoniazid is the hydrazide of isonicotinic acid, often called INH. It is a white crystalline powder, freely soluble in water. The structural similarity to pyridoxine is shown below.

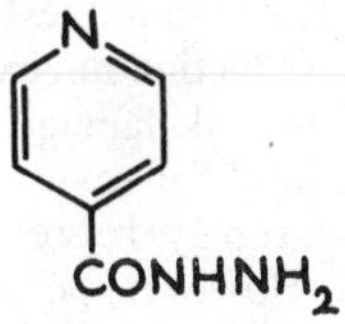

Isoniazid

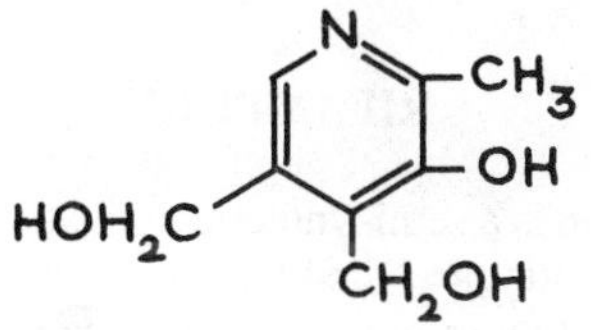

Pyridoxine

Antimycobacterial Activity
In vitro, INH inhibits most tubercle bacilli in a concentration of 0.2 μg/mL or less and is bactericidal for actively growing tubercle bacilli. However, INH is ineffective against many atypical mycobacteria. INH reaches similar concentrations both inside and outside animal cells and thus is able to act on intracellular mycobacteria as well as extracellular ones. Resistant mutants occur in susceptible bacterial populations and tend to be selected out both in vitro and in vivo in the presence of INH. There is no cross-resistance between INH, rifampin, and ethambutol. The simultaneous use of any 2 of these drugs markedly delays the emergence of resistance to one of them. Some isoniazid-resistant tubercle bacilli possess greatly reduced virulence for guinea pigs, but they nonetheless remain virulent for humans.

The mechanism of action of INH is not known. INH apparently combines with an enzyme that is peculiar to INH-susceptible strains of *Mycobacterium tuberculosis*, displacing a pigment precursor molecule and leading to a variety of disorders in cellular metabolism. INH may inhibit the synthesis of mycolic acids. INH exerts competitive antagonism in pyridoxine-catalyzed reactions in *Escherichia coli*. INH and pyridoxine are structural analogs. However, this mechanism is not involved in the antituberculosis action. The administration of large doses of pyridoxine to patients receiving INH does not interfere with tuberculostatic action of INH.

Absorption, Metabolism, & Excretion
INH is readily absorbed from the gastrointestinal tract. The administration of 8 mg/kg/d to children results in blood levels of about 2 μg/mL or more. INH diffuses readily into all body fluids and tissues, including the central nervous system and cerebrospinal fluid. Its intracellular and extracellular levels are the same.

The metabolism—particularly the acetylation—of INH is under genetic control. Two groups of people can be recognized: the "slow" and the "rapid" inactivators of the drug, through acetylation. The "slow" inactivator appears to have an autosomal homozygous recessive hereditary trait, whereas the allele controlling the dominant character (rapid inactivation) shows intermediate dominance. Six hours after ingestion of 4 mg/kg of INH, plasma concentrations of more than 0.8 μg/mL are found in persons who acetylate INH slowly, whereas plasma concentrations are 0.2 μg/mL or less in persons who acetylate INH rapidly. "Slow" inactivators tend to develop polyneuritis more often than "rapid" inactivators (see Direct Toxicity, below). About half of white and black persons in the USA are slow inactivators, whereas many Eskimos, Native Americans, and Orientals are rapid inactivators. The rate of acetylation has little influence in daily dose regimens but may impair antimycobacterial activity in intermittent (2–3 times weekly) administration of INH.

INH is excreted mainly in the urine—partly as unchanged drug, partly as the acetylated form, and partly as other conjugates. The amount of unchanged, free INH in the urine is higher in the "slow" inactivators; the amount of acetylated form is higher in the "rapid" inactivators. In renal failure, normal doses of INH can be given.

Clinical Uses
Isoniazid is probably the most widely useful drug in tuberculosis. In active, clinically manifest disease, it is given in conjunction with ethambutol, rifampin, or streptomycin. A dose of 8–10 mg/kg/d orally or more (20 mg/kg/d in small children) is employed in tuberculous meningitis, miliary dissemination, or wide-spread active pulmonary tuberculosis. Following initial improvement, the dosage is usually reduced to 5–7 mg/kg/d orally (10 mg/kg/d in small children) or 15 mg/kg 2 or 3 times per week.

Children or young adults converting from tuberculin negative to positive skin tests may be given INH, 5–10 mg/kg/d (maximum 300 mg/d), for 1 year as prophylaxis against the 5–15% risk of meningitis or miliary dissemination. For "prophylaxis," INH is given as the sole drug. In addition to skin test converters without active disease, "prophylactic" INH is also suggested for household and other very close contacts (especially children) of freshly recognized active cases; and for skin test-positive persons who undergo immunosuppressive or antineoplastic chemotherapy and have not received "adequate" antimycobacterial treatment in the past.

INH is usually given by mouth but can be injected parenterally in the same dosage.

Adverse Reactions

The incidence and severity of untoward reactions to INH are related to dosage and duration of administration.

A. Allergic Reactions: Fever, skin rashes, and hepatitis are occasionally seen.

B. Direct Toxicity: The most common toxic effects are on the peripheral and central nervous systems. These have been attributed to a relative pyridoxine deficiency, perhaps resulting from competition of INH with pyridoxal phosphate for an enzyme (apotryptophanase). These toxic reactions include peripheral neuritis, insomnia, restlessness, muscle twitching, urinary retention, and even convulsions and psychotic episodes. Most of these complications can be prevented by the administration of pyridoxine, 100 mg daily.

INH can reduce the metabolism of phenytoin, increasing its blood level and toxicity. With prolonged use on a large scale in chemoprophylaxis, isoniazid has been associated with hepatotoxicity. Abnormal liver function tests, clinical jaundice, and multilobular necrosis have been observed. In large groups, about 1% of persons develop clinical hepatitis and up to 10% subclinical abnormalities. Some fatalities have occurred. Hepatitis with progressive liver damage is age-dependent. It occurs rarely under age 20, in 1.5% of those between 30 and 50, and in 2.5% of older persons. The risk of hepatitis with permanent damage is an important determinant in the "prophylactic" use of INH.

In G6PD deficiency, INH may cause hemolysis.

ETHAMBUTOL

This is a synthetic, water-soluble, heat-stable compound, the D isomer of the structure shown below, dispensed as the hydrochloride.

$$\text{H}-\underset{\underset{\text{C}_2\text{H}_5}{|}}{\overset{\overset{\text{CH}_2\text{OH}}{|}}{\text{C}}}-\text{NH}-(\text{CH}_2)_2-\text{HN}-\underset{\underset{\text{CH}_2\text{OH}}{|}}{\overset{\overset{\text{C}_2\text{H}_5}{|}}{\text{C}}}-\text{H}$$

Ethambutol

Many strains of *Mycobacterium tuberculosis* and other mycobacteria are inhibited in vitro by ethambutol, 1–5 μg/mL. The mechanism of action is not known.

Ethambutol is well absorbed from the gut. Following ingestion of 25 mg/kg, a blood level peak of 2–5 μg/mL is reached in 2–4 hours. About 20% of the drug is excreted in feces and 50% in urine, in unchanged form. Excretion is delayed in renal failure. About 15% of absorbed drug is metabolized by oxidation and conversion to a dicarboxylic acid. In meningitis, ethambutol appears in the cerebrospinal fluid.

Resistance to ethambutol emerges fairly rapidly among mycobacteria when the drug is used alone. Therefore, ethambutol is given in combination with other antituberculosis drugs.

Ethambutol, 15 mg/kg, is usually given as a single dose in combination with INH or rifampin. At times, the dose is 25 mg/kg/d.

Hypersensitivity to ethambutol occurs infrequently. The commonest side-effects are visual disturbances: reduction in visual acuity, optic neuritis, and perhaps retinal damage occur in some patients given 25 mg/kg/d for several months. Most of these changes apparently regress when ethambutol is discontinued. However, periodic visual acuity testing is desirable during treatment. With doses of 15 mg/kg/d, visual disturbances are very rare.

RIFAMPIN

Rifampin is a semisynthetic derivative of rifamycin, an antibiotic produced by *Streptomyces mediterranei*. It is active in vitro against some gram-positive and gram-negative cocci, some enteric bacteria, mycobacteria, chlamydiae, and poxviruses. While many meningococci and mycobacteria are inhibited by less than 1 μg/mL, highly resistant mutants occur in all microbial populations in a frequency of 1 in 10^7 or greater. The prolonged administration of rifampin as a single drug permits the emergence of these highly resistant organisms. There is no cross-resistance to other antimicrobial drugs. Rifampin resistance may be due to a permeability barrier or to a chemical modification of the microbial RNA polymerase.

Rifampin binds strongly to DNA-dependent RNA polymerase and thus inhibits RNA synthesis in bacteria and chlamydiae. It blocks a late stage in the assembly of poxviruses, perhaps interfering with envelope formation.

Rifampin is well absorbed after oral administration, widely distributed in tissues, excreted mainly through the liver and to a lesser extent in the urine. With oral doses of 600 mg, serum levels exceed 5 μg/mL for 4–6 hours and urine levels may be 10–100 times higher.

In tuberculosis, a single oral dose of rifampin, usually 600 mg daily (10–20 mg/kg), is administered together with INH, ethambutol, or another antituberculosis drug in order to delay the emergence of rifampin-resistant mycobacteria. A similar regimen may apply to atypical mycobacteria. Rifampin is effective in leprosy.

An oral dose of 600 mg twice daily for 2 days can eliminate a majority of meningococci from carriers. Unfortunately, some highly resistant meningococcal strains are selected out by this procedure. Up to 10% of meningococcus carriers may exhibit rifampin-resistant organisms after 5 days. A combination of minocycline and rifampin avoids this effect. In urinary tract infections and in chronic bronchitis, the use of rifampin rapidly selects resistant mutants.

Rifampin imparts a harmless orange color to urine, sweat, tears, and contact lenses. Occasional adverse effects include rashes, thrombocytopenia, nephritis, and impairment of liver function. Rifampin commonly causes light chain proteinuria and may impair antibody response. Rifampin increases the elimination of anticoagulants (eg, warfarin) and thus may impose a need for a higher dose of anticoagulant. Rifampin increases the urinary excretion of methadone, lowers its plasma concentration, and may thus result in "methadone withdrawal" signs.

Caution: The indiscriminate use of rifampin for minor infections may favor the widespread selection of rifampin-resistant mycobacteria and thus deprive the drug of most of its usefulness.

ALTERNATIVE DRUGS IN TUBERCULOSIS TREATMENT

Because of their antimicrobial efficacy and their relative clinical safety, the drugs of first choice in tuberculosis in 1979–1980 are isoniazid, rifampin, ethambutol, and streptomycin. The alternative drugs listed below are usually considered only (1) in the case of resistance to the drugs of first choice, which occurs with increasing frequency; (2) in case of failure of clinical response to conventional therapy; and (3) when expert guidance is available to deal with the toxic side-effects. In most of the second choice drugs listed (alphabetically) below, the dosage, emergence of resistance, and long-term toxicity have not been fully established.

Capreomycin

Capreomycin is a peptide antibiotic obtained from *Streptomyces capreolus*. Daily injection of 1 g intramuscularly results in blood levels of 10 μg/mL or more. Such concentrations in vitro are inhibitory for several mycobacteria. There is some cross-resistance between capreomycin, viomycin, and kanamycin. Capreomycin (20 mg/kg/d) can perhaps take the place of streptomycin in combined antituberculosis therapy. The most serious toxicity is for the kidney, resulting in nitrogen retention, and for the eighth nerve, resulting in deafness and vestibular disturbances.

Cycloserine

Cycloserine is an antibiotic analog of D-alanine. Oral doses of 250 mg 3 times daily result in blood levels of 15–25 μg/mL. This is sufficient to inhibit many strains of tubercle bacilli. The most serious toxic reactions are various central nervous system dysfunctions and psychotic reactions. These can be controlled

by phenytoin, 100 mg/d orally.

The dosage of cycloserine in tuberculosis is 0.5–1 g/d. Cycloserine has been used in urinary tract infections in doses of 15–20 mg/kg/d.

Cycloserine is discussed further in Chapter 56.

Ethionamide

This yellow crystalline substance is stable and almost insoluble in water. It is a close chemical relative of isoniazid.

In spite of this similarity, there is no cross-resistance between isoniazid and ethionamide. Most tubercle bacilli are inhibited in vitro by ethionamide, 2.5 μg/mL, or less. Many photochromogenic mycobacteria are also inhibited by ethionamide, 10 μg/mL. Such concentrations in plasma and tissues are achieved by daily oral doses of 1 g. This dosage is effective in the clinical treatment of tuberculosis, but is poorly tolerated because of the intense gastric irritation and neurologic symptoms it causes. A dose of 0.5 g orally per day is better tolerated but not very effective. Resistance to ethionamide develops rapidly in vitro and in vivo. Consequently, this drug can be used only in combination with other antituberculosis drugs.

Ethionamide

Pyrazinamide (PZA)

This relative of nicotinamide is stable and sparingly soluble in water.

Pyrazinamide (PZA)

At neutral pH, it is inactive in vitro, but at pH 5.0 it strongly inhibits the growth of tubercle bacilli within cells in concentrations of 15 μg/mL. Such concentrations are achieved by daily oral doses of 20–30 mg/kg, given as 0.5 g 4 times daily or 0.75 g twice daily. Pyrazinamide is well absorbed from the gastrointestinal tract and widely distributed in body tissues. Tubercle bacilli develop resistance to pyrazinamide fairly readily, but there is no cross-resistance with isoniazid. Satisfactory clinical effects can be achieved with this drug, but toxicity is marked. The most serious toxic effect is the hepatic injury that frequently results. Pyrazinamide should be considered only as part of a combined drug regimen in patients harboring tubercle bacilli resistant to first choice drugs.

Aminosalicylic Acid (PAS)

Among several derivatives of salicylic and benzoic acids, p-aminosalicylic acid has the most marked effect on tubercle bacilli.

The structural formula of PAS reveals its close similarity to p-aminobenzoic acid (PABA) and to the sulfonamides (see Chapter 53).

PAS is a white crystalline powder only slightly soluble in water and rapidly destroyed by heat. The sodium salt is freely soluble in water and relatively stable at room temperature.

Aminosalicylic acid (PAS)

Most bacteria are not affected by PAS. Tubercle bacilli are usually inhibited in vitro by PAS, 1–5 μg/mL, but "atypical" mycobacteria are resistant. In susceptible mycobacterial populations, resistant mutants occur and tend to emerge in vitro and in vivo during exposure to PAS. The simultaneous use of a second drug with antimycobacterial activity tends to delay this emergence of resistance.

It is likely that PAS and PABA compete for the active center of an enzyme involved in converting PABA to dihydropteroic acid. The receptors for PABA attachment must be quite specific, because PAS is ineffective against most bacteria whereas sulfonamides are ineffective against tubercle bacilli.

PAS is readily absorbed from the gastrointestinal tract. Average daily doses (8–12 g) tend to give blood levels of 10 μg/mL or more. The drug is widely distributed in tissues and body fluids except the cerebrospinal fluid. PAS is rapidly excreted in the urine, in part as active PAS and in part as the acetylated compound and other metabolic products. Very high concentrations of PAS are reached in the urine. To avoid crystalluria, the urine must be kept alkaline.

Aminosalicylic acid was employed together with isoniazid or streptomycin, or both, in the long-term treatment of tuberculosis. It is used infrequently now because other oral drugs are better tolerated. The dosage is 8–12 g daily orally for adults and 300 mg/kg/d for children.

Gastrointestinal symptoms often accompany full doses of PAS. Anorexia, nausea, diarrhea, and epigastric pain and burning may all be diminished by giving PAS with meals and with antacids. Peptic ulceration and hemorrhage may occur. Kidney or liver damage, thyroid gland injury (goiter with or without myxedema), and metabolic acidosis are rare.

Drug fever, joint pains, skin rashes, granulocytopenia, and a variety of neurologic symptoms—all probably due to hypersensitivity—often occur after 3–8 weeks of PAS therapy, making it necessary to stop PAS administration temporarily or permanently.

Viomycin

This antibiotic is produced by certain *Streptomyces* organisms. It is an aminoglycoside and a strong base, dispensed as a neutral sulfate which is very soluble in water. Most strains of tubercle bacilli are inhibited in vitro by viomycin, 1–10 μg/mL. Such concentrations can be achieved by the injection of 2 g intramuscularly every third day. Tubercle bacilli resistant to viomycin emerge fairly rapidly. There is also some cross-resistance with streptomycin, kanamycin, and capreomycin. Therefore, viomycin—if used at all—must be used in combination with other drugs to delay the emergence of resistance. The most serious toxic side-effects are damage to the kidney and to the eighth nerve, resulting in loss of equilibrium and deafness. Toxic effects are more serious than with streptomycin.

Other Antimycobacterial Drugs

Kanamycin and **tetracyclines** have been employed in combined therapy of tuberculosis. These drugs can inhibit tubercle bacilli in concentrations which may be achieved in vivo. However, they are much less effective than the drugs of first choice.

SHORT–COURSE TUBERCULOSIS CHEMOTHERAPY

Based on several recent trials, a marked change in chemotherapy for uncomplicated pulmonary tuberculosis is being proposed. Various schemes of drug combinations for 9–12 months, involving daily or twice weekly therapy, have achieved good success in inducing complete remissions at least on short-term follow-up.

It must be stressed that these schemes apply *only* to uncomplicated pulmonary tuberculosis and regimens that contain *both* isoniazid (INH) and rifampin (RIF) with or without other drugs. In adults, 300 mg of INH and 600 mg of RIF are given daily. Children receive INH, 10 mg/kg/d up to 300 mg/d, and RIF, 10–20 mg/kg/d up to 600 mg/d. Ethambutol, 15 mg/kg/d, should be added if the patient resides in or has come from an area with a high level of initial drug resistance. This daily regimen continues for 2–8 weeks, depending on clinical and x-ray response and speed of sputum conversion. Subsequently, INH, 15 mg/kg, can be given twice weekly (eg, INH 900 mg twice weekly for a 60-kg adult) and RIF, 600 mg twice weekly. Intermittently, patients must be monitored for thrombocytopenia. The total treatment time is 9–12 months, at least 6 months beyond conversion of sputum to culture negativity.

Other short-course treatments have been proposed.

●   ●   ●

References

Byrd RB & others: Toxic effects of isoniazid in tuberculosis chemoprophylaxis. JAMA 241:1239, 1979.

Curry FJ: Prophylactic effect of isoniazid in young tuberculin reactors. N Engl J Med 277:562, 1967.

Doster B & others: Ethambutol in the initial treatment of pulmonary tuberculosis. Am Rev Respir Dis 107:177, 1973.

Eickhoff TC: Studies of resistance to rifampin in meningococci. J Infect Dis 123:414, 1971.

Ellard GA, Mitchison DA: The hepatic toxicity of isoniazid among rapid and slow acetylators of the drug. Am Rev Respir Dis 118:628, 1978.

Graber CD & others: Light chain proteinuria and humoral immunoincompetence in tuberculous patients treated with rifampin. Am Rev Respir Dis 107:713, 1973.

Johnston RF, Wildrick KH: Impact of chemotherapy on the care of patients with tuberculosis. Am Rev Respir Dis 109:636, 1974.

Maddrey WC, Boitnott JK: Isoniazid hepatitis. Ann Intern Med 79:1, 1973.

McKenzie MS & others: Drug treatment of tuberculous meningitis in childhood. Clin Pediatr 18:75, 1979.

Mitchell RS: Control of tuberculosis. (2 parts.) N Engl J Med 276:842, 905, 1967.

Newman R & others: Rifampin in initial treatment of pulmonary tuberculosis. Am Rev Respir Dis 109:216, 1974.

Pratt TH: Rifampin induced organic brain syndrome. JAMA 241:2421, 1979.

Steiner P & others: Primary isoniazid-resistant tuberculosis in children: Clinical features, strain resistance, treatment, and outcome in 26 children treated at Kings County Medical Center of Brooklyn between the years 1961 and 1972. Am Rev Respir Dis 110:306, 1974.

US Leprosy Panel: Rifampin therapy of lepromatous leprosy. Am J Trop Med Hyg 24:475, 1975.

Waters MF & others: Rifampicin for lepromatous leprosy: Nine years of experience. Br Med J 1:133, 1978.

Wolinsky E: Nontuberculous mycobacteria and associated diseases. Am Rev Respir Dis 119:107, 1979.

53 | Sulfonamides & Sulfones

SULFONAMIDES

A red dye, prontosil, synthesized in Germany by Klarer and Mietzsch in 1932, was ineffective against bacteria in vitro; but Domagk reported in 1935 that it was strikingly active in vivo against hemolytic streptococcal and other infections. This was due to the conversion in the body of prontosil to sulfanilamide, the active drug. The sulfonamide molecule was chemically altered by the attachment of many different radicals, and there has been a proliferation of active compounds. Perhaps 150 different sulfonamides have been marketed at one time or another, the modifications being designed principally to achieve greater antibacterial activity, a wider antibacterial spectrum, greater solubility, or more prolonged action. In spite of the advent of the antibiotic drugs, the sulfonamides are among the most widely used antibacterial agents in the world today, chiefly because of the low cost and their relative efficacy in some common bacterial diseases. The synergistic action of sulfonamide with trimethoprim has brought about an enormous resurgence in sulfonamide use everywhere during the last decade.

Chemistry

The sulfonamides are a group of compounds whose basic formula and relationship to PABA are shown below.

All have the same nucleus to which various R–radicals in the amido group (SO_2NH_2) have been attached or in which various substitutions of the amino group (NH_2) are made. These changes produce compounds with varying physical, chemical, pharmacologic, and antibacterial properties. In general, the sulfonamides are white, odorless, bitter tasting crystalline powders which are much more soluble at alkaline than at acid pH. In a mixture of sulfonamide drugs, each component drug exhibits its own solubility. Therefore, a mixture may be much more soluble, in terms of total sulfonamide present, than one drug used alone. This is the reason for the use of trisulfapyrimidines, a preparation that permits 3 times higher dosage than a single drug for comparable solubility in urine.

Most sulfonamides can be prepared as sodium salts which are moderately soluble, and these are used for intravenous administration. Such solutions are highly alkaline and not very stable, and may precipitate out of solution with polyionic electrolytes (eg, lactate-chloride-carbonate). Certain sulfonamide molecules are designed for low solubility (eg, phthalylsulfathiazole) so that they will stay in the lumen of the bowel for long periods.

Antimicrobial Activity

Different sulfonamides may show quantitative but not necessarily qualitative differences in activity. Sulfonamides can inhibit both gram-positive and gram-negative bacteria, *Nocardia*, *Chlamydia trachomatis*, and some protozoa. Some enteric bacteria are inhibited but not *Pseudomonas*, *Serratia*, *Proteus*, and other multiresistant organisms. Sulfonamides (alone or in combination with trimethoprim) are drugs of choice in previously untreated, first urinary tract infections, nocardiosis, and toxoplasmosis. Many strains of meningococci, pneumococci, streptococci, staphylococci, and gonococci are now resistant.

The action of sulfonamides is bacteriostatic and is reversible by removal of the drug or in the presence of

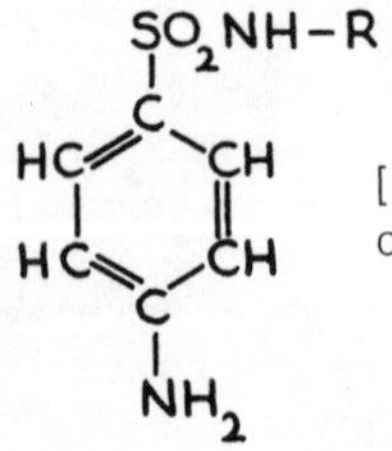

[R = H in the case of sulfanilamide.]

Sulfonamide prototype

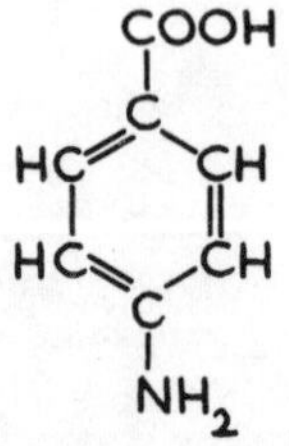

Para-aminobenzoic acid (PABA)

an excess of *p*-aminobenzoic acid (PABA). The mode of action of the sulfonamides is a good example of **competitive inhibition** (see Chapter 47). In brief, susceptible microorganisms require extracellular PABA in order to form folic acid, an essential step in the production of purines and in the ultimate synthesis of nucleic acids. Sulfonamides can enter into the reaction in place of PABA, compete for the enzyme involved, and form nonfunctional analogs of folic acid. As a result, further growth of the microorganisms is prevented. For a given microorganism and a given sulfonamide, the ratio of the inhibitory concentration of drug(s) to varying amounts of PABA is virtually constant. This S:PABA ratio is an index of drug activity and varies from about 30:1 to 2000:1.

Trimethoprim, a trimethoxybenzylpyrimidine, inhibits the dihydrofolic acid reductase of bacteria and some protozoa far more efficiently than the same enzyme of mammalian cells. **Pyrimethamine**, another benzylpyrimidine, inhibits the dihydrofolic acid reductase of protozoa more than that of mammalian cells. Dihydrofolic acid reductases are enzymes which convert dihydrofolic acid to tetrahydrofolic acid, a stage leading to the synthesis of purines and ultimately to DNA. Trimethoprim or pyrimethamine, given together with sulfonamides, produces sequential blocking in this metabolic sequence, resulting in a marked enhancement (synergism) of the activity of sulfonamides (see Chapter 47).

Pyrimethamine

Trimethoprim

Resistance

Animal cells (and some bacteria) are unable to synthesize folic acid but depend upon exogenous sources and for this reason are not susceptible to sulfonamide action. Other cells which produce a large excess of PABA are resistant to sulfonamides, and still others may actually destroy sulfonamides. Sulfonamide-resistant cells occur in most susceptible bacterial populations and tend to emerge under suitable selection pressure. Sulfonamide resistance is under the

genetic control of a transmissible plasmid that may become rapidly and widely disseminated. Thus, the widespread therapeutic use of sulfonamides against gonococci and meningococci has resulted in the establishment of sulfonamide-resistant strains throughout the world. The widespread use of sulfonamides against beta-hemolytic streptococci similarly aided the emergence of resistant strains. Other types of microorganisms—eg, many coliform organisms—are also commonly resistant. It should be specifically mentioned that rickettsiae not only are not inhibited by sulfonamides but are actually stimulated in their growth.

Absorption, Metabolism, & Excretion

Sulfonamides are usually given orally. They are rapidly absorbed from the stomach and small intestine and distributed widely to tissues and body fluids (including central nervous system and cerebrospinal fluid), placenta, and fetus. Absorbed sulfonamides become bound to serum proteins to an extent varying from 20% to over 90%. A varying proportion also becomes acetylated or inactivated by other metabolic pathways. Chemical determinations performed on serum may measure free (active) sulfonamide, the acetylated (inactive) sulfonamide, or the total of both. In order to be therapeutically effective after systemic administration, a sulfonamide must generally achieve a concentration of 8–12 mg/dL of blood. Peak blood levels generally occur 2–3 hours after oral intake.

Soluble sulfonamides are excreted mainly by glomerular filtration into the urine. Different compounds exhibit different degrees of reabsorption in the tubules. A portion of the drug in the urine is acetylated, but enough active drug remains for effective treatment of infections of the urinary tract (usually 10–20 times the concentration present in the blood). In significant renal failure, the dose of sulfonamide and of cotrimoxazole must be reduced.

Sodium salts of sulfonamides are employed for parenteral administration because of their greater solubility. Their distribution and excretion are similar to those of the orally administered drugs.

The "insoluble" sulfonamides (eg, phthalylsulfathiazole) are given orally, are absorbed only slightly in the intestinal tract, and are excreted largely in the feces. Their action is exerted mainly on the intestinal flora.

"Long-acting" sulfonamides, eg, sulfamethoxypyridazine, sulfanilamidomethoxypyrimidine (sulfameter), and sulfadimethoxine, are rapidly absorbed after oral intake and are distributed widely, but urinary excretion—especially of the free form—is very slow. This results in prolonged drug levels in serum. The slow renal excretion is due in part to the high protein binding (more than 85%) and in part to the extensive tubular reabsorption of the free (unacetylated) drug. These drugs are often inadvisable because instances of severe toxicity have resulted from their use. They have been withdrawn in the USA but are still available elsewhere.

Sulfonamides of "intermediate action," eg, sulfamethoxazole, have no clear indication or advantage except convenience of dosage, particularly when formulated in a mixture with trimethoprim (80 mg trimethoprim plus 400 mg sulfamethoxazole per tablet; co-trimoxazole).

Trimethoprim concentrates by nonionic diffusion in prostatic fluid (which is more acid than plasma) and probably also in vaginal fluid. Therefore, it may have more antibacterial activity in prostatic and vaginal fluids than many other antimicrobial drugs.

Laboratory Studies

In order to grow bacteria from specimens obtained from patients receiving sulfonamides, culture media should contain an excess of PABA (5 mg/dL) to overcome the inhibitory effect of the sulfonamide carried in the specimen.

Bacterial susceptibility testing with sulfonamide-containing disks is often unreliable and unsatisfactory because traces of PABA may be present in the medium or because uneven distribution of the bacterial inoculum gravely prejudices the results. PABA-free Mueller-Hinton medium may be satisfactory. Reliable susceptibility testing must be performed in well defined liquid media which are completely free of PABA, contain all nutrients required for fastidious microorganisms (eg, meningococci), and permit the use of a small bacterial inoculum.

Clinical Uses

A. Topical: In general, the application of sulfonamides to the skin, in wounds, or on mucous membranes is undesirable because of their low activity and high risk of allergic sensitization. (An exception to the rule against topical application of sulfonamides may be the use of sodium sulfacetamide solution [30%] or ointment [10%] to the conjunctiva.) Oral administration of the "insoluble" sulfonamides, 8–15 g daily, results in a topical effect—temporary inhibition of the intestinal microbial flora—which is of value in preparing the bowel for surgery; it must be timed so that the lowest microbial levels coincide with the time of the operation (usually on the fourth, fifth, or sixth day after administration). Mafenide acetate (p-amino methyl benzene sulfonamide; Sulfamylon) cream is a sulfonamide topically applied (as 10% cream) to burned skin surfaces. The drug is absorbed in 3 hours into tissue from the vehicle. It has been effective in reducing burn sepsis but has led to an increase of burn infections by fungi and resistant bacteria.

Mafenide causes significant pain on application. Silver sulfadiazine has been applied to burn wounds with relatively little pain. The sulfadiazine is released slowly, and only low systemic levels develop. Silver sulfadiazine appears to be effective in controlling infecting flora of most burn wounds, especially if the burns are not too deep.

Sulfasalazine (salicylazosulfapyridine) is widely used in ulcerative colitis, enteritis, and other inflammatory bowel disease. There is some evidence that this drug is more effective than soluble sulfonamides or other antimicrobials taken orally—all of which may occasionally have a beneficial effect in this type of inflammatory bowel disease. Sulfasalazine is split by intestinal microflora to yield sulfapyridine and 5-aminosalicylate. The latter may be released in the colon in a high concentration and may be responsible for an anti-inflammatory effect. Comparably high concentrations of salicylate cannot be achieved in the colon by oral intake of salicylates. The sulfapyridine is absorbed and may lead to toxic symptoms if more than 4 g of sulfasalazine are taken per day, particularly in persons who are slow acetylators.

B. Oral: The highly soluble and rapidly excreted sulfonamides (eg, sulfadiazine, sulfamerazine, sulfisoxazole) are given in initial doses of 2–4 g (40 mg/kg) followed by a maintenance dose of 0.5–1 g (15 mg/kg) every 4–6 hours. This regimen is indicated in systemic infections and can also be applied to urinary tract infections. In the latter, sulfisoxazole is often preferred because of its high solubility in urine. The urine should be kept alkaline. Alternatively, a mixture of several sulfonamides (in the total doses given above) can be used (eg, trisulfapyrimidines). After an initial attack of urinary tract infection has been treated with sulfonamides, resistant organisms often prevail. Therefore, in relapses, other drugs must be used. The slowly excreted sulfonamides (sulfamethoxypyridazine, sulfadimethoxine, etc) can be given in daily doses of 0.5–1 g (10 mg/kg) for the treatment of minor infections (eg, sinusitis, otitis) or for prolonged maintenance therapy.

The "insoluble" phthalylsulfathiazole is given orally only for preoperative preparation of the bowel (8–15 g daily for 4–7 days).

In protozoal infections, soluble sulfonamides are administered in combination with other agents. Thus, in toxoplasmosis or leishmaniasis, sulfonamides in full systemic doses are combined with pyrimethamine, 50 mg/d. In falciparum malaria, sulfonamides and trimethoprim are given together. In nocardiosis, sulfonamides are the drugs of first choice.

C. Intravenous: Sodium salts of many sulfonamides are available for parenteral injection, but because of their marked alkalinity are best injected intravenously (not intramuscularly) in 5% dextrose in water. Intravenous sulfonamides are generally reserved for comatose patients (most commonly patients with meningitis) or patients who are otherwise unable to take medication by mouth.

D. Pyrimethamine and Trimethoprim: Pyrimethamine is the more toxic drug, and is employed in combination with sulfonamides as a treatment of choice for toxoplasmosis. Trimethoprim plus sulfonamides (co-trimoxazole) has been used in bacterial urinary tract infections, enteric fevers, brucellosis, and many other bacterial infections and in protozoal infections, eg, those due to *Pneumocystis carinii*. Resistance to this combined therapy (inducing a sequential block) emerges very slowly among bacteria or protozoa, but trimethoprim resistance is appearing in coliforms and *Haemophilus*. Supplemental folates may have to be administered with such combined therapy (eg, falciparum malaria) in order to combat folic acid deficiency.

The daily oral dose often includes 240–400 mg of trimethoprim plus 5 times that amount of a sulfonamide. This equals 3–5 tablets of co-trimoxazole. Twice that dose is sometimes administered in severe infection with susceptible organisms. An intravenous form of co-trimoxazole (dose: 33 mg/kg sulfamethoxazole plus 6.7 mg/kg trimethoprim) can be obtained for initial treatment of *Pneumocystis pneumoniae* infection and other life-threatening problems, eg, gram-negative sepsis due to *Serratia*. One-fourth of the dose is given if creatinine clearance is less than 5 mL/min.

The daily oral dose of pyrimethamine is often 25–50 mg in combination with a full dose of a sulfonamide. The ratio of urinary concentrations of sulfonamide to trimethoprim depends on the pH of the urine. Trimethoprim concentrates by nonionic diffusion in prostatic and vaginal fluids, which are more acidic than serum. It may play an antibacterial role in prostatitis and vaginitis.

Co-trimoxazole is used both in prophylaxis of *Pneumocystis* infections in immunosuppressed persons and in prevention of urinary tract infections in particularly susceptible females. Co-trimoxazole has also been accepted for treatment of bacterial exacerbations of chronic respiratory tract disease, in addition to the indications mentioned above.

Adverse Reactions

The sulfonamides can produce a wide variety of side-effects which are due partly to allergy and partly to direct toxicity, and which must be considered whenever unexplained symptoms or signs occur in a patient who may have received these drugs. Up to 5% of patients may exhibit such reactions. The overall incidence of side-effects is higher with the slowly excreted "long-acting" sulfonamides than with the rapidly excreted ones.

The commonest side-effects are fever, skin rashes, photosensitivity, urticaria; nausea, vomiting, or diarrhea; and difficulties referable to the urinary tract (see below). Others include stomatitis, conjunctivitis, arthritis, hematopoietic disturbances (see below), hepatitis, exfoliative dermatitis, polyarteritis nodosa, Stevens-Johnson syndrome, psychosis, and many more.

A. Urinary Tract Disturbances: Sulfonamides may precipitate in urine, especially at neutral or acid pH, producing crystalluria, hematuria, or even obstruction. This is best prevented by using the most soluble sulfonamides (sulfisoxazole, trisulfapyrimidines, sulfacytral), keeping the urine pH alkaline (5–15 g sodium bicarbonate daily), forcing fluids, and performing urinalysis every 3–5 days.

Sulfonamides have also been implicated in various types of nephrosis and in allergic nephritis. Deterioration of renal function can occur with co-trimoxazole.

B. Hematopoietic Disturbances: Sulfonamides can produce anemia (hemolytic or aplastic), granulocytopenia, thrombocytopenia, or leukemoid reactions. In order to prevent these reactions or to be able to withdraw the drug before the reaction has advanced to a severe or life-threatening stage, it is important to check the white blood count and hemoglobin level every 3–5 days. Sulfonamides cause hemolytic reactions, especially in patients whose erythrocytes are deficient in glucose-6-phosphate dehydrogenase. Sulfonamides taken near the end of pregnancy increase the risk of kernicterus in newborns.

Medical & Social Aspects

Sulfonamides can be made and distributed cheaply and are thus among the principal antimicrobial agents available in many developing areas of the world. They continue to be useful for the treatment of such widespread disorders as urinary tract infections and trachoma, but the emergence of drug resistance has impaired their usefulness in streptococcal, gonococcal, meningococcal, *Shigella*, and other infections. Topical use (skin) on a vast scale has contributed heavily to the sensitization of the population.

SULFONES USED IN THE TREATMENT OF LEPROSY

A number of drugs closely related to the sulfonamides have been used effectively in the long-term treatment of leprosy. Some are also employed in malaria. The clinical manifestations of both lepromatous and tuberculoid leprosy can often be suppressed by treatment extending over several years.

Absorption, Metabolism, & Excretion

All of the sulfones are well absorbed from the intestinal tract, are distributed widely in all tissues, and tend to be retained in skin, muscle, liver, and kidney. Skin involved by leprosy contains 10 times more drug than normal skin. Sulfones are excreted into the bile and reabsorbed by the intestine. Consequently, blood levels are prolonged. Excretion into the urine is variable and occurs mostly as a glucuronic acid conjugate. Some persons acetylate sulfones slowly, others rapidly. This may require dosage adjustments. Resistance to sulfones is becoming apparent in leprosy.

Adverse Reactions

The sulfones may cause any of the side-effects listed above for sulfonamides. Anorexia, nausea, and vomiting are common. Hemolysis, methemoglobinemia, or agranulocytosis may occur.

Clinical Uses

Dapsone (diaminodiphenylsulfone, DDS) is the

most widely used and least expensive drug. It is given orally, beginning with a dosage of 25 mg twice weekly and gradually increasing to 100 mg 3–4 times weekly and eventually to 300 mg twice weekly.

Dapsone has also been used in combined drug therapy of chloroquine-resistant malaria.

Sulfoxone sodium is given orally in corresponding dosage.

Solapsone, a complex substituted derivative of dapsone, is given initially in a dosage of 0.5 g 3 times daily orally. The dose is then gradually increased until a total daily dose of 6–10 g is reached.

Other classes of drugs are used when intolerance to sulfones develops. Amithiozone (diphenylthiourea) is given in a dose of 50 mg/d orally, increasing to 200 mg/d. Rifampin is showing great promise as a drug to be used in combination therapy in treatment of leprosy.

• • •

References

Ballin JC: Evaluation of a new topical agent for burn therapy: Silver sulfadiazine (Silvadene). JAMA 230:1884, 1974.

Bose W & others: Controlled trial of co-trimoxazole in children with urinary tract infection. Lancet 2:614, 1974.

Craig WA, Kunin CM: Trimethoprim-sulfamethoxazole: Effects of urinary pH and impaired renal function. Ann Intern Med 78:491, 1973.

Feldman HA: Toxoplasmosis. (2 parts.) N Engl J Med 279:1370, 1431, 1968.

Goldman P, Peppercorn MA: Sulfasalazine. N Engl J Med 293:20, 1975.

Hamilton HE, Sheets RF: Sulfisoxazole-induced thrombocytopenic purpura. JAMA 239:2586, 1978.

Kalowski S & others: Deterioration of renal function with co-trimoxazole. Lancet 1:394, 1973.

Lau WK, Young LS: Trimethoprim-sulfamethoxazole treatment of *Pneumocystis carinii* pneumonia in adults. N Engl J Med 295:716, 1976.

Lawson DH, Jick H: Adverse reactions to co-trimoxazole in hospitalized medical patients. Am J Med Sci 275:53, 1978.

Mihas AA, Goldenberg DJ, Slaughter RL: Sulfasalazine toxic reactions: Hepatitis, fever and skin rash with hypocomplementemia and immune complexes. JAMA 239:2590, 1978.

Richards H & others: Trimethoprim-resistance plasmids and transposons in salmonella. Lancet 2:1194, 1978.

Schiffman DO: Evaluation of an anti-infective combination: Trimethoprim-sulfamethoxazole. JAMA 231:635, 1975.

Schröder H & others: Metabolism of salicylazosulfapyridine. Clin Pharmacol Ther 14:802, 1973.

Stamey TA, Condy M: The diffusion and concentration of trimethoprim in human vaginal fluid. J Infect Dis 131:261, 1975.

US Leprosy Panel: Rifampin therapy of lepromatous leprosy. Am J Trop Med Hyg 24:475, 1975.

US Leprosy Panel: Spaced clofazimine therapy of lepromatous leprosy. Am J Trop Med Hyg 25:437, 1976.

Weinstein L, Madoff MA, Samet CM: The sulfonamides. (2 parts.) N Engl J Med 263:900, 952, 1960.

Yoshikawa TT, Guze LB: Concentrations of trimethoprim-sulfamethoxazole in blood after a single, large oral dose. Antimicrob Agents Chemother 10:462, 1976.

BACITRACIN

Bacitracin is a complex material obtained from a special strain of *Bacillus subtilis* in 1943. It is active against gram-positive microorganisms. Because of its marked toxicity when used systemically, it is now generally limited to topical use.

Chemistry

Bacitracin consists of a group of polypeptides which are highly water-soluble. The material is stable in the dry form or when incorporated into a petrolatum. The unit of activity is defined as the equivalent of 26 μg of a Food and Drug Administration (USA) standard.

Antibacterial Activity

Bacitracin is most active against gram-positive bacteria, including β-lactamase–producing staphylococci, in concentrations of 0.1–20 unit/mL. There is no cross-resistance between bacitracin and other antimicrobial drugs.

Bacitracin inhibits cell wall formation. It interferes with the final dephosphorylation in cycling the phospholipid carrier which transfers mucopeptide to the growing cell wall.

Absorption, Metabolism, & Excretion

Bacitracin is not well absorbed from the gut, from skin, wounds, or mucous membrane surfaces, from pleura, or from synovia. Topical application thus results in local effects without significant systemic toxicity. After intramuscular injection, bacitracin is fairly well absorbed, widely distributed in the body, and excreted by glomerular filtration into the urine.

Clinical Uses

Because of its systemic toxicity, bacitracin is now used mainly for topical treatment. Bacitracin, 500 units/g in an ointment base (often combined with polymyxin or neomycin), is useful for the suppression of mixed bacterial flora in surface lesions of the skin, in wounds, or on mucous membranes. Solutions of bacitracin containing 100–200 units/mL in saline can be employed for instillation into joints, wounds, or the pleural cavity—often in conjunction with other drugs

given systemically. Rarely, bacitracin, 1000 units/ kg/d, is injected intramuscularly into small children with bacterial pneumonia.

Adverse Reactions

Bacitracin is markedly nephrotoxic, producing proteinuria, hematuria, and nitrogen retention. Therefore, systemic use has been virtually abandoned. Topical application only rarely causes hypersensitivity reactions (eg, skin rashes) or produces significant systemic toxicity.

VANCOMYCIN

Vancomycin is an antibiotic produced by *Streptomyces orientalis*. It is active against gram-positive bacteria, particularly staphylococci.

Chemistry

Vancomycin hydrochloride is a crystalline material of high molecular weight (3300). It is soluble in water and very stable. The structural formula has not been established.

Antibacterial Activity

Vancomycin is bactericidal for gram-positive bacteria in concentrations of 0.5–3 μg/mL. Most pathogenic staphylococci are killed by 10 μg/mL or less. Resistant mutants are very rare in susceptible populations, and clinical resistance emerges very slowly. There is no cross-resistance with other known antibiotics.

The mechanism of action involves inhibition of cell wall mucopeptide synthesis. Vancomycin inhibits the utilization of disaccharide(-pentapeptide)-P-phospholipid. Cell membrane function is also damaged.

Vancomycin can be synergistic with aminoglycosides against certain enterococci and other gram-positive bacteria.

Absorption, Metabolism, & Excretion

Vancomycin is not absorbed from the intestinal tract and can be given orally only for the treatment of enterocolitis. Systemic doses must be administered intravenously. After intravenous injection of 0.5 g, blood levels of 10 μg/mL are reached in 5 minutes and maintained for 1–2 hours. The drug is widely distributed in the body. Excretion is mainly through the kidneys into the urine. In the presence of renal insufficiency, striking accumulation may occur and may have serious toxic consequences.

Clinical Uses

The only indication for the use of vancomycin is serious staphylococcal infection or enterococcal endocarditis not responding to other treatment. For antibiotic-associated enterocolitis, 3–4 g are given daily by mouth. For staphylococcal septicemia, 0.5 g is injected intravenously in 20–30 minutes every 6–8 hours (20–40 mg/kg/d for children). Rarely, vancomycin is given with an aminoglycoside in enterococcal endocarditis.

Adverse Reactions

A. Allergic Reactions: Skin rashes and anaphylaxis have been observed infrequently.

B. Direct Toxicity: Vancomycin is highly irritating to tissue. Intramuscular injection is very painful. Thrombophlebitis and chills and fever are common following intravenous injection. Nephrotoxicity and ototoxicity were serious problems with preparations manufactured prior to 1970, so that the drug was limited to patients who failed to respond to or could not tolerate β-lactamase-resistant penicillins. Since the mid 1970s, vancomycin preparations have been remarkably well tolerated, with only limited nephrotoxicity; consequently, the drug can be used with less hesitation considering its great efficacy. For dosage adjustment in renal failure, see p 538.

THE ERYTHROMYCIN GROUP
(Macrolides)

This is a group of closely related compounds characterized by a macrocyclic lactone ring to which sugars are attached. The prototype drug, erythromycin, was obtained in 1952 from *Streptomyces erythreus*. Members of the group include carbomycin, oleandomycin, spiramycin, and many others. Troleandomycin (triacetyloleandomycin) was introduced in 1958.

Chemistry

The formula of erythromycin is $C_{37}H_{67}O_{13}N$. Its general structure is shown below with the macrolide ring and the sugars desosamine and cladinose. The molecular weight of erythromycin is 734. It is poorly soluble in water (0.1%) but dissolves readily in organic solvents. Solutions are relatively stable at 4 C but lose activity rapidly at 20 C and at acid pH. Erythromycins are dispensed as various esters and salts.

Antimicrobial Activity

Erythromycins are effective against gram-positive organisms, especially pneumococci, streptococci, staphylococci, and corynebacteria, in concentrations of 0.02–2 μg/mL. Neisseriae, *Haemophilus*, *Mycoplasma*, *Legionella*, and *Chlamydia trachomatis* are also susceptible.

The antibacterial action of the erythromycins is both inhibitory and bactericidal for susceptible organisms. Activity is enhanced at alkaline pH. Inhibition of protein synthesis occurs by action on the 50S unit of ribosomes. The receptor for erythromycins, lincomycins, and perhaps other drugs is a 23S rRNA on the 50S subunit. Protein synthesis is inhibited as aminoacyl translocation reactions and elongation of the peptide chain are blocked. Resistance to erythromycins results from methylation of the rRNA receptor, which prevents attachment of the drug to the ribo-

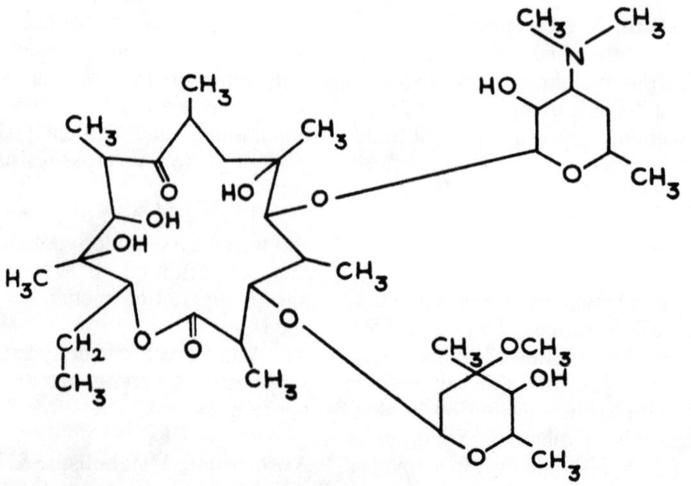

Erythromycin

some. This mechanism is under the control of a plasmid.

Resistance

In most susceptible microbial populations, organisms occur that are highly resistant to erythromycin. Resistance is especially frequent among staphylococci, and their emergence in the course of prolonged treatment with erythromycin is highly predictable. Consequently, erythromycin should never be used as the sole drug in treating severe staphylococcal infections. Erythromycin-resistant pneumococci and streptococci are also being isolated.

There appears to be virtually complete cross-resistance among all members of the erythromycin group. Erythromycin resistance is based on the altered receptor on the 50S unit of the ribosome. Resistance does not involve destruction of drug. There is some cross-resistance to lincomycins.

Absorption, Metabolism, & Excretion

Basic erythromycins are rapidly destroyed by stomach acids. Erythromycin stearate is acid-resistant but not so well absorbed as esters of erythromycin. Oral doses of 2 g/d result in serum levels of up to 2 μg/mL. Large amounts are lost in feces. Absorbed drug is distributed widely in the central nervous system and cerebrospinal fluid and passes the placenta to a limited extent.

Erythromycins are excreted largely in the bile, where levels may be 50 times higher than in the blood. A portion of the drug excreted into bile is reabsorbed from the intestines. Only 5% of the administered dose is excreted in the urine.

Clinical Uses

Erythromycins are the drugs of choice only in some corynebacterial infections (erythrasma, diphtheria carriers, diphtheroid sepsis) and in disease caused by *Mycoplasma pneumoniae* or *Legionella pneumophila*. Erythromycin is active against some chlamydiae and atypical mycobacteria. Otherwise, erythromycins are most useful as penicillin substitutes in individuals with streptococcal or pneumococcal infections who are hypersensitive to penicillin. In this group of drugs, erythromycin estolate (the lauryl sulfate of the propionyl ester of erythromycin) and troleandomycin are absorbed with greatest regularity. However, they also produce the most severe adverse reactions. Therefore, the less well absorbed base, stearate, or succinate may be preferred.

A. Oral Dosage: 0.5 g every 6 hours for adults; 40 mg/kg/d for children. Oral erythromycin base is sometimes combined with oral neomycin or kanamycin for preoperative preparation of the colon.

B. Intravenous Dosage: (Eg, erythromycin glucepate or lactobionate.) 0.5 g every 8–12 hours for adults; 40 mg/kg/d for children.

Adverse Reactions

A. Gastrointestinal Effects: Anorexia, nausea,

vomiting, and diarrhea occasionally accompany oral administration.

B. Liver Toxicity: Erythromycin estolate and troleandomycin can produce acute cholestatic hepatitis with fever and jaundice or subclinical impaired liver function. It is probable that this is a reaction of specific hypersensitivity which can be elicited repeatedly by challenge with the same drugs. Up to 15% of patients receiving these drugs in full doses for more than 2 weeks may have abnormal liver function tests. Some of these abnormal tests (elevated SGOT) may be false positives, but others indicate impairment of liver function. Most patients recover completely, but a few deaths have been reported.

Other salts of erythromycin may also produce cholestatic hepatitis.

LINCOMYCIN & CLINDAMYCIN
(Lincosamines)

Lincomycin is an antibiotic elaborated by *Streptomyces lincolnensis*. Clindamycin is a chlorine-substituted derivative of lincomycin. Both drugs have antimicrobial activity similar to that of erythromycin, but they are chemically quite distinct.

Clindamycin is the more active drug, especially against anaerobes.

Antibacterial Activity

Many gram-positive cocci are inhibited by lincomycins, 0.5–5 μg/mL. Enterococci, *Haemophilus*, neisseriae, and *Mycoplasma* are usually resistant (in contrast to erythromycin). While lincomycins have little or no action on most gram-negative bacteria, *Bacteroides* are usually susceptible. Lincomycins inhibit protein synthesis by interfering with the formation of initiation complexes and with aminoacyl translocation reactions. The receptor for lincomycins on the 50S subunit of the bacterial ribosome is a 23S rRNA, perhaps identical with the receptor for erythromycins. Thus, these 2 drug classes may block each other's attachment and may interfere with each other. Resistance to lincomycins appears slowly, perhaps as a result of chromosomal mutation. Plasmid-mediated resistance has not been established with certainty. Resistance to lincomycin is common among streptococci, pneumococci, and staphylococci. *Clostridium difficile* strains appear to be regularly resistant.

Absorption, Metabolism, & Excretion

Oral doses of lincomycin, 0.5 g every 6 hours, are readily absorbed from the gut if taken away from meals, and yield serum concentrations of 2–5 μg/mL. Similar concentrations are obtained with clindamycin, 0.15 g every 6 hours orally. Both drugs can also be given intramuscularly or intravenously to achieve somewhat higher levels. Lincomycins are widely distributed in the body but do not appear in the central nervous system in significant concentrations. Excretion is mainly through the liver, bile, and urine.

Clinical Uses

Probably the most important indication for clindamycin is the treatment of severe anaerobic infection caused by *Bacteroides* (especially *Bacteroides fragilis*) and other anaerobes which are often resistant to penicillin and which often participate in mixed infections. Clindamycin is given by mouth, 0.15–0.45 g every 6 hours (10–20 mg/kg/d for children). It may, in very severe infections, be given intravenously, 600 mg during 1 hour, every 6–8 hours (10–40 mg/kg/d for children). These doses result in blood and tissue levels in excess of inhibitory concentrations for many anaerobes. Lincomycin may be given by mouth, 0.5 g every 6 hours (30–60 mg/kg/d for children).

The lincomycins have also been suggested for the treatment of gram-positive coccal infections in persons hypersensitive to penicillins, but erythromycins may be preferable for that purpose. An exception may be the use of lincomycins in staphylococcal infections of bone, where successful treatment has been recorded. Meningitis should *not* be treated with lincomycins. Clindamycin crosses the placenta and may reach the fetus in concentrations sufficient for the treatment of anaerobic intrauterine infections. Clindamycin, perhaps combined with an aminoglycoside, has also been considered for penetrating wounds of the abdomen and the gut. Clindamycin has found favor in the management of infections originating in the female genital tract, eg, septic abortion and pelvic abscesses that are populated by a variety of microbes, with heavy participation of anaerobes, including *B fragilis*.

Adverse Reactions

Common side-effects are diarrhea, nausea, and skin rashes. Impaired liver function (with or without jaundice) and neutropenia sometimes occur. Severe diarrhea and enterocolitis—sometimes ending fatally—have followed clindamycin administration and place a serious restraint on its use. The incidence of severe diarrhea has ranged from 2–20% in various studies.

The antibiotic-associated pseudomembranous colitis that has followed administration of clindamycin in some hospitals appears to be caused by toxigenic *C difficile*. This organism is infrequently part of the normal fecal flora but is selected out during administration of clindamycin (and occasionally other drugs). It grows to high numbers in the sigmoid colon and secretes a necrotizing toxin that produces pseudomembranous colitis. This potentially fatal complication must be recognized promptly and treated with oral vancomycin, 0.5 g 4–6 times daily (see above). Local prevalence of *C difficile* may account for the great differences in incidence of antibiotic-associated colitis.

NOVOBIOCIN

Novobiocin (also called streptonivicin, cardelmycin) is an acidic antibiotic produced by *Streptomyces niveus* and purified in 1956. It is active mainly against gram-positive bacteria.

The acidic material is insoluble, but the sodium or calcium salts are soluble in water and fairly stable.

Antibacterial Activity

Many gram-positive cocci are inhibited by novobiocin, 1–5 μg/mL, as are some strains of *Proteus* also. Resistant mutants occur in all susceptible bacterial populations with such frequency (and are of such magnitude) that clinical resistance tends to emerge very rapidly. Therefore, novobiocin can usually not be employed as the sole antimicrobial drug for more than a few days and, if employed at all, must be given in combination with a second drug. There is no known cross-resistance with other antimicrobials.

The mechanism of action of novobiocin is not fully understood. The drug acts at the cell membrane to inhibit synthesis of DNA and teichoic acid. It may have additional mechanisms. Experimentally, novobiocin treatment of cocci carrying plasmids that made them resistant to aminoglycoside resulted in loss of such plasmids.

Absorption, Metabolism, & Excretion

Novobiocin is readily absorbed from the gastrointestinal tract. A major portion of the absorbed drug is bound to serum protein. After ingestion of 0.5 g every 6 hours, the average serum concentration of free (unbound) novobiocin is 2–5 μg/mL. Novobiocin is fairly widely distributed in body fluids and tissues except the central nervous system. Excretion is into the urine and bile. Much of the ingested drug is excreted in the feces.

Clinical Uses

Since the newer penicillins became available, there is no longer an unequivocal indication for the use of novobiocin. Previously, its principal indication was serious staphylococcal infection. At present, novobiocin might occasionally be useful in the treatment of indole-positive *Proteus* infections or of staphylococcal infections in penicillin-hypersensitive persons. The oral dose is 0.5 g every 6 hours (30 mg/kg/d for children). For the prolonged treatment of chronic infection, novobiocin would have to be combined with a second drug to delay emergence of resistance.

Adverse Reactions

The incidence of side-effects is high (10–20%).

A. Direct Toxicity: Nausea, vomiting, and diarrhea occur following oral intake; pain at the site of injection, liver damage with jaundice, and hemolytic anemia occur following parenteral use.

B. Allergic Reactions: Skin rashes, fever, eosinophilia, granulocytopenia, and thrombocytopenia can occur frequently.

METRONIDAZOLE

This nitroimidazole drug has found widespread use as an antiprotozoal agent, particularly for *Trichomonas* and amebic infections. Metronidazole is well absorbed after oral intake, with peak serum levels reaching 5 μg/mL 1 hour after 250 mg orally. The serum half-life is more than 8 hours. The drug diffuses well into all tissues, including the central nervous system, and enters abscesses and empyemas with little protein binding.

In trichomonal vaginitis, both sex partners can be treated with 250 mg 3 times daily by mouth for 7 days. In intestinal or hepatic amebiasis, 750 mg 3 times daily is given for 7–10 days. Metronidazole is strikingly bactericidal for many anaerobes, and in serious anaerobic infections the latter dose has been used.

Metronidazole is also effective in eradicating giardiasis. The drug has been used for preoperative preparation of the colon, and it seems to prevent postoperative anaerobic infections. However, metronidazole has not been approved for this purpose because of laboratory evidence of its carcinogenicity.

Common adverse effects include stomatitis, nausea, diarrhea, and central nervous system disturbances, particularly vestibular reactions with ataxia, vertigo, and headaches. Metronidazole produces disulfiramlike reactions if taken with alcohol.

● ● ●

References

Braun P: Hepatotoxicity of erythromycin. J Infect Dis 119:300, 1975.

Cook FV, Farrar WE: Vancomycin revisited. Ann Intern Med 88:813, 1978.

Eichenwald HF, McCracken GH: Antimicrobial therapy in infants and children. J Pediatr 93:337, 1978.

Fass RR & others: Clindamycin in the treatment of serious anaerobic infections. Ann Intern Med 78:853, 1973.

Feigen RD & others: Clindamycin treatment of osteomyelitis and septic arthritis in children. Pediatrics 55:213, 1975.

Freeark RJ: Penetrating wounds of the abdomen. N Engl J Med 291:185, 1974.

Garrod LP, Lambert HP, O'Grady F: *Antibiotic and Chemotherapy*, 4th ed. Churchill Livingstone, 1973.

Ginsburg CM, Eichenwald HP: Erythromycin: A review of its uses in pediatric practice. J Pediatr 89:872, 1976.

Gorbach SL, Thadepalli H: Clindamycin in pure and mixed anaerobic infections. Arch Intern Med 134:87, 1974.

Hook EW, Johnson WD: Vancomycin therapy of bacterial endocarditis. Am J Med 65:411, 1978.

Keighley MRB & others: Randomised controlled trial of vancomycin for pseudomembranous and postoperative diarrhea. Br Med J 2:1667, 1978.

Ledger WJ & others: Comparison of clindamycin and chloramphenicol in treatment of serious infections of the female genital tract. J Infect Dis 135:S30, 1977.

Pestka S & others: Induction of erythromycin resistance in *Staphylococcus aureus*. Antimicrob Agents Chemother 9:128, 1975.

Tedesco FJ: Clindamycin and colitis: A review. J Infect Dis 135 (Suppl):S95, 1977.

Warner JF & others: Metronidazole therapy of anaerobic bacteremia, meningitis and brain abscess. Arch Intern Med 139:167, 1979.

Willis AT & others: Metronidazole in prevention and treatment of bacteroides infections after appendicectomy. Br Med J 1:318, 1976.

55 | Antifungal Agents

Most fungi are completely resistant to the action of antibacterial drugs. Only a few substances have been discovered which exert an inhibitory effect on the fungi pathogenic for humans, and most of these are relatively toxic. There is a great need for better antifungal drugs.

Amphotericin B and flucytosine are the only antifungal drugs that have been used with any success in the treatment of deep mycoses, meningitis, or sepsis. Other polyene antibiotics are under study. Griseofulvin is effective in dermatophytosis. Nystatin, candicidin, and tolnaftate can only be applied topically. Miconazole is effective topically and has been used systemically on an experimental basis. Penicillin and sulfonamides are used in the treatment of actinomycosis and nocardiosis, respectively.

AMPHOTERICIN B

Amphotericin B is one of 2 antibiotics produced by *Streptomyces nodosus*, purified in 1956. Amphotericin A is not used in therapy.

Chemistry
Amphotericin B is an amphoteric polyene with the empirical formula $C_{46}H_{73}O_{20}N$. The basic moiety is an aminomethylpentose. Amphotericin B is insoluble in water. It is unstable at 37 C, but stable for weeks at 4 C. Microcrystalline preparations can be applied topically but are not absorbed to a significant extent. For systemic use by intravenous injection, a colloidal preparation is employed. This is a yellow powder containing 0.8 mg of sodium deoxycholate for each mg of amphotericin, with a phosphate buffer, to be dissolved in dextrose solution.

Antifungal Activity
Amphotericin B, 0.1–0.8 μg/mL, inhibits in vitro *Histoplasma capsulatum*, *Cryptococcus neoformans*, *Coccidioides immitis*, *Candida albicans*, *Blastomyces dermatitidis*, *Sporothrix schenckii*, and other organisms producing systemic mycotic disease in humans. It has no effect on bacteria. The emergence of resistance to amphotericin B has been observed in vitro.

The mode of action of the polyene antibiotics is fairly well understood. The drug apparently is bound firmly to the cell membrane in the presence of certain sterols and disturbs the permeability and transport characteristics of the membrane. This results in loss of intracellular components (particularly cations) from the cell and produces irreversible damage. Bacteria are insusceptible to polyenes because they lack the sterol which is essential for attachment to the cell membrane. Amphotericin resistance may result from a change in the polyene sterol receptor in the fungal cell membrane. Some attachment of amphotericin B to cholesterol in animal cell membranes probably accounts in part for its toxicity.

Absorption, Metabolism, & Excretion
Amphotericin is poorly absorbed from the gastrointestinal tract. Orally administered amphotericin therefore is effective only on fungi within the lumen of the tract and cannot be used for the treatment of systemic disease. The intravenous injection of 80 mg of amphotericin B per day (0.60 mg/kg/d) results in average blood levels of 0.3–1 μg/mL. Amphotericin is 85% protein-bound and is removed to a very limited extent by hemodialysis. The injected amphotericin is excreted slowly in the urine over a period of several days. The drug is widely distributed in tissues, but only 2–3% of the blood level is reached in cerebrospinal fluid. Consequently, intrathecal administration is necessary in fungal meningitis.

Clinical Uses
For the treatment of systemic fungal infections, amphotericin B is available as a colloidal dry powder to be dissolved with sodium deoxycholate in 5% dextrose in water to a concentration of 0.1 mg/mL; the solution is then given by slow intravenous infusion over a period of 4–6 hours. The initial dose is 1–5 mg/d, increasing daily by 5 mg increments until a final dosage of 0.4–0.8 mg/kg/d is reached. This is usually continued for 6–12 weeks or longer, with a daily dose rarely exceeding 60 mg.

In fungal meningitis, intrathecal injection of 0.5 mg amphotericin B may be given 3 times weekly for up to 10 weeks or longer. Continuous infusion with an Ommaya reservoir is sometimes used. Fungal meningitis relapses commonly. Combined treatment with amphotericin and flucytosine is increasingly used to delay emergence of resistance and in order to reduce toxicity because lower drug doses are required. There is also evidence that true synergism may be involved, with amphotericin enhancing entry of flucytosine into the cell and resulting in markedly increased antifungal activity.

In corneal ulcers caused by fungi, a 0.15% solution dropped onto the conjunctiva every 30 minutes can be curative.

Adverse Reactions

The intravenous injection of amphotericin usually produces chills, fever, vomiting, and headache. This may be minimized by reducing the dosage temporarily, administering aspirin, phenothiazines, antihistamines, or corticosteroids, or stopping injections for several days.

Therapeutically active amounts of amphotericin B commonly impair renal and hepatocellular function and produce anemia. There is a fall in glomerular filtration rate and a change in tubular function. These result in a decrease in creatinine clearance and an increase in potassium clearance. Shocklike fall in blood pressure, electrolyte disturbances (especially hypokalemia), and a variety of neurologic symptoms also occur commonly. In impaired kidney function, the dose of amphotericin must be further reduced.

FLUCYTOSINE

5-Fluorocytosine (flucytosine, 5-FC) is an oral antifungal compound of relatively low toxicity. Flucytosine, 5 μg/mL, inhibits in vitro many strains of *Candida, Cryptococcus,* and *Torulopsis* and some strains of *Aspergillus* and other fungi. Cells are susceptible if they convert fluoropyrimidines into fluoronucleoside triphosphates, which results in the production of nonfunctional RNA. Resistant mutants emerge fairly regularly and rapidly and are selected in the presence of the drug, limiting its usefulness. For this reason, combined treatment with 5-FC and amphotericin B is being explored with some success. True synergism may occur, with enhanced antifungal effect.

Oral doses of 150 mg/kg/d are well absorbed and widely distributed in tissues—including the cerebrospinal fluid—where the drug concentration may be 60–80% of the serum concentration, which tends to be near 50 μg/mL. About 20% of flucytosine is protein-bound. 5-FC is largely excreted by the kidneys, and concentrations in the urine reach 10 times the concentrations in serum. In the presence of renal failure, the drug may accumulate in serum to toxic levels, but hepatic failure has no effect. Flucytosine is removed by hemodialysis.

Flucytosine appears to be relatively nontoxic for mammalian cells (perhaps because they lack a specific permease). Prolonged high serum levels often cause depression of bone marrow, loss of hair, and abnormal liver function. Uracil can inhibit the hematopoietic toxicity, manifested by bone marrow depression, but seems to have no effect on the antifungal activity of 5-FC. The untoward effects of 5-FC have been attributed to conversion to 5-fluorouracil in the body. Nausea, vomiting, and skin rashes occur occasionally. With daily amounts of 6–12 g administered in divided doses, there have been prolonged remissions of fungemia, sepsis, and meningitis caused by susceptible organisms.

HYDROXYSTILBAMIDINE

Hydroxystilbamidine isethionate is an aromatic diamidine active against *Blastomyces dermatitidis* and occasionally against *Nocardia asteroides* in vitro and in vivo. It is administered intravenously in a dosage of 225 mg dissolved in 200 mL of 5% dextrose in water, infused over a 2-hour period once daily. It may be severely toxic for liver and kidneys and has been largely replaced by amphotericin B.

MICONAZOLE

Miconazole, a synthetic imidazole derivative, is an antifungal drug that has long been used as 2% cream in dermatophytosis and in vaginal candidiasis not responding to topical nystatin. Recently miconazole has become available for intravenous use. Up to 3.6 g/d (about 30 mg/kg/d) have been injected intravenously in disseminated candidiasis, coccidioidomycosis, cryptococcosis, paracoccidioidomycosis, blastomycosis, etc. The fungi causing these diseases tend to be inhibited by miconazole, 1–2 μg/mL, in vitro. Serum levels exceeding such concentrations have been achieved, and prolonged remissions have occurred. In meningitis due to these fungi, 10–20 mg/d of miconazole must be given intrathecally or intraventricularly, because little of the drug enters the cerebrospinal fluid from the serum. The relapse rate in fungal meningitis is high. Other imidazoles are being tested as antifungals.

Miconazole produces many significant side-effects, including thrombophlebitis, vomiting, anemia, thrombocytosis, hyponatremia, hyperlipidemia, and, occasionally, leukopenia and hypersensitivity reactions. Miconazole markedly increases the anticoagulant effect of coumarin drugs.

GRISEOFULVIN

Griseofulvin is a substance isolated from *Penicillium griseofulvum* in 1939 and from *Penicillium janczewskii* in 1946. While ineffective against bacteria, it produced shrinking and stunting of fungal hyphae. It was introduced clinically for the treatment of dermatophytoses in 1957.

Chemistry

The structural formula of griseofulvin is shown below.

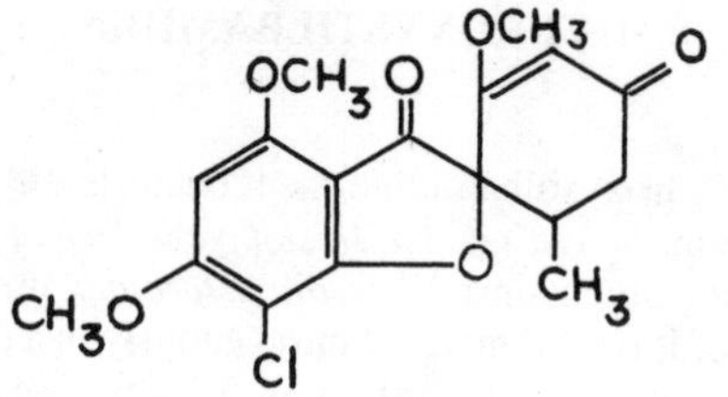

Griseofulvin

The drug is very insoluble in water but quite stable at high temperature, including autoclaving.

Antifungal Activity

Griseofulvin inhibits the growth of dermatophytes, including *Epidermophyton*, *Microsporum*, and *Trichophyton*, in concentrations of $0.5-3$ μg/mL. It has no effect on bacteria, the fungi producing deep mycoses of humans, or certain fungi producing superficial lesions. Resistance can emerge among susceptible dermatophytes.

The mechanism of action has not been established, but it is probable that griseofulvin interferes with nucleic acid synthesis and polymerization. The inhibitory effect may be partially reversed by purines.

Absorption, Metabolism, & Excretion

Absorption of griseofulvin depends greatly on the physical state of the drug and is aided by high-fat foods. Preparations containing microsize particles of the drug are absorbed twice as well as those with larger particles. Microsize griseofulvin, 1 g daily, gives, in adults, blood levels of $0.5-1.5$ μg/mL. Ultramicrosize griseofulvin (Gris-PEG) is absorbed twice as well. The absorbed drug has an affinity for diseased skin and is deposited there, bound to keratin. Thus it makes keratin resistant to fungal growth, and the new growth of hair or nails is freed of infection first. As the keratinized structures are shed, they tend to be replaced by uninfected ones. Little griseofulvin is present in body fluids or tissues. The bulk of ingested griseofulvin is excreted in feces and only a small part in urine.

Clinical Uses

Topical use of griseofulvin has little effect.

The microsize preparations of griseofulvin are given orally, $0.5-1$ g daily, in divided doses ($0.25-0.5$ g for children weighing over 50 lb, or 15 mg/kg/d). An "ultramicrosize" preparation (Gris-PEG) is given in an adult dose of $0.25-0.5$ g. Treatment must be continued for 3–6 weeks if the skin only is involved and for 3–6 months if hair and nails are involved. Griseofulvin is indicated for severe dermatophytosis involving skin, hair, or nails, particularly if caused by *Trichophyton* or *Microsporum*, which respond poorly to other measures. Other topical antifungal drugs may have to be used with griseofulvin.

Griseofulvin may increase the metabolism of coumarin, so that higher doses of the anticoagulant are required. Experimental carcinogenicity has been reported. Phenobarbital reduces absorption of griseofulvin from the gut.

Adverse Reactions

The overall frequency of side-effects is low.

A. Allergic Reactions: Fever, skin rashes, leukopenia, and serum sickness–type reactions occur.

B. Direct Toxicity: Headache, nausea, vomiting, diarrhea, hepatotoxicity, photosensitivity, and mental confusion occur. It is teratogenic and carcinogenic in laboratory animals.

TOPICAL ANTIFUNGAL DRUGS

1. NYSTATIN

Nystatin is a product of *Streptomyces noursei*, described in 1951.

Chemistry

Nystatin is a polyene antibiotic, a very large ring system linked to mycosamine, an amino sugar. The empirical formula is $C_{46}H_{77}NO_{19}$. Nystatin is slightly soluble in water but quickly decomposes in the presence of water or plasma. It is stable in dry form.

Antifungal Activity

Nystatin has no effect on bacteria or protozoa, but in vitro it inhibits many fungi, including *Candida* species, dermatophytes, and organisms producing deep mycoses in humans. In vivo, its action is limited to surfaces where the nonabsorbed drug can be in direct contact with the yeast or mold. Resistance to nystatin does not develop in vivo, but drug-resistant strains of *Candida* species occur.

The mode of action involves binding of nystatin to the cell membrane in the presence of a specific sterol. This results in drastic changes in the permeability of the cell membrane and loss of cations from the cell. Cells that lose the membrane sterol are resistant.

Absorption, Metabolism, & Excretion

Nystatin is not significantly absorbed from skin,

mucous membranes, or the gastrointestinal tract. Virtually all nystatin taken orally is excreted in the feces. There are no significant blood or tissue levels after oral intake.

Clinical Uses

Nystatin can be applied topically to the skin or mucous membranes (buccal, vaginal) in the form of creams, ointments, suppositories, suspensions, or powders for the suppression of local *Candida* infections. Nystatin may be given orally for the suppression of *Candida* in the lumen of the bowel. This may be warranted in very small infants or persons with impaired host defenses (diabetes mellitus, leukemia, high doses of steroids), in whom the possibility of disseminated candidiasis exists. However, the addition of nystatin to oral tetracyclines is of dubious merit.

Nystatin preparations often contain antibacterial drugs.

2. TOLNAFTATE

Tolnaftate—2-naphthyl-N-methyl-N-(3-tolyl)-thionocarbamate—is a topical antifungal drug for use in cream, powder, or solution form in the treatment of dermatophytosis. While *Candida* is resistant, many dermatophytes are suppressed, and clinical efficacy is claimed for treatment courses of 1–10 weeks. With topical application, there appears to be no significant systemic absorption. Toxic and allergic reactions appear to be minimal.

3. CLOTRIMAZOLE

Clotrimazole is a topical antifungal agent which can suppress *Candida* on mucous membranes. It is said to control chronic oral candidiasis when used in the form of buccal troches of 10 mg, 5 times daily. In systemic mycoses, clotrimazole has shown some therapeutic benefit after oral administration of 60–90 mg/kg/d. However, severe gastrointestinal side-effects are common. Clotrimazole is not available for parenteral administration.

4. MICONAZOLE NITRATE

Miconazole nitrate is an imidazole topical antifungal drug (see above), available as 2% cream. It is fungicidal for a majority of common dermatophytes (eg, *Trichophyton, Microsporum, Epidermophyton*) and for *Candida* sp. It appears to be effective in dermatophytosis and is perhaps more effective than nystatin in vaginal candidiasis. Adverse effects of topical application are limited to mucous membrane itching, burning, and some skin rashes.

5. NATAMYCIN

This is a polyene antifungal drug active against many different fungi in vitro. Topical application of 5% ophthalmic suspension can be beneficial in the treatment of keratitis caused by *Fusarium, Cephalosporium*, or other fungi. It is approved for such use but must be combined with appropriate surgical measures.

Natamycin may be effective for oral or vaginal candidiasis. The toxicity after topical application appears to be low.

6. OTHER TOPICAL ANTIFUNGAL DRUGS

Candicidin

Candicidin is a polyene antibiotic proposed solely as a topical drug (in vaginal tablets or ointment) for the treatment of candidal vaginitis. It is not absorbed systemically and produces few toxic effects. Its efficacy is currently being tested.

Fatty Acids

Fatty acids, particularly undecylenic acid and its salts, are effective topical antifungal drugs (see Chapter 58). They are widely useful in tinea pedis and corporis as powders or creams.

Haloprogin

Haloprogin is a topical drug active in vitro against many dermatophytes and in vivo against tinea corporis. It is available as a 1% cream or solution, and 10–20% of the topically applied drug may be absorbed. It occasionally causes local irritation.

●　　●　　●

References

Bennett JE: Chemotherapy of systemic mycosis. (2 parts.) N Engl J Med 290:30, 320, 1974.

Bennett JE: Flucytosine. Ann Intern Med 86:319, 1977.

Bennett JE & others: A comparison of amphotericin B alone and combined with flucytosine in the treatment of cryptococcal meningitis. N Engl J Med 301:126, 1979.

Block ER & others: Flucytosine and amphotericin B: Hemodialysis effects on plasma concentration in man. Ann Intern Med 80:613, 1974.

Burgess JL, Birchall R: Nephrotoxicity of amphotericin B. Am J Med 53:77, 1972.

Chesney PJ & others: Successful treatment of candida meningitis with amphotericin B and 5-fluorocytosine in combination. J Pediatr 89:1017, 1976.

Drutz DJ, Catanzaro A: Coccicioidomycosis. Am Rev Respir Dis 117:727, 1978.

Goldman L: Griseofulvin. Med Clin North Am 54:1339, 1970.

Graybill JR, Levine HB: Successful treatment of cryptococcal meningitis with intraventricular miconazole. Arch Intern Med 138:814, 1978.

Hamilton-Miller JMT: Chemistry and biology of polyene antibiotics. Bacteriol Rev 37:166, 1973.

Hoeprich PD & others: Development of resistance to 5-fluorocytosine in Candida parapsilosis during therapy. J Infect Dis 130:112, 1974.

Kirkpatrick CH, Alling DW: Treatment of oral candidiasis with clotrimazole troches. N Engl J Med 299:1201, 1978.

Koeffler HP, Golde DW: 5-Fluorocytosine: Inhibition of hematopoiesis in vitro and reversal of inhibition by uracil. J Infect Dis 139:438, 1979.

Mandy SJ, Garrott TC: Miconazole treatment for severe dermatoses. JAMA 230:72, 1974.

Medoff G, Kobayashi GS: Amphotericin B. JAMA 232:619, 1975.

Steer PL & others: 5-Fluorocytosine: An oral antifungal compound. Ann Intern Med 76:15, 1972.

Stevens D & others: Miconazole in coccidioidomycosis. Am J Med 60:191, 1976.

Utz JP & others: Therapy of cryptococcosis with a combination of flucytosine and amphotericin B. J Infect Dis 132:368, 1975.

Woods RA & others: Resistance to polyene antibiotics and correlated sterol changes in isolates of Candida tropicalis from a patient with an amphotericin B-resistant funguria. J Infect Dis 129:53, 1974.

Urinary Antiseptics* | 56

Urinary antiseptics are drugs that exert antibacterial activity in the urine but have little or no systemic antibacterial effect. Their usefulness is limited to urinary tract infections. They have no marked antimicrobial activity in the renal parenchyma, but they may have therapeutic usefulness in pyelonephritis—perhaps by preventing ascending reinfection. Prolonged suppression of bacteriuria by means of urinary antiseptics may be desirable in chronic urinary tract infection where eradication of infection by short-term systemic therapy has not been possible.

With indwelling bladder catheters, microorganisms tend to reach the bladder in 2–3 days unless an aseptic closed system is employed. Such a system may also contain acetic acid, 0.25%, or be irrigated with a solution containing polymyxin B, 20 mg/L, and neomycin, 40 mg/L, to prevent ascending infection.

NITROFURANTOIN

Chemistry

Many derivatives of furan possess antibacterial properties. Most of these substances are topical disinfectants (see Chapter 58). Nitrofurantoin is the main urinary antiseptic among nitrofurans.

Nitrofurantoin

Antibacterial Activity

Nitrofurans are bacteriostatic and bactericidal for both gram-positive and gram-negative bacteria in concentrations of 10–500 μg/mL. Although certain strains of microorganisms are resistant (eg, many strains of *Proteus vulgaris* and all strains of *Pseu-*

*The sulfonamides are discussed in Chapter 53.

domonas aeruginosa), resistant mutants are rare in nitrofurantoin susceptible populations. In other words, clinical drug resistance emerges slowly. There is no cross-resistance between nitrofurans and other antimicrobial agents.

The mechanism of action of the nitrofurans is not known. The activity of nitrofurans depends to some extent upon the size of the microbial population. With very high concentrations of bacteria in the urine or in broth, the activity of nitrofurantoin is diminished. The activity of nitrofurantoin is greatly enhanced at pH 5.5 or below.

Absorption, Metabolism, & Excretion

Nitrofurantoin is rapidly and completely absorbed from the gastrointestinal tract, but the absorbed drug is bound so completely to serum protein that no antibacterial effect can be detected in the blood. Nitrofurantoin therefore has no systemic antibacterial activity. In the kidneys, the drug is separated from the carrier protein and excreted in the urine by both glomerular filtration and tubular secretion. Tubular reabsorption occurs, and concentration in hilar lymph is high. Significant nitrofurantoin levels may also be found in interstitial tissue. With average daily doses, concentrations of 200 μg/mL are reached in urine; maximum urine levels may be 300–400 μg/mL. In renal failure, urine levels are insufficient for antibacterial action, but high blood levels may cause toxicity.

Clinical Uses

The average daily dose for urinary tract infection in adults is 400 mg orally in divided doses (5–8 mg/kg/d for children) taken with meals or after eating. Some persons can tolerate up to 600 mg/d, but this higher dose often results in nausea or vomiting. Gastrointestinal disturbance due to nitrofurantoin can be reduced if the drug is taken with food or milk. Nitrofurantoin must never be given to patients with severe renal insufficiency. Oral nitrofurantoin can be given for weeks, months, or even years for the suppression of chronic urinary tract infection. An acidifying agent is desirable to keep urinary pH below 5.5 (see Acidifying Agents, below). Some women are subject to the urethral syndrome or to recurrent manifest urinary tract infection as a result of sexual activity. In many of these cases, daily administration of nitrofurantoin, 100 mg, for months may result in freedom from symptoms and infection.

It is possible to administer the soluble sodium salt of nitrofurantoin intravenously. From 360 to 540 mg are injected daily by continuous infusion for a few days. Even the intravenously injected drug has no systemic antimicrobial activity, but this route reduces severe gastrointestinal disturbances.

Another nitrofuran, furazolidone, 400 mg (5–8 mg/kg in children) daily orally, may reduce diarrhea in cholera and perhaps shorten vibrio excretion. It usually fails in shigellosis.

Adverse Reactions

A. Direct Toxicity: Anorexia, nausea, and vomiting are the principal (and frequent) side-effects of orally administered nitrofurantoin. They occur rarely with intravenous administration. Neuropathies and hemolytic anemias (in G6PD deficiency) are rare.

B. Allergic Reactions: Various skin rashes, pulmonary infiltration, and other hypersensitivity reactions have been reported.

NALIDIXIC ACID & OXOLINIC ACID

These are urinary antiseptics for use in the management of urinary tract infections with gram-negative bacteria. They are effective when taken orally and have no significant systemic activity. Nalidixic acid is the older and better-studied drug.

Chemistry

Nalidixic acid is a synthetic chemical with the formula shown below. It is stable in the dry form and poorly soluble in water. Oxolinic acid is similar.

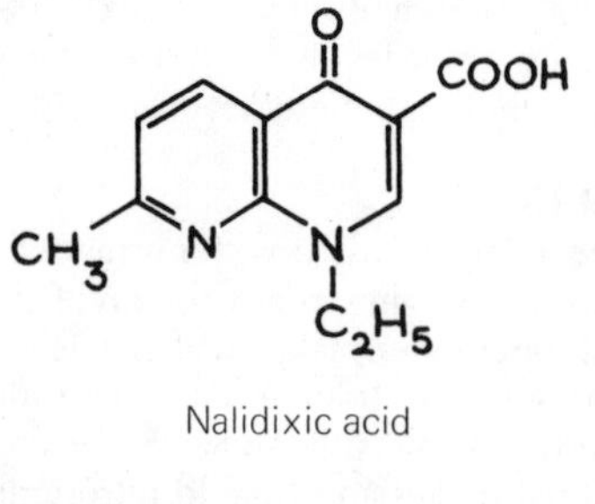

Nalidixic acid

Antibacterial Activity

Nalidixic acid inhibits many gram-negative bacteria in vitro in concentrations of 1–50 μg/mL. Much higher concentrations are necessary to inhibit gram-positive organisms. Most strains of *Escherichia coli* are inhibited, and some strains of *Enterobacter*, *Klebsiella*, and *Proteus*. *Pseudomonas* species are usually resistant.

The mechanism of the chemotherapeutic effect is not entirely clear. Nalidixic acid may lower the pH of the urine sufficiently to result in inhibition of bacteria. Nalidixic acid is also a specific and powerful inhibitor of the DNA synthesis of *E coli* but has little effect on the synthesis of protein or RNA. This inhibition of DNA replication may be the basis of the chemotherapeutic action of this compound.

Resistant microorganisms emerge rapidly during nalidixic acid therapy, both by selection of drug-resistant mutants in the population and by superinfection with drug-resistant microorganisms of another strain or species. Plasmid-mediated resistance to nalidixic acid has not been demonstrated. There is no cross-resistance with other antimicrobial drugs.

Resistance to oxolinic acid can emerge rapidly, as with nalidixic acid.

Absorption, Metabolism, & Excretion

After oral administration, the drug is readily absorbed from the gut. In the blood, virtually all nalidixic acid is firmly bound to protein. Thus, there is no significant systemic antibacterial action. About 20% of the absorbed drug is excreted in the urine in the active form and 80% in an inactive form as a glucuronide conjugate. Levels of active drug in the urine reach 20–250 μg/mL. Increases in concentration above this range result in reduced bactericidal activity.

Clinical Uses

The only indication for these agents is urinary tract infection with coliform organisms. The dose for adults is 1 g orally 4 times daily for 1 week or more. The dose for children is 30–60 mg/kg/d orally in 2–4 divided doses. For prolonged use, the dosage may be reduced.

Adverse Reactions

Nalidixic acid excreted in the urine may give rise to false-positive tests for glucose, but true hyperglycemia and glycosuria may also be produced. There are occasional gastrointestinal disturbances, skin rashes, sensitization to sunlight, visual disturbances, and central nervous system stimulation. Convulsions have been reported following overdosage.

METHENAMINE MANDELATE & METHENAMINE HIPPURATE

Methenamine mandelate is the salt of mandelic acid and methenamine and possesses to some extent the properties of both of these urinary antiseptics. Mandelic acid ($C_6H_5CHOHCOOH$) or hippuric acid taken orally is excreted unchanged in the urine, where these drugs are bactericidal for some gram-negative bacteria if the pH can be kept below 5.5. Methenamine is absorbed readily after oral intake and excreted in the urine. If the urine is strongly acid (pH below 5.5), methenamine releases formaldehyde, which is antibacterial.

Methenamine mandelate, 3–6 g daily orally, or methenamine hippurate, 2–4 g daily orally, are used only as urinary antiseptics. If necessary, acidifying agents (eg, ascorbic acid, 4–12 g daily) may be given to lower urinary pH below 5.5. Sulfonamides cannot be given at the same time because they may form an insoluble compound with the formaldehyde released by methenamine. Persons taking methenamine may exhibit falsely elevated tests for catecholamines.

The action of methenamine mandelate or hippurate is nonspecific against many different microorganisms and consists of the simultaneous effects of formaldehyde and acidity. Microorganisms such as *Proteus* that make a strongly alkaline urine through the release of ammonia from urea usually are insusceptible.

ACIDIFYING AGENTS

In chronic urinary tract infections, eradication of the organisms often fails. It is then important to suppress bacteria for 6–18 months.

Any substance which will produce a urine pH below 5.5 usually inhibits bacterial growth in urine. Ketogenic diets, ammonium chloride, ascorbic acid, mandelic acid, methionine, and hippuric acid (eg, from ingestion of cranberry juice) all can be employed to that end. It is important to check urinary pH frequently and to ascertain by direct microscopic examination that the bacteriuria is actually suppressed. Prolonged suppression (6–18 months) occasionally permits healing of the infection, probably because it blocks the frequent ascending reinfection of the kidneys from the lower tract.

SYSTEMICALLY ACTIVE DRUGS IN URINARY TRACT INFECTION

Many antimicrobial drugs are excreted in the urine in active form. The concentration in urine is often many times higher than the concentration in body fluids or tissues. Effective antibacterial concentrations can therefore be attained in urine with doses too low to be effective in systemic infections. This permits the use of drugs that are relatively toxic. Drugs such as gentamicin, kanamycin, amikacin, or the polymyxins can be administered in doses sufficient to achieve high urine levels without risking significant adverse effects. Even more toxic drugs such as cycloserine (see below) can be administered in a dose of 10–15 mg/kg/d. This produces urine levels sufficient to suppress highly resistant organisms, eg, *Proteus*, with only a moderate risk of serious toxicity. Penicillins in systemic doses

are excreted in the urine to yield concentrations of 100–5000 units/mL. This may be sufficient to suppress not only gram-positive but also many gram-negative bacteria. Ampicillin and carbenicillin are particularly effective against many gram-negative bacteria in the urinary tract unless they are inactivated by high concentrations of β-lactamase in bladder urine.

Soluble sulfonamides (eg, sulfisoxazole, trisulfapyrimidines USP) constitute perhaps the prime choice for initial treatment of urinary tract infection. The dosage (0.5 g 4–6 times daily orally) is substantially smaller than the systemically active amount, yet concentrations in the urine are high. Even better may be the simultaneous use of sulfamethoxazole, 400 mg, with trimethoprim, 80 mg (1 tablet of co-trimoxazole). Four tablets daily is an adequate urinary dose.

Co-trimoxazole also has demonstrated usefulness as a prophylactic drug to be taken by some sexually active women who are subject to recurrent urinary tract infections or the urethral syndrome.

Cycloserine

Cycloserine (D-4-amino-3-isoxazolidinone) is an antibiotic produced by *Streptomyces orchidaceus* in 1955 and later synthesized.

Cycloserine

The substance is water-soluble and very unstable at acid pH. Cycloserine inhibits many microorganisms, including coliforms, *Proteus*, and mycobacteria. The mode of action involves the inhibition of incorporation of D-alanine into mucopeptide of the bacterial cell wall by inhibiting the enzyme alanine racemase. After ingestion of cycloserine, 0.25 g every 6 hours, blood levels reach 20–30 μg/mL—sufficient to inhibit many strains of mycobacteria and gram-negative bacteria. The drug is widely distributed in tissues. Most of the drug is excreted in active form into the urine, where concentrations are sufficiently high to inhibit many organisms causing urinary tract infections.

Cycloserine may produce serious central nervous system toxicity manifested by headaches, tremor, vertigo, acute psychosis, and convulsions. With careful management of oral dosage (below 0.75 g/d), these symptoms can usually be avoided. Cycloserine is occasionally employed for the treatment of tuberculosis or urinary tract infections. The dosage is usually 0.25 g 2–3 times daily by mouth (for children, 20 mg/kg/d). In nocardiosis, cycloserine, 0.25 g 4 times daily with full systemic doses of a sulfonamide, has been occasionally curative.

TOPICAL USE OF ANTIMICROBIAL DRUGS IN THE URINARY TRACT

Indwelling catheterization of the urinary bladder has a high risk of producing urinary tract infection. This risk can be markedly reduced if a closed, sterile collection system is employed with strictest asepsis. This is often combined with the use of an irrigating solution that contains bactericidal concentrations of polymyxins and neomycins, administered by 3-way catheter. Such systems may delay infection with indwelling catheterization for several weeks. They have no place in the treatment of urinary tract infections. Occasionally, amphotericin B, 20 μg/mL, is instilled into the urinary bladder for control of *Candida* infection.

•　•　•

References

Bose W & others: Controlled trial of co-trimoxazole in children with urinary tract infection. Lancet 2:614, 1974.

Crumplin GC, Smith JT: Nalidixic acid: An antibacterial paradox. Antimicrob Agents Chemother 8:251, 1974.

Fang LST & others: Efficacy of single dose and conventional amoxicillin therapy in urinary tract infections localized by the antibody-coated bacteria technic. N Engl J Med 298:413, 1978.

Freeman RB & others: Long-term therapy for chronic bacteriuria in men. Ann Intern Med 83:133, 1974.

Kleeman CR, Hewitt WL, Guze LB: Pyelonephritis. Medicine 39:3, 1960.

Kunin CM: *Detection, Prevention, and Management of Urinary Tract Infections,* 3rd ed. Lea & Febiger, 1979.

Lohr JA & others: Prevention of recurrent urinary tract infections in girls. Pediatrics 59:562, 1977.

Shapera RM, Matsen JM: Oxolinic acid therapy for urinary tract infections in children. Am J Dis Child 131:34, 1977.

Turck M, Anderson KN, Petersdorf RG: Relapse and reinfection in chronic bacteriuria. N Engl J Med 275:70, 1966.

Vosti KL: Recurrent urinary tract infections: Prevention by prophylactic antibiotics after sexual intercourse. JAMA 231:934, 1975.

In many viral infections, replication of the virus reaches a maximum before any clinical symptoms appear. In order to be clinically effective, chemicals that block viral replication must be administered prior to the appearance of disease, ie, as chemoprophylaxis. Some outstanding practical examples (amantadine in influenza A, methisazone in smallpox) are discussed in Chapter 60, Chemoprophylaxis, and also below. In some other viral diseases (eg, herpes simplex keratitis), replication of the agent continues for prolonged periods, and partial inhibition of virus replication may enhance healing. This is the case with idoxuridine and vidarabine in herpetic keratitis.

Only a few clinically applicable agents are available for antiviral therapy, but active research in this area is making some progress. At present, most chemicals that inhibit virus replication also disturb host cell function significantly and therefore are too toxic to be used in chemotherapy.

Inhibitors of viral replication are presented here according to the steps they inhibit in the replicative process. These steps are (1) adsorption, (2) penetration into susceptible cells, (3) synthesis of early (nonstructural) proteins (eg, nucleic acid polymerases), (4) synthesis of nucleic acids (RNA or DNA), (5) synthesis of late (structural) proteins, (6) maturation (assembly) of viral particles, and (7) release from the cell.

INHIBITION OF PENETRATION INTO SUSCEPTIBLE CELLS

Gamma Globulin (See Chapter 61.)

If gamma globulin contains specific antibodies directed against superficial antigens of a given virus, it can interfere with entry of that virus particle into a cell, probably by blocking penetration rather than adsorption. The intramuscular injection of pooled gamma globulin, 0.01–0.1 mL/lb body weight, during the early incubation period can modify infection with the viruses of measles, hepatitis, rabies, poliomyelitis, and possibly other diseases. The protective effect of a gamma globulin injection lasts 2–3 weeks. For infections that have prolonged incubation periods, injec-

tions may have to be given every 2–3 weeks.

It often happens that viral replication is only partially inhibited, so that the development of active immunity may accompany the temporary passive protection conferred by gamma globulin.

Amantadine (Adamantanamine)

Amantadine, a tricyclic symmetric amine, inhibits the penetration into susceptible cells or the uncoating of certain myxoviruses, eg, influenza A (but not influenza B), rubella, and some tumor viruses. It therefore inhibits the replication of these viruses in vitro and in experimental animals. In humans, a daily oral dose of 200 mg of amantadine hydrochloride for 2–3 days before and 6–7 days after influenza A infection reduces the incidence and severity of symptoms and the magnitude of the serologic response. There may also be a slight therapeutic effect if amantadine is started within 18 hours of the onset of symptoms of influenza.

The most marked untoward effects are insomnia, slurred speech, dizziness, ataxia, and other central nervous system signs. Amantadine may accumulate to toxic levels in persons with renal failure.

INHIBITION OF INTRACELLULAR SYNTHESIS

Inhibition of Synthesis of "Early" Proteins

Guanidine and hydroxybenzylbenzimidazole are both capable of inhibiting the replication of certain RNA enteroviruses but not of others. Both substances inhibit the formation of RNA polymerases at concentrations that appear to be harmless to host cells in vitro. Mutants resistant to the action of these compounds are frequent and are rapidly selected out in the presence of the drugs. Therefore, as expected, these compounds do not have significant therapeutic activity in vivo. Trials of biguanidines in RNA virus infections in humans were not encouraging.

Inhibition of Synthesis of Nucleic Acids

Dactinomycin (actinomycin D, Cosmegen) inhibits DNA-dependent RNA synthesis (ie, synthesis of messenger RNA) and thus inhibits the multiplication of DNA viruses. However, the effect is not sufficiently specific to permit its application in vivo, as the drug is severely cytotoxic.

Ribavirin (ribofuranosyl-triazole-carboxamide) can inhibit the replication of both RNA and DNA viruses in experimental models. The compound acts by interfering with guanidine monophosphate formation and subsequent nucleic acid synthesis. A therapeutic action has been noted in some experimental animal virus infections, but the effects in human infections have not been encouraging.

Several **halogenated pyrimidines** can inhibit the replication of DNA viruses because they are analogs of the bases that are DNA building blocks. The incorporation of some pyrimidine analogs results in the formation of nonfunctional DNA and noninfectious virus. Other pyrimidine analogs inhibit specific enzymes. All halogenated pyrimidines with antiviral activity possess marked toxic properties for animal cells and therefore cannot be given systemically without significant adverse effects. However, topical administration is possible and can be used as chemotherapy in special circumstances.

5-Fluorouracil and **5-bromouracil** effectively block the replication of DNA viruses in cell culture systems, but they are relatively ineffective in vivo. **Idoxuridine** (5-iodo-2′-deoxyuridine, IDU, IUDR) can inhibit the replication of most DNA viruses in vitro in cell culture. In vivo it inhibits the replication of herpes simplex virus in the cornea and thus aids in the healing of herpetic keratitis in humans. This is a special circumstance, since herpesvirus proliferates in the avascular corneal epithelium and the topically applied drug remains local and is not rapidly removed by the bloodstream. In the vascular conjunctiva the drug has little therapeutic effect; although adenoviruses are readily inhibited by idoxuridine in vitro, adenovirus conjunctivitis cannot be controlled by idoxuridine in vivo.

For the treatment of herpetic keratitis, idoxuridine is applied to the cornea (every 2 hours around the clock) by instilling 1 drop of a 0.1% aqueous solution into the conjunctival sac. This tends to accelerate spontaneous healing. However, DNA synthesis of host cells is also affected, and some toxic effects on corneal cells are occasionally observed, especially if treatment is continued for more than 10 days. Ointments containing 0.5% idoxuridine have been prepared in order to provide higher drug concentrations. Idoxuridine may induce allergic contact dermatitis.

Most isolates of herpesvirus from untreated cases of herpetic keratitis are strongly inhibited in vitro by idoxuridine, 2 μg/mL. Upon prolonged exposure to idoxuridine in vitro, occasional drug-resistant mutants are selected out that are not inhibited by idoxuridine, 20 μg/mL or more. ''Drug-resistant'' cases of herpetic keratitis occur relatively frequently. Such patients fail to improve with prolonged idoxuridine treatment.

However, many of the virus isolates from such cases appear to be intrinsically susceptible to idoxuridine inhibition in vitro. It is probable that many such strains escape the inhibitory effect of idoxuridine in vivo because they rapidly penetrate into the depth of the corneal stroma and thus become inaccessible to idoxuridine applied to the corneal surface.

In deep herpetic stromal keratitis there is little virus replication in the stroma. Corticosteroids help to reduce the inflammatory response. Idoxuridine is given simultaneously to prevent herpesvirus proliferation in the superficial epithelium.

Vaccinal keratitis responds irregularly to idoxuridine.

In early cases of herpetic encephalitis, the intravenous administration of idoxuridine, 0.3%, was claimed to have curative effects. However, this treatment has been abandoned because of doubtful efficacy and great systemic toxicity. Topically applied idoxuridine has no effect on skin lesions of herpes simplex or zoster, but therapeutic claims are made for idoxuridine in dimethyl sulfoxide or injected by jet gun.

A second purine analog, **cytarabine** (arabinofuranosylcytosine hydrochloride, cytosine arabinoside), also inhibits DNA synthesis and interferes with the replication of DNA viruses. By weight it is about 10 times more effective than idoxuridine, but it is also 10 times more toxic for host cells. Idoxuridine-resistant herpesviruses can be inhibited by cytarabine. Because of its higher toxicity for the cornea, cytarabine has been employed topically only for patients with herpetic keratitis who have failed to respond to idoxuridine. Cytarabine, 0.3–2 mg/kg intravenously as a single daily dose for 5 days, has been used in severe disseminated herpes simplex and in disseminated varicella, but controlled studies have failed to support this use. It did not prove to be effective in treatment of smallpox.

A third purine analog, arabinofuranosyl adenine (adenine arabinoside, **vidarabine**), appears in 1979 to be the least toxic and most effective of the group. It is substantially more active than idoxuridine when used topically as a 3% ointment for suppressing herpetic infections of the cornea. Vidarabine as a 3% ointment is significantly more active against herpesvirus type 1 than type 2. It cannot prevent recurrences but is effective treatment for vaccinial keratitis. The activity of vidarabine is increased by the simultaneous use of an adenosine deaminase inhibitor; normally, vidarabine rapidly loses activity because of deamination. Topical vidarabine has no effect on skin or mucous membrane lesions (including genital lesions) of herpes simplex.

Vidarabine is also currently the most promising analog for systemic administration because of its relatively low toxicity. There are limited effects on bone marrow and on liver and renal function, and immunosuppression appears to be minimal. Doses of 10–15 mg/kg/d intravenously over a 12-hour period result in substantial suppression of clinical systemic herpesvirus activity. In herpetic encephalitis proved by biopsy, use of this systemic treatment for 10 days resulted in a significant reduction in the mortality rate. However, only 40% of the treated survivors were able to resume normal life; the rest suffered from severe neurologic sequelae. The most encouraging results were observed in patients with herpetic encephalitis whose treatment was begun before onset of coma.

Current trials suggest that systemic vidarabine may also be beneficial in neonatal disseminated herpes infection.

Systemic vidarabine can also inhibit the viremia in chronic active hepatitis and can inhibit the dissemination of herpes zoster in immunosuppressed cancer patients. However, prolonged systemic administration of vidarabine may produce more marked adverse gastrointestinal or neurologic side-effects.

Another analog, **trifluorothymidine**, is more effective than idoxuridine in herpetic keratitis and appears to be less toxic, but the cost is high.

Phosphonic acid derivatives can block the synthesis of virus DNA polymerase. Phosphonoacetic acid is effective as an inhibitor of herpesvirus proliferation in vitro and in some experimental systems. Its clinical potential is unknown.

The latest addition to potentially effective antiviral drugs is **acyclovir** (acycloguanosine). By interfering with viral DNA polymerase far more than with host cell polymerase, this drug inhibits DNA synthesis of herpesviruses relatively specifically. In various experimental herpesvirus infections, acyclovir exhibits striking therapeutic efficacy. Preliminary results suggest that it is of low toxicity for humans.

Photodynamic Inactivation

Some viruses can be inactivated if exposed to one of several dyes and irradiated with ordinary white light. Heterotricyclic dyes, eg, neutral red or proflavine, have an affinity for the guanine base portions of DNA and are bound firmly to the DNA of some viruses. Exposure to ordinary white light then leads to inactivation of the virus by producing breaks in the viral DNA.

On this theoretic basis, photodynamic inactivation has been widely applied as topical treatment to skin and mucous membrane lesions caused by herpes simplex. Controlled clinical trials have failed to show a significant benefit from this treatment. There is experimental evidence that photodynamic inactivation may result in neoplastic transformation of cells in vitro and in some animal models. While the risk incurred by treatment of humans is not defined, there is no justification for the use of this method at present.

Interferon

Interferons are a group of glycoproteins produced by cells and capable of inhibiting virus production in tissues. They do so by acting on host cell ribosomes to produce at least 3 cellular enzymes that subsequently block viral reproduction by inhibiting the translation of viral messenger RNA into viral proteins. The 3 known enzymes are a protein kinase, an oligonucleotide synthetase, and an inhibitor of elongation of polypeptide chains. Interferons are host–species specific but not virus-specific—eg, interferon made in chick cells inhibits the synthesis of different viruses in chick but not in mouse or human cells. Inducers of interferon may be viruses, nucleic acids, endotoxins, large polysaccharides, bacteria, synthetic polyanions, and other substances.

In view of the broad range of viruses that are susceptible to interferon inhibition, interferon can be considered a potentially valuable chemotherapeutic agent. Many inducers of **endogenous** interferon (eg, double-stranded RNA, synthetic polymers, small molecules such as tilorone) have been tested for topical application to mucous membranes or for systemic parenteral administration. In general, the results have been less than satisfactory. The amounts of interferon induced (or released) were small, and progressively smaller with daily inducer administration; most inducers have exhibited some type of toxic effect. While harmless and potent inducers of endogenous interferon are being sought, the research emphasis has been to increase production of **exogenous** human interferon on a large scale.

Human interferon is now being produced in milligram quantities, in either pooled blood leukocytes, fibroblasts in culture, or lymphoblastoid cells in culture. In the current literature, interferons are classed as type I if they are induced by virus infection of cultivated cells. Leukocyte interferon and fibroblast interferon, each with somewhat distinct chemical and physiologic characteristics, are type I interferons. Type II interferons (also called ''immune'') are generated by lymphoid cells derived from a host sensitized to a specific antigen when the cells are reexposed to the same antigen in vitro or in vivo. It appears that interferon is one of the immunomodulators released by such lymphoid cells. Its potential usefulness in human neoplasms may rest upon this quality.

Clinical studies have been performed mainly with human leukocyte interferon. If given early, interferon prevented dissemination of herpes zoster in cancer patients, reduced cytomegalovirus shedding after renal transplantation, and prevented reactivation of herpes after trigeminal root section. In chronic active hepatitis, interferon could suppress viremia with hepatitis B virus. Currently, the impression is being explored that interferon might have an adjunctive role in the management of certain neoplasms and might provide effective therapy in rabies and hemorrhagic fevers.

Inhibition of Synthesis of ''Late'' Proteins

A number of different amino acid analogs (eg, **fluorophenylalanine**) inhibit the synthesis of structural proteins for the coats of virus particles. The antibiotic **puromycin** does likewise. However, these inhibitors of protein synthesis show no specificity for the synthesis of virus protein and impair protein synthesis of the host cell to such a degree that they are intensely toxic. Consequently, none of these substances are useful in chemotherapy at present.

In many poxviruses, various **thiosemicarbazones** inhibit virus replication by interfering with the synthesis of a "late" structural protein. As a result, the assembly of normal particles is impaired or blocked. **Methisazone** (N-methylisatin-β-thiosemicarbazone) can block replication of smallpox (variola) virus in humans if administered to contacts within 1–2 days after exposure. Methisazone, 2–4 g orally daily (100 mg/kg/d for children) for 3–4 days, gives striking protection against clinical smallpox, as shown in controlled trials. The availability of methisazone was an important consideration in abolishing smallpox vaccination.

The above application to smallpox is chemoprophylaxis rather than therapy. In addition, the replication of vaccinia virus can be inhibited by methisazone after symptoms have started, eg, in generalized vaccinia or in progressive vaccinia in immunologically deficient individuals. This is a valid form of antiviral chemotherapy restricted to poxviruses only.

Certain sugar analogs can inhibit the synthesis of virus-specific glycoproteins and glycolipids. Thus, 2-deoxy-D-glucose is incorporated into glycoproteins of herpes simplex virus and appears to block the cellular synthesis of major glycosylated polypeptides of herpesvirus. Clinical benefit has been claimed for the topical application of this substance to early lesions of genital herpes in women.

INHIBITION OF MATURATION

The assembly of intact particles can be inhibited by many agents (eg, **5-fluoro-2'-deoxyuridine** [**floxuridine**] or **puromycin**) that induce the synthesis of defective viral constitutents—whether nucleic acids or structural proteins.

Rifampin (see Chapter 52) inhibits DNA-dependent RNA polymerase in bacteria and mammalian cells. It also inhibits poxviruses, but by a different mechanism. Rifampin prevents the assembly of enveloped mature particles. The block apparently occurs during the stage of envelope formation and is reversible upon removal of the drug.

Rifampin has not been used in treatment of human poxvirus infections, but topical application can inhibit human vaccinia lesions.

●   ●   ●

References

Bauer DJ: Clinical experience with the antiviral drug Marboran. Ann NY Acad Sci 130:110, 1965.

Blough HA & others: Successful treatment of human genital herpes infections with 2-deoxy-D-glucose. JAMA 241:2798, 1979.

Cheesman SH & others: Controlled clinical trial of prophylactic human leukocyte interferon in renal transplantation: Effects on cytomegalovirus and herpes simplex virus infections. N Engl J Med 300:1345, 1979.

Greenberg HB & others: The effect of human leukocyte interferon on hepatitis B virus infection in patients with chronic active hepatitis. N Engl J Med 295:517, 1976.

Hirsch MS, Swartz MN: Antiviral agents. (2 parts.) N Engl J Med 302:903, 949, 1980.

Hyndiuk RA & others: Trifluridine in resistant human herpetic keratitis. Arch Ophthalmol 96:1839, 1978.

Jawetz E: Antiviral chemotherapy. In: *Viral Infections: A Clinical Approach*. Drew WL (editor). Davis, 1976.

Johnson KP & others: Herpes simplex encephalitis. Arch Neurol 27:103, 1972.

Juel-Jensen BE & others: Treatment of zoster with idoxuridine in dimethylsulfoxide. Br Med J 4:776, 1970.

Kaufman RH & others: Treatment of genital herpes simplex virus infection with photodynamic inactivation. Am J Obstet Gynecol 132:861, 1978.

Merigan TC & others: Human leukocyte interferon for the treatment of herpes zoster in patients with cancer. N Engl J Med 298:981, 1978.

Meyers MG & others: Failure of neutral-red photodynamic inactivation in recurrent herpes simplex virus infections. N Engl J Med 293:945, 1975.

Nolan DC, Carruthers MM, Lerner AM: *Herpesvirus hominis* encephalitis: Thirteen cases, six treated with idoxuridine. N Engl J Med 282:10, 1970.

Pavan-Langston D, Buchanan RA, Alford CA Jr: *Adenine Arabinoside: An Antiviral Agent*. Ravee Press, 1975.

Pazin GJ & others: Prevention of reactivated herpes simplex infection by human leukocyte interferon after operation on the trigeminal root. N Engl J Med 301:225, 1979.

Pollard RB & others: Effect of vidarabine on chronic hepatitis B infection. JAMA 239:1648, 1978.

Sacks, SL & others: Toxicity of vidarabine. JAMA 241:28, 1979.

Stevens DA & others: Cytosine arabinoside in disseminated zoster. N Engl J Med 289:873, 1973.

Whitley RJ & others: Adenine arabinoside therapy of biopsy-proved herpes simplex encephalitis. N Engl J Med 297:289, 1977.

Whitley RJ & others: Adenine arabinoside therapy of herpes zoster in the immunosuppressed: NIAID collaborative antiviral study. N Engl J Med 294:1193, 1976.

Disinfectants & Antiseptics | 58

The antiseptics and disinfectants differ fundamentally from systemically active chemotherapeutic agents in that they possess little or no selective toxicity. Most of these substances are toxic not only for microbial parasites but for host cells as well. Therefore, they may be used to reduce the microbial population in the inanimate environment, but they can usually be applied only topically, not systemically, to humans.

The terms disinfectants, antiseptics, or germicides have been used interchangeably by some, and the definitions overlap greatly in the literature. The term **disinfectant** often denotes a substance that kills microorganisms in the inanimate environment. The term **antiseptic** often is applied to substances that inhibit bacterial growth both in vitro and in vivo when applied to the surface of living tissue under suitable conditions of contact.

The antibacterial action of antiseptics and disinfectants is largely dependent on concentration, temperature, and time. Very low concentrations may stimulate bacterial growth, higher concentrations may be inhibitory, and still higher concentrations may be bactericidal for certain organisms.

Evaluation of the antiseptics and disinfectants is difficult. Methods of testing are controversial and results are subject to different interpretations. There is a need for effective, nontoxic agents to neutralize disinfectants in vitro. Ideally, disinfectants should be lethal for microorganisms in high dilution, noninjurious to tissues or inanimate substances, inexpensive, stable, nonstaining, odorless, and rapid-acting even in the presence of foreign proteins, exudates, or fibers. No preparation now available combines these characteristics to a high degree.

Many antiseptics and disinfectants were at one time used in medical and surgical practice. Most have now been displaced by chemotherapeutic substances. The 2 remaining areas of use are urinary antiseptics (see Chapter 56) and topical antiseptics. Most topical antiseptics do not aid wound healing but, on the contrary, often impair healing. In general, cleansing of abrasions and superficial wounds by washing with soap and water is far more effective and less damaging than the application of topical antiseptics. Substances applied topically to skin or mucous membranes are absorbed irregularly and often unpredictably. Occlusive dressings with plastic films often greatly enhance absorption. Penetration of drugs through skin epithelium is also greatly influenced by relative humidity and temperature.

A few chemical classes of disinfectants and antiseptics are briefly characterized in the following paragraphs.

Alcohols

Aliphatic alcohols are antimicrobial in varying degree. Ethyl alcohol in 70% concentration is bactericidal in 1–2 minutes at 30 C but less effective at lower and higher concentrations. Ethyl alcohol, 70%, and isopropyl alcohol, 70–90%, are at present the most satisfactory general disinfectants for skin surfaces. They may be useful for sterilizing instruments but have no effect on spores, and better agents are available for this purpose. Aerosols of 70% alcohol with 1 μm size droplets may be the best disinfectants for mechanical respirators.

Propylene glycol and other glycols have been used as vapors to disinfect air. Precise control of humidity is necessary for good antimicrobial action. Glycol vapors are rarely employed at present.

Aldehydes

Formaldehyde in a concentration of 1–10% effectively kills microorganisms and their spores in 1–6 hours. It acts by combining with and precipitating protein. It is too irritating for use on tissues, but it is widely employed as a disinfectant for instruments. Formaldehyde solution USP contains 37% formaldehyde by weight, with methyl alcohol added to prevent polymerization.

Glutaraldehyde as a 2% aqueous alkaline solution (pH 7.5–8.5) serves as a liquid disinfectant for some optical and other instruments and for some valve grafts. It kills viable microorganisms in 10 minutes and spores in 2–3 hours. Contact with tissue must be avoided.

Methenamine taken orally can release formaldehyde into acid urine. It is employed as a urinary disinfectant (see Chapter 56).

Acids

Several inorganic acids have been used for cauterization of tissue. Although they are effective antimicrobial agents, the tissue destruction they cause precludes their use. Benzoic acid, 0.1%, is employed as a food preservative. Esters of benzoic acid are used as antimicrobial preservatives of certain other drugs. Acetic acid, 1%, can be used in surgical dressings as a topical antimicrobial agent; 0.25% acetic acid is a useful antibacterial agent for irrigation of the lower urinary tract. This can also be used with an indwelling catheter and a closed system for urinary drainage. It is particularly active against *Pseudomonas aeruginosa*. Boric acid, 5% in water, or as powder, can be applied to a variety of skin lesions as an antimicrobial agent. However, the toxicity of absorbed boric acid is high, particularly for small children, and its use is not advisable. Salicylic and undecylenic and other fatty acids can serve as fungicides on skin.

Mandelic acid is excreted unchanged in the urine after oral intake; 12 g daily taken orally can lower the pH of urine to 5.0, sufficient to be antibacterial. (See Urinary Antiseptics, Chapter 56.)

Halogens & Halogen-Containing Compounds

A. Iodine: Elemental iodine is an effective germicide. Its mode of action is unknown. A 1:20,000 solution of iodine kills bacteria in 1 minute and spores in 15 minutes, and its tissue toxicity is relatively low. Iodine tincture USP contains 2% iodine and 2.4% sodium iodide in alcohol. It is the most effective disinfectant available for intact skin and should be used to disinfect skin when obtaining blood cultures by venipuncture. Its principal disadvantage is the occasional dermatitis that can occur in hypersensitive individuals. This can be avoided by promptly removing the tincture of iodine with alcohol.

Iodine can be complexed with polyvinylpyrrolidone to yield povidone-iodine NF. This is a water-soluble complex that liberates free iodine in solution (eg, 1% free iodine in 10% solution). It is widely employed as a skin disinfectant, particularly for preoperative skin preparation. It is an effective local antibacterial substance, killing not only vegetative forms but also clostridial spores. Hypersensitivity reactions are infrequent. Povidone-iodine (Betadine) is available in many forms: solution, ointment, aerosol, surgical scrub, shampoo, skin cleanser, vaginal gel, vaginal douche, and individual cotton swabs.

B. Chlorine: Chlorine exerts its antimicrobial action in the form of undissociated hypochlorous acid (HOCl), which is formed when chlorine is dissolved in water at neutral or acid pH. Chlorine concentrations of 0.25 ppm are effectively bactericidal for many microorganisms except mycobacteria, which are 500 times more resistant. Organic matter greatly reduces the antimicrobial activity of chlorine. The amount of chlorine bound by organic matter in an environment (eg, water) and thus not available for antimicrobial activity is called the "chlorine demand." The chlorine demand of relatively pure water is low, so that the addition of 0.5 ppm chlorine is sufficient for disinfection. The chlorine demand of grossly polluted water may be very high, so that 20 ppm or more of chlorine may have to be added for effective bactericidal action.

Chlorine gas causes severe poisoning in concentrations of 1:100,000 or less. It was one of the earliest agents employed in chemical warfare and acts as an intense lung irritant.

Chlorine is used mainly for the disinfection of inanimate objects and particularly for the purification of water. Chlorinated lime forms hypochlorite solution when dissolved. It is a cheap (but unstable) form of chlorine used mainly for disinfection of excreta in the field. Halazone USP is a chloramine employed in tablet form for the sterilization of drinking water. The addition of 4–8 mg halazone per liter will sterilize water in 15–60 minutes unless a large quantity of organic material is present. It may not inactivate cysts of *Entamoeba histolytica*.

Sodium hypochlorite solution, 0.5% NaOCl (diluted sodium hypochlorite [modified Dakin's] solution NF), contains about 0.1 g of available chlorine per 100 mL and can be used as an irrigating fluid for the cleansing and disinfecting of contaminated wounds. Household bleaches containing chlorine can serve as disinfectants for inanimate objects.

Oxidizing Agents

Some antiseptics exert an antimicrobial action because they are oxidizing agents. Most are of no practical importance, and only hydrogen peroxide, sodium perborate, and potassium permanganate are occasionally used.

Hydrogen peroxide solution USP contains 3% H_2O_2 in water. Contact with tissues releases molecular oxygen and there is a brief period of antimicrobial action. There is no penetration of tissues, and the main applications of hydrogen peroxide are as a mouthwash and for the cleansing of wounds. Hydrogen peroxide can probably be used to disinfect smooth glass or plastic contact lenses that are subsequently applied to the eye.

Potassium permanganate USP consists of purple crystals that dissolve in water to give deep purple solutions that stain tissues and clothing brown. A 1:10,000 dilution of potassium permanganate kills many microorganisms in one hour. Higher concentrations are irritating to tissues. The principal use of potassium permanganate solution is in the treatment of weeping skin lesions.

Heavy Metals

A. Mercury: Mercuric ion precipitates protein and inhibits sulfhydryl enzymes. Microorganisms inactivated by mercury can be reactivated by thiols (sulfhydryl compounds). Mercurial antiseptics inhibit the sulfhydryl enzymes of tissue cells as well as those of bacteria. Therefore, most mercury preparations are highly toxic if ingested. Mercury bichloride NF (1:100) can be used as a disinfectant for instruments or unabraded skin.

Yellow mercuric oxide ointment NF contains 1% of insoluble HgO and can be applied to superficial infected skin lesions. Ammoniated mercury ointment USP contains 5% of the active insoluble compound

(HgNH$_2$Cl). It is a skin disinfectant in impetigo.

Some organic mercury compounds are less toxic than the inorganic salts and somewhat more antibacterial. Nitromersol NF, thimerosal NF, and phenylmercuric nitrate NF (1:1000–1:100,000) serve as bacteriostatic antiseptics. They are also used as "preservatives" in various biologic products to reduce the chance of accidental contamination. Merbromin NF (Mercurochrome) is used as a 2% solution that is a feeble antiseptic but stains tissue a brilliant red color. The psychologic effect of this stain has lent support to the (otherwise almost negligible) antiseptic properties of this material.

B. Silver: Silver ion precipitates protein and also interferes with essential metabolic activities of microbial cells. Inorganic silver salts are strongly bactericidal. Silver nitrate, 1:1000, destroys most microorganisms rapidly upon contact. Silver nitrate ophthalmic solution USP contains 1% of the salt, to be instilled into the eyes of newborns to prevent gonococcal ophthalmia. It is effective for this purpose but may cause chemical conjunctivitis by being quite acid; therefore, antibiotic ointment has been used instead at times. Other inorganic silver salts are rarely used for their antimicrobial properties because they are strongly irritating to tissues. In burns, compresses of 0.5% silver nitrate can reduce infection of the burn wound, aid rapid eschar formation, and reduce mortality. If silver nitrate is reduced to nitrite by bacteria in the burn, methemoglobinemia may result. Silver sulfadiazine 1% cream slowly releases sulfadiazine and also silver (see p 572) and effectively suppresses microbial flora in burns. It may have some advantages and causes less pain than mafenide acetate (Sulfamylon) in the treatment of burns, but it has occasionally produced leukopenia.

Colloidal preparations of silver are less injurious to superficial tissues and have significant bacteriostatic properties. Mild silver protein NF contains about 20% silver and can be applied as an antiseptic to mucous membranes. Prolonged use of any silver preparation may result in argyria.

Other Metals

Other metal salts (eg, zinc sulfate, copper sulfate) have significant antimicrobial properties but are rarely employed in medicine at present.

Soaps

Soaps are anionic surface-active agents, usually sodium or potassium salts of various fatty acids. They vary in composition depending on the specific fats or oils and on the particular alkali from which they are made. Since NaOH and KOH are strong bases, whereas most fatty acids are weak acids, most soaps when dissolved in water are strongly alkaline (pH 8.0–10.0). Thus, they may irritate skin, which has a pH of 5.5–6.5. Special soaps (eg, Neutrogena) use triethanolamine as a base and, when dissolved, are near pH 7.0. While most common soaps are well tolerated, excessive use will dry normal skin. Ad-

mixed synthetic fragrances may cause irritation or photosensitization of skin.

Most common soaps remove dirt as well as surface secretions, desquamated epithelium, and bacteria contained in them. The physical action of thorough handwashing with plain soaps is quite effective in removing transient bacteria and other contaminating microorganisms from skin surfaces. For additional antibacterial action, certain disinfectant chemicals (hexachlorophene, phenols, carbanilides, etc) have been added to certain soaps. These chemicals may be both beneficial and potentially harmful and are discussed below.

Phenol & Related Compounds

Phenol denatures protein. It was the first antiseptic employed, as a spray, during surgical procedures by Lister in 1867. Concentrations of at least 1–2% are required for antimicrobial activity, whereas a 5% concentration is strongly irritating to tissues. Therefore, phenol is used mainly for the disinfection of inanimate objects and excreta. Substituted phenols are more effective (and more expensive) as environmental disinfectants. Among them are many proprietary preparations containing cresol and other alkyl-substituted phenols.

Other phenol derivatives such as resorcinol, thymol, and hexylresorcinol have enjoyed some popularity in the past as antiseptics. Several chlorinated phenols are much more active antimicrobial agents.

Hexachlorophene USP is a white crystalline powder which is insoluble in water but soluble in organic solvents, dilute alkalies, and soaps and is an effective bacteriostatic agent. Hexachlorophene liquid soap USP and many proprietary preparations are used widely in surgical scrub routines and as deodorant soaps. Single applications of such preparations are no more effective than plain soaps, but daily use results in a deposit of hexachlorophene on the skin which exerts a prolonged bacteriostatic action. Thus the number of resident skin bacteria is lower on the surgeon's hands if hexachlorophene soap is used daily and if other soaps, which promptly remove the residual hexachlorophene film, are not employed.

Soaps or detergents containing 3% hexachlorophene are effective in delaying or preventing colonization of the newborn's skin with pathogenic staphylococci in hospital nurseries. However, repeated bathing of newborns (and particularly premature infants) with such preparations may permit sufficient absorption of hexachlorophene to result in toxic effects to the nervous system, especially a spongiform degeneration of the white matter in the brain. For this reason, the "routine prophylactic use" of 3% hexachlorophene preparations was discouraged. Stopping the use of hexachlorophene-containing preparations for bathing of newborns has been accompanied by a resurgence of staphylococcal infections in nursery populations.

Other antiseptics have been added to soaps and detergents, eg, carbanilides or salicylanilides. Trichlorcarbanilide now takes the place of hexachlorophenes in several "antiseptic soaps." Regular use of such antiseptic soaps may reduce body odor by preventing bacterial decomposition of organic material in apocrine sweat. All antiseptic soaps may induce allergic reactions or photosensitization.

Chlorhexidine is a bisdiguanide antiseptic employed as a skin cleanser and as a constituent of disinfectant soaps. A 4% solution of chlorhexidine gluconate can be used to cleanse wounds. When incorporated into soaps it is used as an antiseptic handwashing preparation, especially in hospitals and for surgical scrub and preparation of skin sites for operative procedures. Repeated application of chlorhexidine-containing soap results in persistence of the chemical on the skin to give a cumulative antibacterial effect. Chlorhexidine is somewhat less effective against *Pseudomonas* and *Serratia* strains than against coliform and gram-positive organisms.

Gamma benzene hexachloride (Gamene, Kwell) is employed as a 1% lotion, shampoo, or cream to treat scabies, mites, or lice. Usually it is used just twice: It is applied after the skin or hairy areas have been washed with soap and water, and the treatment is repeated one week later. Up to 10% of the chemical may be absorbed from application to the skin, and it may produce toxic effects (skin rashes, blood dyscrasias, or convulsions), especially if ingested accidentally by infants. To prevent reinfestation with mites and lice it is necessary to treat all contacts and wash all clothes of the afflicted individual. When employed in agriculture as lindane, it has given rise to poisoning after inhalation of spray or liquid.

Cationic Surface-Active Agents

Surface-active compounds are widely used as wetting agents and detergents in industry and in the home. They act by altering the energy relationship at interfaces. Cationic surface-active agents are bactericidal, probably by altering the permeability characteristics of the cell membrane. Cationic agents are antagonized by anionic surface-active agents and thus are incompatible with soaps. Cationic agents are also strongly adsorbed onto porous or fibrous materials, eg, rubber or cotton, and are effectively removed by them from solutions.

A variety of cationic surface-active agents are employed as antiseptics for the disinfection of instruments, mucous membranes, and skin, eg, benzalkonium chloride USP (Roccal, Zephiran) and cetylpyridinium chloride NF. Aqueous solutions of 1:1000–1:10,000 exhibit good antimicrobial activity but have some disadvantages. These quaternary ammonium disinfectants are antagonized by soaps, and soaps should not be used on surfaces where the antibacterial activity of quaternary ammonium disinfectants is desired. They are adsorbed onto cotton and thereby removed from solution. When applied to skin, they form a film under which microorganisms can survive. Because of these properties, these substances have given rise to outbreaks of serious infec-

tions due to *Pseudomonas* and other gram-negative bacteria. They cannot be employed safely as skin disinfectants and can only rarely be used as disinfectants of instruments.

Nitrofurans

Many derivatives of furan have antimicrobial properties, especially if a nitro group is in the 5 position of the furan ring. Such compounds are markedly bactericidal for many bacteria in concentrations of 1:20,000 or less. The mechanism of action is not known. Strains of *Pseudomonas* and *Proteus* are often resistant.

Nitrofurantoin USP (Furadantin) is a urinary antiseptic (see Chapter 56). Nitrofurazone NF (Furacin) is used as a topical antimicrobial agent on superficial wounds or skin lesions and as a surgical dressing. The preparations contain about 0.2% of the active drug and do not interfere with wound healing. However, about 5% of patients may become sensitized and may develop reactions, eg, allergic pneumonitis.

Miscellaneous Antiseptics

Lysostaphin, a peptide enzyme, prepared for topical application, can eliminate staphylococci from the nostrils of carriers.

Many synthetic organic dyes have antimicrobial properties. Gentian violet is bacteriostatic and inhibits yeast growth, but it is aesthetically unappealing. Acridine dyes have been used as topical antiseptics in 1:2000 concentration. Methylene blue was formerly used as a urinary antiseptic. Pyridium, an azo dye, was used as a urinary antiseptic although it acts primarily as an analgesic in the bladder. Local anesthetics (eg, procaine, lidocaine) have some inhibitory effect on the growth of bacteria and fungi. Thus, they may interfere with culture of an etiologic agent in specimens from tissues or surfaces exposed to these agents.

Sulfur, in various preparations, is employed as a fungicide and parasiticide for topical use. Many fatty acids, especially propionic and undecylenic acids, are important topical antifungal drugs. Undecylenic acid NF, 5%, and zinc undecylenate NF, 20%, are among the least irritating and most fungistatic drugs available for treatment of dermatophytosis.

STERILIZATION PROCEDURES

It is the purpose of sterilization to make materials free from viable microorganisms, spores, or viruses. This is accomplished commonly by the application of heat under controlled conditions.

Incineration, using controlled burning, is used to dispose of infectious materials. Dry heat (160–170 C for more than 1 hour) is employed to sterilize dry glassware, ceramics, and other materials. Moist heat or autoclaving (121 C for 15 minutes or more at 15 lb/in^2) is used for many instruments, dressings, linens, and bacteriologic media. All of these procedures must be carefully controlled with respect to time, temperature, size of materials, air circulation, displacement of cold air by steam, permeability of packaging materials, and other features that determine the efficacy of the application of heat.

Many materials that must be sterilized do not tolerate high heat, eg, plastics, optical devices, pump oxygenators, and extracorporeal circulation devices. These materials are "gas sterilized" by exposure to **ethylene oxide**, because irradiation is not readily controllable. Ethylene oxide can destroy the viability of microorganisms, probably by the alkylation of sulfhydryl groups of proteins.

Since ethylene oxide is a highly flammable gas, it is usually employed in combination with either 90% CO_2 or fluorinated hydrocarbons. With such a mixture at a temperature of about 50 C and a relative humidity of 50%, about 4–6 hours are required for sterilization. Ethylene oxide rapidly penetrates many types of materials exposed to it in a vacuum, and sterilization is accomplished in 4–12 hours; it then must be removed because it leaves toxic residues, eg, ethylene glycol and ethylene chlorohydrin. For proper ethylene oxide sterilization, materials must be wrapped in cloth, paper, or polyethylene; exposed to the gas for a proper period under controlled temperature; and then evacuated to remove gas and toxic residues and aerated for a prescribed time (often 8–16 hours) before being used.

In most sterilization procedures, indicators of adequate time and temperature exposure and of sterility ("spore strips") must be employed. Careful records are essential and must be kept for years. Chemical indicators for ethylene oxide exposure must be employed.

• • •

References

Aly R, Maibach HI: Comparative study on the antimicrobial effect of 0.5% chlorhexidine gluconate and 70% isopropyl alcohol on the normal flora of hands. Appl Environ Microbiol 37:610, 1979.

Ballin JC: Evaluation of a new topical agent for burn therapy. JAMA 230:1184, 1974.

Block SS: *Disinfection, Sterilization and Preservation*, 2nd ed. Lea & Febiger, 1977.

Cason JS, Lowbury EJL: Mortality and infection in extensively burned patients treated with silver-nitrate compresses. Lancet 1:651, 1968.

Drewett SE & others: Skin distribution of *Clostridium welchii*: Use of iodophor as sporicidal agent. Lancet 1:1172, 1972.

Fraser GL, Beaulieu JT: Leukopenia secondary to sulfadiazine silver. JAMA 241:1928, 1979.

Gezon HM & others: Control of staphylococcal infections in the newborn through the use of hexachlorophene bathing. Pediatrics 51:331, 1973.

Kaslow RA & others: Nosocomial pseudobacteremia: Positive blood cultures due to contaminated benzalkonium antiseptic. JAMA 236:2407, 1976.

Kimbrough RD: Review of evidence of toxic effects of hexachlorophene. Pediatrics 51:391, 1973.

Orkin M & others: Treatment of today's scabies and pediculosis. JAMA 236:1136, 1976.

Perkins JJ: *Principles and Methods of Sterilization in Health Sciences*, 2nd ed. Thomas, 1969.

Reddish GF (editor): *Antiseptics, Disinfectants, Fungicides, and Chemical and Physical Sterilization*. Lea & Febiger, 1957.

59 | Combinations of Antimicrobial Drugs

For 3 decades, physicians have been so justifiably impressed with the efficacy and the relative harmlessness of the antimicrobial drugs that many were tempted to reason that, "If one drug is good, 2 should be better, and 3 should cure almost anybody of almost anything." As a result, multiple antibiotic administration flourished. About one-fifth of all patients admitted to hospitals in the USA receive an antibiotic, and about half of these are given 2 or more antimicrobial drugs simultaneously. The use of fixed drug combinations has been promoted by the pharmaceutical industry vigorously and at times unscrupulously.

The indiscriminate use of antimicrobial drugs has several important disadvantages (see Chapter 48). The use of combinations has obvious additional drawbacks. Among them are the increase in adverse reactions and in sensitization to several drugs simultaneously, and the temptations they offer to relax efforts to arrive at an accurate diagnosis promptly. The problems of antibiotic abuse are discussed in Chapter 48. It is the purpose of this chapter to review some basic features of combined antimicrobial drugs.

POSSIBLE INDICATIONS FOR COMBINED ANTIMICROBIAL DRUGS

The possible reasons for employing 2 or more drugs simultaneously instead of a single drug are as follows:

(1) In certain desperately ill patients with suspected infections of unknown etiology it might be desirable to administer more than one antimicrobial drug immediately in an effort to "cover" the most likely pathogenic organisms. Before such treatment is begun it is essential to take appropriate samples so that laboratory tests can be performed to establish an etiologic diagnosis. The drugs are aimed at the organisms most likely to cause the clinical picture observed, and they are administered only until the establishment of an etiologic diagnosis permits specific therapy. Thus, in suspected septicemia, an antistaphylococcal drug (eg, nafcillin) might be combined with a drug aimed at gram-negative rods (gentamicin, tobramycin, or amikacin) until blood cultures yield a specific microorganism.

(2) In mixed infections it is possible that 2 or more drugs, each acting on a separate portion of a complex microbial flora, may be more effective than one. This applies occasionally to infections of skin, particularly when poorly absorbed antibacterial drugs with narrow spectra are used topically (eg, polymyxin, neomycin, bacitracin). It applies to infections of the peritoneum following perforation of a viscus, in which both anaerobic (bacteroides) and aerobic gram-negative organisms usually participate. Clindamycin (for bacteroides) is sometimes combined with an aminoglycoside (for gram-negative enteric rods). It may at times apply also to mixed systemic infections, particularly of the cardiovascular system, the respiratory tract, or the urinary tract.

(3) In some clinical situations the rapid emergence of bacteria resistant to one drug may impair the chances for cure. The addition of a second drug sometimes delays the emergence of that resistance. This effect has been demonstrated unequivocally in tuberculosis and is the basis for the frequent use of combinations of isoniazid, ethambutol, rifampin, or other drugs. It may apply to other chronic infections, eg, systemic involvement or meningitis due to *Candida*, *Cryptococcus*, or *Torulopsis*. Flucytosine, 150 mg/kg/d, is effective but permits the rapid emergence of resistance. This can be greatly delayed or prevented by the simultaneous use of amphotericin B in low doses (eg, 0.3 mg/kg/d), thus extending the period of useful chemotherapy that may lead to cure. This is one reason for sometimes giving carbenicillin together with gentamicin in *Pseudomonas* sepsis.

(4) The simultaneous use of 2 drugs may at times achieve an effect not obtainable by either drug alone. One drug enhances the antibacterial activity of the second drug against a specific microorganism. Such an effect could be considered "synergism," a term which has been much abused. Unfortunately, such "synergism" is unpredictable: A given combination of drugs must be specifically tailored, by laboratory test, to fit a certain isolate of a given microorganism. A synopsis of the dynamics of combined antibiotic action is given below. One of the best established examples of "synergism" is the cure of bacterial endocarditis caused by enterococci (*Streptococcus faecalis*) by a combination of a penicillin with an aminoglycoside, as

compared to the frequent treatment failure with a penicillin alone.

(5) Drug combinations may occasionally reduce the incidence or intensity of adverse reactions. A given microorganism may be susceptible to each of 2 drugs, but only in dosages which are likely to cause severe adverse reactions. If the drugs are used simultaneously, each can be used in half the dosage—below the threshold of adverse reaction. For example, a *Pseudomonas* strain might be inhibited by polymyxin, 5 μg/mL, or chloramphenicol, 30 μg/mL, used singly, or by a combination of polymyxin, 2 μg/mL, and chloramphenicol, 15 μg/mL. The latter levels can be achieved by reasonably well tolerated doses of each drug, whereas a dose of polymyxin sufficient to yield blood levels of 5 μg/mL will give rise to severe adverse effects.

PROBLEMS IN DEFINING & MEASURING COMBINED ANTIMICROBIAL DRUG EFFECTS

Even when technically feasible, chemical estimates of antimicrobial drug concentration usually do not mirror the antibacterial activity. Direct evaluation of bacteriostatic or bactericidal activity is the only meaningful way of measuring the effects of these drugs. Several methods can be employed, and all may be applicable to the measurement of combined drug action.

(1) **Bacteriostatic effect:** Endpoints are expressed as the minimum amount of drug necessary to suppress visible growth for a given time.

(2) **Bactericidal effect as shown by the rate of killing:** Results are expressed as the bactericidal rate, ie, the slope of the plot of viable survivors at various time intervals.

(3) **Bactericidal effect as shown by the completeness of killing:** The results are expressed as the smallest concentration of drug resulting in a given number of viable survivors in a given time.

(4) **Curative effect as shown in therapeutic trials in vivo.**

The results of any one type of examination need not coincide with those of any other type because the different methods may measure different events in the test system. For example, drug A may be markedly inhibitory but only slightly bactericidal in a certain concentration against a given organism. Drug B may have a slow early bactericidal rate but may kill completely at the end of 24 or 48 hours. One result is not necessarily "better" than another. The test may have to be fitted, by experience, to the clinical problems. Even within a given test system the results may depend on concentration of drugs, duration of action, etc, and on the importance attached to a given event. An example, applied to the measurement of combined antibiotic action, is shown in Fig 59–1.

It is evident that at time I fewer bacteria have survived exposure to drug A than to the combination of A + B. Thus, the early bactericidal effect of A + B is less than that of A alone, an example of antibiotic antagonism. At time II, however, there are fewer survivors of A + B than of A alone—perhaps an additive effect. The interpretation of such test results obviously depends on the importance attached to early bactericidal action and to completeness of killing, respectively.

DYNAMICS OF COMBINED ANTIBIOTIC ACTION

Often, the interaction of 2 antimicrobial drugs is judged from the plot of drug activity in an isobologram (Fig 59–2). From the results of measurements (according to any of the methods described in ¶¶ 1–4 above)

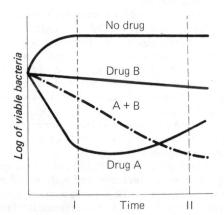

Figure 59–1. Number of viable bacteria after various times of exposure to a single drug or a combination of drugs.

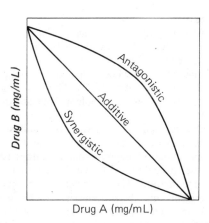

Figure 59–2. Isobologram showing the interaction of 2 antimicrobial drugs.

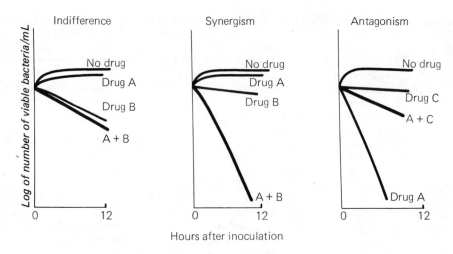

Figure 59–3. Types of combined action of antimicrobial drugs.

with different doses of each drug alone and in combination acting on a given microbial population, it can be determined whether the drugs are additive, synergistic, or antagonistic. These terms can be applied to bacteriostatic or curative effects as well as to bactericidal effects. Bactericidal action in vitro and in vivo is important, and the 3 main results which are observed are illustrated in Fig 59–3.

Indifference or Additive Effect

The most common result is indifference. The combined effect of drugs A and B is equal to that of the single more active component of the mixture A + B, or it is equal to the arithmetic sum of the effects of the individual drugs in their chosen doses. The same total effect could be obtained by the use of a single drug in a dose equivalent to that of the mixture. Undoubtedly, the use of drug mixtures by physicians most often belongs in this category. (It must also be recognized, however, that the simultaneous use of 2 drugs in the "indifferent" category may be justified for one of the reasons given above.)

Synergism

At times the simultaneous action of 2 drugs results in an effect (A + B) which is far greater than that of either A alone or B alone in much larger dosages and also greater than could be expected from simple addition of individual drug effects. The measurement of such an event presents problems that are discussed above.

One type of "synergism" is manifested by a striking increase in rate of bactericidal action of the drug combination beyond that accomplished with twice the concentration of each single drug participating in the mixture. The characteristics of this type of "synergism" may be summarized briefly here:

When such "synergism" is found for a given pair of drugs acting on a given microorganism, it usually extends over a fairly wide range of concentrations of each member of the drug pair and is not greatly influenced by the proportion in the mixture. Conditions must be suitable for the organism to multiply in order to demonstrate "synergism." Only one member of the drug pair need exhibit inhibitory activity in the concentration employed in the mixture; the other may appear to be ineffective by itself.

In at least 3 types of antimicrobial synergism, the mechanism is fairly well understood (see Chapter 47):

(1) Blocking successive steps in metabolic sequence: *Example:* Sulfonamide + trimethoprim. Sulfonamides compete with para-aminobenzoic acid, which is required by some bacteria for the synthesis of dihydrofolate. Folate antagonists such as trimethoprim inhibit the enzyme (dihydrofolic acid reductase) that reduces dihydrofolate to tetrahyhydrofolate. Trimethoprim inhibits the enzyme of bacteria 10^4 times more efficiently than the same enzyme of mammalian cells. The simultaneous presence of a sulfonamide and trimethoprim results in the simultaneous block of sequential steps leading to the synthesis of purines and nucleic acid and can result in a much more complete inhibition of growth than either component of the mixture alone.

(2) One drug inhibits an enzyme that can destroy the second drug: The best example of this mechanism is the binding of β-lactamase by clavulanic acid or other substances. Organisms that produce β-lactamase are resistant to the action of penicillin G because the drug is hydrolyzed by the β-lactamase. However, if the β-lactamase is bound (by clavulanic acid, methicillin, or cloxacillin), the penicillin G is protected and can inhibit or kill the microorganism. This mechanism is attractive but has not yet reached the level of practical therapy.

(3) One drug promotes the entry of a second drug through the microbial cell wall or cell membrane: This appears to be a widely applicable mechanism of synergism of considerable clinical importance. *Examples:* (a) Many streptococci exhibit a relative permeability barrier to aminoglycosides. If a cell wall inhibitory drug is also present, it enhances the penetration of the aminoglycoside, which then acts on ribosomes and kills the cell. Enterococci (*Streptococcus faecalis*) tend to be inhibited by penicillin G but are not killed by it. Aminoglycosides by themselves have virtually no action on streptococci. However, if a penicillin and an aminoglycoside are present together, the penicillin markedly enhances the entry of the aminoglycoside and (if the ribosomes are susceptible to that aminoglycoside) rapid killing results. This occurs with some viridans streptococci, group B streptococci, and group D enterococci. Combined therapy permits cure of sepsis or endocarditis caused by these organisms, whereas each drug alone fails. At times, vancomycin plus an aminoglycoside has a synergistic effect on enterococci or staphylococci. However, cephalosporins cannot be substituted for penicillins in this combined action—perhaps because they do not achieve sufficient concentrations in endocardial vegetations. In sepsis due to many gram-negative drug-resistant bacteria, carbenicillin or ticarcillin may enhance the entry of an aminoglycoside in a synergistic manner. This has been shown particularly for *Pseudomonas* and *Enterobacter* infections.

Cell membrane–active drugs may enhance transport into microbial cells. Thus, polymyxins may facilitate the entry of sulfonamides or rifampin into *Serratia* and markedly enhance the antibacterial effect. Amphotericin B may enhance the entry of flucytosine into fungal cells, and the resulting synergism may permit cure of cryptococcal meningitis not responsive to either drug alone.

Clinical evidence for "synergism": No fixed drug combination regularly results in desirable "synergism." To obtain a "synergistic" combination for use in treating a given patient with an infection, the drugs have to be fitted specifically to the organism isolated from the infection. The best clinical evidence for antibiotic synergism comes from the treatment of bacterial endocarditis, a disease that can be cured only if the infecting organisms are eradicated by bactericidal drugs. The bactericidal action of penicillin on many viridans streptococci is enhanced and accelerated in vitro by the simultaneous presence of an aminoglycoside. Combined treatment with penicillin for 3 weeks and an aminoglycoside for half that period may be optimal for *Streptococcus viridans* endocarditis. Endocarditis caused by enterococci (*S faecalis*) can usually not be cured by penicillin alone, since penicillin is inhibitory but not bactericidal for enterococci. The addition of an aminoglycoside is strikingly bactericidal for many strains of enterococci, and the cure of many such patients with a combination of penicillin or ampicillin with an aminoglycoside is an accepted example of clinical "synergism." Some patients with endocarditis or sepsis caused by β-lactamase–producing staphylococci are cured by drug combinations specifically selected in vitro for their "synergistic" activity. In sepsis caused by gram-negative bacteria, drug pairs specifically selected in the laboratory provided "synergistic" effects in the patient as described above.

There is good clinical evidence from controlled trials that in cryptococcal meningitis, amphotericin B plus flucytosine is superior to either drug alone. Other examples can be found: sulfonamide + minocycline in some nocardioses; penicillin G + tobramycin in some listerioses. However, in each instance, the synergistic effect needs to be established by laboratory studies.

Antagonism

At times the addition of a second drug (C) actually diminishes the antibacterial effectiveness of the first drug (A) (Fig 59–3). This "antagonism" can be manifested by a decrease in the inhibitory activity or in the early bactericidal rate of a drug mixture below that of one or both of its components. Such "antagonism" exhibits the following characteristics.

Antagonism can be demonstrated only when the drugs act on organisms capable of multiplication. Antagonism is most marked when a barely active amount of a bacteriostatic drug is added to a minimal bactericidal amount of a second drug. The bacteriostatic drug (tetracycline, chloramphenicol, erythromycin, etc) acts as an inhibitor of protein synthesis; the bactericidal drug (a penicillin, cephalosporin, or aminoglycoside) seems to require active protein synthesis to exhibit its bactericidal action. In the case of cell wall–active drugs, it has been suggested that the inhibition of protein synthesis by chloramphenicol or tetracycline interferes with the autolytic enzyme system postulated to be an important final step in cell lysis.

Antagonism is obscured by a large excess of either one of the participating agents. Antagonism is limited also by time relationships. The interfering agent must act either before or simultaneously with the bactericidal drug—not after. Antagonism is manifested most readily in clinical situations where host defenses alone are incapable of controlling the infection and where bactericidal drug action is a prerequisite for cure.

Clinical evidence for antimicrobial drug "antagonism": Antagonism is sharply limited by time-dose relationships in vitro and in vivo. It is readily demonstrated with single dose treatment of animal infections but only with difficulty in multiple dose treatment, where the ever-changing blood and tissue levels make it unlikely that the stringent requirements for antagonism will be met. In clinical practice it is usual to give a large excess of antimicrobial drug in multiple doses. Consequently, antagonism cannot be expected to be a frequent outcome of clinical antimicrobial therapy.

There are few documented examples of clinical antagonism. The combination of penicillin and chlortetracycline cured fewer patients with pneumococcal meningitis than did the same dose of penicillin alone. Similarly, the addition of chloramphenicol to ampicillin resulted in more treatment failures in bacterial meningitis than did ampicillin alone. In urinary tract infections caused by gram-negative rods, antagonistic drug combinations failed to eradicate the causative organisms, whereas synergistic drug combinations succeeded. In all of these instances the observed antagonism fitted into the concepts outlined above. The strict time-dose requirements for the demonstration of antagonism make its observation difficult and suggest that it plays only a minor role in determining the end result of treatment in most infections.

THE SELECTION OF DRUG COMBINATIONS IN CLINICAL PRACTICE

As described above, combined drug action is a specific effect of a given drug combination for a given microorganism. It is completely misleading to describe a given drug pair as "synergistic" without specifying a given microorganism. Thus, desirable drug combinations have to be selected for each strain by appropriate laboratory methods. However, a few general guidelines can be formulated to serve as a basis for initial drug selection and for laboratory testing.

The need for combinations of drugs is most notable in the treatment of immunosuppressed patients receiving antineoplastic chemotherapy. Such persons are specifically susceptible to opportunistic infections when the count of polymorphonuclear cells falls below 1000 per microliter of circulating blood. Septicemia in such circumstances arises insidiously but progresses rapidly to death. If the lives of such persons are to be prolonged, a given episode of infection (usually of gram-negative rod sepsis) must be treated promptly and intensively. Commonly, a cell wall inhibitory drug (eg, a penicillin) is combined with the latest aminoglycoside available, one to which widespread resistance has not yet developed. The cell wall inhibitory drug both acts against hypothetical gram-positive invaders and facilitates the entry of aminoglycosides into the cells of gram-negative opportunistic microorganisms. This approach has the double aim of treating mixed infection and of providing hypothetical synergism.

It is acknowledged that most anaerobic infections of body cavities (eg, pelvis, abdomen) following perforation of a viscus are caused by mixtures of anaerobes and gram-negative aerobic enteric bacteria. Enterococci participate only to a minor extent. Initial treatment is directed at the most likely organisms: clindamycin or chloramphenicol against *Bacteroides fragilis*, and gentamicin, tobramycin, or amikacin against enteric aerobic bacteria. Thus, the best drugs available at a given time are aimed against the most likely participants in the mixed infection.

In other situations, the need for combinations of antimicrobial drugs arises infrequently. Apart from enterococcal endocarditis, infections with gram-negative rods, tuberculosis, and fungi are the most likely candidates for combined antimicrobial therapy. In contrast, most staphylococcal infections can be handled well with the β-lactamase–resistant penicillins, and *Brucella, Klebsiella,* and *Pasteurella* infections often respond as well to single drugs as to combinations. Above all, the indiscriminate use of drug combinations must never take the place of proper diagnosis or specifically directed antimicrobial therapy.

Whenever drug combinations are employed and a clinical microbial isolate is available, it is highly desirable to establish the adequacy of drug levels in serum by performing bactericidal assays of serum against the isolate in vitro.

● ● ●

References

Bennett JE & others: A comparison of amphotericin alone and combined with flucytosine in the treatment of cryptococcal meningitis. N Engl J Med 301:126, 1979.

Durack DT & others: Chemotherapy of experimental streptococcal endocarditis: Synergism between penicillin and streptomycin against penicillin-sensitive streptococci. J Clin Invest 53:829, 1974.

EORTC International Antimicrobial Therapy Project Group: Three antibiotic regimens in the treatment of infection in febrile granulocytopenic patients with cancer. J Infect Dis 137:14, 1978.

Fass RJ & others: Clindamycin and gentamicin for aerobic and anaerobic sepsis. Arch Intern Med 137:28, 1977.

Jackson RT & others: Sodium clavulanate potentiation of cephalosporin activity against clinical isolates of cephalothin-resistant *Klebsiella pneumoniae*. Antimicrob Agents Chemother 14:118, 1975.

Jawetz E: Synergism and antagonism among antimicrobial drugs: A personal perspective. West J Med 123:87, 1975.

Klastersky J & others: Gram-negative infections in cancer: Study of empiric therapy comparing carbenicillin-cephalothin with and without gentamicin. JAMA 227:45, 1974.

Krogstad DJ & others: Plasmid-mediated resistance to antibiotic synergism in enterococci. J Clin Invest 61:1645, 1978.

Lindberg J & others: Long term outcome of *Haemophilus influenzae* meningitis related to antibiotic treatment. Pediatrics 60:1, 1977.

Moellering RC & others: Studies on antibiotic synergism against enterococci. J Lab Clin Med 77:821, 1971 (part 1). J Clin Invest 50:2580, 1971 (part 2).

Ostenson RC & others: Polymyxin B and rifampin: New regimen for multiresistant *Serratia marcescens* infections. Antimicrob Agents Chemother 12:655, 1977.

Rahal JJ: Antibiotic combinations: The clinical relevance of synergy and antagonism. Medicine 57:179, 1978.

Sande MA, Overton JW: In vivo antagonism between gentamicin and chloramphenicol in neutropenic mice. J Infect Dis 128:247, 1973.

Saravolatz LD & others: *Staphylococcus aureus* endocarditis: Combined therapy with vancomycin and rifampin. JAMA 240:1963, 1978.

Schauf V & others: Antibiotic killing kinetics of group B streptococci. J Pediatr 89:194, 1976.

Anti-infective chemoprophylaxis is the administration of drugs to prevent the acquisition and establishment of pathogenic microorganisms. In a broader sense, it also includes the use of drugs soon after the acquisition of pathogenic microorganisms but before the development of symptoms and disease.

The administration of one or several antimicrobial agents cannot remove all microorganisms or keep away the entire "microbial world." The useful effect of chemoprophylaxis is limited to the action of a specific drug against a specific microorganism. Thus, only sharply "aimed" chemoprophylaxis can be effective. An effort to prevent all types of microorganisms in the environment from establishing themselves invariably fails and only selects the most drug-resistant organism as the cause of the resulting infection. In all forms of proposed prophylaxis, the risk of the patient's acquiring an infection must be weighed against the toxicity, cost, and inconvenience of the proposed prophylactic drug.

ANTIBACTERIAL & ANTIRICKETTSIAL CHEMOPROPHYLAXIS

SPECIFIC PROPHYLAXIS IN PERSONS OF NORMAL SUSCEPTIBILITY EXPOSED TO A SPECIFIC PATHOGEN

The outstanding examples of this type of chemoprophylaxis are the prevention of streptococcal, meningococcal, and gonococcal infections in both military and civilian populations. Syphilis, plague, malaria, and the rickettsioses will also be considered here.

Streptococci

Group A *Streptococcus* infections may produce

---

*Antiviral prophylaxis is discussed in Chapter 57; antiparasitic prophylaxis in Chapters 62 and 63.

acute illness, suppurative complications, and late nonsuppurative complications such as rheumatic fever or glomerulonephritis. Prevention of primary infection can prevent illness or complications. Treatment of established infection with group A beta-hemolytic streptococci can prevent nonsuppurative complications if the responsible streptococcal antigens are eliminated quickly and completely. Prevention of reinfection with any type of group A streptococci in persons with a past history of rheumatic fever may prevent exacerbations of the latter and development of rheumatic heart disease. Because of the small number of nephritogenic types and the existence of type-specific postinfectious immunity, prevention of reinfection with streptococci is not indicated in nephritis.

Sulfonamides were first employed on a large scale in military populations to prevent streptococcal infections. This was effective for only a short time because of the rapid emergence and selection of sulfonamide-resistant streptococci. Subsequently, penicillin was introduced for mass prophylaxis in military populations, and it has maintained its efficacy: no penicillin-resistant strains of group A beta-hemolytic streptococci have emerged to date. At present, the preferred method is the intramuscular injection of benzathine penicillin G, 1.2 million units, once each month.

Reinfection with streptococci in rheumatic patients can be prevented with benzathine penicillin G, 1.2–2.4 million units intramuscularly every 3–4 weeks; with oral penicillin, 250,000 units twice daily; or (less certainly) with sulfonamides, eg, sulfadiazine, 1 g orally daily on arising. The optimal duration of such prophylaxis in rheumatic subjects has not been established. Some authorities believe that in rheumatic children it should be continued for at least 5 years after a rheumatic attack, and perhaps indefinitely. With advancing age, the chance of a damaging reactivation of rheumatic activity diminishes; therefore, the duration of prophylaxis may be shortened. There must be continuous reassessment of this question. Children on continuous penicillin prophylaxis for rheumatic fever regularly carry penicillin-resistant normal flora in their respiratory tract.

Nonsuppurative poststreptococcal complications can be prevented by the prompt eradication of the infecting streptococci from the respiratory tract. Drugs that suppress streptococcal growth but do not kill them (eg, sulfonamides or tetracyclines) should *never* be used in spite of the apparent clinical improvement they produce in streptococcal sore throat. The treatment of choice is benzathine penicillin G, 1.2 million units (600,000 units for children under 10 years) given intramuscularly once. If procaine penicillin G or other salts are used, repeated intramuscular or oral doses must be given to maintain adequate penicillin levels for 10 days. If such eradication of streptococci begins within 5–8 days after the onset of infection, poststreptococcal complications can be prevented. If eradication of streptococci is started later, it is significantly less effective. Penicillin administration in established acute rheumatic fever does not prevent valvular heart disease.

As an alternative to penicillin, erythromycin may be used.

Many streptococcal infections are asymptomatic. The continuous prophylaxis used in rheumatic subjects is directed largely (and effectively) at subclinical infections. Among nonrheumatics, this is not feasible. However, the attack rate of rheumatic fever is about 3% following symptomatic clinical streptococcal infections and only about 0.3% following asymptomatic or very mild streptococcal infections. The attack rate is somewhat proportionate to the severity of the attack preceding the poststreptococcal complication. Thus, early treatment of symptomatic infections will have a major prophylactic effect. The attack rate of acute glomerulonephritis among children with mild or asymptomatic streptococcal infection is near 0.17%.

Neonatal infection with group B streptococci can probably be prevented either by giving ampicillin intrapartum to the mother—preventing transmission—or by injecting the neonate with penicillin G—preventing their colonization.

Meningococci

Meningococcal infections are a particularly severe problem in closed population groups such as military units. In such groups, there is a high exchange of respiratory microbial flora and establishment of a high carrier rate of pathogenic meningococci. This in turn is followed by a rise in the incidence of meningococcemia and meningitis.

After World War II, the administration of sulfadiazine, 3 g orally daily for 3 days, effectively reduced the carrier rate in military units and eliminated meningitis because virtually all meningococci were sulfonamide-sensitive. Since 1963, sulfonamide-resistant meningococci of groups A, B, and C have produced repeated outbreaks in military groups and in civilian populations. Consequently, sulfonamide prophylaxis lost much of its previous effectiveness. All known meningococci remain susceptible to penicillin G to date. Aqueous penicillin G, 20 million units (12 g) daily, can cure infection with sulfonamide-resistant meningococci. However, short-term penicillin administration does not usually eradicate the carrier state. Since very close household contacts or close medical contacts are significantly more at risk of acquiring

meningococci from patients, prophylaxis is indicated in such instances.

Rifampin, 600 mg orally twice daily for 2 days, can eliminate streptococci from 90% of carriers, but in the remaining ones the streptococci are rifampin-resistant. Minocycline, 100 mg orally every 12 hours for 5 days, can also eliminate the carrier state in most persons. However, minocycline in this dosage may induce major vestibular disturbances.

Gonococci

Gonococcal infection occurs principally after one of 2 types of contact: the passage of the fetus through the mother's infected cervix, and sexual contact. Infection resulting from either type of exposure can be prevented with drugs because of the superficial location of the infecting organisms and their susceptibility to drugs.

Ophthalmia neonatorum is prevented by instilling a bactericidal substance into the conjunctival sac of the newborn immediately after delivery. In many countries, 1% silver nitrate is prescribed by law for this purpose. This is effective.

The implantation of gonococci in the mucous membranes of adult genitalia can be prevented by the presence of sufficient tissue levels of penicillin. Two tablets of 800,000 units penicillin G taken 1–2 hours before or after sexual contact can provide tissue levels sufficient to kill the limited number of gonococci acquired during contact in some instances. However, the rising resistance of gonococci to penicillin makes it less likely that such prophylaxis will succeed, and the widespread "prophylactic" use of penicillins by the most sexually promiscuous individuals has contributed to the maintenance of high levels of β-lactamase-producing gonococci in selected areas (Philippines and West Africa). A single dose of minocycline, 200 mg orally, after sexual intercourse with prostitutes in these areas resulted in moderately successful prophylaxis of gonorrhea in exposed men but led to the selection of the most highly tetracycline-resistant gonococci.

Penicillin prophylaxis of gonorrhea may have an effect on the acquisition of syphilis. Multiplication of *Treponema pallidum* may be inhibited by antigonorrheal prophylaxis, so that the development of clinical syphilis is masked. Prolonged follow-up (serology) is therefore necessary to rule out subclinical syphilitic infection.

Syphilis

Syphilis can be prevented by chemoprophylaxis. The administration of therapeutic doses of benzathine penicillin G (2.4 million units intramuscularly) within 24 hours of exposure has a good chance of preventing or aborting infection. Because of the risk of subclinical infection in spite of chemoprophylaxis, prolonged follow-up is mandatory, with serologic tests on blood and spinal fluid.

Plague

Plague is an extremely serious epidemic threat

when primary cases of human pneumonic plague have occurred. Under such circumstances, the administration of tetracyclines to the entire exposed population (tetracycline hydrochloride, 1 g/d for 4 days) has successfully controlled outbreaks.

Rickettsioses

Certain rickettsial infections (eg, scrub typhus) are not always amenable to vector control (eg, elimination of mites). Since rickettsial multiplication can be inhibited by several antibacterial drugs, chemoprophylaxis is feasible. Chloramphenicol or tetracycline, 1 g orally daily, can provide drug levels that will inhibit rickettsial multiplication in humans after infection has occurred. This chemoprophylaxis serves to avoid serious clinical illness in persons who are forced to spend a short time in a hyperendemic area. It does not prevent infection, but prevents the unrestricted multiplication of the rickettsiae that may result in symptoms. Thus, disease is avoided during drug prophylaxis but the individual remains infected. After drugs are discontinued, multiplication of rickettsiae may begin and may result in disease unless a second and more aggressive therapeutic course of the drugs is begun soon after the symptoms have started.

In many tropical areas, *Anopheles* mosquitoes infected with *Plasmodium vivax* are prevalent. Residents and travelers in such areas can prevent malarial infection by taking 300 mg chloroquine phosphate orally once weekly.

SPECIFIC PROPHYLAXIS IN PERSONS OF INCREASED SUSCEPTIBILITY

Certain individuals with anatomic or functional abnormalities are predisposed toward infections of a serious or even life-threatening nature. It may be feasible to prevent or abort such infections by means of chemoprophylactic drugs given at specific times for short periods.

Prevention of Bacterial Endocarditis

Persons with congenital or acquired (eg, rheumatic) abnormalities of heart valves are unusually susceptible to the implantation of viridans streptococci and other organisms circulating in the bloodstream. If recognized promptly, the resulting endocarditis can often be cured with proper treatment. Nevertheless, endocarditis remains an exceedingly serious disease and efforts to prevent it are worthwhile. Viridans streptococci enter the bloodstream from the respiratory tract. Large numbers of these organisms are pushed into the circulation during chewing and especially during dental procedures and operations on the throat (eg, tonsillectomy). At such times, the increased risk warrants the use of a chemoprophylactic drug. A committee of the American Heart Association (Kaplan & others, 1977) has formulated comprehensive pro-

phylactic drug regimens for adults and children. For example, oral penicillin V, 2 g, is taken 1 hour prior to the procedure and then 0.5 g every 6 hours for 8 doses. The simultaneous use of streptomycin (to enhance the killing of streptococci) is under discussion.

Oral erythromycin, 1 g (20 mg/kg in children) prior to the procedure and 0.5 g every 6 hours for 8 doses, is substituted in persons hypersensitive to penicillin and in those receiving oral penicillin for long-term rheumatic fever prophylaxis. These individuals carry penicillin-resistant viridans streptococci in the throat.

Enterococci *(Streptococcus faecalis)* cause about 10% of cases of bacterial endocarditis. These organisms reach the bloodstream from the urinary or gastrointestinal tract or from the female genital tract. During surgical procedures in these areas, persons with heart valve lesions can be given chemoprophylactic drugs directed against enterococci. This involves the administration of penicillin G, 5 million units, and streptomycin, 1.5 g intramuscularly daily, or another aminoglycoside, beginning on the day of surgery and continuing for 2 days.

During and after cardiac catheterization, blood cultures are positive in 10–20% of patients; and many of these subsequently have fever. Prophylactically administered antibiotics do not influence this sequence.

Persons With Functional & Anatomic Abnormalities of the Respiratory Tract

Persons with emphysema, bronchiectasis, and other chronic pulmonary disorders are subject to attacks of "chronic bronchitis," a recurrent bacterial infection that precipitates respiratory decompensation. The commonest organisms involved in "chronic bronchitis" are pneumococci and *Haemophilus influenzae*. Chemoprophylaxis aimed at these and similar organisms consists of the administration of tetracycline or ampicillin, 1 g daily, during the season of highest bronchitis incidence. This is successful only if patients are not in a hospital environment, where superinfection with *Pseudomonas, Proteus*, or yeasts is very common.

Mucoviscidosis (cystic fibrosis) in children predisposes to frequent and severe bronchopulmonary infections. Before antibiotics became available, such infections were a principal cause of early death. The continuous or intermittent administration of tetracyclines has been remarkably effective in prolonging life and reducing the frequency and severity of respiratory tract infections. Children with mucoviscidosis still get infections even with tetracycline prophylaxis, but their life span is markedly extended. The mechanism of this effect is not established. The complicating infections now are mainly caused by *Pseudomonas* and staphylococci.

Chronic Corticosteroid Administration

Patients who are chronically ill with diseases such as systemic lupus erythematosus or pemphigus that are being controlled only by continuous high doses of corticosteroids may be given antibacterial chemoprophylaxis as long as they are outside the hospital environment; in these circumstances the risk of bacterial infection can perhaps be diminished by continuous or intermittent administration of antimicrobial drugs. There is no uniform or accepted method for such "prophylaxis," however, and its efficacy is not established. Such an approach always fails in hospitalized patients because superinfection with drug-resistant bacteria occurs promptly.

Opportunistic Infections in Severe Granulopenia

Patients with leukemia or other neoplasms who receive antineoplastic chemotherapy usually develop profound neutropenia. When the granulocyte count falls below $500-1000/\mu L$, these patients are unusually susceptible to opportunistic infections, most often staphylococcal and gram-negative bacteremias, or fungemias. In some cancer centers, such individuals are placed on oral insoluble drug prophylaxis consisting of gentamicin, vancomycin, and nystatin during the period of granulocytopenia and until their neutrophil count begins to rise again. In other centers, such patients are given systemic drugs, ranging from oral trimethoprim/sulfamethoxazole (co-trimoxazole) to parenteral cephalosporins, aminoglycosides, or penicillins (eg, amikacin plus cephazolin or ticarcillin plus gentamicin). Some benefits have been shown for each of these forms of antimicrobial prophylaxis in terms of prolonged intervals between infectious episodes, or extended periods of disease remission. Since most of these patients are desperately ill, the risk-benefit ratio is often difficult to evaluate.

Patients with organ transplants are subject to the same risks described above, and similar attempts are made to tide them over the period of maximal immunosuppression with antimicrobials to prevent lethal opportunistic infection. Co-trimoxazole has proved an effective chemoprophylactic against *Pneumocystis carinii* pneumonia. The choice of individual drugs directed against the most dangerous opportunistic organisms varies from month to month and place to place.

Postcoital Cystitis

Some women suffer from acute exacerbations of symptoms of urinary tract infection 24–48 hours after sexual intercourse. In some of these women, the "urethral syndrome" is unequivocally caused by bacteriuria with high counts. In them, the ingestion of 1–3 oral doses of nitrofurantoin, co-trimoxazole, or ampicillin soon after intercourse may have a prophylactic effect. Prolonged daily administration of one tablet of co-trimoxazole may at times reduce the frequency of recurrent urinary tract infection by reducing the colonization of the vaginal introitus with fecal organisms.

ANTIMICROBIAL DRUG PROPHYLAXIS IN SURGERY

Several well-controlled studies have established that the overall incidence of postoperative infection is not diminished by the prolonged administration of antimicrobial drugs before, during, or after surgery in either "clean" or potentially contaminated types of operations. Such drug administration may delay the onset of the symptoms and signs of infection and often tends to select out the more drug-resistant types of microorganisms. Thus, it is well accepted that general "antibiotic prophylaxis" to protect against all types of postoperative infection does not exist. However, some specialized, limited forms of "prophylaxis" listed below enjoy favor with surgeons. In general, "prophylactic" antimicrobials should be given only if the risk of infection is more than 5%; the "prophylactic" should be given for only 1 day; and effective antimicrobial concentrations of the drug should be in the wound area at the time of the surgical procedure. Thus, a cephalosporin (eg, cefazolin), 1 g intramuscularly given 1–2 hours before and 4, 8, and 12 hours after the operation, enjoys some favor and minimizes risks.

Lower Gastrointestinal Tract Surgery

Before elective operations on the lower gastrointestinal tract, it has been the custom to use a low-residue diet for 3 days, cleanse the colon by enemas or the use of saline catharsis for 2 days, and reduce the bowel flora by the preoperative oral administration of either insoluble sulfonamides or neomycin. It is assumed that the reduction in numbers of intestinal bacteria will reduce the hazard of peritoneal infection after accidental contamination with bowel contents at the site of surgery. It is probable that the skill of the surgeon and strict aseptic technic are more important in preventing such infections than the action of these drugs. Two particular problems must be considered:

(1) Oral administration of prophylactic drugs suppresses the bowel flora only transiently and partially. The lowest numbers of bacteria are present within 48 hours after starting neomycin, and within 5–6 days after starting sulfonamides. Soon thereafter, the numbers return to normal levels even when drugs are continued, but the composition of the flora is changed. Neomycin-erythromycin mixtures taken orally are presently in favor.

(2) Preoperative administration of neomycin may lead to implantation of neomycin-resistant staphylococci in the bowel and increase the chances of the development of staphylococcal enterocolitis, with high morbidity and mortality.

In many operations on the lower intestinal tract or the biliary tract or in the repair of a ruptured viscus, contamination with members of the normal flora occurs frequently. The administration of cefazolin (4 g in 24 hours) or gentamicin (7 mg/kg/d)—beginning just before surgery in order to establish effective tissue levels of the drug—has shown some success in reducing postoperative peritonitis. Clindamycin is sometimes added when the likelihood of contamination with anaerobes from the colon or the female genital tract is great. High tissue concentrations of the drug must exist at the time of surgery. "Prophylactic" drug administration should not continue for more than 24–48 hours after surgery.

Cardiovascular Surgery

In minor cardiovascular procedures such as cardiac catheterization or implantation of transvenous pacemakers, bacteria in small numbers are probably introduced but very rarely lead to infection. Systemic antibiotic prophylaxis has no effect in these circumstances. In major cardiac surgery, however, endothelial trauma, placement of sutures, and prosthetic materials all predispose to the local implantation of respiratory or intestinal flora transiently passing through the bloodstream. A high incidence of viridans streptococcal and other infections can be expected to occur. When penicillin G is administered during and for 2–4 days after surgery, this complication is virtually unknown, but staphylococcal endocarditis or pericarditis does occur. If nafcillin is given postoperatively to prevent staphylococcal implantation, gram-negative bacteria (including *Pseudomonas* or *Serratia*) may produce infectious complications. If drugs like gentamicin are aimed at such gram-negative bacteria, infections caused by fungi may occur. Thus, each drug can prevent the development of infection by a particular microorganism but favors the selection of a more resistant organism. Nevertheless, some form of chemoprophylaxis (eg, nafcillin plus gentamicin or cefazolin) during surgery and for 2–3 days afterward is common practice.

Orthopedic Surgery

The considerations mentioned above for cardiac surgery are applicable to orthopedic surgery also. Procedures of increasing magnitude are performed—often with exposure of the wound for hours and implantation of complex foreign bodies as prostheses. Infection by even a few accidentally introduced microorganisms may defeat a major elective procedure. Therefore, the temptation is great to administer antimicrobials to "ban the microbial world." In a majority of controlled studies, this attempt has not succeeded. Occasional studies, however, have proposed a rational form of chemoprophylaxis, ie, the administration of a specific drug to suppress a specific bug. Since the most frequent organisms producing deep infection of the operative site in orthopedics are staphylococci, the administration of a specific antistaphylococcal drug has had prophylactic effectiveness in controlled studies. Ultimately, however, superb surgical technic and asepsis are probably the most important means of preventing infection following surgery.

"PROPHYLAXIS" WITH TOPICALLY APPLIED DRUGS

The local application of drugs directed against common infecting organisms has been proposed for certain surgical sites, eg, the eyes and joints. It is reasoned that these are highly susceptible tissues with poor host defenses and that the locally applied drugs may inactivate the few organisms that inevitably contaminate the operative field during long procedures. There is no conclusive evidence to support this belief.

Local application of poorly absorbed bactericidal drugs (bacitracin-polymyxin-aminoglycoside) to the skin site where indwelling polyethylene tubes or intravenous needles are inserted may delay the introduction of microorganisms that ultimately result in thrombophlebitis with infection. This form of "prophylaxis" must not be permitted to interfere with the all-important principle that intravenous infusion sites must be changed every 48–72 hours if possible.

The local introduction of ampicillin into the surgical wound as a final step in appendectomy or colorectal surgery can significantly reduce the incidence of wound infections, although it probably does not influence the possible development of intraperitoneal infection that might follow contamination.

"PROPHYLAXIS" AGAINST MICROBIAL DISEASE THROUGH TREATMENT OF EARLY, ASYMPTOMATIC INFECTION

Optimal treatment may consist of the administration of effective drugs very early in infection when the microbial population is small and symptoms or signs of disease are still absent. This early treatment is sometimes considered "prophylaxis" of disease, eg, in tuberculosis. An asymptomatic person converts from a negative to a positive tuberculin skin test. Physical and radiologic examinations are entirely normal. To prevent later clinical tuberculosis, such a person is given isoniazid, 5–10 mg/kg/d (up to 300 mg/d), for 6–12 months on the assumption that this treatment will suppress or even eradicate the small population of tubercle bacilli (see Chapter 52).

Similar reasoning applies to early contaminated wounds soon after trauma. If an abdominal viscus is injured (eg, gunshot wound), the leakage of fecal matter is likely to lead to microbial infection. In attempts to limit such infection, most surgeons administer antimicrobial drugs during and after operation when the perforations are closed. The difficulty, obviously, is the selection of drugs most likely to suppress the most invasive microorganisms. Sometimes gentamicin with clindamycin or a penicillin with an aminoglycoside is chosen in the hope of limiting the progression of the infection so that host defenses can localize it.

ANTIVIRAL CHEMOPROPHYLAXIS

An increasing number of chemicals are becoming available that interfere with the multiplication of certain specific viruses in humans. While their use is sometimes referred to as antiviral chemotherapy, they are really active prophylactically because they succeed only if administration of the drug precedes major replication of the virus.

Amantadine hydrochloride (adamantanamine, Symmetrel; see Chapter 57) in a daily dose of 200 mg taken 2–3 days before and 6–7 days after infection with influenza A viruses may reduce the incidence and severity of symptoms and the magnitude of the serologic response. This drug is ineffective against influenza B viruses and most other respiratory agents.

Methisazone (N-methyl-isatin-β-thiosemicarbazone, Marboran; see Chapter 57) in a daily dose of 2–4 g (100 mg/kg/d for children) administered for 3 days to smallpox contacts beginning 1–2 days after exposure has effectively reduced subsequent morbidity and mortality due to smallpox. The drug inhibits viral replication to a limited extent and permits the development of active immunity. It was strikingly effective in areas where smallpox was endemic.

• • •

References

Andersen B & others: Topical ampicillin against wound infection after colorectal surgery. Ann Surg 176:129, 1972.

Clark H: Antibiotic prophylaxis in cardiac catheterization. Am Heart J 77:767, 1969.

Conte JE & others: Antibiotic prophylaxis and cardiac surgery. Ann Intern Med 76:943, 1972.

Ericson C & others: Cloxacillin in the prophylaxis of postoperative infections of the hip. J Bone Joint Surg 55A:808, 1973.

Goodman JS & others: Infection after cardiovascular surgery. N Engl J Med 278:117, 1968.

Gurwith MJ & others: A prospective controlled investigation of prophylactic trimethoprim/sulfamethoxazole in hospitalized granulocytopenic patients. Am J Med 66:248, 1979.

Harrison WO & others: A trial of minocycline given after exposure to prevent gonorrhea. N Engl J Med 300:1074, 1979.

Hughes WT & others: Successful chemoprophylaxis for *Pneumocystis carinii* pneumonitis. N Engl J Med 297:1419, 1977.

Hunt TK & others: Antibiotics in surgery. Arch Surg 110:148, 1975.

Kaplan EL & others: Prevention of bacterial endocarditis. (AHA Committee Report.) Circulation 56:139A, 1977.

Kaplan EL & others: Prevention of rheumatic fever. (AHA Committee Report.) Circulation 55:1, 1977.

Levine AS & others: Protected environments and prophylactic antibiotics in the therapy of acute leukemia. N Engl J Med 288:477, 1973.

McGowan JE Jr, Finland M: Usage of antibiotics in a general hospital: Effect of requiring justification. J Infect Dis 130:165, 1974.

Phelan JP, Pruyn SC: Prophylactic antibiotics in cesarean section: Double blind study of cefazolin. Am J Obstet Gynecol 133:474, 1979.

Roberts NJ, Douglas RG: Gentamicin use and *Pseudomonas* and *Serratia* resistance: Effect of a surgical prophylaxis regimen. Antimicrob Agents Chemother 13:214, 1978.

Sivonen A & others: The effect of chemoprophylactic use of rifampin and minocycline on rates of carriage of *Neisseria meningitidis* in Army recruits in Finland. J Infect Dis 137:238, 1978.

Stone HH & others: Antibiotic prophylaxis in gastric, biliary and colonic surgery. Ann Surg 184:443, 1976.

Stone HH & others: Prophylactic and preventive antibiotic therapy: Timing, duration and economics. Ann Surg 189:691, 1979.

Storring RA & others: Oral non-absorbed antibiotics prevent infection in acute non-lymphoblastic leukemia. Lancet 2:837, 1977.

Veterans Administration Ad Hoc Interdisciplinary Advisory Committee on Antimicrobial Drug Usage: Prophylaxis in surgery. JAMA 237:1003, 1977.

Vosti KL: Recurrent urinary tract infections: Prevention by prophylactic antibiotics after sexual intercourse. JAMA 231:934, 1975.

Yow MD & others: Ampicillin prevents intrapartum transmission of group B streptococcus. JAMA 241:1245, 1979.

Some biologic products are used for the purpose of inducing active immunity to an infectious disease and are administered before symptoms or signs of that disease appear or even before the individual has been exposed to the infectious agent. Other products are administered for the purpose of providing passive immunity to a toxic or infectious agent; these usually consist of preformed antibodies which have short-lived biologic activity.

Whenever biologic products are administered, the physician must be prepared to recognize and manage their untoward effects. Biologic products are usually labile, with a limited shelf life and a definite expiration date, and require specialized storage. The manufacturer's directions must be followed because changes in dosage schedules occur frequently.

THE INDUCTION
OF PASSIVE IMMUNITY
WITH PREFORMED ANTIBODIES

These products are more or less purified and concentrated antibody solutions derived either from man or animals actively immunized against a given antigen. If the source of antibody is human serum, no precautions against hypersensitivity reactions are usually necessary. However, if the antibodies were derived from animal sera, hypersensitivity reactions are common and must be guarded against. These reactions are of the immediate type, ranging from anaphylaxis to serum sickness. In order to avoid anaphylactic reactions, careful tests for hypersensitivity to the animal serum must be performed. If the tests give evidence of hypersensitivity, it is best to avoid that specific type of foreign protein (eg, horse serum) and obtain antibodies made in another animal (eg, goat, rabbit). If an alternative preparation is not available and administration of the specific antibody is deemed essential and potentially lifesaving, desensitization can be carried out. A summary of tests for hypersensitivity and desensitization with antibody-containing proteins is given on p 616.

Antibodies derived from human serum not only avoid the risk of hypersensitivity reactions but also have a much longer half-life in man (about 23 days for IgG antibodies) than those from animal sources. Consequently, much smaller doses of human than of animal antibody can be administered to provide therapeutic concentrations for several weeks. These advantages point to the desirability of using human antibodies for passive protection whenever possible.

HUMAN GAMMA GLOBULIN
(Immune Serum Globulin USP)

Immune serum globulin USP is a commercial preparation of gamma globulin derived from large pools of human plasma by low-temperature ethanol fractionation. The preparation contains about 165 mg of gamma globulin per mL of solution (representing a 25-fold concentration of antibody-containing immunoglobulins of plasma), glycine as stabilizer, and thimerosal as preservative. Such immune serum globulin can be injected intramuscularly or subcutaneously but not intravenously. It has been employed clinically in the following circumstances:

(1) Hypogammaglobulinemia: Deficient antibody production occurs in various degrees and in various clinical forms on the basis of defects in antibody-producing cells. There may also be enhanced catabolism of immunoglobulins. Most of these disorders have a genetic basis and manifest themselves in childhood, leading to recurrent bacterial infections, predominantly of the respiratory tract. Such complications can usually be prevented by the injection of 0.3–0.45 mL/lb immune serum globulin (ie, 150 mg gamma globulin per kg) once each month. Antimicrobial drugs are used to control individual episodes of bacterial infection.

(2) Viral hepatitis: The manifestations of infectious hepatitis A (HA) can be minimized or prevented with immune serum globulin, and the infection can often be kept subclinical. Persons intending to travel to areas where HA is endemic can be given immune serum globulin, 0.01 mL/lb (0.02 mL/kg) every 4–6 weeks, to provide partial passive protection. For nonimmune persons residing in areas where HA is highly endemic, the injection of 0.05 mL/lb (0.1 mL/kg) once every 4–6 months has been recommended.

After suspected or known exposure to HA, immune serum globulin, 0.01 mL/lb (0.02 mL/kg), is injected as promptly as possible, and the injection is repeated 3 weeks later to prevent or modify the disease.

The administration of immune serum globulin does not stop viral multiplication but restricts it somewhat. This favors the development of mild or subclinical disease, which tends to induce active immunity. There is no evidence that passive immunization against viral hepatitis prevents infection; it only modifies the disease.

Pooled human gamma globulin does not regularly contain sufficient anti-hepatitis B antibodies to have any proved effect prophylactically in hepatitis B. Nevertheless, it is suggested that upon definite exposure (needle stick, exposure to blood or other materials from a suspected HbsAg-positive individual), immune serum globulin, 0.06 mL/kg, be injected intramuscularly. If the HbsAg is confirmed as positive and the exposed individual does not have anti-HBs antibodies, hepatitis B immune globulin (see below) is advised. Pooled human gamma globulin has been incriminated as an occasional source of epidemic hepatitis B.

(3) Measles: This disease should be prevented by universal vaccination in early childhood. When vaccinating with the "attenuated" (Edmonston) live strain of measles virus (no longer used in the USA), untoward reactions (ie, manifestations of infection such as fever and rash) can be minimized by the simultaneous injection of immune serum globulin, 0.01 mL/lb (0.02 mL/kg), into a separate site. With more highly attenuated measles vaccine strains (eg, Schwarz), globulin is unnecessary.

In nonvaccinated susceptibles, measles can be either prevented or attenuated with immune serum globulin. To *prevent* clinical measles in susceptible persons, give 0.25 mL/kg of immune serum globulin as soon as possible after exposure. This may be indicated in very young or debilitated unvaccinated children, but it interferes with the development of active immunity.

To *attenuate* clinical measles, give 0.04 mL/kg of immune serum globulin within 8 days of exposure. This results in a modified, mild disease, and permits the development of active immunity which is usually lifelong. Administration of immune serum globulin between the eighth and the tenth days after exposure may produce some attenuation of disease, but after the onset of rash there is no effect.

(4) Rubella: The injection of 0.2–0.5 mL/kg serum immune globulin into pregnant women soon after exposure to rubella may modify or prevent the disease. However, such treatment does not prevent infection of the fetus with rubella virus.

SPECIFIC HYPERIMMUNE HUMAN GAMMA GLOBULINS

Tetanus

A specific hyperimmune gamma globulin has been prepared from persons repeatedly immunized with tetanus toxoid. This human gamma globulin eliminates the problem of hypersensitivity to animal proteins in persons who must receive passive immunization against tetanus. For prophylaxis after injury in nonimmunized persons, 250–500 units of human tetanus immune globulin injected intramuscularly yield levels of 0.03 unit or more of antitoxin per milliliter of serum for several weeks.

Ideally, every individual should have active immunization against tetanus, with boosters at suitable intervals (see immunization schedule, Table 61–2). Human tetanus immune globulin, 3000–6000 units, has been administered for the treatment of clinical tetanus, but proof of its efficacy is lacking. In tetanus of the newborn, 500 units of human hyperimmune tetanus globulin has some therapeutic benefit.

Vaccinia

Hyperimmune gamma globulin (VIG) prepared from the plasma of persons recently and successfully revaccinated with vaccinia virus is available from the American Red Cross. Injection of 0.6–1 mL/kg intramuscularly can arrest the dissemination of vaccinia lesions in patients with eczema and can stop progressive vaccinia in certain persons.

Chickenpox (Varicella)

Specific immune globulin (ZIG) is prepared from the serum of persons recently recovered from herpes zoster and exhibiting high antibody titer. A dose of 0.12 mL/kg injected into leukemic or immunodeficient children within 72 hours of exposure can prevent both infection and disease.

Rabies

Specific human immune globulin has been prepared from the serum of persons repeatedly vaccinated against rabies. The dose is 20 IU/kg; half of the dose is infiltrated around the wound and the rest is injected intramuscularly. Vaccine is started at the same time. (Available from Cutter Laboratories distribution centers. Phone Dallas Distribution Center, [214] 661-5850.)

Rh Sensitization; Erythroblastosis Fetalis

When an Rh-negative mother has an Rh-positive child by an Rh-positive father, she may become sensitized by Rh-positive fetal cells—usually at the time of delivery—and develop antibodies to them. A subsequent Rh-positive fetus may suffer hemolytic disease when these anti-Rh antibodies lyse its red cells. Rh sensitization can usually be prevented when an unsensitized Rh-negative mother is injected with specific immune human $Rh_o(D)$ globulin within 72 hours of delivery. The usual dose is 1 vial containing 1–1.5 mL of high titer IgG globulin injected intramuscularly. This antibody inhibits active antibody formation to the Rh-positive red blood cell antigens which entered the mother's circulation at delivery.

Hepatitis B

Persons suspected of having been exposed to hepatitis B virus–containing materials (see above) may receive hepatitis B immune globulin prepared from serum pools with high-titer anti-HBs antibodies. The dose is 0.06 mg/kg in children and 5 mL in adults, injected intramuscularly twice 1 month apart.

Pertussis

Specific hyperimmune globulins containing antibodies to *Bordetella pertussis* and to various other bacteria have been prepared. The clinical efficacy of these preparations is not fully established, and they are used only in young (< 2 years) nonimmunized children.

Mumps

Mumps hyperimmune globulin has been employed for the protection of susceptible individuals against such complications as orchitis. Its effectiveness is uncertain.

ANTITOXINS & ANTISERA FOR PASSIVE PROTECTION OF HUMANS PREPARED IN ANIMALS

These are concentrated antibody preparations derived from specifically immunized animals, usually horses, sheep, rabbits, or goats, standardized as units. For the production of antitoxins, animals are injected repeatedly with toxoids, ie, toxins detoxified by formaldehyde. The resulting antitoxins can neutralize toxins prior to their attachment to a receptor site. Thus, antitoxins must be administered as promptly as possible to neutralize toxins *before* they are irreversibly bound. The following antitoxins are available:

Diphtheria Antitoxin

A concentrated globulin fraction of pooled sera of animals (horses, sheep, goats, etc) immunized with diphtheria toxoid. When the presumptive clinical diagnosis of diphtheria is made, antitoxin, 10,000–100,000 units, is injected intramuscularly or intravenously after suitable tests for hypersensitivity. Except for the mildest cases, the antitoxin is given without waiting for laboratory confirmation of diphtheria infection.

Botulism Antitoxin

Concentrated globulin fraction of sera of animals immunized with the toxin of *Clostridium botulinum*, type A, B, or E. Antitoxin is usually available as pooled trivalent antitoxin. It must be injected as promptly as possible after the diagnosis of botulism is strongly suspected. After testing for hypersensitivity, give in the dosage and by the route directed by the manufacturer, or contact the Center for Disease Control, Atlanta. (Phone: [404]-633-3311.)

Tetanus Antitoxin

Concentrated globulin fractions of sera of horses or cattle immunized with the toxoid of *Clostridium tetani*. This preparation should be employed only if human hyperimmune antitetanus globulin is not available. Furthermore, under ideal circumstances, all persons should receive active immunization with tetanus toxoid in childhood and suitable booster injections thereafter, so that the need for antitoxin does not arise.

Antivenins

Concentrated globulin fraction of sera of animals immunized with the venoms of poisonous snakes (rattlesnakes, vipers, cobras, and others), spiders, and scorpions. Follow the manufacturer's directions for dosage and route of administration and test for hypersensitivity.

Gas Gangrene Antitoxin

Concentrated globulin fraction of sera of animals immunized with the toxins of various clostridia, including *C welchii (perfringens)*, *C septicum*, and *C oedematiens*. These trivalent or polyvalent preparations have been injected into patients who are suspected of developing gas gangrene as a result of sustaining contaminated wounds. However, their efficacy is very doubtful. It is probably preferable to rely on thorough surgical debridement and treatment with penicillin or other antimicrobial drugs. Hyperbaric oxygen therapy is a possibly useful adjunct.

Rabies Antiserum

Rabies antiserum is a concentrated globulin fraction of serum of horses immunized with rabies virus. It must be injected soon after the bite of a rabid animal, both systemically and into the area of the wound. Directions on dosage are given by the World Health Organization. This material should only be used if human immune rabies serum cannot be obtained.

THE INDUCTION OF ACTIVE IMMUNITY

A variety of products are used in the induction of active immunity to infectious agents or their toxic products. The method of preparation of these biologic products, their nature, and their effects change frequently. Consequently, the manufacturer's directions must be consulted regarding dosage regimen and anticipated untoward effects. The following pages offer only a general description of these biologic products and a summary of recommendations for 1980 regarding immunization of children and travelers.

Products for the induction of active immunity fall into 3 general categories: (1) toxoids, (2) inactivated (killed) vaccines, and (3) live attenuated vaccines. Each of these categories is briefly summarized below.

TOXOIDS

Toxoids are prepared from the exotoxins of bacteria by treatment with formaldehyde and purification. This treatment results in a material which has lost its toxic properties but maintains the antigenic specificity of the active toxin. Antitoxins formed against toxoids will neutralize the active toxins. Toxoids can be dispensed as fluid toxoids, as toxoids adsorbed onto aluminum hydroxide or similar colloid for slower absorption from tissues, or as toxoids alum-precipitated from the original solution and resuspended in saline.

The most universally employed toxoids are those of diphtheria and tetanus. They are often used together (DT), and sometimes combined with pertussis vaccine (DTP). In the immunization of children, alum-precipitated or adsorbed toxoids are injected intramuscularly 3 times at intervals of 4–6 weeks during the first year of life, with subsequent boosters. Children tolerate such slowly absorbed preparations well, but many adults develop fairly severe local and systemic reactions. These reactions can be anticipated by prior testing by means of intradermal injection of 0.1 mL of a 1:20 dilution of diphtheria toxoid (Moloney test). Because of the relative frequency of such reactions, adults should be given (with caution) only specially purified toxoids (Td adult) designated "for adult immunization." Following the primary course of immunization with toxoids, antitoxin levels rise and then fall, but booster injections induce a rapid secondary rise of antibody levels to clinically protective levels (for tetanus, more than 0.02 unit/mL of serum) which persist for long periods. Consequently, years after initial immunization, persons at risk from tetanus or diphtheria are protected by an additional booster injection given immediately after injury or exposure. Thus, booster injections of tetanus toxoid are commonly given to injured persons.

INACTIVATED (KILLED) VACCINES

1. BACTERIAL INACTIVATED VACCINES

Pertussis (Whooping Cough)

Suspensions of inactivated phase I *Bordetella pertussis*, adsorbed onto aluminum hydroxide or precipitated with alum, are injected intramuscularly into children during the first year of life. This usually prevents or modifies disease due to this organism. Pertussis vaccine is usually combined with diphtheria and tetanus toxoids. The vaccine may produce febrile reactions but is usually well tolerated.

Plague

Suspensions of inactivated *Pasteurella pestis* are injected intramuscularly repeatedly in order to stimulate partial resistance to plague infection in areas where epidemiologic control of plague is not feasible. The vaccine often induces marked local pain, swelling, and heat, and a febrile response. Its efficacy is probably not great.

Cholera

Suspensions of inactivated cholera and El Tor vibrios can be injected repeatedly intramuscularly to stimulate partial resistance to cholera infection in countries where the disease is likely to occur. The vaccine often induces marked local pain, swelling, and heat, and a febrile response. Protection depends largely on frequent booster injections (the WHO certificate is valid for only 6 months) and is, at best, of intermediate degree. Cholera toxoids and new types of vaccine are being investigated.

Typhoid

Suspensions of acetone-killed *Salmonella typhi* are injected repeatedly subcutaneously to stimulate partial resistance to typhoid infection in countries where the disease is likely to occur. The vaccine often induces marked local pain, swelling, and heat, and a febrile response. The degree of protection against *S typhi* infection is fairly good; paratyphoid vaccines are almost worthless.

Anthrax

A purified extract of culture filtrate can be given to highly exposed persons but is not generally available.

Pneumococcus

Capsular polysaccharides from 12–14 types of pneumococci have been pooled into polyvalent vaccines. Each 0.5 mL dose contains 50 μg of each capsular type. The types were selected to represent about 80% of the present pneumococcal infections. Adults and children over the age of 2 years generally respond with antibody formation to most or all of the type-specific antigens in the vaccine following a single subcutaneous or intramuscular injection of 0.5 mL. The vaccine appears to be indicated for high-risk individuals, for splenectomized or sickle cell anemia patients, perhaps for persons with chronic obstructive respiratory disease, and perhaps for children with frequently recurring otitis media. The response of children under age 2 years may be irregular, and more than one immunizing dose may be required. The vaccine may result in a shift of the types of pneumococci more commonly producing disease. Some sickle cell or Hodgkin's patients are not fully protected by vaccine against homotypic pneumococcal infection, so that continued penicillin prophylaxis may have to be considered for them.

Meningococcus
Polysaccharides from meningococcus groups A and C can stimulate specific antibodies to protect against disease. Such preparations are used for the control of epidemics or in highly susceptible groups (eg, military recruits) for prophylaxis. One or 2 injections are given subcutaneously.

2. RICKETTSIAL INACTIVATED VACCINES

Epidemic Typhus
Suspensions of inactivated *Rickettsia prowazeki* grown in the yolk sacs of embryonated eggs and purified to reduce the content of egg antigens are injected repeatedly intramuscularly. This vaccine can induce a moderate degree of protection against louse-borne typhus. The efficacy of this vaccine is relatively good provided frequent booster injections are given. The vaccine is indicated only for persons likely to have contact with louse-borne typhus. A live attenuated vaccine (strain E) has been used during typhus epidemics in Africa. It produces a mild, symptomatic infection and induces good immunity.

Rocky Mountain Spotted Fever
Suspensions of inactivated purified *Rickettsia rickettsii* grown in embryonated eggs can be injected repeatedly intramuscularly into persons likely to be exposed to tick bites in endemic areas. This vaccine and others against spotted fevers in other parts of the world are moderately effective in protecting against severe disease.

Other Vaccines
Other vaccines against rickettsial infections (eg, Q fever, scrub typhus) have been prepared. These inactivated preparations probably have moderate protective value in very specialized situations. They are not commercially available.

3. VIRAL INACTIVATED VACCINES

A variety of inactivated viral vaccines have been prepared and proposed for general use. Most have little merit when compared to effective live vaccines.

Adenovirus
Suspensions of inactivated cell culture grown adenovirus types 3, 4, and 7 were proposed for the prevention of respiratory disease in military recruits and children. They are not available in the USA at present because of fears of oncogenicity, SV40 contamination, etc.

Arbovirus
Suspensions of inactivated Japanese B, western equine, and eastern equine encephalomyelitis viruses have been prepared. They are used principally in occupationally exposed persons and are probably not highly protective. They are not commercially available.

Influenza
Suspensions of inactivated egg-grown influenza viruses of the prevailing types and subtypes can be injected intramuscularly to provide a limited degree of protection against natural infection. Such vaccines induce little nasal IgA antibody response in spite of good circulating antibody response. They are recommended mainly for high-risk patients, eg, elderly persons with chronic respiratory disease, patients with serious mitral valve disease, and children with cystic fibrosis. Such individuals should be injected every year with polyvalent vaccine.

Influenza vaccines are usually designed to contain viral antigens of currently prevailing strains. The vaccine for 1979–1980 consists of A/Brazil/78 (H1N1), A/Texas/77 (H3N2), and B/Hong Kong/72.

When a swine influenza strain (Hs1N1) appeared in New Jersey in 1976, a nationwide campaign was undertaken to vaccinate millions of persons against this type of virus, which was suspected to have been involved in the epidemics of 1919–1921. The campaign was not successful because of side-effects to the vaccine, including the neurologic Guillain-Barré syndrome; fortunately, the feared swine influenza virus did not reappear in the population at all.

Influenza vaccine is available in "split-virus" and "whole-virus" preparations. Split-virus vaccines, which contain antigens produced by chemically disrupting the influenza virus, have been associated with somewhat fewer side-effects than whole-virus vaccines, particularly in children. However, the split-virus vaccines appear to be somewhat less effective in eliciting antibodies when given as a single dose to persons who have not been "primed" by exposure to related viruses in nature or through vaccination.

Measles
Inactivated measles virus vaccine should not be used because it induces significant hypersensitivity

without causing effective immunity. Use live virus vaccine.

Mumps

Suspensions of inactivated mumps virus repeatedly injected intramuscularly may induce partial resistance to natural infection. However, the inactivated vaccine is not very effective, and live virus vaccine should be used. Inactivated mumps vaccine has been used as a skin test: A positive delayed reaction (maximum at 18–30 hours) suggests that the person has experienced mumps before and, therefore, may be immune if exposed to the natural disease. However, skin test results are less reliable than serum neutralization tests as indicators of immunity. Inactivated vaccine has also been used in adults to demonstrate that the individual is capable of giving a positive delayed skin reaction.

Poliomyelitis

Suspensions of cell culture grown, formalin-inactivated poliovirus of types I, II, and III (Salk vaccine) can be injected repeatedly intramuscularly. This can induce effective circulating antibodies and gives protection against the central nervous system manifestations of poliomyelitis if boosters are given regularly. However, this vaccine does not alter the susceptibility to intestinal infection with poliovirus and does not tend to eradicate poliovirus from the community. Oral, live virus vaccines are preferable because they can accomplish these ends.

Rabies

Suspensions of tissues from rabies infected animals, inactivated with phenol, are used for repeated injection into persons bitten by animals suspected of having rabies. Occasionally rabies vaccines are given prior to exposure. The efficacy of inactivated rabies vaccine is not established, and all preparations may induce an allergic encephalomyelitis because of their content of central nervous system tissue. At present, rabies virus vaccine is prepared in embryonated duck eggs. Because of low antigenicity, 14–21 doses of duck embryo vaccine are recommended after probable exposure to rabies. If rabies immune serum is administered also, 2 additional booster doses of vaccine are desirable (a total of 23 injections).

A new vaccine of much greater potency and safety has been prepared from rabies virus grown in human diploid cells (WI 38) and inactivated with tri-n-butylphosphate or beta-propiolactone. The immunogenicity of this new preparation is such that measurable serum antibody develops in virtually all persons receiving 4–6 injections. This vaccine was licensed in the USA in June, 1980. It can be obtained through a state health department or by telephoning (800) 327-8387.

LIVE ATTENUATED VACCINES

These consist of suspensions of infectious bacteria or viruses which are attenuated and proved to produce infection but only in a mild, self-limited form or one with no clinical manifestations of illness at all. The aim of such vaccines is to stimulate all aspects of cellular and humoral immunity which occur as part of the response to the natural infection but to avoid the risk of serious disease from fully virulent microorganisms. Thus, a planned mild infection is substituted for an unpredictable, possibly severe one. The most effective vaccines for the induction of active immunity are in this category.

Possible disadvantages of such live vaccines are the difficulty of maintaining a stable, attenuated strain of living agent; manufacturing, standardization, and storage problems; control over contaminating living agents; the threat of mutation toward virulence; and the production of disease in debilitated recipients. In spite of these difficulties, more and more viral vaccines employ live attenuated infectious agents.

1. BACTERIAL LIVE VACCINES

Live attenuated bacteria are used to immunize animals against anthrax and brucella infections. These vaccines are not used for humans.

Plague

While the most widely accepted plague vaccines are killed bacterial suspensions, live attenuated plague bacillus vaccines have been used for immunization campaigns in hyperendemic areas, particularly in the face of threatened epidemics. They appear to be fairly effective live vaccines but are not widely available.

Tuberculosis

Live, avirulent tubercle bacilli, strain BCG (bacille Calmette-Guérin), have been injected into many millions of persons in an attempt to induce partial resistance to infection with virulent tubercle bacilli. Such vaccination usually results in conversion of the tuberculin skin test from negative to positive, and BCG organisms may survive for 3–7 years in the subject. Thus, vaccination results in the loss of the tuberculin test as a sensitive indicator of primary virulent infection and its possible prompt treatment. In many developed countries, BCG vaccination is now recommended only for tuberculin-negative persons who are heavily exposed to infectious cases of tuberculosis (eg, children in a family with active disease) who can be observed medically at frequent intervals. The use of BCG in leprosy has been suggested on the basis of experimental evidence. BCG is also used as a nonspecific stimulant of cell-mediated immunity in certain tumors (eg, melanoma). Live suspensions of *Propionibacterium acnes* have been similarly used.

2. VIRAL LIVE VACCINES

Most effective viral vaccines are in this category at present.

Smallpox

Active vaccinia virus in the form of glycerolated calf lymph or grown in chick embryos is dispensed in capillary tubes. The virus loses viability unless stored below 0 C. After cleansing, the dry skin is inoculated by the multiple pressure method. For proper immunization, the virus must multiply locally, producing vesicles or pustules. Properly performed vaccination results in resistance to smallpox for up to 3 years (WHO certificate).

A contraindication to vaccination is the presence of eczema or other widespread skin disease in the patient or family contacts, because this may predispose to generalized vaccinia, a serious disease. Vaccination must also be avoided in persons with known defects of humoral or cellular immunity (agammaglobulinemia, Hodgkin's disease, etc).

Smallpox vaccine was so effective in protecting against infection that a worldwide eradication campaign has eliminated the virus and the disease in 1979. Consequently, the need for smallpox vaccination no longer exists. However, military personnel in the USA and some other individuals are still being vaccinated and occasionally manifest the untoward effects of vaccinia.

Poliomyelitis

Attenuated strains of poliomyelitis virus types 1, 2, and 3, grown in cell culture, are administered orally either as single types or, usually, as a trivalent mixture to small children. A trivalent booster dose is given orally 1–2 years later and another 3–5 years later. The ingested live virus replicates in the intestine, and some is excreted in feces and spread to contacts. Intestinal virus multiplication is accompanied by both systemic and intestinal antibody formation and induces solid immunity to subsequent virulent poliovirus exposure.

Measles (Rubeola)

Attenuated strains of measles virus, grown in cell culture, are injected intramuscularly once. This produces a mild systemic infection which results in long-term resistance to the natural infection. With the "Edmonston" strain, fever and rash often occur as untoward effects. This can be minimized by the simultaneous injection of human immune serum globulin. Immune serum globulin is not required with the further attenuated strains (eg, Schwarz) of measles virus, which usually result in asymptomatic infection and are now almost universally employed. Live measles vaccines are highly effective if given at age 15 months or later. Inactivated measles vaccines induce hypersensitivity without permanent immunity and are undesirable.

German Measles (Rubella)

Attenuated strains of rubella virus, grown in cell culture, are injected subcutaneously. This produces a systemic infection followed by some immunity to the natural disease. Children tolerate the vaccine well, but fever and arthralgia are common in adults. Rubella vaccine must not be given to pregnant women because the vaccine strain may infect the fetus.

Some physicians prefer to administer rubella vaccine only to prepubertal girls. If given to seronegative adolescent girls and women, it must be ascertained that pregnancy will not occur for 3 months after immunization. Vaccine strains reach the placenta and produce lesions there. Rubella vaccine is not likely to eradicate rubella infection because naturally or artificially immunized persons can become reinfected and can spread the virus via the respiratory route.

Mumps

Attenuated strains of mumps virus, grown in cell culture and dispensed in lyophilized form, are injected subcutaneously or intramuscularly. This produces an asymptomatic infection which probably induces long-term systemic immunity to natural infection. The vaccine is well tolerated by children and young adults.

Yellow Fever

An attenuated strain (17D) of yellow fever virus grown in embryonated eggs is dispensed in lyophilized form and injected subcutaneously. It produces an asymptomatic infection and solid immunity to natural infection and disease for 10 years or more. It has been used in many millions of persons and is an excellent immunizing vaccine. The vaccine approved for administration in the USA is manufactured by the Merrell-National Laboratories and made available through local health departments.

Rabies

An attenuated strain of rabies virus grown in embryonated eggs (high egg passage Flury strain) has been widely used for immunization of animals. After injection, this virus produces an asymptomatic systemic infection and good immunity to natural infection and disease for at least 1–2 years. This live vaccine is not now accepted for human use, but its efficacy is much greater than that of the traditional inactivated rabies vaccines. Live rabies vaccines (eg, cell culture grown) might be very valuable for persons at high risk of exposure to virulent rabies, an almost invariably fatal infection.

Adenovirus

Strains of adenovirus type 4 and type 7 grown in cell culture and ingested in an enteric-coated capsule produce asymptomatic intestinal infection. This infection induces systemic immunity to the potentially debilitating respiratory infection and pneumonitis caused by the same type of adenovirus. This vaccine is being used only in military personnel, where adenovirus respiratory disease is a serious problem.

Varicella

An experimental live attenuated strain of varicella-zoster virus can protect immunodeficient individuals against disease.

HYPERSENSITIVITY TO ANIMAL PROTEINS & DESENSITIZATION

Many persons are hypersensitive to animal proteins or drugs. If they are given such material by injection, there is a chance that anaphylaxis may develop. Therefore, tests for hypersensitivity are indicated prior to any such injection. Serum sickness can develop in anyone, independently of prior sensitization. The following steps are desirable as a safeguard against anaphylactic reactions, and must be observed with biologic products administered for prophylaxis or therapy, particularly with animal sera.

(1) Past history: Has the patient received a similar material before? Does the patient have known allergy, eg, to egg protein?

(2) Materials available must include: Epinephrine, 1:1000 solution, in sterile syringe; airway, soluble corticosteroid, tourniquet, antihistamine drug (eg, diphenhydramine) for injection, oxygen.

(3) Intradermal test: Diluted test material (eg, 1:10 diluted animal serum) is injected intradermally so that 0.1 mL raises a bleb, and the site is observed for 15 minutes. The appearance of erythema and edema with wheal formation suggests specific hypersensitivity.

(4) Conjunctival test: May be done as an alternative to the intradermal test. Instillation of 1 drop of 1:10 dilution of test material into a normal conjunctiva results in itching, lacrimation, and redness within 5 minutes if the person is hypersensitive. One drop of physiologic saline is instilled into the other eye as a control.

When the skin test or conjunctival test indicates hypersensitivity, it is preferable to avoid injection of the material in question and substitute another product. Thus, in place of diphtheria antitoxin in horse serum, diphtheria antitoxin in goat serum might be administered. If an alternative product is not available, desensitization may be attempted as follows:

Inject gradually increasing doses of the product every 30-60 minutes, observing for possible significant reactions. Begin with 0.1 mL of product diluted 1:100. If there is no reaction, give 0.1 mL diluted 1:10. If there is still no reaction, inject 0.1 mL undiluted. If a significant local reaction occurs, inject the same dose, or a smaller dose together with epinephrine, 1:1000, 0.5 mL. Increase the doses of the product gradually but steadily until 2 or 3 mL of undiluted product have been administered without significant reaction. Repeat this dose every 30-60 minutes until the full prophylactic or therapeutic dose has been given.

Desensitization often permits the administration of an animal protein to which the person exhibits moderate hypersensitivity. However, if major reactions occur during the procedure, desensitization attempts should be abandoned.

SKIN TESTS TO DETERMINE DELAYED HYPERSENSITIVITY

In many disease states—or as a result of administration of immunosuppressive drugs—the ability is lost to mount delayed hypersensitivity reactions to antigens to which the individual has been exposed. The following skin test antigens are often employed to test for the ability to react with delayed type hypersensitivity reactions: *Candida,* trichophytin, mumps, PPD-tuberculin, and streptokinase-streptodornase. Most adults can be expected to respond with positive skin tests to one or more of the antigens, thus establishing their competence in cell-mediated reactions.

A skin test may also be a useful indicator of past contact with—and infection by—a microbial or fungal agent; or it may differentiate between closely related infecting agents such as *Mycobacterium tuberculosis* (tested with PPD-S) and *Mycobacterium intracellulare* (PPd-B). The possible diagnostic benefits of such skin tests must be weighed against their disadvantages, eg, sensitization, raising of antibodies, and the occurrence of nonspecific misleading reactions.

ACTIVE IMMUNIZATION AGAINST INFECTIOUS DISEASES

Biologic products used for active immunization are frequently modified. The schedule of administration, dose, and recommended route vary with the product and change often. Always consult the manufacturer's package insert and follow its recommendations. A possible schedule for active immunization of children is shown in Table 61–1.

RECOMMENDED IMMUNIZATION OF ADULTS FOR TRAVEL

Every adult, whether traveling or not, must be immunized with tetanus toxoid. Purified toxoid "for adult use" must be used to avoid reactions. Every adult should also have primary vaccination for poliomyelitis (oral live trivalent vaccine), for diphtheria (use purified toxoid "for adult use"), and perhaps for smallpox. Every traveler must fulfill the immunization requirements of the health authorities of the countries visited. These are listed in *Health Information for International Travel 1976*, HEW Publication No. (CDC) 76–8280. Available from the Director, Quarantine Division, Center for Disease Control, Atlanta 30333.

The following are suggestions for travel in different parts of the world.

Tetanus

Booster injection of 0.5 mL tetanus toxoid, for adult use, every 5–7 years, assuming completion of primary immunization. (All countries.)

Smallpox

Although natural smallpox was declared eradicated from the world in 1979, some military personnel continue to receive vaccinia virus vaccine. The USA requires no vaccination certificate, but some countries do. Travelers may carry a WHO certificate valid for 3 years, which requires registration of batch number. Complications of vaccinia continue to occur in 1979 in vaccinated individuals and their contacts.

Typhoid

Suspension of killed *Salmonella typhi*. For primary immunization, inject 0.5 mL subcutaneously twice at intervals of 4–6 weeks (0.25 mL for children under 10 years). For booster, inject 0.5 mL subcuta-

Table 61–1. Recommended schedule for active immunization and skin testing of children.

Age	Product Administered	Test Recommended
2 months	DTP[1] Oral poliovaccine[2], trivalent	
4 months	DTP Oral poliovaccine, trivalent	
6 months	DTP Oral poliovaccine, trivalent	
15–19 months	DTP Measles vaccine[3] Oral poliovaccine, trivalent Mumps vaccine[4]	
4–6 years	DTP Oral poliovaccine, trivalent	Tuberculin test[5]
12–14 years	Rubella vaccine[6] Td[7]	Tuberculin test[5]

[1] **DTP:** Toxoids of diphtheria and tetanus, alum-precipitated or aluminum hydroxide adsorbed, combined with pertussis bacterial antigen. Suitable for young children. Three doses of 0.5 mL intramuscularly at intervals of 4–8 weeks. Fourth injection of 0.5 mL intramuscularly given about 1 year later.

[2] **Oral live poliomyelitis virus vaccine:** Trivalent (types 1, 2, and 3 combined) given 3 times at intervals of 6–8 weeks and then as a booster 1 year later. Monovalent vaccine is rarely used now; it can be given at 6-week intervals, followed by a booster of trivalent vaccine 1 year later. Inactive (Salk type) trivalent vaccine is available but not recommended. *Note:* One sequence of monovalent vaccines (type 2, then 1, then 3) is in accord with the recommendations of the US Public Health Service Advisory Committee on Immunization Practices. The American Academy of Pediatrics recommends the sequence 1, 3, 2.

[3] **Live measles virus vaccine,** 0.5 mL intramuscularly. When using attenuated (Edmonston) strain, give human gamma globulin, 0.01 mL/lb, injected into the opposite arm at the same time, to lessen the reaction to the vaccine. This is not advised with "further attenuated" (Schwarz) strain vaccine. Inactivated measles vaccine should not be used.

[4] **Live mumps virus vaccine (attenuated),** 0.5 mL intramuscularly.

[5] The frequency with which **tuberculin tests** are administered depends on the risk of exposure, ie, the prevalence of tuberculosis in the population group.

[6] **Rubella live virus vaccine (attenuated)** can be given between age 1 year and puberty. Some physicians recommend rubella vaccine only for prepubertal girls. The entire contents of a single dose vaccine vial, reconstituted from the lyophilized state, are injected subcutaneously. The vaccine must *not* be given to women who are pregnant or are liable to become pregnant within 3 months of vaccination. Women must be warned that there is a possibility of developing arthralgias or arthritis after vaccination. The cell culture–grown RA 27/3 rubella virus vaccine was licensed in USA in 1979. No live vaccine should be given to immunodeficient patients.

[7] **Tetanus toxoid and diphtheria toxoid,** purified, suitable for adults, given every 7–10 years.

neously (or 0.1 mL intradermally) every 3 years. (All countries.) Paratyphoid vaccines are probably ineffective and not recommended at present.

Yellow Fever

Live attenuated yellow fever virus, 0.5 mL, injected subcutaneously. WHO certificate requires registration of batch number of vaccine. Vaccination available in USA only at approved centers. Vaccination must be repeated at intervals of 10 years or less. (Africa, South America.)

Cholera

Suspension of killed vibrios, including prevalent antigenic types. Two injections of 0.5 and 1 mL are given intramuscularly 4–6 weeks apart. This must be followed by 0.5 mL booster injections every 6 months of possible exposure. Protection depends largely on booster doses. WHO certificate is valid for 6 months only. (Middle Eastern countries, Asia, occasionally others.)

Plague

Suspension of killed plague bacilli given intramuscularly, 2 injections of 0.5 mL each, 4–6 weeks apart, and a third injection 6 months later. (Middle Eastern countries, Asia, occasionally South America and others.)

Typhus

Suspensions of inactivated typhus rickettsiae given intramuscularly, 2 injections of 0.5 mL each, 4–6 weeks apart. Booster doses of 0.5 mL every 6 months may be necessary. (Southeastern Europe, Africa, Asia.)

Hepatitis A

No active immunization available. Temporary passive immunity may be induced by the intramuscular injection of human gamma globulin, 0.01 mL/lb every 2–3 months. It is better to give 0.05 mL/lb every 4–6 months if a sojourn in a hyperendemic area is prolonged.

Rabies

For travelers to rural areas of countries where rabies is prevalent, preexposure vaccination should be considered. This involves at least 2 weekly injections of inactivated vaccine plus a booster 1 month later.

● ● ●

References

Ahonkhai VI & others: Failure of pneumococcal vaccine in children with sickle-cell disease. N Engl J Med 301:26, 1979.

Ascari WQ & others: Rh₀(D) immune globulin (human): Evaluation in women at risk of Rh immunization. JAMA 205:1, 1968.

Brunel PA & others: Prevention of varicella by zoster immune globulin. N Engl J Med 280:1191, 1969.

Committee on Control of Infectious Diseases: *Report*, 18th ed. American Academy of Pediatrics, 1977.

Fudenberg HH & others (editors): *Basic & Clinical Immunology*, 2nd ed. Lange, 1978.

Gotschlich EC: Bacterial meningitis: The beginning of the end. Am J Med 65:719, 1978.

Hayden GF & others: Current status of mumps and mumps vaccine in United States. Pediatrics 62:965, 1978.

Health information for international travel, 1976. Morbid Mortal Wkly Rep 25 (Suppl), Oct 1976.

Horstmann DM: Controlling rubella: Problems and perspectives. Ann Intern Med 83:412, 1975.

John TJ & others: Epidemic hepatitis B caused by commercial human immunoglobulin. Lancet 1:1074, 1979.

Johnson RH, Ellis RJ: Immunobiologic agents and drugs available from the Center for Disease Control. Ann Intern Med 81:61, 1974.

Krugman S, Katz SL: Childhood immunization procedures. JAMA 237:2228, 1977.

Lane JA & others: Complications of smallpox vaccination, 1968. N Engl J Med 281:1201, 1969.

Nikoskelainene J & others: Is group-specific meningococcal vaccination resulting in epidemics caused by other groups of virulent meningococci? Lancet 2:403, 1978.

Peltola H & others: Clinical efficacy of meningococcus group A capsular polysaccharide vaccine in children 3 months to 5 years of age. N Engl J Med 297:686, 1977.

Plotkin SA, Wiktor T: Rabies vaccination. Ann Rev Med 29:583, 1978.

Plotkin SA, Wiktor T: Vaccination of children with human cell culture rabies vaccine. Pediatrics 63:219, 1979.

Rimland D & others: Immunization for the internist. Ann Intern Med 85:622, 1976.

Antiprotozoal Drugs | 62

J.F. Catchpool, MB, BS (Lond), LRCP, MRCS, MD

THE CHEMOTHERAPY & CHEMOSUPPRESSION OF MALARIA

The choice of a drug or combinations of drugs for the chemotherapy or chemosuppression of malaria depends on the following factors:

The Prevalence of Drug-Resistant Strains of Plasmodia

During the 1960s, strains of malaria resistant to chloroquine and other antimalarials spread rapidly through Southeast Asia and Latin America. The preferential emergence of chloroquine-resistant strains was caused by a combination of heavy drug pressure, the introduction of large numbers of nonimmune military personnel, and the partial eradication of the disease, which had destabilized the ecology of malaria. However, in Africa, where much of the black population is still exposed to malaria from birth and has acquired a considerable degree of immunity and where the use of antimalarial drugs is not so widespread, chloroquine-resistant strains of malaria are still extremely rare. Chloroquine-resistant strains are now frequently encountered in Southeast Asia, New Guinea, South America, Meso-America, and all of the Indian subcontinent, but they have not yet become established in Africa or the Middle East. All symptomatic *Plasmodium falciparum* infections occurring in refugees from Southeast Asia should be assumed to be chloroquine-resistant and therefore should be treated with oral or parenteral quinine. The best available country-by-country information listing the prevalence of malaria and the risk of chloroquine-resistant *P falciparum* infections is contained in USPHS Publication 79-8280, *Health Information for International Travel 1979*, published by the Center for Disease Control (CDC), Atlanta, Georgia 30333.

In emergencies, information may be obtained by telephoning (404) 633-3311 (days) or (404) 633-2176 (nights and weekends). The CDC keeps stocks of parenteral chloroquine and quinine.

J.F. Catchpool is Assistant Research Epidemiologist, G.W. Hooper Foundation, University of California, San Francisco.

The Species of the Infecting Parasite

Human malaria can be caused by 4 species of protozoal parasites. Three of the 4, *Plasmodium vivax*, *Plasmodium malariae*, and *Plasmodium ovale*, are classified as "relapsing malarias" because they have a secondary or persisting stage of their life cycle. This secondary exoerythrocytic stage of development provides a reservoir of parasites for the reinfection of the erythrocytes that can give rise to a recrudescence of symptoms months or even years after a clinical cure has been obtained by the destruction of the asexual forms in the blood.

P falciparum, the most lethal form of malaria, has no exoerythrocytic stages. Prompt diagnosis and treatment are essential. An average of 4 deaths a year from malaria are reported in the USA; most are due to *P falciparum*. If the strain is not resistant, it readily responds to treatment and a radical cure can be achieved. Malaria caused by this parasite is sometimes called "malignant tertian malaria" because it produces a fulminating infection in nonimmune victims, with spikes of fever every third day corresponding to the bursting of the erythrocytes and the release of the merozoites. Untreated falciparum malaria in nonimmune individuals may rapidly progress to a fatal conclusion.

The disease caused by *P malariae* is sometimes called "quartan malaria" because the spikes of fever come every fourth day. In West Africa, quartan malaria is associated with a high incidence of nephrotic syndrome. *P malariae* is unique because infection can remain dormant for many years.

A rare form of relapsing malaria is caused by *P ovale* (common in West Africa). Its periodicity is similar to that of *P vivax*, but it runs a milder course and is more easily treated.

Chemosuppression for the relapsing malarias must be continued for several weeks after the last exposure to infection.

The Stage of Parasitization

Different antimalarials exert their effects at different stages of the parasite's life cycle. Chemoprophylaxis or therapy of acute attacks by chemosuppression of the clinical manifestations of the disease—or the elimination of all parasites at all stages (a radical cure)—may be achieved by drugs attacking at (1) the

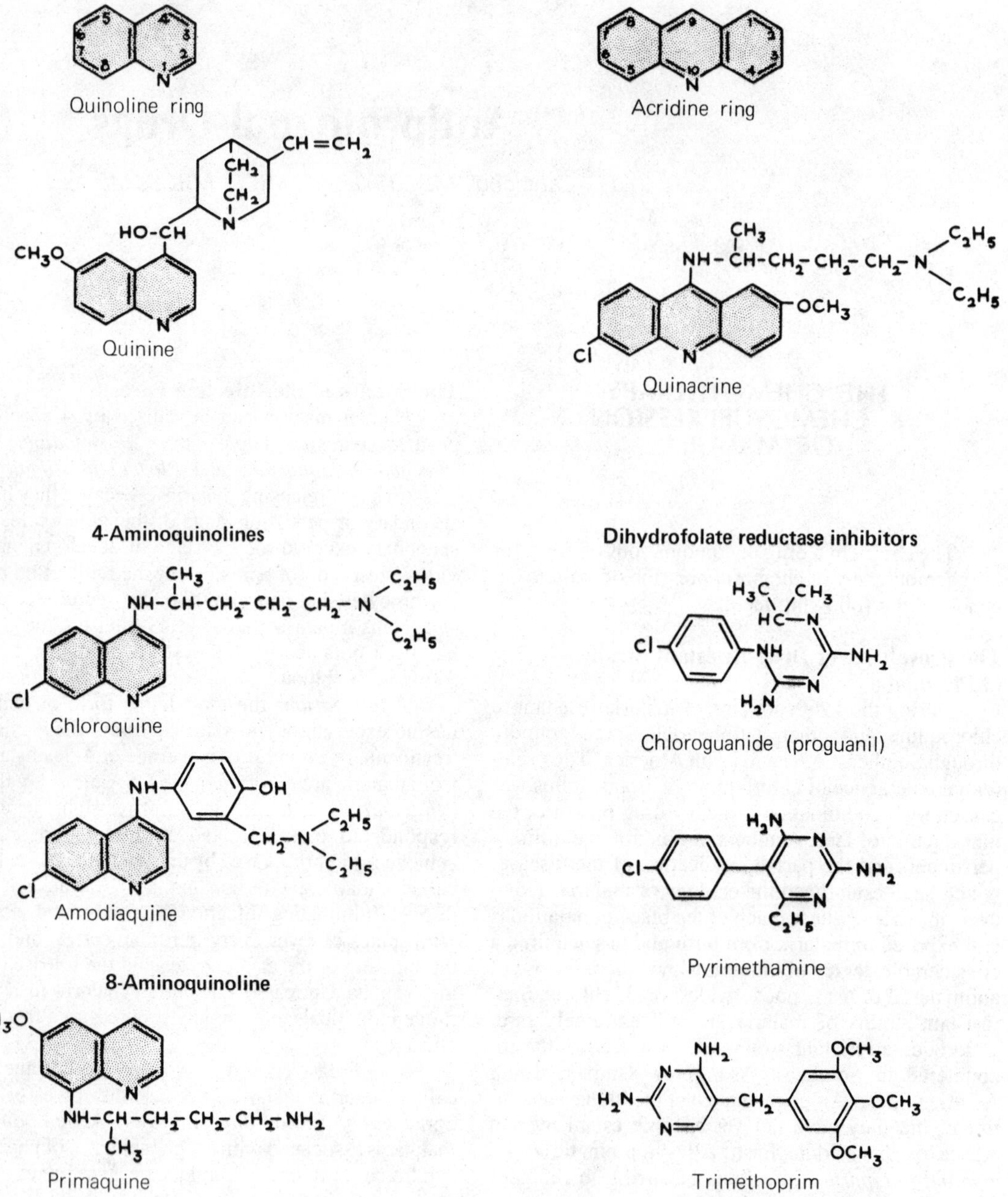

Quinoline ring

Acridine ring

Quinine

Quinacrine

4-Aminoquinolines

Chloroquine

Amodiaquine

8-Aminoquinoline

Primaquine

Dihydrofolate reductase inhibitors

Chloroguanide (proguanil)

Pyrimethamine

Trimethoprim

Sulfones and Sulfonamides

Sulfadiazine

Dapsone
(diaminodiphenylsulfone, DDS)

Figure 62 –1. Structural formulas of antimalarial drugs. Arranged to show structural relationships and historical development of the compounds.

pre-erythrocytic stages (sometimes called "primary exoerythrocytic" or "tissue" stages), which take place in the liver; (2) the erythrocytic stages, in which the parasites multiply rapidly in erythrocytes; or (3) the exoerythrocytic or secondary tissue stages of the relapsing malarias *(P vivax, P malariae,* and *P ovale),* which also take place in the liver. In addition, some drugs may have a selectively toxic effect on the gametocytes that form in the erythrocytes and are responsible for transferring the infection to the mosquito. Other drugs, when ingested in the blood by the mosquito, may prevent the transmission of malaria to another victim by preventing multiplication (sporogony) in the mosquito gut and salivary glands.

Antimalarial drugs are sometimes classified as follows:

(1) Primary tissue schizonticides: Drugs that destroy the primary (pre-erythrocytic) tissue schizonts in the liver soon after infection (eg, primaquine).

(2) Blood schizonticides: ("Chemosuppressive" or "clinically curative" drugs.) Drugs that suppress the symptoms of malaria by destroying the schizonts and merozoites in the erythrocytes (eg, quinine, quinacrine, chloroquine, and amodiaquine).

(3) Gametocides: Drugs that prevent infection of mosquitoes and therefore the spread of infection by mosquitoes by destroying gametocytes in the blood (eg, primaquine).

(4) Sporonticides: Drugs that could help to eradicate the disease by preventing sporogony and multiplication of the parasites in the mosquito when ingested with the blood of the human host (eg, chloroguanide and pyrimethamine).

(5) Secondary tissue schizonticides: ("Radically curative" drugs.) Drugs used to cure the chronic relapsing fevers due to infection by *P vivax, P malariae,* and *P ovale* by destroying the secondary (exoerythrocytic) tissue schizonts developing in the liver (eg, primaquine).

The Frequency of Administration

The antimalarial drugs presently available offer a range in speed and duration of drug action. Rapid-acting drugs are needed for therapy of acute attacks. For suppressive therapy (see Table 62–1), drugs taken once a week or once a month are convenient, but drugs taken daily may have advantages. It is usually easier to form a daily habit than to remember a weekly or biweekly drug dose. The dangers of double dosage or of dose omission are fewer, and a more constant blood level is likely to be obtained.

The Race of the Recipient

Certain unfavorable genetic polymorphisms have been maintained in populations living in malarial areas by conferring a greater tolerance to *P falciparum* malaria. For example, heterozygosity for the sickle cell gene provides a measure of protection against *P falciparum* infection, and it is likely that glucose-6-phosphate dehydrogenase (G6PD) deficiency, hemoglobin C disease, hemoglobin E disease, and β-thalassemia do so also.

US blacks not previously exposed to malaria are notably less susceptible to *P vivax* malaria than US whites. Fifteen percent of US blacks are liable to suffer an acute self-limiting hemolysis when treated with primaquine.

The Degree of Host Immunity

In many parts of the world, the malaria death rate of children under age 4 is frequently as high as 15%. Chronic malarial infection may significantly impair the growth and development of the survivors. However, neonates born to immune mothers are partially immune by virtue of transplacentally acquired antibodies. This protection decreases in the first few months of life, and a partial immunity is acquired by repeated mild attacks of malaria. By age 5, this ability to acquire immunity largely disappears. Chemosuppression of malaria during these first few years may deprive a child of the ability to form active immunity.

Continuous protection of nonimmune persons with antimalarial drugs is mandatory. Continuous regular chemosuppression in children born in malarious areas will not only reduce the high morbidity and mortality rates due to malaria but will also enhance their physical development.

Epidemiologic Factors

Mass chemosuppression of malaria must also take into account the danger of resistant strain emergence. Intermittent and inadequate chemosuppression of nonimmune and partially immune populations who are constantly being reinfected from indigenous reservoirs of parasites greatly favors the emergence and spread of drug-resistant strains of malaria.

Immune populations should not be given chemosuppressive drugs unless the dosage regimens are adequate and strictly adhered to. Areas now cleared of malaria but having suitable anopheline mosquitoes may become reinfected by individuals carrying inadequately treated resistant strains of relapsing malaria. Therefore, travelers leaving areas in which malaria is common should be adequately treated with a tissue schizonticide (such as primaquine) for 4 weeks to obtain a radical cure of the relapsing malarias. In areas with (as yet) only rare cases of chloroquine-resistant malaria, most epidemiologists recommend that chloroquine be reserved for therapy and that it not be used for mass chemoprophylaxis.

Malaria Following Blood Transfusion

An increasing number of cases of malaria (some fatal) have resulted from transfusions of infected blood. In most cases, a donor is incriminated by the presence in the serum of fluorescent antibodies to malaria, but often no parasites can be found in the donor's blood. Subsequent inquiry always reveals that the infected donor once lived in a malarious area. Most of these infections are due to *P vivax* malaria, but infections with *P malariae* and *P ovale,* and even *P falciparum,* have been reported.

Table 62–1. Indications for malaria chemoprophylaxis (modified from: MMWR 27 [Suppl] :81, Mar 10, 1978).

Purpose	Drugs of Choice	Alternative Drugs
To prevent acquisition of malaria in areas without known chloroquine-resistant malaria	Chloroquine phosphate Amodiaquine Hydroxychloroquine Chloroquine sulfate	Pyrimethamine Chlorguanide†
To prevent acquisition of malaria in areas with known chloroquine-resistant strains of *P falciparum*	Pyrimethamine-sulfadoxine†	Since pyrimethamine-sulfadoxine is not available in the USA and must be obtained overseas, travelers should take weekly chloroquine or a comparable drug until pyrimethamine-sulfadoxine can be obtained.
To prevent relapses of *P vivax* and *P ovale*	Primaquine‡	

*Malaria chemoprophylaxis in pregnant women: Pregnancy is not a contraindication for malaria chemoprophylaxis. The most suitable agent for use during pregnancy is chloroquine or one of the other 4-aminoquinolines, because they have not been associated with teratogenic effects when administered for malaria suppression. Neither pyrimethamine nor pyrimethamine-sulfadoxine should be used in pregnant women because of reports of congenital defects associated with the administration of pyrimethamine to animals. To avoid excessive use of drugs during pregnancy, prophylaxis with primaquine, if indicated, should be withheld until after delivery.

†Not available in the USA.

‡Not recommended for all travelers to malarious areas.

QUININE

History

Quinine is the principal alkaloid found in the bark of the South American cinchona tree. The use of cinchona bark for the treatment of malarial fevers dates back to the 17th century. Its discovery and introduction into Europe is usually credited to the Jesuits. Without quinine, the European colonization of tropical Africa would have been impossible. For 300 years, until the Japanese occupation of the Javanese cinchona plantations early in World War II intensified the search for synthetic antimalarial drugs, the powdered bark was the only drug that could effectively suppress the symptoms of malaria. Although quinine can now be synthesized, it and the other cinchona alkaloids are still extracted from cinchona bark.

Of the more than 20 alkaloids found in cinchona bark, only quinine and quinidine are now in use. Both have schizonticidal activity, but because of its superior absorption, only quinine is used for the treatment of malaria. Quinidine is the D-isomer of quinine (see Chapter 16).

Absorption, Metabolism, & Excretion

Quinine is rapidly absorbed from the small intestine, and peak plasma concentrations are obtained 1–3 hours after ingestion. Excretion reaches a maximum after 4 hours, tapers off after another 4 hours, and is almost complete in 24 hours. Only 10% of the oral dose is excreted in the urine; the rest is metabolized. Subcutaneous or intramuscular quinine is poorly absorbed, and inflammation and sloughing may occur at the site of injection. Quinine given intravenously results in significantly higher plasma levels than quinine given orally.

Pharmacologic Effects

A. Mechanism of Action: The exact mechanism of quinine's antimalarial action is uncertain. Quinine can form a hydrogen-bonded complex with double-stranded DNA that inhibits protein synthesis by preventing strand separation and therefore DNA replication and transcription to RNA. Quinine has been observed to depress so many enzyme systems that it has in the past been described as a "general protoplasmic poison."

B. Effects on Malaria: Quinine, along with quinacrine, chloroquine, and amodiaquine, is classed as a "blood schizonticide." It has no effect on the primary or secondary exoerythrocytic "tissue" forms of the parasites and cannot therefore bring about a radical cure of malaria caused by *P vivax, P malariae,* or *P ovale;* neither is it effectively gametocidal or sporonticidal to *P falciparum.* Although quinine cannot prevent infection, it can suppress the symptoms of malaria and also bring about rapid control of an acute attack. Quinine by intravenous drip is now once again the treatment of choice for acute attacks of falciparum malaria in areas where chloroquine-resistant strains of *P falciparum* exist.

C. Other Effects: The actions of quinine on the cardiovascular system are similar to those of quinidine (see Adverse Reactions, below). Quinine has little effect on smooth muscle other than a slight oxytocic action on the gravid uterus, especially during the third trimester of pregnancy. Clinically, it has no effect until labor has started, although dangerously toxic amounts may cause abortion.

In skeletal muscle, quinine has a curarelike effect on the motor end-plate and causes a lengthening of the refractory period. Tetanic contractions associated with various conditions may be diminished by quinine, and the drug has been used to lessen the contractions of myotonia congenita and to provide a diagnostic test for myasthenia gravis by aggravating the symptoms. Quinine was used for centuries to abate fevers due to any cause; its antipyretic action was due mostly to peripheral vasodilation.

Clinical Uses

A. Use in Acute Malaria: For 300 years, quinine was the drug of choice for the treatment and chemosuppression of malaria. By 1959, quinine as an antimalarial had been totally superseded by synthetic antimalarials. However, 3 years later, chloroquine-resistant strains of *P falciparum* were being reported from Colombia and Brazil, and later from Southeast Asia.

By 1965, 80% of US servicemen treated in Vietnam for malaria with chloroquine showed a persisting parasitemia that could only be brought under control with intravenous quinine. Relapses were frequent until, in 1969, quinine therapy was combined with use of pyrimethamine. Unfortunately, in 1968 a strain of *P falciparum* (the Smith strain) appeared that does not respond to quinine-pyrimethamine treatment. Infections with the Smith strain induced in volunteers in US prisons either relapsed after or were completely refractory to treatment with combinations of quinine, chloroquine, pyrimethamine, proguanil, and trimethoprim but were sensitive to a combination of quinine and sulfametopyrazine (sulfalene). For cerebral malaria, which occurs in 2% of attacks of *P falciparum* malaria occurring in nonimmune individuals, intravenous quinine should be preceded by corticosteroids such as dexamethasone, 4–6 mg every 4–6 hours.

B. Other Uses: Quinine (Quinam) is used to relieve leg cramps occurring during recumbency at night. In many parts of the world, quinine is still used as an all-purpose antipyretic. Many tonic waters and cocktail mixes contain quinine in trace amounts.

Adverse Reactions

A. Side-Effects:

1. Cinchonism–This term denotes the mild toxic state that usually develops when the plasma level of quinine exceeds 10–12 mg/L. Symptoms include flushed and sweaty skin, tinnitus, blurred vision, impaired hearing, dizziness, nausea and vomiting, and diarrhea. With severe cinchonism, there may be papular or urticarial skin rashes, deafness, somnolence, diminished visual acuity or blindness (toxic amblyopia) due to ischemia of the retinal vessels, abdominal pain, and disturbances in cardiac rhythm or conduction. Marked hypotension is common, especially with intravenous therapy, and on the ECG, lengthening of the P–R interval and the QRS complex is frequently observed.

2. Local irritant effect–Quinine is an irritant to the gastric mucosa, causing nausea and pain. Painful sterile abscesses frequently result from intramuscular injections. Intravenous injections may cause thrombophlebitis.

3. Hematologic effects–Hemolysis directly attributable to quinine occurs in 0.05% of people treated for acute malaria. Quinine inhibits phagocytosis and may rarely cause leukopenia, agranulocytosis, thrombocytopenic purpura, and Schönlein-Henoch purpura.

4. Blackwater fever–Blackwater fever is the dread syndrome of massive intravascular hemolysis, hemoglobinuria, azotemia, intravascular sludging and coagulation, renal failure, uremia, and death in 25–50% of cases. It is seldom seen in immune populations unless they have been treated with quinine. Hemoglobinuria occurs most often in patients who are also G6PD-deficient. However, irregular or heavy therapy with any antimalarial, repeated and inadequately treated infections, sensitization to the parasite, fatigue, chilling, and perhaps idiosyncrasy to quinine may all be predisposing factors. It is at times necessary to continue quinine therapy in spite of the hemolytic reaction if the infection is due to a resistant strain that cannot be treated with another drug.

B. Overdosage Toxicity: The lethal dose of quinine for adults is about 8 g, but survival has been reported after much larger doses. After overdosage, prompt gastric lavage with an alkaline solution is imperative because the drug is rapidly absorbed and death may ensue within a few hours. There is usually a profound fall of blood pressure owing to peripheral vasodilatation and myocardial depression. Respiration becomes slow and shallow, and cyanosis develops. The quinidinelike action produces the expected electrocardiographic changes and arrhythmias. Doses greater than 4 g in 24 hours usually lead to visual impairment, which may be reversed by discontinuing the drug.

Preparations & Dosages for Chloroquine-Resistant Malaria*

Because of the high proportion of chloroquine-resistant *P falciparum* in Southeast Asia, all falciparum infections seen in refugees should be assumed resistant, and one of the following regimens should be used:

(1) Quinine sulfate, 650 mg, 3 times a day for 3 days plus pyrimethamine, 25 mg, 2 times a day for 3 days plus sulfadiazine, 500 mg, 4 times a day for 5 days; these 3 drugs must be administered concurrently.

(2) Quinine sulfate, 650 mg, 3 times a day for 3 days plus Bactrim Double Strength (160 mg trimethoprim and 800 mg sulfamethoxazole), 2 tablets, 2 times a day for 5 days, administered concurrently.

(3) Quinine sulfate, 650 mg, 3 times a day for 3 days plus tetracycline, 250 mg, 4 times a day for 10 days, administered concurrently.

Several points above the above therapy should be noted. Sulfonamides are used in combination with a folic acid antagonist (eg, pyrimethamine or trimethoprim) because they are synergistic. The type of sulfonamide used is not critical provided that a sufficient blood level is maintained for at least 5 days. While combinations of sulfonamide, a folic acid antagonist, and a tetracycline are effective schizonticides, their rate of action is slow. Thus, at least 3 days of quinine therapy is important to rapidly reduce the parasite density to safe levels. Treatment of *P falciparum* malaria is effective in up to 95% of cases; however, such patients should be carefully followed for at least

*Reproduced from MMWR 28:389, Aug 24, 1979.

90 days to detect recurrent symptoms or parasitemia. Recurrences are usually within the first 30 days but may occur later. Re-treatment may be with the same or another drug combination.

THE 4-AMINOQUINOLINE DERIVATIVES

1. CHLOROQUINE

History

Originally synthesized in 1934 in Germany (Resochine), chloroquine was tested for antimalarial activity, but in 1935 it was reported to be too toxic for human use. In April 1942, following the fall of the Javanese cinchona plantations to the Japanese, the US War Production Board instigated a crash program of research for synthetic antimalarial drugs. By late 1944, US workers had synthesized 25 different 4-aminoquinoline derivatives, finally selecting a compound designated SN 7618 (later named chloroquine) as the most promising—only to discover a few months later that it was identical with the compound patented in Germany and the USA under the name of Resochine. From 1946 to 1966, chloroquine was the drug of choice for the treatment of malaria the world over. In 1966, chloroquine-resistant malaria began to devastate the nonimmune troops in Southeast Asia.

Chemistry & Nomenclature

Chloroquine (Aralen) is 7-chloro-4-(4'-diethylamino-1'-methylbutylamino)quinoline. Trade names and code designations are as follows:

Chloroquine diphosphate: Aralen, Avloclor, Bemaphate, Chinamine, Gontochin, Imagon, Iroquine, Klorokin, Luprochin, Resochin, Resoquine, Sanoquin, Tanakan, Tresochin, Trochin.

Chloroquine sulfate: Nivaquine, Nivaquine B.

Hydroxychloroquine sulfate: Plaquenil, Plaquinol.

Chloroquine diphosphate is a bitter, colorless, dimorphic crystalline powder soluble in water at pH 4.5 but with diminishing solubility at more neutral or alkaline pH. The D and L isomers are equally potent, but the D isomer is slightly less toxic. Chloroquine has a quinoline ring like that of quinine with a side chain identical to that of quinacrine. The Cl atom in the seventh position appears to be crucial to the antimalarial activity of the 4-aminoquinolines and quinacrine.

Absorption, Metabolism, & Excretion

Absorption of chloroquine from the gastrointestinal tract is rapid and complete; maximum plasma concentrations are reached in 1–2 hours. The half-life of chloroquine in the body is about 5 days. Chloroquine is rapidly removed from the plasma and concentrated in those tissues where active protein synthesis and cell multiplication are greatest. The liver, spleen, kidneys, lungs, and leukocytes often contain 200–700 times the plasma concentration (whereas the brain and spinal cord contain only 10–30 times the plasma concentration). For this reason, whenever an effectively schizonticidal plasma level is urgently needed, a loading dose should be given. The concentration of chloroquine in the erythrocytes is about 10–20 times greater than in the plasma and in parasitized erythrocytes about 25 times greater than in normal erythrocytes. Only 10–25% of the oral dose is excreted in the urine. The rate of excretion may be increased by acidification of the urine or decreased by alkalinization of the urine. Concomitant administration of other 4-aminoquinolines or 8-aminoquinolines prolongs and potentiates plasma levels of chloroquine.

Pharmacologic Effects

A. Mechanism of Action: Chloroquine and its congeners block the enzymatic synthesis of DNA and RNA. These drugs form a complex with DNA that prevents DNA from acting as a template for its own replication or transcription to RNA. It has been postulated that the quinoline ring of chloroquine is inserted between the base pairs of the DNA double helix so that the chlorine atom in position 7 of the quinoline ring lies in close proximity to the 2-amino group of guanine in a guanine-cytosine base pair. The diaminoaliphatic side chain of chloroquine lying across the minor groove of the DNA helix ties the 2 strands together by interacting ionically with the phosphoric acid groups of both strands. The electronegativity of the substituent at position 7 of the quinoline ring appears to be critical to the stability of the complex. The length of the side chain bridging the minor groove of the DNA helix is also critical; antimalarial activity is maximal when there are 4 carbon atoms between the 2 N atoms in the side chain, whereas a side chain with 3 or 5 carbon atoms instead of 4 has only two-thirds of the antimalarial activity of chloroquine, and a chain with 2 or 6 carbon atoms instead of 4 exhibits only one-third the activity. The selective toxicity for the malarial parasites must therefore depend on a chloroquine-concentrating mechanism.

B. Effects:

1. In malaria–Chloroquine is an excellent blood schizonticidal drug for all 4 types of malaria. The fever and parasitemia produced by non–drug-resistant strains of plasmodia are usually controlled within 24–48 hours, and in *P falciparum* infections a complete cure can be obtained. However, the drug has no effect on secondary tissue schizonts of relapsing malarias and thus cannot effect a "radical" cure of malaria caused by *P vivax, P malariae,* or *P ovale.*

Chloroquine, like quinine, is not lethal to the gametocytes or sporozoites of *P falciparum,* so that the blood of falciparum-infected chloroquine-treated humans can remain infective to mosquitoes for months. This may favor the emergence of drug-resistant strains of *P falciparum* in endemic areas.

Mechanism of chloroquine resistance. Parasites grown for many months in the presence of steadily increasing but sublethal doses of chloroquine will eventually become partially or totally resistant to the drug, and no concentration of chloroquine in the parasitized red cells can be demonstrated.

Plasmodial resistance to chloroquine is probably due to an impaired mechanism of drug transport across the parasite cell wall, so that the concentration of chloroquine in resistant schizonts never reaches a level sufficient to arrest nucleic acid synthesis.

2. On cardiovascular system–Chloroquine has a slight quinidinelike effect on the cardiovascular system, and changes in the T wave of the ECG may be noticeable during therapy. Chloroquine depresses myocardial excitability to approximately the same extent as quinidine, but it has hardly any effect on the conduction velocity. It has on occasion been used in place of quinidine. Toxic doses depress vasomotor function and induce circulatory collapse, shock, respiratory paralysis, and death.

3. Anti-inflammatory effects–Chloroquine has anti-inflammatory effects that have been useful in the treatment of rheumatoid arthritis and discoid lupus erythematosus. The mechanism is not understood.

The mechanism of chloroquine's therapeutic effect on extraintestinal amebiasis (see below) is presumably the same as the mechanism of its effect on the erythrocytic schizonts.

Clinical Uses

A. Malaria, Acute Attacks: Chloroquine usually terminates the fever and parasitemia of acute attacks of nonresistant strains of falciparum malaria within 24–48 hours, and complete cures are usually obtained because *P falciparum* has no secondary tissue stage. Severe malaria with more than 100,000 parasites/μL of blood or with cerebral, renal, or pulmonary complications requires immediate treatment with slow intravenous infusions of quinine. If an acute attack does not respond to chloroquine within 24 hours, a resistant strain may be involved and other antimalarial drugs must be tried (see p 628). For acute attacks of *P vivax* malaria, chloroquine is the drug of choice; however, because it has no effect on the exoerythrocytic stages, a radical cure is not possible and the symptoms are likely to recur after chloroquine therapy is stopped.

The recommended treatment for *P vivax* infections (MMWR 28:389, Aug 24, 1979) is a total dose of 1.5 g of chloroquine (base) over a 3-day period (600 mg initial dose, followed by 300 mg at 6, 24, and 48 hours). There have been no reports of resistance of this species to chloroquine, and this regimen should eliminate the parasitemia and symptoms within 24–72 hours. Radical curative therapy is administered to eliminate the exoerythrocytic schizonts in the liver; the 2 accepted regimens are as follows:

(1) Primaquine, 15 mg (base) daily for 14 days. The initial dose should be in association with chloroquine, either with the normal therapeutic course or, if administered later, with a single dose of 600 mg (base) of chloroquine.

(2) Primaquine, 45 mg (base) weekly for 8 weeks.

For a closely supervised patient, the 14-day regimen may be preferable because regular drug taking would be assured and the likelihood of missing doses during the longer 8-week course of treatment would be avoided.

The administration of primaquine or chloroquine-primaquine mixtures may cause gastrointestinal symptoms in some patients. Patients with glucose-6-phosphate dehydrogenase (G6PD) deficiency may experience mild to severe hemolysis during primaquine therapy. It is recommended that all patients be screened for G6PD deficiency before primaquine treatment is begun and that periodic determinations of hematocrit be done during therapy. Those with a G6PD deficiency should be placed on the once-weekly dosage schedule rather than the daily regimen. The hemolysis is reversible upon cessation of the drug, and a significant and persistent fall in hematocrit should dictate cessation of treatment.

Most authorities believe that *P malariae* is not a relapsing species of malaria. There are no reports of *P malariae* resistance to chloroquine. Therefore, this species may be treated with chloroquine in the doses outlined above for *P vivax;* no primaquine therapy is indicated.

B. Suppression of Malaria: Chloroquine effectively suppresses all types of malaria except the resistant strains of *P falciparum* (see Table 62–1). If the drug is discontinued too soon after *P vivax* infections, parasitemia may recur after several days. Chloroquine is more potent, less toxic, better tolerated, and more easily administered than quinine or quinacrine. Complete suppression may be obtained with a plasma level of 5–8 μg/L. The prophylactic use of chloroquine or other 4-aminoquinolines involves the risk of the development of resistant strains. Perhaps chloroquine should be used only for the treatment of acute disease and chloroguanide or pyrimethamine for routine prophylaxis except in areas where resistance to these drugs has been reported.

C. Amebiasis: Chloroquine can bring about rapid and complete clinical cures of hepatic amebiasis, although it is slightly less effective than emetine, which is directly toxic to the myocardium (see p 634).

D. Fluke Infections: See Chapter 63.

E. Other Uses: Chloroquine has been used in lupus erythematosus and arthritis, but the danger of prolonged high dosages outweighs the therapeutic advantages. Chloroquine may suppress skin cancers induced by ultraviolet light. It has been used for the treatment of cardiac arrhythmias, but tolerance quickly develops and quinidine is much more effective.

Adverse Reactions

A. Side-Effects: When used for the chemosuppression of malaria, chloroquine has essentially no toxic effects. During chloroquine therapy, there is occasionally vertigo, malaise, anorexia, diarrhea, headache, blurring of vision, pruritus, and urticaria.

These effects may be reduced by taking the drug after meals. The mechanism of this toxicity is unknown, and it resembles mild cinchonism. Oral ammonium chloride, given to acidify the urine, increases renal excretion of chloroquine.

After high dosage there may be macropapular eruptions, desquamation, or exfoliative lesions of the skin, and alopecia or graying of the hair. Lupus erythematosus, lichenoid skin eruptions, and leukopenia induced by chloroquine have been reported.

Toxic psychoses with hallucinations and agitation and peripheral neuropathies with loss of reflexes and muscle power in the lower limbs can occur. Electrocardiographic changes, particularly flattening or inversion of the T waves, are frequent with high doses.

Congenital deafness and mental retardation have been reported in children born to mothers who were taking large doses of chloroquine during pregnancy. Permanent nerve deafness in adults has followed high-dose chloroquine therapy.

B. Ocular Toxicity: Severe and often permanent eye damage may be caused by the prolonged administration of chloroquine in high dosage.

1. Corneal changes–Chloroquine, secreted in tears, is absorbed by the corneal epithelium. The cornea at first becomes insensitive, and diffuse white granules appear in the epithelium. These granules later aggregate into curved lines just below the center of the cornea. Between 10 and 33% of patients taking large doses of chloroquine develop these symptomless corneal deposits, which always regress when the drug is discontinued.

2. Retinal changes–These are nearly always permanent and often progress after withdrawal of the drug. Early symptoms include halos around lights and ill-defined blurring of vision. Ophthalmoscopic examination at this time may reveal a slight edema with fine degrees of pigment clumping, and frequently small pericentral scotomas causing reading discomfort. These scotomas later coalesce into ring scotomas causing large visual field defects. A characteristic ophthalmoscopic picture consists of a granular or stippled hyperpigmentation of the macula, surrounded by a clear zone of depigmentation encircled by another ring of pigment, much like a bull's eye. Most cases occur after more than 300 mg have been given daily for more than a year. Retinal thresholds have been abnormal in all patients given a total of more than 100 g of chloroquine. More than 13% of patients with rheumatoid arthritis treated with chloroquine have retinal changes. All patients on prolonged, high-dose chloroquine must have vision tested and retinas examined at least every 3 months.

C. Overdosage Toxicity: Each year the number of sudden deaths after accidental or intentional overdosage with chloroquine increases. At least 40 recorded suicides have been attributed to chloroquine. After a toxic dose, there are visual disturbances, hyperexcitability, convulsions, atrioventricular block, and death within 2 hours. At autopsy, no abnormalities can be demonstrated except (sometimes) the presence of undissolved tablets in the stomach and tissue levels of chloroquine that are 20 times as high as the prophylactic tissue levels.

There is no antidote. Because chloroquine is rapidly absorbed, gastric lavage must be done before symptoms occur if it is to be of any value. Peritoneal dialysis or hemodialysis is usually unsuccessful.

Contraindications & Cautions

Chloroquine crosses the placenta and may damage the fetus when large doses have been taken during pregnancy. Patients with porphyria and psoriasis should not use chloroquine because it may precipitate an acute attack, and chloroquine should not be combined with other drugs known to cause dermatitis. Gold or phenylbutazone therapy should be discontinued during chloroquine therapy.

Chloroquine should be used with caution in patients with a history of liver damage, or neurologic or hematologic disorders.

Many malariologists condemn the use of chloroquine for mass chemotherapy because of the danger of resistant strain selection. Resistance to chloroquine always extends to the other 4-aminoquinolines and quinacrine, and often to chlorguanide and pyrimethamine as well.

Therapy of acute attacks should never be attempted with combined chloroquine-primaquine tablets, because an adequate therapeutic dose of chloroquine cannot be achieved without also giving toxic amounts of primaquine.

Dosages

A. Malaria Chemoprophylaxis: See Tables 62–1 and 62–2. A blood level of at least 10 μg/L must be maintained.

B. Acute Attacks of Malaria: Because chloroquine is rapidly concentrated in the tissues, a 1-g (600 mg base) priming dose of chloroquine is necessary to achieve effective plasma levels. This should be followed by 500 mg (300 mg base) 6 hours later and 500 mg on 2 successive days. For critically ill patients with intractable vomiting, delirium, or coma, one 250-mg ampule of chloroquine hydrochloride (150 mg base in 5 mL distilled water) may be given intramuscularly (2.5 mL in each buttock). Repeat in 6 hours, and follow with oral therapy. For pediatric emergencies, 5 mg chloroquine per kg may be given intramuscularly followed 6 hours later by an equal oral dose. The total daily dose should not exceed 10 mg/kg.

Pediatric dosages. The WHO recommended loading dose for infants and children is 10 mg/kg body weight followed by 5 mg/kg/d.

All cases of malaria showing no reduction of parasitemia after 12 hours of chloroquine therapy must be assumed to be due to a resistant strain, and quinine therapy should be started. Advice can be obtained from the Center for Disease Control in Atlanta, Georgia.

C. Other Uses: For extraintestinal amebiasis, 500 mg of chloroquine are given twice daily for 2 days followed by 250 mg twice daily for 2–3 weeks.

Table 62—2. Drugs and doses for malaria chemoprophylaxis (modified from: MMWR [Suppl] 27:81, Mar 10, 1978).

Generic Name	Brand Names	Adult Dose	Pediatric Dose
Amodiaquine	Camoquin Flavoquine Basoquin	520 mg (400 mg base) once weekly and continued for 6 weeks after last exposure in a malarious area	< 1 year: 65 mg (50 mg base) 1—3 years: 130 mg (100 mg base) 4—6 years: 195 mg (150 mg base) 7—10 years: 260 mg (200 mg base) 11—16 years: 390 mg (300 mg base)
Chloroquanide (Proguanil)	Paludrine	100—200 mg daily and continued for 6 weeks after last exposure in a malarious area	2 years and under: 25—50 mg 3—6 years: 50—75 mg 7—10 years: 100 mg
Chloroquine phosphate	Aralen Avloclor Resochin	500 mg (300 mg base) weekly and continued for 6 weeks after last exposure in a malarious area	< 1 year: 62 mg (37.5 mg base) 1—3 years: 125 mg (75 mg base) 4—6 years: 165 mg (100 mg base) 7—10 years: 250 mg (150 mg base) 11—16 years: 375 mg (225 mg base) or 5 mg/kg base
Chloroquine sulfate	Nivaquine	500 mg (300 mg base) weekly and continued for 6 weeks after last exposure in a malarious area	< 1 year: 62 mg (37.5 mg base) 1—3 years: 125 mg (75 mg base) 4—6 years: 165 mg (100 mg base) 7—10 years: 250 mg (150 mg base) 11—16 years: 375 mg (225 mg base) or 5 mg/kg base
Hydroxychloroquine	Plaquenil	400 mg (310 mg base) weekly and continued for 6 weeks after last exposure in a malarious area	< 1 year: 50 mg (37.5 mg base) 1—3 years: 100 mg (75 mg base) 4—6 years: 130 mg (100 mg base) 7—10 years: 200 mg (150 mg base) 11—16 years: 290 mg (225 mg base) or 5 mg/kg base
Primaquine	None	26.3 mg (15 mg base) daily for 14 days or 79 mg (45 mg base) once weekly for 8 weeks; start during the last 2 weeks of or following a course of suppression with chloroquine or a comparable drug	0.3 mg/kg base/d for 14 days or 0.9 mg/kg base/d weekly for 8 weeks
Pyrimethamine	Daraprim	25 mg weekly and continued for 6 weeks after last exposure in a malarious area	2 years and under: 6.25 mg 3—10 years: 12.5 mg Over 10 years: Adult dosage
Pyrimethamine- sulfadoxine*	Fansidar Falcidar Antemal Methipox	50 mg pyrimethamine and 1000 mg sulfadoxine every other week and continued for 6 weeks after last exposure in a malarious area†	In terms of sulfadoxine: 6—11 months: 125 mg 1—3 years: 250 mg 4—8 years: 500 mg 9—14 years: 750 mg

*Countries where pyrimethamine-sulfadoxine can be obtained: Belgium, Brazil, Burma, Cambodia, Germany, Hong Kong, Indonesia, Laos, Malaysia, Philippines, Singapore, Switzerland, Thailand, Venezuela, Viet Nam.
†Use of this drug for more than 6 months is discouraged until more information becomes available on its chronic toxicity.

2. THE CHLOROQUINE CONGENERS

None of the 200 known derivatives of 4-amino-quinoline with proved schizonticidal activity have been conclusively shown to be superior to chloroquine; therefore, chloroquine, whose potency and side-effects have been abundantly documented, is the preferred preparation.

The 1972 WHO scientific group on the chemotherapy of malaria lists only 3 other 4-aminoquinolines "in common use": (1) **Amodiaquine dihydrochloride** (Basoquin, Camoquin, Flavoquine), a 7-chloro-4-(3′-diethylaminomethyl-4′-hydroxyanilino)quinoline. For the prophylactic dose of amodiaquine see Table 62—2; (2) **cycloquine** (Ciklochin, Halochin), a 7-chloro-4-(3′,5′,-bis[diethylaminomethyl]-4′-hydroxyanilino)quinolone; and (3) **amopyroquin**

(Propoquin), a 7-chloro-4-(3′-pyrrolidyl-4′-hydroxyanilino)quinoline.

THE 8–AMINOQUINOLINES

History & Chemical Characteristics

Guttmann and Ehrlich observed in 1891 that methylene blue had a weak activity against vivax malaria. German workers in 1926 replaced the acridine ring of methylene blue with a quinoline ring similar to that of quinine to create an 8-aminoquinoline (pamaquine) that was 60 times more potent than quinine but too toxic for prophylactic use. Later, Atabrine (designated quinacrine in the USP and mepacrine in the BP) was synthesized by combining the side chain of pamaquine with the acridine ring of methylene blue. During World War II, Atabrine became the first synthetic to be used for the mass chemosuppression of malaria.

In the search for an effective cure of the relapsing malarias, the 8-aminoquinolines were restudied. Primaquine was found to have the highest therapeutic index of the 8-aminoquinolines synthesized and tested. It is the only antimalarial now in use that is able to accomplish a radical cure of malaria due to *P vivax*.

1. PRIMAQUINE

Chemistry

Primaquine diphosphate is a 6-methoxy-8-(4'-amino-1'-methylbutylamino)quinoline. It is an orange-red crystalline powder with a solubility of 6 g/dL of water.

Absorption, Metabolism, & Excretion

Absorption from the intestine is essentially complete, and peak plasma levels are reached in 6 hours. Only trace amounts can be detected in the plasma 24 hours later, and only about 1% is excreted in the urine unchanged.

Effective clearance of the tissue schizonts does not begin until primaquine has undergone biodegradation by demethylation and oxidation to quinoline-quinone derivatives, which are the active antimalarial and hemolytic agents. The highest tissue concentrations of primaquine are found in the liver and lungs, but primaquine is also concentrated in brain, heart, and skeletal muscles.

Pharmacologic Action

A. Mechanism of Action: Unlike the 4-aminoquinolines, the 8-aminoquinolines do not inhibit DNA replication and transcription.

Primaquine undergoes biotransformation to quinoline-quinone intermediates that are electron-carrying redox compounds capable of acting as oxidants. The intermediate metabolites probably account for the hemolysis and methemoglobinemia as well as the schizonticidal action of the drug.

B. Effects: Although the 8-aminoquinolines structurally resemble the 4-aminoquinolines, their actions on malaria parasites are quite different. The 8-aminoquinolines act on the exoerythrocytic stages and have practically no effect on the erythrocytic stages. Their mode of action is probably related to the mechanism by which they produce an acute self-limiting intravascular hemolysis in individuals with an inherited glucose-6-phosphate dehydrogenase (G6PD) deficiency.

It is postulated that, in contrast to the erythrocytic schizonts, both the tissue schizonts and the G6PD-deficient erythrocytes have a deficiency of an enzyme or cofactor involved in the pentose phosphate path-

way, making them especially susceptible to oxidative damage.

Primaquine also has an effect on the gametocytes; some are destroyed in the blood, and others cannot later mature in the mosquito gut. Primaquine is therefore a "tissue schizonticide" and the only antimalarial able to bring about "radical cures" of the relapsing malarias. Its gametocidal activity also makes it the best available drug to interrupt the transmission of malaria.

Primaquine given orally in therapeutic doses has no pharmacologic effects other than its antimalarial action and its toxic effect on erythrocyte metabolism. It is never given parenterally because it can produce electrocardiographic changes and a profound fall of blood pressure.

Clinical Uses

Primaquine is highly active against the primary exoerythrocytic stages of falciparum and vivax malaria and the secondary exoerythrocytic forms of the relapsing malarias *(P vivax, P malariae,* and *P ovale).* It is also highly active against the gametocytes of all 4 species of human malaria and is therefore used to limit the transmission of malaria. It has only a slight effect on the blood schizonts and cannot be used to relieve the fever and parasitemia of acute attacks. Primaquine is at the moment the only drug able to attack the late tissue stages of *P vivax, P malariae,* or *P ovale* and therefore able to effect a radical cure. Unfortunately, strains of *P vivax* have now appeared in Southeast Asia that are partially resistant to primaquine.

Several programs of mass chemoprophylaxis with primaquine have been carried out in areas of heavy malaria endemicity by WHO and other public health authorities.

Adverse Reactions

A. Primaquine Sensitivity: G6PD deficiency, sometimes called primaquine sensitivity, is an inherited error of metabolism, transmitted by a gene of partial dominance located on the X chromosome. It is estimated that over 100 million people are affected. Red cells deficient in G6PD are sensitive in various degrees to the 8-aminoquinolines and many other drugs, eg, sulfonamides, PAS, aspirin, certain vitamin K derivatives, nitrofurans, and fava beans.

Normal red cells require glucose for survival. Of the glucose metabolized by red cells, 90% is broken down via the Embden-Meyerhof pathway and the other 10% is metabolized by the pentose phosphate pathway. The enzyme G6PD is necessary for the regeneration of NADPH, which in turn is required for the reduction of oxidized glutathione. One of the functions of reduced glutathione is to protect sulfhydryl-dependent enzymes and other cellular proteins against oxidation. The level of reduced glutathione in the red cells of G6PD-deficient individuals fluctuates and is usually lower than normal. Cells with a low level of reduced glutathione and an impaired mechanism for the regeneration of NADPH are particularly vulnerable to the oxidizing effects of substances such as the quinoline-quinones derived from primaquine. When primaquine brings about a further reduction of the level of reduced glutathione in cells that already have an impaired mechanism for the regeneration of NADPH, glucose metabolism may be so deranged that the red cells undergo hemolysis.

The amount of hemolysis occurring with primaquine therapy is therefore dependent on the following 3 factors:

1. The degree of G6PD deficiency–Because the disease is carried on the X chromosome, affected males and the rare females who are homozygous for the trait have the full expression of the disease. Female carriers of the disease are heterozygous for the trait and have a variable expression of the disease. For some reason not yet fully understood, affected whites (especially those whose ancestors inhabited the Mediterranean littoral) have a much more severe expression of primaquine sensitivity than G6PD-deficient blacks.

2. Age of the erythrocyte population–The older erythrocytes have a lower level of G6PD than younger cells and will be the first to hemolyze. Therefore, if aging susceptible cells have already been removed by hemolysis, the remaining younger population of red cells, which are relatively more resistant, will suffer less hemolysis. For this reason, the hemolysis produced by small doses, eg, 15 mg of primaquine per day, is usually self-limiting. Hemolysis occurring at the inception of primaquine therapy can cause a flulike febrile episode consisting of malaise, weakness, and chills lasting 2–3 days.

3. Dose size–The amount of primaquine-induced hemolysis is dose-dependent and self-limiting. Daily doses of 15 mg of primaquine are well tolerated by young G6PD-deficient blacks, and only minor hemolytic disturbances are encountered; with a daily dose of 30 mg, the incidence and severity of the reactions increase sharply.

In some populations, over 20% of those who live in (or whose ancestors came from) areas of endemic falciparum malaria carry the G6PD deficiency trait. The distribution of this potentially lethal gene can be explained by the fact that it confers a small degree of protection against falciparum malaria.

Other less common types of inherited enzyme deficiencies involving erythrocyte metabolism (eg, glutathione reductase deficiency) may also be expressed as primaquine sensitivity.

B. Side-Effects: Toxic reactions, often seen when large doses (60–240 mg) are given, include nausea, headache, disturbances of visual accommodation, pruritus, and abdominal cramps (which may be relieved with antacids). Severe reactions associated with high-dose therapy include leukopenia and methemoglobinemia usually presenting as cyanosis. All patients receiving primaquine should be told to report any signs of hemolysis, such as reddening or darkening of the urine.

Contraindications & Cautions

Blacks, Greeks, Sephardic Jews, Sardinians, and Iranians who are known to have a high incidence of G6PD deficiency should be watched for signs of hemolysis during primaquine therapy. Before initiating treatment with primaquine, it is recommended that all patients should be screened for erythrocyte G6PD deficiency. Periodic determinations of the hematocrit or hemoglobin are essential during therapy. Patients with active rheumatoid arthritis, lupus erythematosus, or any grave systemic disease should not receive primaquine therapy. Nor should primaquine be given at the same time as quinacrine or other drugs known to have depressant effects on the bone marrow.

When primaquine was used for mass chemosuppression, drug resistance of *P falciparum* was induced. In the laboratory, strains of *P berghei* made resistant to primaquine show significant cross-resistance to cycloguanil, pyrimethamine, and dapsone.

Dosages

For primaquine malaria chemoprophylaxis for adults and for children, see Table 62–2.

There are no indications or preparations for intravenous or intramuscular primaquine therapy.

QUINACRINE
(Mepacrine)

Quinacrine, also known as Atabrine and mepacrine, was the first effective synthetic antimalarial of low toxicity. Until the introduction of chloroquine, it was the principal drug used for antimalarial prophylaxis by both the Allied and the Axis armies in World War II.

The standard World War II malaria suppressive was quinacrine, 100 mg orally. It is readily absorbed from the intestinal tract, and peak plasma levels are reached 8 hours later. Four to 6 weeks after discontinuing therapy, quinacrine can still be detected in the pancreas, lungs, bone marrow, liver, and erythrocytes. Quinacrine crosses the placenta, and fetal tissue levels are nearly the same as the maternal levels.

Quinacrine, like quinine and the 4-aminoquinolines, is a blood schizonticide. Continuous therapy can effectively suppress all 4 types of human malaria and can effect a radical cure of nonresistant strains of *P falciparum*. Malaria due to *P vivax, P malariae,* and *P ovale* will relapse a few weeks or months after discontinuing the drug because quinacrine has no effect on the exoerythrocytic schizonts. There is cross-resistance between chloroquine and quinacrine.

Quinacrine can be a cerebrocortical stimulant, producing heightened awareness, increased physical activity, restlessness, and insomnia.

Clinical Uses
A. Treatment and Chemosuppression of Malaria: Quinacrine as an antimalarial agent was

superseded in 1945 by the far more potent and less toxic 4-aminoquinolines.

B. Other Uses: See Chapters 29, 45, and 63.

Adverse Reactions

When quinacrine was used in low dosages as an antimalarial, it produced yellow staining of the skin and infrequent incidence of psychotic reactions. A grayish-blue discoloration of the ears, nasal cartilages, and fingernail beds that can be mistaken for cyanosis was sometimes seen.

THE ANTIFOLS (DIHYDROFOLATE REDUCTASE INHIBITORS): CHLOROGUANIDE (PROGUANIL), PYRIMETHAMINE, & TRIMETHOPRIM

History

British wartime research for a completely nontoxic antimalarial for mass chemoprophylaxis resulted, in 1946, in chloroguanide (proguanil); however, its effectiveness was soon compromised by the emergence of resistant strains. In 1948, a number of 2,4-diaminopyrimidines had been shown, like guanidine, to antagonize folic acid metabolism. Pyrimethamine, because of its resemblance to the active metabolite of guanidine (see structural formulas, p 620), was tested and found to be a highly effective antimalarial. Trimethoprim, an antifolic originally developed as an antibacterial agent, was not tested for antimalarial activity until the desperate search in 1968 and 1969 for drugs effective against the Southeast Asian strains of *P falciparum* resistant to chloroguanide, chloroquine, and pyrimethamine. The discovery of the synergistic potentiation of the antimalarial activity of the antifols when combined with sulfonamides such as sulfamethoxypyridazine and sulfamethoxazole and with sulfones such as dapsone (DDS) has opened a whole new field of antimalarial therapy. However, because of the rapid development of resistance, with cross-resistance to other combinations of antifols and sulfonamides, it is now recommended that these combinations be used only for the treatment of chloroquine-resistant strains.

Chemistry & Nomenclature

A. Chloroguanide (Proguanil) Hydrochloride: Chloroguanide is N^1-(p-chlorophenyl)-N-isopropylbiguanide hydrochloride (Balusil, bigumal, biguanide, chlorguanide, Chloroguanil, Diguanyl, Drinupal, Guanatol, Lepadina, Paludrine, Palusil, Plasin, Proguanide, and Tirian). For prophylaxis, see Table 62–2.

B. Pyrimethamine: Pyrimethamine is a 2,4-diamino-5-p-chlorophenyl-6-ethylpyrimidine. It is also known by the proprietary names Chloridin, Darapram, Daraprim, Erbaprelina, and Malocide.

C. Trimethoprim: Trimethoprim is a 2,4,-di-amino-5-(3,4,5,-trimethoxybenzyl)pyrimidine. It is available as a combination of one part trimethoprim and 5 parts sulfamethoxazole, known as Bactrim or Septra (or co-trimoxazole).

D. Pyrimethamine-Sulfadoxine (Fansidar, Falcidar, Antemal, Methipox): This preparation is the recommended chemoprophylactic antimalarial (by WHO and CDC) for use in parts of the world where chloroquine-resistant *P falciparum* malaria is now endemic. It is a fixed-combination tablet of a long-acting sulfonamide, (sulfadoxine 1000 mg) combined with pyrimethamine 50 mg.

Pediatric dose: In terms of sulfadozine: 6 to 11 months, 125 mg; 1 to 3 years, 250 mg; 4 to 8 years, 500 mg; 9 to 14 years, 750 mg. See Table 62–2.

Fansidar, not yet available in the USA, should replace chloroquine prophylaxis when the traveler enters areas reported to be harboring chloroquine-resistant strains of *P falciparum* (see Table 62–2). Fansidar is principally effective against the erythrocytic stages of the malarial parasite. It can procure adequate suppression of most *P falciparum, P ovale,* and *P vivax* malarias, but not if they are also pyrimethamine-resistant. For these cases, chloroquine must be added. It is also possible that the "relapsing malarias" will relapse after fansidar therapy is discontinued. Therefore, it is advisable to follow fansidar prophylaxis with several weeks of primaquine prophylaxis.

Absorption, Metabolism, & Excretion

Chloroguanide, pyrimethamine, and trimethoprim are slowly but adequately absorbed from the gastrointestinal tract. Peak plasma levels are reached in 3–7 hours after an oral dose, and loading doses are not necessary. Chloroguanide is so rapidly eliminated from the body that it must be administered daily; pyrimethamine is excreted more slowly. Trimethoprim is excreted more slowly than sulfamethoxazole, with which it is combined.

Unlike the quinoline drugs, chloroguanide, pyrimethamine, and trimethoprim do not accumulate in the tissues. Only very low levels of chloroguanide can be detected in the plasma 24 hours after an oral dose, but significant quantities of pyrimethamine and its metabolites—and of trimethoprim—can be found in the tissues 9 days after an oral dose. Between 40–60% of the oral dose of chloroguanide is excreted in the urine and 10% in the feces; 60% is excreted unchanged and 30% as the triazine metabolite. Sufficient pyrimethamine is excreted in maternal milk so that chemosuppressive levels of the drug may be reached in wholly breast-fed infants.

Pharmacologic Effects

When the antifols are given in therapeutic doses, no effects are seen other than the intended antiprotozoal or antibacterial effects. In excessive doses, abdominal pain, diarrhea, hematuria, and a macrocytic anemia like that of folic acid deficiency may occur.

Antimalarial Effects

All 3 of these drugs are strongly sporonticidal. Pyrimethamine, the most potent of the three, has been calculated to be 2000 times as toxic to the malarial parasite as to the host. These drugs can also prevent sporogony in the mosquito gut, and a single dose of pyrimethamine given to a nonimmune person can interrupt transmission for several weeks. All 3 can provide effective and nontoxic antimalarial chemoprophylaxis provided they are continued for at least 10 weeks after the last infected mosquito bite and that there are no resistant strains in the area. They should not be used for the treatment of acute attacks because their blood schizonticide action is too slow. *P falciparum* malaria resistant to pyrimethamine is increasing and has been found not only in Southeast Asia and East Africa but also in West Africa. Pyrimethamine-resistant strains are usually also resistant to proguanil.

Mode of Action of the Antifols

Chloroguanide itself is not active, only its triazine metabolite, which is rapidly excreted. The selective toxicity of all 3 antifols depends on the fact that plasmodia, unlike man and many other animals, have not lost the enzymes needed for the synthesis of folic acid from para-aminobenzoic acid (PABA), glutamic acid, and pteridine but yet cannot make use of preformed folic acid. The plasmodicidal effects of these 3 antimalarials are due to a deficiency of tetrahydrofolate that results in the inhibition of cell division and schizogony. This interference with folic acid metabolism therefore explains the marked synergistic enhancement of potency that occurs when any of these drugs are combined with sulfonamides or sulfones, causing a sequential blockade of folic acid synthesis at 2 different stages along the metabolic pathway (see Chapter 53).

Clinical Uses

A. Malaria Chemosuppression: Chloroguanide is the least toxic of all the antimalarials, but it must be taken in daily 100 mg doses because of its rapid excretion. Pyrimethamine is the most potent chemoprophylactic available (requiring only 25 mg weekly), but, like chloroguanide, it must be taken for 10 weeks after leaving the endemic area. Cures of acute attacks of malaria in nonimmune patients should not be attempted with these drugs because their ability to reduce fever and parasitemia is much too slow.

B. Combination Therapy of Chloroquine-Resistant Falciparum Malaria: In 1969, 12 cases of agranulocytosis occurred among 200,000 soliders in Vietnam who were taking the standard CP (chloroquine, 300 mg base, primaquine, 45 mg base) tablet once a week plus 25 mg of dapsone weekly. Various other combinations such as pyrimethamine plus quinine and pyrimethamine plus sulfadoxine are advocated and have been found to be effective, but malaria resistance to these new combinations soon develops. For this reason, combinations of antifols and sulfonamides should only be used for chloroquine-resistant malaria.

C. Endemic Malaria: Pyrimethamine has been used to interrupt the transmission of malaria in communities of partially immune patients. Such eradication programs should always follow a course of a quick-acting blood schizonticide to minimize the risk of resistant strain emergence. Endemic malaria control has been attempted by the addition of pyrimethamine to cooking salt supplies. However, when this is done, the dosage levels in children under 6 are extremely variable and the emergence of resistant strains is practically assured.

D. Toxoplasmosis: Pyrimethamine, 25 mg, combined with trisulfapyrimidines, 1 g, given orally 4 times a day for 6 weeks, can be used for the treatment of toxoplasmosis. However, if toxoplasmic chorioretinitis is present or if there is a danger of congenital toxoplasmosis, corticosteroids should also be given.

Adverse Reactions

Chloroguanide occasionally induces anorexia but is the least toxic of all the antimalarials.

Pyrimethamine is also well tolerated. Large doses of pyrimethamine given for long periods sometimes lead to folic acid deficiency. Supplementary folic acid can correct the hematologic defect without impairing the drug's therapeutic effect.

Contraindications & Cautions

Cross-resistance to chloroguanide and pyrimethamine may develop when these drugs are given singly in low doses and for long periods of chemosuppression.

Preparations & Dosages

Chloroguanide hydrochloride (proguanil, Paludrine) is available as tablets of 25, 50, 100, and 300 mg containing 87% of the base. For the chemosuppression of malaria, 100–200 mg daily are usually sufficient.

Pyrimethamine is available as 25 mg tablets. For the chemosuppression of malaria, the dosage is 1 or 2 tablets per week. For children under 14, give pyrimethamine elixir (6.25 mg/mL), 2 mL weekly. The first dose should be taken before entering endemic areas, and suppressive therapy must be continued for 10 weeks after leaving the area.

For the treatment of drug-resistant falciparum malaria, 25 mg of pyrimethamine can be given every 8 hours for the first 3 days of a 14-day course of quinine (650 mg every 8 hours). One gram of sulfadoxine, a long-acting sulfonamide, has been combined with 50 mg of pyrimethamine to produce a single-dose cure of chloroquine-resistant malaria. Because of the true synergism between these 2 drugs, one-tenth of the curative dose of pyrimethamine plus one-fourth of the curative dose of sulfadiazine add up to one curative dose for the treatment of *P falciparum* malaria.

OTHER DRUGS WITH ANTIMALARIAL ACTIVITY

For chloroquine-sensitive falciparum malaria, chloroquine therapy remains the treatment of choice. Therapy should always be followed by a 6-week course of primaquine to prevent relapses due to possible concomitant *P vivax* infections.

For chloroquine-resistant malaria, quinine by intravenous infusion followed by a single dose of sulfadoxine and pyrimethamine are highly effective.

Maloprim is a fixed combination tablet containing 100 mg dapsone with 12.5 mg pyrimethamine. The recommended prophylactic dose is 2 tablets for the week preceding exposure, followed by 1 tablet per week.

Cycloguanil embonate (Camolar), the active metabolite of proguanil, is so poorly soluble in the embonate form that it can be used as an intramuscular repository drug. A single injection provides protection for up to 3 months. However, resistance to cycloguanil has been reported.

Tetracycline, 250 mg every 6 hours for 7 days, can clear asexual forms of the parasites of chloroquine-resistant *P falciparum* infections, but tetracycline has no effect against the gametocytes. Tetracycline may have value as an adjunctive agent to achieve radical cures of drug-resistant infections.

Minocycline is a tetracycline analog. Doses of 540 mg quinine base plus 100 mg minocycline 3 times a day for 3 days, followed by minocycline, 100 mg daily for 7 days, have produced radical cures in 97% of patients with *P falciparum* infections.

Clindamycin and **lincomycin** have also proved effective against resistant *P falciparium*.

THE TREATMENT OF AMEBIASIS*

Amebiasis may present as a severe intestinal infection (dysentery), a mild to moderate symptomatic intestinal infection, an asymptomatic intestinal infection, an ameboma or liver abscess, or in the form of other extraintestinal infections.

Drugs available for therapy can be classified according to their site of antiamebic action. Luminal amebicides such as diiodohydroxyquin and diloxanide furoate are active against luminal organisms but are ineffective against parasites in the bowel wall or tissues. The parenterally administered tissue amebicides dehydroemetine and emetine are effective against

*Section on amebiasis contributed by Robert S. Goldsmith, MD, DTM&H, Professor of Tropical Medicine & Epidemiology, University of California, San Francisco.

parasites in the bowel wall and tissues but not against luminal organisms. Chloroquine acts only against organisms in the liver. Antibiotics taken orally are indirect-acting luminal amebicides that exert their effects against bacterial associates of *Entamoeba histolytica* in the bowel lumen and in the bowel wall but not in other tissues. Given parenterally, antibiotics have little antiamebic activity at any site. Paromomycin, however, has a direct effect on amebas. Metronidazole is uniquely effective against organisms at 3 sites: the bowel lumen, bowel wall, and tissues. However, metronidazole used alone is not sufficient as a luminal amebicide.

The following is a partial list of useful antiamebic drugs:

(1) Tissue amebicides (drugs that act primarily in the bowel wall, liver, and other extraintestinal tissues):

(a) Dehydroemetine, emetine.

(b) Chloroquine (active principally in the liver).

(2) Luminal amebicides (drugs that act primarily in the bowel lumen):

(a) Halogenated hydroxyquinolines: Diiodohydroxyquin (iodoquinol), iodochlorhydroxyquin (clioquinol, Entero-Vioform), dibromohydroxyquinoline (Intestopan).

(b) Pentavalent arsenicals: Glycobiarsol, carbarsone, difetarsone.

(c) Alkaloids: Emetine-bismuth-iodide (EBI).

(d) Amides: Diloxanide furoate (Furamide), clefamide (Mebinol), teclozan, etofamide.

(e) Antibiotics: Tetracyclines, paromomycin (Humatin), erythromycin.

(3) Tissue and luminal amebicides: Nitroimidazoles: Metronidazole (Flagyl), tinidazole (Fasigyn), ornidazole.

Treatment may require the concomitant or sequential use of several drugs. Table 62–3 outlines a preferred and an alternative method of treatment for each clinical type of amebiasis. No drugs are recommended as safe or effective for chemoprophylaxis.

In the past few years, the increasing association of several of the most useful antiamebic drugs with serious or potentially serious adverse reactions has required the reevaluation and reassignment of the drugs of choice and alternative drugs. Metronidazole has been found to induce neoplasms in rodents and to be mutagenic for certain bacteria; thus, it is potentially hazardous for humans. In addition, the halogenated hydroxyquinolines have been increasingly implicated in the production of neurotoxicity. The tetracyclines should not be used for children under age 12 years. Such findings reinforce the need for accurate identification of *E histolytica* before drug therapy is initiated.

Asymptomatic Intestinal Infection

When infection is confined to the bowel lumen, cure may often be obtained by use of luminal amebicides alone; but of the drugs in use, none is completely reliable in eradicating the infection. When available, diloxanide furoate is recommended as the

Table 62–3. Treatment of amebiasis.

	Drug(s) of Choice	Alternative Drug(s)
Asymptomatic intestinal infection	Diloxanide furoate[1,2]	Diiodohydroxyquin (iodoquinol)
Mild to moderate intestinal infection	(1) Diloxanide[1,2] or diiodohydroxyquin[3] **plus** (2) A tetracycline[5] **followed by** (3) Chloroquine[6]	(1) Metronidazole[4] **plus** (2) Diloxanide furoate[1,2] or diiodohydroxyquin[3] **or** (1) Paromomycin[7] **followed by** (2) Chloroquine[6]
Severe intestinal infection (dysentery)	(1) Metronidazole[8] **plus** (2) Diloxanide furoate[1,2] or diiodohydroxyquin[3] **If parenteral therapy is needed initially** (1) Intravenous metronidazole[9] until oral therapy can be started (2) Then give oral metronidazole[8] plus diloxanide furoate[1,2] or diiodohydroxyquin[3]	(1) A tetracycline[5] **plus** (2) Diloxanide furoate[1,2] or diiodohydroxyquin[3] **or** (1) Dehydroemetine[1,10] or emetine (see text for dosage) **followed by** (2) A tetracycline[5] plus diloxanide furoate[1,2] or diiodohydroxyquin[3] **followed by** (3) Chloroquine[6]
Hepatic abscess	(1) Metronidazole[8,9] **followed by** (2) Diloxanide furoate[1,2] or diiodohydroxyquin[3] **plus** (3) Chloroquine[6]	(1) Dehydroemetine[1,11] or emetine (see text for dosage) **plus** (2) Chloroquine[12] **plus** (3) Diloxanide furoate[1,2] or diiodohydroxyquin[3]
Ameboma or extraintestinal infection	As for hepatic abscess, but not including chloroquine	As for hepatic abscess, but not including chloroquine

[1] Available in the USA only from the Parasitic Disease Drug Service, Center for Disease Control, Atlanta, Georgia 30333. Telephone requests may be made by calling (404)329-3670.

[2] Diloxanide furoate, 500 mg 3 times daily for 10 days.

[3] Diiodohydroxyquin (iodoquinol), 650 mg 3 times daily for 21 days.

[4] Metronidazole, 750 mg 3 times daily for 10 days.

[5] A tetracycline, 250 mg 4 times daily for 10 days; in severe dysentery, give 500 mg 4 times daily for the first 5 days.

[6] Chloroquine, 250 mg (salt) twice daily for 14 days.

[7] Paromomycin, 25–30 mg/kg (maximum 3 g) daily for 5–10 days.

[8] Metronidazole, 750 mg 3 times daily for 5–10 days.

[9] An intravenous metronidazole is available. See manufacturer's recommendation for dosage.

[10] Dehydroemetine, 1 mg/kg IM or subcut daily for the least number of days necessary to control severe symptoms (usually 3–5 days) (maximum daily dose 0.1 g).

[11] Dehydroemetine, 1 mg/kg daily IM or subcut for 10 days (maximum daily dose 0.1 g) or emetine (see text for dosage).

[12] Chloroquine, 500 mg (salt) twice daily for 2 days and then 250 mg twice daily for 26 days.

most effective and least toxic. The alternative drug is diiodohydroxyquin (iodoquinol). Other alternatives for treatment or retreatment are paromomycin, paromomycin plus diiodohydroxyquin, or metronidazole plus diiodohydroxyquin or diloxanide furoate. Usually in asymptomatic infection drugs are not given to prevent liver infection.

Mild to Moderate Intestinal Infection

In addition to clearing amebas from the bowel lumen by use of the luminal amebicides diloxanide furoate or diiodohydroxyquin, treatment of mild intestinal disease should eradicate trophozoites potentially carried to the liver. When diiodohydroxyquin is used, concomitant use of a tetracycline probably increases intestinal cure rates. It is less well established that adding a tetracycline to diloxanide furoate also increases effectiveness. Chloroquine is used to destroy

trophozoites in the liver or to eradicate an undetected, early stage of amebic liver abscess; the minimum dose needed to accomplish this is not known. Metronidazole is an alternative drug; although it is highly effective against tissue parasites, a course of a luminal amebicide must also be given to enhance the likelihood of intestinal cure. A second alternative treatment is a course of paromomycin followed by chloroquine.

Severe Intestinal Infection

The treatment of choice is metronidazole plus a concurrent course of diloxanide furoate or diiodohydroxyquin. For patients requiring initial parenteral therapy, an intravenous preparation of metronidazole is available.

A tetracycline plus diloxanide furoate or diiodohydroxyquin usually provides an excellent alternative form of treatment. An additional alternative method, particularly for patients requiring initial parenteral therapy, is to give emetine (or dehydroemetine) intramuscularly or subcutaneously for the minimum number of days (usually 3–5; significant toxicity usually does not occur in this period) needed to control severe symptoms. Then start an oral course of a tetracycline plus diloxanide furoate or diiodohydroxyquin; follow these with a course of chloroquine.

Fluid and electrolyte therapy and opiates to control bowel motility are necessary adjuncts in severe amebic dysentery.

Hepatic Abscess

When metronidazole, the drug of choice, is given for 10 days, early or late treatment failure occurs rarely. If a satisfactory clinical response has not occurred within 2–3 days, especially if the abscess has been adequately drained, therapy should be changed to the alternative mode of treatment: emetine (or dehydroemetine) plus chloroquine. When the clinical response to metronidazole is adequate, it is suggested that a 2-week course of chloroquine follow to prevent late failures. The need for adding this course of chloroquine remains to be evaluated.

Since a comparative trial of metronidazole with and without aspiration has not been reported, the need for therapeutic aspiration is still controversial. Aspiration is clearly indicated, however, when the diagnosis is in doubt, if rupture of a large abscess is impending, or if there is a lack of response to therapy.

Concurrent with the either mode of abscess treatment, a course of diloxanide furoate or diiodohydroxyquin should be given to eradicate intestinal infection.

Ameboma or Extraintestinal Disease

Metronidazole is the drug of choice. Emetine (or dehydroemetine) is an alternative drug; chloroquine is not included because it does not reach sufficiently high tissue concentrations (except in the liver) to be effective. A simultaneous course of a luminal amebicide should also be given.

DEHYDROEMETINE

Racemic 2-dehydroemetine dihydrochloride, available since 1964, is a synthetic substance that can substitute for emetine as an equally effective and probably less toxic drug. However, marked myocardial toxicity has been reported following use of the drug. Although not approved for use in the USA, it is available from the Parasitic Disease Drug Service, Center for Disease Control, Atlanta 30333, on an investigational basis.

In laboratory animals, dehydroemetine is less toxic on an equal weight basis than emetine, although qualitatively their toxicities are alike. In humans, the therapeutic action of dehydroemetine is equal to that of emetine.

In experimental animals, dehydroemetine disappears more rapidly from the heart (but not from the liver) than emetine and is excreted more rapidly. If this also occurs in humans, it could account for the fewer electrocardiographic changes that dehydroemetine causes when identical doses of the 2 drugs are given as reported in some studies. However, Sharad and Vakil reported comparable cardiovascular toxicity for the 2 drugs. Thus, greater comparative clinical experience is needed to establish that dehydroemetine is indeed less toxic.

The clinical uses of dehydroemetine are similar to those of emetine: treatment of severe intestinal amebiasis and treatment of amebic liver abscess in conjunction with chloroquine.

The adverse reactions, cautions, and contraindications are the same as for emetine.

Dehydroemetine is available for injection in 1- and 2-mL ampules containing 30 mg/mL. The dosage for severe intestinal disease is 1 mg/kg intramuscularly or subcutaneously daily for the least number of days necessary to control symptoms (usually 3–5 days). The maximum daily dose is 0.1 g. A tetracycline and diloxanide furoate should be given in conjunction with or after dehydroemetine, and chloroquine should follow.

For liver abscess, dehydroemetine is given in conjunction with chloroquine; a course of a luminal amebicide should follow. The dosage of dehydroemetine is 1 mg/kg/d intramuscularly or subcutaneously for 10 days. The maximum daily dose is 0.1 g.

EMETINE HYDROCHLORIDE

Emetine hydrochloride, used for more than 50 years for the treatment of *E histolytica* infection, remains one of the principal drugs for the treatment of severe intestinal infection (amebic dysentery), liver abscess, and other forms of extraintestinal amebiasis. Emetine should not be used to treat asymptomatic or mild intestinal infections.

When available, use dehydroemetine rather than emetine, since the former is equally effective and may be safer.

Chemistry

Emetine can be derived from ipecac or synthesized. Since emetine has 4 asymmetric centers, several stereoisomers are possible, but the structure below is generally accepted as the configuration of the natural (−) alkaloid.

Emetine is usually prepared as the hydrochloride. To prevent deterioration, it should be protected from light.

Absorption, Metabolism, & Excretion

Emetine is administered parenterally, not orally, because it is absorbed erratically from the gastrointes-

Emetine

tinal tract and may induce emesis. When given parenterally, it is stored primarily in the liver, lungs, spleen, and kidneys; only a small amount is found in other tissues, including cardiac, striated, and intestinal muscle. Because emetine is eliminated slowly via the kidney, the drug is cumulative; trace amounts are detectable in the urine 1–2 months after stopping therapy.

Pharmacologic Effects

Emetine affects almost all tissues. In experimental animals, emetine given parenterally in toxic doses causes cellular damage in the liver, kidneys, and skeletal and cardiac muscle. In the myocardium, cloudy swelling and necrosis of myocardial fibers occurs, with focal areas of cellular infiltration and interstitial proliferation resembling Aschoff bodies. Cardiac conduction and contraction are depressed, which may result in a variety of atrial and ventricular arrhythmias, cardiac dilatation, and death.

In vitro, emetine has adrenergic and cholinergic blocking actions. A similar action of the drug in vivo may be responsible for the hypotension and diarrhea that frequently accompany its use. The nausea and vomiting common during therapy are considered central in origin. Emetine may reduce serum potassium levels in some patients. Elevated transaminase levels sometimes occur, but they do not correlate well with clinical or electrocardiographic findings.

Antiamebic Effects

Emetine in therapeutic dosages acts only against trophozoites. At high doses (beyond those tolerated by humans), the drug may be active against cysts.

Clinical Uses

A. Severe Intestinal Disease (Amebic Dysentery): Parenterally administered emetine rapidly alleviates severe intestinal symptoms but is rarely curative even if a full course is given. For this reason and because of its toxicity, emetine should be given for the minimum period needed to relieve severe symptoms (usually 3–5 days). Marked toxicity is unlikely when the drug is used for less than 7 days.

In addition to a short course of emetine, the regimen for severe intestinal amebiasis includes a tetracycline and diloxanide furoate or diiodohydroxyquin. These are followed by a course of chloroquine.

B. Amebic Liver Abscess: Emetine plus chloroquine is an alternative treatment for amebic liver abscess. A course of diloxanide furoate or diiodohydroxyquin should follow.

C. Amebomas and Extraintestinal Amebiasis: Emetine is effective in treating other forms of extraintestinal amebiasis and amebomas.

D. Other Parasites: Emetine has occasionally been useful in the treatment of infections with *Balantidium coli, Fasciola hepatica,* and *Paragonimus westermani,* but safer drugs should be used first.

Adverse Reactions

Emetine is cumulative in its toxic action. Side-effects develop in most patients but are usually not severe if the dosage does not exceed 65 mg daily for 10 days. Few and (usually) mild side-effects appear if the drug is given for 3–5 days; additional mild to severe side-effects appear if the drug is given for up to 10 days; serious toxicity is common if it is given for more than 10 days. Therefore, use of emetine for more than 10 days is contraindicated.

A. Local Reactions: Pain, tenderness, and muscle weakness in the area of the injection are frequent, often starting 24–48 hours after the injection, and may persist for 1–2 weeks. Occasionally, sterile abscesses develop.

B. Gastrointestinal Effects: Diarrhea is induced or exacerbated in many patients, generally beginning several days after the onset of therapy. In the treatment of severe intestinal symptoms, there may be a short period of emetine-induced improvement followed by a relapse of diarrhea with abdominal cramps, and blood and mucus in the stools. Transient nausea occurs in over 30% of patients, but vomiting is rare. A course of treatment can usually be completed in spite of gastrointestinal symptoms. If they are too severe, therapy must be discontinued.

C. Cardiovascular Effects: Minor electrocardiographic changes occur frequently, but severe cardiac toxicity with significant conduction defects is rare. The most serious symptoms and findings are tachycardia and other arrhythmias, precordial pain, and congestive heart failure with dyspnea and hypotension. Most deaths from emetine have been in patients given total doses over 1200 mg; some deaths have been reported in patients given the standard total dose of 650 mg or less. Electrocardiographic changes induced in more than 50% of patients include flattening and inversion of P and T waves, lengthening of the P–R and Q–T intervals, ST elevation, premature beats, and transient atrial fibrillation. These changes usually appear about 7 days after the onset of treatment but occasionally not until 2–3 weeks after the last injection. They are generally reversible, requiring about 6 weeks to return to normal. In rare instances, emetine-induced abnormalities have persisted for several years.

D. Neuromuscular Effects: Generalized muscular weakness—sometimes associated with tenderness, stiffness, aching, or tremors—is reported by many patients. At therapeutic doses, the weakness is usually mild and reversible, but it may persist for several weeks after treatment is stopped. These symptoms are attributed to a direct action of emetine on the muscles and not to neuritis. Although mild paresthesias are reported by patients, a true polyneuritis with objective signs of nerve damage occurs rarely, if ever.

E. Other Side-Effects: Many other mild and often transient side-effects may occur, including fatigue, headache, dizziness, and urticarial, eczematous, or purpuric skin lesions. Proteinuria may also be present.

Contraindications & Cautions

Since emetine is a potentially dangerous drug, careful hospital supervision is essential. Considerable caution should be observed to avoid dangerous inadvertent intravenous administration.

Patients should be kept at bed rest with bathroom privileges during treatment and for several days afterward. They should be examined daily for cardiovascular, neuromuscular, and gastrointestinal signs or symptoms. Pulse and blood pressure should be recorded 3 times a day and electrocardiograms taken prior to the first injection, on the fifth and tenth days of therapy, and weekly for 2 weeks after the last injection.

The drug should be discontinued if the resting pulse (or, particularly, the sleeping pulse) exceeds 110/min (correct for fever) or if marked hypotension, precordial pain, marked gastrointestinal symptoms, or generalized weakness or other neuromuscular symptoms develop. Generalized weakness and muscular aching (to be distinguished from local reactions due to injections) tend to develop before more serious toxic symptoms and thus can be used as a guide for avoiding overdosage.

Electrocardiographic criteria for discontinuing therapy have not been established. Some clinicians believe that prolongation of the P–R, QRS, or Q–T interval is an indication for stopping treatment; ectopic rhythms, although rare, clearly require cessation of therapy.

Patients should remain sedentary for about 4 weeks after completion of therapy, and surgery is inadvisable for at least 6 weeks after administration of emetine.

Great care should be exercised in administering the drug to aged or debilitated people; dosage is usually reduced by half for such patients.

Emetine should not be used in pregnancy or in patients with cardiac or renal disease or with a recent history of polyneuritis. The drug is also contraindicated in young children unless alternative drugs have not been effective in controlling severe dysentery or liver abscess.

Preparations & Dosages

Aqueous solutions of emetine hydrochloride are supplied in ampules containing 32 or 65 mg.

The daily dose of emetine for adults and children is 1 mg/kg subcutaneously (preferred) or intramuscularly. The maximum daily dose for adults is 65 mg; for children under 8 years, 10 mg.

For the treatment of severe intestinal disease, injections are generally given for the minimum number of days needed to control severe symptoms, generally 3–5 days. See under Clinical Uses for additional drugs needed to complete the course of therapy.

For the treatment of hepatic abscess, other extraintestinal disease, and ameboma, the same doses of emetine are used but for a total of 10 days. Patients should not be treated beyond 10 days.

If a second course of therapy is needed, an intervening period of 6 weeks is required.

DILOXANIDE FUROATE
(Furamide)

Diloxanide furoate was introduced in 1957 and has since been extensively used outside the USA for the treatment of intestinal amebiasis. The drug is not effective in the treatment of extraintestinal amebiasis. In the USA, diloxanide furoate is available on an investigational basis from the Parasitic Disease Drug Service, (404) 329-3670.

Chemistry

Diloxanide furoate (Furamide), a substituted acetanilide, is the furoic acid ester of diloxanide (Entamide). It is nearly insoluble in water. For stability, it should be protected from light.

Diloxanide furoate

Pharmacology & Anthelmintic Action

Diloxanide furoate is directly amebicidal, but its mode of action is not known. The acute oral toxicity in rats is a function of age and sex; the LD_{50} ranges from 0.5 to 9.6 g/kg. A dose of 0.75 g/kg to pregnant rats or rabbits resulted, for some animals, in abortion or death. No teratogenic effects were observed.

Absorption, Metabolism, & Excretion

In the gut, diloxanide furoate is split into diloxanide and furoic acid; about 90% of the diloxanide is rapidly absorbed and then conjugated to form the glucuronide. The glucuronide reaches a peak blood level within about 1 hour, drops to low levels within 6 hours, and is rapidly excreted in the urine. The unabsorbed diloxanide is the active antiamebic substance and is not attacked by gut bacteria.

Clinical Uses

Diloxanide furoate is only effective in the treatment of intestinal amebiasis. Although sufficient comparative studies are not available, the drug's effectiveness is apparently not appreciably different from the other luminal amebicides, diiodohydroxyquin (iodoquinol) and paromomycin; but it is probably the least toxic of the three.

Diloxanide furoate is most effective in asymptomatic to mild intestinal infection and is less effective in moderate to severe intestinal disease. It is used alone as a drug of choice in the treatment of asymptomatic infections. For patients having intestinal symptoms, diloxanide furoate is used in conjunction with other drugs as shown in Table 62-3. It is not yet clear if diloxanide furoate combined with a tetracycline is more effective than when it is used alone. Chloroquine is given with diloxanide furoate to prevent the development of amebic liver abscess. In the treatment of liver abscess, diloxanide is added to the regimen in order to eradicate intestinal infection.

When diloxanide furoate was used alone in the treatment of asymptomatic and mildly symptomatic cyst-passers at a dosage of 20 mg/kg for 5–10 days, reported cure rates were 90–100% for studies conducted in temperate areas and 80–90% for studies in tropical areas. In studies of patients with moderate to severe intestinal disease, cure rates were 75–90%; however, when diloxanide furoate and metronidazole were combined, Powell and others (1973) reported a cure rate of 98%.

Adverse Reactions, Contraindications, & Cautions

Diloxanide furoate is free of serious side-effects. Flatulence is common. Nausea and abdominal cramps are infrequent. Esophagitis, dryness of the mouth, vomiting, persistent diarrhea, pruritus, urticaria, proteinuria, and a vague tingling sensation are rarely reported.

The drug should not be used in pregnancy or administered to children under 2 years of age.

Preparations & Dosages

Diloxanide furoate (Furamide) is given orally with meals, 500 mg 3 times daily for 10 days. The drug is supplied as 500-mg tablets. The dosage for children is 20 mg/kg orally divided into 3 doses and given for 10 days. A course of treatment may be repeated in several weeks if necessary.

THE HALOGENATED HYDROXYQUINOLINES
Diiodohydroxyquin (Iodoquinol), Iodochlorhydroxyquin (Clioquinol)

The halogenated hydroxyquinolines were among the first synthetic drugs active in amebiasis. Iodochlorhydroxyquin (introduced in 1931) and diiodohydroxyquin (introduced in 1936) are effective against organisms in the bowel lumen but not against trophozoites in the intestinal wall or extraintestinal tissues.

Chemistry

Three synthetic halogen-substituted 8-hydroxyquinolines have had extensive clinical use—chiniofon (8-hydroxy-7-iodoquinoline-5-sulfonic acid), iodochlorhydroxyquin (clioquinol) (5-chloro-8-hydroxy-7-iodoquinoline), and diiodohydroxyquin (iodoquinol) (8-hydroxy-5,7-diiodoquinoline). Iodochlorhydroxyquin contains approximately 40% iodine and 12% chlorine, and diiodohydroxyquin contains approximately 64% iodine.

Iodochlorhydroxyquin   Diiodohydroxyquin

Absorption, Metabolism, & Excretion

Knowledge is incomplete on the pharmacokinetics of the hydroxyquinolines. Iodochlorhydroxyquin is more readily absorbed than diiodohydroxyquin. Metabolic studies in humans using ^{14}C-iodochlorhydroxyquin indicated that maximal plasma concentrations were reached at 4 hours after administration of a single dose and then decreased, with an apparent half-life of between 11 and 14 hours. Approximately 25% of a single 750-mg oral dose was excreted in the urine over 72 hours. Use of radioactive iodochlorhydroxyquin in animals showed high uptake of the drug in visceral tissues.

The drugs may interfere with certain thyroid function tests by increasing protein-bound serum iodine levels, leading to a decrease in ^{131}I uptake.

Antiamebic Effects

The mechanism of action of diiodohydroxyquin and iodochlorhydroxyquin against amebas is not known. Opinions vary on whether the drugs act only against trophozoites or against cysts as well.

Clinical Uses

A. Intestinal Amebiasis: Diiodohydroxyquin and iodochlorhydroxyquin are alternative drugs for the treatment of asymptomatic or mild to moderate intestinal amebiasis. However, until the question of the association of iodochlorhydroxyquin with the SMON syndrome is resolved, only diiodohydroxyquin should be used in therapy. The drugs are not effective in the initial treatment of severe intestinal disease but are used in the subsequent eradication of the infection. They are not effective against amebomas or extraintestinal forms of the disease, including hepatic amebiasis, but are used in the eradication of concurrent intestinal infection. Reported cure rates for each of the 2 compounds are as high as 80%. Diiodohydroxyquin may cause less diarrhea and gastric irritation than iodochlorhydroxyquin.

B. *Trichomonas vaginalis* Vaginitis: Iodochlorhydroxyquin, given in vaginal inserts or insufflation powders, has been used for the topical treatment of this infection.

C. Other Intestinal Parasites: Diiodohydroxyquin (650 mg 3 times daily for 10 days) when used alone or in conjunction with a tetracycline (250 mg 4 times daily for 7 days) provides adequate treatment for *Dientamoeba fragilis* infections. Diiodohydroxyquin has been reported also to be effective in the treatment of some cases of *Giardia lamblia* and *Balantidium coli* infection.

D. Travelers' Diarrhea and Nonspecific Diarrhea: Neither drug should be used in the prophylaxis and treatment of travelers' diarrhea or for the treatment of chronic nonspecific diarrhea in children and adults.

Adverse Reactions

Evidence is increasing that certain halogenated hydroxyquinolines can produce neurotoxicity, particularly if the drugs are given at greater than recommended doses and for long periods of time. The principal findings associated with this level of use are optic atrophy, visual loss, and peripheral neuropathy. Although these adverse reactions usually improve when the drug is discontinued, some patients have experienced irreversible neurologic damage.

Diiodohydroxyquin has not been implicated in producing neurotoxic side-effects when used at the standard dosage of 650 mg 3 times daily for 21 days. Mild and infrequent side-effects at the standard dosage include diarrhea, which usually stops after several days, and nausea and vomiting, gastritis, abdominal discomfort, constipation, pruritus ani, headache, malaise, and slight enlargement of the thyroid gland. Rarely reported side-effects have been agranulocytosis, discoloration of hair or nails, hair loss, and iodine sensitivity characterized by furunculosis, chills, fever, and a variety of mild to severe skin reactions. Diiodohydroxyquin may be more toxic for infants and young children.

Formerly, when diiodohydroxyquin was given at high doses and for long periods of time to young children with acrodermatitis enteropathica (1200–3300 mg daily for 2–24 months), at least 7 cases of optic atrophy occurred, with decreased visual acuity or blindness.

Iodochlorhydroxyquin was considered nearly free of significant side-effects at the standard dosage (250 mg 3 times daily for 10 days) until the question arose—as yet unresolved—about the drug's etiologic relationship to the SMON syndrome (described below). Infrequent side-effects from iodochlorhydroxyquin are the same as described for diiodohydroxyquin. The risk of neurotoxicity, however, appears to be

greater and to increase with increasing dosage. At dosages of 750–1500 mg/d for less than 2 weeks, about 1% of patients had neurotoxic symptoms; at the same dosages given for over 2 weeks, symptoms appeared in approximately 35% of patients.

Controversy continues about whether a serious new neurologic disease reported from Japan was due to the widespread use there of iodochlorhydroxyquin, to a newly isolated virus, or to other factors. The syndrome is subacute myelo-optic neuropathy (SMON), characterized by chronic abdominal symptoms, peripheral polyneuritis with dysesthesia and weakness in the lower extremities, optic atrophy, and disturbances of vision. Evidence for the association of the drug with the disease included retrospective studies, animal experimental studies, the improvement of symptoms in individual patients when use of the drug was stopped, and the abrupt cessation of the epidemic with withdrawal of hydroxyquinoline drugs from the market. It is not yet possible to reach a conclusion about the cause of SMON syndrome or the risk to be attributed to the use of iodochlorhydroxyquin.

Contraindications & Cautions

The halogenated hydroxyquinolines should no longer be used for the prophylaxis or treatment of travelers' diarrhea or nonspecific diarrhea, and world-wide the drugs should be made available only on a prescription basis. When used for the treatment of amebiasis, they should be taken for the prescribed period of time and dosage.

The drugs should be discontinued when they produce a persistent diarrhea or signs of iodine reactions. They are contraindicated in patients with known intolerance to iodine, in renal and thyroid disease, and probably in severe liver disease not due to amebiasis.

When the drugs are used for young children, careful ophthalmologic assessment should be made before and during the course of therapy.

Preparations & Dosages

The drugs are taken orally after meals. A course should not be repeated without an intervening period of 2–3 weeks.

A. Diiodohydroxyquin, iodoquinol (Embequin, Lanodoxin, Savorquin, Sebaquin, Yodoxin): Diiodohydroxyquin is available as uncoated tablets containing 210 mg and 650 mg. The adult dosage is 650 mg orally 3 times a day for 21 days. The pediatric dosage is 10 mg/kg 3 times a day for 21 days. The medication is well accepted by young children when it is crushed and mixed with applesauce or chocolate syrup.

B. Iodochlorhydroxyquin, Clioquinol (Entero-Vioform, Nioform, Vioform): Iodochlorhydroxyquin is available as enteric-coated tablets or vaginal inserts containing 250 mg and as a powder for vaginal insufflation. The oral dosage is 250 mg 3 times a day for 10 days. In the USA, the drug has been withdrawn from the market pending further study of its toxicity.

THE ARSENICALS

The pentavalent arsenical drugs carbarsone and glycobiarsol have been used for many years for the treatment of amebiasis, but their potential toxicity no longer warrants their inclusion as alternative drugs for the treatment of intestinal infections.

The side-effects of glycobiarsol and carbarsone are due to arsenical reactions. Although infrequent, the most common signs and symptoms are nausea and vomiting, diarrhea, epigastric distress, and skin rashes, which start after several days of therapy. More severe toxicity includes weight loss and polyuria. Exfoliative dermatitis, agranulocytosis, encephalitis, and hepatitis are very rare; a few fatalities have been reported.

METRONIDAZOLE
(Flagyl)

Metronidazole, introduced in 1959 for the treatment of trichomoniasis, was approved in the USA in 1971 for the treatment of amebiasis. Metronidazole is an excellent drug for the eradication of amebic tissue infections (liver abscess, intestinal wall and extraintestinal infections), but it requires the concomitant use of a luminal amebicide to achieve satisfactory cure rates for luminal infections.

In 1971, metronidazole was first reported to increase significantly the incidence of certain naturally occurring tumors in mice and rats given high doses over long periods of time. Subsequently, the drug was shown to induce mutagenic changes in bacterial test systems. A metabolite of metronidazole found in human urine is more mutagenic than the parent drug. It is known that many chemicals that produce mutations in bacteria are also carcinogenic in animals. The extrapolation of such findings to humans is difficult; at present there is no way to determine a safe level in humans for a substance known to produce cancer in animals. A recent report of a retrospective study of women who received metronidazole between 1960 and 1969 and were followed for up to 10 years showed no increase in cancer. This negative finding is encouraging but does not establish the safety of metronidazole, in part because the latent period for chemical carcinogenesis in humans may be 20 years or more. Metronidazole has not been shown to be teratogenic in animals or humans, but the data are not sufficient to rule this out.

It appears prudent to judge metronidazole as a potentially hazardous drug. Therefore, it has been assigned here as an alternative drug in the treatment of mild to moderate intestinal amebiasis, to be used if the drugs of choice fail. However, for the treatment of severe colitis, hepatic abscess, and extraintestinal amebiasis, metronidazole remains the drug of choice; the use of the alternative drugs may entail greater risk.

The chemistry, pharmacokinetics, adverse reactions, and contraindications and cautions of this drug are described on pp 643–644.

In vitro studies show that metronidazole inhibits the growth of trophozoites but does not kill cysts of *E histolytica*. It must be emphasized to the patient that if alcohol is taken concurrently with metronidazole an acute confusional state may follow.

A number of nitroimidazole derivatives (nitrimidazine, tinidazole, and others) are undergoing clinical trials. However, all of those tested have shown the same mutagenic action in *Salmonella* test systems as metronidazole.

Clinical Uses

A. Severe Intestinal Disease (Amebic Dysentery): The suggested dosage is 750 mg 3 times daily for 10 days, plus a course of a luminal amebicide.

B. Liver Abscess: For the treatment of hepatic abscess, a standard regimen of metronidazole is 750 mg 3 times daily for 10 days; however, 5-day courses are also highly effective. A course of a luminal amebicide should be added to enhance eradication of luminal organisms. Metronidazole has 2 advantages over emetine, dehydroemetine, and chloroquine for the treatment of liver abscess. It has less short-term toxicity than emetine or dehydroemetine and, unlike them, is moderately effective against luminal organisms. In Powell's report on amebic liver abscess therapy, 58 of 60 patients were cured by the combination of metronidazole treatment plus aspiration. Subsequent case reports by others suggest occasional metronidazole failures within a few days of starting treatment or weeks later—whether or not the abscess was aspirated.

C. Ameboma and Extraintestinal Infections: Treat as for intestinal disease. However, cure rates for these conditions using metronidazole have not been well determined.

Preparations & Dosage

Metronidazole (Flagyl) is marketed as 250-mg tablets for oral use. The dosage for children is 35–50 mg/kg of body weight divided into 3 doses and given orally for 10 days. The tablets have a bitter taste and are often difficult for children to accept. A tasteless oral suspension of benzoyl metronidazole appears to be equally effective. An intravenous preparation, available elsewhere, is undergoing clinical trials in the USA and may be obtained from the manufacturer for investigational use. It should be used only until the patient can resume taking the medication orally. The effectiveness of metronidazole administered by rectal suppository remains to be determined.

PAROMOMYCIN SULFATE

Paromomycin sulfate, a broad-spectrum antibiotic, is also used in the treatment of intestinal amebiasis and tapeworm infections. It is an aminoglycoside derived from *Streptomyces rimosus* and is closely related to neomycin, kanamycin, and streptomycin in properties and structure. Paromomycin is directly amebicidal in addition to its indirect effect through the inhibition of normal bacteria.

Because paromycin is not significantly absorbed from the gastrointestinal tract, it can only be used as a luminal amebicide and has no effect in extraintestinal amebic infections. The small amount absorbed is excreted slowly and unchanged, mainly by glomerular filtration; some excretion also occurs in the bile. In the presence of ulcerative lesions of the bowel, however, and perhaps with impaired gastrointestinal motility, increased absorption may occur. In renal insufficiency, the drug may accumulate and reach a toxic level.

Mild gastrointestinal side-effects are not uncommon. The number of stools increase; diarrhea, sometimes intense, has been reported in up to 16% of patients. Less frequent are anorexia, nausea and vomiting, epigastric pain, abdominal cramps, and pruritus ani. Other occasional side-effects are headache, dizziness, rashes, and arthralgia. Paromomycin can cause malabsorption as well as overgrowth of nonsusceptible organisms, particularly fungi. The aminoglycosides as a group can be ototoxic (auditory and vestibular) and nephrotoxic as a result of unexpected absorption; theoretically, paromomycin has similar potential, but such reactions have apparently not been reported.

Paromomycin, used alone, is an alternative drug in the treatment of asymptomatic and mild intestinal infection. It has also been used, with variable success, in more severe intestinal disease. The drug is contraindicated in patients with impaired renal function, ulcerative bowel lesions, and intestinal obstruction. In intestinal amebiasis with severe ulceration, paromomycin should not be used because of the risk of increased absorption.

Paromomycin sulfate (Humatin) is administered orally, after meals, at 25–30 mg/kg body weight (maximum 3 g); the daily dose is divided into 3 parts and given for 5–10 days. The pediatric dose is the same as the adult dose. The drug is supplied in 250-mg capsules and as syrup containing 125 mg/5 mL. The above doses are expressed as the base.

THE TREATMENT OF LEISHMANIASIS

Leishmaniasis includes a variety of diseases produced by protozoal parasites of the genus *Leishmania* of the family Trypanosomidae. They are transmitted to humans by the bite of several different species of phlebotomine (flesh-eating) flies, which carry the parasites directly from human to human or from infected rodents or canines to humans. Different varieties of *Leishmania* produce different lesions and require different treatments. The diseases produced by *Leishmania tropica* and *Leishmania mexicana* are characterized by cutaneous lesions only, which usually undergo a spontaneous cure. Infection with *Leishmania braziliensis* (mucocutaneous leishmaniasis) causes large destructive ulcers of the mucous membranes that rarely undergo spontaneous cure. *Leishmania donovani* (visceral leishmaniasis, dumdum fever, tropical splenomegaly, black sickness, ponos) produces a small primary sore, often ignored, followed by hematogenous spread, causing massive enlargement of the spleen and often of the liver and recurring bouts of fever resembling brucellosis. Disease caused by *L donovani* requires hospitalization, correction of the accompanying malnutrition, and specific drug therapy (the choice of drug depending on the geographic location where the disease was encountered) with one or a combination of pentavalent antimonials and one of the aromatic diamidines. The pentavalent antimonial drugs are discussed in Chapter 63.

OTHER DRUGS USED FOR THE TREATMENT OF LEISHMANIASIS

Amphotericin B (Fungizone), 25–50 mg in 500 mL 5% glucose-saline solution, given by slow intravenous drip on alternate days for periods of weeks and even months, has led to complete healing of the lesions of mucocutaneous leishmaniasis that were resistant to antimony therapy.

The suggested daily dose of amphotericin B is 0.25–1 mg/kg. (For toxicity, see Chapter 55.) Amphotericin B may be more potent as a leishmanicide than the antimonials.

Cures of *L braziliensis* and *L tropica* infections have also been obtained with intramuscular injections of the antimalarial repository drug **cycloguanil embonate** (cycloguanil pamoate), an insoluble salt of the dihydrotriazine metabolite of chloroguanide (proguanil). One or 2 intramuscular injections of 350 mg (2.5 mL) of the base have given cure rates of up to 85%.

Oral dehydroemetine resinate (Mebadin) in doses of 1.5 mg/kg orally after meals (to a total dose of 0.85–7 g) gave a 70% cure rate of *L tropica* infections in a study carried out in Iraq.

Metronidazole (Flagyl), 250 mg twice daily orally for 15 days, produced an excellent cure rate of Mexican cutaneous leishmaniasis.

Local injection of mepacrine or antimony compounds into the edges of mucocutaneous ulcers, accompanied by 10 injections of neostibosan on alternate days, is often used.

Nifurtimox (Lampit),* a nitrofurazone derivative, now used to destroy the extracellular trypanosomes in trypanosomiasis, has also been successfully used to treat mucocutaneous leishmaniasis in doses of 8–10 mg/kg daily for 3–5 weeks.

THE TREATMENT OF TRYPANOSOMIASIS

THE AROMATIC DIAMIDINES: PENTAMIDINE, STILBAMIDINE, & PROPAMIDINE

History

Pentamidine, stilbamidine, and propamidine are the only aromatic diamidine derivatives that are sufficiently potent as trypanosomicides and have toxicities low enough to be used for the treatment of trypanosomiasis (sleeping sickness). Pentamidine is now the drug of choice for the treatment and prevention of *Trypanosoma rhodesiense* and *Trypanosoma gambiense* infection and is an alternative to sodium stibogluconate for the treatment of leishmaniasis. Propamidine and the dihydroxyl derivative of stilbamidine are occasionally used.

Chemistry

Pentamidine isethionate (Lomidine, M&B 800) is a 4,4′-diamidinophenoxypentane. It is a white, hydroscopic, crystalline powder soluble 1:10 in water.

The in vitro trypanosomicidal activity of the guanidine derivatives is associated with the terminal amidine and guanidine groups, and the activity is maximal when the amidine groups are connected by an undecane methylene chain.

Absorption, Metabolism, & Excretion

Diamidine compounds are not well absorbed from the gastrointestinal tract, but absorption after parenteral administration is satisfactory. Following intravenous injection, the drug rapidly leaves the circulation and only small amounts appear in the urine. The liver, spleen, kidneys, and adrenals maintain high levels of the diamidines for months after treatment. Single injections of pentamidine can prevent infection by *T gambiense* for up to 6 months. A portion of the drug is metabolized in the body, and part is excreted in the urine. Intermediary metabolic products are not known.

Diamidine compounds cross the placenta but are not excreted in milk. Only trace amounts appear in the central nervous system, so that other trypanosomicides

such as tryparsamide or one of the melanyl arsenicals must be used for the treatment of late stages of African trypanosomiasis with central nervous system involvement.

Pharmacologic Effects

The aromatic diamidines are highly toxic to certain species of protozoa and only slightly toxic to others. *T rhodesiense* and *T gambiense* infections in humans and *T donovani* infections in hamsters can be cured with pentamidine, but the drug has no effect on *Trypanosoma cruzi* infection in mice. The diamidines have some plasmocidal, bactericidal, and fungicidal activity and have been used for the treatment of systemic blastomycosis (see p 581).

Intravenous injections of the diamidines produce a sharp fall of blood pressure that can be only partially blocked by atropine. The peripheral vasodilatation is probably due to a release of tissue-bound histamine and peripheral adrenergic blockade.

After injection of a diamidine drug, the trypanosomes quickly take up the drug to a concentration about 1400 times that of the surrounding tissues. Trypanosomicidal effects appear only after a long latent period. The trypanosomicidal action of the diamidines is antagonized by glucose, and the addition of insulin to cultures slows trypanosome multiplication. Diamidines may interfere with glycolysis in a susceptible protozoon.

Clinical Uses

Pentamidine is the drug of choice for the prevention and treatment of *T gambiense* infections. In the early stages, pentamidine can clear the organisms from the blood and lymph nodes. Diamidines cannot be given intrathecally, and do not reach the central nervous system in sufficient quantities to have any therapeutic effect. Thus, other drugs such as melarsoprol or suramin must be used. In early trypanosomiasis, propamidine and stilbamidine can also be employed.

The diamidines are also used for visceral leishmaniasis (kala-azar) in patients who do not respond to or cannot tolerate antimonials.

Adverse Reactions

The diamidines may result in initial respiratory stimulation followed by respiratory depression. Intravenous injections usually produce a fall of blood pressure, dizziness, and headache together with breathlessness, tachycardia, and vomiting. Respiratory failure and death occur rarely.

The diamidines are nephrotoxic and occasionally neurotoxic, causing nystagmus, ataxia, convulsions, and death.

Delayed toxicity of stilbamidine (but not pentamidine) consists of paralysis of the trigeminal nerve and other peripheral neuropathies.

Preparations & Dosages

Pentamidine isethionate (Lomidine) is not li-

*In the USA, nifurtimox is called Bayer 2502 and is available only from the CDC.

Pentamidine

censed in the USA, although it is available in countries where trypanosomiasis is still endemic. Both pentamidine and Bayer 2502 (nifurtimox) may be obtained from CDC for use on an investigational basis with CDC acting as the "investigator."

For the early stages of *T rhodesiense* and *T gambiense* infections, pentamidine, 4 mg/kg intramuscularly, is given every 1–2 days for 10 doses. For chemoprophylaxis, give 3 mg/kg intramuscularly every 3–6 months.

For *L donovani* infections (kala-azar, visceral leishmaniasis), give pentamidine, 2–4 mg/kg intravenously or intramuscularly daily for up to 15 days.

For the late central nervous system stages of *T rhodesiense* and *T gambiense* infections, melarsoprol must be given.

Nifurtimox (Bayer 2502, Lampit), a nitrofurazone derivative, is the drug of choice for acute Chagas' disease *(T cruzi)*. However, serious allergic skin reactions, gastrointestinal disturbances, and neurologic toxicities are frequently noted. In chronic forms of Chagas' disease, the toxicity may outweigh its usefulness.

MELARSOPROL

Melarsoprol (Mel B), an organic arsenical, is a 2-*p*-(4,6-diamino-1,3,5-triazin-2-ylamino)phenyl-4-hydroxymethyl-1,3,2-dithoarsolan.

Pharmacologic Effects

Melarsoprol is formed by condensing a toxic trivalent arsenical trypanosomicide (melarsen oxide) with an arsenic antagonist (BAL). In the product, the trypanosomicidal activity is retained while the toxicity of arsenic is mitigated. Its mode of action is probably related to an interaction with the sulfhydryl groups of enzymes essential to trypanosome metabolism.

Absorption, Metabolism, & Excretion

Melarsoprol is well absorbed from the gastrointestinal tract, but it is given only intravenously. The drug is quickly excreted.

Clinical Uses

Melarsoprol has now replaced tryparsamide (a pentavalent arsenical) as the drug of choice for the treatment of *T gambiense* infection (African sleeping sickness). Tryparsamide, used for 50 years to control epidemics of trypanosomiasis, had an unfortunate tendency to cause optic atrophy.

Unlike pentamidine, melarsoprol appears in the cerebrospinal fluid in sufficient amounts to exert a trypanosomicidal effect on the late meningoencephalitic stages of human trypanosomiasis. It is also effective in the earlier stages of the disease, but it is used only for the rare pentamidine-refractory cases.

Adverse Effects

The most serious side-effect of melarsoprol therapy, usually occurring at the end of the first week of therapy, is a reactive encephalopathy that may be fatal. Patients in the most advanced stages of the disease are most severely affected.

If the intravenous injections are given too fast, vomiting and colicky abdominal pains occur.

Hypersensitivity reactions can be relieved with corticosteroids.

Preparations & Dosages

Melarsoprol (Mel B) is available for intravenous injection as a solution containing 3.6% (w/v) in propylene glycol. For the therapy of the late stages of *T rhodesiense* and *T gambiense* infections, three 3-day courses are given with an interval of 7 days between courses. Daily injections of 90 mg are given very slowly for the first 3 days; 90–180 mg for the second 3-day course; and 180 mg for the last 3-day course.

Leakage at injection sites causes intense pain and sometimes sloughing.

In the USA, melarsoprol is available only from the Center for Disease Control, Atlanta, Georgia 30333.

OTHER TRYPANOSOMICIDAL DRUGS

SURAMIN
(Bayer 205, Belganyl, Germanin, Naphuride)

Suramin sodium, an organic urea compound available in the USA only from the Center for Disease Control, is the drug of choice for the early stages of trypanosomiasis before there is any central nervous system involvement. It is also the treatment of choice for the adult forms of the filarial parasite *Onchocerca volvulus* (see Chapter 63).

THE TREATMENT OF TRICHOMONIASIS & GIARDIASIS

METRONIDAZOLE
(Flagyl)

Chemistry

Metronidazole, 1-(2-hydroxyethyl)-2-methyl-5-nitroimidazole, is a crystalline nonhygroscopic powder, slightly soluble in water and alcohol. In 1959, the trichomonacidal properties of metronidazole were demonstrated, and human trials showed that the drug is excreted in the semen and urine, making possible high cure rates of chronically infected but asymptomatic males.

Metronidazole (Flagyl)

Pharmacologic Actions

Apart from the trichomonacidal effect achieved by the recommended doses on human infections of *Trichomonas vaginalis,* the drug has so few actions that it appears to be pharmacologically inert. It may produce disulfiramlike aversion to alcohol and thus may also inhibit several enzymes concerned with the metabolism of alcohol. In vitro studies have demonstrated that alcohol dehydrogenase (an NAD-linked enzyme), xanthine oxidase (an FAD-linked enzyme), and uricase (the enzyme converting uric acid to allantoin in subprimate mammals) are all reversibly inhibited by metronidazole. Because metronidazole can inhibit 3 different classes of oxidases but not monoamine oxidase and diamine oxidase, it has been postulated that the drug acts as a nonspecific electron trap.

In humans, metronidazole (10 mg/kg orally) is a highly effective systemic trichomonacide that does not disturb the normal vaginal flora. In vitro, metronidazole in concentrations of 2.5 μg/L destroys 99% of the parasites in cultures of *T vaginalis* within 24 hours, but concentrations as high as 250 μg/L do not affect the growth of Döderlein's bacillus (*Lactobacillus acidophilus*) or *Candida albicans.*

In dogs, large doses (125–150 mg/kg) have produced tremor, ataxia, muscle spasticity, convulsions, and death within 7–28 days. In humans, metronidazole is pharmacologically inert, and doses of up to 800 mg 3 times a day for 10 days for the treatment of intestinal and extra-intestinal amebiasis are commonly used without any major side-effects. It is possible that metronidazole is acting on a metabolic pathway in

nonprimate mammals that has no counterpart in humans (eg, the uricase enzyme system).

Absorption, Metabolism, & Excretion

Metronidazole is rapidly and almost completely absorbed from the gastrointestinal tract. Although only trace amounts of the ingested dose can be recovered in the feces, metronidazole is a potent amebicide for the hepatic forms of *E histolytica.*

After ingestion, the plasma level rises rapidly; effective serum levels are reached in 2–3 hours and maintained for 12 hours after a single oral dose. About 69% of the drug is excreted in the urine unchanged, 26% as a carboxylic metabolite and 5% as a glucuronic acid-ether conjugate of metronidazole. The urine is often colored a deep reddish brown. There is no evidence of metabolic reduction of the nitroimidazole group. Metronidazole crosses the placenta and is excreted in saliva, milk, semen, and vaginal secretions but probably does not reach the cerebrospinal fluid.

Clinical Uses

A. Extraintestinal Amebiasis: Metronidazole is now the drug of choice. See p 633.

B. Urogenital Trichomoniasis: Systemic therapy makes possible the delivery of effective trichomonacidal concentrations of the drug to foci of infections in the genitourinary tract that cannot be reached by local applications. Approximately 90% of *T vaginalis* infections can now be cured with a single course of metronidazole. Although partial resistance has recently been reported, about 90% of the treatment failures will respond to retreatment. Most recrudescences are due to a failure to eradicate the organism from the paraurethral glands of sexual partners; therefore, the treatment of asymptomatic sexual consorts is advised.

C. Giardiasis: Although quinacrine hydrochloride, 100 mg orally 3 times daily for 5–7 days, results in a 90% cure, metronidazole, 250 mg 3 times daily for 10 days, is a useful alternative.

D. Other Uses: In studies purporting to show that metronidazole has a disulfiramlike effect, control of the withdrawal symptoms of chronic alcoholism is claimed.

Acute ulcerative gingivitis of Vincent's stomatitis has been cured with 200 mg orally 3 times daily for 7 days. The drug also appears to be effective for dracunculiasis and for some anaerobic infections.

Adverse Reactions

Metronidazole is known to be carcinogenic in rats and mice and mutagenic in bacteria. Therefore, it should not be used during pregnancy or for asymptomatic trichomonas infections in females until topical agents, vinegar douches, etc, have been given an adequate trial. However, metronidazole remains the only known cure for *T vaginalis* infection and is still the drug of choice for amebic liver abscesses and "mild to moderate" intestinal infections.

Metronidazole has been extensively used for over 20 years; side-effects rarely are severe enough to warrant cessation of therapy. Gastrointestinal symptoms may occur, including an unpleasant metallic taste, furred tongue, glossitis, stomatitis, an overgrowth of candida in the mouth, nausea and vomiting, diarrhea, epigastric pain, and cramping. Headache, insomnia, and dizziness may occur. Rarely reported are ataxia, vertigo, paresthesias, confusion, and other mental effects, urticaria, dysuria, proctitis, and a dark brown discoloration of the urine. Mild leukopenia may occur but is reversible. Hematologic studies have failed to reveal any evidence of persistent leukopenia or blood dyscrasias despite the fact that the nitro group of the imidazole rings has, in other compounds, been associated with serious blood dyscrasias. If a patient receiving metronidazole drinks alcohol, an acute confusional state may follow. Most apparent treatment failures and relapses of *T vaginalis* infections are due to reinfection. Trichomonads taken from seemingly resistant cases have all thus far proved to have the usual in vitro sensitivity to metronidazole; however, certain organisms, including *Proteus vulgaris, Proteus mirabilis, Streptococcus faecalis, Escherichia coli, Pseudomonas aerugunosa,* and mimeae, can inactivate metronidazole. Several instances of attempted suicide with doses of 4–10 g attest to the low toxicity of this drug.

Contraindications & Cautions

Although dogs develop severe neurologic disorders with large doses of metronidazole and rats develop testicular damage, there are no reports of serious toxicity to humans. Moderate leukopenias returning to normal after completion of treatment have been reported. Other careful studies have failed to confirm this finding.

Alcohol should be avoided during treatment. Coexistent candidiasis may be aggravated during therapy, especially when vaginal inserts are used.

Metronidazole is contraindicated in the first trimester of pregnancy and in patients with a blood dyscrasia or organic central nervous system disease. When administered to nursing mothers, metronidazole is secreted in breast milk; it is not known if it can be injurious to the newborn.

Preparations & Dosages

Metronidazole is available in uncoated cream-colored 250 mg tablets for oral administration and 500 mg vaginal inserts. For *T vaginalis* infections, metronidazole, 250 mg 3 times a day for 10 days for females or 250 mg twice a day for 10 days for males, will effect a radical cure in 90% of cases. Should re-treatment be necessary, intervals of 4–6 weeks should be allowed between courses. There is no evidence that the concurrent use of vaginal inserts with oral therapy brings about any improvement in the cure rate.

The drug has been approved by the FDA for use in the USA for amebiasis and trichomoniasis but not for giardiasis. For amebiasis dosages, see p 633.

● ● ●

References

Malaria

General

Clyde DF & others: Treatment of falciparum malaria caused by strain resistant to quinine. JAMA 213:2041, 1970.

Hall AP: The treatment of malaria. Br Med J 1:323, 1976.

Jelliffe DB: The therapy of cerebral malaria in children. Trop Pediatr 69:483, 1966.

Sitprija V: Renal involvement in malaria. Trans R Soc Trop Med Hyg 64:695, 1970.

Transfusion-induced malaria: Georgia. Morbid Mortal Weekly Rep, Oct 21, 1972.

US Departments of the Army, the Navy, and the Air Force: *Malaria (Clinical Features, Treatment, Control and Prevention).* Pages 1–27. Washington, DC, July 14, 1967.

World Health Organization: *Chemotherapy of Malaria and Resistance to Malarials.* Report of a WHO Scientific Group. Technical Report Series No. 529, 1973.

Quinine

Hall AP & others: Human plasma and urine quinine levels following tablets, capsules, and intravenous infusion. Clin Pharmacol Ther 14:580, 1973.

Powell RD: Treatment of malaria. Ration Drug Ther 6:1, Apr 1972.

Sheehy TW, Reba RC: Complications of falciparum malaria and their treatment. Ann Intern Med 66:807, 1976.

Chloroquine

Blount RD: Chloroquine-resistant falciparum malaria. JAMA 200:886, 1967.

Burns RP: Delayed onset of chloroquine retinopathy. N Engl J Med 275:693, 1966.

Carson JW, Barringer ML, Jones RE Jr: Fatal chloroquine ingestion: An increasing hazard. Pediatrics 40:449, 1967.

Ciak J, Hahn FE: Chloroquine: Mode of action. Science 151:347, 1966.

McCann WP, Permisohn R, Palmisano PA: Fatal chloroquine poisoning in a child: Experience with peritoneal dialysis. Pediatrics 55:536, 1975.

Congeners of Chloroquine

Booth K, Larkin K, Maddocks I: Agranulocytosis coincident with amodiaquine therapy. Br Med J 3:32, 1967.

Lucasse C: Single-dose treatment of acute malaria. J Trop Med Hyg 66:280, 1963.

8-Aminoquinolines

Cahn MM, Levy EJ: The tolerance to large weekly doses of primaquine and amodiaquine in primaquine-sensitive and non-sensitive subjects. Am J Trop Med Hyg 11:605, 1962.

Peters W: The possible role of primaquine in inducing multiple drug resistance in *Plasmodium falciparum.* Trans R Soc Trop Med Hyg 60:140, 1966.

Quinacrine

Sapp OL III: Toxic psychosis due to quinacrine and chloroquine. JAMA 187:373, 1964.

Proguanil, Pyrimethamine, & Trimethoprim

Bushby SRM, Hitchings GH: Trimethoprim, a sulphonamide potentiator. Br J Pharmacol 33:72, 1968.

Laing ABG: Treatment of acute falciparum malaria with sulphorthodimethoxine (Fanasil). Br Med J 1:905, 1965.

McGregor IA, Williams K, Goodwin LG: Pyrimethamine and sulphadiazine in treatment of malaria. Br Med J 2:728, 1963.

Pearlman EJ, Hall AP: Prevention of chloroquine-resistant falciparum malaria. (Correspondence.) Ann Intern Med 82:590, 1975.

Amebiasis

General

Adams EB, MacLeod IN: Invasive amebiasis: 1. Amebic dysentery and its complications. 2. Amebic liver abscess and its complications. (2 parts.) Medicine 56:315, 325, 1977.

Juniper K: Amoebiasis. Clin Gastroenterol 7:3, 1978.

Powell SJ: Latest developments in the treatment of amebiasis. Adv Pharmacol Chemother 10:92, 1972.

Symposium on amebiasis. Bull NY Acad Med 47:435, 1971.

Wilmot AJ: *Clinical Amoebiasis.* Blackwell, 1962.

World Health Organization Expert Committee: Amoebiasis. Technical Report Series No. 421, 1969.

Emetine & Dehydroemetine

Klatskin G, Friedman H: Emetine toxicity in man: Studies on the nature of early toxic manifestations, their relation to the dose level, and their significance in determining safe dosage. Ann Intern Med 28:892, 1948.

Lister GD: Delayed myocardial intoxication following the administration of dehydroemetine hydrochloride. J Trop Med Hyg 71:219, 1968.

Miletich DJ & others: The effect of emetine on myocardial catecholamine metabolism. J Pharm Pharmacol 26:101, 1974.

Pain A, Wingfield A: Electrocardiographic changes due to emetine therapy. Trans R Soc Trop Med Hyg 62:221, 1968.

Powell SJ & others: A comparative trial of dehydroemetine and emetine hydrochloride in identical dosage in amoebic liver abscess. Ann Trop Med Parasitol 61:26, 1967.

Sharad CS, Vakil BJ: Cardiovascular toxicity of emetine and dehydroemetine. Indian Pract 24:237, 1971.

Turner PP: The effects of emetine on the myocardium. Br Heart J 25:81, 1963.

Wilmot AJ, Powell SJ, Adams EB: Chloroquine compared with chloroquine and emetine combined in amebic liver abscess. Am J Trop Med Hyg 8:623, 1959.

Diloxanide Furoate

Bell S: An investigation of carriers of *Entamoeba histolytica.* Trans R Soc Trop Med Hyg 61:506, 1967.

Botero RD: Treatment of intestinal amoebiasis with diloxanide furoate, tetracycline and chloroquine. Trans R Soc Trop Med Hyg 61:769, 1967.

Gubey MP, Gupta PS, Chuttani HK: Entamide furoate in the treatment of intestinal amoebiasis. J Trop Med Hyg 68:63, 1965.

Wolfe MS: Nondysenteric intestinal amebiasis: Treatment with diloxanide furoate. JAMA 224:1601, 1973.

Halogenated Hydroxyquinolines & Arsenicals

Committee on Drugs: Blindness and neuropathy from diiodo-hydroxyquin-like drugs. Pediatrics 54:378, 1974.

Inoue YK: An avian-related new herpesvirus infection in man—subacute myelo-optico-neuropathy (SMON). Prog Med Virol 21:35, 1976.

Jack DB, Riess W: Pharmacokinetics of iodochlorhydroxyquin in man. J Pharm Sci 62:1929, 1973.

Kono R: The S.M.O.N. virus theory. (Correspondence.) Lancet 2:370, 1975.

Oakley GP Jr: The neurotoxicity of the halogenated hydroxyquinolines. JAMA 225:395, 1973.

Worden AN, Heywood R: Clioquinol toxicity. (Correspondence.) Lancet 1:212, 1978.

Metronidazole

Beard CM & others: Lack of evidence for cancer due to use of metronidazole. N Engl J Med 301:519, 1979.

Friedman GD: Cancer after metronidazole. (Letter.) N Engl J Med 302:519, 1980.

Kanani SR, Knight R: Experiences with the use of metronidazole in the treatment of non dysenteric intestinal amoebiasis. Trans R Soc Trop Med Hyg 66:244, 1972.

Lindmark DG, Müller M: Antitrichomonad action, mutagenicity, and reduction of metronidazole and other nitroimidazoles. Antimicrob Agents Chemother 10:476, 1976.

Metronidazole (Flagyl). Med Lett Drugs Ther 21:89, 1979.

Powell SJ: Metronidazole in the treatment of amoebic dysentery. Medicine Today 3:48, 1969.

Powell SJ, Stewart-Wynne EJ, Elsdon-Dew R: Metronidazole combined with diloxanide furoate in amoebic liver abscess. Ann Trop Med Parasitol 67:367, 1973.

Roe FJC: Metronidazole: Review of uses and toxicity. J Antimicrob Chemother 3:205, 1977.

Scragg JN, Proctor EM: Tinidazole treatment of acute amebic dysentery in children. Am J Trop Med Hyg 26:824, 1977.

Weber DM: Amebic abscess of liver following metronidazole therapy. JAMA 216:1339, 1974.

What do the bacterial tests of mutagenicity mean? Med Lett Drugs Ther 18:75, 1976.

Paromomycin Sulfate

Courtney KO & others: Paromomycin as a therapeutic substance for intestinal amoebiasis and bacterial enteritis. Ann Biochem Exper Med 20(S):449, 1960.

Keusch GT, Troncale FJ, Buchanan RD: Malabsorption due to paromomycin. Arch Intern Med 125:273, 1970.

Simon M & others: Paromomycin in the treatment of intestinal amebiasis: A short course of therapy. Am J Gastroenterol 48:504, 1967.

Woolfe G: The chemotherapy of amoebiasis. Prog Drug Res 8:13, 1965.

Leishmaniasis

Beltran HF, Gutierrez FM, Biagi FF: [Treatment of Mexican cutaneous leishmaniasis with metronidazole.] Bull Soc Pathol Exot 60:61, 1967.

Chavarria AP, Kotcher E: Preliminary evaluation of cycloguanil pamoate in dermal leishmaniasis. JAMA 194:1142, 1965.

Hassan Abd-Rabbo: Dehydroemetine in leishmaniasis (Oriental sore). J Trop Med Hyg 69:171, 1966.

Prata A: Treatment of kala-azar with amphotericin B. Trans R Soc Trop Med Hyg 57:266, 1963.

Reinhard M, Wacker H: [Treatment of cutaneous leishmaniasis with cycloguanil pamoate.] Dtsch Med Wochenschr 95:2380, 1970.

Salem HH & others: The treatment of cutaneous leishmaniasis with oral dehydroemetine. Trans R Soc Trop Med Hyg 61:776, 1967.

Trypanosomiasis

Gutteridge WE: Chemotherapy and drug sensitivity: Further investigations on the mode of action of pentamidine. Trans R Soc Trop Med Hyg 60:120, 1966.

Trichomoniasis

Metronidazole

Baker RM, Kennan AL: Therapy of trichomoniasis. Wis Med J 66:370, 1967.

Diddle AW: *Trichomonas vaginalis:* Resistance to metronidazole. Am J Obstet Gynecol 98:583, 1967.

Is Flagyl dangerous? Med Lett Drugs Ther 17:53, 1975.

McLoughlin DK: Drug tolerance by *Trichomonas foetus*. J Parasitol 53:646, 1967.

Minnesota Department of Health: Communicable Disease Newsletter 2(9), Nov 1975.

Robert S. Goldsmith, MD, DTM&H

CHEMOTHERAPY OF HELMINTHIC INFECTIONS

Anthelmintic drugs are a group of compounds used to eradicate or reduce in numbers helminthic parasites in the intestinal tract or tissues of humans. Table 63–1 lists the major helminthic infections and provides a guide to the drug of choice and alternative drugs for each infection. In the text that follows, these drugs are arranged alphabetically, with the exception of several drugs that are used in the treatment of schistosomiasis and are presented under antimonial compounds.

Most anthelmintics in use today are active against specific parasites, and some are toxic. Therefore, parasites must be identified before treatment is started, usually by finding the parasite, ova, or larvae in the feces, urine, blood, sputum, or tissues of the host.

Administration of Anthelmintic Drugs

Unless otherwise indicated, oral drugs should be taken with water during or after meals. If pre- or posttreatment purges are necessary in conjunction with a specific drug, magnesium or sodium sulfate may be used. The usual dose, 15–30 g for an adult and 0.2–0.4 g/kg body weight for children, is dissolved in a glass of water. The intensely bitter taste may be partially masked by giving the salts in lemon juice. Magnesium sulfate must not be given to individuals with impaired renal function, and sodium sulfate may be contraindicated in patients with congestive heart failure. Other contraindications to severe purgation are signs of intestinal obstruction, debilitation, and pregnancy.

Dosages for Children

Dosages for infants and children are on a less secure basis than for adults; when not shown in milligrams per kilogram of body weight (or otherwise specified), the dosage may be calculated as a fraction of the adult dose based on Clark's rule or Young's rule (see p 24).

Robert S. Goldsmith is Professor of Tropical Medicine and Epidemiology, University of California, San Francisco.

Contraindications

Pregnancy and ulcers of the gastrointestinal tract are contraindications for most of the drugs listed. Specific contraindications are given in the discussions that follow.

New Drugs

During the past 2 decades, many older anthelmintic drugs have been replaced by far safer and more effective compounds. Although excellent drugs are now available for the treatment of most individual intestinal parasites, efforts continue toward the development of a broad-spectrum anthelmintic that would permit simultaneous treatment of many intestinal parasites, particularly on a mass basis. For many of the parasites found in the tissues, however, we are still without highly effective nontoxic drugs. New remedies are particularly needed for onchocerciasis, clonorchiasis, and hydatid disease.

ANTIMONY COMPOUNDS

The trivalent antimony compounds were for many years the principal drugs for the treatment of schistosomiasis (bilharziasis). They continue to be of importance, but, because of their toxicity, safer drugs should be used as drugs of first choice.

Research efforts over 50 years to combine high cure rates with safety have resulted in the synthesis and screening of thousands of antimonial compounds. The successful antischistosomal agents all have trivalent antimony chelated to oxygen or sulfur. The drugs currently used are antimony potassium tartrate (tartar emetic), introduced in 1918; antimony pyrocatechol sodium disulfonate (stibophen), in 1929; and antimony sodium dimercaptosuccinate (stibocaptate), in 1954. Other trivalent preparations include antimony sodium tartrate, antimony lithium thiomalate (anthiomaline), antimony thioglycollamide, and antimony sodium gluconate (triostam).

Each of the antimony drugs has one or more major defects, including severe toxicity, difficulty with administration, the necessity for prolonged treatment, or low effectiveness. Tartar emetic is superior to the other

Table 63–1. Drugs for the treatment of helminthic infections.

Infecting Organism	Drug of Choice	Alternative Drugs
Roundworms (nematodes)		
Ascaris lumbricoides (roundworm)	Pyrantel pamoate	Piperazine, mebendazole, levamisole,* or bephenium*
Trichuris trichiura (whipworm)	Mebendazole	Hexylresorcinol by retention enema* or oxantel pamoate*†
Necator americanus (hookworm)	Pyrantel pamoate§ or mebenda-	Bephenium,* tetrachloroethylene, or thia-
Ancylostoma duodenale (hookworm)	zole	bendazole
Strongyloides stercoralis (threadworm)	Thiabendazole	Mebendazole,‡§ niridazole,‡** or pyrvinium pamoate‡§
Enterobius (Oxyuris) vermicularis (pinworm)	Pyrantel pamoate or mebendazole	Pyrvinium pamoate
Trichinella spiralis (trichinosis)	ACTH, corticosteroids, and thiabendazole‡ or mebendazole†§	None
Trichostrongylus species	Pyrantel pamoate§ or mebendazole§	Bephenium,* levamisole,* or thiabendazole§
Cutaneous larva migrans (creeping eruption)	Thiabendazole	Diethylcarbamazine‡
Visceral larva migrans	Thiabendazole‡	Diethylcarbamazine‡
Angiostrongylus cantonensis	Levamisole*‡	None
Wuchereria bancrofti (filariasis)	Diethylcarbamazine	None
Wuchereria (Brugia) malayi (filariasis)		
Tropical eosinophilia		
Loa loa (loiasis)		
Onchocerca volvulus (onchocerciasis)	Suramin** plus diethylcarbamazine	None
Dracunculus medinensis (guinea worm)	Niridazole** or metronidazole§	Thiabendazole§ or mebendazole‡
Intestinal capillariasis	Mebendazole	Thiabendazole
Flukes (trematodes)		
Schistosoma haematobium (bilharziasis)	Metrifonate**	Niridazole,** stibocaptate** or stibophen (see antimony compounds), or praziquantel*†
Schistosoma mansoni	Oxamniquine	Niridazole,** stibocaptate** or stibophen (see antimony compounds), or praziquantel*†
Schistosoma japonicum	Niridazole**	Tartar emetic, stibophen or stibocaptate** (see antimony compounds) or praziquantel*†
Clonorchis sinensis (liver fluke)	Chloroquine phosphate‡	Bithionol*‡
Opisthorchis species		
Paragonimus westermani (lung fluke)	Bithionol**	Niclofolan*†
Fasciola hepatica (sheep liver fluke)	Bithionol**	Emetine or dehydroemetine**
Fasciolopsis buski (large intestinal fluke)	Hexylresorcinol*	Tetrachloroethylene or niclosamide**
Heterophyes heterophyes	Tetrachloroethylene	Hexylresorcinol* or bephenium*
Metagonimus yokogawai		
Tapeworm (cestodes)		
Taenia saginata (beef tapeworm)	Niclosamide**	Paromomycin,§ mebendazole,†§ or dichlorophen*
Diphyllobothrium latum (fish tapeworm)		
Taenia solium (pork tapeworm)	Niclosamide**	Mebendazole†§
Cysticercosis (pork tapeworm larval stage)	Mebendazole§‡	None
Hymenolepis nana (dwarf tapeworm)	Niclosamide**	Paromomycin,§ dichlorophen,* or praziquantel*†
Hymenolepis diminuta (rat tapeworm)		
Dipylidium caninum		
Echinococcus granulosus (hydatid disease)	Mebendazole†§‡	None
Echinococcus multilocularis		

*Not available in the USA.
†Undergoing clinical investigation.
‡Effectiveness not established.
§Available in the USA but not approved for this indication.
**Available in the USA only from the Parasitic Disease Drug Service, Parasitic Diseases Branch, Center for Disease Control, Atlanta, Georgia 30333. Telephone (404)329-3670 during the day, (404)329-3644 at night.

antimonials for the treatment of *Schistosoma japonicum* infection but is the most toxic drug of the group, is unstable in solution, requires intravenous administration, and requires that patients be hospitalized. Stibophen and stibocaptate are preferred antimonials for the treatment of *Schistosoma mansoni* and *Schistosoma haematobium* infections because they are stable, are moderately effective, can be given intramuscularly, are less toxic than comparably effective doses of tartar emetic, and can be given on an outpatient basis. Stibocaptate is more convenient than stibophen because the course of treatment is shorter.

Although standardization of methodology for clinical trials and the number of comparative drug studies are increasing, it continues to be difficult to compare the effectiveness and safety of antischistosomal drugs (antimonial and nonantimonial agents) given in different parts of the world. Discrepancies reflect varying criteria of cure, differences in the drug susceptibility of parasitic strains from widely separated regions, and host factors such as sex, race, intensity and duration of infection, and immunity and nutritional status. Quantitative methods such as multiple ovum counts and tests for ovum viability are essential. Therapeutic results become significant only after long follow-up periods (12 months) and when reinfection does not occur, but these objectives are difficult to accomplish.

Pharmacologic Effects

A. Action in Humans: Relatively little information is available on the physiologic and biochemical effects of the trivalent antimonials or the mechanisms of their toxicity, which affects many tissues. When the drugs are given parenterally, the intense vomiting and coughing that may occur are thought to be due both to central effects and to local irritation of antimony excreted on the gastrointestinal and bronchial mucosa.

B. Anthelmintic Action: Trivalent antimony compounds inhibit phosphofructokinase in schistosomes, an enzyme necessary for glycolysis, which is a major source of energy for the parasite. Within minutes to several hours after administration, worm paralysis occurs, followed by relaxation of the suckers that hold the helminth in place in terminal veins. As a result, the schistosomes are carried by the venous flow to the liver or to the lungs, depending upon their original location (bladder or bowel wall) and whether portal bypass occurs via extrahepatic collaterals in advanced liver disease. After the initial injections, the enzyme inhibition and paralysis are reversible and the worms may return to the terminal venules, but repeated administration of the drugs will ultimately result in the death of many of the parasites. Still undetermined is whether significant liver or lung damage occurs when dead worms accumulate in these tissues. Antimony compounds also both affect the reproductive organs of schistosomes, impairing deposition of eggs, and produce morphologic changes in eggs before and after deposition.

Absorption, Distribution, & Excretion

Trivalent antimonials must be given parenterally because of their strong emetic action and slow absorption when given orally. Parenteral administration results in high but transient blood levels because the agents have a high affinity for blood cells and for thyroid, liver, renal, and other tissues. The return of antimony to the blood plasma is slow, thus permitting accumulation. In humans, antimony is excreted mainly via the kidneys; a small amount appears in the feces. Excretion is slow and varies according to the drug, dosages, and the individual responsiveness of the patient. After a single parenteral dose of tartar emetic (2.5 mg/kg), 49% of the antimony was excreted in the urine in 24 hours and 56% in 1 week. After a single injection of stibocaptate (3.1 mg/kg), 14% of the antimony was excreted in 24 hours and 27% in 1 week. Following a full course of tartar emetic, antimony was detected in the urine after 100 days.

Adverse Reactions

Under physiologic conditions the trivalent antimonials dissociate, releasing a small amount of antimonial ions; the frequency and intensity of toxic reactions appears to be associated with the degree of this dissociation. Side-effects occur in most patients, but the drugs are often better tolerated by children than by adults. Most side-effects are mild and disappear within 1–2 days after the last injection; however, many are so severe that up to 50% of patients will be unwilling to complete a course of treatment. The most frequent adverse reactions are pain at the site of injection (for the intramuscular compounds), anorexia, nausea and vomiting, diarrhea, abdominal pain, coughing (less frequent for stibocaptate), myalgia, arthralgia, dizziness, headache, and fatigue.

Frequent cardiovascular side-effects include bradycardia appearing shortly after injections, and hypotension. Electrocardiographic changes occur in most patients; they usually return to normal within 4 weeks after therapy is stopped but may persist longer. These changes include increased amplitude of P waves, prolonged Q–T intervals, depressed ST segments, inverted T waves, and fusion of the ST segment with the T wave. There is no evidence that these changes correlate with abnormal cardiac function or that they are precursors of serious toxicity. The exception is the appearance of extrasystoles and other arrhythmias or symptoms suggesting a Stokes-Adams attack.

Less common side-effects are skin rash, substernal pain, pyrexia, prostration, conjunctivitis, pruritus, depression, and a metallic taste. Rare side-effects include hepatomegaly with laboratory evidence of liver dysfunction, peripheral neuritis, herpes zoster, retrobulbar neuritis with central scotomas, hematuria, thrombocytopenia, and hemolytic anemia (of the autoimmune type).

Pain at the injection site when stibophen and stibocaptate are used can be reduced by prior administration of 1% lidocaine through the same needle used for giving the drug. Vomiting tends to start late in the course of treatment and usually 2–4 hours after injection. Mild nausea and vomiting may sometimes be reduced by giving 6–10 mL of aluminum hydroxide gel before the injection or 15–20 drops of tincture of belladonna orally 3 times a day before meals. Hypotension responds to subcutaneous injections of epinephrine.

Mild muscle or joint pains and nausea are not indications to stop or modify treatment. However, if pain or nausea and vomiting are increasing, the interval between injections should be increased or the dosage reduced. Treatment should be suspended temporarily if skin rashes, marked fatigue, or temperature elevation appears. Urine and blood should be examined at frequent intervals. Therapy should be discontinued in the event of severe and persistent vomiting, substernal pain, continued fever, hematuria, progressive proteinuria, thrombocytopenia, falling hematocrit, signs of hemolytic anemia, or electrocardiographic evidence of arrhythmias. The electrocardiographic changes described above are not an indication to stop treatment.

Among the millions of patients treated with antimonial compounds, sudden and unpredictable deaths have occurred with all of the agents but are considered to be most frequent with tartar emetic and least frequent with stibocaptate. Two mechanism of death have been recognized: cardiac arrhythmias and shock.

Contraindications & Cautions

Intestinal helminth infections, particularly ascarids, should be eradicated before starting treatment. For stibophen and stibocaptate, inadvertent intravenous administration may intensify side-effects; therefore, the needle and syringe should be observed carefully and their position changed if blood appears on aspiration.

Antimonial drugs should be used with caution or not at all in debilitated and malnourished individuals. They are contraindicated in the presence of tuberculosis; acute febrile conditions; herpes simplex and zoster; severe anemia; cardiac, renal, and hepatic insufficiency (except that due to schistosomiasis); terminal forms of schistosomiasis; and for patients treated with antimonials within the previous 2 months. Medication containing iron salts should not be given concurrently with antimonial compounds.

1. STIBOCAPTATE
(Astiban, Antimony Sodium Dimercaptosuccinate)

Chemistry

Stibocaptate is antimony sodium dimercaptosuccinate (antimony III sodium meso 2,3-dimercaptosuccinate; TWSb; Astiban). It is a trivalent antimonial that differs from antimony tartrate in that the oxygen atoms of the hydroxyl groups are replaced by sulfur. Stibocaptate contains 25–26% antimony and is provided as a powder which is stable. It is readily soluble but unstable in water and should be used shortly after being placed in solution.

Clinical Uses

Stibocaptate is an alternative drug for the treatment of schistosomiasis. Most patients can be treated on an outpatient basis.

A wide range of effectiveness has been reported for stibocaptate in different clinical trials. Reported cure rates for S mansoni infection are 29–91%; for S

haematobium infection, 12–100%; usually there has been a significant drop in the ovum count in those not cured. There have been relatively few studies on the use of stibocaptate for S japonicum infections, but cure rates of 50–87% have been reported.

Adverse Reactions, Contraindications, & Cautions

As described above under Antimony Compounds.

Preparations & Dosages

Stibocaptate (Astiban) is supplied in vials containing 0.5 g of the lyophilized drug, to be dissolved in 5 mL of sterile water or normal saline. The resultant 10% solution should be refrigerated and used within 24 hours. Cloudy or discolored solutions should be discarded. The intramuscular route is preferred for stibocaptate. The drug is not marketed in the USA but can be obtained from the Parasitic Disease Drug Service, Center for Disease Control, Atlanta 30333, for investigational use.

The total dose for treatment of S haematobium or S mansoni infections is 40 mg/kg (maximum total 2.5 g) and for S japonicum infection 50 mg/kg (maximum total 2.5 g). The total dose is divided into 5 equal injections given once a week for 5 weeks. After each injection, the patient should rest for half an hour. If necessary, a course of treatment may be repeated in 2 months. If individual doses are given at shorter intervals, such as twice weekly, side-effects are often more severe.

For suppressive management, some form of spaced dosage, such as one dose given monthly for 5–6 months, should be used. Mass treatment becomes possible because side-effects are markedly reduced; patients are unlikely to be effective transmitters of ova, and many become symptom-free or are cured.

2. STIBOPHEN
(Antimony Pyrocatechol Sodium Disulfonate)

Chemistry

Stibophen (sodium antimony III bis[pyrocatechol-2,4-disulfonate]) contains 13.6% trivalent antimony. It is freely soluble and stable in water, may dissociate and become toxic after prolonged storage, and oxidizes when exposed to the air.

Clinical Uses

Most patients can be treated on an outpatient basis.

A. S mansoni and S haematobium: Shookhoff reported 74 cures among 81 adult Puerto Rican patients treated for S mansoni infection who were given 70–100 mL of stibophen. Most & others observed no relapses in 28 Puerto Rican patients infected with S mansoni who were treated with 70 mL of stibophen.

B. *S japonicum:* Stibophen can be used if tartar emetic (the drug of choice) is not well tolerated, but an intensive course of treatment involving administration of a highly toxic amount of stibophen is required. Most & others reported that when 100 mL of stibophen were given during a 14-day period, the drug failed to cure 13 of 64 patients.

Adverse Reactions, Contraindications, & Cautions

As described under Antimony Compounds.

Preparations & Dosages

Stibophen (Fuadin, Fouadin, Neoantimosan, Repodral) is available in ampules, each containing 5 mL of a 6.3% aqueous solution with not more than 0.1% sodium bisulfite as preservative. Each milliliter contains the equivalent of 8.5 mg of trivalent antimony. Once an ampule has been opened, the solution should be used promptly, as it oxidizes when exposed to the air; unused portions should be discarded.

Treatment is generally on an outpatient basis. A test dose of 1.5 mL intramuscularly should be given on the first day to detect the occasional patient who may have an idiosyncratic reaction. Give 3.5 mL the second day, 5 mL the third day, and then 5 mL every second or third day into alternate buttocks until 40 mL have been given. After a rest period of 1–2 weeks the course should be repeated.

If stibophen is used for the treatment of *S japonicum* infection, an intensive (and very toxic) course is required. Inject the drug daily into alternate buttocks as follows: 2, 4, and 6 mL on days 1–3 inclusive, followed by 8 mL daily for 11 doses, the entire course taking 14 days. If needed, a course of treatment may be repeated in 2 months.

3. TARTAR EMETIC
(Antimony Potassium Tartrate)

Chemistry

Antimony potassium tartrate (tartar emetic) contains 36.5% of trivalent antimony. It is soluble 1:12 in water. The sodium salt may be more stable and less toxic than the potassium preparation but requires the same precautions in its use.

Clinical Uses

Patients should be hospitalized for treatment.

A. *S japonicum:* Tartar emetic is an alternative drug for treatment of *S japonicum* infection. Most & others reported 13 failures among 79 patients treated with a total of 1.8 g and 2 failures among 50 patients treated with 2.08 g during a course of 25–33 days. Ata & Mousa reported the use of a longer course of 12–16 injections given at weekly intervals; the drug was well tolerated and the therapeutic results were similar to those of the standard course. A WHO Expert Committee (1972) summarized the efficacy of tartar emetic as resulting in 40–75% cure rates, with a comparable reduction in ovum count in the uncured.

B. *S mansoni* and *S haematobium:* Although tartar emetic is effective for the treatment of *S mansoni* and *S haematobium* infections, other less toxic drugs are preferred. Most reported that a total of 1.8 g of tartar emetic would cure more than 90% of infections with *S mansoni* and that 1.5–1.7 g would cure more than 90% of *S haematobium* infections.

Adverse Reactions

Each injection must be given subcutaneously with scrupulous care, since leakage of even small amounts into the perivascular tissues causes severe necrosis. Phlebitis is a frequent sequel of subcutaneous administration. The speed of injection should be very slow to reduce the incidence of immediate side-effects: cough, dyspnea, a sense of chest constriction, tachycardia, dizziness, vomiting, and hypotension. Paroxysms of coughing occur in most patients but usually subside within a few minutes after the injection. Hypotension responds promptly to stopping the injection and giving epinephrine subcutaneously. Acute vascular collapse is rare. Many other side-effects occur as described above under Antimony Compounds.

Contraindications & Cautions

The drug must be given very slowly by the intravenous route, taking care to avoid leakage into the perivascular tissues. Patients should be under continuous observation during administration, and a syringe containing epinephrine (1:1000) should be immediately available during each injection.

For other essential comments regarding cautions and contraindications, see above under Antimony Compounds.

Preparations & Dosages

Antimony potassium tartrate (tartar emetic) is available as a granular powder. A 0.5% solution that contains 1.8 mg of metallic antimony or 5 mg of tartar emetic per milliliter should be freshly prepared in 5% glucose, physiologic saline solution, or distilled water and sterilized by filtration or by gentle boiling for 5 minutes. Boiling for more than 5 minutes and autoclaving should be avoided. The resultant solution should be used within 2 hours and should be crystal clear and free of sediment.

Patients should refrain from vigorous exercise during the course of treatment. The drug is best given 2–3 hours after a light meal, and the patient should remain recumbent for several hours afterward.

The drug is administered intravenously very slowly through a fine needle over a 10-minute period. The initial dose is 8 mL of the 0.5% solution. Subsequent doses of 12, 16, 20, 24, and 28 mL are given on alternate days. Thereafter, continue 28 mL on alternate days for 9 additional doses until a total of 360 mL (1.8 g of the drug) has been given. If a second course is required, a few months should elapse before resuming treatment.

ASPIDIUM OLEORESIN
(Extract of Male Fern)

One dose of aspidium oleoresin, formerly the major drug for the treatment of tapeworm infections, will eradicate *Taenia saginata, Taenia solium,* and *Diphyllobothrium latum* in more than 80% of patients. However, because of its unpredictable and often severe toxicity (including death rarely), the drug was superseded first by quinacrine and, more recently, by niclosamide and dichlorophen. Aspidium should no longer be used.

BEPHENIUM HYDROXYNAPHTHOATE
(Alcopar)

Bephenium hydroxynaphthoate, synthesized in 1958, is an alternative drug for the treatment of hookworm infections but is less effective against necatoriasis than against ancylostomiasis. The drug is moderately effective for treating ascariasis and trichostrongyliasis, has a low order of activity in trichuriasis, and is ineffective in strongyloidiasis. The drug is no longer marketed in the USA.

Chemistry
The bephenium salts are quaternary ammonium compounds. Bephenium hydroxynaphthoate (benzyldimethyl[2-phenoxyethyl]ammonium 3-hydroxy-2-naphthoate) has an aqueous solubility of 0.02–0.03%. It must be stored in an airtight container.

Bephenium base

Absorption, Metabolism, & Excretion
Bephenium hydroxynaphthoate is poorly absorbed after oral administration. In humans, less than 0.5% of an oral dose of 1 g (of base) was recovered in the urine within 24 hours.

Pharmacologic Effects
Embryopathy was observed when 250–500 mg/kg was given to pregnant rabbits. The water-soluble chloride salt, when inoculated parenterally into dogs and cats, had ganglion blocking properties and caused a brief fall in blood pressure. In humans, no abnormal effects on the liver or kidney have been noted.

Anthelmintic Actions
The effects of bephenium hydroxynaphthoate on ascarid musculature are those of excitation followed by paralysis, associated with a loss of muscular reactivity to acetylcholine. These effects are not reversible.

Clinical Uses
Bephenium hydroxynaphthoate is a safe, moderately well tolerated drug. It may be used in the very young and also in the presence of diarrhea or marked anemia, either of which may accompany severe hookworm disease. The drug's deficiencies are its bitter taste, a high incidence of vomiting after its use, and a higher frequency of side-effects than for other drugs used in the treatment of ascariasis and hookworm infection.

A. *Ancylostoma duodenale:* Bephenium hydroxynaphthoate is an alternative drug for the treatment of hookworm infections due to *A duodenale.* Many studies indicate that a single course of treatment results in a cure rate of 76–98% and that the worm burden in the remaining patients is markedly reduced.

B. *Necator americanus:* Hookworm infections due to *N americanus* are more resistant than those due to *A duodenale* and therefore require treatment on 3 successive days to achieve about 80% reduction in worm loads.

C. *Ascaris lumbricoides:* Bephenium hydroxynaphthoate is moderately effective against roundworms. The reported cure rate after one dose varies from 30 to 82%, which is less satisfactory than the results obtained with piperazine.

D. Mixed *Ascaris* **and Hookworm Infections:** Bephenium hydroxynaphthoate paralyzes roundworms. Therefore, it can be used to treated mixed infestations of hookworms and roundworms without stimulating ascarid migration as reported for tetrachloroethylene, mebendazole, and thiabendazole.

E. *Trichostrongylus orientalis:* Single treatments have resulted in the eradication of the infection from 75–82% of patients.

Adverse Reactions
Bephenium hydroxynaphthoate has a very low toxicity at therapeutic doses. Nausea and vomiting, the common side-effects, are mild and short lasting and occur more frequently in young children. Other symptoms—dizziness, headache, cramping abdominal pain, and diarrhea—are less frequent. Variations in tolerance by ethnic groups have been described.

Contraindications & Cautions
Patients with marked anemia, diarrhea, or dehydration should have the condition partially corrected before the drug is given. In the presence of severe diarrhea due to hookworm disease, it may be necessary to use smaller daily doses and to continue daily treatments for 4–7 days.

The drug should not be used in pregnancy, hypertension, or ulcerative conditions of the gastrointestinal tract not due to hookworms.

Dosages

The drug should be given orally on an empty stomach and food then withheld for 2 hours. Since it is bitter when mixed with water, it can be made more palatable (and less vomiting occurs) when mixed in chocolate milk, orange juice, flavored syrups, or milk. No purgatives should be used.

The dosage for adults and older children is 5 g of the granules (one packet), mixed with water or other liquid, taken twice a day; children weighing less than 22 kg take half of the adult dosage. One day of treatment results in a high cure rate for *A duodenale* and *T orientalis* infections. The same daily dosage should be repeated for 3 days if the drug is used for *N americanus* infections or if the species of hookworm is not known. Two weeks later, reexamine the stools and re-treat if necessary. It is not always possible or essential to completely eradicate hookworm infection. If iron deficiency anemia accompanies severe hookworm disease, it should be treated with iron medication and a high-protein diet.

Preparations Available

Bephenium hydroxynaphthoate (Alcopar) is prepared as granules in 5-g packets (5 g of the granules contain 4.3 g of bephenium hydroxynaphthoate equivalent to 2.5 g of bephenium base).

BITHIONOL
(Actamer, Bithin, Lorothidol)

Bithionol is the drug of choice for the treatment of *Paragonimus westermani* (lung fluke) and *Fasciola hepatica* (liver fluke) infections. It needs further evaluation for its effectiveness in the treatment of clonorchiasis, opisthorchiasis, and infection with the large tapeworms. The drug is not marketed in the USA, but it can be obtained from the Parasitic Disease Drug Service, Center for Disease Control, Atlanta 30333, for investigational use. Topical bithionol was formerly used in soaps and cosmetics in the USA but was withdrawn from the market because it produced contact dermatitis and photodermatitis.

Bithionol (bis[2-hydroxy-3,5-dichlorophenyl]-sulfide) reaches peak blood levels in humans in 4–8 hours. At a daily dosage of 50 mg/kg in 3 divided doses for 5 days, a serum level of 50–200 μg/mL is maintained. Excretion appears to be mainly via the kidney. The mode of action of bithionol against *P westermani* has not been established, but the drug does inhibit oxidative phosphorylation.

The recommended dosage for pulmonary, cerebral, and subcutaneous paragonimiasis and for fascioliasis is 30–50 mg/kg orally on alternate days for 10–15 doses. The daily dose should be divided into a morning and evening dose. A series of clinical reports from 1961 to 1967 indicated that 97% of 420 patients with pulmonary paragonimiasis were cured using a dosage schedule ranging from 10 to 50 mg/kg, on alternate days, for a total of 5–15 doses. The drug should be used with caution in children under about 8 years of age because of limited experience with that age group. Bithionol is often useful in acute cerebral paragonimiasis, sometimes requiring more than one course of treatment, but has little effectiveness in chronic cerebral infections.

Side-effects are frequent but are generally mild and transient. Gastrointestinal symptoms, particularly diarrhea, occur in most patients but may decrease or stop after several days of treatment. Headache and dizziness are common. Urticaria and skin rash are infrequent and usually occur between the fourth and seventh days of treatment. Patients taking bithionol should have serial liver function tests.

CHLOROQUINE PHOSPHATE
(Aralen)

For general pharmacologic discussion, see Chapter 62.

Clinical Uses

No satisfactory treatment is available for clonorchiasis or opisthorchiasis, and the use of chloroquine for these infections is controversial. Many other drugs have been used, including bithionol, gentian violet, antimony preparations, dithiazanine, and hexachloroparoxylol.

The recommended course of treatment with chloroquine is 250 mg 3 times a day for 6 weeks. The drug may be useful in reducing the worm burden in relatively new infections, but in chronic infections it is unlikely to do more than temporarily decrease egg production and lessen symptoms. Patients should not be regarded as cured until at least a 6-month follow-up has been completed.

Adverse reactions at the recommended dosage are frequent, particularly in the first few weeks, and may necessitate temporary reduction in dosage or discontinuation of therapy. Side-effects include nausea, headache, pruritus, dizziness, and diarrhea. The ocular damage that may develop during long-term administration of the drug for other conditions has not been reported when chloroquine is used for 6 weeks, but this possibility should be kept in mind in using this drug without established merits.

DICHLOROPHEN
(Anthiphen)

Dichlorophen (bis[5-chloro-2-hydroxyphenyl]-methane) is effective and safe for the treatment of several tapeworm infections. Reported cure rates for *T saginata* infection range from 70 to 90% for doses greater than 5 g. Cure rates for *T solium* infection are probably similar, but few reports are available. Treatment of 64 patients infected with *Hymenolepis nana* with 62 mg/kg resulted in a 70% reduction in egg counts in 80% of patients. Waris reported 64% of 73 patients cured of *D latum* infection using 6 g daily for 2 days.

Dichlorophen has a consistent laxative effect; colic and mild nausea and vomiting may also occur. Lassitude and rash are rare, and jaundice has been reported.

The same cautions should be observed for the treatment of *T solium* infection with dichlorophen, especially the posttreatment purge, as are described for niclosamide with respect to the theoretic risk of cysticercosis after release of ova from disintegrating tapeworm segments. Because of the risk of drug-induced vomiting, in *T solium* infection it is preferable to use an alternative drug. Dichlorophen is contraindicated in the presence of liver disease. Alcoholic beverages should be avoided during treatment.

Dichlorophen (Anthiphen) is prepared as 0.5-g tablets. The dosage is 70 mg/kg taken on an empty stomach in the morning, without prior dietary restrictions or purgatives. Breakfast may follow in 2 hours. Some physicians repeat the dose the following morning. Except for *T solium* infection, no posttreatment purge is necessary even if a search for the scolex is intended, because the drug itself has a laxative action. Since the disintegrated scolex can rarely be identified, the results of treatment are not known with certainty until stools are reexamined 3–4 months later, when worms, if not expelled, will have regenerated and begun to shed new segments.

Dichlorophen is not marketed in the USA.

DIETHYLCARBAMAZINE CITRATE
(Banocide, Caricide, Hetrazan, Notézine)

Diethylcarbamazine, discovered in 1947, is the drug of first choice for the treatment of filariasis infections.

Chemistry

Diethylcarbamazine citrate, 1-diethylcarbamyl-

Diethylcarbamazine base

4-methylpiperazine dihydrogen citrate, is a piperazine derivative. The citrate salt contains 51% of the active base.

Absorption, Metabolism, & Excretion

When given orally, diethylcarbamazine is rapidly absorbed from the gastrointestinal tract. A single oral dose of 200 mg of base produces a peak blood level of 1.6 μg/mL in 1–2 hours. The minimum effective blood concentration appears to be 0.8–1.0 μg/mL.

Distribution studies indicate that the drug rapidly equilibrates with all tissues (including blood cells) except fat. It is excreted within 30 hours in the urine, either as unchanged drug or as a variety of degradation products. There is no tendency to accumulation with repeated doses.

Pharmacologic Effects

A. Actions on Humans: The headache, sleepiness, and vomiting that may accompany administration of the drug are probably due to stimulating effects of the compound on the central nervous system. In high concentrations, diethylcarbamazine has antiinflammatory or blocking action in some anaphylactic reactions; the mechanism is imperfectly understood. Oral doses of 100–200 mg/kg to pregnant rats and rabbits had no teratogenetic effects. Diethylcarbamazine is absorbed when applied to the conjunctiva and has a microfilaricidal effect in the aqueous humor. However, in heavily infected patients, a severe anterior uveitis may follow. Ocular inserts with varying concentrations of diethylcarbamazine are undergoing clinical trials. The drug is also absorbed topically when applied as a 1% lotion. However, reports vary on its effectiveness and freedom from significant side-effects.

B. Anthelmintic Actions: Microfilariae disappear from the blood when a therapeutic course of diethylcarbamazine is administered to patients infected with *Wuchereria bancrofti, Brugia malayi,* or *Loa loa.* Microfiliariae also disappear from the skin of patients infected with *Dipetalonema streptocerca,* but the drug is less effective or inactive against microfilariae of *Dipetalonema perstans.* In the course of treatment, many microfilariae are killed on the first day, but others die in subsequent days. Thus, antigen may be released from dying worms over several days.

Diethylcarbamazine causes a shift in location of microfilariae. In nocturnally periodic *W bancrofti* infection, if the drug is given in the daytime, the microfilariae apparently lose their position in the lung and appear in increased numbers in the peripheral circulation. In onchocerciasis, the drug flushes microfilariae from the dermis into the epidermis; and in some patients microfilariae may then be found in blood, urine, sputum, aqueous humor, and cerebrospinal fluid.

Diethylcarbamazine also kills adult worms of *W bancrofti, B malayi, L loa,* and *D streptocerca* but not those of *Onchocerca volvulus* or *Dirofilaria immitis.* The drug may have some lethal or sterilizing effect on *D perstans* and *Mansonella ozzardi.* The drug is highly effective against adult worms of *L loa*. The extent to which adult worms of *W bancrofti* and *B malayi* are killed in humans is not known. However, if therapy is adequate, microfilariae do not reappear in the majority of patients, which suggests that the adult worms are killed or at least permanently sterilized. The death of adult worms has been confirmed by experimental studies on *B malayi* infection in cats, by direct observation of *L loa* infection in humans, and by biopsies of *W bancrofti* infections in humans. No conclusion can be drawn, however, about the mode of action of diethylcarbamazine against adult worms.

Clinical Uses

A. *W bancrofti, B malayi, L loa:* Diethylcarbamazine is the drug of choice for treatment of these parasites, given its high order of therapeutic efficacy and relative lack of serious toxicity. Microfilariae are rapidly killed by diethylcarbamazine. Adults are killed more slowly, often requiring several courses of treatment.

B. *O volvulus:* Treatment must be individualized for each patient to determine if clinical findings require treatment and if the patient can tolerate drug side-effects. Although diethylcarbamazine kills microfilariae in the skin, it causes severe, sometimes violent reactions. Furthermore, the reduction in microfilariae is only temporary, since diethylcarbamazine does not kill adult worms. However, weekly doses of 200 mg of diethylcarbamazine may theoretically be useful in keeping infected persons symptom-free and preventing microfilariae from invading the eye.

The preferred treatment of onchocerciasis consists of surgical removal of accessible nodules (particularly those on the head), the use of suramin in selected patients to kill adult worms, and use of a course of diethylcarbamazine before suramin to slowly destroy microfilariae. If suramin is given alone, without a preliminary course of diethylcarbamazine, it may cause sufficiently rapid death of microfilariae to result in severe symptoms.

C. Other Parasites: Diethylcarbamazine is effective against tropical eosinophilia when given orally in a variety of dosage schedules. As much as 6 mg/kg 3 times daily, for 5–10 days or longer, may be necessary.

Diethylcarbamazine may have some effect against *D perstans* and *M ozzardi* infections, but it is not effective against *D immitis*. It has been used in the treatment of *Ascaris* infections and cutaneous larva migrans, but other drugs are superior.

D. Mass Therapy: One important application of diethylcarbamazine therapy has been its use for mass treatment of *W bancrofti* infections to reduce transmission and, it is hoped, to achieve eradication in some areas. Various regimens have been used, a common one being 5–6 mg/kg orally 1 day each week or month for 6–12 doses. Often, because of side-effects, patients will not return for repeated doses.

E. Prevention of *L loa* Infection: For the prevention of *L loa* infections, a regimen of 2.5 mg/kg twice daily for 3 consecutive days once a month may be tried.

Adverse Reactions

Diethylcarbamazine is a safe drug at therapeutic levels. Only a few mild, occasional side-effects can be attributed directly to the drug: headache, malaise, anorexia, and weakness. Nausea and vomiting, sleepiness, and skin rashes occur less often. However, mild to severe allergic symptoms (the "Mazzotti reaction" in onchocerciasis) are frequent as a result of the release of foreign protein from dying microfilariae or adult worms. These reactions are usually absent or mild for *W bancrofti* infection, more intense for *B malayi* infection, occasionally severe for *L loa* infection, and often very severe for *O volvulus* infection. Allergic side-effects that may start within 30 minutes after the initial dose of diethylcarbamazine are hyperpyrexia (up to 39 C), headache, tachycardia, cough, tachypnea, nausea and vomiting, malaise to prostration, joint pains, papular rash, intense pruritus, urticaria and edema of the skin, and inflammatory reactions of lymph nodes and lymphatics. In *W bancrofti* and *B malayi* infections, tenderness, inflammation, and small nodules may develop in sites in the groin or thighs. In *L loa* infection, small wheals may appear on the skin. In onchocerciasis, vertigo and hypotension may occur; eye findings include pain, photophobia, lacrimation, itching, visual field defects, and posterior segment changes.

These symptoms may persist for 3–7 days. Leukocytosis and an intensification of eosinophilia are usually present. If allergic reactions are severe, the dosage should be reduced or treatment interrupted. Thereafter, treatment may be continued and new reactions may not occur, except for an occasional local reaction at the site of a dying adult worm.

Allergic encephalitis has been described rarely in loiasis and in patients heavily infected with onchocerciasis (skin concentrations of 100–500 microfilariae per mg). In onchocerciasis some deaths have occurred in debilitated patients. After taking a small amount of the drug and without the usual allergic symptoms, the patients lapsed into shock and coma followed by death. However, diethylcarbamazine has been administered to several million persons having other infestations, with no reported fatalities.

Contraindications & Cautions

In patients infected with onchocerciasis, severe reactions may be provoked early in therapy, and damage to the eye may result as microfilariae are killed. Particular caution should be employed if microfilariae are producing symptoms in the skin or if microfilariae or nodules are close to the eyes. Patients with heavy loads of microfilariae in the ocular tissues should be hospitalized and treated by a physician with adequate ophthalmologic knowledge and the necessary equipment for eye examination, including a slitlamp.

Patients with attacks of lymphangitis due to *W*

bancrofti or *B malayi* infection should be treated in a quiescent period between attacks.

In loiasis, reactions are more likely in patients with pretreatment microfilariae counts greater than 50/mm^3 of blood; exchange transfusion has been suggested to reduce such counts.

Patients suspected of having malaria should be treated with chloroquine before they are given diethylcarbamazine, since the latter drug may provoke a relapse in nonsymptomatic malaria infections.

There are no absolute contraindications to the use of diethylcarbamazine, but caution is advised in patients with hypertension.

Preparations & Dosages

Diethylcarbamazine citrate (Banocide, Caricide, Hetrazan, Notézine) is available as 50-mg tablets or as a syrup containing 24 mg/mL.

A. W bancrofti, B malayi, L loa: These infections are treated with 2 mg of the citrate salt per kg body weight given orally 3 times a day after meals for 21 days. To reduce the incidence of allergic reactions from dying microfilariae, a single dose (2 mg/kg) is administered on the first day, 2 doses on the second day, and 3 doses on the third day and thereafter. For *B malayi* or for loiasis (with its risk of encephalopathy), the same schedule should be used, but individual doses should start at 1 mg/kg once on the first day and gradually increase to 2 mg/kg 3 times daily by the fourth to fifth day.

Antihistamines may be given for the first 4–5 days of diethylcarbamazine therapy to reduce the incidence of "allergic" reactions. Corticosteroids should be started and doses of diethylcarbamazine temporarily lowered if severe reactions occur.

Blood should be checked for microfilariae several weeks after treatment is completed; if any are still present, a course may be repeated at intervals of 3–4 weeks. However, since the initial treatment does not kill all adult worms, microfilariae may reappear in 3–12 months. Cure may require subsequent courses of treatment over 1–2 years.

B. O volvulus: Severe reactions due to the death of microfilariae may occur when diethylcarbamazine is used in the treatment of onchocerciasis, particularly if microfilariae are producing symptoms in the skin or are found near the eyes, and also if skin concentrations of microfilariae are high (over 100/mg). If possible, treatment should be started in the hospital, with low doses that are increased progressively. The following is one type of dosage schedule for heavy infections, with the drug to be given after meals: initially, give 25 mg once and wait several days for the reaction to subside; then give 25 mg twice daily for 2 days; then 50 mg twice daily for 2 days; then 100 mg twice daily for 2 days; then 200 mg twice daily for 7 days. When reactions to diethylcarbamazine have nearly ceased, suramin treatment is started. If suramin is not used, continue treatment with diethylcarbamazine indefinitely at weekly intervals in a dosage of 200 mg. In these treatments, allergic reactions will be smaller or absent.

In mild infections, symptomatic relief of treatment side-effects is often attempted with antihistamines and analgesics; but corticosteroids may be necessary. However, all patients with heavy infections should receive corticosteroids starting 1 day before treatment and continuing for 3–7 days, at which time the dosage is to be reduced gradually. If keratoconjunctivitis or iridocyclitis occurs, administer betamethasone eye drops.

EMETINE HYDROCHLORIDE

Emetine is an alternative drug for the treatment of *Fasciola hepatica* infection. It is administered by deep subcutaneous injection in doses of 1 mg/kg (maximum 65 mg daily) for 10 days. This treatment program is fairly effective in removing the parasite and, in this dosage schedule, is relatively safe. General pharmacologic information and the precautions necessary in treatment with emetine are presented in Chapter 62.

HEXYLRESORCINOL
(Crystoids)

Chemistry, Absorption, Metabolism, & Excretion

Hexylresorcinol (1,3-dihydroxy-4-hexylbenzene), a phenol derivative, was used for many years as a broad-spectrum anthelmintic but has been superseded for most indications by drugs that are more effective and easier to use. It continues to be an alternative drug for trichuriasis and for several intestinal fluke infections. The drug is not available in the USA.

After ingestion, approximately one-third of hexylresorcinol is absorbed from the gastrointestinal tract and then eliminated rapidly in the urine. Since the drug is soluble in fat and combines with protein, food should not be present in the upper gastrointestinal tract.

Adverse Reactions

Hexylresorcinol is nearly devoid of systemic toxicity at therapeutic levels, but topically it is corrosive to the oral mucosa and perianal skin. When given orally, mucosal ulceration may occur in the mouth unless the crystals are incorporated into hard gelatin-coated pills. Although the mucosa of the intestinal tract is protected by its mucous secretions, the drug may cause epigastric discomfort, vomiting, or diarrhea in a few individuals.

Contraindications & Cautions

To protect the oral mucosa, considerable care must be taken to ensure that pills are swallowed immediately and not chewed. Children should be supervised to be certain that the pills are not retained between the teeth and cheeks or under the tongue. For uncooperative children, hexylresorcinol crystals dissolved in 20 mL of water may be delivered through a duodenal tube. Hexylresorcinol is contraindicated in the presence of peptic ulcers, ulcerative colitis, and intestinal obstruction.

Clinical Uses, Preparations, & Dosages

Hexylresorcinol is prepared as gelatin-coated pills (Crystoids) for oral use or in bulk form for preparation of enemas. The pills contain 0.2 g of the drug. Hexylresorcinal is no longer marketed in the USA.

A. Treatment of Trichuriasis (Whipworm, Trichocephaliasis): Hexylresorcinol by retention enema is an alternative drug in the treatment of trichuriasis. However, it is recommended only for patients with significant symptoms and if the preferred drug, mebendazole, is not available.

In the evening, a warm soapsuds enema is followed by a 0.2% hexylresorcinol enema (volume, 20–30 mL/kg of body weight up to 1200 mL). The enema should be retained for 30 minutes; retention is facilitated by taping the buttocks together. If necessary, a small saline enema may be used to initiate expulsion. Two or more treatments at weekly intervals may be necessary to reduce worm loads and stop symptoms, but removal of all the parasites is not necessary and should not be attempted. *Caution:* Perianal skin irritation that develops when hexylresorcinol is used as a retention enema is preventable by the application of a film of petrolatum.

B. Treatment of *Fasciolopsis buski, Heterophyes heterophyes*, and *Metagonimus yokogawai* Infections: Alcohol should be avoided for 24 hours before and after treatment. Pretreatment purges are generally omitted except in the treatment of fasciolopsiasis. The day before treatment, the total diet should be reduced and the evening meal limited to soft, fat-free foods. Breakfast should be omitted on the morning of treatment and the drug administered with water. No food should be taken for 5 hours, but water is permissible. A saline purge (for adults use 30 g magnesium sulfate) should be given 2 hours after treatment. An additional course of treatment can be given a week later.

Adults and children over age 12 years receive 1 g; children age 8–12 years, 0.8 g; children age 6–8 years, 0.6 g; and infants and children up to age 6 years, 0.1 g per year of age. A minimum dose of 0.4 g is usually necessary for small children, who tolerate it well.

HYCANTHONE METHANESULFONATE
(Etrenol)

Hycanthone has been undergoing clinical trials since 1968 for the treatment of schistosomiasis. It is effective against *Schistosoma mansoni* and *S haematobium* but not *S japonicum*. The drug's important contribution is its high effectiveness with only a single intramuscular injection. However, its hepatotoxicity in some patients is sufficiently severe to cast doubts on its continued usefulness for individual or mass therapy. Furthermore, data are accumulating that cause concern about the drug's potential for teratogenicity and carcinogenicity and about acquired drug resistance. Hycanthone is not available in the USA.

Chemistry

Hycanthone methanesulfonate, 1-([2-diethylaminoethyl]amino)-4-hydroxymethyl-thioxanthen-9-one methanesulfonate, a thioxanthone compound and the hydroxymethyl analog of lucanthone, is believed to be both the natural metabolite of lucanthone and the metabolite responsible for the latter's schistosomicidal activity. Hycanthone has been used as the base for oral administration and as the methanesulfonate salt for intramuscular administration.

Absorption, Metabolism, & Excretion

After intramuscular administration, hycanthone reaches peak blood levels in 30 minutes and peak tissue levels in 60 minutes. The half-life of the drug in the blood is 1 hour; tissue clearance is nearly complete in 24 hours. Eighty percent of hycanthone is excreted in 48–72 hours, most through the bile and feces in the form of conjugated metabolites and about 10–15% in the urine.

Pharmacologic Effects

High doses (12 mg/kg) of hycanthone have produced signs of acute liver damage in cats. Therapeutic doses of hycanthone in humans have not produced the neuropsychiatric side-effects of lucanthone, although doses of 25 mg/kg in a variety of animal species have produced restlessness, excitement, and convulsions.

The effect of hycanthone on adult worms is to cause a shift of the parasites from terminal venules to the liver, followed by degenerative changes and death in a few days. Hycanthone also inhibits ovulation.

Clinical Uses

The only indications for hycanthone are *S mansoni* or *S haematobium* infections; the drug is not effective against *S japonicum*. Cure rates 6–12 months after a single intramuscular injection of 2.5–3 mg/kg have been variously reported as 42–95% *(S mansoni)* and 39–81% *(S haematobium)*. In patients not cured, many investigators report more than 90% reduction in the excretion of viable ova. In oral therapy trials, 3–5 days of treatment were necessary to provide the effectiveness of one intramuscular injection, but oral administration produced more side-effects.

Adverse Reactions

The frequency of reported side-effects has ranged from 40 to 60%. Generally, they clear within 24 hours. Vomiting, which was experienced by more than 50% of patients, began 4–6 hours after administration, but was usually mild and short-lasting. Dimenhydrinate or meclizine may be used to relieve the vomiting. *Caution:* Do *not* give phenothiazines. Pain at the site of injection, although frequent, is not severe if the drug is injected deep into the gluteus minimus muscle. Other mild and brief side-effects include nausea, abdominal cramps, diarrhea, constipation, headache, dizziness, weakness, myalgia, rash, itching, eosinophilia, and transient T wave changes on the ECG. Rarely reported are low-grade fever, sterile abscess at the injection site, insomnia, and tremors. The severe central nervous system symptoms (vertigo, convulsions, psychosis) seen with lucanthone are not found with hycanthone therapy. Low-grade transaminase elevations that return to normal within a few days have been described in approximately 15% of patients. Transient rises in bilirubin may also occur.

Early confidence in the safety of hycanthone was shaken by reports of 21 deaths associated with its use among approximately 400,000 patients treated in Brazil and Africa. These deaths occurred within 2–5 days after treatment and were characterized by acute hepatic necrosis. An additional 13 nonfatal reactions with jaundice were reported. It is possible that many of the deaths could have been avoided had current contraindications been observed.

A recent report indicated that by reducing the dosage to 1.5 mg/kg, most of the immediate symptoms were eliminated but the marked effect of the drug in reducing the worm burden was retained. Whether the lower dosage will reduce the incidence of fatalities is unknown. At least 72 deaths have now been reported in spite of the adoption of the contraindications listed below.

Mutagenicity of hycanthone has been demonstrated in *Drosophila melanogaster* and in several bacterial and mammalian cell culture systems. Increased numbers of intrauterine deaths and abnormal fetuses have been demonstrated in mice and rabbits following intramuscular administration of hycanthone. Experimental studies have shown an increased frequency of hepatomas in hycanthone-treated mice as compared to controls. Whether hycanthone has significant teratogenic and carcinogenic potential for humans needs to be determined.

Acquired resistance of schistosomes to hycanthone has been demonstrated in mice; whether the mechanism might be an induced mutation or the selecting-out of a preexisting resistant strain of schistosomes is unsettled. Limited evidence suggests the development of drug-resistant strains in humans. A recent study has also shown differences in susceptibility to hycanthone of different strains of *S mansoni*.

In June 1972, a WHO consultant group recommended that the use of hycanthone be continued, but urged that comparable data for antischistosomal drugs be obtained to establish their relative hazards.

Contraindications & Cautions

Contraindications to the use of hycanthone are recent or present jaundice, liver tenderness, nonschistosomal liver disease, severe malnutrition, and the concurrent use of drugs known to cause liver malfunction, such as phenothiazines, broad-spectrum antibiotics, nitrofurantoin, streptomycin, or antituberculosis drugs. Hycanthone should not be used in pregnancy, should not be given to children under age 3 years, and perhaps should not be used concurrently with oral contraceptives.

Treatment should be deferred during the acute phase of schistosomiasis and in the presence of acute infection—with the exception of protracted *Salmonella* infection seen with some cases of schistosomiasis. Treatment should also be deferred for 1 month or longer in patients who have been under chronic medication for other diseases or who have recently had general anesthesia. Patients with anemia, malnutrition, malaria, and tuberculosis should have these conditions corrected or controlled before undergoing hycanthone treatment. Caution should also be exercised and the patient hospitalized if the patient has the hepatosplenic form of schistosomiasis, advanced renal or cardiac disease, or tuberculosis.

Preparation & Dosages

Hycanthone methanesulfonate (Etrenol) is supplied as a powder in 200-mg vials. It is prepared for injection by adding 2 mL of sterile distilled water, resulting in a solution containing 100 mg of base per mL that is stable for 24 hours at 5–37 C. The dosage is a single intramuscular injection containing 2.5 mg of base per kg (± 0.5 mg/kg) up to a maximum adult dose of 200 mg of base. Hycanthone should not be injected into the arm or the leg but is given deep into the gluteus minimus, high under the iliac crest, with care taken to avoid intravascular injection. Most patients can be treated as outpatients but should be seen for follow-up on at least the second and third days after the injection. Patients may be re-treated in 3 months.

For children who have severe symptoms, the manufacturers recommend hospitalization and only one-half the standard dosage initially, followed by the second half 1 week later.

LEVAMISOLE & TETRAMISOLE
(Ketrax, Decaris)

Levamisole hydrochloride and tetramisole hydrochloride are synthetic imidazothiazole derivatives, levamisole being the L-isomer of DL-tetramisole. Since most of the anthelmintic activity of the compounds is limited to the L-isomer, use of levamisole rather than tetramisole permits a reduction in dosage and hence in side-effects. Tetramisole, introduced in 1966, has been extensively studied in humans. Levamisole was introduced subsequently and continues under active clinical investigation for its anthelmintic and immunologic properties. Neither drug is marketed in the USA. The drugs are highly effective in eradicating *Ascaris* and *Trichostrongylus* from most patients with a single course of treatment. They are only moderately effective in hookworm infections due to *A duodenale* and have a low effectiveness in *N americanus, Trichuris trichiura,* and pinworm infections. Their usefulness in strongyloidiasis remains to be determined.

Chemistry

Levamisole hydrochloride (L-tetramisole HCl), (−)-2,3,5,6-tetrahydro-6-phenylimidazo[2,1-b]-thiazole hydrochloride, is normally given orally but may be injected subcutaneously.

Absorption, Metabolism, & Excretion

Levamisole is rapidly and extensively absorbed. In humans, a single oral dose of 150 mg produces a peak plasma level of 0.5 μg/mL in 2 hours. (This is the same order of concentration needed to produce in vitro immunologic effects.) Levamisole is widely distributed to the tissues, with a high concentration in the liver, where it is extensively metabolized. Although blood levels fall rapidly—the plasma half-life is 4 hours—the pharmacologic and immunologic effects are prolonged. Within 24 hours, 60% of the oral dose is found in the urine, mostly as metabolites. Almost the entire dose is eliminated from the body within 2 days. Apparently levamisole crosses the blood-brain barrier, for it is effective against *Angiostrongylus cantonensis* in rats.

Pharmacologic Effects and Anthelmintic Actions

Pharmacologically, levamisole has a reversible ganglion-stimulating effect on mammalian tissue at both parasympathetic and sympathetic sites. In general, this results in stimulation of the central and autonomic nervous systems and skeletal muscle. Levamisole also has a positive inotropic and chronotropic effect on the fatigued heart muscle and is a strong inhibitor of mammalian alkaline phosphatases, except for intestinal and placental isoenzymes.

Levamisole is an immunomodulating and immunostimulating agent (see p 525). It affects host defenses by modulating cell-mediated immune responses, including polymorphonuclear leukocyte, macrophage, or T cell functions. The immune reactivity increases promptly after only a single dose and is thought to persist from days to months. The drug is under intensive clinical investigation to determine its mechanism of action and effectiveness in a variety of clinical conditions.

In nematodes, levamisole stimulates ganglionlike structures, causing contraction of muscle and then neuromuscular inhibition of the depolarizing type, resulting in paralysis. The worms are then eliminated by peristalsis. There is some indication that the anthelmintic action of levamisole may also stem from its inhibiting action on fumarate reductase.

Adverse Reactions

When levamisole is used in a single dose for the treatment of *Ascaris* and hookworm infections, side-effects are mild and transient. They include nausea and vomiting, mild abdominal cramping pain, headache, dizziness, weakness, and skin rash. In Moens' 1978 report on 1734 patients tested in 10 studies, 12% had one or more of these symptoms, yet 15% of the group receiving placebos also had these symptoms. In other studies, reported side-effects ranged from none to 23%; workers were in agreement that the symptoms were mild. Transient optic neuritis after a single dose and an anaphylactic reaction in a patient receiving the third of 3 doses given at intervals of 2–4 weeks have recently been reported.

When levamisole is used for its immunologic properties in long-term treatment at dosages of 150 mg/d, 2–4 times a week for several months, side-effects have occurred in about 5% of patients. The adverse reactions include a flu-like syndrome with fever, gastrointestinal symptoms, central nervous stimulation (nervousness, irritability, insomnia, sensory stimulation, and vertigo), skin rash, thrombocytopenia, and nonfatal and fatal agranulocytosis.

Contraindications & Cautions

Do not use in patients with advanced renal or hepatic disease.

Clinical Uses, Preparations, & Dosages

Levamisole (Ketrax, Decaris, Ethnor, Solaskil) is available in 40- or 50-mg tablets and as a syrup. Adults receive a single dose of 150 mg and children a single dose of 3 mg/kg. Stools should be checked 2 weeks later and treatment repeated until all ascarids are removed.

A. Treatment of Ascariasis: With a single oral dose, studies have shown an average cure rate of 91% (range 86–100%), with marked reduction (98%) in ova count in those not cured.

B. Treatment of Hookworm Infection: Single doses of levamisole have produced cure rates of 64–100% in the treatment of *Ancylostoma* infections. However, cure rates reported for *Necator* infections were much lower—27–68%. Further studies are needed to evaluate efficacy and side-effects of higher doses or longer courses of treatment.

C. Treatment of Other Infections: In *Trichostrongylus* infections, a single dose is curative in over 95% of patients. In filariasis studies in animals and humans, levamisole has microfilaricidal effects but is not macrofilaricidal at doses that can be tolerated.

MEBENDAZOLE
(Vermox)

Mebendazole has a wide spectrum of anthelmintic activity and is nearly free of side-effects. It is the drug of choice in trichuriasis infections and is particularly useful in mixed infections with trichurids, ascarids, hookworms, and pinworms, but it does not produce satisfactory cure rates in strongyloidiasis. Clinical trials suggest that mebendazole may be the first drug useful in the treatment of some cases of echinococcosis and possibly cysticercosis. Flubendazole, the parafluoro analog of mebendazole, is undergoing early clinical trials. It is similar to mebendazole in its anthelmintic spectrum and few side-effects, but in addition it appears to be active in the treatment of strongyloidiasis.

Chemistry

Mebendazole (methyl 5-benzoylbenzimidazole-2-carbamate) is a synthetic benzimidazole. Unlike the benzimidazole anthelmintic thiabendazole, mebendazole is substituted in position 5 and has a carbamate function.

Mebendazole

Absorption, Metabolism, & Excretion

Mebendazole is poorly absorbed. Following oral administration, peak plasma levels are reached in 2–4 hours. The drug is excreted in urine as unchanged drug or as a primary metabolite. With administration of 100 mg of mebendazole twice daily for 3 days, plasma levels of the drug and its principal metabolite, the 2-amine, never exceeded 0.03 μg/mL and 0.09 μg/mL, respectively. These studies led to the estimation that less than 1% of the administered dose was absorbed.

Pharmacologic Effects & Anthelmintic Actions

Mebendazole irreversibly blocks uptake of exogenous glucose by nematodes, leading to glycogen depletion and reduced generation of ATP required for survival. As a result, the parasites die or are immobilized only slowly, and their clearance from the gastrointestinal tract may not be complete until several days after treatment. Mebendazole does not affect blood glucose levels in animals or humans. Efficacy of the drug varies with gastrointestinal transit time and intensity of infection, and possibly with the strain of parasite and whether or not the drug is chewed.

Acute and chronic toxicologic studies in animals indicate a wide range between therapeutic and toxic doses. The LD_{50} (mg/kg orally) was more than 640 in rabbits and dogs and more than 1280 in mice and rats. Significant hematologic, biochemical, or pathologic abnormalities were not found in animals given 40 mg/kg daily for 13 weeks but were noted in rats given a daily dosage of 130 mg/kg. In pregnant rats the drug had embryotoxic and teratogenic activity at single oral doses as low as 10 mg/kg.

Clinical Uses

A. *Trichuris trichiuria* (Whipworm): Most studies indicate that when mebendazole is given at a dosage schedule of 100 mg twice daily for 3–4 days, cure rates are 60–80%, with marked reduction in ovum counts in those not cured. However, lower cure rates have also been reported. The heavier the infection, the more difficult it becomes to eradicate with only one course of treatment.

B. *Enterobius vermicularis* (Pinworm): Reports from various studies indicate cure rates of 90–100%. Thus, mebendazole compares favorably with the single-dose regimen of pyrvinium pamoate and pyrantel pamoate.

C. *Ascaris lumbricoides*, Hookworm, and *Trichostrongylus* Infections: A 3-day course produces cure rates of 90–100% for ascariasis and *Trichostrongylus* infections, with a marked reduction in the worm burden in those not cured. Reported cure rates for hookworm infections of both species range from about 35 to 95%.

D. Tapeworms: Mebendazole at a dosage of 300 mg twice daily for 3 days appears to be effective therapy for *T solium* infection; the drug has a theoretic advantage over niclosamide because proglottids are expelled intact after therapy. Reports have varied on the effectiveness of mebendazole for *T saginata* infection.

E. Hydatid Disease: In hydatid disease, when mebendazole was used at high dosages for several months, marked regression and apparent death of cysts occurred for some patients. Rarely, allergic reactions have occurred during the course of therapy and are thought to be due to liberation of antigen.

F. Other Infections: For treatment of **intestinal capillariasis,** mebendazole is the drug of choice at a dosage of 400 mg daily in divided doses for 21 or more days.

In **trichinosis,** initial reports suggest therapeutic efficacy against both the adult worms in the intestine and larvae in muscle. The suggested dosage is 1 g daily for 14 days.

Although reported cure rates in **strongyloidiasis** range from 40 to 75% with a standard 3-day course of therapy, a longer course may be more effective and should be tried. The efficacy of mebendazole in **dracontiasis** needs further study, as does the combined usage of mebendazole plus levamisole in **filariasis.**

Adverse Reactions

Mebendazole therapy has been remarkably free of side-effects even in debilitated patients. Mild nausea and vomiting, diarrhea, and abdominal pain have been reported infrequently. In children heavily parasitized by *Ascaris,* abdominal cramps are not uncommon; oral passage of ascarids in those under age 5 years has been reported from some countries.

Contraindications & Cautions

The drug is contraindicated in pregnant women. It

should be used with caution in children under age 2 years because of limited experience.

Preparations & Dosages

Mebendazole (Vermox) is prepared as tablets containing 100 mg of the drug. It may be therapeutically advantageous to advise that the tablets be chewed before swallowing; they can be taken before or after meals.

The same dosage schedule is used for adults and for children over age 2 years. For the treatment of ascariasis, trichuriasis, and hookworm infections, give 100 mg twice daily for 3 days. In severe trichuriasis infections, a longer course (up to 6 days) or a repeat course will often be necessary. No pretreatment or posttreatment purging is used. Reexamine stools for ova in 2–3 weeks to determine if a second course of treatment is necessary.

For the treatment of pinworms, give 100 mg one time only. Repeat the dose at 2 and 4 weeks.

METRIFONATE
(Bilarcil)

Metrifonate was introduced in 1952 as the insecticide trichlorfon (Dipterex) and then in 1960 as an oral drug for the treatment of *Schistosoma haematobium* infections. It is not effective against *S mansoni* or *S japonicum*. In the USA, metrifonate is only available from the Center for Disease Control, Atlanta 30333 (telephone number [404] 329-3670), on an investigational basis.

Chemistry, Absorption, Metabolism, & Excretion

Metrifonate, an organophosphorus compound, is O,O-dimethyl-1-hydroxy-2,2,2-trichloroethyl-phosphonate.

In humans, metrifonate is rapidly absorbed after oral administration and rapidly broken down, although the metabolic pathway is not yet understood. In various animal species, a peak of radioactive ^{32}P-labeled substance is found in plasma, kidneys, lungs, liver, and adrenals 2 hours after administration and is no longer detectable after 24–48 hours.

Pharmacologic Effects & Anthelmintic Actions

The mode of action of metrifonate as a cholinesterase inhibitor appears to be indirect, possibly as a result of its being transformed into the active metabolite dichlorvos (2,2-dichlorovinyl dimethyl phosphate). Dichlorvos was formerly used in the treatment of humans with hookworm infections and ascariasis.

In acute toxicity studies in experimental animals, the oral LD$_{50}$ was between 400 and 674 mg/kg. In chronic toxicity studies, unresolved discrepancies regarding toxicity of the compound for specific organs

may be caused by differences in the purity of the test material. Some studies show no abnormalities; others indicate potential for hepatotoxicity and hematologic toxicity.

Some organophosphorus compounds are known to have mutagenic properties. Similar claims have been made for metrifonate, including a report that it was weakly carcinogenic in rats and that it altered DNA in vitro. There was no evidence that low doses of metrifonate increased the rate of lethal mutations in *Drosophila*. Dichlorvos, however, was mutagenic in some microtest systems but not in mammalian test systems.

Studies using therapeutic dosages in humans or comparable doses in animals produced no untoward physiologic or chemical abnormalities except for cholinesterase inhibition, which results in the accumulation of acetylcholine at nerve synapses and may produce some short-lasting signs and symptoms. Following oral ingestion of 7.5–12.5 mg/kg of metrifonate by infected persons, there is an almost complete inhibition of plasma cholinesterase and a marked reduction (about 50%) of erythrocytic cholinesterase. Plasma recovery is usually 70% or more by 2 weeks and is completed by 4 weeks, but erythrocyte recovery may take up to 15 weeks. Prolonged depression of cholinesterase activity in the blood is not known to be associated with any disturbance of organ structure or function.

The mode of action of metrifonate against schistosomes is unknown, but it is assumed to act on both the immature and mature stages of the parasites by cholinesterase inhibition. One result is a shift of adult schistosomes from the bladder venous plexus to small arterioles of the lungs, where they are trapped and encased and then die.

Clinical Uses

In the treatment of *S haematobium* infections, cure rates in various clinical trials ranged from 44 to 93% when 3 doses of 7.5–10 mg/kg were given orally at 14- to 28-day intervals. Those not cured showed a marked reduction in ova counts. Recent work by Jewsbury and others (1977) has shown that metrifonate is also effective as a prophylactic against urinary schistosomiasis when given monthly to children in a highly endemic area.

Metrifonate is being tested as a microfilaricidal drug in the treatment of onchocerciasis. It appears to produce fewer side-effects than diethylcarbamazine, but it is also less effective.

Adverse Reactions

In clinical trials in over 6000 persons, tolerance has been excellent. Some studies report no side-effects; others note mild and transient findings including nausea and vomiting, diarrhea, abdominal pain, bronchospasm, headache, weakness, and vertigo. These symptoms may begin within 30 minutes and persist up to 12 hours. The drug was well tolerated by patients in advanced stages of the disease.

Contraindications & Cautions

Metrifonate should not be used after recent exposure to insecticides or drugs that might potentiate cholinesterase inhibition. General anesthetics should be avoided for 48 hours after administration of the drug. The drug is contraindicated in pregnancy. In the USA, it is required that plasma cholinesterase levels be determined before each dose of the drug.

Preparations & Dosages

Metrifonate (Bilarcil) is supplied in 100-mg divided tablets and is taken orally at a dosage of 7.5–10 mg/kg once, and then repeated twice at 2-week intervals. The drug is not marketed in the USA but can be obtained from the Parasitic Disease Drug Service, Center for Disease Control, Atlanta 30333 (telephone number [404] 329-3670).

NICLOFOLAN
(Menichlopholan, Bilevon, Bayer 9015)

Niclofolan is a hydroxylated biphenyl compound that may prove to be useful in the treatment of paragonimiasis. When used in Nigeria as a single dose of 2 mg/kg, it gave a cure rate of 73–90% in patients infected with *Paragonimus uterobilateralis*. Bone and joint pain and skin rash were frequent side-effects, but were mild and disappeared within 3 days. Further studies are needed to determine the effectiveness of niclofolan in treating paragonomiasis in other parts of the world. The advantage of niclofolan over bithionol is that treatment consists of a single dose.

NICLOSAMIDE
(Yomesan)

Niclosamide, introduced in 1960, is the drug of choice for the treatment of infection with several tapeworm species. It is not available for use in the USA except from the Parasitic Disease Drug Service, Center for Disease Control, Atlanta 30333.

Chemistry

Niclosamide is N-(2'-chloro-4'-nitrophenyl)-5-chlorosalicylamide.

Niclosamide

Absorption & Metabolism

Niclosamide is apparently not absorbed from the gastrointestinal tract. The unaltered drug has not been recovered from the blood or urine.

Pharmacologic Effects & Anthelmintic Actions

Following oral administration in animals and humans, no hematologic, renal, or hepatic abnormalities have been noted.

The scoleces and segments of cestodes, but not the ova, are rapidly killed on contact with niclosamide. This may be due to the drug's inhibition of oxidative phosphorylation. Associated with the death of the parasite is release of the scolex from the intestinal wall. Even if a purge is used to expel the tapeworm, the scolex may be partially digested and difficult to identify.

Clinical Uses

Niclosamide has far fewer and less severe side-effects than quinacrine or aspidium oleoresin and is equally or more effective. Dichlorophen, another taeniacide, is also highly effective but has given variable results. Its side-effects are also mild but may be more frequent than those of niclosamide.

A. *Taenia saginata* (Beef Tapeworm): The cure rate for 781 documented cases reported in the literature was 89%.

B. *T solium* (Pork Tapeworm): Niclosamide is considered equally effective for *T solium* infection.

C. *Diphyllobothrium latum* (Fish Tapeworm): In a group of 297 adult patients receiving 2 g in a single dose, the cure rate was 73% when the tablets were swallowed whole and 87% when they were chewed.

D. *Hymenolepis nana* (Dwarf Tapeworm): In a series of approximately 350 cases, the overall cure rate for niclosamide was 75%.

E. Other Tapeworms: Results have been promising in patients treated for *Hymenolepis diminuta* and *Dipylidium caninum* infections. Niclosamide is not effective against tapeworm species that are parasites of extra-intestinal tissues (cysticercosis or hydatid disease in humans).

F. Other Parasites: Niclosamide can be used as an alternative drug for the treatment of *Fasciolopsis buski* infection, although it is not as effective as tetrachloroethylene or hexylresorcinol.

Adverse Reactions

The drug rarely produces side-effects. Nausea, vomiting, and intestinal colic have been reported.

Contraindications & Cautions

Niclosamide should be used cautiously in children under age 2 years, since experience with the drug in this age group is limited. The consumption of alcohol should be avoided on the day of treatment and for 1 day afterward.

There are no contraindications to the use of niclosamide. The drug can probably be given safely after the first 3 months of pregnancy.

Preparations & Dosages

Niclosamide (Yomesan) is prepared as chewable tablets, each containing 0.5 g of the drug. Tablets are flavored with saccharin and vanilla. The adult dosage is 4 tablets (2 g). Children weighing more than 34 kg are given 3 tablets; children 11–34 kg, 2 tablets.

Pre- and posttreatment purges are not necessary, except for an occasional patient with chronic constipation requiring a pretreatment laxative. Niclosamide should be given in the morning on an empty stomach. The tablets must be chewed thoroughly and then swallowed with water. For small children, pulverize the tablets and then mix with water. The patient may eat 2 hours later. In the treatment of the large tapeworms, segments will continue to pass for several days with normal peristalsis.

A. T saginata, D latum, and D caninum: Treatment requires only a single dosage. Although not usually necessary, for the large tapeworms, a purge may be given 2 hours after treatment in an attempt to recover and identify the scolex before it disintegrates, thus indicating that the entire worm has passed and will not regenerate. If the scolex is not found or is not searched for, cure can be presumed only if regenerated segments have not reappeared 3–5 months after treatment.

B. T solium: Niclosamide is taken at the same dosage and in the same manner as for *T saginata* infection. However, 2 hours after treatment, an effective purge (such as 15–30 g of magnesium or sodium sulfate) must be given to eliminate all mature segments before ova can be released. Since niclosamide does not kill ova released from disintegrating tapeworm segments, cysticercosis is theoretically possible after treatment of *T solium* infections. It is unknown whether larvae are released from ova in the large bowel. If so, they could penetrate the intestinal wall and reach the tissues. The hazard is apparently overemphasized, since no cases of cysticercosis have been reported after use of niclosamide.

C. H nana: Hymenolepiasis requires extended treatment because both internal and external autoinfection occurs, and humans harbor both the larval and adult forms of the parasite. One mode of therapy is to treat daily for 7 days and to recheck stools at 3 weeks. On the first day of treatment the dosage is as given above; on days 2–7 give one-half that dosage. Purgatives should not be given.

D. H diminuta: Treat as for *H nana*.

NIRIDAZOLE
(Ambilhar)

Niridazole when given orally is active against all 3 species of schistosomes. Most persons experience side-effects, sometimes severe; but if the cautions and contraindications are followed, the drug appears safe to use. However, mutagenic and carcinogenic properties have been reported. Niridazole is also effective in the treatment of dracontiasis. The drug is not marketed in the USA but may be obtained from the Parasitic Disease Drug Service, Center for Disease Control, Atlanta 30333, for use on an investigational basis.

Chemistry,

Niridazole is 1-(5-nitro-2-thiazolyl)-2-imidazolidinone, a nitrothiazole derivative.

Niridazole

Absorption, Metabolism, & Excretion

Following oral administration, niridazole is absorbed slowly; the maximum blood concentration is reached in 6 hours. Greater blood levels are reached if the drug is given in 2 divided doses 12 hours apart rather than in one single larger dose. The concentration of the unmetabolized drug (the active agent against the parasite) is 5 times higher in the portal blood than in the peripheral circulation because most of the drug is metabolized in the first cycle through the liver. Elimination is mostly through urine and through bile into feces.

However, high blood concentrations of the unmetabolized drug are found in the peripheral circulation in patients with hepatic dysfunction (because metabolic degradation is impaired) and in the presence of portal-systemic shunts (because the drug bypasses the liver). The many side-effects of niridazole are thought to occur when this unmetabolized drug reaches a threshold level in the peripheral circulation.

Pharmacologic Effects

A. Actions in Experimental Animals and Humans: The drug produces temporary inhibition of spermatogenesis in experimental animals, but inhibition is reversible, with no subsequent interference with fertility and no posttreatment teratogenic effect. Present evidence indicates that the drug does not have permanent effects on spermatogenesis in humans. Niridazole has been shown to have a glycogen-lowering effect in monkey muscle; such glycogen depletion may be responsible for some of the side-effects in humans. Niridazole also has uricosuric effects.

In addition to its antiparasitic actions, niridazole has antibacterial and anti-inflammatory properties and suppresses delayed hypersensitivity. Manifestations of the latter have included depression of skin test reactivity and lymphocyte transformation in humans, and retardation of allograft rejection and granuloma formation in mice. In animals, signs of damage to the hematopoietic system have been noted following several weeks of niridazole therapy, but in humans there have been no reports of adverse effects on peripheral blood counts or bone marrow, nor have there been reports of increased susceptibility to infection. Thus, niridazole is potentially useful as an immunosuppressive drug.

B. Anthelmintic Actions: In experimental animals infected with *S mansoni,* adequate oral doses of niridazole cause a "liver shift" of adult worms that is followed by their death. Niridazole is rapidly concentrated in adult worms, resulting in the inhibition of phosphorylase inactivation followed by glycogen depletion of the parasite. Niridazole also inhibits or interrupts egg production.

Clinical Uses

A. *S haematobium, S mansoni,* and *S japonicum:* Of the three species, *S haematobium* is the easiest to eradicate with niridazole treatment and *S japonicum* the most difficult. Since it is not uncommon for live ova to be undetectable for 2–6 months after treatment and then to reappear at 6–12 months, cure rates are best based on the longer follow-up period. In clinical trials based on a 12-month follow-up, cure rates of 78–82% have been reported for *S haematobium,* 38–80% for *S mansoni,* and 26–48% for *S japonicum.* Among patients not cured, marked reduction in ovum counts (80–90%) usually occurs. Efforts to reduce side-effects but retain effectiveness by giving niridazole over longer periods than the standard course and at reduced daily doses have had variable success.

In the treatment of *S mansoni* infections, relatively recent infections appear to be more difficult to treat than older infections; perhaps for this reason, children with this infection sometimes appear to be more refractory to treatment than adults. Despite niridazole's moderate effectiveness against *S japonicum,* the drug is often so poorly tolerated that alternative drugs must be used.

In the treatment of *S haematobium* infections, evidence suggests that short courses of standard doses given for only 3 days result in cure rates of two-thirds or more of patients and marked reduction in ovum counts in the others. Further studies with long-term follow-up are needed to establish the effectiveness of this approach.

B. *Dracunculus medinensis:* Niridazole provides effective treatment for dracontiasis (guinea worm infection). Reduction of swelling and rapid relief of pain follow treatment, and the worms can then be pulled out relatively easily.

C. *Entamoeba histolytica:* Niridazole and metronidazole (Flagyl) given orally are the first drugs that are effective against both intestinal and extra-intestinal amebiasis. Because of its toxicity, niridazole should not be used for amebiasis except when no other drugs can be used. The recommended dosage is 25 mg/kg (maximum 1.5 g) for 7–10 days in divided daily doses.

Adverse Reactions

Side-effects are transient and occur in more than 70% of patients. They are often more intense in the first 3–5 days and then diminish as therapy continues. Children generally tolerate the drug better than adults; patients with *S japonicum* infections are most likely and patients infected with *S haematobium* least likely to have significant side-effects.

The most common adverse reactions are anorexia, nausea and vomiting, diarrhea, abdominal pain, fatigue, headache, dizziness, myalgia, arthralgia, sweating, palpitation, and skin rashes. The urine may become dark brown, with an unpleasant musty odor. Liver function tests may become abnormal. Cough, pulmonary infiltrates, and marked eosinophilia may occur. Niridazole can provoke hemolysis in persons with red cells deficient in glucose-6-phosphate dehydrogenase. In animal experiments, damage to the hematopoietic system has been observed. In humans, the drug has not been incriminated as a cause of bleeding tendencies, yet epistaxis and gastrointestinal hemorrhage have rarely been reported during niridazole therapy, and Stevens-Johnson syndrome and hemolytic syndromes have been described.

Niridazole also produces temporary inhibition of spermatogenesis in some men. Concern has been expressed about possible teratogenic effects, but none have been observed in limited follow-ups of patients. Tachycardia and minor electrocardiographic changes (flattening or inversion of T waves and ST depression) occur frequently but have not been associated with impairment of cardiac function.

Headache and myalgia may be relieved by aspirin. Antispasmodics may relieve gastrointestinal symptoms. Antihistamines may be helpful in controlling allergic reactions caused by release of foreign proteins from disintegrating worms.

Neuropsychiatric symptoms in patients who appear to be free of hepatic dysfunction have been reported in 1–2% of those infected with *S haematobium* and in up to 5% of those infected with *S mansoni;* however, in advanced schistosomal liver disease, up to 60% may have symptoms. Central nervous system symptoms tend to reach a maximum about the third day and may decrease after that. Initial central nervous system symptoms may include mild headache, paresthesias, insomnia, and anxiety. Electroencephalographic changes are also common but have not been useful in predicting more serious side-effects. If headache persists for more than 24 hours, treatment should be stopped for 12–48 hours, and then it may be possible to resume at the same dosage or a reduced dosage. If the following symptoms occur, the drug should be discontinued: marked mood changes (agitation, anxiety, depression), slurred speech, confusion, psychosis (auditory or visual hallucinations, violent behavior), and convulsions. These symptoms will usually subside within 48 hours after discontinuation of medication. However, in rare instances a normal mental state may not be reached for about 3 weeks. Administration of phenobarbital throughout niridazole therapy may diminish the central nervous system reactions.

Liver function tests and blood counts should be

followed during the course of therapy.

Niridazole has recently been shown to have both mutagenic and carcinogenic properties. Niridazole itself, and metabolic derivatives in the urine of patients treated with the drug, have been shown to have mutagenic activity in *Salmonella* test systems. In addition, niridazole has been reported to induce both benign and malignant tumors in mice. Although in the 10 years of its use in human infections there have been no reports implicating niridazole in causing cancer, the agent must be considered potentially hazardous for humans.

Contraindications & Cautions

Niridazole should always be used under close daily medical supervision. The drug is generally given on an outpatient basis, but hospitalization is required in the USA. The following patients should always be hospitalized for treatment: debilitated patients, the elderly and very young, and patients with any degree of impairment of hepatic function. In advanced cases of schistosomal liver disease there is some evidence to support the use of much smaller doses given over an extended period of time. Patients should be tested for G6PD deficiency; if positive, observe carefully for hemolysis during the course of treatment.

Patients with the following conditions generally should not receive the drug: history of liver disease; impaired liver function; the hepatosplenic form of schistosomiasis; caridac or renal disease; hypertension; age over 50; or a history of psychiatric disorders, epilepsy, or gastrointestinal hemorrhage or ulcer. Patients with severe malnutrition, anemia, infections, and other debilitating conditions should have these problems corrected before therapy is begun. Niridazole should not be administered concurrently with isoniazid.

Preparations & Dosages

Niridazole (Ambilhar) is prepared as 100- and 500-mg tablets. The dosage for schistosomiasis and dracontiasis is 25 mg/kg (maximum 1.5 g) daily for 7 days, divided into 2–3 fractions and given with meals. Although the evidence for its effectiveness is not fully convincing, some workers recommend that adult patients receive phenobarbital, 100–150 mg daily in divided doses, to reduce the incidence of central nervous system side-effects. For the treatment of *S japonicum* infections, it is currently recommended that the course of treatment be stopped in 5 days.

Children infected with *S mansoni* receive the adult dosage. However, for children infected with *S haematobium*, the duration of treatment can be reduced to 5 days if daily doses of 30–35 mg/kg are administered in divided doses.

OXAMNIQUINE
(Vansil)

Oxamniquine has been undergoing clinical trials for about 8 years. It is highly effective and the drug of choice for treating *Schistosoma mansoni* infections, but it is not effective against *S haematobium* or *S japonicum*.

Chemistry, Absorption, Metabolism, & Excretion

Oxamniquine, a synthetic tetrahydroquinoline derivative, is 6-hydroxymethyl-2-isopropylaminomethyl-7-nitro-1,2,3,4-tetrahydroquinoline.

Oxamniquine is readily absorbed after oral administration; a 1-g test dose reached a peak serum level of about 900 ng/mL after 2 hours and was nearly cleared after 10 hours. The drug is converted into inactive metabolites that are largely excreted in the urine. Although oxamniquine is effective when given parenterally, parenteral administration is no longer used because it induces severe local pain.

Anthelmintic Actions

Oxamniquine is active against both the mature and immature stages of *S mansoni*. Although the exact mechanism of action is not known, in experimental animals the drug stops oviposition; in animals and humans, it induces a shift of the worms from the mesentery to the liver.

Clinical Uses

Oxamniquine is effective only against *S mansoni*. Following a single dose of 15–20 mg/kg, an 80–90% cure rate was reported in Brazil; in those not cured, a 90–95% reduction in egg excretion was observed. In Egypt and parts of Africa, however, a larger dose—about 60 mg/kg given over 2–3 days—was needed to achieve the same cure rates. In East Africa, cure rates are somewhat lower. The drug is generally less effective in children than in adults.

The advantage of oxamniquine over niridazole, the other effective oral drug, is the absence of severe side-effects when it is used in the hepatosplenic stage of the disease.

Adverse Reactions

In clinical trials the drug has been safe and free of significant side-effects. Dizziness persisting for about 6 hours is common. A low-grade fever starting on the second day of treatment or several days later is frequently reported in Egypt but occurs less often in Brazil. Drowsiness, nausea and vomiting, diarrhea, abdominal colic, headache, and pruritus are less frequently reported. An orange to red discoloration of the urine may appear. A transient drop in leukocytes and lymphocytes may be seen, and liver function abnormalities, particularly transaminase elevations, may appear as late as one week after treatment. Observations that require further confirmation are individual or rare reports of skin rash, nephrotic syndrome, and central nervous system stimulation, including psychic excitement, hallucinations, and seizures.

Oxamniquine showed no evidence for mutagenicity in the Ames test and, when given to animals and humans, produced no chromosomal abnormalities.

Contraindications & Cautions

Patients with a history of epilepsy should be treated in hospital; further experience with the drug in such patients may show that an alternative drug should be used.

Preparations & Dosages

Oxamniquine (Vansil, Mansil) is prepared for oral use in 250-mg capsules and as a syrup containing 50 mg/mL. Optimal dosage schedules are still to be determined, but they clearly vary for different regions of the world. A suggested dosage for Brazil is 15 mg/kg given once after eating in the evening; for Egypt, 15 mg/kg given twice daily after meals for 2 days. Higher dosages are being tested in children.

OXANTEL PAMOATE

Oxantel pamoate, a m-oxyphenol analog of pyrantel pamoate, is undergoing clinical evaluation for the treatment of trichuriasis. It is not effective in the treatment of ascariasis, strongyloidiasis, or hookworm infection. The pamoate salt is nearly insoluble in water and is very poorly absorbed after oral administration.

For patients with light to moderate trichuriasis, the following cure rates were obtained using only a single dose of oxantel: at 10 mg/kg, 57–75% were cured; at 15 mg/kg, 88%; and at 20 mg/kg, 100%. A dosage of 15 mg/kg daily for 2 days is suggested for moderate and heavy infections. The drug is free of significant side-effects; rarely, nausea and vomiting and abdominal cramps were noted.

Therapeutic trials have recently been reported for the preparation combining oxantel and pyrantel. Because pyrantel is effective against Ascaris and hookworm, the combination has shown such a level of effectiveness in mixed infections with Ascaris, hookworm, and trichurids that it rivals mebendazole as a broad-spectrum anthelmintic. Unfortunately, neither drug is effective in strongyloidiasis.

PAROMOMYCIN
(Humatin)

Paromomycin, a member of the kanamycin-neomycin group of antibiotics that has a broad spec-

trum of antibacterial activity (see Chapter 51), has been shown to be effective against tapeworms. Because it is poorly absorbed from the gastrointestinal tract, it has been used for the reduction of intestinal bacteria and for the treatment of amebiasis. Although nephrotoxicity, ototoxicity, and central nervous system toxicity are possible with paromomycin as with other members of the neomycin group, such complications have not been reported. A 1-day course of treatment produces abdominal pains and diarrhea in more than 30% of patients, with nausea and vomiting reported less often. The dosage for adults is 1 g every 15 minutes for 4 doses; for children 11 mg/kg every 15 minutes for 4 doses. Botero cured 14 of 15 patients and Wittner & Tanowitz cured all of 15 patients with T saginata, T solium, or D latum infections by using paromomycin. The authors also effected cures in 10 cases of H nana infection in children and adults by using a dosage of 45 mg/kg for 5–7 days.

Because of the risk of drug-induced vomiting, it would be preferable in T solium infections to use an alternative drug. However, if paromomycin is used, it should be followed by an intense posttreatment purge (15–30 g magnesium or sodium sulfate) 2 hours later in order to rapidly eliminate the tapeworm segments before they disintegrate.

Paromomycin (Humatin) is available as 250-mg capsules and as a pediatric syrup containing 125 mg/5 mL. It should be administered after meals. Although the drug is marketed in the USA for other indications, in its use for tapeworm infections it is considered an investigational drug by the FDA.

PIPERAZINE

Piperazine salts, introduced in 1949, have been drugs of choice in the treatment of roundworms. Piperazine is not useful for treatment of hookworm infection, trichuriasis, or strongyloidiasis and is no longer recommended in this text for the treatment of pinworms.

Chemistry

Piperazine is available as a hexahydrate (which contains about 44% of the base) and as a variety of neutral salts: citrate, phosphate, adipate, tartrate, and others.

Piperazine base

Absorption, Metabolism, & Excretion

A portion of the absorbed salt is metabolized in the body. The remainder is excreted in the urine, but the rate of excretion varies widely for different persons.

Orally administered piperazine is almost free of pharmacologic action.

Anthelmintic Actions

In vivo studies indicate that piperazine causes a paralysis of *Ascaris* by blocking the stimulating effects of acetylcholine at the myoneural junction. Piperazine has a similar myoneural blocking action on mammalian skeletal muscle, but of a low order. When the drug is used in humans, the paralyzed roundworms are unable to maintain their position in the host and are expelled by normal peristalsis. The worms passed are alive.

Clinical Uses

Several properties of the piperazine salts combine to make these drugs nearly ideal for the treatment of *Ascaris* infections: palatability, a high order of effectiveness, low cost, a low toxicity at therapeutic levels, and the lack of need for pretreatment or posttreatment purges.

A. *Ascaris lumbricoides:* Piperazine is an alternative drug for roundworm infections. When patients are treated once daily for 2 days, cure rates are over 90%. Longer courses are needed for equivalent cure rates in patients with heavy infections. Piperazine syrup, administered via an intestinal drainage tube, is used in the nonsurgical management of intestinal obstruction due to heavy *Ascaris* infection.

B. *Enterobius (Oxyuris) vermicularis:* Piperazine is no longer recommended here for pinworm infections. Although 95% cure rates are achieved by the 7-day course of treatment, equivalent cure rates are possible with only a single dose of pyrvinium pamoate, pyrantel pamoate, or mebendazole.

Adverse Reactions

There is a wide range between the therapeutic and toxic doses of piperazine. Mild side-effects occur occasionally, including nausea and vomiting, diarrhea, abdominal pain, and headache. Neurotoxic side-effects, including vertigo, incoordination, difficulty in focusing, muscular weakness, lethargy, and confusional states, are rarely reported. Patients with a predisposition to grand mal or petit mal epilepsy may have an exacerbation of seizures. Although piperazine is potentially allergenic, only rarely have the following allergic symptoms been attributed to it: urticaria, erythema multiforme, purpura, fever, and arthralgia.

Contraindications & Cautions

Piperazine compounds should not be given to patients with impaired renal or hepatic function or with a history of epilepsy or chronic neurologic disease. Piperazine may be used during the last trimester of pregnancy. Piperazine and phenothiazines should not be given together.

Preparations & Dosages

The therapeutic effectiveness of the various piperazine salts is about the same; in solution, all form piperazine hexahydrate. Among the many preparations available as tablets, wafers, or syrups are piperazine citrate (Antepar, Anthecole, Multifuge, Vermago, Vermidol, Pipizan), piperazine phosphate (Antepar wafers, Pripsen), piperazine calcium edetate (Perin), piperazine tartrate (Piperat, Veroxil), piperazine adipate (Entacyl, Oxurasin, Oxyzin), and piperazine hexahydrate (Arpezine, Dispermin).

Piperazine citrate (Antepar) is prepared as a syrup containing 110 mg/mL (the equivalent of 100 mg of piperazine hexahydrate) or as tablets containing 550 mg (the equivalent of 500 mg of piperazine hexahydrate).

A. Treatment of Ascariasis: The dosage for piperazine (as the hexahydrate) is 75 mg/kg body weight (to a maximum dose of 3.5 g) for 2 days in succession, giving the drug orally before or after breakfast. For heavy infestations, treatment should be continued for 4 days in succession. No pre- or posttreatment cathartics are used. In most cases, cure is obtained, but stools should be reexamined at 2-week intervals and treatment repeated until ova are no longer found.

B. Treatment of Enterobiasis: The daily oral dose of piperazine (as the hexahydrate) is 65 mg/kg up to a maximum dose of 2.5 g. This dosage should be given daily for 7 days, before or after breakfast. Cathartics are not used. The course of treatment should be repeated after 2 weeks. Because of its long course of treatment, piperazine is no longer recommended in this text for enterobiasis if the drugs of choice are available.

PRAZIQUANTEL
(Droncit, Biltricide, EMBAY 8440)

Praziquantel is currently undergoing clinical trials for the treatment of schistosomiasis, tapeworm infections, and cysticercosis. It is a synthetic compound, given orally, and has the unique characteristic of being effective in animals against all species of schistosomes pathogenic to humans. No teratogenic or mutagenic activity has been observed.

Praziquantel, a pyrazino isoquinoline compound, is 2-cyclohexylcarbonyl-1,3,4,6,7,11b-hexahydro-2H-pyrazino [2,1-a] isoquinoline-4-one. It is a crystalline powder, is nearly insoluble in water, and has a bitter taste. After oral administration, the drug is rapidly absorbed, reaches a maximum serum concentration in 1–3 hours, is metabolized extensively and rapidly, and then is excreted mainly via the kidneys — approximately 70% in the first day, and 90% by 4 days.

Early clinical reports from a multicenter study (Groll, 1977) indicated infrequent (4%) and "transient and negligible" side-effects. A single dose of 10–25 mg/kg resulted in cure of large tapeworm infections: *Taenia saginata,* 125 patients; *T solium,* 31 patients; *Diphyllobothrium* spp, 53 patients. At a dosage of 25 mg/kg, 44 of 45 patients were cured of *Hymenolepis nana* infections.

PYRANTEL PAMOATE
(Antiminth, Combantrin)

Pyrantel pamoate is a highly effective drug for the treatment of pinworm, ascarid, and *Trichostrongylus orientalis* infections. It is moderately effective against both species of hookworm, but less so against *Necator americanus.* It is not effective in trichuriasis or strongyloidiasis. Oxantel, an analog of pyrantel, has been used successfully in the treatment of trichuriasis (see p 666).

Chemistry
Pyrantel pamoate, a tetrahydropyrimidine, is *trans*-1,4,5,6-tetrahydro-1-methyl-2-(2-[2-thienyl]-vinyl)-pyrimidine hydrogen pamoate.

Pyrantel base

Absorption, Metabolism, & Excretion
Pyrantel is poorly absorbed from the gastrointestinal tract. Over half of the administered dose is recovered unchanged in the feces, and only 7% or less of the dose is found in the urine unchanged or as a metabolite of the drug.

Pharmacologic Effects & Anthelmintic Actions
The anthelmintic action of pyrantel is due to an inhibitory action on neuromuscular transmission. In the helminth, a spastic neuromuscular paralysis occurs and the worm is subsequently expelled from the host's intestinal tract. In both vertebrate neuromuscular preparations and strip preparations of *Ascaris,* pyrantel shows the activity typical of depolarizing neuromuscular blocking agents. Pyrantel also inhibits cholinesterases.

Clinical Uses
A. *Enterobius vermicularis:* In most reports, pyrantel given as a single dose and repeated in 2 weeks is effective in curing pinworms in over 95% of pa-

tients. In 3 comparative studies of pyrantel and pyrvinium pamoate, both drugs were equally effective, but pyrantel may have produced fewer side-effects. Unlike pyrvinium, pyrantel does not stain stool or clothing red. Mebendazole is equally effective and is without significant side-effects. Piperazine, which is effective and safe, has the disadvantage of requiring a 7-day course of treatment.

B. *Ascaris lumbricoides:* Pyrantel given only once in a dosage of 10 mg/kg has been reported in different studies to be curative in 85–100% of patients.

C. Hookworm and *T orientalis:* Pyrantel has a high order of effectiveness against *T orientalis.* In *Ancylostoma duodenale* infections, pyrantel given as a single dose produces cures in over 90% of cases and a marked reduction in the worm burden in the remainder. However, for *N americanus* infections, the cure rate depends on the intensity of infection. A single dose may give a satisfactory cure rate in light infections, but for moderate or heavy infections (over 2000 ova per g of feces) a 3-day course is necessary.

Adverse Reactions, Contraindications, & Cautions
Side-effects are infrequent, mild, and transient. Reports vary on their incidence; 4–20% of adults and children may experience one or more of the following: nausea and vomiting, diarrhea, abdominal cramps, drowsiness, and headache. Less frequently reported were dizziness, insomnia, rash, fever, and weakness. No important effects on hematologic, renal, or hepatic function have been recorded.

There are no contraindications to pyrantel, but it should be used with caution in patients with liver dysfunction, since low, transient SGOT elevations have been noted in a small number of patients. Experience with the drug in children under age 2 years is limited.

Preparations & Dosages
Pyrantel pamoate (Antiminth, Combantrin) is prepared as a suspension containing 50 mg of pyrantel base per mL and as tablets containing 125 mg of the base.

For the treatment of pinworm infections and ascariasis, give a single oral dose of 10 mg of pyrantel base per kg of body weight (maximum 1 g). Treatment may be given before or after meals; purges are not used. For pinworm infections, repeat the dose at 2 and 4 weeks; for ascariasis, repeat only if ova are still found 2 weeks after treatment.

For hookworm infections due to *A duodenale,* give a single oral dose of 10 mg of pyrantel base per kg of body weight (maximum 1 g). For infections due to *N americanus* or when the species is unknown, a single dose may be sufficient for light infections, but for moderate or heavy infections repeat the dose daily for 3 days. Recheck stools in 2 weeks. In the USA, pyrantel is considered an investigational drug by the FDA when used for hookworm infections.

Pyrvinium base

PYRVINIUM PAMOATE
(Povan)

Pyrvinium pamoate, a cyanine dye, is a highly effective drug for the treatment of pinworm. Although the drug may be useful for the treatment of *Strongyloides stercoralis* infection, it has only a low order of anthelmintic action against *Trichuris trichiura* and hookworm infections and is not effective against *Ascaris lumbricoides* infection.

Chemistry, Absorption, Metabolism, & Excretion,

Pyrvinium pamoate (viprynium embonate, pyrvinium embonate) is the bis-6-dimethylamino-2(2-[2, 5-dimethyl-1-phenyl-3-pyrrolyl]vinyl)-1-methylquinolinium salt of pamoic acid.

Pyrvinium pamoate is not appreciably absorbed from the gastrointestinal tract when taken orally.

Anthelmintic Actions

As a group, the cyanine dyes contain the amidinium ion system, which may be responsible for their anthelmintic activity. Pyrvinium pamoate is highly effective against *E vermicularis;* it appears to exert its effect by preventing the parasite from using exogenous carbohydrates. The parasite dies when its endogenous reserves are depleted. The drug does not kill *Enterobius* ova.

Clinical Uses

A. *Enterobius vermicularis* **(Pinworm):** Pyrvinium is an alternative drug for pinworm infections. Reported cure rates after a single dose range from 90 to 100%. Thus, it is as effective as pyrantel and mebendazole; each of the drugs requires only one treatment (followed by repeat doses at 2 and 4 weeks), but pyrvinium produces more side-effects. Although piperazine is equally effective and causes few side-effects, it requires a 7-day course of treatment.

When one member of a household is treated for pinworms, diagnosis and treatment of all other members may be considered. However, reinfection from the outside occurs so frequently in families with young children that a pragmatic approach to therapy for such families may be to offer treatment only to symptomatic persons and to eradicate infections in all members of the household only when children are older.

B. *Strongyloides stercoralis* **(Dwarf Threadworm):** There are few reports of the use of pyrvinium pamoate for the treatment of strongyloidiasis. Wang & Galli reported clearing larvae from the stools of 11 of 12 patients using 2–6.4 mg/kg of pyrvinium pamoate suspension for 7 days. The safety and effectiveness of this extended treatment have yet to be confirmed.

Adverse Reactions

Pyrvinium pamoate is well tolerated, but it may cause nausea and vomiting, diarrhea, or dizziness in some persons, particularly older children and adults. Emesis occurs more often with the suspension than the tablet formulation. Photosensitization and other allergic reactions have been reported. Parents and patients should be told that posttreatment stools are often stained red for several days and the suspension, if spilled, will stain most materials red.

Contraindications & Cautions

Tablets should be swallowed intact to avoid staining the teeth. The drug should be used cautiously in children weighing less than 10 kg (22 lb), for experience with the drug is limited in young children.

There are no contraindications to the use of pyrvinium pamoate. However, it is preferable not to use the drug in the presence of inflammatory conditions of the gastrointestinal tract that theoretically might facilitate absorption.

Dosage

For the treatment of pinworms, a single dose is administered orally before or after meals. The dosage is 5 mg of pyrvinium base per kg body weight up to a maximum of 250 mg. No pre- or posttreatment purges are used. Treatment should be repeated at 2 and 4 weeks.

Preparations Available

Pyrvinium pamoate (Povan) is available in tablets containing 50 mg of pyrvinium base and as a suspension (Povan Suspension) containing 10 mg of base per mL.

QUINACRINE HYDROCHLORIDE
(Mepacrine, Atabrine)

Quinacrine was formerly an alternative drug for the treatment of tapeworm infections. Because of its toxicity, it should no longer be used unless the drug of choice (niclosamide) or alternative drugs (mebendazole, paromomycin, or dichlorophen) are not available. For a fuller description of the properties and use of quinacrine, consult earlier editions of this textbook.

Quinacrine commonly causes nausea and vomiting in the high dosage used for tapeworm therapy. Additional side-effects include dizziness, mild diarrhea, colic, headache, urticaria, and central nervous system stimulation. The latter may be manifested by restlessness, confusion, anxiety, euphoria, aggressive behavior, or psychotic reactions.

SURAMIN
(Antrypol, Bayer-205, Belganyl, Germanin, Naphuride)

Suramin, introduced in 1921 for the treatment of African trypanosomiasis, is the drug of choice to eradicate adult parasites of *Onchocerca volvulus* infections. The drug is not marketed in the USA but can be obtained from the Parasitic Disease Service, Center for Disease Control, Atlanta 30333, for use on an investigational basis.

Pharmacologic & Anthelmintic Actions

Suramin's general tendency to firmly bind to serum proteins results in nonspecific inhibition of many enzymes. As a result, it is a potent ATP inhibitor, and it has multiple actions on clotting through its effects on complement, on fibrinolysis, and on kinin formation. The drug's specific action on enzymes concerned with DNA and RNA metabolism may be the basis for its antiparasitic action. The drug acts principally on adult female worms, causing them to die and degenerate by the fifth week of treatment; male worms live much longer. Some microfilariae (but not all) are also killed.

Suramin has an abortive action on pregnant rats and is teratogenic in mice. No cases of abortion or fetal malformation have been noted following use of the drug in pregnant women.

Chemistry, Absorption, Metabolism, & Excretion

Suramin, a complex derivative of urea, is freely soluble in water. Because it is poorly absorbed from the gastrointestinal tract and causes intense local irritation when given subcutaneously or intramuscularly, it should be given intravenously. Suramin persists in the plasma firmly bound to plasma proteins; only small amounts are taken up by reticuloendothelial cells and the epithelium of the renal proximal convoluted tubules. The plasma concentration falls during the first few hours to become constant for several days; this is followed by a low concentration for up to 6 months. Sequential doses have a cumulative effect. The drug appears to be relatively resistant to catabolism, and active metabolites are not known. After a single dose a small amount is excreted in the urine in the first few days, but thereafter most of the dose cannot be recovered. Because suramin does not cross the blood-brain barrier, it is effective only in the early stage of African trypanosomiasis.

Clinical Uses

Suramin and Mel W (melarsonyl potassium) are the only effective drugs against adult *Onchocerca* worms. Unpredictable deaths have occurred with both compounds, but suramin is the safer of the two and the only drug that should be considered for treatment. An effective therapeutic program for individual patients consists of nodulectomy for accessible *Onchocerca* nodules (particularly those on the head) plus drug therapy in the form of suramin against adult worms and diethylcarbamazine to kill the microfilariae. Before starting suramin, all patients should receive a course of diethylcarbamazine to eliminate most microfilariae. However, treatment must be individualized to determine whether the patient can tolerate the side-effects and whether clinical findings require treatment. Hawking (1978) concluded, "Probably suramin should be given to all heavily infected patients with considerable pruritus or with danger of ocular complications, eg, microfilariae in the skin of the head." If the eyes are not endangered, many authorities limit treatment to nodulectomy and an initial intensive course of diethylcarbamazine, followed by weekly doses of 200 mg indefinitely.

Adverse Reactions

Side-effects of suramin are attributable both to the drug and to allergic reactions from release of antigen following death of adult worms or microfilariae. Immediate reactions may include nausea and vomiting, colic, urticaria, and, rarely, circulatory collapse and loss of consciousness. Beginning a few hours after the injection, a new set of reactions may occur: fever, malaise, headache, joint pains, pain around nodules, abdominal cramps, myalgia, ocular symptoms (photophobia, lacrimation, burning, itching, iritis), edema of the face or limbs, pruritic or papular rash, and cutaneous hyperesthesia of the soles and palms that may be accompanied by fissuring and peeling. Proteinuria is common after several doses and is not an indication for stopping therapy. After the fourth or fifth weekly treatment, other allergic symptoms may occur as adult parasites die or degenerate and foreign proteins are released. Weakness may persist for up to 10 weeks. Deep abscesses centered about dying adult worms may occur and require drainage.

In addition to the systemic reactions, there may be an aggravation of ocular lesions, especially anterior uveitis and a punctate and sclerosing keratitis. Recently, a hypothesis has been presented that suramin treatment of ocular onchocerciasis may be associated with a risk of optic atrophy. Agranulocytosis, jaundice, renal shutdown, and hemolytic anemia have been observed very rarely. Rare and sometimes fatal reactions have been recorded in patients who develop prolonged high fever, severe prostration, arthritis, exfoliative dermatitis, severe ulceration of the mouth and pharynx, or severe diarrhea. When very large doses of suramin have been used for the treatment of pemphigus, fatalities associated with degeneration of the adrenal cortex have been reported, but similar pathologic findings have not been described in patients treated for onchocerciasis.

Most reactions are not severe but are so annoying that many patients refuse to complete a course of treatment. Antihistamines may partially relieve allergic reactions due to dying parasites. Severe reactions can usually be controlled by giving corticosteroids.

Contraindications & Cautions

Patients receiving suramin must be closely watched, preferably in the hospital. Those with heavy loads of microfilariae in the ocular tissues should be treated under the supervision of a physician with adequate ophthalmologic experience and the necessary equipment for eye examination, including a slitlamp. The drug is contraindicated for those intolerant to a test dose, for pregnant patients, and for patients with hypertension or preexisting hepatic and renal insufficiency; it should be used with caution in children under age 10 years, in those with a history of allergy, and in the aged or debilitated. Malnutrition should be corrected before initiating therapy.

Urine should be examined for protein, red cells, and casts before each treatment. Slight proteinuria is not an indication to stop therapy, as it usually clears within 2 months and there is no residual damage to the kidneys. However, the presence of considerable protein or formed elements in the urine calls for skipping a dose, reducing subsequent doses, or ceasing therapy. Other indications for discontinuation of treatment are prolonged high fever, severe prostration, marked arthritis, exfoliative dermatitis, ulceration of the buccal mucosa, and severe diarrhea.

Preparations & Dosages

Suramin (Antrypol, Bayer-205, Belganyl, Germanin, Naphuride) is marketed in ampules containing 0.5 and 1 g dry powder that must be kept dry, cool, and sealed in dark bottles during storage. A 10% solution should be prepared for injection in cold, pyrogen-free distilled water or saline and must be used within 30 minutes.

An initial dose of 0.1 g is given intravenously to test for rare intolerance to the drug—recognized by the immediate reactions noted above. If the drug is tolerated, the course for adults over 60 kg in weight is 1 g (10–15 mg/kg in children) weekly for 5–6 weeks. Light infections may require only 1 g weekly for 4 weeks, heavy infections 1 g weekly for 7 weeks. Injections must be given intravenously and slowly over a period of 1 minute, with great care to avoid leakage outside the vein, which is very painful, but the drug can be tolerated and is effective by deep intramuscular injection if no vein can be found. A second course of treatment cannot be given earlier than 3 months after the first course.

TETRACHLOROETHYLENE

Tetrachloroethylene was introduced in 1925 for the treatment of hookworm infections due to *Necator americanus* or *Ancylostoma duodenale* and remains an effective alternative drug.

Chemistry

Tetrachloroethylene (perchloroethylene; $Cl_2C=CCl_2$), an unsaturated halogenated hydrocarbon, is a colorless, volatile liquid that is slowly decomposed by light and by various metals. A major problem with tetrachloroethylene, and one that may have affected its efficacy in clinical trials, is its deterioration in tropical climates. To preserve its potency, it should be stored in a cool dark place.

Although the drug is nearly insoluble in water, its solubility is increased by the presence of alcohol or lipids in the gastrointestinal tract.

Absorption, Metabolism, & Excretion

Absorption of tetrachloroethylene is minimal in a normal gastrointestinal tract if the drug is taken in the absence of lipids or alcohol. The small amount absorbed is excreted in the expired air.

Anthelmintic Actions

Tetrachloroethylene is more effective against *N americanus* than against *A duodenale*. Its mode of action has not been clearly established; it may depress muscle cells or neighboring nerve structures. Paralysis results, causing the hookworms to release their attachment to the intestinal mucosa.

Tetrachloroethylene does not paralyze or kill *Ascaris lumbricoides* but is thought to stimulate them, causing their migration; this effect is not established.

Clinical Uses

A. *N americanus*: Up to 80% of patients infected with this hookworm species will be cured after one treatment with tetrachloroethylene; the worm load in the remaining patients is reduced.

B. *A duodenale*: The reported cure rates for *Ancylostoma* infection after a single treatment with tetrachloroethylene are 25–65%. Several additional treatments with tetrachloroethylene at 4- to 7-day intervals are usually required if it is used for this parasite.

C. Intestinal Flukes: Tetrachloroethylene is

often effective in the eradication of the small intestinal flukes, *Heterophyes heterophyes* and *Metagonimus yokogawai;* the large intestinal fluke, *Fasciolopsis buski; Echinostoma* species; and *Gastrodiscoides hominis.* The drug is used in the same dosages and in the same manner as for hookworm infections.

Adverse Reactions

Tetrachloroethylene has had extensive use without serious side-effects. However, mild gastrointestinal symptoms (nausea and vomiting, epigastric burning, and abdominal cramps) and central nervous system symptoms (dizziness, vertigo, headache, and drowsiness) occur frequently. Transient loss of consciousness has been reported, and hypotensive episodes have occurred in severely anemic patients. Therefore, when feasible, the patient should be kept at bed rest and under observation for 4 hours after administration of the drug.

Contraindications & Cautions

It is not well established whether the presence of *Ascaris* infections contraindicates the use of tetrachloroethylene. Therefore, in mixed infections with both roundworms and hookworms, the roundworms should be eliminated first.

The drug is contraindicated in the treatment of small, severely ill children. It should be avoided in pregnancy, hepatic diseases, gastroenteritis, alcoholism, severe constipation, and patients undergoing heavy metal therapy.

Patients with severe anemia should have this partially corrected before administration of the drug.

Preparations & Dosages

Tetrachloroethylene USP, while approved for human use, is available in the USA only as a veterinary preparation (Nema worm capsules); however, this preparation is safe and effective for use in humans. It is available in a liquid form or in soft gelatin capsules containing 0.2, 1, and 5 mL. The gelatin capsules prevent irritation of the oral mucous membranes.

The patient should be told to avoid alcohol and fatty foods for 24 hours before and 3 days after medication. Food, but not water, is withheld the morning the drug is administered. The dosage is 0.12 mL/kg up to a maximum of 5 mL, and is taken orally in capsule form. The patient should be kept at bed rest for 4 hours following treatment, and then food may be started. Purgation following treatment is no longer advised, for it may increase side-effects and decrease the effectiveness of the drug. An alternative (and probably preferable) time to give the drug is at bedtime, but 6 hours after the last meal. Stool specimens should be examined at the end of 2 weeks. Two or more treatments at intervals of 4–7 days may be required to clear the infection or reduce the worm burden to levels at which the remaining parasites cause no significant blood loss. If iron deficiency anemia is present, it should be treated with ferrous sulfate and a high-protein diet.

THIABENDAZOLE
(Mintezol)

Thiabendazole is the drug of choice for the treatment of strongyloidiasis and cutaneous larva migrans and may also be useful in trichinosis and visceral larva migrans infections. Although it has a broad spectrum of anthelmintic activity, because of its frequent and sometimes severe toxicity it should not be a drug of first choice for the treatment of pinworm, ascarid, or hookworm infections. It is not effective for the treatment of trichuriasis.

Chemistry

Thiabendazole (2-[4-thiazolyl]-1H-benzimidazole) is a benzimidazole compound. It is tasteless and nearly insoluble in water. Although a chelating agent that forms stable complexes with a number of metals, including iron, it does not bind calcium.

Thiabendazole

Absorption, Metabolism, & Excretion

Studies in humans have shown that thiabendazole is rapidly absorbed after an oral dose. Drug concentrations in plasma peak within 1 hour and are barely detectable after 8 hours. Excretion is mainly via the urine, 90% appearing in 1 hour. The drug is almost completely metabolized to the 5-hydroxy form, which appears in the urine largely as the glucuronide or sulfate conjugate. Thiabendazole can also be absorbed from the skin.

Pharmacologic Effects & Toxicity

Thiabendazole given to cats and dogs in large doses orally (4 g/kg) and intravenously (40 mg/kg) did not produce significant effects on the cardiovascular or respiratory system. Thiabendazole has anti-inflammatory properties, which may be an important factor in its ability to relieve symptoms in some parasitic diseases. Thiabendazole also has immunomodulating effects on T cell function similar to those of levamisole.

Clinical Uses

A. *Strongyloides stercoralis:* Thiabendazole is the drug of choice for the treatment of strongyloidiasis. Of 134 patients treated in 9 studies, 125 (93%) were cured with a dosage of 25 mg/kg twice daily for 2–3 days.

B. *Enterobius vermicularis* (Pinworm): Thiabendazole eradicates pinworms in over 95% of patients treated. However, because of its potential toxicity, the equally effective drugs pyrvinium pamoate, pyrantel pamoate, or mebendazole should be used instead.

C. Cutaneous Larva Migrans (Creeping Eruption): Thiabendazole is the first effective systemic drug for the treatment of cutaneous larva migrans, an infection caused by *Ancylostoma braziliense* or *Ancylostoma caninum.*

D. *Trichuris trichiura* (Whipworm): Reported cure rates for whipworm infections range from 5 to 35% when thiabendazole is used for 2 days. In those not cured, the worm load is substantially reduced. Cure rates increase when the drug is continued for 3–5 days, but side-effects also increase.

E. Trichinosis: Information is limited on the effect of thiabendazole on the intestinal phase of trichinosis in humans. During the invasive stage, however, biopsy evidence is increasing that the drug destroys some (though not all) larvae in muscle, especially during the first 2 months of the disease. In this acute phase, amelioration or remission of signs and symptoms is usual without equivalent improvement in abnormal laboratory findings.

ACTH and corticosteroids are also effective in controlling the clinical manifestations of trichinosis and may be lifesaving in severe infections.

F. *Ascaris lumbricoides:* When a dosage of 25 mg/kg is used twice daily for 2–3 days, the mean cure rate as reported by various investigators is 75%. Pyrantel will clear over 90% of *Ascaris* infections when used for 1 day and causes fewer side-effects than thiabendazole.

G. Other Infections: When 25 mg/kg of thiabendazole was used twice daily for 2–3 days for the treatment of **hookworm infections,** the mean cure rate among 488 patients in 14 trials was 77% (range 30–100%).

Intestinal capillariasis has been successfully treated with thiabendazole at a dosage of 12 mg/kg given twice daily for 30 days.

For the treatment of **dracunculiasis,** Sastry and others (1978) report high effectiveness when the drug is used at a dosage of 50–75 mg/kg in divided doses for one day. Local inflammation subsides rapidly, followed by death of the worms in 4–6 days. Most worms are then spontaneously extruded or can be extracted manually. Re-treatment is occasionally needed.

The effectiveness of thiabendazole in **visceral larva migrans** has not been determined. Several reports have indicated the usefulness of topical thiabendazole for the treatment of **scabies** and **tinea nigra palmaris.**

Adverse Reactions

Side-effects from thiabendazole are common but generally mild and transient. They tend to occur 3–4 hours after ingestion of the drug and last 2–8 hours. Reports on their incidence vary from 7% to more than 50% of patients treated with 25 mg/kg twice daily for 2 days. Higher doses or extension of treatment beyond 2 days increases symptoms.

The most common side-effects are dizziness, anorexia, and nausea and vomiting. Less frequent are epigastric pain, abdominal cramping pain, diarrhea, headache, drowsiness, giddiness, lethargy, and pruritus. Perianal rashes, tinnitus, paresthesias, bradycardia, hypotension, and visual disturbances are rare.

Other side-effects have been reported, but some may represent manifestations of the disease or reactions to dying parasites rather than drug reaction. They include fever, chills, conjunctival injection, angioneurotic edema, lymphadenopathy, skin rashes, toxic epidermal necrolysis, and anaphylaxis.

Seven cases of erythema multiforme have been associated with thiabendazole therapy in children; in 2 severe cases (Stevens-Johnson syndrome), fatalities occurred.

Rarely seen during therapeutic use in humans are hyperglycemia, jaundice, and liver function abnormalities. Severe intrahepatic cholestasis due to thiabendazole hypersensitivity has been reported.

Some patients may excrete a metabolite that imparts an asparaginelike odor to the urine during therapy and for 24 hours thereafter.

Occasionally reported during thiabendazole treatment have been leukopenia, crystalluria, and hematuria, all of which subsided when therapy was discontinued.

Contraindications & Cautions

Experience with thiabendazole is limited in children weighing less than 15 kg. It may be best to use alternative drugs in patients with hepatic or renal dysfunction. The drug should be used with caution where drug-induced vomiting may be dangerous. There are a few reports of ascarids becoming hypermotile after treatment and appearing at the nose or mouth.

Since the drug makes some patients dizzy or drowsy, it should not be used during the day for patients whose work or activity requires complete mental alertness.

Discontinue the drug immediately if hypersensitivity symptoms appear—including fever, chills, conjunctival injection, skin rashes, and lymphadenopathy.

Preparations & Dosages

Thiabendazole (Mintezol) is available as a suspension containing 100 mg of the drug per mL and as tablets containing 500 mg of the drug. It should be given after meals, and the tablet formulation should be chewed well. Pre- and posttreatment purges and dietary restrictions are not necessary.

In the treatment of strongyloidiasis and cutaneous larva migrans, the dosage is 25 mg/kg twice daily for 2 days. The maximum single dose should not exceed 1.5 g, and the total daily dose should not exceed 3 g. The same dosage may be used for ascariasis or hookworm infection if the preferred drugs are not available. A second course may be given one week later if indicated. In disseminated strongyloidiasis, the drug should be given for 5 days. In the treatment of cutaneous larva migrans, excellent results have followed daily application for about 5 days of a cream containing 15% thiabendazole in a hygroscopic base. An easily prepared cream can also be made from a ground 0.5-g tablet mixed with 5 g of petroleum jelly.

The current recommendation for the treatment of trichinosis is 25 mg/kg twice daily for 5 days. However, as experience is gained, longer courses of therapy may be shown to be necessary. The total daily dose should not exceed 3 g.

Thiabendazole is no longer recommended in this text for pinworms or trichuriasis.

•   •   •

References

Antischistosomal Compounds

Friedheim E: Chemotherapy of schistosomiasis. Pages 29–144 in: *Chemotherapy of Helminthiasis*. Vol 1 in: *International Encyclopedia of Pharmacology and Therapeutics*. Pergamon Press, 1973.

Katz N: Chemotherapy of schistosomiasis mansoni. Adv Pharmacol Chemother 14:2, 1977.

Long-term toxicity of antischistosomal drugs. J Toxicol Environ Health 1:173, 1975. [Entire issue.]

McMahon JE: Treatment of schistosomiasis: Factors affecting chemotherapy and reflections on ideal drug treatment. Trop Geog Med 30:161, 1978.

WHO reports on schistosomicidal drugs. Bol of Sanit Panam 6:82, 1972.

WHO: Schistosomiasis control. WHO Tech Rep Series No. 515, 1973.

Antimony Compounds

Ata A-H, Mousa AH: Treatment of bilharziasis by the slow method. J Egypt Med Assoc 43:746, 1960.

Davis A: Comparative trials of antimonial drugs in urinary schistosomiasis. Bull WHO 38:197, 1968.

El-Shabrawy M & others: Intestinal schistosomiasis: A comparative therapeutic trial. J Egypt Med Assoc 55:69, 1972.

Most H & others: Schistosomiasis japonicum in American military personnel: Clinical studies of 600 cases during the first year after infection. Am J Trop Med Hyg 30:239, 1950.

Also see references under Antischistosomal Compounds.

Bephenium

Cavier R: Chemotherapy of intestinal nematodes. Chap 4, pages 215–436, in: *Chemotherapy of Helminthiasis*. Vol 1 in: *International Encyclopedia of Pharmacology and Therapeutics*. Pergamon Press, 1973.

Davis A: *Drug Treatment in Intestinal Helminthiases*. World Health Organization, 1973.

Senewiratne B & others: A comparative study of the relative efficacy of pyrantel pamoate, bephenium hydroxynaphthoate and tetrachlorethylene in the treatment of *Necator americanus* infection in Ceylon. Ann Trop Med Parasitol 69:233, 1975.

Bithionol

D'Sa CJ: Human fascioliasis. Proc R Soc Med 63:285, 1970.

Grados O, Berrocal LA: Chemotherapy of fascioliasis with bithionol. Revta Inst Med Trop S Paulo 19:425, 1977. [English summary.]

Kim JS: Treatment of *Paragonimus westermani* infections with bithionol. Am J Trop Med Hyg 19:940, 1970.

Miyazaki I, Nishimura K: Cerebral paragonomiasis. Pages 109–132 in: *Topics on Tropical Neurology*. Hornabrook R (editor). Davis, 1975.

Yokogawa M: *Paragonimus* and paragonimiasis. Pages 99–158 in: *Advances in Parasitology*. Vol 3. Dawes B (editor). Academic Press, 1965.

Bitoscanate

Symposium on bitoscanate. Prog Drug Res 19:1–107, 1975. [Entire issue.]

Chloroquine Phosphate

Komiya Y: *Clonorchis* and clonorchiasis. Pages 53–106 in: *Advances in Parasitology*. Vol 4. Dawes B (editor). Academic Press, 1966.

Yokogawa M: *Paragonimus* and paragonimiasis. Pages 99–158 in: *Advances in Parasitology*. Vol 3. Dawes B (editor). Academic Press, 1965.

Dichlorophen

Biagi F, Gómez Orozco L, Robledo E: [Efficacy of dichlorophen against *Hymenolepis nana*.] Bol Med Hosp Infant Mex 16:113, 1959.

Seaton DR: On the use of dichlorophen as a taenifuge for *Taenia saginata*. Ann Trop Med Parasitol 54:338, 1960.

Standen OD: Chemotherapy of helminthic infections. Chap 20, pages 701–892, in: *Experimental Chemotherapy*. Vol 1. Schnitzer RJ, Hawking F (editors). Academic Press, 1963.

Turner PP: The treatment of tapeworm infestation with "Antiphen." J Trop Med Hyg 66:259, 1963.

Diethylcarbamazine

Anderson J, Fuglsang H: Further studies on the treatment of ocular onchocerciasis with diethylcarbamazine and suramin. Br J Ophthalmol 62:450, 1978.

Bird AC & others: Visual loss during oral diethylcarbamazine treatment for onchocerciasis. (Correspondence.) Lancet 2:46, 1979.

Bryceson ADM, Warrell DA, Pope HM: Dangerous reactions to treatment of onchocerciasis with diethylcarbamazine. Br Med J 1:742, 1977.

Hawking F: Diethylcarbamazine and new compounds for the treatment of filariasis. Adv Pharmacol Chemother 16:129, 1979.

Jones BR, Anderson J, Fuglsang H: Effects of various concentrations of diethylcarbamazine citrate applied as eye drops in ocular onchocerciasis, and the possibilities of improved therapy from continuous non-pulsed delivery. Br J Ophthalmol 62:428, 1978.

Emetine

Hadden JW, Pascarelli EF: Diagnosis and treatment of human fascioliasis. JAMA 202:149, 1967.

Hexylresorcinol

Jung RC: Use of a hexylresorcinol tablet in the enema treatment of whipworm infection. Am J Trop Med Hyg 3:918, 1954.

Hycanthone

Buchanan N & others: Fatal hepatic necrosis in association with the use of hycanthone: A case report. S Afr Med J 53:257, 1978.

Cohen C: Liver pathology in hycanthone hepatitis. Gastroenterol 75:103, 1978.

Cook JA & others: A controlled trial of hycanthone and placebo in schistosomiasis mansoni in St. Lucia. Ann Trop Med Parasitol 71:197, 1977.

Hatchuel W: Fatal hepatic necrosis in association with hycanthone. (Correspondence.) S Afr Med J 54:808, 1978.

Ong TM: Genetic activities of hycanthone and some other antischistosomal drugs. Mutat Res 55:43, 1978.

Warren KS & others: Hycanthone dose-response in Schistosoma mansoni infection in Kenya. Lancet 1:352, 1978.

Also see references under Antischistosomal Compounds.

Levamisole & Tetramisole

Farahmandian I & others: Comparative studies on the evaluation of the effect of new anthelminthics on various intestinal helminthiases in Iran. Chemotherapy 23:98, 1977.

Forbes LS: Toxicological and pharmacological relations between levamisole, pyrantel and diethylcarbamazine and their significance in helminth chemotherapy. Southeast Asian J Trop Med Public Health 3:235, 1972.

Janssen PAJ: The levamisole story. Prog Drug Res 20:347, 1976.

Levamisole: A cautionary note. (Editorial.) Lancet 3:291, 1979.

Moens M & others: Levamisole in ascariasis: A multicenter controlled evaluation. Am J Trop Med Hyg 27:897, 1978.

Mebendazole

Chongsuphajaisiddhi T & others: Treatment of soil-transmitted nematode infections in children with mebendazole. Ann Trop Med Parasitol 72:59, 1978.

Farahmandian I & others: Comparative studies on the evaluation of the effect of new anthelminthics on various intestinal helminthiases in Iran. Chemotherapy 23:98, 1977.

Keystone JS, Murdoch JK: Diagnosis and treatment. Drugs five years later: Mebendazole. Ann Intern Med 91:582, 1979.

Scragg JN, Proctor EM: Mebendazole in the treatment of severe symptomatic trichuriasis in children. Am J Trop Med Hyg 26:198, 1977.

Sonnett JJ, Thienpont D: The treatment of trichinosis with mebendazole. Acta Clin Belg 32:297, 1977.

Wilson JF, Davidson M, Rausch RL: A clinical trial of mebendazole in the treatment of alveolar hydatid disease. Am Rev Respir Dis 118:747, 1978.

Metrifonate

Holmstedt B & others: Metrifonate: Summary of toxicological and pharmacological information available. Arch Toxicol 41:3, 1978.

Jewsbury JM, Cooke MJ, Weber MC: Field trial of metrifonate in the treatment of prevention of schistosomiasis infection in man. Ann Trop Med Parasitol 71:67, 1977.

Lamb MJ: Mutagenicity tests with metrifonate in Drosophila melanogaster. Mutat Res 56:157, 1977.

Plestina R, Davis A, Bailey DR: Effect of metrifonate on blood cholinesterases in children during the treatment of schistosomiasis. Bull WHO 46:747, 1972.

Niclofolan

Nwokolo A, Volkmer KJ: Single dose therapy of paragonomiasis with menichlopholan. Am J Trop Med Hyg 26:688, 1977.

Niclosamide

Jones WE: Niclosamide as a treatment for Hymenolepis diminuta and Dipylidium caninum infection in man. Am J Trop Med Hyg 28:300, 1979.

Kahra A, Veharanta T: [Expelling the broad tapeworm with Yomesan.] Suom Laak 8:325, 1963. [Finnish.]

Most H & others: Yomesan (niclosamide) therapy of Hymenolepis nana infections. Am J Trop Med Hyg 20:206, 1971.

Perera DR & others: Niclosamide treatment of cestodiasis: Clinical trials in the United States. Am J Trop Med Hyg 19:610, 1970.

Niridazole

Bassily S & others: Low-dose niridazole in the treatment of Schistosoma mansoni. Ann Trop Med Parasitol 73:295, 1979.

Bulay O & others: Carcinogenic effects of niridazole on rodents infected with Schistosoma mansoni. J Natl Cancer Inst 59:1625, 1977.

The pharmacological and chemotherapeutic properties of niridazole and other antischistosomal compounds. Conference. Ann NY Acad Sci 160:426, 1969.

Saif M & others: On the treatment of urinary bilharziasis with niridazole. J Egypt Med Assoc 57:83, 1974.

Solbach W, Wagner H, Röllinghoff M: Effect of niridazole in cellular immunity in vivo and in vitro. Clin Exp Immunol 32:411, 1978.

Sy FS: Niridazole in the treatment of schistosomiasis japonica. J Philippine Med Assoc 53:151, 1977.

Also see references under Antischistosomal Compounds.

Oxamniquine

Bassily S & others: Treatment of complicated schistosomiasis mansoni with oxamniquine. Am J Trop Med Hyg 27:1284, 1978.

Clarke V de V & others: Dose-finding trials of oral oxamniquine in Rhodesia. S Afr Med J 50:1867, 1976.

Katz N & others: Clinical trials with oxamniquine, by oral route, in schistosomiasis mansoni. Revta Inst Med Trop S Paulo 18:371, 1976.

Omer AHS: Oxamniquine for treating Schistosoma mansoni infection in Sudan. Br Med J 2:163, 1978.

Silva LC & others: Further clinical trials with oxamniquine (UK 4271): A new anti-schistosomal agent. Revta Inst Med Trop S Paulo 17:307, 1975.

Oxantel Pamoate

Dissanaike AS: A comparative trial of oxantel-pyrantel and mebendazole in multiple helminth infection in school children. Drugs 15 (Suppl 1):11, 1978.

Garcia EG: Treatment for trichuriasis with oxantel. Am J Trop Med Hyg 25:914, 1976.

Lee EL & others: Therapeutic evaluation of oxantel pamoate (1,4,5,6-tetrahydro-1-methyl-2-[trans-3-hydroxy-styryl] pyrimidine pamoate) in severe *Trichuris trichiura* infection. Am J Trop Med Hyg 25:563, 1976.

Paromomycin

Botero D: Paromomycin as effective treatment of *Taenia* infections. Am J Trop Med Hyg 19:234, 1970.

Pawlowski Z, Schultz AG: Taeniasis and cysticercosis *(Taenia saginata)*. Adv Parasitol 10:292, 1972.

Tanowitz HB, Wittner M: Paromomycin in the treatment of *Diphyllobothrium latum* infection. Am J Trop Med Hyg 76:151, 1973.

Ulivelli A: Paromomycin and taeniasis. Lancet 1:696, 1968.

Wittner M, Tanowitz H: Paromomycin therapy of human cestodiasis with special reference to hymenolepiasis. Am J Trop Med Hyg 20:433, 1971.

Piperazine

Berger JR & others: Acute transitory cerebellar dysfunction associated with piperazine adipate. Arch Neurol 36:180, 1979.

Brown HW, Chan KF, Hussey KL: Treatment of enterobiasis and ascariasis with piperazine. JAMA 161:515, 1956.

Bumbalo TS, Plummer LJ: Piperazine (Antepar) in the treatment of pinworm and roundworm infections. Med Clin North Am 41:575, 1957.

Farid Z & others: Single-dose treatment for *Ascaris* infection with piperazine citrate: With a study of the egg-parasite ratio. Am J Trop Med Hyg 15:516, 1966.

Fernando MA, Balasuriya S: Control of ascariasis by mass treatment with piperazine citrate. Ceylon Med J 22:120, 1977.

McCullagh SF: Allergenicity of piperazine: A study in environmental aetiology. Br J Ind Med 25:319, 1968.

Praziquantel

Gönnert R, Andrews P: Praziquantel, a new broad-spectrum antischistosomal agent. Z Parasitenkd 52:129, 1977.

Groll E: Panaroma general del tratamiento de las infecciones humanas por cestodes con praziquantel (Embay 8440). Bol Chil Parasitol 32:27, 1977.

Leopold G & others: Clinical pharmacology in normal volunteers of praziquantel, a new drug against schistosomes and cestodes. Europ J Clin Pharmacol 14:281, 1978.

Praziquantel: Data on the efficacy against *Schistosoma mansoni, S haematobium,* and *S japonicum* in experimentally infected animals. Z Parasitenkd 52:117, 1977.

Pyrantel Pamoate

Bell WJ, Nassif S: Comparison of pyrantel pamoate and piperazine phosphate in the treatment of ascariasis. Am J Trop Med Hyg 20:584, 1971.

Botero D, Castanõ A: Comparative study of pyrantel pamoate, bephenium hydroxynaphthoate, and tetrachlorethylene in the treatment of *Necator americanus* infections. Am J Trop Med Hyg 22:45, 1973.

Davis A: *Drug Treatment in Intestinal Helminthiases*. World Health Organization, 1973.

Farahmandian I & others: Comparative studies on the evalua-

tion of the effect of new anthelminthics on various intestinal helminthiases in Iran. Chemotherapy 23:98, 1977.

Senewiratne B & others: A comparative study of the relative efficacy of pyrantel pamoate, bephenium hydroxynaphthoate and tetrachlorethylene in the treatment of *Necator americanus* infection in Ceylon. Ann Trop Med Parasitol 69:233, 1975.

Pyrvinium Pamoate

Beck JW & others: The treatment of pinworm infections in humans (enterobiasis) with pyrvinium chloride and pyrvinium pamoate. Am J Trop Med Hyg 8:349, 1959.

Buchanan RA & others: Pyrvinium pamoate. Clin Pharmacol Ther 16:716, 1974.

Turner JA, Johnson PE Jr: Pyrvinium pamoate in the treatment of pinworm infection (enterobiasis) in the home. J Pediatr 60:243, 1962.

Wang CC, Galli GA: Strongyloidiasis treated with pyrvinium pamoate. JAMA 193:847, 1965.

Suramin

Anderson J, Fuglsang H: Further studies on the treatment of ocular onchocerciasis with diethylcarbamazine and suramin. Br J Ophthalmol 62:450, 1978.

Bell D: Treatment of onchocerciasis. (Correspondence.) Br Med J 1:1213, 1979.

Hawking F: Suramin: With special reference to onchocerciasis. Adv Pharmacol Chemother 15:289, 1978.

Thylefors B, Rolland A: The risk of optic atrophy following suramin treatment of ocular onchocerciasis. Bull WHO 57:479, 1979.

Tetrachloroethylene

Bueding E, Swartzwelder C: Anthelmintics. Pharmacol Rev 9:329, 1957.

Carr HP, Sardá MEP, Nuñez NA: Anthelmintic treatment of uncinariasis. Am J Trop Med Hyg 3:495, 1954.

Senewiratne B & others: A comparative study of the relative efficacy of pyrantel pamoate, bephenium hydroxynaphthoate and tetrachlorethylene in the treatment of *Necator americanus* infection in Ceylon. Ann Trop Med Parasitol 69:233, 1975.

Thiabendazole

Arguedas JA & others: Community control of *Strongyloides stercoralis* by thiabendazole. Tex Rep Biol Med 33:265, 1975.

Campbell WC, Cuckler AC: Thiabendazole in the treatment and control of parasitic infections in man. Tex Rep Biol Med 27 (Suppl 2):665, 1969.

Casali AJ, Costa EA: Investigacion clinica y anatomopatologica del tratamiento de la triquinosis aguda con tiabendazol. Bol Chil Parasitol 32:66, 1977.

Harland PSEG, Meakins RH, Harland RH: Treatment of cutaneous larva migrans with local thiabendazole. (Correspondence.) Br Med J 2:772, 1977.

Perrin J & others: Thiabendazole treatment of presumptive visceral larva migrans. Clin Pediatr 14:147, 1975.

Sastry SC, Kumar KJ, Lakshminarayana V: The treatment of dracontiasis with thiabendazole. J Trop Med Hyg 81:32, 1978.

Thiabendazole. Tex Rep Biol Med 27 (Suppl 2):1, 1969.

Management of Acute Intoxications | 64

The acute and chronic toxicity of the various classes of drugs have been discussed in earlier chapters, and these data about therapeutic agents provide a significant fraction of the information needed by the physician in handling cases of poisoning. However, a large number of poisons that are not used in therapy are encountered in the environment because they are used in household, factory, or farm or are present in food, air, or water. Data on such environmental toxins will be presented in Chapters 65 and 66, and a distinction between acute and chronic effects will often be made.

The treatment of definite or possible acute intoxication is a frequent demand on all physicians and must often be carried out with limited or only presumptive information about the nature of the poison and the severity of exposure. Actual or possible poisoning is always an emergency, and a routine for management must be established before the need arises. A procedure generally applicable to the management of acute poisonings is therefore presented in this chapter.

SOURCE & INCIDENCE OF ACUTE POISONINGS

Considering not only accidental but also suicidal, criminal, and industrial exposures, there are about 1½ million cases—8000 of which are fatal—each year in the USA in which a physician will have to initiate treatment for poisoning or decide that emergency treatment is or is not necessary. Of these, about half will be accidental and account for at least 1500 deaths in children, of which 80% will be children 1–4 years of age. Children under age 5 account for 65% of the reported accidental poisonings. The agents involved are those accessible to the normally curious child. In half of the cases, medicines are involved—most often those commonly around the home, eg, aspirin, iron pills, tranquilizers, sedatives, oral contraceptives, and thyroid. Bleaches and other cleaning products, pesticides, and petroleum products are also common toxic agents despite their unpleasant flavors and aromas.

PREVENTION OF ACCIDENTAL POISONING

A large percentage of acute poisonings, including even suicides, are preventable. Most accidental poisonings conform to familiar patterns, and the home can be made much safer if the physician provides (and the parents accept) some commonsense safety instructions designed to prevent selection of the wrong container by an adult and to keep potential poisons out of the reach of children. Keeping aspirin on a high shelf and taking bleaches out of the cabinet under the sink would by themselves reduce the incidence of poisonings significantly. Parents should be asked to search the home for dangerous chemicals before a child begins to creep.

Rules for Prevention of Poisoning

(1) Medicines should be stored in a high or locked cabinet. Medications used regularly—eg, aspirin, sedatives, iron, and contraceptive pills—should not be kept in an easily accessible handbag or on a table or low shelf if young children are in the home.

Medication should be left in the safety packages usually provided. "Child-proof" closures have demonstrated usefulness.

(2) Patients should be told not to save unused prescription medications. Because very few will act on this advice, prescribed medications should be labeled with the name of the drug, prescribed in the smallest practical amount, and stored with care.

(3) Children should not be cajoled into taking medicine by comparing it with candy. "Candy" medicine tablets and flavored syrups are dangerous for children.

(4) Do not store poisons (cleaners, etc) in the same cabinet as foodstuffs.

(5) Do not store poisons (paint thinner, insecticides, etc) in cups, soft drink bottles, or other food containers. Do not bring insecticides or other chemicals home from work in such containers.

(6) Label all stored materials carefully.

(7) Use the following checklist to locate dangers and warn children and parents. These items should be kept locked up or stored out of reach.

Table 64—1. Management of acute intoxications (summary).

When Not in Attendance (Phone Call)	When in Attendance (Hospital or Emergency Room)

1. Brief history.
2. Disposition:
  a. Treatment or close observation not necessary.
  b. Immediate home treatment followed by hospitalization.
  c. Meet patient at hospital or emergency room.
  d. Call to emergency service (fire department or ambulance service).
3. Immediate home treatment:
  a. Remove from exposure—
    (1) Skin—Remove contaminated clothing, wash skin. Flood acid or alkali burns with water for 5 minutes.
    (2) Eyes—Flood with water 5 minutes (20 minutes if alkali) with lids held apart.
    (3) Inhalation—Remove from contaminated area.
  b. Give artificial respiration if necessary.
  c. Dilute caustic or irritant poisons with water or milk. Otherwise, give fluid only in anticipation of emesis.
  d. Attempt to induce emesis unless the patient is comatose or convulsing or has ingested a corrosive substance (acid or alkali) or petroleum distillate.
	1. Remove any source of continuing exposure—eg, remove contaminated clothing, wash skin, wash eyes.
	2. Maintain patent airway and support respiration and circulation.
	3. Brief history and necessary physical examination.
	4. Consider gastric lavage or induced emesis for orally ingested toxins if there are no contraindications.
	5. Specific therapy if available.
	6. Increase rate of excretion of poisons—eg, fluids, osmotic diuretics, alkalies.
	7. Symptomatic treatment of shock, convulsions, etc.
	8. Definitive history and physical examination. Identify agent if possible.
	9. Collect laboratory samples for identification and determination of levels of poison, both for control of treatment and for legal purposes.
	10. Preach prevention.

a. In the kitchen or laundry—
  All medicines
  Ammonia
  Bleach
  Caustics (lye, Drano, Liquid-Plumr, washing soda, etc)
  Disinfectants
  Furniture polish and wax
  Moth balls
  Oven cleaner
  Spot remover, rug cleaner

b. In the garage—
  Fire starter
  Gasoline, kerosene, etc
  Insecticide
  Paint, shellac, etc
  Paint remover
  Paint thinner
  Rodenticide
  Snail and slug bait
  Turpentine
  Weed killer
  Wood bleach (oxalic acid)

c. In the bathroom and bedroom—
  All medicines
  Cold wave preparations
  Hair dyes and bleaches
  Lighter fluid
  Nail polish remover

(8) All gas heaters and stoves should be vented.

(9) Write down emergency phone numbers before the need arises.

(10) If occupational exposure is a hazard, follow the manufacturer's cautions about the storage and handling of toxic materials and the use of protective equipment.

TREATMENT OF ACUTE POISONING

Treatment may begin when the patient is brought to the physician or when a parent phones for advice. The points discussed below are summarized in Table 64–1.

WHEN NOT IN ATTENDANCE

Disposition

The history provided by the parent or other person phoning the physician will usually establish what poison has been taken. The container will usually be at hand, and, if the product is unfamiliar to the physician, the label will usually identify toxic ingredients. The parent will less often be able to provide dependable information on the amount taken but can often describe how quickly the symptoms (if any) appeared.

The most common decision at this point is to suggest that no treatment or only a period of close observation is necessary. Not every child who has alarmed a mother by chewing on crayons need be hospitalized.

At the other extreme is the situation that is so grave (because of respiratory depression or convulsions) that the immediate response is to phone the emergency service in order to provide equipment to support respiration.

Unless some unusual difficulty with transport or distance exists or unless there is an indication for the immediate home treatment outlined below, the patient should be brought to the hospital or emergency room for definitive treatment.

Immediate Home Treatment

A. Remove From Continued Exposure: Treatment should not be delayed but should be started at home if the skin or eyes have been in contact with a corrosive substance or if contamination of the clothing or skin is resulting in continued contact with the poison. Contaminated clothing should be removed and the skin washed. Acid or alkali burns should be flooded with water for 5 minutes. If the eyes have been exposed to a caustic substance, they should be washed while the lids are held apart for 5 minutes (acid) or 20 minutes (alkali) before the patient is moved to the hospital.

In cases of inhalation poisoning (most commonly carbon monoxide), removal to open air is obviously of first importance.

B. Give artificial respiration if necessary.

C. Dilute and Adsorb Poison: The administration of oral fluids, except in the case of ingested caustic or irritant poisons, should be avoided because the additional fluid promotes gastric emptying. When emptying has occurred, the poison cannot be removed by lavage or emesis, and greater quantities may be absorbed.

Activated charcoal is an effective adsorbent for some poisons and can be given *after* emesis is induced, but it is seldom available when needed. "Universal antidote" (powdered charcoal, tannic acid, and magnesium oxide) should not be used because the ingredients are mutually inactivating.

D. Induce Emesis: Most authorities agree that efforts to induce emesis at home merely delay treatment and that the patient should instead be brought promptly to the hospital. Stimulating the back of the throat with a finger or the handle of a spoon or giving salt or mustard are not dependable ways of causing vomiting. If syrup of ipecac is immediately available, it should be given at once.

WHEN IN ATTENDANCE

The order in which the following procedures are carried out will vary with the nature of the poison and with the urgency of the situation.

Terminate Exposure

If the skin or eyes are contaminated, there is more urgency in carrying out this step. If the poison has been taken orally and is not a caustic, termination of continuing exposure is accomplished by inducing emesis or by gastric lavage as described below.

A. Skin Contamination: Water, from whatever source available (shower, faucet, hose, or bucket), should be used to remove poisons from the skin and to dilute and neutralize corrosive substances. Clothing should be removed with concern for the operator—ie, with the protection of gloves or running water. Acids and alkalies should be removed by using large amounts of water but not by chemical neutralization, since the exothermic reaction may add damage by heat to the chemical injury.

Eyes: Chemical neutralization of acids or alkalies should not be attempted. Any delay in removing caustic substances from the eye is extremely dangerous. Treatment should be started immediately and close to the place of exposure by washing the corneal surface for 5 minutes with flowing water with the lids held apart. As soon as the patient is brought to the emergency service, irrigation should be resumed with sterile saline solution or water for 5 minutes if the substance is acid and 20 minutes if an alkali.

Artificial Respiration

Maintain a patent airway and support respiration in depressed or comatose patients.

Brief History & Cursory Physical Examination

Eliciting the history and performing a physical examination should not unduly delay gastric emptying or other treatment but must provide enough information to allow a decision about whether or not lavage should be performed.

Gastric Lavage or Emesis

The conditions under which the stomach should be emptied are not clearly defined, and opinion also differs about whether gastric lavage or induced emesis is preferable.

A. Gastric Lavage: Lavage is performed with the patient lying head down on the left side. A soft rubber tube is passed into the stomach, and 4-oz portions of tap water are repeatedly added and withdrawn. Once the toxic material has left the stomach, of course, lavage is of no value. It is generally held that lavage should not be done if more than 2–4 hours have elapsed since exposure, but many poisons cause pylorospasm and slow gastric emptying, and lavage may be profitable up to 12 hours after ingestion of the poison.

There appears to be a growing preference for emptying the stomach by inducing vomiting with syrup of ipecac, a procedure that is less difficult for physician and patient.

The value of gastric lavage is not supported by some experimental studies, which suggest that gastric emptying into the intestine is hastened by lavage. However, in these studies a small (nasogastric) tube was used rather than a tube of adequate size (30 gauge) passed through the mouth. Critics of the use of syrup of ipecac point out that the mere occurrence of vomiting tells nothing about the completeness of gastric emptying.

The decision to perform lavage or induce vomiting is often based on a desire to protect the physician from recrimination and possible legal action rather than on any belief in its value. When the time from ingestion to treatment is brief enough to justify emptying the stomach, the use of an emetic is convenient and requires no equipment. In the emergency room, conservative practice probably still favors a properly performed gastric lavage.

Clear **contraindications** to the performance of gastric lavage are the following:

1. If more than 30 minutes have elapsed since ingestion of acid or alkali. Necrosis of the esophagus results in an increased hazard of perforation.

2. Ingestion of petroleum distillate (kerosene, paint thinner, spot remover, etc). Regurgitated amounts of these hydrocarbons are aspirated into the lungs and cause chemical pneumonia.

3. Coma, stupor, and delirium are contraindications because of the hazard of aspiration. If, however, a cuffed endotracheal tube is put in place, lavage may be performed on comatose patients.

4. Convulsions, unless or until they are controlled by other medication. The stimulation associated with intubation may precipitate convulsions.

B. Induced Emesis: The indications for and contraindications to inducing emesis are the same as listed above for gastric lavage. The question of which of the 2 technics is preferable is not completely resolved.

1. Ipecac syrup–Syrup of ipecac, 15–20 mL, is given by mouth, followed in 2–5 minutes by milk, water, or fruit juice. The dose may be repeated in 15–20 minutes if the first dose is without effect. Vomiting usually occurs within 10 minutes even if the poison is a drug generally credited with antiemetic properties, eg, antipsychotic tranquilizers.

Syrup of ipecac may be sold without a prescription in 1-oz bottles with directions for use in causing vomiting. It should be kept in every home. Only the specially labeled syrup of ipecac should be used in order to avoid any possible confusion with fluidextract of ipecac. Inadvertent use of the fluidextract has been responsible for at least 7 deaths.

2. Apomorphine–Ipecac syrup has been characterized as a slow emetic, and it has been suggested that apomorphine is preferable because of its more rapid action after injection. Apomorphine is, of course, a narcotic, and many patients will be sleepy following its use. More severe depression or continued vomiting can be terminated by administering a narcotic antagonist. The dosage of apomorphine in adults is 6 mg intramuscularly; in children, 0.05 mg/kg intramuscularly. The action of apomorphine can be terminated with levallorphan (Lorfan), 0.02 mg/kg intramuscularly; nalorphine (Nalline), 0.1 mg/kg intramuscularly; or naloxone (Narcan), 0.01 mg/kg intramuscularly.

C. Adsorbent or Antidote in Stomach: In specific situations, lavage may be carried out with fluids other than tap water—eg, phosphate to remove iron, ammonium nitrate or hydroxide to detoxify formaldehyde, or sodium thiosulfate to detoxify iodide. In the case of hypochlorite bleach, the use of sodium thiosulfate by mouth obviates the need for lavage.

Following lavage or emesis, one of the above antidotes may be left in the stomach or a suspension of activated charcoal may be added through the lavage tube or swallowed in an effort to adsorb and slow absorption of the poison. Activated charcoal—properly prepared, carefully stored, and used in adequate amounts—has been shown in animal experiments to absorb some common poisons and drugs but not ferrous sulfate, alcohols, or caustics.

Specific Therapy If Available

The specific antidote should be employed in those few cases in which one is available. These include the following:

Antisera
Ethyl alcohol for methanol
Amyl nitrite for cyanide
Atropine and pralidoxime for phosphate insecticides
Calcium salts for fluoride, oxalate
Epinephrine for anaphylactic reactions
Methylene blue for methemoglobinemia
Naloxone, etc for narcotic analgesics
Chelating agents for metals including iron
Oxygen for carbon monoxide

Symptomatic & Supportive Treatment

If no specific therapy is available, treatment is designed to support the patient during the period of detoxification and to shorten this period by increasing the rate of excretion of the poison. Ill-advised or unduly vigorous symptomatic treatment can be quite damaging to the patient and should be based on experience in treating the specific poison. Pain, vomiting, diarrhea, fluid and electrolyte derangements, and other symptoms are controlled in the usual ways. There are, in addition, a few special problems in treating acute intoxication.

A. Shock: Since the phenothiazine tranquilizers and the related antidepressant drugs are common causes of intoxication, it must be emphasized that hypotension is not necessarily the same as shock. Patients with a predominantly postural hypotension associated with a dilated, warm periphery usually require no treatment other than the recumbent position. Shock or impending shock frequently occurs in intoxication with barbiturates and other depressant drugs and should be treated by reexpansion of the plasma volume rather than with vasopressors such as norepinephrine. Experience with vasodilators such as isoproterenol is still limited and investigational, but preliminary reports are promising.

B. Coma: The treatment of intoxication with barbiturates or other hypnotics has been discussed in Chapter 23, where the rationale for the conservative or physiologic method of treatment is presented in detail. Analeptic or stimulant drugs are not used because their use is both hazardous and ineffective.

C. Convulsions: Convulsions must be distinguished from the violent dystonias seen in children after intoxication with one of the antipsychotic tranquilizers. Convulsions must then be classified into one or the other of 2 large classes: those that originate in the spinal cord, as after strychnine poisoning or during tetanus; and the more common type that is suprasegmental in origin.

Local anesthetic toxicity is perhaps the most familiar example of convulsions that originate in a suprasegmental site. The treatment of such convulsions is discussed in Chapter 22, where it is emphasized that convulsions are usually well tolerated, especially if oxygen is available between paroxysms, and that treatment with central nervous system depressants to control the convulsions may add dangerously to the postconvulsant depression. If an anesthetist and the requisite equipment are available, succinylcholine may be used to control convulsions through its peripheral action. An inhalation anesthetic or intravenous thiopental may be used if convulsions persist. If the convulsant poison has a very prolonged duration of action, phenytoin may be given as an anticonvulsant.

D. Toxic Psychosis: The most common cause of toxic psychosis or paranoid or hallucinatory states today is the deliberate use of LSD or methamphetamine (see Chapter 7). A toxic psychosis can be caused by other central nervous system stimulants; by parasympatholytics such as are in stramonium leaves; by bromides; by abrupt withdrawal of alcohol or other sedatives; by some industrial poisons; and by infection and fever. Experience with people who take drugs in search of hallucinatory experiences has shown that reassurance and explanation can greatly reduce the intensity of the reaction. Chlorpromazine can be used to reduce hallucinatory, paranoid, or excited behavior if necessary and if the state is due to a stimulant drug. Chlorpromazine will intensify the effects of the atropinelike drugs, and the sedatives are preferable to the antipsychotic tranquilizers in such situations. The sedatives are also preferable if anxiety rather than distortion of perception is the predominant symptom and in the withdrawal states.

Definitive History & Physical Examination; Identification of Agent

The history and physical examination are developed to the extent that the need for emergency treatment permits and the need for information requires. After essential therapy has been given, a detailed history should be taken and a careful examination performed.

Determination of the extent and mechanism of exposure may require a long period of investigation. Trade names, ingredients, and much additional useful information are included in the references listed at the end of this chapter. If the physician has no references available, the nearest Poison Control Center can usually provide the information. The labeling of most substances encountered in industry or in the household provides some approximation of their toxicity. Highly toxic substances, ie, those with an estimated oral LD_{50} of 0–50 mg/kg, must bear the signal word "danger" or "poison" as well as an antidote statement, directions

to call a physician immediately, and a skull and crossbones. The label of moderately toxic (LD_{50} of 50–500 mg/kg) or less toxic (500–5000 mg/kg) substances must bear the signal words "warning" and "caution," but no antidote statement is required.

Suspected criminal poisoning must always be reported, and occupational exposures must be reported in most states.

Increase Rate of Excretion of Poison

The use of osmotic diuretics and alkalies to shorten the period of detoxification has been discussed in the sections on the barbiturates and the salicylates.

Peritoneal dialysis or hemodialysis (artificial kidney) may be used in special situations to remove a drug or poison. The procedures are themselves slightly hazardous and are used only in very severe intoxications and usually only when acute renal failure is also present. Table 64–2 lists some of the drugs and toxins that have been shown to be dialyzable.

Collect Samples for Laboratory

The poison can usually be identified on clinical grounds and the conclusion supported by simple urine tests for the most common agents done in the

Table 64–2. Partial list of drugs and poisons removed by peritoneal dialysis or hemodialysis.

Sedative-hypnotics	
Alcohols:	Piperidinedione derivatives:
Chloral hydrate	Methyprylon (Noludar)
Ethanol	(but not glutethimide
Ethchlorvynol (Placidyl)	[Doriden])
Ethylene glycol	Others:
Methanol	Methaqualone
Barbiturates	Paraldehyde
Carbamates:	
Ethinamate (Valmid)	
Meprobamate (Equanil, Miltown)	
Nonnarcotic analgesics	
Aspirin	Phenacetin
Methyl salicylate	
Narcotic analgesics *(Note:* Specific antagonist available.)	
Heroin	Propoxyphene (Darvon)
CNS stimulants and antidepressants	
Amitriptyline (Elavil)	Pargyline (Eutonyl)
Dextroamphetamine	Phenelzine (Nardil)
(Dexedrine)	Tranylcypromine (Parnate)
Imipramine (Tofranil)	
Metals and metal ions	
Arsenic	Mercury
Calcium	Potassium
Iron	Sodium
Lead	Strontium
Magnesium	
Halides	
Bromide	Iodide
Fluoride	
Miscellaneous	
Boric acid	Ergotamine
Carbon tetrachloride	Nonhalogenated aromatic
Chlorates	hydrocarbons

emergency room. In chronic intoxications definitive laboratory work may be of great importance, but in acute poisonings most decisions are made before laboratory data become available. Nevertheless, vomitus or lavage fluid and urine should be collected in clean containers and carefully labeled, sealed, and refrigerated in the event that they are needed for legal purposes or to identify the agent. Blood and urine samples should be collected in known or suspected poisoning with agents for which analytic methods are useful, especially alcohol, barbiturates, and salicylates, or when the results of laboratory tests influence treatment decisions (eg, possible iron intoxication). Data on blood gases and electrolytes are of value in managing intoxications.

• • •

References

Texts & Manuals for Identification of Agents

Dreisbach RH: *Handbook of Poisoning: Diagnosis & Treatment,* 10th ed. Lange, 1980.

Gosselin RE: *Clinical Toxicology of Commercial Products,* 4th ed. Williams & Wilkins, 1976. [Composition of 17,000 products.]

Griffenhage GB, Hawkins LL (editors): *Handbook of Nonprescription Drugs.* American Pharmaceutical Association. [Annual publication.]

Kingsbury JM: *Poisonous Plants of the United States and Canada.* Prentice-Hall, 1964.

Moeschlin S: *Poisoning.* Grune & Stratton, 1965.

Patty FA (editor): *Industrial Hygiene and Toxicology.* 2 vol. Interscience, 1963.

Physician's Desk Reference. Medical Economics, Inc. [Annual publication.]

Plunkett ER: *Handbook of Industrial Toxicology.* Chemical Publishing Co, 1966.

Treatment

Activated charcoal rediscovered. (Editorial.) Br Med J 3:487, 1972.

Arena JM: Poisoning: Treatment and prevention. (3 parts.) JAMA 232:1272; 233:358, 900, 1975.

Baselt RC, Wright JA, Cravey RH: Therapeutic and toxic concentration of more than 100 toxicologically significant drugs in blood, plasma, or serum. Clin Chem 21:44, 1975.

Clarke A: Effect of safety packaging on aspirin ingestion by children. Pediatrics 63:687, 1979.

Gosselin RE, Smith RP: Trends in the therapy of acute poisonings. Clin Pharmacol Ther 7:279, 1966.

Matthew H & others: Gastric aspiration and lavage in acute poisoning. Br Med J 2:1333, 1966.

Matthew H: Acute poisoning: Some myths and misconceptions. Br Med J 1:519, 1971.

Matthew H, Lawson AAH: *Treatment of Common Acute Poisonings,* 3rd ed. Churchill Livingstone, 1975.

Proudfoot AT, Park J: Changing pattern of drugs used for self-poisoning. Br Med J 1:90, 1978.

Thoman ME, Verhulst HL: Ipecac syrup in antiemetic ingestion. JAMA 196:433, 1966.

Dangerous Metals & Chelating Agents | 65

The metallic poisons or heavy metals are discussed separately from other environmental poisons to simplify the presentation of the many toxic agents that must be identified and to emphasize chelation as a mechanism of drug action. Chelating or sequestering agents remove metallic ions from solution, and the resulting nonionic organometallic complex is often less toxic and more rapidly excreted than the metallic ions.

CHELATION

In the formation of the covalent (ionic) bond, each atom contributes one electron to the shared pair in the common molecular orbital. In $PtCl_2$, for example, the ordinary valence of Pt^{2+} is satisfied.

In addition, through coordinate-covalent bonding, metals may have auxiliary valences and form complexes or coordination compounds with electronegative atoms. A coordinate-covalent bond is formed when both shared electrons are contributed by one atom. For example, platinum in the above salt may accept electron pairs from the nitrogen of ammonia, forming cisplatin, a coordination compound used in cancer chemotherapy.

When the ligand contains at least 2 donor atoms, chelate formation may occur. Chelate formation involves formation of ordinary covalent bonds or, more commonly, of coordinate-covalent bonds between an electrophilic, electropositive atom of a metal and nucleophilic atoms or ligands (usually N, O, or S) of an organic molecule so as to form a heterocyclic ring containing the metal atom and 2, 3, or 4 atoms from the organic molecule.

Fig 65–1, for example, represents a common chelating or sequestering agent. The polycarboxylic acid can form salts utilizing covalent or ionic bonds as

A

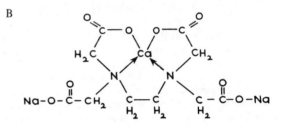

B

C

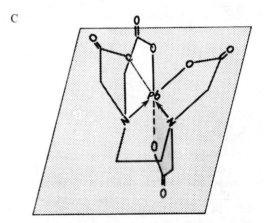

Figure 65–1. Salt and chelate formation with ethylenediamine-tetraacetic acid (EDTA). *A:* In a solution of the disodium salt of EDTA, the sodium and hydrogen ions are chemically and biologically available. *B:* In solutions of calcium disodium edetate, calcium is bound by coordinate-covalent bonds with nitrogen as well as by the usual ionic bonds. Calcium ions are effectively removed from solution. *C:* In the lead-edetate chelate, lead is incorporated into 5 heterocyclic rings.

683

in the disodium salt (A). However, when the disodium-calcium salt is formed (B), additional bonding is possible. Calcium has unfilled **d** orbitals that can accept electron pairs from the nitrogen. The calcium is then held firmly in the heterocyclic organometallic rings that result and can no longer provide calcium ions. In fact, if the tetrasodium salt is added to blood or other material, calcium ions are sequestered by the "clawlike" hold of the chelate and clotting is prevented. The lead-EDTA chelate is even more stable and is formed preferentially even in the presence of calcium ions. In the compound shown in C, all 6 of the ligands of EDTA have contributed to the formation of partially fused, 5-membered rings.

The stability of metal chelates depends upon properties of the metal and of the chelating agent, and compounds can therefore be selected to bind certain metals with a degree of specificity sufficient to make them therapeutically useful in the treatment of intoxications. The stability of the chelate is greatest—ie, the dissociation into metal ion and ligand is least—when the ligand molecule contains more than one electron-donating atom, in which case it is said to be polydentate. Stability is also increased if the metal becomes part of several fused rings when the chelate is formed, and complex, naturally occurring chelates such as hemoglobin are very stable.

The chelate formed has chemical and biologic properties different from either of the precursors. The metal is no longer present in an ionized form and is not biologically available. The chelates formed in the course of therapy must be nontoxic and very water-soluble so that they may be more rapidly excreted than the offending metal. All chelating agents remove or inactivate some of the trace metals present in the organism, and it has been suggested (but not yet established) that some drugs may exert their pharmacologic action through this mechanism.

CHELATING AGENTS
(Table 65–1.)

A variety of chelating agents are available. In some cases—eg, deferoxamine and iron—a single chelating agent is related to a single metal. As a rule, however, several possible pairs are involved. The pharmacology of the individual chelating agents will, therefore, be discussed separately before the discussion of heavy metal toxicity.

1. DIMERCAPROL (BAL)

Chemistry

Arsenical vesicants were developed late in World War I to supplement sulfur mustard gases. Early in

Table 65–1. Summary of metallic poisons, and chelating agents effective against each.

	Chelating Agent of Choice	Alternative Chelating Agent or Other Antidotal Therapy
Antimony	Dimercaprol	...
Arsenic	Dimercaprol	...
Barium	...	Precipitate with sulfate
Beryllium	...	...
Bismuth	Dimercaprol	...
Cadmium	Dimercaprol	Edetate
Calcium	...	Sulfate, phosphate, furosemide
Chromium	Dimercaprol	...
Cobalt	...	...
Copper	Penicillamine	...
Gold	Dimercaprol	...
Iron	Deferoxamine	Edetate
Lead	Dimercaprol and edetate	Penicillamine
Manganese	...	Edetate (?)
Mercury	Dimercaprol	N-Acetylpenicillamine
Nickel	Dithizon,* Dithiocarb*	...
Plutonium	DTPA*	...
Silver	...	Precipitate with chlorides
Thallium	Dithizon (?)*	...
Uranium	Edetate (?)	Bicarbonate prevents renal damage
Vanadium	Edetate (?)	Ascorbic acid
Zinc	Edetate	Dimercaprol

*Investigational drug.

World War II, before it became apparent that the nitrogen mustards would replace the arsenical vesicants should chemical warfare be attempted, the British developed an antagonist to the toxic effects of arsenic. Since the prototype of the arsenic mustard gas was lewisite, the new compound was called British antilewisite, or BAL.

The reaction of arsenic with sulfhydryl groups, especially those in the keratin of skin, nails, and hair, was well known, Ehrlich having suggested that the thiol group was the "arsenic receptor." In studying the combination of arsenic with the protein keratin, the British workers observed that, generally, one equivalent of arsenic reacted with 2 equivalents of sulfhydryl groups. They introduced dimercaprol, a simple dithiol (Fig 65–2), to react similarly with arsenic, neutralizing its toxic effects and hastening its excretion. It is still the primary agent used in the treatment of arsenic and mercury poisoning.

Dimercaprol has an offensive odor similar to that of other mercaptans or thiols. It is not soluble in water and is dispensed as a solution in peanut oil.

Adverse Reactions

Dimercaprol may reactivate sulfhydryl-containing enzymes that have been inactivated by a heavy metal, but it may inactivate other enzymes, presumably by chelating trace metals. Perhaps for this reason it causes a great variety of side-effects when given in more than the minimal dose described below.

However, its acute effects are not dangerous, and chronic toxic effects have not been reported. Side-effects include local pain at the injection site, fever, nausea, salivation, and paresthesias in the mouth and throat.

Dosages

Dimercaprol is given by deep intramuscular administration. The dose usually recommended is 2.5 mg/kg (or 0.25 mL/10 kg) every 4 hours for the first 2 days and then every 12 hours for a total of 10 days or until recovery. Treatment can be less intensive if the situation permits—eg, 100 mg 4 times on the first day; 2 times on days 2, 3, and 4; and once on days 5 and 6.

2. CALCIUM DISODIUM EDETATE

Chemistry

Ethylenediaminetetraacetic acid itself—ie, the acid rather than any salt—is the form of this agent most potent in removing calcium from solutions. It may be added to shed blood to prevent clotting, but when so used it is a chemical reagent rather than a drug. Salts of the acid when used as drugs are known under their generic names as edetates. Disodium edetate and trisodium edetate also bind calcium and for this reason have only investigational uses. Given acutely and in large amounts, they are toxic because they lower serum calcium. During chronic administration, the calcium chelate formed may be damaging to the kidneys. During administration of a dose of intermediate size, the plasma calcium level may be maintained by mobilization of calcium from the skeleton and other stores.

Calcium disodium edetate will, on the other hand, exchange calcium for lead and a few other heavy metals. It is still used parenterally in combination with dimercaprol in the treatment of lead poisoning. Given orally, it either is ineffective or adds toxicity.

Adverse Reactions

CaNa₂ EDTA should be given in dilute solutions to prevent thrombophlebitis and should be given in interrupted dosage to prevent depletion of essential metals. Dosage should not exceed that recommended in order to avoid the renal tubular damage observed in experimental situations. If these precautions are observed, the side-effects will be limited to an occasional febrile flu-like state appearing some hours after the injection.

Dosages

For intravenous administration, 15–25 mg/kg of edetate (Versenate) (0.08–0.125 mL/kg of a 20% solution) are added to 250 or 500 mL of 5% dextrose and given over a period of 1–2 hours twice daily. The daily dose should not exceed 50 mg/kg/d in adults or 30 mg/kg in children. The drug should be given in 5-day

courses with a rest period of at least 2 days between courses. Urinalyses should be done during the treatment period, and the dosage reduced if changes appear in the urinary sediment.

3. PENICILLAMINE

Chemistry

Penicillamine (Fig 65–2) is an amino acid that occurs only as a product of the hydrolysis of penicillin. It can be considered a dimethylcysteine or a thiovaline. The D-isomer is much less toxic than the racemate and is the form used as a drug. Penicillamine is well absorbed after oral administration, and very little is metabolized in the body. Its prime advantage is its suitability for chronic oral administration.

Clinical Uses

Penicillamine was first introduced for the treatment of Wilson's disease (hepatolenticular degeneration), to remove copper from and prevent accumulation of copper in tissues. It may be effective as a chelator of lead and probably of mercury.

In addition, it combines chemically with cysteine to form a cysteine-penicillamine disulfide that is much more soluble than cystine (cysteine-cysteine disulfide). It is, therefore, used in the treatment of cystinuria. In controlled studies, it is also active in early rheumatoid arthritis. Its place in therapy, which appears similar to that of gold, is limited (see Chapter 27).

N-Acetylpenicillamine is even more stable than the parent compound and offers advantages over penicillamine, especially as a chelator of mercury.

Adverse Reactions

The side-effects inherent in this drug have limited its usefulness. Animal toxicity studies have shown inhibition of wound healing and evidence of muscle and blood vessel damage. Penicillamine may interfere with the synthesis of DNA, collagen, and mucopolysaccharides. In humans, side-effects tend to be reduced when lower doses are employed and when maintenance levels are more slowly reached. Proteinuria, a serious side-effect, is encountered in 20% of patients. An immune complex nephritis, usually with subepithelial deposits (membranous nephropathy), occurs rarely but may be reversible when the drug is withdrawn. Continued administration of penicillamine in the presence of significant proteinuria may lead to renal insufficiency. Leukopenia and thrombocytopenia may occur at any time and may herald aplastic anemia. Because of these hematologic consequences, sequential blood counts are required, with prompt cessation of the drug initiated if the platelet count falls below 100,000/μL or the white count below 3000/μL. Marrow aplasia may be self-limited after medication is stopped. However, most deaths related

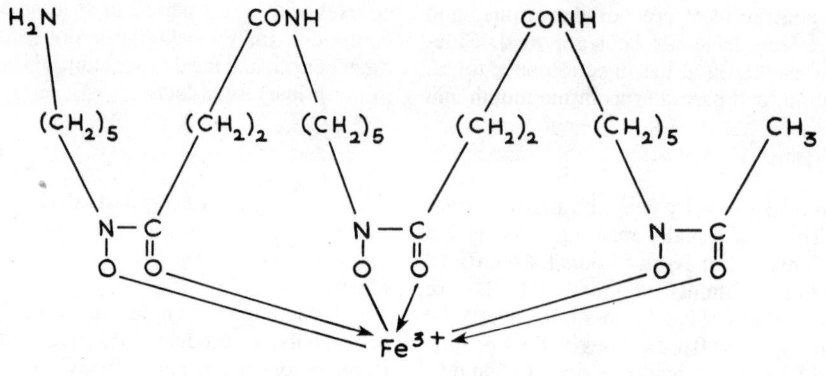

Ferroxamine

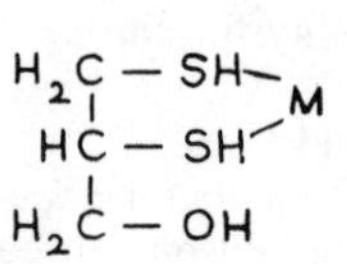

Dimercaprol
(2,3-dimercaptopropanol)

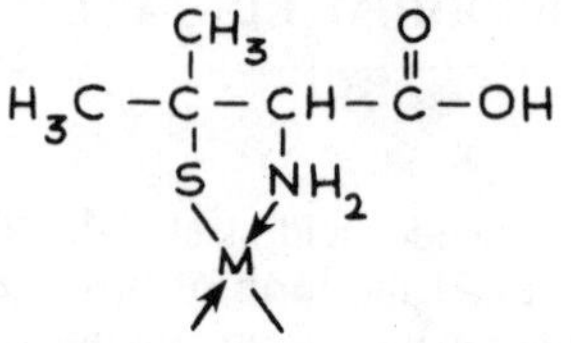

Penicillamine

Figure 65–2. Chemical structures of several metal chelates. Ferroxamine without the chelated iron is deferoxamine (Desferal). It is represented here to show the functional groups; the iron is actually held in a caged system. Dimercaprol incorporates the metal into a stable heterocyclic ring by covalent bonding. A single molecule of copper or other metal may be held by 2 molecules of penicillamine. M = metal molecules.

to penicillamine administration are due to aplastic anemia. Skin reactions, the most common side-effect, may occur at any time during the course of drug therapy. They may respond to lowering the dose and sometimes to antihistamines.

Pemphigus and pemphigoid reactions have been seen, and oral ulcers are sometimes observed. Drug fever, which may be seen as an early response to penicillamine, is often associated with cutaneous eruptions.

Loss of taste or a metallic taste may develop. The blunting of taste reception may relate to zinc chelation by the drug. Anorexia and nausea and vomiting may also occur.

A variety of autoimmune diseases, presumably mediated through immune complexes, have been observed, including myasthenia gravis, Goodpasture's syndrome, lupus erythematosus, hemolytic anemia, and thyroiditis. The drug must be discontinued permanently when any of these conditions is encountered.

Dosages

Penicillamine (Cuprimine) is administered orally 1½ hours after meals. The usual course of treatment begins with 125 mg or 250 mg once a day for 1 month; if no side-effects occur, the dose is doubled the second month. If therapeutic effects in rheumatoid arthritis are

not seen after 3 months, the dose is increased at monthly intervals up to 750 mg daily (250 mg 3 times a day). It is rarely necessary to exceed this maximum. In the treatment of Wilson's disease, the dose may be increased to 250 mg 4 times a day, but the optimal dose must be determined with the aid of urinary copper determinations. The medication should not be given to pregnant women or for any articular disease except rheumatoid arthritis. Improvement can be expected in about 70% of patients but is observed only after a latent period of about 3 months. Side-effects that usually necessitate discontinuing the drug occur in approximately 40% of patients. Blood counts, including a platelet count, and urinalysis should be performed twice a month for 4–6 months and then monthly. A history of allergy to penicillin is not a contraindication to penicillamine. Patients who develop renal involvement, drug fever, autoimmune syndromes, and hematologic problems should not be rechallenged with the drug.

4. OTHER CHELATING AGENTS

Deferoxamine (Desferal) is used in the treatment of intoxication with iron (see Chapter 42). Sodium dithiocarb (sodium diethyldithiocarbamate) and diphenylthiocarbazone (Dithizon) are investigational drugs used in the treatment of nickel and thallium poisoning. DTPA (diethylenetriaminepentaacetic acid) is available where plutonium contamination may occur and has been used effectively intravenously or by inhalation in several hundred people.

METALLIC POISONS

LEAD

Inhalation of lead is a hazard in industry when metals or painted metals are cut or burned. Lead pigments are no longer present in the usual house paints, but many old buildings in slum and rural areas have peeling layers of old paint, plaster, and putty that may be eaten by children. Lead from pipes or ceramic glaze has contaminated water and food, and potentially dangerous amounts have been detected near smelters.

About 10% of ingested lead is absorbed. Its immediate distribution is widespread, but, if the amount ingested exceeds the maximal rate of excretion, lead is deposited in bone, where it is inactive insofar as toxicity is concerned. The half-life of lead is, for convenience, said to be 20 days in blood and soft tissues and 20 years in bone.

The usual adult intake (dietary and from the air) is about 300 μg/d. Toxicity may occur if the daily intake reaches 1000 μg/d. Children during their creeping and exploring phase can easily ingest dangerous amounts of lead from a single daily chip of paint, plaster, or putty. In some slum areas, 5–10% of children age 1–5 years may show increased blood levels of lead without symptoms.

Clinical Findings

A. Acute Intoxication: When a soluble, rapidly absorbed compound of lead is ingested or when lead vapors are inhaled, the symptoms—eg, lead encephalopathy or abdominal pain—may be rapid in onset. However, the manifestations are the same as those described for chronic intoxication. The onset of symptomatic chronic lead poisoning may be very slow or acute, and a chronic course may be interrupted by acute episodes. Therefore, the usual distinction between acute and chronic intoxication is not easily made.

B. Chronic Intoxication:

1. Red blood cells–Anemia is usually present due in part to an inhibition by lead of at least 2 steps in the synthesis of heme: (1) Delta-aminolevulinic acid (ALA) is not converted to porphobilinogen and appears in the urine in abnormal and diagnostically useful amounts. (2) Protoporphyrin is not converted to heme and hemoglobin, and its immediate precursor, protoporphyrin IX, appears in the urine in increased amounts. In addition, the period of survival of red cells is reduced. The increased turnover of red cells leads to the appearance of increased numbers of reticulocytes and of stippling of erythrocytes by the inclusion of basophilic remnants of mitochondria.

2. Smooth muscle–Intestinal smooth muscle is stimulated. Spasm and hypermotility cause intense cramping pain, or "lead colic." Blood vessel constriction causes pallor and an acute, reversible hypertension.

3. Encephalopathy–In adults, symptoms may be limited to irritability and slowed mentation.

In children, the impending encephalopathy is not easily anticipated because the earliest symptoms are nonspecific: decreased appetite, irritability, fatigue, abdominal pain, and possibly vomiting. These are followed by drowsiness or stupor, persistent vomiting, and convulsions as cerebral edema and intracranial pressure increase.

Blood levels of lead above 80 μg/dL clearly show a threat of acute toxicity in children, and those below 40 μg/dL are accepted as safe. Levels between these figures are found in children in old urban areas and in areas near ore processing installations. Selected tests of motor performance and intelligence show that these functions are depressed in such children.

4. Lead palsy or myopathy– It is still not established whether changes in muscle function are neural or muscular in origin. Fatigability and weakness are common. Wrist drop, foot drop, and involvement of the extraocular muscles occur. Sensory changes do not occur.

5. Lead line–A finely stippled deposit may occur in the margins of the gingival tissues. The procedure for identification consists of expressing blood from the area, as with pressure from a glass slide, and observing with a hand lens.

6. X-ray findings–Radiopaque material may be demonstrable upon x-ray examination of the abdomen. A chronic increase in lead absorption, with the deposition of lead in long bones, leads to "lead lines" as the radiopacity increases at the metaphyses.

7. Laboratory findings–The following technics are available:

a. Lead in blood. Determination of lead in the blood is the most useful test for diagnosis or screening.

b. Response of urinary lead to test dose of penicillamine or edetate.

c. Increased amount of erythrocyte stippling.

d. Increase in amounts of coproporphyrin excreted in urine.

e. Increase in amounts of aminolevulinic acid excreted in urine.

Treatment

A. Chelation: If the intoxication is acute, treatment should be initiated with injections of both dimercaprol and edetate in order to avoid the increased toxic effects sometimes precipitated by edetate. Thereafter, treatment can be continued with edetate or the combination of both drugs.

In less acute situations, deleading can be accomplished with repeated courses of a chelating agent—eg, edetate—given as described above. Oral penicillamine (Cuprimine) is far more convenient, but its use is still investigational. It appears to be an effective deleading agent in adults, but its usefulness in children remains to be established.

B. Calcium Gluconate: In the past, calcium was given to hasten the deposition of lead with the extra calcium in bone. There is no question but that lead is retained in bone, but the relief of colic afforded by injected calcium salts is apparently due to its action on smooth muscle.

C. Encephalopathy: Chelating agents are of doubtful immediate value. Urea or a similar osmotic diuretic may be used to reduce cerebral edema (see Chapter 17). A single attack leaves 25% of the children retarded, and each recurrence increases the number with retardation, convulsive states, spasticity, or blindness. Obviously, the child cannot be returned to the same environment.

ORGANIC LEAD

Organic lead, encountered in the form of tetraethyl lead added to gasoline, is a powerful and prolonged central nervous system stimulant and convulsant. About 10% of the lead emitted in automobile exhaust is still organic lead; the balance becomes inorganic lead that can be inhaled and that accumulates in the surface waters of areas of the ocean close to concentrations of automobiles. The marketing of leaded gasoline is now being phased out.

ARSENIC

Arsenic is a transition element, or metalloid. Its oxides are hydrated to acids, but it also reacts with nonmetals.

Inorganic arsenicals were for several hundred years the favorite agents of poisoners. Paris green (copper acetoarsenite) was the first pesticide, and organic arsenicals were the primary agents in the therapy of syphilis until penicillin became available. The toxicology of arsenic has lost much of its practical importance, but of the metals only lead causes more deaths. Industrial exposure still occurs during the refining and smelting of other metals, and some pesticides (rat bait, herbicides) contain arsenic.

Clinical Findings & Treatment
A. Acute Intoxication: Because arsenic damages all capillaries, many organ systems are affected, but gastrointestinal symptoms are most prominent. Symptoms following overwhelming doses reflect a violent gastroenteritis: pain and difficulty in swallowing, epigastric and abdominal pain, vomiting, and watery or bloody diarrhea. Blood pressure falls, and death is due to shock. Jaundice or oliguria may appear in 1–3 days. Smaller single doses cause some of the same symptoms together with muscle cramps, irritability, dizziness, and weakness that last for about 2 weeks.

Specific treatment is with dimercaprol.

B. Chronic Intoxication: The onset may be insidious and may simulate many diseases. Appetite is well maintained; thus, when arsenic was used criminally, ingestion continued to the end. The manifestations include peripheral or optic neuritis, pigmentation of the skin, localized edema, conjunctivitis, diarrhea, nausea and vomiting, nephritis, jaundice, cirrhosis, anemia, and dependent edema.

Specific treatment is with dimercaprol.

C. Carcinogenicity: Arsenic has long been said to cause palmar and plantar keratoses and subsequent carcinomas. Most observations are in conflict with the traditional belief, and many of the cases reported earlier were probably due to coal tar. Arsenic is not carcinogenic in animal experiments. Nevertheless, accumulating epidemiologic evidence suggests that some groups of workers and some groups who live near smelters have a higher than normal incidence of carcinomas of the respiratory tract.

D. Arsine: Arsine is a gas that results from the action of acid on arsenic metal or arsenic compounds in the presence of a reducing agent—eg, another active metal. It can cause severe hemolysis.

MERCURY

Opportunities for contact with salts of mercury are fortunately becoming rare. Mercuric (bi)chloride is now rarely used as a disinfectant or homicidal agent. Metallic mercury has become comparatively more important as a toxic agent. Orally ingested, it is poorly absorbed and virtually nontoxic in adults. However, it volatilizes at room temperature and is a hazard in laboratories. Metallic mercury from the clinical laboratory has also been accidentally and suicidally injected.

Mercury is excreted by the kidneys, colon, salivary glands, and liver. Many of the toxic effects appear at these sites of greatest concentration.

Clinical Findings & Treatment
A. Acute Intoxication: The immediate danger (first day) is shock due to fluid loss from local damage to the gastrointestinal tract. Colitis with bloody diarrhea follows when mercuric ions are excreted by the large bowel. Necrosis of the proximal renal tubule may follow. Recovery begins in about 1 week.

Specific treatment is with dimercaprol as described above.

B. Chronic Intoxication: Signs are related to the kidney (eg, proteinuria), the mouth (eg, stomatitis, excessive salivation, and blue gum line), and the central nervous system (eg, anxiety, depression, headache, weakness, insomnia, and irritability). Treatment consists of dimercaprol, 2.5 mg/kg intramuscularly twice daily for a prolonged period as determined by the course of the patient.

C. Acrodynia: Small amounts of mercury in infants and young children—eg, from teething powders, diaper rinses, ammoniated mercury ointment, or paint—may cause a hypersensitivity reaction with generalized erythema. It is responsive to treatment with dimercaprol.

D. Monoalkyl Mercury Poisoning: A group of methyl and ethyl mercury compounds in which the carbon-mercury bond is not easily split causes toxic effects different from those of inorganic mercury.

Ingestion of these compounds causes, after a latent period of weeks, damage to the cerebellum and to specific areas of the cerebral cortex. Symptoms include paresthesia, ataxia, slurred speech, constricted visual fields, and deafness, with progression to blindness, coma, and death.

Antifungal seed coatings or dressings—eg, methylmercury dicyandiamide—have caused sporadic cases of poisoning and a few disastrous epidemics when treated wheat intended for seed use was milled and used in bread. During the last of 3 epidemics in Iraq (in 1972), there were 459 hospital deaths.

In the 1950s, methyl mercury was discharged from a plastics plant into Minamata Bay (Japan) and taken up by fish and shellfish. Among the families who depended upon the seafood, there were 121 intoxications with 46 deaths plus 22 deformed and retarded neonates.

It has since been demonstrated that mercury and many of its compounds can be transformed by bacteria into methyl mercury, which enters the food chain and appears in potentially dangerous levels in fish. The concentration of methyl mercury in fish taken from waters near many industries is elevated, but fish concentrate naturally occurring mercury as well, and the levels currently causing concern have probably been present for millenia.

The excretion of methyl mercury, which has a half-life in the human of about 70 days, is hastened by the systemic administration of penicillamine or acetylpenicillamine or the oral administration of a thiol resin available as an investigative drug. Dimercaprol is ineffective.

ANTIMONY

Antimony occurs in type metal and other alloys, batteries, ceramics, and drugs such as tartar emetic. Its properties are similar to those of arsenic. Like arsenic, upon reaction with acid it evolves a gas, stibine (SbH_3), that causes hemolysis. The MLD of antimony is 100 mg.

Clinical Findings & Treatment

A. Acute Intoxication: Antimony is more irritating locally than arsenic but is more rapidly excreted. Manifestations include nausea, vomiting, diarrhea, nephritis, and hepatitis. In addition to general measures, treat with dimercaprol; its effectiveness is established for inorganic antimonial and trivalent organic compounds.

B. Chronic Intoxication: Manifestations include itching skin pustules, bleeding gums, conjunctivitis, laryngitis, headache, weight loss, and anemia.

BERYLLIUM

Beryllium salts were used until 1949 in the phosphors of fluorescent lamps. Contact also occurs during its smelting. Beryllium and its alloys are being used more and more in airframes, but no problems of toxicity have yet been reported.

The hazards of even minimal contact with beryllium salts were acknowledged only reluctantly and after needless delay had prolonged an epidemic of intoxications.

Clinical Findings & Treatment

Beryllium acts locally to produce a granulomatous response. Three clinical patterns are seen:

A. Indolent Ulcers: Contact with beryllium salts causes an eczematoid dermatitis. With heavier exposure or (especially) if some of the material is deposited in the tissue, an indolent ulcer occurs that does not heal until the irritant material is excised.

B. Respiratory Tract Irritation: Signs of upper respiratory tract irritation and acute pulmonary edema occur.

C. Chronic Pulmonary Granulomatoses: Over 200 fatal cases of chronic obliterative pulmonary disease have been identified. The extent of the underlying exposure may be very slight; some cases resulted from handling the clothes of workers. Treatment with corticosteroids may have a temporary effect but does not alter the variable and unpredictable course.

The properties of beryllium should be related to those of silica and other particulate matters that cause pulmonary fibrosis.

BISMUTH

Soluble bismuth compounds are a very rare cause of chronic intoxication. Manifestations include skin eruptions, weakness, joint pains, diarrhea, metal line on the gums, and stomatitis.

Treatment is with dimercaprol.

CADMIUM

Poisoning by ingestion of cadmium is rare now that cadmium-plated cooking utensils are no longer used. Cadmium poisoning still occurs following the inhalation of cadmium oxide dusts or fumes during the smelting of zinc ores or welding or cutting cadmium-plated metal.

Clinical Findings & Treatment

A. Acute Inhalation: Initial symptoms are as for other metal fume fevers, followed in a few hours by dyspnea, chest pain, and pulmonary edema. Permanent pulmonary fibrotic changes may follow.

B. Chronic Intoxication: The onset is insidious and is delayed at least 2 years after first exposure. Symptoms may first become apparent when exposure is no longer present. Progressive obstructive respiratory disease may develop. Renal tubular damage with proteinuria is less threatening but more common. One epidemic of severe osteomalacia due to cadmium occurred in a population conditioned by repeated pregnancies and a diet low in calcium and vitamin D.

Chelating agents do not influence the chronic state. During acute intoxication, cadmium excretion is increased by administration of dimercaprol or EDTA. The complex may, however, cause additional renal damage.

CHROMIUM & CHROMATES

Chromium, chromium salts, and chromates are used in alloying, in tanning, in the manufacture of rust- and corrosion-resistant paints, and in many other industrial processes.

No treatment of established value is available for the acute or the topical reaction.

Clinical Findings

A. Topical Effects: Skin contact, especially with the strongly oxidizing chromates, leads to incapacitating eczematous dermatitis and ulceration. Ulceration and perforation of the nasal septum also occur.

B. Carcinogenicity: The incidence of lung cancer is increased up to 15 times normal in workers exposed to chromite, chromic oxide, and chromium ores.

C. Acute Intoxication: Gastroenteritis, nephritis, hepatitis.

GOLD

Various gold salts are still occasionally used in the treatment of the active inflammatory stage of rheumatoid arthritis. The effectiveness of gold compounds is established, but allergic toxic reactions are common and serious. See Chapter 27.

MANGANESE

Manganese toxicity occurs as a consequence of exposure to dusts in mining or alloying.

Clinical Findings

A. Acute Intoxication: Metal fume fever.

B. Chronic Pulmonary Effects: Recurrent chemical pneumonitis.

C. Chronic Neurologic Effects: Damage to basal ganglia, with permanent changes similar to those of parkinsonism. After the worker leaves the source of the exposure, the manganese excess is excreted but the neurologic defect persists. Chelating agents are then of no value, but levodopa is effective as in other parkinsonian states.

NICKEL & NICKEL CARBONYL

Metallic nickel can cause a contact (allergic) dermatitis and is commonly present in watch cases and jewelry. Nickel and its salts have negligible toxicity for humans.

However, nickel carbonyl—$Ni(CO)_4$—is a volatile pulmonary irritant and carcinogenic substance generated during the purification of nickel. Exposures have been rare since 1920.

Immediate symptoms are cough, dizziness, and weakness; these are followed by dyspnea and pulmonary edema. Treat dyspnea with 100% oxygen by mask. Treat pulmonary edema. Sodium diethyldithiocarbamate (Dithiocarb), 50–100 mg/kg orally or intramuscularly, is an investigational drug.

THALLIUM

The oral administration of thallium salts as depilatories in the treatment of ringworm led to many cases of toxicity prior to 1940. Sporadic cases of intoxication still occur from the mistaken ingestion of rodent or ant bait that contains thallium sulfate or acetate.

With large doses, signs of intense gastrointestinal irritation, headache, and tachycardia appear in 12 hours. Delirium, convulsions, coma, and respiratory paralysis can occur in 2–7 days.

With smaller doses, the onset of signs of intoxication may be delayed. They include ataxia, paresthesias and neuropathy, lethargy, confusion, and depilation.

No specific treatment is available. Claims are made that large doses of dimercaprol are effective. Diphenylthiocarbazone (Dithizon) is used in veterinary practice.

• • •

References
(See also texts and manuals listed in Chapter 64.)

Chelating Agents

Catsch A, Hartmuth-Hoehne AE: Pharmacology and therapeutic applications of agents used in heavy metal poisoning. Pharmacol Ther [A] 1:1, 1976.

Gordon MH: Penicillamine for treatment of rheumatoid arthritis. JAMA 229:1342, 1974.

Penicillamine: More lessons from experience. Br Med J 3:120, 1975.

Lead

Chisolm J: Treatment of acute lead intoxication: Choice of chelating agents and supportive therapeutic measures. Clin Toxicol 3:527, 1970. (Also see N Engl J Med 289:1016, 1973.)

Hardy HL & others: Lead as an environmental poison. Clin Pharmacol Ther 12:982, 1971.

Jacobziner H: Lead poisoning in childhood: Epidemiology, manifestations, and prevention. Clin Pediatr 5:277, 1966.

Klein M & others: Earthenware containers as a source of fatal lead poisoning. N Engl J Med 283:669, 1970.

Landrigan PJ & others: Neuropsychological dysfunction in children with chronic low-level lead absorption. Lancet 1:708, 1975.

Needleman HL & others: Deficits in psychologic and classroom performance of children with elevated dentine lead levels. N Engl J Med 300:689, 1979.

Mercury

Bakir F & others: Methylmercury poisoning in Iraq. Science 181:230, 1973.

Buxton JT Jr & others: Metallic mercury embolism: Report of cases. JAMA 193:573, 1965.

Goldwater LJ, Nicolau A, Da Madeira SJ: Absorption and excretion of mercury in man. Arch Environ Health 12:196, 1966.

Hill DM: Self-administration of mercury by subcutaneous injection. Br Med J 1:342, 1967.

Kark RAP & others: Mercury poisoning and its treatment with N-acetyl-D,L-penicillamine. N Engl J Med 285:10, 1971.

Pierce PE & others: Alkyl mercury poisoning in humans: Report of an outbreak. JAMA 220:1439, 1972.

Other Metals (See Chapter 42 for iron and deferoxamine.)

American Rheumatism Association, Cooperating Clinics Committee. Arthritis Rheum 16:353, 1973. (Gold)

Bair WJ, Thompson RC: Plutonium: Biomedical research. Science 183:715, 1974.

Browning E: *Toxicity of Industrial Metals,* 2nd ed. Appleton-Century-Crofts, 1969.

Carruthers M, Smith B: Evidence of cadmium toxicity in a population living in a zinc-mining area. Lancet 2:845, 1979.

Cotzias GC: Chronic manganese poisoning: Clearance of tissue manganese concentrations with persistence of neurological picture. Neurology 18:376, 1968.

Frost DV: Arsenicals in biology: Retrospect and prospect. Fed Proc 26:194, 1967.

Gumpel JM: Deaths associated with gold treatment: A reassessment. Br Med J 1:215, 1978.

Hardy HL: Beryllium poisoning: Lessons in control of man-made disease. N Engl J Med 273:1188, 1965.

Jenkins RB: Inorganic arsenic and the nervous system. Brain 89:479, 1966.

Lauwerys RR & others: Investigations on lung and kidney function in workers exposed to cadmium. Environ Health Perspect 28:137, 1979.

McCarty DJ & others: Aplastic anemia secondary to gold-salt therapy: Report of fatal case and a review of literature. JAMA 179:655, 1962.

Nickel. National Academy of Sciences, 1975.

Ott MG, Holder BB, Gordon HL: Respiration cancer and occupational exposure to arsenicals. Arch Environ Health 29:250, 1974.

Prasad AS: Clinical, biochemical and pharmacologic role of zinc. Annu Rev Pharmacol 19:393, 1979.

Sternlieb I, Scheinberg IH: Prevention of Wilson's disease in asymptomatic patients. N Engl J Med 278:352, 1968.

66 | Common Environmental Toxic Agents

Much of the material in prior chapters is relevant to a discussion of toxicology. For convenience in organizing our approach to the practical problems that arise, the toxicity of agents used in therapy was discussed in Chapter 6 independently of other environmental hazards. Therapeutic agents are, of course, involved in many accidental poisonings as well as in therapeutic misadventures. Furthermore, a study of the effects of therapeutic agents is an essential preliminary to the study of environmental poisons that may act through the same mechanism—eg, cholinesterase inhibition and central nervous system stimulation or depression.

At this point, the problem is to somehow organize the many poisons not anticipated by the discussions of therapeutic agents. It will become obvious that an organized discussion cannot include the name, composition, and special properties of the thousands of industrial and household products involved; for such data practitioners, no matter what their specialties, will have to keep at hand one of the books listed at the end of the chapter and use other resources such as the nearest Poison Control Center. The properties of the most common industrial and household poisons are presented in an outline that can be expanded by experience and need.

A number of aspects of toxicology are not discussed below, and mention of them would serve to emphasize the many disciplines participating in this field. Analytical chemists, industrial hygienists, agricultural engineers, and criminologists supplement the work of physicians in this field, and other public health workers and regulatory agencies deal with populations as well as with individual patients. The establishment of permissible levels of toxic contaminants in the environment, the use of protective equipment, and the surveillance of exposed workers are problems too varied to be dealt with here.

AGRICULTURAL CHEMICALS

The agricultural resources and methods of many countries are unable to meet the needs of the population involved. In other countries—notably the USA—the agricultural industry provides large amounts of fresh food throughout the year for the domestic population and a surplus for export as well. In the USA, this feat of productivity is accomplished even though 50% of our total crops are fed to livestock—ie, we are able to burn amino acids for calories—and only 2.2% of the labor force is engaged in agriculture. Fertilizers, insecticides, weed killers, and preservatives are utilized in tremendous amounts. The resulting acute toxicity is minimal (considering, for example, that in the state of California alone 125 million pounds of pesticides were used in 1970), but problems of chronic toxicity and environmental damage have led to emotional interactions between groups representing the agricultural industry, "citizens' lobbies" and others concerned with ecology and the "quality of life," appointed and elected officials concerned with formulating and implementing public policy, and scientists and technologists engaged in responding to the sometimes conflicting demands of all voices raised in controversy.

INSECTICIDES

The use of insecticides increases yields and provides the unblemished products now demanded by the consumer. Insecticides are also used to keep households free of pests and to control vectors of disease. There are 3 general classes of insecticides:

(1) Botanical insecticides: The pyrethrins are esters that occur in the flowers of daisy plants. Synthetics—eg, piperonyl butoxide and other ethers—are equivalent. These insecticides kill rapidly but act only briefly. They are present in household sprays, either alone or in combination with an organic phosphate.

(2) Organic phosphate or carbamate cholinesterase inhibitors: The organic phosphate and carbamate types of insecticide—parathion, malathion, demeton, and many others—are irreversible inhibitors of cholinesterase (see Chapter 8). The acute toxicity of the cholinesterase inhibitors is great, but they are not stable in the presence of water and thus are not persistent. Exceptions to that generalization are parathion, which is not water-soluble and may be present for 1–3 weeks after application; and demeton, which may persist for a month and be present as a residue on harvested foods.

(3) **Chlorinated hydrocarbons:** This group must now be discussed in detail.

Chlorinated Hydrocarbon Insecticides

The chlorinated hydrocarbon insecticides (introduced in 1939) act slowly to kill insects and are persistent; residues from a single application to an open surface remain active for 2–12 months. They have been valuable in the control of disease vectors—eg, body lice and mosquitoes—and huge amounts have been applied to food plants.

A. Chemistry and Identification: The compounds are cyclic hydrocarbons that contain a large amount of chlorine. They are very soluble in fat but water-insoluble and comparatively stable.

They can be placed in several chemical classes and their names listed (Fig 66–1).

1. Chlorobenzene derivatives–Chlorophenothane (DDT), DDD, TDE, DFDT (parafluoro analog of DDT), Neotrane, Dimite (DMC), Dilan.

2. Benzene hexachloride–There are 4 isomers of this compound. The pure gamma isomer is called lindane. Benzene hexachloride and DDT are used topically as parasiticides (see Chapter 5).

3. Chlorinated camphenes–Toxaphene and a closely related mixture, Strobane.

4. Chlorinated polycyclic hydrocarbons–Chlordane (a mixture), heptachlor (a component of chlordane), aldrin, mirex, dieldrin, endrin, isodrin, and methoxychlor.

B. Pharmacokinetics: In the organism or in the environment, the chlorinated hydrocarbons are very stable. The trichloroethane moiety of DDT (Fig 66–1) is dechlorinated to a dichloroethylene analog (DDE). DDT and DDE are stored in the fat of animals. Only a small fraction is oxidized to a water-soluble acetic acid derivative (DDA) and excreted.

C. Properties as Insecticides: The water-insoluble hydrocarbons may be applied as a dust or prepared for use as sprays by dissolution in kerosene or by emulsification. They are rapidly absorbed across the chitinous exoskeleton of the insect and act on its nervous system to cause convulsions. Different insects and different stages of the life cycle may be susceptible only to a particular insecticide. Mites (scabies) are controlled by benzene hexachloride but not by DDT.

D. Human Toxicity: Acute human toxicity is not a common or serious problem, especially when compared with that of the organophosphates. The chlorinated hydrocarbon insecticides cause a generalized stimulation of the central nervous system. The sequence of effects may include vomiting, paresthesias, irritability, undue reactions to auditory and other stimuli, tremors, convulsions, and death from respiratory paralysis.

Treatment is general rather than specific—ie, gastric lavage and control of convulsions.

The above description applies to DDT and related chlorobenzenes. Reactions to toxaphene proceed to convulsions without intervening signs. The estimated oral lethal dose of DDT is probably around 0.3 g/kg; for toxaphene, pure lindane, or chlordane, about 50 mg/kg.

Recovery from an acute episode may take 2 or more months.

The clinical picture during a possible acute toxic reaction is often complicated by the effects of the solvents—usually petroleum distillate—simultaneously ingested or inhaled.

No pattern of chronic human intoxication has been established—ie, the above state of acute intoxication may be reached slowly, but no separate chronic effects are authenticated.

Understandably, there has been great concern about the chronic effects of insecticides. Residues on food are controlled, but DDT and its metabolite DDE (and BHC and dieldrin) accumulate in the fat of individuals until equilibrium between the slow rate of ingestion and slow metabolism is reached. In the USA, this point of equilibrium has apparently been reached, and the concentration in the fat of humans remained at about 9–12 parts per million of DDT plus its metabolite until the restrictions on its use were recently imposed.

Volunteers have been given DDT in dosages about 200 times the usual dietary intake for as long as 18 months without detectable toxicity.

E. Effect in the Ecosystem: One of the great advantages of these fat-soluble substances—and also the basis for ecologic damage—is their chemical stability and biologic persistence. Applied to a wall or other surface, they may persist in concentrations lethal

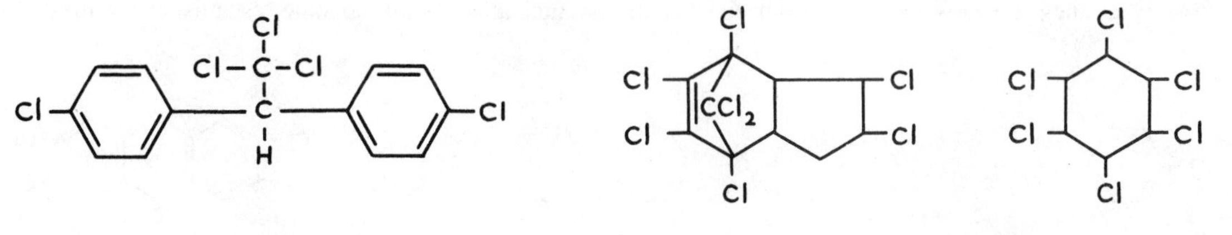

DDT   Chlordane   Benzene hexachloride

Figure 66–1. Chemical structure of representative chlorinated hydrocarbon insecticides.

to insects for 2–12 months; they may also remain as residues on food plants and in the meat and dairy products of animals that ingest the plants. They are destroyed by microorganisms in the soil only over a period of years; leaching by water, of course, simply contaminates another phase of the environment—eg, the soil from one estuary studied contained 32 lb of DDT and its metabolite DDE per acre. In one test, 37% of applied DDT was still in the soil of the test plot after 17 years.

The persistent insecticides are concentrated as they are carried up the food cycle. Fish and reptiles probably are affected. Fish-eating birds (brown pelicans on one island close to the outflow of the Los Angeles River) and bird-eating birds (peregrine falcon) have definitely been damaged.

F. Regulation: The use of DDT in the USA has been forbidden from the last day of 1972. Manufacture of aldrin and dieldrin, which are more toxic and more persistent than DDT, was stopped in 1975. The questionable carcinogenicity of the latter 2 compounds was invoked to justify the prohibition of their use. The use of cholinesterase inhibitors has, of course, increased, but chlorinated hydrocarbons less persistent in the body and environment will presumably come into use.

In California, where half of the insecticides used in the USA are applied, each operator using any but the safest agricultural chemicals must be licensed and each application approved. In California in 1974, there were no deaths and 1150 illnesses in which pesticides were suspected as the cause among workers.

HERBICIDES

Selective herbicides (weed killers) are efficient in reducing competition for fertilizer and require little labor in their application.

Phenoxy Herbicides

Phenoxy or chlorphenoxy herbicides are "2,4-D" and "2,4,5-T"—ie, 2,4-dichlorophenoxyacetic acid or 2,4,5-trichlorophenoxyacetic acid or their less volatile esters. They are related to plant growth regulators or auxins and act selectively to kill broad-leafed plants by stimulating excessive and disorganized growth.

Interest in these compounds stems not from their toxicity as they are now used but from an episode

during the Vietnam conflict. About 12% of the area of South Vietnam was sprayed with various combinations of 2,4,5-T and other herbicides to destroy food crops and jungle growth. The "agent orange" of some manufacturers contained a contaminant, 2,3,7,8-tetrachloro-dibenzodioxin (TCDD, dioxin), that has amazing acute toxicity (0.6 μg/kg is lethal in guinea pigs) and in animals is by far the most potent teratogen known. Whether there was or was not an epidemic of congenital defects in Vietnam as a result of this contaminant will probably never be known.

Interest in TCDD continues because of the possibility that it was a contaminant responsible for deaths of newborns after the use of hexachlorophene and because it is formed when pentachlorophenol, a wood preservative, is burned.

Paraquat

Paraquat, a bipyridilium compound (Fig 66–2), is a nonselective weed killer. It is used in the household as "spot" weed and grass killer and is widely used in farming because it can be applied at seeding, can exert its effect, and can be inactivated before the seed germinates. It is highly toxic, and the deaths that have so far occurred suggest a lethal dose of 4 mg/kg in humans, or, operationally defined, less than one swallow of the usual 20% solution. In large doses it can cause acute pulmonary edema. The usual pattern, however, is an interstitial pulmonary fibrosis ending in death after a few days. No effective treatment is known. Renal damage also occurs.

FOOD ADDITIVES & RESIDUES

Food additives may defer the time at which a foodstuff becomes stale or spoiled and thus prevent wastage and add enjoyment. They may also be used to mislead the consumer—eg, the use of nitrites to maintain the red color of meat—or to compensate for poor processing methods. There is, therefore, a Food Additive Amendment to the Food and Drug Act, and pretesting of new additives for safety is required and product surveillance constantly carried out. The regulatory agency determines, for example, that food colorings are not carcinogenic, establishes the limits for

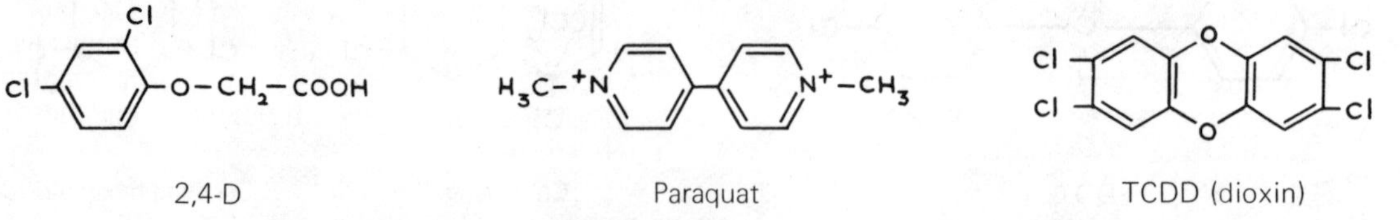

Figure 66–2. Chemical structure of representative herbicides.

residues of insecticides, and prescribes the time before slaughter when a medicated feed must be discontinued.

The discretion of the regulatory agency in the USA is severely limited by the Delaney Amendment (1958) to the Food and Drug Act. This legislation forbids the use as a food additive of any substance found to induce cancer in animals or humans—ie, no tolerance level can be set. This law explains the controversial actions on the 2 additives next discussed.

Artificial Sweeteners

Sodium or calcium cyclamate has advantages over saccharin, the only previously available non-caloric sweetener or sugar substitute. It leaves no bitter aftertaste, and, since it is stable to acid and heat, it can be added to processed foods. Its use had consequently grown until 3.5% of the sugar intake in the USA had been replaced by this synthetic substance. Use of the cyclamates was not limited to individuals with a clear need to restrict total calories or calories from carbohydrate but was extended to foods for general use, including even meats such as bacon and ham.

The only clearly established adverse effect of cyclamate or the cyclamate-saccharin mixtures during the period of common use was the appearance of soft stools or even diarrhea. No chronic toxic effects have been demonstrated in humans. However, feeding experiments established that cyclamate is carcinogenic in animals, and its use was suspended. The demonstration that it is in part metabolized to cyclohexylamine, a known inducer of bladder cancer, intensified the concern.

Saccharin has also been shown to be carcinogenic in animals, but the problem has been met by legislation that forbids its exclusion from the market but requires a warning label.

Another sweetener, a dipeptide of aspartic acid and phenylalanine methyl ester (aspartame), was marketed briefly and then withdrawn when one of its metabolites was shown to be possibly carcinogenic in rats.

Diethylstilbestrol

Diethylstilbestrol (DES) injected into or added to the feed of cattle and chickens significantly increases the efficiency with which feed is converted to meat. The estrogens are, however, clearly carcinogenic, and as soon as analytic methods became sufficiently sensitive to detect DES in the carcass, the use of DES was prohibited. The effect on the cost of producing beef was perceptible (about 8%), and this prohibition was stayed by court action for some time. The prohibition finally became effective early in 1976.

HYDROCARBONS

The hydrocarbons are all general anesthetics but may in addition have toxic effects on the lungs, liver, heart, and bone marrow. Because of these secondary effects, they are classified here into 3 groups.

1. PETROLEUM DISTILLATES

Petroleum distillates with various boiling points are used in a variety of industrial and household solvents. The many cleaning and polishing preparations are second only to therapeutic agents as causes of accidental intoxication.

Source of Exposure

Petroleum ether (naphtha, benzine, mineral spirits), kerosene, and gasoline are the aliphatic hydrocarbons included in this class. They are used as such and in paint thinner, dry cleaners or spot removers, furniture polish, and countless other products. They may be combined with other toxic solvents—eg, methanol in gun cleaner—or contain toxic solutes such as insecticides.

Mechanism of Action

These hydrocarbons are general anesthetics and also pulmonary irritants. They have low surface tensions; even a small amount will spread over a wide area, causing a chemical interstitial pneumonitis or acute pulmonary edema. The hydrocarbon can reach the lung by aspiration during ingestion of the irritant substance or during vomiting, whether caused by the gastric irritation of the toxin or by efforts to pass a stomach tube or induced to empty the stomach. The danger of aspiration is greatest with the low boiling point petroleum ether and less with kerosene.

Acute Intoxication

A. Manifestations: Nausea, vomiting, cough, pulmonary edema, pneumonitis, and, with large doses, central nervous system depression.

B. Treatment: Lavage adds to the risk of aspiration. It may be used if the less volatile substances have been ingested or if a cuffed endotracheal tube can be placed.

The central nervous system depression may require that respiration be assisted. Pneumonitis should be treated with oxygen and antibiotics.

Corticosteroids are often given to reduce pulmonary fibrosis. There is no evidence for or against their effectiveness. If the patient survives, resolution of the pulmonary infiltrate is usually complete regardless of the treatment.

Chronic Intoxication

A state of chronic intoxication occurs in workers

exposed for long periods to low concentrations and possibly in individuals who inhale hydrocarbons habitually. The resulting state is variable, but general slowing (depression), loss of memory, ataxia, and disturbances of speech are reported. Treatment consists entirely of removal from exposure.

2. AROMATIC HYDROCARBONS

Other hydrocarbons are generally anesthetics but lack the specific pulmonary toxicity.

Benzol

Benzol (benzene) and possibly toluene, an ingredient of the cement used in glue sniffing, can cause aplastic anemia. The bone marrow aplasia is not allergic in origin (see Chapter 6) but graded and dose-related. Long exposure is required, and a long latent period may be present.

Naphthalene

Naphthalene is a solid, and significant exposure requires ingestion. In individuals with a deficiency of glucose-6-phosphate dehydrogenase, it can cause hemolysis with anemia and renal tubular damage. Naphthalene can also cause dermatitis after industrial exposure. Toxicity is now uncommon since dichlorobenzene balls or insecticide sprays have replaced naphthalene as moth repellents.

3. HALOGENATED (CHLORINATED) HYDROCARBONS

These solvents are general anesthetics and are also hepatotoxic. Moreover, as was discussed in relation to halogenated hydrocarbons used as general anesthetics, they may be cardiotoxic. High concentrations in inspired air at the beginning of exposure may cause bradycardia or cardiac arrest. They also may sensitize the myocardium to the effects of epinephrine and norepinephrine in causing ventricular arrhythmias. However, the danger of arrhythmias after the use of sympathomimetic amines should be assumed to be present after the ingestion or inhalation of any of the hydrocarbons, whether halogenated or not.

Carbon Tetrachloride

Carbon tetrachloride is a nonflammable solvent, cleaner, and degreaser that is dangerous when inhaled, ingested, or absorbed through the skin. Its use in products sold for household use is now prohibited.

A. Acute Toxicity: The immediate effects are nausea and vomiting, signs of central nervous system depression ranging from confusion to coma, and respiratory depression. After 2 days to 2 weeks, signs of liver and kidney damage may appear. Fat accumulation in liver cells and centrilobular necrosis are manifest as jaundice and an enlarged, tender liver. Necrosis may be massive enough to be fatal. Oliguria or anuria results from renal tubular damage.

B. Chronic Toxicity: The above changes may occur following repeated smaller exposures.

C. Treatment: No specific treatment is available. As little as one swallow—perhaps as little as 4 mL by mouth—of carbon tetrachloride may be fatal. The toxicity is greatly increased by prior or concurrent ingestion of alcohol.

Other Halogenated Hydrocarbons

Trichloroethylene, which is used to some extent as a general anesthetic (or at least analgesic), is a substitute for carbon tetrachloride in household cleaners and in industry. It has caused hepatic damage but only after heavy exposure in industrial situations.

Tetrachloroethylene is a more potent central nervous system depressant than carbon tetrachloride and is also hepatotoxic.

Ethylene dichloride is a laboratory and industrial solvent as toxic as carbon tetrachloride. It is also a pulmonary irritant and can cause pulmonary edema.

Methyl bromide, a fumigant for grain, is also a pulmonary irritant.

The Freons used as propellants in spray cans are similar in effect to halothane (see Chapter 20). They are occasionally inhaled from a plastic bag for the pleasurable disinhibition provided. In at least 40 cases, death has resulted, presumably because the high initial concentration led to cardiac arrest.

ESTERS, KETONES, ETHERS

These compounds all produce some degree of central nervous system depression. Most cause irritation of the skin and mucous membranes. The number of compounds that may be encountered is very large, and one of the references listed at the end of Chapter 64 should be consulted for the toxicity of a specific poison. Innocuousness should not be assumed, although serious intoxication is unusual.

CAUSTICS & CORROSIVES

Many substances are local irritants but also exert important systemic effects. Identification of an environmental poison as having only local effects greatly simplifies treatment, but unfortunately some substances cause prolonged morbidity or death by a purely local action.

Substances that act as pulmonary or upper respiratory tract irritants are discussed in the next section. The remaining agents act on the cornea, the skin, or the gastrointestinal tract depending upon the nature of the exposure.

STRONG ACIDS & BASES

Ingestion of strong acids invariably causes death or prolonged morbidity; the estimated lethal dose is about 1 mL. Drain cleaners (Drano) contain sodium hydroxide; washing powders and dishwashing machine powders contain strongly alkaline phosphates; and ammonia is found in most households.

Ingestion

The results of ingestion of any caustic substance include burning pain in the mouth, pharynx, and abdomen; vomiting of material that contains blood; stains or burns around the mouth; shock; and (later) signs of perforation and peritoneal irritation.

Treatment must be immediate. Dilute the acid or alkali by forcing the patient to swallow large amounts of whatever is available—eg, water or milk. Fluids should be given repeatedly, even if the patient is vomiting, until the poison is diluted several hundred times. Gastric lavage can be performed only within the first hour; thereafter, the risk of perforation is too great. If a gastric tube is passed, it should be left in place until the possibility of perforation has been assessed. After extensive lavage or oral fluids, the poison can be neutralized with milk of magnesia (acid) or with fruit juice (alkali). Chemical neutralization applied prematurely will generate heat and increase damage.

Treat pain and shock as required. A demulcent such as milk or beaten eggs can be given hourly.

The danger of esophageal or gastric perforation is present for several weeks until the tissue destroyed by the caustic is replaced. Corticosteroids should be given (parenterally if necessary) to reduce fibrosis and the chance of an esophageal stricture.

Eye & Skin Contact

Follow the general directions provided in Chapter 64—eg, flood the eyes with water for 15 minutes while holding the lids apart.

OTHER LOCAL IRRITANTS

Bleaches

Common bleaching solutions are 3–6% sodium hypochlorite in water and are less dangerous than the strong bases just discussed. Esophageal damage is rare, and stricture has not been reported. The lethal dose for children is estimated as 15–30 mL. Bleaching solutions are discussed separately from the other alkalies to emphasize that a specific treatment is available. Sodium thiosulfate, 5–10 g in 200 mL of water, decomposes hypochlorite in the stomach and obviates the need for lavage. Bleach is an alkali, but no attempt should be made to neutralize it, since in the presence of acid, the even more irritant hypochlorous acid is formed.

Soaps & Detergents

Because they are easily accessible in every household, soaps and detergents are often accidentally ingested. Serious reactions are very rare.

A. Anionic and Nonionic Detergents: Anionic detergents are the ordinary soaps—ie, sodium or potassium salts of fatty acids—or the sulfonated hydrocarbon type of detergent found in many familiar household brands. In these compounds the anion rather than the sodium or other cation is responsible for the lowering of surface tension. By themselves they have not been dangerous. Nonionic detergents or surfactants are even less toxic.

However, these detergents are sold as mixtures with other ingredients, and in any individual case it must be determined whether the product contains dangerous amounts of alkali. Liquid detergents (for dishwashing) and granules (for laundry and general purposes) contain phosphate, silicates, and carbonates and are alkaline enough to cause gastroenteritis. It is difficult to imagine the ingestion of a dose large enough to justify lavage, but the material should be diluted with water or milk. Persistent vomiting or diarrhea may require care.

Powders for electric dishwashers contain more alkali, and immediate dilution with large volumes of fluid is required. Ingestion of large amounts of polyphosphate may bind calcium and cause tetany.

B. Cationic Detergents: These substances are used as disinfectants rather than cleaners. They are quaternary ammonium derivatives—ie, the surface active cation contains a charged nitrogen. Examples are methylbenzethonium (Diaparene) and benzalkonium (Zephiran). They are absorbed after ingestion and can cause systemic toxicity due to central nervous system stimulation (restlessness, confusion, convulsions, and coma) and muscle weakness progressing to respiratory paralysis. The effects are to some degree suggestive of the action of nicotine.

The cation of this type of detergent can be neutralized by the anion of soaps just as the germicidal action of one is destroyed by the other. A mild soap solution should be given by mouth. Other treatment is symptomatic.

AGENTS ACTING ON THE RESPIRATORY TRACT

GASES

An inhaled gas may simply be absorbed across the alveolar membrane and exert a systemic effect. However, there are gases that can act on the respiratory tract to cause serious or even lethal local effects without the appearance of systemic toxicity. It is these irritant gases that are emphasized in this section.

Gases may be classified according to their toxic effects as follows:

(1) Gases that are absorbed and exert anesthetic or other systemic effects.

(2) Asphyxiant gases: Simple asphyxiants exclude oxygen from the atmosphere and the lungs. Chemical asphyxiants—eg, cyanide or carbon monoxide—interfere with the transport or utilization of oxygen.

(3) Pulmonary irritants—eg, phosgene or nitric oxide—are agents that act on the lungs after a latent period to produce acute pulmonary edema with minimal or no irritation to the upper respiratory tract or other structures.

(4) Upper respiratory tract irritants—eg, ammonia, formaldehyde, sulfur dioxide—are irritant at once to the upper airway, the eyes, and even the skin.

(5) Upper respiratory tract and pulmonary irritant gases—eg, chlorine—can act in both ways.

1. PULMONARY IRRITANT GASES

Nitric oxide (brown N_2O_4 at room temperature; colorless NO_2 at elevated temperatures) is present in the smoke or fumes from some fires. It is evolved from fresh silage from heavily fertilized fields, and exposure in the confines of a silo can cause "silo-filler's disease." It is formed at the high temperatures reached in the cylinders of gasoline engines. The oxides of nitrogen emitted by automobile exhaust probably do not act as pulmonary irritants. They do, however, react with hydrocarbon fragments in the presence of ozone and sunlight to form the eye irritants of smog. **Chlorine** is not only used in industry but is occasionally generated in potentially dangerous amounts in the home by mixing bleach (hypochlorite) and vinegar or acid type toilet bowl cleaners. In a partially closed space—eg, a shower stall—dangerous concentrations can be reached. **Methyl bromide** (a fumigant), **ozone,** and **phosgene** are also pulmonary irritants.

Following exposure there is a latent period of 3 or more hours during which areas of hyperemic consolidation develop in the lungs that are apparent on x-ray as diffuse, granular changes. If the exposure was minimal, the patient may experience some dyspnea and feelings of tightness or oppression in the chest but will recover quickly. After greater exposures, the dyspnea may become intense and be accompanied by cyanosis and the production of frothy, bloody fluid as transudation fills the alveoli.

No specific treatment is agreed upon for this state. Oxygen and bronchial dilators may be used.

Recovery, if it occurs, involves a period of severe bronchial pneumonia. In a few patients who receive an exposure that is barely sublethal, a chronic form of obliterative pulmonary fibrosis may occur. This state is beginning to be designated adult respiratory distress.

2. UPPER RESPIRATORY TRACT IRRITANTS

Chlorine, ammonia, and sulfur dioxide cause conjunctivitis, pharyngitis, laryngitis, and tracheitis. With some concentrations, the irritation may be so intense that laryngospasm may occur. The mucosa may be edematous and hyperemic or, in the most severe cases, may slough.

3. CYANIDE

The cyanide ion stops cellular respiration and causes death so quickly that, practically speaking, treatment is possible only if the exposure is expected and treatment is at hand.

Hydrogen cyanide is used as a fumigant. Its salts are used in industry in synthetic, photographic, plating, and other processes. Exposure may be by ingestion or by inhaling hydrogen cyanide gas generated by the action of acids on sodium or potassium cyanide.

Cyanide can be released from glycosides that occur in plants. Other industrial or laboratory compounds may release cyanide—eg, cyanogen. Cyanide is not liberated by cyanamide, ferricyanide, or ferrocyanide.

The cyanide ion complexes with many metals. It combines with the ferric iron of cytochrome oxidase, which can then no longer act in electron transport. In the absence of cytochrome oxidase activity, oxygen is not utilized and organ function persists only as long as anaerobic metabolism can sustain it. Other metalloenzymes are less sensitive, but inhibition does occur.

Treatment

A. Inhalation: The crucial treatment for inhalation of hydrocyanic acid vapors is removal from the contaminated atmosphere. If the victim has a perceptible pulse or both a pulse and spontaneous respiration, recovery is probable if oxygen and assisted respiration are provided. If the victim is apneic and pulseless, resuscitation is attempted before the specific treatment (nitrites, sodium thiosulfate) described below is initiated.

B. Ingestion: After a brief period of respiratory stimulation due to an action on carotid chemoreceptors, dizziness, headache, fall in blood pressure, unconsciousness, convulsions, and respiratory arrest follow. Depending upon the dose, 1–15 minutes may be available for treatment.

Cyanide ingestion is one of the few situations in which specific treatment precedes general measures. Treatment includes the following:

1. Oxygen–Oxygen (100%) by mask should be provided. If the period of hyperpnea has passed, the victim should receive artificial respiration. There is no theoretic reason why oxygen should be of value in this situation, but both laboratory and clinical experience support its use.

2. Inhalation of amyl nitrite–Amyl nitrite is given by inhalation from a crushed ampule. The nitrite is rapidly absorbed in the lungs and converts some hemoglobin to methemoglobin, an oxidized form with iron in the ferric form. Cyanide complexes with such ferric iron and is not transferred to intracellular cytochrome oxidase.

3. Sodium nitrite–Amyl nitrite acts rapidly but forms methemoglobin less actively than sodium nitrite. As soon as possible, give sodium nitrite, 10 mL of 3% solution intravenously over a period of 2 minutes.

4. Sodium thiosulfate–Cyanide is converted in the liver to thiocyanate, which is virtually nontoxic. The reaction is governed by a transsulfurase, and the rate depends upon the amount of sulfur available. Thiosulfate permits the rapid transformation of cyanide (CN^-) to thiocyanate (SCN^-). Give 50 mL of 25% sodium thiosulfate intravenously over a period of 10 minutes.

4. CARBON MONOXIDE

Carbon monoxide is still among the most common causes of death by poisoning. Furthermore, it may be or may become an environmental hazard affecting whole populations.

The automobile engine and unvented gas heaters are the important nonindustrial sources of carbon monoxide. Smoking cigarettes or cigars adds to the exposure of the individual. Following explosions or fires, accumulation of carbon monoxide is more often a danger than is exhaustion of oxygen.

Carbon monoxide combines reversibly with hemoglobin at the same site (the ferrous iron) needed for the transport of oxygen. The affinity of carbon monoxide for this site is 200 times greater than that of oxygen. Carbon monoxide can therefore accumulate in the blood even when ambient concentrations are low.

The carboxyhemoglobin formed cannot carry oxygen and, in addition, further reduces the supply of oxygen to the tissues by shifting the dissociation curve of the remaining oxyhemoglobin to reduce transfer of oxygen to tissues. As a result, the dysfunction caused by changing 50% of the hemoglobin to carboxyhemoglobin is much greater than the effect of reducing the hemoglobin concentration 50% in an ordinary anemia.

The principal signs of carbon monoxide intoxication are those of hypoxia. The bright pink color imparted to the skin and mucous membranes by high concentrations of carboxyhemoglobin is seen only at autopsy. With prolonged severe exposure, bullous skin lesions may appear.

The symptoms of acute intoxication depend upon the fraction of hemoglobin converted to carboxyhemoglobin. The progression can be approximated as follows: (1) Decreased psychomotor ability. (2) Headache and a feeling of tightness in the temporal area. (3) Headache progresses and becomes throbbing, with confusion and loss of visual acuity. (Approximately 20–30% carboxyhemoglobin, or exposure to 500 ppm.) (4) Tachycardia, tachypnea, syncope, coma. (5) Deep coma, convulsions, shock, respiratory failure. (Approximately 60–90% carboxyhemoglobin, or exposure to 1000 ppm.)

Carbon monoxide and smoking. Cigarette smokers often reach 8% carboxyhemoglobin levels and, depending upon how many cigarettes they smoke each day and how much and how short they smoke each cigarette, may have twice that level. If the toxic action of CO is due entirely to a decrease in oxygen-carrying capacity, the amount of CO from cigarette smoking should be without toxic effect. The effect on oxygen dissociation in the tissues or combination with myoglobins is a possible additional factor because there are data that can be interpreted as incriminating CO in the well-established association between cigarette smoking and atherosclerotic heart disease. There is a better correlation with carboxyhemoglobin levels and the degree of atherosclerotic disease than with the smoking history expressed in number of cigarettes per day.

Treatment

The patient should be removed from exposure and put at rest to reduce oxygen need. Oxygen should be given under positive pressure. Hyperbaric oxygen is the best treatment, but the equipment required for its administration is not generally available.

The half-time for CO desaturation in room air is 4–6 hours, but in 100% oxygen even at atmospheric pressure it is less than 40 minutes. Recovery from the effects of prolonged hypoxia is not necessarily as rapid or as complete. Some patients (10% in a recent series) will be left with gross neurologic damage, and many appear to have persistent personality changes and impaired memory.

DUSTS

Dusts may settle on the surface of the body and cause local irritation or allergic reactions, or they may be inhaled and absorbed from the mucous membranes of the upper respiratory tract and cause systemic toxicity. There are, however, important problems in environmental medicine that are due to suspended dust particles small enough to be carried to the alveoli with inhaled air. In this context, dusts can be defined as solid particles 0.5–10 μm in size dispersed in air.

Dusts are classified according to toxic effects:

(1) Dusts causing systemic poisoning: If the solid is soluble or the particle small enough, it may be absorbed and thus cause systemic toxicity—eg, the dusts of the heavy metals and the insecticides already discussed.

(2) Dusts causing a febrile reaction—eg, the several metal fume fevers already discussed or the reaction to cotton dust.

(3) Dusts causing extensive pulmonary fibrosis—eg, silica and asbestos.

(4) Dusts causing minimal or no pulmonary fibrosis.

The states due to the inhalation of dusts that remain in the lungs are called pneumoconioses. A given pneumoconiosis may be malignant—eg, silicosis—or may not be symptomatic. The malignant pneumoconiosis or pulmonary fibrosis of berylliosis was discussed in the previous chapter with the metallic poisons. Silicosis and asbestosis are the other dangerous forms of dust disease.

Silicosis

Dusts of silica (silicon dioxide, SiO_2, quartz) are thrown into the air during rock cutting or grinding, abrasive manufacture, sandblasting, hard rock mining or tunneling, and pottery making. With the exception of the silicates in asbestos, mica, and talc, only silica causes progressive pulmonary fibrosis.

To be damaging, particles must be small enough to be carried to the alveolus—ie, less than 5–10 μm in size and most dangerous in the range 1–3 μm. If the particles are less than 0.5 μm in size, they are dissolved rapidly and a pulmonary reaction does not

occur. Depending upon the concentration and characteristics of the dust, exposure of 6 months to 25 years may lead to symptomatic silicosis, sometimes 5 years after the end of exposure.

Silica particles are removed from the circulation by phagocytic cells. Not all of the silica ingested by phagocytes reaches the lymph nodes, but some particles accumulate in the peribronchial and perivascular spaces. A fibrotic reaction is stimulated as the silica dissolves over a period of many years. The process, as seen on x-ray, is first diffusely granular, then more linear, and finally nodular.

The clinical picture is that of progressive obliterative pulmonary disease—ie, cough and exertional dyspnea. Tuberculosis superimposed on silicosis is more likely to be progressive.

There is no specific treatment. Positive pressure breathing with bronchial dilators may be helpful. Exposure to silica should be reduced to permissible levels. Silicosis is only very slowly progressive.

Silicate Dusts

Asbestos (various hydrated magnesium silicates) causes a pneumoconiosis in which the fibrosis is dense but linear rather than nodular. Asbestos bodies are found in the lungs and sputum. Asbestos is widely used as a fireproofing and insulating material, and recent studies of groups of construction workers establish not only that asbestosis is far more common than was previously realized but that the presently established limit (maximal allowable concentration of fibers in the air) is dangerously high. Asbestos or ferruginous bodies are seen in the lungs of urban residents who have had no known exposure.

Workers exposed to asbestos in the mines or working with asbestos insulation have an unexpectedly high incidence of mesothelioma of the pleura or peritoneum and of bronchogenic carcinoma. If they also smoke cigarettes, the incidence of carcinomas of the lung is about 92 times the expected rate.

Mica dust (aluminum silicates and other metals) and talc (magnesium silicate) can also cause pulmonary fibrosis.

Coal Workers' Pneumoconiosis

The idea that coal dust containing no silica could

Table 66–1. Effects of inhalation of miscellaneous dusts not discussed in the text.

	Clinical Findings	X-Ray Pattern	Prognosis
Barium sulfate (barite) Iron oxide Tin oxide	None	Stippled or nodular pattern due to radiopacity of insoluble metal salt	Nonprogressive
Cotton dust	Emphysema, bronchitis (byssinosis)	Emphysema	Nonprogressive if exposure terminated
Mold hay or grain*	Dyspnea, fever, bronchial pneumonia (farmer's lung)	Diffuse mottling	Nonprogressive
Sugar cane dust (bagasse*)	Chills and fever, pneumonitis, dyspnea	Diffuse mottling	Nonprogressive after acute episode
Glass fiber, rock wool	Dermatitis, folliculitis	. . .	Tolerance develops

*Reaction, probably allergic, to contaminating actinomycete.

lead to slowly progressive, fatal pulmonary disease has been difficult to establish. Yet the "black lungs" of coal miners show a high incidence of pulmonary fibrosis, dilated respiratory bronchioles in areas of deposited dust, and emphysema. For many years in this country, the relation to occupation was generally denied and compensation withheld, probably because the grave clinical picture was associated with disproportionately minor radiologic changes. In 1969, however, federal legislation acknowledged the relationship to employment that had been accepted in Britain since 1934 and at the same time required programs of dust suppression in the mines.

Other Dusts

Bauxite (an aluminum ore) is converted in electric furnaces to alundum or corundum (Al_2O_3). Inhalation of fumes from this source has caused a progressive, linear fibrosis complicated by episodes of pneumothorax. Silica is present in the fumes and in the lungs, and the role of the aluminum oxide is not known.

The effects of some additional dusts are summarized in Table 66–1.

•   •   •

References
(See also texts and manuals listed in Chapter 64.)

Hydrocarbons

Baldachin BJ, Melmed RN: Clinical and therapeutic aspects of kerosene poisoning: A series of 200 cases. Br Med J 2:28, 1964.

Jamison KE, Wallace ER: Kerosene pneumonitis treated with adrenal steroids. Calif Med 100:43, 1964.

Knox JW, Nelson JR: Permanent encephalopathy from toluene inhalation. N Engl J Med 275:1494, 1966.

Vigliani EC, Saita G: Benzene and leukemia. N Engl J Med 271:872, 1964.

Dusts & Gases

Bodansky O: Methemoglobinemia and methemoglobin-producing compounds. Pharmacol Rev 3:144, 1951.

Cope C: The importance of oxygen in the treatment of cyanide poisoning. JAMA 175:1061, 1961.

Finck PA: Exposure to carbon monoxide: Review of the literature and 567 autopsies. Milit Med 131:1513, 1966.

Ivanhoe F, Meyers FH: Phosgene poisoning as an example of neuroparalytic acute pulmonary edema: The sympathetic vasomotor reflex involved. Dis Chest 46:211, 1964.

Kleinfeld M, Messite J, Shapiro J: Clinical, radiological, and physiological findings in asbestosis. Arch Intern Med 117:813, 1966.

Lave LB, Seskin EP: Air pollution and human health. Science 169:723, 1970.

Murphy RLH & others: Effects of low concentrations of asbestos. N Engl J Med 285:1271, 1971.

Naeye RL: Black lung disease: The anthracotic pneumoconioses. Pathol Annu 8:349, 1973.

Ryder R & others: Emphysema in coal workers' pneumoconiosis. Br Med J 2:481, 1970.

Selikoff IJ, Hammond EC, Churg J: Asbestos exposure, smoking, and neoplasia. JAMA 204:106, 1968.

Smith JS, Brandon S: Morbidity from acute carbon monoxide poisoning at three-year follow-up. Br Med J 1:318, 1973.

Waldbott GL: *Health Effects of Environmental Pollutants.* Mosby, 1973.

Pesticides

Frazer AC: Pesticides. Annu Rev Pharmacol 7:319, 1967.

Hayes WJ Jr, Dale WE, Pirkle CI: Evidence of safety of long-term, high, oral doses of DDT for man. Arch Environ Health 22:119, 1971.

Hoffman WS & others: The relation of pesticide concentrations in fat to pathological changes in tissues. Arch Environ Health 15:758, 1967.

Quinby GE & others: DDT storage in the US population. JAMA 191:175, 1965.

Upholt WM, Kearney PC: Pesticides. N Engl J Med 275:1419, 1966.

Woodwell GM, Wurster CF Jr, Isaacson PA: DDT residues in an east coast estuary: A case of biological concentration of a persistent insecticide. Science 156:821, 1967.

Other Agents

Arena JM: Poisonings and other health hazards associated with use of detergents. JAMA 190:56, 1964.

Coon JM, Maynard EA (editors): Problems in toxicology. Fed Proc 19(3) (Suppl):1, 1960.

Fairshter RD, Wilson AF: Paraquat poisoning. Am J Med 59:751, 1975.

Gerarde HW: Toxicology: Organic. Annu Rev Pharmacol 4:223, 1964.

Roush G Jr, Kehoe RA: Toxicology: Inorganic. Annu Rev Pharmacol 4:247, 1964.

Appendix

THE EFFECTS OF DRUGS ON COMMON CLINICAL LABORATORY PROCEDURES
(Table 1)

With the increasing number of available drugs and the increasing number and complexity of tests performed by the clinical laboratory, drug-induced interference with test results is occurring with greater frequency. Table 1 has been prepared to assist clinicians and laboratory personnel in identifying such drug effects. In an effort to keep the information clinically relevant, no information from in vitro or animal studies has been included.

Although an effort has been made to cover each area thoroughly, it is inevitable that a listing of this type will be incomplete. The reader may wish to add to the chart on the basis of personal reading and experience.

Types of Drug Interference

Alterations in clinical laboratory results caused by drugs may be grouped into 2 general categories:

A. Effects Due to Pharmacologic or Toxic Properties of Drugs: Here, a physiologic change is produced in the level of the parameter being measured. In Table 1, changes of this nature are designated as increase (+) or decrease (−). The magnitude of the change depends upon a variety of factors such as dosage of drug, duration of administration, condition of patient, etc.

B. Effects Due to Interference With the Testing Procedure: In this case, the drug or its metabolite becomes a contaminant that may alter the value obtained or interfere with the measurement. This type of interference is indicated in Table 1 as increase (●) or decrease (○). It should be noted that drugs may affect one method of performing a given laboratory procedure and have no effect on another. For this reason, the specific testing method affected has been specified whenever possible.

Arrangement of Table 1

Table 1 lists the drugs that may affect the results of the laboratory tests indicated at the top. Tests less commonly influenced by drug administration are included in the column headed Other Tests.

All drugs are listed alphabetically by generic name, with common trade names and other names in parentheses. Some general drug classifications have been used. If a drug falls into one of the categories listed below, it should be sought under that general classification.

Aluminum antacids
Aminoglycosides
Anabolic steroids
Barbiturates
Calcium antacids
Cephalosporins
Contrast media, iodine-containing
Corticosteroids
Digitalis glycosides
Estrogens
Gold salts
Indandiones
Inorganic iodides
Iron, oral
Mercurial kiuretics
Monoamine oxidase inhibitors
Oral contraceptives
Phenothiazines
Progestogens
Salicylates
Sulfonamides
Tetracyclines
Thiazide diuretics
Tricyclic antipressants

DRUGS HAZARDOUS FOR USE DURING PREGNANCY
(Table 2)

The teratogenic and other ill effects on the fetus of drugs taken during pregnancy are of concern to obstetricians and other physicians and to the regulatory agencies that must authorize the manufacture and distribution of drugs that may be used by this group of patients. Evidence of safety during pregnancy may be more difficult to establish than evidence of teratogenicity, and a conservative attitude toward the use of drugs in pregnant women errs, if at all, in the right direction.

Drugs that have been shown or are assumed to be dangerous during pregnancy are listed in Table 2.

Table 1 is prepared by Philip Hansten, PharmD, Associate Professor of Clinical Pharmacology, College of Pharmacy, Washington State University, Pullman, Washington; and Lisa Lybecker, BPharm, College of Pharmacy, Washington State University, Pullman, Washington.

Table 1. Effects of drugs on common laboratory tests.

+ = Increase (pharmacologic or toxic effect) ● = Increase (test interference)
− = Decrease (pharmacologic or toxic effect) ○ = Decrease (test interference)
N = See notes (below) ★ = Present or positive

	BLOOD, SERUM, OR PLASMA													URINE										OTHER TESTS
	Amylase	Bilirubin	Cholesterol	Coombs (Direct)	CPK	Glucose	Thyroxine	Phosphatase, Alk.	Potassium	Prothrombin Time	SGOT and SGPT	Urea Nitrogen	Uric Acid	Color	Catecholamines	Glucose (Benedict)	5-HIAA	Ketones	Porphyrins	Protein	Steroids	Urobilinogen	VMA	
Acetaminophen		N		★		N											N							
Acetazolamide (Diamox)		+				−		−		+	+		+							●		+		Blood ammonia +
Acetohexamide (Dymelor)		−				−	+						−				−							
Alcohol, ethyl	+	−		N	N				N	N	N		N	N	+				N					Serum aldolase (N); Serum lactate +
Allopurinol (Zyloprim)		+					+			+	+		−											
Aluminum antacids								+			+	+												Serum phosphate −
Aminocaproic acid (Amicar)			N	+																				
Aminoglycosides										+									N	★		N		Blood ammonia (N); Serum magnesium (N); Urine estriol (N)
Aminophylline	N												N		+									
Aminosalicylic acid (PAS)		−						−	+	+		+		N		●		N						
Amphotericin B (Fungizone)	+	+		+	N	−		−	+	+	+	+	N											
Ampicillin			★	N	N					+	+	N							N	★				Urine estriol −
Anabolic steroids									N	+		N	N								N			
Ascorbic acid	+	+				−						N	N								N			
Azathioprine (Imuran)	N	−					+		N	+														
Barbiturates	N						N												N					
Bromsulphalein (BSP)							N											N				●		Metyrapone response −
Caffeine					+		+						N	+	+							●		
Calcium antacids																								
Carbamazepine (Tegretol)	N	N					+		N	+		N								N				Serum calcium (N)

Acetaminophen:
Overdose may produce liver damage with hyperbilirubinemia.
Hypoglycemia has been reported with large doses, but false decreases have also been reported (glucose oxidase-peroxidase method).
May cause false increases in urinary 5-HIAA (screening methods using nitrosonaphthol reagent).

Alcohol, ethyl:
Acute intoxication may produce myopathy, with elevation of serum aldolase, CPK, and SGOT.
Acute intoxication may enhance hypoprothrombinemic effect of oral anticoagulants.
Acute intoxication may increase serum uric acid, while chronic alcoholism may result in hypouricemia.
The diuresis produced results in a lighter urine.
Attacks of acute intermittent porphyria may be precipitated by ethanol.

Allopurinol:
May enhance hypoprothrombinemic effect of oral anticoagulants.

Aminoglycosides:
Oral aminoglycosides may decrease serum cholesterol.
Oral aminoglycosides may reduce urinary urobilinogen.
Oral aminoglycosides may decrease blood ammonia in patients with hepatic disease.
Gentamicin has been associated with decreased serum magnesium.
Oral aminoglycosides may decrease urinary estrogen excretion.

Aminophylline:
May produce false increases in serum uric acid when done by an adaptation of the method of Bittner (Am J Clin Pathol 40:423, 1963).

Aminosalicylic acid:
Reportedly may produce acute pancreatitis with elevated serum amylase.
May cause reddening of the urine if toilet bowl recently cleaned with hypochlorite bleach.
Will produce yellow color with Ehrlich's reagent test for porphobilinogen or urobilinogen.

Ampicillin:
Intramuscular ampicillin may result in increased serum CPK levels.

Anabolic steroids:
May decrease blood glucose in diabetic patients.
May enhance hypoprothrombinemic effect of oral anticoagulants.
Norethandrolone (Nilevar) may elevate SGOT.
Testosterone treatment increases urinary excretion of 17-ketosteroids, whereas methyltestosterone does not appear in the urine.

Ascorbic acid:
May produce false elevations in uric acid determinations (except enzymatic methods).
Large doses may produce false-positives by copper reduction methods (eg, Clinitest), and false negatives by glucose oxidase methods (eg, Clinistix, Tes-Tape).
May interfere with the determination of urinary 17-hydroxycorticosteroids by a modification of the Reddy, Jenkins, Thorn procedure (Metabolism 1:511, 1952; 3:489, 1954).

Azathioprine:
Pancreatitis has been reported following azathioprine administration.
May decrease serum uric acid in patients with gout.

Barbiturates:
Serum amylase may be decreased in barbiturate poisoning.
Prolonged use of barbiturates as anticonvulsants has resulted in osteomalacia with elevated serum alkaline phosphatase.
May inhibit hypoprothrombinemic effect of oral anticoagulants.
Attacks of acute intermittent porphyria may be precipitated by barbiturates.

Bromsulphalein (BSP):
May interfere with alkaline phosphatase determinations.
May produce false-positive tests for acetone by reacting with sodium nitroprusside (as found in some reagent strips).

Caffeine:
Coffee reportedly may result in spurious elevations in serum uric acid as done by an adaptation of the method of Bittner (Am J Clin Pathol 40:423, 1963).

Calcium antacids:
Large doses of calcium carbonate may produce hypercalcemia.

Carbamazepine:
Jaundice has occurred; incidence must await further trials.
May inhibit hypoprothrombinemic effect of oral anticoagulants.
May produce false-positive Zimmermann reaction for 17-ketosteroids and 17-hydroxycorticosteroids.

Table 1 (cont'd). Effects of drugs on common laboratory tests.

Legend:

+ = Increase (pharmacologic or toxic effect)
− = Decrease (pharmacologic or toxic effect)
N = See notes (below)
● = Increase (test interference)
○ = Decrease (test interference)
★ = Present or positive

	BLOOD, SERUM, OR PLASMA													URINE										OTHER TESTS
	Amylase	Bilirubin	Cholesterol	Coombs (Direct)	CPK	Glucose	Thyroxine	Phosphatase, Alk.	Potassium	Prothrombin Time	SGOT and SGPT	Urea Nitrogen	Uric Acid	Color	Catecholamines	Glucose (Benedict)	5-HIAA	Ketones	Porphyrins	Protein	Steroids	Urobilinogen	VMA	
Carbenicillin (Geopen, Pyopen)									−															
Cephalosporins				★	N			+		+		N			N	N			N	★	N			
Chloral hydrate (Noctec)										N		N			N	●			N		N	−		
Chloramphenicol (Chloromycetin)																●								
Chlordiazepoxide (Librium)		+												N										
Chloroquine (Aralen)																								
Chlorpropamide (Diabinese)		+	−	★	N			+		+									N					Serum calcium +
Chlorthalidone (Hygroton)						+						+	+											Blood ammonia +
Chlorzoxazone (Paraflex)		+												N										
Cholestyramine (Cuemid)			−							+														Serum chloride (N)
Cimetidine (Tagamet)										N														Serum creatinine +; Serum prolactin +
Cisplatin (Platinol)											+	+	+											Serum magnesium −
Clindamycin (Cleocin)					N						+													
Clofibrate (Atromid-S)			−		+	N				N	+		−											Serum aldolase +
Clonidine (Catapres)															N								−	Plasma growth hormone +
Cloxacillin (Tegopen)										+	N													
Codeine	N																							
Colchicine			−																					
Colistin (Coly-Mycin)	N	N																		★				
Contrast media, iodine-containing	N	N							N			−			N	N				N	N		−	
Corticosteroids		+	+		+	+			N		+	N			+	+					N			Urine estriol −
Cyclophosphamide (Cytoxan)									N															Serum cholinesterase −

Carbenicillin:
Intramuscular administration may result in increased serum CPK levels.

Cephalosporins:
Larger doses may adversely affect renal function, with elevation of the BUN. Cephalothin may form an interfering dark color in Benedict's test for urinary glucose.
Large doses of cephalothin may produce false increases in urinary 17-ketosteroids (Zimmermann reaction).

Chloral hydrate:
May transiently increase the hypoprothrombinemic response to oral anticoagulants.
Large doses reportedly may cause false elevation of BUN (nesslerization technic), but more study is needed.
Attacks of acute intermittent porphyria may be precipitated.
May interfere with fluorimetric test for urine catecholamines.
May interfere with the determination of urinary 17-hydroxycorticosteroids by a modification of the Reddy, Jenkins, Thorn procedure (Metabolism 1:511, 1952; 3:489, 1954).

Chloroquine:
May color urine rusty yellow or brown.
May be a precipitating factor for porphyria.

Chlorpropamide:
May be a precipitating factor in porphyria.

Chlorthalidone:
Has produced pancreatitis, with resultant increase in serum amylase. Excessive use has produced hypokalemic myopathy with elevated CPK.

Chlorzoxazone:
May color urine orange or purplish-red.

Cholestyramine:
Has produced hyperchloremic acidosis in children.
Absorption of orally administered thyroid hormones is decreased if cholestyramine is given within several hours.

Cimetidine:
May enhance hypoprothrombinemic effect of oral anticoagulants.

Clindamycin:
Intramuscular administration of clindamycin appears to increase serum CPK levels in a majority of patients.

Clofibrate:
Glucose tolerance tends to improve in diabetics receiving clofibrate.
May enhance the hypoprothrombinemic effect of oral anticoagulants.

Clonidine:
Chronic therapy reduces urine catecholamines, but abrupt withdrawal may increase them.

Codeine:
May elevate serum amylase, but less potent than other opiates (eg, morphine) in this regard.
May produce elevated transaminase levels in certain patients.

Colchicine:
Reported to have an unpredictable antithyroid effect.

Contrast media, iodine-containing:
Cholangiography may result in transient elevations of serum amylase.
Cholecystographic media can result in increased serum bilirubin.
May see false decreases in urinary metanephrines (Crout modification of Pisano method).
Sodium diatrizoate (Hypaque) may form a black color in Benedict's tests for glucose.
Iodoalphionic acid (Priodax), iopanoic acid (Telepaque), and sodium diatrizoate (Hypaque) may give false-positives with sulfosalicylic acid and nitric acid, but not with heat and acetic acid.
May decrease values for 17-ketogenic steroids (Rutherford-Nelson method).

Corticosteroids:
Have produced pancreatitis, with resultant increase in serum amylase.
May increase the requirement for coumarin anticoagulants.
Corticosteroids are weak uricosurics, but may produce severe hyperuricemia in patients with acute leukemia.
Potent corticosteroids decrease urinary 17-ketosteroid and 17-hydroxycorticosteroid excretion.

Cyclophosphamide:
Rapid lysis of tumor cells in patients with lymphomas or leukemias may result in hyperkalemia.

Table 1 (cont'd). Effects of drugs on common laboratory tests.

+ = Increase (pharmacologic or toxic effect)
− = Decrease (pharmacologic or toxic effect)
N = See notes (below)
● = Increase (test interference)
○ = Decrease (test interference)
★ = Present or positive

Drug	Amylase	Bilirubin	Cholesterol	Coombs (Direct)	CPK	Glucose	Thyroxine	Phosphatase, Alk.	Potassium	Prothrombin Time	SGOT and SGPT	Urea Nitrogen	Uric Acid	Color	Catecholamines	Glucose (Benedict)	5-HIAA	Ketones	Porphyrins	Protein	Steroids	Urobilinogen	VMA	Other Tests
Cyproheptadine (Periactin)	+					N																		
Dextrothyroxine (Choloxin)			−			+	+																	
Diazoxide (Hyperstat)						+			N		N	+	+			+								
Dicumarol										+			−			+								
Digitalis glycosides					N																			
Disulfiram (Antabuse)		+	N			+	+	+		N	+													Serum estrogen +
Epinephrine						+									−								N	
Erythromycin		N													N									
Estrogens	N	+	N			+	+	+		N	N	+	+		N	+				N	N			Serum ceruloplasmin + ; Plasma cortisol +
Ethacrynic acid (Edecrin)	N					N		−	−			N	N							N	N			
Ethchlorvynol (Placidyl)																								
Ethinamate (Valmid)									N											N	N			
Ethionamide (Trecator)		+				−	+				+													
Ethoxazene (Serenium)																								
Furazolidone (Furoxone)								+		+	+	+		N										Urine bilirubin (N)
Furosemide (Lasix)	N					+	+	+	−			+	+	N					N					
Glucagon						+		−	N															Blood ammonia +
Glucose infusions						+						−	−		N									Serum calcium −
Glutethimide (Doriden)							N		N															Blood ammonia (N)
Glyceryl guaiacolate (Robitussin)												−	−										N	
Gold salts		+					+									●			★					Serum proteins (N)
Griseofulvin (Fulvicin, Grifulvin)									N									N	★			N		

Cyproheptadine

Although depression of fasting blood glucose has been reported, subsequent studies have not confirmed this.

Dextrothyroxine:

Enhances hypoprothrombinemic effect of oral anticoagulants.

Digitalis glycosides:

Intramuscular digoxin may increase serum CPK.

Disulfiram:

Inhibits decrease in serum cholesterol which normally occurs when alcoholics abstain.

Enhances hypoprothrombinemic effect of oral anticoagulants.

Epinephrine:

Epinephrine and related agents used in asthma by inhalation may increase urinary catecholamines and urinary VMA.

Erythromycin:

The estolate salt may produce cholestatic hepatitis with elevated bilirubin levels.

May cause false increase of transaminases done by colorimetric methods. The estolate salt may produce true increases in transaminase due to hepatic toxicity.

May produce false elevation in fluorimetric determinations for urinary catecholamines.

Estrogens:

Oral contraceptives have been associated with pancreatitis and elevated serum amylase.

Cholesterol usually unchanged or decreased in postmenopausal women. Massive elevation of cholesterol and triglyceride occasionally reported.

May increase cortisol-binding proteins, resulting in moderate decrease in urinary 17-ketosteroids and 17-hydroxycorticosteroids.

Ethacrynic acid:

Has been implicated in the production of pancreatitis, with resultant increase in serum amylase.

Both hypoglycemia (in uremic patients) and hyperglycemia (in diabetics) have been reported.

May cause uricosuria if given intravenously and urate retention if given orally.

May slightly decrease urinary cortisol excretion.

Ethchlorvynol:

May depress the anticoagulant activity of the coumarin anticoagulants.

Ethinamate:

May markedly increase the absorption in 17-ketosteroid determinations (modified Zimmermann reaction).

Ethoxazene:

May color urine orange to orange-red.

May produce falsely high readings in the assay of porphyrins by spectrophotofluorimetry.

May produce interfering color for urine bilirubin by Bili-Labstix or Ictotest.

Furazolidone:

May color urine brown.

Furosemide:

Has precipitated pancreatitis, with resultant increase in serum amylase.

Glucagon:

May enhance response to oral anticoagulants.

Glucose:

Intravenous glucose may produce glycosuria in some patients.

Some studies have shown that a large glucose load may increase blood ammonia in patients with cirrhosis and portasystemic shunts; however, further studies have indicated that this effect is small.

Glutethimide:

Long-term use occasionally results in osteomalacia with elevated alkaline phosphatase.

May enhance metabolism of coumarin anticoagulants.

Glyceryl guaiacolate:

May cause a color change during screening methods for VMA, but final measurement apparently is not affected.

Gold:

Gold-induced nephrotic syndrome of colitis may lower serum albumin, globulins, or both.

Griseofulvin:

May depress anticoagulant activity of coumarin anticoagulants.

May precipitate acute attack in patients with porphyria.

Table 1 (cont'd). Effects of drugs on common laboratory tests.

+ = Increase (pharmacologic or toxic effect)
− = Decrease (pharmacologic or toxic effect)
N = See notes (below)

● = Increase (test interference)
○ = Decrease (test interference)
★ = Present or positive

Drug	Amylase	Bilirubin	Cholesterol	Coombs (Direct)	CPK	Glucose	Thyroxine	Phosphatase, Alk.	Potassium	Prothrombin Time	SGOT and SGPT	Urea Nitrogen	Uric Acid	Color	Catecholamines	Glucose (Benedict)	5-HIAA	Ketones	Porphyrins	Protein	Steroids	Urobilinogen	VMA	Other Tests
Guanethidine (Ismelin)						N									−								−	
Heparin			−	N		N											N							
Hydralazine (Apresoline)				★					+															
Hydroxyzine (Atarax, Vistaril)		+																			N			
Imipramine (Tofranil)		+			+		+																	
Indandiones								+		+	+			N										
Indomethacin (Indocin)				★					+		+	+	−			−			★	★				
Insulin						−																		Serum calcium −
Iodides, inorganic							N																	Stool blood (N)
Iron, oral						+																		Blood ammonia (N)
Isoniazid (INH)				★		+					+													Blood lactate (N)
Levodopa (L-dopa)				★									N	N	N	N	N							
Levothyroxine (Synthroid)						N	+						N		N	−	N					N	N	
Lidocaine					N																			
Lithium carbonate						+	−								+									
Mefenamic acid (Ponstel)				N					N	N						●			★	★				Urine bilirubin ●
Meperidine (Demerol)	+					+	−								N								N	
Mephenesin (Sinan, Tolserol)	+																			N				
Meprobamate (Equanil, Miltown)										N														Metyrapone response −
Mercurial diuretics												+			N									

Guanethidine:
Has antidiabetic activity and may decrease insulin requirements.

Heparin:
In acquired hemolytic anemia, heparin may cause the direct Coombs test to become negative.
Reportedly may increase blood glucose; confirmation is needed.
May decrease urinary 5-HIAA excretion in patients with carcinoid syndrome.

Hydroxyzine:
May falsely increase the reading for 17-hydroxycorticosteroids (modified Glenn-Nelson technic).

Indandiones:
May color the urine orange.

Indomethacin:
Has produced pancreatitis, with resultant increase in serum amylase.
Hyperkalemia has occurred in some patients, and in others the hypokalemia of Bartter's syndrome has improved.

Inorganic iodides:
Occasionally produce thyrotoxicosis with elevated serum thyroxine.
May interfere with the determination of urinary 17-hydroxycorticosteroids by a modification of the Reddy, Jenkins, Thorn procedure (Metabolism 1:511, 1952; 3:489, 1954).

Insulin:
Insulin-induced hypoglycemia results in release of epinephrine, thus increasing urinary excretion.

Iron, oral:
Administration of ferrous sulfate and ferrous fumarate has resulted in false-positive benzidine tests for occult blood in the stools.

Isoniazid:
Both true glycosuria and false-positive Benedict's tests have been reported. Acetonuria may occur with isoniazid intoxication.
Although isoniazid is reported to increase blood ammonia, some studies have failed to confirm this.
Isoniazid intoxication may increase serum lactate.

Levodopa:
May produce false increases for serum uric acid by colorimetric methods but not when uricase is used. True increases also reported.
Urine may darken on standing.
Both false-positive Clinitest and false-negative glucose oxidase reactions may occur, especially with large doses.
May interfere with ferric chloride tests for urine ketones, Ketostix, and possibly Acetest.
Small increase in urinary VMA excretion, but VMA measured by Pisano method may be falsely decreased.

Levothyroxine:
Serum thyroxine levels increased to normal or above normal in adequately treated patients.
Increasing thyroid hormone activity enhances anticoagulant effect of coumarins.

Lidocaine:
Intramuscular lidocaine may increase serum CPK.

Lithium carbonate:
Preliminary studies indicate that urinary VMA excretion may be somewhat increased.

Mefenamic acid:
Autoimmune hemolytic anemia may occur after prolonged therapy.
May increase response to oral anticoagulants.

Meperidine:
May elevate transaminase levels in certain patients.

Mephenesin:
May cause color changes during screening methods for VMA, but final measurement apparently is not affected.

Meprobamate:
May increase the absorbance in measurements for 17-ketosteroids (Zimmermann reaction).

Mercurial diuretics:
Meralluride (Mercuhydrin) may produce false-negatives for urinary glucose as measured by glucose oxidase methods (eg, Clinistix, Tes-Tape).

Table 1 (cont'd). Effects of drugs on common laboratory tests.

+ = Increase (pharmacologic or toxic effect)   ● = Increase (test interference)
− = Decrease (pharmacologic or toxic effect)   ○ = Decrease (test interference)
N = See notes (below)   ★ = Present or positive

Drug	Amylase	Bilirubin	Cholesterol	Coombs (Direct)	CPK	Glucose	Thyroxine	Phosphatase, Alk.	Potassium	Prothrombin Time	SGOT and SGPT	Urea Nitrogen	Uric Acid	Color	Catecholamines	Glucose (Benedict)	5-HIAA	Ketones	Porphyrins	Protein	Steroids	Urobilinogen	VMA	Other Tests
Metaxalone (Skelaxin)																	●			N				
Methenamine (Mandelamine, Uritone)																●				★	N	N		Urine estriol ○
Methicillin (Dimocillin, Staphcillin)												+											N	
Methocarbamol (Robaxin)												N	N	N										
Methotrexate		+									+	+												
Methyldopa (Aldomet)	N	+		★			+	+		+	+	N		N	●	−							N	
Methylene blue											+			N										
Metronidazole (Flagyl)									N					N			−		N					
Miconazole (Monistat i.v.)	+	+	+			−										−	−							Serum triglycerides +
Monoamine oxidase inhibitors (MAOI)									N								−						−	Blood ammonia (N); Metyrapone response (N); Serum cholinesterase (N)
Morphine	+	+								N	N				●					N				
Nafcillin (Unipen)	+									+	+													
Nalidixic acid (NegGram)		−				N				+	+				●									
Nicotinic acid (large doses)	+	+				+				+	+		+		N	●								
Nitrofurantoin (Furadantin)	N	N				+	+	+		+	+	+		N	N									
Nitroglycerin	+										+				+								+	
Novobiocin (Albamycin)	N	N																						
Oral contraceptives	N	N	N			+	+			+	N					−		N	N		N			Metyrapone response −
Oxacillin (Prostaphlin)										+	+									N				
Pargyline (Eutonyl)						−										−								
Penicillamine (Cuprimine)								N											★	★			−	
Penicillin G				★											●	●				N				

Metaxalone:
Implicated in the production of proteinuria.

Methenamine:
Produces false elevation in urinary 17-hydroxycorticosteroids by method of Reddy (Metabolism 3:489, 1954).
May interfere with tests for urinary urobilinogen.

Methocarbamol:
Parenteral preparations may contain polyethylene glycol, which may increase urea retention in patients with renal impairment.
Urine may darken on standing.
May produce false increases in urinary VMA by screening method of Gitlow but not in quantitative procedure of Sunderman.

Methotrexate:
Nephropathy with elevated urea nitrogen has been reported.
Hyperuricemia may occur due to rapid lysis of tumor cells.

Methyldopa:
May produce sialadenitis with increased amylase.
Urine may darken on standing.
Does not appreciably affect VMA determinations.

Methylene blue:
Colors the urine blue.

Metronidazole:
Enhances hypoprothrombinemic effect of oral anticoagulants.
May cause darkening of urine.

Miconazole:
May enhance hypoprothrombinemic effect of oral anticoagulants.

Monoamine oxidase inhibitors:
Although MAO inhibitors have been reported to reduce blood ammonia, some of these agents have produced hepatotoxicity and thus could be dangerous in patients with impaired liver function.
Nialamide may decrease the response to metyrapone.
Phenelzine (Nardil) may decrease serum cholinesterase levels.

Morphine:
May elevate transaminase levels in certain patients.
Attacks of acute intermittent porphyria may be precipitated.

Nafcillin:
Large doses may produce false-positives for urine protein (sulfosalicylic acid method).

Nalidixic acid:
Large doses or overdoses may produce false elevations in blood glucose (Somogyi-Nelson procedure).
May cause false elevation of urinary 17-ketosteroids (Zimmermann reaction).

Nicotinic acid:
May impair glucose tolerance, resulting in glycosuria.

Nitrofurantoin:
Cholestatic jaundice occasionally occurs following nitrofurantoin.
May tint urine brown.

Novobiocin:
May produce jaundice with an increase in unconjugated but not conjugated bilirubin in plasma; also, a yellow pigment may occur in the plasma which interferes with icterus index and bilirubin determinations.

Oral contraceptives:
Hyperlipidemic patients have developed pancreatitis following initiation of oral contraceptive use.
Oral contraceptives have been reported to elevate serum cholesterol.
A decrease in the hypoprothrombinemic effect of bishydroxycoumarin may occur.
May affect the handling of porphyrins by the liver; urinary coproporphyrin excretion may be increased.
The estrogenic component may increase cortisol-binding proteins, resulting in a moderate decrease in urinary 17-ketosteroids and 17-hydroxycorticosteroids.

Oxacillin:
High doses in infants may cause azotemia and proteinuria.

Penicillin G:
Massive intravenous doses of penicillin G sodium may produce hypokalemia.
Penicillin G potassium can produce hyperkalemia.
Massive doses may yield false-positive results for proteinuria when turbidity measures are used (eg, heat and acetic acid, sulfosalicylic acid).
Intravenous doses may produce false elevations of 17-ketogenic steroids (Norymberski method) and a less marked increase in 17-ketosteroid determinations (Zimmerman reaction).

Table 1 (cont'd). Effects of drugs on common laboratory tests.

+ = Increase (pharmacologic or toxic effect)
− = Decrease (pharmacologic or toxic effect)
N = See notes (below)
● = Increase (test interference)
○ = Decrease (test interference)
★ = Present or positive

Drug	BLOOD, SERUM, OR PLASMA													URINE										OTHER TESTS
	Amylase	Bilirubin	Cholesterol	Coombs (Direct)	CPK	Glucose	Thyroxine	Phosphatase, Alk.	Potassium	Prothrombin Time	SGOT and SGPT	Urea Nitrogen	Uric Acid	Color	Catecholamines	Glucose (Benedict)	5-HIAA	Ketones	Porphyrins	Protein	Steroids	Urobilinogen	VMA	
Pentazocine (Talwin)	N																							Urine bilirubin ●
Phenazopyridine (Pyridium)														N				N	N	N	N	N		
Phenolphthalein	+	+												N										
Phenothiazines					N	+								N		○					N	●		Metyrapone response −
Phensuximide (Milontin)	N	N					+				+		N										N	
Phenylbutazone (Butazolidin)	N	N					+			N			−											
Phenytoin (Dilantin)						+	−							N										Metyrapone response −; Serum calcium −
Polymyxin B (Aerosporin)												+								★				
Primaquine															●									
Probenecid (Benemid)	+												−								N			
Procainamide (Pronestyl)							+			+								N	N					
Procaine																						N		
Progestogens							+																	
Propoxyphene (Darvon)	+	+			N	−	+			+				N							N			
Propranolol (Inderal)	N					−			+	+														
Propylthiouracil							−			+														
Pyrazinamide (PZA)	+									N			+											
Quinacrine (Atabrine)														N										
Quinethazone (Hydromox)							+		N	+		+	+											
Quinidine	+	+		★						+				●	●						N			
Reserpine														N		N					N		N	
Riboflavin														N							N	N		
Rifampin (Rifadin, Rimactane)	+	+		★			+		N	+	N			●							N			

714 Appendix

Pentazocine:
Causes sphincter of Oddi spasm, indicating that elevations of serum amylase may occur.

Phenazopyridine:
May color urine orange to orange-red.
May produce interfering colors for urine ketones by Ketostix or Gerhardt ferric chloride method.
May produce falsely high readings in the assay of porphyrins by spectrophotofluorimetry.
May interfere with Ames reagent strips for urine protein as well as the nitric acid ring test.
May yield a pink to red color in Ehrlich's test for urobilinogen.

Phenolphthalein:
May impart a red to purple color to an alkaline urine.

Phenothiazines:
Intramuscular chlorpromazine may result in increased CPK levels.
Chlorprothixene may result in significant uricosuria.
May color urine pink to red or red-brown.
Chlorpromazine may result in high apparent values for urine metanephrines (Pisano method).
May interfere with diacetic acid determinations.
May cause false increases in 17-ketosteroids (Zimmermann reaction).
Chlorpromazine may produce moderate decreases in urinary VMA excretion.

Phensuximide:
May color urine pink to red or red-brown.

Phenylbutazone:
May occasionally produce hepatitis with hyperbilirubinemia.
Parotitis, with resultant elevation of serum amylase, is a rare complication of phenylbutazone therapy.
Markedly enhances hypoprothrombinemic effect of oral anticoagulants.
Phenylbutazone is a weak uricosuric.

Phenytoin:
Jaundice is a rare complication of phenytoin therapy.
May color urine pink or red to red-brown.
Slightly decreases excretion of 17-ketosteroids and 17-hydroxycorticosteroids.

Probenecid:
May decrease urinary 17-ketosteroid excretion.

Procaine:
May react with Ehrlich's reagent in test for porphyrins or urobilinogen.

Propoxyphene:
Has produced hypoglycemia in a patient with impaired renal function.
Preliminary evidence indicates that propoxyphene may cause false decreases in urinary 17-hydroxycorticosteroids (Porter-Silber) and 17-ketosteroids (Zimmermann reaction).

Propranolol:
False increases in serum bilirubin (by SMA 12/60) in uremic patients taking propranolol.

Pyrazinamide:
May decrease plasma prothrombin levels owing to its hepatotoxicity.
Urinary 17-ketosteroids may be decreased, followed by a return to normal.

Quinacrine:
May color the urine yellow.

Quinidine:
May interfere with the determination of urinary 17-hydroxycorticosteroids by a modification of the Reddy, Jenkins, Thorn procedure.

Reserpine:
May cause slight initial increase in excretion of 5-HIAA.
May cause slight increase in absorbance in 17-hydroxycorticosteroid measurements (modified Glenn-Nelson technic).
Chronic administration decreases urinary catecholamine and VMA excretion; however, increases in both may be seen during the first day or 2 of therapy.

Riboflavin:
Large doses may produce yellow discoloration in urine.

Rifampin:
Inhibits hypoprothrombinemic effect of oral anticoagulants.
May produce acute renal failure with elevated urea nitrogen.
May produce red-orange color in urine.

Table 1 (cont'd). Effects of drugs on common laboratory tests.

Legend:

- + = Increase (pharmacologic or toxic effect)
- − = Decrease (pharmacologic or toxic effect)
- N = See notes (below)
- ● = Increase (test interference)
- ○ = Decrease (test interference)
- ★ = Present or positive

Drug	Amylase	Bilirubin	Cholesterol	Coombs (Direct)	CPK	Glucose	Thyroxine	Phosphatase, Alk.	Potassium	Prothrombin Time	SGOT and SGPT	Urea Nitrogen	Uric Acid	Color	Catecholamines	Glucose (Benedict)	5-HIAA	Ketones	Porphyrins	Protein	Steroids	Urobilinogen	VMA	OTHER TESTS
Salicylates	N	+	N			N	−	−	−	+	+		N		−	N	N	N		★			N	Urine estriol −
Spironolactone (Aldactone)								+	+						●	●								Plasma cortisol ●
Succinylcholine (Anectine)									+		+													
Sulfinpyrazone (Anturane)								+	+				−											
Sulfonamides	N		N		N	N			N	N	+	+		N	●	N			N	N		N		
Tetracyclines	N	N	N		N	N			N	N	+	+			N	N		N	N			−		
Thiabendazole (Mintezol)																					N			Blood ammonia + Serum calcium +
Thiazide diuretics	+	+			+	+		−	−				+	N	N	−								
Thyroglobulin (Proloid)			−			N			N															
Thyroid, desiccated			−			N			N															
Tolazamide (Tolinase)							+	+		+														
Tolbutamide (Orinase)					−	−	−				+			N										
Triamterene (Dyrenium)					+	+		+			+	+	+	N					N					
Tricyclic antidepressants		+														−								
Triiodothyronine (Cytomel)			−				−		N													−		
Trimethadione (Tridione)																				N				
Troleandomycin (TAO)		+						−		+			N						★	★				
Viomycin (Vanactane, Viocin)								−																Serum calcium −
Vitamin A	N		N				N			N										★				Serum calcium (N)

Salicylates:

Salicylism has resulted in pancreatitis, with resultant increase in serum amylase.

Large doses may decrease serum cholesterol.

The salicylates have variable effects on blood glucose; a hypoglycemic action may be seen (especially in diabetics), and both hyperglycemia and hypoglycemia have occurred from salicylate intoxication.

Large doses (eg, 3–5 g/d) can cause uricosuria; smaller doses result in urate retention.

Aspirin may interfere with fluorescence methods for urinary 5-HIAA.

May produce an interfering color in ferric chloride test for acetoacetic acid.

False increases with various methods for urinary VMA, but false *decreases* may occur with Pisano method.

Sulfonamides:

Reports have appeared describing pancreatitis with elevated serum amylase following sulfasalazine and sulfamethizole.

Jaundice has been produced, owing to both acute hemolytic anemia and hepatotoxicity.

Some sulfonamides enhance the hypoprothrombinemic effect of oral anticoagulants.

May color urine rusty yellow or brownish.

May react with Ehrlich's reagent in test for porphyrins or urobilinogen. May also precipitate an attack of acute intermittent porphyria.

Sulfisoxazole may lead to false-positive results for proteinuria by turbidity and by heat and acid methods; also, many sulfonamides may result in crystalluria with true proteinuria.

Tetracyclines:

Prolonged high doses have resulted in pancreatitis in certain patients.

Oral chlortetracycline may reduce serum cholesterol.

Oxytetracycline has produced hypoglycemic effects in diabetics but apparently not in normal subjects.

Intravenous tetracycline may decrease plasma prothrombin activity; also, tetracyclines may reduce the vitamin K-producing bacteria in the gut.

Parenteral forms containing ascorbic acid may cause false-negatives in urinary glucose by glucose oxidase methods (eg, Clinistix, Tes-Tape).

Thiabendazole:

Hyperglycemia may occur (incidence is low).

Thiazide diuretics:

May cause hyperglycemia and glycosuria in patients predisposed to diabetes.

May cause slight decrease in urinary cortisol excretion.

Thyroglobulin; desiccated thyroid:

Effects on serum thyroxine should be consistent with metabolic effects.

Increasing thyroid hormone activity increases anticoagulant effect of coumarins.

Tolbutamide:

A metabolite may cause false-positive tests for proteinuria when turbidity procedures are used (eg, heat and acetic acid, sulfosalicylic acid).

Triamterene:

May produce a pale blue fluorescence in the urine.

Triiodothyronine:

Increasing thyroid hormone activity increases hypoprothrombinemic effect of coumarins.

Troleandomycin (triacetyloleandomycin):

May cause false elevations of 17-ketosteroids (Drekter) and 17-hydroxycorticosteroids (Porter-Silber).

Vitamin A:

Intoxication may produce hepatotoxicity with increased bilirubin, alkaline phosphatase, and transaminase.

Intoxication may produce hypercalcemia.

Table 2. Drugs hazardous for use during pregnancy.

During First Trimester
  A. Antineoplastic agents:
    Aminopterin
    Chlorambucil (Leukeran)
    Melphalan (Alkeran)
    Methotrexate
    Radioiodine
  B. Antinauseants (Antihistamines): OTC preparations containing these drugs must bear a warning against their use by women who are pregnant or who may become pregnant:
    Chlorcyclizine (Perazil)
    Cyclizine (Marezine)
    Meclizine (Bonine)
  C. Incompletely Studied Drugs: Animal studies do not establish risk or freedom from risk of teratogenicity. Adequate epidemiologic studies are available for only a few drugs. The labeling of a large number of drugs, therefore, includes a statement that the safety of use during pregnancy has not been established or that significant information is not available. The physician is cautioned to weigh the need for any drug during pregnancy against the possible hazard. Such a disclaimer is almost invariably present in the package insert or manufacturer's prescribing information of recently introduced drugs, eg–
    Carbamazepine (Tegretol)
    Cholestyramine (Questran)
    Furosemide (Lasix)
    Pargyline (Eutonyl)
    Phenylbutazone (Butazolidin)
    Propranolol (Inderal)
  D. Phenytoin (Dilantin)
  E. Coumarin Type Anticoagulants

Throughout Pregnancy
  A. Antidiabetic Agents (Oral):
    Acetohexamide (Dymelor)
    Chlorpropamide (Diabinese)
    Phenformin (DBI)
    Tolbutamide (Orinase)
  B. Anti-infective Agents:
    Ethionamide (Trecator)

    Streptomycin
    Tetracyclines
  C. Endocrine Agents:
    Androgens
    Anti-inflammatory (adrenocortical) steroids
    Antithyroid drugs
      Methimazole (Tapazole)
      Propylthiouracil
    Diethylstilbestrol
    Progestins
    Protein anabolic steroids
      Oxandrolone (Anavar)
      Oxymetholone (Adroyd, Anadrol)
      Stanozol (Winstrol)

Late in Pregnancy
    Ergot alkaloids
    Laxatives (except for mild agents)
    Quinine, quinidine

Close to Time of Delivery
    Some drugs transferred to the fetal circulation may have adverse effects on the newborn.
  A. CNS Depressants:
    Barbiturates and other sedative-hypnotics if given in larger than sedative doses
    General anesthetics (except nitrous oxide) if given in more than analgesic concentrations
    Narcotic analgesics
  B. Vitamin K
  C. Chemotherapeutic Agents:
    Chloramphenicol (Chloromycetin)
    Long-acting (protein-bound) sulfonamides, eg, sulfamethoxpyridazine (Kynex, Midicel)
    Novobiocin (?)
  D. Rauwolfia Alkaloids
  E. Anticoagulants:
    Dicumarol (bishydroxycoumarin)
    Ethyl biscoumacetate (Tromexan)
    Warfarin (Coumadin)
  F. Agents Listed Above as Hazardous Throughout Pregnancy.

FDA EVALUATION OF
EFFECTIVENESS OF DRUGS

Drugs first marketed after 1962 have been approved by the FDA under the expanded authority—ie, evidence of efficacy was presumably supplied. Following the advice of the consultants, the FDA has reclassified the drugs in the following categories:

(1) Effective: A drug may be judged effective for at least one of its claimed indications for use, and no question of its continued marketing is raised. For other suggested uses, the drug may be placed in one of the categories described below, in which case the manufacturer must either provide additional information or change the labeling at some future time.

(2) Probably effective: The presumption is that the drug is effective for the claimed indication but adequate data are lacking. The manufacturer is given 12 months to provide additional data or develop a protocol for collecting the information.

(3) Possibly effective: There is little evidence of effectiveness and small expectation that such evidence can be collected. The manufacturer is given 6 months to develop a satisfactory protocol for further study. The drug may remain on the market in the meantime.

(4) Ineffective, or–

(5) Ineffective in fixed combination: In these cases, the data are available and establish that the claims are unsubstantiated or that a hazard exists. The product has either been removed from the market or is in the process of being removed.

Apothecary Equivalents

Metric		Approximate Apothecary Equivalents		Metric		Approximate Apothecary Equivalents	
30	g	1	oz	25	mg	3/8	gr
6	g	90	gr	20	mg	1/3	gr
5	g	75	gr	15	mg	1/4	gr
4	g	60	gr	12	mg	1/5	gr
3	g	45	gr	10	mg	1/6	gr
2	g	30	gr	8	mg	1/8	gr
1.5	g	22	gr	6	mg	1/10	gr
1	g	15	gr	5	mg	1/12	gr
0.75	g	12	gr	4	mg	1/15	gr
0.6	g	10	gr	3	mg	1/20	gr
0.5	g	7 ½	gr	2	mg	1/30	gr
0.4	g	6	gr	1.5	mg	1/40	gr
0.3	g	5	gr	1.2	mg	1/50	gr
0.25	g	4	gr	1	mg	1/60	gr
0.2	g	3	gr	0.8	mg	1/80	gr
0.15	g	2 ½	gr	0.6	mg	1/100	gr
0.12	g	2	gr	0.5	mg	1/120	gr
0.1	g	1 ½	gr	0.4	mg	1/150	gr
75	mg	1 ¼	gr	0.3	mg	1/200	gr
60	mg	1	gr	0.25	mg	1/250	gr
50	mg	3/4	gr	0.2	mg	1/300	gr
40	mg	2/3	gr	0.15	mg	1/400	gr
30	mg	1/2	gr	0.12	mg	1/500	gr
				0.1	mg	1/600	gr

Units of Small Measurement (Weights)

In keeping with the decision of several scientific societies to employ a uniform system of metric nomenclature, *Review of Medical Pharmacology* has been converted to such a uniform system. Equivalents of present and past measurements are listed below.

gram	g
10^3 g	kg (kilogram)
10^{-3} g	mg (milligram)
10^{-6} g	μg (microgram, replaces γ)
10^{-9} g	ng (nanogram; replaces mμg)
10^{-12} g	pg (picogram; replaces $\mu\mu$g)
10^{-6} meter	μm (micrometer; replaces μ)

Index

When the British and USA generic names differ only by a consistent and recognizable convention (eg, British phenobarbitone, USA phenobarbital) or spelling (eg, British oestradiol, USA estradiol), the British name has not been indexed. The British generic name has been indexed when it varies markedly from the USA name—eg, Pethidine (Brit): *See* Meperidine.

Norflex, 323
dl-Norgestrel, 402
Norinyl, 404
Norlestrin, 404
Noroxine, 346
Norpace, 153
Norpramin, 296
D-Norpseudoephedrine, 302
Nortriptyline, 296
Noscapine, 334
Notezine, 654, 666
Notice of Claimed Investigational Exemption for a New Drug, 20
Novobiocin, 532, **578**
    effects on laboratory tests, 712
Novothyral, 346, 347
Novotiral, 346, 347
Nozinan, 258
NPH insulin, 385
NSAID, 280
Nubain, 265, 272
Null cells, 517
Numorphan, 265, 272, 276. *See also inside front cover.*
Nupercaine, 219, 225
Nutritional toxicity due to alcohol, 247
Nutrition, total parenteral, 452
Nux vomica, 4
Nylidrin, 80, 93, 122
Nystatin, 37, 531, 580, **582**

Obesity, 300
Octamethyl pyrophosphoramide, 62
Oily lotion, 35
Ointments, 34, 35
Oleandomycin, 532, 576
OMPA, 62
Onchocerca volvulus, 648, 655, 656
Onchocerciasis, 648, 655, 656
Oncovin, 490, 494
o,p-DDD, 366, 497
Ophthaine, 218
Opiate receptor, 269
Opiates
    in drug abuse, 48
    semisynthetic, 265
Opisthorchiasis, 653
Opisthorchis, 648, 653
Opium. *See inside front cover.*
    alkaloids of, 265
    tincture of, 276
Optimine, 191
Oral administration of drugs, 25
Oral contraceptives, **403–409**
    carcinoma due to, 408
    effects on laboratory tests, 712
    spotting due to, 407
Oral hypoglycemic agents, **385–389**
Orchitis, prophylaxis for, 611
Orenzyme, 181
Oretic, 164
    in hypertension, 114
    structure of, 161
Organ, transplantation of, 523
Organic phosphate inhibitors, 692
Organo-lead, 688
Orinase, 386
    effects on laboratory tests, 716
Ornipressin, 433
Ornithine vasopressin, 433
Orphenadrine, 323

Ortho-Novum, 404
Orthopedic surgery, antimicrobial prophylaxis in, 607
Osmolality, 460, 462
Osmotic diuretics, 77, **168**
Osteomalacia, 466
Osteoporosis, 413
    and fluoride, 458
Osteosclerosis, 458
OTC drugs, 29
Otosclerosis, 458
Ouabain, 137, 140, 142, 145
Ovary, **393–411**
    carcinoma of, 498, **508**
    function of, disturbances in, 395
    hormones of, 393
    mammalian, diagram of, 393
Ovcon, 404
Overhydration, 461
Over-the-counter drugs, 29
Ovine prolactin, 422
Ovral, 404
Ovrette, 404
Ovulating hormone, 417, 427
Ovulation-inducing agents, 393, **409**
Ovulen, 404
Oxacillin, 540, 543, 546
    effects on laboratory tests, 712
Oxalate, 370
Oxamniquine, 665
Oxandrolone, 415
Oxantel pamoate, 666
Oxazepam, 230, 237. *See also inside front cover.*
Oxazole, 239
Oxazolidinedione, 310, 313
Oxidation, by liver microsomal system, 11
Oxidative deamination, 11
Oxidizing agents, 594
Oxolinic acid, 532, 586
Oxprenolol, 102
Oxurasin, 667
Oxycodone, 265, 272, **276**. *See also inside front cover.*
Oxygen
    hyperbaric, 332, 333, 699
    preparations of, 333
    therapy with, 332
        adverse reactions in, 333
Oxygen tent, 332
Oxymetholone, 415
Oxymorphone, 265, 272, **276**. *See also inside front cover.*
Oxyphenbutazone, 289
Oxyphencyclimine, 78
Oxyphenonium, 78
Oxytetracycline, 553
Oxytocics, **128–134**
Oxytocin, 131, 417, **432**, 433
    effects of drugs on, 432
Oxyuris vermicularis, 648, 667
Oxyzin, 667
Ozone, 698

PABA, 471, 532, 570
Pachycurares, 211
Paget's disease, 374, 458
Pagitane, 323
Painful shoulder, 290
Paint thinner, 680

PALA, 489
    as anticancer agent, 480
    as investigational anticancer agent, 499
Paludrine, 630
    in malaria chemoprophylaxis, 627
    preparations and dosages, 631
Palusil, 630
PAM, 68
Pamine, 78
Pancreas, carcinoma of, 498, 509
Pancreatin, 330
Pancreatitis, acute, 74
Pancrelipase, 330
Pancuronium, 215
Pangamic acid, 448
Panparnit, 334
Pantothenic acid, 446
Panwarfin, 171
Papanicolaou smear, 507
Papase, 181
Papaverine, 122, 183, 265, 267
Papaver somniferum, 264
Papillary necrosis, renal, 288
Para-aminobenzoic acid, 349, 570
    esters of, 218
Para-aminophenol derivatives, 280, 287
Para-aminosalicylic acid, 568
    effects on laboratory tests, 704
Paracetamol (Brit): *See* Acetaminophen.
Parachloramphetamine, 195
Parachlormethamphetamine, 195
Parachlorophenylalanine, 195
Paracodin, 265
Paradione, 310, 313
Paraflex, 239, 240
    effects on laboratory tests, 706
Paragonimiasis, 653
Paragonimus westermani, 635, 648, 653
Paraldehyde, 236, 237, 681. *See also inside front cover.*
Paralysis agitans, 319
Paramethadione, 310, 313
Paramethasone, 357
Paraoxon, 62
Paraquat, 694
Parasiticidal action of topical drugs, 38
Parasiticidal dermatologic preparations, 37
Parasitization, stage of, 619
Parasympathetic or craniosacral division of autonomic nervous system, 58
Parasympatholytic drugs, **71–79**
    dosages and preparations available, 78
    as hallucinogens, 52
    list of, 78
    in parkinsonism, 323
    sedative effects of, 229
Parasympathomimetic agents, **56–70**
    action of, 59
    toxicity due to, treatment of, 77
Parathion, 62
Parathormone, 371
Parathyrin, 371
Parathyroid gland
    extract of, 372
    function of, disorders of, 372
    hormone of, **369–378**
        human, bovine, and porcine, amino acid sequence of, 371
Parathyroid injection, 372